CW00573580

Tolley's
Health and Safety
at Work
Handbook
1994

Sixth Edition

by
Malcolm Dewis LLB, MIOSH

Tolley Publishing Company Limited
A UNITED NEWSPAPERS PUBLICATION

Published by
Tolley Publishing Company Limited
Tolley House
2 Addiscombe Road
Croydon Surrey CR9 5AF England
081-686 9141

Typeset in Great Britain by
Letterpart Limited
Reigate, Surrey

Printed in Great Britain by
Mackays of Chatham plc
Chatham, Kent

Foreword

Successful companies are usually safe and healthy ones. This is no coincidence. Most will have included the management of safety as an integral part of their management responsibilities on a par with their marketing strategy or business plans.

They will have looked at their duties under health and safety law, assessed any risks within their organisation, taken the necessary measures to minimise those risks and drawn up a well thought out and relevant safety policy statement. What's more, they would not have treated health and safety in isolation but would have integrated it into the daily running of their business.

Yet this message of good health and safety management practice has yet to percolate fully throughout industry. Why? Inspectors find that while companies are willing to manage safety, many of them are daunted by the prospect of obtaining, sifting through and digesting the necessary information. This highlights the vital importance of being able to gain access easily to health and safety information especially in the light of recent new regulations resulting from European Community directives on health and safety.

I am therefore delighted that this revised sixth edition of Tolley's Health and Safety at Work Handbook has been produced. It provides the reader with information on duties under current health and safety law and guidance on good practice, set out in an easily readable and accessible format.

This handbook should help not only employers to practise good safety management but will also be of help to safety practitioners, union safety representatives and members of the public.

Sir John Cullen, FEng, PhD
Chairman
Health & Safety Commission
5 May 1993

Preface

Herewith is the Sixth Edition of this popular Handbook on workplace health, safety and welfare law, with accompanying housekeeping procedures and best practices. The latest edition, which states the law as at 31 October 1993, has been updated and altered to accommodate changes in statute, regulations, repeals, revocations and cumulative case law.

The past working year has brought in train some significant changes (and proposed changes) in the following areas of workplace activity. These changes affect particularly

(i) management of health and safety at work, with the introduction of the *Management of Health and Safety at Work Regulations 1992* – requiring employers to prepare risk assessments and have regular safety audits by competent safety personnel;

(ii) provision, use and maintenance of work equipment, with the introduction of the *Provision and Use of Work Equipment Regulations 1992* – themselves dependent for efficacy on compliance by suppliers with their new safety duties under the *Supply of Machinery (Safety) Regulations 1992*;

(iii) use and maintenance of VDU terminals and workstations, courtesy of the *Health and Safety (Display Screen Equipment) Regulations 1992* and provision for eyesight tests for operators on request;

(iv) manual handling of loads, with the introduction of the *Manual Handling Operations Regulations 1992*, requiring employers to prepare risk assessments of likely hazards to employees from such activities;

(v) provision, correct use and maintenance of personal protective equipment, with the introduction of the *Personal Protective Equipment at Work Regulations 1992*, themselves dependent for efficacy on the *Personal Protective Equipment (EC Directive) Regulations 1992*, requiring designers and manufacturers of such equipment to comply with EC standards;

(vi) provision and maintenance of safe workplaces, free from health risks, and with satisfactory and suitable welfare facilities, including, for the first time, safe internal and pedestrian traffic routes, escalators and travelators, smoke-free rest rooms and areas, windows that can be opened and cleaned safely, and doors and gates that are openable and operate safely, courtesy of the *Workplace (Health, Safety and Welfare) Regulations 1992*.

With the exception of the *Management of Health and Safety at Work Regulations*, all these 'Six Pack' regulations carry attendant civil liability, which will in time come to replace the existing common law duties.

(vii) the on-going dissemination of information to the public concerning environmental pollution, in the form of the *Environmental Information Regulations 1992*, the *Public Information for Radiation Emergencies Regulations 1992* and the *Radioactive Substances Act 1993*. Moreover, by dint of the *Clean Air Act 1993*, occupiers of premises can be required by environmental health departments to specify emission of pollutants into the air from their premises;

(viii) modification of control limits for certain types of asbestos, courtesy of the *Control of Asbestos at Work (Amendment) Regulations 1992*;

(ix) the need, on the part of operators, to prepare and revise Safety Cases, in the case of offshore installations, by virtue of the *Offshore Installations (Safety Case) Regulations 1992*;

(x) the classification, preparation and labelling and packaging of information concerning dangerous chemicals for supply and transportation, courtesy of the *Chemicals (Hazard Information and Packaging) Regulations 1993* (*CHIP*);

(xi)   the right of employees not to be victimised for participation and involvement in health and safety activities, courtesy of the *Trade Union Reform and Employment Rights Act 1993* – an important milestone in the enshrinement of employee safety rights. Under this Act, where employees are dismissed for involvement, dismissal is deemed to be unfair; in addition, they can present a complaint to an industrial tribunal. Employees are also entitled to a 'shopping list' of employment particulars.

Moreover, the proposed introduction – probably sometime in 1994 – of the *Fire Precautions (Places of Work) Regulations* promises to extend requirements currently applicable to fire-certificated premises to other workplaces and premises. The forthcoming *Construction, Design and Management Regulations*, imposing duties on those who manage building operations, will, hopefully, contribute to a reduction in accidents and injuries in construction and related activities. And the Safety Signs Directive, harmonising safety signs at the workplace, the Product Safety Directive, requiring manufacturers to market and circulate safe products as well as the Physical Agents Directive, laying duties in connection with sources of non-ionising radiation, all foreshadow greater awareness of health and safety on the part of workers and consumers and greater vigilance on the part of employers, managers and manufacturers.

Developments in civil law have not been exactly prosaic, either. The decision of the Court of Appeal in *Larner v British Steel plc, The Times, 19 February 1993* which emphasised that the duty on employers to provide and maintain a safe place of work 'so far as reasonably practicable' was a strict one and not referable to reasonable foreseeability, has obvious risk management implications for employers. So, too, does the incipient 'no win no fee', or contingency fee system, long associated with American product liability litigation, suggestive of awards of increased damages. In tandem with this, maximum fines (on summary conviction) of £20,000 for breach of certain workplace and environmental duties guarantee to concentrate the managerial mind on health and safety and the environment.

In addition, there have been some structural alterations to the latest edition. In particular, Chapter 9 'Dangerous Substances I – at the Workplace' has been re-worked to reflect a more practical approach to the spate of regulatory controls applicable to dangerous substances in use at the workplace; Chapter 12 has been updated to include latest civil liability developments relating to statutory undertakers and environmental pollution; Chapter 13 has been revamped to include the *Trade Union Reform and Employment Rights Act 1993* and Chapters 18, 28 and 46 modified (and augmented) to accommodate the requirements of the *Provision and Use of Work Equipment Regulations 1992* and the *Workplace (Health, Safety and Welfare) Regulations 1992*.

Given this mixture, the Handbook still aims, as originally, to provide clear and concise guidance on statute and case law, accompanying codes of practice, as well as practical safety criteria and procedures, for industrial managers, company directors, safety practitioners, enforcement officers, liability insurance assessors, safety representatives, occupational health personnel and legal practitioners. Trainees involved in safety management, appreciation, refresher or introduction courses may also find the handbook useful.

Malcolm Dewis, LLB, MIOSH
1 November 1993

Contents

Contents

Contents

Acknowledgements

The author wishes to acknowledge the debt owed to the contributors of the first edition, some of whose chapters have been reproduced, either wholly or in part.

All Crown Copyright material is reproduced by kind permission of Her Majesty's Stationery Office. Use of VDU Equipment (Chapter 27) and the Pressure Systems and Transportable Gas Containers (Chapter 37) are reproduced with the kind permission of the Controller of Her Majesty's Stationery Office and are Crown copyright.

Extracts from 'The Complete Idiot's Guide to CHIP' are reproduced by kind permission of the Health and Safety Executive.

Extracts from BS 5378: Part 1:1980 and from BS 5304:1988 are reproduced by kind permission of the British Standards Institution. Complete copies of the documents can be obtained from the British Standards Institution, Linford Wood, Milton Keynes MK14 6LE; telex 825777 BSIMK G; telefax 0908 320856.

The publishers are grateful to the Oil and Chemical Plant Constructors' Association and their publishers, the Building Advisory Service, for permission to reproduce figure 3 (Chapter 7) from the OCPCA Safety Manual; to GW Sparrow & Sons plc for their permission to reproduce figure 6 and Tables 20 and 21 (Chapter 26); to Butterworths for permission to reproduce some case material from North's 'Occupiers' Liability' in Chapter 32; to Paramount Publishing for permission to reproduce the unreported cases on civil liability for injury by fire (Chapter 19) from 'Fire Safety and the Law'; to Pitman for permission to reproduce the permit to work certificate (Chapter 1) from 'The Handbook of Health and Safety Practice', Second Edition; and to RoSPA for permission to reproduce the resuscitation procedure chart in Chapter 20.

For checking scripts and proofs thanks also to the British Safety Council and RoSPA.

List of Tables

List of Illustrations/Diagrams

Abbreviations and References

Many abbreviations occur only in one chapter of the book and are set out in full there. The following is a list of abbreviations used more frequently or throughout the book.

Organisations/Publications

ACAS	=	Advisory, Conciliation and Arbitration Service
ACOP	=	Approved Code of Practice
BS	=	British Standard
BSC	=	British Safety Council
CBI	=	Confederation of British Industry
Cmnd	=	Command Paper
COIT	=	Central Office of the Industrial Tribunals
DSS	=	Department of Social Security
EC	=	European Community
HMIP	=	HM Inspectorate of Pollution
HSC	=	Health and Safety Commission
HSE	=	Health and Safety Executive
HMSO	=	Her Majesty's Stationery Office
HSIB	=	Health and Safety Information Bulletin
ILO	=	International Labour Office
IOSH	=	Institution of Occupational Safety and Health
JCT	=	Joint Contracts Tribunal
RoSPA	=	Royal Society for the Prevention of Accidents
TUC	=	Trades Union Congress

Statutes/Statutory Instruments

CHIP	=	Chemicals (Hazard Information and Packaging) Regulations 1993
COSHH	=	Control of Substances Hazardous to Health Regulations 1988
CPA	=	Consumer Protection Act 1987
EPA 1990	=	Environmental Protection Act 1990
EPCA	=	Employment Protection (Consolidation) Act 1978
FA	=	Factories Act 1961
FSA 1990	=	Food Safety Act 1990
HSWA	=	Health and Safety at Work etc. Act 1974
OLA	=	Occupiers' Liability Act 1957
OSRPA	=	Offices, Shops and Railway Premises Act 1963
TULRA	=	Trade Union and Labour Relations Act 1974 (as amended)
TURERA	=	Trade Union Reform and Employment Rights Act 1993
UCTA	=	Unfair Contract Terms Act 1977
Reg	=	Regulation (or Statutory Instrument)
SI	=	Statutory Instrument
SR&O	=	Statutory Rule and Order
Sch	=	Schedule
s or Sec	=	Section

Case citations

AC	=	Appeal Cases
AER	=	All England Reports
CB, NS	=	Common Bench, New Series (ended 1865)
CL	=	Current Law

CLJ	=	Current Law Journal
CLY	=	Current Law Year Book
CMLR	=	Community Law Reports
Con LR	=	Construction Law Reports
F & F	=	Foster & Finlayson (ended 1867)
HSIB	=	Health and Safety Information Bulletin
ICR	=	Industrial Cases Reports
IRLR	=	Industrial Relations Law Reports
JP	=	Justice of the Peace and Local Government Review
KB/QB	=	Law Reports, King's (Queen's) Bench Division
KIR	=	Knight's Industrial Reports
Lloyd's Rep	=	Lloyd's List Reports
LR CP	=	Law Reports, Common Pleas Cases
LR Ex	=	Law Reports, Exchequer Cases
LT	=	Law Times Reports
Macq	=	Macqueen (Scot) (ended 1865)
NLJ	=	New Law Journal
RTR	=	Road Traffic Reports
SC	=	Session Cases (Scot)
SJ	=	Solicitors' Journal
SLT/SLT (Notes)	=	Scots Law Times/(Notes)
TLR	=	Times Law Reports
WLR	=	Weekly Law Reports

Legal terminology

ECJ	=	European Court of Justice
HL	=	House of Lords
CA	=	Court of Appeal
EAT	=	Employment Appeal Tribunal
IT	=	Industrial Tribunal
J	=	Mr Justice, a junior judge, normally sitting in a court of first instance
LJ	=	Lord Justice, a senior judge, normally sitting in a court of appeal
plaintiff	=	the person presenting a claim in a civil action
defendant	=	the person against whom a claim is brought in a civil action
appellant	=	the person bringing an appeal in a civil action
respondent	=	the person against whom an appeal is brought in a civil action
tort	=	a species of civil action for injury or damage where the remedy or redress is an award of unliquidated damages
'volenti non fit injuria'	=	'to one who is willing no harm is done'; a complete defence in a civil action
obiter dicta	=	words said by the way
ratio decidendi	=	principle of a case

Chapter 1

Introduction

1.1 Health and safety at work used justifiably to be labelled as the Cinderella of the legal, medical and business worlds. Lawyers were on balance lethargic about it, doctors regarded occupational health as the poor relation of disease proper, whilst businesses only got involved when, ominously, an inspector called – an occurrence less likely now than in previous years. This is a situation which is rapidly changing. Following the tragedies in the chemical industry in Mexico City and Bhopal, and the nuclear catastrophe in Chernobyl, not to mention the disastrous fire at King's Cross tube station, London, in 1987 and the Piper Alpha debacle in July 1988 – underlining, as they all clearly do, the need for good health and safety management and maintenance – health and safety has suddenly been catapulted into the cockpit of social legislation by the EC. Indeed, the overriding inference is that new employment law will find its inexorable way into our internal legal system by the circuitous route of health and safety, the latter being subject to Qualified Majority Voting (QMV) rather than unanimity of agreement. Hence, a continuing flow of directives, resulting in subsequent legislation, on health and safety can be expected in the short term. On the other hand, however, older regulations, particularly where they might duplicate duties in parent legislation of more recent origin, may well be shortly excised, or, at least, subject to strenuous critical assessment, as part of the recent Government review of health and safety legislation.

Hitherto, there has been a succession of directives concerned with dangerous substances, industrial major accident hazards, prescribed occupational diseases, product liability, hours of work of drivers of goods and passenger vehicles as well as training of drivers of vehicles carrying dangerous substances – all trickling into a stream of regulations imposing strict controls on employers and managers, accompanied by ever-escalating penalties. Thus, the maximum penalty, on summary conviction, for health and safety offences, as from 1 October 1992, is £5,000, under the *Criminal Justice Act 1991*; whilst breaches of *Secs 2–6* of the *Health and Safety at Work etc. Act 1974* (duties on employers, occupiers and manufacturers), as well as failure to comply with improvement/prohibition notices or a remedial court order under *Sec 42*, attract maximum fines, on summary conviction, of £20,000, as from 6 March 1992, by dint of the *Offshore Safety Act 1992* (see 17.1, 17.7, 17.8, 17.29 ENFORCEMENT and Chapter 34 'Offshore Operations').

As for civil liability or entitlement to compensation, awards of damages in personal injury cases continue to mount with a widening of the liability net. Victims of nervous shock may recover damages in group actions, following Hillsborough; bereavement has a higher 'premium' placed on it, namely £7,500; whilst victims of pneumoconiosis, byssinosis and diffuse mesothelioma can get lump sum awards, irrespective of proof of fault, where their former employers have gone out of business; and group actions have begun to characterise litigation regarding defective products, especially drugs.

A wide-ranging review of the law of damages by the Law Commission suggests that:

1

—   disaster victims may be entitled to punitive damages from negligent companies (as well as facing possible manslaughter charges (see 15.45 EMPLOYERS' DUTIES)) – this would equate to the US situation where negligent manufacturers have punitive damages awarded against them in product liability actions in addition to a straight compensatory award for injury-causing defect;

—   structured settlements for accident victims may become the norm, that is, payment of compensation monthly for a victim's lifetime instead of by way of lump sum, similar to payments of social security benefits (see 6.11 COMPENSATION FOR WORK INJURIES/DISEASES);

—   in class actions, such as disaster claims or drugs' side-effects claims, award of a global sum for the whole of the class is emerging as a possibility;

—   damages may fulfil a retributive function as well as being compensatory (that is, deprive wrongdoers of gain and punish perpetrators).

Moreover, proposed introduction of a full-blown conditional fee system (i.e. no win no fee) in (*inter alia*) personal injuries litigation, although not entirely parallel with the American contingency fee system (which latter entitles the successful attorney to a slice of the litigant's damages) will undoubtedly have a considerable effect on levels of damages, resulting, almost certainly, in increased awards.

1.2   Recent key statutory developments are the *Control of Substances Hazardous to Health Regulations 1988 (COSHH)*, as amended in 1991 and 1992; the *Noise at Work Regulations 1989*, requiring employers to keep noise at work levels to 85dB; the *Public Information for Radiation Emergencies Regulations 1992* requires employers, from which radiation emergencies are reasonably foreseeable, to inform the general public; the *Personal Protective Equipment at Work Regulations 1992* and the *Personal Protective Equipment (EC Directive) Regulations 1992* requires employers to provide and manufacturers to produce suitable personal protective equipment for use at work; the *Construction Products Regulations 1991* requiring construction products to incorporate certain basic health and safety features; the *Provision and Use of Work Equipment Regulations 1992* and the *Supply of Machinery (Safety) Regulations 1992* requiring employers to provide and manufacturers to produce machinery for use at work with health and safety designed in; the *Management of Health and Safety at Work Regulations 1992* requiring employers to assess the health and safety needs of employees and make use of competent safety personnel for audit purposes; the *Offshore Safety Act 1992*, introducing maximum penalties of £20,000 on summary conviction and converting the *Mineral Workings (Offshore Installations) Act 1971* into an 'existing statutory provision', within the scope of *HSWA 1974* (see further 17.2(*c*) ENFORCEMENT; as well as the *Radioactive Substances Act 1993* and the *Chemicals (Hazard Information and Packaging) Regulations 1993 (CHIP)*, requiring suppliers of dangerous substances to classify such substances and prepare and revise safety data sheets.

Equally important is the *Environmental Protection Act 1990*, specifying 'integrated pollution control' and which has brought in a regime of 'prior authorisations' for an augmented number of 'prescribed processes' (from fuel/power to acid manufacturing), coupled with legally binding emission limits and a residual duty to use 'best practicable environmental options' to control pollution, accompanied by a requirement on operators of such plant and processes to use 'best available techniques not entailing excessive cost' (BATNEEC) as a condition precedent to authorisation. In addition, under the *Clean Air Act 1993*, occupiers of premises can be required to quantify emissions of pollutants into the air and the *Environmental Information*

Regulations 1992 (SI 1992 No 3240) require that environmental information be disclosed on request, unless unduly sensitive.

Employees are given important new rights and remedies in the *Trade Union Reform and Employment Rights Act 1993*; in particular, the right not to be 'victimised' for involvement in health and safety activities, the right to present a complaint to an industrial tribunal on such grounds and introduction of the presumption that dismissal for safety reasons is deemed to be unfair.

Consumers are also catered for by the *Food Safety Act 1990* and regulations passed under it, the *Gas Safety (Installation and Use) Regulations 1984* (as recently amended), requiring employers to ensure that gas fitters are competent and are members of an HSE-approved body, and the *Gas Appliances (Safety) Regulations 1992 (SI 1992 No 711)*.

Moreover, the overlap between health and safety and social security goes on apace. Industrial injury benefit has been replaced by statutory sick pay (SSP), payable by employers for up to a maximum of 28 weeks following an injury-causing accident at work, after which disablement benefit may be payable; the list of prescribed occupational diseases continues to grow, with hydiatiosis and carpal tunnel syndrome recently added and the distinct likelihood that emphysema and bronchitis in the case of coal mining will shortly be added and, still more important, following the introduction of the *Social Security Act 1989*, all earlier disablement benefits, paid or payable for five years immediately after work injury, are deductible (except for fatal injuries) from subsequently awarded damages, with its knock-on effect on employers' liability insurance premiums (see Chapter 16 'Employers' Liability Insurance'). Currently, social security administration is governed by the *Social Security Administration Act 1992*, whilst contributions and benefits are the subject of the *Social Security (Contributions and Benefits) Act 1992*, replacing the *Social Security Act 1975*.

Parameters of health and safety at work

1.3   The law on health and safety at work cannot realistically be considered in isolation. Interrelated are EC social law, safety management, insurance, loss control, environmental protection, product liability and social security (this last is covered in Chapter 6 'Compensation for Work Injuries/Diseases', whilst liability insurance is dealt with in Chapter 16 'Employers' Liability Insurance', environmental protection in Chapter 12 'Emissions into the Atmosphere', EC directives below (see 1.4) and product liability in Chapter 38 'Product Safety').

Given this mix, the Handbook is predominantly concerned with the law on health and safety at work but, more specifically, the substantive law of England and Wales (i.e. English law), including offshore installations. The book is not, however, intended to be an authoritative guide to the law in either Scotland or Northern Ireland. Whilst much of the legislation applies to Scotland, the markedly different basic legal tradition of that country has not been incorporated. By contrast, Northern Ireland has a very similar legal tradition to that of England and Wales but a separate system of legislation, that is similar but not always identical. Legislation applicable to Northern Ireland has not been included. EC institutions and their relationship with UK law are discussed directly below (see 1.4).

The European dimension – EC law and institutions

1.4   Involvement of the European Community (EC), formerly the European Economic Community (EEC), in social legislation, including health and safety, is on-going if not hectic, emanating in a spate of directives on employment law, health and safety at work and the environment, dangerous substances through product liability to training of drivers of vehicles carrying dangerous substances, carcinogens etc.

Apart from being a free trade agreement between twelve (as yet) independent members, the EC has its own institutions and legislative powers. The constitution of the EC is laid down in treaties, which specify its internal and external powers, i.e. principally the Treaty of Rome 1957, as amended by later agreements, such as the *Single European Act 1986* and the Maastricht Treaty 1991.

EC legislative institutions

1.5   The main legislative institutions of the EC are the Commission, the Council of Ministers, the European Parliament and the European Court of Justice (ECJ).

(a) EC Commission

This is the supreme EC executive, consisting of seventeen independent members appointed by Member States, two each from the five larger states of Germany, France, United Kingdom, Spain and Italy, and one each from the remainder. Its main function is to propose EC legislation and as such is divided into several directorates. Its deliberations are in secret. Its proposals to the Council of Ministers normally take the form of directives.

(b) Council of Ministers

A political body, this is the final decision-making organ of the EC, that is, the EC government. It considers proposals from the Commission, after which it must consult with the European Parliament. Most EC legislation must be agreed unanimously, though some legislation is subject to Qualified Majority Voting (QMV), e.g. significantly, health and safety legislation.

(c) European Parliament

The European Parliament is (at the moment) consultative and advisory and debates on proposals for legislation are the only open part of the EC's decision-making process. Failure, on the part of the Council of Ministers, to consult with the European Parliament, means that any legislation is void. Parliament can reject or propose amendments to legislation subject to Qualified Majority Voting (QMV).

(d) European Court of Justice (ECJ)

Based in Luxembourg and consisting of thirteen judges, appointed by Member States, and assisted by six advocates-general, this court has supreme authority on matters of EC law and interpretation of treaties. Its proceedings are rather different from those of our internal courts, with more accent on written submissions than oral argument and proceedings are more inquisitorial. The court delivers a single judgment with no dissents. Its main function is to hear referrals from national courts for a ruling on the interpretation of provisions of Community law. Under Article 177 (of the Rome Treaty) any court or tribunal of a Member State can refer any matter of EC law to the European Court, which tends to look at the spirit rather than the letter of the law (unlike our own appeal courts). Both the High Court and the Court of Appeal can interpret EC law and are not obliged to grant right of appeal to the European Court of Justice, but, if requested, either of our appeal courts is so bound to refer an appeal to the European Court, consistent with Article 177 (above) (*HP Bulmer Ltd v J Bollinger SA [1974] 2 AER 1226*). Sec 3(1) of the *European Communities Act 1972*, as amended by the *European Communities (Amendment) Act 1986*, explains that interpretation of treaties concerning the EC and Community instruments, if not referred to the European Court, is to be decided in accordance with principles established by any relevant decision of the European Court.

(Because the United Kingdom did not sign up to the social chapter of the Maastricht Agreement in 1991, subsequent EC social and employment law cannot apply here as a result of decisions of the European Court. This is not, however, the case with health and safety legislation, which will extend to the United Kingdom, since it is subject to Qualified Majority Voting (QMV) (see above).)

Community law

1.6   EC law is contained in treaties (e.g. the Treaty of Rome 1957, the *Single European Act 1986*), legislation proposed by its institutions and case law and principles of law formulated by the European Court of Justice. In the event of a conflict between EC law and national law, EC law prevails, even if national law is later in time (*R v Secretary of State for Transport, ex parte Factortame Ltd [1990] 3 CMLR 86; [1991] 1 AER 70*). Moreover, national legislation must be interpreted consistently with EC law, if national legislation is passed to implement it (*Litser v Forth Dry Dock & Engineering Co Ltd [1989] 2 WLR 634*).

Approximately 90% of Community law is made by the EC Commission, much of which concerns common agricultural policy. More substantial Community law comes from the Council of Ministers, acting on proposals made by the Commission and published in draft form months or even years before a decision is taken. The UK Parliament has set up a Committee in the House of Commons and House of Lords to scrutinise Community proposals. Only the European Court of Justice can declare Community legislation invalid.

Types of EC law

1.7   Hierarchically, EC law consists of the following.

(a) Provisions of the Treaty of Rome (as amended by later Treaties)

Under *Sec 2* of the *European Communities Act 1972*, such provisions are not enforceable in the United Kingdom in the absence of an internal statute expressly detailing the rights conferred in the United Kingdom as a response to the general requirements of the Treaty.

(b) Regulations

Under Article 189 (of the Rome Treaty) these become part of domestic law without the need of legislation to implement them. Regulations are legislative acts of general application and have, practically, no role in health and safety.

(c) Directives

Directives are a remarkably fertile source of EC law and, as far as health and safety are concerned, the most important source of UK legislation. Under Article 189 (of the Rome Treaty), directives are binding, though it is left to Member States to decide upon the means of giving them legal and/or administrative effect. Directives must generally be implemented, though this is not invariably essential (*Van Duyn v The Home Office [1974] 3 AER 178*), the normal period of implementation being two years. In the United Kingdom implementation usually takes the form of statutory instrument (or regulation), as required by *Sec 2* of the *European Communities Act 1972*; but occasionally may be an Act of Parliament (e.g. the *Consumer Protection Act 1987*, implementing the directive on product liability). In the field of health and safety, EC directives have been responsible for most of the recent statutory additions to protective industrial and environmental legislation, with controls over lead, asbestos, industrial major accident hazards and defective products.

Occasionally a directive is 'directly effective', that is, does not require formal implementation and comes into effect after its time limit has expired. This can only happen when the directive is aimed at the State or a public body rather than a private organisation, e.g. a company.

Types of directives

1.8   Key directives are framework directives. These lay down a framework or raft of controls in a general way, to which more specific controls may later be annexed in the form of daughter or satellite directives – rather in the way that a parent Act of Parliament is subsequently fleshed out by regulations. This has happened in the case of health and safety (see the *Single European Act 1986* at 1.12 below).

Compliance with directives

1.9   Under Article 5 (of the Rome Treaty) Member States are required to take all appropriate measures, general or particular, to ensure fulfilment of obligations arising out of the Treaty or resulting from action by institutions of the Community. Thus, Member States must comply with directives, generally by implementing them (see above). Failure to implement a directive on the part of a Member State entitles the EC Commission to initiate infringement proceedings and, if necessary, under Article 169 it can bring a Member State before the European Court of Justice in order to achieve compliance, or alternatively, withhold funds.

Approximation of laws

1.10   Article 100 (of the Rome Treaty) enables directives to be issued for the purpose of approximation or harmonisation of laws and practices of the Member States, which directly affect the establishment or functioning of the Common Market. With the addition of Article 100A, the *Single European Act 1986* introduced Qualified Majority Voting (QMV) for many proposals of this nature, e.g. proposals relating to health and safety, product controls and environmental protection, with the object of expediting the advent of a single internal market. For that reason, health and safety and environmental legislation will come 'on stream' more quickly than would otherwise have been the case, since national veto is outlawed (e.g. the directive on emissions from large combustion plants (i.e. acid rain)). Moreover, the implication appears to be that failure to implement health and safety/environmental directives may be regarded as a distortion of trade or disguised subsidy to the offending Member State. Indeed, it may sometimes be permissible to interfere with the requirement of free trade (under Article 30) on environmental grounds (*Disposable Beer Cans, Re EC Commission v Denmark [1989] 54 CMLR 619*). By extension, therefore, this may come to duplicate in the case of health and safety, which may be a justifiable ground for discrimination against foreign manufacturers.

Challenging EC legislation

1.11   Directives can be challenged within two months of issue, under Article 173, basically on the ground that they are *ultra vires* (i.e. unconstitutional). The only recorded instance of this to date is the directive on the titanium dioxide industry in 1991 (*Commission of the European Communities v Council of the European Communities, The Times, 21 August 1991*).

The Single European Act 1986 (SEA)

1.12 An important step towards an integrated Europe was realised by the *Single European Act 1986* (*SEA*), which came into effect on 1 July 1988. This had the effect of putting health and safety proposals high on the list of priorities of the Council of Ministers. This Act makes new internal market and social policy objectives, introduced into the Treaty of Rome, more easily attainable.

Articles 8A, 8B and 8C in the Treaty specify that the EC must adopt measures to dismantle progressively social barriers, such as varying standards of health and safety. Thus, Article 118A provides that Member States must pay particular attention to encouraging improvements, especially in the working environment, as regards health and safety of workers. Prior to this, there had been no specific provision in the Treaty for health and safety, and most directives in that area had been adopted under Article 100, concerned with the 'approximation of laws affecting the . . . functioning of the common market'.

In order to facilitate achievement of these new objectives, the Act provides for Council decisions in these areas to be reached via a new decision-making procedure, namely, on the basis of a Qualified Majority Vote (QMV), each Member State having a vote weighted according to the size of its population. This contrasts with the previous position relating to 'approximation' under Article 100, which required unanimity of agreement. This latter procedure will expedite legislation on health and safety at work.

After a decade during which the EC Commission has been almost entirely restricted to control of health hazards, such as lead, asbestos and noise, the Safety Framework Directive is significant, as envisaging a programme of directives concerned with accident prevention and occupational health, e.g. personal protective equipment, manual handling and display screens equipment directives.

The Framework Directive

1.13 The Framework Directive, although reflecting the broad-brush approach of the *Health and Safety at Work etc. Act 1974*, by laying general duties on employers and employees, requires, in addition, employers to assess risks at work to employees and others and take steps to prevent and reduce them. This includes the key (new) requirement on employers to 'appoint competent personnel' to monitor health and safety at the workplace – an already common practice in certain parts of industry but not (to date) a statutory requirement (see further Safety officers, Chapter 15 'Employers' Duties') including the health and safety of temporary workers. Both assessment and consequential health and safety arrangements will have to be recorded by employers employing five or more employees, and groups of employees at risk identified in writing. In addition, employers will have to formulate procedures to be carried out in the event of serious and imminent danger to employees – again, a practice followed in many industries already. (For details of the recent *Management of Health and Safety at Work Regulations 1992 (SI 1992 No 2051)*, see Chapter 15 'Employers' Duties'.)

7

Elements of health and safety law

Statute law and common law

1.14   *Statute law* consists principally of statutes or primary legislation. This has been the main source of law in modern times. Statutes lay down a framework of a system, the details of which are filled in later by a series of regulations or statutory instruments (SIs), though sometimes statutes lay down a complete system of law, e.g. *Finance Acts* and some of the *Companies Acts*. They generally introduce new law (e.g. the *Health and Safety at Work etc. Act 1974*, the *Consumer Protection Act 1987*, the *Environmental Protection Act 1990*) but sometimes they are passed to codify previous (often confused) common law (e.g. the *Sale of Goods Acts 1893* and *1979*) or to consolidate previous statute law, e.g. the *Factories Act 1961*, consolidating earlier *Factories Acts*. Important statutes tend to come into operation at various times by means of Commencement Orders (e.g. the *Fire Safety and Safety of Places of Sport Act 1987*, the *Consumer Protection Act 1987* and the *Environmental Protection Act 1990*) followed by a series of specific regulations. When statute and common law happen to conflict, statute prevails.

In the field of health and safety, many statutes confer power on a Secretary of State (usually the Secretary of State for Employment) or Minister of the Crown to make statutory instruments (SIs) which specify more detailed rules for the implementation of the broad parent Act. These statutory instruments/regulations must be within the scope of or *intra vires* the parent Act; otherwise they will be invalid. Today, statutory instruments tend to take the form of regulations, though others are called 'orders'. This has not always been so. Prior to 1948, statutory instruments were collectively known as 'statutory rules and orders' (SR&Os). Thus, most of the specific substantive law on health and safety at work will be found in this second layer of legislation, or 'delegated' or 'subordinate' legislation. More particularly, specific health, safety and welfare requirements are to be found in regulations passed pursuant (mainly) to the *Health and Safety at Work etc. Act 1974* (*HSWA*), e.g. the *Ionising Radiations Regulations 1985*, the *Control of Substances Hazardous to Health Regulations 1988* (*COSHH*), and (secondarily) to the *Factories Act 1961* (e.g. the *Abrasive Wheels Regulations 1970*, the *Power Presses Regulations 1965*) or the *Offices, Shops and Railway Premises Act 1963*.

By virtue of *Sec 6* of the *Statutory Instruments Act 1946*, a regulation/statutory instrument becomes law after a period of 40 days of being laid before Parliament, if no resolution to the contrary is passed against it in either House, and a breach of regulations is actionable, even though the regulations are silent (see 1.18, 1.44 below), unless the regulations state otherwise.

1.15   *Common law* is the English traditional law that remains in areas where Acts of Parliament have not penetrated or intervened. It is predominantly judge-made and accounts for much of the law of contract and tort. Common law systems characterise not only the United Kingdom but also the Commonwealth and North America. Law has evolved from the determination of particular cases to the formulation of a general principle. This contrasts with the position in Continental Europe and other countries with legal systems based on Roman law. Here the law tends to be set out in a general way in a code, civil or penal, and expressed in mandatory terms, e.g. employers shall do so and so. . . . In practice, however, provisions of codes are interpreted liberally and hedged with provisos. Case law is authoritatively bound together by precedent, binding or persuasive; that is, the court hierarchical structure is such that lower courts must follow decisions of higher courts on the same point of law and higher courts, or appeal courts, must generally follow their earlier decisions on the same point – an exception being the

House of Lords, which is not bound by its earlier decisions. Where a previous decision must be followed, this is known as binding precedent; where it may be followed, this is known as persuasive precedent. The binding element in a case is the *ratio decidendi* (or reason for the decision) and must be distinguished from *obiter dicta* (words said by the way), often introduced by a preamble, on the part of the judge, to the effect '. . . if I were called to decide . . . I should be inclined to say . . .'. *Ratio decidendi* is the application of a legal principle or principles to the facts of a particular case.

The distinction between statutory and common law duties, in the field of occupational health and safety, may be expressed as follows. *Statutory duties* are contained in Acts of Parliament and/or statutory instruments and are enforceable by the State through its executive arm, the Health and Safety Executive (HSE). Breach of statutory duty gives rise, principally, to criminal liability, though it can also give rise to civil liability where breach has resulted in injury, disease or death (see 1.16, 1.17 below). *Common law duties* have their origin in court decisions and are principally concerned with civil liability (see 1.17 below).

Criminal liability and civil liability

1.16   *Criminal liability* arises from the commission of a crime or 'criminal offence'. The accused is liable to be prosecuted before a criminal court (i.e. normally the magistrates' court but sometimes the Crown Court) and, if found guilty, sentenced to a specific punishment – most often a fine but sometimes (though this is rare) imprisonment. A standard scale of fines for many statutory offences including health and safety offences was introduced by the *Criminal Justice Act 1982, s 37*, ranging from £25 – £1,000, and has recently been updated by the *Criminal Justice Act 1991*, increasing the maximum fine on summary conviction, in health and safety cases, from £2,000 to £5,000, except for breaches of *Secs 2–6* of the *Health and Safety at Work etc. Act 1974*, which attract a maximum fine, on summary conviction, of £20,000, courtesy of the *Offshore Safety Act 1992, s 4(2)*. However, on conviction on indictment, the court can impose an indefinite or unlimited fine on an employer – which is exactly what happened recently when the Scottish High Court imposed fines of £250,000 and £500,000 respectively on BP Oil Refinery Ltd, in two separate incidents involving the deaths of three workers, at its Grangemouth refinery (*The Times, 22 March 1988*). These fines are huge compared with previous 'record' fines (see *R v Swan Hunter Ltd*, Chapter 17 'Enforcement'). The origin of most criminal offences associated with health and safety lies in statute/statutory instrument. Although certain crimes are still governed by common law (e.g. murder, manslaughter) these are not particularly relevant in health and safety. However, in light of certain recent tragedies involving the travelling public, manslaughter prosecutions (including possible corporate responsibility) may become a reality (see further Chapter 15 'Employers' Duties'). Statutes or statutory instruments specifying statutory duties will also specify if a breach is a criminal offence. In addition, criminal proceedings (i.e. prosecutions) are always initiated by the State, or in the name of the State, by a member of one of its executive departments, e.g. a health and safety inspector. The purpose of prosecution is to obtain conviction and sentence, that is, a penal aim. It is not possible to insure against sentence; indeed, it is illegal to request cover from insurers in respect of payment of fines and/or for insurers to attempt to provide cover for penalties (see Chapter 16 'Employers' Liability Insurance'). (As for gradations of statutory duties, see further 15.16-15.19 EMPLOYERS' DUTIES.)

1.17   *Civil liability* arises from an act or omission which the law regards as entitling one individual, company or organisation to present a legal claim against another. Civil claims are heard in civil courts (principally the county courts or the High Court). In particular, the two areas of civil law most relevant to health and safety at work are (*a*) *torts* (a collective name for certain rights of action, especially negligence (see 1.22 below)) and *breach of statutory duty* (see 1.18 below) and (*b*) *breach of contract* (i.e. contract of employment, see 1.19 below). Although there are signs of an awakening of a contractual approach towards health and safety at work, the normal civil claim where injury/disease and/or death has occurred, remains a claim in tort for negligence (but see *Johnstone v Bloomsbury Health Authority* (15.9 EMPLOYERS' DUTIES)).

Where there is a civil claim in respect of injury, disease or death, the following features are present (in contrast with criminal proceedings).

(*a*)   The proceedings are brought by an individual (the plaintiff). If the case involves a fatal accident, the proceedings are normally brought by the dependants of the deceased, normally the widow. Under the *Administration of Justice Act 1982* a statutory maximum sum (currently £7,500) is now payable for bereavement, in addition to death. Such solace compensation was never payable at common law.

(*b*)   The purpose of the claim is to secure an award of damages, i.e. money compensation, for suffering and disablement. In the case of a fatal accident, compensation is related to the degree of financial support provided to the dependants by the deceased. The aim is, therefore, compensatory.

(*c*)   Civil liability in 'tort' can be insured against – indeed such insurance against liability is compulsory for most classes of employers (see Chapter 16 'Employers' Liability Insurance'). In contrast, it is not normally possible to insure against civil liability for breach of contract.

Much of this part of civil law, i.e. the law relating to civil duties and civil liability, is contained in common law. Acts of Parliament have intervened from time to time to modify specific aspects, especially where common law has become obsolescent or equivocal, e.g. the *Occupiers' Liability Act 1957*, clarifying the civil duties of occupiers, or the *Fatal Accidents Acts* extending the rights of dependants to claim in fatal injury cases. Civil liability for breach of statutory duty represents the interface between civil and criminal liability.

Civil action for breach of statutory duty

1.18   Quite apart from allowing a civil claim under the law of negligence (i.e. in 'tort'), the courts have sometimes recognised that a breach of duty imposed by statute may give rise to a civil claim for damages. This applies in cases where a statute imposes a duty but (apart perhaps from stipulating criminal liability as a consequence of breach) says nothing about civil liability for injury/loss caused by breach. In such a case, the approach of the courts has been to ask: 'Was the duty imposed specifically for the protection of a particular class of persons, or was it intended to benefit the general public at large?'. If the answer is the former, a civil claim may be allowed. More particularly, the courts have regarded the safety provisions of the *Factories Acts* as being protective of a particular class and have accordingly allowed a civil action for damages by a person belonging to the protected class (e.g. employees) who has been injured as a result of breach of duty (*Groves v Lord Wimborne [1898] 2 QB 402*; *Solomons v R Gerzenstein Ltd [1954] 2 AER 625*). However, certain of the 'health and welfare' duties under the *Factories Acts* appear to be regarded as being directed towards public health in general, and therefore not capable of giving rise to an action for breach of statutory duty. Moreover, where a breach of statutory duty is alleged, a breach of common law duty may be alleged as well (the 'double-barrelled' action, see 1.45 below). The principle of liability for breach of statutory duty does not, however, apply where the Act itself provides an alternative remedy, or, on the other hand, expressly states that an action for breach of its duties does not lie (as is the case with the general duties in *Secs 2-8* of the *Health and Safety at Work etc. Act 1974*). Moreover, safety regulations, even if silent as to civil liability, are actionable. [*Health and Safety at Work Act 1974, s 47(2); Consumer Protection Act 1987, s 41*]. (See also 1.43 and 1.44 below.)

Employers, employees and the contract of employment

1.19   The law on health and safety at work is normally concerned with employers and employees (though other types of people, such as occupiers of premises, may also come within its scope). The legal relationship between an employer and employee is a complex one, but it essentially arises out of the 'contract of employment'. Since contracts of employment are often not in writing (that is, all their terms) (see 13.3 EMPLOYEE SAFETY RIGHTS, DISCIPLINARY PROCEDURES AND UNFAIR DISMISSAL), it becomes necessary to apply certain criteria in order to ascertain whether there is a contract of employment or some other form of contract such as a contract for services (self-employment). It is necessary to know whether there is a contract of employment because many of the duties in health and safety law are owed by employers to employees; employers are only vicariously liable for the negligent acts of employees and it is only in respect of liability to employees that insurance is compulsory; in addition, only employees can complain of unfair dismissal. The recent *Trade Union Reform and Employment Rights Act 1993* (*TURERA*) has elevated the importance of safety in employment (see further Chapter 13 'Employee Safety Rights, Disciplinary Procedures and Unfair Dismissal').

Key criteria for determining the existence of a contract of employment are as follows.

(*a*)   Does the person for whom the work is being done *control* the way in which the work is done – specifying hours, the work to be done, manner of work, transfers from one task to another, general discipline etc.?

(*b*)   Is the worker, working as part of the person's business, *integrated into the organisation?*

(*c*)   Alternatively, are there indications that the worker is trading in his own right (i.e. is self-employed), e.g. does he take a degree of financial control? Is he insured? Does he provide his own tools and equipment and his own assistants?

(*Yewens v Noakes [1880] 6 QBD 530; Stevenson, Jordan and Harrison Ltd v Macdonald & Evans Ltd [1952] 1 TLR 101; Market Investigations Ltd v Minister of Social Security [1969] 2 QB 173; Ferguson v John Dawson & Partners (Contractors) Ltd [1976] 1 WLR 1213*, see Chapter 7 'Construction and Building Operations').

Health and safety duties at common law

Duties of employers

1.20   The common law position is, and always was, that employers must take reasonable care to protect their employees and their immediate family (see 15.1 EMPLOYERS' DUTIES) from risk of foreseeable injury, disease or death at work. The effect of this is that if an employer actually knows of a health and/or safety risk to the workforce, or ought in the light of current state of the art to have known of the existence of a hazard, he will be liable if an employee is injured or killed or suffers illness as a result of the risk, if the employer failed to take the required reasonable care.

1.21   An employer's duties at common law were identified in general terms by the House of Lords in *Wilsons & Clyde Coal Co Ltd v English [1938] AC 57*. The common law requires that all employers provide and maintain:

(*a*)   a safe place of work; and

(*b*)   a safe system of work; and

(*c*)   safe plant and appliances.

(See further Chapter 15 'Employers' Duties'.)

In addition, employers are liable for injury-causing accidents to employees as a consequence of the negligence of their other employees, provided that the negligent act arises 'out of and in the course of employment'. This is the effect of the application of the principle of vicarious liability at common law (see Chapter 15 'Employers' Duties').

Duty under the law of negligence

1.22   The duty of care required by common law, if civil liability for negligence is to be avoided, can, and does apply to anybody in any situation. The duty seeks to ensure simply that a person takes 'reasonable care' if he is in a situation where, if he were to fail to take such care, it could be foreseen that somebody else might suffer injury or loss. Negligence can thus arise out of a positive act or, alternatively, an omission or failure to act. The relevant question in all cases is: would a reasonable person have taken a greater degree of care in what he did than the particular person did? If the answer is in the affirmative, then, irrespective of the person's subjective state of mind, he will be found liable for any injury resulting from his failure to meet the standards of the reasonable man. In practice, the standards of the mythical reasonable man are assessed by the judge. Hence, health and safety standards are continually subject to critical judicial surveillance, and in consequence, gradually upgraded. ('The standard goes up as men become wiser. It does not stand still as the law sometimes does' per Denning LJ, as he then was, in *Qualcast Ltd v Haynes [1959] 2 AER 38*.)

In order to establish liability for negligence, an injured person (e.g. injured employee) must prove:

(*a*)   existence of duty of care owed to him by (e.g.) his employer; and

(*b*)   breach of that duty; and

(*c*)   that his injury/disease was caused (i.e. materially, although not exclusively, contributed to) by the breach of duty.

1.23   The burden of proving a case in a civil action is on a balance of probabilities, i.e. it is more likely than not that the injury occurred in the way alleged. To this extent it is a lesser burden of proof than in criminal cases, where proof beyond a reasonable doubt is required. An example of this is shown in *Bonnington Castings Ltd v Wardlaw [1956] 1 AER 615* where a worker contracted pneumoconiosis as a result of being exposed to two sources of dust in the course of his employment. One source of dust was under the control of his employer, whilst the other was outside the employer's control. As a steel dresser the worker was exposed to silica dust from pneumatic hammers and there was no known means (then) of preventing the escape of dust from such machines. In addition, he was exposed to dust from swing grinders, which could have been made harmless. The appellant's claim succeeded on the second ground that dust from the swing grinders was a material cause of his illness. 'The employee must in all cases prove his case by the ordinary standard of proof in civil actions; he must make it appear at least that on a balance of probabilities the breach of duty caused or materially contributed to his injury' (per Lord Reid). Though a short while later in *Gardiner v Motherwell Machinery & Scrap Co Ltd [1961] 3 AER 831*, where a worker engaged on demolishing buildings and boilers had contracted dermatitis, Lord Reid said, 'In my opinion, when a man who has not previously suffered from a disease contracts that disease after being subjected to conditions likely to cause it, and when he shows that it starts in a way typical of disease caused by such conditions, he establishes a *prima facie* presumption that his disease was caused by those conditions'. This statement by Lord Reid is virtually tantamount to 'prescription of diseases' at common law (see further test of prescription in Chapter 31 'Occupational Health'). Compliance with usual trade professional practices or received professional wisdom, has traditionally been a cast-iron defence to negligence (*Pearson v North Western Gas Board [1968] 2 AER 669* where a gas mains fractured owing to severe frost, causing an explosion which destroyed the plaintiff's home. Expert evidence showed that there was no way then of protecting the public from such damage. It was held that such evidence rebutted negligence. How far this position will obtain now that gas/electricity are 'products' for the purpose of product liability, is more doubtful (see further Chapter 22 'Gas Safety' and Chapter 38 'Product Safety')). Moreover, compliance with the *Construction Products Regulations 1991* is a defence to proceedings, concerning the same matter, under the *Health and Safety at Work etc. Act 1974*. *[Construction Products Regulations 1991, Reg 33(1)]*.

The common law duty of care, and liability for breach of it, applies to everyone, but in the field of occupational health and safety law, the duty is laid particularly on:

(*a*)   employers;

(*b*)   occupiers of premises;

(*c*)   employees and other workers;

(*d*)   designers/manufacturers of tools and machinery for use at work.

Where negligence is self-evident – res ipsa loquitur

1.24   There are limited circumstances in which a court may be prepared to say that the 'facts speak for themselves' (i.e. *res ipsa loquitur*), and as such are evidence of negligence. Here it is for the defendant (normally the employer) to show that he has taken reasonable care. If he cannot do this, he will be adjudged negligent (see further Chapter 40 'Shops').

Statutory duties before the Health and Safety at Work etc. Act 1974

Factories Acts

1.25   'The history of occupational safety legislation in Britain is to a great extent, though not exclusively, the history of legislative control over manufacturing industry'. (*Cmnd 5034, Appendix 5*). Indeed, until *HSWA* was introduced in 1974, creating a consensual approach towards occupational health and safety, legislation consisted of a series of statutes passed on an ad hoc basis in an endeavour to control safety hazards and, to a lesser extent, health hazards as well. The first statute to be passed was the *Health and Morals of Apprentices Act 1802*. This sought to combat the appalling conditions in which children worked in the textile industry by limiting the number of hours apprentices worked in the cotton industry and specifying minimum standards of heating, lighting and ventilation. It was enforced (indifferently) by visitors appointed to factories by local magistrates.

The first *Factory Act* was introduced in 1833, principally to control the excessively long hours worked by children in the textile industry. It established four factory inspectors who had statutory powers of entry and enforcement in factories and mills. In 1864 the matchmaking and pottery industries were given statutory protection, and in 1867 enforcement of safety began in workshops (i.e. smaller working establishments than factories), with the passing of the *Workshop Regulation Act*. In 1878 the distinction, for enforcement purposes, between factories and workshops was removed by the *Factory and Workshop Act*, both being merged into 'factories'. A significant measure was the *Factory and Workshop Act 1901*. This introduced a pattern of legislation which, to this day, characterises health and safety legislation, i.e. a built-in power enabling the Minister (or Secretary of State) to pass ad hoc regulations to deal with hazards in certain industries/processes.

In more recent times there have been three *Factories Acts* (excluding the current one), i.e. the *Factories Act 1937*, with additions to it made in 1948 and 1959. The *Factories Act 1937* was important because it eliminated the distinction between the various types of factories (i.e. workshops, textile factories etc.). It also, for the first time, laid down *detailed* provisions in respect of health, safety and welfare at work.

Present day factory legislation is contained in the *Factories Act 1961*, which consolidated much of the earlier statute law. This Act, though, in conjunction with other legislation (see 1.26 below) is currently being replaced by *HSWA* and regulations passed under it – though the transition is a gradual one.

Other protective legislation

1.26   Following protective legislation for factories, similar legislation has come to apply also to coal mines, offices and shops and agriculture. Coal mining was an early candidate for protective legislation. In 1842 the *Mines and Collieries Act* was passed, regulating the conditions and hours of work of children in mines. In 1843 the first Inspectorate of Mines was established. Working conditions in quarries were subsequently regulated by the *Metalliferous Mines Regulation Act 1872*. The law was consolidated with the *Coal Mines Act 1911*. Current law on health and safety in mines and quarries is contained in the *Mines and Quarries Act 1954* (which is currently being revised).

Protective legislation for office and shop workers began in 1886 with the *Shop Hours Regulation Act*. This regulated the hours of employment of young persons (i.e. persons over 16 but under 18), but it was not until 1963, when the *Offices, Shops and Railway Premises Act* (*OSRPA*) was passed that the health, safety and welfare of workers in offices, shops and (some) railway premises came to be controlled through enforcement. Working conditions, as distinct from health and safety, for shop workers are currently contained in the *Shops Act 1950*.

Agriculture received its first general protective Act, the *Agriculture (Safety, Health and Welfare Provisions) Act* as late as 1956, under which umbrella many sets of regulations have been passed; though as early as 1878 the *Threshing Machines Act* had been passed and in 1897 the *Chaff-cutting Machines (Accidents) Act* was passed.

Other protective legislation, in chronological order, includes the *Prevention of Accidents Rules 1902–1931*, regarding safety on the railways; the various *Merchant Shipping Acts*, regarding safety on ships; the *Civil Aviation Acts*, regarding aviation safety, and more recently, the *Mineral Workings (Offshore Installations) Act 1971*, now enforceable by HSE, courtesy of the *Offshore Safety Act 1992*, regarding safety in the offshore oil industry, and the *Safety at Sea Act 1986*, regarding the carrying of lifeboats and training of crew members in safety procedures.

The Health and Safety at Work etc. Act 1974 (HSWA)

1.27   This Act is the most revolutionary in the history of health and safety legislation. It adopted many of the recommendations of the Robens Report. Its most significant provisions are the following.

(a)   It laid down broad general duties applicable to *all* workplaces, thus allowing for the future introduction of more specific regulations and codes of practice. (The importance of the supporting role of 'approved' or voluntary codes of practice supplementing these new regulations, or even operating independently of them, cannot be overstressed. Indeed, the overall scheme of *HSWA* is largely dependent on them, see 1.28 below.) This new system of statutory and non-statutory standards was intended to replace, in a gradual, stage-by-stage process, the earlier protective statutes and regulations, and *HSWA* accordingly provides for their repeal, but many of these repeals have not yet been given legal effect.

(b)   It established the Health and Safety Commission (HSC) and gave it power to propose health and safety regulations and approve codes of practice (see Chapter 23 'Health and Safety Commission and Executive').

(c)   It set up the Health and Safety Executive (HSE) as the unified executive arm of the HSC with the responsibility for enforcing health and safety laws (see Chapter 23 'Health and Safety Commission and Executive').

(d)   It gave health and safety inspectors the enforcement powers proposed by the Robens Committee (see Chapter 17 'Enforcement').

(e)   Recognising that the workforce was the most valuable source of information on hazards and health and safety matters in the workplace, it made provision, subsequently implemented by regulations, for the appointment of safety representatives on behalf of the workforce to monitor health and safety on the shopfloor, and for the appointment of safety committees (see Chapter 25 'Joint Consultation – Safety Representatives and Safety Committees').

(f)   It imposed duties for the first time on the self-employed. Self-employed persons must carry out work activities in such a way as to ensure, so far as reasonably practicable, that they (and others who are not their employees) are not exposed to health/safety risks. [*HSWA s 3(2)*]. Failure to comply with this duty may lead to criminal liability (*Jones v Fishwick, COIT 10155/89* where a butcher who failed to use a protective apron whilst boning out, was liable for breach of *Sec 3(2)*).

(g)   The application of *Secs 2–6* of the *Health and Safety at Work etc. Act 1974* (duties on employers, occupiers and manufacturers) as well as the general objectives of *HSWA* (securing health and welfare of persons at work, as set out in *Sec 1*), to offshore installations, by dint of the *Offshore Safety Act 1992, s 1*.

Voluntary standards, codes of practice and guidance notes

1.28   Apart from specific regulations, *HSWA* is also (and equally importantly) supported by codes of practice issued or approved by the HSC, and guidance notes published by the HSE. It must be emphasised that both codes of practice and guidance notes, although important to the proper maintenance of health and safety, are non-statutory standards (see further 1.30, 1.31 below). Examples of regulations supplemented in this way are the *Safety Representatives and Safety Committees*

15

Regulations 1977 (see Chapter 25 'Joint Consultation – Safety Representatives and Safety Committees'), the *First-Aid Regulations 1981* (see Chapter 20 'First-Aid') and the *Noise at Work Regulations 1989*.

National/international standards

1.29   Standards promote industrial efficiency and competitiveness and compliance is generally voluntary (though for legal effect, see below), though some directives, such as public utilities directives, require contracting authorities to define specification requirements by reference to national standards implementing European standards. A standard is a technical specification for the guidance of manufacturers and/or operators, and for purchasers in choosing a product which is safe and fit for its intended purpose. In the United Kingdom standards normally emanate from the British Standards Institution (BSI). Sometimes the safety standards of the BSI receive statutory support, though not all industrial and consumer products are so covered. That a product or class of products satisfies a particular BSI standard is frequently denoted by certification and marking, e.g. Kitemark. Safety certification is also available for electrical products from the British Electrotechnical Approvals Board (BEAB) and for gas appliances from the Gas Corporation. It should be emphasised, however, that certification does not mean that a given product is safe, as required by law. Ultimately, it would have to be left to a court to determine whether a given product or class of products is safe, as required by statute and/or common law. Conversely, however, failure on the part of a manufacturer to conform with a British Standard would, almost certainly, mean that a legal requirement had not been complied with. In this respect, recognised safety standards, such as British Standards, have an effect in law similar to approved codes of practice (see above); their importance as regards statutory requirements should never, therefore, be underestimated.

In addition, manufacturers may increasingly have to meet mandatory sets of standards specified by the country for which the product is destined, and sometimes these standards can be more strict than in the United Kingdom, e.g. North America. Thus, there is a steady move towards international standards, through the European Standards Committee (CEN) and the International Standards Organisation (ISO) (see, for example, CENELEC and the certification of electrical products to IEC standards (11.9 ELECTRICITY)). The EC has produced directives relating to the safety of products, the purpose of which is to harmonise consumer law throughout the EC, e.g. the Product Liability Directive (see Chapter 38 'Product Safety'). To this end, manufacturers and importers who sell products/equipment without a 'CE' mark, commit a criminal offence. The 'CE' mark means that a given product complies with the essential requirements of the Product Safety Directive. In sum, a manufacturer could not argue that he had complied with a legal requirement unless he had, *inter alia*, conformed with a relevant British/international standard/CE mark; though conversely, compliance with such a standard would not *invariably* mean that he had conformed with the statute/common law – though it would go a long way towards it. Failure to follow a specification of a British Standard can involve a manufacturer in liability for negligence (*Greaves & Co (Contractors) Ltd v Baynham Meikle and Partners [1975] 3 AER 99* (see also 18.28 FACTORIES AND WORKPLACES)).

Guidance Notes

1.30   The Health and Safety Executive publish eight main sets of Guidance Notes. These are:

(1)   CS – Chemical series;

(2)   EH – Environmental hygiene series;

(3)   GS – General series;

(4)   MS – Medical series;

(5)   PM – Plant and machinery;

(6)   HS(G) – Health and Safety (Guidance) series;

(7)   HS(R) – Health and Safety (Regulations) series;

(8)   BPM – Best practicable means (in so far as still relevant).

The importance of Guidance Notes can be seen from remarks in *Stokes v GKN Sankey Ltd* (see 15.20 EMPLOYERS' DUTIES).

Legal effect of an approved code of practice

1.31   A provision in an 'approved' code of practice (i.e. approved by the HSC, see Chapter 23 'Health and Safety Commission and Executive') is not a statutory duty and so cannot of itself be enforced by HSE inspectors. Nor can it of itself give rise to civil liability. [*HSWA s 17(1)*]. Nevertheless, failure on the part of a person to whom its provisions apply to comply with it can have serious consequences, as it may bring into effect a *presumption* that he was in breach of the statutory requirements. This is laid down by *HSWA s 17(1)(2)* and only applies to *criminal* proceedings for breach of duty. That section stipulates that, in criminal proceedings for a contravention of a requirement of *HSWA ss 2–7* or any regulations made under *HSWA* or any other health and safety legislation still in effect, if there is an approved code of practice relevant to the requirement and the person accused had not complied with the provisions of the code, proof of breach of the code is evidence of guilt. In such a case, it is incumbent on the accused to satisfy the court that he was able to comply with the statutory requirement in some way other than by observing the code. (This does not, however, alter the general burden of proof, which remains on the prosecution, see Chapter 17 'Enforcement'.) Ideally, codes should state legal and quasi-legal obligations simply, without accumulating too much legalism, thereby requiring that the code be constantly updated.

Permits to work – quasi-law

1.32   Emanating (though not expressly mentioned therein) from certain requirements of the *Factories Act 1961* (e.g. *Sec 30* concerning work in confined spaces, involving dangerous substances/fumes, where there is a lack of oxygen), permits to work provide a formal safety control system against accidental injury to personnel/plant/products, when foreseeably hazardous work is undertaken. The permit to work, consisting of a document detailing the work to be done/precautions to be taken (see *fig. 1*), is a statement that all foreseeable hazards have been noted and precautions defined. It does not, in itself, make the job safe but relies for effectiveness on specified personnel implementing it conscientiously under supervision and control.

Requirements of permits to work

1.33   1.   The permit must specify clearly who is to do the work, the time for which it is valid, the work to be done and the necessary precautions.

2.   Until the permit is cancelled, it supersedes all other instructions.

3.   During the currency of the permit, no person must work at any place or on any plant not earmarked as safe by the permit.

17

4.   No person must carry out any work not covered in the permit. If there is a change in work rotation, the permit must be amended/cancelled. This latter can only be done by the originator of the permit.

5.   Where another person takes over a permit, as, for instance, in an emergency, that person must assume full responsibility for the work, either until the work is complete or he has formally returned the permit to the originator.

6.   There must be liaison with other work areas whose activities could be affected by permit work.

7.   Where permit work is to be carried out on part of a site or on specific plant, the limits of the work area must be clearly marked.

8.   Permits to work must take into account on-site contractors who should be briefed prior to commencement of work. Moreover, compliance with safety regulations and procedures, including permits to work, should be a condition of contract (see Chapter 7 'Construction and Building Operations').

Use of permits

1.34   Permits to work should be used for the following activities:

(*a*)   entry into confined spaces/closed vessels/vats;

(*b*)   work involving demolition of pipelines or opening of plant containing steam, ammonia, chlorine, hazardous chemicals, vapours, gases or liquids under pressure;

(*c*)   work in certain electrical systems;

(*d*)   welding and cutting work (other than in workshops);

(*e*)   work in isolated locations or where access is difficult, or at heights;

(*f*)   work near or requiring use of highly flammable/explosive/toxic substances;

(*g*)   work causing atmospheric pollution;

(*h*)   pressure testing;

(*j*)   fumigation operations using gases;

(*k*)   ionising radiations work;

(*l*)   any of the above activities involving on-site contractors.

Cancellation of permit

1.35   Once scheduled work is complete, the permit to work certificate should be cancelled and returned to the originator, who should see that all permit work has been carried out satisfactorily. The originator should then sign the declaration to the effect that all personnel/equipment/plant has been removed from the area. The plant/equipment should then be returned to service and the person responsible for the plant should check that the permit has been properly cancelled and then make a final entry on the certificate, accepting responsibility for the plant.

Documentation

1.36   Permits should be printed in triplicate, self-carbonned and serial-numbered. The originator should distribute them as follows:

(i)   the original to the person undertaking the work (and possibly posted at place of work);

(ii) first copy to be given to the person responsible for the area in which work is to be carried out;

(iii) second copy should be retained by the originator.

Competent/authorised persons

1.37   Not infrequently, health and safety legislation requires certain duties, normally involving a high degree of expertise, to be carried out only by 'competent' or, less often, 'authorised' persons. Examples abound as follows.

1.   *Construction Regulations 1961-1966*

   (*a*)   supervision of demolition work;

   (*b*)   supervision/handling/use of explosives;

   (*c*)   inspection of scaffold materials before erection;

   (*d*)   supervision of erection/alteration/dismantling of scaffolds;

   (*e*)   inspection of scaffolds every seven days and after adverse weather conditions;

   (*f*)   daily inspection of excavations;

   (*g*)   supervision of erection of cranes.

2.   *Electricity at Work Regulations 1989, Reg 16* – persons to be competent to prevent danger and injury.

3.   *Abrasive Wheels Regulations 1970, Reg 9* – mounting of abrasive wheels.

4.   *Power Presses Regulations 1965, Reg 6* – carrying out inspections and testing safety devices.

5.   *Factories Act 1961, s 22(2)* – examination of hoists/lifts.

6.   *Offshore Installations (Operational Safety, Health and Welfare) Regulations 1976, Reg 23* – helicopter operations.

7.   *Offshore Installations (Operational Safety, Health and Welfare) Regulations 1976, Reg 6* – examination of lifting machinery.

8.   *Management of Health and Safety at Work Regulations 1992, Reg 6* – all employers.

9.   *Pressure Systems and Transportable Gas Containers Regulations 1989, Regs 8–10, 13.*

It is, therefore, unfortunate that 'competence', obviously a key requirement, has generally not been defined either by statute or case law – an exception being the *Management of Health and Safety at Work Regulations 1992 (SI 1992 No 2051)*, which refer to a person as being 'competent' where he has sufficient training and experience or knowledge as to enable him to assist in securing compliance, on the part of the employer, with the necessary safety legislation and maintenance procedures. [*Regs 6(5), 7(3)*].

PERMIT TO WORK CERTIFICATE

LOCATION: **ORIGINATOR:**   **DATE:**

PART A
Valid from .... (time) to .... (time) on .... (date)
Issued by .... to ....
This permit is issued for the following work ....
in .... department/area/section.

PART B – PRECAUTIONS	YES/NO	N/A	SIGNATURE
1 The above plant has been removed from service and persons under my supervision have been informed.			
2 The above plant has been isolated from all sources of: (a) ingress of dangerous fumes, flammable and toxic substances (b) electrical and mechanical power; (c) heat, steam and/or hot water.			
3 The above plant has been freed of dangerous substances.			
4 Atmospheric tests have been carried out and the atmosphere is safe.			
5 The area is roped off or otherwise segregated from adjacent areas.			
6 The appropriate danger/caution notices have been displayed.			
7 The following additional safety precautions have been taken: (a) the use of safety belt and life line; (b) the use of goggles and/or gloves; (c) the use of flameproof lamps; (d) the use of fresh air/self-contained breathing apparatus; (e) prohibition on naked lights/sources of ignition; (f) .... (g) .... (h)			

Part C – DECLARATION
I hereby declare that the operations detailed in Parts A and B have been completed and that the above particulars are correct.
Signed .... Date .... Time ....

PART D – RECEIPT/ACCEPTANCE OF CERTIFICATE
I have read and understand this certificate and will undertake to work in accordance with the conditions in it.
Signed .... Date .... Time ....

PART E – COMPLETION OF WORK
The work has been completed and all persons under my supervision, materials and equipment have been withdrawn.
Signed .... Date .... Time ....

PART F – REQUEST FOR EXTENSION
The work has NOT been completed and permission to continue is requested.
Signed .... Date .... Time ....

PART G – EXTENSION
I have re-examined the plant detailed above and confirm that the certificate may be extended to expire at .... (time).
Further precautions ....
Signed .... Date .... Time ....

PART H – CANCELLATION OF PERMIT
I hereby declare this Permit to Work cancelled and that all precautionary measures specified have been withdrawn.
Signed .... Date .... Time ....

PART I – RETURN TO SERVICE
I accept the above plant back into service.
Signed .... Date .... Time ....

PART J – REMARKS, SPECIAL CONDITIONS AND EXTRA INFORMATION

---

fig. 1

Maintenance operations

1.38 Many work activities, processes, plant and machinery involve periodical compulsory maintenance – that is, repair, restoration or cleaning of process machinery or plant – either dictated by statutory requirement (see 1.41 below) or current best practice (or both). Maintenance operations account for a high proportion of accidents, incidents and near misses as well as typically endangering persons and premises in the nearby vicinity not engaged in a work activity or present in a work situation. All industries are affected but particularly 'vulnerable' are chemical processes, offshore operations, buildings and construction work, food and food processing, factory production work – with over three-quarters of accidents and dangerous occurrences arising during repair, renovation or cleaning. Constantly recurring incidents with chemicals include splashing through contact; escape of harmful substances; gassing as a result of exposure to fumes; falls from heights; injury caused by moving machinery; fire or explosion, whether causing injury or not; and incidents connected with overpressure. The principal causes behind maintenance-related accidents/incidents are:

(1) absence of permit to work (see 1.32 above) or inadequacy of system;

(2) absence or inadequacy of protective equipment (see Chapter 36 'Personal Protective Equipment');

(3) unsafe system of work (see 15.28 EMPLOYERS' DUTIES);

(4) defective equipment (see 15.13 EMPLOYERS' DUTIES, 28.6, 28.46 MACHINERY SAFETY);

21

(5) unsafe place of work (e.g. working platform, access/egress provision, housekeeping) (see Chapter 2 'Access');

(6) inadequate training/supervision (see 15.31 EMPLOYERS' DUTIES).

Maintenance work subdivides into three distinct parts, namely,

(1) preparation,

(2) job itself, and

(3) return of plant to operation.

If accidents/near misses are to be averted or minimised, more attention needs to be focussed by management and operatives on the hazards involved in maintenance operations, with particular regard being paid to introduction of permit to work systems and protective clothing and equipment.

Checklist for maintenance operations

1.39 (1) *Permit to work system*

    (a) what is the job?

    (b) what are the dangers?

    (c) is a permit necessary?

    (d) what checks should be carried out?

    (e) who carries out the checks?

    (f) are isolation procedures satisfactory and suitable?

    (g) who authorises the permit?

    (h) who is the recipient of the permit?

    (j) are there re-checking procedures?

    (k) is there a time limit?

    (l) is there a shift change procedure?

    (m) is there a hand-back procedure?

    (n) are spot checks carried out by supervision?

(2) *Protective equipment*

    (a) have all foreseeable risks been identified?

    (b) does protective equipment provide adequate protection?

    (c) has it been properly maintained and checked prior to use?

    (d) is it readily accessible?

    (e) do employees know when it should be used?

    (f) have employees been properly trained?

    (g) is there adequate supervision to ensure that it is used?

(3) *Safe equipment*

    (a) is plant designed to be safe in view of known/foreseeable risks?

    (b) has it been installed as per specifications?

(c) are there procedures for ensuring that specification is not departed from by maintenance?

(d) are steps taken to ensure that work is properly carried out under supervision?

(4) *Machinery maintenance*

(a) are all dangerous parts securely fenced?

(b) does maintenance work foreseeably bring operatives near unguarded machinery?

(c) are guards removed for routine maintenance cleaning?

(d) are interlock systems checked and regularly maintained?

(e) are there effective isolation systems?

(5) *Access/place of work*

(a) is there fixed access for routine maintenance?

(b) does maintenance work require additional access?

(c) has proper training been given on use of temporary access equipment?

(d) is suitable temporary access readily available for emergency work?

(e) has training been given on safe use of ladders? (see 7.45 CONSTRUCTION AND BUILDING OPERATIONS, 46.34 WORK AT HEIGHTS)

(f) does supervision ensure that temporary access is correctly used?

(g) are working platforms regularly inspected for deterioration/dislodgement?

(Adapted from Dangerous Maintenance (HSE 1985)).

Main statutory requirements relating to maintenance – classified lists

(A) All workplaces

1.40 (1) plant/systems of work [*HSWA s 2(2)(a)*] (also at common law);

(2) places of work under employer's control/means of access and egress [*HSWA s 2(2)(d)*] (also at common law);

(3) working environment [*HSWA s 2(2)(d)*] (also at common law);

(4) access to electrical equipment and adequate lighting facilities [*Electricity at Work Regulations 1989, Reg 15*];

(5) control measures/protective equipment [*Control of Substances Hazardous to Health Regulations 1988, Reg 9*];

(6) equipment/devices/systems [*Workplace (Health, Safety and Welfare) Regulations 1992, Reg 5*], but not construction sites;

(7) floors/surfaces of traffic routes to ensure freedom of obstruction and to prevent slipping, falling and tripping [*Workplace (Health, Safety and Welfare) Regulations 1992, Reg 12*], but not construction sites;

(8) work equipment [*Provision and Use of Work Equipment Regulations 1992, Reg 7*];

23

(9)   guards on machinery [*Provision and Use of Work Equipment Regulations 1992, Reg 12*];

(10) safe means of access to areas of maintenance [*Supply of Machinery (Safety) Regulations 1992, 3 Sch*];

(11) all personal protective equipment (including offshore installations [*Personal Protective Equipment at Work Regulations 1992, Reg 7*];

(12) pressure systems [*Pressure Systems and Transportable Gas Containers Regulations 1989, Reg 12*] – wherever such equipment may be found;

(13) ear protection [*Noise at Work Regulations 1989, Reg 10*].

(B) Factories Act 1961 and Offices, Shops and Railway Premises Act 1963

(14) access to places of work [*Factories Act 1961, s 29(1)*];

(15) floors, steps, stairs, passages, gangways [*Factories Act 1961, s 28*];

(16) stairs affording means of exit [*Factories Act 1961, s 28(2)*];

(17) staircases with two open sides or liable to cause accidents [*Factories Act 1961, s 28(2); OSRPA s 16(2)*];

(18) ladders [*Factories Act 1961, s 28(5)*];

(19) reasonable temperature [*Factories Act 1961, s 3; OSRPA s 6*];

(20) effective means of drainage [*Factories Act 1961, s 6*];

(21) parts of machinery in use or motion [*Factories Act 1961, s 16*];

(22) guards on abrasive wheels [*Abrasive Wheels Regulations 1970, Reg 11*];

(23) guards on horizontal milling machines [*Horizontal Milling Machines Regulations 1928/1934, Reg 6*];

(24) woodworking machines [*Woodworking Machines Regulations 1974, Reg 42*];

(25) hoists/lifts (for carrying goods and people) [*Factories Act 1961, s 22*];

(26) effective devices for supporting platform/cage (hoists for carrying people only) [*Factories Act 1961, s 23(3)*];

(27) fencing of teagle openings [*Factories Act 1961, s 24(2)*];

(28) all parts of lifting machinery other than hoists and lifts (e.g. cranes) [*Factories Act 1961, s 27*];

(29) lifting tackle [*Factories Act 1961, s 26*];

(30) hoists/lifts suspended by ropes and chains [*Offices, Shops and Railway Premises (Hoists and Lifts) Regulations 1968, Reg 5*];

(31) efficient devices (automatic) for lifts for carrying people (either in addition to or in exclusion of goods) [*Offices, Shops and Railway Premises (Hoists and Lifts) Regulations 1968, Reg 9*];

(32) adequate lighting facilities [*Factories Act 1961, s 5*];

(33) adequate lighting facilities [*OSRPA s 8*];

(34) adequate lighting facilities [*Woodworking Machines Regulations 1974, Reg 43*];

(35) effective and suitable ventilation [*Factories Act 1961, s 4; OSRPA s 7*];

(36)   approved breathing apparatus, belts, ropes, reviving apparatus and oxygen cylinders [*Factories Act 1961, s 30(6)*].

(C) Fire risks

(37)   fire certificates – means of escape [*Fire Precautions Act 1971, ss 6, 12*];

(38)   means of escape, exempt premises [*Fire Precautions Act 1971, s 9A*];

(39)   gas appliances in industrial, commercial and domestic premises [*Gas Safety (Installation and Use) Regulations 1984, Reg 28*];

(40)   means of escape in the case of fire/fire fighting equipment [*Highly Flammable Liquids and Liquified Petroleum Gases Regulations 1972, Regs 12, 17*] – factories and other places where HFL and LPG is present;

(41)   storage tanks/vessels [*Highly Flammable Liquids and Liquefied Petroleum Gases Regulations 1972, Regs 5, 7*] – workplaces where HFL/LPG is present;

(42)   fire fighting equipment/safety curtain [*Theatres Act 1968*] – theatres;

(43)   fire appliances and safety curtains [*Cinematograph (Safety) Regulations 1955*] – cinemas.

(D) Building and construction sites

(44)   access to places of work [*Construction (Working Places) Regulations 1966, Reg 6*];

(45)   scaffolds, ladders [*Construction (Working Places) Regulations 1966, Regs 7, 11, 30, 31*];

(46)   head protection [*Construction (Head Protection) Regulations 1989, Reg 3*];

(47)   lifting operations [*Construction (Working Places) Regulations 1966, Reg 17*];

(48)   lighting of access/openings [*Construction (Working Places) Regulations 1966, Reg 47*];

(49)   ventilation in excavations/pits [*Construction (General Provisions) Regulations 1961, Reg 21*];

(50)   crawling boards [*Construction (Working Places) Regulations 1966, Reg 35*];

(51)   crawling ladders [*Construction (General Provisions) Regulations 1961, Reg 35*];

(52)   safety nets/sheets [*Construction (General Provisions) Regulations 1961, Reg 38*];

(53)   safe means of access/egress [*Construction (Health and Welfare) Regulations 1966, Reg 16*];

(54)   scaffolds/ladders [*Construction (General Provisions) Regulations 1961, Regs 7, 11*];

(55)   trestle scaffolds [*Construction (General Provisions) Regulations 1961, Reg 21*];

(56)   platforms/gangways for affording safe footholds [*Construction (General Provisions) Regulations 1961, Reg 30*];

(57)   ladders/folding step ladders [*Construction (General Provisions) Regulations 1961, Reg 31*];

(58)   locomotives [*Construction (General Provisions) Regulations 1961, Reg 26*];

(59)   mechanically propelled vehicles/trailers [*Construction (General Provisions) Regulations 1961, Reg 34*];

(60)   lifting appliances [*Construction (Lifting Operations) Regulations 1961, Reg 10*];

(61)   unobstructed passageways on stages/gantries [*Construction (Lifting Operations) Regulations 1961, Reg 12*];

(62)   cabins for drivers of power-driven lifting appliances [*Construction (Lifting Operations) Regulations 1961, Reg 14*];

(63)   rail-mounted cranes [*Construction (Lifting Operations) Regulations 1961, Reg 20*];

(64)   crane mountings [*Construction (Lifting Operations) Regulations 1961, Reg 21*];

(65)   platforms/cages in event of failure of hoists/ropes [*Construction (Lifting Operations) Regulations 1961, Reg 42*];

(66)   cofferdams [*Construction (General Provisions) Regulations 1961, Reg 15*];

(67)   Vessels for transporting water [*Construction (General Provisions) Regulations 1961, Reg 23*].

(E) Special cases

(68)   clean premises and hygienic handling methods [*Food Hygiene Regulations 1970*] – food manufacturing premises, wholesale and retail premises and premises catering to the public;

(69)   exhaust equipment [*Control of Asbestos at Work Regulations 1987, Reg 13*] – all workplaces involving asbestos processes;

(70)   control measures, personal protective equipment at work or other things or facilities in workplaces that may be affected by asbestos [*Control of Asbestos at Work Regulations 1987, Reg 10*];

(71)   all parts of offshore installations and their equipment [*Offshore Installations (Operational Safety, Health and Welfare) Regulations 1976, Reg 5*] – offshore installations;

(72)   guards on machinery on offshore installations [*Offshore Installations (Operational Safety, Health and Welfare) Regulations 1976, Reg 12*] – offshore installations;

(73)   sick bays on offshore installations [*Offshore Installations (Health, Safety and Welfare) Regulations 1976, Reg 27*];

(74)   drinking water [*Offshore Installations (Health, Safety and Welfare) Regulations 1976, Reg 25*];

(75)   field machinery [*Agriculture (Field Machinery) Regulations 1962, Reg 15*];

(76)   all cooling towers and evaporative condensers require notification to the local authority [*Notification of Cooling Towers and Evaporative Condensers Regulations 1992, Reg 3*] and there is a special need for high-level maintenance of this equipment [*Provision and Use of Work Equipment Regulations 1992*].

Maintenance on machinery

1.41   Recent legislation, in the form of the *Supply of Machinery (Safety) Regulations 1992*, and the *Provision and Use of Work Equipment Regulations 1992*, by way of acknowledgment of the number of accidents arising from maintenance operations on machinery, provides:

(a) in new workplaces as from 1 January 1993 and existing workplaces as from 1 January 1997, employers must ensure that machines are constructed or adapted for use so that, so far as is reasonably practicable, they can be maintained while the machine is shut down. Where this is not reasonably practicable, they must ensure that maintenance operations on the machine can be carried out without risk to the health and safety of persons involved, or, alternatively, there must be measures to protect them whilst carrying out maintenance on moving machines [*Provision and Use of Work Equipment 1992, Reg 22*];

(b) machinery must be designed/manufactured so as to enable maintenance to be carried out without the guard being dismantled (if possible) [*Supply of Machinery (Safety) Regulations 1992, 3 Sch*] – all workplaces (duty on manufacturer);

(c) if possible, maintenance should be carried out only when machinery is at a standstill [*Supply of Machinery (Safety) Regulations 1992, 3 Sch*] (duty on manufacturer).

Interrelationship of statutory and common law duties

Having examined the source and development of statutory and common law duties, it is now possible to consider certain aspects of the relationship between them.

'Statutory negligence'

1.42 Negligence, as we have seen, applies a general, universal duty of care. Many of the detailed statutory duties are no more than a specific statement of this duty in a particular context. For example, many of the specific duties contained in the *Factories Act 1961* relating to ventilation, access, safe place of work etc. formed part of the all-embracing duty of every employer to take reasonable care of his employees (see 1.20 above). However, certain statutory duties may require a higher standard of care than that required by the common law of negligence (for example, *Factories Act 1961, s 12(1)* which states simply that every flywheel directly connected to every prime mover, and every moving part of any prime mover, 'shall be securely fenced' – no test of foreseeable danger).

How far is breach of governmental standards a breach of common law duty?

1.43 It is tempting to assume that breach of statutory duty implies civil liability at common law for negligence. Indeed, although some American courts (addressing themselves to product liability actions) have styled breach of a governmental standard as being negligence *per se*, English courts seem less convinced. Thus, in *Boyle v Kodak Ltd [1969] 2 AER 439* Lord Diplock said, 'When considering the civil liability engrafted by judicial decision upon the criminal liability which has been imposed by statute, it is no good looking to the statute and seeing from it where the criminal liability would lie, for we are concerned only with civil liability. We must look to the cases.' This seems to mean that criminal liability is not evidence of negligence (nor *res ipsa loquitur*, see 1.24 above), and that a claimant must prove the three conditions for negligence (see 1.22 above) if he is to succeed in his action for damages on the ground of negligence alone. This notwithstanding, breach of safety regulations, even if silent, are actionable (i.e. give rise to civil liability *per se*) (see 1.18 above).

Breach of statutory duty — the 'double-barrelled' action

1.44   The recognition of a civil action for damages for breach of statutory duty, irrespective of any right of action for negligence, has led to the so-called 'double-barrelled' action against an employer, traceable back to the decision in *Kilgollan v Cooke & Co Ltd [1956] 1 AER 294* (a case concerning the fencing requirements of the *Factories Act 1937*). In such a 'double-barrelled' action, the employee sues for damages simultaneously but separately on grounds of:

(a)   negligence; and

(b)   breach of a relevant statutory duty.

Exclusion of civil liability for breach of general statutory duties
Sec 47 of the *Health and Safety at Work etc. Act 1974* provides that:

(a)   a breach of any of the general duties in *Secs 2-8* will *not* give rise to civil liability (though, as these provisions are drawn from the negligence rules at common law, it seems likely that there would in any case, in the event of breach, be a corresponding liability for negligence); and

(b)   breach of any duty contained in health and safety regulations made under the Act *will* give rise to civil liability, unless the regulations state otherwise (see 1.18 above).

How far are the detailed standards minimal requirements?

1.45   Finally, it is very much arguable that specific safety requirements, e.g. those laid down in the regulations, should be regarded as minimum standards (unless by their very terms they impose a standard far in excess of the standard of care likely to be taken by the reasonable man). The general duties of the common law, and of *HSWA*, are not limited in scope and may thus require rather more than the specific standard. The case of *Bux v Slough Metals Ltd [1974] 1 AER 262* provides a clear example – the employer was held to have complied with his specific statutory duty to 'provide' goggles for the employee, but was held liable for damages for breach of his general common law duties in failing to supervise the employee adequately to ensure that the employee wore them. Employers should accordingly bear in mind that compliance with any specific statutory standards should be their minimum aim, and may not of itself be enough to avoid liability.

Effect of insurance on civil liability

1.46   Given that it is only possible to insure against civil liability, as distinct from criminal liability (and then only against tortious as distinct from contractual liability), it seems no exaggeration to concede that, since the introduction of compulsory employers' liability insurance for work injuries/diseases by the *Employers' Liability (Compulsory Insurance) Act 1969*, civil liability has been growing progressively stricter. In consequence, damages have been awarded in circumstances where, at times at any rate, it seems that the risk of injury was not reasonably foreseeable (see test of negligence, 1.22 above). Indeed, one cannot avoid the conclusion that, given the 'guarantee' of the deposit of a fund of insurance moneys (in the wake of compulsory liability insurance), judges are much more predisposed to 'invite' insurers to shell out to the victims of work (and road and medical) injuries. This shift in emphasis was quintessentially identified by Lord Denning MR in *Nettleship v Weston [1971] 3 AER 581* (a road traffic injury case, involving a learner driver): 'Thus we are moving away from the concept "No liability without fault". We are beginning to apply the test – "On whom should the risk fall?"'

Morally the learner driver is not at fault but legally she is liable to be because she is insured and the risk should fall on her'. This then is a clear signpost on the road towards 'no fault' compensation.

No fault compensation

1.47 Recently, the British Medical Association (BMA) has argued for a £100 million no fault compensation scheme for victims of (most) medical accidents in order to ensure quicker and fairer settlements. Aimed at avoiding lengthy and expensive litigation, under such a scheme capital sums could be paid to claimants, based on the injured victim's *needs*, irrespective of fault or negligence. Given that medical accidents are generally more serious than other classes of accidents, most medical accident victims would be eligible for up to £25,000 to compensate for pain/suffering and temporary absence from work; whilst those with permanent disabling injuries (e.g. brain damage) would be awarded a capital sum large enough to generate a minimum of £10,000 annually for the rest of their lives. A similar no fault system is also planned for some road injuries.

As for non-medical injuries, particularly work injuries, it has been recommended that the main source of compensation be social security payments, whilst tort/negligence moneys be retained only as a means of topping up social security benefits (Report of the Royal Commission on Civil Liability and Compensation for Personal Injury, Vol 1, para 937). More particularly, the 'existence of a substantial no fault scheme for industrial accidents, and the significant body of opinion which has drawn attention to the adverse effects of the tort system in the field of accident prevention, prompt serious consideration of the abolition of the tort action as a means of providing compensation for work accidents' (para 906).

Main shortcomings of the negligence (or fault) system

1.48 1. It lays too much emphasis on the behaviour of the defendant (i.e. culpability) rather than the suffering of the plaintiff.

2. It is liability-oriented rather than accident-compensation oriented, and so adversarial.

3. It is not related to the need of the plaintiff or to the defendant's ability to pay, but relies on liability insurance.

4. It aspires to deter the defendant from further acts of negligence, by imposition of damages; imposition of 'penalties', however, is the hallmark of criminal law.

5. Since social security benefits are payable almost immediately after injury at work (see Chapter 6 'Compensation for Work Injuries/Diseases'), whilst personal injury damages are payable much later, the fault system would probably have collapsed in the absence of a framework of compulsory liability insurance. However, structured settlements may eventually become the norm for accident victims, whereby they would receive monthly payments (see 6.11 COMPENSATION FOR WORK INJURIES/DISEASES).

Recent health and safety regulations

Latest statutory developments

1.49 1. The *Health and Safety (Enforcing Authority) Regulations 1989 (SI 1989 No 1903)* added the following 'activities' to the list of premises specified in the original

Health and Safety (Enforcing Authority) Regulations 1977 which are inspected (for enforcement purposes), by local authorities:

(*a*)   display or demonstration of goods at exhibitions;

(*b*)   cosmetic or therapeutic treatments;

(*c*)   sports, cultural or recreational activities;

(*d*)   hiring out of pleasure craft for use on inland waters;

(*e*)   care, treatment, accommodation or exhibition of animals;

(*f*)   funeral parlours and undertaking activities;

(*g*)   church worship or religious meetings.

(For a full list of 'activities' enforced currently by HSE and local authorities, see Chapter 17 'Enforcement'.)

2.   The *Noise at Work Regulations 1989 (SI 1989 No 1790)* require employers, where noise exposure exceeds 85 dB(A) over a working day, to make formal noise assessments, give employees information about their working conditions and issue personal ear protection on request. Where exposure levels exceed 90 dB(A), employers must reduce noise, where reasonably practicable, designate ear protection zones and ensure employees have and wear ear protectors. Correspondingly, employees must co-operate, by wearing ear protectors above exposures of 90 dB(A), as well as using properly any other noise control equipment and report any defects in it (see Chapter 30 'Noise and Vibration').

3.   The *Electricity at Work Regulations 1989 (SI 1989 No 635)* impose health and safety requirements with regard to electricity at work, thereby replacing the previous *Electricity Regulations 1908-1944* (see Chapter 11 'Electricity').

4.   Arguably the most important regulations since the *Health and Safety at Work etc. Act 1974* itself, the *Control of Substances Hazardous to Health Regulations 1988 (SI 1988 No 1657)* (otherwise known as *COSHH*), require employers to protect employees from 'substances hazardous to health' (other than lead, radiation and asbestos – covered elsewhere) by carrying out formal assessments, monitoring exposure, providing on-going instruction to employees and health surveillance, including regular medical checks and keeping health records (see Chapter 9 'Dangerous Substances I'). Amendment *SI 1990 No 2026* introduces new maximum exposure limits for benzene, acrylamide and an additional maximum exposure limit for man-made mineral fibres; maximum exposure limits for ethylene dibromide, arsenic and rubber fumes are amended; and the maximum exposure limit for 1-methoxy-2-propanol is removed. Amendment *SI 1991 No 2431* adds benzene to the list of prohibited carcinogens; whilst amendment *SI 1992 No 2382* seeks to control exposure to carcinogens. Biological agents are to be added by the new *Schedule 11* by 1 January 1994.

5.   All sickness and disablement benefits paid or payable to an injured worker, within five years immediately following his injury, are deductible *in full* from subsequently awarded damages including general damages, except damages for fatal injuries. [*Social Security Act 1989, s 22*]. This does not, however, affect insurance moneys paid or payable under a personal accident insurance policy (*Bradburn v Great Western Railway (1874) LR 10 Exch 1*). In addition, the person making compensation (usually an insurance company) must pay to the Secretary of State an amount equal to that which is required to be deducted. [*Sec 22(1)(b)*].

6.   Public registers must be kept of notices served on premises by HSE inspectors and environmental health officers, under the requirements of the *Environment*

and Safety Information Act 1988 (see further Chapter 17 'Enforcement'). There is similar provision regarding operations breaching the *Environmental Protection Act 1990* (see further Chapter 12 'Emissions into the Atmosphere').

7. The *Health and Safety (Emissions into the Atmosphere) (Amendment) Regulations 1989 (SI 1989 No 319)* increase the classes of premises from which emissions into the atmosphere can be controlled to include certain asbestos works, large combustion works, electricity works above a specified capacity, fibre works, large glass works, large paper pulp works and large general purpose incinerators, including those owned and operated by public authorities. There are also additions to the list of 'noxious or offensive substances' (see Chapter 12 'Emissions into the Atmosphere').

8. The *Control of Industrial Air Pollution (Registration of Works) Regulations 1989 (SI 1989 No 318)* modify the system of registration of works specified by the *Alkali etc. Works Regulation Act 1906*, requiring applications for certificates of registration of such works to be advertised as well as giving the general public access to such applications (see Chapter 12 'Emissions into the Atmosphere').

9. The *Environmental Protection Act 1990* establishes a system of integrated pollution control, to be administered by HM Inspectorate of Pollution and (in the case of air pollution) local authorities, for certain specified processes, as well as a system of prior authorisations in place of the former presumptive limits and best practicable means (see further Chapter 12 'Emissions into the Atmosphere').

10. The *Environmental Protection (Prescribed Processes and Substances) Regulations 1991 (SI 1991 No 472)* specify processes which require prior authorisation for operation.

11. The *Health and Safety Information for Employees Regulations 1989 (SI 1989 No 682)* stipulate that information relating to health, safety and welfare be given to employees, by means of posters or leaflets, including the name/address of the relevant local enforcing authority.

12. The *Health and Safety at Work etc. Act 1974 (Application outside Great Britain) Order 1989 (SI 1989 No 840)* extends the operation of the *Health and Safety at Work Act* to offshore installations and pipelines.

13. The *Offshore Installations (Safety Representatives and Safety Committees) Regulations 1989 (SI 1989 No 971)* provide for the elections of safety representatives on offshore installations, with powers similar to their on-shore counterparts.

14. The *Fire Precautions (Factories, Offices, Shops and Railway Premises) Order 1989 (SI 1989 No 76)* requires that a fire certificate must be applied for when more than 20 people are at work, or more than 10 elsewhere than on the ground floor; the *Fire Precautions (Application for Certificate) Regulations 1989 (SI 1989 No 77)* prescribed a new form of application for a fire certificate under the *Fire Precautions Act 1971* (see Chapter 19 'Fire and Fire Precautions'); and the *Fire Precautions (Non-Certificated Factory, Office, Shop and Railway Premises) (Revocation) Regulations 1989 (SI 1989 No 78)* revoked the *Fire Precautions (Non-Certificated Factory, Office, Shop and Railway Premises) Order 1976 (SI 1976 No 2010)* (see Chapter 19 'Fire and Fire Precautions').

15. The *Pressure Systems and Transportable Gas Containers Regulations 1989 (SI 1989 No 2169)* repeal *Secs 32, 33, 35* and *36* of the *Factories Act 1961* relating to steam boilers, steam receivers, air receivers etc. and require periodic examination of pressure systems.

16. The *Construction (Head Protection) Regulations 1989 (SI 1989 No 2209)* require the wearing of head protection on construction sites (with the exception of Sikhs).

17. The *Road Traffic (Carriage of Explosives) Regulations 1989 (SI 1989 No 615)* impose certain requirements and prohibitions on persons carrying explosives by road.

18. The *Food Safety Act 1990* places tighter controls on unfit and unsafe food and enforcement procedures are extended to possession for sale as well as sale itself.

19. The *Food Premises (Registration) Regulations 1991 (SI 1991 No 2825)* provide for the registration of food premises, creating criminal offences in relation to the use of unregistered premises.

20. The *Gas Safety (Installation and Use) (Amendment) Regulations 1990 (SI 1990 No 824)* require that gas fitters, whether employees or self-employed persons, be competent and members of an HSE-approved body (e.g. CORGI).

21. The *Health and Safety (Training for Employment) Regulations 1990 (SI 1990 No 1380)* extend the protection of *HSWA* to trainees, though not if training is provided in an educational establishment or training is part of the contract of employment.

22. The *Damages for Bereavement (Variation of Sum) (England and Wales) Order 1990 (SI 1990 No 2575)* increases the statutory sum for bereavement to £7,500 (from £3,500).

23. The *Control of Explosives Regulations 1991 (SI 1991 No 1531)* place new requirements on persons keeping explosives, including making and keeping satisfactory records.

24. The *Road Traffic (Training of Drivers of Vehicles Carrying Dangerous Goods) Regulations 1992 (SI 1992 No 744)* require operators of vehicles carrying dangerous goods/substances (chemicals, explosives, radioactive material) to ensure that drivers have received adequate instruction/training in the dangers involved.

25. The *Construction Products Regulations 1991 (SI 1991 No 1620)* require that construction products, when incorporated in design and building, satisfy the following criteria (namely, (*a*) mechanical resistance and stability, (*b*) safety in case of fire, (*c*) hygiene, health and environment, (*d*) safety in use, (*e*) noise protection and (*f*) energy economy and heat retention).

26. The *Environmental Protection (Controls on Injurious Substances) Regulations 1992 (SI 1992 No 31)* prohibit the supply and use of lead carbonate/lead sulphate for use as paint as well as mercury compounds for use in heavy duty industrial textiles.

27. The *Road Traffic (Carriage of Dangerous Substances in Road Tankers and Tank Containers) Regulations 1992 (SI 1992 No 743)* impose new controls on operators of vehicles carrying dangerous substances in bulk by road.

28. The *Road Traffic (Carriage of Dangerous Substances in Packages, etc.) Regulations 1992 (SI 1992 No 742)* impose updated controls on operators of vehicles carrying dangerous substances in packages.

29. The *Packaging of Explosives for Carriage Regulations 1991 (SI 1991 No 2097)* impose requirements on operators packaging explosives for road transportation.

30. The *Management of Health and Safety at Work Regulations 1992 (SI 1992 No 2051)* require employers to assess risks to employees, provide them with necessary health surveillance and appoint competent persons to monitor the health and safety of employees.

31. The *Offshore Safety Act 1992* increases maximum fines, on summary

conviction, for breach of *Secs 2–6* of the *Health and Safety at Work etc. Act 1974*, to £20,000 (as from £5,000); and makes the *Mineral Workings (Offshore Installations) Act 1971* (and regulations made under it) enforceable by HSE.

32. The *Health and Safety (Display Screen Equipment) Regulations 1992 (SI 1992 No 2792)* require employers to assess the risks to users of display screens (VDUs), provide software which is suitable and carry out eyesight tests for employees free of charge.

33. The *Manual Handling Operations Regulations 1992 (SI 1992 No 2793)* (by way of replacement of *Factories Act 1961, s 72* and *OSRPA s 23*) require employers to obviate the need for employees to lift heavy loads.

34. The *Personal Protective Equipment at Work Regulations 1992 (SI 1992 No 2966)* require employers to assess the personal protection needs of their employees and provide them with suitable personal protective equipment to EC certification level.

35. The *Personal Protective Equipment (EC Directive) Regulations 1992 (SI 1992 No 3139)* require manufacturers to produce personal protective equipment to EC certification level.

36. The *Provision and Use of Work Equipment Regulations 1992 (SI 1992 No 2932)* require employers to provide machinery that is free from health and safety risks during foreseeable use.

37. The *Supply of Machinery (Safety) Regulations 1992 (SI 1992 No 3073)* require manufacturers to design and produce machinery for use at work which, during the course of foreseeable use, is safe and free from health risks.

38. The *Workplace (Health, Safety and Welfare) Regulations 1992 (SI 1992 No 3004)* impose requirements on employers with respect to structural safety in workplaces and hygiene and welfare provision.

39. The *Offshore Installations (Safety Case) Regulations 1992 (SI 1992 No 2885)* require operators of offshore installations to prepare and revise safety cases (i.e. information relating to management of general health and safety and control of major accident hazards), submitting same to HSE.

40. The *Public Information for Radiation Emergencies Regulations 1992 (SI 1992 No 2997)* require operators of nuclear sites to inform the public about the dangers of possible radiation leaks, in conjunction with local authorities.

41. The *Offshore Safety Act 1992* increases maximum fines, on summary conviction, for breach of *Secs 2–6* of the *Health and Safety at Work etc. Act 1974*, to £20,000 (as from £5,000); and makes the *Mineral Workings (Offshore Installations) Act 1971* (and regulations made under it) enforceable by HSE.

42. The *Trade Union Reform and Employment Rights Act 1993 (TURERA)*, apart from specifying written particulars which employers must supply to employees within two months of commencement of employment, prevent employees from being 'subjected to detriment' for participation in health and safety activities and for drawing dangers to their employer's attention; in addition, dismissal for health and safety involvement is generally deemed to be unfair.

43. The *Radioactive Substances Act 1993* requires occupiers of premises to register premises containing radioactive substances and mobile radioactive apparatus and acquire authorisation for disposal; penalties include a maximum fine of £20,000 on summary conviction, and an indefinite fine and/or up to five years' imprisonment on conviction on indictment.

44. The *Chemicals (Hazard Information and Packaging) Regulations 1993 (SI 1993 No 1746)*, which came into force on 1 September 1993, require suppliers of dangerous substances to classify them and prepare and revise safety data material.

45. The *Social Security (Industrial Injuries) (Prescribed Diseases) Amendment (No 2) Regulations 1993 (SI 1993 No 1985)*, which came into force on 13 September 1993, provide for the prescription of chronic bronchitis and emphysema as occupational diseases, where either or both conditions have been contracted as a result of working underground in a coal mine for twenty years.

Chapter 2

Access

Introduction

2.1 With the regular daily flow of labour to and from the workplace and vehicles making deliveries and collecting, access and egress points constitute potentially hazardous situations. For this reason there is a duty on employers and factory occupiers to 'provide and maintain' safe access to and egress from a place of work both under statute and at common law. As part and parcel of compliance with the *Building Regulations 1991*, this includes access facilities for disabled workers and visitors (that is, persons who have difficulty walking or are in a wheelchair, or, alternatively, have a hearing problem or impaired vision) (see further 18.13 FACTORIES AND WORKPLACES). Statutory requirements consist of general duties under *HSWA*, which apply to all employers, and the more specific duties of the *Workplace (Health, Safety and Welfare) Regulations 1992*; in addition, existing factories are 'serviced' by the relevant provisions of the *Factories Act 1961* until 1 January 1996.

2.2 The term 'access' is a comprehensive one and refers to just about anything that can reasonably be regarded as means of entrance/exit to a workplace, even if it is not the usual method of access/egress. Unreasonable means of access/egress would not be included, such as a dangerous short-cut, particularly if management has drawn a worker's attention to the danger, though the fact that a worker is a trespasser does not prevent his recovering damages (*Westwood v The Post Office [1973] 3 AER 184*) (see further 33.4 OFFICES). The proper procedure is for the employer/factory occupier to designate points of access/egress for workers and see that they are safe, well-lit, maintained and (if necessary) manned and de-iced. Moreover, the statutory duties apply to access/egress points to any place where any employees have to work, and not merely their normal workplace.

This chapter summarises the key duties, both at common law and statutory, in connection with safe means of access and egress and vehicular traffic routes for both internal traffic and deliveries. Requirements relating to work in confined spaces are also summarised, as necessarily involving access and egress points.

Common law duty of care

2.3 At common law every employer owes all his employees a duty to provide and maintain safe means of access to and egress from places of work. Moreover, this duty extends to the workforce of another employer/contractor who happens to be working temporarily on the premises, by analogy with *Mersey Docks & Harbour Board v Coggins & Griffiths (Liverpool) Ltd [1947] AC 1* (see further Chapter 15 'Employers' Duties'). Although specifically referred to in the leading case on employers' common law liability of *Wilsons & Clyde Coal Co Ltd v English [1938] AC 57 (at p 80)* by Lord Wright, this common law duty is part of the general duty placed by common law upon everyone (not just employers) to take reasonable care in respect of others who may be foreseeably injured (*Donoghue v Stevenson [1932] AC 562*) (see further 38.17 PRODUCT SAFETY). Hence the common law duty covers all workplaces, out of doors as well as indoors, above ground or below and extends to factories, mines, schools, universities, aircraft, ships, buses and even fire engines and appliances (*Cox v Angus [1981] ICR 683* where a fireman injured in a cab was entitled to damages at common law).

Internal traffic and deliveries

2.4   There should be sufficient traffic routes to allow vehicles to circulate safely and without difficulty. As for internal traffic, lines in buildings should clearly indicate where vehicles are to pass, e.g. fork lift trucks. Obstructions, such as limited headroom (existing prior to 1993), are acceptable so long as clearly indicated. Temporary obstacles should be brought to the attention of drivers by warning signs or hazard cones or, alternatively, access prevented or restricted. Both internal traffic and delivery traffic should be subject to sensible speed limits (e.g. 10 mph), which should be clearly displayed. Speed ramps (sleeping policemen), preceded by a warning sign or mark, are a wise investment, save for fork lift trucks, on workplace approaches. The traffic route should be wide enough to allow vehicles to pass oncoming or parked traffic and it may be advisable to introduce one way systems or parking restrictions.

Checklist for deliveries

2.5   1.   Avoid sharp or blind bends – if not possible, indicate hazard (e.g. blind corner).

2.   Give prominent warning of limited headroom.

3.   Shield overhead obstructions (e.g. electric cables).

4.   Fence or otherwise protect any edges/slopes along the route.

5.   If possible, use one way traffic flow systems.

6.   Restrict reversing to places/bays where it can be done safely.

7.   Employ banksmen to supervise safe movement of vehicles.

8.   Fit reversing alarms to alert drivers of obstruction or obstacle.

9.   Ensure that pedestrians and disabled persons are well away.

10.   Provide high visibility clothing for people permitted in the area (e.g. bright jackets/overalls).

11.   Try not to use routes at shift times when they are more likely to be crowded.

12.   Segregate vehicular from pedestrian traffic through tunnels, bridges, gateways.

13.   Provide loading bay with at least one exit point from lower level; wide loading bays should have at least two exit points, one at each end.

14.   Install adequate lighting along external roadways, particularly in winter, in loading bays, pedestrian walkways and parking areas.

Thus, as from 1 January 1993, every new workplace and, as from 1 January 1996, every existing workplace (so far as reasonably practicable) must be so organised that pedestrians and vehicles can circulate in a safe manner. [*Workplace (Health, Safety and Welfare) Regulations 1992, Reg 17(1)*].

Traffic routes

2.6   Traffic routes must be

(*a*)   suitable for vehicles;

(*b*)   in a suitable position;

(*c*)   of sufficient number;

(*d*)   of sufficient size.

[*Workplace (Health, Safety and Welfare) Regulations 1992, Reg 17(2)*]. (This requirement applies in *existing* factories/workplaces, as far as reasonably practicable only.)

More particularly,

(i)   vehicles must be able to use route without endangering persons working near it;

(ii)   vehicular traffic route must be segregated from (*a*) doors, (*b*) gates or (*c*) pedestrian traffic routes leading onto it;

(iii) where vehicles and pedestrians use the same route, they must be sufficiently segregated;

(iv)   traffic routes must be clearly indicated.

[*Workplace (Health, Safety and Welfare) Regulations 1992, Reg 17(3)–(5)*].

Existing factories – statutory duties under the Factories Act 1961 – requirement until 1 January 1996

2.7   Specific provision is made in the *Factories Act 1961, s 29(1)* (remaining in force until 1 January 1996) for safe access to places of work in factories (for the definition of 'factory', see Chapter 18 'Factories and Workplaces'). This section requires that, so far as is reasonably practicable (see Chapter 15 'Employers' Duties'), factory occupiers must 'provide and maintain' safe means of access to every place at which any person has at any time to work. The duty to keep a place of work safe is strict and liability is not referable to reasonable foreseeability (*Larner v British Steel plc, The Times, 19 February 1993*, concerning an experienced mechanical fitter injured when working on equipment in the steel-making process, which the respondents knew to be cracked. It was held that the employer was strictly liable for breach of statutory duty; nor was it necessary for an employee to show that the danger was reasonably foreseeable). In order for employers to avert liability, it is necessary for them to show that it was not reasonably practicable to make and keep the place of work safe. There is, therefore, a distinction between statutory and common law liability in relation to a safe place of work.

Access must be 'to' a place of work (*Davies v de Havilland Aircraft Ltd [1950] 2 AER 582* where the employee was injured when he slipped on a patch of oily water in a passageway leading from the shopfloor to the works canteen. His claim for damages for breach of (what is now) *Factories Act 1961, s 29(1)* failed on the ground that the passageway was not a means of access *to* a place of work. It would have been otherwise had the employee been coming from the canteen to the workbench). The duty relates to access to and egress from all places at which any person (e.g. indirect employee) *has at any time to work*. Thus, ditches, roofs, chimneys, window-sills, planks, stairways will all qualify. Temporary as well as permanent means of access must be safe, so far as reasonably practicable. Thus, in *Darby v GKN Screws & Fasteners [1986] ICR 1* the plaintiff fell on ice in front of the entrance to a factory door at 7.45 a.m. This entrance had not been salted. The salting gang had come on duty at 7.30 a.m. and had salted the most dangerous parts first, which did not include the entrance to the door. It was held that failure to salt all approaches to the factory was not a breach of the *Factories Act 1961, s 29(1)*. Although the means of access need not be to the normal place of work, access and/or egress must be to some place incidental to work (see *Hemmings v British Aerospace Ltd* below). In *Hemmings v British Aerospace Ltd, The Times, 2 May 1986* the employee slipped on ice and injured himself whilst using a path to attend a union meeting at a factory canteen. He sued the employer for failing to institute and maintain a system of ice-clearance, in breach of the *Factories Act 1961, s 29(1)*. It was held that the path was access to a place of work and the employer was liable. Safe means of access/egress must be 'provided and maintained'. 'Maintained' means 'maintained in an efficient state, in working order, and in good repair'. [*Factories Act 1961, s 176(1)*]. However, not every area need be gritted by the start of the working day (*Gitsham v CH Pearce & Sons plc, The Times, 11 February 1991* where an employee fell on an ungritted roadway at 8.45 am. The employers had an extensive procedure for clearing snow and ice on access roads. It was held that the employer was not liable).

2.8 Moreover, means of access/egress can be or become unsafe, not merely structurally but owing to dangerous activities and equipment carried on or operating there. It has been shown that liability arises not only in respect of physical injuries but also occupational deafness, if not too remote (*Nixon v Searle & Co, The Times, 21 December 1981* where a defective cylinder exploded, causing the employee partial deafness. It was held that the cylinder was permanent equipment, having been in situ in the factory for nine years, and the employer was liable for breach of *Sec 29(1)*). Although the scope of *Sec 29(1)* is potentially quite wide, the means of access/egress must have been approved by the employer; otherwise it is not regarded as 'provided' (*Smith v British Aerospace Ltd [1982] ICR 98* where an aircraft inspector used a set of portable steps instead of fixed steps. He struck his head and lacerated his scalp. The employer was held not to be liable).

Persons protected by the Factories Act 1961, s 29(1)

2.9 Means of access/egress must be safe for any person working in the factory (for the meaning of 'factory', see Chapter 18 'Factories and Workplaces'). As with *Sec 28(1)*, this extends protection to persons other than direct employees. It includes employees of outside contractors and labour-only subcontractors working on factory premises (*Dexter v Tenby Electrical Accessories Ltd, The Times, 10 March 1991* where an employee of a contractor was injured on a roof, where he had been told to work. It was held that the occupier was liable). It (almost certainly) does not include persons doing their own work on factory premises, e.g. firemen, policemen, factory inspectors. Although, particularly in the case of firemen, the law cannot be considered settled (see *Flannigan v British Dyewood Co Ltd 1970 SLT 285* where a fireman was seriously injured whilst fighting a fire on factory premises). Such persons, essentially doing their own work on factory premises, would be advised to sue under the *Occupiers' Liability Act 1957* (see Chapter 32 'Occupiers' Liability'). They are, of course, owed a duty of care under *HSWA s 3(1)*, but breach of this section does not give rise to civil liability.

Access and egress hazards

2.10 *HSWA s 2(2)(d)* is concerned with regulating access and egress to 'any place of work'. That place of work could be the machine shop of a factory, the working platform to a scaffold 50 metres above ground level or a coal face a mile or more below ground level. Typical hazards associated with a failure to provide safe means of access and egress to a workplace include defective floors and staircases, inadequate factory traffic systems, the risk of falls from heights and down unfenced shafts in mines. The legal requirements relating to these aspects are dealt with in Chapter 7 'Construction and Building Operations' and Chapter 46 'Work at Heights'.

Confined spaces

2.11   Accidents and fatalities (see, for instance, the case of *Baker v Hopkins* (15.39 EMPLOYERS' DUTIES)), such as drowning, poisoning by fumes or gassing, have happened as a result of working in confined spaces. Normal safe practice is a formalised permit to work system (see 1.32–1.37 INTRODUCTION) or checklist tailored to a particular task together with appropriate and sufficient variety of personal protective equipment. Hazards typical of this sort of operation are:

(*a*)   atmospheric hazards – oxygen deficiency, enrichment (see *R v Swan Hunter Shipbuilders Ltd* (7.37 CONSTRUCTION AND BUILDING OPERATIONS)), toxic gases (e.g. carbon monoxide) (see also 10.11 DANGEROUS SUBSTANCES II), explosive atmospheres (e.g. methane in sewers);

(*b*)   physical hazards – low entry headroom or low working headroom, protruding pipes, wet surfaces underfoot as well as any electrical or mechanical hazards;

(*c*)   chemical hazards – concentration of toxic gas can quickly build up, where there is a combination of chemical cleaning substances and restricted air flow or movement.

In order to combat this variety of hazards peculiar to work in confined spaces, use of both gas detection equipment and suitable personal protective equipment are a prerequisite, since entry/exit paths are necessarily restricted.

Prior to entry, gas checks should test for (*a*) oxygen deficiency/enrichment, then (*b*) combustible gas and (*c*) toxic gas, by detection equipment being lowered into the space. This will determine the nature of personal protective equipment necessary. If gas is present in any quantity, the offending space should then be either naturally or mechanically ventilated. Where gas is present, entry should only take place in emergencies, subject to the correct respiratory protective equipment being worn. Assuming gas checks establish that there is no gaseous atmosphere, entry can then be made without use of respiratory equipment; any atmospheric change subsequently registering on the gas detection equipment.

Statutory requirements relating to work in confined spaces – Factories Act 1961, s 30 (not repealed)

2.12   A confined space is any

(i)   chamber,

(ii)   tank,

(iii)   vat,

(iv)   pit,

(v)   flue etc.

Hence typical spaces are tunnels, silos, storage tanks, sewers and manholes. In addition to a formalised permit to work system, the following precautions must be taken:

(*a*)   where there is no adequate means of egress from the confined space, a manhole must be provided of a minimum size [*Sec 30(2)*];

(*b*)   a responsible person must certify that the space is safe for entry for a specified length of time without the use of breathing apparatus [*Sec 30(4)*];

(*c*)   where the space is not certified as safe, no one must enter or remain in the space unless he is wearing breathing apparatus, has authority to enter and, where practicable, is wearing a safety belt attached to a rope under the control of a person outside the space who keeps watch [*Sec 30(3)*];

(*d*)   there must be sufficient trained persons to use the apparatus available during the operation [*Sec 30(7)*];

(*e*)   a supply of approved breathing apparatus, belts, ropes, reviving apparatus and oxygen must be kept available and adequately maintained, including thorough examination at least once per month [*Sec 30(6)*].

(See also Chapter 36 'Personal Protective Equipment'.)

Checklist for entry

2.13   1. Gas detection equipment.

2. Respiratory protective equipment.

3. Other suitable additional personal protective equipment (e.g. alarm).

4. Communications equipment (for contacting the outside world).

5. Harnesses (for hiking up).

6. Rescue and resuscitation equipment.

Access/egress requirements for particular industries/processes

The following access/egress requirements apply to specific industries/processes.

Construction sites

2.14   So far as reasonably practicable, there must be suitable and sufficient safe access to and egress from every place at which any person at any time works; moreover, such access/egress must be properly maintained (for the meaning of 'properly maintained', see Chapter 15 'Employers' Duties'). [*Construction (Working Places) Regulations 1966, Reg 6(1)*].

In addition, every place at which any person at any time works, must, so far as is reasonably practicable, be made and kept safe for any person working there. [*Construction (Working Places) Regulations 1966, Reg 6(2)*].

A means of access is not sufficient and safe 'if it is a possible cause of injury to anybody acting in a way in which a person of the type who will use the means of access may reasonably be expected to act in circumstances which may reasonably be expected to occur' (*Trott v W E Smith* [*1957*] *1 WLR 1154*) (see also the definition of 'dangerous' machinery in *Walker v Bletchley-Flettons Ltd* in Chapter 28 'Machinery Safety').

Employers (who are also contractors) do not owe duties under *Regulation 6* to the employees of subcontractors, local authorities etc. (see further 7.11 CONSTRUCTION AND BUILDING OPERATIONS).

Lifting operations on construction sites

2.15 Where any person is engaged on the examination, repair or lubrication of any lifting appliance and is liable to fall more than two metres, there must be provided and maintained safe means of access to/egress from the place at which the person has to work, including adequate handholds and footholds (where necessary). [*Construction (Lifting Operations) Regulations 1961, Reg 17 as amended*].

Operations with electricity

2.16 In order to avoid injury, adequate working space and adequate means of access must be provided at all electrical equipment on which or near which work is being done which could cause danger. [*Electricity at Work Regulations 1989, Reg 15*].

Chapter 3

Accident Reporting

Scope of problem

3.1 Large scale losses, such as King's Cross and Piper Alpha, along with hefty compensation payments for injury/disease at work, are automatically mediagenic and grab headlines. This, however, is only the tip of a jumbo-sized iceberg. The fact is that incidence of reported routine accidents, which injure but do not kill, damage plant, cause business interruption losses and result in lost time and lost orders, costs industry annually some £700 million. In 1990, for instance,1.6 million injury-causing accidents occurred and 750,000 workers took time off through ill-health. The *overall* cost involved (excluding social security payments) lay somewhere between £4,000 and £9,000 million, including liability insurance payments, costs of recruitment and training and property losses.

Reporting of Injuries, Diseases and Dangerous Occurrences Regulations 1985 (RIDDOR)

3.2 There are obligations on employers and other 'responsible persons' who have control over employees and work premises to notify and report to the relevant enforcing authorities accidents, both fatal and non-fatal, which occur at work, as well as occupational diseases and dangerous occurrences. Approximately 1.5 million work-related injuries occur per year, some half million of which are caught by *RIDDOR* (below). Of these 60% went to hospital and 4% were detained for more than 24 hours. Work-related injuries and ill-health are responsible for around 29 million days off work per annum – that is, just over one day for every worker. Over two-fifths of reported major injuries are caused by falls from a height and a third of reported over-3-day injuries are caused by handling accidents. In sum, there are about 360 fatal accidents per working year.

The *Reporting of Injuries, Diseases and Dangerous Occurrences Regulations 1985 (RIDDOR) (SI 1985 No 2023)* specify reportable work injuries, including occupational diseases (3.12 below) and some gas injuries (3.17 below). There is also a duty on an employer to keep an Accident Book (form BI 510). However, the procedure whereby any absences from work over three days due to work injury were reported to the DSS has been changed, and such absences are now directly reportable to the HSE or enforcing authority (see 3.10 below). In addition, the *Regulations* apply not only to accidents but to 'near accidents' or 'dangerous occurrences' (see 3.9 and Appendix A below).

There are also existing obligations to notify the HSE of accidents caused by dangerous substances. These requirements are covered at 8.8 CONTROL OF INDUSTRIAL MAJOR ACCIDENT HAZARDS. If, in relation to such an accident, the requirements in this chapter are followed, it will be deemed to be sufficient compliance for the purposes of the *Control of Industrial Major Accident Hazards Regulations 1984 (CIMAH) (SI 1984 No 1902)*.

Duty to report/notify

Duty to report

3.3   Whenever any of the following occurs, a responsible person (see 3.6 below) must

(i)   report it in writing to the enforcing authority [*Reg 3(1)*] (see 3.7 and 3.14 below),

(ii)   keep a record of it for at least three years (see further 3.19 below):

   (*a*)   the death of any person (whether or not at work) as a result of an accident arising out of or in connection with work [*Reg 3(1)*] (see 3.8 and 3.15 below);

   (*b*)   a person suffering a major injury or condition as a result of an accident at work [*Reg 3(2)*] (see 3.8 below);

   (*c*)   a specified dangerous occurrence arising out of or in connection with work [*Reg 3(1)*] (see 3.9 below);

   (*d*)   a person at work being incapacitated for more than three days as a result of an injury caused by an accident at work [*Reg 3(3)*] (see 3.10 below);

   (*e*)   the death of an employee if it occurs after a reportable injury (see 3.8 and 3.15 below) leading to the employee's death, but not more than one year afterwards [*Reg 4*];

   (*f*)   a person at work being affected by a specified disease (see Appendix B 'List of Reportable Diseases'), provided that

      (i)   a doctor diagnoses the disease, and

      (ii)   the person's job involves a prescribed work activity [*Reg 5*] (see 3.12 below);

   (*g*)   certain gas incidents [*Reg 6*] (see 3.17 below);

   (*h*)   certain road accidents [*Reg 10(2)*] (see 3.16 below).

The report must be made on the prescribed form (see Appendices C1 and C2 below).

Duty to notify

3.4   In addition to reporting an incident, a responsible person must notify the enforcing authority by the quickest means practicable (normally by telephone) in the following cases: (*a*) death of any person; (*b*) major injury/condition; and (*c*) specified dangerous occurrence [*Reg 3(1)*] (see 3.9 below for the occurrences mentioned in (*c*)).

Exceptions to reporting

3.5   It is not necessary to report injuries/conditions/deaths in the cases of

(*a*)   a patient undergoing treatment in a hospital or in the surgery of a doctor or dentist, or

(*b*)   a member of the armed forces of the Crown on duty when the injury/death occurred.

[*Regs 10(1) and (3)*].

An accident which has to be reported under one of the following provisions does not also have to be notified under the *Reporting of Injuries etc. Regulations*:

(*a*)   the *Regulation of Railways Act 1871* and Orders and Regulations made thereunder;

(*b*)   the *Explosives Act 1875*;

(*c*)   the *Merchant Shipping Acts 1894-1979* and Orders and Regulations made thereunder;

(*d*)   the *Railway Employment (Prevention of Accidents) Act 1900*;

(*e*)   the *Nuclear Installations Act 1965* and Orders and Regulations made thereunder;

(*f*)   the *Civil Aviation (Investigation of Combined Military and Civil Air Accidents) Regulations 1969 (SI 1969 No 1437)*;

(*g*)   the *Ionising Radiations Regulations 1985 (SI 1985 No 1333)*.

[*Reg 10(4), 6 Sch*].

Responsible person

3.6   The duty to report/notify accidents, deaths and dangerous occurrences falls upon a 'responsible person'. [*Reg 2(1)*]. The status of a 'responsible person' varies according to whether an injured person is an employee, trainee or self-employed and, in some cases, according to where the injury occurs, as follows:

Table 1

Persons responsible for reporting accidents

Death, specified major injury or condition, or over-3-day injury;	of an employee at work	that person's employer
	of a person receiving training for employment	the person whose undertaking makes immediate provision of the training
	of a self-employed person at work in premises under the control of someone else	the person for the time being having control of the premises in connection with the carrying on by him of any trade, business or undertaking
Specified major injury or condition, or over-3-day injury:	of a self-employed person at work in premises under his control	the self-employed people themselves or someone acting on their behalf

Death, or specified major injury or condition:	of a person who is not himself at work (but is affected by the work of someone else), e.g. a member of the public, a student, a resident of a nursing home	the person for the time being having control of the premises in connection with the carrying on by him of any trade, business or undertaking at which, or in connection with the work at which, the accident causing the injury happened
A dangerous occurrence on the railway:		the person for time being having control of the premises in connection with the carrying on by him or her of any trade, business or undertaking at which, or in connection with the work at which, the dangerous occurrence happened
A dangerous occurrence involving a pipe-line (see Appendix A)		the owner of the pipe-line
A dangerous occurrence involving a dangerous substance being conveyed by road (see Appendix A)		the operator of the vehicle

A dangerous occurrence in
  mines
  quarries
  closed tips
		the manager of the mine
		the owner of the quarry
		the owner of the mine or quarry with which that tip is associated

In the case of dangerous occurrences 13 and 14 in Appendix A (transport by road of dangerous substances, see also 3.4 above) the operator of the vehicle, i.e. the person currently holding an operator's licence is the responsible person. Where no operator's licence is required, the keeper of the vehicle is the responsible person. In all other cases (with the exception of dangerous occurrences 13 and 14 in Appendix A, see also 3.4 above) the responsible person is the person in control of work premises. This will often be the employer, but on a construction site where there are main and subcontractors, the principal responsible person is the main contractor.

[*Reg 2(1)(a)*].

Enforcing authority

3.7   Health and safety law is separately enforced by (*a*) the Health and Safety Executive (HSE), (*b*) local authorities, through their environmental health departments, and to a lesser extent (*c*) local fire authorities. In the case of the HSE, the enforcing officer is an HSE inspector; in the case of the local authority the enforcing officer is an environmental health officer. Fire officers are also enforcement officers in the case of fire precautions (see further 17.3, 17.4 ENFORCEMENT, 19.6 FIRE AND FIRE PRECAUTIONS for fire authorities and also Appendix D at the end of this chapter for list of relevant HSE addresses).

Major injuries/conditions

3.8   Where any person dies or suffers major injuries/conditions as a result of an accident arising out of or in connection with work, such incident must be reported (and in certain cases, notified). The person who dies or suffers injury etc. need not be at work; it is enough if his death or injury arose from a work activity. Thus, someone shopping who fell and was injured on an escalator, could sue the person in control of the escalator, so long as the injury was connected with the design of the escalator; similarly, a member of the public who was overcome by fumes on a visit to a factory and who lost consciousness, as well as a patient in a nursing home who fell over an electrical cable lying across the floor, or even a pupil or student killed or injured whilst performing an activity in connection with his curriculum which was participated in/supervised by his teacher/lecturer.

Reportable major injuries/conditions are as follows:

(*a*)   fracture of the skull, spine or pelvis;

(*b*)   fracture of any bone

    (i)   in the arm or wrist (but not a bone in the hand), or

    (ii)   in the leg or ankle (but not a bone in the foot);

(*c*)   amputation of

    (i)   a hand or foot, or

    (ii)   a finger, thumb or toe, or any part if the joint or bone is completely severed;

(*d*)   loss of sight of an eye, penetrating injury to an eye, or a chemical or hot metal burn to an eye;

(*e*)   either

    (i)   injury (including burns) requiring immediate medical treatment, or

    (ii)   loss of consciousness,

    resulting (in either case) from an electric shock from any electrical circuit/equipment, whether or not due to direct contact;

(*f*)   loss of consciousness resulting from lack of oxygen;

(*g*)   decompression sickness (unless suffered during diving operations at work) requiring immediate medical treatment;

(*h*)   either

    (i)   acute illness requiring medical treatment, or

    (ii)   loss of consciousness,

    resulting (in either case) from absorption of any substance by inhalation, ingestion or through the skin;

(*j*)   acute illness requiring medical treatment where there is reason to believe that this resulted from exposure to a pathogen or infected material;

(*k*)   any other injury resulting in the person injured being admitted immediately into hospital for more than 24 hours.

[*Reg 3(1)(2)*].

Specified dangerous occurrences

3.9   There are four categories of reportable dangerous occurrences (set out in *Schedule 1*), ranging from general dangerous occurrences (e.g. collapse/overturning of a lift, explosion of a pressure vessel, dangerous occurrences on public highways and on private roads) to specific dangerous occurrences in mines, quarries and on the railways (see Appendix A at the end of this chapter).

The most commonly reported 'dangerous occurrences' are the failure, collapse or overturning of lifting machinery (21%) and the uncontrolled or accidental release of a potentially harmful substance/pathogen (18.5%) (i.e. Nos 1 and 9 in Appendix A 'List of Reportable Dangerous Occurrences' at the end of this chapter).

Injuries incapacitating for more than three days

3.10   Where a person at work is incapacitated for more than three consecutive days from their normal contractual work (excluding the day of the accident but including any days which would not have been working days) owing to injury resulting from accident at work, a report of the accident in writing on form F 2508 (revised) must be sent to the enforcing authority within seven days [*Reg 3(3)*] (see further Appendix C1 at the end of this chapter). This procedure also applies in the case of road accidents in connection with work activities (see further 3.16 below).

Notification of further matters

3.11   If the Health and Safety Commission approves of notification of further matters relating to an incident, the Executive may require further details

(*a*)   of the circumstances leading up to the reported incident;

(*b*)   about the nature or design (or both) of any plant involved in the reported incident; and

details of

(*c*)   safety systems and procedures for the control of the plant or substance involved in the reported incident;

(*d*)   qualifications, experience and training of staff having use or control of any plant or substance or concerned with safety systems or procedures;

(*e*)   design and operation documentation;

(*f*)   arrangements for the protection of personnel from any plant or substance connected with the reported incident;

(*g*)   results of any examination of, or tests carried out on, any plant or installation involved in the reported incident;

(*h*)   any available information about levels of exposure of persons at the work place to airborne substances.

[*5 Sch*].

Specified diseases

3.12   Where a person at work suffers from any occupational disease, which is related to a particular activity (as set out in *Schedule 2, column 2*), a report must be sent to the enforcing authority [*Reg 5(1)*] (see further Appendix C2 at the end of this chapter).

This presupposes written diagnosis of the disease by a doctor and that the employee is currently involved in that work-related activity. (Many of these conditions are those in respect of which disablement benefit is payable (see further 31.42 OCCUPATIONAL HEALTH).)

This applies where:

(*a*)   in the case of an employee or person undergoing training, the responsible person has received a written statement prepared by a doctor diagnosing the disease as one of those specified in *Schedule 2, column 1* of the *Regulations*; and

(*b*)   in the case of a self-employed person, that person has been informed by a doctor that he is suffering from such a disease.

[*Reg 5(3)*].

Under the *Industrial Diseases (Notification) Act 1981* and the *Registration of Births and Deaths Regulations 1987 (SI 1987 No 2088)* particulars are to be included on the death certificate as to whether death might have been due to or contributed to by the employment of the deceased. These particulars are to be supplied by the doctor who attended the deceased during his last illness.

Who is covered?

3.13   Protected by the regulations are

(*a*)   employees;

(*b*)   self-employed persons;

(*c*)   trainees (i.e. YT trainees, sandwich students, trainees other than YT trainees on courses administered by the Department of Employment);

(*d*)   a person, not an employee or trainee, on premises under the control of another, or who was otherwise involved in an accident (see 3.8 above).

Actions to be taken by employers when accidents at work occur
3.14

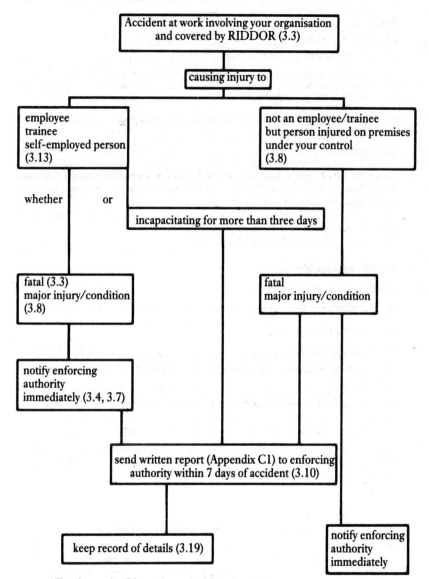

Accident at work involving your organisation
and covered by RIDDOR (3.3)

causing injury to

employee
trainee
self-employed person
(3.13)

not an employee/trainee
but person injured on premises
under your control
(3.8)

whether   or

incapacitating for more than three days

fatal (3.3)
major injury/condition
(3.8)

fatal
major injury/condition

notify enforcing
authority
immediately (3.4, 3.7)

send written report (Appendix C1) to enforcing
authority within 7 days of accident (3.10)

keep record of details (3.19)

notify enforcing
authority
immediately

(For Appendix C1 see the end of this chapter.)

Reporting the death of an employee

3.15   Where an employee, as a result of an accident at work, has suffered a reportable
injury/condition which is the cause of his death within one year of the date of the
accident, the employer must inform the enforcing authority in writing of the death
as soon as it comes to his attention, whether or not the accident has been reported
under *Regulation 3*. [*Reg 4*].

This requirement to report a death also applies to those situations (see 3.16 below) arising out of accidents on the road. [*Reg 10(2)*].

Road accidents

3.16   Road traffic accidents are governed by *RIDDOR* if death or major injury/condition (3.8 above) is caused by or connected with

(*a*)   exposure to any substance conveyed by road,

(*b*)   loading/unloading vehicles,

(*c*)   construction/demolition/alteration/repair/maintenance activities on or along public roads,

and this irrespective of whether the employee/self-employed person/trainee was engaged in (*a*), (*b*) or (*c*), or, alternatively, some other person. Thus, injury of an employee, struck by a passing vehicle, or a motorist injured by falling scaffolding alongside a road, are covered. [*Reg 3(1)*]. In addition, dangerous occurrences on public highways and private roads are covered.

Duty to report gas incidents

Actual gas incidents

3.17   Where:

(*a*)   a supplier of flammable gas through a fixed pipe distribution system; or

(*b*)   a filler; or

(*c*)   an importer; or

(*d*)   a supplier (not by way of retail trade) of a refillable container containing liquified petroleum gas (LPG)

receives notification of any death, injury or condition (see 3.3 above) which has arisen out of or in connection with the gas supplied, filled or imported, he must first notify the HSE and then send a report of the incident within 14 days. [*Reg 6(1)*].

Such incidents occur mainly in domestic premises and exclude injuries to people at work caused by a work activity. Average deaths from carbon monoxide poisoning are three times those due to explosion and fire.

Likely gas incidents

3.18   Where a supplier of flammable gas through a fixed pipe distribution system, acting on information, decides that a gas fitting, or any flue or ventilation, on account of its (*a*) design, (*b*) construction, (*c*) manner of installation, (*d*) modification or servicing is or has been likely to cause death, injury or a condition (mentioned in 3.3 above) in consequence of:

(*a*)   accidental leakage of gas;

(*b*)   inadequate combustion of gas; or

(*c*)   inadequate removal of the products of combustion of gas,

he must send a report to the HSE within 14 days, unless he has earlier reported the incident. [*Reg 6(2)*].

(For further information, see Chapter 22 'Gas Safety'.)

Duty to keep records

3.19   Records must be kept of injuries/conditions, dangerous occurrences and diseases for up to three years.

Such records must contain:

(*a*)   in the case of injuries/conditions/dangerous occurrences:

    (i)   date and time of accident or dangerous occurrence,

    (ii)   name of person, occupation, nature of injury/condition,

    (iii)   place where accident or dangerous occurrence happened,

    (iv)   brief description of circumstances;

(*b*)   in the case of occupational diseases:

    (i)   date of diagnosis of disease,

    (ii)   occupation of person affected,

    (iii)   name or nature of disease.

[*Reg 7*].

(For further duties in connection with gas containers, see Chapter 37 'Pressure Systems and Transportable Gas Containers'.)

Penalties

3.20   Contravention of any of the provisions of *RIDDOR* is an offence. The maximum penalty on summary conviction is a fine of £5,000. Conviction on indictment in the Crown Court carries an unlimited fine.

Defence in proceedings for breach of Regulations

3.21   It is a defence under the Regulations for a person to prove that:

(*a*)   he was not aware of the event requiring him to notify or send a report to the enforcing authority; and

(*b*)   he had taken all reasonable steps to have all such events brought to his notice.

[*Reg 11*].

Objectives of accident reporting

3.22   There should be an effective accident reporting and investigation system in all organisations. Accident reporting procedures should be clearly established in writing with individual reporting responsibilities specified. Staff should be trained in the system and disciplinary action may have to be taken where there is a failure to comply with it. Moreover, there is a case for all accidents, no matter how trivial they may seem, being reported through the internal reporting procedures.

The principal objectives of an accident reporting procedure are:

(*a*)   to ensure compliance with current legislation, e.g. *RIDDOR*;

(*b*)   to enable prompt remedial action to be taken;

(*c*)   to assist in monitoring the implementation of statements of health and safety policy (see further Chapter 41 'Statements of Health and Safety Policy');

(*d*)   to assist decision-making, planning and future resource allocation;

(*e*)   to provide feedback information which can be used in the development of future safety strategies and safe systems of work; and

(*f*)   to provide information to other interested parties.

Items (*b*) to (*f*) above are considered separately below in 3.23-3.26.

Remedial action

3.23   To ensure that prompt remedial action is taken in order to prevent future recurrences of the accident, a detailed investigation of the accident should be undertaken. This investigation will enable data to be collected for use in future safety strategies and assess compliance with legislation. Fundamentally, it should aim at establishing the sequence of events identifying, in particular, the direct and indirect causes of the accident.

Such an investigation should be undertaken initially by the departmental manager or supervisor accompanied by the safety specialist and safety representative (if appointed). The investigation report should, in addition to the basic factual information required, indicate what action has been taken to prevent a recurrence, including any dates agreed for completion of work or action to be taken by management. Further detailed investigation may be undertaken by the safety specialist, an insurance company representative and enforcement officer (HSE inspector or local authority environmental health officer) depending upon the particular circumstances of the accident. The results of all such investigations together with action taken, should be recorded and communicated, perhaps through a company accident bulletin, to all concerned. At the same time, any notifications and recordings as required by legislation should be completed.

Monitoring implementation of Statement of Health and Safety Policy

3.24   Accurate reporting, recording and investigation of accidents is one of the factors to be considered when assessing the implementation by a company of its Statement of Health and Safety Policy (see Chapter 41 'Statements of Health and Safety Policy'). An analytical examination of all accident statistics by type, injury site, extent of plant and property damage, department/section, direct and indirect causes, and by time of day and even season of the year, may all serve to highlight existing deficiencies, lack of clear identification of responsibilities in the Statement and also suggest possible improvements in the current implementation programme, e.g. a need for specific health and safety training. However, findings from statistical analyses should be examined in conjunction with data resulting from other safety monitoring exercises, such as safety audits, safety sampling exercises, surveys and inspections.

Decision-making, planning and resource allocation

3.25   By examining accident data, together with data from safety monitoring activities, a clear indication of health and safety problem areas may be obtained. The utilisation of such accident data will provide for an objective assessment of each problem area, identify deficiencies in management performance, enable future management objectives to be established and agreed, including the system for measuring the relative achievement of such objectives, and will form a reference point for assessing performance. In this way all levels of management will have an improved perception of their role in accident prevention, as a result of which they should be able to plan and budget for health and safety improvement.

Informing other interested parties

3.26 There is a need to provide information concerning certain accidents, occupational diseases and dangerous occurrences to interested parties, other than enforcement agencies. These interested parties are insurance companies, safety representatives, trade associations and legal representatives of the organisation.

Insurance companies

3.27 Generally, insurance companies will need to be notified of any accident, occupational disease or dangerous occurrence which is likely to result in a claim. This aspect is usually a condition of the insurance contract. Notification is normally achieved through completion of the relevant insurance company accident claim form and may well involve further investigation by a representative of the insurance company or the insurance broker, once the completed form has been passed via the insurance broker to the insurance company. Certain insurance companies are now accepting a copy of the form BI 76 as first notification of the accident whereas receipt of a copy of the company accident notification form may be the case otherwise.

Safety representatives

3.28 An employer must make available to safety representatives the information within the employer's knowledge necessary to enable them to fulfil their functions. [*Safety Representatives and Safety Committees Regulations 1977 (SI 1977 No 500)*]. The safety representatives must be allowed to go where it is safe to make an inspection where a notifiable accident or dangerous occurrence has happened or a prescribed disease has been contracted. The employer and his representatives may be present at the inspection. [*Reg 6*]. The approved code of practice produced by the HSC in association with these Regulations states that such information should include information which the employer keeps relating to the occurrence of any accident, dangerous occurrence or notifiable industrial disease and any associated statistical records. [*Code of Practice: Safety Representatives and Safety Committees 1976, para 6(c)*]. See Chapter 25 'Joint Consultation – Safety Representatives and Safety Committees'.

Trade associations

3.29 Many trade associations require their member firms to supply them with statistical information on accidents on an annual basis. These statistics are used mainly to aid comparisons and to monitor performance on an industry-wide basis.

Legal representatives

3.30 The organisation's legal representatives commonly expect notification of accidents and occupational diseases contracted, particularly where there is a potential civil action for negligence against the company. Additionally, legal representatives of an injured party would expect reasonable access to such information (see further *Waugh v British Railways Board* at 25.10 JOINT CONSULTATION – SAFETY REPRESENTATIVES AND SAFETY COMMITTEES).

Appendix A

List of Reportable Dangerous Occurrences

PART I — GENERAL

Lifting machinery etc.

1. The collapse of, the overturning of, or the failure of any load bearing part of —

(*a*) any lift, hoist, crane, derrick or mobile powered access platform, but not any winch, teagle, pulley block, gin wheel, transporter or runway;

(*b*) any excavator; or

(*c*) any pile driving frame or rig having an overall height, when operating, of more than 7 metres.

Passenger carrying amusement device

2. The following incidents at a fun fair (whether or not a travelling fun fair) while the relevant device is in use or under test —

(*a*) the collapse of, or the failure of any load bearing part of, any amusement device provided as part of the fun fair which is designed to allow passengers to move or ride on it or inside it; or

(*b*) the failure of any safety arrangement connected with such a device, which is designed to restrain or support passengers.

Pressure vessels

3. Explosion, collapse or bursting of any closed vessel, including a boiler or boiler tube, in which the internal pressure was above or below atmospheric pressure, which might have been liable to cause the death of, or any of the injuries or conditions covered by Regulation 3(2) to, any person, or which resulted in the stoppage of the plant involved for more than 24 hours.

Electrical short circuit

4. Electrical short circuit or overload attended by fire or explosion which resulted in the stoppage of the plant involved for more than 24 hours and which, taking into account the circumstances of the occurrence, might have been liable to cause the death of, or any of the injuries or conditions covered by Regulation 3(2) to, any person.

Explosion or fire

5. An explosion or fire occurring in any plant or place which resulted in the stoppage of that plant or suspension of normal work in that place for more than 24 hours, where such explosion or fire was due to the ignition of process materials, their by-products (including waste) or finished products.

Escape of flammable substances

6. The sudden, uncontrolled release of one tonne or more of highly flammable liquid.

Collapse of scaffolding

7. A collapse or partial collapse of any scaffold which is more than 5 metres high which results in a substantial part of the scaffold falling or over-turning and where the scaffold is slung or suspended, a collapse or partial collapse of the suspension arrangements (including any outrigger) which causes a working platform or cradle to fall more than 5 metres.

Collapse of building or structure

8. Any unintended collapse or partial collapse of —

    (*a*) any building or structure under construction, reconstruction, alteration or demolition, or of any false-work, involving a fall of more than 5 tonnes of material; or

    (*b*) any floor or wall of any building being used as a place of work, not being a building under construction, reconstruction, alteration or demolition.

(On average, a worker is killed in the construction industry every three days. On an average day, 59 construction workers are reported injured.)

Escape of a substance or pathogen

9. The uncontrolled or accidental release or the escape of any substance or pathogen from any apparatus, equipment, pipework, pipe-line, process plant, storage vessel, tank, in-works conveyance tanker, land-fill site, or exploratory land drilling site, which having regard to the nature of the substance or pathogen and the extent and location of the release or escape, might have been liable to cause the death of, any of the injuries or conditions covered by Regulation 3(2) to, or other damage to the health of, any person.

Explosives

10. Any ignition or explosion of explosives, where the ignition or explosion was not intentional.

Freight containers

11. Failure of any freight container or failure of any load bearing part thereof while it is being raised, lowered or suspended.

Pipe-lines

12. (*a*) the bursting, explosion or collapse of a pipe-line or any part thereof; or

    (*b*) the unintentional ignition of anything in a pipe-line, or of anything which immediately before it was ignited was in a pipe-line.

Conveyance of dangerous substances by road

13. — (1) Any incident —

    (*a*) in which a road tanker or tank container used for conveying a dangerous substance by road —

        (i)   overturns; or

(ii) suffers serious damage to the tank in which the dangerous substance is being conveyed; or

(*b*) in which there is, in relation to such a road tanker or tank container —

(i) an uncontrolled release or escape of the dangerous substance being conveyed; or

(ii) a fire which involves the dangerous substance being conveyed.

14. — (1) Any incident involving a vehicle conveying a dangerous substance by road, other than a vehicle to which paragraph 13 applies, where there is —

(*a*) an uncontrolled release or escape from any package or container of the dangerous substance being conveyed; or

(*b*) a fire which involves the dangerous substance being conveyed.

Breathing apparatus

15. Any incident where breathing apparatus, while being used to enable the wearer to breathe independently of the surrounding environment, malfunctions in such a way as to be likely either to deprive the wearer of oxygen or, in the case of use in a contaminated atmosphere, to expose the wearer to the contaminant, to the extent in either case of posing a danger to his health, except that this paragraph shall not apply to such apparatus while it is being —

(*a*) used in a mine; or

(*b*) maintained or tested.

Overhead electric lines

16. Any incident in which plant or equipment either comes into contact with an uninsulated overhead electric line in which the voltage exceeds 200 volts, or causes an electrical discharge from such an electric line by coming into close proximity to it, unless in either case the incident was intentional.

Locomotives

17. Any case of an accidental collision between a locomotive or a train and any other vehicle at a factory or at dock premises which might have been liable to cause the death of, or any of the injuries or conditions covered by Regulation 3(2) to, any person.

PART II — DANGEROUS OCCURRENCES WHICH ARE REPORTABLE IN RELATION TO MINES

Fire or ignition of gas

1. The ignition, below ground, of any gas (other than gas in a safety lamp) or of any dust.

2. The accidental ignition of any gas in part of a firedamp drainage system on the surface or in an exhauster house.

3. The outbreak of any fire below ground.

4. An incident where any person in consequence of any smoke or any other indication that a fire may have broken out below ground has been caused to leave any place.

5. The outbreak of any fire on the surface endangering the operation of any winding or haulage apparatus installed at a shaft or unwalkable outlet or of any mechanically operated apparatus for producing ventilation below ground.

Escape of gas

6. Any violent outburst of gas together with coal or other solid matter into the mine workings except when such outburst is caused intentionally.

Failure of plant or equipment

7. The breakage of any rope, chain, coupling, balance rope, guide rope, suspension gear or other gear used for or in connection with the carrying of persons through any shaft or staple shaft.

8. The breakage or unintentional uncoupling of any rope, chain, coupling, rope tensioning system or other gear used for or in connection with the transport of persons below ground, or breakage, while men are being carried, of any belt, rope or other gear used for or in connection with a belt conveyor designated by the mine manager as a man-riding conveyor.

9. An incident where any conveyance being used for the carriage of persons is overwound; or any conveyance not being so used is overwound and becomes detached from its winding rope; or any conveyance operated by means of the friction of a rope on a winding sheave is brought to rest by the apparatus provided in the headframe of the shaft or in the part of the shaft below the lowest landing for the time being in use, being apparatus provided for bringing the conveyance to rest in the event of its being overwound.

10. The stoppage of any ventilating apparatus (other than an auxiliary fan) causing a substantial reduction in ventilation of the mine lasting for a period exceeding 30 minutes, except when for the purpose of planned maintenance.

11. The collapse of any headframe, winding engine house, fan house or storage bunker.

Breathing apparatus

12. At any mine an incident where —

    (*a*) breathing apparatus or a smoke helmet or other apparatus serving the same purpose or a self-rescuer, while being used, fails to function safely or develops a defect likely to affect its safe working; or

    (*b*) immediately after using and arising out of the use of breathing apparatus or a smoke helmet or other apparatus serving the same purpose or a self-rescuer, any person receives first-aid or medical treatment by reason of his unfitness or suspected unfitness at the mine.

Injury by explosion of blasting material etc.

13. An incident in which any person suffers an injury (not being an injury covered by Regulation 3(2) or one reportable under Regulation 3(3) (see 3.9 above)) resulting from an explosion or discharge of any blasting material or device.

Use of emergency escape apparatus

14. An incident where any apparatus is used (other than for the purpose of training and practice) which has been provided at the mine in accordance with any scheme or any other arrangements are carried out in accordance with the scheme whereby persons employed below ground in the mine use means of egress therefrom in an emergency.

Inrush of gas or water

15. Any inrush of noxious or flammable gas from old workings.

16. Any inrush of water or material which flows when wet from any source.

Insecure tip

17. Any movement of material or any fire or any other event which indicates that a tip is or is likely to become insecure.

Locomotives

18. Any incident where an underground locomotive when not used for shunting or testing purposes is brought to rest by means other than its safety circuit protective devices or normal service brakes.

PART III — DANGEROUS OCCURRENCES WHICH ARE REPORTABLE IN RELATION TO QUARRIES

1. The collapse of any storage bunker.

2. The sinking or overturning of any waterborne craft or hovercraft.

3. An incident in which any person suffers an injury (not being an injury covered by Regulation 3(2) or one reportable under Regulation 3(3) (see 3.9 above)) resulting from an explosion or discharge of any blasting material or device for which he receives first-aid or medical treatment at the quarry.

4. An occurrence in which any substance is ascertained to have been projected beyond a quarry boundary as a result of blasting operations in circumstances in which any person was, or might have been, endangered.

5. Any movement of material or any fire or any other event which indicates that a tip is, or is likely to become, insecure.

Part IV — Dangerous Occurrences which are Reportable in Relation to Railways

1. — (1) Any of the following incidents which, taking into account the circumstances, might have been liable to cause the death of, or any of the injuries or conditions covered by Regulation 3(2) to, any person —

(*a*) failure of —

(i) a locomotive;

(ii) a railway vehicle; or

(iii) a rope haulage system used in working an inclined railway; or any part thereof;

(*b*) failure of a structure or part of the permanent way or formation, including any tunnel or cutting; or

(*c*) any train or railway vehicle striking an obstruction on the line.

(2) Any case of collision, derailment, or a train unintentionally becoming divided, except one occurring on a siding or during shunting operations when there were no passengers on the train or other vehicles involved.

(3) Failure of the equipment of any level crossing or a train running onto a level crossing when not authorised to do so.

[*The Reporting of Injuries, Diseases and Dangerous Occurrences Regulations 1985, Reg 2(1), 1 Sch*].

Appendix B

List of Reportable Diseases

COLUMN 1	COLUMN 2

Poisonings

1.   Poisonings by any of the following: Any activity.

(a)   Acrylamide monomer;
(b)   Arsenic or one of its compounds;
(c)   Benzene or a homologue of benzene;
(d)   Beryllium or one of its compounds;
(e)   Cadmium or one of its compounds;
(f)   Carbon disulphide;
(g)   Diethylene dioxide (dioxan);
(h)   Ethylene oxide;
(i)   Lead or one of its compounds;
(j)   Manganese or one of its compounds;
(k)   Mercury or one of its compounds;
(l)   Methyl bromide;
(m)   Nitrochlorobenzene, or a nitro- or
       amino- or chloro-derivative of benzene or
       of a homologue of benzene;
(n)   Oxides of nitrogen;
(o)   Phosphorus or one of its compounds.

Skin diseases

2. Chrome ulceration of: Work involving exposure to chromic
   (a) the nose or throat; or   acid or to any other chromium com-
   (b) the skin of the hands or forearm.   pound.

3. Folliculitis.   Work involving exposure to mineral
4. Acne.   oil, tar, pitch or arsenic.
5. Skin cancer.

6. Inflammation, ulceration or   Work with ionising radiation.
   malignant disease of the skin.

Lung diseases

7. Occupational asthma.   Work involving exposure to any of the
                                    following agents —

                                    (a) isocyanates;

                                    (b) platinum salts;

(c) fumes or dusts arising from the manufacture, transport or use of hardening agents (including epoxy resin curing agents) based on phthalic anhydride, tetrachlorophthalic anhydride, trimellitic anhydride or triethylenetetramine;

(d) fumes arising from the use of rosin as a soldering flux;

(e) proteolytic enzymes;

(f) animals or insects used for the purposes of research or education or in laboratories;

(g) dusts arising from the sowing, cultivation, harvesting, drying, handling, milling, transport or storage of barley, oats, rye, wheat or maize, of the handling, milling, transport or storage of meal or flour made therefrom.

8. Extrinsic alveolitis (including Farmer's lung).

Exposure to moulds or fungal spores or heterologous proteins during work in —

(a) agriculture, horticulture, forestry, cultivation of edible fungi or maltworking; or

(b) loading or unloading or handling in storage mouldy vegetable matter or edible fungi; or

(c) caring for or handling birds; or

(d) handling bagasse.

9. Pneumoconiosis (excluding asbestosis).

1. (a) The mining, quarrying or working of silica rock or the working of dried quartzose sand or any dry deposit or dry residue of silica or any dry admixture containing such materials (including any activity in which any of the aforesaid operations are carried out incidentally to the mining or quarrying of other minerals or to the manufacture of articles containing crushed or ground silica rock);

(b) the handling of any of the materials specified in the foregoing subparagraph in or incidental to any of the operations mentioned therein, or substantial exposure to the dust arising from such operations.

2. The breaking, crushing or grinding of flint or the working or handling of broken, crushed or ground flint or materials containing such flint, or substantial exposure to the dust arising from any of such operations.

3. Sand blasting by means of compressed air with the use of quartzose sand or crushed silica rock or flint, or substantial exposure to the dust arising from such sand blasting.

4. Work in a foundry or the performance of, or substantial exposure to the dust arising from, any of the following operations:

   (a) the freeing of steel castings from adherent siliceous substance;

   (b) the freeing of metal castings from adherent siliceous substance:

      (i) by blasting with an abrasive propelled by compressed air, by steam or by a wheel; or

      (ii) by the use of power-driven tools.

5. The manufacture of china or earthenware (including sanitary earthenware, electrical earthenware and earthenware tiles), and any activity involving substantial exposure to the dust arising therefrom.

6. The grinding of mineral graphite, or substantial exposure to the dust arising from such grinding.

7. The dressing of granite or any igneous rock by masons or the crushing of such materials, or substantial exposure to the dust arising from such operations.

8. The use, or preparation for use, of a grind-stone, or substantial exposure to the dust arising therefrom.

9. (a) Work underground in any mine in which one of the objects of the mining operations is the getting of any mineral;

   (b) the working or handling above ground at any coal or tin mine of any minerals extracted therefrom, or any operation incidental thereto;

(*c*) the trimming of coal in any ship, barge, or lighter, or in any dock or harbour or at any wharf or quay;

(*d*) the sawing, splitting or dressing of slate, or any operation incidental thereto.

10. The manufacture, or work incidental to the manufacture, of carbon electrodes by an industrial undertaking for use in the electrolytic extraction of aluminium from aluminium oxide, and any activity involving substantial exposure to the dust arising therefrom.

11. Boiler scaling or substantial exposure to the dust arising therefrom.

10. Byssinosis.

Work in any room where any process up to and including the weaving process is performed in a factory in which the spinning or manipulation of raw or waste cotton or of flax, or the weaving of cotton or flax, is carried on.

11. Mesothelioma.
12. Lung cancer.
13. Asbestosis.

(*a*) The working or handling of asbestos or any admixture of asbestos;

(*b*) the manufacture or repair of asbestos textiles or other articles containing or composed of asbestos;

(*c*) the cleaning of any machinery or plant used in any of the foregoing operations and of any chambers, fixtures and appliances for the collection of asbestos dust;

(*d*) substantial exposure to the dust arising from any of the foregoing operations.

14. Cancer of a bronchus or lung.

Work in a factory where nickel is produced by decomposition of a gaseous nickel compound which necessitates working in or about a building or buildings where that process or any other industrial process ancillary or incidental thereto is carried on.

Infections

15. Leptospirosis.	Handling animals, or work in places which are or may be infested by rats.
16. Hepatitis.	Work involving exposure to human blood products or body secretions and excretions.
17. Tuberculosis.	Work with persons or animals or with human or animal remains or with any other material which might be a source of infection.
18. Any illness caused by a pathogen referred to in column 2, opposite.	Work involving a pathogen which presents a hazard to human health.
19. Anthrax.	Any activity.

Other conditions

20. Malignant disease of the bones. 21. Blood dyscrasia. }	Work with ionising radiation.
22. Cataract.	Work involving exposure to electro-magnetic radiation (including radiant heat).
23. Decompression sickness. 24. Barotrauma. }	Breathing gases at increased pressure.
25. Cancer of the nasal cavity or associated air sinuses.	1. (*a*) Work in or about a building where wooden furniture is manufactured; (*b*) work in a building used for the manufacture of footwear or components of footwear made wholly or partly of leather or fibre board; or (*c*) work at a place used wholly or mainly for the repair of footwear made wholly or partly of leather or fibre board.

2. Work in a factory where nickel is produced by decomposition of a gaseous nickel compound which necessitates working in or about a building or buildings where that process or any other industrial process ancillary or incidental thereto is carried on.

26. Angiosarcoma of the liver.

(*a*) Work in or about machinery or apparatus used for the polymerization of vinyl chloride monomer, a process which, for the purposes of this provision, comprises all operations up to and including the drying of the slurry produced by the polymerization and the packaging of the dried product; or

(*b*) work in a building or structure in which any part of that process takes place.

27. Cancer of the urinary tract.

Work involving exposure to any of the following substances —

(*a*) alpha-naphthylamine, beta-naphthylamine or methylene-bisorthochloroaniline;

(*b*) diphenyl substituted by at least one nitro or primary amino group or by at least one nitro and primary amino group (including benzidine);

(*c*) any of the substances mentioned in sub-paragraph (*b*) above if further ring substituted by halogeno, methyl or methoxy groups, but not by other groups;

(*d*) the salts of any of the substances mentioned in sub-paragraphs (*a*) to (*c*) above;

(*e*) auramine or magenta.

28. Vibration white finger.

(*a*) The use of hand-held chain saws in forestry; or

(b) the use of hand-held rotary tools in grinding or in the sanding or polishing of metal, or the holding of material being ground, or metal being sanded or polished, by rotary tools; or

(c) the use of hand-held percussive metal-working tools, or the holding of metal being worked upon by percussive tools, in riveting, caulking, chipping, hammering, fettling or swaging; or

(d) the use of hand-held powered percussive drills or hand-held powered percussive hammers in mining, quarrying, demolition, or on roads or footpaths, including road construction; or

(e) the holding of material being worked upon by pounding machines in shoe manufacture.

*(Legionnaire's disease (see further 9.26, 9.27 DANGEROUS SUBSTANCES I) is not reportable in England and Wales (though it is so in Scotland). It will probably become reportable when the Biological Agents Directive has been implemented by the end of 1994.)

Appendix C1

Prescribed Form for Making Reports

A **Subject of report** *(tick appropriate box or boxes)* – *see note 2*

| Fatality ☐ 1 | Specified major injury or condition ☐ 2 | "Over three day" injury ☐ 3 | Dangerous occurrence ☐ 4 | Flammable gas incident (fatality or major injury or condition) ☐ 5 | Dangerous gas fitting ☐ 6 |

B **Person or organisation making report** (ie person obliged to report under the Regulations) – *see note 3*

Name and address –

Post code – ☐

Name and telephone no. of person to contact –

Nature of trade, business or undertaking –

If in construction industry, state the total number of your employees – ☐

and indicate the role of your company on site *(tick box)* –

| Main site contractor ☐ 7 | Sub contractor ☐ 8 | Other ☐ 9 |

If in farming, are you reporting an injury to a member of your family? *(tick box)* ☐ Yes ☐ No

C **Date, time and place of accident, dangerous occurrence or flammable gas incident** – *see note 4*

Date ☐ ☐ 19 ☐
day month year

Time – ☐

Give the name and address if different from above –

Where on the premises or site –
and
Normal activity carried on there

ENV ☐

☐

Complete the following sections D, E, F & H if you have ticked boxes, 1, 2, 3 or 5 in Section A. Otherwise go straight to Sections G and H.

D **The injured person** – *see note 5*

Full name and address –

| Age ☐ | Sex ☐ (M or F) | Status *(tick box)* – | Employee ☐ 10 | Self employed ☐ 11 | Trainee (YTS) ☐ 12 |
| | | | Trainee (other) ☐ 13 | | Any other person ☐ 14 |

☐

Trade, occupation or job title –

☐

Nature of injury or condition and the part of the body affected –

☐

F2508 (rev 1/86)   *continued overleaf*

E Kind of accident - *see note 6*

Indicate what kind of accident led to the injury or condition (*tick one box*) —

Contact with moving machinery or material being machined ☐ 1	Injured whilst handling lifting or carrying ☐ 5	Trapped by something collapsing or overturning ☐ 8	Exposure to an explosion ☐ 12
Struck by moving, including flying or falling, object. ☐ 2	Slip, trip or fall on same level ☐ 6	Drowning or asphyxiation ☐ 9	Contact with electricity or an electrical discharge ☐ 13
Struck by moving vehicle ☐ 3	Fall from a height* ☐ 7	Exposure to or contact with a harmful substance ☐ 10	Injured by an animal ☐ 14
Struck against something fixed or stationary ☐ 4	*Distance through which person fell [____] (metres)	Exposure to fire ☐ 11	Other kind of accident (give details in Section H) ☐ 15

Spaces below are for office use only. [____]

F Agent(s) involved — *see note 7*

Indicate which, if any, of the categories of agent or factor below were involved (*tick one or more of the boxes*) —

Machinery/equipment for lifting and conveying ☐ 1	Process plant, pipework or bulk storage ☐ 5	Live animal ☐ 9	Ladder or scaffolding ☐ 13
Portable power or hand tools ☐ 2	Any material, substance or product being handled, used or stored. ☐ 6	Moveable container or package of any kind ☐ 10	Construction formwork, shuttering and falsework ☐ 14
Any vehicle or associated equipment/ machinery ☐ 3	Gas, vapour, dust, fume or oxygen deficient atmosphere ☐ 7	Floor, ground, stairs or any working surface ☐ 11	Electricity supply cable, wiring, apparatus or equipment ☐ 15
Other machinery ☐ 4	Pathogen or infected material ☐ 8	Building, engineering structure or excavation/underground working ☐ 12	Entertainment or sporting facilities or equipment ☐ 16
			Any other agent ☐ 17

Describe briefly the agents or factors you have indicated —

[_____]

G Dangerous occurrence or dangerous gas fitting — *see notes 8 and 9*

Reference number of dangerous occurrence [_____]   Reference number of dangerous gas fitting [_____]

H Account of accident, dangerous occurrence or flammable gas incident - *see note 10*

Describe what happened and how. In the case of an accident state what the injured person was doing at the time —

[_____]

Signature of person making report [_____]   Date [_____]

68

Appendix C2

Prescribed Form for Making Reports

A **Person or organisation making report**
(ie person obliged to report under the Regulations)

Name and address
Post code
Name of person to contact for further inquiry
Tel. No.

Nature of trade, business or undertaking

B **Details of the person affected**

Surname _____ Forenames _____

Date of birth [| | 1 9   ]   Sex (M or F) [   ]
          day *month*   *year*

Occupation _____

Please indicate whether Employee [   ]
(tick box)
                Other person [   ]

If not an employee, what is the ill person's status?
(eg self-employed or trainee)

F2508A (1/86)

continued overleaf

C Details of the disease which is being reported
(a full list of diseases which are reportable is given| in the accompanying notes)

For HSE Use

Name or schedule number of the disease

Date of doctor's statement which
first diagnosed the disease

		19	
day	month		year

Doctor's name and address, if known

Post code

D Description of work giving rise to this report

Describe any work of the affected person which might be relevant to the onset
of the disease. If the disease is thought to have been caused by the ill person's
exposure to an agent at work (eg a specific chemical) please state what the suspected
agent is.

ENV

E Any other relevant information

Signature of person making report   Date

Appendix D

Health and Safety Executive Area Offices

South West
Inter City House, Mitchell Lane,
Victoria Street
Bristol BS1 6AN
Telephone: (0272) 290681

South
Priestley House, Priestley Road
Basingstoke RG24 9NW
Telephone: (0256) 473181

South East
3 East Grinstead House, London Road
East Grinstead
West Sussex RH19 1RR
Telephone: (0342) 326922

London North
Maritime House, 1 Linton Road, Barking
Essex IG11 8HF
Telephone: (081) 594 5522

London South
1 Long Lane
London SE1 4PG
Telephone: (071) 407 8911

East Anglia
39 Baddow Road, Chelmsford, Essex
CM2 0HL
Telephone: (0245) 284661

Northern Home Counties
14 Cardiff Road, Luton, Beds LU1 1PP
Telephone: (0582) 34121

East Midlands
Belgrave House, 1 Greyfriars,
Northampton NN1 2BS
Telephone: (0604) 21233

West Midlands
McLaren Building, 2 Masshouse Circus
Queensway, Birmingham B4 7NP
Telephone: (021) 200 2299

Wales
Brunel House, Fitzalan Road
Cardiff CF2 1SH
Telephone: (0222) 473777

Marches
The Marches House, Midway
Newcastle-under-Lyme, Staffs ST5 1DT
Telephone: (0782) 717181

North Midlands
Birbeck House, Trinity Square
Nottingham NG1 4AU
Telephone: (0602) 470712

South Yorkshire and Humberside
Sovereign House, 40 Silver Street
Sheffield S1 2ES
Telephone: (0742) 739081

West and North Yorkshire
8 St Paul's Street, Leeds LS1 2LE
Telephone: (0532) 446191

Greater Manchester
Quay House, Quay Street
Manchester M3 3JB
Telephone: (061) 831 7111

Merseyside
The Triad, Stanley Road
Bootle L20 3PG
Telephone: (051) 922 7211

North West
Victoria House, Ormskirk Road
Preston PR1 1HH
Telephone: (0772) 59321

North East
Arden House, Regent Centre
Gosforth
Newcastle-upon-Tyne NE3 3JN
Telephone: (091) 284 8448

Scotland East
Belford House, 59 Belford Road
Edinburgh EH4 3UE
Telephone: (031) 225 1313

Scotland West
314 St Vincent St, Glasgow G3 8XG
Telephone: (041) 204 2646

Chapter 4

Asbestos

Introduction

4.1 Asbestos (Greek meaning 'unburnable', 'unquenchable') is the classic example of a naturally-occurring dangerous substance found throughout industry. It is a generic term for a variety of silicates of iron, magnesium, calcium, sodium and aluminium which naturally exist in fibrous form. Defined as 'any of the following minerals . . . crocidolite, amosite, chrysotile, fibrous anthophyllite and any mixture containing any of the said minerals' and 'fibrous actinolite and fibrous tremolite' (by the *Asbestos (Licensing) Regulations 1983* and the *Control of Asbestos at Work Regulations 1987* as amended), asbestos has emerged in the last decade as one of the most significant occupational health hazards worldwide (asbestosis together with mesothelioma: 32 deaths in 1968, 74 in 1976 and 88 in 1983; mesothelioma of the pleura: 98 deaths in 1968, 198 in 1976 and 400 in 1983). More spectacularly, in North America the avalanche of product liability litigation involving asbestosis/mesothelioma resulted in America's biggest manufacturer of asbestos, Johns-Manville Corporation of Denver, filing for voluntary liquidation in the early eighties. As usual developments have been more prosaic over here but asbestosis/mesothelioma claims, the flagship of 'long tail liability', have caused major headaches for liability insurance companies, including Lloyds.

Pathological effects of exposure to asbestos

4.2 Health risks are associated with the inhalation of fibrous dust and its dispersion within the lungs and other parts of the body. Workers engaged in extracting the fibre and processing it, along with those manufacturing asbestos products, are particularly vulnerable. However, exposure to asbestos alone is uncommon; in practice other mineral dusts are normally inhaled along with asbestos and the effect of these and other pollutants, such as cigarette smoke, often combine to produce diseases such as asbestosis etc. Inhalation of asbestos can give rise to the following three medical conditions namely, asbestosis, cancer of the bronchial tubes and cancer of the pleural surface (see further 4.30 below).

Asbestos social security awards peaked in 1986 at 329, whereas mesothelioma awards escalated from 93 in 1981 to 462 in 1990.

Unlike many occupational diseases, asbestos-related diseases manifest themselves tardily over an incubation period of anything from 20 to 30 years. In consequence, current incidence of asbestos-related disease is not a measure of the effects of present dust levels, but rather of past dust exposures, which were (obviously) too high. In addition, this 'long tail' liability has caused havoc with normal time limitation periods and strained the application of the three year rule for personal injury claims operating under the *Limitation Act 1980* (see 4.31 below and Limitation of actions at 15.11 EMPLOYERS' DUTIES).

Control of exposure – control limits

4.3 Exposure to all forms of asbestos should be reduced to the minimum reasonably practicable (for the meaning of this expression, see Chapter 15 'Employers' Duties'). But more particularly, personal exposure should not exceed the *control limits* (formerly TLVs – threshold limit values). Control limits are the *upper* level of permitted exposure, for each species of asbestos, above which the risk to health is unacceptable. The following control limits apply (see also 4.8 below):

(*a*)   for dust consisting of/containing (i) crocidolite or (ii) amosite:
– 0.2 fibres per millilitre of air averaged over a continuous period of 4 hours,
– 0.6 fibres per millilitre of air averaged over any continuous period of 10 minutes;

(*b*)   for dust consisting of/containing chrysotile:
– 0.5 fibres per millilitre of air averaged over 4 hours,
– 1.5 fibres per millilitre of air averaged over a continuous period of 10 minutes.

[*Reg 2 as amended by Control of Asbestos at Work (Amendment) Regulations 1992 (SI 1992 No 3068), Sch*].

(N.B. These measurements represent the concentration of fibres per millilitre of air sampled by routine atmospheric monitoring, e.g. by use of a static sampling device.)

Control limits

4.4   Replacing TLVs, a control limit is the limit which is 'judged, after detailed consideration of the available evidence, to be "reasonably practicable" for the whole spectrum of work activities in Great Britain'. They are 'those exposure limits contained in regulations, approved codes of practice and EC Directives, or those agreed by the Health and Safety Commission'. (For the legal effect of approved codes of practice as distinct from regulations, see 1.31 INTRODUCTION and Chapter 17 'Enforcement'.) Characteristically, they

(*a*)   are set at a level which it would be reasonably practicable for relevant sectors of industry to achieve;

(*b*)   provide a clear indication of what the law requires as a maximum standard, so that when they are exceeded, employers know that they are in breach of *HSWA*;

(*c*)   are based on a full review of medical/scientific evidence by the HSE and agreed by employers'/employees' organisations as acceptable.

4.5   Hence, as distinct from TLVs or recommended limits (which indicate the highest tolerable level of exposure), control limits represent the lowest exposure technically and economically possible. For this reason, control limits are not synonymous with safe levels of exposure which, once attained, make further improvements in dust control unnecessary. Rather they are gradually self-updating (see further, *Qualcast Ltd v Haynes* at 1.22 INTRODUCTION). Failure to comply with control limits, or to put it another way, reduce exposure to the minimum reasonably practicable, can result in prosecution or some other form of enforcement action (see Chapter 17 'Enforcement').

Statutory requirements governing exposure to asbestos

4.6   Compliance with exposure limits is only part of an employer's duty towards his employees under *HSWA* and the *Control of Asbestos at Work Regulations 1987*. The detailed statutory requirements are as follows.

(a)   *General.* All employers must provide a safe working environment for their employees. [*HSWA s 2(2)(e)*]. This includes provision, so far as is reasonably practicable (see Chapter 15 'Employers' Duties') of an environment to which exposure of employees to asbestos dust is reduced to levels minimally reasonably practicable.

(b)   *Specific.* Specific statutory requirements relating to protection against exposure to asbestos dust are contained in the *Control of Asbestos at Work Regulations 1987 (SI 1987 No 2115)* as amended, the *Asbestos (Licensing) Regulations 1983 (SI 1983 No 1649)* and the *Control of Pollution (Special Waste) Regulations 1980 (SI 1980 No 1709).* Moreover, labelling of asbestos products used at work is specified in the *Chemicals (Hazard Information and Packaging) Regulations 1993* (formerly the *Classification, Packaging and Labelling of Dangerous Substances Regulations 1984* and the *Road Traffic (Carriage of Dangerous Substances in Road Tankers and Tank Containers) Regulations 1992 (SI 1992 No 743)* (see 4.25 below)).

Environmentally, the *Control of Pollution (Special Waste) Regulations 1980* are important. The '*Special Waste' Regulations 1980* govern the disposal of asbestos and are designed to protect the general public from exposure to asbestos dust by providing that, on disposal, no dust escapes or will escape from buried deposits, thereby causing health hazards. The regulations do not, however, apply to asbestos cement unless broken up or containing crocidolite (see 4.39 below).

History of statute law on asbestos

4.7   The first regulations on asbestos, the *Asbestos Industry Regulations 1931*, were passed to control asbestosis in asbestos textile factories. These regulations were confined to asbestos factories handling and processing raw fibre. The purpose of these regulations was to prevent workers contracting asbestosis (see Chapter 31 'Occupational Health'), since the dangers of lung cancer and mesothelioma were not then fully documented, nor were the varying levels of hazard associated with the three different species of asbestos, i.e. crocidolite, amosite and chrysotile – and so the regulations applied to all three species. The *Asbestos Industry Regulations 1931* protected workers in asbestos textile factories, manufacture of brake linings and asbestos cement works, usually against the least harmful species of asbestos, namely chrysotile. Significantly, however, workers in the thermal insulation industry exposed to the most harmful kind of asbestos, namely crocidolite, were not covered by statute and their employers were under no statutory duties. Indeed, it was not until the *Asbestos Regulations 1969* were passed that these workers were covered for the first time.

Action levels and control limits

4.8   Being limited in operation to factories, the *Asbestos Regulations 1969* were replaced by the wider *Control of Asbestos at Work Regulations 1987*, extending to all workplaces where asbestos is made, used or handled. The basic duty of employers, whose employees are, or are liable to be exposed to above 'action level' asbestos, is to *prevent* the exposure of employees to asbestos. However, this may in many cases represent an ideal situation towards which employers should aim in the long term. Hence, where *prevention* of exposure is not reasonably practicable in cost/benefit terms, employers should *reduce* exposure of their employees, by means other than use of respiratory protective equipment, to the lowest level reasonably practicable. 'Action level' refers to one of the following cumulative exposures to asbestos over a continuous twelve-week period, namely:

(*a*)   where exposure is to asbestos consisting of or containing any crocidolite (blue asbestos) or amosite (brown asbestos) either alone or in conjunction with chrysotile (white asbestos), 48 fibre-hours per millilitre of air;

(*b*)   where exposure is to asbestos consisting of or containing any other types of asbestos (e.g. chrysotile – white asbestos), 96 fibre-hours per millilitre of air;

(*c*)   where both types of exposure occur separately during a twelve-week period, a proportionate number of fibre-hours per millilitre of air.

[*Reg 2(1) as amended by Control of Asbestos at Work (Amendment) Regulations 1992, Sch*].

But where reduction below the specified 'control limits' is not reasonably practicable in cost/benefit terms, employees must be supplied additionally with suitable and approved respiratory protective equipment in order to reduce the concentration of airborne asbestos inhaled by employees to a level below the specified 'control limit' (see further 4.3 above).

4.9   In addition, all employers whose employees are, or are liable to be affected, must designate asbestos areas and respirator zones, monitor the exposure of employees to asbestos, ensure that employees undergo regular periodic medical checks and keep health records for a minimum of forty years. Penalties for breach of these regulations are the same as those for breach of the *Health and Safety at Work etc. Act 1974* itself, that is, a maximum fine of £5,000 on summary conviction and an indefinite fine and/or up to two years' imprisonment on conviction on indictment. Moreover, many of the duties exist for the benefit not just of employees but also of indirect workers and the general public who may be affected by exposure to asbestos. The duties also apply to self-employed persons. [*Reg 3*].

Control of Asbestos at Work Regulations 1987 (SI 1987 No 2115) (as amended)

Prohibitions on asbestos activities

4.10   No employer must carry out work which:

(*a*)   exposes, or

(*b*)   is liable to expose,

his employees to asbestos, unless first:

(i)   he has identified the type of asbestos involved in the work activity; or

(ii)   he has assumed that the asbestos is not chrysotile alone and treated it accordingly (see 4.14, 4.15 below)

[*Reg 4*];

(iii)   he has made and regularly reviewed an assessment of exposure. Such assessment must:

(*a*)   identify the type of asbestos;

(*b*)   determine the nature and degree of exposure expected in the course of the work;

(*c*)   specify the steps necessary to prevent or reduce exposure to the lowest level reasonably practicable (see Chapter 15 'Employers' Duties' for meaning of this expression). The assessment must be reviewed regularly where there is a significant change in working conditions or if the assessment does not seem to be still valid

[*Reg 5(4) as amended by Control of Asbestos at Work (Amendment) Regulations 1992, Sch*];

(iv)   he has prepared a written plan prior to the commencement of removal activities, a copy to be retained for at least two years following completion of the work [*Reg 5A as inserted by Control of Asbestos at Work (Amendment) Regulations 1992, Sch*] (see 4.14, 4.15 below);

(v)   he has notified the 'enforcing authority' (see Chapter 17 'Enforcement' for the meaning of this expression) at least 28 days before commencing work, of:

(*a*)   his name, address and telephone number;

(*b*)   his usual place of business;

(*c*)   types of asbestos used or handled;

(*d*)   maximum quantity of asbestos on the premises (see 4.14 below);

(*e*)   activities/processes involved on the premises;

(*f*)   products (if any) manufactured (see 4.16 below);

(*g*)   date when work activity is to start.

Also any material change(s) in work activity involving asbestos must be notified. [*Reg 6, 1 Sch*].

Notification of work with asbestos: specimen form

4.11 To comply with regulation 6 of the Control of Asbestos at Work Regulations 1987 the following particulars are to be sent to the relevant Enforcing Authority.

Name ....

Company ....

Usual place of business ....

....

Telephone number ....

Brief description of work with asbestos

1 Type(s) of asbestos used or handled (crocidolite, amosite, chrysotile or other)

....

....

....

2 Maximum quantity of asbestos held on the premises at any one time

....

....

....

3 Activities or processes involved

....

....

....

4 Products manufactured

....

....

....

5 Date of commencement of work activity where work has yet to begin

....

....

....

Duties in connection with asbestos activities

Employers

4.12 All employers whose employees are, or are liable to be, affected by exposure to above 'action level' asbestos (see 4.8 above), must:

(*a*) provide adequate information, instruction and training to such employees, so that they are aware of the risks and can take the necessary precautions (see 4.20 below) [*Reg 7*];

(*b*) (i) (ideally) prevent exposure of employees to asbestos, but where prevention of exposure is not reasonably practicable, reduce exposure to the lowest level reasonably practicable by means other than use of respiratory protective equipment (that is, by substituting for asbestos a substance not creating a health risk or lesser health risk to employees) [*Reg 8(1A) as inserted by Control of Asbestos at Work (Amendment) Regulations 1992, Sch*], and inform workers of unforeseen events arising from abnormal exposure to asbestos,

(ii) where reduction to below specified 'control limits' (see 4.8 above) is not reasonably practicable, supply employees in addition with suitable and HSC approved respiratory protective equipment in order to reduce the concentration of airborne asbestos inhaled by employees to a level below the specified 'control limit'

[*Reg 8 as amended by Control of Asbestos at Work (Amendment) Regulations 1992, Sch*],

(iii) if an unforeseen event occurs, resulting in escape of asbestos, ensure that only persons responsible for carrying out repairs are permitted into an affected area and are provided with respiratory protective equipment/clothing *and* that employees are notified (see 4.17–4.20 below)

[*Reg 8(4) as amended by Control of Asbestos at Work (Amendment) Regulations 1992, Sch*];

(*c*) ensure that personal protective equipment is properly used or applied [*Reg 9*];

(*d*) and is maintained in a clean and efficient state and in good working order and is regularly examined/tested by a competent person (see 1.37 INTRODUCTION). A record of such maintenance must be kept for at least five years [*Reg 10*];

(*e*) provide adequate and suitable protective clothing and see that such clothing is disposed of as asbestos waste or, alternatively, cleaned at regular intervals. The clothing must first be packed in a suitable container labelled 'Warning. Contains asbestos. Breathing asbestos dust is dangerous to health. Follow safety instructions' [*Reg 11, 2 Sch*];

(*f*) (ideally) prevent the spread of asbestos, but where prevention is not reasonably practicable, reduce its spread to the lowest level reasonably practicable [*Reg 12*] (see 4.16 below);

(*g*) keep work premises clean and, in the case of new premises, ensure that they are:

(i) designed/constructed to facilitate cleaning, and

(ii)   equipped with an adequate and suitable vacuum cleaning system which ideally should be a fixed system

[*Reg 13*].

Designated areas/air monitoring/health records

Designated asbestos areas/respirator zones

4.13   All employers must:

(*a*)   designate as asbestos any area where exposure to asbestos of an employee exceeds, or is liable to exceed, the 'action level' (see 4.8 above);

(*b*)   designate respirator zones in any zone where the concentration of asbestos exceeds, or is liable to exceed, the 'control limit' (see 4.8 above);

(*c*)   ensure that employees (other than employees whose work so requires) do not either (i) enter or (ii) remain in any designated areas/zones;

(*d*)   ensure that employees do not eat/drink/smoke in designated areas/zones.

Both (*a*) asbestos areas and (*b*) respirator zones must be separately demarcated and identified by notices, and in the case of a respirator zone, the notice must require an employee entering the zone to wear respiratory protective equipment. [*Reg 14*].

Written assessments

4.14   Written assessments should specify:

(i)   type of work involved;

(ii)   reasons for not using a substitute material;

(iii)   type and quantity of asbestos and results of analysis;

(iv)   details of expected exposure – and, in particular,

(*a*)   likelihood of action level being exceeded (see 4.8 above),

(*b*)   likelihood of control limit being exceeded (see 4.8 above),

(*c*)   if above relevant control limits, expected exposure for provision of respiratory protective equipment,

(*d*)   frequency and duration of exposure,

(*e*)   expected exposure of non-employees,

(*f*)   air monitoring results,

(*g*)   measures to reduce exposure to lowest level reasonably practicable (see 4.16 below),

(*h*)   procedures relating to provision and use of respiratory protective equipment and other protective equipment,

(*j*)   in case of demolition, procedures for asbestos to be removed prior to demolition,

(*k*)   procedures for dealing with emergencies,

(*l*)   procedures for disposal of asbestos waste.

(ACOP to these Regulations).

Plan of work

4.15   In the case of demolition and construction work or asbestos removal work, a plan of work should be prepared, prior to work commencement, specifying

(i)   nature/duration of work;

(ii)   address/location of work;

(iii)   methods for handling asbestos;

(iv)   personal protective equipment for protection and decontamination of employees, including those living nearby.

The plan, which must be submitted to HSE on request, should indicate that, so far as reasonably practicable, asbestos/asbestos products have been removed prior to work commencement. [*Reg 5A as inserted by Control of Asbestos at Work (Amendment) Regulations 1992, Sch*].

Reduction of exposure to asbestos

4.16   Exposure to asbestos dust can be avoided or minimised both by local exhaust ventilation and a suitable work system – the latter varying according to whether the working environment is construction or manufacturing. In the case of *construction*, a suitable work system consists of:

(i)   removal of asbestos materials prior to work commencement;

(ii)   methods of work involving minimum breakage, abrasion, machining or cutting of asbestos;

(iii)   suppression of dust by wetting;

(iv)   segregation of work with asbestos;

(v)   removal of off-cuts, waste and dust.

In the case of *manufacturing*, similar results are achievable by:

(i)   limiting quantity of asbestos used;

(ii)   limiting number of persons exposed;

(iii)   ensuring collection of waste and removal from work area as soon as possible in suitably labelled containers;

(iv)   ensuring that damaged containers of raw fibre and waste are repaired forthwith or placed inside another suitable container;

(v)   avoiding manual handling of raw fibre or intermediate products;

(vi)   cleaning/sealing all products containing asbestos, as well as premises and plant (see 4.20 below).

Maintenance and inspection

4.17   Exhaust ventilation equipment should be regularly checked and, in particular, hoods, air movement and dampers. If there are any defects, these should be reported immediately. Moreover, equipment should be

(i)   inspected weekly, and

(ii)   examined and tested by a competent person every six months.

Weekly inspections

4.18   Weekly inspections consist of a check on position, condition of hoods and any visible signs of malfunction (e.g. dust deposits).

In particular,

     (i)   if dust seems to be escaping, this should be confirmed by means of a dust lamp;

    (ii)   pressure drop across the filter should be checked in the case of manometers fitted to dust collectors;

  (iii)   filter hoppers/bins should be checked to ensure proper routine emptying;

  (iv)   record of weekly inspection should be kept and any faults logged;

   (v)   faults should be rectified quickly.

Six-monthly examination and test

4.19   This consists of:

   (a)   *New equipment – Part I examination*

        (i)   confirmation that system is operating to specification;

       (ii)   measurement of pressures and air velocities (i.e. static and dynamic pressures, face and duct velocities as well as static pressure differences across fans and filters);

     (iii)   checks on dust collection.

   (b)   *Previously examined machinery – Part II examination*

        (i)   visual check for deterioration/leakage;

       (ii)   verification that method of use of system is satisfactory;

     (iii)   check on dust collection;

    (iv)   measurement of pressures/velocities.

This done, a report of the examination should be completed and signed within 14 days.

Maintenance schedules

4.20   Apart from inspections, the following maintenance on controls (and personal protective equipment) is necessary, namely,

   (a)   cleaning equipment – particularly vacuum cleaners (to BS 5145);

   (b)   washing and changing facilities;

   (c)   controls (especially enclosures) to prevent contamination.

The maintenance schedule should specify:

   (i)   which controls require maintenance;

  (ii)   how maintenance is to be carried out;

 (iii)   who is responsible for maintenance and remedying defects.

Asbestos premises and hot work

4.21   Cleaning of asbestos-contaminated premises should be frequent, and for inside walls and ceilings at least once a year, though not by dry manual brushing or sweeping. Hosing is permissible if residues are suitably disposed of (see 4.24 below). Ideally, a fixed vacuum system should be installed, using high efficiency filters and venting (preferably) outside. Small amounts of asbestos dust can be removed with a well-dampened cloth.

Asbestos stripping should not be carried out on hot plant until absolutely necessary, and preferably on a scheduled basis during shutdowns or holidays, since the risk of heat stress is greater at such times, leading possibly to heat stroke (see 31.42 OCCUPATIONAL HEALTH), which can be fatal. The main reason for this is that, as insulation material is progressively removed, heat input into the working area will increase; in addition, protective equipment is normally hooded with elasticated cuffs and ankles, restricting air movement over the body and minimising evaporation of sweat. Moreover, respiratory protective equipment often restricts breathing. Work in such high temperatures can cause burns, swelling of ankles and feet, fainting, muscle cramps, heat exhaustion, breathing difficulties and thirst; and so periodical break-offs are advisable as follows:

Work at 26.0°C – 27.5°C – 15 minutes rest after 45 minutes work

Work at 27.5°C – 29.0°C – 30 minutes rest after 30 minutes work

Work at 29.0°C – 31.0°C – 45 minutes rest after 15 minutes work

Air monitoring

4.22   All employers must monitor the exposure of employees to asbestos and keep a record of such monitoring for:

(*a*)   forty years, if a health record (see 4.23 below);

(*b*)   otherwise, five years.

[*Reg 15 as amended by Control of Asbestos at Work (Amendment) Regulations 1992, Sch*].

Health records/medical surveillance

4.23   All employers must:

(*a*)   keep health records of all employees exposed to asbestos exceeding 'action level' (see above) for at least forty years (the incubation period of many asbestos-related diseases) [*Reg 16(1) as amended by Control of Asbestos at Work (Amendment) Regulations 1992, Sch*];

(*b*)   require employees exposed to above 'action level' asbestos, to undergo a periodic medical examination at least every two years.

Employers must be issued with a certificate of examination and keep it for at least four years, giving a copy to the employee. Such medical examinations, carried out by Employment Medical Advisers (EMAs), during working hours and on work premises, are at the expense of the employer, who must therefore provide suitable facilities. On being given reasonable notice, employers must allow employees access to health records. [*Reg 16*].

Washing facilities/storage/distribution/labelling etc.

4.24   All employers must:

(*a*)   provide employees exposed to asbestos with adequate and suitable facilities for

(i) washing/changing,

(ii) storage of protective clothing and personal clothing not worn during working hours, and

(iii) separate storage of respiratory protective equipment

[*Reg 17*];

(*b*) ensure that raw asbestos or asbestos waste is not

(i) stored,

(ii) received into or despatched from the place of work, or

(iii) distributed (unless in a totally enclosed distribution system) within the place of work,

unless it is in a suitable and sealed container clearly labelled and marked [*Reg 18*].

Labelling/marking of asbestos products

4.25 (*a*) Raw asbestos must be labelled: 'Warning. Contains asbestos. Breathing asbestos dust is dangerous to health. Follow safety instructions'. Additionally, chrysotile will have to be labelled 'R 45 – May Cause Cancer'.

(*b*) Waste containing asbestos must be:

(i) labelled in accordance with the *Chemicals (Hazard Information and Packaging) Regulations 1993* (see Chapter 9 'Dangerous Substances I'); or

(ii) if conveyed by road in a road tanker or tank container, in accordance with the *Road Traffic (Carriage of Dangerous Substances in Road Tankers and Tank Containers) Regulations 1992* (see Chapter 10 'Dangerous Substances II').

(*c*) Where asbestos is supplied as a product for use at work, it must be labelled: 'Warning. Contains asbestos. Breathing asbestos dust is dangerous to health. Follow safety instructions'.

[*Reg 19*].

(For the effect of 'warnings' on civil liability in connection with defective products, see further Chapter 38 'Product Safety'.)

Employees' duties

4.26 Every employee exposed to asbestos above 'action level' must:

(*a*) make full and proper use of any control measures, personal protective equipment or other facility provided by the employer;

(*b*) report any defect to the employer in personal protective equipment or control measures [*Reg 9(2)*];

(*c*) not enter/remain in (i) asbestos areas (ii) respirator zones (unless his work permits him to do so) [*Reg 14*];

(*d*) when required by his employer, present himself during working hours for medical examination/checks [*Reg 16(4)*].

Prohibitions on asbestos products – the Asbestos (Prohibitions) Regulations 1992 (SI 1992 No 3067)

(a) Amphibole asbestos

4.27   The *Asbestos (Prohibitions) Regulations 1992 (SI 1992 No 3067)* prohibit importation and supply of amphibole and use/supply of chrysotile asbestos. No-one must use amphibole asbestos or any product containing it, unless products containing

(*a*)   crocidolite or amosite, were in use before 1 January 1986, or

(*b*)   other forms of amphibole asbestos, were in use before 1 January 1993.

[*Regs 4, 5*].

Asbestos spraying is also prohibited [*Reg 6*].

(b) Chrysotile asbestos

Supply and use of products containing chrysotile is prohibited as follows:

(*a*)   materials/preparations for spraying;

(*b*)   paints/ varnishes;

(*c*)   filters for liquids – medical filters (after 31 December 1994);

(*d*)   road surfacing material with more than 2% fibre content;

(*e*)   mortars, protective coatings, filters, sealants, jointing compounds, mastics, glues, decorative products/finishes;

(*f*)   insulating or soundproofing materials with a low density;

(*g*)   air filters, filters used in transport and distribution of natural/town gas;

(*h*)   underlays for plastic floors/wall coverings;

(*j*)   textiles unless treated to avoid fibre release – diaphragms for electrolysis after 31 December 1998;

(*k*)   roofing felt (after 1 July 1993).

[*Reg 7(1), Sch*].

Asbestos stripping by contractors – Asbestos (Licensing) Regulations 1983 (SI 1983 No 1649)

4.28   A system of licensing coupled with notification in advance applies to work with asbestos insulation or coating. (Asbestos-based insulating boards, ceiling tiles or other low-density products are no longer in use in the United Kingdom.)

The only situation where a licence is not necessary for such work is where:

(*a*)   the whole job will only take two hours (or less) *and* no one will spend more than one hour on the work in seven consecutive days; or

(*b*)   a self-employed person, or an employer using his own employees, is doing the work on his own premises; or

(*c*)   the work consists solely of air monitoring or collecting samples.

[*Reg 3*].

Even though a licence is not necessary, employers (or self-employed persons) must still comply with the *Control of Asbestos at Work Regulations 1987* and in particular, should:

(i) give to employees the necessary instruction and training;

(ii) provide adequate information to others (e.g. workforce of an outside contractor) who may be affected by the work;

(iii) achieve the lowest level of asbestos dust reasonably practicable (for the meaning of 'reasonably practicable', see Chapter 15 'Employers' Duties');

(iv) ensure that employees are under medical surveillance.

Issue of licence

4.29 All licences are issued by the Health and Safety Executive (HSE), even if the premises have previously been inspected by the local authority. Enforcing authorities (i.e. HSE/local authority) must be given at least 28 days' notice of any proposed stripping work for any type of asbestos. [*Reg 4(1)(b)*].

The HSE can:

(*a*) impose a time limit on the period for which a licence is issued;

(*b*) impose other conditions; or

(*c*) refuse to issue a licence.

[*Reg 4(2)*].

There is an appeal to the Secretary of State under *HSWA s 44*.

Any conditions imposed will depend upon the applicant's previous track record with asbestos work; and companies with limited experience will receive more restrictive licences than companies with greater experience. In particular,

(i) new applicants will receive one year licences;

(ii) renewal licensees will receive a licence for 30 months;

(iii) licensees who have been the recipient of enforcement action but who are considered likely to improve, will be required to comply with an agreed method statement for each job;

(iv) licensees with a poor first year record, but not bad enough for refusal, will receive a similar restrictive licence, but for one year.

For medical surveillance requirements, see 4.23(*b*) above.

Occupational diseases associated with asbestos

4.30 There are three occupational diseases associated with working with asbestos, i.e.:

— diffuse mesothelioma (D3);

— primary carcinoma of the lung (D8); and

— bilateral diffuse pleural thickening (D9).

The occupations for which these three conditions are prescribed are as follows:

(*a*) working or handling asbestos, or any admixture of asbestos;

(*b*) manufacture or repair of asbestos textiles or other articles containing or composed of asbestos;

(*c*) cleaning of any machinery or plant used for (*a*) and (*b*), and of any chambers, fixtures and appliances for the collection of asbestos dust;

(*d*)   substantial exposure to dust arising from operations (*a*), (*b*) and (*c*).

[*Social Security (Industrial Injuries) (Prescribed Diseases) Regulations 1985 (SI 1985 No 967), 1 Sch*].

Actions against the employer for asbestos-related diseases

4.31   In addition to being prescribed occupational diseases, asbestosis/mesothelioma are also actionable at common law against the employer (*Bryce v Swan Hunter Group [1987] 2 Lloyd's List Rep 426*). It is exactly this type of action i.e. damages for insidious occupational disease, which has caused judges to ponder as to whether such tortious action begins either when (*a*) exposure to asbestos/asbestos dust takes place or (*b*) symptoms of asbestosis/mesothelioma manifest themselves. Symptom manifestation can take anything from 20-30 years after exposure and consequently the possibility arises that actions for damages, being actions in respect of 'personal injuries', may become statute-barred (see 'time limitation periods' at 15.11 EMPLOYERS' DUTIES).

Time limitation problems

4.32   The first indication that strict adherence to time limitation statutes might not be the best approach to entitlement to compensation for asbestosis/mesothelioma occurred in *Central Asbestos Co Ltd v Dodd [1973] AC 518*. Here the respondent was employed by the appellant in a workshop where various processes connected with asbestos were carried out from 1952 to 1965. Throughout that period the employer was in breach of the *Asbestos Regulations 1931* and, in consequence, the employee was exposed to asbestos dust and contracted asbestosis, leading eventually to his death. The employee's condition was diagnosed in January 1964, when he was advised by the Pneumoconiosis Medical Panel not to carry on working with asbestos. He did not, however, feel ill then and so continued working for the company. In March 1964 he was awarded disablement benefit based on 10% disablement. In September 1965 the respondent left the company on his doctor's advice. By then he knew that (*a*) he was suffering from asbestosis, (*b*) the company had been convicted for breach of the *Asbestos Regulations 1931* during all the period he had worked there, and (*c*) the nature of his condition meant that he had to stop working with asbestos. He did not, however, know he had a good cause of action against his employer, having been told by the works manager (who was also suffering from asbestosis) that there was a panel which awarded compensation for asbestosis, but that it was impossible to sue his employer. When he learned that a co-employee was suing the company in April 1967, he also started legal action.

The appellant argued that the claim was statute-barred under the *Limitation Act 1963*. It was held (by the House of Lords) that the action was not statute-barred. It was exactly this sort of situation that the *Limitation Act 1963* was intended to remedy. Explaining why, Lord Reid said, 'In this disease (pneumoconiosis), as in asbestosis, the sufferer's lungs may have been damaged many years before any symptoms develop or even many years before any X-ray or other examination can disclose that there is anything wrong. So the men only discovered that they had the disease at various dates from 1955 onwards; and this House was compelled by the terms of the statute (*Limitation Act 1939*) to reach the absurd result that a man's claim may be time-barred before it is possible for him to know that he has suffered any damage'. Significantly, claims for asbestosis/mesothelioma cannot begin to run before a claimant has knowledge, both medical and legal, of his condition and liability for it. Current law is contained in the *Limitation Act 1980*, which states that the period for initiating action is three years from:

(*a*)   the date on which the cause of action accrued; or

(*b*)   the date of knowledge (if later) of the person injured.

[*Limitation Act 1980, s 11(4)*].

Although employers can be sued for the death of employees caused by asbestos-related conditions, this does not necessarily extend to wives of asbestos workers (*Gunn v Wallsend Slipway and Engineering Co Ltd, The Times, 23 January 1989* where the wife of the plaintiff died as a result of mesothelioma caused by inhalation of asbestos from the plaintiff's working clothes, and it was held that when the plaintiff began to be exposed to asbestos dust (that is in the mid-fifties), medical knowledge did not extend to an appreciation that the condition could be contracted in that way, that is, by washing contaminated clothes). Had the wife's condition begun to be contracted in that way after 1965, it might well have been possible for the plaintiff to have recovered damages, since the damages associated with asbestos were better known and so such a risk would have been foreseeable. (A similar 'prohibition' applies in the case of lead, see 15.1 EMPLOYERS' DUTIES and 36.1 PERSONAL PROTECTIVE EQUIPMENT.)

Discretionary exclusion of time limits

4.33   Statutory time limits can be excluded if the court thinks it equitable to allow an action to proceed. [*Limitation Act 1980, s 33*]. (See 'time limitation periods' at 15.11 EMPLOYERS' DUTIES.)

Practical control measures

4.34   Asbestos has been the standard form of thermal insulation since the turn of the century and may be found in numerous locations in industrial, commercial and domestic premises. In its various forms, it may be present in lagging to pipework, tanks and boilers, or as a component of structural finishes, such as walls and ceilings. In most cases, the presence of asbestos is not considered until it is actually exposed through normal wear and tear on plant and structural finishes, through structural damage or during redevelopment work.

In order to prevent further exposure, a practical control system is necessary, which incorporates procedures for sampling, treatment or removal, and disposal of asbestos waste.

Asbestos has been used widely for the following industrial purposes:

(*a*)   as fire protection on structures, protected exits, doors and in fire breaks in service ducts;

(*b*)   in the construction of inner walls and partitions;

(*c*)   in switchgear areas;

(*d*)   in ceiling tiles and linings for semi-exposed areas e.g. loading bay canopies;

(*e*)   for thermal and acoustic insulation of buildings; and

(*f*)   for thermal insulation of cold stores.

It may be applied in several forms, namely:

—   *Sprayed asbestos coating.* The asbestos content is not normally less than 55%, and such coating usually contains amosite or crocidolite.

—   *Thermal insulation material.* Thermal insulation of services or process plant frequently consists of sectional insulation, such as asbestos insulation board, which may contain a considerable proportion of asbestos. In some cases asbestos may be a minor constituent of the mixture together with materials such as magnesia and diatomaceous earth. The asbestos content of insulation board is typically 16.25%, amosite being the most common form of asbestos used.

Sampling

4.35   An asbestos removal contractor should initially commence operation by taking a series of 10 gm samples in areas where asbestos is suspected. In large buildings this may entail taking several hundred samples for analysis. Once the results of these samples have been received a decision to remove or seal the asbestos must be taken. The actual sampling procedure needs a high degree of control in terms of site preparation for sampling, the use of personal protective equipment, the actual sampling process and despatch of samples. Specific provisions apply to those persons taking the sample, in exactly the same way as those engaged in removal or sealing of the asbestos.

Disposal of asbestos waste

4.36   A number of aspects must be considered here:

(a)   the provision and use of suitable receptacles;

(b)   transfer procedures from surface to receptacles;

(c)   transfer procedures from working area to disposal point; and

(d)   action to be taken in the event of asbestos spillage.

Asbestos waste must be disposed of only at a licensed disposal site and in accordance with specific requirements laid down by the licensing authority i.e. county council. The requirements relate to information on the premises from which the waste is removed, the address of the licensed site, the nature and composition of the waste, the quantity to be deposited, and the size, number and type of waste containers (see also 4.39 below).

Transportation of asbestos waste

4.37   Before transporting any asbestos waste, the haulier must ensure that, so far as is reasonably practicable:

(a)   suitable vehicles are available;

(b)   the release of asbestos dust is prevented;

(c)   effective arrangements exist for dealing with accidental spillage; and

(d)   effective arrangements exist for decontamination of the vehicle used for transport.

Such arrangements should ensure that asbestos dust is not released during decontamination.

HSE Guidance Notes

4.38   A number of Guidance Notes dealing with this subject are available and should be consulted, together with the Approved Code of Practice and Guidance Note mentioned earlier, before any work involving asbestos is undertaken. These Guidance Notes are:

EH 10 – Asbestos – Control limits. Measurement of airborne dust concentrations and assessment of control measures.

EH 35 – Probable asbestos dust concentrations on construction processes.

EH 36 – Work with asbestos cement.

EH 37 – Work with asbestos insulating board.

EH 41 – Respiratory protective equipment for use against asbestos.

EH 47 – The provision, use and maintenance of hygiene facilities for work with asbestos insulation and coatings.

EH 50 – Training operatives and supervisors for work with asbestos insulation and coatings.

EH 51 – Enclosures provided for work with asbestos insulation, coatings and insulation board.

EH 52 – Removal techniques for asbestos insulation.

Disposal of asbestos/asbestos products

4.39 Disposal of asbestos is governed by the *Control of Pollution (Special Waste) Regulations 1980 (SI 1980 No 1709)*, passed under the *Control of Pollution Act 1974* and the *Environmental Protection Act 1990* (see further Chapter 12 'Emissions into the Atmosphere'). Duties under the *Special Waste Regulations* are placed on (*a*) producers, (*b*) carriers and (*c*) disposers (though not on disposal authorities disposing within their own area). The main duties are as follows:

(*a*)   any producer of special waste (e.g. asbestos) must prepare six copies of a 'consignment note' (see *fig. 2* below), complete parts A and B of the note and send a copy to (i) the disposal authority and (ii) the carrier, retaining a copy for himself [*Reg 4*];

(*b*)   the carrier must transmit copies to the disposer, retaining a copy of the consignment note on which parts A, B, C, D and E have been completed [*Reg 5*];

(*c*)   the disposer, on receiving a consignment of special waste, must:

   (i)   complete part E of the consignment note on three of the remaining copies,

   (ii)   retain a copy,

   (iii) send a copy to the disposal authority, and

   (iv)   send a copy to the carrier

   [*Reg 6*];

(*d*)   (i) producers and (ii) carriers must keep on site a register containing copies of all consignment notes for at least two years; moreover, a disposer must keep a register containing copies of all consignment notes until the disposal licence is surrendered/revoked [*Reg 13*];

(*e*)   any person who deposits special waste on land must record the location of each deposit and keep records until the disposal licence is surrendered/ revoked, and then send the records to the local disposal authority [*Reg 14*].

Offences/penalties

4.40 Any producer, disposer or carrier who fails to comply with the regulations is liable:

(*a*)   on summary conviction, to a fine of not more than £5,000; and

(*b*)   on conviction on indictment, to imprisonment for up to two years and an indefinite fine.

[*Reg 16* (as subsequently amended)].

Form for consignment notes for disposal of hazardous waste

4.41

<table>
<tr>
<td colspan="2">
Department of the Environment/Welsh Office/
Scottish Development Department

CONSIGNMENT NOTE FOR THE CARRIAGE
& DISPOSAL OF HAZARDOUS WASTES
</td>
<td>Serial No.</td>
</tr>
<tr>
<td>Producer's
Certificate

A</td>
<td colspan="2">
(1) The material described in B is to be collected from...........................
....

and (2) taken to..
....

Signed.. Name ....
On behalf of... Position...................................
Address and telephone...................... Date ....
.... Estimated date of collection..........
</td>
</tr>
<tr>
<td>Description
of the
Waste

B</td>
<td colspan="2">
(1) General description and physical nature of waste

(2) Relevant chemical and biological components and maximum
    concentrations

(3) Quantity of waste and size, type and number of containers

(4) Process(es) from which waste originated
</td>
</tr>
</table>

Carrier's Collection Certificate **C**	I certify that I collected the consignment of waste and that the information given in A(1) & (2) and B(1) & (3) is correct, subject to any amendment listed in this space: I collected this consignment on............................at.............:............hours Signed................................Name............................Vehicle Registration No.... On behalf of... Address and telephone...Date............................ ....
Producer's Collection Certificate **D**	I certify that the information given in B & C is correct and that the carrier was advised of appropriate precautionary measures. Signed................................Name............................Telephone................Date................
Disposer's Certificate **E**	I certify that Waste Disposal Licence No.........................issued by.................. .... Council, authorises the treatment/disposal at this facility of the waste described in B (and as amended where necessary at C). Name and address of facility... .... This waste was delivered in vehicle (Reg. No.).. at...............:.............hours on (date)............................and the carrier gave his name as...on behalf of .... Proper instructions were given that the waste should be taken to.. Signed................................Name............................Position........................ Date...on behalf of...
For use by Producer/ Carrier/ Disposer	

fig.2

Chapter 5

Children and Young Persons

Introduction

5.1   Health and safety legislation understandably lays great emphasis upon the need for safety consciousness, supervision, and training in safe methods of work for young people (*Kerry v Carter* [*1969*] *3 AER 723*). In particular, there are specific restrictions relating to the employment of children (see 5.4 below), and no child under the age of 13 can be employed in any capacity, paid or otherwise. In addition, there are special provisions relating to young persons operating machinery (although most of these will eventually be repealed by the *Provision and Use of Work Equipment Regulations 1992 (SI 1992 No 2932)* and replaced by regulations therein (see 5.6-5.10)); and restrictions on the employment of young persons in certain processes (5.11) and in agriculture (5.15), but the former requirements governing hours of work, rest breaks, meal times, shift work and night work, have been removed by the *Employment Act 1989, 3 Sch Pt II* and *8 Sch.* (For further information on the removal of restrictions relating to women workers, see Chapter 45 'Women Workers'.) This chapter outlines the provisions regulating employment of children and young persons, cross-referencing, where appropriate, to parallel protection in Chapters 28 'Machinery Safety' and 45 'Women Workers'.

Definition of 'child'

5.2   A child is a person under compulsory school-leaving age, i.e., at present, under 16. [*Education Act 1944, s 58(1); Education (School-Leaving) Dates Act 1976*].

Definition of 'young person'

5.3   A young person is a person who has ceased to be a child but who has not attained 18. [*Employment of Women, Young Persons and Children Act 1920, s 4; Factories Act 1961, s 176(1)*].

Prohibitions on the employment of children

5.4   It is forbidden to employ any child, whether paid or not, in any of the following circumstances:

(*a*)   where the child is under the age of 13;

(*b*)   before the end of school hours;

(*c*)   before 7 a.m. or after 7 p.m. on any day;

(*d*)   for more than two hours on any school day;

(*e*)   for more than two hours on Sunday;

(*f*)   to lift, carry or move anything heavy enough to cause him injury.

[*Children and Young Persons Act 1933, s 18(1); Children Act 1972, s 1(2); Employment of Children Act 1973, 1 Sch Pt II*].

The prohibitions set out above are general, applying to shops, offices and factories. In addition, there is the specific provision that no child can be employed in an industrial undertaking, i.e. mines, quarries, factories, building and works of engineering construction and transportation. [*Employment of Women, Young Persons and Children Act 1920, s 1(1)*].

Local authorities have the power to make bye-laws relevant to the employment of children, although a similar power relating to young persons was revoked by the *Employment Act 1989*. [*Children and Young Persons Act 1933, s 18*].

Trainees

5.5   Certain trainees, who are not employees, are given the protection of the *Health and Safety at Work Act* as follows:

(*a*)   YT trainees (provided the training is not in an educational establishment or part of the contract of employment (see 1.19 INTRODUCTION));

(*b*)   employment training;

(*c*)   employment rehabilitation;

(*d*)   job training scheme;

(*e*)   individual training with an employer;

(*f*)   voluntary projects programme;

(*g*)   community programme;

(*h*)   wider opportunities training programme;

(*j*)   management extension programme;

(*k*)   graduate gateway programme;

(*l*)   professional training scheme;

(*m*)   special training provision; and

(*n*)   community industry scheme.

[*Health and Safety (Training For Employment) Regulations 1990 (SI 1990 No 1380)*].

RIDDOR also applies to trainees and apprentices (see further Chapter 3 'Accident Reporting').

Young persons and work involving machinery

5.6   No young person may work with certain specified machines unless he has been fully instructed as to the dangers and the precautions to be taken, and

(*a*)   he has received sufficient training in working the machine; and

(*b*)   he is under adequate supervision from a person who has a thorough knowledge and experience of the machine.

[*Factories Act 1961, s 21(1)*].

Employers must send a written notice of the employment of young people, within seven days of their commencing work, to the local careers office. The object of this duty is selective medical examinations of those who may benefit from this. [*Employment Medical Advisory Service Act 1972, s 5*].

Machines for which training is specifically required

5.7   The following machines are those for which a young person must be specifically trained.

Mechanically powered machines

(a)   brick and tile presses;

(b)   machines used for opening or teasing in upholstery or bedding works;

(c)   carding machines in use in the wool textile industry;

(d)   corner staying machines;

(e)   dough brakes;

(f)   dough mixers;

(g)   worm pressure extruding machines;

(h)   gill boxes in use in the wool textile trades;

(j)   machines in use in laundries, i.e.:

    (i)   hydro-extractors,

    (ii)   calenders,

    (iii)   washing machines,

    (iv)   garment presses;

(k)   meat mincing machines;

(l)   milling machines in metal trades;

(m)   pie and tart making machines;

(n)   power presses, both hydraulic and pneumatic;

(o)   loose knife punching machines;

(p)   wire stitching machines;

(q)   semi-automatic wood turning lathes.

Machines used without mechanical power

(r)   guillotine machines;

(s)   platen printing machines.

[*Dangerous Machines (Training of Young Persons) Order 1954 (SI 1954 No 921)*].

Prohibition on the use of power presses and circular saws

5.8   There is a general prohibition on the operation of power presses by young persons. [*Power Presses Regulations 1965 (SI 1965 No 1441), Reg 4(1)(4)*]. Moreover, there is a similar prohibition on the operation of circular saws by young persons in *existing* factories until 1 January 1997. [*Woodworking Machines Regulations 1974 (SI 1974 No 903), Reg 13(1)(3)*]. This prohibition does not apply in new workplaces, since the *Woodworking Machines Regulations 1974* have been revoked by the *Provision and Use of Work Equipment Regulations 1992, Reg 27* (see Chapter 28 'Machinery Safety').

Fencing/cleaning/general maintenance of machinery by young persons – all new workplaces

5.9 In all new workplaces, employers must ensure that

(1) all work equipment is constructed and adapted so that, so far as reasonably practicable, maintenance operations, involving risks to health and safety, can be carried out while work equipment is shut down; or

(2) (*a*) maintenance operations can be carried out without exposing a person carrying them out to danger, or

(*b*) appropriate measures can be taken to protect such person.

[*Provision and Use of Work Equipment Regulations 1992, Reg 22*]. (See further Chapter 28 'Machinery Safety'.)

In practice, this means that maintenance work will be carried out whilst machinery is inactive. If, however, equipment has to be running or working during maintenance operations and this is attendant with risks, safeguards should be instituted, e.g. provision of temporary guards, limited movement controls, crawl speed operated by hold-to-run controls.

Fencing/cleaning of machinery by young persons in existing workplaces

5.10 Existing factories are unaffected by *Reg 22* of the *Provision and Use of Work Equipment Regulations 1992* until 1 January 1997. In the meantime, the following requirements continue to apply (although technically revoked by *Reg 27*):

(1) Young persons not to lubricate/adjust machine parts whilst in motion – factories. [*Factories Act 1961, s 15(2)*].

(2) Young persons not to lubricate/adjust machinery whilst in motion – offices and shops. [*OSRPA s 17(5)*].

(3) (*a*) no examination of any part of machinery in motion not securely fenced;

(*b*) no lubrication/adjustment of machine parts while part of machinery is in motion.

[*Operations at Unfenced Machinery Regulations 1938/1946/1976, Reg 1*].

(4) No person to be a machine attendant unless 18 years. [*Operations at Unfenced Machinery Regulations, Reg 3*].

'In motion' can carry a different meaning, for the purposes of *Sec 15* of the *Factories Act 1961*, from the corresponding expression in *Sec 16* (see 28.15 MACHINERY SAFETY).

Restrictions on the employment of young persons — specific processes

5.11 Persons under 18 are prohibited from working in the following processes and occupations:

(*a*) (i) any lead process;

(ii) work in any room where manipulation of raw oxide of lead or pasting is carried out

[*Electric Accumulator Regulations 1925 (SR&O 1925 No 28), Reg 1*];

(*b*) any enamelling process [*Vitreous Enamelling of Metal or Glass Regulations 1908 (SR&O 1908 No 1258), Reg 7*] (persons under 16);

(*c*) certain work in the pottery industry [*Pottery (Health and Welfare) Special Regulations 1950 (SI 1950 No 65), Reg 6, as amended by Employment Act 1989, 8 Sch*];

(*d*) work on offshore installations [*Offshore Installations (Operational Safety, Health and Welfare) Special Regulations 1976 (SI 1976 No 1091), Reg 28*];

(*e*) certain agricultural activities (see 5.15 below);

(*f*) painting any part of a factory building with lead paint [*Factories Act 1961, s 131*] (for further controls over work with lead in any workplace, not just a factory).

Supply and use of lead paint has been prohibited from 28 February 1992 except in connection with historic buildings and works of art (*Environmental Protection (Controls on Injurious Substances) Regulations 1992 (SI 1992 No 31)* (see also 9.34 DANGEROUS SUBSTANCES I)).

Power of inspector to require factory employment to cease

5.12 Where a factory inspector is of the opinion that the employment of a young person in a factory or particular process is either prejudicial to his health, or to the health of other persons, he may serve a notice on the factory occupier informing him accordingly, and recommending that the employment of the young person be discontinued after the period named in the notice. After the expiry of that period, the factory occupier must not employ the young person, unless either the factory doctor, or the employment medical adviser has personally examined the young person and certified him fit to work in the factory or at the process. [*Factories Act 1961, s 119*]. This section, in effect, empowers an inspector to require a fitness for work certificate.

Provisions regulating the employment of young persons in offices and shops

5.13 Where a young person is employed in a shop, his employer must exhibit on the premises a notice specifying the weekday on which the young person is not to be employed after 1 p.m. [*Young Persons (Employment) Order 1938 (SR&O 1938 No 1501), Art 1*]. This is because all shops must give a weekly half-day holiday to employees and notice of this must be displayed in the shop. [*Shops Act 1950, s 1(1)*].

There is no equivalent statutory requirement in *OSRPA* to *Factories Act 1961, s 21* (see 5.6 above), regarding the training and supervision of young persons. *OSRPA s 19* relates to the training and supervision of persons generally working at dangerous machines. (See further Chapter 33 'Offices'.)

Employer's duty to record details of hours worked by a young person

5.14 The employer of a young person working in a shop (as defined in Chapter 40 'Shops') must keep records of the following details relating to that employee:

(*a*) his name;

(*b*) particulars of hours worked;

(c)   rest and meal intervals and a record of any overtime.

[Shops Act 1950, s 32].

Agriculture

5.15   Agriculture is the only major industry which has to take into account the constant presence of children and young persons. A considerable proportion of people killed in agricultural activities are children and young persons, particularly the former. Strict compliance with statutory requirements is, therefore, essential to combat this.

Main statutory prohibitions on jobs carried out by children and young persons

Children

5.16   (a)   *Children under 13 years.* A child under 13 must not:

   (i)   drive or ride on a tractor when used in the course of agricultural operations [*Agriculture (Avoidance of Accidents to Children) Regulations 1958, Regs 3, 4*];

   (ii)   ride on agricultural implements, while they are being towed or propelled [*Reg 5*].

   It is also an offence for a person to cause or permit a child under 13 to ride on or drive a tractor or machine, or to ride on an agricultural implement. [*Agriculture (Safety, Health and Welfare Provisions) Act 1956, s 7(3)*].

   (b)   *Children under 16 years.* A child under 16 must not:

   (i)   operate or assist at a circular saw [*Agriculture (Circular Saws) Regulations 1959, Reg 2, 2 Sch*];

   (ii)   remove a guard from a field machine [*Agriculture (Field Machinery) Regulations 1962, 1 Sch Pt IV*];

   (iii)   remove a guard from a stationary machine or prime mover [*Agriculture (Stationary Machinery) Regulations 1959, Sch Pt II*] (revoked by the *Provision and Use of Work Equipment Regulations 1992, Reg 27* but applicable to existing equipment until 1 January 1997).

Young persons

5.17   A young person must not:

   (a)   feed produce into a drum feeding mouth of a thresher [*Agriculture (Threshers and Balers) Regulations 1960, Sch Pt III*];

   (b)   operate a circular saw, except under the supervision of a person over 18 with a thorough knowledge of its working [*Agriculture (Circular Saws) Regulations 1959, Reg 1, 2 Sch*].

Chapter 6

Compensation for Work Injuries/ Diseases

Introduction

6.1 Compensation for work injuries, diseases and death is payable under two interrelated but nevertheless independent systems, namely, under the social security system (or national insurance, as it used to be known) and in the form of damages for civil wrongs (torts). The former is a form of public insurance, funded by employers/employees and taxpayers, and benefit is payable irrespective of liability on the part of an employer, i.e. 'no fault' – though connection with employment must be established. The social security system is bound by legislation, such as the various *Social Security Acts*, culminating in the present *Social Security Administration Act 1992* and the *Social Security Contributions and Benefits Act 1992*, the *Social Security (Industrial Injuries) (Prescribed Diseases) Regulations 1985* and sundry other legislation.

The tort system is a form of private insurance, funded by employers' liability insurance premiums (see Chapter 16 'Employers' Liability Insurance') and awards of damages depend on proof of negligence against an employer (see further Chapter 1 'Introduction' and Chapter 15 'Employers' Duties'). Current law is to be found in a variety of Acts, such as the *Law Reform (Personal Injuries) Act 1948*, the *Employers' Liability (Compulsory Insurance) Act 1969*, the *Employers' Liability (Defective Equipment) Act 1969* and the common law of tort, particularly negligence. Strictly speaking, the expression 'compensation' is reserved for 'benefits', whereas tort moneys are normally referred to as 'damages'. This chapter examines the two concurrent systems and interaction between them.

Social security benefits – background

6.2 As from 1948, when national (state) insurance came into being, two types of social security benefits were traditionally payable in relation to work injuries and/or diseases, i.e. (*a*) injury benefit and (*b*) disablement benefit. (Death benefit is also payable to the widow of a deceased worker.) Both these benefits were payable to employees (not self-employed persons) irrespective of contribution record (or absence of it). Injury benefit served to replace loss of earnings whilst an employee was off work for more than three days following an injury-causing accident 'arising out of and in the course of his employment'. [*Social Security Contributions and Benefits Act 1992, s 94*]. Disablement benefit, taking the form of a pension or, in less severe cases, a gratuity, was payable in respect of loss of faculty/amenity, whether or not an employee was prevented by injury/disease from working, and normally in respect of a prescribed occupational disease (see 6.7 below). Half the value of both injury and disablement benefit was deducted from any subsequently awarded damages. [*Social Security (Consequential Provisions) Act 1975, 2 Sch Pt VIII; Law Reform (Personal Injuries) Act 1948*]. (See 6.25 below for the current position.)

6.3   There were two key conditions attached to entitlement to benefit, i.e., that an employee suffered:

(*a*)   personal injury caused by accident arising out of and in the course of employment [*Social Security Contributions and Benefits Act 1992, s 94(1)*];

(*b*)   a prescribed occupational disease [*Social Security Contributions and Benefits Act 1992, s 108(1)*]; or

(*c*)   a prescribed personal injury (other than one caused by accident). [*Social Security Contributions and Benefits Act 1992, s 108*] (see further 6.4 below).

Generally, injury benefit was payable for injuries of type (*a*) and disablement benefit for occupational diseases, type (*b*). In addition, and less important in practice, was a third hybrid condition, known as a 'process' disease (see below), which, for historical reasons, was classified as part of 'personal injury caused by accident'. The key, therefore, to benefit under both schemes was causation – in the case of injury benefit, between employment and injury-causing accident, and in the case of disease, between employment(s) and disease. Many diseases are prescribed in relation to occupation, by reference to physical, biological and chemical agents, and current law is to be found in the *Social Security (Industrial Injuries) (Prescribed Diseases) Regulations 1985 (SI 1985 No 967)* (see Chapter 31 'Occupational Health'). In particular, if a disease was not prescribed, benefit was not payable, unless an employee could bring his case within 'personal injury by accident' parameters, as required by *Sec 94* of the *Social Security Contributions and Benefits Act 1992*. Alternatively, of course, he could sue his employer(s) for damages at common law for negligence (see Chapter 15 'Employers' Duties'), establishing on a balance of probabilities connection between occupation(s) and disease.

Process injuries/diseases

6.4   The original *Workmen's Compensation Act 1897* (the first 'no fault' statute) did not acknowledge the connection between employment(s) and disease, though gradually diseases came to be recognised as employment-related and hence deserving of compensation, a fact which led to prescription of diseases (see Chapter 31 'Occupational Health'). If, however, a disease was not prescribed, an employee, short of suing his employer in tort, would have to bring his claim within 'personal injury caused by accident' parameters. Thus, 'The accidental character of the injury is not . . . removed or displaced by the fact that, like many other accidental injuries it set up a well known disease, which was immediately the cause of death, and would no doubt be certified as such in the usual death certificate' (per Lord Macnaghten in *Brintons Ltd v Turvey* [*1905*] *AC 230* where the respondent's husband, formerly employed in sorting wool in the appellant's factory, was infected by anthrax, from which he died. It was held that it was injury by accident, within the meaning of the *Workmen's Compensation Act 1897*). This led to a distinction between 'accident' illnesses and 'process' illnesses, the former attracting benefit, the latter being compensatable only if negligence could be proved at common law.

6.5   The essential difference between the two was (and still is) that, with 'accident' illnesses, the illness derives from an identifiable incident or incidents (i.e. accidents), e.g. the case of an underground fireman who died from broncho-pneumonia as a result of having to work in cold water waist deep was held to be 'injury by accident' and so the employer was liable (*Walker v Bairds & Dalmellington Ltd (1936) 153 LT 322*); in another case a miner was exposed to cold down-draught on one occasion as a result of being kept waiting at a mid-landing for one and a half hours where it was held to be 'injury by accident' and so the employer was liable

(*Coyle v John Watson Ltd [1915] AC 1*). It was always difficult to bring a successful case on 'process' grounds. 'The distinction between accidents and disease has been insisted upon throughout the authorities and is . . . well founded . . . I do not know . . . that any explicit formula can be adopted with safety. There must, nevertheless, come a time when the indefinite number of so-called accidents and the length of time over which they occur take away the element of accident and substitute that of process' (per Lord Porter in *Roberts v Dorothea Slate Quarries Co Ltd [1948] 2 AER 201* where a worker's claim for compensation for silicosis failed on the ground that he could not prove that each particle of silica which he had inhaled over a lengthy period, was an 'accident'). Similarly, 'Unless the applicant can indicate the time, the day, and circumstance, and place, in which the accident has occurred by means of some definite event, the case cannot be brought within the general purview of the Act, and does not entitle a workman or his dependants to compensation' (per Cozens-Hardy MR in *Eke v Hart-Dyke [1910] 2 KB 677* where the employer was not liable for ptomaine poisoning of his gardener). Most recently, however, anxiety was held not to be 'injury by accident' for the purposes of the *Social Security Act 1975* (*Fraser v Secretary of State for Social Services 1986 SLT 386* in which acute anxiety tension resulted in a civil servant being off work for 19 months; injury benefit was refused).

Passively inhaled smoke *per se* does not qualify for benefit under *Sec 94* of the *Social Security Contributions and Benefits Act 1992*; however, sudden inhalations of considerable quantities of smoke constitute 'personal injury by accident'. Thus, in *Clay v Social Security Commissioners, The Times, 31 August 1990*, an asthma sufferer suffered painful injury to lungs, nausea, headaches and extreme breathlessness, on account of colleagues smoking in her office. It was held that she suffered 'personal injury by accident' after inhaling her colleagues' tobacco smoke. Moreover, action for damages against the employer will also lie in the case of employees who have to suffer the adverse effects of passively inhaled smoke (*Bland v Stockport Metropolitan Council, The Times, 28 January 1993* where an employee suffered pharyngitis, painful glands and eventually chronic bronchitis, requiring surgery, as a result of passively inhaled cigarette smoke. It was held that the employer was liable for damages of £15,000). (On smoking at work, see further 13.13 EMPLOYEE DISCIPLINE, SAFETY AND UNFAIR DISMISSAL.)

Social security cover

6.6 Current law on administration of social security is contained in the *Social Security Administration Act 1992*. More particularly, industrial injuries benefit is payable where an employee suffers personal injury caused by an accident or suffers from a prescribed disease (see 31.42 OCCUPATIONAL HEALTH) (after 4 July 1948) arising out of and in the course of employment. [*Social Security Contributions and Benefits Act 1992, ss 94(1), 108(1)*].

Such benefit consists of:

(*a*)   sickness benefit;

(*b*)   invalidity benefit;

(*c*)   industrial injuries benefit;

(*d*)   constant attendance allowance;

(*e*)   disablement pension;

(*f*)   severe disablement pension.

Some other benefits are paid to existing beneficiaries who were entitled to them before 1988.

By dint of regulation, under the *Social Security Administration Act 1992*, employees will be required to:

(*a*) notify employers of work accidents, in respect of which benefit is payable, within a specified period;

(*b*) provide information concerning possible determination of claims;

(*c*) facilitate notification of accidents and the making of claims.

Disablement benefit claimants will be required to:

(*a*) submit, from time to time, to medical examination in order to determine the effect of a relevant accident or the appropriate treatment, and

(*b*) submit to appropriate medical treatment.

Compensation for travelling and loss of earnings will be allowed in suitable cases. [*Social Security Administration Act 1992, s 9*].

Injury benefit was merged into mainline sickness benefit (both being payable for loss of earnings related to sickness at work) in 1983. Disablement benefit for loss of amenity, payable normally as a weekly pension on top of earnings or some other social security benefit, was retained, but with modifications in favour of lower percentage pensions for minor disablement (e.g. 25% for 30% disablement) and higher percentage pensions for more severe disablement (e.g. 95% for 90% disablement). Moreover, benefit is also payable to UK subjects from the date of the employee's return to the country for industrial injuries arising out of work accidents occurring in any country of the world and not merely EC countries provided that his employer has been paying UK national insurance contributions. There are special provisions for airmen, mariners and continental shelf workers.

(For more detailed information on state benefits for industrial injuries see 'Tolley's Social Security and State Benefits'.)

Prescribed occupational diseases

6.7   The advisability (or otherwise) of an occupational disease being prescribed, is the remit of the Industrial Injuries Advisory Council (IIAC), under the *Social Security Administration Act 1992, s 171*.

A disease must be prescribed before benefit will be payable (i.e. disablement benefit). If a disease is not prescribed, an employee seeking compensation will have to sue his employer for negligence. A disease may be prescribed if:

(*a*) it ought to be treated, having regard to its causes and incidence and other relevant considerations, as a risk of occupation and not as a risk common to all persons; and

(*b*) it is such that, in the absence of special circumstances, the attribution of particular cases to the nature of the employment can be established with reasonable certainty.

[*Social Security Contributions and Benefits Act 1992, s 108*].

The current list of prescribed occupational diseases is to be found in the *Social Security (Industrial Injuries) (Prescribed Diseases) Regulations 1985 (SI 1985 No 967)* as subsequently amended by *Amendment Regulations 1989 (SI 1989 No 1207)* (see Chapter 31 'Occupational Health') (and *SI 1990 No 2269, SI 1991 No 1938* and *SI 1993 No 1985*).

Presumptions

6.8 (*a*) A presumption in favour of work-related injury exists in favour of the employee. Thus, an accident arising in the course of employment is deemed, in the absence of evidence to the contrary, to have arisen out of employment. [*Social Security Contributions and Benefits Act 1992, s 94(3)*]. This would not normally include playing sports (other than professionally) unless the employee was obliged (not merely encouraged) to play sport (*R v National Insurance Commissioner ex p Michael [1977] 1 WLR 109* where a policeman was injured playing football; the claim failed). Acts incidental to employment would, however, normally be covered (as in the tort system – see Chapter 15 'Employers' Duties') (*R v National Insurance Commissioner, ex p East [1976] ICR 206* where an employee was injured in the factory canteen before clocking on; the claim succeeded).

(*b*) The fact that an employee is acting contrary to statutory duties/regulations or an employer's instructions does not prevent any accident taking place 'in the course of employment'. [*Social Security Contributions and Benefits Act 1992, s 98*]. (This is again similar to the tort system.)

(*c*) An accident which occurs while an employee is travelling to/from work is deemed to arise out of employment if (and only if):

   (i) the accident happened in a vehicle being operated by or on behalf of his employer, e.g. minibus belonging to firm or works bus, so long as members of the public were excluded; and

   (ii) the vehicle was not being operated in the ordinary course of public transport.

[*Social Security Contributions and Benefits Act 1992, s 99*].

The fact that the employer pays a mileage allowance or for travelling time does not mean the injury arises out of employment (*R v Industrial Injury Benefits Tribunal, ex p Fieldhouse (1974) 17 KIR 63* and R(I) 1/91, see further Chapter 15 'Employers' Duties').

(*d*) An accident is deemed to arise out of and in the course of employment if it happens when the employee, in an actual or supposed emergency, goes to rescue or protect persons thought to be injured or endangered, or to minimise damage to property. [*Social Security Contributions and Benefits Act 1992, s 100*].

(*e*) An accident is deemed to arise out of and in the course of employment if caused by:

   (i) another person's misconduct, skylarking or negligence (or action taken in consequence thereof), e.g. quarrel, if connected with work;

   (ii) the behaviour or presence of an animal, bird, fish or insect (e.g. wasp in a jam factory);

   (iii) an employee being struck by an object or by lightning.

[*Social Security Contributions and Benefits Act 1992, s 101*].

(*f*) Even though employment is illegal or void, benefit for injury or disease may still be payable. [*Social Security Contributions and Benefits Act 1992, s 97(2)*].

Moreover, there is a presumption that an occupational disease is employment-related, though this is not universal (see 31.30 OCCUPATIONAL HEALTH).

Successive accidents

6.9 Where a person suffers two or more successive accidents arising out of and in the course of employment, an employee is not entitled, for the same period, to receive industrial injuries benefit by way of two or more disablement pensions at an aggregate weekly rate exceeding:

£88.40 – persons over 18
£54.15 – persons under 18

[*Social Security Contributions and Benefits Act 1992, s 107*].

Current work injury benefit rates

6.10 As from 6 April 1992 the following weekly work injury benefit rates take effect.

Table 2

1. Sickness benefit

Under pensionable age

i.e. man under 65, woman under 60

single person	£42.70
adult dependant	£25.50
dependent child	£9.65

Over pensionable age

the pensioner	£51.95
adult dependant	£31.20
dependent child	£10.85

2. Disablement benefit

extent of disability	over 18	under 18
100%	£91.60	£56.10
90%	£82.44	£50.49
80%	£73.28	£44.88
70%	£64.12	£39.27
60%	£54.96	£33.66
50%	£45.80	£28.05
40%	£36.64	£22.44
30%	£27.48	£16.83
20%	£18.32	£11.22

As from 1 October 1986, disablement below 14% does not attract benefit (except in the case of pneumoconiosis, byssinosis and diffuse mesothelioma). The maximum disablement gratuity is £6,080.

[*Social Security Benefits Uprating Order 1993 (SI 1993 No 349), 1 Sch, Part V*].

Damages for occupational injuries and diseases

6.11 When a person is injured or killed at work in circumstances indicating negligence on the part of an employer, he may be entitled to an award of damages. Damages are normally of two kinds, i.e. liquidated and unliquidated damages. *Liquidated damages* are damages where the amount and circumstances of payment have been agreed in advance by the contracting parties; awards are generally confined to cases of breach of contract.

Where negligent injury and/or death occur, compensation by way of prior agreement is not possible. In other words, employers and employees cannot agree beforehand a set amount of damages for injury, disease or death at work. Such damages, i.e. *unliquidated damages*, are assessed by judges in accordance with precedent; very exceptionally they may be assessed by a jury. Damages are also categorised as general and special damages, according to whether they reflect pre-trial or post-trial losses.

Damages normally take the form of a lump sum; however, 'structured settlements', whereby accident victims are paid a monthly sum for the rest of their lives, are being seriously considered as a more practical alternative (see 1.1 INTRODUCTION). This may well involve greater reliance on actuarial evidence and a rate of return of interest provided by index-linked government securities. Moreover, the rule in *British Transport Commission v Gourley* (see 6.12 below), to the effect that damages are paid *net* of tax, may have to be modified, as offering a fiscal subsidy to defendants. In addition, introduction of a conditional fee system (no win no fee) in personal injuries cases, similar to the American contingency fee system (although not entitling lawyers to a share of the litigant's damages), may well result in increased damages.

Basis of claim for damages for personal injuries at work

6.12   The basis of an award of unliquidated damages is that an injured employee should be entitled to recoup the loss which he has suffered in consequence of the injury/disease at work. 'The broad general principle which should govern the assessment in cases such as this is that the Tribunal should award the injured party such a sum of money as will put him in the same position as he would have been in if he had not sustained the injuries' (per Earl Jowitt in *British Transport Commission v Gourley [1955] 3 AER 796*). Normally, a lump sum must be awarded. Courts cannot order periodical payments instead of a lump sum, unless both parties consent (*Burke v Tower Hamlets Health Authority, The Times, 10 August 1989*).

It is not necessary that a particular injury be foreseeable, although it normally would be (see further *Smith v Leech Braine & Co Ltd*, at 15.36 EMPLOYERS' DUTIES). Moreover, if the original injury has left the plaintiff susceptible to further injury (which would not otherwise have happened), damages will be awarded in respect of such further injuries, unless due to the negligence of the plaintiff himself (*Wieland v Cyril Lord Carpets Ltd [1969] 3 AER 1006* where a lady, who had earlier injured her neck, was fitted with a surgical collar. She later fell on some stairs, injuring herself, because her bifocal glasses had been dislodged slightly by the surgical collar. It was held that damages were payable in respect of this later injury, by the perpetrator of the original act of negligence). Conversely, where, in spite of having suffered an injury owing to an employer's negligence, an employee contracts a disease which has no causal connection with the earlier injury, and the subsequent illness prevents the worker from working, any damages awarded in respect of the injury will at that point stop, since the supervening illness would have prevented (and, indeed, has prevented) the worker from going on working.

6.13   Listed below are the various losses for which the employee can expect to be compensated. Losses are classified as non-pecuniary and pecuniary.

Non-pecuniary losses

The principal non-pecuniary losses are:

(*a*)   pain and suffering prior to the trial;

(*b*)   disability and loss of amenity (i.e. faculty) before the trial;

(*c*)   pain and suffering in the future, whether permanent or temporary;

(*d*)   disability and loss of amenity in the future, whether permanent or temporary;

(*e*)   bereavement.

(Damages for loss of expectation of life were abolished by the *Administration of Justice Act 1982, s 1(1)* (see further 'Loss of amenity' at 6.19 below).)

There are four main compensatable types of injury, namely (*a*) maximum severity injuries (or hopeless cases), e.g. irreversible brain damage, quadraplegia; (*b*) very serious injuries but not hopeless cases, e.g. severe head injuries/loss of sight in both eyes/injury to respiratory and/or excretory systems; (*c*) serious injuries, e.g. loss of arm, hand, leg; (*d*) less serious injuries, e.g. loss of finger, thumb, toe etc. There is a scale of rates applicable to the range of disabilities accompanying injury to workers but it is nowhere as precise as the scale for social security disablement benefit. The general (perhaps obvious) principle is that the more serious the disability the greater the damages. Damages for maximum severity cases can vary between £750,000 and £1 million, whereas damages for loss of non-index finger or toe would probably be not much more than £1,000. (Readers should consult latest *'Quantum'* cases.)

Pecuniary losses

These consist chiefly of:

(*a*)   loss of earnings prior to trial (i.e. special damages);

(*b*)   expenses prior to the trial, e.g. medical expenses;

(*c*)   loss of future earnings (see below);

(*d*)   loss of earning capacity, i.e. the handicap on the open labour market following disability.

In actions for pecuniary losses, employees can be required to disclose the general medical records of the whole of their medical history to the employer's medical advisers (*Dunn v British Coal Corporation, The Times, 5 March 1993*).

General and special damages

General damages

6.14   General damages are awarded for loss of future earnings, earning capacity and loss of amenity. They are, therefore, awarded in respect of both pecuniary and non-pecuniary losses. An award of general damages normally consists of:

(*a*)   damages for loss of future earnings;

(*b*)   pain and suffering (before and after the trial); and

(*c*)   loss of amenity (including disfigurement).

Special damages

Special damages are awarded for itemised expenses and loss of earnings incurred prior to the trial. Unlike general damages, this amount is normally agreed between the parties' solicitors. When making an award, judges normally specify separately awards for general and special damages.

Assessment of pecuniary losses (i.e. loss of future earnings)

6.15   Assessing loss of future earnings can be a chancy affair, subject, as it is, to the vagaries and vicissitudes of human life. As was authoritatively said, 'If (the plaintiff) had not been injured, he would have had the prospect of earning a continuing income, it may be, for many years, but there can be no certainty as to what would have happened. In many cases the amount of that income may be doubtful, even if he had remained in good health, and there is always the possibility that he might have died or suffered from some incapacity at any time. The loss which he has suffered between the date of the accident and the date of the trial (i.e. special damages (see above)) may be certain, but his prospective loss is not. Yet damages must be assessed as a lump sum once and for all (see, however, 'Provisional awards' at 6.22 below), not only in respect of loss accrued before the trial but also in respect of a prospective loss' (per Lord Reid in *British Transport Commission v Gourley* [*1955*] *3 AER 796*). Moreover, if, at the time of injury, a worker earns at a particular rate, it is presumed that this will remain the same. If, therefore, he wishes to claim more, he must show that his earnings were going to rise, for example, in line with a likely increase in productivity – a probable rise in *national* productivity is not enough.

Capitalisation of future losses

6.16   Loss of future earnings, often spanning many years ahead, particularly in the case of a relatively young employee, is awarded normally as a once-and-for-all capital sum for the maintenance, sometimes for life, of the injured victim. Here it is important to understand that the award of damages is calculated on the basis of the *present* value of future losses – a sum less than the aggregate of prospective earnings because the final amount has to be discounted (or reduced) to give the *present* value (of future losses). And where injury shortens the life of a worker, he can recover losses for the whole period for which he would have been working (net of income tax and social security contributions, which he would have had to pay), if his life had not been shortened by the accident. The present value of future losses can be gauged from actuarial or annuity tables. Indeed, it is necessary to identify a capital sum which, as income is progressively and periodically deducted for maintenance of the injury victim (with the necessary statutory deductions for income tax and social security contributions), will equate with the net loss of earnings over the working life of the injured victim.

More particularly, the net annual loss (based on rate of earnings at the time of trial and not allowing for inflation) (the multiplicand) has to be multiplied by a suitable number of years' purchase (i.e. multiplier), and often ranging between 8 and 15, and set out in actuarial tables. The multiplier will represent the number of years' purchase necessary to buy an annuity at between 4% and 5% (e.g. 4½%) – a low rate of interest because, in times of inflation, this gives a greater number of years' purchase (or multiplier). However, there is no increase in multiplier for higher rates of tax or as provision for subsequent changes in tax rates.

Example

In the case of a male worker, aged 30 at the date of trial, and earning £10,000 per year net, on a 4½% interest yield, the multiplier will be 17.1. Hence, general damages will be about £170,000, assuming incapacity to work up to age 65.

In the case of a male worker, aged 50 at date of trial, earning £20,000 net, on a 4½% interest yield, the multiplier will be 10.1. Hence, general damages will be about £200,000 assuming incapacity to work until age 65. (The corresponding multipliers for similar female workers are 19.3 (£190,000) and 15.4 (£300,000), assuming same earnings (which is unlikely).)

Institutionalised accident victims

6.17   Injury victims can claim all expenses reasonably and foreseeably incurred by way of treatment in a hospital, convalescent home etc. Where, however, the injury is grave and long-term institutionalised maintenance is necessary, the victim cannot claim both loss of earnings and medical/institutional expenses, since, being in a hospital, the injured worker no longer has normal living expenses, that is, the expense of maintaining himself and his family. Such living expenses, saved by maintenance in a public hospital, are, therefore, deducted from loss of earnings [*Administration of Justice Act 1982, s 5*] (see further 'Set-off' at 6.26 below).

Medical expenses reasonably incurred are also recoverable. An injured worker is not bound to opt for free NHS medical treatment; if, however, he does, he cannot claim for free NHS treatment in his damages; though he could for medical expenses incurred in *private* health care. Similarly, damages cannot be claimed in respect of nursing care which is free. However, damages can be claimed in respect of services voluntarily rendered (by the defendant), out of a combination of affection and duty, since, if they had not been freely provided, paid assistance would have been necessary, and this would have to have been compensated (*Hunt v Severs, The Times, 13 May 1993* (road accident victim cared for by defendant, whom she later married, entitled to damages for his voluntary services)). Indeed, in cases of very severe injuries, courts often refrain from calculating future pecuniary losses, where the victim is likely to spend the remainder of his life in institutionalised care.

In addition, if nursing and constant attendance is necessary, claims can be made for these items as well as the cost of adapting a house and/or car to meet the needs of the disabled person – though not for the *basic* cost of a house or car. And where a marriage breaks down following injuries to a spouse, the extra cost involved in attending to the accident victim's needs is recoverable, though this cannot include a calculation for maintenance sums payable and the cost of the divorce settlement (*Pritchard v JH Cobden Ltd [1987] 1 AER 300*).

Moreover, injury damages are regarded as a matrimonial asset, for the purposes of the *Matrimonial and Family Proceedings Act 1984*, and so can be proceeded against by the wife following separation or divorce (*Wagstaff v Wagstaff, The Times, 26 November 1991*).

Non-pecuniary losses (i.e. loss of amenity)

6.18   It is generally accepted by the courts that quantification of non-pecuniary losses is considerably more difficult than computing pecuniary losses. Clearly, it is more difficult to attach a figure to the loss of a foot or eye than to two years' wages or salary. This becomes even more difficult where loss of sense of taste and smell are involved, or loss of reproductive or excretory organs. Unlike pecuniary losses, loss of amenity generally consists of two awards, i.e. an award for (i) actual loss of amenity and (ii) the impairment of the quality of life suffered in consequence (i.e the psychic loss). That judges recognise the inadequacy of damages here is much in evidence. (In the case of a plaintiff who had suffered grave injuries, 'He is deprived of much that makes his life worthwhile. No money can compensate for the loss. Yet compensation has to be given in money. The problem is insoluble' (per Lord Denning MR in *Ward v James* [*1965*] *1 AER 563*).)

Victims are generally conscious of their predicament but in very serious cases they may not be, a distinction underlined in the leading case of *H West & Son Ltd v Shephard* [*1963*] *2 AER 625*. Thus, damages are payable for loss of amenity, whether or not a plaintiff is aware of his predicament. In other words, it is not just subjective or psychic losses which are compensatable. If, however, a victim's injuries are of the maximum severity kind (e.g. tetraplegia) and he is conscious of his predicament, his damages will be greater, since a person who is mentally anguished about his condition, suffers more than one who is not. However, where, as is often, the injuries shorten the life of an accident victim, his damages for non-pecuniary losses will be reduced to take into account the fact of shortened life.

Types of non-pecuniary losses recoverable

6.19   The following are the non-pecuniary losses which are recoverable by way of damages:

(*a*)   pain and suffering;

(*b*)   loss of amenity;

(*c*)   bereavement.

Pain and suffering

This refers principally to actual pain and suffering at the time of the injury and later. Since, however, modern drugs can easily remove acute distress, actual pain and suffering is not likely to be great and so damages awarded will be relatively small.

Additionally, 'pain and suffering' includes 'mental distress' and related psychic conditions; more specifically (i) nervous shock, (ii) concomitant pain or illness following post-accident surgery and embarrassment or humiliation following disfigurement.

(i)   *Nervous shock*

Nervous shock refers to actual and quantifiable damage to the nervous system, affecting nerves, glands and blood. Originally, damages for nervous shock were unavailable unless nervous shock was accompanied by actual physical injury (*Bourhill v Young* [*1942*] *2 AER 396*). This position has now changed, a development traceable back to the case of *Hinz v Berry* [*1970*] *1 AER 1074*. The appellant left her husband and children in a car in a layby while she crossed over the road to pick bluebells. The respondent negligently drove his car into the rear of the appellant's car. The appellant heard the crash and later saw her husband and children lying severely injured, the former fatally injured. She became ill from nervous shock and successfully sued the respondent for damages.

In *McLoughlin v O'Brian* [*1982*] *2 AER 298*, it was held that the class of people who may sue for damages for nervous shock depends on the proximity of the plaintiff's relationship with the deceased or injured person. This was confirmed and expanded by the House of Lords in *Alcock v Chief Constable of South Yorkshire Police* [*1991*] *3 WLR 1057*. They stated that the class of persons to whom this duty of care was owed as being sufficiently proximate was not limited by reference to particular relationships such as husband and wife or parent and child, but was based on ties of love and affection, the closeness of which would need to be proved in each case except that of a spouse or parent when this closeness would be assumed.

The law also requires that the plaintiff seeking damages for nervous shock must prove that the shock resulted from being within sight or hearing of the relevant event or its immediate aftermath. It was held in *McLoughlin v O'Brian* (above) that the immediate aftermath included the visit to hospital of a wife and mother after she had been told by a motorist of the accident in which her family were injured and her daughter was killed. The immediate aftermath does not include viewing a disaster involving relatives or friends on television (*Alcock v Chief Constable of South Yorkshire Police* (above)).

In *Ravenscroft v Rederiaktiebologet Transatlantic, The Times, 6 April 1992*, the House of Lords reversed the Court of Appeal decision on this case. An employee was crushed to death by a runaway forklift truck and the mother of the employee sought damages for a psychiatric illness resulting from nervous shock. It was held that this action was not sustainable unless the shock had arisen from sight or hearing of the relevant event or its immediate aftermath. The mother had not seen the accident, nor was she present at his death in hospital and she did not see the body immediately afterwards. There is no duty of care to relatives. The exact extent of the shock need not be foreseen (*Brice v Brown [1984] 1 AER 997*).

(ii) *Illness following post-accident surgery*

The plaintiff was employed by the defendant as a train driver. Whilst operating a passenger train, he saw two employees less than thirty yards away on the line he was passing along. He blew the horn but the employees only moved when the train was a few yards away. As a result, the plaintiff suffered shock and was admitted to hospital where he was diagnosed as having suffered a heart attack. He was off work for nine months. When he returned to work he was not able to drive main-line trains because of his heart condition, and was engaged on shunting operations. This in turn revived a serious back injury from which he had suffered for a long time. Eighteen months later he stopped work and several months afterwards he was readmitted to hospital for a laminec-tomy. Following this back surgery, the plaintiff suffered a further heart attack. It was held that nervous shock was a reasonably foreseeable consequence of the employer's breach of duty; in addition, the employer had to take his victim as he found him, i.e. with a pre-existing symptomless back condition, pre-disposing him to heart attacks, and the employer had to pay damages in respect of both these conditions as well (*Galt v British Railways Board (1983) 133 NLJ 870*).

Loss of amenity

This is a loss, permanent or temporary, of a bodily or mental function, coupled with gradual deterioration in health, e.g. loss of finger, eye, hand etc. Traditionally, there are three kinds of loss of amenity, ranging from maximum severity injury (quadraplegias and irreversible brain damage), multiple injuries (very severe injuries but not hopeless cases) to less severe injuries (i.e. loss of sight, hearing etc.). Obviously, the more grave the injury the greater the award of damages. Moreover, it is clear that, on balance, damages reflect the actual amenity loss rather than the concomitant psychic loss, at least in hopeless cases. Though, if a plaintiff is aware that his life has been shortened, he will be compensated for this loss. Thus, the *Administration of Justice Act 1982, s 1(1)* states:

'(i) damages are not recoverable in respect of loss of expectation of life caused to the injured person by the injuries; but

(ii) if the injured person's expectation of life has been reduced by injuries, there shall be taken into account any pain and suffering caused or likely to be caused by awareness that his expectation of life has been reduced.'

Bereavement

A statutory sum of £7,500 is awardable for bereavement by the *Fatal Accidents Act 1976, s 1A* (as amended by the *Administration of Justice Act 1982, s 3(1)* and the *Damages for Bereavement (Variation of Sum) Order 1990 (SI 1990 No 2575)*). This sum is awardable at the suit of husband or wife, or of parents provided the deceased was under eighteen at the date of death if the deceased was legitimate; or of the deceased's mother, if the deceased was illegitimate. (In *Doleman v Deakin, The Times, 30 January 1990* it was held that where an injury was sustained before the deceased's eighteenth birthday, but the deceased actually died after his eighteenth birthday, bereavement damages were not recoverable by his parents.)

Fatal injuries

6.20 Death at work can give rise to two types of action for damages, i.e.

(*a*) damages in respect of death itself, payable under the *Fatal Accidents Act 1976* (as later amended); and

(*b*) damages in respect of liability which an employer would have incurred had the employee lived; here the action is said to 'survive' for the benefit of the deceased worker's estate, payable under the *Law Reform (Miscellaneous Provisions) Act 1934*.

Actions of both kinds are, in practice, brought by the deceased workman's dependants, though actions of the second kind technically survive for the benefit of the deceased's *estate*. Moreover, previously paid state benefits are *not* deductible from damages for fatal injuries. [*Social Security Act 1989, s 22(4)(c)*]. Nor are insurance moneys payable on death deductible e.g. life assurance moneys. [*Fatal Accidents (Damages) Act 1908 as re-enacted by the Administration of Justice Act 1982, s 4*]. This also includes any amounts passing to dependants as a result of intestacy (*Wood v Bentall Simplex Ltd, The Times, 3 March 1992* in which an annual income of £5,000, receivable on intestacy, was not to be deducted from damages for fatal accident).

Damages under the Fatal Accidents Act 1976

'If death is caused by any wrongful act, neglect or default which is such as would (if death had not ensued) have entitled the person injured to maintain an action and recover damages, the person who would have been liable if death had not ensued, shall be liable . . . for damages. . .'. [*Administration of Justice Act 1982, s 3(1), amending the Fatal Accidents Act 1976*].

Only dependants, which normally means the deceased's widow (or widower) and children and grandchildren can claim – the claim generally being brought by the bereaved spouse on behalf of him/herself and children. The basis of a successful claim is *dependency*, i.e. the claimant must show that he was, prior to the fatality, being maintained out of the income of the deceased. If, therefore, a widow had lived on her own private moneys prior to her husband's death, the claim will fail, as there is no dependency.

Originally at common law if a widow remarried, or if her marriage prospects were good, this was taken into account in assessing damages for fatal injuries, since remarriage or its prospects lessened the financial hardship caused by death of a breadwinner. This rule has, however, been abolished. The *Fatal Accidents Act 1976, s 3* provides that remarriage or remarriage prospects are not to be taken into account in assessing fatal damages though likelihood of divorce will (see *Martin v Owen* at 6.21 below).

However, contributory negligence (see further Chapter 15 'Employers' Duties') on the part of the deceased, will result in damages on the part of the dependants, being reduced. [*Fatal Accidents Act 1976, s 5*].

Assessment of damages in fatal injuries cases

6.21   Damages in respect of a fatal injury are calculated by multiplying the net annual loss (i.e. earnings minus tax, social security contributions and deductions necessary for personal living (i.e. dependency)) by a suitable number of years' purchase, as in the case of non-fatal injuries (see 6.16 above). There is no deduction for things used jointly, such as a house or car. But where a widow also works, this will reduce the dependency and she cannot claim a greater dependency in future on the ground that she and her deceased husband intended to have children (*Malone v Rowan* [*1984*] *3 AER 402*). Moreover, if, at the time of death, a widow is separated from her husband, her claim for dependency depends on the likelihood of either being reconciled, or, alternatively, receiving maintenance (*Davies v Taylor* [*1972*] *3 AER 836*). Under *Sec 3* (see 6.20 above) what has to be valued is the expectation of continuing dependency on the deceased, had he lived. Anything that might affect that expectation was relevant including the likelihood of divorce (*Martin v Owen, The Times, 21 May 1992*).

Where both parents are dead as a result of negligence or a mother dies, dependency is assessed on the cost of supplying a nanny (*Watson v Willmot* [*1991*] *1 AER 473; Cresswell v Eaton* [*1991*] *1 AER 484*).

Moreover, benefits accruing to a person, such as a widow's pension, are not taken into account in assessing damages. [*Fatal Accidents Act 1976, s 4*].

Provisional awards

6.22   Because medical prognosis can only *estimate* the chance of a victim's recovery, whether partial or total, or alternatively, deterioration or death, it is accepted that there is too much chance and uncertainty in the system of lump sum damages paid on a once-and-for-all basis. 'Chance' refers to 'measurable probabilities' rather than 'fanciful probabilities'. Serious deterioration denotes clear risk of deterioration beyond the norm that could be expected, ruling out pure speculation (*Wilson v Ministry of Defence* [*1991*] *1 AER 638*). Similarly in the case of dependency awards under the *Fatal Accidents Act 1976* it can never be known what the deceased's future would have been, yet courts are expected and called upon to make forecasts as to future income. Therefore, if the doctors get it wrong and a seriously ill victim makes a miraculous recovery, or a victim who was expected to do well suddenly and unforeseeably deteriorates, injustice results from the previous over and under compensation. To meet this problem it is provided that provisional awards may be made. Thus, 'This section applies to an action for damages for personal injuries in which there is proved or admitted to be a chance that at some definite or indefinite time in the future the injured person will, as a result of the act or omission, which gave rise to the cause of action, develop some serious disease or suffer some serious deterioration in his physical or mental condition'. [*Administration of Justice Act 1982, s 6(1)*]. Moreover, 'Provision may be made by rules of the court for enabling the court to award the injured person:

(*a*)   damages assessed on the assumption that the injured person will not develop the disease or suffer the deterioration in his condition; and

(*b*)   further damages at a future date if he develops the disease or suffers the deterioration'.

[*Administration of Justice Act 1982, s 6(2)*].

The mere fact that there is a disagreement over future medical prognosis, does not necessarily prevent a sufficient basis of agreement for provisional damages (*Hurditch v Sheffield Health Authority [1989] 2 AER 869* where the plaintiff, suffering from asbestosis, claimed provisional damages against his employer. Part of the medical statement was disputed. It was held that the offer and acceptance of a 'provisional figure' was sufficient for the purposes of *Sec 6* of the *Administration of Justice Act 1982*).

Interim awards

6.23   In certain limited circumstances a successful plaintiff can apply to the court for an interim payment. This enables a plaintiff to recover *part* of the compensation to which he is entitled before the trial rather than waiting till the result of the trial is known – which may be some time away. This procedure is provided for in Order 29, Part II of the Rules of the Supreme Court, but it only applies where the defendant is either (*a*) insured, (*b*) a public authority, or (*c*) a person whose resources are such as to enable him to make the interim payment. Interim orders cannot be made in 'chance' and 'forecast' cases (see 6.22 above).

Interest on damages

6.24   Damages constitute a judgment debt; such debt carries interest at 8% (currently) up to date of payment. Courts have a discretion to award interest on any damages, total or partial, prior to date of payment (and this irrespective of whether part payment has already been made [*Administration of Justice Act 1982, s 15*]), though this does not apply in the case of damages for loss of earnings, since they are not yet due. Moreover, a plaintiff is entitled to interest at 2% on damages relating to non-pecuniary losses (except bereavement), even though the actual damages themselves take into account inflation (*Wright v British Railways Board [1983] 2 AC 773*). Under *Sec 17* of the *Judgments Act 1838* (and *Sec 35A* of the *Supreme Court Act 1981* and *Schedule 1* of the *Administration of Justice Act 1982*), interest runs from the date of the damages judgment. Thus, where, as sometimes happens, there is a split trial, interest is payable from the date that the damages are quantified or recorded, rather than from the date (earlier) that liability is determined (*Thomas v Bunn, Wilson v Graham, Lea v British Aerospace plc, The Times, 17 December 1990*). Moreover, interest at the recommended rate (of 8%) is recoverable only after damages have been assessed, and not (earlier) when liability had been established (*Lindop v Goodwin Steel Castings Ltd, The Times, 21 May 1990*). The current rate of interest has been reduced from 15% to 8% [*Judgment Debts (Rate of Interest) Order 1993 (SI 1993 No 564)*] – this interest being tax-free [*Administration of Justice Act 1982, s 74*].

Awards of damages and state benefits for work injuries

6.25   As with awards of damages in tort actions, compensation is available from the DSS for illness and disability associated with work, i.e. sickness benefit and disablement benefit, the former being payable for loss of earnings (including the old industrial injury benefit), and the latter for loss of amenity. An injured employee is entitled to both state benefits and damages for personal injury. However, *all* of the state benefits, paid or payable in respect of the work injury, must be deducted from subsequently awarded damages of £2,500 or more (the so-called 'set-off' rule) (see 6.26 below) from 3 September 1990 [*Social Security Administration Act 1992, ss 81–88*]. Where the damages awarded are reduced by reason of contributory negligence or under any other statutory provision or contract, the set-off has to be deducted from the full amount of damages. [*Law Reform (Personal Injuries) Act 1948, s 2(3)*]. For example, if a plaintiff was awarded £10,000 damages and he had received £3,000 of social security benefits and was also 50% contributorily negligent, he would receive £10,000 minus £3,000 = £7,000 minus 50% (for his contributory negligence), that is, £3,500. The compensator must pay to the Secretary of State a sum equivalent to the State benefit paid to the plaintiff. There are certain exempt payments:

(*a*)   from the Macfarlane Trust for haemophilia victims;

(*b*)   from the NCB Pneumoconiosis Compensation Scheme;

(*c*)   to victims suffering from sensorineural loss, where the loss is less than 50 dB in one or both ears;

(*d*)   contractual sick pay;

(*e*)   under the *National Health Service (Injury Benefit) Regulations 1974*;

(*f*)   under the Scheme established by the Secretary of State on 24 April 1992.

Unlike the other state benefits, 80% of statutory sick pay will be deductible. [*Social Security (Recoupment) Regulations 1990, Reg 2*].

Set-off

6.26 The current position relating to set-off is as follows:

Non-deductible items

(*a*)   contractual pension (including payment by a friendly society or trade union) (*Parry v Cleaver [1969] 1 AER 555*), nor is a contractual pension deductible from damages for wrongful dismissal (*Hopkins v Norcros plc, The Times, 21 April 1992*);

(*b*)   state subsistence benefits;

(*c*)   retirement pension;

(*d*)   accident insurance payable under a personal accident policy taken out by the employee (*Bradburn v Great Western Railway Co (1874) LR 10 Exch 1*). If the employer agreed to pay sick pay for a period and covered this with insurance, this amount would have to be deducted (*Hussain v New Taplow Paper Mills Ltd [1988] 1 AER 541* (see below));

(*e*)   savings attributable to care and maintenance in a public hospital/nursing home [*Administration of Justice Act 1982, s 5*];

(*f*)   involuntary redundancy payment;

(*g*)   moneys from a benevolent fund, paid through trustees (and not directly to the injured person or dependant), in respect of injuries;

(*h*)   widow's allowance;

(*j*)   ill-health awards and higher pension benefits provided by the employer (*Smoker v London Fire & Civil Defence Authority, The Times, 18 April 1991*);

(*k*)   pension scheme to which employer contributed (*Wood v British Coal Corporation [1991] IRLR 271*);

(*l*)   moneys paid under employer's insurance policy, for injury regardless of fault (*McCamley v Cammell Laird Shipbuilders Ltd [1990] 1 AER 854* concerning a personal accident group insurance policy where the sum was to be paid by reference to the annual wage of the injured person);

(*m*)   ex gratia payments by employer (*Bews v Scottish Hydro-Electric plc, The Times, 25 March 1992*).

Deductible items

(*a*)   sickness benefit (though not in the case of fatal injuries);

(*b*)   invalidity benefit (though not in the case of fatal injuries);

(*c*)   disablement benefit (though not in the case of fatal injuries);

(*d*)   severe disablement benefit (though not in the case of fatal injuries);

(*e*)   statutory sick pay (SSP);

(*f*)   contractual sick pay (payable for a longer period);

(*g*)   any remuneration or earnings from employment;

(*h*)   unemployment benefit;

(*j*)   benevolent moneys paid directly to the injured person or relative;

(*k*)   payments made to an employee under the employer's permanent health insurance scheme (*Hussain v New Taplow Paper Mills Ltd* (see above));

(*l*)   family income supplement;

(*m*)   voluntary redundancy payments (*Colledge v Bass Mitchells and Butlers Ltd [1988] 1 AER 536*);

(*n*)   attendance/mobility allowances (*Hodgson v Trapp [1989] AC 807*);

(*o*)   job release scheme payments (*Cranby v Mercer, The Times, 6 March 1984*).

Pneumoconiosis

6.27   Pneumoconiosis is compensatable under different heads; first, as a ground for disablement benefit, under the *Social Security Contributions and Benefits Act 1992* (see 6.3 above), and, secondly, by way of claim made under the *Pneumoconiosis etc. (Workers' Compensation) Act 1979* – the latter being in addition to any disablement benefit previously paid.

(A) Pneumoconiosis/tuberculosis-pneumoconiosis/emphysema – disablement benefit

Where a person is suffering from pneumoconiosis accompanied by tuberculosis, then, for benefit purposes, tuberculosis is to be treated as pneumoconiosis. [*Social Security Contributions and Benefits Act 1992, s 110*]. This applies also to pneumoconiosis accompanied by emphysema or chronic bronchitis, provided that disablement from pneumoconiosis, or pneumoconiosis and tuberculosis, is assessed at, at least, 50%. [*Social Security Contributions and Benefits Act 1992, s 110*]. However, a person suffering from byssinosis is not entitled to disablement, unless he is suffering from loss of faculty which is likely to be permanent. [*Social Security Contributions and Benefits Act 1992, s 110*].

(B) Pneumoconiosis – payment of compensation under the Pneumoconiosis etc. (Workers' Compensation) Act 1979

Claims made under the *Pneumoconiosis etc. (Workers' Compensation) Act 1979* are in addition to any disablement benefit paid or payable under the *Social Security (Industrial Injuries) (Prescribed Diseases) Regulations 1985 (SI 1985 No 967)*. Indeed, whereas the latter consists of periodical payments, the former resemble damages awarded against an employer at common law and/or for breach of statutory duty, except that under the above Act fault (or negligence) need not be proved. Claims made under the *Pneumoconiosis etc. (Workers' Compensation) Act 1979* must be made in the manner set out in the *Pneumoconiosis etc. (Workers' Compensation) (Determination of Claims) Regulations 1985 (SI 1985 No 1645)*. The claim must be made (except in the case of a 'specified disease' – see 6.28 below) within 12 months from the date on which disablement benefit (under the *Social Security Regulations*) first become payable; or if the claim is by a dependant, within 12 months from the date of the deceased's death. [*Pneumoconiosis etc. (Workers' Compensation) (Determination of Claims) Regulations 1985, Reg 4(1), (2)*]. Awards for pneumoconiosis/byssinosis have declined slowly recently (from 723 in 1978 to 508 in 1987).

Claims for specified diseases

6.28   Claims for a 'specified disease', i.e.:

(*a*)   pneumoconiosis, including (i) silicosis, (ii) asbestosis and kaolinosis;

(*b*)   byssinosis (caused by cotton or flax dust);

(*c*)   diffuse mesothelioma;

(*d*)   primary carcinoma of the lung coupled with evidence of (i) asbestosis and/or (ii) bilateral diffuse pleural thickening

[*Pneumoconiosis etc. (Workers' Compensation) (Specified Diseases) Order 1985 (SI 1985 No 2034)*], must be made within 12 months from the date when disablement benefit first became payable, or, in the case of a dependant, within 12 months from the date of the deceased's death [*Pneumoconiosis etc. (Workers' Compensation) (Determination of Claims) Regulations 1985, Reg 4(3)(4)*]. These time periods can be extended at the discretion of the Secretary of State. Moreover, where a person has already made a claim and has been refused payment, he can apply for a reconsideration of determination, on the ground that there has been a material change of circumstances since determination was made, or that determination was made in ignorance of, or based on, a mistake as to material fact.

6.29   The *Pneumoconiosis etc. (Workers' Compensation) (Payment of Claims) (Amendment) Regulations 1992 (SI 1992 No 403)* updated the 'principal regulations' (that is, the *1988 Regulations*) by increasing the amount of payment by 5%. Amounts of payment to the three categories of claimants are as follows:

(A) Payments to sufferers of a specified disease (i.e. pneumoconiosis, byssinosis etc.)

Age of disabled person	Percentage assessment for the relevant period									
	10% or less	11-20%	21-30%	40%	50%	60%	70%	80%	90%	100%
	£	£	£	£	£	£	£	£	£	£
37 and under	20,018	35,749	41,944	43,136	44,327	45,280	46,235	47,187	48,141	49,093
38	19,446	34,318	40,681	42,137	43,373	44,327	45,280	46,235	47,187	48,141
39	18,874	32,887	39,418	41,133	42,422	43,373	44,327	45,280	46,235	47,187
40	18,303	31,457	38,156	40,132	41,466	42,422	43,373	44,327	45,280	46,235
41	17,731	30,028	36,892	39,130	40,515	41,466	42,422	43,373	44,327	45,280
42	17,157	28,599	35,629	38,132	39,561	40,515	41,466	42,422	43,373	44,327
43	16,301	26,930	34,365	37,369	38,895	40,038	40,990	41,944	42,897	43,852
44	15,443	25,261	33,102	36,606	38,226	39,561	40,515	41,466	42,422	43,373
45	14,586	23,593	31,840	35,843	37,560	39,084	40,038	40,990	41,944	42,897
46	13,727	21,926	30,577	35,081	36,892	38,608	39,561	40,515	41,466	42,422
47	12,870	20,257	29,313	34,318	36,225	38,132	39,084	40,038	40,990	41,944
48	12,130	19,588	28,313	32,792	35,081	36,795	37,750	38,703	39,655	40,611
49	11,391	18,923	27,311	31,267	33,938	35,461	36,415	37,369	38,323	39,276
50	10,654	18,255	26,330	29,743	32,792	34,126	35,081	36,033	36,986	37,940
51	9,915	17,588	25,308	28,217	31,649	32,792	33,755	34,698	35,653	36,606
52	9,175	16,921	24,309	26,692	30,504	31,457	32,413	33,364	34,318	35,270
53	8,483	15,730	22,783	25,357	29,360	30,504	31,457	32,413	33,364	34,318
54	7,793	14,538	21,257	24,024	28,217	29,552	30,504	31,457	32,413	33,364
55	7,102	13,346	19,734	22,688	27,072	28,599	29,552	30,504	31,457	32,413
56	6,410	12,154	18,207	21,354	25,930	27,645	28,599	29,552	30,504	31,457
57	5,720	10,962	16,683	20,018	24,789	26,692	27,645	28,599	29,552	30,504
58	5,267	9,963	14,896	17,968	22,305	24,070	25,095	26,097	27,072	28,026
59	4,813	8,960	13,107	15,921	19,827	21,448	22,544	23,593	24,595	25,546
60	4,362	7,959	11,320	13,869	17,351	18,828	19,994	21,092	22,117	23,070
61	3,908	6,958	9,533	11,820	14,872	16,206	17,443	18,589	19,638	20,590
62	3,456	5,958	7,746	9,770	12,394	13,584	14,896	16,087	17,157	18,112
63	3,216	5,386	6,958	8,736	11,023	12,201	13,441	14,586	15,633	16,587
64	2,982	4,813	6,172	7,698	9,652	10,820	11,988	13,084	14,108	15,061
65	2,742	4,242	5,386	6,663	8,282	9,437	10,533	11,583	12,584	13,537
66	2,503	3,672	4,600	5,623	6,913	8,055	9,080	10,080	11,059	12,011
67	2,265	3,098	3,812	4,587	5,541	6,674	7,626	8,580	9,533	10,486
68	2,204	3,001	3,682	4,396	5,352	6,410	7,328	8,317	9,234	10,176
69	2,145	2,907	3,552	4,207	5,161	6,150	7,032	8,055	8,939	9,865
70	2,085	2,813	3,419	4,016	4,969	5,886	6,733	7,793	8,639	9,558
71	2,026	2,716	3,290	3,824	4,778	5,623	6,435	7,532	8,342	9,249
72	1,967	2,622	3,158	3,636	4,587	5,363	6,136	7,269	8,042	8,939
73	1,918	2,576	3,111	3,564	4,516	5,243	6,018	7,079	7,805	8,675
74	1,871	2,525	3,063	3,491	4,446	5,123	5,899	6,887	7,568	8,407
75	1,825	2,479	3,016	3,419	4,372	5,005	5,780	6,697	7,328	8,150
76	1,776	2,430	2,966	3,349	4,301	4,887	5,661	6,507	7,089	7,889
77 and over	1,728	2,383	2,920	3,276	4,230	4,766	5,541	6,318	6,851	7,626

(B) Payments to dependants of a person who has died from a specified disease (other than diffuse mesothelioma)

Age of disabled person at his last birthday preceding death	Percentage assessment for the relevant period				
	10% or less	11%-20%	21%-30%	40%	50% and over
	£	£	£	£	£
37 and under	9,414	18,352	20,972	21,688	22,284
38	9,128	17,541	20,257	20,972	21,734
39	8,843	16,730	19,543	20,257	21,187
40	8,554	15,921	18,828	19,543	20,638
41	8,269	15,111	18,112	18,828	20,090
42	7,985	14,302	17,396	18,112	19,543
43	7,470	13,251	16,753	17,469	19,019
44	6,958	12,201	16,109	16,825	18,488
45	6,447	11,154	15,467	16,182	17,968
46	5,933	10,103	14,768	15,537	17,443
47	5,422	9,055	14,181	14,896	16,921
48	5,029	8,769	13,705	14,395	16,277
49	4,635	8,483	13,226	13,895	15,633
50	4,242	8,198	12,751	13,393	14,990
51	3,849	7,912	12,274	12,893	14,347
52	3,456	7,626	11,797	12,394	13,705
53	3,276	6,958	10,892	11,702	13,178
54	3,098	6,291	9,985	11,011	12,655
55	2,920	5,623	9,080	10,320	12,130
56	2,742	4,957	8,174	9,629	11,605
57	2,561	4,291	7,269	8,939	11,081
58	2,394	3,812	6,233	7,723	9,629
59	2,226	3,336	5,196	6,507	8,174
60	2,062	2,861	4,158	5,291	6,721
61	1,896	2,383	3,122	4,076	5,267
62	1,728	1,907	2,085	2,861	3,812
63	1,728	1,871	2,015	2,632	3,397
64	1,728	1,835	1,941	2,407	2,982
65	1,728	1,800	1,871	2,180	2,561
66	1,728	1,765	1,800	1,954	2,145
67 and over	1,728	1,728	1,728	1,728	1,728

(C) Payments to dependants of persons who have died as a result of diffuse mesothelioma

Age of disabled person at his last birthday preceding death	Payment
	£
37 and under	22,284
38	21,734
39	21,187
40	20,638
41	20,090
42	19,543
43	19,019
44	18,488
45	17,968
46	17,443
47	16,921
48	16,277
49	15,633
50	14,990
51	14,347
52	13,705
53	13,178
54	12,655
55	12,130
56	11,605
57	11,081
58	9,629
59	8,174
60	6,721
61	5,267
62	3,812
63	3,397
64	2,982
65	2,561
66	2,145
67 and over	1,728

[*Pneumoconiosis etc. (Workers' Compensation) (Payment of Claims) (Amendment) Regulations 1993 (SI 1993 No 1158), Sch*].

Chapter 7

Construction and Building Operations (including Subcontractors)

Introduction

7.1 Statistically a worker is killed in the construction industry every three days. One member of the public is killed by construction activities every month. For someone working in the construction industry for twenty years, there is a 1 in 600 risk that he will die as a result of an accident at work; and a 1 in 2 risk that he will suffer a reportable injury. Half the fatal injuries are caused by falls from heights; and two-fifths of reported major injuries are caused by falls from heights.

That health and safety considerations are crucial to construction activities and the tendering which precedes them is obvious (*General Building and Maintenance plc v Greenwich London BC, The Times, 9 March 1993 – Reg 16(1)(b)* of the *Public Works Contracts Regulations 1991 (SI 1991 No 2680)*, empowered local authorities to require contractors to provide a list of works and a certificate of satisfactory completion, which included health and safety. A contractor who disregarded health and safety considerations had his tender rejected by the local authority, as it did not make satisfactory provision therefor).

Health and safety law relating to construction and associated activities can be complicated, embracing, as it does, certain general requirements of the *Health and Safety at Work Act 1974*, a series of regulations passed under the *Factories Act 1961*, namely, the quartet of *Construction Regulations 1961-1966*, as well as civil liability at common law and under the *Occupiers' Liability Act 1957*, not to mention any contractual variants under the JCT Standard Form of Contract and any standard form subcontracts. In addition, the role of subcontractors is a dominant one in the building industry, and the reciprocal health and safety duties of contractors/ subcontractors towards main occupiers (and vice versa) has long been underspotlighted, together with the overall need for a standard form of contract for manufacturing industry generally, comparable with that used in the building industry.

Moreover, there is a tendency to identify liability for accidents/injuries on construction sites with those in overall control of activities, as evinced by the (proposed) *Construction (Design and Management) Regulations*, coming into force in 1994, which impose specific duties on clients, designers, project supervisors and contractors. Thus, the (draft) regulations require employers – or project supervisors – to appoint health and safety co-ordinators at all construction sites where building and civil engineering works are carried on and to prepare a health and safety plan. More particularly, (*a*) where work is scheduled to last longer than 30 working days and where more than 20 workers are engaged simultaneously, or (*b*) is scheduled to exceed 500 person-days, a notice of the work to be undertaken must be sent to the enforcing authority, together with (*inter alia*) the name/address of the project supervisor, the health and safety co-ordinator during preparation stage and during execution stage.

This chapter consists of:

— definitions of 'building operations' and 'works of engineering construction' and associated case law (see 7.2, 7.3 below);

— general statutory requirements for health and safety in all types of building operations and works of engineering construction (see 7.5 below);

— principal health and safety duties laid down by the *Construction (Working Places) Regulations 1966*. (The *Construction (Lifting Operations) Regulations 1961* are dealt with in Chapter 26 'Lifting Machinery and Equipment' (see 7.8-7.18 below));

— an examination of contractors, subcontractors and main occupiers together with reciprocal health and safety duties; the importance of negotiations in subcontract work; contract compliance and the consequences of non-compliance on the part of contractors; *Sec 3(1)* of the *Health and Safety at Work Act 1974*; and joint civil liability of occupiers and contractors/ subcontractors under the *Occupiers' Liability Act 1957* (see 7.28-7.41 below);

— duties specified in the *Construction (Head Protection) Regulations 1989* (discussed at 7.19-7.28 below);

— structural safety requirements, as specified by the *Construction (Working Places) Regulations 1966*, and requirements concerning gangways, ladders and sloping roofs (see 7.41-7.51 below);

— consideration of the *Construction Products Regulations 1991* which require that construction products satisfy certain criteria as far as design and building are concerned (see 7.52 below);

— practical safety criteria and matters in connection with construction, demolition, working at heights, scaffolding, temporary works, earthworks and falsework etc. (see also Chapter 46 'Work at Heights' and 7.53-7.62 below).

Building operations and works of engineering construction are notorious for their high accident frequency. This is largely accounted for by the often temporary nature of the work and the changing face of the workplace; for instance, in steel erection the actual workplace may often exist for minutes rather than months, even less years.

Definitions

'Building operations'

7.2   'Building operations' is a wide term (though does not include 'work of engineering construction', see 7.3 below), including:

(*a*)   construction, structural alteration and repair or maintenance of a building (including repointing, redecoration and the external cleaning of the structure);

(*b*)   demolition of a building;

(*c*)   preparation and laying the foundations of an intended building.

[*Factories Act 1961, s 176(1)*].

'Work of engineering construction'

7.3   'Work of engineering construction' means:

(*a*)   the construction of any railway line or siding (but not to an existing railway);

(*b*)   the construction, structural alteration or repair (including repointing and repainting), or demolition of any of the following: (i) dock, (ii) harbour, (iii) inland navigation, (iv) tunnel, (v) bridge, (vi) viaduct, (vii) waterworks, (viii) reservoir, (ix) pipe-line, (x) aqueduct, (xi) sewer, (xii) sewage works, and (xiii) gasholder;

unless carried on upon a railway or tramway. [*Factories Act 1961, s 176(1)*];

(*c*)   all the above activities on any steel or reinforced concrete structures (other than buildings), roads, airfields, sea defence works or river works;

'steel structure' includes the repainting of a mobile crane mounted on a platform and moving on rails (*British Transport Docks Board v Williams [1970] 1 AER 1135*);

(*d*)   any construction or work of civil engineering or like nature, i.e. (i) construction, (ii) demolition, (iii) repair of a pipe-line (carrying anything other than water) but not work on factory premises or on a railway.

[*Engineering Construction (Extension of Definition) Regulations 1960 (SI 1960 No 421); Engineering Construction (Extension of Definition) (No 2) Regulations 1968 (SI 1968 No 1530)*].

Thus, the *Extension of Definition Regulations* specifically exclude works carried on:

(i)   in factories (as defined in Chapter 18 'Factories and Workplaces');

(ii)   in electrical stations;

(iii)   on a railway or tramway (*1960 Regulations*); or

(iv)   on a pipe-line for the conveyance of water (*1968 Regulations*).

Main case law on statutory definitions

7.4   The following points have been established by case law in relation to some statutory definitions:

(*a*)   'external cleaning' (see definition of Building operations, 7.2 above), does not include window cleaning, but does include cleaning of a glass roof, itself forming part of the roof area (*Bowie v Great International Plate Glass Insurance Cleaning Co [1981] CLY 1207*);

(*b*)   preliminary dusting of roof trusses by painters constitutes 'construction' (*O'Brien v UDEC Ltd (1968) 5 KIR 449*);

(*c*)   measuring of windows by a glazier in houses under construction constitutes 'construction' (*Vineer v Doidge & Sons Ltd [1972] 2 AER 794*);

(*d*)   installation of plant in a building is not a 'building operation'; but if the plant is installed in a building in connection with construction work, this will qualify as a 'building operation' (*Baxter v CEGB [1964] 2 AER 815* where the installation of a calor gas heater at a power station was held to be a 'building operation');

(*e*)   scaffold erection (and dismantling) qualifies as a 'building operation' (*Smith v Vange Scaffolding and Engineering Co Ltd [1970] 1 AER 249*).

Allocation of statutory requirements

7.5   Safety of building operations and works of engineering construction is governed generally by *HSWA*. In particular,

(1)   contractors (as employers) owe health and safety duties to their employees [*Sec 2*];

(2)   employees owe such duties to their employers (i.e. contractors/ subcontractors) [*Sec 7*];

(3)   building owners (i.e contractors' employers) owe health and safety duties to subcontractors and their employees [*Sec 3(1)*];

(4)   self-employed contractors/workmen owe health and safety duties to other self-employed persons (e.g. building owners to main contractors), and to employees (but who are not their own) [*Sec 3(2)*].

In this connection, self-styled 'labour-only' subcontractors have been held to be employees of a large main contractor and so are entitled to the protection of some of the *Construction Regulations* (*Ferguson v John Dawson & Partners Ltd [1976] IRLR 346* where a nominated subcontractor was liable to a 'self-employed labour-only subcontractor' for breach of *Reg 28(1)* of the *Construction (Working Places) Regulations 1966*, requiring provision of guard-rails and toe-boards at working platforms and places).

Building owners and occupiers have duties to employees of contractors and subcontractors. [*Sec 4(1)(2)*].

Thus, *HSWA s 4* states that anyone 'having control to any extent' of premises, must take reasonable care in respect of persons working there, who are *not* employees. This duty can be subject to indemnity clauses in a lease and/or contract (see further Chapter 32 'Occupiers' Liability'). This duty is strict and must be carried out so far as is reasonably practicable, that is, subject to cost-effective constraints (see further *Larner v British Steel plc*, 2.7 ACCESS).

However, although ostensibly applicable to all workplaces, the *Workplace (Health, Safety and Welfare) Regulations 1992 (SI 1992 No 3004)* do not extend to building operations and works of engineering construction, unless some other activity is being carried on (see further 18.3 FACTORIES AND WORKPLACES) but the *Construction (Design and Management) Regulations* are due to come into operation early in 1994, placing key new duties upon:

(*a*)   clients;

(*b*)   designers;

(*c*)   planning supervisers;

(*d*)   principal (or main) contractors;

(*e*)   contractors (including both employers and the self-employed).

These new regulations are intended to ensure that effective direction and co-ordination of health and safety characterises every phase of the construction/ development project, from drawing-board to handover.

Common law requirements

7.6   Like all other employers, building contractors must take reasonable care of their employees (see Chapter 15 'Employers' Duties'). This duty extends to 'labour-only' subcontractors (*Ferguson v Dawson* (see 7.5 above)). It is, however, important to realise that liability for injury and/or death on a construction site is often shared by those in occupation, with the result that an injured employee of a main contractor or subcontractor could, if necessary, sue the building owner(s), main contractor(s) and subcontractor(s) and any architect who has also been negligent (see Chapter 32 'Occupiers' Liability'). In addition, there is liability based on occupation under the *Occupiers' Liability Act 1957*.

Multiple occupation of construction sites

7.7   Where, as is normal on large construction sites, standard form (JCT) building work is being carried out, multiplicity of occupation (or control) is not uncommon. Here control will be shared among building owner(s), main contractor(s) and subcontractor(s). It has been decided that the legal nature of the relationship between a building owner and main contractor is that of licensor and licensee (*Hounslow London Borough Council v Twickenham Garden Developments Ltd [1970] 3 AER 326*).

This vests in the building owner some degree of control over the works (inviting potential application of the (new) *Construction (Design and Management) Regulations* due in 1994), e.g. if the contractor does not carry out and complete the works (in accordance with the requirements of Clause 2(1) of the JCT Standard Form Contract) the licence can, subject to certain exceptions, be terminated. Moreover, (given that some statutory duties can be modified) Clause 20(1) of the Conditions of Contract states that 'the contractor shall be liable for, and shall indemnify the employer against any expense, liability, loss or claim or proceedings whatsoever arising under any statute or at common law in respect of personal injury to or the death of any person whomsoever arising out of, or in the course of, or caused by the carrying out of the works, unless due to any act or neglect of the employer or of any person for whom the employer is responsible' (e.g. employee). The proviso to the clause 'unless due to any act or neglect of the employer' is limited solely to common law negligence and does not extend to statutory negligence. This means that the contractor will have to indemnify the employer (i.e. building owner) where the claim by the injured person is based on a breach of statutory duty by the employer (*Hosking v de Havilland Aircraft Ltd [1949] 1 AER 540* where a building contractor dug a ditch in the grounds of a factory, using an unsound plank to bridge the ditch. In consequence, a person on the factory premises was injured. It was held that the factory occupier was liable under the *Factories Act 1961, s 29(1)* (as it is now)).

In consequence, the building owner can insist that the main contractor(s) take out insurance to meet that indemnity, and likewise the main contractor(s) can insist that the subcontractor(s) do the same (Clause 21.1 JCT Standard Form Contract). Thus, for the purposes of common law liability, based on occupation, persons injured on building sites can sue the building owner, main contractor and any subcontractor who may be responsible, the question of indemnity as between the liable parties being governed and determined by the terms of the JCT Contract.

Specific Regulations made under the Factories Act 1961

7.8   Certain provisions of the *Factories Act 1961* are applied to building operations and works of engineering construction (see 7.2, 7.3 above for definitions), since they are both regarded as 'notional' factories. [*Factories Act 1961, s 127(1)(4)*]. Sec 127(4) is important, as it empowered the Minister to pass specific regulations relating to construction and works of engineering construction. The result has been the quartet of *Construction Regulations*, as follows:

(*a*)   the *Construction (General Provisions) Regulations 1961 (SI 1961 No 1580)*;

(*b*)   the *Construction (Lifting Operations) Regulations 1961 (SI 1961 No 1581)*;

(*c*)   the *Construction (Working Places) Regulations 1966 (SI 1966 No 94)*; and

(*d*)   the *Construction (Health and Welfare) Regulations 1966 (SI 1966 No 95)*.

These regulations apply whether or not a building operation (but not a work of engineering construction) is being carried on inside a factory (for definition of 'factory' see Chapter 18 'Factories and Workplaces'). It is proposed, in the near future, to replace part of the *Construction Regulations* with regulations placing more emphasis on the *management* of safety in construction, namely, the draft *Construction (Design and Management) Regulations* (see 7.1 above).

The following observations specifically regarding the *Building (Safety, Health and Welfare) Regulations 1948*, could be said to characterise in a general way the whole gamut of construction regulations: 'I find it necessary to make some general observations about the interpretation of regulations of this kind. They are addressed to practical people skilled in the particular trade or industry, and their primary purpose is to prevent accidents by prescribing appropriate precautions. Any failure to take prescribed precautions is a criminal offence. The right to compensation which arises when an accident is caused by a breach is a secondary matter. The regulations supplement but in no way supersede the ordinary common law obligations of an employer to care for the safety of his men, and they ought not to be expected to cover every possible kind of danger . . .' (*Gill v Donald Humberstone & Co Ltd [1963] 3 AER 180*, per Lord Reid).

Statutory defence of employer/factory occupier not available to contractors

7.9 Although the common law defences open to a factory occupier (see Chapter 15 'Employers' Duties') are available also to contractors and civil engineering firms when sued for injuries to employees, the principal defence under the *Factories Act 1961* is not so available. This defence is contained in *Sec 155(2)*, which states that where there is a contravention by any person of any regulation or order under the *Factories Act 1961*, 'that person (is) guilty of an offence, and the occupier or owner (is) not guilty of an offence, by reason only of contravention of the provision . . . unless it is proved that he failed to take all reasonable steps to prevent the contravention'. This means that the factory occupier is only liable (in addition to the other person) if he failed to take reasonable steps to prevent the breach, *and it must be proved that he failed to take such steps*, if he is to be considered liable. In the case of a building contractor, however, who has separate duties under *Reg 3(1)* of the *Construction (Working Places) Regulations 1966* (see 7.11(*b*) below), the occupier is not guilty by reason *only* of contravention of the provision in question but because of his duties in another (dual) capacity under these regulations. This has the (unfortunate) consequence that building contractors are subject to the *Factories Act 1961* but cannot raise the general statutory defence open to the normal factory occupier (*Davies v Camerons Industrial Services Ltd [1980] 2 AER 680*). However, conviction of employees under *Sec 155(2)* probably does not prejudice a subsequent claim for damages by them, since that section is concerned only with criminal liability. 'Criminal and civil liability are two separate things . . . The legislation (*Factories Act 1937*) might well be unwilling to convict an owner who failed to carry out an absolute statutory duty of a crime with which he was not himself directly concerned, but still be ready to leave the civil liability untouched' (*Potts v Reid [1942] 2 AER 161*).

Notional factories within factories

7.10 Where building operations or works of engineering construction are carried on inside a regular factory, both (*a*) the *Construction Regulations 1961-1966*, and (*b*) the *Factories Act 1961* apply. [*Factories Act 1961, s 127(8)*].

Moreover, this will also be the position in the case of a dock where a work of engineering construction is being carried out, since docks are within the *Factories Act 1961* by virtue of *Sec 125*. Here, if an employee of a building contractor was injured, he could sue either (i) his own employer under the *Construction Regulations*, or (ii) the actual factory occupier under the *Factories Act 1961* or, possibly, both.

Allocation of duties under the Construction Regulations

7.11   Two separate categories of persons are subject to duties under the *Construction (Working Places) Regulations 1966*, as follows:

(*a*)   employers; and

(*b*)   contractors.

Duties in *Regulation 3* are owed by both employers and contractors who may have employees. The duties are owed by each of them to their own employees, except in the case of the scaffolding provisions (see 7.17 below), which are owed by both to the employees of either of them. However, building owners are not liable under *Reg 3* and contractors do not owe a duty thereunder to subcontractors (*Kealey v Heard [1983] 1 AER 973*). But a self-employed person masquerading as an employee can sue under *Reg 3*, by way of analogy with *Ferguson v John Dawson* (see 7.5 above).

Employers may additionally be contractors. Employers and contractors are liable for breach of the regulations set out for reference in Tables 3 and 4 below, in so far as there is risk of injury to their own employees (i.e. not to the workforce of a subcontractor (*Smith v Wimpey Ltd [1972] 2 AER 723*)) (see 7.17, 7.18 below for liability relevant to scaffolding).

Table 3

Working Places Regulations specified for compliance by employers and contractors to their employees including slipping or falling risks

[*Construction (Working Places) Regulations 1966, Reg 3(1)(a)*]

Reg	Subject matter	Reg	Subject matter
6	Working places and access to work	23	Scaffolds used by workmen of different employers
7	Provision and maintenance of scaffolds, ladders or other means of support	24	Construction of working platforms, gangways and runs – persons falling
8	Supervision of scaffolding and inspection of material	25	Boards and planks in working platforms, gangways and runs
9	Construction and material of scaffolds	26	Width of working platforms – persons slipping and falling
10	Defective scaffold material	27	Widths of gangways and runs – persons slipping and falling
11	Maintenance of scaffolds	28	Guard-rails and toe-boards at working platforms and places – persons falling
12	Partly erected or dismantled scaffolds		
13	Standards or uprights, ledgers and putlogs	29	Guard-rails, etc., for gangways, runs and stairs, etc. – persons falling
14	Ladders used in scaffolds		
15	Stability of scaffolds	30	Platforms, gangways, runs and stairs, etc.
16	Slung scaffolds		
17	Cantilever, jib, figure and bracket scaffolds	31	Construction and maintenance of ladders and folding step ladders
18	Support for scaffolds		
19	Suspended scaffolds (not power operated)	32	Use of ladders and folding step ladders
20	Boatswain's chairs, cages, skips etc.	33	Openings, corners, breaks, edges and open joisting – persons falling
21	Trestle scaffolds		
22	Inspection of scaffolds, boatswain's chairs etc.		

Reg	Subject matter	Reg	Subject matter
34	Exceptions from *Reg 33* (guard-rails, toe-boards, barriers and coverings may be removed or remain unerected in certain cases) – persons falling	35	Sloping roofs – persons slipping and falling
		36	Work on or near fragile materials
		38	Prevention of falls and provision of safety nets and belts

Employers and contractors owe the following duties set out for reference in Table 4 below to all persons on site, not just employees.

Table 4

Working Places Regulations specified for compliance by all employers and contractors in respect of falling objects

[*Construction (Working Places) Regulations 1966, Reg 3(1)(b)*].

Reg	Subject matter	Reg	Subject matter
24	Construction of working platforms, gangways and runs – falling materials	34	Exceptions from *Reg 33* (guard-rails, toe-boards, barriers and coverings; may be removed or remain unerected in certain cases) – falling articles and materials;
26	Width of working platforms – falling articles and materials		
27	Widths of gangways and runs – falling articles and materials	35	Sloping roofs – falling articles and materials
28	Guard-rails and toe-boards at working platforms and places – falling materials	37	Loads on scaffolds
		38	Prevention of falls and safety nets and belts
29	Guard-rails etc. for gangways, runs and stairs – falling articles and materials	39	Reports required by *Reg 22* in respect of scaffolds, boatswain's chairs, cages, skips and similar plant
33	Openings, corners, breaks, edges and open joisting – falling materials		

Moreover, it is important to note that the duties in Table 3 and Table 4 must be carried out even though an employee has not complied with them, under *Reg 3(2)* of the *Construction (Working Places) Regulations 1966*.

Duty of employees to comply with regulations

7.12   Under the *Construction (Working Places) Regulations 1966* every employee involved in building operations or works of engineering construction must:

(*a*)   comply with such of the regulations as affect them;

(*b*)   co-operate in all other cases; and

(*c*)   report defects to his employer or his foreman.

[*Construction (Working Places) Regulations 1966, Reg 3(2)*].

7.13   Failure on the part of an employee to comply, leading to his injury, constitutes contributory negligence (*Boyle v Kodak Ltd [1969] 2 AER 439*).

No duties are owed to self-employed persons under the above regulations (*Herbert v Shaw Ltd [1959] 2 AER 189*), but self-styled labour-only subcontractors are normally treated as employees under the above regulations (see *Ferguson v Dawson*, 7.5 above). Also, there are special provisions relating to scaffolding (see 7.17 below).

Working at heights

7.14   The *Construction (Working Places) Regulations 1966* are predominantly concerned with preventing injury to persons who might fall whilst working at heights and, to a lesser extent, with injury from articles falling from a height. The regulations, therefore, apply to (principally) scaffolds and other means of access to work at heights, such as ladders and crawling boards. (Other regulations and criteria relating to work at heights are considered in Chapter 46 'Work at Heights'.)

Means of access and egress to place of work

7.15   Suitable and sufficient safe access to and egress from every place of work, at which any person (not just an employee) has at any time to work, must be provided and properly maintained, so far as is reasonably practicable [*Reg 6(1)*]; and must be made and kept safe for any person working there, so far as is reasonably practicable [*Reg 6(2)*]. Where a plaintiff alleges failure to provide safe means of access, the defendant must specifically plead that it was not 'reasonably practicable' and prove it, if he wishes to avail himself of that defence (*Bowes v Sedgefield DC [1981] ICR 234*, where a carpenter, an employee of a local authority, was instructed to secure an empty house which was boarded up but had been damaged by trespassers. He climbed through a window and fell, injuring himself. It was held that there was a duty on the employer to prove that it was not reasonably practicable to provide/maintain safe means of access, which he had not discharged). Such duty is comparable with that placed on employers by the *Factories Act 1961* (see further *Larner v British Steel plc* at 2.7 ACCESS).

Scaffolding

Definition of a scaffold

7.16   A scaffold means any structure provided temporarily, on or from which persons carry out work in connection with:

(*a*)   a building operation; or

(*b*)   work of engineering construction; and which enables

   (i)   persons to obtain access to, or

   (ii)   materials to be taken to,

any place at which such work is carried out.

[*Construction (Working Places) Regulations 1966, Reg 4*].

More particularly, scaffolds are:

(*a*)   a working platform;

(*b*)   gangway;

(*c*)   run;

(*d*)   ladder or step-ladder (but not ones that are independent of the structure);

(*e*)   guard-rail;

(*f*)   toe-board;

(*g*)   other safeguards, including all fixings.

[*Construction (Working Places) Regulations 1966, Reg 4*].

Scaffolds are not:

(*a*)   a lifting appliance (see Chapter 26 'Lifting Machinery and Equipment' for definition); or

(*b*)   a structure used to support

   (i)   a lifting appliance; or

   (ii)   other plant or equipment.

The definition of scaffold is, therefore, wide and is not necessarily limited to scaffolds which are actually being used rather than erected or assembled. It will also apply to simple as well as elaborate scaffolds, e.g. temporary staging. Most of the regulations relating to scaffolds can refer to either situation, of use or erection (e.g. *Reg 9* – construction and material; *Reg 12* – partly erected or dismantled scaffolds; *Reg 14* – ladders used in scaffolds; but *Reg 11* – maintenance of scaffolds, seems to contemplate actual erection of a scaffold).

Duties of scaffolders generally

7.17   Every contractor or employer who:

(*a*)   erects or alters scaffolding; or

(*b*)   erects, installs or uses any other plant or equipment;

must comply with the regulations relating to scaffolding and to the erection, installation or use of such plant. [*Construction (Working Places) Regulations 1966, Reg 3(1)*].

(For the detailed provisions relating to duties of scaffolders, see Chapter 46 'Work at Heights'.)

The purpose of this provision is to impose an additional duty on those specialising in scaffold erection, which is owed to *all* workmen, whoever employs them (*Smith v Vange Scaffolding and Engineering Co Ltd [1970] 1 AER 249*).

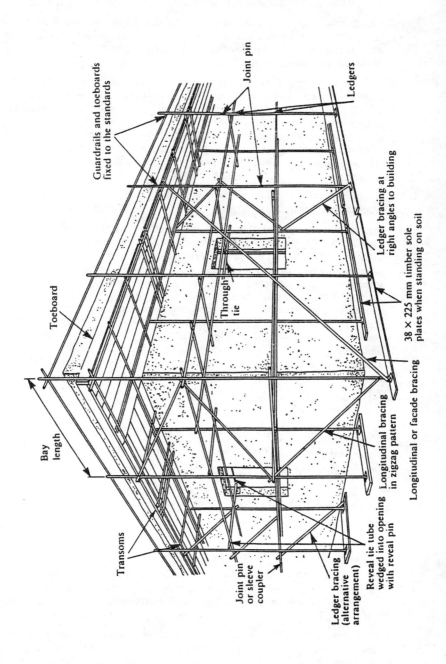

Joint pin

Ledgers

Guardrails and toeboards fixed to the standards

Ledger bracing at right angles to building

Toeboard

Through tie

38 × 225 mm timber sole plates when standing on soil

Bay length

Longitudinal bracing in zigzag pattern

Longitudinal or facade bracing

Transoms

Joint pin or sleeve coupler

Reveal tie tube wedged into opening with reveal pin

Ledger bracing (alternative arrangement)

fig. 3 Independent tied scaffold

Compliance with scaffolding regulations

7.18   The duty of compliance with the scaffolding regulations (i.e. *Regs 6-38* of the *Construction (Working Places) Regulations 1966*) falls upon both (i) employers, whether they have erected scaffolding or not, and (ii) contractors who have erected or altered the scaffolding. [*Reg 3*].

Moreover, every contractor who takes over a scaffold which he has not erected, must check its stability and the soundness of material used in it before use. [*Reg 23*]. This regulation applies even when the employee who is injured on the scaffold is competent (*Vineer v Doidge & Sons Ltd [1972] 2 AER 794* where glazing subcontractors sent an employee to measure for windows and the latter was injured when using scaffolding provided by the main contractor. It was held that the glazing subcontractors were in breach of *Reg 23*, even though the injured employee was competent).

Head Protection Regulations

7.19   Head injuries account for nearly one-third of all construction fatalities, but fell significantly after the introduction of the *Construction (Head Protection) Regulations 1989 (SI 1989 No 2209)*. These regulations specify requirements for head protection during construction work (for definition, see 7.2 and 7.3 above), including offshore operations (see Chapter 34 'Offshore Operations'), but not diving operations at work. These regulations place duties on employers, persons in control of construction sites, self-employed persons and employees regarding the wearing of head protection. The purpose of head protection is to prevent/mitigate head injury caused by: falling/swinging objects, e.g. materials and/or crane hooks; and striking the head against something, as where there is insufficient headroom. Circumstances where head injury is not reasonably foreseeable on construction sites are limited, but it probably would not be required on/in:

(a)   sites where buildings are completed and there is no risk of falling materials/objects;

(b)   site offices, cabins, toilets, canteens or mess rooms;

(c)   cabs of vehicles, cranes etc.;

(d)   work at ground level, e.g. road works.

Duties of employers

7.20   The following duties are laid on employers:

Provision/maintenance of head protection

Every employer (that is, main contractor, subcontractor etc.) must provide each employee, while at work on building/construction operations, with suitable head protection, and keep it maintained/replaced (as recommended by the manufacturer). [*Reg 3(1)*].

Moreover, head protection equipment must be kept in good condition and stored, when not in use, in a safe place, though not in direct sunlight or hot or humid conditions. It should be inspected regularly and have defective harness components replaced, and sweatbands regularly cleaned or replaced.

Ensuring head protection is worn

So far as reasonably practicable (for meaning, see Chapter 15 'Employers' Duties'), every employer must ensure that each of his employees, whilst on construction work, wears suitable head protection, unless there is no foreseeable risk of injury to his head (other than by falling). [*Reg 4(1)*].

Moreover, every employer (or employee) who has control (for meaning, see below) over any other person engaged in construction work, must ensure, so far as is reasonably practicable, that such persons wear suitable head protection, unless there is no foreseeable risk of injury to the head, other than by falling. [*Reg 4(2)*].

Persons in control of construction sites

7.21   For the purposes of these regulations, the following persons may be deemed to be 'in control' of construction sites:

(*a*)   main contractor;

(*b*)   managing contractor;

(*c*)   contractor bringing in subcontractors;

(*d*)   contract manager;

(*e*)   site manager;

(*f*)   subcontractor;

(*g*)   managers, including foremen, supervisors;

(*h*)   engineers and surveyors;

(*j*)   (sometimes) clients and architects with control over persons at work.

Procedures and rule making

7.22   Employers and others in control must:

(*a*)   identify when/where head protection should be worn;

(*b*)   inform site personnel procedurally when/where to wear head protection and post suitable safety signs to that effect (see *fig. 4* below);

(*c*)   provide adequate supervision;

(*d*)   check that head protection is, in fact, worn.

Supervision by those responsible for ensuring head protection is worn, is an on-going requirement, including looking out for helmet use at all times, starting early in the day and taking in arrivals on site.

Persons in control of construction works can (and should) make rules regulating the wearing of suitable head protection. Such rules must be in writing and be brought clearly to the attention of those involved. Such procedure is particularly useful to main/managing contractors on multi-contractor sites, and rules/regulations on head protection should form part of overall site safety procedures (see further Chapter 13 'Employee Discipline, Safety and Unfair Dismissal').

Wearing suitable head protection – duty of employees

7.23   Employees must also make full and proper use of head protection and must return it to the accommodation provided for it after use. [*Construction (Head Protection) Regulations 1989, Reg 6 as amended by the Personal Protective Equipment at Work Regulations 1992, 2 Sch 23*]. They must also comply with the rules and regulations made for the wearing of head protection mentioned in 7.22 above (see also 36.7

PERSONAL PROTECTIVE EQUIPMENT). All employees, provided with suitable head protection, must take reasonable care of it and report any loss of it or obvious defect in it, to the employer etc. [*Reg 7*].

'WEAR YOUR HEAD PROTECTION'

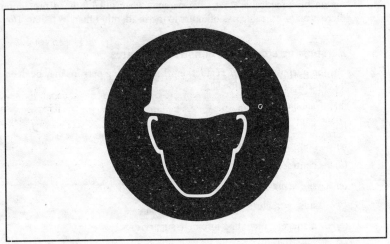

fig. 4 Head protection safety sign

Suitable head protection

7.24   Suitable head protection refers to an industrial safety helmet conforming to British Standard BS 5240: Part 1: 1987 Industrial Safety Helmets – Specification for construction and performance (or an equivalent standard). Helmets to BS 5240 can include optional comfort features (which, from a purely industrial relations viewpoint, are highly advisable, see further Chapter 13 'Employee Safety Rights, Disciplinary Procedures and Unfair Dismissal'). For work in confined spaces, 'bump caps' to BS 4033 are more suitable – BS 4033: 1968 Specification for industrial scalp protection (light duty).

Suitability of head gear involves the following factors: fit, comfort, compatibility with work to be done and user choice.

Fit

Head protection should be of an appropriate shell size for the person who is to wear it, and have an easily adjustable headband, nape and chin strap. The range of size adjustment should be sufficient to accommodate thermal liners in cold weather.

Comfort

Head gear should be as comfortable as possible, including:

(*a*)   a flexible headband of adequate width and contoured vertically and horizontally to fit the forehead;

(*b*)   an absorbent, easily cleanable or replaceable sweatband;

(*c*)   textile cradle straps;

(*d*)   chin straps (when fitted) which

(i)   fit round the ears,

(ii)   are compatible with any other personal protective equipment needed (see further Chapter 36 'Personal Protective Equipment'),

(iii)   are fitted with smooth, quick release buckles which do not dig into the skin,

(iv)   are made from non-irritant materials,

(v)   are capable of being stowed on the helmet when not in use.

Compatibility with work to be done

Head gear should not impede work to be done. For instance, an industrial safety helmet with little or no peak is functional for a surveyor taking measurements, using a theodolite or to allow unrestricted upward vision for a scaffold erector. If a job involves work in windy conditions, at heights, or repeated bending or constantly looking upwards, a secure retention system is necessary. Flexible headbands and Y-shaped chin straps can help to secure the helmet on the head. If other personal protective equipment, such as ear defenders or eye protectors, are required, the design must allow them to be worn safely and in comfort.

User choice

In order to avoid possibly unpleasant industrial relations consequences or a possible action for unfair dismissal (see further Chapter 13 'Employee Discipline, Safety and Unfair Dismissal'), it is sensible and advisable to allow the user to participate in selection of head gear.

Duties of self-employed personnel

7.25   Every self-employed person involved in construction/building operations, must:

(i)   provide himself with suitable head protection and maintain/replace it, whenever necessary. (Although it does not actually say so in the regulations, failure to do so can lead to the person being refused work on site or being ordered off site (see 7.33 below, Contract compliance).) [*Reg 3(2)*];

(ii)   ensure that any person over whom he has control, wears suitable head gear, unless there is no foreseeable risk of injury [*Reg 4(2)*];

(iii)   give directions to any other self-employed person regarding wearing of suitable head gear [*Reg 5(4)*];

(iv)   wear properly suitable head protection, unless there is no foreseeable risk of injury to the head, and make full and proper use of it and return it to the accommodation provided for it after use. [*Reg 6(2)–(4)*].

(v)   where the presence of more than one risk to health or safety makes it necessary for him to wear or use simultaneously more than one item of personal protective equipment, see that such equipment is compatible and continues to be effective against the risk or risks in question [*Personal Protective Equipment at Work Regulations 1992 (SI 1992 No 2966), Reg 5(2)*].

Exceptions

7.26   The following categories of workers on construction sites are exempt from the regulations:

(a)   divers actually diving or preparing to dive [*Diving Operations at Work Regulations 1981*];

(b)   Sikhs wearing turbans on construction sites [*Employment Act 1989, ss 11, 12*], though the regulations do apply to Sikhs not normally wearing turbans at work.

Visitors on site

7.27   It is not necessary that visitors are provided with, or even less wear head protection, under these regulations. Nevertheless, in order to satisfy their general duty under *Sec 2* of the *Health and Safety at Work Act 1974*, and additionally avoid any civil liability for injury at common law in an action for negligence (see further Chapter 15 'Employers' Duties') and/or under the *Occupiers' Liability Act 1957*, employers should provide visitors to the site with suitable head protection where there is a reasonably foreseeable likelihood of injury.

Subcontractors

7.28   Most industrial/commercial organisations delegate corporate functions and duties, placed on them by statute, regulation and common law, to contractors and subcontractors. This practice is particularly common in the construction industry, where a main contractor, in order the more competently and expeditiously to discharge his contractual obligations towards his employer (or builder owner), sublets performance of parts of the contract to specialists, e.g. steel erection. Not infrequently such specialists are selected or nominated by an architect who acts as an umpire between conflicting interests of employer and contractor, and contractor and subcontractor. Main contractors are legally responsible to employers and subcontractors to main contractors. If, therefore, there is a breach of contract, e.g. delay in completion, owing, say, to liquidation of a subcontractor, the employer's remedy is to sue the main contractor who, in turn, would exercise his contractual rights against the subcontractor, for whose performance of the contract (though not the actual way in which the work was done) he is responsible. In *Padbury v Holliday & Greenwood Ltd (1912) 28 TLR 494*, owing to the negligence of an employee of a subcontractor, a tool fell off a casement and struck a passer-by, causing him injury. It was held that the main contractor was not liable for this act of collateral negligence on the part of the workforce of the subcontractor. Alternatively, had the injury suffered by the passer-by been caused by faulty workmanship involved in the project, for which the main contractor was responsible, e.g. a lamp falling in consequence of faulty repair, the main contractor would have been liable (see *Tarry v Ashton* (7.38 below)).

Significantly, this practice of subletting performance of parts of the entire contract is regarded as sufficiently important in the building industry to justify the existence of a Standard Form of Building Contract (the JCT Standard Form). This means that the rights/obligations of all interested parties, namely, the employer, main contractors and subcontractors, both nominated and domestic, are specified in a formal jointly witnessed contract, known as the Joint Contracts Tribunal (JCT). When a dispute arises between any of the interested parties, for example, who is liable for an injury to an employee of a subcontractor, reference is made to the Conditions of Contract (or Subcontract). If necessary, such a dispute will be decided by arbitration, since the contract provides for independent arbitration machinery in the form of the RIBA (Royal Institute of British Architects). RIBA arbitration does not exclude jurisdiction of the courts but, in practice, that is often the result, since arbitration is quicker and cheaper. In other words, the building industry has its own quasi-judicial internal disputes machinery and procedures.

This is preferable to no machinery at all, since all interested parties know where they stand – at least, that is the theory.

Moreover, given the increasing delays in both systems and escalating costs of retaining legal teams, the Confederation of British Industry (CBI) has advocated 'alternative dispute resolution' (ADR), which has worked particularly well in the United States and Australia, for the speedy resolution of disputes. This is a consensual process whereby the parties agree that they wish to get together and resolve a dispute, in contrast with the adversarial technique of litigation. Its main features are:

(1)   control by the parties themselves;

(2)   a consensual process;

(3)   cost-effectiveness, in terms of legal costs and managerial time;

(4)   speed;

(5)   confidentiality of commercial information;

(6)   commercial settlements can be achieved with terms outside what a court or arbitrator can order;

(7)   a continuing commercial relationship is possible between the parties.

Importance of contract

7.29   This situation does not duplicate throughout manufacturing industry. This does not mean, however, that employers in the manufacturing industry do not enter into similar contractual arrangements, even though perhaps not so elaborate, to their counterparts in construction. Frequently manufacturing employers delegate the performance of contractual obligations and statutory duties to specialist contractors (e.g. window cleaning, machinery guarding, electrical maintenance – all duties placed on employers by the *Factories Act 1961* and the *Electricity Regulations*). In many instances, such 'orders' are placed and accepted verbally and informally over the telephone or socially over a meal or drink. This is not a wise practice! The unpalatable truth is that, unless both parties clearly spell out their legal rights and liabilities in an order form (or some similar contractual document), the normal liabilities of common law and statute will govern their relationship. This can have unpleasant consequences, particularly for employers (or occupiers), where, for instance, use of machinery is involved, or where some of the employer's workforce is informally transferred to work with the contractor, and is subsequently injured. The fact is that employers have a collection of duties and liabilities placed on them by statute, regulation and common law, simply because they are employers, have control of work premises and are insured. In addition, both statutory and common law duties are placed on companies or organisations as occupiers of premises. Assuming that employers (or occupiers) wish to limit their liability, at least for their own acts of negligence or obtain an indemnity from a contractor in respect of a breach of statutory duty, they should take steps to do so before allowing contractors on site – in other words, as part of the preliminary negotiations. Indeed, since a lot of contractors are 'engaged' on the basis of informal oral communication, followed (often) by completion of an order form, it is doubtful whether much thought is always given to legal 'niceties', such as the principles of contract formation (see also 7.5 above).

Terms to be negotiated

7.30   It is a tenet of contract law that all conditions and exemptions must be agreed during the period of contract formation, except such terms as might be implied into the contract anyway by statute, common law or previous dealings. For example, a husband and wife arrived at a hotel as guests and paid for a room in advance. They went up to the room. On one of the walls was the following notice: 'The proprietors will not hold themselves responsible for articles lost or stolen unless handed to the manageress for safe custody'. The wife closed the self-locking door of the bedroom and took the key downstairs to the reception desk. A third party took the key and stole certain of the wife's furs. In the ensuing action the defendants sought to rely on the notice as a term of the contract. It was held that the contract was completed at the reception desk and no subsequent notice could affect the plaintiff's rights (*Olley v Marlborough Court Ltd [1949] 1 KB 532*).

Where the employer and the contractor have done business together before over a period of time, however, so that the terms on which business was done could be ascertained with some certainty, then, reference to continuation of business on the 'usual terms' may be sufficient to cover any possible liability that might arise. Here both parties could be taken to know the situation regarding liability and compliance with legal duties (though this does not necessarily extend to employees of the contractor (see *Burnett v British Waterways Board* below)). At least this will probably be the case in business transactions, where the two parties, as employer and contractor, are at arm's length (though it would not be so in consumer transactions). For example, the plaintiff company and the defendant company were both engaged in the business of hiring out earth moving equipment. The defendant was also involved in drainage work on marshy ground and, in urgent need of a crane, agreed to hire a crane from the plaintiff; terms of payment being agreed but no reference being made to the plaintiff's conditions of hire. The plaintiff sent the defendant a copy of such conditions which provided (*inter alia*) that the hirer would be responsible for all expenses arising from use of the crane. Before the defendant signed the form containing the conditions, the crane sank into a marsh through no fault of the defendant and the plaintiff claimed from the defendant the cost of recovering the crane. Held: the plaintiff succeeded. The plaintiff company's conditions of hire applied, since both parties were in the trade and of equal bargaining power and both parties understood that the plaintiff's conditions of hire would apply (*British Crane Hire Corporation Ltd v Ipswich Plant Hire Ltd [1974] 1 AER 1059*). This will probably not be the position where one of the parties is a consumer. In *Hollier v Rambler Motors Ltd [1972] 1 AER 399*, the plaintiff, a consumer, telephoned the defendant company and asked if the company would repair his car at the company's garage. The garage manager agreed so long as the plaintiff had it towed to the garage. While in the garage the car was damaged by a fire which started as a result of the garage employee's negligence and the plaintiff claimed damages from the defendant. On three or four occasions in the previous five years the plaintiff had had repairs carried out at the garage and on each of these occasions had signed a form which, under the place for the signature stated 'The company is not responsible for damage caused by fire to customers' cars on the premises'. In an action for negligence against the company, the defendant said that, although the plaintiff had not signed the form on this occasion, the exemption clause, as set out in the form, had been incorporated into the unwritten contract by a previous 'course of dealing', and this had the effect of excluding liability for negligence. It was held that the plaintiff succeeded. The exemption clause had not been incorporated by a 'course of dealing'. Before a term could be implied into a consumer contract by a previous course of dealing, it was necessary to show that the consumer had actual and not merely constructive knowledge of the term.

Employees excluded

7.31   Although both parties may be in business and so at arm's length, contract conditions and exemption clauses would probably not bind their employees, particularly the contractor's employees. In *Burnett v British Waterways Board [1973] 2 AER 631*, a lighterman employed by a contractor was injured in consequence of the negligence of one of the employer's workmen when they were moving his barge from the river into the dock belonging to the employer, British Waterways Board. When the accident happened the barge was still in the tidal way a little way from the dock gates. The rope supplied by the employer, which was being used to pull in the barge, was defective. The rope snapped and knocked the contractor's employee over, injuring him. The employer admitted negligence but argued that he was absolved from liability by a notice, saying 'Lightermen . . . availing themselves of the facilities and assistance of the servants of British Waterways Board do so at their own risk and upon the understanding that no liability whatsoever shall attach to British Waterways Board or its servants for any loss, damage or injury from whatever cause arising to the craft or to any person on board. . . '. During his long period of employment as a lighterman the plaintiff had become aware of and had read the notice. It was held by the Court of Appeal that the occupier could not rely on the notice to absolve him from liability for injury. The fact was that the workman had been sent onto the employer's premises and there he had been compelled to accept the 'facilities'. He had no freedom of choice in the matter and could not have agreed to the terms of the notice and so the defence of assumption of risk of injury (i.e. *volenti non fit injuria*) was unavailable to the occupier.

Need to communicate contract terms

7.32   To this extent, therefore, reliance on the 'usual terms' may prove to be hazardous. In addition, the law changes and is constantly being updated by cases, and it will, therefore, be necessary to modify existing arrangements in the light of this from time to time. For these reasons the prudent employer/occupier, in his dealings with contractors, will specify the 'terms and conditions' applicable to the latter's entry and occupation, and ensure that, as far as health and safety is concerned, these conditions are understood by the contractor and his workforce. More particularly, the contractor must be aware of and understand the 'terms' before signing the order form, i.e. before completing the contract which contains the 'terms and conditions', or before committing his signature to some contractual document which refers to such terms and conditions elsewhere, because if the contractor signs the order form without understanding the 'terms and conditions' applicable between him and the employer, he will subsequently, nevertheless, be bound by them. For example, the defendant sold to the plaintiff a slot machine, inserting in the order form the following clause 'Any express or implied condition, statement or warranty, statutory or otherwise, is hereby excluded'. The plaintiff signed the order form but did not read the relevant clause. She now sued in respect of the defective nature of the slot machine. It was held that the exemption clause was binding on her, although the defendant had made no attempt to read the document to her nor had drawn her attention to the clause (*L'Estrange v Graucob [1934] 2 KB 394*). However, any exemption clause would be inapplicable if it was contained in a document coming into existence after the contract was made. In *Chapelton v Barry UDC [1940] 1 KB 532* the plaintiff wished to hire deck chairs and went to a pile owned by the defendant behind which there was a notice stating 'Hire of chairs 2d per session of three hours'. The plaintiff took two chairs, paid for them, and received two tickets which he put into his pocket after merely glancing at them. One of the chairs collapsed, injuring him. A notice on the back of the ticket provided that 'The council will not be liable for any accident or damage arising from hire of chairs'. The plaintiff sued for damages and the council sought to rely on the clause in the ticket. It was held that the clause was not binding on the plaintiff. The billboard by the chairs made no attempt to limit the liability of the council and it was unreasonable to communicate conditions by means of a mere receipt, i.e. evidence that the contract had already taken place.

Contract compliance

7.33   The contractor should, moreover, ensure that his workforce is familiar with the 'terms and conditions', compliance with which, in many cases, is designed to protect the employer from liability. More particularly, there are several statutes which make employers liable for breach of statutory duty to both their own employees and the workforce of an incoming independent contractor (e.g. fencing requirements of the *Factories Act 1961*; access to work requirements and *HSWA s 3(1)*). In addition, any contract entered into between employer and contractor would normally provide that the contractor should indemnify the employer for any breach of common law/statutory duty, regulation etc. and the contractor should take out insurance to meet this contingency, unless the breach is due to negligence on the part of the employer. In the case of the Standard Form of Building Contract, in such a situation, it has been held that the proviso 'unless due to any act or neglect of the employer' is limited to common law negligence, with the result that the contractor would still have to indemnify the employer against breach of statutory duty, that is, unless the breach was due to negligence on the part of the employer (see further *Hosking v de Havilland* at 7.7 above). It is not unnatural, therefore, that the employer should impress upon the contractor the importance of compliance with steps designed to ensure that the employer is not exposed to such liability. This is often referred to as 'contract compliance'.

Contract compliance arises where an outside workforce enters the premises of an employer to carry out a particular operation (or operations) ancillary to the general function of the employer. It does not apply to the situation where an employee is transferred temporarily off company premises to another employer, e.g. contractor. Quintessentially, it refers to the situation where an employer enters into a contract with a contractor in order to ensure, not that the employer is absolved from liability where otherwise there would be liability, but that contractors do not involve employers in such liability, i.e. activate such liability. (The specific circumstances in which contractors can involve employers in liability, are mentioned below.)

Definitions

7.34   The principal protagonists in this scenario are (*a*) the occupier (or employer), (*b*) the contractor and, possibly, the subcontractor.

(*a*)   *Occupier.* This refers to a factory occupier or the occupier of some other industrial organisation. An 'occupier' is a person who is in *control* of and has the duty of safe management of work premises.

(*b*)   *Contractor.* This refers to the person or company invited by the occupier onto his premises to carry out some corporate function, or to whom performance of some statutory duty has been delegated, for example, window cleaning, electrical maintenance. There is a tendency to suppose that such person is self-employed and so is not owed some of the safety duties owed to employees. This may not always be the case (see *Ferguson v Dawson* at 7.5 above).

Liability of employer in connection with contract work

7.35   In practice, two sorts of situation give rise to liability:

(*a*)   injuries/diseases, or the risk of them, to employees of the contractor as a result of working on the occupier's premises; or, alternatively, injuries or the risk of them to the employer's own workforce as a result of the employer failing to acquaint the contractor's workforce with dangers, thereby endangering his own employees (see *R v Swan Hunter Shipbuilders Ltd* below);

(*b*)   injuries/damage to members of the public, or pollution or nuisance to neighbouring landowners.

Such liability can be both criminal and civil (often strict).

(a) Criminal liability

7.36   This can arise under several statutes and at common law (e.g. where, owing to gross negligence, employers commit manslaughter – in practice, this is rare). Particularly relevant are the *Factories Act 1961* and the *Health and Safety at Work Act 1974, ss 3(1), 4(2)*. (It should be added, in fairness, that the situation can reverse, in favour of the employer, owing to a breach of safety legislation by the contractor, see *R v Mara* at 7.37 below.)

Health and Safety at Work Act 1974

7.37   In particular, *Sec 3(1)* states: 'It shall be the duty of every employer to conduct his undertaking in such a way as to ensure, so far as is reasonably practicable, that persons not in his employment who may be affected thereby are not thereby exposed to risks to their health or safety'.

An instructive case involving this section was *R v Swan Hunter Shipbuilders Ltd* [*1982*] *1 AER 264*. During construction of a ship at a shipbuilder's yard, subcontractors, who had no contract with the shipbuilders, were working on the ship while it was being fitted out. The shipbuilders were aware that, because of use of oxygen hoses with fuel gases in welding, there was a risk of fire due to the atmosphere in confined and poorly ventilated spaces in the ship becoming oxygen enriched. In regard to that danger they had, so far as was reasonably practicable, provided a safe system of work by providing information and instruction for their own employees by compiling and distributing to them a book of rules on the use of fuel gases and oxygen (which stipulated that at the end of the day's work, all oxygen hoses should be returned from the lower decks to an open deck, or, where impracticable, the hoses should be disconnected at the cylinder or manifold) and by introducing a system of checks by night patrolmen to ensure that the rules were being observed. This rule book was *not* distributed to the subcontractor's employees working on the ship. At the end of the day's work, an employee of the subcontractor failed to disconnect the oxygen hose which was being used in a poorly ventilated lower deck and oxygen was discharged from the hose during the night. In consequence, on the next morning, when a welder working in the lower deck lit his welding torch, a fierce fire escaped. The shipbuilders were charged with:

(*a*)   failing to provide/maintain a safe system of work, contrary to *Sec 2(2)(a)* by reason of failure to provide/maintain a system of work whereby, at the end of the day's work, all oxygen hoses used in any lower decks, were taken to the topmost deck or some other safe and ventilated place, or, if impracticable, disconnected from the manifolds;

(*b*)   failing to provide such information/instruction as was necessary to ensure the health/safety of their employees, contrary to *Sec 2(2)(c)*;

(*c*)   failing to conduct their undertaking in such a way as to ensure that persons not in their employment, who might be affected thereby, were not exposed to risks to health and safety, contrary to *Sec 3(1)*, by reason of their failure to inform and instruct subcontractor's employees of the dangers of oxygen-enriched atmosphere and the necessity, after work, to take all oxygen hoses to the topmost deck or disconnect them.

On appeal against conviction on all three counts, it was held by the Court of Appeal that:

(i)   duties imposed on an employer by *Secs 2 and 3* followed the common law duty of care of the main contractors to co-ordinate operations at a place of work so as to ensure not only the safety of his own employees but also that of the subcontractor's employees. The main contractor had to prove, on a balance of probabilities, that it was not reasonably practicable for him to carry out the duties under *Secs 2* and *3*;

(ii) the shipbuilders were under a duty, under *Sec 2(2)(a)*, to provide/maintain a safe system of work for the subcontractor's employees, so far as was reasonably practicable, and provide them with information/instruction so as to ensure their safety.

Accordingly, the main contractor, Swan Hunter Shipbuilders Ltd, was fined £3,000 and the subcontractor, Telemeters Ltd, £15,000 after eight men were trapped and killed on board HMS Glasgow.

Furthermore, if the main contractor fails, as in *Swan Hunter*, to comply with *Sec 3(1)*, in his duties towards subcontracted labour, it is likely that he would be in breach of his duty towards his own employees, under *Sec 2*. Thus, anyone who is responsible for co-ordinating work has to ensure that reasonable safety precautions are taken for the workmen of a contractor or subcontractor.

This rule can work in reverse against the contractor and in favour of the employer's workforce. In *R v Mara* [1987] *1 AER 478* the director of a company providing cleaning services placed a contract with International Stores Ltd to clean its premises on weekday mornings. It was agreed that cleaning machines provided by the cleaning company would be left at IS's premises and that IS's employees could use the machines to clean the loading bay at IS's premises. An employee of IS was electrocuted by a faulty cable on one of the company's machines, while using it to clean the loading bay. The director was charged with breach of *Sec 33(1)* of the *Health and Safety at Work Act 1974* (see further Chapter 17 'Enforcement'). It was held that failure to remove/replace the unsafe cable was a breach by the company of its duty to its own employees, under *Sec 2(2)*, since it had not, so far as was reasonably practicable, provided and maintained plant which was safe and/or made arrangements for ensuring safety in connection with the use/handling of articles. Since the cable would (or might) have been used by employees of IS, the occupier, it followed that they might be exposed to risks resulting from the way in which the company carried out its undertaking, under *Sec 3(1)*. The director's appeal was, therefore, dismissed. Other sections giving rise to criminal liability under the *Health and Safety at Work Act 1974* and involving occupiers and contractors, are *Secs 4(2)* and *5* (see further Chapter 32 'Occupiers' Liability' and Chapter 12 'Emissions into the Atmosphere').

(b) Civil liability

7.38   Normally employers are only liable for the negligent acts/omissions of their own employees or agents but there are certain important exceptions. The following are the main circumstances in which an employer can be liable for the torts of contractors or their employees, causing injury/death to any other worker on site or to a member of the public. Much of this civil liability of employers is based on occupation, viz.

(*a*)   Where statute makes the occupier liable even though the contractor is at fault (see 7.7 above, *Hosking v de Havilland Aircraft Ltd*).

(*b*)   Where work is being carried on on or near a public highway or thoroughfare. An employer contracted a contractor to put up a lamp overhanging the highway. Later the lamp fell because the work had not been done properly. The employer, not the contractor, was held to be liable (*Tarry v Ashton (1876) 1 QB 314*).

(*c*)   Where the rule in *Rylands v Fletcher* applies. Here the defendant employed an independent contractor to build a reservoir on his land. The contractor was competent and employed competent workers. Later water escaped from the reservoir, percolating through some disused mine shafts and flooded the plaintiff's mine. It was held that, although he had not been negligent, nevertheless, the defendant was liable for the negligence of the contractors (see further Chapter 19 'Fire and Fire Precautions').

(*d*)   Where an employee of an occupier is injured by the contractor's negligence but overall control rests with the occupier. Normally where an occupier's employee is negligently injured by a contractor's employee, the contractor would be liable, on the basis of vicarious liability. But where overall control rests with the occupier, he may be liable for injury to his own employee negligently caused by the contractor's workmen. For example, the respondents employed the appellant as a deckhand in the course of dredging operations carried out by the respondents and their parent company. Whilst working on a tug owned by the parent company, under the control of a tug master employed by the parent company, the appellant was seriously injured and sued the defendants. At first instance it was held that the defendants were vicariously liable for the tug master's negligence. The defendants appealed, arguing that they were not responsible for the actions of the tug master, because he was not under their control but that of the parent company. The Court of Appeal held that the tug master was not an employee of the defendants, but, since the defendants had put the plaintiff who was young and inexperienced under the care and control of the tug master, he was their agent or delegate and was required to take reasonable care to devise a safe system of work for the plaintiff. The defendants appealed. It was held by the House of Lords that the duty to provide/maintain a safe system of work on the employer was personal and non-delegable. In other words, if the duty was not performed, it was no defence for the employer to show that he had delegated its performance to a person, employee or not, whom he reasonably believed was competent to perform it. The defendants had delegated the duty to the tug master, who was negligent in failing to operate that system. 'The defendants did not, and could not, dispute the existence of such a duty of care, nor that it was "non-delegable" in the special sense in which the phrase is used in this connection. This special sense does not involve the proposition that the duty cannot be delegated . . . but only that the employer cannot escape liability if the duty has been delegated and then not properly performed' (per Lord Hailsham) (*McDermid v Nash Dredging & Reclamation Co Ltd [1987] 2 AER 878*).

(*e*)   Where the employer ratifies the tort of the contractor. For example, a manufacturer supplies safety equipment which does not meet the requirements of an improvement notice served on the employer, and the employer agrees to use the equipment, with the result that an employee is injured.

(f)   Where the employer does not exercise reasonable care in selecting a competent contractor. For example, he fails to make inquiries of the contractor or uses a contractor with a bad reputation.

(g)   Joint liability under the *Occupiers' Liability Act 1957*. Occupation of premises is not normally exclusive to employers (though, to some extent, exclusiveness of occupation can be secured by creating a separate factory or workplace (see 7.39 below)). Where contractors and subcontractors are on site, part of the site or premises will be occupied by them. To this extent there is joint liability under the *Occupiers' Liability Act 1957* and both employer and contractor could be sued simultaneously if an injury occurred in a 'common part'. Occupation is synonymous with control or management and anyone who has control 'to any extent' will be deemed to be in joint occupation. In *Wheat v Lacon & Co Ltd [1966] 1 AER 582*, the appellant's husband was killed when he fell down some steps at a public house managed by a third party and owned by the respondents. The judgment of the House of Lords made clear that both the respondents and the manager were in occupation, the third party because he was managing the premises and the owners because they defined the scope of his managing activity in a lease. Joint liability under the *Occupiers' Liability Act 1957* extends to damage to property as well as personal injury (*AMF International Ltd v Magnet Bowling Ltd and Trentham [1968] 2 AER 789* where the property of a subcontractor was damaged owing to the negligence of an employee of the main contractor. It was held that there was liability under the *Occupiers' Liability Act 1957*). This joint statutory liability, or the risk of it, should be separately insured against, otherwise the occupier may well find that he is not covered (*Gold v Patman & Fotheringham Ltd [1958] 2 AER 497*, a building case). Another example is where garage owners employed demolition contractors to demolish an old building and building contractors to erect an extension to a garage. An architect was also employed to prepare plans and supervise both operations. The old building and the gable wall at the end of the existing garage were to be demolished to allow for an extension which would lengthen the existing building. Having demolished the old building, the demolition contractors were told to leave the gable wall for the time being. Before the demolition contractors left the site, two walls supporting the gable wall had been knocked down and the earth had been dug out from the foundations of the gable wall, so exposing unsafe foundations. The architect inspected the site just before the demolition contractors left and could, had he carried out a proper inspection, have seen that the wall was unsafe. He advised the building owners that it was safe. The foreman of the demolition company also declared the wall safe. The building contractors did not examine the wall in any detail because they relied, as the architect and demolition contractors should have assumed that they would, on the wall being left safe. The plaintiff was a labourer employed by the building contractors, and while he was on the site, the gable wall collapsed, injuring him. He sued the demolition contractors, the architect and the building contractors. It was held that all three were liable in negligence to the plaintiff, the damages being apportioned 42% against the architect, 38% against the demolition contractors and 20% against the building contractors (*Clay v A J Crump & Sons Ltd and Others [1963] 3 AER 687*).

Separate factories/workplaces

7.39   It is clearly advisable in the interests of good mutual housekeeping (and, incidentally, to minimise the possible incidence of joint civil liability based on occupation) to segregate the part of the operation that is in the hands of the contractor. The legal effect of doing this is as follows.

(*a*)   Segregation constitutes a 'separate factory' for the purposes of the *Factories Act 1961*. This means that the contractor becomes an independent factory occupier and can be prosecuted, separately from the main occupier. This includes building contractors, since building operations qualify as 'notional factories'. [*Factories Act 1961, s 127(4)*]. An example of this occurred in the case of a construction site inside factory premises where steam-boilers were being installed (*Street v British Electricity Authority [1952] 1 AER 679*). Before there can be a separate factory, for the purposes of the *Factories Act 1961, s 175(6)*, the following conditions must be satisfied:

  (i)   the area must be clearly definable and physically separated, e.g. by a fence, wall or barrier;

  (ii)   the organisation in control of the area must be closely identified and control must be acknowledged by both employer and contractor;

  (iii)   the contractor must be allowed to be in control of the segregated area;

  (iv)   the segregated site must be used for a purpose wholly different from the general purpose of the organisation.

(*b*)   In addition to separate liability under the *Factories Act 1961, s 175(6)*, the contractor (and the employer) can incur additional criminal liability under the *Health and Safety at Work Act 1974, s 4(2)*: 'It shall be the duty of each person who has, to any extent, control of premises . . . or of means of access thereto or egress therefrom or any plant or substance in such premises to take measures as it is reasonable for such a person in his position to take to ensure, so far as is reasonably practicable, that the premises . . . means of access and egress available for use by persons using the premises, and any plant or substance in the premises, or provided for use there, is or are safe and without risk to health'.

(*c*)   Even though a 'separate factory/workplace' is created, for the purposes of the *Factories Act 1961, s 175(6)*, it is extremely doubtful whether this would entirely eliminate the possibility of joint civil liability between occupier and contractor under the *Occupiers' Liability Act 1957*, and employers (i.e. occupiers) would still be liable for equipment, plant, buildings, furniture and services in that area and as such should warn the contractor of hazards associated with them, particularly latent hazards, e.g. faulty electrical circuit (see 7.38(*g*) above).

Construction plant – statutory requirements until 1 January 1996

7.40   The following types of construction plant (to which the *Supply of Machinery (Safety) Regulations 1992 (SI 1992 No 3073)* do not extend) (see 28.46, 28.47 MACHINERY SAFETY) must have an EC-type examination certificate and certificate of conformity and an approved body must carry out EEC inspections in Great Britain before they can be marketed, namely:

(*a*)   roll-over protective structures (ROPS) cannot be marketed unless they satisfy the above criteria [*Roll-over Protective Structures for Construction Plant (EEC Requirements) Regulations 1988 (SI 1988 No 363)*];

(*b*)   falling-object protective structures (FOPS) for construction plant likewise cannot be marketed unless they satisfy the above criteria [*Falling-Object*

Protective Structures for Construction Plant (EEC Requirements) Regulations 1988 (SI 1988 No 362)].

If a ROPS or FOPS does not conform with the examination requirements the approved body will give notice of the decision to the manufacturer who then has a right of appeal within 14 days from the receipt of the decision. [*Reg 8 of both SIs*]. Certificates may be suspended or withdrawn immediately. In the case of FOPS the certificate may be suspended temporarily so long as the manufacturer conforms with the requirement in a given period. If the manufacturer applies for a review, copies of the documents submitted to the approved body and the decision must accompany the application. The Secretary of State may then hold an inquiry. [*Reg 9 of both SIs*].

In addition, the *Self-Propelled Industrial Trucks (EEC Requirements) Regulations 1988 (SI 1988 No 1736*, as subsequently amended by *SI 1989 No 1035)* provide for stability, visibility and functional tests to be carried out on self-propelled industrial trucks (not exceeding 10,000 kilograms) by the manufacturer and/or an approved body, to ensure that such trucks comply with Annex 1 of the Special Directive. [*Regs 5 and 6*]. Also, the marketing of any self-propelled industrial truck is prohibited unless accompanied by a certificate of conformity [*Regs 3, 10 and 11*] (see also Chapter 26 'Lifting Machinery and Equipment').

Stairs, gangways and ladders – Construction (Working Places) Regulations 1966 (SI 1966 No 94)

7.41   Stairs, gangways and ladders on construction sites are governed by the *Construction (Working Places) Regulations 1966 (SI 1966 No 94).*

Width of gangways

Every gangway and run from any part of which a person (not merely an employee) is liable to fall more than two metres must:

(*a*)   if used for the passage of *persons* only, be at least 430 mm wide;

(*b*)   if used for the passage of *materials*, be adequate in width for the passage of materials and, in any case, be at least 600 mm wide.

[*Construction (Working Places) Regulations 1966, Reg 27(1)*].

A gangway between holes in the floor qualifies as a 'working place', for the purposes of the regulations (*Boyton v Willmont Bros [1971] 3 AER 624*).

Reg 27(1) does not apply to a gangway or run where it is impracticable (for limitation of space) to provide a gangway or run of the width required. In such a case, the gangway or run should be as wide as is reasonably practicable. [*Reg 27(2)*]. The fact that erecting guard-rails is unreasonable and senseless does not make it 'impracticable' (*Boyton v Willmont Bros* (see above)).

Stairs and gangways fitted with hand-rails

7.42   Stairs must be provided throughout their length with hand-rails or other efficient means to prevent the fall of persons. If necessary, in order to prevent danger to any person (not merely an employee but also lawful visitors), the hand-rails or other means must be continued beyond the end of the stairs. [*Reg 29(1)*].

Guarding stairs and gangways

7.43   Where a person (see 7.41 above) is liable to fall more than two metres, every side of any gangway, run or stairs must be provided:

(*a*)   with a suitable guard-rail or guard-rails of adequate strength to a height of between 910 mm and 1.15 metres above the gangway, run or stairs; and

(*b*)   except in the case of stairs, with toe-boards or other barriers up to a sufficient height of at least 150 mm to prevent the fall of persons, materials and articles.

[*Reg 29(2)*].

Temporary gangways can be exempted from this requirement. This requirement applies to scaffold materials and tools, bricks and the like, which have not become affixed to the structure but which it is intended should become affixed to the structure, as well as builders' debris. It is designed to protect persons working at sites from falling materials and not from collapse of the structure, whether a chimney, roof or part of the shaft (*Bailey v Ayr Engineering Co Ltd* [*1958*] *2 AER 222* by way of analogy with the *Building (Safety, Health and Welfare) Regulations 1948, Reg 90*). In addition, where building operations or works of engineering construction are being carried out, safety helmets to BS 5240: 1987 should be worn by personnel on site to protect them from falling objects [*Construction (Head Protection) Regulations 1989*] (see further Chapter 36 'Personal Protective Equipment').

Obstructions and slippery substances

7.44   If a platform, gangway, run or stair becomes slippery, action must be taken by way of sanding, cleaning or otherwise, to rectify the condition as soon as is reasonably practicable. [*Reg 30(1)*].

Moreover, every platform, gangway and stairway must be kept free from any unnecessary obstruction and material as well as from rubbish and projecting nails. [*Reg 30(2)*]. (For the meaning of 'obstruction', see 18.32 FACTORIES AND WORKPLACES.) An employee who was injured whilst trying to remove an obstruction recovered damages for breach of this regulation. (It was very likely that a person finding an obstruction would try to remove it so the chain of causation was not broken.) (*McGovern v British Steel Corporation* [*1986*] *ICR 608 (CA)*).

Ladders on construction sites

7.45   A ladder or folding step-ladder must be:

(*a*)   of good construction, suitable and sound material and adequate strength for the purpose for which it is used; and

(*b*)   properly maintained.

[*Reg 31(1)*]. (This corresponds to the *Factories Act 1961, s 28(5)*, see 18.42 FACTORIES AND WORKPLACES.)

Under the *Building (Safety, Health and Welfare) Regulations 1948 (SI 1948 No 1145), Reg 29* (the predecessor of *Regs 31* and *32* of the current regulations), this duty was held to be delegable, on the part of the main contractor, to his steel erector foreman, with the result that when a foreman was injured through not using a suitable ladder (he used a fruit-picking ladder!), the main contractor was not liable (*Johnson v Croggan & Co Ltd* [*1954*] *1 WLR 195*). This would appear to be one of the few situations where a statutory safety duty can be delegated by an employer to an employee without there being a residuum of liability on the employer (see also Chapter 17 'Enforcement').

Specific safety requirements relating to ladders on construction sites

Ladders on bases

7.46   Except in the case of ladders less than three metres in length (see also 7.45 above), no ladder standing on a base must be used unless:

(*a*)   it is securely fixed near to its upper resting place, or, in the case of a vertical ladder, near to its upper end, except where such fixing is impracticable (for the meaning of this expression, see further 7.41 above). The ladder must be securely fixed at or near its lower end (*Boyle v Kodak Ltd [1969] 2 AER 439* is a case turning on the *Building (Safety, Health and Welfare) Regulations 1948, Reg 29(4)*, the predecessor of *Reg 32(2)*, in which both employer and employee were held in breach of the regulation); and

(*b*)   it has a level and firm footing and is not standing on loose bricks or other loose packing; and

(*c*)   it is secured where necessary to prevent undue swaying or sagging; and

(*d*)   it is equally and properly supported on each stile or side.

[*Reg 32(2)*].

This regulation does not apply to:

(i)   ladders on roofs (see Chapter 46 'Work at Heights');

(ii)   crawling boards (see Chapter 46 'Work at Heights');

(iii) crawling ladders (see Chapter 46 'Work at Heights');

(iv)   ladders less than three metres in length if it is secure from slipping or falling and is not used for communication.

[*Reg 32(1)(b)*].

Other requirements

7.47   (*a*)   No ladder must be used unless:

(i)   it extends to at least 1.05 metres above the place of landing or the highest rung to be reached by the feet of any person using the ladder; or

(ii)   if this is impracticable, to the greatest practicable height; or

(iii) unless there is other adequate hand-hold; and

(iv)   there is sufficient space at each rung to provide adequate foothold.

(*b*)   No folding step-ladder must be used:

(i)   unless it has a level and firm footing; or

(ii)   while it is standing on loose bricks or other loose packing.

(*c*)   No ladder must be used in which a rung is missing or is defective.

[*Regs 31(2), 32(5)(7)*].

(See also Chapter 46 'Work at Heights'.)

All ladders on construction sites

7.48 With the exception of ladders standing on bases, which are governed by *Reg 32(2)* (see 7.46 above), all ladders prior to use must be:

(*a*)   securely suspended;

(*b*)   secured, where necessary, to prevent undue swinging and swaying;

(*c*)   equally and properly suspended by each stile or side.

[*Reg 32(6)*].

Sloping roofs

7.49 Where a sloping roof is used as a means of access to or egress from (for the meaning of these expressions, see Chapter 2 'Access') work on a roof, or part of it, crawling ladders or crawling boards must be provided (for the meaning of 'provide', see Chapter 15 'Employers' Duties') on the sloping roof. [*Reg 35(3)*]. (For more detail on working at heights, see Chapter 46 'Work at Heights'.)

Crawling ladders and crawling boards must be:

(*a*)   of good construction, suitable and of sound material, as well as of adequate strength;

(*b*)   free from patent defect, and properly maintained (for the meaning of 'maintain', see Chapter 15 'Employers' Duties' and Chapter 18 'Factories and Workplaces');

(*c*)   properly supported;

(*d*)   securely fixed or anchored to the sloping surface, or over the roof ridge, or securely fixed in some other effective way, to prevent slipping.

[*Reg 35(5)*].

Crawling ladders and crawling boards are not necessary on a sloping roof where batten handholds and footholds make the roof as safe as if they had been provided. [*Reg 35(6)*].

Ladders and work on fragile materials

7.50 If a person would be liable to fall more than two metres when passing across or working on or from material which would be liable to fracture under his weight, crawling ladders or crawling boards, or duck boards, must be *provided* to support that person, unless his weight is supported by other equally safe means (e.g. lightweight staging). [*Reg 36(1)*].

General health and safety requirements relating to floors etc.

7.51 All employers (whether factory occupiers or occupiers of offices and shops, or of other premises) have a general duty under *HSWA s 2(2)(d)* to maintain a place of work in a condition which is safe and without health risks. This includes floors and gangways, passageways and even ladders. Moreover, all employers owe a similar duty to persons on their premises for reasons not connected with the work process, e.g. firemen and factory inspectors, by virtue of *HSWA s 3(1)*.

Composition of construction products

7.52   Products must be suitable for construction works and works of civil engineering and can then carry the 'CE' mark. To that end, when incorporated into design and building, construction products should satisfy the following criteria, namely,

(*a*)   mechanical resistance and stability;

(*b*)   safety in case of fire;

(*c*)   hygiene, health and the environment;

(*d*)   safety in use;

(*e*)   protection against noise; and

(*f*)   energy economy and heat retention.

[*Construction Products Regulations 1991 (SI 1991 No 1620), Reg 3, 2 Sch*].

Manufacturers must show that their products conform to these specifications, if necessary, by submitting to third party testing (see also 36.11 PERSONAL PROTECTIVE EQUIPMENT for products generally).

Practical safety criteria

7.53   Falling from a height is the most frequent cause of fatal accidents in the construction industry, hence the considerable attention paid to aspects such as the erection, inspection and maintenance of scaffolds, and the more general aspects of roof work in the *Construction (Working Places) Regulations 1966*. Accidents associated with ladders are also a common feature of this industry.

Although not statutory requirements the following criteria should be considered in any assessment of construction site safety.

Ladders

7.54   (*a*)   Only ladders in a sound condition should be used.

(*b*)   The 'one out four up' rule should be strictly adhered to in all situations (i.e. that the vertical height from the ground to the ladder's point of rest should be four times the distance between the base of the vertical dimension and the foot of the ladder).

(*c*)   Ladders should be securely fixed near to their upper resting place or, where this is impracticable, 'footed' by an individual or securely fixed at the base to prevent slipping.

(*d*)   Ladders should be inspected on a regular basis and a record of such inspections maintained.

Working platforms

7.55   (*a*)   Working platforms should be adequately fenced by means of guard-rails and toe-boards.

(*b*)   Platforms should be adequately covered with sound boards.

(*c*)   Where mobile platforms are used, they should be stationed on a firm level base and, where possible, tied to the structure to prevent sideways movement. Wheel-locking devices should be provided and used.

(*d*)   The following height to base ratios should be applied for all mobile working platforms:

outdoor work – 3:1; indoor work – 3.5:1.

Materials

7.56   (*a*)   Meticulous standards of housekeeping must be maintained on working platforms and other elevated working positions to prevent materials, tools and other items falling on to people working directly below. The correct positioning of toe-boards is most important here.

(*b*)   Lifting operations should ensure correct hooking and slinging prior to raising, correct assembly of gin-wheels and a high degree of supervision.

(*c*)   Catchment platforms or 'fans' should be installed to catch small items which may fall during construction, particularly where work is undertaken above a public thoroughfare.

Excavations

7.57   (*a*)   Trenches should be adequately timbered with regard to the depth and width of the trench, the nature of the surrounding ground and the load imposed by subsoil.

(*b*)   Excavated ground and building materials should be stored well away from the verge of any excavation.

Powered hand tools and machinery

7.58   (*a*)   Electrically operated hand tools, such as drills, should comply with British Standard 2769: 1964 and, unless 'all insulated' or 'double insulated', must be effectively earthed.

(*b*)   Portable tools and temporary lighting arrangements should operate through reduced voltages, using 110 volt mains isolation transformers with the secondary winding centre tapped to earth.

(*c*)   Power take-offs, cooling fans, belt drives and other items of moving machinery should be securely fenced to prevent workers coming into contact with them. All woodworking machinery, such as planing machines and circular saws, should comply with the *Woodworking Machines Regulations 1974* (see Chapter 28 'Machinery Safety').

Site transport

7.59   (*a*)   Employees should not travel on site transport, such as dumper trucks, and notices should be affixed to such vehicles to that effect.

(*b*)   All vehicle movement and tipping operations on site should be supervised by a person outside the driver's cab.

(*c*)   Site vehicles should be subject to regular maintenance, particular attention being paid to braking and reversing systems.

(*d*)   Only competent and trained drivers should be allowed to drive site vehicles.

(*e*)   Site roadways should be maintained in a sound condition, free from mud, debris, obstructions and large puddles. The verges of the roadway should be clearly defined and adequate lighting provided, particularly at tipping points, reversing and turning areas.

Demolition

7.60   (*a*)   A pre-demolition survey should always be undertaken, making use of the original plans if available.

(*b*)   Catching platforms should be installed not more than 6 m below the working level wherever there is a risk to the public.

(*c*)   Employees should be provided with safety helmets incorporating chin straps, goggles, heavy duty gloves and safety boots with steel insoles. In certain cases, respiratory protection, safety belts or harnesses may also be necessary.

(*d*)   Demolition should be undertaken, wherever possible, in the reverse order of erection.

(*e*)   When using working platforms, all debris should be removed on a regular basis.

(*f*)   Independently supported working platforms over reinforced concrete slabs should be demolished.

(*g*)   Members of framed structures should be adequately supported and temporary props, bracing or guys installed to restrain remaining parts of the building.

(*h*)   Employees should not work from the floor of a building which is currently being demolished.

(*j*)   Where pulling arrangements, demolition ball, explosives or pusher arms are to be used, employees should be kept well away until these stages have been completed.

(*k*)   Frequent inspections must be made of the demolition site to detect dangers which may have arisen following commencement of demolition.

Fire

7.61   (*a*)   All sources of ignition should be carefully controlled, e.g. welding activities, the use of blow lamps, gas or liquid fuel fired appliances.

(*b*)   All flammable materials, including waste materials, should be carefully stored away from the main construction activity.

(*c*)   All employees should be aware of the fire warning system, training sessions being undertaken according to need.

(*d*)   There should be sufficient access for fire brigade appliances in the event of fire.

(*e*)   There should be adequate space between buildings, e.g. site huts, canteen, etc.

(*f*)   High-risk buildings should be separated from low-risk buildings.

(*g*)   Controlled areas, where smoking and the use of naked lights are forbidden, should be established and suitably marked with warning signs.

(*h*)   An adequate supply of water should be available for fire brigade appliances and on-site fire-fighting.

(*j*)   Fire wardens should be appointed to undertake routine site inspections, together with the operation of a fire patrol, particularly at night and weekends.

(See also 'Fires on construction sites' at 19.79 FIRE AND FIRE PRECAUTIONS.)

HSE Guidance Notes in connection with demolition and safe erection of structures

7.62   GS 28/1 –   Safe erection of structures: Part 1: initial planning and design.

GS 28/2 –   Safe erection of structures: Part 2: site management and procedures.

GS 28/3 –   Safe erection of structures: Part 3: working places and access.

GS 28/4 –   Safe erection of structures: Part 4: legislation and training.

GS 29/1 –   Health and safety in demolition work: Part 1 – Preparation and planning.

GS 29/2 –   Health and safety in demolition work: Part 2 – Legislation.

GS 29/3 –   Health and safety in demolition work: Part 3 – Techniques.

GS 29/4 –   Health and safety in demolition work: Part 4 – Health hazards.

Chapter 8

Control of Industrial Major Accident Hazards

Introduction

8.1   In the last 25 years or so there has been a substantial change in traditional industrial processes. Industry has become more sophisticated, with the introduction of robots, computerised fully automatic processes and a reduced, but more highly skilled labour force. Whilst the more traditional risks to workers associated with, for example, machinery and plant, have been reduced, the major hazard potential of many installations has increased, with resultant risk not only to the labour force but to people living in the immediate vicinity of the installation. The risk of catastrophic harm from potentially ultra-hazardous plants, is provided for in the *Control of Industrial Major Accident Hazards Regulations 1984* (which are to be completely revised by the end of 1994) as a result of which plants catering for storage and manufacture of explosives, waste incineration and chemical risks at nuclear sites, will be covered. Some of these high-powered operations may also be subject to pollution control measures and procedures specified in the *Environmental Protection Act 1990*, failure to comply with which, and hence resulting in service of notice/prosecution/conviction, will result in an (unwanted) entry in a public register (see further Chapter 12 'Emissions into the Atmosphere'). In addition, some 250 industrial sites have been 'upgraded' and subject to more stringent safety requirements, courtesy of the *Control of Industrial Major Accident Hazards (Amendment) Regulations 1990*; these latest regulations also give similar public access to information about hazards on site. This chapter considers the legislation dealing with major industrial hazards and the factors to be considered at the planning stage of new and potentially dangerous installations. Altogether about 550 installations are involved, but not nuclear or MOD establishments.

Public disclosure of radiation emergency

8.2   In the wake of Chernobyl, the *Public Information for Radiation Emergencies Regulations 1992 (SI 1992 No 2997)* require employers in control of nuclear installations, from which radiation emergencies are reasonably foreseeable, to apprise the general public of the danger in tandem with local authorities. Ministry of Defence installations are exempt from these requirements if the national interest so dictates. [*Reg 3*].

(1) Potential radiation emergency

Any employer (or self-employed person) who conducts an undertaking, where a radiation emergency is reasonably foreseeable, must:

(a)   furnish and update (at least, once in three years) members of the public likely to be in the area, *without their having to request it*, with information concerning

      (i)   basic facts about radioactivity and its effects on persons/ environment,

   (ii)   various types of radiation emergency covered and their conse-
          quences for people/environment,

   (iii) emergency measures to alert, protect and assist people in the event
          of a radiation emergency,

   (iv)   action to be taken by people in the event of an emergency,

   (v)   authority/authorities responsible for implementing emergency
          measures; and

(*b*)   make the above information publicly available.

[*Public Information for Radiation Emergencies Regulations 1992, Reg 3(1)(4), 2 Sch*].

Employers must liaise with district councils and London borough councils in order
for the latter to disseminate the necessary information. [*Reg 3(3)*].

(2) Actual radiation emergency

It is incumbent on county councils to prepare and update regularly information
relating to an emergency, to members of the public actually affected by a radiation
emergency, and advise on appropriate health measures. [*Reg 4*]. The following
information should be supplied:

   (i)   nature of the emergency that has occurred, its origin, extent and probable
          development;

   (ii)   health protection measures, including:

          (*a*)   restrictions on consumption of foodstuffs and contaminated water,

          (*b*)   hygiene and decontamination,

          (*c*)   recommendation to stay indoors,

          (*d*)   distribution/use of protective substances,

          (*e*)   evacuation arrangements,

          (*f*)   special warning for certain population groups;

   (iii) announcements concerning co-operation with instructions or compliance
          with competent authorities;

   (iv)   if there has been no release of radioactivity/ionising radiations, but this is
          likely, advice to

          (*a*)   listen to radio/television,

          (*b*)   brief establishments with particular collective responsibilities,

          (*c*)   brief occupational groups particularly affected;

   (v)   if possible, resumé of basic facts of radioactivity and its effects on
          persons/environment.

[*Reg 4, 3 Sch*].

Control of Industrial Major Accident Hazards Regulations 1984 (SI 1984 No 1902)

8.3   Certain accidents, if they occur, are considered to be so potentially catastrophic that
those in control of operations must *demonstrate* to the HSE (the enforcing authority for
the purpose of these regulations) that they are able to control the hazards involved,

whether to the immediate workforce or the neighbouring area and environment. Thus, following the scenes of major industrial disasters at Flixborough, Seveso, Minamata, Mexico City and most recently, Bhopal, those in charge of chemical and petrochemical plants must prepare and update, as often as is necessary, an on-site emergency plan in conjunction with the local authority. More particularly, the law is to be found in the *Control of Industrial Major Accident Hazards Regulations 1984 (SI 1984 No 1902) (CIMAH)*, otherwise known as the 'Seveso Directive' (as amended by *SI 1988 No 1462* and *SI 1990 No 2325*; which require written safety reports (see 8.9 below) by 1 June 1994, and on- and off-site emergency plans (see 8.12 below) from 31 March and 30 September 1991 respectively).

8.4   Before undertaking activities at the following installations, using the substances listed in Table 5 below, manufacturers must prepare a written report and send a copy to the HSE at least three months before commencing that activity. The installations are as follows:

(*a*)   for the production, or treatment, or processing of organic or inorganic chemicals, using, amongst others:

    (i)   alkylation;

    (ii)   amination by ammonolysis;

    (iii)   carbonylation;

    (iv)   condensation;

    (v)   dehydrogenation;

    (vi)   esterification;

    (vii)   halogenation and manufacture of halogens;

    (viii)   hydrogenation;

    (ix)   hydrolysis;

    (x)   oxidation;

    (xi)   polymerization;

    (xii)   sulphonation;

    (xiii)   desulphurization, manufacture and transformation of sulphur-containing compounds;

    (xiv)   nitration and manufacture of nitrogen-containing compounds;

    (xv)   manufacture of phosphorous-containing compounds;

    (xvi)   formulation of pesticides and pharmaceutical products;

    (xvii)   distillation;

    (xviii)   extraction;

    (xix)   solvation;

    (xx)   mixing;

(*b*)   for the purposes of distillation, refining or other processing of petroleum or petroleum products;

(*c*)   for the total or partial disposal of solid or liquid substances by incineration or chemical decomposition;

(*d*)   for the production, processing or treatment of energy gases, e.g. LPG, LNG, SNG;

(*e*)   for the dry distillation of coal or lignite;

(*f*)   for the production of metals or non-metals by a wet process or through electrical energy.

[*Control of Industrial Major Accident Hazards Regulations 1984, 4 Sch*].

8.5   Where the following substances are used (see Table 5 below):

Table 5

Toxic Substances specified under the Control of Industrial Major Accident Hazards Regulations 1984

(*a*)   Very toxic substances:

— substances which correspond to the first line of the table below,

— substances which correspond to the second line of the table below and which, owing to their physical and chemical properties, are capable of producing major accident hazards similar to those caused by the substance mentioned in the first line:

	LD50 (oral)[1] mg/kg body weight	LD50 (cutaneous)[2] mg/kg body weight	LC50[3] mg/1 (inhalation)
1	LD50 ≤ 5	LD50 ≤ 10	LC50 ≤ 0.1
2	5 < LD50 ≤ 25	10 < LD50 ≤ 50	0.1 < LC50 ≤ 0.5

[1] LD50 oral in rats.
[2] LD50 cutaneous in rats or rabbits.
[3] LC50 by inhalation (four hours) in rats.

(*b*)   Other toxic substances:

The substances showing the following values of acute toxicity and having physical and chemical properties capable of producing major accident hazards:

LD50 (oral)[1] mg/kg body weight	LD50 (cutaneous)[2] mg/kg body weight	LC50[3] mh/1 (inhalation)
25 < LD50 ≤ 200	50 < LD50 ≤ 400	0.5 < LC50 ≤ 2

[1] LD50 oral in rats.
[2] LD50 cutaneous in rats or rabbits.
[3] LC50 by inhalation (four hours) in rats.

(*c*)   Flammable substances:

(i)   flammable gases: substances which in the gaseous state at normal pressure and mixed with air become flammable and the boiling point of which at normal pressure is 20°C or below;

> (ii)   highly flammable liquids: substances which have a flash point lower than 21°C and the boiling point of which at normal pressure is above 20°C;
>
> (iii) flammable liquids: substances which have a flash point lower than 55°C and which remain liquid under pressure, where particular processing conditions, such as high pressure and high temperature, may create major accident hazards.
>
> (*d*)   Explosive substances: substances which may explode under the effect of flame or which are more sensitive to shocks or friction than dinitrobenzene.
>
> (*e*)   Oxidising substances: substances which give rise to a highly exothermic reaction when in contact with other substances, particularly flammable substances. [*(Amendment) Regulations 1990 (SI 1990 No 2325), 2 Sch*].

or

8.6   where quantities of the following dangerous substances/preparations (see column 1 in Table 6 below) are stored at any place, installation (other than those in 8.4(*a*) above and corresponding substances in Table 7), premises, building or area of land, in isolation or within an establishment:

Table 6
Isolated storage of dangerous substances

Substances or groups of substances *Column 1*	Quantities (tonnes)	
	For application of Regulation 4 *Column 2*	For application of Regulations 7 to 12 *Column 3*
Acetylene	5	50
Acrolein (2-propenal)	20	200
Acrylonitrile	20	200
Ammonia	50	500
Ammonium nitrate[a]	350	2,500
Ammonium nitrate in the form of fertilisers[b]	1,250	10,000
Bromine	50	500
Carbon disulphide	20	200
Chlorine	10	75
Diphenyl methane di-isocyanate (MDI)	20	200
Ethylene dibromide (1,2 Dibromoethane)	5	50
Ethylene oxide	5	50
Formaldehyde (concentration $\geqslant$90%)	5	50
Hydrogen	5	50

Hydrogen chloride (liquefied gas)	25	250
Hydrogen cyanide	5	20
Hydrogen fluoride	5	50
Hydrogen sulphide	5	50
Methyl bromide (Bromomethane)	20	200
Methyl isocyanate	0.15 (150 kilograms)	0.15 (150 kilograms)
Oxygen	200	2,000
Phosgene (Carbonyl chloride)	0.75 (750 kilograms)	0.75 (750 kilograms)
Propylene oxide	5	50
Sodium chlorate	25	250
Sulphur dioxide	25	250
Sulphur trioxide	15	100
Tetraethyl lead or tetramethyl lead	5	50
Toluene di-isocyanate (TDI)	10	100

(a) This applies to ammonium nitrate and mixtures of ammonium nitrate where the nitrogen content derived from the ammonium nitrate is ›28% by weight and to aqueous solutions of ammonium nitrate where the concentration of ammonium nitrate is ›90% by weight.

(b) This applies to straight ammonium nitrate fertilisers which comply with Council Directive 80/876/EEC 'on the approximation of laws of the Member States relating to straight ammonium nitrate fertilisers of high nitrogen content' and to compound fertilisers where the nitrogen content derived from the ammonium nitrate is ›28% by weight (a compound fertiliser contains ammonium nitrate together with phosphate and/or potash).

[*(Amendment) Regulations 1990 (SI 1990 No 2325), 3 Sch*].

the following duties apply under the regulations.

Duties of manufacturers

Demonstrate safe operation

8.7   Manufacturers in control of major accident potential (MAP) industrial activities must:

(*a*)   identify major accident hazards; and

(*b*)   take steps to:

(i)   prevent major accident hazards and limit their consequences to persons and the environment;

(ii)   provide those working on site with information, training and equipment, and, if necessary, produce documentation of this.

[*Reg 4(2)*].

Notify major accidents

8.8   If a major accident occurs on site, a manufacturer must notify the HSE of the accident; the latter must then obtain from the manufacturer the following:

(a)   information relating to: (i) the circumstances of the accident, (ii) dangerous substances involved, (iii) data available for assessing the effects of the accident on man/environment, (iv) emergency measures taken;

(b)   action considered necessary to:

   (i)   alleviate medium or long-term effects of accident; and

   (ii)   prevent its recurrence.

[Reg 5(1)].

A Major Hazards Co-ordinating Unit has been set up within the HSE to develop a policy on the control of all installations presenting large-scale hazards to public safety and to co-ordinate the work of other government departments.

Prepare and update reports

8.9   In the case of industrial activities involving a quantity of the following substances equal to or more than the quantity specified in column 2 of Table 7 below reports must be prepared and updated (see 8.11 below for the information to be contained in the report).

Table 7

Reportable substances

The quantities set out below relate to each installation or group of installations belonging to the same manufacturer where the distance between the installations is not sufficient to avoid, in foreseeable circumstances, any aggravation of major accident hazards. These quantities apply in any case to each group of installations belonging to the same manufacturer where the distance between the installations is less than 500 metres.

Substance (Column 1)	Quantity (for application of Regulations 7-12) (Column 2)	see Note* CAS Number (Column 3)	see Note* EEC Number (Column 4)
Group 1 — Toxic substances (quantity ≤ 1 tonne)			
Aldicarb	100 kilograms	116-06-3	006-017-00-X
4-Aminodiphenyl	1 kilogram	92-67-1	
Amiton	1 kilogram	78-53-5	
Anabasine	100 kilograms	494-52-0	
Arsenic pentoxide, Arsenic (V) acid and salts	500 kilograms		
Arsenic trioxide, Arsenious (III) acid and salts	100 kilograms		
Arsine (Arsenic hydride)	10 kilograms	7784-42-1	
Azinphos-ethyl	100 kilograms	2642-71-9	051-056-00-1
Azinphos-methyl	100 kilograms	86-50-0	015-039-00-9
Benzidine	1 kilogram	92-87-5	612-042-00-2
Benzidine salts	1 kilogram		
Beryllium (powders, compounds)	10 kilograms		
Bis(2-chloroethyl) sulphide	1 kilogram	505-60-2	
Bis(chloromethyl) ether	1 kilogram	542-88-1	603-046-00-5
Carbofuran	100 kilograms	1563-66-2	006-026-00-9
Carbophenothion	100 kilograms	786-19-6	015-044-00-6
Chlorfenvinphos	100 kilograms	470-90-6	015-071-00-3
4-(Chloroformyl) morpholine	1 kilogram	15159-40-7	
Chloromethyl methyl ether	1 kilogram	107-30-2	
Cobalt metal, oxides, carbonates, sulphides as powders	1 tonne		
Crimidine	100 kilograms	535-89-7	613-004-00-8
Cyanthoate	100 kilograms	3734-95-0	015-070-00-8
Cycloheximide	100 kilograms	66-81-9	
Demeton	100 kilograms	8065-48-3	
Dialifos	100 kilograms	10311-84-9	015-088-00-6

Substance (Column 1)	Quantity (Column 2)	CAS Number (Column 3)	EEC Number (Column 4)
OO-Diethyl *S*-ethylsul- phinylmethyl phosphoro- thioate	100 kilograms	2588-05-8	
OO-Diethyl *S*-ethylsul- phonylmethyl phosphoro- thioate	100 kilograms	2588-06-9	
OO-Diethyl *S*-ethylthio- methyl phosphorothioate	100 kilograms	2600-69-3	
OO-Diethyl *S*-isopropylthio- methyl phosphorodithioate	100 kilograms	78-52-4	
OO-Diethyl *S*-propylthio- methyl phosphorodithioate	100 kilograms	3309-68-0	
Dimefox	100 kilograms	115-26-4	015-061-00-9
Dimethylcarbamoyl chloride	1 kilogram	79-44-7	
Dimethylnitrosamine	1 kilogram	62-75-9	
Dimethyl phosphoramido- cyanidic acid	1 tonne	63917-41-9	
Diphacinone	100 kilograms	82-66-6	
Disulfoton	100 kilograms	298-04-4	015-060-00-3
EPN	100 kilograms	2104-64-5	015-036-00-2
Ethion	100 kilograms	563-12-2	015-047-00-2
Fensulfothion	100 kilograms	115-90-2	015-090-00-7
Fluenetil	100 kilograms	4301-50-2	607-078-00-0
Fluoroacetic acid	1 kilogram	144-49-0	607-081-00-7
Fluoroacetic acid, salts	1 kilogram		
Fluoroacetic acid, esters	1 kilogram		
Fluoroacetic acid, amides	1 kilogram		
4-Fluorobutyric acid	1 kilogram	462-23-7	
4-Fluorobutyric acid, salts	1 kilogram		
4-Fluorobutyric acid, esters	1 kilogram		
4-Fluorobutyric acid, amides	1 kilogram		
4-Fluorocrotonic acid	1 kilogram	37759-72-1	
4-Fluorocrotonic acid, salts	1 kilogram		
4-Fluorocrotonic acid, esters	1 kilogram		
4-Fluorocrotonic acid, amides	1 kilogram		
4-Fluoro-2-hydroxybutyric acid	1 kilogram		
4-Fluoro-2-hydroxybutyric acid, salts	1 kilogram		
4-Fluoro-2-hydroxybutyric acid, esters	1 kilogram		
4-Fluoro-2-hydroxybutyric acid, amides	1 kilogram		

Substance (*Column 1*)	Quantity (*Column 2*)	CAS Number (*Column 3*)	EEC Number (*Column 4*)
Glycolonitrile (Hydroxyacetonitrile)	100 kilograms	107-16-4	
1,2,3,7,8,9-Hexa-chlorodibenzo-*p*-dioxin	100 kilograms	19408-74-3	
Hexamethylphosphoramide	1 kilogram	680-31-9	
Hydrogen selenide	10 kilograms	7783-07-5	
Isobenzan	100 kilograms	297-78-9	602-053-00-0
Isodrin	100 kilograms	465-73-6	602-050-00-4
Juglone (5-Hydroxynaph-thalene-1,4-dione)	100 kilograms	481-39-0	
4,4'-Methylenebis (2-chloro-aniline)	10 kilograms	101-14-4	
Methyl isocyanate	150 kilograms	624-83-9	615-001-00-7
Mevinphos	100 kilograms	7786-34-7	015-020-00-5
2-Naphthylamine	1 kilogram	91-59-8	612-022-00-3
Nickel metal, oxides, carbonates, sulphides as powders	1 tonne		
Nickel tetracarbonyl	10 kilograms	13463-39-3	028-001-00-1
Oxydisulfoton	100 kilograms	2497-07-6	015-096-00-X
Oxygen difluoride	10 kilograms	7783-41-7	
Paraoxon (Diethyl 4-nitrophenyl phosphate)	100 kilograms	311-45-5	
Parathion	100 kilograms	56-38-2	015-034-00-1
Parathion-methyl	100 kilograms	298-00-0	015-035-00-7
Pentaborane	100 kilograms	19624-22-7	
Phorate	100 kilograms	298-02-2	015-033-00-6
Phosacetim	100 kilograms	4104-14-7	015-092-00-8
Phosgene (Carbonyl chloride)	750 kilograms	75-44-5	006-002-00-8
Phosphamidon	100 kilograms	13171-21-6	015-022-00-6
Phosphine (Hydrogen phos-phide)	100 kilograms	7803-51-2	
Promurit (1-(3,4-Dichloro-phenyl)-3-triazenethio-carboxamide)	100 kilograms	5836-73-7	
1,3-Propanesultone	1 kilogram	1120-71-4	
1-Propen-2-chloro-1,3-diol diacetate	10 kilograms	10118-72-6	
Pyrazoxon	100 kilograms	108-34-9	015-023-00-1
Selenium hexafluoride	10 kilograms	7783-79-1	
Sodium selenite	100 kilograms	10102-18-8	034-002-00-8
Stibine (Antimony hydride)	100 kilograms	7803-52-3	
Sulfotep	100 kilograms	3689-24-5	015-027-00-3

Substance (*Column 1*)	Quantity (*Column 2*)	CAS Number (*Column 3*)	EEC Number (*Column 4*)
Sulphur dichloride	1 tonne	10545-99-0	016-013-00-X
Tellurium hexafluoride	100 kilograms	7783-80-4	
TEPP	100 kilograms	107-49-3	015-025-00-2
2,3,7,8-Tetrachlorodibenzo-*p*-dioxin (TCDD)	1 kilogram	1746-01-6	
Tetramethylene-disulphotetramine	1 kilogram	80-12-6	
Thionazin	100 kilograms	297-97-2	
Tirpate (2,4-Dimethyl-1,3-dithiolane-2-carboxalde-hyde *O*-methyl-carbamoyloxime)	100 kilograms	26419-73-8	
Trichloromethanesulphenyl chloride	100 kilograms	594-42-3	
1-Tri(cyclohexyl)stannyl-1 *H*-1,2,4-triazole	100 kilograms	41083-11-8	
Triethylenemelamine	10 kilograms	51-18-3	
Warfarin	100 kilograms	81-81-2	607-056-00-0
Group 2 — Toxic substances (quantity > 1 tonne)			
Acetone cyanohydrin (2-Cyanopropan-2-ol)	200 tonnes	75-86-5	608-004-00-X
Acrolein (2-Propenal)	200 tonnes	107-02-8	605-008-00-3
Acrylonitrile	200 tonnes	107-13-1	608-003-00-4
Allyl alcohol (2-Propen-1-ol)	200 tonnes	107-18-6	603-015-00-6
Allylamine	200 tonnes	107-11-9	612-046-00-4
Ammonia	500 tonnes	7664-41-7	007-001-00-5
Bromine	500 tonnes	7726-95-6	035-001-00-5
Carbon disulphide	200 tonnes	75-15-0	006-033-00-3
Chlorine	25 tonnes	7782-50-5	017-001-00-7
Ethylene dibromide (1,2-Dibromoethane)	50 tonnes	106-93-4	602-010-00-6
Ethyleneimine	50 tonnes	151-56-4	613-001-00-1
Formaldehyde (concentration ≥ 90%)	50 tonnes	50-00-0	605-001-01-2
Hydrogen chloride (liquefied gas)	250 tonnes	7647-01-0	017-002-00-2
Hydrogen cyanide	20 tonnes	74-90-8	006-006-00-X
Hydrogen fluoride	50 tonnes	7664-39-3	009-002-00-6
Hydrogen sulphide	50 tonnes	7783-06-4	016-001-00-4
Methyl bromide (Bromomethane)	200 tonnes	74-83-9	602-002-00-3

Substance (*Column 1*)	Quantity (*Column 2*)	CAS Number (*Column 3*)	EEC Number (*Column 4*)
Nitrogen oxides	50 tonnes	11104-93-1	
Propyleneimine	50 tonnes	75-55-8	
Sulphur dioxide	250 tonnes	7446-09-5	016-011-00-9
Sulphur trioxide	75 tonnes	7446-11-9	
Tetraethyl lead	50 tonnes	78-00-2	
Tetramethyl lead	50 tonnes	75-74-1	
Group 3 — Highly reactive *substances*			
Acetylene (Ethyne)	50 tonnes	74-86-2	601-015-00-0
Ammonium nitrate[a]	2,500 tonnes		
Ammonium nitrate in the form of fertilisers[b]	5,000 tonnes	6484-52-2	
2,2-Bis(*tert*-butyl- peroxy)butane (concentra- tion ⩾ 70%)	50 tonnes	2167-23-9	
1,1-Bis(*tert*-butyl- peroxy)cyclohexane (concentration ⩾ 80%)	50 tonnes	3006-86-8	
tert-Butyl peroxyacetate (concentration ⩾ 70%)	50 tonnes	107-71-1	
tert-Butyl peroxyisobutyrate (concentration ⩾ 80%)	50 tonnes	109-13-7	
tert-Butyl peroxy isopropyl carbonate (concentration ⩾ 80%)	50 tonnes	2372-21-6	
tert-Butyl peroxymaleate (concentration ⩾ 80%)	50 tonnes	1931-62-0	
tert-Butyl peroxypivalate (concentration ⩾ 77%)	50 tonnes	927-07-1	
Dibenzyl peroxydicarbonate (concentration ⩾ 90%)	50 tonnes	2144-45-8	
Di-*sec*-butyl peroxydi- carbonate (concentration ⩾ 80%)	50 tonnes	19910-65-7	
Diethyl peroxydicarbonate (concentration ⩾ 30%)	50 tonnes	14666-78-5	
2,2-Dihydroperoxypropane (concentration ⩾ 30%)	50 tonnes	2614-76-8	
Di-isobutyryl peroxide (concentration ⩾ 50%)	50 tonnes	3437-84-1	
Di-*n*-propyl peroxydicarbon- ate (concentration ⩾ 80%)	50 tonnes	16066-38-9	

Substance (Column 1)	Quantity (Column 2)	CAS Number (Column 3)	EEC Number (Column 4)
Ethylene oxide	50 tonnes	75-21-8	603-023-00-X
Ethyl nitrate	50 tonnes	625-58-1	007-007-00-8
3,3,6,6,9,9-Hexamethyl-1,2,4,5-tetroxacyclononane (concentration ≥ 75%)	50 tonnes	22397-33-7	
Hydrogen	50 tonnes	1333-74-0	001-001-00-9
Liquid oxygen	2,000 tonnes	7782-44-7	008-001-00-8
Methyl ethyl ketone peroxide (concentration ≥ 60%)	50 tonnes	1338-23-4	
Methyl isobutyl ketone peroxide (concentration ≥ 60%)	50 tonnes	37206-20-5	
Peracetic acid (concentration ≥ 60%)	50 tonnes	79-21-0	607-094-00-8
Propylene oxide	50 tonnes	75-56-9	603-055-00-4
Sodium chlorate	250 tonnes	7775-09-9	017-005-00-9
Group 4 — Explosive substances			
Barium azide	50 tonnes	18810-58-7	
Bis(2,4,6-trinitrophenyl)-amine	50 tonnes	131-73-7	612-018-00-1
Chlorotrinitrobenzene	50 tonnes	28260-61-9	610-004-00-X
Cellulose nitrate (containing > 12.6% nitrogen)	100 tonnes	9004-70-0	603-037-00-6
Cyclotetramethylene-tetranitramine	50 tonnes	2691-41-0	
Cyclotrimethylene-trinitramine	50 tonnes	121-82-4	
Diazodinitrophenol	10 tonnes	7008-81-3	
Diethylene glycol dinitrate	10 tonnes	693-21-0	603-033-00-4
Dinitrophenol, salts	50 tonnes	609-017-00-3	
Ethylene glycol dinitrate	10 tonnes	628-96-6	603-032-00-9
1-Guanyl-4-nitrosamino-guanyl-tetrazene	10 tonnes	109-27-3	
2,2',4,4',6,6'-Hexanitro-stilbene	50 tonnes	20062-22-0	
Hydrazine nitrate	50 tonnes	13464-97-6	
Lead azide	50 tonnes	13424-46-9	082-003-00-7
Lead styphnate (Lead 2,4,6-trinitroresorcinoxide)	50 tonnes	15245-44-0	609-019-00-4
Mercury fulminate	10 tonnes	20820-45-5 628-86-4	080-005-00-2
N-Methyl-N,2,4,6-tetranitroaniline	50 tonnes	479-45-8	612-017-00-6

Substance (Column 1)	Quantity (Column 2)	CAS Number (Column 3)	EEC Number (Column 4)
Nitroglycerine	10 tonnes	55-63-0	603-034-00-X
Pentaerythritol tetranitrate	50 tonnes	78-11-5	603-035-00-5
Picric acid (2,4,6-Trinitro-phenol)	50 tonnes	88-89-1	609-009-00-X
Sodium picramate	50 tonnes	831-52-7	
Styphnic acid (2,4,6-Trinitroresorcinol)	50 tonnes	82-71-3	609-018-00-9
1,3,5-Triamino-2,4,6-trinitrobenzene	50 tonnes	3058-38-6	
Trinitroaniline	50 tonnes	26952-42-1	
2,4,6-Trinitroanisole	50 tonnes	606-35-9	609-011-00-0
Trinitrobenzene	50 tonnes	25377-32-6	609-005-00-8
Trinitrobenzoic acid	50 tonnes	$\left\{\begin{array}{l} 35860\text{-}50\text{-}5 \\ 129\text{-}66\text{-}8 \end{array}\right.$	
Trinitrocresol	50 tonnes	28905-71-7	609-012-00-6
2,5,6-Trinitrophenetole	50 tonnes	4732-14-3	
2,4,6-Trinitrotoluene	50 tonnes	118-96-7	609-008-00-4
Group 5 — Flammable substances			
Flammable substances as defined in Schedule 1, paragraph (c)(i)	200 tonnes		
Flammable substances as defined in Schedule 1, paragraph (c)(ii)	50,000 tonnes		
Flammable substances as defined in Schedule 1, paragraph (c)(iii)	200 tonnes		

* CAS Number (Chemical Abstracts Service Number) means the number assigned to the substance by the Chemical Abstracts Service, details of which may be obtained from the Service itself at PO Box 3012, Columbus, Ohio, USA 43210/0012, or by telephoning, at the first instance, the Royal Society of Chemistry, The Science Block, Milton Road, Cambridge CB4 4WF, Tel: 0223 4200 66.

EEC Number means the number assigned to the substance by the Commission of the European Communities, details of which can be obtained from its office at 20 Kensington Palace Gardens, London W8 4QQ.

(a) This applies to ammonium nitrate and mixtures of ammonium nitrate where the nitrogen content derived from the ammonium nitrate is › 28% by weight and to aqueous solutions of ammonium nitrate where the concentration of ammonium nitrate is › 90% by weight.

> (b) This applies to straight ammonium nitrate fertilisers which comply with Council Directive 80/876/EEC 'on the approximation of laws of the Member States relating to straight ammonium nitrate fertilisers of high nitrogen content' and to compound fertilisers where the nitrogen content derived from the ammonium nitrate is › 28% by weight (a compound fertiliser contains ammonium nitrate together with phosphate and/or potash).
>
> [*3 Sch; (Amendment) Regulations 1990 (SI 1990 No 2325), 1 Sch, Pt II*].

or

8.10   where quantities of dangerous substances mentioned in 8.5 above, manufacturers must, before undertaking the activity, prepare a written report containing the following information and send a copy to the HSE at least three months before commencing that activity or before such shorter time as the Executive may agree in writing. [*Reg 7(1), 3 Sch*].

The HSE can require a manufacturer to supply additional information to this, if necessary. [*Reg 9(1)*].

Information to be submitted in the report

8.11   Information relating to every dangerous substance involved in the activity in a relevant quantity as listed in 8.6, 8.9 above, namely:

(*a*)   the name of the dangerous substance or, for a dangerous substance a general designation, the name corresponding to the chemical formula of the dangerous substance;

(*b*)   a general description of the analytical methods available to the manufacturer for determining the presence of the dangerous substance, or references to such methods in the scientific literature;

(*c*)   a brief description of the hazards which may be created by the dangerous substance;

(*d*)   the degree of purity of the dangerous substance, and the names of the main impurities and their percentages.

Information relating to the installation, namely:

(*a*)   a map of the site and its surrounding area to a scale large enough to show any features that may be significant in the assessment of the hazard or risk associated with the site;

(*b*)   a scale plan of the site showing the locations and quantities of all significant inventories of the dangerous substance;

(*c*)   a description of the processes or storage involving the dangerous substance and an indication of the conditions under which it is normally held;

(*d*)   the maximum number of persons likely to be present on site;

(*e*)   information about the nature of the land use and the size and distribution of the population in the vicinity of the industrial activity to which the report relates.

Information relating to the management system for controlling the industrial activity, namely:

(*a*)   the staffing arrangements for controlling the industrial activity with the name of the person responsible for safety on the site and the names of those who are authorised to set emergency procedures in motion and to inform outside authorities;

(*b*)   the arrangements made to ensure that the means provided for the safe operation of the industrial activity are properly designed, constructed, tested, operated, inspected and maintained;

(*c*)   the arrangements for training of persons working on the site.

Information relating to the potential major accidents, namely:

(*a*)   a description of the potential sources of a major accident and the conditions or events which could be significant in bringing one about;

(*b*)   a diagram of any plant in which the industrial activity is carried on, sufficient to show the features which are significant as regards the potential for a major accident or its prevention or control;

(*c*)   a description of the measures taken to prevent, control or minimise the consequences of any major accident;

(*d*)   information about the emergency procedures laid down for dealing with a major accident occurring at the site;

(*e*)   information about prevailing meteorological conditions in the vicinity of the site;

(*f*)   an estimate of the number of people on site who may be exposed to the hazards considered in the report.

[*6 Sch*].

Moreover, manufacturers must not carry out any modifications to the industrial activity unless a further report is made, detailing those changes, and sent to the HSE at least three months before making the modifications. [*Reg 8(1)*].

Prepare an emergency plan

8.12   Manufacturers on such sites must prepare and update an adequate on-site emergency plan, detailing how major accidents will be dealt with on site and the person responsible for safety and the names of those authorised to take action. [*Reg 10(1)*]. The local authority must prepare an off-site emergency plan. [*Regs 11(1), 15(1)*].

The manufacturer must assist the local authority with the information the authority reasonably requires. The local authority may charge a fee for the preparation and keeping up to date of this emergency plan. [*Regs 11(1), 15(1)*].

Information to be communicated to the public

8.13   A manufacturer occupying a site which may cause a major accident hazard must make this information available to the public in the area which is likely to be affected by such an accident. He must consult the local authority for the area about making this information available but the manufacturer is responsible for the accuracy, completeness and form of the information. The information to be supplied appears below. [*Reg 12, as substituted by (Amendment) Regulations 1990, Reg 4*].

(*a*)   Name of manufacturer and address of site.

(*b*)   Identification, by position held, of person giving the information.

(c)   Confirmation that the site is subject to these regulations and that the report referred to in *Regulation 7(1)* or at least the information required by *Regulation 7(3)* has been submitted to the Executive.

(d)   An explanation in simple terms of the activity undertaken on the site.

(e)   The common names, or in the case of storage covered by *Part II* of *Schedule 2* the generic names or the general danger classification, of the substances and preparations involved on site which could give rise to a major accident, with an indication of their principal dangerous characteristics.

(f)   General information relating to the nature of the major accident hazards, including their potential effects on the population and the environment.

(g)   Adequate information on how the population concerned will be warned and kept informed in the event of an accident.

(h)   Adequate information on the actions the population should take and on the behaviour they should adopt in the event of an accident.

(j)   Confirmation that the manufacturer is required to make adequate arrangements on site, including liaison with the emergency services, to deal with accidents and to minimise their effects.

(k)   A reference to the off-site emergency plan drawn up to cope with any off-site effects from an accident. This should include advice to co-operate with any instructions or requests from the emergency services at the time of an accident.

(l)   Details of where further relevant information can be obtained, subject to the requirements of confidentiality laid down in national legislation.

[*8 Sch as amended by (Amendment) Regulations 1990, 4 Sch*].

Penalties

8.14   The penalties for breach are the same as in the *Health and Safety at Work etc. Act 1974*.

Major hazard analysis

8.15   The potential for major hazard situations arising must be considered by manufacturing management. Management should be asking itself the following questions:

(a)   'What is the worst possible event or situation that could arise in this location?'

For instance, a major rapidly escalating fire,

a sudden release of large quantities of toxic gases,

a pressure vessel explosion,

collapse of a major structure, or

a nuclear radiation incident.

(b)   'What procedures have been established to prevent such an incident?'

(c)   'What procedures have been established in the event of such an incident taking place?'

The events of Flixborough and Bhopal have focused people's minds on this potential for major hazards, particularly in the chemical industry where many manufacturing installations are located close to centres of population. There is a need, therefore, for occupiers of such installations to undertake a form of major hazard analysis for both existing installations and at the project design stage of new installations.

The major hazards audit shown in 8.16–8.25 below should assist management and safety specialists in the assessment necessary, taking into account, of course, the information requirements outlined in *CIMAH Regulations, 6 Sch* (see 8.11 above).

Major hazard audit

Dangerous substances

8.16   (*a*)   List all substances which are:

      (i)   flammable;

      (ii)   explosive;

      (iii)   corrosive;

      (iv)   toxic (state their effects); and

      (v)   otherwise harmful (state specific hazards).

(*b*)   State whether these substances are:

      (i)   raw materials;

      (ii)   intermediate products;

      (iii)   final products;

      (iv)   by-products; or

      (v)   waste products.

(*c*)   List the points where identified dangerous substances are encountered in the process by reference to:

      (i)   specific part of the process; and

      (ii)   specific plant and equipment.

Indicate these points by cross-reference to the process operating manual.

(*d*)   List the significant physical properties of identified dangerous substances, including:

      (i)   incompatibility with other chemical substances;

      (ii)   chemical reaction rates;

      (iii)   conditions of instability; and

      (iv)   other significant properties.

(*e*)   Show data sources and list available information sources on critical points raised.

(See also Chapters 9 and 10 'Dangerous Substances I and II'.)

Potential process hazards

(*a*)   List maximum operating pressures of all pressure vessels and systems under both normal and abnormal operating conditions.

(*b*)   State (i) the form, (ii) the location, (iii) the condition, and (iv) the date of testing of each pressure relief device.

(*c*)   State whether operators are exposed to risk of injury by the discharge of pressure relief devices.

(*d*)   List the maximum permissible operating temperatures and sources of heat. Identify the over-temperature controls that are provided in the event of abnormal operating conditions. State the form of protection provided to hot surfaces to protect operators from burns.

(*e*)   State the dangers that may arise if process reaction conditions are deviated from in the manner below, and the necessary protection procedures:

    (i)   abnormal temperatures;

    (ii)   abnormal reaction times;

    (iii)   instrument failure;

    (iv)   addition of materials at the wrong stage;

    (v)   addition of the wrong materials;

    (vi)   materials flow stoppage;

    (vii)   equipment leaks, both out of the process and into the process;

    (viii)   agitation failure;

    (ix)   loss of inert gas blanket;

    (x)   errors in valve or switch operation;

    (xi)   clubbed relief line;

    (xii)   failure of relief device;

    (xiii)   material spillage on floor or dispersal to air.

(See also Chapter 37 'Pressure Systems and Transportable Gas Containers' for detailed requirements.)

Waste disposal

8.17   (*a*)   List gaseous stack effluents/discharges and concentrations together with smoke characteristics.

(*b*)   State the approved height of stacks.

(*c*)   State whether scrubbers, electrostatic or centrifugal removal of stack effluents are needed.

(*d*)   State the direction of prevailing winds as they relate to exposed areas and residential areas.

(*e*)   State the effluents which are run through the waste disposal system, from each point in the process, and the method of transfer.

State their:

    (i)   pH value;

    (ii)   relative toxicity;

    (iii)   flammability; and

    (iv)   miscibility with water.

(f)   State the procedure for preventing flammable liquids from reaching sewers.

(g)   List any specific hazardous solid waste products and the procedure for handling, removal and disposal of them.

(See also Chapter 24 'Highly Flammable Liquids'.)

Piping systems

8.18   (a)   Confirm that piping systems are adequately supported with permanent hangers.

(b)   Confirm that pipework is of correct material and scheduled thickness for service.

(c)   Confirm that pressure tests for critical services and processes are scheduled on a regular basis.

(d)   Confirm that safe access is provided to all valves.

Electrical equipment

8.19   (a)   Confirm that all hazardous locations are classified.

(b)   Confirm that location of all electrical equipment is classified, including:

    (i)   lighting;

    (ii)   wiring and switches;

    (iii)   motors;

    (iv)   instrumentation;

    (v)   intercoms, telephones, clocks, etc.

(c)   Confirm all grounding meets the required standard.

(d)   Identify the persons responsible for monitoring the equipment and frequency of monitoring.

(See also Chapter 11 'Electricity'.)

Fire protection

8.20   (a)   Confirm all fire exit doors are checked on a regular basis.

(b)   Confirm exposed steel supporting major items of equipment are fireproofed.

(c)   Confirm whether automatic or manually-operated sprinkler system is installed.

(d)   Confirm whether any special fire extinguishing equipment is installed/provided.

(e)   State the number, type and location of all fire appliances and the system for ensuring regular servicing of such appliances.

(f)   Identify the location of fire hydrants and hose reel appliances.

(g)   Identify the location of fire alarm points and building evacuation alarms.

(h)   State the system for storage of flammable substances and whether flammable liquids are handled in the open.

(*j*)   Specify the amount of flammable liquids stored, their specific locations and precautions for such storage, both internally and externally.

(*k*)   State current procedure for fire drills.

(See also Chapter 19 'Fire and Fire Precautions'.)

Ventilation

8.21   (*a*)   State the frequency of air changes required at particular operating areas.

(*b*)   State the frequency of checking of ventilation system and responsibility for it.

(*c*)   State whether specific exhaust ventilation is required for a certain process or processes. List the flow rates to be achieved and the responsibility for checking.

(*d*)   State the degree of risk of ventilation intakes recirculating contaminated air.

(See also Chapter 43 'Ventilation'.)

Structural safety

8.22   (*a*)   Confirm safety rails with toe-boards are provided on all working platforms over 1 m high and on all occupied enclosed parts of the roof space.

(*b*)   Confirm all parts of the buildings are readily accessible.

(*c*)   Confirm all staircases and landings are fitted with handrails, and are adequately lit.

(*d*)   Confirm all fixed vertical ladders are fitted with backrings at 1 m intervals, with safe access to elevated landings.

(See also Chapter 18 'Factories and Workplaces'.)

Personnel, equipment and facilities

8.23   (*a*)   Specify the type and form of protective overclothing provided.

(*b*)   Confirm that safety boots/shoes are provided.

(*c*)   Confirm that gloves/gauntlets are provided for certain tasks.

(*d*)   Confirm that the appropriate type of eye protection is provided for certain tasks.

(*e*)   Confirm that safety helmets/bump caps are provided for all operators.

(*f*)   Confirm that respirator stations are adequately identified and maintained.

(*g*)   State the frequency of overall changing, particularly where there is heavy soiling.

(*h*)   Confirm that a rest room is provided.

(See also Chapter 36 'Personal Protective Equipment'.)

Machinery and plant

8.24   (*a*)   Confirm that all machinery and plant is adequately guarded or fitted with the appropriate safety devices in accordance with BS 5304: 1988.

(*b*)　Confirm that all machinery and plant is examined on a regular basis to ensure compliance with BS 5304: 1988.

(See also Chapter 28 'Machinery Safety'.)

Training

8.25　(*a*)　Confirm that operating manuals have been produced and provided.

(*b*)　Confirm that general and specific training needs of all grades of staff have been identified, with specific reference to safe systems of work, individual responsibilities, the use of personal protective equipment and scheduled high risk operations/activities.

(*c*)　Confirm there is a training programme, qualified trainers to implement the programme and that all staff are adequately trained.

(*d*)　Confirm all new operators receive health and safety induction training within 14 days of commencing work.

(*e*)　Confirm that the effectiveness of training activities is monitored.

(*f*)　Confirm that occupational health and first-aid practices are adequately covered in training.

(*g*)　Confirm that safety rules and procedures, e.g. permit to work systems, have been established, publicised and are enforced.

(See also Chapter 1 'Introduction' and Chapter 15 'Employers' Duties'.)

Chapter 9

Dangerous Substances I – at the Workplace

Background and classification

9.1 Originally many dangerous substances used at the workplace were attended with tragic and often fatal consequences. Occupational diseases like hatter's shakes, potter's rot and grinder's lung were not untypical, not to mention the acutely depressant and sometimes suicidal effect of inhaling quantities of carbon disulphide fumes used in the manufacture of rainwear. Over the last hundred years the number of dangerous substances used at the workplace has multiplied enormously (e.g. fibreglass, cement, compressed and flammable gases, epoxy and polyester resins etc.) as well as the concomitant variety of processes, machinery and gadgetry generating dusts, fumes, gases and vapours. In tandem with technological development came a series of *ad hoc* regulations aimed at controlling the effects of dangerous substances in particular industries. For instance, lead (see 9.40 below) was targeted by a raft of regulations traceable back to the turn of the century; similarly silica in regulations relating to potteries as well as the *Grinding of Metals (Miscellaneous Industries) Regulations 1925*. As a new danger manifested itself, so combative measures appeared in its wake. This was the pattern effectively for the last 75 years. Following inception of the *Health and Safety at Work etc. Act 1974*, however, earlier legislation and regulations were replaced by regulations containing codes of practice (see 1.28 and 1.31 INTRODUCTION), requiring employers to *assess* the health risks to employees and implement health-oriented and risk-preventive strategies – a classic example being the *Control of Substances Hazardous to Health Regulations 1988* (*COSHH*) (see 9.20 below). In this way, employers can match controls to the perceived dangers rather than have to abide by statutory requirements which might well be too rigid.

The great majority of dangerous substances used in industry/commerce as well as in research establishments, are chemical compounds, though there are several naturally occurring substances, such as asbestos (see Chapter 4), heavy metals, silica dust and mineral oils. In addition, workers may be exposed to hazards from biological agents (see 9.31 below), such as micro-organisms and cell cultures as well as respiratory sensitisers (see 9.39 below).

To date, regulations applicable to dangerous substances are:

(1)   *Notification of New Substances Regulations 1982* (see 9.2);

(2)   *Notification of Installations Handling Hazardous Substances Regulations 1982* (see 9.3);

(3)   *Chemicals (Hazard Information and Packaging) Regulations 1993* (see 9.8);

(4)   *Control of Substances Hazardous to Health Regulations 1988 (as amended)* (see 9.20);

(5)   *Notification of Cooling Towers and Evaporative Condensers Regulations 1992* (see 9.27);

(6)   *Control of Lead Regulations 1980* (see 9.40);

(7)   *Ionising Radiations Regulations 1985* (see 9.44) and the *Ionising Radiations (Outside Workers) Regulations 1993* (see 9.50);

(8)   *Dangerous Pathogens Regulations 1981* (see 9.59);

(9)   *Control of Explosives Regulations 1991* (see 9.64);

(10)   *Road Traffic (Carriage of Dangerous Substances in Road Tankers and Tank Containers) Regulations 1992* (see Chapter 10 'Dangerous Substances II');

(11)   *Road Traffic (Carriage of Dangerous Substances in Packages etc.) Regulations 1992* (see Chapter 10 'Dangerous Substances II');

(12)   *Control of Asbestos at Work Regulations 1987* (see Chapter 4 'Asbestos');

(13)   *Highly Flammable Liquids and Liquefied Petroleum Gases Regulations 1972* (see Chapter 24).

Exposure to a whole range of dangerous substances at work can lead to the onset of identifiable diseases and adverse health effects, including some diseases which are prescribed and for which disablement benefit is payable (see 31.42 OCCUPATIONAL HEALTH). However, legionnaire's disease is neither notifiable (except in Scotland) nor is it prescribed, though it is serious enough to have resulted in fatalities and comes within the ambit of the Biological Agents Directive (see 9.31). More particularly, this chapter examines:

(1)   notification of new substances (9.2);

(2)   notification of sites handling hazardous substances (9.3);

(3)   marking of hazardous sites (9.4);

(4)   classification, packaging and labelling of dangerous substances (9.8 and Appendix C);

(5)   control of substances hazardous to health (including carcinogens) (9.19, 9.36);

(6)   controls over lead (9.40);

(7)   controls over dangerous pathogens (9.59);

(8)   proposed controls over biological agents (9.31);

(9)   proposed controls over respiratory sensitisers (9.39);

(10)   controls over radioactive substances (9.42);

(11)   controls over explosives (9.60).

Notification of dangerous chemicals – draft Notification of New Substances Regulations 1993

New and existing substances

9.2   The European Inventory of Existing Commercial Chemical Substances (EINECS) lists all 100,000 substances marketed for commercial purposes between 1 January 1971 and 18 September 1981 – that is, existing substances. These 'existing substances' are controlled by the *EC Existing Substances Regulations 1993*. By contrast, a new substance is one *not* listed in EINECS and to date these are controlled by the *Notification of New Substances Regulations 1982 (SI 1982 No 1496)*. These regulations, which apply only to a limited number of specialist importers and chemical manufacturers, are to be replaced by the *Notification of New Substances Regulations 1993* which adopt directive 92/69/EEC as the test method for such substances.

Scope of New Substances Regulations 1993

The regulations will not be applicable to certain pesticides (which are subject to a similar rigorous notification procedure under other legislation) and substances used in research and development or circulated only in small quantities. The draft *Notification of New Substances Regulations*, which should appear in November 1993, aim to protect persons and the environment from the possible adverse effects of new substances. More particularly,

(*a*)   the 'competent authority' to be notified of the existence of new substances is both HSE and the Department of the Environment (DoE);

(*b*)   the competent authority will have to carry out an independent risk assessment for newly notified substances in order to determine how best to manage them;

(*c*)   suppliers/manufacturers will have to share data where more than one intends to notify;

(*d*)   the new regulations will extend to offshore operations;

(*e*)   HSE/DoE will be able to charge for notification/assessment work;

(*f*)   time scales for placing substances on the market are to be:

    (i)   after 60 days – full notification substances (i.e. 1 tonne or more per year),

    (ii)   after 30 days – reduced notification substances (i.e. less than 1 tonne per year).

Notification of sites handling hazardous substances – Notification of Installations Handling Hazardous Substances Regulations 1982 (SI 1982 No 1357)

9.3   Activities involving a notifiable quantity (or more) of a dangerous substance (hereafter referred to as 'hazardous substance') must not be carried on at any site or in (most) pipe-lines, unless the HSE has been notified in writing at least three months before such activity commences, or within such shorter time as the HSE specifies, of the following matters:

(*a*)   *In the case of sites:*

    (i)   the name and address of the person making the notification;

    (ii)   the address of the site where the notifiable activity will take place;

    (iii)   the area of the site in question;

    (iv)   the date when it is anticipated that the notifiable activity will commence, or, if already commenced, a statement to that effect;

    (v)   a general description of the activities carried on or intended to be carried on;

    (vi)   the name and address of the planning authority;

(vii)   the name and maximum quantity of each hazardous substance liable to be on site.

[*Notification of Installations Handling Hazardous Substances Regulations, 2 Sch Pt I*].

(*b*)   *In the case of pipe-lines:*

(i)   the name and address of the person making the notification;

(ii)   the address of the place from which the pipe-line activity is controlled and the addresses of the places where the pipe-line starts and finishes and a map showing the pipe-line route;

(iii) the date when it is anticipated that the notifiable activity will commence, or, if already commenced, a statement to that effect;

(iv)   the name and address of the planning authority;

(v)   the total length of the pipe-line, its diameter and normal operating pressure, coupled with the name and maximum quantity of each hazardous substance liable to be in the pipe-line.

[*2 Sch Pt II, Reg 3(1)*].

Regulation 3(1) applies in the case of hazardous substances:

(i)   within 500 metres of the site of a pipe-line and connected to it;

(ii)   any other site controlled by the same person within 500 metres of the site; and

(iii) in any vehicle, vessel, aircraft or hovercraft under the control of the same person, used for storage purposes at the site, or within 500 metres of it, but *not* if used for transporting hazardous substances (for regulations and requirements relating to transportation of hazardous substances, see Chapter 10 'Dangerous Substances II').

Activities involving the following quantities of hazardous substances on sites or in pipelines must be notified to the HSE:

Table 8

Notifiable quantities of named hazardous substances in relation to sites

1 Substance	2 Notifiable quantity tonnes
Liquefied petroleum gas, such as commercial propane and commercial butane, and any mixture thereof held at a pressure greater than 1.4 bar absolute	25
Liquefied petroleum gas, such as commercial propane and commercial butane, and any mixture thereof held under refrigeration at a pressure of 1.4 bar absolute or less	50
Phosgene	2
Chlorine	10
Hydrogen fluoride	10
Sulphur trioxide	15
Acrylonitrile	20
Hydrogen cyanide	20
Carbon disulphide	20
Sulphur dioxide	20
Bromine	40
Ammonia (anhydrous or as solution containing more than 50% by weight of ammonia)	100
Hydrogen	2
Ethylene oxide	5
Propylene oxide	5
tert-Butyl peroxyacetate	5
tert-Butyl peroxyisobutyrate	5
tert-Butyl peroxymaleate	5
tert-Butyl peroxy isopropyl carbonate	5
Dibenzyl peroxydicarbonate	5
2,2-Bis(*tert*-butylperoxy)butane	5
1,1-Bis(*tert*-butylperoxy)cyclohexane	5
Di-sec-butyl peroxydicarbonate	5
2,2-Dihydroperoxypropane	5
Di-*n*-propyl peroxydicarbonate	5
Methyl ethyl ketone peroxide	5
Sodium chlorate	25

Some cellulose nitrate	50
Some ammonium nitrate	500
Aqueous solutions containing more than 90 parts by weight of ammonium nitrate per 100 parts by weight of solution	500
Liquid oxygen	500

[*1 Sch Pt I*].

Table 9

Classes of substances not specifically named in Part I above

1 Class of Substance	2 Notifiable quantity tonnes	
1. Gas or any mixture of gases which is flammable in air and is held in the installation as a gas.	15	
2. A substance or any mixture of substances which is flammable in air and is normally held in the installation above its boiling-point (measured at 1 bar absolute) as a liquid or as a mixture of liquid and gas at a pressure of more than 1.4 bar absolute.	25	being the total quantity of substances above the boiling points whether held singly or in mixtures.
3. A liquefied gas or any mixture of liquefied gases, which is flammable in air, has a boiling point of less than 0°C (measured at 1 bar absolute) and is normally held in the installation under refrigeration or cooling at a pressure of 1.4 bar absolute or less.	50	being the total quantity of substances having boiling points below 0°C whether held singly or in mixtures.
4. A liquid or any mixture of liquids not included in items 1 to 3 above, which have a flash point of less than 21°C.	10,000	

[*1 Sch Pt II*].

Marking of sites by signs – Dangerous Substances (Notification and Marking of Sites) Regulations 1990 (SI 1990 No 304)

9.4   Where there is a total quantity of 25 tonnes (or more) of dangerous substances present on site as defined now by *Schedule 3* of the *CHIP Regulations 1993* (see 9.8 below) [*CHIP Regulations 1993, Reg 21(11)*], the *Dangerous Substances (Notification and Marking of Sites) Regulations 1990 (SI 1990 No 304)* require the *notification* and *marking* of such sites with appropriate safety signs. These regulations require that those in control of sites ensure that there are not more than 25 tonnes of 'dangerous substances' on site, unless there has first been notification to (*a*)   the local fire authority, and

(*b*)   HSE,

of

   (i)   name and address of person notifying;

  (ii)   full postal address of site;

 (iii)   general description of nature of business;

 (iv)   list of classifications of dangerous substances;

  (v)   date when it is anticipated that total quantity of 25 tonnes (or more) of dangerous substances will be present.

[*Reg 4, 2 Sch*].

A further notification is required when there is a cessation or reduction of dangerous substances already notified or if there is a change in the list of any classifications of dangerous substances. [*Reg 4*].

The following substances are excluded from these requirements:

(*a*)   radioactive substances (see 9.42 below);

(*b*)   Class I explosives (see 9.60 below);

(*c*)   substances in aerosol dispensers;

(*d*)   substances buried/deposited in the ground as waste.

[*2 Sch*].

Signs are to be kept clean and free from obstruction so far as reasonably practicable. [*Reg 7*].

Exceptions to duty to notify

9.5   The following sites have their own notification procedure, namely,

   (i)   sites notifiable to HSE, in accordance with the *Notification of Installations Handling Hazardous Substances Regulations 1982* (see 9.3 above);

  (ii)   sites controlled by *Reg 7* of the *Control of Industrial Major Accident Hazards Regulations 1984* (see 8.10 CONTROL OF INDUSTRIAL MAJOR ACCIDENT HAZARDS);

 (iii)   sites controlled by the *Petroleum Spirit (Consolidation) Act 1928*;

 (iv)   sites controlled by *Reg 27* of the *Dangerous Substances in Harbour Areas Regulations 1987*;

  (v)   sites for which there exists a disposal licence under *Sec 5* of the *Control of Pollution Act 1974*; and

 (vi)   nuclear sites.

Marking requirements

9.6   Where there are 25 tonnes (or more) of dangerous substances present on site, safety signs to BS 5378: 1980/1982 must be displayed, as specified in *Schedule 3*, so as to give adequate warning to firemen before entering a site in an emergency. Moreover, safety signs are required to be displayed at such locations on site as an inspector may direct, carrying the appropriate hazard warning symbol and text, e.g.

skull and crossed bones – Toxic. In the case of substances with mixed classifications, the sign must carry the exclamation mark symbol (!) plus the words 'Dangerous Substance'. [*Reg 5*]. (These requirements are not applicable to petrol filling stations.)

Table 10

Classifications and Hazard Warnings – Site markings (as per Marking of Sites Regulations 1990)

1 *Classification*	2 *Hazard warning symbol and text*
Non-flammable compressed gas	 COMPRESSED GAS
Toxic gas	 TOXIC GAS

1 *Classification*	2 *Hazard warning symbol and text*
Flammable gas	FLAMMABLE GAS
Flammable liquid	FLAMMABLE LIQUID
Flammable solid	FLAMMABLE SOLID

1 *Classification*	2 *Hazard warning symbol and text*
Spontaneously combustible substance	SPONTANEOUSLY COMBUSTIBLE
Substance which in contact with water emits flammable gas	DANGEROUS WHEN WET
Oxidizing substance	OXIDIZING AGENT

1 *Classification*	2 *Hazard warning symbol and text*
Organic peroxide	 ORGANIC PEROXIDE
Toxic substance	 TOXIC
Corrosive substance	 CORROSIVE

1 *Classification*	2 *Hazard warning symbol and text*
Harmful substance Other dangerous substance Mixed hazards	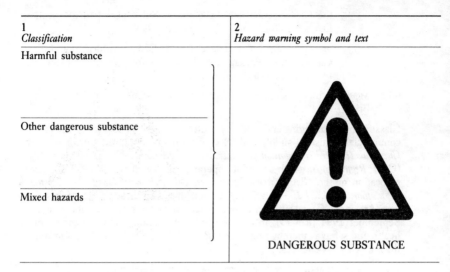 DANGEROUS SUBSTANCE

[*3 Sch*].

Enforcement and penalties

9.7   (*a*)   Enforcement of notification requirements is by HSE;

       (*b*)   enforcement of marking requirements is by the fire authority, except as follows:

           (i)   cessation of presence of dangerous substances on site,

           (ii)   reduction of quantity of dangerous substances below 25 tonnes, and

           (iii)   change in list of classifications notified

       when notification must be to (*a*) HSE and (*b*) fire authority.

[*Reg 8, 2 Sch Part II*].

Penalties for breach are as in the case of a breach of *HSWA* (see further Chapter 17 'Enforcement').

Classification, packaging and labelling of dangerous substances – the Chemicals (Hazard Information and Packaging) Regulations 1993 (SI 1993 No 1746) (CHIP)

Definitions

9.8   (*a*)   *Substance* – chemical elements and their compounds in the natural state or obtained by production process, including additives and impurities but generally not solvents. [*Reg 2(1)*].

       (*b*)   *Preparation* – mixtures or solutions of two or more substances. [*Reg 2(1)*].

       (*c*)   *Dangerous substances* – are those

           (i)   on the Approved Supply List (ASL) – 'Information Approved for the Classification and Labelling of Substances and Preparations Dangerous for Supply' (16 February 1993);

(ii)   on the Approved Carriage List (ACL) – 'Information for the Classification, Packaging and Labelling of Substances Dangerous for Carriage' (16 February 1993).

(*d*)   *Supplier* – includes importers of dangerous substances established in Great Britain.

Classification, packaging and labelling controls over substances dangerous for (*a*) commercial/industrial supply and (*b*) conveyance by road, are contained in the *Chemicals (Hazard Information and Packaging) Regulations 1993 (SI 1993 No 1746)* (*CHIP Regulations*), which came into operation on 1 September 1993, by way of revocation of the *Classification, Packaging and Labelling of Dangerous Substances Regulations 1984 (SI 1984 No 1244)*. Compliance with these revoked regulations (see Appendix C) is sufficient compliance with the new regulations until 1 September 1994 [*Reg 19*]; in addition, HSE can grant exemption, if no-one's health and safety is thereby prejudiced [*Reg 17*]. The *CHIP Regulations* introduce the following key changes:

(i)   preparation of safety data sheets in addition to labelling;

(ii)   new classifications of dangerous substances, i.e. carcinogenic, mutagenic, teratogenic (as per EC 92/69/EEC, which will be the basis of the forthcoming approved code of practice on *CHIP Regulations*);

(iii)   suppliers will be expected to know of the classification of a substance; not to do so is to risk committing an offence.

(A) Substances/preparations dangerous for supply – classification requirements

9.9   A supplier must not supply a substance/preparation dangerous for supply, unless

(*a*)   it has first been duly classified (see 9.8 above),

(*b*)   a record is kept of such classification for, at least, three years, and

(*c*)   if necessary, such record is made available, on request, to the enforcing authorities (see 9.17 below).

[*Regs 5(1), 15 and 1 Sch*] – substances; [*Regs 5(5), 15 and 4 Sch*] – preparations.

Provision of safety data sheets

9.10   Suppliers of dangerous substances/preparations must provide recipients with dated safety data sheets, updated as and when necessary, containing the following information:

(i)   identification of substance/preparation and company;

(ii)   composition/information on ingredients;

(iii)   hazards identification;

(iv)   first-aid measures;

(v)   fire-fighting measures;

(vi)   accidental release measures;

(vii)   handling and storage;

(viii) exposure controls/personal protection;

 (ix) physical/chemical properties;

 (x) stability and reactivity;

 (xi) toxicological data;

(xii) ecological data;

(xiii) disposal considerations;

(xiv) transport information;

 (xv) regulatory information;

(xvi) other matters.

[Reg 6, 6 Sch].

This is not necessary in cases where substances/preparations are sold to the general public from a shop (e.g. medicines), if sufficient information is given with the product to enable users to take the necessary health and safety measures but this exception does not apply if the product is to be used at work. *[Reg 6(5)]*. Safety sheets have to be supplied free of charge and with data in English except where recipient is in another Member State, when it should be in that language. *[Reg 6(4)(6)]*.

9.11

Table 11

Indications of danger for substances dangerous for supply

Column 1 Indication of danger	Column 2 Symbol-letter	Column 3 Symbol
Explosive	E	
Oxidizing	O	
Extremely flammable	F+	
Highly flammable	F	
Very toxic	T+	
Toxic	T	
Harmful	Xn	
Corrosive	C	
Irritant	Xi	
Dangerous for the environment	N	

[*Chemicals (Hazard Information and Packaging) Regulations, 2 Sch*].

(B) Substances dangerous for carriage

9.12 With the exception of:

(*a*) a vehicle (in which the substance is being carried) not being used for, or in connection with, work;

(*b*) a tank container of more than 3 cubic metres;

(*c*) a substance carried within the meaning of the Convention concerning International Carriage by Rail (COTIF);

(*d*) a substance carried on an international transport operation within the meaning of the European Agreement concerning the International Carriage of Dangerous Goods by Road (ADR);

(*e*) an international transport operation subject to any special bilateral or multilateral agreement made under Article 43 of the European Agreement (ADR);

(*f*) a vehicle not for the time being subject to the European Agreement (ADR), because it belongs to the armed forces; or

(*g*) a substance packaged and labelled in accordance with the Technical Instructions for the Safe Transport of Dangerous Goods by Air issued by the International Aviation Organisation.

[*Reg 3(3)*].

A consignor must not consign (either as principal or agent) a substance dangerous for carriage before first classifying it (see 9.8 above) *as per* Approved Carriage List (ACL). [*Reg 7(1), 3 Sch*]. The substances which have been classified as dangerous for carriage appear at 10.17 DANGEROUS SUBSTANCES II.

Packaging requirements for substances dangerous for supply and carriage

9.13 Such substances must not be supplied/consigned, unless packaged suitably for the purpose. In particular,

(*a*) the receptacle containing the substance/preparation must be designed/ constructed/maintained and closed, so as to prevent escape/spillage of contents – a requirement which can be satisfied by fitting a suitable safety device;

(*b*) the receptacle, if likely to come into contact with the substance/preparation, must be made of materials which are not liable to be adversely affected nor, in combination, constitute a health and safety risk;

(*c*) where the receptacle is fitted with a replaceable closure, the closure must be designed so that the receptacle can be repeatedly re-closed, without allowing escape of contents.

[*Reg 8*].

Substances/preparations dangerous for supply – labelling requirements

(*a*) *Substances*

9.14 With the exception of

(i) gas (compressed, liquefied or dissolved under pressure), unless

    (*a*) a preparation,

    (*b*) in an aerosol dispenser,

    (*c*) a pesticide

    [*Reg 9(5)*];

(ii) substances transferred from one workplace to another [*Reg 9(6)*];

(iii) substances supplied in small quantities – except those which are (*a*) explosive, (*b*) very toxic and (*c*) toxic [*Reg 9(7)*],

suppliers must not supply substances, unless the following particulars are clearly shown:

(i) name/full address/telephone number of supplier (whether manufacturer, importer, distributor);

(ii) name of substance;

(iii) (*a*) indication(s) of danger and danger symbol(s),

    (*b*) risk phrases (not necessary on packages containing fewer than 125 millilitres [*Reg 9(8)*]),

    (*c*) safety phrases (not necessary on packages containing fewer than 125 millilitres, unless (i) explosive, (ii) very toxic, (iii) toxic, (iv) corrosive and (v) extremely flammable),

    (*d*) the EEC number (if any) and if the substance is dangerous for supply in the 'Approved Supply List', the words 'EEC label',

The safety phrases can appear on a separate label, if more convenient. [*Reg 9*].

(*b*) *Preparations*

(i) name/address/telephone number of supplier (whether manufacturer, importer, distributor);

(ii) trade name or designation;

(iii) (*a*) identification of constituents,

    (*b*) indication(s) of danger and danger symbol(s),

    (*c*) risk phrases,

    (*d*) safety phrases,

    (*e*) if a pesticide,

        (i) trade name,

        (ii) name and concentration of active ingredients – to be expressed as percentage by weight (pesticides supplied as solids, in aerosol dispensers or as volatile/viscous liquids);

    (*f*) in the case of a preparation intended for sale to the general public, in a nominal quantity, risk phrases and safety phrases may be omitted so long as the substance is not classified as harmful and they may also be omitted in certain other cases involving less dangerous substances.

[*Reg 9(8)*].

Misleading phrases such as 'non-harmful', 'non-toxic' should be avoided (*Vacwell v BDH Chemicals Ltd [1969] 3 AER 1681*) (see further Chapter 38 'Product Safety').

Substances/preparations dangerous for carriage – labelling requirements

9.15   Consignors must not consign substances/preparations dangerous for carriage, unless the package in which either is carried clearly shows, or permits to be shown on the receptacle or inner packagings, the following:

(i)   name/full address/telephone number of the consignor;

(ii)   (*a*)   designation of substance etc.,

(*b*)   substance identification number (if any),

(*c*)   hazard warning sign;

(iii)   where the quantity is more than 25 litres

(*a*)   the nature of dangers to which the substance may give rise,

(*b*)   emergency action

(if necessary, on a separate statement accompanying the package and, in the case of a gas cylinder, partly on the label and partly on a separate statement; and in the case of a package containing two or more dangerous substances in separate receptacles, separate labels). [*Reg 10(1)(3)*].

Excluded substances

The following are excluded from the operation of the regulations:

(i)   (*a*)   receptacles containing any toxic gas – 25 millilitres or less;

(*b*)   receptacles containing any flammable gas – 500 millilitres or less;

(*c*)   receptacles containing any non-flammable compressed gas – 5.5 litres or less (with no account taken of an individual receptacle having a volume of 1.4 litres or less); or

(ii)   in any other case, where the total quantity is 1 litre or less.

[*Reg 10(4)*].

Carriage in a single receptacle

9.16   In cases where *Regs 9* and *10* would need to be complied with, it is possible to label the package with the following particulars in the case of carriage in a single receptacle.

(i) *Substances which weigh less than 250 litres*

(*a*)   name, address, telephone number,

(*b*)   name of substance,

(*c*)   risk phrases,

(*d*)   safety phrases,

(*e*)   EEC number,

(*f*)   substance identification number (SIN) (if any),

(*g*)   hazard warning sign.

(ii) *Substances which weigh 250 litres or more*

(*a*)   name, address, telephone number,

(*b*)   trade name or other designation,

(*c*)   indications of danger with corresponding symbol (if any),

(*d*)   risk phrases,

(*e*)   safety phrases,

(*f*)   substance identification number,

(*g*)   hazard warning sign,

(*h*)   information relating to dangers associated with substance and the emergency action necessary (as per the 'Approved Carriage List') – where the quantity of any substance in any receptacle exceeds 25 litres. (This can appear on a separate statement accompanying the package.)

[*Reg 11(2)(a)(b)*].

(iii) *Preparations which weigh less than 250 litres*

(*a*)   name, address and telephone number of supplier,

(*b*)   trade name of preparation,

(*c*)   indications of danger with corresponding symbols (if any),

(*d*)   nominal quantity (if to be sold to the public),

(*e*)   safety phrases,

(*f*)   EC number,

(*g*)   substance identification number,

(*h*)   hazard warning sign,

or all of the requirements of *Reg 9* and the hazard substance number.

(iv) *Preparations weighing 250 litres or more*

(*a*)   name and address,

(*b*)   trade name of preparation,

(*c*)   identification of constituents of preparation,

(*d*)   risk phrases,

(*e*)   safety phrases,

(*f*)   nominal quantity (if for sale to the public),

(*g*)   substance identification number,

(*h*)   hazard warning sign,

(*j*)   if quantity of substance is more than 25 litres; the nature of the danger the substance may cause and emergency action to be taken, as in substances above.

Other exceptions are made for one or more receptacles in outer packaging. They can either be labelled as in the single receptacle derogations above or may follow the requirements of *Reg 10*. Certain other variations are possible relevant to controlled drugs, micro-organisms and samples taken by enforcement authorities.

Labelling requirements for particular preparations dangerous for supply

9.17   In the case of

(*a*)   preparations which are (i) very toxic, (ii) toxic, (iii) corrosive or (iv) intended to be sold to the general public;

(*b*)   paints/varnishes containing lead;

the following safety phraseology should appear on the labelling:

(*a*)   'Keep locked up' – substances/preparations that are very toxic, toxic, corrosive or to be sold/supplied to the general public.

(*b*)   'Contains lead. Should not be used on surfaces that are liable to be chewed or sucked by children'. (Paints and varnishes containing lead). In the case of packages containing less than 125 millilitres of such preparation – 'Warning, contains lead'.

(*c*)   'Cyanoacrylate. Danger. Bonds skin and eyes in seconds. Keep out of reach of children' – cyanoacrylate based adhesives (appropriate safety advice must accompany the packet).

(*d*)   'Contains isocyanates. See information supplied by manufacturer' – isocyanates.

(*e*)   'Contains epoxy constituents. See information supplied by manufacturer' – epoxy constituents with an average molecular weight >700.

(*f*)   'Do not breathe gas/fumes/vapour/spray'
'In case of insufficient ventilation wear suitable respiratory equipment'
'Use only in well-ventilated areas'
– sprays.

(*g*)   'Warning! Do not use with other products. May release dangerous gases (active chlorine)' – supply to the general public.

(*h*)   'Warning! Contains cadmium.
Dangerous fumes are formed during use.
See information supplied by the manufacturer.
Comply with safety instructions'
– cadmium (alloys) intended to be used for brazing or soldering.

[*Reg 13, 7 Sch, Part II*].

Further labelling requirements

9.18   All labels for supply purposes and for substances dangerous for carriage must be indelibly marked and securely fixed to the package and the hazard warning sign must stand out from its background so that it is clearly noticeable. It must be possible to read the label horizontally when the package is set down normally and it must have a side length of 100 square millimetres. If it is not possible to comply with any of the requirements because of the shape of the package, it should be attached in some other appropriate manner.

The dimensions of the label for substances and preparations dangerous for supply and for carriage are reproduced below.

In the case of substances dangerous for carriage, the symbol must be at least one tenth of the size of the label which must itself conform with the requirements below. In the case of substances dangerous for carriage, the symbol must be printed on an orange-yellow background and it must not measure less than one-tenth of the label size and also must not be less than 100 square millimetres in size.

Capacity of package	*Dimensions of label*
(*a*) not exceeding 3 litres	if possible at least 52 × 74 millimetres
(*b*) exceeding 3 litres but not exceeding 50 litres	at least 74 × 105 millimetres
(*c*) exceeding 50 litres but not exceeding 500 litres	at least 105 × 148 millimetres
(*d*) exceeding 500 litres	at least 148 × 210 millimetres

[*Reg 14*].

Enforcement/penalties and civil liability

Enforcement

9.19   HSE is the enforcing authority for *CHIP Regulations*, except where the dangerous substance is supplied from a registered chemist, where the Pharmaceutical Society of Great Britain is the enforcing authority. If the supply is from a shop, mobile vehicle or market stall, or to members of the public, the local Weights and Measures Authority is the enforcing authority. [*Reg 18(2)*].

Penalties

Breach of the provisions of the *Chemicals (Hazard Information and Packaging) Regulations 1993* carries the same penalties as breach of *HSWA* itself (see further Chapter 17 'Enforcement').

Defence

It is a defence to a charge under *CHIP* that a person took all reasonable care and exercised all due diligence to avoid commission of that offence [*Reg 18(4)*] – a difficult test to satisfy (see Chapter 33 'Offices' and *Dewhurst (JH) Ltd v Coventry Corporation* [*1969*] *3 AER 1225*).

Civil liability

Where breach of duty causes damage/injury, this can give rise to civil liability. [*Reg 18(1)(b)*].

Control of substances hazardous to health – Control of Substances Hazardous to Health Regulations 1988 (as amended) (COSHH)

9.20   The scope of these regulations is wide – from chemicals to petroleum, to dust, micro-organisms and carcinogens (see 9.35) to prospectively biological agents (see

9.30) and respiratory sensitisers (see 9.38) – imposing a considerable remit on employers. More particularly, a substance hazardous to health is

(*a*)   a substance

    (i)   on the Approved Supply List (ASL) (see 9.8 above),

    (ii)   on the Approved Carriage List (ACL);

(*b*)   a substance for which there is

    (i)   a maximum exposure limit (MEL) (specified in the *COSHH (Amendment) Regulations 1992, 2 Sch*) (see Appendix A), e.g. acrylonitrile, carbon disulphide, benzene,

    (ii)   an occupational exposure standard (OES) (see Appendix A);

(*c*)   a micro-organism (see 9.31);

(*d*)   substantial concentration of airborne dust (see Chapter 43 'Ventilation');

(*e*)   a substance otherwise residually hazardous to health;

(*f*)   a carcinogen (see 9.36);

[*Control of Substances Hazardous to Health Regulations 1988, Reg 2(1); COSHH (Amendment) Regulations 1992 (SI 1992 No 2382)*];

and shortly

(*g*)   certain biological agents (see 9.31); and

(*h*)   respiratory sensitisers (see 9.39);

    but not

  (i)   asbestos – covered by the *Control of Asbestos at Work Regulations 1987* (see Chapter 4 'Asbestos');

  (ii)   lead – covered by the *Control of Lead at Work Regulations 1980* (see 9.40);

  (iii)   ionising radiations – covered by the *Ionising Radiations Regulations 1985* (see 9.44);

  (iv)   highly flammable liquids and liquefied petroleum gases – covered by the *Highly Flammable Liquids and Liquefied Petroleum Gases Regulations 1972* (see Chapter 24);

  (v)   dangerous pathogens (see 9.59).

Revoking a spread of time-honoured regulations applicable to a wide range of specific industries and processes, passed in an age when control techniques were much more elementary (see 9.1 above) and on an ad hoc basis, the *COSHH Regulations* require employers to assess and update health risks to employees – in other words, to keep and record an on-going inventory of risks to the workforce.

Duties under COSHH

(a) Employers

9.21   Employers have been given a range of duties to their employees. These duties also apply to other persons, so far as is reasonably practicable, who may be affected by the work. However, the duties mentioned below relevant to health surveillance, monitoring and instruction and training duties under *Regs 10, 11, 12(1)* and *(2)* apply exclusively to employees.

The following main duties are as follows:

(1)   to carry out (and review) a formal independent assessment of health risks to employees [*Reg 6*] (see 9.22);

(2)   to prevent/control exposure of employees to health risks [*Reg 7*] (see 9.23);

(3)   to institute proper use of controls and personal protective equipment [*Regs 8, 9*] (see also Chapter 36 'Personal Protective Equipment');

(4)   to maintain, examine and test controls and keep records [*Reg 9*] (see 9.24);

(5)   to monitor workplace exposure of employees [*Reg 10*] (see 9.25);

(6)   provide health surveillance for employees, where necessary [*Reg 11*] (see 9.26);

(7)   provide information, instruction and training regarding hazardous substances [*Reg 12*].

(b) Employees

(1)   to make full and proper use of control measures and personal protective equipment [*Reg 8(2)*];

(2)   at the cost of the employer, to present himself for health surveillance [*Reg 11(9)*].

Risk assessments

9.22   The object of a risk assessment is to enable budgetary decisions to be made regarding measures deemed necessary to impose the requisite controls on 'substances hazardous to health'; in addition, a formal assessment system is proof that a particular organisation has taken cognisance of health hazards and has implemented, or is about to do so, steps to eliminate/minimise their incidence. More particularly, assessments should identify:

(i)   risks posed to the health of the workforce;

(ii)   steps necessary to control exposure to those hazards;

(iii)   other action necessary to achieve compliance with regulations relating to maintenance requirements and personal protective equipment;

(iv)   extent of exposure.

Merely following suppliers' product data is not necessarily sufficient for compliance purposes; HSE Guidance Notes and manufacturers' standards should also be consulted. Not to do so is to be left open to the charge that one has not done all that was 'reasonably practicable' – this statutory requirement implying that employers should keep up to date with the latest HSE, industrial and technical publications (*Stokes v GKN (Bolts and Nuts) Ltd* [*1968*] *1 WLR 1776*) (see Chapter 15 'Employers' Duties').

Controlling exposure

9.23   Employers must ensure that employees are not exposed to substances which are hazardous to health where this may be prevented, or if not, the exposure must be adequately controlled. Other measures which do not require the use of personal protective equipment must be used as far as is reasonably practicable.

Whilst maximum exposure must be below the Maximum Exposure Limits, control will only be adequate if exposure is reduced to the lowest that is reasonably practicable. The approved methods for averaging over the specified reference periods are reproduced in the Guidance Note EH 40.

If exposure occurs no greater than the approved occupational standard, or if the employer acts quickly to remedy any excess as soon as is reasonably practicable, he will not be liable.

Respiratory equipment, if used, must conform with either the EC standard or be of a type approved by the HSE. The Guidance shows that respiratory protection requires a big back-up in training, supervision and maintenance and that correct fitting is crucial. [*Reg 7*].

Checking that control measures are properly and fully used is vital, together with periodic checks to make sure there are no defects in control measures. Regular testing of equipment is necessary with time-tables for this. Records of control measures, which are required to be kept for five years, need to be made. Depending on the size of the business, a simple book, or computer records may be suitable. (For the express requirements for control of exposure to carcinogens see 9.38 below.) A Guidance: 'Step by Step to COSHH Assessment' (from which these recommendations have been derived) and a Code of Practice: 'The Control of Substances Hazardous to Health 1988 and Control of Carcinogenic Substances' are available from HMSO.

The fact that a substance is not in the list does not mean that it can be safely inhaled. In such a case exposure should be controlled to a level at which nearly all the population could be exposed, day after day, without adverse effects on health.

'Measures for preventing or controlling exposure

Measures could be any combination of the following:

(*a*)   for preventing exposure;

    (i)   elimination of the use of the substance;

    (ii)   substitution by a less hazardous substance or by the same substance in a less hazardous form;

(*b*)   for controlling exposure:

    (i)   totally enclosed process and handling systems;

    (ii)   plant or processes or systems of work which minimise generation of, or suppress or contain, the hazardous dust, fume, micro-organisms etc. and which limit the area of contamination in the event of spills and leaks;

    (iii)   partial enclosure, with local exhaust ventilation;

    (iv)   local exhaust ventilation;

    (v)   sufficient general ventilation;

    (vi)   reduction of numbers of employees exposed and exclusion of non-essential access;

    (vii)   reduction in the period of exposure for employees;

    (viii)   regular cleaning of contamination from, or disinfection of, walls, surfaces etc;

    (ix)   provision of means for safe storage and disposal of substances hazardous to health;

    (x)   suitable personal protective equipment;

(xi)   prohibition of eating, drinking, smoking etc. in contaminated areas;

(xii)   provision of adequate facilities for washing, changing and storage of clothing, including arrangements for laundering contaminated clothing.

In existing work situations, the present control measures should be carefully reviewed, and improved, extended or replaced as necessary to be capable of achieving, and sustaining, adequate control.

If, in spite of the above control measures, leaks, spills or uncontrolled releases of a hazardous substance could still occur, means should be available for limiting the extent of risks to health and for regaining adequate control as soon as possible. The means should include, where appropriate, established emergency procedures, safe disposal of the substance and sufficient suitable personal protective equipment to enable the source of the release to be safely identified and repairs to be made. All persons not concerned with the emergency action should be excluded from the area of contamination.'

(ACOP).

Engineering controls – records of examination and test

9.24   Engineering controls should be subject to regular examination and test and records kept as follows:

(*a*)   local exhaust ventilation plant – every 14 months;

(*b*)   local exhaust ventilation plant in the following specific industries:

—	blasting for the cleaning of metal castings	– every month
—	grinding/polishing/abrading of metal processes in any room for more than 12 hours in any week (not gold, platinum or iridium):	– every 6 months
—	non-ferrous metal castings	– every 6 months
—	jute cloth manufacture	– every month

(*c*)   any other case   – at suitable intervals

[*Control of Substances Hazardous to Health Regulations 1988, Reg 9, 3 Sch*].

Monitoring exposure at the workplace

9.25   Where employees are exposed to substances hazardous to health, employers must ensure that there is adequate monitoring of exposure and records kept for 40 years. In particular, in the case of exposure to

(*a*)   vinyl chloride monomer – monitoring must be continuous;

(*b*)   vapour/spray emitted by electrolytic chromium processes (except trivalent chromium) – every 14 days.

[*Control of Substances Hazardous to Health Regulations 1988, Reg 10 (as amended by SI 1992 No 2382), 1 Sch*].

Provision of health surveillance

9.26   Health surveillance must be arranged by employers as follows:

(A)   Schedule 5 employees;

(B)   where exposure is associated with either an identifiable disease (see Chapter 31 'Occupational Health') or adverse health effects (see, for instance, legionella at 9.27 below).

(A) Schedule 5 employees

Schedule 5 requires that health surveillance of employees under an employment medical adviser or appointed doctor must be arranged by employers at intervals of not more than 12 months, i.e. employees exposed to:

(i)   vinyl chloride monomer (VCM) whilst engaged in

    (*a*)   manufacture,

    (*b*)   production,

    (*c*)   reclamation,

    (*d*)   storage,

    (*e*)   discharge,

    (*f*)   transport,

    (*g*)   use,

    (*h*)   polymerisation,

    (unless exposure is insignificant);

(ii)   nitro/amino derivatives of phenol/benzene (or its homologues) whilst engaged in

    (*a*)   manufacture of nitro/amino derivatives of phenol/benzene, and

    (*b*)   making of explosives with such substances;

(iii)   potassium or sodium chromate or dichromate, whilst engaged in manufacture;

(iv)   1-naphthylamine, orthotolidine, dianisidine, dichlorbenzidine, whilst engaged in manufacture;

(v)   auramine, magenta, whilst engaged in manufacture;

(vi)   carbon disulphide, disulphur dichloride, benzene (and benzol), carbon tetrachloride, trichlorethylene, whilst engaged in processes in which these substances are

    (*a*)   used,

    (*b*)   given off as vapour,

    in the manufacture of indiarubber or its articles or goods;

(vii)   pitch, whilst engaged in manufacture of blocks of fuel consisting of

    (*a*)   coal,

    (*b*)   coal dust,

    (*c*)   coke/slurry,

    with pitch as a binding ambience.

(B) Exposure-related identifiable diseases

Exposure to a whole range of substances at work can lead over a period of time to the onset of identifiable diseases and/or adverse health effects. Indeed, exposure to certain substances can lead to diseases which are prescribed, that is, for which disablement benefit is payable, without the employee having to establish negligence against his employer(s) (see 31.42 OCCUPATIONAL HEALTH); or to non-notifiable diseases (e.g. legionnaire's disease). Legionnaire's disease is neither notifiable (except in Scotland) (see App.B ACCIDENT REPORTING) nor is it a prescribed occupational disease (see 31.42 OCCUPATIONAL HEALTH) though it is serious enough to have resulted in fatalities.

Legionella (for medical aspects, see 31.12 OCCUPATIONAL HEALTH)

9.27   Between 100 and 200 cases of legionella are reported each year in England and Wales. *COSHH Regulations* extend to the prevention and control of risks from hazardous micro-organisms, including legionella. Occupiers of non-domestic premises must inform the local authority in writing where a 'notifiable device' exists on their premises. [*Notification of Cooling Towers and Evaporative Condensers Regulations 1992 (SI 1992 No 2225), Reg 3(1)*]. A 'notifiable device' is a cooling tower or an evaporative condenser, but not one

(*a*)   containing no water exposed to air; or

(*b*)   whose water/electricity supply is not connected.

[*Notification of Cooling Towers and Evaporative Condensers Regulations 1992, Reg 2*].

So far as reasonably practicable, employers (and occupiers), as regards factories, hospitals, laboratories, schools and construction sites with

(i)   water systems incorporating a cooling tower,

(ii)   water systems incorporating an evaporative condenser,

(iii) hot water services (except where the volume of water does not exceed 300 litres),

(iv)   hot/cold water services (irrespective of size) in particularly susceptible premises (e.g. health care premises),

(v)   humidifiers/air washers, creating water droplets, where water temperature is likely to exceed 20°C,

(vi)   spa baths/pools where warm water is recirculated,

must

(*a*)   identify/assess sources of risk;

(*b*)   prepare schemes for preventing/controlling risk;

(*c*)   implement precautions;

(*d*)   keep records of precautions.

All systems (particularly those in nursing homes/hospitals) susceptible to colonisation by legionella should be assessed, with particular regard to

(i)   droplet formation potential;

(ii)   water temperature;

(iii) risk to anyone inhaling water droplets;

(iv)   means of preventing/controlling risk.

Vulnerable areas of the workplace

9.28   The two most vulnerable areas of the workplace are (*a*) hot (and sometimes cold) water services and (*b*) air conditioning and industrial cooling systems.

(*a*)   *Hot (and cold) water systems*

Colonising typically storage tanks, calorifiers, pipework, dead legs, water softeners and filters, as well as taps and showers, legionella can proliferate in warm water temperatures. Cold water services normally are not so vulnerable, except in the case of large cold water systems where use is intermittent or where water temperatures can exceed 20°C.

(*b*)   *Air conditioning/industrial cooling systems*

Typically heated to 30°C, water from the cooling tower can become heavily contaminated by dust, slime and sludge, thereby providing ideal conditions for legionella to breed. Emanating from cooling towers, legionnaire's disease has resulted to date in a number of fatalities at work, and passers-by, as well as employees, are also at risk. Indeed, most industrial cooling systems operate at temperatures ideal for germination of legionella. Also, evaporative condensers have an industrial cooling function and are used for air conditioning purposes. Since the volume of water in such condensers is less than in a cooling tower, control of water quality is more difficult.

Suitable precautions

9.29   (*a*)   *Hot water systems*

Water services should be checked regularly and well maintained, particularly

  (i)   water temperatures at calorifiers;

  (ii) water temperatures at taps after one minute's running (in any case, all taps should be inspected at least once a year);

  (iii) tanks, for organic/bacteriological material (should be inspected at least annually);

  (iv) calorifiers, for organic/bacteriological material;

  (v)   accessible pipework and insulation.

Where there is risk of legionnaire's disease, water systems should be disinfected, to BS 6700 'Specification for the design, installation, testing and maintenance of services supplying water for domestic use within buildings'. This can be achieved chemically, by chlorination, or thermally, by simply raising the temperature of the water to such level that legionella cannot survive.

In addition,

  (vi)   avoid water temperatures between 20°C and 45°C;

  (vii) avoid water stagnation;

  (viii) avoid use of materials that harbour bacteria;

  (ix)   keep system clear so as to avoid accumulation of sediment harbouring bacteria;

  (x)   make use of water treatment systems and chemicals;

  (xi)   ensure the whole system operates safely.

(*b*)   *Cooling towers/air conditioning systems*

Precautions here include

(i)   designing cooling towers to ensure that aerosol release is minimised;

(ii)   locating towers away from ventilation inlets, opening windows and populated areas (in practice, cooling towers and air inlets are often situated together at roof level);

(iii)   maintaining the system in a clean and sound condition;

(iv)   controlling water quality.

Prosecutions for legionella

9.30   Where an employer is prosecuted (under *Sec 3(1)* of the *Health and Safety at Work etc. Act 1974*) with exposing members of the public to health risks from legionella, it is not necessary to show that members of the public had actually inhaled bacterium, or that it had been there to be inhaled; it was enough that there had been a risk of its being there (*R v Board of Trustees of the Science Museum, The Times, 15 March 1993*).

Protection against biological agents

9.31   A fourth amendment to *COSHH*, in the form of a new *Schedule 11* to the original regulations, to be operational as from 1 January 1994, is to implement the Biological Agents Directive. The amendment aims to extend protection to workers liable to infection from biological agents. A biological agent (for compensation purposes, see 31.42 (B) OCCUPATIONAL HEALTH) consists of (*a*) a micro-organism, (*b*) cell cultures or (*c*) human endoparasites (including ones genetically modified) which might cause infection, allergy, toxicity or generally constitute a health hazard, including colonisation of a worker by cells derived from tumours. Most biological agents are micro-organisms (including bacteria, fungi, viruses and microscopic parasites – hence legionella is within scope (see 9.27 above). They are classified into four categories of ascending level of risk, according to their propensity to cause infection to both individuals and the community, gravity of disease and availability of vaccine and treatment. (An Approved List of Biological Agents is shortly to be published.) Importantly, a distinction is made between activities involving a deliberate intention to work with or use biological agents (e.g. laboratory) and those where exposure is incidental (e.g. health care). In the latter case, employers will not be expected to keep a list of employees exposed to the two most hazardous categories of agents (C and D); whereas, in the former case, this is mandatory. [*para 11*].

Schedule 11 to COSHH – Duties of employers

The following are the main duties of employers in respect of biological agents.

(1)   To carry out a risk assessment based on the approved classification of the agent (see above 'Approved Classification List'); if an agent is not so classified, it is assignable to category 3 – 'can cause severe human disease'.

(2)   Where possible, to prevent exposure of employees to hazardous biological agents by substitution of a less hazardous agent.

(3)   Notwithstanding, if there is residual risk of exposure and prevention is not reasonable, exposure to be variously controlled, principally by

(*a*)   reduction of the number of employees likely to be exposed;

(*b*)　　design/engineering out release of biological agents;

(*c*)　　use of biohazard sign.

(4)　　To provide written instructions and display notices specifying procedure(s) to be followed in case of

　　(*a*)　　serious accident/incident involving handling of a biological agent; or

　　(*b*)　　a Group 4 biological agent – 'causes severe human disease'.

(5)　　To inform employees (or safety representatives) of

　　(*a*)　　any accident/incident resulting in release of a biological agent of Group 3 or 4;

　　(*b*)　　causes of accident/incident;

　　(*c*)　　steps already taken/to be taken to remedy the situation.

(6)　　To keep for 40 years a list of employees exposed to Group 3 or 4 agents, indicating type of work done, agents to which they have been exposed, records of exposures/accidents, available for inspection by an employment medical adviser and/or individual employee affected.

(7)　　To notify HSE at least 30 days in advance in writing if they propose to store for the first time biological agents of Groups 2, 3 and 4; including formerly 'listed pathogens', since the *Health and Safety (Dangerous Pathogens) Regulations 1981* are to be revoked by the *COSHH Amendment Regulations* (see 9.59 below).

Categories of biological agents

There are four categories of biological agents, namely,

(*a*)　　Group 1 – unlikely to cause human disease;

(*b*)　　Group 2 – can cause human disease;

(*c*)　　Group 3 – can cause severe human disease; and

(*d*)　　Group 4 – causes severe human disease.

Medical examinations

9.32　　Medical examination must be carried out by employment medical advisers or appointed doctors in the case of *Schedule 5* employees, e.g. exposure to VCM, and, preferably, in other (non-*Schedule 5*) cases as well. In the case of *Schedule 5* employees, medical examinations must take place annually. They must be paid for by employers and employees are entitled to see employment health records, on giving reasonable notice. Correspondingly, employees must submit to medical examination, when required to do so by the employer, during working hours. [*Reg 11(g)*]. If the employment medical adviser concludes that an employee should no longer be engaged in such work or only under specified conditions, the employer must not permit the employee to do such work or, alternatively, only under specified conditions. [*Reg 11(b)*]. In such circumstances, employees may be entitled to paid leave following suspension on medical grounds (see 31.13 OCCUPATIONAL HEALTH). Employers (or employees) who are dissatisfied with such suspension order, can apply to the HSE within 28 days for a review of the decision. Medical records must be kept by the employer for at least 40 years. [*Reg 11(3) and SI 1992 No 2382, 1 Sch*].

Disclosure of information to employees regarding hazardous substances

9.33   Given that prevention is better than cure, the regulations oblige employers to acquaint their employees with the dangers arising from working with substances hazardous to health, and, in consequence, the precautions that they should take.

Specific information

Specifically, information must

(*a*)   include the results of monitoring exposure;

(*b*)   be given to the employees (or safety representative) where the maximum exposure (MEL) is exceeded in the case of *Schedule 1* substances, e.g. cadmium, carbon disulphide, isocyanates; and

(*c*)   be given about the collective results of health surveillance.

[*Reg 12*].

Prohibition on use at work of certain hazardous substances

9.34   Certain substances are prohibited from importation which are also not to be used at work, namely:

(*a*)   2-naphtylamine, benzidine, 4-aminodiphenyl, 4-nitrodiphenyl, their salts and any substance containing any of those compounds in a total concentration [equal to or greater than 0.1 per cent by mass];

(*b*)   matches filled with white phosphorus.

Benzene must not be supplied for use at work if its use is prohibited by Item 11 in the table below. [*Reg 4*].

In addition to specifying preventive measures, *COSHH* imposes prohibitions on the use at work of the following hazardous substances:

PROHIBITION OF CERTAIN SUBSTANCES HAZARDOUS TO HEALTH FOR CERTAIN PURPOSES

Item No.	Column 1	Column 2
	Description of substance	*Purpose for which the substance is prohibited*
1.	2-naphthylamine; benzidine; 4-aminodiphenyl; 4-nitrodiphenyl; their salts and any substance containing any of those compounds, in any other substance in a total concentration equal to or greater than 0.1 per cent by mass.	Manufacture and use for all purposes including any manufacturing process in which a substance described in column 1 of this item is formed.
2.	Sand or other substance containing free silica.	Use as an abrasive for blasting articles in any blasting apparatus.

Item No.	Column 1	Column 2
	Description of substance	*Purpose for which the substance is prohibited*
3.	A substance– (a) containing compounds of silicon calculated as silica to the extent of more than 3% by weight of dry material; or (b) composed of or containing dust or other matter deposited from a fettling or blasting process.	Use as a parting material in connection with the making of metal castings.
4.	Carbon disulphide.	Use in the cold-cure process of vulcanising in the proofing of cloth with rubber.
5.	Oils other than white oil, or oil of entirely animal or vegetable origin or entirely of mixed animal and vegetable origin.	Use for oiling the spindles of self-acting mules.
6.	Ground or powdered flint or quartz other than natural sand.	Use in relation to the manufacture or decoration of pottery for the following purposes– (a) the placing of ware for the biscuit fire; (b) the polishing of ware; (c) as the ingredient of a wash for saggars, trucks, bats, cranks, or other articles used in supporting ware during firing; and (d) as dusting or supporting powder in potters' shops.
7.	Ground or powdered flint or quartz other than– (a) natural sand; or (b) ground or powdered flint or quartz which forms part of a slop or paste.	Use in relation to the manufacture or decoration of pottery for any purpose except– (a) use in a separate room or building for– (i) the manufacture of powdered flint or quartz; or (ii) the making of frits or glazes or the making of colours or coloured slips for the decoration of pottery; (b) use for the incorporation of the substance into the body of ware in an enclosure in which no person is employed and which is constructed and ventilated to prevent the escape of dust.
8.	Dust or powder of a refractory material containing not less than 80 per cent. of silica other than natural sand.	Use for sprinkling the moulds of silica bricks, namely bricks or other articles composed of refractory material and containing not less than 80 per cent. of silica.
9.	White phosphorus.	Use in the manufacture of matches.
10.	Hydrogen cyanide.	Use in fumigation except when– (a) released from an inert material in which hydrogen cyanide is absorbed; (b) generated from a gassing powder; or (c) applied from a cylinder through suitable piping and applicators other than for fumigations in the open air to control or kill mammal pests.
11.	Benzene and any substance containing benzene in a concentration equal to or greater than 0.1 per cent., other than motor fuels and waste.	Use for all purposes except use in industrial processes and for the purposes of research, development and analysis.

Item No.	Column 1	Column 2
	Description of substance	*Purpose for which the substance is prohibited*

12.	Lead carbonate and sulphate in paint.	No persons must
		  (a) sell, or
		  (b) use in business or a manufacturing process
		lead carbonate or lead sulphate for use as paint (cxcept for use in restoration/ maintenance of historical buildings).

13.	Mercury compounds.	A similar prohibition applies to mercury compounds in heavy duty textiles [*Reg 4*]; or mercury/arsenic compounds for use in treatment of industrial waters [*Reg 5*]. The maximum penalty for breach, on summary conviction, is a fine of £20,000.
14.	DBB or substance containing DBB in a concentration equal to or greater than 0.1 per cent by weight.	
15.	Ugilec 121 (monomethyl-dichloro-diphenyl methane) and DBBT (monomethyl-dibromo-diphenyl methane) (as from 31 July 1992). Ugilec 141 (except in relation to plant and machinery already in service on that date) (as from 18 June 1994).	

16.	Pentachlorophenol (PCP), unless for use as
	(a) an authorised pesticide; or
	(b) in industrial installation
	   (i) for impregnation of fibres/heavy
	        duty textiles, or
	   (ii) as a synthesising/processing agent.	

17.	Cadmium in
	(a) polyvinyl chloride (PVC) CN code
	    nos 3904 10, 3904 21, 3904 22
	(b) polyurethane (PUR) CN code no
	    3909 50
	(c) low-density polyethylene (ld PE) CN
	    code no 3901 10
	(d) cellulose acetate (CA) CN code nos
	    3912 11, 3912 12
	(e) Cellulose acetate butyrate (CAB) CN
	    code nos 3912 11, 3912 12
	(f) epoxy resins CN code no 3907 30
		Use of cadmium in pigmentation, and marketing of such products as from 31 July 1993

		and as from 31 December 1995.

	(a) finished products made from
	   (i) melamine-formaldehyde (MF)
	          resins CN code no 3909 20
	   (ii) urea-formaldehyde (UF) resins
	          CN code no 3909 10
	   (iii) unsaturated polyesters (UP) CN
	          code no 3907 91
	   (iv) polyethylene terephthalate
	          (PET) CN code no 3907 91
	   (v) polybutylene terephthalate (PBT)
	   (vi) transparent/general purpose
	          polystyrene CN code nos 3903
	          11, 3903 19
	   (vii) acrylonitrile methylmethacrylate
	          (AMMA)
	   (viii) cross-linked polyethylene (VPE)
	   (ix) high-impact polystyrene
	   (x) polypropylene (PP) CN code no
	          3902 10, or	

Item No.	Column 1	Column 2
	Description of substance	*Purpose for which the substance is prohibited*

	(b) paints CN code nos 3208/3209.	
18.	Paints containing cadmium CN code nos 3208/3209 if cadmium content exceeds 0.01 per cent by mass, and CN code nos 3208/3209 for paints which have a high zinc content, unless residual content of cadmium does not exceed 0.1 per cent by mass.	Not to be marketed after 31 December 1995.

19.	Cadmium as a stabiliser in the following finished products
	  (i) packaging materials CN code nos 3923 29 10, 3920 41, 3920 42
	  (ii) office/school supplies CN code no 3926 10
	  (iii) furniture fittings CN code no 3926 30
	  (iv) apparel and clothing accessories (including gloves) CN code no 3926 20
	  (v) floor/wall coverings CN code no 3918 10
	  (vi) impregnated, coated, covered or laminated textile fabrics CN code no 3903 10
	  (vii) imitation leather CN code no 4202
	  (viii) gramophone records CN code no 8524 10
	  (ix) tubes/pipes CN code no 3917 23
	  (x) swing doors
	  (xi) vehicles for road transport (interior, exterior, underbody)
	  (xii) coating of steel sheet in construction or industry
	  (xiii) insulation for electrical wiring.
		Use of cadmium as a stabiliser and marketing of finished products as from 30 June 1994.

20.	Cadmium plating in
	  (i) equipment/machinery for
	    (a) food production CN code nos 8210, 8417 20, 8419 81, 8421 11, 8421 22, 8422, 8435, 8437, 8438, 8476 11
	    (b) agriculture CN code nos 8419 31, 8424 81, 8432 to 8434 and 8436
	    (c) cooling and freezing CN code no 8418
	    (d) printing and book binding CN code nos 8440, 8442 and 8443
	  (ii) equipment/machinery for production of
	    (a) household goods CN code nos 7321, 8421 12, 8450, 8509 and 8516
	    (b) furniture CN code nos 8456, 8466 and 9401 to 9404
	    (c) sanitary ware CN code no 7324
	    (d) central heating and air conditioning plant CN code nos 7322, 8403, 8404 and 8415
		Use of cadmium plating and marketing of products plated with cadmium as from 31 July 1993.

Item No.	Column 1	Column 2
	Description of substance	*Purpose for which the substance is prohibited*
(iii)	(a) paper and board CN code nos 8419 32, 8439 and 8441 (b) textiles and clothing CN code nos 8444, 8445, 8447 to 8449, 8451 and 8452 (c) industrial handling equipment and machinery CN code nos 8425 to 8431 (d) road and agricultural vehicles CN code nos 8701 to 8716 (e) rolling stock CN code nos 8601 to 8609 (f) vessels CN code nos 8901 to 8908.	Use of cadmium plating and marketing of products plated with cadmium as from 30 June 1995.

[*COSHH Regulations 1988 (SI 1988 No 1657), 2 Sch; COSHH (Amendment) Regulations 1991 (SI 1991 No 2431) 2 Sch; Environmental Protection (Controls on Injurious Substances) Regulations 1992 (SI 1992 No 31), Reg 3; Environmental Protection (Controls on Injurious Substances) (No 2) Regulations 1992 (SI 1992 No 1583), Regs 2–4; Environmental Protection (Controls on Injurious Substances) Regulations 1993 (SI 1993 No 1), Regs 2–5; Environmental Protection (Controls on Injurious Substances) (No 2) Regulations 1993 (SI 1993 No 1643), Regs 2–5].*

Prohibition on importation of carcinogens

9.35 Importation of the following substances/articles into the United Kingdom is forbidden as being carcinogenic, nor must any such substance/article be supplied for use at work:

(*a*) 2-naphthylamine,
benzidine,
4-aminodiphenyl,
4-nitrodiphenyl,
(and their salts and substances containing any of those compounds in a total concentration exceeding 0.1 per cent);

(*b*) matches made with white phosphorous

[*Reg 4*];

(*c*) benzene (except in industrial processes or research).

[*Control of Substances Hazardous to Health (Amendment) Regulations 1991 (SI 1991 No 2431)*].

Carcinogens

9.36 Every employer must ensure that exposure of his employees to substances hazardous to their health is prevented, or if this is not reasonably practicable, is adequately controlled. If it is not reasonably practicable to prevent exposure of any employees to a *carcinogen* by using an alternative substance or process, then these measures must be taken:

(*a*) the total enclosure of the process and handling systems unless this is not reasonably practicable;

(*b*) plant, process and systems of work which minimise the generation of, or suppress and contain, spills, leaks, dust, fumes and vapours of carcinogens;

(c)   limitation of the quantities of a carcinogen at the place of work;

(d)   keeping the number of persons who might be exposed to a carcinogen to a minimum;

(e)   prohibiting eating, drinking and smoking in areas that may be contaminated by carcinogens;

(f)   the provision of hygiene measures including adequate washing facilities and regular cleaning of walls and surfaces;

(g)   the designation of those areas and installations which may be contaminated by carcinogens, and the use of suitable and sufficient warning signs; and

(h)   the safe storage, handling and disposal of carcinogens and use of closed and clearly labelled containers.

[*COSHH Regulations 1988, Reg 7(2A) inserted by the Personal Protective Equipment at Work Regulations 1992*].

If control measures fail and this results in the escape of carcinogens into the workplace, only persons charged with repairs must be allowed into the affected area and they must be provided with appropriate respiratory equipment. Employees must be informed immediately of the risk. [*COSHH Regulations 1988, Reg 7(6A) inserted by the Personal Protective Equipment at Work Regulations 1992*].

A carcinogen is any substance/preparation classified as per the *Chemicals (Hazard Information and Packaging) Regulations 1993 (CHIP), Reg 5* and *10 Sch*, and requiring to be labelled with risk phrase R 45 (may cause cancer) or R 49 (may cause cancer by inhalation), whether or not the substance/preparation requires to be classified anyway under *CHIP* [*COSHH Regulations 1988, Reg 2, as amended by SI 1992 No 2382*], namely:

(i)   any of the substances listed in 9.37 below, and

(ii)   any of the following substances/processes, namely,

    (a)   aflatoxins;

    (b)   arsenic and inorganic compounds;

    (c)   arsenic and beryllium compounds;

    (d)   bichromate manufacture;

    (e)   electrolytic chromium processes (excluding passivation) involving hexavalent chromium compounds;

    (f)   mustard gas;

    (g)   calcining, sintering or smelting of nickel copper matte or acid leaching or electro-refining of roasted matte;

    (h)   ortho-toluidine;

    (j)   coal soots, coal tar, pitch and coal tar fumes;

    (k)   the following mineral oils:

        (i)   unrefined and mildly refined vacuum distillates,

        (ii) catalytically cracked petroleum oils with final boiling points above 320°C,

        (iii) used engine oils;

    (l)   auramine manufacture;

(m)   leather dust in boot/shoe manufacture;

(n)   hard wood dusts;

(o)   isopropyl alcohol manufacture;

(p)   rubber manufacturing giving rise to rubber process dust and rubber fume;

(q)   magenta manufacture;

(r)   4-Nitrobiphenyl.

[*Chemicals (Hazard Information and Packaging) Regulations 1993, Reg 5, 10 Sch*].

Apart from specific requirements relating to the labelling of carcinogens (see 9.37 below), where it is not reasonably practicable to prevent exposure to a carcinogen, employers should institute certain controls.

Substances that must be labelled as carcinogenic

9.37   The following substances must be labelled 'R 45; may cause cancer' or 'R 49; may cause cancer by inhalation', for the purposes of the *Chemicals (Hazard Information and Packaging) Regulations*, namely,

Acrylonitrile
4-aminobiphenyl
Salts of 4-aminobiphenyl
Arsenic and inorganic arsenic compounds
Arsenic trioxide
Benzene
Benzidine
Beryllium and compounds
Salts of benzidine
Benzo-(a)-anthracene
Benzo-(a)-pyrene
Benzo-(b)-fluorathene
Benzo-(j)-fluorathene
Benzo-(k)-fluorathene
Bis(chloromethyl)ether
Cadmium chloride
Calcium chromate
2-chloroallyl diethly dithiocarbamate (Sufallate ISO)
Chlorodimethyl ether
1-chloro-2,3-epoxypropane (Epichlorohydrin)
Chromium III chromate
o-Dianisidine
Salts of o-dianisidine
1,2-Dibromo-3-chloropropane
1,2-Dibromoethane (Ethylene dibromide)
3,3'-Dichlorobenzidine
Salts of 3,3'-dichlorobenzidine
1.2-Dichloroethane (Ethylene dichloride)
2,2'-Dichloro-4,4' methylenedianiline (MbOCA)
1,3-Dichloro-2-propanol
Diethyl sulphate
Dimethylcarbamoyl chloride
NN-Dimethylhydrazine
Dimethylnitrosamine

Dimethyl sulphate
Distillate aromatic extracts
Ethylene oxide
1,2-Epoxypropane (Proplyene oxide)
Hexamethylphosphoric triamide
2-Methylazridine
Methyl-ONN-azoxymethyl acetate (Methyl azoxy methyl acetate)
1-Methyl-3-nitro-1-nitrosoguanidine
2-Naphthylamine
Salts of 2-Naphthylamine
5-Nitroacenaphthene
4-Nitrobiphenyl
2-Nitronaphthalene
2-Nitropropane
Ortho-toluidine
1,3-Propanesultone
3-Propaneolide (Propiolactone)
Strontium chromate
Styrene oxide
o-Tolidine
Salts of o-Tolidine
Vinyl chloride (Chloroethylene)
Zinc chromates (including zinc potassium chromate)

[EH 40/94]. [*CHIP Regulations 1993, Reg 5*].

Defence

9.38   It is a defence that an accused took all reasonable precautions and exercised all due diligence to avoid commission of the offence. [*Reg 16*].

Respiratory sensitisers

9.39   A respiratory sensitiser is a substance which can cause the respiratory system to develop a condition liable to make it over-react – sensitisation – if the substance is inhaled again; as well as causing serious chronic diseases, such as asthma and farmer's lung (see 31.42 OCCUPATIONAL HEALTH). Significantly, since sensitisation affects only a minority of workers (or categories of workers), control can be difficult if not elusive, principally because employers may often not recognise the health hazard when present. Particular culprits are allergens and isocyanates, but not untypical are certain anhydrides, reactive dyes and platinum salts. Industries potentially at risk are polyurethane manufacture, food packaging, adhesives, plastics, resins, textile processes and platinum refining. Sensitisation can also occur from nickel in the plating industry, henna in hairdressing, hardwood dust in woodworking and furniture making, as well as in pharmaceutical manufacture, enzyme preparations and foodstuffs – such as egg proteins in food processing and crustaceans in sea-food processing.

In order to comply with *COSHH Regulations*, employers should prevent exposure of sensitive employees to respiratory sensitisers but, if this is not reasonably practicable, control it. This involves both formal assessment of risks and inventory of necessary control measures as well as provision of adequate information and training. Sensitised employees should be medically advised about the sort of work they can do without further risk to health.

Control of lead at work – Control of Lead at Work Regulations 1980 (SI 1980 No 1248)

9.40   Approximately 10,000 workers are exposed significantly to lead through occupation. Many processes can lead to lead poisoning, most commonly lead smelting, melting and burning, vitreous enamelling on glass and metal, pottery glazing, manufacture of lead compounds and accumulators, painting, plumbing, soldering and rubber production. The long-standing industry-by-industry regulations (going back to the turn of the century) applicable to lead, have largely been superseded by the current *Control of Lead at Work Regulations 1980* and accompanying code of practice. These regulations reflect a new approach to the problem of exposure of employees to lead, in that employers have to ensure that employees under threat of significant exposure are under surveillance by an Employment Medical Adviser or appointed doctor, or, alternatively, if either of the latter so certify should not be employed on such work, or only on conditions mentioned in the certificate.

Statutory requirements

(A) Duties of employers

9.41   Employers must:

(i)   assess the nature and degree of exposure of employees to lead, where any work may expose persons to lead [*Reg 4(1)*];

(ii)   provide controls through plant, materials, processes (as distinct from provision of personal protective equipment) over exposure of employees to lead [*Reg 6*];

(iii) provide employees with adequate information, instruction and training regarding the dangers of lead [*Reg 5*];

(iv)   provide employees, liable to exposure from airborne lead, with respiratory protective equipment, unless control strategies are adequate, which must comply with EC requirements [*Reg 7; Personal Protective Equipment (EC Directive) Regulations 1992 (SI 1992 No 3139)*];

(v)   provide employees with suitable personal protective clothing which must comply with EC requirements [*Reg 8; Personal Protective Equipment (EC Directive) Regulations 1992 (SI 1992 No 3139)*];

(vi)   prevent the spread of contamination of lead from the workplace [*Reg 12*];

(vii) ensure that respiratory equipment or protective clothing is properly used as well as any other control measure [*Reg 13*];

A wife who suffers lead poisoning, as a result of cleaning an employee's overalls, may have an action against the employer, but her illness must be foreseeable (*Hewett v Alf Brown's Transport Ltd* – see further 15.1 EMPLOYERS' DUTIES and 36.1 PERSONAL PROTECTIVE EQUIPMENT).

(viii) ensure that employees do not eat, drink or smoke in a place liable to be contaminated [*Reg 10(1)*];

(ix)   provide employees, liable to exposure, with

(*a*)   adequate washing facilities,

(*b*)   adequate changing facilities,

    (*c*)   adequate storage facilities for protective clothing and personal clothing not worn during working hours

[*Reg 9*];

  (x) ensure cleanliness of the work place, premises, plant, respiratory equipment and protective clothing [*Reg 11*];

  (xi) maintain control measures, respiratory protective equipment and protective clothing in an efficient state and good repair [*Reg 14*];

  (xii) provide adequate monitoring procedures to measure concentrations of lead, unless exposure is not significant; and measure concentrations [*Reg 15*];

  (xiii) ensure that any employees exposed are under medical surveillance by an Employment Medical Adviser or appointed doctor [*Reg 16*].

(*B*) *Duties of employees*

Employees must

  (i) prevent the spread of contamination of lead from the workplace [*Reg 12*];

  (ii) make full and proper use of control measures, respiratory protective equipment and protective clothing, report defects and return the equipment/clothing to its accommodation after use [*Reg 13*];

  (iii) not eat, drink or smoke in a place liable to be contaminated by lead [*Reg 10(2)*].

Failure to comply with these requirements could lead to prosecution and possibly job dismissal, or, in cases of injury, reduction in compensation (see further Chapter 14 'Employees' Duties').

Radioactive substances

9.42   Radiation is energy released variously as gamma rays, X-rays, visible light, infra-red and ultraviolet light and microwaves, in the form of waves or particles. The length and frequency of waves (the electromagnetic spectrum) is determined by the quantity of energy released by an atom. It is inherently harmful to people but has also been indispensable in the treatment of certain illnesses and has important industrial uses, such as lasers and welding. Radiation can be natural or of artificial origin; an example of the former is a gamma ray, of the latter an x-ray, such as is used in hospitals, clinics and dental practices. The main danger associated with exposure to radiation is cancer, with exposure to natural radiation being less controllable. To date, however, radiation workers are on par with textile and food workers in a relatively safe industry – 1 in 57,000 deaths per year (HSE statistics 1982).

There are two main kinds of radiation, namely, (*a*) ionising radiations, which are potentially more dangerous (ion – Greek – charged atom) as producing a chemical effect, and (*b*) non-ionising radiations, that is, sources lacking the energy to shatter or ionise atoms. Occupationally, the main example of ionising radiation is an x-ray; whilst examples of non-ionising radiations, in the form of visible, ultraviolet and infra-red light, microwave heat and radio frequency, characterise industries as various as textiles, furniture, paper, automotive, rubber, plastics, construction, communications and power. Legislation has grafted itself onto the distinction between ionising and non-ionising radiations, the former being controlled currently by the *Ionising Radiations Regulations 1985*, whilst the latter are the subject of a draft EC directive on Physical Agents.

Effect of radiation exposure

(a) Ionising radiations

9.43   Ionising radiations cause tissue damage and the extent of tissue reaction depends on the density of ionisation in the path of radiation – a linear energy transfer (LET). Direct action of radiation on cells can cause cell death or induce mutation. Health effects of radiation can be genetic or somatic, the former affecting offspring, the latter the irradiated individual. Somatic effects take the form of early or late responses, the latter sometimes resulting in induction of malignant disease. Here there may be a latency of several decades between irradiation and tumour appearance.

Workers in hospitals, medical establishments, dental departments, laboratory staff and university researchers are vulnerable to hazards from ionising radiations. Radiation hazards can be emitted from two kinds of sources (*a*) a sealed source, and (*b*) an unsealed source. With the former, a sealed source, the source is contained so that the radioactive material cannot be released, e.g. an X-ray machine. Such radioactive material is usually solid, whereas unsealed sources take the form of gases, liquids or particulates and, because they are unsealed, entry into the body is fairly easy.

(b) Non-ionising radiations

Non-ionising radiations – such as lasers used in welding and cutting, ultraviolet radiation associated with arc welding and infra-red radiation emitted by radiant fires – particularly threaten the eye. Laser beams can cause blindness and exposure to ultraviolet radiation 'arc eye', if goggles or protective glasses are not worn.

Statutory requirements relating to radiation safety

Ionising radiations – the Ionising Radiations Regulations 1985 (SI 1985 No 1333)

(A) Duties of employers

9.44   (1)   Not to undertake for the first time work with ionising radiation (except in the case of exposure to the short-lived daughters of radon 222 – where notification after commencement of work is sufficient), unless at least 28 days prior to commencement of work, he

    (*a*)   has notified HSE of the intention to carry out such work;

    (*b*)   has supplied the following particulars:

        (i)   name/address of employer;

        (ii)   address of premises where work is to be carried out;

        (iii)   nature of business;

        (iv)   on type of radiation, e.g. sealed source, unsealed radioactive substance, radiation generator, atmosphere containing the short-lived daughters of radon 222;

        (v)   whether any source is to be used at other premises;

        (vi)   dates of notification and commencement of work.

[*Reg 5(2), 4 Sch*].

There are certain exceptions to the general duty to notify, e.g. nuclear installations, radioactive substances having an activity concentration of more than 100 Bqg^{-1}. Material changes in work activity have to be notified, though not cessation, except where (*a*) the site has been or is to be vacated, and (*b*) the work involves a radioactive substance other than a radioactive substance solely in the form of a sealed source.

Defence to notification requirement

It is a defence for a person to prove that

(*a*)   he neither knew nor had reasonable cause to believe that he had undertaken (or might be required to undertake) work with ionising radiation, and

(*b*)   where he had discovered that he had undertaken (or was undertaking) work with ionising radiation, he had forthwith notified HSE of the necessary details.

[*Reg 5*].

(2)   To restrict, so far as is reasonably practicable (for the meaning of this expression, see Chapter 15 'Employers' Duties'), the exposure of employees, and other persons foreseeably affected, to ionising radiations. [*Reg 6(1)*]; this is to be done preferably by engineering controls and shielding and ventilation containment of radioactive substances; warning devices and safety features are only ancillary protection. [*Reg 6(2)*].

(3)   To provide employees and others (e.g. outside maintenance workers) with adequate and suitable personal protective equipment. [*Reg 6(3)*].

(4)   To prevent any radioactive substance, in the form of a sealed source (see 9.43 above) from being held in the hand or manipulated directly by hand, unless the instantaneous dose rate to the skin of the hand is less than 75 μSvh^{-1}. [*Reg 6(5)*].

(5)   So far as is reasonably practicable, to prevent any unsealed radioactive substance (or article containing a radioactive substance) from being held in the hand or directly manipulated by hand. [*Reg 6(5)*].

(6)   To ensure that employees (and others foreseeably affected) are not exposed to dose limitations of ionising radiations greater than the following:

(*a*)   for employees of 18 or over   50

(*b*)   for trainees under 18   15

(*c*)   for any other person (e.g. member of the public)   5

[*Reg 7, 1 Sch*].

(7)   To designate as *controlled areas* any area where doses are likely to exceed 30% of any dose limit for employees aged 18 or more [*Reg 8(1)*] (controlled area).

(8)   To designate as a *supervised area* any area (not being a controlled area) where any person is likely to be exposed to more than 30% of ionising radiations than he would be exposed to in a controlled area. [*Reg 8(2)*] (supervised area).

(9)   Not to permit employees (or others) to enter or remain in a controlled area, unless the employee (or other person)

(*a*)   is a classified person (see (10) below);

217

(*b*)   enters or remains in the area under a written system of work preventing:

    (i)   an employee of 18 or more from receiving a dose of ionising radiations more than 30% of any relevant dose limit (see (6) above),

    (ii)   any other person from receiving a dose of ionising radiations greater than the statutory dose limit (see (6) above).

[*Reg 8(6)*] (permit to work system).

(10)   In the case of employees of 18 or over, who are likely to receive a dose of ionising radiations greater than 30% of any relevant dose limit, to designate them as '*classified persons*'. [*Reg 9(1)*] (classified persons).

No such designation may be made, however, unless the medical adviser or appointed doctor has certified in the health record that in his professional opinion a person is fit to be classified. [*Reg 9(3)*]. He must also inform the employees of relevant health hazards, precautions to be taken and the importance of complying with medical and technical requirements. He must also provide the employees with appropriate training in radiation protection. [*Reg 12(c)*].

(11)   To appoint qualified persons as radiation protection advisers where

(*a*)   any employees are exposed to an instantaneous dose rate of more than $7.5 \ \mu Svh^{-1}$ and provide them with adequate information and facilities [*Reg 10(5)*]; or

(*b*)   a controlled area has been designated (see (7) above)

[*Reg 10(1)*] (radiation protection advisers).

(12)   In the case of classified persons, to ensure that all significant doses of ionising radiations received are assessed (preferably by use of personal dosemeters), and that health records of (*a*) classified persons and (*b*) employees who have been overexposed, are kept for at least 50 years. [*Reg 13(2)(3)*] and to send to the Executive within three months of the end of each calendar year or other agreed period summaries of all dose records for the year.

(13)   To control radioactive substances (see 9.46 below).

(14)   To assess radiation hazards to employees and the general public and to prepare a contingency plan in order to minimise exposure (see below).

(15)   In the case (mainly) of

(*a*)   classified persons;

(*b*)   employees who have received overexposure (but are not classified persons);

(*c*)   employees engaged in work with ionising radiation on conditions imposed by an employment medical adviser (see above) or appointed doctor;

    (i)   to provide adequate medical surveillance, and

    (ii)   to have and maintain a health record (or copy) for at least fifty years from the date of the last entry and make it available to the Employment Medical Adviser or appointed doctor.

[*Reg 16(1)–(3) and (9)*].

(B) Duties of employees

9.45 Employees are required to

(1) (in the case of women), inform the employer as soon as they discover that they are pregnant [*Reg 12(d)*];

(2) present themselves for medical examination and tests during working hours (for medical surveillance purposes) (see above) [*Reg 16(7)*];

(3) not to expose themselves (or any other persons) to ionising radiation more than is reasonably necessary for carrying out the work [*Reg 6(4)(a)*];

(4) exercise reasonable care while working [*Reg 6(4)(a)*];

(5) make full and proper use of personal protective equipment [*Reg 6(4)(b)*];

(6) report to the employer any defects in personal protective equipment [*Reg 6(4)(c)*];

(7) not to eat, drink or smoke, take snuff or apply cosmetics in a controlled area, but can drink from a drinking fountain, if the water is not contaminated [*Reg 6(6)*];

(8) knowingly expose himself (or any other person) to ionising radiation to an extent greater than is necessary for work purposes.

(For further information relating to employees' failure to take care for their own health and safety and the possible legal consequences, see Chapter 14 'Employees' Duties'.)

Designation of controlled areas

(a) External radiation

9.46 Employers must designate as a *controlled area*, any area in which the instantaneous dose rate exceeds (or is likely to do so) $7.5 \mu Svh^{-1}$ but, where the dose rate does not exceed that amount, this designation need not be made because a radioactive substance is in the area (and certain other conditions are satisfied which are beyond the scope of this publication).

[*6 Sch*].

(b) Internal radiation

Employers must designate as a *controlled area* any area where either:

(i) the air concentration of radionuclide, averaged over any 8-hour working period, exceeds (or is likely to do so) the concentration specified for that radionuclide in Column 3 of *Schedule 2*; or

(ii) the level of contamination of any surface by a radionuclide, as determined by a suitable method, exceeds (or is likely to do so) the contamination level for that radionuclide specified in Column 4 of *Schedule 2*.

An area is not required to be designated as a *controlled area* if the only potential or actual source of contamination is a radioactive substance present in the area and the total activity of the radionuclide in the area does not exceed the quantity for that radionuclide specified in Column 5 of *Schedule 2*.

[*6 Sch*].

(c) Short-lived daughters of radon 222

Employers must designate as a *controlled area* any area in which the concentration in the air of short-lived daughters of radon 222, averaged over an 8-hour working period, exceeds 2×10^{-6} Jm^{-3} (~0.1 working levels).

Control of radioactive substances

9.47   Control over radioactive substances must be exercised as follows:

(a)   so far as reasonably practicable, the substance should be in the form of a sealed source (see 9.43 above); the design, construction and maintenance of articles containing and embodying radioactive substances, must prevent leakage [*Reg 18(1)(2)*];

(b)   records relating to quantity and location of radioactive substances, should be kept for at least two years [*Reg 19*];

(c)   radioactive substances must be kept in suitable receptacles in a suitable store [*Reg 20*]; during transportation, radioactive substances must be kept in a suitably labelled receptacle [*Reg 21*].

Assessments and notifications

9.48   (1)   Work must not be carried out with ionising radiations, unless employers have first made an assessment identifying the nature and magnitude of radiation hazards to (*a*) employees and (*b*) the general public. [*Reg 25*].

(2)   Where the assessment reveals that employees or the general public are likely to receive a dose of ionising radiations above the statutory dose limit (see 9.44(6) above) the employer must prepare a contingency plan in order to minimise exposure. [*Reg 27*].

(3)   Where overexposure to radiation has already taken place, the employer must carry out an investigation to determine whether there are circumstances which show beyond reasonable doubt that no overexposure could have occurred. Failing this, he must notify

(a)   the HSE;

(b)   the employee's employer;

(c)   in the case of his own employee, an employment medical adviser.

[*Reg 29*].

Penalties

Penalties under the *Ionising Radiations Regulations 1985* are as in *HSWA* (see further Chapter 17 'Enforcement').

Persons undergoing medical examinations

9.49   In the interest of persons (or patients) undergoing medical examination, employers must ensure that their employees, carrying out such examinations with ionising radiation, are qualified and can produce a certificate to that effect. Employers must also retain a record of their training. [*Ionising Radiation (Protection of Persons Undergoing Medical Examination or Treatment) Regulations 1988 (SI 1988 No 778)*].

Ionising Radiations (Outside Workers) Regulations 1993 (SI 1993 No 2379)

9.50 Regulations, namely, the *Ionising Radiations (Outside Workers) Regulations 1993 (SI 1993 No 2379)* affecting the health and safety of outside workers, that is, those who work in an EC country other than their own and who work in a controlled area will come into force on 1 January 1994. The outside employer will have to provide those of his employees who may be exposed to radiation in a controlled area with a uniquely identified radiation passbook containing prescribed particulars. The person in charge of the works on site (the operator) will have to ensure that the employee is able to undertake the work safely, that he is suitably monitored and that the estimated radiation doses are entered in the radiation passbook.

The outside undertaking will also have to obtain information about the risks and estimated doses from the operator and will have to arrange instruction and training for the employees.

Duties of outside contractors

9.51 Outside contractors must ascertain what radiation hazards outside workers will be exposed to and accordingly send only workers who are suitable. Outside workers must have received the necessary information and training regarding risks and an estimate must be made of the dose receivable by the worker. [*Reg 4*]. Following this, the worker must be issued with an individual radiation passbook and a record kept of its issue. This should contain

(*a*)   individual serial number;

(*b*)   date of issue;

(*c*)   name/address of outside contractor, signed by authorised person;

(*d*)   name, date, birth, gender of outside worker;

(*e*)   date of last medical review of outside worker and his classification;

(*f*)   name of organisation where work is undertaken, period of assignment, latest dose assessment prior to assignment and estimated dose information.

[*Reg 5; Schedule*].

Duties of operators

9.52 Operators of organisations receiving outside workers must disclose to outside contractors details relating to radiological and other risks involved; and ensure, by reference to the passbook, that workers have received the necessary training, are medically fit and know how to use personal protective equipment. Upon completion of work, operators must enter details of the dose received by the outside worker in the passbook. (This may not be necessary in the case of short duration visits.) [*Reg 6*]. Where overexposure has occurred, the operator must carry out an investigation to show that there are no circumstances in which overexposure could have occurred; failing this, the operator must notify

(i)   the HSE;

(ii)   the outside worker's employer.

[*Ionising Radiations Regulations 1985, Reg 29*].

Duties of outside workers

9.53   Outside workers must take reasonable care of passbooks, must not falsify information in it, must return the passbook on leaving their employment and make it available to the operator. [*Reg 7*].

Defence

9.54   It is a defence for outside contractors to show that breach of duty arose because the *operator* did not fulfil a term of a written contract entered into by him; and for an operator to show that an *outside* contractor failed to fulfil such term. [*Reg 8*].

Non-ionising radiations

9.55   Regulation for both optical and non-optical radiation is proposed as follows:

(i)   *Optical radiation* (i.e. infra-red, visible and ultraviolet light) – threshold level to be *half* the ceiling value (the ceiling value equating with exposure limits recommended by the American Congress of Governmental Industrial Hygienists (ACGIH)). At threshold value, workers

(a)   must be given adequate information and training;

(b)   must be supplied with personal protective equipment, on request;

(c)   are entitled to health surveillance.

At ceiling level

(a)   employers would have to establish a regime of control strategies – copies being sent to safety representatives;

(b)   personal protective equipment would have to be used;

(c)   hazard areas would have to be designated; and

(d)   systematic health surveillance would have to be carried out.

(ii)   *Non-optical radiation* (electric and magnetic fields with frequencies up to 300 GHz) – threshold level to be *one-fifth* of the ceiling level, ceiling values of electric currents and specific absorption rate of energy in the human body as well as contact current being tabulated. In addition, there are three action levels. At first action level, employers must

(a)   carry out a risk assessment;

(b)   provide workers with information and training;

(c)   provide workers with personal protective equipment, on request (in the case of electric fields).

At second action level (1.6 times the value of fields serving as first action levels), employers will have to

(a)   establish a regime of control strategies;

(b)   designate hazard areas, restricting access;

(c)   train operators and check their competence.

At third action level (three times the value of first action level) offending work activities must be notified to HSE. Equipment producing this level will have to be marked.

Radioactive substances and the environment – Radioactive Substances Act 1993

9.56   Radioactive material – defined mainly as actinium, lead, polonium, protoactinium, radium, radon, thorium and uranium – must not be kept on premises, or permitted or caused to be kept, for trade purposes, unless the premises are registered, following application to the Chief Radiation Inspector [*Sec 6*], who must copy same to all interested local authorities. The Chief Inspector can grant or refuse such application, the former conditionally or unconditionally. [*Sec 7*]. Following registration (and/or authorisation for disposal purposes (see 9.57 below)), copies of registration/authorisation documents must be posted at the premises in a prominent position so as to be accessible to employees and members of the public. [*Sec 19*]. On registration, copies of registration documents must be circulated to all interested local authorities, though there is an exemption from registration during currency of a nuclear site licence. [*Secs 7, 8*]. Copies of registration and authorisation documents must be made available for inspection by the general public at all reasonable times on payment of a reasonable fee; and they are entitled to take copies. [*Sec 39*]. Moreover, documentation concerning site and disposal authorisation must be retained, if necessary, for production to an inspector on demand. [*Sec 20*]. Registration requirement extends to use of mobile radioactive apparatus, such as might be used in testing or measuring radioactive substances or emitting them into the environment. [*Sec 9*]. In the case of registration or authorisation (for disposal) being refused, cancelled or revoked, an aggrieved operator can appeal directly to the Secretary of State [*Sec 26*]; this also applies where he wishes to appeal against enforcement and/or prohibition notices (see 9.58 'Enforcement' below).

Disposal of radioactive waste

9.57   Disposal of radioactive waste can be a contentious matter and for that reason the *Radioactive Substances Act 1993* prohibits disposal of radioactive waste from trade premises – save in the case of waste from clocks and watches [*Sec 15*] – except in accordance with authorisation granted by the Chief Radiation Inspector [*Secs 13, 14*]. Such authorisation can be revoked or varied at any time, with or without conditions. In some cases, prior to grant of authorisation, consultation with public and local authorities may be necessary. [*Sec 18*].

Enforcement

9.58   Failure to comply with a registration or authorisation, or with one or more of its conditions can lead to service of an enforcement notice against an offender – a copy being sent to interested local authorities. [*Sec 21*]. However, where retention, use, accumulation or disposal of radioactive material or apparatus – even in furtherance of registration or more particularly disposal – involves *imminent* risk of environmental pollution or harm to human health, the offending operator can be served with a prohibition notice. [*Sec 22*]. The purpose of an enforcement notice is remedial; that of a prohibition notice to stop the offending activity (see further 17.6 ENFORCEMENT). Inspectors (who are indemnified against any subsequent criminal and civil liability) are empowered to enter premises on which there are, or are suspected to be, radioactive substances, at all reasonable times, to carry out tests, require co-operation and assistance on the part of occupiers and to compel occupiers to leave premises undisturbed. [*Sec 31*].

Offences and penalties

Offences are mainly concerned with (*a*) registration and disposal authorisation, (*b*) display of documentation concerning registration and disposal authorisation and (*c*) retention of documentation concerning site suitability and disposal. More particularly:

(*a*)   Violation of registration and/or authorisation requirements (or attaching conditions) carries

   (i)   on summary conviction, a maximum fine of £20,000 or up to six months' imprisonment (or both);

   (ii)   on conviction on indictment, an indefinite fine, or up to five years' imprisonment (or both).

   [*Sec 32*].

(*b*)   Failure to display the necessary documents (relating to registration and authorisation) carries

   (i)   on summary conviction, a maximum fine of £5,000;

   (ii)   on conviction on indictment, an indefinite fine.

   [*Sec 33(1)*].

(*c*)   Failure to retain site and disposal documents carries

   (i)   on summary conviction, a maximum fine of £5,000;

   (ii)   on conviction on indictment, an indefinite fine.

   [*Sec 33(2)*].

Companies and other bodies corporate, whether nationalised or not, are subject to the same penalties as individual functional directors, managers and secretaries found guilty of consent, connivance or neglect. So, too, 'other persons', who are not the 'alter ego' of the organisation and generally lower down the corporate tree [*Secs 36, 37*] (see further 17.34 ENFORCEMENT). The *Radioactive Substances Act 1993* binds the Crown, although the latter cannot be liable in any criminal proceedings, with the exception of Crown employees. [*Sec 42*].

Dangerous pathogens

9.59   The *Health and Safety (Dangerous Pathogens) Regulations 1981 (SI 1981 No 1011)* – to be replaced by the *COSHH Amendment Regulations*, implementing the Biological Agents Directive (see 9.31 above) – prohibit the keeping, handling and transportation of a listed pathogen (see below for meaning), unless the HSE has been notified at least 30 days in advance [*Reg 3(1)*]; nor must a diagnostic service be carried out involving a listed pathogen, unless similar notice has been given [*Reg 4(1)*].

Listed pathogens

Crimean haemorrhagic fever virus (Congo)
Ebola virus
Junin haemorrhagic fever virus
Lassa fever virus
Machupo haemorrhagic fever virus
Marburg virus
Rabies virus
Simian herpes B virus
Smallpox virus
Venezuelan equine encephalitic virus.

Controls over explosives at work

(A) Classification and labelling of explosives

9.60 Classification and labelling of explosives is governed by the *Classification and Labelling of Explosives Regulations 1983 (SI 1983 No 1140)*. Explosive articles and substances fall into one of five categories, namely, those with

		division
(i)	mass explosion hazard	1.1
(ii)	projection hazard (but not mass explosion hazard)	1.2
(iii)	fire hazard and either	1.3

     (*a*)   minor blast hazard, or

     (*b*)   minor projection hazard, or

     (*c*)   both

     (but not mass explosion hazard)

(iv)	no significant hazard	1.4
(v)	very insensitive substances with mass explosion hazard	1.5

Explosive articles/substances must not be conveyed, kept or supplied, unless

(*a*) they have been classified according to composition, and in the form and packaging necessary, and

(*b*) they and their packaging are correctly labelled.

[*Classification and Labelling of Explosives Regulations 1983, Reg 3*].

Exceptions

(i) explosives being manufactured/tested [*Reg 4(2)*];

(ii) fireworks, small arms ammunition kept by a retailer, or so obtained [*Reg 4(3)*].

Moreover, both the explosives themselves and their inner and outer packagings must be correctly labelled.

Labelling requirements of explosives

9.61 (*a*) Packaged explosives of divisions 1.1, 1.2 and 1.3 must be labelled as follows:

[*3 Sch 1*].

(*b*)   Packaged explosives of divisions 1.4 and 1.5 as follows:

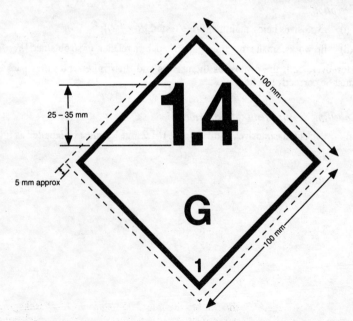

[*3 Sch 4*].

The same labelling requirements apply to unpackaged explosives, except that the hazard classification code is that for the article when not packaged, e.g. flammable; in the case of 'fireworks', the packaging must be labelled 'Firework'.

[*3 Sch 7*].

Labelling of packaging

9.62   The following are the main

(*a*)   explosive *articles* in respect of which outer packaging must be labelled:

    (i)   explosive articles (not specified),

    (ii)   boosters without detonator,

    (iii)   demolition charges,

    (iv)   detonating cord,

    (v)   igniter cord,

    (vi)   electric detonator,

    (vii)   non-electric detonator,

    (viii)   igniter fuse,

    (ix)   safety fuse,

    (x)   detonating fuse,

    (xi)   igniters,

    (xii)   sounding devices

[*Reg 8(1), 4 Sch*];

(*b*)   explosive *substances*, in respect of which both inner and outer packaging must be labelled:

barium azide
gunpowder
diazodinititrophenol (wetted)
blasting explosives
lead azide (wetted)
mercury fulminate
nitrocellulose
nitroglycerin
nitrostarch
pentolite
powder cake
explosive samples
explosive substances (not specified)
trinitrotoluene (TNT)
tritonal

[*Reg 8(1)(2), 5 Sch*].

In all cases, labelling should be durable and fixed on the packaging and article/substance or on a piece of paper securely fixed to the packaging and article/substance. [*Reg 10*].

Defence

9.63   It is a defence that a person charged took all reasonable precautions *and* exercised all due diligence to comply. [*Reg 12*]. Generally speaking, this 'due diligence' defence has not been invoked with much success (see Chapter 40 'Offices').

(B) Control of explosives at work (enforcement agency: the police)

9.64   Control of explosives at work is governed by the *Control of Explosives Regulations 1991 (SI 1991 No 1531)*.

Duties of employers

With the exception of *Schedule 1* explosives (see 'Exempt explosives' below), before an employer can acquire and keep explosives, he must

(*a*)   possess a valid explosives certificate to the effect that he is a fit person (i.e. free from criminal conviction);

(*b*)   acquire and keep

   (i)   no more than the specified quantity, and

   (ii)   only specified explosives

      (*a*)   in a specified place, and

      (*b*)   for specified purposes

   [*Reg 7*].

(*c*)   keep up-to-date records of the explosives and their source for at least three years, which must be made available for inspection by a police officer [*Reg 12, 3 Sch*];

(*d*)   report the loss of any explosive [*Reg 13*];

and he must not

(*e*)   transfer explosives, unless the transferee is in possession of a valid explosives licence and is a fit person [*Reg 8*].

Certificate for the purposes of acquiring/keeping explosives

9.65   FORM OF EXPLOSIVES CERTIFICATE

HEALTH AND SAFETY AT WORK ETC. ACT 1974
CONTROL OF EXPLOSIVES REGULATIONS 1991

CERTIFICATE TO *ACQUIRE/ACQUIRE AND KEEP EXPLOSIVES

1. I the undersigned *being/being duly authorised by the chief officer of police for ....police force, do hereby certify that (name)....................................of (address) ....is a fit person to *acquire/acquire and keep explosives in accordance with this certificate.

Alternative A—acquisition only

2. The maximum amount of explosives acquired on any one occasion shall not exceed ....

3. The only explosives which may be acquired are those of the following descriptions, namely ....

4. Explosives may only be acquired for the purpose(s) of ....

5. This certificate shall be valid until ....(maximum one year), unless notice of revocation by or on behalf of the chief officer of police has been served on the certificate holder at an earlier date.

(Notes:
(a) If this certificate relates to acquisition only, this section must be completed in accordance with these Notes and "alternative B" deleted.
(b) Each of paragraphs 2, 3 and 4 may be completed or deleted.
(c) Paragraph 5 must be completed.)

Alternative B—acquisition and keeping

2. The explosives may only be kept at the

*licensed factory
*licensed magazine
*registered premises   at ....
*store
*premises occupied by the Secretary of State
*premises used for keeping for private use

3. The only explosives which may be acquired or kept are those of the following descriptions, namely ....

4. The amount of explosives kept may not exceed the amount which may lawfully be kept at the said premises.

5. This certificate shall be valid until ....(maximum three years), unless notice of revocation by or on behalf of the chief officer of police has been served on the certificate holder at an earlier date.

(Notes:
(a) If this certificate relates to acquisition and keeping, this section must be completed in accordance with these Notes and "alternative A" deleted.
(b) In paragraph 2 all but one of the alternatives marked with a * must be deleted. No address should be inserted if the explosives are to be kept at premises used for keeping for private use. An address must be inserted in all other cases.
(c) If paragraph 2 allows explosives to be kept at a store, registered premises or premises used for keeping for private use paragraph 3 must be completed. If paragraph 2 refers to keeping explosives at premises used for keeping for private use, the description of explosives in paragraph 3 must not include any explosives other than one or more of those mentioned in regulation 10(1) of the Regulations.
(d) Paragraph 4 needs no change.
(e) Paragraph 5 must be completed.)

Signed..

Date ....

* Delete as applicable

Placing of explosives on the market

9.66 The impending *Placing on the Market and Supervision of Transfers of Explosives Regulations* require that explosives, placed on the market, present a minimal risk to human life and health and to property. Each explosive must have the performance characteristic specified by the manufacturer and be disposable in such a way as not to damage the environment.

Appendix A

Maximum exposure limits and occupational exposure standards – COSHH Regulations

(a) Maximum exposure limits

A maximum exposure limit (MEL) is the maximum concentration of a substance, averaged over a reference period, to which employees may be exposed, e.g. by inhalation, as specified in *Schedule 2* of the *Control of Substances Hazardous to Health (Amendment) Regulations 1992* (as amended). The combined effect of *Regs 7(4)* and *16* is to require all employers to take reasonable precautions not to exceed MELs. Thus, in the case of substances with an 8-hour long-term reference period (unless statutory assessment shows that the level of exposure is unlikely to exceed MEL), in order to comply, an employer should carry out a monitoring programme (in accordance with *Reg 10*) as proof that MEL is not *normally* exceeded. Alternatively, where a substance has a short-term MEL (e.g. 10 minutes to be increased to 15 minutes as from 1 January 1994), brief exposure is likely to have acute effects. Here short-term exposure limits should *never* be exceeded.

LIST OF SUBSTANCES ASSIGNED TO MAXIMUM EXPOSURE LIMITS

Current maximum exposure limits (MELs) are specified in the *Control of Substances Hazardous to Health (Amendment) Regulations 1991 (SI 1991 No 2431)* and the *Control of Substances Hazardous to Health (Amendment) Regulations 1992 (SI 1992 No 2382)*, as follows:

		Reference periods			
		Long-term maximum exposure limit (8-hour TWA reference period)		Short-term maximum exposure limit (10-minute reference period)	
Substance	Formula	ppm	mg m^{-3}	ppm	mg m^{-3}
Acrylamide	$CH_2{=}CHCONH_2$	—	0.3	—	—
Acrylonitrile	$CH_2{=}CHCN$	2	4	—	—
Arsenic & compounds except arsine (as As)	As	—	0.1	—	—
Asbestos (see 4.3 ASBESTOS)					
Benzene	C_6H_6	5	15	—	—
Bis(chloromethyl) ether	$ClCH_2OCH_2Cl$	0.001	0.005	—	—
Buta-1.3-diene	$CH_2{=}CHCH{=}CH_2$	10	22	—	—
2-Butoxyethanol	$C_4H_9OCH_2CH_2OH$	25	120	—	—
Cadmium & cadmium compounds, except cadmium oxide fume and cadmium sulphide pigments (as Cd)	Cd	—	0.05	—	—
Cadmium oxide fume (as Cd)	CdO	—	0.05	—	0.05
Cadmium sulphide pigments (respirable dust as Cd)	CdS	—	0.04	—	—
Carbon disulphide	CS_2	10	30	—	—
Chromium (VI) compounds (as Cr)	Cr	—	0.05	—	—
1,2-Dibromoethane (Ethylene dibromide)	$BrCH_2CH_2Br$	0.5	4	—	—
Dichloromethane	CH_2Cl_2	100	350	—	—

Substance	Formula	Reference periods			
		Long-term maximum exposure limit (8-hour TWA reference period)		Short-term maximum exposure limit (10-minute reference period)	
		ppm	mg m^{-3}	ppm	mg m^{-3}
2.2'-Dichloro–4.4'-methylene dianiline (MbOCA)	$CH_2(C_6H_3ClNH_2)_2$	—	0.005	—	—
2-Ethoxyethanol	$C_2H_5OCH_2CH_2OH$	10	37	—	—
2-Ethoxyethyl acetate	$C_2H_5OCH_2CH_2OOCCH_3$	10	54	—	—
Ethylene oxide	CH_2CH_2O	5	10	—	—
Formaldehyde	HCHO	2	2.5	2	2.5
Grain dust		—	10	—	—
Hydrogen cyanide	HCN	—	—	10	10
Isocyanates, all (as-NCO)		—	0.02	—	0.07
*Man-made mineral fibre		—	5	—	—
2-Methoxyethanol	$CH_3OCH_2CH_2OH$	5	16	—	—
2-Methoxyethyl acetate	$CH_3COOCH_2CH_2OCH_3$	5	24	—	—
Nickel and its inorganic compounds (except nickel carbonyl):	Ni	—	—	—	—
water-soluble nickel compounds (as Ni)		—	0.1	—	—
nickel and water-insoluble nickel compounds (as Ni)		—	0.5	—	—
Rubber process dust		—	8	—	—
† Rubber fume		—	0.6	—	—
Silica, respirable crystalline	SiO_2	—	0.4	—	—
Styrene	$C_6H_5CH=CH_2$	100	420	250	1050
1,1,1-Trichloroethane	CH_3CCl_3	350	1900	450	2450
Trichloroethylene	$CCl_2=CHCl$	100	535	150	802
‡ Vinyl chloride	$CH_2=CHCl$	7	—	—	—
Vinylidene chloride	$CH_2=CCl_2$	10	40	—	—
Wood dust (hard wood)		—	5	—	—

[*Control of Substances Hazardous to Health (Amendment) Regulations 1992 (SI 1992 No 2382), 2 Sch*].

As from 1 January 1994, short-term maximum exposure limit will increase to 15 minutes, applying additionally to:

Substance	Formula	Long-term maximum exposure limit (8-hour TWA reference period)		Short-term maximum exposure limit (10-minute reference period)	
		ppm	mg m^{-3}	ppm	mg m^{-3}
Acetaldehyde	CH_3CHO	25	45	50	90
Beryllium/compounds	Be	—	0.002	—	—
Cadmium/compounds (but not cadmium oxide fume/cadmium sulphide pigments)	Cd	—	0.025	—	—
Cadmium oxide fume	CdO	—	0.025	—	0.5
Cadmium sulphide/pigments	CdS	—	0.04	—	—
Cobalt	Co	—	0.1	—	—
1,2-Dichloroethane	$ClCH_2CH_2Cl$	5	20	—	—
Dichloromethane	CH_2Cl_2	100	350	300	1050

Substance	Formula	Long-term maximum exposure limit (8-hour TWA reference period)		Short-term maximum exposure limit (10-minute reference period)	
		ppm	mg m^{-3}	ppm	mg m^{-3}
1/-Chloro-2,3-epoxy-propane	OCH$_2$-CH-CH$_2$Cl	0.5	2	1.5	6
4,4'-Methylenedianiline	CH$_2$(C$_6$H$_4$NH$_2$)$_2$	0.01	0.08	—	—
2-Nitropropane	CH$_3$CH(No$_2$)CH$_3$	5	18	—	—
Rubber process dust		—	6	—	—

(b) Occupational exposure standards

An occupational exposure standard (OES), as approved by the HSC, is the concentration of a substance, daily exposure to which over a given period, is not, according to present knowledge, likely to have injurious effects on employees. Where a substance has been assigned an OES, employers should do what is reasonably practicable (see further Chapter 15 'Employers' Duties') to reduce exposure to that standard. Nevertheless, if exposure exceeds OES, control is still adequate if the employer has indicated why OES has been exceeded *and* is doing all that is reasonably practicable to comply with OES. In all cases, employers should endeavour to comply with good occupational hygiene criteria. (See further EH40/93.)

Appendix B

HOW CHIP WORKS

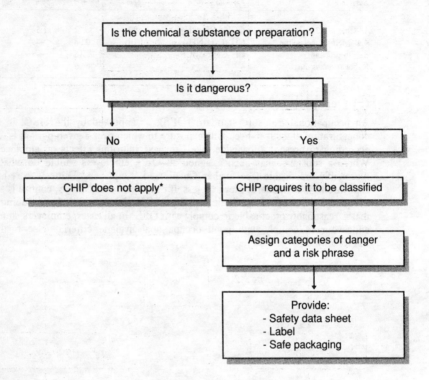

Is the chemical a substance or preparation?

Is it dangerous?

No

Yes

CHIP does not apply*

CHIP requires it to be classified

Assign categories of danger
and a risk phrase

Provide:
- Safety data sheet
- Label
- Safe packaging

* But see regulation 13 of CHIP for preparations which are special cases

HOW CLASSIFICATION WORKS

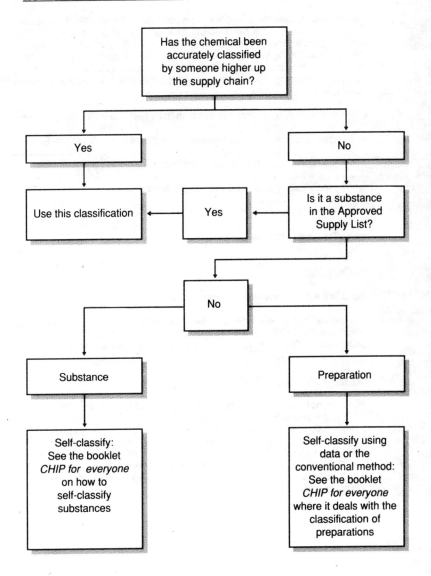

LABELLING

If a dangerous chemical is supplied in a package, the package must be labelled. You do not have to label the chemical if it is going through a pipe or is being supplied in bulk. The aim is to tell anyone handling the package or using the chemicals about the hazards and to give brief advice on suitable precautions. For workers, the label is a supplement to information provided by the employer, for others (including the general public) it is a major way of getting the information across.

CHIP specifies exactly what has to go on the label. The main elements are:

● the name, address and telephone number of a supplier in the EC;

● the name of the substance or the trade name if it is a preparation;

● the indication of danger and associated symbol;

● the risk phrases; and

● the safety phrases.

PACKAGING

Suppliers are responsible for getting the label right.

If you want to know what the law says about packaging, you will need to look at regulation 8 of CHIP. We think it is quite clear. Let us know if you do not understand it. Our address can be found at the end of the guide.

SO HOW DO I GET STARTED?

First, do not panic. If you already comply with CPL, you have until 1 September 1994 to get yourself sorted out to comply with CHIP. This is when the 12 month transition period between CPL and CHIP runs out. For packages of 25 litres or less, you may have another six months. However, we strongly advise you to get up to date as soon as you can. All the supply requirements stem from EC directives which are constantly being amended. More changes are on their way next year and more the year after. We will be keeping the guidance up to date and will try to make it easy for you.

METHANOL

Highly flammable

Toxic

200-659-6
EEC label

Toxic by inhalation and if swallowed
Keep out of reach of children
Keep container tightly closed
Keep away from sources of ignition
No smoking
Avoid contact with skin

Supplied by
Sykes, Warner and Foster Ltd
Rue de Hart, Derrickville
Brussels Belgium
Tel 000 1111 2222

Example of a supply label for a substance

AUNTIE MARY'S PATENT CLEANSER
Contains trichloretheylene

Harmful
1 litre

Possible risk of irreversible effects
Do not breathe vapour
Wear suitable protective clothing and gloves

Mixed by:
Sykes, Warner and Foster Formulations Ltd
Rond Point Mosselmans, Derrickville
Brussels, Belgium
Tel 000 1111 2222

Example of a supply label for a preparation

Supplied by HSE (071/243/6000) 'The complete idiot's guide to CHIP'

Appendix C

Classification, packaging and labelling of dangerous substances – Classification, Packaging and Labelling of Dangerous Substances Regulations 1984 (SI 1984 No 1244) (as amended by SI 1990 No 1255)

I   The *Classification, Packaging and Labelling of Dangerous Substances Regulations 1984 (SI 1984 No 1244)* as amended by *SI 1990 No 1255*, were introduced principally to extend statutory control, in the form of packaging and labelling requirements, to (*a*) conveyance in bulk by road of dangerous substances, and (*b*) supply of dangerous substances in the normal course of industry and commerce. For these purposes 'dangerous substances' are specifically those on the 'approved list', i.e. the list published by the Health and Safety Commission on 24 April 1990. [*Classification, Packaging and Labelling of Dangerous Substances (Amendment) Regulations 1990 (SI 1990 No 1255)*]. (There is a separate Road Tanker Approved List 1992 (see 10.3 DANGEROUS SUBSTANCES II).)

The 'approved list' consists of:

(*a*)   substances dangerous for commercial and industrial supply, e.g. white phosphorus;

(*b*)   substances dangerous for conveyance by road, e.g. petroleum fuel;

(Part 1A)

(*c*)   substances dangerous for conveyance by road not specified in Part 1A as dangerous for conveyance by road, e.g. liquid arsenical pesticides;

(*d*)   articles specified in Part 1C (of the approved list), e.g. firelighters, tear gas candles;

(*e*)   dangerous solvents, e.g. benzene.

[*Classification, Packaging and Labelling of Dangerous Substances Regulations 1984, Reg 4*].

Substances not covered by the regulations

II   The following substances are outside the scope of the regulations:

(*a*)   *When conveyed by road*:

(i)   radioactive substances (but these are covered by the new *Radioactive Material (Road Transport) Act 1991*, enabling transport inspectors to serve enforcement notices in respect of vehicles carrying radioactive packages, and, if necessary, to enter such vehicles or premises containing such vehicles; breach carries with it a maximum fine of £1,000 on summary conviction, and, on indictment, up to two years' imprisonment and/or an indefinite fine [*Sec 6*]);

(ii)   a substance in a tank container with a capacity of more than three cubic metres;

(iii)   a substance intended for use as a food (but not an 'additive', which is caught by the regulations);

(iv)   an animal feeding stuff;

(v)   a cosmetic;

        (vi)   a medicine;

      (vii)   a controlled drug;

    (viii)   a disease-producing micro-organism;

      (ix)   a sample taken by an enforcing authority, e.g. HSE.

    [Reg 3(1)].

(b)   *When supplied*:

        (i)   munitions;

       (ii)   a substance imported into the UK and which is in transit through the UK under customs control;

      (iii)   a gas compressed, liquefied or dissolved under pressure (but not a gas in an aerosol dispenser or a pesticide);

      (iv)   a substance: intended for export to a non-EC state; or intended for supply to an EC state which has not implemented these regulations;

       (v)   a pesticide (approved under the pesticides safety precaution scheme);

      (vi)   a substance transferred from one part of a factory or workplace to another part;

      (vii)   a new substance not yet fully tested but containing the warning 'Caution – substance not yet fully tested';

    (viii)   a fertiliser;

      (ix)   any substance to which *Reg 3(1)* (see (a) above) applies.

    [Reg 3(2)].

III   Certain methods of bulk conveyance are also outside the scope of the regulations; these include:

(a)   vehicles not used for work purposes;

(b)   vehicles conveying explosives (see 10.24 DANGEROUS SUBSTANCES II below);

(c)   substances being conveyed as part of an international transport operation;

(d)   substances packaged and labelled in accordance with the requirements of either

        (i)   the international maritime dangerous goods code, or

       (ii)   the report of the Department of Trade's Standing Advisory Committee on the carriage of dangerous goods in ships;

(e)   substances packaged and labelled in accordance with the technical instructions for the safe transport of dangerous goods by air;

(f)   petroleum spirit conveyed by road;

(g)   substances being conveyed by road in a vehicle used on public roads but only for the delivery of goods between private premises.

[Reg 3(3)].

The HSE can grant exemption in respect of dangerous substances or classes, so long as the health and safety of persons involved is not likely to be prejudiced. *[Reg 14]*.

Classification of dangerous substances

IV   (*a*)   *Substances dangerous for supply*. These are set out for reference in the Table below.

Table

Classification of dangerous substances (substances dangerous for supply)

Table of characteristic properties, indications of general nature of risk and symbols

1 Characteristic properties of the substance	2 Classification and indication of general nature of risk	3 Symbol
A substance which may explode under the effect of flame or which is more sensitive to shocks or friction than dinitrobenzene.	Explosive.	
A substance which gives rise to highly exothermic reaction when in contact with other substances, particularly flammable substances.	Oxidizing.	
A liquid having a flash point of less than 0 degrees Celsius and a boiling point of less than or equal to 35 degrees Celsius.	Extremely flammable.	
A substance which— (*a*) may become hot and finally catch fire in contact with air at ambient temperature without any application of energy; (*b*) is a solid and may readily catch fire after brief contact with a source of ignition and which continues to burn or to be consumed after removal of the source of ignition; (*c*) is gaseous and flammable in air at normal pressure; (*d*) in contact with water or damp air, evolves highly flammable gases in dangerous quantities; or (*e*) is a liquid having a flash point below 21 degrees Celsius.	Highly flammable.	

1	2	3
Characteristic properties of the substance	Classification and indication of general nature of risk	Symbol
A substance which is a liquid having a flash point equal to or greater than 21 degrees Celsius and less than or equal to 55 degrees Celsius, except a liquid which when tested at 55° in the manner described in Schedule 2 to the Highly Flammable Liquids and Liquefied Petroleum Gases Regulations 1972 (a) does not support combustion.	Flammable	No symbol required.
A substance which if it is inhaled or ingested or it penetrates the skin, may involve extremely serious acute or chronic health risks and even death.	Very toxic.	
A substance which if it is inhaled or ingested or it penetrates the skin, may involve serious acute or chronic health risks and even death.	Toxic.	
A substance which if it is inhaled or ingested or if it penetrates the skin, may involve limited health risks.	Harmful.	
A substance which may on contact with living tissues destroy them.	Corrosive.	
A non-corrosive substance which, through immediate, prolonged or repeated contact with the skin or mucous membrane, can cause inflammation.	Irritant.	

[*1 Sch*].

Substances dangerous for supply

Packaging requirements

V   Dangerous substances must not be supplied (or conveyed by road), unless:

(a)   they are in a package suitable for that purpose; and

(b)   the receptacle containing the dangerous substance:

(i)   is designed, constructed, maintained and closed so as to prevent any of the contents of the receptacle from escaping when subjected to the 'stresses and strains' of normal handling (this requirement may be met by fitting a suitable safety device);

(ii)   is made of materials which are neither liable to be adversely affected by that substance or, in conjunction with that substance, to form any other substance which is a health and safety risk; or

(iii)   if fitted with a replaceable closure, has a closure which is designed so that the receptacle can be repeatedly reclosed, without its contents escaping.

[*Reg 7*].

Labelling requirements

Substances dangerous for supply

VI   A substance dangerous for supply must contain the following information clearly shown and readable and indelibly marked, either:

(*a*)   on the receptacle containing the substance; or

(*b*)   on the outside of the packaging containing the receptacle:

(i)   the name and address of the manufacturer, importer, wholesaler or other supplier;

(ii)   designation of the substance;

(iii)   indication of the general nature of the risk and symbols illustrative of the risk(s), e.g. 'harmful', 'corrosive';

(iv)   risk phrases, e.g. 'toxic by inhalation';

(v)   safety phrases, e.g. 'keep away from heat', 'do not empty into drains'.

[*Regs 8(1), 13*].

If it is not reasonably practicable (for the meaning of this expression, see Chapter 15 'Employers' Duties') to provide safety information on the main label, such information can be given on a separate label or on a sheet accompanying the package. [*Reg 8(7)*]. Even so, misleading and/or unhelpful terminology, such as 'non-harmful', 'non-toxic' should be avoided, as this can give rise to expensive civil liability if injury is caused in consequence (see Chapter 38 'Product Safety' and *Vacwell v BDH Chemicals Ltd* [*1969*] *3 AER 1681*).

Labelling requirements for particular preparations

VII   In the case of:

(*a*)   paints and varnishes containing more than 0.5% lead;

(*b*)   cyanoacrylate-based adhesives;

(*c*)   preparations containing isocyanates;

(*d*)   preparations containing sensitisers; and

(*e*)   sprays;

the following risk and safety phraseology should appear on the labelling:

(*a*)   *paints/varnishes*:

242

    (i)   'Contains lead. Should not be used on surfaces liable to be chewed or sucked by children' (receptacles containing 125 mls or more of paint/varnish);

    (ii)   'Warning. Contains lead' (receptacles containing less than 125 mls);

(*b*)   *cyanoacrylate-based adhesives*: 'Cyanoacrylate. Danger. Bonds skin and eyes in seconds. Keep out of reach of children';

(*c*)   receptacle containing preparation containing *isocyanates* must include on the label: 'Contains isocyanates' and 'See information supplied by manufacturer';

(*d*)   *sensitisers*: 'May cause sensitisation by inhalation' and/or 'May cause sensitisation by skin contact';

(*e*)   *sprays*: e.g. paint, varnish, printing ink, adhesive: 'Do not breathe gas/fumes/vapour/spray' and 'In case of insufficient ventilation, wear suitable respiratory equipment'.

[*Reg 12*].

Compliance with these 'descriptions' does not necessarily relieve the supplier from civil liability (see Chapter 38 'Product Safety').

Enforcement and penalties

VIII   Breach of the *Classification, Packaging and Labelling of Dangerous Substances Regulations* carries with it the same penalties as breach of *HSWA* (see Chapter 17 'Enforcement').

Enforcement

HSE is the enforcing authority for these regulations, except where the dangerous substance is supplied from a registered chemist, where the Pharmaceutical Society of Great Britain is the enforcing authority. If the supply is from a shop, mobile vehicle or market stall, or to members of the public, the local Weights and Measures Authority is the enforcing authority.

Defence to prosecution

It is a defence to prosecution under these regulations that a person took all reasonable care and exercised all due diligence to avoid the commission of that offence. [*Reg 15(4)*]. This is a difficult test to satisfy (see Chapter 33 'Offices' and *Dewhurst (JH) Ltd v Coventry Corporation* [*1969*] *3 AER 1225*).

Civil liability

Where breach of duty under the regulations causes damage, this can give rise to civil liability. [*Reg 15(1)(b)*].

Chapter 10

Dangerous Substances II – Transportation

Introduction

10.1 Because a truck driver can, in principle, (unlike a train driver) drive through almost any street he likes, the need for compliance with statutory requirements relating to the transportation of dangerous substances is paramount. In the United Kingdom, unlike certain other countries, there have been few serious transport accidents involving dangerous substances, though, given the quantities and varieties of substances carried, there is clearly potential for some. Urban and suburban streets and roads present a direct potential hazard to people, houses and shops; rural roads to the environment and wildlife. Typical accidents that can be envisioned involve, say, collision of a road tanker carrying liquefied toxic gas, such as ammonia or chlorine, puncture of an LPG tanker, leaving a trail of fire or torch flame, or even a fire in a vehicle carrying high explosives. The consequences of such an accident could be severe or even fatal to other road users and people living in the immediate vicinity and, bearing in mind, for example, that there are about one million deliveries of LPG (propane and butane) to both industrial and domestic sites in both urban and outlying areas, the scope of the risk begins to emerge.

The list of substances dangerous for conveyance by road in a road tanker is contained in the (new) Road Tanker Approved List (1992). Classification, packaging and labelling requirements in connection with such substances are specified in the *Chemicals (Hazard Information and Packaging) Regulations 1993 (SI 1993 No 1746)* (see Chapter 9 'Dangerous Substances I').

Transportation of dangerous substances by road

10.2 Under *HSWA s 2*, as well as at common law, employers are under a general duty to protect members of the public from dangers arising from their activities/operations at work. In view of spillages from transportation by road of dangerous substances, this duty is particularly relevant to such operations, a view reinforced by the *Road Traffic (Carriage of Dangerous Substances in Road Tankers and Tank Containers) Regulations 1992 (SI 1992 No 743)*, the *Road Traffic (Carriage of Dangerous Substances in Packages etc.) Regulations 1992 (SI 1992 No 742)* and the *Road Traffic (Training of Drivers of Vehicles Carrying Dangerous Goods) Regulations 1992 (SI 1992 No 744)*. Indeed, so potentially serious are the possible consequences of transportation of dangerous products, gases and substances in bulk containers, that the *Road Traffic (Training of Drivers of Vehicles Carrying Dangerous Goods) Regulations 1992* require operators of vehicles carrying dangerous goods to ensure that drivers are adequately trained and instructed in the dangers involved (see 10.4 below). Moreover, transportation of explosives by road, which comes within the ambit of the *Road Traffic (Carriage of Explosives) Regulations 1989 (SI 1989 No 615)* and radioactive material, as governed by the *Radioactive Material (Road Transport) Act 1991* and regulations, are also considered in the chapter (10.23–10.26 below).

Importance of approved list

10.3   The Road Tanker Approved List 1992 (Health and Safety Executive) contains the updated list of substances dangerous for conveyance in road tankers and tank containers and can be obtained from HMSO; in addition, it contains substance identification numbers (SIN), emergency action codes and classifications. Part 2 specifies the method for ascertaining the multi-load action code (see 10.14 below).

A substance is classified either by the HSC (and so appears on the approved list) or, for a substance not on the list, by reference to *Schedule 1* of the regulations. Substances referred to in the approved list are normally single chemical substances (e.g. ethylene, sulphuric acid). But other substances, mixtures or preparations, which possess one or more of the characteristic properties listed in Column 1 of the list, are classified by reference to *Schedule 1* of the regulations. In such cases, the classification will be determined by whichever is the most hazardous property. The approved code of practice on 'Classification of Dangerous Substances for Conveyance in Road Tankers and Tank Containers' gives practical guidance on how to determine the most hazardous characteristic property.

The emergency action code informs the emergency services of the action to be taken in the event of an accident. Codes approved by the HSC for dealing with dangerous substances are specified in the approved list and must appear on the hazard warning panel, fitted to such vehicles. [*Road Traffic (Carriage of Dangerous Substances in Road Tankers and Tank Containers) Regulations 1992 (SI 1992 No 743), Reg 18, 3 Sch*]. If a substance is not on the approved list, the hazard warning panel must not show an emergency warning action code. [*3 Sch*]. The hazard warning panel must be kept clean and free from any obstruction. [*Reg 24*]. It should be positioned as close as possible to the middle of both the front and rear of the vehicle, should be vertical, weather resistant, indelibly marked and securely fixed. [*Reg 18*].

fig. 5 – Hazard warning panel

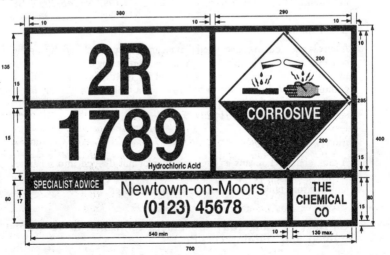

[*SI 1992 No 743, 3 Sch*].

Training of drivers of vehicles carrying dangerous products

10.4   The *Road Traffic (Training of Drivers of Vehicles Carrying Dangerous Goods) Regulations 1992 (SI 1992 No 744)*, came into effect on 1 July 1992. They require that operators of vehicles carrying dangerous substances must ensure that drivers have received adequate instruction/training so as to appreciate the dangers involved and their duties under these regulations, associated regulations and *HSWA*; and that they keep records of training so provided. [*Regs 4(1)(2)*]. There are, however, certain defences (see 10.22 below). Enforcement is by the HSE except in the case of petroleum transportation.

Definitions

10.5   (i) *Operator*

An operator is defined as:

(*a*)   in relation to a road tanker, the person who holds, or should hold an operator's licence for the use of the vehicle for the carriage of goods by road or, if no licence is required, the keeper of the vehicle or, if the vehicle is not registered in the UK, the driver of the vehicle;

(*b*)   in relation to a tank container:

(i)   the owner of the tank container or his agent, if that person has a place of business in Great Britain and is identified on the tank or document carried in the vehicle as the owner or agent of the owner; or

(ii)   in other cases, the operator of the vehicle on which the tank container is conveyed.

[*SI 1992 No 742, Reg 4; SI 1992 No 743, Reg 5*].

(ii) *Road tanker*

A road tanker refers to both (i) rigid and articulated road tankers and (ii) draw-bar trailers having a tank structurally or otherwise attached to the trailer frame which is not intended to be removed from the vehicle. [*SI 1992 No 743, Reg 2(1)*].

(iii) *Tank*

A tank is a vehicle so constructed that it can be securely closed during the course of conveyance by road (except for the purpose of relieving excessive pressure) and, for the purpose of these regulations, is used for the carriage of a liquid, gaseous or granular material or sludge in bulk. Hence a tank which has any opening (other than for relieving excessive pressure) which cannot be securely closed by valves or covers, is not a 'tank'. [*SI 1992 No 743, Reg 2(1)*].

(iv) *Tank container*

A tank container means a 'tank, whether or not divided into separate compartments, having a total capacity of more than 3 cubic metres (other than the carrying tank of a road tanker) and includes a tube container'. [*SI 1992 No 743, Reg 2(1)*].

Carriage of dangerous substances for which drivers must be trained and training certificates

10.6   The dangerous substances involved (with reference to the approved list, i.e. the list published by HSE on 24 April 1990, entitled 'Information approved for the classification, packaging and labelling of dangerous substances') are

(*a*)   dangerous substances contained in Part I of the approved list (unless in such diluted form as not to create a risk); or

(*b*)   any other substance which, by reason of its characteristics, creates a risk to the health and safety of any person in the course of conveyance by road, which is comparable with the risk created by substances specified in the approved list. Such characteristic properties are detailed in *Schedule 1* of the regulations.

Key substances covered are

(i)   petroleum, commercial butane/propane;

(ii)   flammable solids;

(iii)   flammable/toxic gases;

(iv)   asbestos;

(v)   special waste (see 4.39 ASBESTOS);

(vi)   organic peroxide (including carriage in transformers/capacitators);

(vii)   explosives (see also 10.23 below);

(viii)   radioactive material.

But not

(i)   flammable liquids with a flashpoint between 55°C and 100°C;

(ii)   food;

(iii)   medicines, dangerous drugs;

(iv)   obnoxious/infectious substances.

[*SIs 1992 Nos 742, 743, Regs 2(1)*].

In addition, drivers must possess a valid vocational training certificate [*Reg 5*] or even a provisional vocational training certificate [*Reg 6*]; though an existing training certificate may well be sufficient [*Reg 7*]. Such certificates must be available for production (to the police or goods vehicle examiner) throughout the whole of a particular journey. [*Regs 9, 10*].

Penalties

10.7   Penalties for breach duplicate those for breach of *HSWA*, that is, a maximum fine of £5,000 on summary conviction, and, on conviction on indictment, up to two years' imprisonment and an indefinite fine.

Transportation of dangerous substances/products by road

10.8   Both the *Road Traffic (Carriage of Dangerous Substances in Road Tankers and Tank Containers) Regulations 1992 (SI 1992 No 743)* and the *Road Traffic (Carriage of Dangerous Substances in Packages etc.) Regulations 1992 (SI 1992 No 742)*, by way of revocation of earlier similar regulations (*SI 1981 No 1059* and *SI 1986 No 1951*), whilst re-enacting much of the earlier regulations, stipulate some key new requirements, particularly regarding written instructions/information to be provided by consignors to operators and how it is to be used; precautions to be taken against fire/explosion; prohibitions against overfilling; and supervision of vehicles. Both sets of regulations apply to vehicles from the time they have been loaded or filled until the time of unloading or cleaning or purging, irrespective of whether the vehicle is on the road (*SI 1992 No 743, Reg 3(2)* and, by implication, *SI 1992 No 742* relating to packaged transportation).

The main thrust of both sets of regulations is to specify substance identification numbers, emergency action codes and classifications; require the marking of vehicles, training of drivers (see 10.4 above) and precautions against fire and explosion. Particularly, however, in the case of road tankers, there are new requirements in connection with (*a*) unloading petrol at filling stations and (*b*) hazard warning panels being fitted to the ends of tank containers as well as to the sides. Whereas, in the case of packaged substances, the new regulations extend to substances at the lowest level of risk (packing group 1.1 substances), which are now covered if they are carried in receptacles of 200 litres or more.

Transportation of radioactive materials

10.9   Transportation of radioactive material by road is outside the ambit of the new regulations, though drivers of vehicles carrying such materials must be trained in the dangers involved (see 10.4 above). Since, however, there are obvious dangers involved in transporting radioactive materials in packages, such transportation is controlled separately by the *Radioactive Material (Road Transport) Act 1991* and regulations to be made thereunder (see 10.26 below). A radioactive package is a 'package comprising radioactive material which has been consigned for transport and its packaging'. [*Radioactive Material (Road Transport) Act 1991, s 1(2)*].

Road Traffic (Carriage of Dangerous Substances in Road Tankers and Tank Containers) Regulations 1992 (SI 1992 No 743)

10.10   These regulations impose duties on consignors, operators and drivers.

(a) Consignors

Consignors of dangerous substances must provide operators with written information identifying risks involved in carrying such substances in order to enable operators to comply with their duties (below); and operators break the law if they undertake carriage without being in receipt of such information. Once in receipt, operators should enter it on computer, keeping it, at least, two weeks after completion of the journey. [*Reg 10*]. If the consignor has no place of business in the UK, the consignee has the same responsibilities as the consignor.

(b) Operators

The following are the main duties of operators:

   (i)   to ensure that drivers are given adequate written information identifying substances carried, quantity and nature of hazards. Such information must be kept in the cab and it must be readily available (for production to the police/goods vehicle examiner) during the journey. It should refer to action taken in the event of persons being exposed to the substances carried, and also spillage; measures to be taken in the event of fire and also the fire-fighting equipment to be used, as well as instructions on protective clothing [*Reg 12*];

   (ii)   precautions against fire/explosion [*Reg 13*];

(iii) contact with other substances – to ensure, before loading, that dangerous substances, when coming into contact with other substances, do not significantly increase risks to health and safety [*Reg 14*];

(iv) prohibition against overfilling – to ensure that tanks are not overfilled through liquid expansion or over-pressurisation and, since operators are generally not present when tanks/containers are being filled, the prohibition against overfilling will have to be clearly communicated to drivers [*Reg 15*];

(v) to ensure that openings in tanks and valves are closed before the journey starts [*Reg 16*];

(vi) hazard warning panels – to ensure that each vehicle has and displays *three* hazard warning panels, one at the *rear* and one on each *side*, which must be weather-resistant and indelibly marked [*Reg 18(1)*];

(vii) (*a*) tank containers to carry hazard warning panels – *greater than 6 cubic metres* – to ensure that such tank containers display *four* hazard warning panels, one fitted to each *side* of the tank container and one fitted to each *end* of the tank container,

(*b*) tank containers to carry hazard warning panels – *less than 6 cubic metres* – to ensure that such tank containers display *two* hazard warning panels, one of which must be fitted to each *side* of the tank container.

In both cases, hazard warning panels must be weather-resistant and indelibly marked on one side [*Reg 19(1)*];

(viii) to ensure that hazard warning panels are kept clean and free from obstruction – hazard warning panels/labels must be kept clean and free from obstruction (but can be mounted behind a ladder, which does not obstruct vision) [*Reg 24*];

(ix) to ensure that drivers receive adequate instruction/training – drivers must receive adequate instruction/training in the dangers involved and in comprehending their duties under *HSWA* and these and associated regulations [*Reg 26*];

(x) to ensure that each uncompartmented carrying tank/compartment is provided with two weather-resistant labels, in the case of *multi-loads* [*Reg 20*] (see 10.13 below).

(*c*) Drivers

The following are the main duties of drivers:

(i) to keep written information provided by the operator in the cab readily available at all times when the substance is being carried [*Reg 12(2)*];

(ii) where a tractor unit is uncoupled from an articulated vehicle, to attach the written information to the trailer in a readily visible position; or, alternatively, to give to the occupier of premises where the trailer is situate [*Reg 12(6)*];

(iii) to make available, on request to the police/fire or ambulance services written information during the journey [*Reg 12(7)*];

(iv) to observe all precautions for preventing fire/explosion [*Reg 13(2)*];

(v) to park the vehicle in a safe place, except when

(*a*) it is being supervised by a competent person over 18, or

(b)   if no competent person is present, when the vehicle has been damaged or broken down and the driver has gone for assistance

[*Reg 17(1)*];

(vi)   to display hazard warning panels at all times required – road tankers [*Reg 18(2)*];

(vii)   to display hazard warning panels at all times required – tank containers [*Reg 19(2)*];

(viii)   to keep hazard warning panels clean and free from obstruction [*Reg 24*];

(ix)   to produce on request (to a policeman or goods vehicle examiner) written information provided by the operator [*Reg 27(1)*];

(x)   to display two weather-resistant labels indelibly marked, in the case of multi-loads [*Reg 20*] (see 10.13 below).

Petroleum deliveries at filling stations

10.11   There are new procedures under driver-controlled petrol deliveries. A Part III licence from a petroleum licensing authority will be required for this type of delivery. (Part II lays down the procedure for licence-controlled deliveries and is not covered here.)

Drivers must (*inter alia*):

(a)   *Before commencing delivery*

(i)   verify that the quantity to be delivered can be safely received by the storage tank by visually checking ullage*,

(ii)   verify that there is a dialling tone on each telephone,

(iii)   place a fire extinguisher close to the unloading point,

(iv)   test the high level alarm to check that the audible signal functions correctly,

(v)   check that the delivery hose is securely connected to the appropriate outlet on the road tanker and to the filling point of the storage tank;

(b)   *During delivery*

(i)   shut off engine of road tanker,

(ii)   ensure that it remains stationary,

(iii)   ensure that no petrol overflows from the storage tank, or escapes from the hose connection,

(iv)   keep constant watch on the filling point of the storage tank, carrying tank of the road tanker, delivery hose, vapour balance hose and connections at both ends;

(c)   *After delivery*

(i)   secure caps on the filling point,

(ii)   disconnect the vapour balance hose (where necessary),

(iii)   securely replace manhole covers.

[*Part III, 4 Sch*].

* 'ullage' is the difference (expressed in litres) between the maximum working capacity of a storage tank and the quantity of petrol in it at a given time.

Entry into confined spaces on forecourts – current best practice

10.12   The dangers associated with entry into man-holes by staff working on forecourts, can be minimised, if not averted, by compliance with the *Factories Act, s 30* (see 2.12 ACCESS) – specifying restrictions for entry into confined spaces – and COSHH (see 9.20 DANGEROUS SUBSTANCES I).

More particularly, the flammability limit of petrol vapour in air is 15,000 ppm. Good hygiene standards dictate 300 ppm for an eight-hour all day every day exposure, and 750 ppm for ten minutes, as the short-term exposure (e.g. man-hole chamber working). Man-hole chambers downwind of vehicles filling up can be dangerous, as displaced vapour ends up in the chamber causing unacceptably high levels of petrol vapour. In the case of chambers of medium-sized depth (more than 29″ and less than 49″) a continuous triple gas monitor (for petrol vapour, carbon monoxide and oxygen) should be used along with an extract fan. A company employee should be in attendance above the chamber. In the case of the deepest man-holes (more than 49″) there must be a similar monitor and extractor fan, together with a resuscitator, checked and in working order, on standby. Also a lifting tripod and lifting gear should be set up over the man-hole and the employee entering the man-hole should put on a lifting harness and be connected to the lifting gear. The second employee should stay in attendance above the man-hole ready, if necessary, to winch out the employee below.

Multi-loads/multi-load emergency action

10.13   Operators (and drivers) of road tankers/tank containers carrying a multi-load must ensure that two weather-resistant labels, indelibly marked, are at all times displayed. [*Reg 20*].

A multi-load is a load consisting of two or more dangerous substances in

(*a*)   separate uncompartmented carrying tanks of a tank container,

(*b*)   separate compartments of a compartmented carrying tank of a road tanker, or

(*c*)   separate compartments of a compartmented tank container,

whether or not carried in tandem with a non-dangerous substance. [*Reg 2(1)*].

Multi-load emergency action

10.14   Part 2 of the approved list specifies the method for ascertaining the multi-load emergency action code, i.e. a number 1 to 4, followed by a letter, followed in certain cases by the letter 'E'.

Emergencies

The emergency action code – use and interpretation

10.15   Part 4 of the approved list provides the interpretation of the emergency action code as follows.

The upper set of figure and letters in the hazard warning panel provides the following information to emergency services:

(*a*)   the number indicates the equipment suitable for fire fighting and, where appropriate, for dealing with spillages, thus:

251

1 – water jet; 2 – water fog; 3 – foam; 4 – dry agent.

(b)   the first letter indicates the precautions to be taken in the event of a fire or a spillage as indicated in the Table to Part 4 of the approved list. Typical examples are set out for reference in Table 12 below:

Table 12

Typical examples of precautions to be taken in event of fire/spillage

Letter	Danger of violent reaction or explosion	Protective clothing and breathing apparatus	Measures to be taken
P	Yes	Full protective clothing	Dilute
R	No	Full protective clothing	Dilute
S	Yes	Breathing apparatus	Dilute
X	No	Full protective clothing	Contain

For the purposes of this Table:

(i)   'full protective clothing' includes breathing apparatus;

(ii)   where 'breathing apparatus' is indicated, protective gloves are appropriate;

(iii)   'dilute' indicates that the substance may be washed to a drain with a large quantity of water; and

(iv)   'contain' indicates a need to avoid spillages from entering drains or water courses.

(c)   where the letter 'E' occurs at the end of an emergency action code, evacuation of people from the neighbourhood of an incident should be considered.

The four figure number in the hazard warning panel is the substance identification number, for instance:

1961 – ethane, refrigerated liquid;   1935 – cyanide solutions;

2416 – trimethyl borate;   2941 – fluoroanilines.

Numbers commencing with a figure '7' are specifically hazardous wastes, for instance:

7008 – hazardous waste, liquid, containing alkali;

7023 – hazardous waste, containing organo-lead compounds.

For an example of an emergency warning action code see *fig.5* above.

Defence and penalties

10.16   It is a defence for a person to prove that he took all reasonable precautions and exercised all due diligence to avoid the commission of the offence (see Chapter 33 'Offices' and the case of *Dewhurst (JH) Ltd v Coventry Corporation* in 33.19 OFFICES). Penalties are the same as in *HSWA*.

Table 13

Labelling requirements for substances dangerous for conveyance by road

Table of characteristic properties, classification and hazard warning signs

1 Characteristic properties of the substance	2 Classification	3 Hazard warning sign
A substance which— (a) has a critical temperature below 50°C or which at 50° has a vapour pressure of more than 3 bars absolute; and (b) is conveyed by road at a pressure of more than 500 millibars above atmospheric pressure or in liquefied form, other than a toxic gas or a flammable gas.	Non-flammable compressed gas.	COMPRESSED GAS
A substance which has a critical temperature below 50°C or which at 50°C has a vapour pressure of more than 3 bars absolute and which is toxic.	Toxic gas.	TOXIC GAS
A substance which has a critical temperature below 50°C or which at 50°C has a vapour pressure of more than 3 bars absolute and is flammable.	Flammable gas.	FLAMMABLE GAS

1 Characteristic properties of the substance	2 Classification	3 Hazard warning sign
A liquid with a flash point of 55°C or below except a liquid which— (a) has a flash point equal to or more than 21°C and less than or equal to 55°C; and (b) when tested at 55°C in the manner described in Schedule 2 to the Highly Flammable Liquids and Liquefied Petroleum Gases Regulations 1972 (a) does not support combustion.	Flammable liquid.	

(a) S.I. 1972/917.

A solid which is readily combustible under conditions encountered in conveyance by road or which may cause or contribute to fire through friction.	Flammable solid.	
A substance which is liable to spontaneous heating under conditions encountered in conveyance by road or to heating in contact with air being then liable to catch fire.	Spontaneously combustible substance.	

1 Characteristic properties of the substance	2 Classification	3 Hazard warning sign
A substance which in contact with water is liable to become spontaneously combustible or to give off a flammable gas.	Substance which in contact with water emits flammable gas.	
A substance other than an organic peroxide which, although not itself necessarily combustible, may by yielding oxygen or by a similar process cause or contribute to the combustion of other material.	Oxidizing substance.	
A substance which is— *(a)* an organic peroxide; and *(b)* an unstable substance which may undergo exothermic self-accelerating decomposition.	Organic peroxide.	

1 Characteristic properties of the substance	2 Classification	3 Hazard warning sign
A substance known to be so toxic to man as to afford a hazard to health during conveyance or which, in the absence of adequate data on human toxicity, is presumed to be toxic to man.	Toxic substance.	 TOXIC
A substance known to be toxic to man or, in the absence of adequate data on human toxicity, is presumed to be toxic to man but which is unlikely to afford a serious acute hazard to health during conveyance.	Harmful substance.	 HARMFUL – STOW AWAY FROM FOODSTUFFS
A substance which by chemical action will— (a) cause severe damage when in contact with living tissue; (b) materially damage other freight or equipment if leakage occurs.	Corrosive substance.	 CORROSIVE
A substance which is listed in Part 1A of the approved list and which may create a risk to the health or safety of persons in the conditions encountered in conveyance by road, whether or not it has any of the characteristic properties set out above.	Other dangerous substance.	 DANGEROUS SUBSTANCE

1 Characteristic properties of the substance	2 Classification	3 Hazard warning sign
Packages containing two or more dangerous substances which have different characteristic properties.	Mixed hazards.	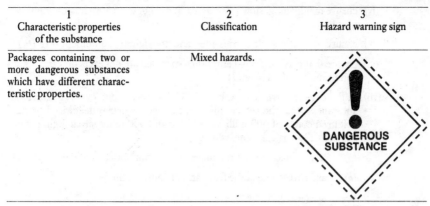

[*Chemicals (Hazard Information and Packaging) Regulations 1993, 3 Sch*].

Road Traffic (Carriage of Dangerous Substances in Packages etc.) Regulations 1992 (SI 1992 No 742)

10.18   These regulations impose duties on consignors, operators and drivers of vehicles carrying dangerous substances in receptacles, in bulk, or in transformers or capacitators.

(a) Consignors

Consignors must provide operators with written information to enable operators to comply with their statutory duties and be aware of the hazards involved; and operators are in breach of the law if they carry dangerous substances in the absence of such information. If the consignor has no place of business in the UK, these responsibilities devolve on the consignee. [*Reg 6(1)(2)(3)*].

(b) Operators

Operators must

   (i)   keep written information for at least two weeks after completion of the journey either in written form or on computer [*Reg 6(4)*];

   (ii)   ensure that drivers have received adequate instruction/training and know the risks involved and understand mutual statutory duties [*Reg 8(1)*];

   (iii)   in the case of vehicles used for carriage (where the total mass is at least 3 tonnes) of (*inter alia*)

      (*a*)   dangerous substance in bulk,

      (*b*)   organic peroxide/flammable/toxic gas,

      (*c*)   asbestos,   5 litres or more

      (*d*)   special waste,

      (*e*)   organic peroxide – self-accelerating decomposition temperature of 50°C or below,

      (*f*)   any flammable solid – self-accelerating decomposition temperature of 55°C or below,

keep a record of training and make a copy available to the driver [*Reg 8(2)*];

(iv) ensure that loading, stowing or unloading is not to create a health/safety risk [*Reg 9*];

(v) ensure that the vehicle carries adequate fire-fighting equipment [*Reg 10(1)*];

(vi) ensure that maximum concentrations specified are not exceeded and/or any conditions satisfied [*Reg 11*];

(vii) in the case of carriage of at least 500 kilograms of one or more dangerous substances, that the vehicle displays two rectangular reflectorised orange-coloured plates of 400 millimetres base and 300 millimetres high, set in a substantially vertical plane, which

   (*a*)   have a black border not more than 15 mm wide,

   (*b*)   are affixed one at the front and the other at the rear,

   (*c*)   are clearly visible

   [*Reg 12(3)*];

(viii) when the dangerous substances have been removed from the vehicle, these plates must be covered or removed from the vehicle [*Reg 12(5)*] and they must not be displayed when the vehicle is not being used for the carriage of dangerous substances [*Reg 13*];

PGR Hazard Warning Vehicle Plates

If you carry dangerous substances by road new regulations may affect you.....

The Road Traffic (Carriage of Dangerous Substances in Packages etc.) Regulations, 1986 - known as PGR, require the use of reflective warning plates:
To be used when quantities of 500 Kg or more of a dangerous substance is being conveyed.
The operator must ensure that the vehicle displays 2 orange plates, one at the front and one at the rear of the vehicle. These plates must be reversed when the goods are unloaded.

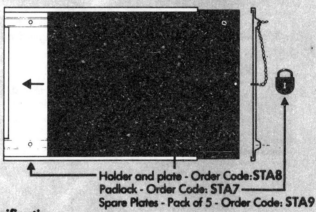

Holder and plate - Order Code: STA8
Padlock - Order Code: STA7
Spare Plates - Pack of 5 - Order Code: STA9

Specifications

Size: 400mm x 300mm

Material: Holder - Aluminium, black finish
Plate 2mm styrene with orange reflective material on one side with 15mm black border, black on reverse

Fastening: Chain and clip to secure plate to holder

Fixing: Four pre-drilled holes to enable bolting/rivetting

Padlock: For extra security we offer a small padlock to fix the plate to the holder

Signs are guaranteed to comply with current legislation

(ix) ensure that the vehicle used for carriage of toxic/harmful substances, does not carry food, unless food is carried separately and adequately protected from the risk of contamination [*Reg 16(1)*];

(x) ensure that the vehicle carrying the dangerous substance (and, where necessary, the freight container)

    (*a*) is properly designed, of adequate strength, and of good construction,

    (*b*) is suitable for the purpose for which it is being used, having regard to the nature of the journey and the characteristic properties and quantity of both the dangerous substance and any other substance being carried. Any parts of the vehicle likely to come in contact with the substance and fittings should be made from materials not likely to be affected by the substance.

[*Reg 5*]. (See 10.19 below.)

(*c*) Drivers

Drivers must

(i) observe precautions for preventing fire/explosion [*Reg 10(2)*];

(ii) in the case of carriage of organic peroxide with self-accelerating decomposition temperature of 50°C or below, see that the control temperature is not exceeded [*Reg 11(2)*];

(iii) in the case of carriage of a flammable solid with self-accelerating decomposition temperature of 55°C or below, see that the control temperature is not exceeded [*Reg 11(3)*];

(iv) display the hazard warning plates [*Reg 12(4)*];

(v) when the dangerous substances have been removed from the vehicle, these plates must be covered, or removed from the vehicle [*Reg 12(5)*] and they must not be displayed when the vehicle is not being used for the carriage of dangerous substances [*Reg 13*];

(vi) park the vehicle in a safe place except when

    (*a*) supervised at all times by a competent person over 18, or

    (*b*) the vehicle is damaged or broken down and the driver has gone for assistance [*Reg 14*];

(vii) produce, on request (to a policeman or goods vehicle examiner) written information provided by the operator [*Reg 15(1)*];

(viii) see that food is carried separately or protected from risk of contamination [*Reg 16(1)*].

Construction of vehicles

10.19 Vehicles or tanks must be properly designed, of adequate strength and of good construction, made from sound and suitable material. [*SI 1992 No 743, Reg 6; SI 1992 No 742, Reg 5*].

Marking of packages

10.20 Packages containing substances dangerous for conveyance by road must disclose the following information:

(a)   the name and address or telephone number (or both) of the person who consigns the substances by road;

(b)   designation of substance, e.g. sodium cyanide;

(c)   substance identification number, e.g. sodium cyanide 1689;

(d)   hazard warning sign;

(e)   where the quantity of the substance exceeds 25 litres, the nature of the dangers arising from the substance and the emergency action that should be taken – this can be provided on a separate sheet.

[*Reg 9*].

Labelling is not required where the volume of the receptacle or total volume of all receptacles in a package is:

(a)   in the case of toxic gas, 25 mls or less;

(b)   in the case of flammable gas, 500 mls or less;

(c)   in the case of non-flammable compressed gas, 5.5 litres or less;

(d)   in any other case (total quantity of the dangerous substance), 1 litre or less.

[*Chemicals (Hazard Information and Packaging) Regulations 1993, Reg 10(4)*].

For more details of carriage packaging requirements, see 9.8 DANGEROUS SUBSTANCES I.

Penalties

10.21   Penalties for breach of these regulations duplicate those for breach of *HSWA*.

Defence

10.22   It is a defence that a person charged took all reasonable precautions and exercised all due diligence to avoid commission of the offence. [*Reg 17*].

Transportation of explosives by road

10.23   Explosives can be activated by fire, impact or bad packaging, assembly or manufacture. They present a range of potential hazards, from mass explosion hazard, in which the entire load can be affected immediately (e.g. dynamite cartridges in wooden boxes), through projection hazards (e.g. mortar bombs) to more insignificant hazards (e.g. small arms).

Transportation of explosives, which is both civilian and military, is patently a potentially extremely hazardous operation, as demonstrated by the explosion on an industrial estate at Peterborough in March 1989, involving an unplacarded vehicle, without a radio-telephone (essential in such vehicles), carrying 800 kg of mixed explosives, and resulting in the death of a firefighter and injuries to 107 other people. The problem of safe transportation of explosives is compounded by the fact that placarding, particularly of military vehicles, is not an ideal solution, and a balance has to be struck between safety, on the one hand, and security, on the other.

Packaging of explosives is governed by the *Packaging of Explosives for Carriage Regulations 1991 (SI 1991 No 2097)*, which came into effect on 1 March 1992, whilst transportation of explosives by road is regulated by the *Road Traffic (Carriage of Explosives) Regulations 1989 (SI 1989 No 615)*, both sets of which (unlike the *Control of Explosives Regulations 1991*) are enforced by the HSE.

Packaging of Explosives for Carriage Regulations 1991 (SI 1991 No 2097)

10.24　The main requirements of these regulations are:

(1)　(most) explosives must not be transported unless suitably packaged [*Reg 4*];

(2)　the packaging must be designed/constructed so that it will

　　(*a*)　protect the explosives,

　　(*b*)　prevent the escape of explosives,

　　(*c*)　avoid increased risk of ignition,

　　(*d*)　be able to be safely handled,

　　(*e*)　be able to withstand loading in the course of foreseeable stacking,

　　and so that

　　(*f*)　the inner packaging and interior of the outer packaging is free from grit and rust,

　　(*g*)　the explosives are not likely to come into contact with another substance or article that could cause an explosion.

[*Reg 5*].

Road Traffic (Carriage of Explosives) Regulations 1989 (SI 1989 No 615)

10.25　These regulations lay requirements on consignors (i.e. persons entrusting explosives for carriage), actual transporters (i.e. operators) and, to a lesser extent, drivers of vehicles carrying explosives. It is possible to obtain certificates of exemption from the HSE. [*Reg 17(1)*].

Duties of transporters

These duties encompass safe carriage, exchange information, correct marking of vehicles and the training of drivers.

(i)　*Safe carriage*

Operators of vehicles must ensure that

(*a*)　vehicles are suitable for safety and security of explosives, and vehicles for carrying passengers must not be used [*Reg 5(2)*];

(*b*)　not more than the specified quantity of explosives is carried, namely,

Division	Compatibility group	Maximum
1.1	A	500 kilograms
1.1	B,F,G or L	5 tonnes
1.1	C,D,E or J	16 tonnes
1.2	Any	16 tonnes
1.3	Any	16 tonnes

[*Reg 6, 2 Sch*].

(*c*)   employees and others actually transporting explosives take reasonable care

    (i)   to prevent accidents/minimise harmful effects of accidents (see 9.60 DANGEROUS SUBSTANCES I), and

    (ii)   prevent unauthorised access to and/or removal of load;

(*d*)   when the driver is not present, a competent person normally attends the vehicle (but see *Schedule 1*);

(*e*)   when the most dangerous explosives are being carried (group 1.1 – those with mass explosion hazard potential (see 9.60 DANGEROUS SUBSTANCES I)), drivers follow a route agreed with the police [*Reg 11*];

(*f*)   drivers and/or their attendants are over 18 years (except in the case of carriage of *Schedule 1, Part I* explosives, and *Schedule 1, Part II* if the total quantity carried does not exceed 50 kilograms). [*Reg 15*].

(ii)   *Marking of vehicles*

Both operators and drivers of vehicles used for the carriage of explosives must ensure that such vehicles are marked with

(*a*)   two black rectangular reflectorised orange-coloured plates at the front and back, having a black border not more than 15 millimetres wide

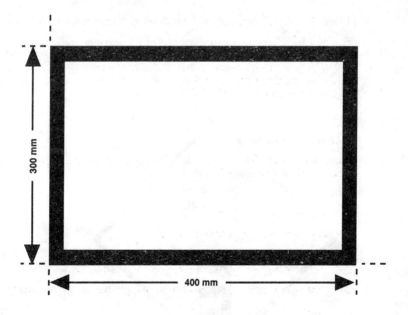

[*4 Sch*]

and in the case of explosives of divisions 1.1, 1.2 or 1.3 (i.e. more dangerous varieties);

(*b*)   two placards on each side of the vehicle, with orange-coloured background, having a black border

[*4 Sch*]

or, in the case of explosives of divisions 1.4 or 1.5 (less powerful)

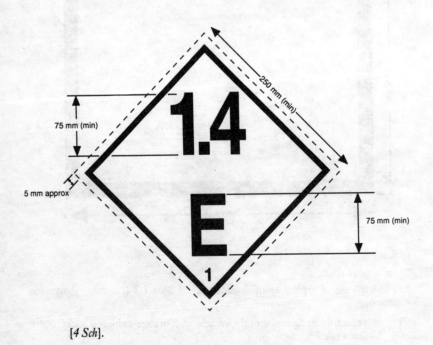

[*4 Sch*].

(iii)   *Training of drivers*

Operators must ensure that drivers and their attendants are adequately trained and instructed, so as to understand

(*a*)   the dangers associated with particular explosives;

(*b*)   their duties under these regulations and the *Health and Safety at Work Act* generally.

Records of such training must be kept and a copy given to drivers/attendants, except in the case of explosives under *Parts I* and *II* of *Schedule 1* (see below) and gunpowder/smokeless powder less than 5 kilograms. [*Reg 14*].

(iv)   *Provision of information*

Consignors must furnish operators with accurate and up-to-date written information about explosives to be carried, so that operators can comply with their duties. [*Reg 9*].

In turn, operators must ensure that drivers (or their attendants) possess written information, at the start of the journey (*a*) about the type and quality of explosives, (*b*) the names/addresses of consignor, consignee and operator, and (*c*) the nature of the dangers associated with explosives carried. [*Reg 10(6), 1 Sch*].

The requirement for written information does not apply to those explosives listed under *Schedule 1, Parts I–III* (see below), nor to those listed under *Parts II* and *III* provided the load does not exceed 50 kilograms and it is accompanied by a person who knows the relevant information:

PART I

1 *Explosives*	2 *UN Number*
Articles, pyrotechnic for technical purposes	0432
Cartridges, power device	0323
Cartridges, signal	0405
Cartridges, small arms	0012
Cartridges small arms, blank	0014
Cases cartridge, empty, with primer	0055
Cutters, cable, explosive	0070
Fireworks	0337
Flares, aerial	0404
Fuse, safety	0105
Igniters	0454
Lighters, fuse	0131
Primers, cap type	0044
Signal devices, hand	0373
Signals, railway track, explosive	0193

PART II

1 *Explosives*	2 *UN Number*
Cartridges, small arms	0328
Cartridges, small arms	0339
Cartridges, small arms, blank	0327
Cartridges, small arms, blank	0338

Cases, cartridge, empty with primer	0379
Fireworks	0333
Fireworks	0334
Fireworks	0335
Fireworks	0336
Signal devices, hand	0191
Signals, distress, ship	0195

PART III

1 *Explosives*	2 *UN Number*
Articles, pyrotechnic for technical purposes	0428
Articles, pyrotechnic for technical purposes	0429
Articles, pyrotechnic for technical purposes	0430
Articles, pyrotechnic for technical purposes	0431
Cartridges, oil well	0277
Cartridges, oil well	0278
Cartridges, power device	0275
Cartridges, power device	0276
Cartridges, power device	0381
Cartridges, signal	0054
Cartridges, signal	0312
Cases, combustible empty, without primer	0446
Cases, combustible empty, without primer	0447
Cord, igniter	0066
Dinitrosobenzene	0406
Flares, aerial	0093
Flares, aerial	0403
Flares, surface	0092
Flash powder	0094
Flash powder	0305
Fuse, instantaneous non-detonating: (quickmatch)	0101
Igniters	0121
Igniters	0314
Igniters	0315
Igniters	0325
5-Mercapto-tetrazole-l-acetic acid	0448
Potassium salts of aromatic nitro-derivatives, explosive	0158
Primers, cap type	0377
Primers, cap type	0378
Rockets, line throwing	0238
Rockets, line throwing	0240
Rockets, line throwing	0453
Signals, distress, ship	0194
Signals, railway track, explosive	0192
Signals, smoke with explosive sound unit	0196
Signals, smoke without explosive sound unit	0197
Sodium dinitro-o-cresolate, dry or wetted with less than 15% water by mass	0234
Sodium picramate, dry or wetted with less than 20% water by mass	0235
Tetrazole-l-acetic acid	0407
Zirconium picramate dry or wetted with less than 20% water by mass	0236

[Road Traffic (Carriage of Explosives) Regulations 1989 (SI 1989 No 615), 1 Sch].

Transportation of radioactive packages by road

10.26　The *Radioactive Material (Road Transport) Act 1991*, envisaging the introduction of regulations to 'prevent injury to health/damage to property and/or the environment', enables transport inspectors and examiners to issue enforcement notices in respect of vehicles carrying radioactive packages, in breach of regulations; to enter such vehicles or premises housing them; to remove vehicles to a specified place; to prohibit transport of such packages, or to prohibit the driving of the vehicle. Breach carries with it a maximum fine of £1,000 on summary conviction or imprisonment for a term not exceeding three months or both; on conviction on indictment, there is a maximum penalty of up to two years' imprisonment and/or an indefinite fine.

The export of dangerous chemicals outside the EC

10.27　The *Export of Dangerous Chemicals Regulations 1992 (SI 1992 No 2415)* came into force on 29 November 1992. These regulations relate to the EC common notification system for dangerous chemicals being imported from non-EC countries. These regulations ban an exporter from providing false or misleading information relating to any requirement or prohibition relating to this form of export. The Health and Safety Executive is the enforcing authority and enforcement follows the *HSWA* rules (see further Chapter 17 'Enforcement').

Chapter 11

Electricity

Introduction

11.1　Electricity, properly used, is a safe, convenient and efficient source of energy for heat, light and power at the place of work. Misused, or if allowed to get out of control, it can cause damage and kill – as can any other form of energy. In an average year, up to 1,000 people are injured and about 50 are killed in electrical accidents at work. Although these numbers are relatively small in comparison with the casualties attributed to other accident classifications, the injuries sustained are usually more severe, and those responsible for safety at work should provide high standards of electrical installations, plant and apparatus, and ensure that they are adequately controlled and maintained. It is also necessary that those who work on such installations, plant and apparatus, or who are affected thereby, should be trained, instructed and supervised to the standards required. This chapter considers the main electrical hazards and how to avoid them (see 11.2, 11.3 below), the general requirements of the *Health and Safety at Work etc. Act 1974 (HSWA)* (see 11.5 below), and then deals with specific requirements of the *Electricity at Work Regulations 1989 (SI 1989 No 635)* as well as the *Electrical Equipment for Explosive Atmospheres (Certification) Regulations 1990 (SI 1990 No 13)* (see 11.10 below). The wide range of relevant British Standards and codes of practice are listed in Appendix 2.

In general, urban supplies of electricity from electricity boards are by underground cable systems and rural supplies are by overhead lines. Sub-stations are used by the statutory bodies, and also by certain large industrial and commercial users, to transform the supply voltages to the level required, e.g. 400/275kV to 132kV; 132kV to 33kV; 33kV to 11kV and 11kV to 415V and 240V. Contact with electricity board overhead lines and underground cables is the cause of a number of serious accidents every year. Precautions for the avoidance of danger from such lines and cables, by contractors and others working in the vicinity are given in the following documents:

— 　'Avoidance of danger from overhead lines' GS 6 (available from the HSE or local electricity boards).

— 　'Recommendations on the avoidance of danger from underground electricity cables' (available from Post Office Telecommunications, electricity boards, British Gas or the National Water Council).

Electrical hazards

11.2　Electrical hazards may arise from bad design, construction and installation, inadequate standards of protection and maintenance, or from misuse and incorrect operation. Such hazards are liable to result in damage to equipment, in the initiation of explosion or even more general fire propagation, or in electric shock or burns. Good design and construction of electrical apparatus and conductors can be expected if they comply with recognised standards. Good installation, protection and maintenance require the employment of competent staff or contractors. Correct operation and use also depend on competence, achieved through adequate training, instruction and supervision of people to enable them to work safely with electricity.

Electric shock is caused by an electric current flowing through the body, affecting the nervous system and upsetting bodily organs and functions. The value of the current and the time during which it flows are the most important factors in determining the effect on the body. The heart is particularly susceptible to a condition known as ventricular fibrillation at currents as little as 50 milliamps (0.05 Amp) flowing for a few seconds. The maximum current that is accidentally passed through a body should not normally exceed 2 milliamps (0.002A) but even a minor shock, if received by someone working at a height, could result in a serious fall. Calculations of current flow depend upon the resistance of the fault path (including the resistance of the body) and on the applied voltage. However, if a person receives a shock from standard mains voltage (240V) and is in direct contact with earthed metal, there is a high chance of a serious injury. Burns, often extensive and deep-seated, are caused by the intense heating effects of an electric current flow – usually when there is electric arcing between broken conductors or contacts, or between hand tools and live terminals.

Preventive action

11.3   Preventive action against shock and burns includes the following: inspection of portable hand-held tools and lamps; regular checking of fuses and other means of circuit protection to ensure correct size and setting; regular tests of earth continuity; regular inspection of rubber gloves, mats, insulated tools and test instruments; avoidance of work near live conductors; the use of proper systems and methods of work including, for special hazards, the use of 'permit to work' cards or similar safety control documentation (see 1.32 INTRODUCTION). Moreover, precautions against danger from electricity must be seen in relation to legal requirements and also to the relevant standards and codes of practice (see 11.12, 11.13 below).

Legal requirements

11.4   Safety of electrical installations and work on and with electricity, either in one's own workplace or at that of a third party, is controlled generally by the *Health and Safety at Work etc. Act 1974* and specifically by the *Electricity at Work Regulations 1989 (SI 1989 No 635)*, as well as *Reg 44* of the *Construction (General Provisions) Regulations 1961* (electrical installations/equipment in relation to construction work); and also, the *Electrical Equipment for Explosive Atmospheres (Certification) Regulations 1990 (SI 1990 No 13)* (as amended).

General duties under the Health and Safety at Work Act 1974

11.5   *HSWA* provides a comprehensive legal framework for occupational health and safety. Although nothing is said directly in the Act about electricity, its general requirements regarding, for example, safe methods of work, safe access and egress and the training, instruction and supervision of employees, have relevance to activities involving electricity. (For a fuller consideration of these duties, see Chapter 15 'Employers' Duties'.)

The Electricity at Work Regulations 1989 (SI 1989 No 635)

Format and philosophy

11.6   The *Electricity at Work Regulations 1989* apply to all workplaces including, in addition to factories, installations in shops, offices, educational establishments and laboratories. The regulations are aimed at *users*, not manufacturers and suppliers of electrical equipment. In conformity with the philosophy of *HSWA* (see Chapter 1 'Introduction'), these regulations lay down only the general principles of electrical safety; more detailed guidance being found in the IEE Wiring Regulations (currently 16th edition), HSC/HSE Guidance Notes, as well as British, European and International Standards (see 11.12 below).

Unlike the earlier *Regulations 1908-1944*, these regulations do not distinguish between systems of different voltages. Thus, there are no regulations specifically applicable to high voltage installations; indeed, they apply equally at all system voltages in the interests of preventing 'danger' or 'injury'. Rather, the regulations specify duties to prevent 'danger' or 'injury'. 'Danger' is synonymous with risk of injury; hence, where the regulations exist to 'prevent danger', they must be complied with to avoid risk of foreseeable injury. The regulations distinguish between 'danger' and 'injury' to accommodate the fact that work is carried out on live conductors, and as such is dangerous; a situation which cannot be prevented. Nevertheless, there is still a requirement to prevent 'injury' arising from such danger. [*Reg 14*].

The regulations importantly specify different levels of duty. Some regulations impose an absolute duty, e.g. *Reg 5* relating to strength/capability of electrical equipment; others require employers to do what is 'reasonably practicable' (for the meaning of which, see 15.18 EMPLOYERS' DUTIES), e.g. *Reg 4*; whilst others still specify 'reasonableness', e.g. *Reg 14*. In the case of alleged breach of an 'absolute' duty, it is a defence that reasonable measures have been taken *and* all due diligence observed [*Reg 29*] – a defence that has not, in other contexts, been successfully invoked (see further *Dewhurst (JH) Ltd v Coventry Corporation* at 33.19 OFFICES).

Safe system of work – general requirement

11.7   There is an overriding need to provide/maintain a proper safe system of work in connection with work on electrical systems, whether alive or if they have been made dead. [*Regs 4, 13 and 14*].

Unlike the earlier *Electricity Regulations*, there are no in-built exemptions. Because the regulations specify *principles* of electrical safety, there is no requirement for exemptions, in spite of *Reg 30* (providing for exemptions), which is designed to 'mop up' any unforeseen defects arising in connection with the new regulations. Nor is there a requirement to post electric shock notices, although it may well be helpful to do so at places where persons may be under a greater risk of electric shock [*Reg 14*]; though there is such a requirement in the case of a mine.

Design/construction/maintenance of electrical systems – general requirement

11.8   All systems must be constructed and maintained so as to prevent danger, so far as reasonably practicable (for the meaning of 'reasonably practicable', see Chapter 15 'Employers' Duties'). 'Construction' includes design of the system and selection of equipment used on it. Moreover, electrical systems must be effectively and regularly maintained. [*Reg 4(2)*]. However, the regulations are essentially user-orientated and do not impose duties on manufacturers and designers of electrical equipment, though there is a general duty on the latter to make/design and supply safe equipment under *HSWA s 6* (see further Chapter 38 'Product Safety').

As regards design of electrical systems, compliance with the IEE Wiring Regulations (currently 16th edition) (see 11.12 below) will go a long way towards satisfying *Reg 4(2)*. This will include periodical inspection. More particularly, Appendix 16 of the IEE Wiring Regulations advises on maximum recommended periods between inspections of fixed electrical installations. In the case of portable electrical tools, manufacturers' directions/recommendations should be followed.

Specific duties on users of electrical installations

Strength and capability of electrical equipment

11.9   No electrical equipment must be put into use where its strength and capability can be exceeded, thereby causing danger. [*Reg 5*]. This is an absolute requirement (for the meaning of 'absolute duty', see further Chapter 15 'Employers' Duties'), which must be complied with, irrespective of whether risk of injury is foreseeable, though it is a defence to breach of this duty that 'reasonable steps have been taken and all due diligence observed to avoid breach'. [*Reg 29*]. Thus, electrical equipment must be properly selected and adequately rated before being put into use.

Siting of equipment in adverse/hazardous environments

Electrical equipment that can reasonably foreseeably be exposed to

(*a*)   mechanical damage;

(*b*)   the effects of weather, natural hazards, temperature or pressure;

(*c*)   the effects of wet, dirty, dusty or corrosive conditions; or

(*d*)   any flammable or explosive substance (including dusts, vapours or gases),

must be so constructed or protected so as to prevent, so far as reasonably practicable, danger from exposure. [*Reg 6*].

This requirement is aimed at protecting electrical equipment from reasonably foreseeable adverse/hazardous conditions, both indoors and used outside (e.g. weatherproofing of switchboards housing electrical equipment). In particular, users should select with care electrical equipment to be used on construction sites, where conditions can be particularly adverse and/or hazardous.

Insulation, protection and placement of conductors

All conductors in a system giving rise to danger, must either

(*a*)   be suitably covered with insulating material and protected, so far as is reasonably practicable, to prevent danger; or

(*b*)   have such precautions taken as will prevent danger, including being suitably placed.

[*Reg 7*].

The purpose of this requirement is to prevent danger from conductors in a system that can give rise to danger, as from electric shock, by resort to permanently safeguarding live conductors. In situations where it is not possible to insulate fully (e.g. electric overhead travelling crane), this requirement is satisfied where live conductors are out of reach and so safe by position. If they intermittently come within reach, or where a ladder is being used, the safe system of work should limit or control access.

Earthing

Precautions must be taken, either by earthing or other suitable means, to prevent danger arising when any conductor (other than a circuit conductor, which may reasonably foreseeably become charged as a result of use of a system, or a fault in a system) becomes charged. [*Reg 8*].

This requirement, to avoid risk of electric shock from conductive parts of a system which may inadvertently become charged owing to a fault in the system, is absolute. (As such, however, *Reg 29* (see 11.6 above) provides a defence.) This notwithstanding, such risk is normally avoided by earthing, i.e. ensuring that outer conductive parts which can be touched are connected to earth. In addition, it may be necessary to 'cross-bond' water, gas or oil carried in metallic pipes to the central earthing terminal at the electrical supply intake, thus avoiding incidence of dangerous voltages between different items of exposed metal.

To this end, every earthing or bonding conductor must be of adequate cross-sectional area for safe carriage of any expected fault current for the time that it takes the fuse to operate and disconnect the supply.

In addition, this regulation requires installation of residual current devices, use of all-insulated/double-insulated equipment, reduced voltage systems (240/110V in connection with portable electrical tools used, for example, on construction sites), thus reducing current flow through the body in case of shock, and earth free systems.

Integrity of referenced connectors

Where a circuit conductor is connected to earth, or other reference point, nothing that might foreseeably be expected to cause danger, by breaking electrical continuity or introducing high impedance, must be placed in that conductor, unless suitable precautions are taken to prevent that danger. [*Regs 9, 10*].

This requirement is especially important in the case of three-phase supplies, where the neutral conductor is connected to earth at source on the distribution system, so that phase voltages are not adversely affected by unbalanced loading. However, the requirement does not prevent all electrical devices from being placed in referential circuit conductors, e.g. a joint/bolted link, so long as precautions ensure that such objects do not cause danger, when being operated/removed. But fuses and transistors should not be so placed, since there would be a risk of danger, through forming an open circuit or introducing a high impedance into the circuit.

Moreover, every joint or connection must be mechanically and electrically suitable for use in order to avoid danger. [*Reg 10*]. Again, this duty is absolute and so the defence enshrined in *Reg 29* applies (see 11.6 above). The requirement extends to connections to plugs, sockets and any other means of joining or connecting conductors, whether connections are permanent or temporary.

Excess current protection

Efficient means, suitably located, must be provided for protecting from excess of current every part of a system necessary to prevent danger. [*Reg 11*]. This duty is absolute but *Reg 29* (see 11.6 above) provides a defence. The duty requires installation of protective devices, such as fuses/circuit breakers, to ensure that all parts of an electrical system are safeguarded from the consequences of fault conditions.

The main fault conditions are (*a*) overloads, (*b*) short circuits and (*c*) earth faults, the difference being that (*b*) and (*c*) present immediate danger, whilst, in the case of (*a*), some time passes before danger occurs. In all cases, the protective device aims to detect abnormal current flows and interrupt the fault current in anticipation of danger. As with earlier requirements, the IEE Wiring Regulations give detailed guidance on selection and rating of protective devices.

Cutting off supply and isolation of electrical equipment

Suitable means (including methods of identifying circuits) must exist for

   (i)   cutting off the supply of electrical energy to any electrical equipment; and

   (ii)   the isolation of any electrical equipment.

[*Reg 12*].

This requirement is dual – namely, that there exist facilities for (*a*) cutting off the supply of electrical energy and (*b*) isolating electrical equipment. 'Isolation' is disconnection/separation of electrical equipment from all sources of electrical energy.

Quite a few accidents occur in connection with work on a de-energised system, but which is inadvertently still live. Designed to ensure both disconnection of live supplies from all sources and that de-energised plant cannot inadvertently become live, this requirement (in tandem with *Regs 4, 14* and *16*) underlines the need for provision and maintenance of a safe system of work. This would consist of:

(*a*)   isolation from all points of supply;

(*b*)   securing each point of isolation, e.g. by fuses;

(*c*)   earthing, where necessary;

(*d*)   proving dead at point of work;

(*e*)   demarcation of safe work zone;

(*f*)   safeguarding from adjacent live conductors (e.g. by screening);

(*g*)   issue of permit to work (see further Chapter 1 'Introduction').

Work on or near live conductors

No person must carry out work on or so near to any live conductor (other than one suitably covered with insulating material to prevent danger) that danger may arise, unless

(*a*)   it is unreasonable for it to be dead; and

(*b*)   it is reasonable for him to be at work on or near it, while it is live; and

(*c*)   suitable precautions (including provision of suitable protective equipment) are taken to prevent danger.

[*Reg 14*].

There are limited circumstances where live working is permitted, as where it is not practicable to carry out work with the equipment dead, e.g. testing; or where making the equipment dead might endanger other users of the equipment. This requirement imposes an absolute duty not to work on live electrical equipment, unless the circumstances justify it. Moreover, if such work proceeds, suitable precautions must be taken to prevent injury, including a written company policy specifying the criteria for live working and the precautions to be taken.

Precautions

Typically, live work should only be done by trained or competent employees (see further *Reg 16* (below)) in possession of adequate information about the nature of the work and system. Appropriately insulated tools, equipment and protective clothing (e.g. rubber gloves/rubber mats) should be used, as well as screens. Such work should be done with another 'competent' person present, if this would minimise the risk of injury (see *Reg 16* below). In addition, access to the work area should be restricted and earth-free work areas established.

Working space/access/lighting

In order to prevent injury, adequate working space, adequate means of access and adequate lighting must be provided at all electrical equipment on which or near which work is being done that can cause danger. [*Reg 15*]. (For 'Access' and 'Lighting' provisions, see further Chapters 2 and 27 respectively.)

Competent staff

No person must carry out a work activity where technical knowledge or experience is necessary to prevent danger or injury, unless he has such knowledge or experience or is under the appropriate degree of supervision. [*Reg 16*].

Re-enacting *Reg 28* of the *Electricity Regulations 1908-1944* (with, however, important differences), this requirement specifies that, where accompaniment on electrical work takes place, such *accompanying person* must be competent to supervise the work (overruling *Vosper Thorneycroft (UK) Ltd v HSE (1979 unreported)*). This is particularly true in the case of work on live conductors or on high voltage systems.

Use of electrical equipment in explosive atmospheres

11.10 The *Electrical Equipment for Explosive Atmospheres (Certification) Regulations 1990 (SI 1990 No 13)* (as amended by *SI 1990 No 2377* and *SI 1991 No 2826*) are concerned with electrical equipment for use in potentially explosive atmospheres and provide for the appointment of certification bodies. [*Reg 3*]. Manufacturers of such equipment may apply to a certification body for a certificate of conformity to the effect that the electrical equipment conforms to the standards specified in the directive and the certification bodies are empowered to carry out checks. [*Reg 4*]. In addition, manufacturers may apply to an appropriate certification body for an inspection certificate to the effect that the equipment offers a degree of safety equivalent to EC standards.

On being issued with a conformity/inspection certificate, manufacturers can affix to electrical equipment the appropriate distinctive community mark, namely,

(a)   that specified in Annex II to the First Specific Directive – in the case of the Framework Directive;

(b)   that specified in Annex C – in the case of the Gassy Mines Directive.

[*Reg 11(1)*].

Affixation of community marks, otherwise than in accordance with *Reg 11(1)*, is punishable as a breach of health and safety regulations.

Where a certification body refuses to issue a certificate of conformity or inspection, or withdraws one already issued, the certification body must forthwith send a written notice of the decision to the manufacturer. [*Reg 6*]. In such a case, a manufacturer can apply to the Secretary of State for a review of the decision of the certification body within 60 days of receipt of the written notice. [*Reg 7*]. The application has to be made in writing, stating the grounds on which it is made and copies of the documents supplied by the manufacturer to the certification body and a copy of the notice of decision should be included with the application. The Secretary of State then has a discretion to direct the holding of an inquiry. [*Reg 8*].

Product liability

11.11   In addition to electrical stations being factories for the purposes of the *Factories Act 1961, s 123* (see further Chapter 18 'Factories and Workplaces'), 'electricity' is also a product for the purposes of the *Consumer Protection Act 1987*. [*Consumer Protection Act 1987, s 1(2)*]. Consequently, where a defect in an electrical installation/system results in injury, damage and/or death, liability is strict (see further Chapter 38 'Product Safety').

Non-statutory standards and codes

11.12   The Institution of Electrical Engineers (IEE) produced the first set of what has become known as the 'IEE Wiring Regulations' in 1882. The current edition of the IEE Wiring Regulations includes requirements for design, installation, inspection, testing and maintenance of electrical installations in or about buildings generally. The regulations as such have no statutory force, though they provide an indication of good industrial practice for the purposes of the *Electricity Regulations 1989*.

11.13   The National Inspection Council for Electrical Installations Contracting (NICEIC) enrols contractors whose work is of an approved standard. NICEIC surveys work to check that it complies with IEE Wiring Regulations.

The British Standards Institution (BSI) has issued many British Standards and codes of practice for electrical equipment and practice. Such standards and codes are subject to revision and supplementation. The standards range from insulation, earthing terminals and electrical connections of small equipment, to a complex set of precautions and specialised electrical equipment, based on the IEC concepts of flameproofing, intrinsic safety and other types of protection for electrical equipment in flammable atmospheres.

Examples of codes of practice topics issued by BSI include the subjects of earthing, street lighting, electrical equipment of industrial and office machines and distribution of electricity on construction and building sites (see further Appendix 2). The British Approvals Service for Electrical Equipment in Flammable Atmospheres (BASEEFA), linked with the HSE, is the official UK body for testing and certificating electrical apparatus for use in hazardous atmospheres, to IEC standards as accepted by CENELEC and BSI. The British Electrical and Allied Manufacturers' Association (BEAMA) issues a specialised range of standards and codes drawn up in consultation with users and others and the British Electrical Approvals Board for Household Equipment (BEAB) gives its seal of approval to such domestic type equipment as satisfies design and safety standards.

The *Electricity (Standards of Performance) Regulations 1993 (SI 1993 No 1193)* which came into force on 8 June 1993, provide for compensation to be payable by electricity suppliers for interruptions to supply and breach of other performance standards. These regulations have been made under the *Competition and Service (Utilities) Act 1992* (see Chapter 12 'Emissions into the Atmosphere') which itself introduced information on each public electricity supplier's performance standards and for each of them to establish a complaints procedure. Regulations are to be made relevant to billing disputes also. [*Secs 21–23*].

Emissions into the Atmosphere

Introduction

12.1 Statutory controls over industrial pollution have existed since the *Alkali Act 1863* (and its amendment in 1887), both designed to eliminate or, at least, minimise the worst effects of Victorian smokestack industries and their foul emissions. Laying emphasis, as it did, on control of (mainly) smoke emission, legislation has traditionally identified industrial pollution with air pollution. Water pollution, toxic waste, litter, oil and radiation pollution came to be regulated later (e.g. *Control of Pollution Act 1974*, the *Radioactive Substances Act 1960* (now the *Radioactive Substances Act 1993*, which came into effect on 27 August 1993; see further 9.56 DANGEROUS SUBSTANCES I) and the *Litter Act 1983*). Indeed, the main regulatory machinery for controlling *industrial* pollution (until, that is, the *Environmental Protection Act 1990*), was the *Alkali and Works Regulation Act 1906* (particularly *Sec 9*), in association (much later) with *Sec 5* of the *Health and Safety at Work etc. Act 1974* and, on the public health side, the *Public Health Act 1936, s 92(1)(d)* (now repealed) which provided that manufacturing dust/effluvia were statutory nuisances (see 'Statutory nuisances' at 12.27 below).

More recently, controls over pollution, emissions and escapes of potentially harmful substances have underscored prevention of damage to the environment rather than punishment and compensation for individual offences committed and injuries suffered in connection with occupation of land (e.g. common law nuisance). Indeed, prior to the introduction of the *Environmental Protection Act 1990* the law made no provision for protection of an integrated environment, preferring to focus on a patchwork quilt of its constituent but individual elements, e.g. water, air, radiation etc. To some extent, this trend is continued by legislation today, with emphasis still being lent to creation of offences associated with occupation of premises (e.g. the recent *Clean Air Act 1993*) but there the resemblance ends, with an identifiable shift away, in favour of access to environmental information and public accountability (e.g. the *Competition and Services (Utilities) Act 1992* and the *Environmental Information Regulations 1992*). In tandem therewith, archaic controls imposed by the law of tort on environmental pollution, caused by statutory undertakers, have been replaced by a raft of consumer-orientated duties and prescribed standards in connection with supply of water, gas and electricity (e.g. the *Competition and Services (Utilities) Act 1992* and the *Water Resources Act 1991*). This alterophobia towards pollution and contamination crystallises in the EC draft directive on Civil Liability for Waste, with its threat of strict liability hovering over producers and transporters of (non-nuclear) waste (see 12.31 below).

This apart, civil liability for environmental damage exists, generally, in the form of strict liability at common law under the rule in *Rylands v Fletcher* (see 19.44 FIRE AND FIRE PRECAUTIONS) and, more specifically, by dint of a succession of statutes concerned with 'statutory undertakers' such as the *Water Industry Act 1991* and the *Water Resources Act 1991*, the *Merchant Shipping (Oil Pollution) Act 1971* and the *Control of Pollution Act 1974*. In addition, under the *Consumer Protection Act 1987*, gas and electricity are classed as products with attendant strict liability for injury-causing defects (see Chapter 38 'Product Safety'). Finally, many aspects of civil liability for environmental damage are likely to involve strict liability, following the introduction of the (draft) EC Civil Liability Waste Directive, OJ C 251 Vol 32, Oct 1989, not yet implemented, which enshrines the principle of 'polluter pays'.

Earlier statutory controls over industrial pollution

12.2   Certain industrial processes, giving off potentially considerable emission of atmospheric pollutants, or which were technically difficult to control, were subject to *Sec 9* of the *Alkali Act 1906* (specific controls) and *Sec 5* of the *Health and Safety at Work etc. Act 1974* (general control). Control took the form of supervision of operations, involving emission of noxious substances, by HM Air Pollution Inspectorate, Controlled Waste Inspectorate and Radiochemical Inspectorate. Breach, resulting in injurious dust/effluvia, might have led to prosecution for statutory nuisance under *Sec 92(1)(d)* of the *Public Health Act 1936*; though, in practice, this was rare, since ministerial consent had to be obtained before local authorities could institute summary proceedings for nuisance, if proceedings could have been instituted by an air pollution inspector under the *Alkali and Works Regulation Act 1906*. There was provision for such prosecution in *Sec 22* of the *1906 Act* but it was very rarely used.

Currently, the *Control of Industrial Air Pollution Regulations 1989*, coupled with the *Health and Safety (Emissions into the Atmosphere) Regulations 1983* and *1989* require certain scheduled processes not to be operated until a certificate of registration had been issued by the particular Inspectorate of Pollution. Moreover, the *Control of Industrial Air Pollution Regulations 1989* provide for public access, on payment of a nominal fee, to the register of scheduled processes (this equating with the requirements of the *Environment and Safety Information Act 1988* in the field of workplace health and safety (see 17.22 ENFORCEMENT)).

Recent anti-pollution statutory controls

12.3   Recent anti-pollution measures have emerged in the form of both parent and subordinate legislation. In particular, the *Competition and Services (Utilities) Act 1992* provides for imposition by regulation of prescribed standards on suppliers of water, gas, electricity as well as sewerage undertakers, with compensation payable to consumers (including loss caused by environmental damage), as a civil debt, for breach. Secondly, the *Clean Air Act 1993*, a consolidation statute, by way of repeal of the *Clean Air Act 1956* and the *Control of Smoke Pollution Act 1989*, as well as partially repealing the *Control of Pollution Act 1974* [*Secs 75–84*] and the *Environmental Protection Act 1990* [*Sec 85*], prohibits the following emissions:

(*a*)   dark smoke from chimneys [*Sec 1*],

(*b*)   dark smoke from industrial trade premises [*Sec 2*],

and provides

(i)   that new furnaces, so far as practicable, are to be smokeless, and

(ii)   for (*a*) smoke control areas – prohibiting emissions of smoke and (*b*) adaptation of fireplaces in private dwellings.

[*Secs 18, 20 and 24*].

In addition, thereunder, air pollution can be limited/reduced by regulations controlling the composition/contents of motor fuel [*Sec 30*] and occupiers of premises can be required to specify/quantify emission of pollutants into the air, from their premises [*Sec 36*]. Failure, without reasonable cause, to comply with

Sec 36, can lead, on conviction, to imposition of a maximum fine of £5,000. Thirdly, the *Environmental Information Regulations 1992 (SI 1992 No 3240)* underline the desirability of individuals being allowed to access environmental information if not too sensitive. Thus, government departments, local authorities, Crown Ministers, with environmental responsibilities, are required, subject to certain exceptions, to make available, on request, and at reasonable times and places, information on the environment, subject to a charge. [*Reg 3*].

Fourthly, offences of polluting 'controlled waters' are included in the *Water Resources Act 1991*. More particularly, a person who 'causes or knowingly permits' poisonous, noxious or polluting matter or solid waste to enter controlled waters, is guilty of an offence punishable

(a)   on summary conviction, with imprisonment for up to three months or a fine of up to £20,000 (or both),

(b)   on conviction on indictment, with imprisonment for up to two years, or to an indefinite fine (or both).

There are several designated defences, including

(i)   authorisation, for prescribed processes purposes (see 12.14 below);

(ii)   consent given under the *Control of Pollution Act 1974*; and

(iii)   waste management or disposal licence.

[*Secs 85, 88*].

Damage consequent upon escape of water from a pipe renders the Water Authority liable to civil proceedings. Defences are identical with those specified in the *Water Industry Act 1991*. [*Water Resources Act 1991, s 208*] (see above).

Integration of inspectorate

12.4   As with workplace health and safety prior to the *Health and Safety at Work etc. Act 1974*, this piecemeal expansion of regulations relating to pollution was accompanied by the establishment in 1987 of HM Inspectorate of Pollution (in England and Wales but not Scotland). Thus, the pre-existing Industrial Air Pollution Inspectorate, Controlled Waste Inspectorate and Radiochemical Inspectorate, were amalgamated into a system of 'integrated pollution control' (IPC) – a process which reached its nadir in the *Environmental Protection Act 1990 (EPA)*, which is substantially in force (see further 12.13 below).

Summary of current legislation

12.5   The *Alkali and Works Regulation Act 1906* having been repealed by *EPA 1990, Part IX, 16 Sch*, current statutory controls over atmospheric emissions are contained in

(a)   the *Health and Safety (Emissions into the Atmosphere) Regulations 1983* and *1989 (SIs 1983 No 943 and 1989 No 319)*;

(b)   *Control of Industrial Air Pollution (Registration of Works) Regulations 1989 (SI 1989 No 318)*;

(c)   *Control of Asbestos in the Air Regulations 1990 (SI 1990 No 556)*;

(d)   the *Environmental Protection Act 1990, Part I*;

(e)   the *Radioactive Substances Act 1993* (see 9.56 DANGEROUS SUBSTANCES I);

(f)   the *Air Quality Standards Regulations 1989 (SI 1989 No 317)*, introducing fixed air quality standards (in place of the more informal and flexible structures of the *Alkali Acts*);

(g)   the *Clean Air Act 1993* (see 12.3 above);

(h)   the *Competition and Services (Utilities) Act 1992* (see 12.1 and 12.3 above); and

(j)   the *Water Industry* and *Water Resources Acts 1991* (see 12.30 below).

Health and Safety (Emissions into the Atmosphere) Regulations 1983 and 1989

12.6   These regulations identify 62 registrable/scheduled processes (ranging from acetylene to zinc works) and 82 specified noxious substances (ranging from acetic acid to volatile organic sulphur compounds). Operators of such plant/processes are required to obtain consent (to operate) by means of annual registration/re-registration.

Consent of pollution authorities depended (and still does until *EPA 1990* comes into effect fully) on equipment and working procedures satisfying the requirements of the 'best practicable means' (bpm) test. In other words, the *presumption* was that processes/plants complied with regulations if they conformed with Bpm Guidance Notes published by HMIP and, in particular, 'numerical emission limits' and 'best practicable means'. Moreover, breach of these Guidance Notes was *not* necessarily tantamount to breach of regulations. This, together with the limited number of prosecutions for breach of the *Alkali Act 1906* precipitated the introduction of *EPA 1990*.

Prescribed premises/scheduled processes

12.7   Some 2,000 registrable works, covering some 3,000 scheduled processes, are now controlled by inspectors, either centrally or locally (see 12.17 below). These are as follows:

Acetylene works

Works in which acetylene is made and used in any chemical manufacturing process.

Acrylates works

Works in which acrylates are–

(a)   made or purified; or

(b)   made and polymerised; or

(c)   purified and polymerised; or

(d)   stored and handled in fixed tanks with an aggregate capacity exceeding 20 tonnes.

Aldehyde works

Works in which formaldehyde, acetaldehyde or acrolein or the methyl, ethyl or propyl derivatives of acrolein are made.

Aluminium works

Works in which–

(a)   oxide of aluminium is extracted from any ore; or

(b)   aluminium is extracted from any compound containing aluminium by a process evolving any noxious or offensive gases; or

(c)   aluminium swarf is degreased by the application of heat; or

(d)   aluminium or aluminium alloys are recovered from aluminium or aluminium alloy scrap fabricated metal, swarf, skimmings, or other residues by melting under flux; or

(e)   aluminium is recovered from slag or drosses; or

(f)   molten aluminium or aluminium alloys are treated by chlorine or its compounds; or

(g)   materials used in the above processes or the products thereof are treated or handled by methods which cause noxious or offensive gases to be evolved.

Amines works

Works in which–

(a)   any methylamine or any ethylamine is made; or

(b)   any methylamine or any ethylamine is used in any chemical process.

Ammonia works

Works in which ammonia is–

(a)   made or recovered; or

(b)   used in the ammonia-soda process; or

(c)   used in the manufacture of carbonate, hydroxide, nitrate or phosphate of ammonia, or urea or nitriles; or

(d)   stored and handled in anhydrous form in fixed tanks with an aggregate capacity exceeding 100 tonnes.

Anhydride works

Works in which acetic, maleic or phthalic anhydrides or the corresponding acids are made or recovered.

Arsenic works

Works for the preparation of arsenious acid, or where nitric acid or a nitrate is used in the manufacture of arsenic acid or an arsenate and works in which any volatile compound or arsenic is evolved in any manufacturing process and works in which arsenic is made.

Asbestos works

Works in which–

(a)   raw asbestos is produced, but excluding any process directly associated with the mining of ore; or (*b*)   asbestos is used in the manufacture and industrial finishing of

    (i)   asbestos cement,

    (ii)   asbestos cement products,

    (iii)   asbestos fillers,

    (iv)   asbestos filters,

    (v)   asbestos floor coverings,

    (vi)   asbestos friction products,

    (vii)   asbestos insulating board,

    (viii)   asbestos jointing, packaging and reinforcement materials,

    (ix)   asbestos packing,

    (x)   asbestos paper and card, or

    (xi)   asbestos textiles; or

(*c*)   crocidolite is stripped from railway vehicles, other than as a part of repair or maintenance or during vehicle recovery after an accident; or

(*d*)   railway vehicles containing crocidolite are destroyed by burning at purpose-built installations.

[*Health and Safety (Emissions into the Atmosphere) (Amendment) Regulations 1989 (SI 1989 No 319)*]. (For the new provisions relating to the emission of asbestos dust see 12.12 below.)

Benzene works

Works (not being tar works or bitumen works) in which–

(*a*)   any wash oil used for the scrubbing of coal gas is distilled; or

(*b*)   any crude benzol is distilled; or

(*c*)   benzene is distilled or recovered.

Beryllium works

Works in which–

(*a*)   any ore or concentrate or any material containing beryllium or its compounds is treated for the production of beryllium or its alloys or its compounds; or

(*b*)   any material containing beryllium or its alloys or its compounds is treated, processed or fabricated in any manner giving rise to dust or fume.

Bisulphite works

(*a*)   Works in which sulphurous acid is used in the manufacture of acid sulphites of the alkalis or alkaline earths; or

(*b*)   works in which oxides of sulphur are–

    (i)   made; or

    (ii)   used or evolved in any chemical manufacturing operation; or

    (iii)   used in the production of sulphurous acid.

Bromine works

Works in which bromine is made or used in any manufacturing operation.

Cadmium works

Works in which–

(*a*)   metallic cadmium is recovered; or

(*b*)   cadmium alloys are made or recovered; or

(*c*)   any compound of cadmium is made by methods giving rise to dust or fume.

Carbon disulphide works

Works for the manufacture, use or recovery of carbon disulphide.

Carbonyl works

Works in which metal carbonyls are manufactured or used in any chemical or metallurgical manufacturing process.

Caustic soda works

Works in which black liquor produced in the manufacture of paper is calcined in the recovery of caustic soda.

Cement works

Works in which–

(*a*)   argillaceous and calcareous materials are used in the production of cement clinker; or

(*b*)   cement clinker is handled and ground.

Ceramic works

Works in which–

(*a*)   heavy clay or refractory goods are fired by coal or oil in any kiln in which a reducing atmosphere is essential; or

(*b*)   salt glazing of any earthenware or clay material is carried on.

Chemical fertiliser works

Works in which the manufacture of chemical fertiliser is carried on, and works in which any mineral phosphate is subjected to treatment involving chemical change through the application or use of any acid and works for the granulating of chemical fertilisers involving the evolution of any noxious or offensive gas.

Chlorine works

Works in which chlorine is made or used in any manufacturing process.

Chromium works

Works in which–

(*a*)   any chrome ore or concentrate is treated for the production therefrom of chromium compounds; or

(*b*)   chromium metal is made by methods giving rise to dust or fume.

Copper works

Works in which–

(*a*)   by the application of heat

    (i)   copper is extracted from any ore or concentrate or from any material containing copper or its compounds; or

    (ii)   molten copper is refined; or

    (iii)   copper or copper alloy swarf is degreased; or

    (iv)   copper alloys are recovered from scrap fabricated metal, swarf or residues by processes designed to reduce the zinc content; or

    (v)   copper alloys are recovered from scrap fabricated metal, swarf or residues; or

(*b*)   copper or copper alloy is melted and cast,

excluding works in which the aggregate casting capacity does not exceed 10 tonnes per day.

Di-isocyanate works

Works in which–

(*a*)   di-isocyanates or partly polymerised di-isocyanates are made; or

(*b*)   di-isocyanates or partly polymerised di-isocyanates are used in the manufacture of flexible or rigid polyurethane foams or elastomers; or

(*c*)   polyurethane foams are subjected to hot-wire cutting or flame-bonding.

Electricity works

Works in which solid liquid or gaseous fuel is burned–

(*a*)   for the generation of electricity solely for distribution to the general public or for the purposes of public transport (but excluding compression ignition engines burning distillate fuel with a sulphur content of less than 1%); or

(*b*)   for the generation of electricity for any purpose where the net rated thermal input of the works is 50 megawatts or more (other than works mentioned in (*a*)).

Fibre works

Works in which glass fibre or mineral fibre (other than asbestos fibre) is made.

Fluorine works

Works in which fluorine or its compounds with other halogens are made or used in the manufacture of any product, or works for the manufacture of fluorides, borofluorides or silicofluorides.

Gas liquor works

Works (not being sulphate of ammonia works and chloride of ammonia works) in which hydrogen sulphide or any other noxious or offensive gas is evolved by the use of ammoniacal liquor in any manufacturing process, and works in which any such liquor is desulphurised by the application of heat in any process connected with the purification of gas.

Gas and coke works

Works (not being producer gas works) in which–

(a)   coal, oil, or mixtures of coal or oil with other carbonaceous materials or products of petroleum refining, or natural gas, or methane from coal mines, or gas derived from fermentation of carbonaceous materials are handled or prepared for carbonisation or gasification or reforming and in which these materials are subsequently carbonised or gasified or reformed; or

(b)   water gas is produced or purified; or

(c)   coke or semi-coke or other solid smokeless fuel is produced and quenched, cut, crushed or graded; or

(d)   gases derived from any process in (a) are subjected to purification processes.

Hydrochloric acid works

(a)   hydrochloric acid works or works (not being alkali works) where hydrogen chloride is evolved, either during the preparation of liquid hydrochloric acid, or for use in any manufacturing process, or as the result of the use of chlorides in a chemical process;

(b)   tinplate flux works, in which any residue or flux from tinplate works is calcined for the utilisation of such residue or flux, and in which hydrogen chloride is evolved; and

(c)   salt works (though not works in which salt is produced by refining rock salt, otherwise than by the dissolution of rock salt at the place of deposit) in which the extraction of salt from brine is carried on, and in which hydrogen chloride is evolved.

Hydrofluoric acid works

Works in which–

(a)   hydrogen fluoride is evolved either in the manufacture of liquid hydrofluoric acid or its compounds, or as the result of the use of fluorides in a chemical process; or

(b)   mineral phosphates are treated with acid other than in fertiliser manufacture; or

(c)   mineral phosphates are defluorinated; or

(d)   anhydrous hydrogen fluoride is stored and handled in fixed tanks with an aggregate capacity exceeding 1 tonne.

Hydrogen cyanide works

Works in which hydrogen cyanide is made or is used in any chemical manufacturing process.

Incineration works

Works for the destruction by burning of–

(a)   waste produced from chemical manufacturing processes; or

(b)   chemical waste containing combined bromine, cadmium, chlorine, fluorine, iodine, lead, mercury, nitrogen, phosphorous, sulphur or zinc; or

(c)   waste produced in the manufacture of plastics; or

(d)   other waste, where the works are capable of incinerating 1 tonne or more of waste per hour.

Iron works and steel works

Works in which–

(a)   iron ores or iron ores and other materials for the production of iron are handled, stored or prepared, but excluding the winning of iron ores; or

(b)   iron ores for the production of iron are calcined, sintered or pelletised; or

(c)   iron or ferro-alloys are produced in a blast furnace or by direct reduction; or

(d)   iron or steel is melted in

  (i)   electric arc furnaces; or

  (ii)   cupolas employing a heated air blast; or

(e)   steel is produced, melted or refined in Tropenas, open hearth or electric arc furnaces; or

(f)   air or oxygen or air enriched with oxygen is used for the refining of iron or for the production, shaping or finishing of steel; or

(g)   ferro-alloys are made by methods giving rise to dust or fume; or

(h)   iron or ferro-alloys produced in any process described in (c), (d) or (g) are desulphurised by methods giving rise to dust or fume.

Large combustion works

Works in which solid, liquid or gaseous fuel is burned in boilers or furnaces with a net-rated thermal input of 50 megawatts or more.

Large glass works

Works capable of producing 5,000 tonnes or more of glass (other than glass fibre) per year.

Large paper pulp works

Works capable of producing 25,000 tonnes or more of paper pulp by chemical methods per year.

Lead works

Works in which –

(a)   by the application of heat,

(i)   lead is extracted or recovered from any material containing lead or its compounds; or

(ii)   lead is refined; or

(iii)   lead is applied as a surface coating to other metals by spraying; or

(*b*)   compounds of lead are manufactured, extracted, recovered or used in processes which give rise to dust or fume, but excluding the manufacture of electric accumulators and the application of glazes or vitreous enamels; or

(*c*)   organic lead compounds are made.

Lime works

Works in which–

(*a*)   calcium carbonate or calcium-magnesium carbonate is burnt by means of solid, liquid or gaseous fuels; or

(*b*)   lime is slaked on premises where any process described in (*a*) is carried out.

Magnesium works

Works in which magnesium or its alloys or any compound of magnesium is made by methods giving rise to dust or fume.

Manganese works

Works in which manganese or its alloys or any compound of manganese is made by methods giving rise to dust or fume.

Metal recovery works

Works in which metal is recovered from scrap cable by burning in a furnace.

Mineral works

Works in which–

(*a*)   metallurgical slags; or

(*b*)   pulverised fuel ash; or

(*c*)   minerals, other than moulding sand in foundries or coal,

are subjected to any size reduction, grading or heating by processes giving rise to dust.

Nitrate and chloride of iron works

Works in which nitric acid or a nitrate is used in the manufacture of nitrate or chloride of iron.

Nitric acid works

Works in which the manufacture of nitric acid is carried on and works in which nitric acid is recovered from oxides of nitrogen and works where in the manufacture of any product any acid-forming oxide of nitrogen is evolved.

Paraffin oil works

Works in which crude shale oil is produced or refined, and

(*a*)   any product of the refining of crude shale oil is treated so as to cause the evolution of any noxious or offensive gases; or

(*b*)   any such product is used in any subsequent chemical manufacturing process, except as a solvent.

Petrochemical works

Works in which–

(*a*)   any hydrocarbons are used for the production of ethylene or propylene or other olefines; or

(*b*)   (i)   ethylene or propylene or other olefines or mixtures are used in any chemical manufacturing process; or

(ii)   any product of the processes in (*b*)(i) is used, except as a solvent, in any subsequent chemical manufacturing process; or

(*c*)   ethylene, or propylene or other olefines or products of processes in (*b*)(i) and (ii) or mixtures are polymerised.

Petroleum works

Works in which–

(*a*)   crude or stabilised crude petroleum or associated gas, or condensate is

(i)   handled or stored; or

(ii)   refined; or

(*b*)   any product of such refining is subjected to further refining or to conversion; or

(*c*)   natural gas is refined or odorised; or

(*d*)   any product of any of the above operations is used, except as a solvent, in any subsequent chemical manufacturing process; or

(*e*)   used lubricating oil is prepared for re-use by any thermal process.

Phosphorus works

Works in which–

(*a*)   phosphorus is made; or

(*b*)   yellow phosphorus is used in any chemical or metallurgical process.

Picric acid works

Works in which nitric acid or a nitrate is used in the manufacture of picric acid.

Producer gas works

Works in which producer gas is made from coal and in which raw producer gas is transmitted or used.

Pyridine works

Works in which pyridines or picolines or lutidines are recovered or made.

Selenium works

Works in which–

(a)   any ore or concentrate or any material containing selenium or its compounds is treated for the production of selenium or its alloys or its compounds; or

(b)   any material containing selenium or its alloys or its compounds (other than as colouring matter) is treated, processed or fabricated in any manner giving rise to dust or fume.

Smelting works

Works in which sulphides or sulphide ores, including regulus or mattes are calcined or smelted.

Sulphate of ammonia works, and chloride of ammonia works

Works in which the manufacture of sulphate of ammonia or of chloride of ammonia is carried on.

Sulphide works

Works in which–

(a)   hydrogen sulphide is evolved by the decomposition of metallic sulphides; or

(b)   hydrogen sulphide is used in the production of such sulphides; or

(c)   hydrogen sulphide or mercaptans are–

    (i)   made, or

    (ii)   used in any chemical process, or

    (iii)   evolved as part of any chemical process.

Sulphuric acid (Class I) works

Works in which the manufacture of sulphuric acid is carried on by the lead chamber process, namely, the process by which sulphurous acid is converted into sulphuric acid by means of oxides of nitrogen and by the use of a lead chamber or by any other process involving the use of oxides of nitrogen.

Sulphuric acid (Class II) works

Works in which the manufacture of sulphuric acid is carried on by any process other than the lead chamber process, and for the concentration or distillation of sulphuric acid.

Tar works and bitumen works

(a)   works in which gas tar or coal tar or bitumen is distilled or heated in any manufacturing process, and any product of the distillation of gas tar or coal tar or bitumen is distilled or heated in any process involving the evolution of any noxious or offensive gas; or (*b*)   works in which heated materials produced from gas tar or coal tar or bitumen are applied in coating or wrapping of iron or steel pipes or fittings.

Uranium works

Works (not being works licensed under the *Nuclear Installations Acts 1965(a)* and *1969(b)* and not being nuclear reactors or works involving the processing of irradiated fuel for the purpose of removing fission products) in which–

(*a*)   any ore or concentrate or any material containing uranium or its compounds is treated for the production of uranium or its alloys or its compounds; or

(*b*)   any volatile compounds of uranium are manufactured or used; or

(*c*)   uranium or its compounds are manufactured, fashioned or fabricated by methods giving rise to dust or fume.

Vinyl chloride works

Works in which vinyl chloride is made or polymerised or used or stored and handled in fixed tanks with an aggregate capacity exceeding 20 tonnes.

Zinc works

Works in which, by the application of heat, zinc is extracted from the ore, or from any residue containing that metal, and works in which compounds of zinc are made by methods giving rise to dust or fume.

[*Health and Safety (Emissions into the Atmosphere) Regulations 1983 (SI 1983 No 943), Reg 3, 1 Sch as amended by the Health and Safety (Emissions into the Atmosphere) (Amendment) Regulations 1989 (SI 1989 No 319)*].

Noxious/offensive substances

12.8   The following are noxious/offensive substances in respect of which persons in control of prescribed premises must use the 'best practicable means' (see above) to prevent their emission into the atmosphere:

—   acetic acid or its anhydride

—   acetylene

—   acrylic acid

—   acrylates

—   aldehydes

—   amines

—   ammonia or its compounds

—   arsenic or its compounds

—   asbestos

—   bromine or its compounds

—   carbon disulphide

—   carbon dioxide

—   carbon monoxide

— chlorine or its compounds

— cyanogen or its compounds

— di-isocyanates

— ethylene

— fluorine and its compounds

— fumaric acid

— fumes or dust containing aluminium, antimony, arsenic, beryllium, cadmium, calcium, chlorine, chromium, copper, gallium, iron, lead, magnesium, manganese, mercury, molybdenum, nickel, phosphorus, platinum, potassium, selenium, silicon, silver, sodium, sulphur, tellurium, thallium, tin, titanium, uranium, vanadium, zinc or their compounds

— fumes or vapours from benzene works, paraffin oil works, petrochemical works, petroleum works, or tar works and bitumen works

— glass fibres

— hydrocarbons

— hydrogen chloride

— hydrogen sulphide

— iodine or its compounds

— isocyanates

— lead or its compounds

— maleic acid or its anhydride

— mercury or its compounds

— metal carbonyls

— mineral fibres

— nitric acid or oxides of nitrogen

— nitriles

— phenols

— phosphorus or its compounds

— phthalic acid or its anhydride

— products containing hydrogen from the partial oxidation of hydrocarbons

— pyridine or its homologues

— smoke, grit and dust

— styrene

— sulphuric acid or sulphur trioxide

— sulphurous acid or sulphur dioxide

— vinyl chloride

— volatile organic sulphur compounds

[*Health and Safety (Emissions into the Atmosphere) Regulations 1983, Reg 4, 2 Sch; Health and Safety (Emissions into the Atmosphere) (Amendment) Regulations 1989*].

Owners of such 'process' premises must apply annually for certificate of registration/re-registration, under the *Control of Industrial Air Pollution (Registration of Works) Regulations 1989.*

Control of Industrial Air Pollution (Registration of Works) Regulations 1989 (SI 1989 No 318)

12.9   These regulations govern registration of industrial air pollution premises. Thus, owners of such processes must apply for registration, giving

(*a*)   name/address of owner of works, or company etc.;

(*b*)   name/address of premises;

(*c*)   identification (by means of map/plan) of those parts of the premises where work is to be carried on;

(*d*)   name of local authority;

(*e*)   date of application;

(*f*)   nature of work;

(*g*)   nature and amount of noxious/offensive substance;

(*h*)   means by which work is to be carried out in accordance with statutory requirement;

(*j*)   provision for determining nature/amount of noxious/offensive substances emitted.

[*Reg 3*].

Registration of industrial air pollution premises

12.10   The requirements relating to registration of industrial air pollution premises contained in the *Control of Industrial Air Pollution (Registration of Works) Regulations 1989* modify the registration requirements of *Sec 9* of the *Alkali Act 1906* and, in addition, provide for public access to the register of scheduled processes (see 12.3 above).

After fourteen days following receipt of application by the Secretary of State, the applicant must publish, in a local newspaper in each of two successive weeks, a notice containing the following particulars:

(*a*)   name of owner;

(*b*)   address of premises;

(*c*)   brief description of the nature of the work;

(*d*)   address of places where and a statement of the times when the application can be inspected;

(*e*)   a statement that written representations concerning the application can be made to the Secretary of State and that those received by him within 21 days of first publication of the notice, will be relevant in deciding the application;

(*f*)   the address to which representations should be made; and

(*g*)   the date on which the notice was first published.

[*Reg 4*].

Contents of the register of listed works

12.11 The register of a 'listed work' must contain the following particulars:

(*a*)   name and address of the owner of the work or limited company and registered office;

(*b*)   name and address of premises;

(*c*)   identification (by map/plan) of the parts of the premises where the work is or will be carried on;

(*d*)   name of the local authority;

(*e*)   description of the nature of the work to be carried on;

(*f*)   category of work into which the work falls (see Prescribed premises/ scheduled processes at 12.7 above);

(*g*)   description of the means necessary to enable work to be carried on in accordance with the *Alkali Act 1906* and/or the *Health and Safety at Work Act 1974* and the *Environmental Protection Act 1990*;

(*h*)   maximum amount of emission that can be lawfully made;

(*j*)   description of provision to be made for determining the nature and amount of a noxious/offensive substance;

(*k*)   date on which the application is received by the Secretary of State and the date on which the certificate of registration is issued; and

(*l*)   if work is closed for twelve months or more, the date when the work is closed.

[*Reg 7*].

Moreover, changes in particulars in the certificate of registration must be notified to the Secretary of State within one month of the change. [*Reg 10*]. The register is available for public inspection free of charge during normal working hours, and on payment of a fee, members of the public can take copies. Copies of registers and any amendments are also to be sent to local authorities who must also allow inspection and copying of entries. [*Reg 8*].

Control of Asbestos in the Air Regulations 1990

12.12 Emissions of asbestos dust into the atmosphere are governed specifically by the *Control of Asbestos in the Air Regulations 1990 (SI 1990 No 556)*. Thus, any person having control of premises from which asbestos is emitted through discharge outlets into the air, during use of asbestos, must ensure that the concentration of asbestos

(*a*)   discharged, does not exceed 0.1 milligram of asbestos per cubic metre of air; and

(*b*)   emitted, is measured at six-monthly intervals or less.

[*Control of Asbestos in the Air Regulations 1990, Reg 2*].

Moreover, anyone working with products containing asbestos must ensure that significant environmental pollution is not caused by

(i)   asbestos fibres or dust emitted into the air; and/or

(ii)   demolition of buildings, structures and installations containing asbestos and removal from them of asbestos or materials containing asbestos, involving release of asbestos fibres or dust into the air.

[*Control of Asbestos in the Air Regulations 1990, Reg 4*].

Environmental Protection Act 1990 (EPA)

12.13   The *Environmental Protection Act 1990* is the most important piece of environmental legislation to date, introducing a regime of 'integrated pollution control' (IPC) – that is, a unified inspectorate to handle all aspects of the environment. By contrast, earlier regimes had been fragmented in their approach to environmental problems, dealing with them reactively on an ad hoc basis – hence the succession of various statutory controls ranging from the *Alkali Acts*, the *Public Health Acts*, the *Town and Country Planning Acts*, the legislation on noise pollution, the *Clean Air Acts*, the *Radioactive Substances Act*, the *Litter Act*, the *Deposit of Poisonous Wastes Act* etc.

The new unified system of 'integrated control' is administered and policed by Her Majesty's Inspectorate of Pollution (HMIP), and local authority environmental health departments in the case of air pollution control (APC). To this end, HMIP and local authorities have been given wide powers to implement *EPA 1990*, including insisting on 'prior authorisation' procedures in the case of 'specified processes' (see further 12.14, 12.17 and 12.26 below).

In addition, *EPA 1990* reformulates statutory nuisances in connection with noise/smells (Part III), litter (Part IV), radioactive substances (Part V), genetically modified organisms (Part VI), nature conservation (Part VII) and hazardous chemicals/dumping at sea/stubble burning (Part VIII), and, by dint of the *Motor Vehicles (Type Approval) (Amendment) (No 3) Regulations 1991 (SI 1991 No 2830)*, controls are extended to pollution from diesel engines.

Industrial atmospheric pollution – EPA 1990, Part I

12.14   Under *EPA 1990* the system of '*presumptive limits*' and '*best practicable means*' is abolished. Instead, a regime of *prior authorisations* envisages an *augmented number of 'specified processes'* – that is, a considerably greater number of processes than those specified in the *Emissions into the Atmosphere Regulations* are subject to integrated pollution control and enforcement procedures by local authorities; this number is continually expanding in line with updating EC directives. [*Sec 156*]. The Secretary of State has, by regulations (see 12.26 below), prescribed certain processes as requiring authorisation certificates before they can continue in operation, in line with his power to do so, under *Sec 2(1)* (see below and 12.26).

Moreover, *emission limits* are now *legally binding* and operators are under a *residual duty* to use '*best practicable environmental options*' (BPEO) to control pollution. Regulations made under *Sec 2(1)* specifying processes requiring prior authorisation, before they can continue to operate, are the *Environmental Protection (Prescribed Processes and Substances) Regulations 1991* (see 12.26 below). In addition, regulations can also be expected, similar in orientation to the *Air Quality Standards Regulations 1989* (see 12.5 above), specifying emission limits and quality objectives, breach of which will give rise to service of enforcement notices/prosecutions. [*Sec 3*].

Operators of plant, therefore, must now obtain authorisation for their operation [*Sec 6*] – such authorisation being dependent on their preventing specified substances being released into the atmosphere, or, where this is not practicable (here meaning 'reasonably practicable' [*EPA s 79(9)*]), reducing emissions into the atmosphere to a minimum. Moreover, *such residual releases must be rendered harmless by 'best practicable environmental options'*. In other words, even if plant operators meet specific standards in authorisation, they will still have to employ best practicable environmental options to control residual emissions [*Sec 7(4)*], and BPEO applications require operators to submit environmental statements to this effect, evaluating practicable environmental options.

Best available techniques not entailing excessive cost (BATNEEC)

12.15   In order to comply with *Sec 6* (above) and obtain authorisation, operators have to use *'best available techniques not entailing excessive cost'* (BATNEEC) for

(*a*)   preventing release of substances; and

(*b*)   rendering harmless any residual substances.

[*Sec 7(2)*].

In this connection *Sec 7(10)* makes it clear that 'techniques' extend beyond technology and equipment in use, to 'design/construction/layout and maintenance of buildings' as well as 'number, qualifications, training and supervision of persons employed'. This is in sharp contrast with the earlier position under the *Alkali and Works Regulation Act 1906*, whereby process operators had to take 'best practicable means' to comply. 'Best practicable means' took into account the means of operators against whom the law was enforced as well as the economic and social consequences to the community of control, current state of the art and local conditions. Technical limitations of older equipment were not ignored either, though compliance with standard trade practice was not always enough (*Scholefield v Schunck (1855) 19 JP 84*). Needless to say, there were few prosecutions for alleged breach of the *Alkali Act*.

HM Inspectorate of Pollution's (HMIP) Guidance Notes (of quasi-legal force) state: 'the *presumption* will be that the best available techniques will be used, but that presumption can be modified by *economic considerations* when it can be shown that the cost of applying best available techniques would be excessive in relation to the environmental protection achieved. If, for instance, there is one technology which reduces emission of polluting substances by 90% and another which reduces the emissions by 95%, but at four times the cost, it may be a proper judgment to hold that because of the small benefit and the great cost the second technology would entail excessive cost. If, on the other hand, the emissions were particularly dangerous, it may be proper to judge that the additional cost was not excessive.' This is comparable with employers being required to do what is 'reasonably practicable', for the purposes of the *Health and Safety at Work etc. Act 1974* (see Chapter 15 'Employers' Duties'). General Guidance Notes are also available from the Department of the Environment.

An application to an enforcing authority must be in writing, containing

(*a*)   name, address and telephone number of applicant;

(*b*)   where prescribed processes will not be carried on by mobile means:

(i)   name of local authority where the prescribed process is to be carried on,

(ii)   address of premises where process is to be carried on,

(iii)   map/plan showing location of premises,

(iv)   if part of premises only is to be used for carrying out the process, a plan identifying it;

    (c)   in the case of mobile plant:

        (i)   name of local authority in which applicant has his main place of business,

        (ii)   address of that place of business;

    (d)   in both types of plant:

        (i)   description of prescribed process,

        (ii)   description of techniques for preventing release of substance(s) or for reducing release to a minimum,

        (iii)   details of any proposed release of such substances,

        (iv)   proposals for monitoring release,

        (v)   matters on which applicant relies to secure compliance with *Sec 7(2), (4)* and *(7)* of *EPA 1990* (see below and 12.16),

        (vi)   any additional information which applicant wants taken into account.

[*Environmental Protection (Application, Appeals and Registers) Regulations 1991 (SI 1991 No 507), Reg 2*].

National Plan

12.16   Apart from preparation of emission standards by HMIP, the Secretary of State may separately require standards to be inserted in authorisations and produce a National Plan, with which authorisations must comply. [*Sec 7*]. Such Plan will come to assume increasing importance as more and more directives update environmental controls (e.g. Large Combustion Plants Directive). [*Sec 156*].

Enforcement of EPA 1990

12.17   Any regulations passed under *EPA 1990* are subject to enforcement by either HMIP (central control) or environmental health officers of local authorities (local control). [*Sec 2(4)*]. More particularly, industrial air pollution control requirements, as well as 2nd-tier (or Part B) processes (see 'Timetable for air pollution control' at 12.26 below) are enforceable by environmental health departments of local authorities. [*EPA 1990, Part I*].

However, given that an enforcing authority is empowered to vary conditions of authorisation [*Sec 10*] and the Secretary of State to update them [*Sec 3*] – both of which are likely to occur in line with the National Plan (above) and a flow of EC directives, on-going upgrading of processes will take place independently of prosecution and other legal remedies.

This notwithstanding, however, *EPA 1990* gives enforcing authorities considerable enforcement powers analogous with those of HSE inspectors, for the purposes of *HSWA* (see Chapter 17 'Enforcement') as follows.

    (i)   An enforcement notice can be served (by an HMIP inspector or an environmental health officer of a local authority) where an inspector is of the opinion that the conditions of authorisation have been breached, specifying the necessary remedial action within a specified period. [*Sec 13*].

    (ii)   A prohibition notice can be served where there is an 'imminent risk of serious pollution of the environment', relating to any aspects of the process, whether regulated by conditions of authorisation or not. A prohibition notice can suspend an authorisation or specify remedial action necessary before plant can continue to operate. [*Sec 14*].

Appeals against notices

12.18 An operator who has been refused authorisation or who is dissatisfied with conditions attaching to an authorisation, or an operator whose authorisation has been revoked, can appeal to the Secretary of State. [*Sec 15*]. The latter can

(*a*) affirm the decision;

(*b*) grant/vary the authorisation;

(*c*) quash the conditions of the authorisation;

(*d*) quash the decision revoking the authorisation.

[*Sec 15(6)*].

Additional powers of inspectors

12.19 In addition, inspectors can enter 'process' premises and examine equipment, direct that premises/equipment be left undisturbed, take measurements/photographs, require persons to answer questions, dismantle and detain objects. [*Sec 17*]. But *no answer given by a person under examination is admissible against him in criminal proceedings.* [*Sec 17(8)*]. Where an inspector believes that an article on any premises is a cause of imminent danger or serious harm, he can seize it and render it harmless, having first (normally) taken a sample of it. [*Sec 18*].

Public register

12.20 Enforcing authorities must establish and maintain a public register of information, in which records (or, at least, most records) relating to application for authorisation, authorisation itself, enforcement and prohibition notices, revocations and convictions are to be kept. [*Sec 20*]. (This equates with the position under the *Environment and Safety Information Act 1988* regarding notices served under *HSWA* (see 17.22 ENFORCEMENT).) Enforcing authorities must

(*a*) ensure that registers are available, at all reasonable times, for inspection by the public free of charge; and

(*b*) afford members of the public facilities for obtaining copies of entries, on payment of a reasonable charge.

[*Sec 20(7)*].

Offences/penalties/burden of proof

Offences

12.21 The following are the main offences that operators may commit:

(*a*) contravening an authorisation;

(*b*) failing to give due notice to an enforcing authority, on transfer of an authorisation;

(*c*) failing to comply with or contravening a requirement/prohibition of an enforcement or prohibition notice;

(*d*)   failing to comply with an inspector's direction in the normal exercise of his powers;

(*e*)   preventing any person from appearing before or answering a question to which an inspector may require an answer;

(*f*)   intentionally obstructing an inspector;

(*g*)   making false, misleading or reckless statements;

(*h*)   making a false entry in any record connected with authorisations;

(*j*)   failing to comply with a court order to remedy an offence.

[*Sec 23(1)*].

Penalties

12.22   (1)   For breach of (*a*), (*c*) and (*j*) in 12.21 above:

    (i)   on summary conviction, a maximum fine of £20,000;

    (ii)   on conviction on indictment, an indefinite fine or a maximum of two years' imprisonment, or both.

[*Sec 23(2)*].

(2)   For breach of (*b*), (*g*) and (*h*) in 12.21 above:

    (i)   on summary conviction, not more than the statutory maximum;

    (ii)   on conviction on indictment, an indefinite fine or a maximum of two years' imprisonment, or both.

[*Sec 23(3)*].

(3)   For breach of (*d*), (*e*) and (*f*) in 12.21 above, on summary conviction, a fine not greater than the statutory maximum (i.e. £20,000) (see Statutory maximum at 12.27 below). [*Sec 23(4)*].

Burden of proof

12.23   In any proceedings for an offence relating to failure to comply with/contravening a requirement/prohibition of an enforcement/prohibition notice, *it is for the accused to prove that there was no better available technique not entailing excessive cost than was, in fact, used to satisfy the condition.* [*Sec 25(1)*]. (This equates with *HSWA s 40* (see further 17.24 ENFORCEMENT).)

In addition, where an entry is required in a record concerning observance of any condition of authorisation, and entry has *not* been made, this is evidence that the condition has *not* been observed. [*Sec 25(2)*].

Offences of bodies corporate/companies/etc. and 'other persons'

Offences of bodies corporate

12.24   Where an offence under *EPA 1990*, committed by a body corporate, is proved to have been committed with the consent or connivance, or attributable to neglect on the part of

(*a*)   any director,

(*b*)   manager,

(*c*)   secretary, or

(*d*)   other similar officer,

he, as well as the body corporate, is guilty of an offence, whether or not proceedings are taken against the body corporate itself. [*Sec 157(1)*]. (This is analogous with *HSWA s 37(1)* (see 17.32 ENFORCEMENT and 15.45 EMPLOYERS' DUTIES).) This may well lead to disqualification from being a company director, under the *Company Directors' Disqualification Act 1986, s 2*.

Offences of 'other persons'

Where the commission by any person of an offence is due to the act or default of some other person, that other person may be charged with and convicted of the offence, whether or not proceedings are taken against the body corporate. [*Sec 158*].

Analogous with *HSWA s 36(1)* and similar provisions of other similarly-oriented legislation, this requirement applies to corporate officials and employees, such as supervisors, not sufficiently senior to qualify as directors and company secretaries (see 17.32, 17.34 ENFORCEMENT).

Application of EPA 1990 to Crown

12.25   *EPA 1990* applies to the Crown but breach of the Act itself, or any regulations made under it, will *not* give rise to *criminal* liability. [*Sec 159(1) and (2)*]. (This compares with the position of the Crown under *HSWA* (see 17.35 ENFORCEMENT).)

Timetable for process authorisation

These processes are under HMIP control and the application dates for authorisations are as appear below. A substantial proportion are already in force. Part 'B' Processes require applications to the local authority (see below) concerning air pollution.

'Part A' Processes – Integrated pollution control (HMIP)

12.26

Class No. of process	Process	Comes within IPC	Application for authorisation to be submitted between
	Fuel & Power Industry		
1.3	Combustion (>50M Wth): boilers and furnaces	1.4.91	1.4.91 & 30.4.91
1.1	Gasification	1.4.92	1.4.92 & 30.6.92
1.2	Carbonisation	1.4.92	1.4.92 & 30.6.92
1.3	Combustion (remainder)	1.4.92	1.4.92 & 30.6.92
1.4	Petroleum	1.4.92	1.4.92 & 30.6.92
	Waste Disposal Industry		
5.1	Incineration	1.8.92	1.8.92 & 31.10.92
5.2	Chemical recovery	1.8.92	1.8.92 & 31.10.92
5.3	Waste derived fuel	1.8.92	1.8.92 & 31.10.92

Class No. of process	Process	Comes within IPC	Application for authorisation to be submitted between
	Mineral Industry		
3.1	Cement	1.12.92	1.12.92 & 28.2.93
3.2	Asbestos	1.12.92	1.12.92 & 28.2.93
3.3	Fibre	1.12.92	1.12.92 & 28.2.93
3.4	Glass	1.12.92	1.12.92 & 28.2.93
3.6	Ceramic	1.12.92	1.12.92 & 28.2.93
	Chemical Industry		
4.1	Petrochemical	1.5.93	1.5.93 & 31.7.93
4.2	Organic	1.5.93	1.5.93 & 31.7.93
4.7	Chemical pesticide	1.5.93	1.5.93 & 31.7.93
4.8	Pharmaceutical	1.5.93	1.5.93 & 31.7.93
4.3	Acid manufacturing	1.11.93	1.11.93 & 31.1.94
4.4	Halogen	1.11.93	1.11.93 & 31.1.94
4.6	Chemical fertiliser	1.11.93	1.11.93 & 31.1.94
	(chemical fertilisers into granules		1.5.94 & 31.7.94)
4.9	Bulk chemical storage	1.11.93	1.5.94 & 31.7.94
4.5	Inorganic chemical	1.5.94	1.5.94 & 31.7.94
	Metal Industry		
2.1	Iron and steel	1.1.95	1.1.95 & 31.3.95
2.3	Smelting	1.1.95	1.1.95 & 31.3.95
2.2	Non-ferrous	1.5.95	1.5.95 & 31.7.95
	Other Industry		
6.1	Paper manufacturing	1.11.95	1.11.95 & 31.1.96
6.2	Di-isocyanate	1.11.95	1.11.95 & 31.1.96
6.3	Tar and bitumen	1.11.95	1.11.95 & 31.1.96
6.4	Uranium	1.11.95	1.11.95 & 31.1.96
6.5	Coating	1.11.95	1.11.95 & 31.1.96
6.6	Coating manufacturing	1.11.95	1.11.95 & 31.1.96
6.7	Timber	1.11.95	1.11.95 & 31.1.96
6.9	Animal & plant treatment	1.11.95	1.11.95 & 31.1.96

'Part B' Processes – Local authority air pollution control

Combustion (except solid fuel manufactured from waste by heat)	1/4/91 – 30/9/91
	1/4/92 – 30/9/92
Iron and steel and Non-ferrous metals	1/10/91 – 31/3/92
Cement/lime manufacture Asbestos Other mineral processes	1/10/91 – 31/3/92
Glass manufacture Ceramic production	1/4/91 – 30/9/91

Incineration
Timber   } 1/4/92 – 30/9/92
Maggot breeding

Di-isocyanates
Coating and Printing
Rubber   } 1/4/92 – 30/9/92
Release into air of
prescribed substance (see below)

[*Environmental Protection (Prescribed Processes and Substances) Regulations 1991, 1, 3 and 4 Schs; Amendment Regulations 1992 (SI 1992 No 614); Amendment (No 2) Regulations 1993 (SI 1993 No 2405)*].

All applications for authorisation for operation of Part 'B' Processes from local authorities, have been completed.

Some modification of the above regulations can be expected in the foreseeable future, particularly in the case of smaller concerns, with certain processes being removed from IPC altogether or transferred to local authority control.

Prescribed substances

The following substances are prescribed for the purposes of local authority air pollution control:

—   oxides of sulphur

—   oxides of nitrogen

—   oxides of carbon

—   organic compounds and partial oxidation products

—   metals, metalloids

—   asbestos, glass fibres and mineral fibres

—   halogens

—   phosphorus

—   particulate matter

[*4 Sch*].

Statutory nuisances

12.27   Dust, steam, smells or other effluvia emitted from industrial/trade premises and being either (*a*) prejudicial to health or (*b*) a nuisance, are a statutory nuisance. [*Environmental Protection Act 1990, s 79(1)(d)*]. Similarly, smoke, fumes or gas emitted from any premises, are also statutory nuisances [*Environmental Protection Act 1990, s 79(1)(b) and (c)*]; so also is noise [*Sec 79(1)(g)*]. Prosecutions for statutory nuisance are not normally likely where operators have acquired 'authorisation' (see 12.17 above). There are, however, certain processes that do not require 'authorisation' (e.g. non-ferrous metals) that could conceivably give rise to a charge of statutory nuisance – in which case 'best practicable means' would be a defence (see below).

Where a local authority is of the opinion that a statutory nuisance exists, or is likely to recur, it must serve an *abatement notice*, on the person creating the nuisance, or, if of a structural nature, on the owner of premises; or, if the person creating the nuisance cannot be traced, on the owner or occupier of premises. [*Environmental Protection Act 1990, s 80(1), (2)*]. Contravention, without reasonable excuse, of an abatement notice, carries with it a maximum fine, on summary conviction, of £20,000. [*Environmental Protection Act 1990, s 80(6)*]. Appeals against such notices must be lodged within 21 days of service of notice [*Sec 80(3)*]. It is a defence (generally) that 'best practicable means' were used to prevent/minimise the nuisance [*Sec 80(7)*]. A limitation of *Sec 80* is that an abatement notice cannot be served if the nuisance was not committed on 'premises'. In such cases, resort must be had to common law against the offending occupier (*Halsey v Esso Petroleum Co Ltd [1961] 2 AER 145* where noise from the defendants' tankers outside the plaintiff's house was an actionable nuisance and an injunction was granted). (For statutory controls over environmental noise, see Chapter 30 'Noise and Vibration'.) However, the test of 'best practicable means' is to apply only so far as compatible with any duty imposed by law and/or any safe working conditions [*EPA 1990, s 79(9)(c) and (d)*] – cost-effective criteria, given that 'practicable' is synonymous with a duty to do what is 'reasonably practicable' [*Sec 79(9)(a)*]. In addition, occupiers of premises may be required by local authorities to furnish information about emissions of pollutants and substances from their premises (see 12.3 above).

Current civil liability for environmental damage

12.28   Although the main legislation in connection with environmental protection is the *Environmental Protection Act 1990*, this Act does not provide for civil liability for environmental damage and pollution, which are currently dealt with (*a*) (specifically) under a succession of statutes concerned with public utilities and statutory undertakers (e.g. *Water Industry Act 1991, Water Resources Act 1991, Electricity Act 1989*) and (*b*) (generally) at common law under the rule in *Rylands v Fletcher*, as well as under the *Consumer Protection Act 1987*, stipulating strict product liability for injuries caused by defective supply of gas or electricity. [*Consumer Protection Act 1987, ss 1(1) and 2(1)*]. It should be emphasised, however, that there will shortly be a blanket regime of strict civil liability for environmental damage, courtesy of the (draft) EC Civil Liability Waste Directive (see 12.1, 12.31 above).

Statutory liability of public utilities and statutory undertakers

12.29   Originally at common law public utilities and statutory undertakers, creating nuisances and environmental pollution as a result of their activities, could generally not be sued in absence of negligence, since they were under a statutory duty to provide and maintain a public service. Now, however, under the various relevant provisions of the *Competition and Services (Utilities) Act 1992*, regulations made thereunder will require standards of performance to be met by particular suppliers (i.e. gas, electricity, water, sewerage services), with compensation payable to consumers as a civil debt, in cases where prescribed standards are not met. In so far as breach of prescribed standards might constitute environmental damage, it will be so actionable.

Specific statutory utilities

12.30   Statutes specifying civil liability for environmental damage either generally or in certain limited circumstances, are as follows:

(1)   *Water.* There is a duty on water suppliers to supply to domestic or food production premises only water which is wholesome at time of supply [*Water Industry Act 1991, s 68(1)*] – and regulations may well be passed for securing compliance [*s 69*]. Indeed, it is an offence, punishable by fine, for a water

undertaker to supply water unfit for human consumption [*s 70*]. Moreover, occupiers of trade premises must obtain consent on the part of a statutory undertaker to discharge trade effluent into a public sewer [*s 118*]. If damage is caused by escape of water, the water undertaker is liable, subject to certain exceptions, as where

(*a*)   escape is due to the fault of the aggrieved party;

(*b*)   escape is due to any of his employees or agents;

(*c*)   loss is sustainable by the National Rivers Authority, or public gas supplier, or the highway authority.

Moreover, contributory negligence is a defence. [*Sec 209*].

In addition, the *Competition and Services (Utilities) Act 1992* provides for compensation to consumers by way of civil debt for breach of prescribed standards (see above).

(2)   *Electricity.* Environmental damage caused by escape of electricity gives rise to strict product liability, electricity being a 'product'. [*Consumer Protection Act 1987, ss 1(1) and 2(1)*].

(3)   *Gas.* Liability for damage caused by escape of gas is strict, gas being a 'product'. [*Consumer Protection Act 1987, ss 1(1) and 2(1)*].

(4)   *Nuclear installations.* Nuclear installations are generally strictly liable for 'occurrences' involving fissile uranium, plutonium or radioactive material either on site or in transit [*Nuclear Installations Act 1965, ss 7 and 8*]; but this does not extend to economic loss, e.g. reduction in the market value of a house contaminated by nuclear material. If damage is partly caused by the plaintiff doing some act intentionally or recklessly, damages will be reduced. Any environmental damage not actually caused by breach but not reasonably separable from it, is deemed to have been caused by breach.

(5)   *Toxic waste.* Where waste, including scrap metal and effluent, has knowingly been deposited (i) at an unlicensed site and abandoned, or (ii) in breach of terms of a licence permitting deposits, there is liability, subject to the following defences:

(*a*)   the defendant tried to find out whether a deposit of waste would be an offence and had no reason to suppose that he had been misled;

(*b*)   the defendant was acting under his employer's instructions;

(*c*)   in the case of breach of a licence, all reasonable steps had been taken to comply with the conditions of the licence; or

(*d*)   damage was due to the plaintiff's fault or the plaintiff consented to the damage (*volenti*, see further 15.39 EMPLOYERS' DUTIES).

[*Control of Pollution Act 1974, s 88*].

(6)   *Atmospheric pollution.* Prior to the introduction of the *Environmental Protection Act 1990* and the *Air Quality Standards Regulations 1989* (see 12.5(f) above), controls over industrial atmospheric pollution were imposed by the *Alkali etc. Works Regulation Act 1906* and, in a more general way, by *Sec 5* of the *Health and Safety at Work etc. Act 1974* (emissions into the atmosphere). Neither of these Acts dealt with civil liability for atmospheric pollution – and nor does the *Environmental Protection Act 1990* – with the result that liability will be referable to nuisance and/or the rule in *Rylands v Fletcher* at common law, both the latter being examples of strict liability (but see above for the special position of 'statutory undertakers').

(7)   *Oil pollution.* Liability for escape/discharge of oil, whether cargo or fuel, is strict and extends to contamination and cost of remedial action, though not consequent economic loss (e.g. loss of tourism). [*Merchant Shipping (Oil Pollution) Act 1971, s 1*]. It is a defence that escape/discharge was due wholly to the act/omission of a third party, who was not the owner's employee or agent *and* who acted with intent to do damage, or if escape/discharge was due to an act of war.

EC Civil Liability Waste Directive

12.31   Liability at common law for environmental damage and pollution is within the ambit of the rule in *Rylands v Fletcher (1868) LR 3 HL 330* (see further Chapter 19 'Fire and Fire Precautions'), at least, as far as neighbouring land owners and/or occupiers are concerned. Although liability under this rule is strict, its application is nevertheless severely limited. There are two principal reasons for this. First, land usage has to be 'non-natural', before the rule can operate. Second, by way of corollary, a potentially environmentally hazardous use of land normally presupposes grant of planning permission and so its usage can hardly be 'non-natural' (see further *Read v Lyons* at 19.44 FIRE AND FIRE PRECAUTIONS). However, liability for nuisance causing pollution of land (as a result of escape of organochlorides) can be retroactive (*Eastern Counties Leather plc v Cambridge Water Co, The Times, 29 December 1992*, concerning pollution of water 17 years earlier by accidental spillages of perchloroethane (a de-greasing agent) on the part of the appellant. It was held that the appellant was liable (in excess of £1 million). Liability was strict and not referable to negligence – a harsh judgment on those who conducted their undertakings by standards of the time without the aid of a crystal ball!). This seems to underline the need for a restatement of civil liability on environmental damage and pollution. Such is the remit of the (draft) EC Civil Liability Waste Directive.

This proposes the introduction of strict liability (though not for nuclear waste) for personal injury, property damage and purely environmental harm, on the basis of 'polluter pays'. Liability is likely to be visited upon the person, natural or legal, who generates waste (i.e. the producer), or jointly upon the producer and transporter. There are no financial ceilings and both producers and transporters will be required to be comprehensively insured. The fact that a producer/transporter holds a valid permit for waste disposal issued by a public authority, is not a defence, though *force majeure* (act of God) is – as currently at common law. Liability cannot be excluded or modified by contractual provision (i.e. contracting out) and rights of action persist for up to thirty years from date of occurrence of damage-causing incident, subject to expiry of right of action after a three-year period of the plaintiff becoming aware, actually or constructively, of (*a*) environmental damage and (*b*) identity of the producer.

Chapter 13

Employee Safety Rights, Disciplinary Procedures and Unfair Dismissal

Introduction

13.1 Work normally consists of a contractual relationship between employer and employee, in consequence of which the employer agrees to provide the employee with work, remuneration, holidays etc., in return for which the employee agrees to carry out the work with reasonable care and skill and also honesty and loyalty. Contracts are formed in the same (often informal) way as other contracts but, unlike most other types of contract, are heavily regulated by legislation diluting the underlying principle of freedom of contract – as well as also often containing terms imported into the individual contract of employment from a collective agreement struck between an employers' association and a trade union. In this way, employees are protected from, say, racial discrimination and sexual discrimination whilst employment protection is guaranteed by unfair dismissal laws and safety and health at work by statutes such as the *Health and Safety at Work etc. Act 1974* and the *Factories Act 1961*. These various statutory duties are (or become) implied terms of the individual contract of employment and enforceable between employer and employee before industrial tribunals and, if necessary, the Employment Appeal Tribunal (EAT) (see 13.39 below). Indeed, most contentious matters arising out of the employer-employee contract are redressible by industrial tribunals, which have been accorded extended jurisdiction under the *Trade Union Reform and Employment Rights Act 1993* (*TURERA*) (see 13.37 below). Significantly, however, they are not empowered to hear cases involving civil liability for negligence and personal injuries at work, or criminal liability for breach of the *Factories Act 1961* and similar penal legislation (see *Lindsay v Dunlop Ltd* at 13.23 below). In sum, the importance of health and safety in an employment context cannot be over-emphasised, with the concomitant overlap with other equally top-tier industrial relations legislation, such as the *Employment Protection (Consolidation) Act 1978* (*EPCA*), the *Sex Discrimination Acts 1975/1986* and, more recently, the *Trade Union Reform and Employment Rights Act 1993* – this last conferring, for the first time, on employees key *health and safety rights* enforceable before tribunals. The entire relationship of employer and employee is contractual from start to finish; inevitably, therefore, promotion and maintenance of health and safety at work – practices, procedures and accompanying disciplinary measures – will have contractual implications and overtones.

13.2 Apart from instituting health and safety measures and establishing safe working rules and practices for employees, the safety-conscious employer will be delinquent in his duties if he fails to oversee operation of such measures, rules and practices. This can be a complicated affair, involving interaction of overlapping areas of law and disciplinary procedures (which do not themselves have the force of law *per se* but) which, in the interests of good industrial relations, should be implemented and followed by management and workforce. Importantly in this connection, the *Trade Union Reform and Employment Rights Act 1993* (*TURERA*) from 30 August 1993, apart from updating individual contractual rights generally (see 13.3 below), protects employees from victimisation for participation and involvement in health and safety activities and apprising employers of harmful (or potentially harmful) circumstances; similarly if employees refused, during the currency of danger, to return to work or tried to protect themselves and others from danger (see 13.7 below). If so victimised, an employee can present a complaint to an industrial tribunal and, if upheld, is entitled to an award of compensation (see 13.9 below). Equally significant, where an employee is dismissed for involvement in health and safety activities, either as an employee or safety representative, such dismissal will be treated as unfair, under the terms of the amended *EPCA* (see 13.10 below).

This chapter examines

(1)   the importance of, and formalities associated with, the contract of employment (see 13.3);

(2)   the interrelationship of statute/common law health and safety duties with the contract of employment and the consequences of breach (see 13.11);

(3)   the effect of the ACAS Code of Practice: Discipline at Work on health and safety procedures (see 13.19, 13.20);

(4)   the jurisdiction of and procedures before industrial tribunals (as well as the Employment Appeal Tribunal) (see 13.34–13.39);

(5)   statute law relating to unfair dismissal and remedies (including criteria for the calculation of compensation) (see 13.10, 13.25–13.33);

(6)   key cases on actual and constructive dismissal for breach of health and safety laws and procedures (see 13.23, 13.24).

In addition, also considered are smoking and drinking at work, in so far as they may be health and safety hazards, and other forms of deviant and potentially dangerous conduct, such as skylarking and practical joking (see 13.13 below) as well as the common law duties of employers and employees in a contractual context (see 13.3, 13.4 and 13.13 below).

Importance of contract of employment

13.3   A contract of employment is a contract, written or oral, express or implied, establishing the relationship of employer and employee, including an apprenticeship (*Massey v Crown Life Insurance Co [1978] 2 AER 576*). (For the legal implications of this relationship, see further 1.19 INTRODUCTION.) The validity, formation and enforceability of most types of contracts, including contracts of employment, are governed by the principles of common law. This is why common law remedies are still residually available for breach, e.g. wrongful dismissal (see 13.25 below). This notwithstanding, since 1963 most contracts of employment, or, more particularly, the formalities attending them, have been regulated by, first, the *Contracts of Employment Act 1963*, followed by the *Employment Protection (Consolidation) Act 1978* (*EPCA*) – the current principal legislation – as importantly amended by the *Trade Union Reform and Employment Rights Act 1993* (*TURERA*), protecting employees and safety representatives from victimisation and dismissal for health and safety activities – dismissal for health and safety reasons being deemed to be *unfair*. The *Contracts of Employment Act 1963* required an 'irreducible minimum' of written particulars, by way of confirmation of the key points of the contract, to be supplied by employers to employees as a record of what was agreed between them, so as to minimise the potential for dispute, should a misunderstanding subsequently arise. Current employment particulars, including an itemised pay statement, are specified in the *Employment Protection (Consolidation) Act 1978* (*EPCA*) as amended by the *Trade Union Reform and Employment Rights Act 1993, 4 Sch*. If an employer fails or refuses to supply the requisite particulars (see 13.4 below), or one or more of them, within two months of commencement of an employee's employment, the employee can apply to an industrial tribunal, which can determine what particulars should have been given. It cannot, however, interpret such particulars, since this is exclusively within the jurisdiction of the common law courts.

Employment particulars

13.4　All employees, except those

(*a*)　employed for less than one month, or

(*b*)　employed under contract involving fewer than eight hours weekly,

are entitled to the following written particulars of employment, namely, a statement containing:

　(i)　the names of employer and employee;

　(ii)　the date of commencement of employment;

　(iii)　the date of commencement of the period of continuous employment (including any employment with a previous employer);

　(iv)　scale/rate of remuneration;

　(v)　intervals at which remuneration is payable (weekly, monthly etc.);

　(vi)　terms and conditions relating to hours of work;

　(vii)　terms and conditions relating to holidays; incapacity for work owing to sickness – there is no presumption that a contract of employment contains an implied term that sick pay will be paid (*Mears v Safecar Security [1982] 2 AER 865*); pensions;

　(viii)　length of notice which the employee must give and is entitled to receive to terminate the contract;

　(ix)　title of job, job description;

　(x)　if employment is not permanent, the period for which it is expected to continue; or, if for a fixed term, the date when it is to end;

　(xi)　the place of work;

　(xii)　any relevant collective agreements;

　(xiii)　the period for which the employee is required to work outside the United Kingdom and the currency in which he is to be remunerated.

However, no statement is necessary where

(*a*)　the employee's employment began within six months after the end of earlier employment with the same employer;

(*b*)　a statement was duly supplied in respect of that earlier employment;

(*c*)　the terms of his current employment are identical with those of his earlier employment.

[*EPCA 1978, ss 1–6 as substituted by TURERA 1993, s 26, 4 Sch*].

Disciplinary procedures

13.5 In addition, the statement of employment particulars must include a note specifying:

    (i) any disciplinary rules (e.g. ACAS Code of Practice: Discipline at work) applicable to the employee, or, alternatively, referring the employee to a document which

        (*a*) the employee has reasonable opportunities of reading in the course of employment, or

        (*b*) is made accessible to him in some other way specifying such rules;

    (ii) (*a*) a person to whom the employee can apply if he is dissatisfied with any disciplinary decision relating to him, and

        (*b*) a person to whom the employee can apply for the purpose of seeking redress of any grievance relating to his employment,

and the manner in which such application be made. If fewer than 20 people are employed, the note need not include items (i)(*a*) and (*b*) and (ii)(*b*). In effect, these employees are only entitled to have information on the identity of a person they can apply to for redress of grievances. [*Trade Union Reform and Employment Rights Act 1993, 4 Sch*].

By way of confirmation of *EPCA 1978, s 1(5)*, the memorandum specifying disciplinary procedures does *not* extend to health and safety at work matters. [*TURERA 1993, 4 Sch 3(2)*].

Application of principles of contract law to contracts of employment

13.6 Because employment is 'created' by contract, relations between employers and employees are, therefore, determined by application of the general principles of contract law (as modified severely by statutory intervention, e.g. unfair dismissal rules). The following rules of contract law are particularly relevant here.

    (1) A contract is frustrated by incapacity, e.g. sickness, if such incapacity makes the contract substantially impossible of performance at a crucial time (*Hare v Murphy Bros [1974] 3 AER 940*, concerning a foreman sentenced to a year's imprisonment after 25 years of service, who later claimed compensation for unfair dismissal or a redundancy payment. It was held that his imprisonment made performance of his contract of employment impossible and so his employment was terminated as of the date of his sentence. His application for redundancy payment, therefore, failed).

    The implication of this decision is that an employee in such circumstances could not claim unfair dismissal. However, this may not exactly reflect the true position. Arguably, where an employee by his own conduct makes the performance of the contract impossible, the employee is in breach of contract, entitling the employer to repudiate the contract and dismiss the employee (see 13.18 below) (*Norris v Southampton City Council [1982] ICR 177* where an employee, a cleaner employed by the defendant, was convicted of assault and reckless driving and sentenced to imprisonment. His employer dismissed him and he complained that his dismissal was unfair. It was held by the Employment Appeal Tribunal that the contract of employment had not been frustrated. There could only be frustration where there was no fault on the part of both parties. Where there was fault, such as deliberate conduct leading to inability to perform the contract, there was no frustration but a repudiatory breach. In such a case, the employer had the option of treating the contract as repudiated or not and, if he chose the former and decided to dismiss the employee, then, he was entitled to do so; it was then incumbent on the (lower) industrial tribunal to decide whether the dismissal had been fair or otherwise).

(2)   A party to a contract is only bound by those terms which

(*a*)   are in existence; and

(*b*)   he is aware of at the time of formation of the contract.

It is no good expecting, for instance, an employee to be bound by disciplinary procedures and their consequences (e.g. dismissal) if either (*a*) he did not know of the procedure when he entered employment or (*b*) his attention was not subsequently specifically drawn to it (*Systems Floors (UK) Ltd v Daniel* [*1981*] *IRLR 475*).

Not all contract terms are expressly agreed between the parties; some are implied into contracts either by statute or common law or both, e.g. the requirements of the *Factories Act 1961* and the *Health and Safety at Work etc. Act 1974* and an employer's implied duty to take reasonable care for the health and safety of his employees, takes precedence over an express term requiring employees to work specified long hours which may damage their health and safety (*Johnstone v Bloomsbury Health Authority*, see 15.9 EMPLOYERS' DUTIES). In the case of contracts of employment the ACAS Code of Practice, first issued in 1972, has long been regarded as authoritative and comprehensive in the 'minefield' of industrial relations, enabling both managements and unions to formulate procedures for settling disputes. Current disciplinary procedures and practices are set out in the 1991 ACAS Code: Discipline at Work. The provisions of the ACAS Code (the 'Highway Code' of industrial relations) are imported into contracts of employment in the interests of 'promoting and maintaining good industrial relations' [*Employment Protection Act 1975,. s 1(2)*] – which created ACAS in 1975.

As far as the law relating to unfair dismissal is concerned (see 13.15-13.22 below), an employer who fails to follow procedures laid down in the ACAS Code – except in cases of gross misconduct where it is not necessary to follow these procedures (per Lord Denning MR in *Taylor v Alidair Ltd*, see 13.21 below), might well be deemed not to have acted reasonably, as required by the *Employment Act 1980, s 6*. Secondly, employees must be made aware of the existence of disciplinary rules/procedures and the terms of company health and safety policy statements (see Chapter 41 'Statements of Health and Safety Policy'), as well as the consequences for breach of health and safety laws and regulations, and common law liabilities. These should be made clear either on entering employment, through induction training, or at the earliest opportunity during employment – the point being that an employee cannot be expected to co-operate with his employer in health and safety matters, as he is required to do by *HSWA s 7* (see Chapter 14 'Employees' Duties'), if he is unaware of (*a*) his legal duties, (*b*) disciplinary procedures and (*c*) consequences of the breach of both.

(A) Employee's right not to be victimised or dismissed for health and safety activities

13.7   Employees are entitled not to be 'subjected to detriment' (i.e. victimised) for the following:

(*a*)   having been designated to carry out health and safety activities by the employer, carried out (or proposed to carry out) such activities; or

(*b*)   being a safety representative, or member of a safety committee, performed (or proposed to perform) functions as a safety representative or member of a safety committee either

    (i)   in accordance with arrangements established under or by dint of any enactment (e.g. the *Safety Representatives and Safety Committees Regulations 1977*, see Chapter 25 'Joint Consultation'), or

    (ii)   by reason of being acknowledged as such by the employer; or

(*c*)   being an employee at a place where there was

    (i)   no safety representative or safety committee, or

    (ii)   a safety representative or safety committee but it was not reasonably practicable to highlight the matter through the committee or safety representative,

brought to his employer's attention circumstances connected with his work which he reasonably believed were harmful (or potentially harmful) to health and safety.

(*d*)   in circumstances of danger, which he reasonably believed to be serious and imminent and which he could not reasonably have been expected to avert, left (or proposed to leave) or refused to return to his place of work or any dangerous part of such place;

(*e*)   in circumstances of danger, which he reasonably believed to be serious and imminent, took (or proposed to take) appropriate steps to protect himself or others from danger.

[*EPCA 1978, s 22A inserted by TURERA 1993, 5 Sch*].

Importantly, however, an employee is not to be regarded as having been 'subjected to detriment', if the employer shows that it was (or would have been) so negligent for the employee to take the steps he took (or proposed to take) that a reasonable employer might have treated him in that way. [*EPCA 1978, s 22A(3) as inserted by TURERA 1993, 5 Sch*].

In this connection, every employee has a duty to inform his employer (or health and safety nominee) of

    (i)   any work situation representing a serious and immediate danger to health and safety; and

    (ii)   any shortcoming in the employer's protection arrangements.

[*Management of Health and Safety at Work Regulations 1992, Reg 12(2)*].

Presentation of safety complaint

13.8   In the case of a breach of *Sec 22A* of *EPCA 1978*, employees can complain to an industrial tribunal if 'subjected to detriment'. Here it is incumbent on an employer to show the ground on which any act, or deliberate failure to act, was done. Such complaint must be presented either

(*a*)   before the expiry of three months, beginning with the date of the act, or failure to act; or, if the act/failure to act is part of a series of similar acts/failures to act, the last of them;

(b)　where it was not reasonably practicable to present the complaint within the three-month period, within such further period as the tribunal considers reasonable

[*EPCA 1978, s 22B as inserted by TURERA 1993, 5 Sch*].

Employees' remedies for detriment in health and safety cases

13.9　Where a complaint is well-founded, the tribunal will make

(a)　a declaration to that effect, and

(b)　an award of compensation to the employee. Such compensation must be 'just and equitable' and include any expenses incurred as well as loss of any benefit which the employee might reasonably be expected to have had but for the employer's failure to act. However, where the employee's conduct caused or contributed to his detriment, his compensation will be reduced to such extent as is 'just and equitable'.

[*EPCA 1978, s 22C as inserted by TURERA 1993, 5 Sch*] (see also 13.18 below).

(B) Employee's right not to be dismissed for health and safety reasons

(1) Unfair dismissal

13.10　Dismissal of an employee is to be regarded as *unfair* if the reason (or principal reason) for it was that the employee

(a)　having been designated to carry out health and safety activities by the employer, carried out (or proposed to carry out) such activities; or

(b)　being a safety representative, or member of a safety committee, performed (or proposed to perform) functions as a safety representative or member of a safety committee either

　　(i)　in accordance with arrangements established under or by dint of any enactment (e.g. the *Safety Representatives and Safety Committees Regulations 1977*, see Chapter 25 'Joint Consultation'), or

　　(ii)　by reason of being acknowledged as such by the employer; or

(c)　being an employee at a place where there was

　　(i)　no safety representative or safety committee, or

　　(ii)　a safety representative or safety committee (but it was not reasonably practicable to highlight the matter through the committee or safety representative),

brought to his employer's attention circumstances connected with his work which he reasonably believed were harmful (or potentially harmful) to health and safety.

(d)　in circumstances of danger, which he reasonably believed to be serious and imminent and which he could not reasonably have been expected to avert, left (or proposed to leave) or refused to return to his place of work or any dangerous part of such place;

(e)　in circumstances of danger, which he reasonably believed to be serious and imminent, took (or proposed to take) appropriate steps to protect himself or others from danger.

[*EPCA 1978, s 57A as inserted by TURERA 1993, 5 Sch*].

(2) Fair dismissal

Dismissal, on grounds of health and safety, is not to be regarded as unfair if the employer shows that it was (or would have been) so negligent for the employee to take the steps he took (or proposed to take) that a reasonable employer might have dismissed him for taking (or proposing to take) them. [*EPCA 1978, s 57A(3) as inserted by TURERA 1993, 5 Sch*].

Statutory duties as implied terms of a contract of employment

13.11   Many of the contracts in everyday use, such as product sale, hire-purchase agreements etc. have terms implied into them from statute or common law (or both), generally in the interests of maintaining reasonableness between contracting parties. To some extent this has happened – or, at any rate, has started to happen – in the case of contracts of employment. Thus, an employer who was in breach, say, of *HSWA* or the *Factories Act 1961* could be sued for unfair constructive dismissal by an aggrieved employee; similarly, an employee who was in breach of, for example, *HSWA s 7* (duty to co-operate) or of one of the regulations of the *Construction (Working Places) Regulations 1966* (see Chapter 7 'Construction and Building Operations') could be fairly dismissed, assuming that his dismissal had followed a reasonable disciplinary procedure, as recommended by the ACAS Code of Practice (two oral warnings followed by one written one provided that the employee has been employed for at least two years). [*Employment Act 1989, s 15(1); TURERA 1993, s 26, 4 Sch*]. In this way statutory duties become contractual terms and 'enforceable' personally between employer and employee, rather than impersonally through state enforcement agencies, such as the HSE. More particularly, statutory duties laid on employers and employees by protective occupational legislation and regulations, such as *HSWA*, the *Factories Act 1961*, *OSRPA 1963*, the *Construction Regulations*, the *Control of Lead at Work Regulations*, the *Ionising Radiations Regulations 1985* and the *Management of Health and Safety at Work Regulations 1992*, are 'enforceable' in this interparty fashion before industrial tribunals, or, if necessary, on appeal to the Employment Appeal Tribunal (EAT).

Works safety rules

13.12   Based on the *Management of Health and Safety at Work Regulations 1992*, many companies operate, or may wish to operate in-plant rules on safety and health and associated matters, such as smoking, drinking, fighting, skylarking, wearing protective clothing and generally taking precautions in the interests of health and safety. Indeed, these regulations should form the basis of works safety rules. Such 'safety' rules, whether introduced with agreement or not, although perfectly lawful, are not necessarily terms of a contract. Nevertheless, their breach on the part of an employee, to all intents and purposes, will have similar consequences. The law was authoritatively put by Roskill LJ (referring to the employer's rule book, where a 'work to rule' had started) as follows: 'It was not suggested that strictly speaking this formed part of the contract of employment as such. But every employer is entitled within the terms and scope of the relevant contract of employment to give instructions to his employees and every employee is correspondingly bound to accept instruction properly and lawfully given. The rule book seems to me to constitute instructions given by the employer to the employee in accordance with that general legal right' (*Secretary of State for Employment v ASLEF (No 2)* [*1972*] *2 AER 949*). If, therefore, an employee unreasonably refused to obey an instruction in a rule book, arguably he would be construed as having failed to co-operate with his employer in promoting and maintaining health and safety and, after the necessary 'code of practice' procedures had been exhausted, he could be dismissed. Here it should be re-emphasised that employees must be apprised of the consequences of failing to co-operate and, in some cases this may have to be repeated more than once, since certain conduct is (patently) less hazardous than other. Thus, skylarking, practical joking and fighting are more obvious hazards than smoking (see 13.13 below) (except, say, in a petroleum complex), or drinking (see 13.13 below), or failing to wear certain kinds of protective clothing (see Chapter 36 'Personal Protective Equipment'). Here it may well be necessary for employers to 'spell out' the danger more clearly and forcefully – this would apply particularly in the case of risks to hearing, where the dangers are latent and insidious – together, of course, with the consequences (i.e. dismissal).

Smoking, drinking and skylarking

13.13 It is only in cases of gross misconduct that an employer is entitled to dismiss an employee instantly, without following a procedure such as is enshrined within the ACAS Code (see 13.19-13.22 below). Normally, drinking and skylarking would not in themselves qualify as 'gross misconduct', although an employer might well be vicariously liable for any injury caused in consequence (see below and Chapter 15 'Employers' Duties'). Of course if, in combination with other factors, drinking, skylarking, and more particularly, smoking create a serious risk to health and safety, then there could be a justification for instant dismissal, e.g. where smoking constitutes a high fire risk.

Moreover, there are certain regulations which prohibit smoking at work, either totally or partially. So long as employees are made aware of such prohibitions and the consequences of breach of them (i.e. prosecution/dismissal), it is thought that contravention of such prohibitions could qualify for instant dismissal – though this would have to be judged in all the circumstances of the particular case. The regulations are as follows:

(a)   *Explosives Act 1875, s 10*;

(b)   *Celluloid (Manufacture, etc.) Regulations 1921, Regs 6, 12*;

(c)   *Manufacture of Cinematograph Film Regulations 1928, Regs 10, 15*;

(d)   *Magnesium (Grinding of Castings and Other Articles) Special Regulations 1946, Regs 13, 14*;

(e)   *Factories (Testing of Aircraft Engines and Accessories) Special Regulations 1952, Reg 20*;

(f)   *Gas Safety (Installations and Use) Regulations 1984, Reg 5* and *(Amendment) Regulations 1990, Reg 6*;

(g)   *Highly Flammable Liquids and Liquefied Petroleum Gases Regulations 1972, Reg 14*;

(h)   *Control of Lead at Work Regulations 1980, Reg 10*;

(j)   *Control of Asbestos at Work Regulations 1987, Reg 14* (designated area);

(k)   *Road Traffic (Carriage of Dangerous Substances in Road Tankers and Tank Containers) Regulations 1992*;

(*l*)   *Road Traffic (Carriage of Dangerous Substances in Packages etc.) Regulations 1992*; and

(*m*)   *Ionising Radiations Regulations 1985, Reg 6(6).*

The current trend is hostile towards smoking at work, as being a health as well as a fire hazard, and employers may have to establish non-smoking areas. Employees who smoke in such areas in defiance of company policy/regulations could be dismissed (see further 6.5 COMPENSATION FOR WORK INJURIES/ DISEASES).

Statutory duties and common law liabilities – maintenance of discipline

13.14   Employers must also institute and maintain discipline so as to discharge their own statutory duties and common law obligations (see Chapter 15 'Employers' Duties'). It is a statutory (as well as a common law) requirement that employers ensure that both direct and indirect workforces (if any) working on premises under their control, even though shared, are made aware of health and safety rules, practices and procedures. [*Management of Health and Safety at Work Regulations 1992, Regs 8, 10*]. *HSWA s 2(2)(c)* is explicit and adamant on this point (see also the case of *R v Swan Hunter Shipbuilders Ltd*, Chapter 15 'Employers' Duties'). Moreover, this double-headed duty to instruct and disseminate information to the workforce is an on-going one and employers should, through supervisory personnel, encourage and exhort employees to comply with the rules – though this does not extend to 'wet-nursing' experienced 'hands' (*Woods v Durable Suites Ltd [1953] 2 AER 391* – see Chapter 15 'Employers' Duties'). Additionally, some hazards are a good deal less obvious than others, e.g. hazards associated with noise, occupational cancer and failure to use and/or wear correct protective clothing and equipment. Here it is not enough for an employer to provide such equipment/clothing – he must ensure that his employees (and, if necessary, indirect labour) know why they are to wear it; and continuous efforts must be made by supervision to see that they do so (*Bux v Slough Metals Ltd*, see 1.45 INTRODUCTION). Failure to inform, instruct and exhort in such circumstances, as where, for instance, a company doctor failed to warn the workforce of the dangers of rubbing oil into personal clothing (i.e. scrotal cancer) can involve the employer in a costly civil action on the ground of vicarious liability (*Stokes v GKN Sankey Ltd [1968] 1 WLR 1776* and *Pape v Cumbria CC [1991] IRLR 463*, concerning an office cleaner who caught dermatitis and facial eczema after using Vim, Flash and polish. The employer was held liable for damages at common law, since he had not instructed her in the dangers of using chemical materials with unprotected hands and had not made her wear rubber gloves).

Employers are vicariously liable for injury/disease to employees caused by management failing to competently carry out their statutory and common law duties, and it therefore becomes doubly necessary to ensure that discipline is maintained through both line, middle and senior management. Hence, if it is known that a particular employee is a constant source of danger to co-employees, the employer should remove the source of danger – at least, in the last resort. 'If a fellow workman . . . by his habitual conduct is likely to prove a source of danger to his fellow employees, a duty lies fairly and squarely on the employer, to remove the source of the danger.' (*Hudson v Ridge Manufacturing Co Ltd [1957] 2 AER 229*), or at any rate, transfer the offending employee to another shop or department.

Unfair dismissal

Origins

13.15 In order to save employees (and employers) the expense and delay associated with going to court, as well as general 'hassle', the *Employment Protection (Consolidation) Act 1978* and, particularly recently, the *Trade Union Reform and Employment Rights Act 1993* (*TURERA*) allow aggrieved employees dismissed from their jobs to present a claim of unfair dismissal before (more informal) industrial tribunals. This is known as suing for unfair dismissal, and is the normal remedy exercised by dismissed employees. However, because contracts of employment are governed by common law principles (see 13.6, 13.11 above), breaches can be addressed by common law remedies available through the ordinary courts, e.g. county court. These common law remedies are not yet available through industrial tribunals but breach of an employment contract (other than actions for personal injuries) will be able to be heard in industrial tribunals under *EPCA 1978, s 131* and *TURERA 1993, s 38* when an order has been made under that Act. Hence in the case of a disputed dismissal, there is nothing to prevent an employee from suing for damages for wrongful dismissal, the common law remedy, such damages being potentially greater than the statutory sums available for unfair dismissal (the statutory remedy) under the *Employment Protection (Consolidation) Act 1978* and updating regulations and orders. Moreover, an industrial tribunal award is *not* set off against court damages (*O'Laoire v Jackel International Ltd (No 2)* [1991] ICR 718).

Current law relating to unfair dismissal is contained in the *Employment Protection (Consolidation) Act 1978*, as subsequently amended by a series of *Employment Acts*, including particularly, the *Employment Act 1989* and *TURERA 1993*. Here, basically, the law is that in certain cases where an employee is dismissed in circumstances which are automatically deemed to be 'unfair', dismissal for health and safety reasons is also deemed to be automatically unfair – and contrary to statute (see below – reason for dismissal) and he can present a claim before an industrial tribunal. If his complaint is upheld the employer will be ordered either to (*a*) pay compensation (the usual remedy), (*b*) reinstate (unlikely), or (*c*) re-engage the ex-employee in a different capacity from his former employment. [*EPCA 1978, s 69*].

Only an employee can complain of unfair dismissal; it is not open to an independent contractor so to complain (see 1.19 INTRODUCTION and 13.3 above).

Qualifying conditions

13.16 Moreover, employees are prevented from presenting a claim if they

(*a*)   have not worked for the employer for two years as from 1 June 1985 [*Unfair Dismissal (Variation of Qualifying Period) Order 1985*] but this qualifying period does not apply to dismissal on health and safety grounds, or to any of the other inadmissible reasons. [*EPCA 1978, s 64(4) inserted by TURERA 1993, s 29(3)*]. Unless they have been continuously employed for two years, they are not entitled to a written statement of reasons for dismissal [*Employment Act 1989, s 15(1)*];

(*b*)   are part-time workers, working fewer than 16 hours per week; but if they have worked for the employer, or an associated employer, for a minimum of five years, eight hours work per week is enough to qualify.

[*EPCA 1978, 13 Sch, paras 3–6*].

An exception occurs where dismissal is connected with suspension on medical grounds or suspension as a result of health and safety requirements in *EPCA 1978, 1 Sch*, where only four weeks' service is the qualifying period [*EPCA 1978, s 64*] (see 31.13 OCCUPATIONAL HEALTH).

Test of dismissal – actual or constructive

13.17   Generally speaking, it is not difficult to determine whether or not there has been a dismissal – dismissal simply relates to the situation where the employer terminates the contract of employment. Termination of the contract can, in practice, arise in one of two ways and result in two separate kinds of dismissal, i.e. (*a*) actual and (*b*) constructive. (Of the two, the former is much more common.)

(*a*)   *Actual dismissal*

This is where the employer terminates the employee's contract of employment, usually because the employee is considered to be in breach of some express or implied term (see 13.2-13.11 above) of the contract.

(*b*)   *Constructive dismissal*

Here the employee resigns because the employer is in breach of an express or implied term of the contract. Such breach must be a repudiatory breach, going to the root of the contract (*Western Excavating (ECC) Ltd v Sharp* [*1978*] *IRLR 27*). Nothing short of this will do. Thus, the mere fact that an employer acted unreasonably for the purposes of *EPCA s 57(2)* (see 13.18 below) would be insufficient evidence of a fundamental repudiatory breach. Such breach only occurs if the employer has demonstrated by his conduct that he no longer considers himself bound by the terms of the contract.

Reason for dismissal

13.18   In order to establish whether dismissal was fair or unfair, the employer must show:

(*a*)   the main reason for the dismissal; and

(*b*)   that it was one of the statutory reasons, i.e. one of those set out in *EPCA 1978, s 57(2)*; or

(*c*)   some other 'substantial' reason, justifying dismissal (e.g. breach of health and safety requirements, see 14.10 EMPLOYEES' DUTIES and 15.33 EMPLOYERS' DUTIES, or an emergent health risk, e.g. respiratory problems associated with working with polyvinylchloride (PVC). Here an employer will probably be held to have dismissed a worker unfairly, unless the employer first obtains a toxological report from the supplier and has the offending material analysed (per Lord Donaldson in *Piggott Brothers & Co Ltd v Jackson HSIB 188*)).

[*EPCA 1978, s 57(1)*].

The principal reasons which might well be relevant in a health and safety claim (very few unfair dismissal claims are related to health and safety) are those set out in *EPCA s 57(2)*, relating to:

(i)   the capability or qualifications of an employee; or

(ii)   the conduct of an employee.

Dismissal for involvement/participation in health and safety activities is deemed to be unfair. [*EPCA 1978, s 57A as inserted by TURERA 1993, 5 Sch*].

When an employer has established such a reason, the question whether he has acted 'reasonably' in dismissing the employee, is then left to the industrial tribunal. In particular, the tribunal must consider the size and administrative resources of the company. [*Employment Act 1980, s 6*]. Arguably a bigger company with more resources would be expected to do more and be more conscious of detail than a smaller one (see also 13.31 below, the case of *Trusthouse Forte (Catering) Ltd v Adonis*).

Importance of the Advisory, Conciliation and Arbitration Service (ACAS) Code of Practice: Discipline at Work (1991)

13.19   Under *Sec 209* of the *Trade Union and Labour Relations (Consolidation) Act 1992*, ACAS has a general duty to promote improvement of industrial relations and, more particularly, under *Sec 213(1)* of that Act may, on request or otherwise, give employers, employers' associations, workers and trade unions such advice as it thinks appropriate on matters concerned with or affecting or likely to affect industrial relations. Here the ACAS Code: Discipline at Work (1991) has traditionally been regarded as a fulcrum of reliability by employers and trade unions in connection with disciplinary procedures at work (involving *inter alia* health and safety at work). Indeed, failure to follow the procedures in the Code means that, in all probability, an employer did not act reasonably in dismissing an employee.

Disciplinary procedure in action

13.20   An established in-house code of disciplinary practice is essential (see 13.5 above) and no disciplinary procedure is complete without a clearly identifiable appeals procedure. In practice there are always two sides to a story, and it is therefore necessary that employees be allowed to give an explanation of their actions, and correspondingly, management must initiate a thorough examination of all the circumstances leading to the alleged 'offence' in an endeavour to ascertain the truth (*Henry v Vauxhall Motors Ltd* (see below)).

The contract of employment and supporting job title/description (see 13.3, 13.4 above) must identify the requirements and responsibilities of all employees and management. There should be detailed in the company safety policy (see Chapter 41 'Statements of Health and Safety Policy') employees' duties and other relevant protective legislation, together with a reminder that compliance with health and safety laws, regulations and procedures is a condition of employment. Employees should be left in no residual doubt about the form and severity of sanctions available, and should be readily familiar with the appeals procedure. Serious offences involving flagrant and/or habitual infringement or disregard of health and safety precautions and requirements, amounting to 'gross misconduct' should attract instant dismissal (see 13.21 below), and this fact should be underlined in both works' rules and individual contracts of employment. A disciplinary procedure based on the ACAS Code should be in operation before the necessary disciplinary action is commenced: it cannot be introduced at the time disciplinary measures are initiated – a fact which seems to presuppose some degree of joint discussion between management and workers.

In-plant procedure based on the ACAS Code

The following are the essentials of such a procedure:

(*a*)   the procedure should be in writing;

(*b*)   communication of it to employees should also be in writing, supported by verbal briefings;

(*c*)   common breaches, e.g. failure to wear appropriate personal protective clothing, constitute offences within the workplace, though not necessarily gross misconduct (see 13.21 below).

Gross misconduct

13.21   Flagrant and/or habitual disregard for health and safety precautions and requirements constitutes 'gross misconduct' (see *Ashworth v Needham and Sons Ltd* (13.23(*e*) below) and *Taylor v Alidair Ltd [1978] IRLR 82*). Works rules should specify clearly the offences attracting instant and summary dismissal. An exhaustive inventory of such conduct is impossible but the following are likely 'candidates':

(*a*)   habitual/blatant disregard of health and safety laws, regulations and procedures;

(*b*)   breach of specific statutory requirements;

(*c*)   smoking where there is a clear fire/health hazard;

(*d*)   theft of company property;

(*e*)   vandalisation of company property.

Since, however, dismissal is the ultimate sanction, other alternatives, such as suspension (with or without pay) should be examined, but such suspension should be short, and provision for this procedure must be specified in the contract of employment.

Summary of combined effect of EPCA 1978 and the ACAS Code

13.22   The combined effect of the requirements of *EPCA 1978* (as later amended) and the ACAS Code of Practice is to ensure that employers make their employees aware of conduct that can result in dismissal. The employee is entitled to be treated fairly and employers should not seek to impose a discipline unilaterally without an established and mutually understood procedure. The procedure should, therefore, be accepted by all concerned and policy formulated, as far as possible, by representatives from the entire workforce.

Case law illustrating 'fair' and 'unfair' dismissal

Actual dismissal

13.23   Points decided on actual dismissal cases (i.e. where the employer dismisses the employee) are as follows.

(*a*)   An employee who creates danger can be fairly dismissed (*Martin v Yorkshire Imperial Metals Ltd, COIT No 709/147 Case No 32793/77*). In this case an employee who made an adjustment to his machine allowing it to operate without the safety lever being in position, was fairly dismissed even though neither he nor any other employee had suffered injury.

(*b*)   An employee who suffers from mental ill-health may be fairly dismissed (*O'Brien v Prudential Assurance Co Ltd EAT No 271/78*). Here an employee who had a long history of mental illness and who concealed this fact at his interview, was held to have been fairly dismissed.

(*c*)   It is fair to dismiss an employee suffering from an illness which makes it dangerous to his own health to continue and possibly dangerous also to the health of others (*Balogun v Lucas Batteries Ltd 1979 (unreported)*).

(d)   Dismissal was held to be fair where one employee was dismissed for refusing to work normally after face masks had been provided for use in an area where hot rubber fumes were emitted. The unions and employees by a large majority had agreed to work with the masks. In the circumstances the dismissal was fair, and the EAT also said that it was not for the tribunal to decide specifically here whether there had been a breach of the *Factories Act 1961, s 63* (provision for removal of dust and fumes); whether there had been a breach of statutory duty was a matter for the courts (*Lindsay v Dunlop Ltd [1980] IRLR 93*).

(e)   An employee who flagrantly disregards safety duties may be fairly dismissed on the grounds of gross misconduct (see 13.21 above) (*Ashworth v Needham and Sons Ltd 1977 COIT No 681/78, Case No 20161/77*). Here an employee who put up a collapsible fence around a cellar, instead of steel or concrete plates, was held to have been fairly dismissed.

(f)   Failure to investigate thoroughly a safety complaint may mean that dismissal is unfair (*Mayhew v Anderson Ltd 1977 COIT No 670/40, Case No 19799/77*). An employee who had suffered several eye accidents whilst sewing at work, complained that company goggles purchased for 78p were uncomfortable. The union representative said that custom-made eye protectors were available for £33. It was held that the dismissal of the employee for refusal to wear company goggles was unfair since suitable alternative eye protection was available, though the alternative need not necessarily be custom-made protectors.

(g)   In *Henry v Vauxhall Motors Ltd 1977 COIT No 664/85, Case No 25290/77*, an employee who had never complained (before) found the safety helmet provided by the company uncomfortable and refused to wear it. He was dismissed. It was held that his dismissal was unfair, since management had failed to investigate sufficiently the employee's reasons for refusing to wear the helmet provided: 'One suspects that if the company had found out the true reason for the applicant's claim (as they could with reasonable investigation) the whole matter could no doubt have been settled satisfactorily'. Moreover, as the employee was an immigrant with little comprehension of English, management should have taken more pains to investigate.

'Constructive' dismissal cases

13.24   The following cases illustrate the concept of constructive dismissal.

(a)   Failure to investigate a safety complaint may be constructive dismissal (*British Aircraft Corporation Ltd v Austin [1978] IRLR 332*).

(b)   Failure to investigate a freak accident is not constructive dismissal (*Buttars v Holo-Krome Ltd Case No 2188/78*). An employee operating a Waterbury cold header suffered eye injury when a blank flew out of the top of the machine and struck and broke one lens of his safety spectacles injuring one eye. There was no breach of the *Factories Act 1961, s 14*, since that section does not require guards to be provided against material flying out of machines (see further Chapter 28 'Machinery Safety'). Moreover, *HSWA s 2* only requires what is reasonably practicable of the employer. This was a recurrence of something which had happened once in 20 years. It was a freak accident: 'We were not satisfied that the machine was unsafe nor that the respondents had failed in any statutory or other duty. We do not think that in any respect the respondents repudiated the applicant's contract.'

(c)   An employer's duty of care at common law (see further Chapter 15

'Employers' Duties') extends to taking precautions to protect his employees from criminal attack (*Charlton v The Forrest Printing Ink Co Ltd [1978] IRLR 559*). Thus, failure to take precautions to protect employees from criminal attack constitutes constructive dismissal (*Keys v Shoefayre Ltd [1978] IRLR 476*). Here the employee worked part-time in a shop in an area where there was a high crime rate. The shop was robbed by some armed youths. Subsequently the employee requested installation of a telephone, so that police could be notified in future. The employer did nothing. Less than a month later there was another armed robbery and the employee resigned. It was held that there was a constructive dismissal, and it was no answer for the employer to argue that neighbouring shops had not installed telephones.

(*d*)   An employee who was unable to smoke at work, following the introduction of a total smoking ban, was not constructively dismissed (*Dryden v Greater Glasgow Health Board (1991) HSIB 196*) since smoking is not an implied term of a contract of employment but a personal habit 'falling far short of the kind of custom that has been implied into a contract of employment'.

Remedies for unfair dismissal

13.25   There are essentially four separate remedies for breach of contract of employment as follows:

(*a*)   the common law remedy of wrongful dismissal, for which damages are payable. These can be much higher than the sums payable by way of statutory compensation under *EPCA 1978*, amounting to loss of salary, perks, pension rights etc. (*Shove v Downs Surgical plc [1984] ICR 532*). Because of the expense and delay involved in going to court, in practice employees tend to opt for the statutory remedy;

(*b*)   the statutory remedy of unfair dismissal (dismissal for health and safety reasons being deemed unfair);

(*c*)   a declaration that an employee has been subject to detriment (i.e. victimisation);

(*d*)   compensation for an employee being subject to detriment.

(This chapter is concerned only with (*b*), (*c*) and (*d*).)

Statutory remedies under the Employment Protection (Consolidation) Act 1978 (as amended by TURERA 1993)

13.26   A dismissed employee has basically two alternatives open to him:

(*a*)   compensation; or

(*b*)   reinstatement or re-engagement in a different capacity.

The latter remedy, reinstatement/re-engagement, is discretionary and is not frequently granted by the tribunal. Of the two, re-engagement is more common. Re-engagement means that the ex-employee is retained by the employer, but on different terms, and (often) less pay; reinstatement means that the dismissed employee is given back his former job with all its perks, fringe benefits etc. – a situation which is not very likely after dismissal! This notwithstanding, by far the most usual course of action for a dismissed employee is to make a claim for compensation. Here it is important to distinguish between law, on the one hand, and practice, on the other. The legal position is that a tribunal must always first address itself to the feasibility of reinstatement/re-engagement, and only if not feasible, award compensation. In practice, (*a*) employees do not ask for reinstatement/re-engagement and (*b*) employers can often successfully argue that reinstatement/re-engagement are not practicable options; hence compensation is the common remedy.

Time for bringing actions for compensation

13.27   A claim against an employer for compensation must normally be brought before an industrial tribunal within three months of the actual date when the contract was terminated. [*EPCA 1978, s 67(2) and s 22B as inserted by TURERA 1993, 5 Sch*].

In certain circumstances, however, a claim can be brought outside this time period, i.e. if the employee can show that:

(*a*)   it was not reasonably practicable (e.g. through illness) for him to have done so within the time limit; and

(*b*)   he brought the claim within such extended period as was reasonable.

[*EPCA 1978, s 67(2)*].

Compensation for unfair dismissal

13.28   Calculating compensation for unfair dismissal can be a complicated affair. Basically an award consists of (or can consist of): (*a*) a basic award and (*b*) a compensatory award, and (*c*) sometimes an additional award (though this is rare). In particular circumstances, also, a special award can be made (see 13.33 below).

Basic award

13.29   This is calculated in the same way as redundancy payments, but there is no minimum age limit with unfair dismissal. Moreover, in cases of breach of health and safety leading to unfair dismissal, contributory fault on the part of the employee is taken into account (which it is not in cases of redundancy payment). [*EPCA 1978, as amended by the Employment Acts 1980 and 1982, ss 72, 73*]. There is a maximum week's pay for this calculation which is currently £205. Where the reason (or principal reason) is an inadmissible one, then, unless

(*a*)   the employee does not request the tribunal to make an order under *Sec 69* (see 13.15 above), or

(*b*)   the case falls within *Sec 73(2)*,

the award must include a special award (see 13.33 below). [*EPCA 1978, s 72(2) as inserted by TURERA 1993, 5 Sch 7*].

Compensation is based on each year of employment (subject to a maximum of 20 years) as follows:

(*a*)   over 18 but under 22 – ½ week's pay;

(*b*)   22 but under 41 – 1 week's pay;

(*c*)   not below 41 – 1½ weeks' pay.

Example:

In the case of a 45 year old man, continuously employed for the past 20 years, and earning £150 per week at the time of dismissal, his basic award would be:

$$25\text{-}41 = 16 \text{ years @ 1 week's pay} \qquad\qquad = £2,400$$
$$42\text{-}45 = 4 \text{ years @ 1½ weeks' pay} \qquad\quad = £900$$
$$\text{total} \qquad\qquad\qquad\qquad = £3,300$$

(There is a minimum basic award of £2,700, as from 1 April 1992. [*Unfair Dismissal (Increase of Limits of Basic and Special Awards) Order 1992 (SI 1992 No 313)*].)

Compensatory award

13.30   This consists of:

(a)   loss of wages (net of tax and other deductions) up to the date of the hearing (minus any earnings actually paid between dismissal and the date of the hearing);

(b)   calculable future loss from the date of the hearing;

(c)   loss of any benefits, including pension rights. This latter can be a large amount, bringing the final sum to more than statutory maximum of £11,000, as from 1 June 1993.

[*Unfair Dismissal (Increase of Compensation Limit) Order 1993 (SI 1993 No 1348)*].

Both basic and compensatory awards are reducible on the ground of contributory fault.

Contributory fault on the part of an employee

13.31   (a)   The basic award is reduced where there is contributory fault on the part of the employee, to such an extent as is 'just and equitable' and this includes the new health and safety rights [*EPCA 1978, s 22C(5) as inserted by TURERA 1993, 5 Sch*].

(b)   The compensatory award is reduced where the dismissal was 'to any extent caused or contributed to by any action of the employee . . . by such proportion as the tribunal considers just and equitable' [*EPCA 1978, s 74(6)*].

Knowledge on the part of an employee that his conduct is wrong and might well lead to dismissal is tantamount to contributory fault and will result in a reduction of compensation (*Trusthouse Forte (Catering) Ltd v Adonis [1984] IRLR 382* where a wine waiter was summarily dismissed for smoking in a no smoking area of the restaurant. He knew that he was doing wrong in smoking. He was awarded compensation for unfair dismissal (i.e. the 'offence' was not serious enough to justify summary dismissal) but this was reduced by 30% because the employee knew he was doing wrong and could be dismissed).

Additional award

13.32   This sort of award is comparatively rare and is only made where an employer fails to comply with an order to reinstate or re-engage an employee. [*EPCA 1978, ss 71–76 as amended by the Employment Acts 1980 and 1982*].

Special award

13.33   This award is made in circumstances where employees have been dismissed for union membership or activities, unfairly dismissed for non-membership of a trade union, or unfairly selected for redundancy on union membership grounds, or for reasons associated with health and safety matters. Special awards are calculated as follows:

(*a*)   one week's pay multiplied by 104, or

(*b*)   £13,400,

whichever is greater, but not exceeding £26,800. [*EPCA 1978, s 75A as inserted by TURERA 1993, 5 Sch 9*]. However, in cases of 'contributory fault' on the part of the employee (see 13.31 above), where the amount of the basic award is reduced, the amount of the 'special award' is similarly to be reduced. Moreover, if the tribunal considers it 'just and equitable' to reduce or further reduce the amount of special award to any extent, it shall do so. And, if an employee has unreasonably either

(*a*)   prevented compliance with a *Sec 69* order (see 13.15 above), or

(*b*)   refused an offer by the employer, which would have operated to reinstate the employee,

the tribunal is to reduce or further reduce the amount of special award to such extent as is 'just and equitable'. [*EPCA 1978, s 75A(4)(5) as inserted by TURERA 1993, 5 Sch*].

Industrial tribunals – role and jurisdiction

13.34   Industrial tribunals were first established under the *Industrial Training Act 1964* to deal with appeals against industrial training levies by employers. Their jurisdiction has been expanded piecemeal by the *Redundancy Payments Act 1965*, the *Industrial Relations Act 1971*, the *Health and Safety at Work etc. Act 1974*, the *Sex Discrimination Act 1975*, the *Employment Protection Act 1975*, the *Employment Protection (Consolidation) Act 1978*, a subsequent succession of *Employment Acts*, the *Trade Union and Labour Relations (Consolidation) Act 1992* and the *Trade Union Reform and Employment Rights Act 1993*.

About 60 tribunals sit each day up and down the country and consider disputes across the whole spectrum of employment law, including health and safety at work matters, but more particularly, claims of unfair dismissal (both actual and constructive) for breach of health and safety regulations and hygiene regulations (for the law relating to unfair dismissal, see 13.15 above). They were originally intended as speedy, cheap, informal courts – the small claims courts of employment disputes. Their function was to 'provide a quick and cheap remedy for what (the legislature) had decided were injustices in the employment sphere. The procedure was to be such that both employers and employees could present their cases without having to go to lawyers for help'. (*Clay Cross Ltd v Fletcher [1979] ICR 1*).

Constitution and decision

13.35   Industrial tribunals are composed of a legally qualified chairman, appointed by the Lord Chancellor, and two lay members – one from management and one from a trade union, selected from panels kept by the Department of Employment after nominations from employer's organisations and trade unions. There are about 150 chairmen, largely part-time, and about 1,200 lay members. Proceedings are generally to be heard by the chairman and the two other members, or with the parties' consent, one other member. [*EPCA 1978, s 128(2A) as inserted by TURERA 1993, s 36(2)*]. Though some matters can be heard by a chairman sitting alone. [*EPCA 1978, s 128(2C)*]. When all members are sitting, the majority view prevails; though there is, in fact, unanimity in 96% of all cases.

Representation/legal aid

13.36 In spite of the above dictum in *Clay Cross* (see 13.34 above), some of the legislation has become so complicated that there is a tendency to employ lawyers on both sides. Nevertheless, a party is entitled to appear on his own behalf, or to have a friend or indeed anyone else appear for him. The latter is however rather risky, since an unqualified person may not be familiar with the law or procedures involved.

Legal aid is available for advice but not representation in tribunals. Employees with a grievance related to employment, and who are union members, are normally represented by the union.

Jurisdiction

13.37 Industrial tribunals are empowered to hear complaints under the following Acts:

(*a*)   the *Equal Pay Act 1970*;

(*b*)   the *Trade Union and Labour Relations Act 1974* (as amended in 1976) and the *Trade Union and Labour Relations (Consolidation) Act 1992*;

(*c*)   the *Health and Safety at Work etc. Act 1974*;

(*d*)   the *Sex Discrimination Acts 1975* and *1986*;

(*e*)   the *Race Relations Act 1976*;

(*f*)   the *Employment Protection (Consolidation) Act 1978*;

(*g*)   the *Employment Acts 1980-1990*;

(*h*)   the *Trade Union Reform and Employment Rights Act 1993*.

Moreover, jurisdiction over matters connected with contracts of employment, including awards of damages (except for personal injuries) may be subsequently conferred on industrial tribunals by the appropriate Minister. [*TURERA 1993, s 38*].

Complaints relating to health and safety at work matters

13.38 Industrial tribunals deal with the following aspects of matters relevant to health and safety:

(*a*)   appeals against improvement and prohibition notices;

(*b*)   time off for the training of safety representatives [*Safety Representatives and Safety Committees Regulations 1977, Reg 11 (1)(a)*];

(*c*)   failure of employer to pay a safety representative for time off for carrying out his functions and training [*SRSCR 1977, Reg 11 (1)(b)*];

(*d*)   failure of employer to make a medical suspension payment [*EPCA 1978, s 22*];

(*e*)   dismissal for involvement in health and safety activities [*EPCA 1978, ss 57A–57C as inserted by TURERA 1993, s 28, 5 Sch*];

(*f*)   dismissal, actual or constructive, following a breach of health and safety law, regulation and/or term of a contract of employment;

(*g*)   complaints involving an employee being subject to detriment for involvement in health and safety activities. [*EPCA 1978, s 22B as inserted by TURERA 1993, s 28, 5 Sch*].

Appeals – the Employment Appeal Tribunal (EAT)

13.39   Appeals from industrial tribunals lie to the Employment Appeal Tribunal [*EPCA 1978, 11 Sch 20*]; except in health and safety matters, where appeal lies to the Divisional Court of the High Court. Like the EAT, the latter can only interfere where the tribunal has erred in respect of the view of law (not facts) which it took. Appeals from the EAT and the High Court go to the Court of Appeal where litigants must be represented by counsel. After this, there may be an appeal to the House of Lords. On referral by one of our judicial bodies, a case could ultimately be heard in the European Court of Justice (ECJ). This court has power to deal with all employment law laid down in the Treaty of Rome and Regulations and Directives made under it. Its decisions are implemented by the courts.

Proceedings before the Employment Appeal Tribunal are heard by a judge and either two or four appointed members – so that (in either case) there is an equal number of persons whose knowledge and experience of industrial relations is as representatives of employers and/or workers. However, with the parties' consent, proceedings can be heard by a judge and one appointed member, or by a judge and three appointed members. [*TURERA 1993, s 37*].

Chapter 14

Employees' Duties

Introduction

14.1   Perhaps inevitably, by far the greater part of this book deals with the duties of employers (and occupiers of buildings) to ensure the health and safety of employees and other workers. Nevertheless, employees themselves are subject to certain duties (as well as being recipients of certain (new) statutory rights in connection with health and safety maintenance (see further 15.32, 15.35 EMPLOYERS' DUTIES and 14.10 below)).

—   the duty of care owed by an employee under the common law of negligence (see 14.4-14.6 below);

—   the duties owed by an employee under his contract of employment (see 14.7-14.9 below and 13.1 EMPLOYEE SAFETY RIGHTS, DISCIPLINARY PROCEDURES AND UNFAIR DISMISSAL);

—   the general statutory duties owed by employees under the *Health and Safety at Work etc. Act 1974 (HSWA)*, or imposed by specific regulations (see 14.10-14.12 below).

In each case the consequences of breach of duty are also considered.

Meaning of 'employee'

14.2   The term 'employee' does not merely refer to the shopfloor. Everyone working in a particular company or business is likely to be an employee – and this applies up to the highest level of management. The only exceptions will be employers, some company directors (i.e. non-executive), the partners of a firm, and any person working as an independent contractor (see 1.19 INTRODUCTION and 13.3 EMPLOYEE SAFETY RIGHTS, DISCIPLINARY PROCEDURES AND UNFAIR DISMISSAL). Moreover, the principal cause of an accident may sometimes be failure on the part of intermediate or junior management to implement or supervise safety measures/procedures, rather than a failure on the part of the employer. Here the responsible managers may be prosecuted instead of the employer (see further *HSWA s 36* in Chapter 17 'Enforcement'). Moreover, 'employee' for health and safety purposes will soon expressly include temporary workers (it was generally accepted that *HSWA*, by implication, applied to them).

Temporary workers

14.3   Apart from being covered by *Secs 2* and *3* of the *Health and Safety at Work etc. Act 1974*, as from 1 January 1993, all employers (and self-employed persons) must provide temporary workers, actually employed or about to be employed, with relevant information on

(a)   any special skills/qualifications needed to carry out work safely, and (*b*)   any health surveillance to be provided.

[*Management of Health and Safety at Work Regulations 1992, Reg 13(1)(2)*].

Duty of employees at common law

14.4   Like any other person, an employee is bound by the general duty of care imposed by common law negligence (see further 1.22 INTRODUCTION and 15.21 *et seq* EMPLOYERS' DUTIES). The three consequences of an employee not taking reasonable care (or, put another way, acting carelessly) are that:

(*a*)   a co-employee or third party (e.g. member of the public) may be injured or killed; or

(*b*)   the employee may himself be injured or killed; or

(*c*)   both may be injured or killed.

Consequences of breach of common law duty

Injury to co-employee or other third party

14.5   Where, as a result of an employee's carelessness or disobedience (or even some malicious activity), a co-employee or employee of an outside contractor or member of the public is injured or killed, his employer is vicariously liable for such injury or death (see Chapter 15 'Employers' Duties'). This liability arises from an employer's status as an employer and must be insured against (see Chapter 16 'Employers' Liability Insurance'). In such circumstances, the employer's insurer can subrogate or recover damages paid for the negligence of an employee, against that employee (see *Lister v Romford Ice & Cold Storage Co Ltd*, Chapter 15 'Employers' Duties') – though this is rare in practice. Subrogative rights, however, may well be exercised in cases of (*a*) collusion, and/or (*b*) wilful misconduct.

Injury to employee himself

14.6   Where, as a result of his own carelessness or disobedience, an employee is injured or killed, either he or his dependants will lose part of – or sometimes all – the damages on the ground of the worker's own contributory negligence (see further Chapter 15 'Employers' Duties'). Here it should be noted that there can be 100% contributory negligence on the part of a worker, even though the main purpose of a statute/statutory instrument is to protect the worker from his own carelessness (*Jayes v IMI (Kynoch) Ltd [1985] ICR 155*, involving *Factories Act 1961, s 14(1)* and the *Operations at Unfenced Machinery Regulations 1938*). This doctrine is the most usual ground for reducing amounts of damages and is frequently applied by civil courts and in out-of-court settlements. The basic principle is that the more an employee is adjudged to blame, the greater will be the reduction of his damages under the *Law Reform (Contributory Negligence) Act 1945*. Contributory negligence is regarded as a partial defence to an employer sued for negligence (see Chapter 15 'Employers' Duties').

A secondary consequence, much rarer in practice, is that a court may infer that the irresponsible conduct of an employee was such that the employee agreed to run the risk of negligent injury (i.e. *'volenti non fit injuria'*). The dearth of relevant case law reiterating this approach suggests that the *'volenti'* interpretation is out-dated (see further Chapter 15 'Employers' Duties').

Contractual duties of employees

14.7   As far as health and safety are concerned, the principal 'implied terms' in a contract of employment are:

(*a*)   the duty of an employee to carry out his duties with reasonable skill and not to be negligent;

(*b*)   the duty of obedience, or co-operation with an employer.

14.8   Traditionally, employees have been expected to use diligence and reasonable skill in performing their work (*Harmer v Cornelius (1858) 5 CB, NS 236*). This would now appear synonymous with a general duty to take reasonable care (i.e. not to be negligent) while at work (*Lister v Romford Ice & Cold Storage Co Ltd [1957] 1 AER 125*, giving rise to the exercise of subrogative rights on the part of the employer's insurer).

Consequences of breach of contractual duties

14.9   Contractual duties on the part of employees are owed to an employer, and not to any person who may have been injured as a result of the breach. Hence, an employer could sue an employee for breach of a term of his contract of employment. This is, however, extremely rare in practice and the consequences of breach of contractual terms by employees are largely governed by statute law relating to unfair dismissal (see Chapter 13 'Employee Safety Rights, Disciplinary Procedures and Unfair Dismissal'). Misconduct on the part of an employee, whether or not resulting in actual breach of the contract, entitles an employer to take disciplinary action against an employee, and even dismiss him – though in the latter case, there must have been a breach of a contractual term. A case of gross disobedience or breach of discipline may well lead to summary dismissal (see further 13.21 EMPLOYEE SAFETY RIGHTS, DISCIPLINARY PROCEDURES AND UNFAIR DISMISSAL).

Statutory duties of employees

General statutory duties

14.10   It is the duty of every employee, while at work:

(*a*)   to take reasonable care for the health and safety of himself and of other persons (including members of the public) who may foreseeably be affected by his acts or omissions at work; and

(*b*)   as regards any duty or requirement imposed on his employer or any other person (e.g. individual corporate officer or manager – see *HSWA ss 36, 37*), by or under any of the relevant statutory provisions, to co-operate with him to enable that duty or requirement to be performed or complied with; and

(*c*)   not intentionally or recklessly to interfere with or misuse anything provided for the purposes of health and safety in pursuance of a statutory requirement (see Chapter 36 'Personal Protective Equipment')

[*HSWA ss 7, 8*];

(*d*)   not to use machinery, equipment, dangerous substances, transport equipment, means of production or safety device, except in conformity with training and instruction provided by the employer. Employees must notify their employers of any work situation involving immediate danger. [*Management of Health and Safety at Work Regulations 1992, Reg 12(2)*];

(*e*)   to inform his employer (or his employer's safety nominee) unless earlier reported, of

(i)   any work situation involving serious and immediate danger to health and safety, and

(ii)   any shortcoming in protection arrangements.

[*Management of Health and Safety at Work Regulations 1992, Reg 12(2)*].

Specific statutory duties

14.11   In addition to the general statutory duties, there are many regulations laying down specific health and safety duties on employees or selected groups of workers when doing particularly hazardous jobs or involved in similar processes, e.g. the *Power Presses Regulations 1965, Reg 4*; the *Abrasive Wheels Regulations 1970, Reg 9* and the *Control of Lead at Work Regulations 1980*, as well as regulations providing for the wearing of personal protective clothing by employees (see Chapter 36 'Personal Protective Equipment').

Consequences of breach of statutory duties

14.12   The main consequences of breach of statutory duties by employees are as follows:

(*a*)   failure to comply with a statutory duty is a criminal offence, the punishment on conviction normally taking the form of a fine. Such duties are enforced against employees, as against employers, by HSE inspectors (see Chapter 17 'Enforcement');

(*b*)   failure to comply with *Sec 7* or *Sec 8* does not of itself give rise to civil liability; but if it resulted in injury or death, there could be liability for negligence at common law [*HSWA s 47(1) (4)*] (see Chapter 15 'Employers' Duties');

(*c*)   penalties for failure to comply with specific statutory duties, as laid down in regulations, are normally to be found in the parent Act under which the regulations were passed, e.g. *Factories Act 1961* or *HSWA*. As regards civil liability, it is in situations where regulations place specific safety duties on highly skilled and trained employees that it becomes easier for employers to invoke the defence of *volenti non fit injuria* (see Chapter 15 'Employers' Duties');

(*d*)   job dismissal for being in breach of contract of employment (see 13.23, 13.24 EMPLOYEE SAFETY RIGHTS, DISCIPLINARY PROCEDURES AND UNFAIR DISMISSAL).

Chapter 15

Employers' Duties

Introduction

15.1 In order to secure compliance with their extensive statutory and common law duties, as well as relevant codes of practice, maintenance procedures and British Standards, employers are required to appoint competent safety personnel, that is, safety officers, occupational nurses, physicians and hygienists. Appointment of such personnel promotes good industrial relations and establishes an ongoing dialogue and rapport with the workforce, through their representatives. This is now part and parcel of the statutory duty on employers to *manage* health and safety, as enshrined in the *Management of Health and Safety at Work Regulations 1992 (SI 1992 No 2051)* (see further 15.29 and 15.47 below).

Indeed, risk management generally has become a key corporate priority, in keeping with the increasingly onerous responsibility for health and safety placed on employers (see Chapter 38 'Product Safety').

Various EC directives (through their implementing provisions), *HSWA* and regulations made under it, as well as common law in a residual way, set out the basic duties of employers to all of their employees at work, though the significance of many common law duties in this connection has been superseded by the new 'Six Pack' regulations. With the exception of the *Management of Health and Safety at Work Regulations 1992*, the other five regulations envisage an accumulation of possible civil liability, since they do not exclude the right of civil action.

It should be noted that an employer also owes a duty of care to the immediate family of an employee but only in respect of foreseeable risk (*Hewett v Alf Brown's Transport Ltd, The Times, 4 February 1992* where a wife's claim for lead poisoning, as a result of exposure to dust while cleaning her husband's overalls, failed; the husband's exposure to lead, for the purposes of *Reg 8* of the *Control of Lead at Work Regulations 1980*, was insignificant). Other statutes and regulations lay down specific requirements in particular workplaces (see, for example, Chapter 18 'Factories and Workplaces'). This chapter deals with the following matters:

— Action for injuries at common law (see 15.2-15.12);

— Vicarious liability (see 15.3-15.7);

— Limitation periods (see 15.11);

— Compensation for bereavement (see 15.12);

— Defective equipment and the *Employers' Liability (Defective Equipment) Act 1969* (see 15.13, 15.14);

— Nature of statutory duties (see 15.16-15.19);

— Common law duties (see 15.20);

— Legal nature of employers' common law and statutory duties in civil law (see 15.21);

330

—   Negligence (see 15.22);

—   Causation (see 15.23);

—   Liability for consequences of an act of negligence (see 15.25-15.27);

—   Employers' general statutory duties (as extended) (see 15.28, 15.29);

—   Employers' duty to train in health and safety (see 15.31-15.33);

—   Disclosure of information to employees (see 15.34, 15.35);

—   Procedures in the event of serious and imminent dangers (see 15.35);

—   Common law and statutory duties compared (see 15.36);

—   Employers' defences (see 15.37-15.39);

—   Fatal injuries (see 15.40-15.42);

—   Criminal liability (see 15.43-15.45);

—   Remedies for injured employees (see 15.46);

—   Safety officers, occupational hygienists, occupational health services (see 15.47-15.54).

(For the contractual obligations of employers towards employees and industrial relations implications, see Chapter 13 'Employee Safety Rights, Disciplinary Procedures and Unfair Dismissal'.)

Action for injuries at common law and statutory developments – potted history

15.2   Originally the notion of liability on the part of employers for injuries suffered by employees at work met with some judicial hostility. This came, in particular, from two directions, i.e.: (*a*) the doctrine of common employment, traceable to *Priestley v Fowler (1837) 3 M & W 1* where an action in respect of injury suffered by a butcher's employee in the course of employment, caused by a defective van, was unsuccessful. In future, employers were not to be liable for injuries suffered by an employee in the course of employment and caused by a co-employee; (*b*) '*volenti non fit injuria*' (to one who is willing no harm is done). This had the consequence that if a worker were injured at work, it was largely his own fault; he had willingly entered into a contract of employment (no one had forced him to do so) and so he must accept the risks that go with it. Both views were consistent with the prevailing laissez-faire ideology.

The adverse consequences of common employment were 'offset' in the latter half of the 19th and early 20th centuries by the idea, first evolved by Scottish courts, that an employer owed a personal duty to each employee not to expose him to unreasonable risk or harm, i.e. the employee had not consented to run the risk of the employer's personal (as distinct from vicarious) carelessness. This development reached its peak in *Wilsons and Clyde Coal Co Ltd v English [1938] 2 AER 628*. Moreover, there was a statutory incursion into common employment made by the *Employers' Liability Act 1880*, which allowed the worker to sue the employer in a limited range of accidents, though damages were limited to three years' wages.

As far as '*volenti*' was concerned, the turning point was *Smith v Baker & Sons [1891] AC 305* in 1891, where a worker drilling rocks was injured by a stone falling from a crane in the course of his employment. The employer's defence that the worker had agreed to run the risk of injury at work failed, the House of Lords finding that the employer had been liable. The implication of this decision was that workers were no longer expected to put up with prevailing conditions but rather were entitled to protection at work.

The next development of note was the introduction of workmen's compensation for injury at work. The first *Workmen's Compensation Act* was passed in 1897. This was the predecessor of the current social security industrial injury legislation, in that entitlement to compensation was referable to fact of injury, irrespective of fault, suffered during the course of employment. There was also provision, in the event of fatal injuries, for dependants. The maximum amount of compensation awarded was half a worker's wages, payable weekly. This insurance scheme applied originally only to industrial injuries, though eventually (1925) a limited range of occupational diseases was included. Moreover, if in addition a worker had a common law claim, he had to choose which compensation he wanted (i.e. state insurance or damages) – he could not have both. (Further developments in social security are covered in Chapter 6 'Compensation for Work Injuries/Diseases'.)

During the last fifty years of common law litigation the chief landmarks have been:

(*a*)   *vicarious liability* – the notion that an employer, owing to his status as an employer, or organisation is liable for injury at work, in many cases because individual fault cannot be pinpointed (see 15.3-15.7 below);

(*b*)   the gradual recognition of more occupational diseases and their socially handicapping consequences, e.g. vibration white finger, deafness, tenosynovitis (see 15.8, 15.9 below) and repetitive strain injury (RSI) (see Chapter 31 'Occupational Health');

(*c*)   the double-barrelled action for breach of both common law and statutory duty (see 15.10 below);

(*d*)   extension of time limitation periods beyond the three year limit (see 15.11 below);

(*e*)   introduction of compensation for bereavement (see 15.12 below);

(*f*)   compulsory insurance for employers' liability, resulting in more successful claims, and 'egg shell skull rulings' (i.e. injuries to which earlier employments have predisposed the worker) (see 15.15 below and Chapter 16 'Employers' Liability Insurance');

(*g*)   strict liability on the part of employers for defective equipment (see 15.13, 15.14 below);

(*h*)   the discharge of statutory duties relating to health and safety to be judged by cost/benefit criteria (i.e. 'reasonably practicable') (see 15.16-15.19 below).

Vicarious liability

15.3   Because of his status as an employer, an employer is liable for injuries and/or death negligently caused by one employee to another, or to a worker belonging to an outside workforce engaged on the premises, or even to a member of the general public. It is necessary that injury or death arises as the result of a tortious act by an employee in the course of employment. A development of judicial origin, once the rule of common employment law was abolished by the *Law Reform (Personal Injuries) Act 1948*, vicarious liability became the principal ground for actions by employees against employers, since injury-causing accidents rarely arise through the personal negligence of employers. However, an employer is only vicariously liable for an employee's acts if the latter is carrying out a task or duty delegated to him, and not merely acting for the employer's benefit or at his request (*Nottingham v Aldridge Prudential Assurance Co [1971] 2 AER 751* where the employer was not liable for injury to his employee when the latter was driving to a residential training centre, since the employee was under no duty to drive).

Employees' conduct

15.4   It is important nevertheless to realise that an act arises in the course of employment, even though an employee is acting in an unauthorised way or in a manner prohibited by his employer (*Rose v Plenty [1976] 1 AER 97* where a boy was injured on a milk float in circumstances where the driver, an employee, had been forbidden to 'employ' children to deliver milk and collect empties). Similarly, in *Kay v ITW Ltd [1967] 3 AER 22* where a forklift truck driver, finding a lorry in his way, got in and moved it, although not authorised to drive lorries and this was regarded to be in the course of his employment.

Also, a similar employers' liability arises even where an employee has been grossly negligent. In *Century Insurance Co Ltd v Northern Ireland Road Transport Board [1942] AC 509*, an employee of the respondent was employed to deliver petrol in tankers to garages. Whilst delivering petrol at a garage forecourt, and whilst petrol was actually being transferred from the tanker to an underground tank at the garage, the employee decided to have a smoke. Having lit a match, he then threw it away while still alight, and it landed by the underground tank. There was an explosion and considerable damage was done to persons and property. It was held that the employer was liable, since the employee was doing what he was employed to do, namely deliver petrol, even though he was acting in a grossly negligent way.

In addition, where an employee gives orders to a co-employee by way of a practical joke, he is still acting in the course of employment, and the employer is liable. In *Chapman v Oakley Animal Products (1970) KIR 1063* the plaintiff employee was told to put his hand in the nozzle of a machine to clear an obstruction. Fellow employees wanted to spray him with crushed ice out of the machine. Another employee slipped and accidentally turned on the machine. The plaintiff's hand was injured in the machine. The employer was found to be liable. However, employers would not normally be liable for injuries suffered by employees whilst playing sport, unless sport was an integral part of their employment, e.g. a professional footballer.

Training, including safety training is now part of an employee's employment. [*HSWA s 2(2)(c)*]. If an employee is negligently injured by another employee during the course of in-plant training, or off-the-premises training the employer could be liable, but not if the training takes place in an educational establishment. [*Health and Safety (Training for Employment) Regulations 1990*] (see 15.32 below for statutory training requirements). Liability extends to apprentices on a training course (*Duffy v Thanet DC (1984) 134 NLJ 680*).

Travel to work

15.5   An act or omission causing injury arises during the course of employment even if committed before work starts or after it finishes, so long as it is reasonably incidental to work. As regards travelling to and from work, the rule is that an employee is acting in the course of his employment only if he is going about his employer's business at the time. In *Vandyke v Fender [1970] 2 QB 292*, men travelling to work in a car provided by their employers and paid a travelling allowance (but no wages for travelling time) were not on duty and not in the course of their employment. By contrast, an employee required by his employer to travel from his home to a place away from his usual workplace to carry out work there and who was paid wages for the travelling time was acting in the course of his employment while travelling (*Smith v Stages and Another [1989] ICR 272 (HL)*). This equates with the social security position. An employee, in receipt of a flat-rate travelling allowance to compensate for extra travel, was not involved in an 'industrial accident', for the purposes of the *Social Security Act 1975, s 50*, when he was injured on his way home from work ten minutes after he had finished work (R(I)1/91).

Extent of the liability

15.6   An employer's liability also extends to professionals' duties if they are also employees. For example, where a company doctor failed to warn employees of the precautions to be taken against an established health risk (i.e. scrotal cancer from rubbing oil into personal garments), the employer was held to be vicariously liable (*Stokes v GKN (Bolts and Nuts) Ltd [1968] 1 WLR 1776*).

It should also be noted that where a director is an employee of the company, the company will be vicariously liable to him if he is killed or injured at work (*Lee v Lee's Air Farming Ltd [1960] 3 AER 420*).

The real importance of vicarious liability lies in the fact that it imposes liability in circumstances where fault cannot always be located, isolated or pinpointed.

15.7   There is a considerable body of case law on vicarious liability. The other main points which have been established are as follows:

(*a*)   an employee is acting within the course of employment even if he performs his work or a task contravening a statute or regulation (*National Coal Board v England [1954] 1 AER 546*);

(*b*)   an employee who takes a lunch break during the course of a journey whilst at work, is acting within the course of employment (*Harvey v RG O'Dell Ltd [1958] 1 AER 657*);

(*c*)   an employee is acting within the course of employment if injured doing something incidental to work, e.g. having a cup of tea (*Davidson v Handley Page Ltd [1945] 1 AER 255*);

(*d*)   an employee acts within the course of employment if he stays in a dangerous work place, contrary to instructions (*Stapley v Gypsum Mines Ltd [1953] 2 AER 478* – roof of gypsum mine);

(*e*)   an employee is acting within the course of employment if he uses an uninsured private car for company business (*Canadian Pacific Railway Co v Lockhart [1942] AC 591*);

(*f*)   an employee who uses a private car rather than a company lorry on a job, is acting within the course of employment (*McKean v Raynor Bros (Nottingham) Ltd [1942] 2 AER 650*);

(*g*)   by contrast, an employee who does an unauthorised act which is not so connected with an authorised act as to be a mode of doing it, but an independent act, is not acting within the course of his employment (*Aldred v Nacanco [1987] IRLR 292* where an employee pushed an unsteady washbasin against another employee who suffered back injury from turning quickly and was unsuccessful in his action for damages);

(*h*)   an employer is vicariously liable for negligence of an independent contractor, if the latter becomes part of his workforce and causes the death of an employee (*Marshall v Sharp & Sons 1991 SLT 114*);

(*j*)   moreover, recently it has been established that the owner of plant hired to another, in furtherance of the Contractors' Plant Association's model clauses, remains vicariously liable for acts or omissions of the plant operator, if he was not a competent operator (*McConkey v Amee, The Times, 28 February 1990*).

Gradual recognition of occupational diseases

15.8   The record of criminal courts in imposing penalties for breach of health and safety legislation, prior to *HSWA*, showed a marked disparity between penalties imposed for safety offences (averaging £100) and those imposed for health offences (averaging £50). Similarly, as regards civil liability of employers, case law initially identified with liability for physical injuries (accidents), whilst liability for (often much more debilitating, if not fatal) occupational diseases lagged way behind. Thus, liability at common law for deafness originated with the decision in *Berry v Stone Manganese Marine Ltd [1972] 1 Lloyd's Rep 182*; and all employers are considered to have been 'on notice' of risks associated with noise at work as from 1963, when 'Noise and the worker' was published by the (then) Factory Inspectorate (*McGuinness v Kirkstall Forge Engineering Ltd (1979) (unreported)*). Recognition of liability at common law for asbestosis goes back to *Central Asbestos Co Ltd v Dodd (AC 518)* in 1973. Liability for vibration-induced white finger (VWF) is generally associated at common law with *McFaul v Garringtons Ltd (1985) HSIB 113*, employers being on notice of the condition as from 1 January 1971; tenosynovitis became recognised at common law with the decision in *Burgess v Thorn Consumer Electronics Ltd (1983) HSIB 93* and, more recently, repetitive strain injury (RSI) in the case of *McSherry and Lodge v British Telecom [1992] 13 Med LR 129*. This 'discovery' of more and more occupational diseases, giving rise to liability at common law, is likely to be a continuing process. (Many of the diseases recognised at common law are prescribed occupational diseases for the purposes of social security under the *Social Security Contributions and Benefits Act 1992* (see Chapter 6 'Compensation for Work Injuries/Diseases' and the Industrial Injuries Advisory Council (IIAC) is continually reviewing new 'entrants' for prescription, e.g. chronic bronchitis/emphysema in coal miners and metal production workers, and bladder cancer in relation to work in aluminium smelting) in which case employees are entitled to both disablement benefit under the *Social Security (Industrial Injuries) (Prescribed Diseases) Regulations 1985 (SI 1985 No 967)*, and to damages at common law, though in the final calculation all social security benefits paid or payable within five years of the injury, except in the case of fatal injuries will be deducted from the award of damages. [*Social Security Administration Act 1992, ss 81, 82*].) The principal criterion of recognition of liability is employment-related link (i.e. causation); more particularly, it must be established that employment is the material cause of disease and that the disease is not common to all persons, in a way similar to the test of prescription under the *Social Security Contributions and Benefits Act 1992* (see 6.7 COMPENSATION FOR WORK INJURIES/DISEASES).

15.9   More specifically, case law has in more recent times established that there is a duty on an employer to warn a prospective employee of possible health hazards inherent in a job so that the applicant can refuse to take the position if he wishes (*White v Holbrook Precision Castings Ltd [1985] IRLR 215* – Raynaud's phenomenon and/or vibration white finger likely). He may not, however, dismiss an employee for refusing to work with polyvinylchloride (PVC), although causing respiratory problems, without obtaining a toxological report from the supplier and having the material analysed independently (*Piggott Brothers & Co Ltd v Jackson HSIB 188*). Nor may he contractually require an employee to work so much overtime that his health might foreseeably be damaged (*Johnstone v Bloomsbury Health Authority [1991] 2 AER 293* – concerning a junior doctor, required by his contract of employment to work 40 hours per week and 'be available' for overtime of a further

48 hours per week on average. It was held that his employer was in breach of his duty to take reasonable care for the health and safety of his employees, of whom the appellant was one).

Double-barrelled action for breach of common law and statutory duty

15.10   Where an employee is injured at work in circumstances disclosing breach of:

(*a*)   common law; and

(*b*)   statutory duty (e.g. under the *Factories Act 1961*, *OSRPA 1963*, and/or regulations passed thereunder, or under *HSWA*, e.g. *Control of Lead at Work Regulations 1980*); it is customary for the employee to sue the employer in a separate but simultaneous action for both (the 'double-barrelled' action for negligence) i.e. for:

(i)   negligence at common law; and

(ii)   breach of statutory duty.

(This development is traceable back to the decision in *Kilgollan v Cooke & Co Ltd* [*1956*] *2 AER 294*.)

Extension of time limitation periods

15.11   Current law relating to time limitation periods for bringing civil actions is contained in the *Limitation Act 1980*. *Sec 11* lays down a maximum period of three years in the case of personal injuries and death. This period starts to run from:

(*a*)   in the case of non-fatalities:

(i)   the date on which the cause of action accrued; or

(ii)   the date of knowledge (if later) of the person injured

[*Limitation Act 1980, s 11(5)*];

(*b*)   in the case of fatal injuries/diseases:

(i)   the date of death; or

(ii)   the date of the personal representative's knowledge;

whichever is the later [*Limitation Act 1980, s 11(6)*].

If, however, the time limit has expired at the time of death (i.e. the dependant has known of the fatal injury/disease for three years or more), the claim of the dependant is barred. [*Limitation Act 1980, s 12(1)(2)*]. The key issue, therefore, is 'knowledge'. 'Knowledge', for limitation purposes, is defined as knowledge:

(*a*)   that the injury was significant (*Stephen v Riverside Health Authority, Current Law, March 1990* where the plaintiff was held not to have knowledge of a significant injury by reason only that she had some knowledge of radiography and suffered anxiety about the risk of cancer);

(*b*)   that the injury was attributable in whole or in part to negligence, breach of statutory duty; and

(*c*)   of the identity of the defendant (i.e. employer).

Thus, for limitation purposes, time starts to run against a plaintiff once he has knowledge of the above facts, whether or not he knew that they amounted to legal liability. [*Limitation Act 1980, s 14(1)*]. If, for example, a plaintiff did not know which particular company within a group of companies to sue, this would stop time running (*Simpson v Norwest Holst (Southern) Ltd [1980] 2 AER 471*). Time under the *Limitation Act 1980* begins to run against the employee from the time when he has a broad general knowledge that his injuries were referable to an employer's negligence. 'Where the acts and omissions on the part of the defendants which are complained of are, in broad terms, the exposure of their employee to dangerous working conditions and their failure to take reasonable and proper steps to protect him from such conditions, I think that the employee who has this broad knowledge may well have knowledge of the nature referred to in *Sec 14(1)(b)* sufficient to set time running against him, even though he may not yet have the knowledge sufficient to enable him or his legal advisers to draft a fully and comprehensively particularised statement of claim' (per Slade LJ in *Wilkinson v Ancliff Ltd [1986] 3 AER 429* where an employee suffered asthma as a result of inhaling chemicals which he transported in the course of his employment). Thus, where an office cleaner who, after using Vim and Flash for a continuous period of eight years, developed dermatitis of the hands in 1982 and then facial eczema in 1985, but did not bring a claim until 1987, it was held that her claim was not statute-barred, since the doctor had not drawn her attention to the possibility of occupational disease until 1985 (*Pape v Cumbria CC [1991] IRLR 463*) (see also 13.14 EMPLOYEE SAFETY RIGHTS, DISCIPLINARY PROCEDURES AND UNFAIR DISMISSAL).

The courts have a discretionary power to exclude time limits in respect of actions for personal injury and death. Thus, if it appears to the court that it would be equitable to allow an action to proceed, having regard to the degree to which the provisions of *Sec 11* or *Sec 12* of the *Limitation Act 1980* prejudice the plaintiff or any person whom he represents, the court may direct that those provisions shall not apply to the action. [*Limitation Act 1980, s 33*]. Thus, a plaintiff's ignorance of her legal right to seek a civil remedy is relevant to an application under *Sec 33* (*Halford v Brookes, The Independent, 27 November 1990*).

Moreover, a court can exercise discretion (under *Sec 33*) in favour of an injured plaintiff, even though the plaintiff is in receipt of an annuity and other payments under an employer's health insurance scheme (*Eidi v Service Dowell Schlumberger SA, Current Law, March 1990*).

If a writ is issued within the 'limitation period', i.e. three years, it is not prejudiced by *Sec 11*, and so *Sec 33* cannot apply (*Deerness v Keeble & Son [1983] 2 Lloyd's Rep 260*). But 'knowledge' is not a synonym for 'belief' (*Davis v Ministry of Defence, The Times, 7 August 1985* where new action for dermatitis allowed).

Moreover, the court has powers to direct that the period between dissolution of a company and an order declaring the dissolution void (under *Companies Act 1985, s 651*, as amended by *Companies Act 1989, s 141*) shall not count for *Limitation Act* purposes.

The fact that an injured or deceased workman does not start action within the statutory period because, being in receipt of wages and a disability pension, he does not wish to 'sponge' on his employer, is not a good reason for failing to take action. The action can, however, still proceed, if it appears equitable to the court to allow it (*Buck v English Electric Co Ltd [1978] 1 AER 271*). But where the plaintiff could reasonably have had the knowledge to bring the action within the limitation period, receipt of legal advice that her claim would fail did not prevent time running (*Farmer v National Coal Board, The Times, 27 April 1985*). Also, prejudice caused to the defendant by a plaintiff's delay in notifying the defendant of the claim, when the plaintiff could easily have done so, was a ground for not letting a time-barred action proceed under *Sec 33* of the *Limitation Act 1980* (*Donovan v Gwentoys Ltd [1990] 1 AER 1018*).

An action for damages cannot be struck out because of delay in pursuing (within the limitation period) unless the delay makes fair trial impossible or prejudices the defendant (*Department of Transport v Chris Smaller (Transport) Ltd* [*1989*] *1 AER 897*).

The limitation period is extended if the claimant is under a disability when the action accrued. The extension is for a period of six years from when he ceased to be under the disability or died. 'Disability' means infancy or unsoundness of mind. [*Limitation Act 1980, s 28*]. The Court of Appeal stated in *Turner v W H Malcolm Ltd, The Times, 24 August 1992* that there is no limitation period applying to a person who is under a permanent disability, in this case, irreversible brain damage.

Compensation for bereavement

15.12   At common law, damages awarded for fatal injuries suffered at work did not include a sum for bereavement; it was merely a cold cash payment for loss of a breadwinner and there was no built-in element of solace compensation. This has been altered by the *Administration of Justice Act 1982, s 3* (as amended by the *Damages for Bereavement (Variation of Sum) Order 1990 (SI 1990 No 2575)* as from 1 April 1991), which provides that, in the event of a fatal injury at work negligently caused, a maximum sum of £7,500 should be paid for bereavement.

Defective equipment

15.13   Since the introduction of the *Employers' Liability (Defective Equipment) Act 1969*, employers have been strictly liable for injuries to employees caused by defective equipment, where the defect is wholly or in part the result of (indifferent) manufacture. A form of strict liability, this equates with strict liability for manufacturers for product defects, under the *Consumer Protection Act 1987* (see Chapter 38 'Product Safety'). The *Employers' Liability (Defective Equipment) Act 1969* was passed to reverse the effect of the decision in *Davie v New Merton Board Mills Ltd* [*1956*] *1 AER 379*, concerning a worker who had lost the sight of an eye when a drift he was using broke, and a piece flew out. The employer argued that he had obtained the drifts from a well known and reputable supplier and the House of Lords held, therefore, that he had exercised reasonable care.

Employers' Liability (Defective Equipment) Act 1969

15.14   This Act provides that an injury suffered by an employee is to be attributable to negligence on the part of the employer in the following situations:

(*a*)   where an employee suffers personal injury (including death [*Sec 1(3)*]) in the course of employment in consequence of a defect in equipment; and

(*b*)   the equipment was provided by his employer for use in the employer's business; and

(*c*)   the defect is attributable (wholly or in part) to the fault of a third party (whether identified or not, e.g. a manufacturer, British or foreign).

[*Sec 1*].

Employers are, therefore, made liable for defects of supply and manufacture and should protect themselves against this by way of contractual indemnity against the manufacturer. They cannot otherwise contract out of their duties (see 15.24 below). This Act prevents an employer from escaping liability when his employee is injured by faulty equipment, where the fault is that of the supplier of equipment alone. It does not give the employee a new cause of action (*Clarkson v Jackson &*

Sons, The Times, 21 November 1984). A ship is not 'equipment' for the purposes of the *Defective Equipment Act 1969.* An employee's workplace is not 'equipment' (per O'Connor LJ in *Coltman v Bibby Tankers Ltd 'The Derbyshire' [1987] 1 AER 933* but a flagstone is (*Knowles v Liverpool CC (HL) [1993] 1 WLR 1428* where an employee of the respondent, who suffered personal injury in the course of employment, when handling a flagstone which broke, was entitled to damages for breach of the Act). Actions under the *Employers' Liability (Defective Equipment) Act 1969* may be partly superseded by actions under the *Supply of Machinery (Safety) Regulations 1992* which impose health and safety requirements relevant to both machinery for use at work and for private use.

Compulsory employers' liability insurance

15.15 An employer's liability, both at common law and for breach of his various statutory duties, is underwritten by compulsory insurance under threat of penalty (see further Chapter 16 'Employers' Liability Insurance').

Nature of statutory duties

15.16 In the field of occupational health and safety, statutory duties are of three kinds, i.e.: (*a*) absolute, (*b*) practicable, (*c*) reasonably practicable. Most duties fall into categories (*b*) and (*c*).

Absolute requirements

15.17 Where the risk of injury etc. is inevitable if safety precautions are not taken, the statutory duty may well be absolute; that is, liability is not referable to negligence, or failing to take practicable or reasonably practicable precautions. The classic example of an absolute statutory duty used to be the *Factories Act 1961, s 12(1).* This requires that 'every flywheel directly connected to any prime mover and every moving part of any prime mover . . . shall be securely fenced, whether the flywheel or prime mover is situated in an engine house or not'. If, in consequence, a machine became commercially or mechanically unusable when it had been fenced this was irrelevant (*Summers and Sons Ltd v Frost [1955] AC 746*). An absolute requirement does not mean that no defence is available; statute may prescribe a defence or a defence may exist at common law (e.g. act of God). An absolute requirement is one where liability is not referable to negligence or risk of foreseeable injury. In practice, absolute requirements are rare.

Practicable requirements

15.18 More typical is the 'practicable' requirement. A statutory duty which has to be carried out so far as 'practicable' must be carried out if, in the light of current knowledge, technology and invention, it is feasible – and this, even though it may be difficult, inconvenient and costly (*Schwalb v Fass (H) & Son (1946) 175 LT 345*). Hence, although not such a strict requirement as an absolute requirement, it is stricter than a 'reasonably practicable' requirement (see below) or a duty to take reasonable care at common law. A 'practicable' duty is one that can be done, that is feasible of achievement. Hence, if there is an obstruction, for instance, in a gangway or on a workshop floor, it may be feasible or 'practicable' to remove it; whereas the duty to take reasonable care at common law would probably require that attention was drawn to it and that it be isolated. What is 'practicable' takes account of the state of knowledge at the time. In practice, virtually all of the duties under the *Factories Act* and *OSRPA* and regulations passed thereunder have to be carried out as far as 'practicable' or as far as 'reasonably practicable', the current tendency, in light of the 'EC Six Pack' of regulations, being towards imposition of stricter duties rather than ones to be implemented 'so far as reasonably practicable'. This is also a vaguer obligation (see below). However, 'practicable' duties, under the *Environmental Protection Act 1990*, are synonymous with a duty to do what is 'reasonably practicable' (see 12.27 EMISSIONS INTO THE ATMOSPHERE).

Reasonably practicable

15.19   This is a less strict duty than the requirement to do what is 'practicable' but nevertheless can involve imposition of a strict duty. A statutory duty to do what is 'reasonably practicable' (e.g. provide and maintain a safe place of work) does not mean that an employer is only liable where breach gives rise to an injury which is reasonably foreseeable. Indeed, in some cases, the duty is strict (e.g. *Factories Act 1961, s 29(1)* – provision and maintenance of safe place of work) and an employer must show that it was not 'reasonably practicable' to carry it out (see *Larner v British Steel plc* at 2.7 ACCESS). The classic definition of 'reasonably practicable' is that in *Edwards v National Coal Board [1949] 1 AER 743*: ' "reasonably practicable" is a narrower term than "physically possible", and seems to me to imply that a computation must be made by the owner in which the quantum of risk is placed on one scale and the sacrifice involved in the measures necessary for averting the risk (whether in money, time or trouble) is placed in the other, and that, if it be shown that there is a gross disproportion between them – the risk being insignificant in relation to the sacrifice – the defendants discharge the onus on them. Moreover, this computation falls to be made by the owner at a point of time anterior to the accident'.

The duty explaining what is 'reasonably practicable' was masterfully stated as follows: 'If a precaution is practicable it must be taken unless in the whole circumstances that would be unreasonable. And as men's lives may be at stake it should not lightly be held that to take a practicable precaution is unreasonable . . .' (*Marshall v Gotham Co [1954] 1 AER 937* per Lord Reid).

Within the parameters of what is 'reasonably practicable', employers would be expected to know about relevant changes in the law affecting their operation, particularly liability for certain occupational diseases, e.g. arc welder's lung disease (*Cartwright v GKN Sankey Ltd (1973) 14 KIR 349*); vibration-induced white finger (VWF) (*McFaul v Garringtons Ltd (1985) HSIB 113*); occupational deafness, following publication of 'Noise and the Worker' by the (then) Factory Inspectorate (*McGuinness v Kirkstall Forge Engineering Ltd (1979) (unreported)*). Employers would also be expected to be aware of official HSE publications. These fall into six main categories, i.e.: General Safety (GS); Chemical Safety (CS); Environmental Hygiene (EH); Medical Series (MS); Plant and Machinery (PM); and Health and Safety (Guidance) (HS(G)). They should also keep abreast of relevant recent legislation/statutory instruments/codes of practice, published by HMSO (see further Appendix 1).

Moreover, the requirement to do what is 'reasonably practicable' involves employers keeping au fait with current relevant technical publications and developments potentially affecting their product and/or business. 'Whilst I am far from saying that every one of the welter of official and unofficial publications about safety that are published every year should be spotted and perused and followed by an employer even in such a large organisation, I do find that the defendant's organisation should have succeeded in acquiring and distributing this leaflet . . .' (an article in the British Journal of Industrial Medicine 'Skin Cancer in the Engineering Industry from the use of Mineral Oil' (1950) where the plaintiff suffered from scrotal cancer resulting from the use of such oil (*Stokes v Guest Keen & Nettlefold (Bolts and Nuts) Ltd [1968] 1 WLR 1776* per Swanwick J)).

Common law duties

15.20   The duties of employers were formulated against the back-drop of the industrial revolution. Many of the basic rules applicable today originated from decisions of courts in the middle and late 19th century, e.g. vicarious liability (see 15.3-15.7 above). Eventually more duties were placed on employers by the courts and previous immunities eliminated by legislation, e.g. the common employment doctrine, whereby an employer was not liable for injury at work negligently inflicted on one employee by another. Today at common law employers owe a general duty towards all their employees to take reasonable care so as to avoid injuries and diseases and deaths occurring at work. More specifically, all employers must:

(*a*)   provide a safe place of work with safe means of access and egress;

(*b*)   provide and maintain safe appliances and equipment and plant for doing the work;

(*c*)   provide and maintain a safe system for doing work;

(*d*)   provide competent and safety-conscious personnel

(*Wilsons & Clyde Coal Co Ltd v English [1938] 2 AER 628*).

It is important to note that these duties apply even though an employee:

(*a*)   is working away on third party premises. Here the employer remains liable for any injuries arising in connection with the system of work on the third party premises, whilst the occupier of the premises may be responsible for defects in the structure of the premises, which would not ordinarily be apparent to a worker engaged on such work (see Chapter 32 'Occupiers' Liability'). Moreover, an employer's common law duty does not extend to isolated injury-causing incidents to an employee whilst working abroad (*Cook v Square D Ltd, The Times, 23 October 1991* where an employee who was sent to work as a computer consultant in Saudi Arabia was injured on defective flooring; the UK employer was held not to be liable for the injury);

(*b*)   has been hired out to another employer, but control over the job he is performing remains with his permanent employer (*Mersey Docks and Harbour Board v Coggins and Griffiths (Liverpool) Ltd [1947] AC 1* where the Board hired out the services of a skilled crane driver to a firm of stevedores, and the former was held liable for injury negligently caused by the crane driver whilst working for the stevedores; *Morris v Breaveglen Ltd, The Times, 29 December 1992*, concerning a labourer, employed by a subcontractor, whose services were transferred to a main contractor. Having had no training in the use of a dump truck, he was injured when it went over the edge of a site. It was held that the subcontractor was liable for breach of (*a*) statutory duty – *Regs 32* and *37* of the *Construction (General Provisions) Regulations 1961* and (*b*) his common law duty).

The test of whether an employee has been temporarily 'employed' by another employer is 'control'. If the temporary employer, either personally or vicariously, can direct the employee not only what to do but how to do his job, control has passed to the temporary employer. It should be noted here that the mere fact that the services of an employee have been 'extended' to a temporary employer does not mean that control has passed. Indeed, in the case of transfer of (*a*) a skilled operative, or (*b*) an operative with machinery/equipment, control normally remains with the permanent employer (e.g. the crane driver in the *Mersey Docks* case), though this is not so in the case of an non-specialist operator (*Garrard v Southey & Co and Standard Telephones and Cables Ltd [1952] 1 AER 597* where an electrician was loaned and took orders from the temporary employer's foreman, who was

himself an electrician. He was later injured whilst working in the factory. It was
held that the temporary employer was liable for the injury).

Legal nature of employer's common law and statutory duties in civil law

15.21   Claims for damages for injuries/diseases at work are traditionally part of the law of
tort and have been based on negligence (see 15.22 below); though there seems no
reason why they should not also be contractual. Moreover, statutes laying down
duties supported by penalties rarely, if ever, classify such duties in terms of
contractual and tortious liability. Judicial pronouncements must, therefore, be
considered carefully. Referring to the relationship between employer and
employee, Viscount Radcliffe remarked 'Since, in any event, the duty in question is
one which exists by imputation or implication of law and not by virtue of any express
negotiation between the parties, I should be inclined to say that there is no real
distinction between the two possible sources of obligation. But it is certainly, I
think, as much contractual as tortious' (*Lister v Romford Ice and Cold Storage Co Ltd*
[1957] 1 AER 125). However, there is no general duty of care on the part of the
employer to protect the employee's *economic* welfare (by insurance against special
risks or by advising the employee to insure himself) (*Reid v Rush Tompkins Group plc*
[1989] 3 AER 228; see 16.8 EMPLOYERS' LIABILITY INSURANCE).

Moreover, as far as the tortious duty is concerned, this is personal to the employer
and cannot be delegated to a third party. Hence, an employer will be liable for
injuries caused to an employee whilst the employee is working away for the parent
company, by the negligence of a non-employee of his, but an employee of the
parent company (*McDermid v Nash Dredging and Reclamation Co Ltd [1987] 2 AER*
878). *McDermid's* case is an important restatement of the nature of an employer's
common law duties in health and safety towards his employees. During the course
of giving judgment, Lord Brandon made it clear that (*a*) an employer owed his
employee a duty to exercise reasonable care to ensure that the system of work
provided for him was a safe one; (*b*) the provision of a safe system of work had two
aspects (i) the devising of such a system and (ii) the operation of it; and (*c*) the duty
to provide a safe system of work was personal and could not be delegated by the
employer. This has the consequence that if the duty was not performed (as here), it
is no defence for the employer to show that he has delegated its performance to a
person, whether or not an employee, whom he reasonably believes to be competent
to perform it. In spite of such delegation the employer is liable for non-
performance of the duty. This does not, however, apply in the case of employees
sent to work abroad, who are injured at work (*Cook v Square D Ltd* (15.20 above)).
Nevertheless, where several employees are working on a foreign site for some
length of time, the UK employer may well be required to inspect the site and satisfy
himself that the occupiers are conscious of their obligations concerning the safety
of people working there (per Farquharson J).

Employees injured whilst working abroad are not entitled, as a result of the double
actionability rule, to damages from their employer in English law under the English
courts' jurisdiction unless:

(*a*)   the employer and employee are both normally resident in England and
Wales; and

(*b*)   the injury would have been actionable in England; and

(*c*)   the injury would be actionable in the place where it occurred

(*Chaplin v Boys [1971] AC 356*).

For an exception to this where the cause of action is most closely connected with the UK, see the discussion of *Johnson v Coventry Churchill International Ltd* at 16.10 EMPLOYERS' LIABILITY INSURANCE.

Negligence

15.22 The common law duties enunciated above are part of the general law of negligence, and as such are specific aspects of the duty to take reasonable care. Negligence itself has been defined as:

(*a*)   existence of a duty of care owed by the defendant to the plaintiff;

(*b*)   breach of that duty; and

(*c*)   damage, loss or injury resulting from or caused by the breach.

(*Lochgelly Iron & Coal Co Ltd v M'Mullan [1934] AC 1*).

These three factors must be established by an injured employee before he is entitled to damages, though in the case of a breach of statutory duty (see 15.28 below), he merely has to show that breach of the statutory duty/regulation was the material cause of his injury. The damages which he may receive in respect of his injury/disease are known as 'unliquidated' damages (see Chapter 6 'Compensation for Work Injuries/Diseases').

Causation

15.23 It is essential that breach of duty *caused* the injury or disease at work. The fact that an employer admits, even through his solicitor in writing, that he is negligent is not enough; it must be proved that the breach caused injury (*Rankine v Garton Sons & Co Ltd [1979] 2 AER 1185*). Breach of duty need not be the exclusive cause, but it must be a substantial one, i.e. it must materially contribute to the condition/or injury.

The element of causation may be illustrated by the following three cases:

(*a*)   a glazier was carrying a large sheet of glass which required both hands to hold. He overbalanced on a staircase and fell, causing himself serious injury. There was no hand-rail, contrary to *Reg 27* of the (then) *Building (Safety, Health and Welfare) Regulations 1948*. It was shown that, as both hands were used in holding the glass, a hand-rail would have been of no use (*Corn v Weir's Glass (Hanley) Ltd [1960] 2 AER 300*);

(*b*)   a 17-year-old employee was put in charge of a circular saw. He had received training to operate the machine, in particular, he had been instructed in the use of a push-stick to push bits of wood through the saw, as required by what is now *Reg 19* of the *Woodworking Machines Regulations 1974*. While holding a push-stick in his right hand, the employee used his left hand to clear away some of the off-cuts lying on the saw table, and his thumb and three fingers were injured when coming into contact with the saw blade. His claim for damages failed. The material cause was not any breach of statutory duty on the part of the employer, but rather the employee's own deliberate act of not using the push-stick – itself a breach of the regulation (*Lewis v Denye [1940] 3 AER 299*);

(*c*)   if an employee refuses to wear safety devices/equipment, there will be no common law liability even if the employer had not provided them (hypothetical causation). An employee steel erector fell 70 feet from a tower he was erecting in a shipyard and was killed. A safety belt would have saved him. The employer normally made safety belts available, but as they were not being much used by the men, the belts had been removed to another site. The employee was an experienced steel erector and he would not have used belts, if provided. An action, (*inter alia*), against the shipyard occupiers under the *Factories Act 1936, s 26(2)* (applicable in Scotland), failed. The material cause of injury was the fact that, even if safety belts had been provided he would not have worn them (*Cummings v Sir William Arrol & Co Ltd and Another [1962] 1 AER 623*). (Today such a decision is less likely in view of the duty on employers, under the *Personal Protective Equipment at Work Regulations 1992, Regs 4, 5* and *6* to provide suitable PPE etc., and to instruct and train in use of it [*Reg 9*], as well as the duty on employees to wear same [*Reg 10(2)*].)

These cases notwithstanding, certain presumptions have from time to time been invoked, particularly in the case of occupational diseases. Thus, 'When a man who has not previously suffered from a disease contracts that disease after being subject to conditions likely to cause it, and when he shows that it starts in a way typical of disease caused by such conditions, he establishes a *prima facie* presumption that his disease was caused by those conditions' (per Lord Reid in *Gardiner v Motherwell Machinery & Scrap Co Ltd [1961] 3 AER 831*).

No contracting out

15.24   An employer cannot contract out of his liability in negligence relating to personal injuries, whether personal, vicarious or organisational, and it is compulsory for him to insure against this liability (see Chapter 16 'Employers' Liability Insurance'). Various statutes prevent contracting out, as follows:

(a)   the *Law Reform (Personal Injuries) Act 1948, s 1(3)* – invalidating provisions in contracts of employment attempting to exclude employers' liability for personal injury to employees;

(b)   the *Employers' Liability (Defective Equipment) Act 1969, s 1(2)* – imposing liability for the supply of injury-causing defective equipment to employees;

(c)   the *Unfair Contract Terms Act 1977, s 2(1)* – preventing contracting out of liability for negligence causing personal injury.

Liability for consequences of an act of negligence

15.25   Originally, a person responsible for an original act of negligence was also liable for all direct consequences flowing from that act of negligence, whether reasonably foreseeable or not (i.e. liable for total loss) (*Re Polemis and Furness Withy and Co [1921] 3 KB 560*). This was later modified, however, to liability for all reasonably foreseeable consequences (*Overseas Tankship (UK) Ltd v Morts Dock and Engineering Co Ltd (the Wagon Mound) [1961] AC 388*). In the case of employer's liability, however, the employer may well be liable for 'most' direct consequences, whether foreseeable or not, on the principle that a 'wrongdoer takes his victim as he finds him' (and that if he happens to have an egg-shell skull, so much the worse). Even on this basis, however, i.e. egg-shell skull, some consequences will be too remote to attract liability (see 15.27 below, *Meah v McCreamer (No 2)*).

In *Smith v Leech Braine & Co Ltd [1961] 3 AER 1159* the plaintiff's husband had been a galvaniser at the defendant's factory. He suffered a burn on the lip from a splash of molten metal. The injury would not have happened if the employer had taken adequate statutory precautions. The burn led to a terminal cancer, to which the deceased had a predisposition, as he had earlier worked in a gasworks. It was held that the employer was liable for the cancer. 'It has always been the law of this country that a tort feasor takes his victim as he finds him . . . The test is not whether these employers could reasonably have foreseen that a burn would have caused cancer and that he would die. The question is whether these employers could reasonably foresee the type of injury he suffered, namely, the burn' (per Lord Parker).

Moreover, when the act of a third person intervenes between the original act or omission (i.e. original act of negligence) and the damage, the original act or omission is still the direct cause of damage, if the intervention of the third person might reasonably have been expected (*Robinson v The Post Office [1974] 2 AER 737* in which the appellant suffered a minor wound when he slipped on a ladder with an oily rung at work. He was given anti-tetanus serum and later developed encephalitis. The doctor did not administer the test dose. But even if the test dose had been administered, the appellant would have shown no reaction. It was held that although the doctor had been negligent, his negligence had not caused encephalitis). See also *Galt v British Railways* at 6.19 COMPENSATION FOR WORK INJURIES/DISEASES.

In addition, if, through negligence, an employer is responsible for an occurrence affecting the parent of a child, causing the child to be born disabled, he will be liable to the child, if he would have been liable in tort to the parent. But there is no liability for a pre-conceptual occurrence if the parents knew of, and accepted, the particular risk. [*Congenital Disabilities (Civil Liability) Act 1976, s 1*].

Nervous shock

15.26   There are no damages at common law for normal emotional distress following the death of or injury to a loved one. If, however, the bereaved suffers a recognisable psychiatric illness, damages are payable (Lord Bridge in *McLoughlin v O'Brian [1983] AC 410, 421*). Moreover, if nervous shock is reasonably foreseeable (e.g. in the case of an injured employee's wife), it makes no difference that the extent of nervous injury is unforeseeable (*Brice v Brown [1984] 1 AER 997*, following *Smith v Leech Braine* (see 15.25 above)). Grief of the bereaved was considered recently in *Re Herald of Free Enterprise* (arbitration case, *The Guardian*, 2 May 1989). The arbitrators said that 'nervous shock' was an odd legal phrase: a claimant had to establish that he was suffering not merely grief but abnormal or pathological grief. More recently, now that *Ravenscroft's case* has been overruled by *Alcock v Chief Constable of South Yorkshire Police [1991] 3 WLR 1057 (HL)*, it has been confirmed that a claim for damages for psychiatric illness resulting from nervous shock caused by negligence, is not sustainable unless the shock had arisen from sight or hearing of the tragic event or its immediate aftermath (see 6.19 COMPENSATION FOR WORK INJURIES/DISEASES for an account of these cases).

Economic losses too remote

15.27   Where a person suffers purely economic loss as a result of another's negligence, this loss has traditionally been considered to be too remote to be recoverable (*Weller v Foot & Mouth Disease Research Institute [1965] 3 AER 560* where financial loss suffered by auctioneers as a result of negligent escape of African virus which had infected cattle was found too remote to be claimed; and *Spartan Steel & Alloys Ltd v Martin (Contractors) & Co Ltd [1972] 3 AER 557* where the loss of profit from being unable to melt metal in the foundry as a result of an electric cable being negligently damaged was only recoverable loss if there had been physical damage done as well). This has recently been confirmed in *Simaan General Contracting Co v Pilkington Glass Ltd, The Times, 18 February 1988, Merlin v British Nuclear Fuels Ltd [1990] 3*

WLR 383 (breach of *Nuclear Installations Act 1965*) and *Wentworth v Wilts CC, The Times, 22 May 1992* concerning a highway, which was in such a state of disrepair that milk could not be collected from the plaintiff's farm, as a result of which he lost the farm. It was held that this was purely economic loss and he could not recover.

The expenditure arising out of divorce is not recoverable as part of damages in personal injuries cases (*Pritchard v J H Cobden Ltd [1987] 1 AER 300 (CA)*). Moreover, if in consequence of accident causing an injury, a person undergoes a change of personality and attacks and rapes women, he cannot recover from the original 'perpetrator' of the accident (e.g. vehicle driver, employer) damages for sums paid by way of damages to the rape victims (*Meah v McCreamer (No 2) [1986] 1 AER 943*).

Employers' general statutory duties

15.28   General statutory duties of employers are contained in *Sec 2* of the *Health and Safety at Work etc. Act 1974*, as amended by the *Management of Health and Safety at Work Regulations 1992 (SI 1992 No 2051)*. These duties are as follows:

'It shall be the duty of every employer to ensure, so far as is reasonably practicable, the health, safety and welfare at work of all his employees.' [*HSWA s 2(1)*]. Breach of this duty carries a maximum fine, on summary conviction, of £20,000 (see 17.29 ENFORCEMENT). This duty is sub-divided into the following:

(a)   the provision and maintenance of plant and work systems, that are safe and without health risks;

(b)   arrangements for ensuring safety and freedom from health risks in the use, handling, storage and transport of articles and substances;

(c)   provision of information, instruction, training and supervision necessary to ensure health and safety;

(d)   maintenance of a place of work which is under the employer's control and all means of access and egress, in a safe state and without health risks;

(e)   provision and maintenance of a working environment that is safe and without health risks, including arrangements for the welfare of employees whilst at work

[*HSWA s 2(2)*];

(f)   preparation and revision of a safety policy including a no-smoking policy [*HSWA s 2(3)*]. (See further Chapter 41 'Statements of Health and Safety Policy'.)

Moreover, health and safety duties extend to temporary workers as well as apprentices and certain trainees. [*Management of Health and Safety at Work Regulations 1992, Reg 13*]. Thus, employers (and the self-employed) must provide temporary workers and apprentices/trainees, whether on a fixed-term contract or not, with comprehensible information on skills required of them and about the risks to which they may be exposed and health surveillance.

The duties under *Sec 2(2)(a)* – provision of safe system of work, and under *Sec 2(2)(c)* – provision of information, instruction and training, extend to the workforce of an outside contractor, or to any persons working on his premises not in contractual relationship with the employer (Court of Appeal, *R v Swan Hunter Shipbuilders Ltd [1982] 1 AER 264*). (See further Chapter 7 'Construction and Building Operations'.)

In addition, it is the duty of every employer to conduct his undertaking in such a way as to ensure, so far as is reasonably practicable (see 15.19 above), that persons not in his employment, but who may be affected, are not exposed to risks to their health and safety. [*HSWA s 3(1)*]. This duty, too, extends to provision of information, instruction and training to persons working on an employer's premises who are not his employees or in a contractual relationship with him (*R v Swan Hunter Shipbuilders Ltd [1982] 1 AER 264* as above – duties further crystallised in the *Management of Health and Safety at Work Regulations 1992*).

Management of health and safety at work – the Management of Health and Safety at Work Regulations 1992 (SI 1992 No 2051)

15.29   The *Management of Health and Safety at Work Regulations 1992 (SI 1992 No 2051)* impose on all employers (and self-employed persons) the following specific duties (in addition to other duties (see 15.31–15.34, 15.47 below)):

(a) To own employees

(1)   To make a formal assessment of risks so as to identify the protective measures necessary. In the case of five or more employees, the assessment must be in writing (see 15.30 below). [*Reg 3*]. (For a typical risk assessment checklist, see Chapter 39 'Risk Analysis and Safety Monitoring'.)

(2)   To implement arrangements for effective planning, organisation, control, monitoring and review of preventive and protective measures required; taking account of the nature of the activities carried out at the workplace and size of undertaking. In the case of five or more employees, this must be in writing. [*Reg 4(1)(2)*]. This may already be the case in some concerns already familiar with the need to prepare and update company safety policies (see Chapter 41 'Statements of Health and Safety Policy').

(3)   To provide employees (including temporary workers) with health surveillance where necessary (against the range of occupational hazards outlined in Chapter 31 'Occupational Health'). [*Reg 5*].

(b) To indirect workers

(1)   To make and review a formal assessment of risks. [*Reg 3*].

(2)   To provide them (and their employers) with relevant information on risks and preventive/protective measures [*Reg 10*] and to inform their employers of the person nominated to control evacuation procedures and supply information on these procedures (see 15.35 below).

Risk assessments

15.30   Apart from day-to-day routine checks, employers are required to conduct a systematic general examination of their work activity, recording significant findings. The assessment should identify hazards present and quantify risks. In larger organisations such assessments will often be conducted by the company safety officer (see 15.48 below), though specialist outside in-put will be more typical of smaller firms. The purpose of the assessment is to acquaint an employer with such measures as are necessary to comply with his statutory (and common law) duties. And employers controlling a number of workplaces may wish to avail themselves of a 'model' risk assessment prepared by a trade association.

Plan of risk assessment

A risk assessment should

(*a*)   cover all significant risks/hazards, beginning with those hazards having the potential to cause harm – as indicated by relevant legislation, e.g. *Factories Act*, the *Offices and Shops Act* (see further 41.12 STATEMENTS OF HEALTH AND SAFETY POLICY). Obvious 'candidates' are machinery, electrical equipment, kitchens, substances and transport, fire traps and foreseeable consequential loss (see Chapter 19 'Fire and Fire Precautions'). Not so obvious 'candidates' are the type of goods delivered to premises and nature and structure of adjacent premises, with what attendant result if, say, an explosion or fire were to occur;

(*b*)   concentrate on the daily facets of work activity. Not infrequently this differs from descriptions in works manuals; in particular, extra-routine activities should not be overlooked, e.g. maintenance (see further 1.38 INTRODUCTION), loading/unloading and deliveries (see Chapter 2 'Access');

(*c*)   single out groups of workers particularly at risk, e.g. disabled, partially sighted, lone workers, young or inexperienced workers (see further Chapter 5 'Children and Young Persons');

(*d*)   identify all groups potentially at risk, e.g. part-time relief staff, maintenance workers, security staff, cleaning workers, indirect labour (after consultation with their employer) (see 15.29 above) and visitors;

(*e*)   monitor existing precautionary measures. More particularly, they may be adequate for compliance purposes, but checks to ensure that they are in good efficient order are necessary (see 'Maintenance operations' at 1.38 INTRODUCTION). Also, the occurrence of an emergency may spotlight the need for a review of procedures.

Record of assessment (in the case of five or more employees)

Records of assessment are required to be retrievable for reference by management or by an inspector or safety representative. In practice, most such assessments will be in writing and should show

(*a*)   significant hazards identified;

(*b*)   existing control measures;

(*c*)   population potentially affected by significant risks.

Duty to train in health and safety

15.31   The Department of Employment defines 'training' as the 'systematic development of attitude, knowledge and skill patterns required by an individual to perform adequately a given task or job'. The key to safe working and proper maintenance of health and safety at work lies in induction training and refresher courses. This applies across the whole corporate spectrum, from the board of directors down through middle management and onto the shopfloor. Moreover, inspectors will want to see arrangements in the company health and safety policy for provision of safety training (see Chapter 41 'Statements of Health and Safety Policy'). Employers using subcontract labour are under a duty to train and instruct subcontract personnel. The consequences of failure to do so can mean prosecution and, possibly, an action for damages, where failure to train is an element in injury-causation.

Training duties are laid on employers (generally) by the *Health and Safety at Work etc. Act 1974* and the *Management of Health and Safety at Work Regulations 1992*, and, more particularly, by regulations passed under the *Factories Act 1961* and the *Offices,*

Shops and Railway Premises Act 1963. Employees should co-operate with employers in undergoing training and, if necessary, refresher courses in safety training. Moreover, the *Health and Safety (Training for Employment) Regulations 1990 (SI 1990, No 1380)* extend the protection of the *Health and Safety at Work Act* to trainees, though not if the training provider is an educational establishment or if the training is provided under a contract of employment.

General duty on employer to train in job safety

15.32   All employers must, so far as is reasonably practicable, (for meaning, see 15.19 above) provide information, instruction and training so as to ensure the health and safety at work of their employees. [*HSWA s 2(2)(c)*]. They must also take into account employees' capabilities with regard to health and safety. [*Management of Health and Safety at Work Regulations 1992, Reg 11(1)*].

Every employer must ensure that his employees are provided with adequate health and safety training

(*a*)   on recruitment, and/or

(*b*)   on exposure to new/increased risks owing to

    (i)   transfer/change of responsibilities;

    (ii)   introduction of new work equipment or a change to existing work equipment;

    (iii)   introduction of new technology;

    (iv)   introduction of a new system of work or a change to existing systems of work.

Such training should be repeated periodically and should be adapted to take account of new or changed risks, where necessary, and take place during working hours.

[*Management of Health and Safety at Work Regulations 1992, Reg 11(2)(3)*].

Failure to train

Failure to train can have two consequences:

(*a*)   the employer commits a criminal offence and can be prosecuted for breach of *Sec 2(2)(c)*;

(*b*)   in any subsequent civil action at common law or under other health and safety regulations, the employer may have to pay compensation for injury to employees, where lack of training materially contributed to the injury.

Employees' duty to co-operate in training

There is a general duty on all employees to co-operate with their employer in promoting and maintaining health and safety standards at work. [*HSWA s 7(b)*]. Failure to do so can lead to prosecution and/or (more often) dismissal (*Wilson v Stephens and Carter Ltd (1977) COIT No 649/153, Case No 2269/77* where an employee, who refused to attend a safety training course involving a week away from home, was held to have been fairly dismissed). General job safety training would, of necessity, be much less specialised than that necessary for safety officers and safety representatives (see Safety officers at 15.48 below and Chapter 25 'Joint Consultation – Safety Representatives and Safety Committees').

Specific safety training requirements

15.33   Certain specific regulations relating to machinery in factories (and, to a lesser extent, in offices) where the risk of injury to operatives is high in the absence of training, require employers to ensure that such operatives have received the necessary instruction and training. These regulations are (in workplaces)

(a)   the *Power Presses Regulations 1965 (SI 1965 No 1441), Reg 4*;

(b)   the *Abrasive Wheels Regulations 1970 (SI 1970 No 535), Reg 9*;

(c)   the *Personal Protective Equipment at Work Regulations 1992 (SI 1992 No 2966), Reg 9*;

(d)   the *Manual Handling Operations Regulations 1992 (SI 1992 No 2793), Reg 44*;

(e)   the *Provision and Use of Work Equipment Regulations 1992 (SI 1992 No 2932), Reg 9*;

(items (c) to (e) also apply to offices, shops and railway premises) (see further Chapter 28 'Machinery Safety')

and (in offices)

(a)   the *Offices, Shops and Railway Premises Act 1963, s 19(1)*; and

(b)   the *Prescribed Dangerous Machines Order 1964 (SI 1964 No 971)*;

(c)   the *Health and Safety (Display Screen Equipment) Regulations 1992 (SI 1992 No 2792), Reg 6*;

(see further Chapter 33 'Offices')

and (on the road)

(a)   the *Road Traffic (Carriage of Dangerous Substances in Road Tankers and Tank Containers) Regulations 1992 (SI 1992 No 743), Reg 26*;

(b)   the *Road Traffic (Carriage of Dangerous Substances in Packages etc.) Regulations 1992 (SI 1992 No 742), Reg 8*;

(c)   the *Road Traffic (Training of Drivers of Vehicles Carrying Dangerous Goods) Regulations 1992 (SI 1992 No 744), Reg 4*;

(d)   the *Road Traffic (Carriage of Explosives) Regulations 1989 (SI 1989 No 615), Reg 14*;

(see further Chapter 10 'Dangerous Substances II').

Duty to provide relevant information

15.34   The *Health and Safety Information for Employees Regulations 1989 (SI 1989 No 682)* require employers to:

(a)   display approved posters containing up-to-date information on health, safety and welfare legislation, so that it can easily be read by employees at work; or

(b)   give approved leaflets with relevant information to employees.

Such information must contain the address of the local enforcing authority and EMAS. [*Regs 4, 5*]. Exemptions may be granted by HSE. It is a defence to a charge for an employer to prove that he took all reasonable precautions and exercised all due diligence to avoid breach. [*Reg 7*].

In order to demonstrate hands-on management of workplace health and safety maintenance, employers must, in addition, provide employees with relevant, easily understandable, information on

(*a*)   risks to their health and safety identified by the formal assessment (see 15.30 above);

(*b*)   preventive and protective measures necessary;

(*c*)   procedures to be followed in the event of serious and imminent danger (see 15.35 below);

(*d*)   identity of nominated safety personnel (see 15.29 above, 15.47–15.54 below);

(*e*)   risks to employees of another employer sharing the same workplace premises.

[*Management of Health and Safety at Work Regulations 1992, Regs 8, 9(1)(c)*].

Procedures in the event of serious and imminent danger

15.35   All employers from 1 January 1993 must establish, specify and implement procedures under the *Management of Health and Safety at Work Regulations*

(*a*)   to be followed in the event of serious and imminent danger [*Reg 7(1)*].

This refers to

(i)   information relating to the nature of hazards involved and steps to be taken;

(ii)   procedures to enable persons affected to stop work and proceed to a place of safety;

(iii)   preventing persons from resuming work where a danger is still imminent.

[*Reg 7(2)*];

(*b*)   for restricting access to danger areas by employees, unless the latter have received adequate health and safety instruction [*Reg 7(1)*];

(*c*)   for nominating sufficient competent persons to secure evacuation [*Reg 7(1)*].

(See 15.47-15.54 below.)

All employees (including temporary employees and employees employed by another employer present in the workplace) and also the employers of outside employees present in the workplace must, in relation to potential serious and imminent dangers, be kept informed of the name of the competent officer nominated to control evacuation procedures and they must also all be provided with information of the procedures to be adopted in such emergencies and of any changes to them. [*Reg 8*].

Emergency procedures should be in writing, indicating the limits of employees' actions. Information on them should be communicated to

(*a*)   all employees;

(*b*)   indirect workers and/or their employers;

(*c*)   any external health and safety personnel (see 15.47 below).

Periodical exercises simulating emergency situations, so as to familiarise staff with procedures, are advisable.

Common law and statutory duties compared

15.36   Common law duties are general and apply to everybody; they reach many areas which are now (but were not originally) covered by statute, e.g. place of work, access and egress, heating, lighting and ventilation. Statutory duties, on the other hand, tend to be specific. They are also penal and impose a forfeiture for breach. Because of this they are, in general, construed narrowly and in favour of the person against whom the duty is sought to be enforced (*Gorris v Scott (1874) LR 9 Exch 125*). They can also give rise to civil liability, except where this is expressly excluded by statute (*Groves v Lord Wimborne [1898] 2 QB 402*). Although there is an express exclusion of civil liability for breach of the general duties under *HSWA s 47(1)* (see Chapter 1 'Introduction'), yet breach of health and safety regulations, causing injury/damage, are actionable, even if silent (unless stated not to be so actionable) [*Sec 47(2)*] (see 1.18 and 1.44 INTRODUCTION). Since most of the new 'Six Pack' regulations do not expressly exclude civil liability (with the exception of the *Management of Health and Safety at Work Regulations 1992 [Reg 15]*), civil actions can be expected and, since most of the new regulations place statutory duties on employees (as well as employers), the importance of contributory negligence (see below) is likely to increase at the expense of '*volenti*' (see 15.38 below).

Employers' defences

15.37   When sued (in tort) for breach of (*a*) common law and/or (*b*) statutory duty, an employer can raise two defences. These are:

(*a*)   contributory negligence;

(*b*)   assumption of risk of injury (*volenti non fit injuria*).

Contributory negligence

15.38   The defence of contributory negligence on the part of an injured employee is the more common of the two defences. It is defined in the *Law Reform (Contributory Negligence) Act 1945* as follows: 'Where any person suffers damage as the result partly of his own fault and partly of the fault of any other person or persons, a claim in respect of that damage shall not be defeated by reason of the fault of the person suffering the damage, but the damages recoverable in respect thereof shall be reduced to such extent as the court thinks just and equitable having regard to the claimant's share in the responsibility for the damage.' [*Sec 1(1)*]. There can be 100% contributory negligence on the part of a worker (*Jayes v IMI (Kynoch) [1985] ICR 155*). This is so even if the principal purpose of the statute is to protect against the folly of the worker, e.g. *Factories Act 1961, s 14(1)* and the *Operations at Unfenced Machinery Regulations 1938, Reg 5(a)(d)*. Moreover, 'fault' means 'negligence, breach of statutory duty or other act or omission – which gives rise to a liability in tort or would, apart from this Act, give rise to the defence of contributory negligence'. [*Sec 1(4)*].

Since contributory negligence is, in practice, the most common defence it has generated a considerable body of case law. The main points which have been established by cases are the following:

(*a*)   contributory negligence is a defence against:

    (i)   common law negligence (*Butterfield v Forrester (1808) 11 East 60*);

    (ii)   breach of statutory duty (*Caswell v Powell Duffryn Associated Collieries Ltd [1939] 3 AER 722*);

    (iii)   actions under the *Fatal Accidents Acts* (*Purnell v Shields [1973] RTR 414*);

(b)   contributory negligence used to be a complete defence at common law (*Butterfield v Forrester* above), but since 1945 is only a partial defence to the employer, resulting in apportionment of damages for an employee (i.e. reduction);

(c)   now that 'fault' on the part of an employee no longer bars his claim to damages, the courts are much more willing to say that both employer and employee are to blame for an injury and apportion damages accordingly (but see (d) below);

(d)   workers engaged on repetitive or monotonous work are 'foreseeably' inadvertent from time to time; and inadvertence is not negligence (*Norris v Syndic Manufacturing Co Ltd [1952] 1 AER 935* where a machine was tested without a guard in order to save time and there was found to be no contributory negligence). This is particularly true in the case of injuries resulting from inadequate guarding of machinery, as the object of the fencing requirements of the *Factories Act 1961* was to protect the worker from his own acts of carelessness and inadvertence – this applies to skilled and semi-skilled workers (*Summers & Sons Ltd v Frost [1955] 1 AER 870*). Before fault can be shifted from the employer to the employee, the employee's conduct must have been reckless or deliberate (*Stocker v Norprint Ltd (1971) 10 KIR 10* where one of the employee's fingers was cut off by a guillotine and the employer was found liable for breach of *Sec 14(1)*, even though the employee had put his hand too far into the inadequately guarded opening);

(e)   an employee is not guilty of contributory negligence if he uses makeshift equipment when either (i) none or (ii) inadequate equipment/tackle is provided (*Woods v Durable Suites Ltd [1953] 2 AER 391* where a workman provided his own staging; *Machray v Stewarts & Lloyds Ltd [1964] 3 AER 716* where a rigger was injured whilst using makeshift tackle because better tackle was not provided);

(f)   an employee is entitled to assume his employer's compliance with statutory duties (*Westwood v The Post Office [1973] 3 AER 184* where the appellant's husband was killed whilst going through an 'unauthorised' lift motor room to a rooftop to sunbathe – the employer had not secured the trapdoor, as required by *OSRPA s 16*; and hence was liable);

(g)   acting in disobedience of orders is contributory negligence (*National Coal Board v England [1954] 1 AER 546* where an employee was injured whilst assisting shotfirer to set up for shot blasting, contrary to instructions; *Smith v Chesterfield and District Co-operative Society Ltd [1953] 1 AER 447* where an employee was injured putting hand under the guard of a pastry machine, contrary to instructions);

(h)   disregarding obvious dangers is contributory negligence (*Rushton v Turner Bros Asbestos Co Ltd [1959] 3 AER 517* where an employee was injured putting his hand up an exit chute to clear an obstruction, whilst operating an asbestos fibre crushing machine; he had received very thorough training and knew of the danger involved in cleaning the machine whilst in motion). The employer was however liable in *FE Callow (Engineers) Ltd v Johnson [1970] 3 AER 639*, even though an employee used a plastic 'squeezie' bottle to dispense coolant into a lathe instead of operating the automatic system. The employee was contributorily negligent (*Kerry v Carter [1969] 3 AER 723*) where a young apprentice falsely informed a farmer that he knew how to use a circular saw; and also in *Uddin v Associated Portland Cement Manufacturers Ltd [1965] 2 AER 213* where an employee was injured whilst climbing on top of a dust extracting plant where he was not supposed to be (as he was employed on cement packing), in order to retrieve a pigeon;

(j)   failure to use equipment provided for safety is contributory negligence (*Lewis v Denye [1940] 3 AER 299* which involved failure to use a push-stick, as required by the predecessor of the *Woodworking Machines Regulations 1974, Reg 19; Bux v Slough Metals Ltd [1974] 1 AER 262* which involved failure to use goggles, contrary to the *Non-ferrous Metals (Melting and Founding) Regulations 1962, Reg 13(4)*);

(k)   causation determines whether an employee's damages are to be reduced, but not the amount by which they are to be reduced. This is determined by what is 'just and equitable', as required by the *Law Reform (Contributory Negligence) Act 1945, s 1(1) (Davies v Swan Motor Co (Swansea) Ltd [1949] 1 AER 620*, per Denning LJ);

(l)   an employee's breach of a statutory health and safety duty imposed on him *personally* is contributory negligence (*Ginty v Belmont Building Supplies Ltd [1959] 1 AER 414* where crawling boards were not used by an employee when working on an asbestos roof, even though provided);

(m)   an employee's breach of a statutory health and safety duty imposed on his employer is contributory negligence (*Ross v Associated Portland Cement Manufacturers Ltd [1964] 2 AER 452* where an employee was killed when using a long ladder obtained from factory stores to repair a wire safety net 22 feet high suspended below an aerial ropeway; *Boyle v Kodak Ltd [1969] 2 AER 439* where an experienced painter failed to secure a ladder, contrary to the *Building (Safety, Health and Welfare) Regulations 1948, Reg 29* and was injured).

In the last case (*m*), the following conditions must be satisfied before the above rule can apply:

(i)   the employer must have complied with his statutory duties in making all necessary safety arrangements and instructed the employee in the use of them, so that the 'fault' lies in peformance of the duty by the employee (*Boyle v Kodak Ltd* (above) – 'every ladder shall . . . be securely fixed' [*Building (Safety, Health and Welfare) Regulations 1948, Reg 29(4)*]; *Johnson v Croggan & Co Ltd [1954] 1 AER 121* [*Building (Safety, Health and Welfare) Regulations 1948, Reg 29(1)*] – delegation of the duty to select a proper ladder, left to a competent steel erector; *Smith v Baveystock (A) & Co Ltd [1945] 1 AER 531* – delegation of setting up circular saw left to experienced circular saw operator; *Horne v Lec Refrigeration Ltd [1965] 2 AER 898* – delegated procedure of switching off power presses, before re-setting moulds, to competent fitter);

(ii)   before delegation can take place, health and safety duties must be clearly delegated to an employee; and the employee must be sufficiently well trained and experienced to appreciate the gravity of duties transferred to him (*Vyner v Waldenberg Bros Ltd [1945] 2 AER 547* where safety duties regarding circular saws, as laid down in the *Woodworking Machinery Regulations 1922* were not delegated to a wood carver).

Assumption of risk of injury ('volenti non fit injuria' – to one who is willing no harm is done)

15.39   This is a complete defence to negligence by the employer, and means that the employee impliedly agreed to run the risk of accidental harm. The defence has arisen chiefly in connection with injuries to spectators at potentially hazardous activities, e.g. motor racing, ice-hockey etc., or travelling as a passenger in a car or aircraft (*Morris v Murray* [1990] *3 AER 801* where the plaintiff was not entitled to damages for negligent injury, on the ground of *volenti*, since he had knowingly and willingly embarked on a flight with a drunken pilot). It has, however, rarely been successful when used by employers to defend actions brought by injured employees, principally because willingness to accept risk of injury assumes exercise of freedom of choice, which is generally not the case where there is a contract of employment (*Burnett v British Waterways Board* [1973] *1 WLR 700* where a notice had been placed at the dockside saying that persons 'availed themselves of dock facilities at their own risk'. A capstan rope parted while a barge was docking, injuring the plaintiff, who had seen the notice many times and understood it. It was held that the employer was liable). *Volenti* has rarely been successful as a defence in industrial injury actions since the decision in *Smith v Baker & Sons* [1891] *AC 305* where a workman was injured by a rock falling from the jib of a crane. The employer's plea of *volenti* failed.

The demise of *volenti* as a successful defence, associated with *Smith v Baker*, is generally identified with judicial awareness that employees were entitled to protection at work and did not have to look out for themselves. It has not attracted so much case law as contributory negligence but such case law as there is, establishes:

(*a*)   mere knowledge is not consent (*Burnett v British Waterways Board* above and see also *Stephen v Riverside Health Authority* at 15.11 above);

(*b*)   certain occupations are inherently dangerous, e.g. a test pilot, working with bulls. Here, if the employer has taken reasonable care, *volenti* will succeed, but if the danger is not inherent, the defence will not succeed (*Smith v Baker & Sons* above); where an employee is paid extra to take on a risk or a risky operation, the defence will succeed;

(*c*)   *volenti* cannot be pleaded as a defence by an employer who is in breach of a statutory duty, unlike contributory negligence, e.g. the duty to fence machinery (*Wheeler v New Merton Board Mills Ltd* [1933] *2 KB 669*);

(*d*)   it is a defence to breach of statutory duty by an employee, with the result that, if the party injured seeks to make the employer vicariously liable (see above), he will not be liable (*ICI Ltd v Shatwell* [1964] *2 AER 999*, a case which involved two brothers who were experienced and certificated shotfirers. Regulations imposed on them personally, not on the employer, a duty to see that certain precautions were taken before shotfiring began. They knew of risks of premature explosion and of the prohibition. Nevertheless, they decided to test without taking cover. An explosion occurred and both men were injured. It was held that the employers were not liable);

(*e*)   if an employee assumes the risk of injury by going to the aid of a co-employee, who is in foreseeable danger, this is not *volenti* (*Haynes v Harwood* [1935] *1 KB 146* where a policeman was injured whilst going to the aid of a third party run down by a horse and cart out of control – the defence of *volenti* failed; *Baker v Hopkins & Sons* [1959] *3 AER 225* where a doctor was overcome by carbon monoxide fumes while going to rescue two workmen down a well – *volenti* failed).

Fatal injuries

Civil liability

15.40   Originally at common law there was no liability to pay damages for fatal injuries at work (or anywhere else). 'In a civil court the death of a human being cannot be complained of as an injury' (*Baker v Bolton (1808) 1 Camp 493 NP*). With the advent of industrial machinery, however, coupled with steam trains and motor vehicles, this laissez-faire attitude towards the sanctity of human life was challenged. In 1845 the (then) Lord Chancellor, Lord Campbell passed the first *Fatal Accidents Act*, which gave a right of action for damages in the event of 'wrongful death'. The current law is contained in the *Fatal Accidents Act 1976*, as later amended by the *Administration of Justice Act 1982*. Death gives rise to two separate issues in civil law: (*a*) actionability in respect of death itself; and (*b*) survival of civil actions for the benefit of the deceased's estate.

Actionability in respect of death itself

15.41   The *Fatal Accidents Act 1976*, as amended by the *Administration of Justice Act 1982*, s 3(1) states, 'If death is caused by any wrongful act, neglect or default which is such as would (if death had not ensued) have entitled the person injured to maintain an action and recover damages in respect thereof, the person who would have been liable if death had not ensued, shall be liable to an action for damages, notwithstanding the death of the person injured'.

Moreover, this action is for the benefit of the deceased worker's dependants (i.e. normally the widow, widower, children or parents). [*Fatal Accidents Act 1976, s 1(2)*]. The dependant is entitled to sue because of breach of duty owed to the deceased (e.g. negligence). Damages are calculated on the basis of what is lost by way of family maintenance as a result of death of the breadwinner. Although this used to be purely a cold cash transaction, it now includes a statutory sum of £7,500 for bereavement. [*Administration of Justice Act 1982, s 3(1), as amended*]. Nominal damages for loss of expectation of life have been abolished [*Administration of Justice Act 1982, s 1(1)*] and replaced by an action for bereavement (see Chapter 6 'Compensation for Work Injuries/Diseases').

Survival of actions

15.42   Actions for injury at work which the deceased worker might have had, had he lived, survive for the benefit of his estate, normally for the benefit of his widow, but not necessarily, as he might have willed his estate to someone else, e.g. a mistress. This is provided for in the *Law Reform (Miscellaneous Provisions) Act 1934*. Any damages paid or payable under one Act are 'set off' when damages are awarded under the other Act, as in practice actions in respect of deceased workers are brought simultaneously under both Acts.

Criminal liability

15.43   Certain recent tragedies involving the general travelling public have focused attention on corporate liability for manslaughter. Provision exists in the *Health and Safety at Work Act 1974* for prosecution against companies *per se* and individual executive (though not non-executive) directors, in the form of *Sec 37* (see Chapter 17 'Enforcement').

Manslaughter

15.44   Manslaughter is of two kinds (*a*) voluntary and (*b*) involuntary. The former, which is essentially murder but reduced in severity owing to, say, diminished responsibility, is not relevant to health and safety; whereas, the latter is. Involuntary manslaughter extends to all unlawful homicides where there is no 'malice aforethought' or intent to kill. There are two forms of involuntary manslaughter, namely (*a*) constructive and (*b*) reckless manslaughter. The former, constructive manslaughter, applies to situations where death results from an act unlawful at common law or by statute, amounting to more than mere negligence. The latter, reckless manslaughter (sometimes called 'gross negligence') is where death is caused by a reckless act or omission, and a person acts recklessly when he acts '. . . without having given any thought to the possibility of there being any such risk or, having recognised that there was some risk involved, has none the less gone on to take it' (*R v Lawrence [1981] 1 AER 974* – a road traffic case).

Corporate criminal liability

15.45   A company can incur criminal liability in one of two ways. First, it can be vicariously liable for the criminal acts of its agents and servants (see Chapter 17 'Enforcement'). Secondly, it can be personally liable. It is under this second head of liability that a company could be guilty of manslaughter. Here a company can be personally liable for the acts/omissions of its controlling officers, on the ground that their acts/omissions are those of the company itself. But the crime must be one for which imprisonment is not the exclusive penalty, e.g. murder, owing to the (obvious) practical difficulty of imprisoning a company. Being a crime which is punishable by imprisonment or fine, manslaughter is a crime which could be committed by a company. The law was well summed up as follows: 'A company may in many ways be likened to a human body. It has a brain and nerve centre which controls what it does. It also has hands which hold the tools and act in accordance with directions from the centre. Some of the people in the company are mere servants and agents who are nothing more than hands to do the work and cannot be said to represent the mind or will. Others are directors and managers who represent the directing mind and will of the company and control what it does. The state of mind of these managers is the state of mind of the company and is treated by the law as such' (per Lord Denning in *H L Bolton (Engineering) Ltd v T J Graham & Sons Ltd [1956] 3 AER 624*).

On this basis, companies and other bodies corporate could be tried for involuntary manslaughter.

Remedies for injured employees

15.46   The remedy which an injured employee may claim in a civil court action from his employer is damages for:

(*a*)   breach of a common law duty (see 15.20 above) – this liability of the employer may arise vicariously in respect of negligence by another employee (see 15.3–15.6 above); or

(*b*)   breach of statutory duty, where a right of civil action is recognised (e.g. under many sections of the *Factories Act 1961*) – here it should be noted that a breach by an employer of *HSWA ss 1-53*, though probably also constituting a breach of common law duty (see above), does not give rise to an action for breach of the statutory duty [*HSWA s 47*] and this also applies to the new *Management of Health and Safety at Work Regulations 1992, Reg 15*; or

(*c*)   an amalgam of both (*a*) and (*b*) above – the so-called 'double-barrelled' action (see 15.10 above).

An injured or disabled employee may also be entitled to claim social security benefit from the state. These benefits are considered in Chapter 6 'Compensation for Work Injuries/Diseases'.

Actions against employers for negligence are brought in civil courts (assuming there is no out-of-court settlement, which is the common practice), and the form of redress is damages. Civil action may or may not follow prosecution in a criminal court by an HSE inspector. If the injured worker is a member of a trade union, his case will often be taken by the union against the employer's insurer, since employers are covered by compulsory insurance against this liability (see Chapter 16 'Employers' Liability Insurance').

The management of health and safety at work – safety officers, occupational health nurses, occupational physicians, occupational hygienists

15.47   The major impact of the *Health and Safety at Work etc. Act 1974 (HSWA)* was to initiate a change in attitude towards occupational health and safety from that of a purely managerial commitment to one of responsibility on the part of the whole workforce. *HSWA* predicated in a general way that employers had to manage health and safety at work, and this requirement has been underlined and reinforced further by the *Management of Health and Safety at Work Regulations 1992 (SI 1992 No 2051)*.

In particular, employers must

(1)   make regular risk assessments of the health and safety of both direct and indirect workers by way of implementation of the EC Safety Framework Directive (see 1.13 INTRODUCTION) [*Reg 3*];

(2)   make arrangements for effective planning, organisation, control and monitoring of preventive and protective measures [*Reg 4*];

(3)   appoint (though not necessarily employ) competent personnel to enable them to discharge their statutory safety duties and functions [*Reg 6*].

Competence depends on the training and experience received and such personnel, that is, safety officers, occupational health nurses, occupational physicians and hygienists will be responsible for ensuring the health and safety of both direct and indirect workers, including temporary staff. [*Reg 6(4)(b)*]. In larger establishments, where the spectrum of potential risks is wider, this may well involve full-time employment of a team of personnel (such as are mentioned in 15.48–15.54 below); whereas in smaller operations, employers may well avail themselves of outside qualified personnel. [*Management of Health and Safety at Work Regulations 1992, Reg 6*]. Failure to make such appointments is a criminal offence under *HSWA s 33(1)(c)*, under which Act these regulations were made, and it can also entail adverse insurance consequences (see 16.21 EMPLOYERS' LIABILITY INSURANCE).

Safety officers

Legal requirements on employers

15.48   From an early date common law had expected employers, where necessary, to delegate performance of safety duties to competent nominees. 'Thus in the case of a manufacturer employing machinery which might be attended with danger to the persons employed about it . . . the master must either ascertain the state of the machinery or apparatus himself; or employ some competent person to do so' (*Webb v Rennie (1865) 4 F & F 608).* But with more and more rapid advances in technology, the threat of workplace danger ever nearer and greater than before, and a spate of industrial health and safety legislation to contend with, today's health and safety practitioner needs to be a professional and an integral part of the management team, able to draw upon legal, technical and administrative disciplines. Hence, employers are required to appoint competent personnel in the form of safety officers, to oversee the safety of their operation. *[Reg 6(1)].* Safety officers do not need to be employees – and, indeed, in smaller and medium-sized establishments, necessary safety expertise will, in all probability, be called in from an outside specialist pool.

Health and safety managers/advisers

15.49   Many large multi-location organisations employ specialists whose principal function is to advise directors and senior management on policy matters which are translated into action at local unit level. Such persons originate from a range of professional disciplines – law, engineering, chemistry, insurance – and may have transferred to industry following service with one of the enforcement agencies such as the HSE or local authority environmental health department. The majority will have undertaken a period of full-time or part-time education, either to degree or diploma level, of three to six years' duration, or longer.

Within these large organisations health and safety advisers operate on a national basis. They do not generally have executive authority but do have direct access to directors and senior management in their co-ordinating role. They are concerned mainly with the management of health and safety as an integral feature of the business operation, and are involved with policy issues such as the preparation and revision of the company statement of health and safety policy, the measurement of individual unit safety performance, company systems for accident reporting, recording and investigation, joint consultation procedures on a national basis, disaster planning and control, and their formal documentation. The formulation of policy and procedures with regard to environmental working conditions, occupational health and hygiene, and health and safety training at all levels, fall within their brief, together with liaison with enforcement agencies at national level. The health and safety manager/adviser may advise company legal specialists and insurance departments on matters of direct concern, and monitor the performance of unit safety officers.

This role is essentially a promotional one. Through direct contact with directors the health and safety manager's primary task is to ensure that occupational health and safety becomes 'institutionalised' within the organisation and is treated with the same importance as other areas such as marketing, finance and production. In effect, he is 'selling' or promoting the benefits of good standards of safety, health and welfare to directors and senior management to ensure their integration as a prominent feature of the business objectives, concerned with reducing losses, improving management performance and maintaining the organisation's image as a good employer in the market place.

Duties of safety officer

15.50   The duties of a safety officer include:

(*a*)   advising line management in order to assist it to fulfil its responsibility for safety. This entails:

(i)   advising on safety aspects in the design and use of plant and equipment and the checking of new equipment before commissioning;

(ii) carrying out periodic inspections to identify unsafe plant, unsafe working conditions and unsafe practices, to report on the results of such inspections and make recommendations for remedying any defects found;

(b) advising upon the drawing up and implementation of safe systems of work, and the provision and use of appropriate protective equipment;

(c) advising upon legal requirements affecting health and safety;

(d) participating in the work of safety committees and joint consultations affecting the workforce;

(e) promoting and, where appropriate, participating in safety education programmes to assist in safety consciousness at all levels within the organisation and specifically to teach supervisors to develop safe working conditions;

(f) working in collaboration with the training department, where this exists, to secure regular safety training of employees;

(g) providing information about accident prevention techniques, and preparing visual aids, including posters, slides, film strips etc. for safety training purposes;

(h) assessing possible causes of injury and circumstances likely to produce an accident, the compilation of necessary reports, and tendering advice to prevent recurrence;

(j) recording of accident statistics and presenting information in appropriate form for the use of management and others in ensuring safety performance;

(k) maintaining liaison with other departments, including medical and training departments, with official bodies such as government inspectorates, local authorities and fire authorities, and with outside bodies such as RoSPA, British Safety Council and the Fire Protection Association; and

(l) keeping up-to-date with modern processes and techniques, with special reference to safety.

Occupational health nurses

15.51 Employers will shortly have to provide employees with appropriate health surveillance to meet the risks at work to which they may be exposed. Such requirement respects the need, at least in larger establishments, for the provision of access to an occupational nurse, and, possibly, an occupational physician. An occupational health nurse should preferably hold the Occupational Health Nursing Certificate (OHNC) of the Royal College of Nursing (RCN) in addition to a general nursing qualification i.e. SRN.

The occupational health nurse's role consists of eight main elements:

(a) health supervision;

(b) health education;

(c) environmental monitoring and occupational safety;

(d) counselling;

(e) treatment services;

(f) rehabilitation and resettlement;

(g) unit administration and record systems; and

(*h*)   liaison with other agencies.

Duties of the occupational health nurse

15.52   The RCN identifies the following duties which a fully trained occupational health nurse could perform:

(*a*)   health assessment in relation to the individual worker and the job to be performed;

(*b*)   noting normal standards of health and fitness and any departures or variations from these standards;

(*c*)   referring to the occupational physician or doctor such cases which, in the opinion of the nurse, require further investigation and medical, as distinct from nursing, assessment;

(*d*)   health supervision of vulnerable groups, e.g. young persons, disabled workers;

(*e*)   routine visits to and surveys of the working environment, and informing as necessary the appropriate expert when a particular problem requires further specialised investigation;

(*f*)   employee health counselling;

(*g*)   health education activities in relation to groups of workers;

(*h*)   the assessment of injuries or illness occurring at work and treatment or referral as appropriate;

(*j*)   responsibility for the organisation and administration of occupational health services, and the control and safe-keeping of non-statutory personal health records; and

(*k*)   a teaching role in respect of the training of first-aid personnel and the organisation of emergency services.

The RCN further recommends that where a full-time medical officer with occupational health training and management is employed, the doctor assumes overall responsibility for the leadership and organisation of the occupational health service. As a matter of principle in such organisations, nursing staff organised in hierarchies work to one nurse leader who is responsible for the overall organisation and administration of the occupational health nursing services. The most senior nurse should work in close partnership with the doctor in charge.

Occupational physicians

15.53   The British Medical Association (BMA) has identified the duties and responsibilities of doctors holding appointments in occupational medicine as encompassing the following:

The effects of health on the capacity to work

(*a*)   Provision of advice to employees on all health matters relating to their working capacity.

(*b*)   Examination of applicants for employment and advice as to their placement.

(*c*)   Immediate treatment of medical and surgical emergencies occurring at the place of employment.

(*d*)   Examination and continued observation of persons returning to work after absence due to illness or accident and advice on suitable work.

(*e*)   Health supervision of all employees with special reference to young persons, pregnant women, elderly persons and disabled persons.

The effect of work on health

(*a*)   Responsibility for nursing and first-aid services.

(*b*)   The study of the work and working environment and their effects on the health of employees.

(*c*)   Periodical examination of persons exposed to special hazards in respect of their employment.

(*d*)   Advice to management regarding:

    (i)   the working environment in relation to health;

    (ii)   occurrence and significance of hazards;

    (iii)   accident prevention; and

    (iv)   statutory requirements in relation to health.

(*e*)   Medical supervision of health and hygiene of staff and facilities, with particular reference to canteens, kitchens, etc. and those working in the production of foods or drugs for sale to the public.

(*f*)   The arranging and carrying out of such education work in respect of the health, fitness and hygiene of employees as may be desirable and practicable.

(*g*)   Advising those committees within the organisation which are responsible for health, safety and welfare of employees.

Occupational hygienists

15.54   Occupational hygiene is concerned with the identification, measurement, evaluation and control of environmental factors arising from work which might adversely affect the health or well-being of people at work or in the community. The occupational hygienist is concerned with the measurement, monitoring, evaluation and control of health risks associated with occupational and environmental stressors – noise, dust, fumes, radiation, toxic substances, etc. Control methods may be based on a comparison between the analytical results of measurements taken and current hygiene standards e.g. occupational exposure limits. Entry to the profession is controlled by the British Examination Board in Occupational Hygiene (BEBOH).

Chapter 16

Employers' Liability Insurance

Introduction

16.1   Most employers carrying on business in Great Britain are under a statutory duty to take out insurance against claims for injuries/diseases brought against them by employees. When such a compulsory insurance policy is taken out the insurance company issues the employer with a certificate of insurance, and the employer must keep a copy of this displayed in a prominent position at his workplace, so that employees can see it. It is a criminal offence to fail to take out such insurance and/or to display a certificate (see 16.13, 16.14 below). These duties are contained in the *Employers' Liability (Compulsory Insurance) Act 1969* (referred to hereafter as the '*1969 Act*') and in the *Employers' Liability (Compulsory Insurance) General Regulations 1971*, as later amended by *SIs 1971 No 1117; 1974 No 208; 1975 Nos 194, 1443* – referred to hereafter as the *Compulsory Insurance General Regulations*. In addition, the requirements of the *1969 Act* extend to offshore installations (see further Chapter 34 'Offshore Operations') but do not extend to injuries suffered by employees when carried on or in a vehicle, or entering or getting onto or alighting from a vehicle, where such injury is caused by, or arises out of use, by the employer, of a vehicle on the road. [*Employers' Liability (Compulsory Insurance) Exemption (Amendment) Regulations 1992 (SI 1992 No 3172), Reg 2*]. Such employees would normally be covered under the *Road Traffic Act 1988, s 145* as amended by the *Motor Vehicles (Compulsory Insurance) Regulations 1992 (SI 1992 No 3036)*.

Object of compulsory employers' liability insurance

16.2   The purpose of compulsory employers' liability insurance is to ensure that employers are covered for any legal liability to pay damages to employees who suffer bodily injury and/or disease during the course of employment and as a result of employment. It is the liability of the employer towards his employees which has to be covered; there is no question of compulsory insurance extending to employees, since employers are under no statutory and/or common law duty to insure employees against risk of injury, or even to advise on the desirability of insurance (see 15.21 EMPLOYERS' LIABILITY); it is their potential legal liability to employees which must be insured against (see 16.8 below). Such liability is normally based on negligence, though not necessarily personal negligence on the part of the employer. Moreover, case law suggests that employers' liability is becoming stricter. The rule that employers must 'take their victims as they find them' underlines the need for long-tail cover because the employer may find himself liable for injuries/diseases which 'trigger off' or exacerbate existing conditions. (See further Chapter 15 'Employers' Duties'.)

An employers' liability policy is a legal liability policy. Hence, if there is no legal liability on the part of an employer, no insurance moneys will be paid out. Moreover, if the employee's action against the employer cannot succeed, the action for damages cannot be brought against an employer's insurer (*Bradley v Eagle Star Insurance Co Ltd [1989] 1 AER 961* where the employer company had been wound up and dissolved before the employer's liability to the injured employee had been established) (see below for the transfer of an employer's indemnity policy to an employee). The effect of this decision has been reversed by the *Companies Act 1989*, amending *Sec 651* of the *Companies Act 1985* which allows the revival of a dissolved company within two years of its dissolution for the purpose of legal claims and, in personal injuries cases, the revival can take place at any time subject to the existing limitation of action rules contained in the *Limitation Act 1980*. For example, in the recent case of *Re Workvale [1992] 1 WLR 416*, the court exercised its discretion under *Sec 33* of the *Limitation Act 1980* to allow a personal injuries claim to proceed after the three-year limitation period had expired. This meant that the company could also be revived under the provisions of *CA 1985, s 651(5)* and *(6)* (as amended). Thus, proceedings under the *Third Parties (Rights against Insurers) Act 1930, s 1, 1(b)* may be brought in this manner.

If the employer becomes bankrupt or if a company becomes insolvent, the employer's right to an indemnity from his insurers is transferred to the employee who may then keep the sums recovered with priority to his employer's creditors. This is only so if the employer has made his claim to this indemnity by trial, arbitration or agreement before he is made bankrupt or insolvent (*Bradley v Eagle Star Insurance Co Ltd [1989] 1 AER 961*). The employee must also claim within the statutory limitation period from the date of his injury (see 16.7 below for subrogation rights generally).

The policy protects an employer from third party claims; an employee as such is not covered since he normally incurs no liability. Although offering wide cover an employers' liability policy does not give cover to third party non-employees (e.g. independent contractors and members of the public). Such liability is covered by a public liability policy which, though advisable, is not compulsory.

This chapter examines:

—   the general law relating to contracts of insurance (see 16.3-16.6 below);

—   the insurer's right of recovery (i.e. subrogation) (see 16.7 below);

—   the duty to take out employers' liability insurance (see 16.8-16.12 below);

—   issue and display of certificates of insurance (see 16.13 below);

—   penalties (see 16.14 below);

—   scope and cover of policy (see 16.15-16.18 below);

—   'prohibition' of certain terms (see 16.19 below);

—   trade endorsement for certain types of work (see 16.20, 16.21 below).

General law relating to insurance contracts

16.3   Insurance is a contract. When a person wishes to insure, for example, himself, his house, his liability towards his employees, valuable personal property or even loss of profits, he (the proposer) fills in a proposal form for insurance, at the same time making certain facts known to the insurer about what is to be insured. On the basis of the information disclosed in the proposal form, the insurer will decide whether to accept the risk or at what rate to fix the premium. If the insurer elects to accept the risk, a contract of insurance is then drawn up in the form of an insurance policy. (Incidentally, it seems to matter little whether the negotiations leading up to contract took place between the insured (proposer) and the insurance company or between the insured and a broker, since the broker is often regarded as the agent of one or the other, generally of the proposer (*Newsholme Bros v Road Transport &*

General Insurance Co Ltd [1929] 2 KB 356).) However, a lot depends on the facts. If he is authorised to complete blank proposal forms, he may well be the agent of the insurer.

Extent of duty of disclosure

16.4   A proposer must disclose to the insurer all material facts within his actual knowledge. This does not extend to disclosure of facts which he could not reasonably be expected to know. 'The duty is a duty to disclose, and you cannot disclose what you do not know. The obligation to disclose, therefore, necessarily depends on the knowledge you possess. I must not be misunderstood. Your opinion of the materiality of that knowledge is of no moment. If a reasonable man would have recognised that the knowledge in question was material to disclose, it is no excuse that you did not recognise it. But the question always is – Was the knowledge you possessed such that you ought to have disclosed it?' (*Joel v Law Union and Crown Insurance Co [1908] 2 KB 863* per Fletcher Moulton LJ).

An element of consumer protection, in favour of insureds, was introduced into insurance contracts by the Statement of General Insurance Practice 1987, a form of self-regulation applicable to many but not to all insurers. This has consequences for the duty of disclosure, proposal forms (16.5 below), renewals and claims.

Filling in proposal form

16.5   Generally only failure to make disclosure of relevant facts will allow an insurer subsequently to invalidate the policy and refuse to compensate for the loss. The test of whether a fact was or was not relevant is whether its omission would have influenced a prudent insurer in deciding whether to accept the risk, or at what rate to fix the premium.

The arm of *uberrima fides* (i.e. the utmost good faith) is a long one. If, when filling in a proposal form, a statement made by the proposer is at that time true, but is false in relation to other facts which are not stated, or becomes false before issue of the insurance policy, this entitles the insurer to refuse to indemnify. In *Condogianis v Guardian Assurance Co Ltd [1912] 2 AC 125* a proposal form for fire cover contained the following question: 'Has proponent ever been a claimant on a fire insurance company in respect of the property now proposed, or any other property? If so, state when and name of company'. The proposer answered 'Yes', '1917', 'Ocean'. This answer was literally true, since he had claimed against the Ocean Insurance Co in respect of a burning car. However, he had failed to say that in 1912 he had made another claim against another insurance company in respect of another burning car. It was held that the answer was not a true one and the policy was, therefore, invalidated.

Loss mitigation

16.6   There is an implied term in most insurance contracts that the insured will take all reasonable steps to mitigate loss caused by one or more of the insured perils. Thus, in the case of burglary cover of commercial premises, this could extend to provision of security patrols, the fitting of burglar alarm devices and guard dogs. In the case of employers' liability, it will extend to appointment or use of services of an accredited safety officer and/or occupational hygienist, either permanently or temporarily, particularly in light of the *Management of Health and Safety at Work Regulations 1992*, to oversee, for example, application of the *COSHH Regulations 1988*. Again, in the case of fire cover, steps to mitigate the extent of the loss on the part of the insured, might well extend to regular visits by the local fire authority and/or advice on storage of products and materials by reputable risk management consultants. Indeed, it is compliance with this implied duty in insurance contracts that accounts for the growth of the practice of risk management, and good housekeeping on the part of more and more companies.

Subrogation

16.7   Subrogation enables an insurer to make certain that the insured recovers no more than exact replacement of loss (i.e. indemnity). 'It (the doctrine of subrogation) was introduced in favour of the underwriters, in order to prevent their having to pay more than a full indemnity, not on the ground that the underwriters were sureties, for they are not so always, although their rights are sometimes similar to those of sureties, but in order to prevent the assured recovering more than a full indemnity.' (*Castellain v Preston [1883] 11 QBD 380* per Brett LJ). Subrogation does not extend to accident insurance moneys, whereby the insured (normally self-employed) is promised a fixed sum in the event of injury or illness (*Bradburn v Great Western Railway Co (1874) LR 10 Exch 1* where the appellant was injured whilst travelling on a train, owing to the negligence of the respondent. He had earlier bought personal accident insurance to cover him for the possibility of injury on the train. It was held that he was entitled to both damages for negligence *and* insurance moneys payable under the policy (see further 6.26 COMPENSATION FOR WORK INJURIES/ DISEASES)). The right of subrogation does not arise until the insurer has paid the insured in respect of his loss, and has been invoked infrequently in employers' liability cases. In *Morris v Ford Motor Co Ltd [1973] 2 AER 1084* the Ford Motor Co had subcontracted cleaning at one of their plants to the X company, for which the appellant worked. Whilst engaged on this work at the plant, the appellant was injured owing to the negligence of an employee whilst driving a forklift truck. The appellant claimed damages from the respondent company for the negligence of their employee, on the grounds of vicarious liability. X company had, however, entered into a contract of indemnity with the respondent company, agreeing to indemnify the company for all losses or claims for injury arising out of the cleaning operations. Although accepting that they were bound by the terms of this contract of indemnity, the X company argued that they should be subrogated against the negligent Ford employee, on the ground that the employee had carried out his work negligently. It was held that the agreement by the British Insurance Association that they would not sue an employee of an insured employer in respect of injury caused to a co-employee, unless there was either (*a*) collusion and/or (*b*) wilful misconduct on the part of the employee, was binding and that the X company could not recoup its loss from the negligent employee.

Duty of employer to take out and maintain insurance

16.8   'Every employer carrying on business in Great Britain shall insure, and maintain insurance against liability for bodily injury or disease sustained by his employees, and arising out of and in the course of their employment in Great Britain in that business.' [*Employers' Liability (Compulsory Insurance) Act 1969, s 1(1)*].

Such insurance must be provided under one or more 'approved policies'. An 'approved policy' is a policy of insurance not subject to any conditions or exceptions prohibited by regulations (see 16.19 below). [*Sec 1(3)*].

There is no duty under the *1969 Act* to warn or insure the employee against risks of employment outside Great Britain (*Reid v Rush Tompkins Group plc [1989] 3 AER 228 (CA)*) (see further Chapter 15 'Employers' Duties').

Employees covered by the Act

16.9   Cover is required in respect of liability to employees who either:

(*a*)   are ordinarily resident in Great Britain; or

(*b*)   though not ordinarily resident in Great Britain, are present in Great Britain in the course of employment here for a continuous period of not less than 14 days.

[*Sec 2(2)(b); Compulsory Insurance General Regulations, Reg 4*].

Employees not covered by Act

16.10   An employer is not required to insure against liability to an employee who is (*a*) a spouse, (*b*) father, (*c*) mother, (*d*) son, (*e*) daughter, (*f*) other close relative. [*Sec 2(2)(a)*]. Those who are not ordinarily resident in the UK are not covered by the Act except as above. Nor are employees working abroad covered. Such employees can sue under English law in limited circumstances (see 15.21 EMPLOYERS' DUTIES) (*Johnson v Coventry Churchill International Ltd [1992] 3 AER 14* where an employee, working in Germany for an English manpower leasing company, was injured when he fell through a rotten plank. He was unable to sue his employer under German law; although he was working in Germany, it was held that England was the country with the most significant relationship with the claim because he had made the contract in England, his employers had covered him with personal liability insurance and he therefore expected them to compensate him through these insurers for any personal injury sustained in Germany).

Degree of cover necessary

16.11   The amount for which an employer is required to insure and maintain insurance is £2,000,000 in respect of claims relating to any one or more of his employees, arising out of any one occurrence. [*Sec 1(2); Compulsory Insurance General Regulations, Reg 3*].

Most policies, however, have no upper limit, being for an indemnity unlimited in amount.

Exempted employers

16.12   The following employers are exempt from the duty to take out and maintain insurance:

(*a*)   county and local councils;

(*b*)   nationalised industries;

(*c*)   any body holding a Government department certificate that any claim which it cannot pay itself will be paid out of moneys provided by Parliament;

(*d*)   the London Transport Executive;

(*e*)   statutory water undertakers and certain water boards;

(*f*)   Commission for the New Towns;

(*g*)   health service bodies, National Health Service Trusts;

(*h*)   probation and after-care committees, magistrates' court committees;

(*j*)   governments and foreign states or commonwealth countries and some other specialised employers.

There are other types of employer specified in the regulations, but these are the main exceptions.

[Employers' Liability Compulsory Insurance Act 1969, s 3; Employers' Liability (Compulsory Insurance) General Regulations 1971, Reg 3].

Issue and display of certificates of insurance

16.13   The insurer must issue the employer with a certificate of insurance, which has to be issued not later than 30 days after the date on which insurance was commenced or renewed. *[Sec 4(1); Compulsory Insurance General Regulations, Reg 5].*

A copy of the certificate must be displayed at each place of business where there are any employees entitled to be covered by the insurance policy and it must be placed where they can easily see and read it. *[Reg 6].*

An employer must, if a notice has been served on him by the Health and Safety Executive, produce a copy of the policy to the officers specified in the notice and he must permit inspection of the policy by an inspector authorised by the Secretary of State to inspect the policy. *[Reg 7].*

Penalties

Failure to insure or maintain insurance

16.14   Failure by an employer to effect and maintain insurance for any day on which it is required is a criminal offence, carrying a maximum penalty on conviction of £2,500. *[Criminal Justice Act 1991, s 17(1)].*

Failure to display a certificate of insurance

Failure on the part of an employer to display a certificate of insurance in a prominent position in the workplace is a criminal offence, carrying a maximum penalty on conviction of £1,000. *[Criminal Justice Act 1991, s 17(1)].*

Cover provided by a typical policy

Persons

16.15   Cover is limited to protection of employees (for the definition of 'employee', see 14.2 EMPLOYEES' DUTIES). Independent contractors are not covered; liability to them should be covered by a public liability policy. Directors who are employed under a contract of employment are covered, but directors paid by fees who do not work full-time in the business are generally not regarded as 'employees'. Liability to them would normally be covered by a public liability policy. Similarly, since the judicial tendency is to construe 'labour-only' subcontractors in the construction industry as 'employees' (see Chapter 7 'Construction and Building Operations'), employers' liability policies often contain the following endorsement: 'An employee shall also mean any labour master, and persons supplied by him, any person employed by labour-only subcontractors, any self-employed person, or any person hired from any public authority, company, firm or individual, while working for the insured in connection with the business'. The public liability policy should then be amended to exclude the insured's liability to 'employees' so designated.

Scope of cover

16.16   The policy provides for payment of:

(*a*)   costs and expenses of litigation, incurred with the insurer's consent, in defence of a claim against the insured (i.e. civil liability);

(*b*)   solicitor's fees, incurred with the insurer's consent, for representation of the insured at proceedings in any court of summary jurisdiction (e.g. magistrates' court or Crown Court), coroner's inquest, or a fatal accident inquiry (i.e. criminal proceedings), arising out of an accident resulting in injury to an employee. It does *not* cover payment of a fine imposed by a criminal court.

Geographical limits

16.17   Cover is normally limited to Great Britain, Northern Ireland, the Channel Islands and the Isle of Man, in respect of employees normally resident in any of the above, who sustain injury whilst working in those areas. Cover is also provided for such employees who are injured whilst temporarily working abroad, so long as the action for damages is brought in a court of law of Great Britain, Northern Ireland, the Channel Islands or the Isle of Man – though even this proviso is omitted from some policies.

Conditions which must be satisfied

16.18   (*a*)   Cover only relates to bodily injury or disease; it does not extend to employee's property. This latter cover is provided by an employers' public liability policy.

(*b*)   Injury must arise out of and during the course of employment (see Chapter 15 'Employers' Duties'). If injury does not so arise, cover is normally provided by a public liability policy.

(*c*)   Bodily injury must be caused during the period of insurance. Normally with injury-causing accidents there is no problem, since injury follows on from the accident almost immediately. Certain occupational diseases, however, may not manifest themselves until much later, e.g. asbestosis, mesothelioma, pneumoconiosis, deafness. Here legal liability takes place when the disease manifests itself, or is 'discovered' (see further 15.11 EMPLOYERS' DUTIES). Moreover, at least as far as occupational deafness is concerned, liability between employers can be apportioned, giving rise to contribution between insurers (see further Chapter 30 'Noise and Vibration').

(*d*)   Claims must be notified by the insured to the insurer as soon as possible, or as stipulated by the policy.

Regulation 2 does not fetter the freedom of underwriters to apply certain conditions in connection with intrinsically hazardous work; for instance, exclusion of liability for accidents arising out of demolition work, or in connection with use of explosives (*A J Dunbar v A & B Painters and Economic Insurance Co [1986] 2 Lloyd's Rep 38* where an insurer was entitled to repudiate liability for work at a height of more than forty feet, where the policy contained an express clause to this effect).

'Prohibition' of certain terms

16.19   All liability policies contain conditions with which the insured must comply if the insurer is to 'progress' his claim, e.g. notification of claims. Failure to comply with such condition(s) could jeopardise cover under the policy: the insured would be legally liable but without insurance protection. In the case of an employers' liability policy, an insurer might seek to avoid liability under the policy if the condition requiring the insured to take reasonable care to prevent injuries to employees, and/or comply with the provisions of any relevant statutes/statutory instruments (e.g. *HSWA; Ionising Radiations Regulations 1985*), or to keep records, was not complied with.

The object of the *1969 Act* was to ensure that an employer who had a claim brought against him would be able to pay the employee any damages awarded. Regulations made under the Act, therefore, sought to prevent insurers from avoiding their liability by relying on breach of a policy condition, by way of 'prohibiting' certain conditions in policies taken out under the Act. More particularly, insurers cannot avoid liability in the following circumstances:

(*a*)   some specified thing being done or being omitted to be done after the happening of the event giving rise to a claim (e.g. omission to notify the insurer of a claim within a stipulated time);

(*b*)   failure on the part of the policy-holder to take reasonable care to protect his employees against the risk of bodily injury or disease in the course of employment. As to the meaning of 'reasonable care' or 'reasonable precaution' here, 'It is eminently reasonable for employers to entrust . . . tasks to a skilled and trusted foreman on whose competence they have every reason to rely'. (*Woolfall and Rimmer Ltd v Moyle and Another [1941] 3 AER 304*). The prohibition is therefore, not broken by a negligent act on the part of a competent foreman selected by the employer. Where, however, an employer acted wilfully (in causing injury) and not merely negligently (though this would be rare), the insurer could presumably refuse to pay (*Hartley v Provincial Insurance Co Ltd [1957] Lloyd's Rep 121* where the insured employer had not taken steps to ensure that a stockbar was securely fenced for the purposes of the *Factories Act 1937, s 14(3)* in spite of repeated warnings from the factory inspector, with the result that an employee was scalped whilst working at a lathe. It was held that the insurer was justified in refusing to indemnify the employer who was in breach of statutory duty and so liable for damages). This was confirmed in *Aluminium Wire and Cable Co Ltd v Allstate Insurance Co Ltd [1985] 2 Lloyd's Rep 280*;

(*c*)   failure on the part of the policy-holder to comply with statutory requirements for the protection of employees against the risk of injury – the reasoning in *Hartley v Provincial Insurance Co Ltd* (see (*b*) above), that wilful breach may not be covered, probably applies here too;

(*d*)   failure on the part of the policy-holder to keep specified records and make such information available to the insurer (e.g. accident book or accounts relating to employees' wages and salaries (see Chapter 3 'Accident Reporting')).

[*Compulsory Insurance General Regulations 1971, Reg 2(1)*].

Trade endorsements for certain types of work

16.20   There are no policy exceptions to the standard employers' liability cover. Trade endorsements, however, are used frequently in underwriting employers' liability risks, and there is nothing in the Act to prevent insurers from applying their normal underwriting principles and applying trade endorsements where they consider it necessary, i.e. they will amend their standard policy form to exclude certain risks. Thus, there may be specific exclusions of liability arising out of types of work, such as demolition, or the use of mechanically driven woodworking machinery, or work above certain heights, unless the appropriate rate of premium is paid. This does mean that there are still circumstances where an employee will not obtain compensation from his employer based on the employer's insurance cover.

Measure of risk and assessment of premium

16.21   Certain trades or businesses are known to be more dangerous than others. For most trades or businesses insurers have their own rate for the risk, expressed as a rate per cent on wages (other than for clerical, managerial or non-manual employees for whom a very low rate applies). This rate is used as a guide and is altered upwards or downwards depending upon:

(*a*)   previous history of claims and cost of settlement;

(*b*)   size of wage roll;

(*c*)   whether certain risks are not to be covered, e.g. the premium will be lower if the insured elects to exclude from the policy certain risks, such as the use of power driven woodworking machinery;

(*d*)   the insured's attitude towards safety.

Many insurers survey premises with the object of improving the risk and minimising the incidence of accidents and diseases. This is an essential part of their service, and they often work in conjunction with the insured's own safety staff (see Chapter 39 'Risk Analysis and Safety Monitoring').

Extension of cover

16.22   In addition to employers' liability insurance, it is becoming increasingly common for companies to buy insurance in respect of directors' personal liability. Indeed, in the United States, some directors refuse to take up appointments in the absence of such insurance being forthcoming (see further 17.33 ENFORCEMENT).

Chapter 17

Enforcement

Introduction

17.1   In the last decade there has been a movement away from a purely legalistic approach towards health and safety at work to one concerned with loss prevention, asset protection, accountability and consultation with the workforce, a situation without parallel under previous protective legislation. An effective system of enforcement is still, however, essential if workplaces are to be kept safe and accidents prevented. Prior to the *Health and Safety at Work etc. Act 1974 (HSWA)*, the principal sanction against breach of a statutory requirement was prosecution. This preoccupation with criminal proceedings was criticised by the Robens Committee (para 142) as being largely ineffective in securing the most important end result, namely that the breach should be remedied as soon as possible. *HSWA*, therefore, has given HSE inspectors a range of enforcement powers which do not necessarily depend on prosecution for their efficacy. Most important of these are the powers to serve improvement and prohibition notices. Contravention of an improvement/prohibition notice carries with it, on summary conviction, a maximum fine of £20,000; or, alternatively, six months' imprisonment (see 17.29 below). In particular, a prohibition notice may be served by an inspector where he believes there to be a risk of serious personal injury, regardless of whether any offence has actually been committed. Equally important, though less obvious perhaps, HSE inspectors and environmental health officers, the two principal enforcement authorities, can use powers given to them by *HSWA*, i.e. serve improvement and prohibition notices, in order to enforce pre-*HSWA* statutory requirements, e.g. duties under the *Factories Act 1961* and *Offices, Shops and Railway Premises Act 1963 (OSRPA)*, since these qualify as 'relevant statutory provisions' (see 17.2 below). Recently, however, greater enforcement powers have been conferred on local authorities by the *Health and Safety (Enforcing Authority) Regulations 1989* (see 17.4 below). Also, the *Planning (Hazardous Substances) Act 1990* requires consent in respect of hazardous substances on land, the quantity of which exceeds the quantity specified by regulations to be passed under the Act. In addition, hazardous substances authorities can issue hazardous substances contravention notices, which will operate similarly to improvement notices. (See further 17.19 below.)

More recently, the *Environmental Protection Act 1990* has conferred similar notice-serving powers on HM Inspectors of Pollution (HMIP) and environmental health departments of local authorities (see further Chapter 12 'Emissions into the Atmosphere'). The *Radioactive Material (Road Transport) Act 1991* has given transport inspectors powers to detain, search and generally 'quarantine' vehicles carrying radioactive packages in breach of that Act (see further Chapter 10 'Dangerous Substances II') and the *Radioactive Substances Act 1993* similarly empowers inspectors in respect of premises containing radioactive substances and mobile radioactive apparatus (see 9.42 DANGEROUS SUBSTANCES I).

Such enforcement powers apart, breach of a statutory requirement is still a criminal offence. Prosecution, albeit a 'reserve weapon', is an important one. Persons committing a breach, or permitting one to occur, should be in no doubt that they stand to be prosecuted. It is not just the employer who is liable to prosecution: employees and junior and middle management and even visitors to the workplace can also be prosecuted, either in tandem with the employer or alone. If the employer is a company or local authority, the company, its directors and/or officers, as well as councillors may be charged with an offence (see 17.32 below).

Prosecutions and other enforcement procedures are the responsibility of the appropriate 'enforcing authority' (see 17.3-17.5 below) and penalties for breach were increased, under the *Criminal Justice Act 1991* (see 17.28 and 17.29 below) and, more recently, under the *Offshore Safety Act 1992*. In addition, where an employee is injured or killed as a result of negligence or breach of a statutory requirement, a civil action may be brought against the employer for damages. Although possibly an additional form of enforcement, civil liability is mainly discussed in Chapter 15 'Employers' Duties'.

This chapter deals with the following aspects of enforcement:

— The 'relevant statutory provisions' which can be enforced under *HSWA* (see 17.2 below).

— The 'enforcing authorities' (see 17.3-17.5 below).

Part A: Enforcement Powers of Inspectors

— Improvement and prohibition notices (see 17.6-17.11 below).

— Appeals against improvement and prohibition notices (see 17.12, 17.13 below).

— Grounds for appeal against a notice (see 17.14-17.18 below).

— Hazardous substances contravention notice (see 17.19 below).

— Inspectors' powers of search and seizure (see 17.20 below).

— Indemnification by enforcing authority (see 17.21 below).

— Public register of notices (see 17.22 below).

Part B: Offences and Penalties

— Prosecution for contravention of the relevant statutory provisions (see 17.23, 17.24 below).

— Main offences and penalties (see 17.26-17.31 below), including those for breach of the *Planning (Hazardous Substances) Act 1990* (see 17.25 below).

— Offences committed by particular types of persons, including the Crown (see 17.32-17.36 below).

(For offences under the *Environmental Protection Act 1990*, see 12.21-12.25 EMISSIONS INTO THE ATMOSPHERE.)

'Relevant statutory provisions' covered by the Health and Safety at Work etc. Act 1974

17.2   The enforcement powers conferred by *HSWA* extend to any of the 'relevant statutory provisions'. These comprise:

(*a*)   the provisions of *HSWA Part I* (i.e. *Secs 1-53*); and

(*b*)   any health and safety regulations passed under *HSWA*, e.g. the *Ionising Radiations Regulations 1985*, the *Management of Health and Safety at Work*

> *Regulations 1992* and the *Supply of Machinery (Safety) Regulations 1992 (SI 1992 No 3073)*; and

(*c*)   the 'existing statutory provisions', i.e. all enactments specified in *HSWA 1 Sch*, including any regulations etc. made under them, so long as they continue to have effect; that is, the *Explosives Acts 1875-1923*, the *Mines and Quarries Act 1954*, the *Factories Act 1961*, the *Public Health Act 1961*, the *Offices, Shops and Railway Premises Act 1963* and (by dint of the *Offshore Safety Act 1992*) the *Mineral Workings (Offshore Installations) Act 1971*.

[*HSWA s 53(1)*].

Enforcing authorities

The Health and Safety Executive (HSE)

17.3   The HSE is the central body entrusted with the enforcement of health and safety legislation (see Chapter 23 'Health and Safety Commission and Executive'). In any given case, however, enforcement powers rest with the body which is expressed by statute to be the 'enforcing authority'. Here the general rule is that the 'enforcing authority', in the case of industrial premises, is the HSE and, in the case of commercial premises within its area, the local authority (the enforcing authority in over a million premises), except that the HSE cannot enforce provisions in respect of its own premises, and similarly, local authorities' premises are inspected by the HSE. Each 'enforcing authority' is empowered to appoint suitably qualified persons as inspectors for the purpose of carrying into effect the 'relevant statutory provisions' within the authority's field of responsibility. [*HSWA s 19(1)*]. Inspectors so appointed can exercise any of the enforcement powers conferred by *HSWA* (see 17.6-17.11 below) and bring prosecutions (see 17.23, 17.24 below).

The appropriate 'enforcing authority'

17.4   The general rule is that the HSE is the enforcing authority, except to the extent that:

(*a*)   regulations specify that the local authority is the enforcing authority instead; the regulations that so specify are the *Health and Safety (Enforcing Authority) Regulations 1989 (SI 1989 No 1903)* (hereafter referred to as the '*Enforcing Authority Regulations*'); or

(*b*)   one of the 'relevant statutory provisions' specifies that some other body is responsible for the enforcement of a particular requirement.

[*HSWA s 18(1), (7)(a)*].

Table 14

Activities for which the HSE is the enforcing authority

The HSE is specifically the enforcing authority in respect of the following activities (even though the main activity on the premises is listed in *1 Sch*, see below). Note that water and telecommunications systems are now excluded under the *1989 Regs*.

---

1. Any activity in a mine or quarry;

2. fairground activity;

3. any activity in premises occupied by a radio, television or film undertaking, where broadcasting, recording, filming, or video-recording is carried on;

4. (*a*) construction work (with modifications);

    (*b*) installation, maintenance or repair of gas systems or work in connection with a gas fitting;

    (*c*) installation, maintenance or repair of electricity systems;

    (*d*) work with ionising radiations;

5. use of ionising radiations for medical exposure;

6. any activity in radiography premises where work with ionising radiations is carried on;

7. agricultural activities, including agricultural shows;

8. any activity on board a sea-going ship;

9. ski slope, ski lift, ski tow or cable car activities;

10. fish, maggot and game breeding (but not in a zoo).

[*Enforcing Authority Regulations 1989, Reg 4(5)(b) and 2 Sch*].

The HSE is the enforcing authority against the following, and for any premises they occupy, including parts of the premises occupied by others providing services for them. (This is so even though the main activity is listed in *1 Sch*, see below.)

11. Local authorities;

12. parish councils and community councils in England and Wales;

13. police authorities;

14. fire authorities;

15. international HQs and defence organisations and visiting forces;

16. United Kingdom Atomic Energy Authority (UKAEA);

17. the Crown (except where premises are occupied by HSE itself).

The HSE is also the enforcing authority for:

18. indoor sports activity (with conditions);

19. enforcement of *HSWA s 6* (duties of manufacturers/suppliers of industrial products).

[*Enforcing Authority Regulations 1989, Reg 4 and 1 Sch*].

20. Offshore installations. [*Offshore Safety Act 1992, s 1*].

Table 15

Activities for which local authorities are the enforcing authorities

Where the main activity carried on in non-domestic premises is one of the following, the local authority is the enforcing authority (i.e. a district council or London borough council, or in Scotland, the islands or district council). [*Enforcing Authority Regulations 1989*].

1. Sale or storage of goods for retail/wholesale distribution (including sale and fitting of motor car tyres, exhausts, windscreens or sunroofs), except:

    (*a*) where it is part of a transport undertaking;

    (*b*) at container depots where the main activity is the storage of goods in course of transit to or from dock premises, an airport or railway;

    (*c*) where the main activity is the sale or storage for wholesale distribution of any dangerous substances;

    (*d*) where the main activity is the sale or storage of water or sewage or their by-products or natural or town gas;

2. display or demonstration of goods at an exhibition, being offered or advertised for sale;

3. office activities;

4. catering services;

5. provision of permanent or temporary residential accommodation, including sites for caravans or campers;

6. consumer services provided in a shop, except:

    (i)   dry cleaning;

    (ii) radio/television repairs;

7. cleaning (wet or dry) in coin-operated units in launderettes etc.;

8. baths, saunas, solariums, massage parlours, premises for hair transplant, skin piercing, manicuring or other cosmetic services and therapeutic treatments, except where supervised by a doctor, dentist, physiotherapist, osteopath or chiropractor;

9. practice or presentation of arts, sports, games, entertainment or other cultural/recreational activities, unless carried on:

    (*a*) in a museum;

    (*b*) in an art gallery;

    (*c*) in a theatre;

    (*d*) where the main activity is the exhibition of a cave to the public;

10. hiring out of pleasure craft for use on inland waters;

11. care, treatment, accommodation or exhibition of animals, birds or other creatures, except where the main activity is:

(i)   horse breeding/horse training at stables;

(ii)   agricultural activity;

(iii)   veterinary surgery;

12. undertaking, but not embalming or coffin making;

13. church worship/religious meetings.

[*Enforcing Authority Regulations 1989, Reg 3(1) and 1 Sch*].

A new provision states that where premises are occupied by more than one occupier, each part separately occupied is 'separate premises', for the purposes of enforcement. [*Reg 3(2)*]. But this does not apply in the case of:

(*a*)   airport land;

(*b*)   a tunnel system;

(*c*)   offshore installation;

(*d*)   building/construction sites;

(*e*)   university, polytechnic, college, school etc. campuses;

(*f*)   hospitals;

where HSE is the enforcing authority for the whole of the premises. [*Reg 3(1) and 1 Sch*].

Responsibility for all legislation affecting industrial air pollution was, in 1987, transferred from the Health and Safety Executive to the Pollution Inspectorate of the Department of the Environment. [*Control of Industrial Pollution (Transfer of Powers of Enforcement) Regulations 1987 (SI 1987 No 180)*]. (See also 12.7 EMISSIONS INTO THE ATMOSPHERE.)

Transfer of responsibility between the HSE and local authorities

17.5   Enforcement can be transferred (though not in the case of Crown premises), by prior agreement, from the HSE to the local authority and vice versa. The Health and Safety Commission is also empowered to effect such a transfer, without the necessity of such agreement. In either case, parties who are affected by such transfer must be notified. [*Enforcing Authority Regulations 1989, Reg 5*]. Transfer is effective even though the above procedure is not followed (i.e. the authority changes when the main activity changes) (*Hadley v Hancox, The Times, 18 November 1986*, decided under the previous regulations).

Where there is uncertainty, a new provision allows responsibility to be assigned jointly (to either HSE or a local authority). [*Reg 6(1)*].

PART A

ENFORCEMENT POWERS OF INSPECTORS

Improvement and prohibition notices

17.6   It was recommended by the Robens Committee that 'Inspectors should have the power, without reference to the courts, to issue a formal improvement notice to an employer requiring him to remedy particular faults or institute a specified programme of work within a stated time limit.' (Cmnd 5034, para 269). 'The improvement notice would be the inspector's main sanction. In addition, an alternative and stronger power should be available to the inspector for use where he considers the case for remedial action to be particularly serious. In such cases he should be able to issue a prohibition notice.' (Cmnd 5034, para 276). *HSWA* put these recommendations into effect.

Improvement notices

17.7   An inspector may serve an improvement notice if he is of the opinion that a person:

(*a*)   is contravening one or more of the 'relevant statutory provisions' (see 17.2 above); or

(*b*)   has contravened one or more of those provisions in circumstances that make it likely that the contravention will continue to be repeated.

[*HSWA s 21*].

In the improvement notice the inspector must:

(i)   state that he is of the opinion in (*a*) and (*b*) above; and

(ii)   specify the provision(s) in his opinion contravened; and

(iii)   give particulars of the reasons for his opinion; and

(iv)   specify a period of time within which the person is required to remedy the contravention (or the matters occasioning such contravention).

[*HSWA s 21*].

The period specified in the notice within which the requirement must be carried out (see (*d*) above) must be at least 21 days – this being the period within which an appeal may be lodged with an industrial tribunal (see 17.12 below). [*HSWA s 21*].

Failure to comply with an improvement notice can have serious penal consequences (see 17.29 below).

Prohibition notices

17.8   If an inspector is of the opinion that, with regard to any activities to which *Sec 22(1)* applies (see below), the activities involve or will involve a risk of serious personal injury, he may serve on that person a notice (a prohibition notice). [*HSWA s 22(2)*].

It is incumbent on an inspector to show, on a balance of probabilities, that there is a risk to health and safety (*Readmans v Leeds CC [1992] COD 419* where an environmental health officer served a prohibition notice on the appellant regarding shopping trolleys with child seats on them, following an accident involving an eleven-month-old child. The appellant alleged that the industrial tribunal had wrongly placed the burden of proof on them, to show that the trolleys were not dangerous. It was held by the High Court (allowing the appeal), that it was for the inspector to prove that there was a health and/or safety risk).

Prohibition notices differ from improvement notices in two important ways, as follows:

(*a*)   with prohibition notices, it is not necessary that an inspector believes that a provision of *HSWA* or any other statutory provision is being or has been contravened;

(*b*)   prohibition notices are served in *anticipation* of danger.

Sec 22 applies where, in the inspector's opinion, there is a hazardous activity or state of affairs generally. It is irrelevant that the hazard or danger is not mentioned in *HSWA*; it can exist by virtue of other legislation, or even in the absence of any relevant statutory duty. In this way notices are used to enforce the later statutory requirements of *HSWA* and the earlier requirements of the *Factories Act 1961* and other protective occupational legislation.

A prohibition notice must:

(*a*)   state that the inspector is of the opinion stated immediately above;

(*b*)   specify the matters which create the risk in question;

(*c*)   where there is actual or anticipatory breach of provisions and regulations, state that the inspector is of the opinion that this is so and give reasons;

(*d*)   direct that the activities referred to in the notice must not be carried out on, by or under the control of the person on whom the notice is served, unless the matters referred to in (*b*) above have been remedied.

[*HSWA s 22(3)*].

Failure to comply with a prohibition notice can have serious penal consequences (see 17.29 below).

Differences between improvement and prohibition notices

17.9   Unlike an improvement notice, where time is allowed in which to correct a defect or offending state of affairs, a prohibition notice can take effect immediately.

A direction contained in a prohibition notice shall take effect:

(*a*)   at the end of the period specified in the notice; or

(*b*)   if the notice so declares, immediately.

[*HSWA s 22(4) as amended by Consumer Protection Act 1987, 3 Sch*].

Risk of injury need not be imminent, even if the notice is to take immediate effect (*Tesco Stores Ltd v Kippax COIT No 7605-6/90*).

An improvement notice gives a person upon whom it is served time to correct the defect or offending situation. A prohibition notice, which is a direction to stop the work activity in question rather than put it right, can take effect immediately on issue; alternatively, it may allow time for certain modifications to take place (i.e. deferred prohibition notice). Both types of notice will generally contain a schedule of work which the inspector will require to be carried out. If the nature of the work to be carried out is vague, the validity of the notice is not affected. If there is an appeal, an industrial tribunal may, within its powers to modify a notice, rephrase the schedule in more specific terms (*Chrysler (UK) Ltd v McCarthy [1978] ICR 939, DC*).

Effect of non-compliance with notice

17.10   If, after expiry of the period specified in the notice, or in the event of an appeal, expiry of any additional time allowed for compliance by the tribunal, an applicant does not comply with the notice or modified notice, he can be prosecuted. If convicted in the Crown Court of contravening a prohibition notice, he may be imprisoned. [*HSWA s 33(1)(g), (3)(b)(i), (4)(d)*].

Service of notice coupled with prosecution

17.11   Where an inspector serves a notice, he may at the same time decide to prosecute for the substantive offence specified in the notice, e.g. *Factories Act 1961, s 14* or an offence under *OSRPA*. The fact that a notice has been served would not be relevant to the prosecution. Nevertheless, an inspector would not normally commence proceedings until after the expiry of 21 days, i.e. until he was satisfied that there was to be no appeal against the notice or until the tribunal had heard the appeal and affirmed the notice, since it would be inconsistent if conviction by the magistrates were followed by cancellation of the notice by the tribunal. The fact that an industrial tribunal has upheld a notice would not be binding on a magistrates' court hearing a prosecution under the statutory provision of which the notice alleged a contravention; it would be necessary for the prosecution to prove all the elements in the offence (see 17.24 below).

Industrial tribunals are mainly concerned with hearing unfair dismissal claims by employees; only a tiny proportion of cases heard by them relates specifically to health and safety although the new provisions relating to health and safety in the *Trade Union Reform and Employment Rights Act 1993* may increase the number of cases heard (see 13.34 EMPLOYEE SAFETY RIGHTS, DISCIPLINARY PROCEDURES AND UNFAIR DISMISSAL). Moreover, they are not empowered to determine breaches of criminal legislation, e.g. *Factories Act 1961* (see 13.23(*d*) EMPLOYEE SAFETY RIGHTS, DISCIPLINARY PROCEDURES AND UNFAIR DISMISSAL and the case of *Lindsay v Dunlop*).

Appeals against improvement and prohibition notices

17.12   A person on whom either type of notice is served may appeal to an industrial tribunal within 21 days from the date of service of the notice (see Chapter 13 'Employee Safety Rights, Disciplinary Procedures and Unfair Dismissal' for the jurisdiction of industrial tribunals relevant to the *Health and Safety at Work etc. Act 1974*). The tribunal may extend this time where it is satisfied, on application made in writing (either before or after expiry of the 21-day period), that it was not reasonably practicable for the appeal to be brought within the 21-day period. On appeal the tribunal may either affirm or cancel the notice and, if it affirms it, may do so with modifications in the form of additions, omissions or amendments. [*HSWA ss 24(2), 82(1)(c); Industrial Tribunals (Improvement and Prohibition Notices Appeals) Regulations 1974 (SI 1974 No 1925), Reg 3 and 2 Sch*].

Effect of appeal

17.13   Where an appeal is brought against a notice, the lodging of an appeal automatically suspends operation of an improvement notice, but a prohibition notice will continue to apply unless there is a direction to the contrary from the tribunal. Thus:

(*a*)   in the case of an improvement notice, the appeal has the effect of suspending the operation of the notice;

(*b*)   in the case of a prohibition notice, the appeal only suspends the operation of the notice in the following circumstances:

(i)   if the tribunal so directs, on the application of the appellant; and

(ii)   the suspension is then effective from the time when the tribunal so directs.

[*HSWA s 24(3)*].

Grounds for appeal

17.14   The main grounds for appeal are:

(*a*) the inspector wrongly interpreted the law (see 17.15 below);

(*b*) the inspector exceeded his powers, though not necessarily intentionally, under an Act or regulation (see 17.16 below);

(*c*) breach of law is admitted but the proposed solution is not 'practicable' or not 'reasonably practicable', or that there was no 'best practicable means' other than that used (see also 12.27 EMISSIONS INTO THE ATMOSPHERE where 'best practicable means' is also a defence to a charge of statutory nuisance) (depending on the terminology of the particular statute) (see 17.17 below);

(*d*) breach of law is admitted but the breach is so insignificant that the notice should be cancelled (see 17.18 below).

The delay involved in lodging an appeal can have important practical consequences. It is not uncommon for up to four months to elapse before an appeal against an improvement notice can be heard by the tribunal (in the case of prohibition notices it is about one month). For this reason particularly, and in view of the fact that notice of appeal suspends operation of an improvement notice, many companies opt for appealing, since at the time of service of notice they may not be in a position to meet the requirements of the notice; whereas, three or four months later, the position may have changed. If, however, the sole reason for appealing is to gain time and nothing else, the tribunal is not likely to be sympathetic and costs could be awarded against the unsuccessful appellant, though this is rare. [*Industrial Tribunals (Improvement and Prohibition Notices Appeals) Regulations 1974, Reg 3, 13 Sch 1*]. This provision states that: 'a tribunal may make an Order that a party shall pay to another party either a specified sum in respect of the costs of or in connection with an appeal incurred by that other party or, in default of agreement, the taxed amount of those costs'.

Inspector's wrong interpretation of the law

17.15 It is doubtful whether many cases have succeeded, or indeed would succeed on this ground. Two situations are possible. First, a statute or regulation imposes on an employer a strict duty. This occurs in the case of certain sections of the *Factories Act 1961*, e.g. *Secs 12, 13*, dealing with prime movers and transmission machinery. Here there is virtually no scope for argument for the employer (*Ransom v Baird, COIT No 1/23, Case No 10899/75*, involving the *Factories Act 1961, s 1* – 'keeping factory walls smooth and impervious').

The second situation is where a statute permits latitude and requires a duty to be carried out 'so far as reasonably practicable'. The definition of 'reasonably practicable' was authoritatively laid down in *Edwards v National Coal Board* (see 15.19 EMPLOYERS' DUTIES). Here an employer has more scope for argument. For example, in *Roadline (UK) Ltd v Mainwaring, Case No 3869/76* an improvement notice, requiring the employer to provide heating in a transit shed pursuant to *HSWA s 2*, was cancelled by the tribunal on the ground that the cost of heating improvement was excessive in relation to the minimal benefit that might result. Similar decisions have been given under *OSRPA* where many of the sections do not lay down absolute duties but contain the words 'reasonably accessible' (*Davis v Environmental Health Department of Leeds City Council* [*1976*] *IRLR 282*).

Employers should note that contesting a prohibition notice on the ground that there has been no legal contravention is pointless, since valid service of a prohibition notice does not depend on legal contravention (*Roberts v Day, COIT No 1/133, Case No 3053/77*). In addition, inspectors can use their powers under *Secs 21, 22* and *25* ('search and destroy dangerous articles and substances') in respect of one or more of the 'relevant statutory provisions' (see 17.2 above).

Inspector exceeded powers under statute

17.16   This situation often overlaps with that in the above paragraph. It can happen that an inspector exceeds his powers under statute by reason of misinterpretation of the statute or regulation (*Deeley v Effer, COIT No 1/72, Case No 25354/77*). This case involved the requirement that 'all floors, steps, stairs, passages and gangways must, so far as is reasonably practicable, be kept free from obstruction and from any substance likely to cause persons to slip'. [*OSRPA s 16(1)*]. The inspector considered that employees were endangered by baskets of wares in the shop entrance. The tribunal ruled that the notice had to be cancelled, since the only persons endangered were members of the public, and *OSRPA* is concerned with dangers to employees.

Proposed solution not practicable

17.17   The position in a case where, although breach of the law is admitted, the proposed solution is not considered practicable, depends upon the nature of the obligation. The duty may be strict, or have to be carried out so far as practicable or, alternatively, so far as reasonably practicable. In the first two situations cost of compliance is irrelevant; in the last case, where a requirement has to be carried out 'so far as reasonably practicable', cost-effectiveness is the key to liability. Here the key question is: is cost excessive in relation to the improvements which would be brought about if safety measures were taken and devices introduced? In a leading case, the appellant was served with an improvement notice requiring secure fencing on transmission machinery. An appeal was lodged on the ground that the proposed modifications were too costly (£1,900). It was argued that because of the intelligence and integrity of the operators, a safety screen costing £200 would be adequate. The tribunal dismissed the appeal (*Belhaven Brewery Co Ltd v McLean* [*1975*] *IRLR 370*).

Where breaches of the general duties of *HSWA* are concerned, cost is a factor. This is not to be confused with the current financial position of the appellant. In *Harrison (Newcastle-under-Lyme) Ltd v Ramsay* [*1976*] *IRLR 135*, a notice requiring cleaning, preparation and painting of walls had to be complied with even though the company was on a major economy drive. The cost factor is likely to have less weight in the case of a prohibition notice than an improvement notice (*Nico Manufacturing Co Ltd v Hendry* [*1975*] *IRLR 225*, where the company argued that a prohibition notice in respect of the worn state of their power presses should be cancelled on the ground that it would result in a 'serious loss of production'. The tribunal dismissed this argument). Similarly, an undertaking by a company to take additional safety precautions, until a new boiler was installed, against the risk of injury from unsafe plant, as well as accompanying loss of profits, was not a good argument (*Grovehurst Energy v Strawson, HM Inspector, COIT No 5035/90*).

Tribunals are prepared, under their powers under *HSWA s 24*, to alter time limits attaching to improvement and prohibition notices (*Campion v Hughes* [*1975*] *IRLR 291*, where even though there was an imminent risk of serious personal injury, an extension of four months was allowed for erection of fire escapes). Thus, requesting more time in which to carry out improvements or modifications is a cost argument which is heard sympathetically.

Breach of law is insignificant

17.18   Where a notice refers to breach of an absolute duty and the breach is admitted but the appellant argues that the breach is trivial, the cases show that the appellant has little chance of success (*South Suburban Co-operative Society Ltd v Wilcox* [*1975*]

IRLR 292, where a notice had been issued in respect of a cracked wash-hand basin. It was argued by the appellant that, in view of their excellent record of cleanliness, there was no need for officials to visit the premises. The appeal was dismissed).

Contravention of hazardous substances control

17.19 Where there is (or has been) a breach of a hazardous substances consent, issued by a hazardous substances authority, the hazardous substances authority can issue a 'hazardous substances contravention notice', which will, as with improvement notices,

(i) specify the alleged breach, and

(ii) outline the steps necessary to remedy the breach.

This can include a requirement that the hazardous substance(s) be removed from the land. [*Planning (Hazardous Substances) Act 1990, s 24(1)*]. Similar powers are given under *Sec 5* of the *Radioactive Material (Road Transport) Act 1991* and the *Radioactive Substances Act 1993* (see 9.56 DANGEROUS SUBSTANCES I).

Inspectors' powers of search and seizure in case of imminent danger

17.20 Where an inspector has reasonable cause to believe that there are on premises 'articles or substances ("substance" includes solids, liquids and gases – *HSWA s 53(1)*) which give rise to imminent risk of serious personal injury', he can:

(*a*) seize them; and

(*b*) cause them to be rendered harmless (by destruction or otherwise).

[*HSWA s 25(1)*].

Before an article 'forming part of a batch of similar articles', or a substance is rendered harmless, an inspector must, if practicable, take a sample and give to a responsible person, at the premises where the article or substance was found, a portion which has been marked in such a way as to be identifiable. [*HSWA s 25(2)*]. After the article or substance has been rendered harmless, the inspector must sign a prepared report and give a copy of the report to:

(*a*) a responsible person (e.g. safety officer); and

(*b*) the owner of the premises, unless he happens to be the 'responsible person'. (See 3.6 ACCIDENT REPORTING for the meaning of this term.)

[*HSWA s 25(3)*].

Analogous powers are given to transport inspectors under the *Radioactive Material (Road Transport) Act 1991, s 5* in respect of vehicles carrying radioactive packages.

A customs officer may assist the enforcing authority or the inspector in his enforcement duties under the *Health and Safety at Work etc. Act 1974* by seizing any imported article or substance and he may then detain it for not more than two working days and he may disclose information about it to the enforcing authorities or inspectors. [*HSWA ss 25A, 27A, inserted by Consumer Protection Act 1987, 3 Sch*].

Indemnification by enforcing authority

17.21 Inspectors are indemnified against any liability, criminal or civil, that may arise in the exercise of their powers under *HSWA* and other protective occupational legislation. [*HSWA s 26*].

Public register of improvement and prohibition notices

17.22   Improvement (though not in the case of the *Fire Precautions Act 1971*) and prohibition notices have to be entered in a public register as follows:

(*a*)   within 14 days following the date on which notice is served in cases where there is no right of appeal;

(*b*)   within 14 days following the day on which the time limit expired, in cases where there is a right of appeal but no appeal has been lodged within the statutory 21 days;

(*c*)   within 14 days following the day when the appeal is disposed of, in cases where there is a right of appeal.

[*Environment and Safety Information Act 1988, s 3*].

In addition, registers must also be kept of notices served by:

(i)   fire authorities, under the *Schedule* to the *Environment and Safety Information Act 1988* for the purpose of *Sec 10* of the *Fire Precautions Act 1971* (not improvement notices);

(ii)   local authorities, under the *Schedule* to the *Environment and Safety Information Act 1988* for the purpose of *Sec 10* of the *Safety of Sports Grounds Act 1975*;

(iii)   responsible authorities (as defined by *Sec 2(2)* of the *Environment and Safety Information Act 1988*) and the Minister of Agriculture, Fisheries and Food under *Sec 2* of the *Environment and Safety Information Act 1988* for the purpose of *Sec 19* of the *Food and Environment Protection Act 1985*;

(iv)   enforcing authorities, as regards Integrated Pollution Control (HMIP) and air pollution control (local authorities), under *Sec 20* of the *Environmental Protection Act 1990*; and

(v)   enforcing authorities under the *Radioactive Substances Act 1993* (see 9.56 DANGEROUS SUBSTANCES I).

These registers are open to inspection by the public free of charge at reasonable hours and, on request and payment of a reasonable fee, copies can be obtained from the relevant authority. [*Environment and Safety Information Act 1988, s 1*]. Such records can also be kept on computer.

PART B

OFFENCES AND PENALTIES

Prosecution for breach of the 'relevant statutory provisions'

17.23   Prosecutions can, and often do, follow non-compliance with an improvement or prohibition notice. Indeed, inspectors will sometimes prosecute without serving notice. Prosecutions normally take place before the magistrates but there is provision in *HSWA* for prosecution on indictment. [*HSWA s 33(3)(b)*]. The determining factor behind prosecution on indictment is the gravity of the particular offence.

Burden of proof

17.24   Throughout criminal law the burden of proof of guilt is on the prosecution to show that the accused committed the particular offence (*Woolmington v DPP [1935] AC 462*). The burden is a great deal heavier than in civil law, requiring proof of guilt beyond a reasonable doubt as distinct from on a balance of probabilities (see Chapter 15 'Employers' Duties'). While not eliminating the need for the prosecution to establish the general burden of proof of guilt, *HSWA s 40* makes the task of the prosecution easier by transferring the onus of proof to the accused. More particularly, *Sec 40* states that it is incumbent on the accused to show either that it was not (*a*) practicable, or (*b*) reasonably practicable, or (*c*) there was no better practicable means than those used, to satisfy the particular duty or requirement. If the accused cannot discharge this duty, the case will be considered proved against him. However, *Sec 40* does not apply to an offence created by *Sec 33(1)(g)* – failing to comply with an improvement notice (*Deary v Mansion Hide Upholstery [1983] ICR 610 (CA)* where an improvement notice was served on the defendant company, requiring it to provide fire resistant storage for polyurethane foam. The company did not comply, nor did it appeal. The magistrates had ruled that the company had, for the purposes of *Sec 40*, done what was 'reasonably practicable' but the company's failure to appeal meant that they were liable for an offence.). A similar burden of proof exists under the *Environmental Protection Act 1990* (see further Chapter 12 'Emissions into the Atmosphere').

Offences and penalties under the Planning (Hazardous Substances) Act 1990

Offences

17.25   There is a breach of hazardous substances consent if:

(*a*)   a quantity of hazardous substance equal to or exceeding the controlled quantity is, or has been, present on land and either

(i)   there is no hazardous substances consent, or

(ii)   although there is a consent, the quantity present exceeds the maximum quantity permitted by the consent;

or

(*b*)   if there is, or has been, a failure to comply with a condition relating to a hazardous substances consent.

[*Sec 23(2)*].

Main offences and penalties

17.26   Health and safety offences are either (*a*) triable summarily (i.e. without jury before the magistrates), or (*b*) triable summarily and on indictment (i.e. triable either way), or (*c*) triable only on indictment. Most health and safety offences, however, fall into categories (*a*) and (*b*).

Summary offences and offences triable either way

17.27   The main health and safety offences triable (*a*) summarily, or (*b*) summarily or on indictment are the following:

(*a*)   failure to carry out one or more of the general duties of *HSWA ss 2-7*;

(b) contravening either:

    (i) *HSWA s 8* – intentionally or recklessly interfering with anything provided for safety;

    (ii) *HSWA s 9* – levying payment for anything that an employer must by law provide in the interests of health and safety (e.g. personal protective clothing);

(c) contravening any health and safety regulations;

(d) contravening a requirement imposed under *HSWA s 14* (power of the HSC to order an investigation);

(e) contravening a requirement imposed by an inspector;

(f) preventing or attempting to prevent a person from appearing before an inspector, or from answering his questions;

(g) contravening a requirement of a prohibition or improvement notice (*HSWA s 40* is not applicable to this offence (*Deary v Mansion Hide Upholstery* [*1983*] *ICR 610*));

(h) intentionally obstructing an inspector or customs officer in the exercise of his powers;

(j) intentionally or recklessly making false statements, where the statement is made:

    (i) to comply with a requirement to furnish information; or

    (ii) to obtain the issue of a document;

(k) intentionally making a false entry in a register, book, notice etc. which is required to be kept;

(l) falsely pretending to be an inspector;

(m) failing to comply with a remedial court order, made under *Sec 42*.

[*HSWA s 33(1)*].

There is no time limit for bringing prosecutions for offences under *Sec 33(1)(a)* (*Kemp v Liebherr (Great Britain) Ltd, The Times, 5 November 1986*). The time limit for bringing summary proceedings in the magistrates' court therefore applies. The limit is six months from the date of the making of the complaint. That period may be extended in the case of special reports, coroners' court hearings or in cases of death generally. [*HSWA s 34(1)*]. There is no time limit for commencing hearings in the Crown Court.

Summary trial or trial on indictment

17.28 Many of these offences are, for the purposes of the *Magistrates' Courts Act 1980*, triable either way, i.e. summarily before the magistrates, or on indictment before the Crown Court. The offences mentioned in (d), (e), (f) and (g) above, however, are only triable summarily. (Note that in the case of (c) above, it is only an offence consisting of contravening a requirement imposed by an inspector under *Sec 20* which is triable summarily; contravention of a requirement imposed under *Sec 25*, i.e. power to seize and destroy articles and substances, is triable either way.)

Generally, offences triable either way are tried summarily. They could, however, be tried on indictment (e.g. if the magistrates felt that the matter was too serious for them and required a penalty greater than they could impose under their powers under *HSWA s 33(3)(a)*, as amended by the *Criminal Justice Act 1991, s 17(1)* (revision of standard scale of fines 1-5: £200-£5,000)) (as updated by the *Offshore Safety Act 1992* (see 1.1 INTRODUCTION and 17.1, 17.29)).

Penalties on summary conviction

17.29　The maximum fine which can currently be imposed on summary conviction is £5,000 [*Criminal Justice Act 1991, s 17(1)*]. In certain specified cases, however, magistrates can impose fines of £20,000 (see 17.30 below). In this way, health and safety penalties have been brought into line with fines for food safety violations and environmental protection (see Chapter 12 'Emissions into the Atmosphere' and Chapter 21 'Food and Food Hygiene').

Trial on indictment could well take place where an offence created serious risk to life or disclosed flagrant disregard of health and safety duties, or alternatively, the offender was a persistent one. Here the Crown Court can impose an unlimited fine. [*HSWA s 33(3)(b)(ii)*]. In addition, the prosecution may ask for trial on indictment, or the defendant may refuse consent to summary trial.

Penalties for health and safety offences

17.30　Penalties tend to relate to the three main categories of offences characterising breach of health and safety legislation, namely,

(i)　breaches of *Secs 2–6* of the *Health and Safety at Work etc. Act 1974* – serious offences:

(*a*)　summary conviction – a maximum £20,000 fine,

(*b*)　conviction on indictment – an unlimited fine (but no imprisonment);

(ii)　breaches of improvement or prohibition orders, or orders under *Sec 42* of the *Health and Safety at Work etc. Act* to remedy the cause of offence – serious offences:

(*a*)　summary conviction – a maximum £20,000 fine, or imprisonment for up to six months,

(*b*)　conviction on indictment – an unlimited fine or imprisonment for up to two years;

(iii)　offences relating to breaches of various inspectors' duties:

(*a*)　summary conviction – a maximum fine of £2,000,

(*b*)　conviction on indictment – an unlimited fine or up to two years' imprisonment (or both) for licence breaches and explosives offences.

[*Health and Safety at Work etc. Act 1974, s 33(1A), (2) and (2A) as inserted by the Offshore Safety Act 1992*].

Defences

17.31　Although no general defences are specified in the *Health and Safety at Work etc. Act 1974*, specific defences are laid down in the *Factories Act 1961, s 155(2)* and the *Offices, Shops and Railway Premises Act 1963, s 67(1)* (see further 18.26 FACTORIES AND WORKPLACES). In addition, most regulations passed under the *Health and Safety at Work Act* carry the defence of 'due diligence'.

Offences committed by particular types of persons

Offences of companies, corporate bodies and directors

17.32   Many statutes, including *HSWA*, place statutory duties upon limited companies and other bodies corporate, for example local authorities, and prosecutions are brought against the company or body corporate itself and/or individual functional directors. This refers normally to the situation where an offence has been committed or permitted by a person acting as the company itself, e.g. the managing director, individual functional directors or the company secretary, though not exclusively. Thus, a company could be prosecuted where an employee removed a guard and the foreman omitted to tell him to replace it, whether an accident followed or not.

Where an offence is committed by a body corporate, senior persons in the hierarchy of the company may also be individually liable. Thus, where the offence was committed with the consent or connivance of, or was attributable to any neglect on the part of any of the following, that person is himself guilty of an offence and liable to be punished accordingly. Those who may be so liable are:

(*a*)   any functional director;

(*b*)   manager (which does not include an *employee* in charge of a shop while the manager is away on a week's holiday (*R v Boal, The Times, 16 March 1992*, concerning *Sec 23* of the *Fire Precautions Act 1971* – identical terminology to *HSWA s 37*));

(*c*)   secretary;

(*d*)   other similar officer of the company;

(*e*)   anyone purporting to act as any of the above.

[*HSWA s 37(1)*].

Most prosecutions under *HSWA s 37(1)* would be limited to that body of persons who act as the company, i.e. the board of directors and individual functional directors, as well as senior managers (*Tesco Stores Ltd v Nattrass [1971] 2 AER 127* – a case taken on the similar wording of the *Trade Descriptions Act 1968*). The conditions for liability under *Sec 37(1)* are, therefore, as follows:

(*a*)   did the person act as the company? A good test is whether he was able to delegate the performance of a statutory duty placed on the company;

(*b*)   if he acted in that capacity, did he act with neglect (not a synonym for negligence)?

Prosecutions under *Sec 37(1)* are rare.

(See also 'Corporate manslaughter' in Chapter 15 'Employers' Duties'.) Similar duties exist under the *Environmental Protection Act 1990*, see 12.24 EMISSIONS INTO THE ATMOSPHERE. Directors convicted for breach of *HSWA s 37* may also be disqualified, for up to two years, from being a director of a company, under the provisions of the *Company Directors' Disqualification Act 1986, s 2(1)* as having committed an indictable offence connected with (*inter alia*) the *management* of a company (*R v Chapman (1992, unreported)* where a director of a quarrying company was disqualified and fined £5,000 for contravening a prohibition notice on an unsafe quarry where there had been several fatalities and major injuries).

Directors' insurance

17.33   Companies can now buy insurance in order to protect directors. [*Companies Act 1989, s 137*]. Moreover, directors need not contribute towards premiums, as they had to previously. Such insurance, which must be mentioned in the Annual Report and Accounts, protects directors against

(*a*)   civil liability for claims made against them in breach of directorial duties, e.g. by shareholders when directors have acted in breach of their duty of care to the company, as well as legal costs and expenses incurred in defence or settlement of such claim;

(*b*)   legal costs and expenses involved in defending criminal actions (e.g. breach of *HSWA s 37*), but not the fine or other penalty incurred, it being illegal to insure against payment of penalties (see further 16.16 EMPLOYERS' LIABIL-ITY INSURANCE).

Offences due to the act of 'another person'

17.34   As Lord Reid observed in *Tesco Stores Ltd v Nattrass*, 'A board of directors can delegate part of their functions of management so as to make their delegate an embodiment of the company within the sphere of delegation.' This is the situation envisaged by *HSWA s 36(1)*. Where such delegation takes place, the end result will differ according to the nature of the offence created by the statute. Statutes are principally of two kinds: (*a*) those creating strict liability and (*b*) those where liability is based on intent or neglect. *HSWA* is a statute where liability for breach is generally referable to neglect. In the first case, i.e. statutes of strict liability, the fact of delegation does not prevent the employer/company from being vicariously liable (*James & Son Ltd v Smee [1954] 3 AER 273; Allen v Whitehead [1930] 1 KB 211*). In the latter case, i.e. liability referable to neglect, the fact of delegation normally transfers liability away from the company to the person to whom performance of the statutory duty has been delegated. In such cases if there is no fault or neglect on the part of the director who delegated the duty, the person to whom it was delegated, that is, the 'other person', may well be liable. This is the position under much consumer protection legislation. With *HSWA*, however, although provision is separately made for prosecution of less senior corporate persons, e.g. safety officers, training officers, works managers, under *Sec 36(1)*, this does not prevent a further prosecution against the company itself. Thus, *Sec 36(1)* states: 'Where an offence under *HSWA* etc. is due to the act or default of some other person, then:

(*a*)   that other person is guilty of the offence, and (notwithstanding);

(*b*)   a second person (e.g. body corporate) can be charged and convicted, whether or not proceedings are taken against the first-mentioned person.'

[*HSWA s 36(1)*].

Position of the Crown

17.35   The general duties of *HSWA* bind the Crown. [*HSWA s 48(1)*]. (For the position under the *Factories Act 1961* and *OSRPA*, see Chapters 18 'Factories and Workplaces' and 33 'Offices'). However, improvement and prohibition notices cannot be served on the Crown, nor can the Crown be prosecuted. [*HSWA s 48(1)*]. Crown employees, however, can be prosecuted for breaches of *HSWA*. [*HSWA s 48(2)*]. Crown immunity is no longer enjoyed by health authorities, nor premises used by health authorities (defined as Crown premises). [*National Health Service (Amendment) Act 1986, s 2*]. Indeed, hospitals, whether NHS hospitals or NHS trusts or private hospitals, do not enjoy Crown immunity. [*National Health Service and Community Care Act 1990, s 60*]. Since 1 April 1992 they have been subject to the *Food Safety Act 1990*. Most Crown premises can be inspected by authorised officers in the same way as privately-run concerns, though prosecution against the Crown is not possible. [*Food Safety Act 1990, s 54(2)*].

Civil liability of the Crown

17.36   Ever since the *Crown Proceedings Act 1947* (*CPA*) was passed, the Crown has been liable in tort both for:

(*a*)   torts of its own employees; and

(*b*)   torts committed by the Crown as an employer.

[*Crown Proceedings Act 1947, s 2(1)*].

Thus, under the *Crown Proceedings Act 1947, s 2(1)(b)*, the Crown has the same duties to its employees as other employers (see Chapter 15 'Employers' Duties'). Until recently members of the armed forces could not sue the Crown for negligence inflicted by other members of the armed forces, if such injuries were suffered in the course of duty or on premises or vehicles used for military purposes. Now, however, such actions against the Crown can be maintained in respect of acts or omissions causing injury. [*Crown Proceedings (Armed Forces) Act 1987, s 1*]. The Secretary of State may revive the former restrictions by Order at times of imminent national danger or great emergency or for the purposes of any warlike operations in other parts of the world. [*Sec 2*].

Chapter 18

Factories and Workplaces – Health, Safety and Welfare

Introduction

18.1   Five key elements are endemic to workplace integrity, namely, (*a*) structure (based on function), (*b*) health, (*c*) safety, (*d*) welfare and (*e*) hygiene. Originally legislation only insisted on these basic requirements in factories and offices and shops. With the introduction of the *Health and Safety at Work etc. Act 1974*, however, emphasis shifted notionally to workplaces generally. What mattered was contract of employment rather than place of work. As long as a person was at work, permanently or temporarily, sedentary or otherwise, in a managerial capacity or on the shopfloor, indoors or outside, mobile, peripatetic or otherwise, he was entitled to the protection of *HSWA*, and any subsequent regulations. More particularly, following the arrival of the *Workplace (Health, Safety and Welfare) Regulations 1992 (SI 1992 No 3004)*, most workplaces will have to conform to certain minimal standards by 1 January 1996 relating to:

(1)   regular and systematic maintenance [*Reg 5*] (see 18.4 below);

(2)   ventilation [*Reg 6*] (see Chapter 43);

(3)   temperature [*Reg 7*] (see Chapter 42);

(4)   lighting [*Reg 8*] (see Chapter 27);

(5)   cleanliness [*Reg 9*] (see 18.5 below);

(6)   absence of overcrowding [*Reg 10*] (see Chapter 35);

(7)   sedentary comfort [*Reg 11*] (see 18.6 below);

(8)   safety underfoot/floors [*Reg 12*] (see 18.7 below);

(9)   freedom from falls and falling objects [*Reg 13*] (see Chapter 46);

(10)   structural integrity and stability – *Building Regulations 1991* (see 18.12 below);

(11)   doors and gates [*Reg 18*] (see 18.8 below);

(12)   windows and window cleaning [*Regs 14–16*] (see Chapter 46);

(13)   escalators and travelators [*Reg 19*] (see 18.9 below);

(14)   pedestrian traffic routes [*Regs 12, 17*] (see 18.10 below);

(15)   vehicular traffic routes [*Reg 17*] (see Chapter 2);

(16)   sanitary conveniences/washing facilities [*Regs 20, 21*] (see Chapter 44);

(17)   drinking water [*Reg 22*] (see Chapter 44);

(18)   clothing accommodation [*Reg 23*] (see Chapter 44);

(19)   rest/meal facilities [*Reg 25*] (see Chapter 44).

Moreover, as a result of the Safety Signs Directive, all workplace signs erected after mid-1994 will have to conform to the new standardised rules on design and use (92/58/EEC OJ L 245/23).

Existing factories and offices and shops

18.2   Existing factories and offices/shops are still 'serviced' (until 1 January 1996) by the *Factories Act 1961, ss 1–7, 18, 28, 29, 57–60* and *69* and *OSRPA ss 4–16*, although repealed by the *Workplace (Health, Safety and Welfare) Regulations 1992, Reg 27*. This chapter deals specifically with the requirements of the *Workplace (Health, Safety and Welfare) Regulations 1992* concerning (*a*) maintenance, (*b*) cleanliness, (*c*) workstation comfort, (*d*) condition of floors, (*e*) doors and gates, (*f*) escalators and travelators and (*g*) pedestrian traffic routes. Perhaps not entirely coincidentally, certain duties specified in the *Workplace (Health, Safety and Welfare) Regulations 1992* overlap with some of the requirements of the *Building Regulations 1991* – concerned with the health, safety and welfare of building occupants, whether industrial, commercial or private.

Definition of workplace

18.3   A workplace is any non-domestic premises available to any person as a place of work, including

(*a*)   canteens, toilets (see Chapter 44 'Welfare Facilities');

(*b*)   parts of a workroom or workplace (e.g. corridor, staircase, means of access/egress);

(*c*)   modification, extension, conversion of an original workplace;

but excluding

(i)   a workplace in a ship, aircraft, train or road vehicle;

(ii)   building operations/works of engineering construction (see 7.2 and 7.3 CONSTRUCTION AND BUILDING OPERATIONS);

(iii)   mining activities.

[*Workplace (Health, Safety and Welfare) Regulations 1992, Regs 2, 3 and 4*].

General maintenance of workplace

18.4   All workplaces, equipment and devices should be maintained

(*a*)   in an efficient state,

(*b*)   in an efficient working order, and

(*c*)   in a good state of repair.

[*Workplace (Health, Safety and Welfare) Regulations 1992, Reg 5*].

Dangerous defects should be reported and acted on as a matter of good housekeeping (and to avoid possible subsequent civil liability). Defects resulting in equipment/plant becoming unsuitable for use, though not necessarily dangerous, should lead to decommissioning of plant until repaired – or, if this might lead to the number of facilities being less than required by statute, repaired forthwith (e.g. defective toilet).

To this end, a suitable maintenance programme must be instituted, including

(a) regular maintenance (inspection, testing, adjustment, lubrication, cleaning);

(b) rectification of potentially dangerous defects;

(c) record of maintenance/servicing.

(For all activities/systems/processes requiring statutory maintenance, see 1.39 INTRODUCTION.)

General cleanliness

18.5 All furniture and fittings of every workplace must be kept sufficiently clean. Surfaces of floors, walls and ceilings must be capable of being kept sufficiently clean and waste materials must not accumulate otherwise than in waste receptacles. [*Workplace (Health, Safety and Welfare) Regulations 1992, Reg 9*].

The level and frequency of cleanliness will vary according to workplace use and purpose. Obviously a factory canteen should be cleaner than a factory floor. Floors and indoor traffic routes should be cleaned at least once a week, though dirt and refuse, not in suitable receptacles, should be removed at least daily, particularly in hot atmospheres or hot weather. Interior walls, ceilings and work surfaces should be cleaned at suitable intervals and ceilings and interior walls painted and/or tiled so that they can be kept clean. Surface treatment should be renewed when it can no longer be cleaned properly. In addition, cleaning will be necessary to remove spillages and waste matter from drains or sanitary conveniences. Methods of cleaning, however, should not expose anyone to substantial amounts of dust, and absorbent floors likely to be contaminated by oil or other substances difficult to remove, should be sealed or coated, say, with non-slip floor paint (not covered with carpet!).

Workstation and sedentary comfort

18.6 It should be possible to carry out work safely and comfortably with reasonable protection from adverse weather and the likelihood of slips or falls. Work materials and equipment in frequent use (or controls) should always be within easy reach, so that people do not have to bend or stretch unduly. Workstations, including seating and access, should be suitable for special needs, for instance, disabled workers. The workstation should allow people likely to have to do work there adequate freedom of movement and ability to stand upright, thereby avoiding the need to work in cramped conditions. More particularly, seating should be suitable, providing adequate support for the lower back and a footrest provided, if feet cannot be put comfortably flat on the floor.

(a) Workstations

Every workstation must be so arranged that

(1) it is suitable for

    (a) any person at work who is likely to work at the workstation, and

    (b) any work likely to be done there;

(2) so far as reasonably practicable, it provides protection from adverse weather;

(3) enables a person to leave it swiftly or to be assisted in an emergency;

(4) ensures any person is not likely to slip or fall.

[*Workplace (Health, Safety and Welfare) Regulations 1992, Regs 11(1)(2)*].

(b) Workstation seating

A suitable seat must be provided for each person at work whose work (or a substantial part of it) can or must be done seated. The seat should be suitable for

(i)   the person doing the work, and

(ii)   the work to be done.

Where necessary, a suitable footrest should be provided.

[*Workplace (Health, Safety and Welfare) Regulations 1992, Regs 11(3)(4)*].

Condition of floors – safety underfoot

18.7   The principal dangers connected with industrial and commercial floors are slipping, tripping and falling. Slip, trip and fall resistance are a combination of right floor surface and appropriate type of footwear. Manufacturers of such floors and footwear should design and produce floors and footwear with slip resistance uppermost in mind and, should they fail to do so, occupiers sued for damages for breach of statutory/common law duty (see 18.29 and 18.33 below) should obtain indemnity terms in contracts with manufacturers, who will be increasingly under threat once the Product Safety Directive is law (see 38.1 PRODUCT SAFETY). For their part, occupiers should ensure that level changes, multiple changes of floor surfaces, steps and ramps etc. are clearly indicated. Safety underfoot is at bottom a trade-off between slip resistance and ease of cleaning. Floors with rough surfaces tend to be more slip-resistant than floors with smooth surfaces, especially when wet; by contrast, smooth surfaces are much easier to clean but less slip-resistant. Use of vinyl flooring in public areas – basically slip-resistant – is on the increase. Vinyl floors should be periodically stripped, degreased and resealed with slip-resistant finish; linoleum floors similarly. Then, too, in wintry weather, with a risk of injury from ice and snow, gritting and route closure programmes should be instituted (see further 2.7 ACCESS for possible civil liability).

Apart from being safe, floors must also be hygienically clean. In this connection, quarry tiles have long been 'firm favourites' in commercial kitchens, hospital kitchens etc. but can be hygienically deceptive. In particular, grouted joints can trap bacteria as well as presenting endless practical cleaning problems. Hence the gradual transition to seamless floors in hygiene-critical areas. Whichever floor surface is appropriate and whichever treatment is suitable, underfoot safety depends on workplace activity (office or factory), variety of spillages (food, water, oil, chemicals), nature of traffic (pedestrian, cars, trucks).

Thus, floors in workplaces must

(*a*)   be constructed so as to be suitable for use. [*Workplace (Health, Safety and Welfare) Regulations 1992, Reg 12(1)*].

        They should always be of sound construction and adequate strength and stability to sustain loads and passing internal traffic; they should never be overloaded (see *Greaves v Baynham Meikle* (18.28 below) for possible consequences in civil law).

(*b*)   (i)   not have holes or slopes, or

         (ii)   not be uneven or slippery

        so as to expose a person to risk of injury. [*Workplace (Health, Safety and Welfare) Regulations 1992, Reg 12(2)(a)*].

        Holes, bumps or uneven surfaces or areas resulting from damage or wear and tear should be made good and, pending this, barriers should be erected or locations conspicuously marked. Temporary holes, following, say, removal of floorboards, should be adequately guarded. Special needs should be catered for, for instance, disabled walkers or those with impaired sight. (Deep holes are governed by *Reg 13* (see 46.3 WORK AT HEIGHTS).) Where possible, steep slopes should be avoided, and otherwise provided with a secure handrail. Ramps used by disabled persons should also have handrails.

(*c*)   be kept free from

    (i)   obstructions (see 18.29 and 18.32 below), and

    (ii)   articles/substances likely to cause persons to slip, trip or fall (see 18.29 below)

so far as reasonably practicable. [*Workplace (Health, Safety and Welfare) Regulations 1992, Reg 12(3)*].

Floors should be kept free of obstructions impeding access or presenting hazards, particularly near or on steps, stairs, escalators and moving walkways, on emergency routes or outlets, in or near doorways or gangways or by corners or junctions. Where temporary obstructions are unavoidable, access should be prevented and people warned of the possible hazard. Furniture being moved should not be left in a place where it can cause a hazard.

(*d*)   have effective drainage. [*Workplace (Health, Safety and Welfare) Regulations 1992, Reg 12(2)(b)*].

Where floors are likely to get wet, effective drainage (without drains becoming contaminated with toxic, corrosive substances) should drain it away, e.g. in laundries, potteries and food processing plants. Drains and channels should be situated so as to reduce the area of wet floor and the floor should slope slightly towards the drain and ideally have covers flush with the floor surface. Processes and plant which cause discharges or leaks of liquids should be enclosed and leaks from taps caught and drained away. In food processing and preparation plants, work surfaces should be arranged so as to minimise the likelihood of spillage. Where a leak or spillage occurs, it should be fenced off or mopped up immediately.

Doors and gates

18.8   Doors and gates must be suitably constructed and, if necessary, fitted with safety devices. In particular,

(*a*)   sliding, vertically moving or powered doors/gates must not cause injury by falling on or trapping a person,

(*b*)   powered doors/gates must have identifiable and accessible emergency stop controls,

(*c*)   powered doors/gates must operate manually, unless they open automatically if power fails.

[*Workplace (Health, Safety and Welfare) Regulations 1992, Reg 18*].

Doors and gates must be suitably constructed and fitted with safety devices. In particular,

    (i)   a sliding door/gate must have a device to prevent its coming off its track during use;

    (ii)   an upward opening door/gate must have a device to prevent its falling back;

(iii)   a powered door/gate must

(*a*)   have features preventing it causing injury by trapping a person (e.g. accessible emergency stop controls),

(*b*)   be able to be operated manually unless it opens automatically if the power fails;

(iv)   a door/gate capable of opening, by being pushed from either side, must provide a clear view of the space close to both sides.

[*Workplace (Health, Safety and Welfare) Regulations 1992, Reg 18*].

Escalators and travelators

18.9   Escalators and travelators must

(*a*)   function safely;

(*b*)   be equipped with safety devices;

(*c*)   be fitted with emergency stop controls.

[*Workplace (Health, Safety and Welfare) Regulations 1992, Reg 19*].

Pedestrian traffic routes

18.10   (For vehicular traffic routes, see Chapter 2 'Access'.)

Taking the various forms of

(*a*)   stairs;

(*b*)   staircases;

(*c*)   fixed ladders (see Chapter 46 'Work at Heights');

(*d*)   doorways;

(*e*)   gateways

[*Reg 2*];

pedestrian traffic routes must

(i)   be of sound construction;

(ii)   have a surface suitable for use and purpose;

(iii)   not have holes or slopes;

(iv)   not be uneven or slippery;

(v)   be kept free from obstructions and articles/substances likely to cause persons to slip, trip or fall (see also 18.7 above, 18.29 and 18.32 below);

(vi)   be provided with sufficient handrails;

(vii)   in the case of staircases, be provided with guards.

[*Workplace (Health, Safety and Welfare) Regulations 1992, Reg 12*].

Civil liability

18.11   There is no specific reference to civil liability in the regulations. However, safety regulations are actionable, even if silent (as here), and, if a person suffered injury/damage as a result of breach by an employer, he could sue (see 1.18, 1.44

INTRODUCTION). Certainly, there is civil liability for breach of the *Building Regulations* (18.14 below).

Controls over building work – Building Regulations 1991 (SI 1991 No 2768)

18.12   Certain requirements, in the interests of the health, safety, hygiene and welfare, of occupants of buildings (including industrial and commercial premises), are specified in the *Building Regulations 1991* which came into force on 1 June 1992, as follows.

The building must be

(1)   (if it has five or more storeys) constructed so that, in the event of an accident, it will not suffer collapse disproportionate to its cause;

(2)   constructed so that, in the event of failure of any part of a roof (if the roof is in a part of a public building, shop or shopping mall with a roof with a clear span exceeding 9 metres between supports), it will not suffer collapse disproportionate to its cause;

(3)   designed and constructed so that there are means of escape in case of fire to a place of safety outside, and to inhibit the spread of fire internally and externally (see further Chapter 19 'Fire and Fire Precautions');

(4)   designed and constructed to provide facilities to assist firefighters.

Also,

(*a*)   precautions should be taken to avoid danger to health and safety caused by dangerous toxic substances on or in ground on which the building is to stand;

(*b*)   reasonable precautions should be taken to prevent cavity wall insulating material from giving off toxic fumes;

(*c*)   there must be

(i)   adequate means of ventilation for occupants, and

(ii)   adequate sanitary conveniences;

(*d*)   stairs, ramps, floors, balconies and roofs must be guarded with barriers to protect users from the risk of falling.

[*Building Regulations 1991, 1 Sch*].

Access for disabled persons

18.13   As part and parcel of compliance with the *Building Regulations 1991*, access and certain other facilities to both industrial, commercial (and domestic) buildings, in the case of non-domestic buildings, should be made available to disabled persons (though, arguably, compliance can be achieved in other ways), that is, persons who have

(*a*)   difficulty in walking or use a wheelchair, or

(*b*)   impaired hearing or sight.

The provisions apply to

(i)   newly erected buildings,

(ii)   substantially reconstructed buildings, and

    (iii)   extensions to a building with a ground floor.

[Building Regulations 1991, 1 Sch].

To achieve adequate access and use of the premises for the disabled, it is suggested that the following should be provided:

    (i)   grippable handrails (to a height of 900 mm above the surface of a ramp or the pitch line of a flight of steps and 1,000 mm above the surface of a landing);

    (ii)   stairs with neither sharply tapered treads nor open risers;

    (iii)   wheelchair stairlifts (as an alternative to passenger lifts);

    (iv)   platform lifts (as an alternative to a ramp) to enable wheelchair users to move to different levels within a storey;

    (v)   sanitary conveniences located so that a wheelchair user does not have to travel more than one storey to reach a suitable WC (i.e. one which is wheelchair manoeuvrable); as far as ambulant disabled people are concerned, at least one WC compartment should be provided within each range of WCs in storeys not designed to be accessible to the disabled.

Buildings affected

Buildings primarily affected are shops, offices, factories, warehouses, schools and other educational establishments (including student residential accommodation), institutions, premises to which the public is admitted on payment or otherwise.

Civil liability for breach of the Building Regulations 1991

18.14   There is civil liability for breach of the *Building Regulations 1991*. Such action is based on strict liability, though common law actions for negligence for personal injury, arising from occupation of defective premises and caused by breach of the *Building Regulations*, are also possible. *[Building Act 1984, s 38(3)]*. In this connection (i.e. action for negligence at common law), local authorities do not owe a duty of care to a building owner to see that he complies with the *Building Regulations* (*Richardson v West Lindsey District Council [1990] 1 AER 296*).

Factories Act 1961

18.15   Until the requirements of the new regulations are fully operational on 1 January 1996, in respect of pre-1993 workplaces, some current requirements of the *Factories Act 1961* will continue to apply to factories (even after 1 January 1996, though their practical importance may have diminished).

Of all protective occupational legislation prior to the *Health and Safety at Work etc. Act 1974 (HSWA)*, the most important by far was (and still is) the *Factories Act 1961*, itself the successor of a long line of *Factories Acts* and *Factories and Workshops Acts* dating back to 1878. Although traditionally associated with the enforcement of health, safety and welfare duties in manufacturing industry (which is the principal application of the *Factories Act 1961*), the term 'factory' has a more extensive meaning, and applies to building operations and works of civil engineering as well as work carried out in the open air (see Chapter 7 'Construction and Building Operations'). Moreover, following *HSWA*, regulations made thereunder are gradually replacing earlier protective legislation – and this is the broad general policy of the HSE. The repeal of the *Factories Act 1961* is a continuing process and its provisions are being superseded by *HSWA* and the *Workplace (Health, Safety and Welfare) Regulations* and codes of practice. This chapter considers (*a*) premises constituting factories, (*b*) design and structural safety requirements relating to such premises, and (*c*) basic hygiene requirements, as well as (*d*) the welfare of workers.

From the point of view of enforcement, the *Factories Act 1961* has been (and still is) infinitely more important than the *Offices, Shops and Railway Premises Act 1963 (OSRPA)*. Many of its provisions are assiduously enforced by the HSE and civil actions are still brought for breaches of the Act. Actions lie for breach of statutory duty under the *Factories Act 1961*, at least as far as safety and health duties are concerned (the position regarding the welfare provisions is not so clear), whereas actions for breach of statutory duty do not lie in respect of the general duties of *HSWA* (see 'Introduction' above) (which give rise to common law actions only). Moreover, some of the provisions of the *Factories Act 1961* (remaining in force until 1 January 1997) acquired an almost legendary character, e.g. *Sec 14(1)* relating to 'dangerous machinery' which was subject to a plethora of case law because it does not define 'danger', e.g.: 'A part of machinery is dangerous if it is a possible cause of injury to anybody acting in a way in which a human being may be reasonably expected to act in circumstances which may reasonably be expected to occur' (*Walker v Bletchley-Flettons Ltd [1937] 1 AER 170*).

PART A

DEFINITION OF 'FACTORY'

There are two types of factory: (*a*) principal factories and (*b*) subsidiary factories.

Principal factories

18.16   For the purposes of the *Factories Act 1961*, 'factory' means essentially 'any premises in which, or within the close or curtilage or precincts of which, persons are employed in *manual* labour in any process for, or incidental to any of the following:

(*a*)   the making of any article or part of any article; or

(*b*)   the altering, repairing, ornamenting, finishing, cleaning or washing, or the breaking up or demolition of any article; or

(*c*)   the adapting for sale of any article; or

(*d*)   the slaughtering of cattle, sheep, swine, goats, horses, asses or mules; or

(*e*)   the confinement of such animals while awaiting slaughter;

. . . being premises in which . . . work is carried on by way of trade or for the purposes of gain and to or over which the employer of the persons employed therein has the right of access or control'. [*Factories Act 1961, s 175(1)*].

'Close' is a definable area upon which one or more of the activities mentioned in *Sec 175(1)* take place. It is not necessary that there be a boundary wall or fence. Thus, a part of a quayside in the open air, where a floating oil dock was being constructed, was a factory (*Barry v Cleveland Bridge and Engineering Co Ltd [1963] 1 AER 192*). 'Close' or 'precincts' imply a boundary surrounding an enclosure; the boundary might be a line. If the boundary defines land over which special rights of use are granted, which sets the land apart from other land over which only rights of way exist, this can be a 'close, curtilage or precinct' of a factory (*Walsh v Allweather Mechanical Grouting Co Ltd [1959] 2 AER 588* where a concrete apron bounded by a fence in a hangar (itself a factory) was held to be a 'factory').

Open land 250 yards from a factory was held to be a 'factory' (*Hosking v de Havilland Aircraft Co Ltd [1949] 1 AER 540* where a factory employee was injured on a plank placed over a trench by contractors. The plank collapsed. It was held that there was a breach of the predecessor of the *Factories Act 1961*).

A construction site inside factory premises is a 'factory' (*Street v British Electricity Authority [1952] 1 AER 679* where steam-boilers were being installed in an electricity generating plant).

Subsidiary factories

18.17   These are essentially of three kinds and need not be part of or allied to a principal factory; what is important is that they service the principal factory.

(a)   *Processes incidental to any factory*. Premises in which the following processes incidental to 'principal factories' are carried on:

   (i)   sorting articles;

   (ii)   washing bottles, filling bottles, filling containers, packing articles

   [*Factories Act 1961, s 175(2)*];

   also repairing factory machinery (*Thorogood v Van den Bergs & Jurgens Ltd [1951] 1 AER 682*); quarrying sand and gravel and infilling with rubble and refuse where the quarrying area was held to be a 'factory' but the infill site was not (*Ham River Grit Co Ltd v Richmond Rating Authority [1949] 1 AER 286*); a construction site in a factory was held not to be 'incidental' to the factory (*Street v British Electricity Authority [1952] 1 AER 679*); repairing a concrete runway and apron at an aerodrome was not 'incidental' to a factory (*Walsh v Allweather Mechanical Grouting Co Ltd [1959] 2 AER 588*).

(b)   *Processes incidental to special trades*:

   (i)   laundries ancillary to a business, e.g. hotel;

   (ii)   locomotive works, garages, barge depots ancillary to a transport undertaking: this includes railway running sheds where running repairs are carried out (but not premises for housing transport, where cleaning and running repairs and adjustments are done);

   (iii)   workshops ancillary to a cinema or theatre;

   (iv)   workshops handling wood or metal articles ancillary to any business, where mechanical power is in use;

   (v)   workshops incidental to building and engineering operations (see Chapter 7 'Construction and Building Operations');

   (vi)   gasholders with storage capacity of 140 cubic metres or more.

   [*Factories Act 1961, s 175(2)*].

(c)   *Particular undertakings*:

   (i)   shipbuilding or ship-repairing yards and dry docks;

   (ii)   hooking, plaiting, lapping, making-up or packing of yarn or cloth;

   (iii)   printing and binding works;

   (iv)   cinema studios (including theatres).

   [*Factories Act 1961, s 175(2)*].

Factory work

18.18   Factory work is of three kinds:

(*a*)   making an article or part of it;

(*b*)   altering, repairing, ornamenting, finishing, cleaning, washing or the breaking or demolition of any article;

(*c*)   adapting for sale of any article.

[*Factories Act 1961, s 175(1)*].

The term 'article' is not defined in the Act but has been interpreted in a general way as including (*a*) coal, (*b*) gas, (*c*) water (*Longhurst v Guildford, Godalming & District Water Board [1961] 3 AER 545*, though not electricity, but electrical stations are included by dint of the *Factories Act 1961, s 123* (see 18.22(*a*) below)), and animal carcasses (*Fatstock Marketing Corporation Ltd v Morgan [1958] 1 AER 646*).

'Adapting for sale' has been construed as including:

(*a*)   the process to which an article is subjected in a workplace that produces some change in the article, making it saleable when, prior to that, it was not saleable;

(*b*)   separating or sorting articles from a bulk lot, even though the end product consists of the constituent parts of the bulk lot (*Richardson & Son v Middlesbrough Assessment Committee [1947] 1 AER 884*). This has included particularly:

   (i)   crating eggs (*Richardson & Son v Middlesbrough Assessment Committee [1947] 1 AER 884*);

   (ii)   boxing sweets (*Fullers Ltd v Squire [1901] 2 KB 209*);

   (iii)   sorting and baling rags (*Kaye v Burrows [1931] AC 477*);

   (iv)   bulk seed cleaning (*Hines v Eastern Counties Farmers Co-operative Association Ltd [1931] AC 480*);

   (v)   bottling beer delivered in bulk (*Sedgwick v Watney, Coombe Reid & Co Ltd [1931] AC 461*);

   (vi)   freezing food for storage (*Union Cold Storage Co Ltd v Bancroft [1931] AC 488*);

   (vii)   making up floral wreaths (*Hoare v Green (R) Ltd [1907] 2 KB 315*);

(*c*)   testing and certification of articles '*per se*' is not 'adaptation' (*Grove v Lloyds British Testing Co Ltd [1931] AC 466*); but testing of manufactured products by the manufacturer himself, and their subsequent repair, are part of the manufacture and do therefore amount to 'adaptation for sale' (*Acton Borough Council v West Middlesex Assessment Committee and de Havilland Propellers Ltd [1949] 1 AER 409*).

The key point is the main purpose for which the premises are used; if manual labour forms a substantial part of what is done on the premises they may well be a factory; whereas if it plays an ancillary part they probably will not qualify as a factory. Thus, a porter employed in a chemist's shop does not have the protection of the *Factories Act 1961 (Joyce v Boots Cash Chemists (Southern) Ltd [1950] 2 AER 719*, though he will have the protection of *HSWA*) but a room at the rear of a radio shop used to repair faulty radios and televisions qualified as a factory, since manual labour was a principal part of repair work (*Haygarth v J & F Stone Lighting & Radio Ltd [1965] 3 WLR 316*). The fact that only one or two employees work on the premises does not prevent the premises being a factory.

Factory premises

18.19   Factory premises are normally indoors but can be outdoors (*Walsh v Allweather Mechanical Grouting Co Ltd [1959] 2 AER 588* (see 18.16 above)). Premises which, although not part of the factory where industrial workers are engaged in manual labour, are nevertheless used for purposes incidental to the main purpose of the factory, are classed as part of the factory and the provisions of the *Factories Act 1961* extend to them (unless specifically excluded). This would include a canteen, since provision of meals is material to the main purpose of the factory, and so a hand-rail had to be provided in a canteen, consistently with (what is now) *Sec 28(2)* of the Act (*Luttman v ICI Ltd [1955] 3 AER 481*). But a restaurant for administrative staff to which workers were not admitted, and which was sometimes used for management and shop steward conferences, was held not to be 'incidental' to the main purpose of the factory and so not covered by the *Factories Act 1961* (*Thomas v British Thomson-Houston Co Ltd [1953] 1 AER 29*). Such a building today would, almost certainly, come within *HSWA s 2(2)(d)*, as being a building within an employer's control (see Chapter 15 'Employers' Duties').

Premises in which trade or gain results from manual labour cannot be a factory, unless the employer has right of access to them. Normally no problems arise here but there could be difficulties, for example, where there is a sit-in by the workforce and the employer is forbidden to enter, or where the employer is a workers' co-operative, since in the latter case it is difficult to see that there is an employer in the traditional sense. Here presumably enforcement would be against the workers' co-operative.

'Separate factory'

18.20   Sometimes there is a clearly defined area within a factory which is separated from the rest of the factory and whose purpose is not incidental to the purpose or purposes of the factory. Such an area may well qualify as a separate factory in itself. This will often be the position where an independent contractor is engaged on work within the factory, e.g. a construction site inside factory premises where steam-boilers were being installed (*Street v British Electricity Authority [1952] 1 AER 679*). This is provided for by the *Factories Act 1961, s 175(6)*. Here enforcement of the Act would be against the independent contractor.

Crown premises

18.21   The *Factories Act 1961* extends to 'factories belonging to or in the occupation of the Crown, to building operations and works of engineering construction undertaken by or on behalf of the Crown, and to employment by or under the Crown of persons in painting buildings', e.g. hospital painters. [*Factories Act 1961, s 173(1)*].

Special cases

18.22   The *Factories Act 1961* extends to the following by virtue of *Part VII* of the Act relating to 'Special Applications and Extensions' (though in the case of docks and ships the application is limited).

(*a*)   *Electrical stations [Sec 123]*.

(*b*)   *Charitable and reformatory institutions*, where manual labour is carried on for making and adapting articles for sale [*Sec 124*].

(*c*)   *Docks [Sec 125]*. Many provisions of the *Factories Act 1961* were applied to warehouses (particularly where mechanical power was used). Currently, the fencing requirements of the *Factories Act 1961, ss 12–17, 20, 21*, and lifting requirements [*Secs 22–27*], as well as requirements relating to floors and passages [*Sec 28*], apply to all dock premises on the basis that they qualify as 'notional factories'. [*Docks Regulations 1988 (SI 1988 No 1655), Reg 23*]. The fencing requirements remain in force until 1 January 1997 in existing factories and factory premises (see further 28.10 MACHINERY SAFETY).

(*d*)   *Ships*. The provisions of *Sec 126(2)* apply to work carried out in a harbour or wet dock in constructing, reconstructing or repairing a ship, or in scaling, scurfing or cleaning boilers, or in cleaning oil fuel tanks or bilges in a ship or any tank in a ship last used for oil carried as cargo, or any tank or hold that was last used for any substance of a dangerous or injurious nature.

(*e*)   *Premises within the control of the Crown or a municipal or public authority*, even though work is not carried on by way of trade or for the purposes of gain. [*Factories Act 1961, s 175(9)*]. Thus, although a hospital will not qualify as a factory, a workshop within the curtilage of a hospital for mechanical and electrical repairs and minor installation work within the hospital, is a factory (*Bromwich v National Ear, Nose and Throat Hospital [1980] 2 AER 663*).

However, technical colleges and institutes are outside the scope of the *Factories Act 1961* (*Weston v London County Council [1941] 1 AER 555*), though they are covered by *HSWA*, since students are deemed not to be 'employed'.

Building operations and works of engineering construction

18.23   Many of the provisions of the *Factories Act 1961* apply 'to building operations and works of engineering construction undertaken by way of trade or business, or for the purpose of any industrial or commercial undertaking, and to any line or siding which is used in connection therewith and for those purposes, and which is not part of a railway or tramway'. [*Factories Act 1961, s 127(1)*].

More important, however, is *Sec 127(4)* establishing that building works and civil engineering sites are notional factories, empowering the Minister to pass regulations relating to them. The result has been the passing of the quartet of *Construction Regulations 1961-66* (see Chapter 7 'Construction and Building Operations'). These regulations apply whether or not the building or civil engineering operation is being carried on inside a factory itself, as defined in *Sec 175*. In this way a subcontracted worker who was injured would have two or even three civil remedies, against the actual factory occupier, the notional factory occupier (i.e. main contractor) and against his own employer (i.e. subcontractor).

Power to make regulations in relation to factories

18.24   The *Factories Act 1961, s 76* empowered the relevant Minister to make specific regulations in relation to factories, a power which was extensively used, and accounted for a great number of regulations governing dangerous activities and trades, some of which have been partially repealed (e.g. the *Abrasive Wheels Regulations 1970*) and will remain in force only until 1 January 1997, e.g. the *Construction Regulations 1961-66* and the *Power Presses Regulations 1965*. Although *Sec 76* has long been repealed, as from 1 January 1975, by the *Factories Act 1961 etc. (Repeals and Modifications) Regulations 1974 (SI 1974 No 1941)*, many of the regulations passed under its umbrella still remain in force and form a hard residual core of legislation on workplace health and safety.

Enforcement of the Factories Act 1961 and regulations

18.25　By virtue of the *Factories Act 1961, s 155(1)* offences under the Act are normally committed by occupiers rather than owners of factories. Unless they happen to occupy a factory as well, the owners of a factory would not normally be charged. Offences therefore relate to physical occupation or control of a factory (for an extended meaning of 'occupier', see Chapter 32 'Occupiers' Liability'). Hence the person or persons or body corporate having managerial responsibility in respect of a factory are those who commit an offence under *Sec 155(1)*. This will generally be the managing director and board of directors and/or individual executive directors. Moreover, if a company is in liquidation and the receiver is in control, he is the person who will be prosecuted and this has in fact happened (*Meigh v Wickenden [1942] 2 KB 160; Lord Advocate v Aero Technologies 1991 SLT 134* where the receiver was 'in occupation' and so under a duty to prevent 'accidents by fire or explosion', for the purposes of the *Explosives Act 1875, s 23*). Here it is worth noting that, although breaches of *HSWA* and regulations made under it are offences under *Sec 33(1)* of that Act, breaches of the *Factories Act 1961* and its regulations are still charged under *Sec 155(1)*. Clearly, as regulations under *HSWA* begin to supersede the requirements of the *Factories Act 1961*, the importance of *Sec 155(1)* will diminish.

Defence of factory occupier

18.26　The main defence open to a factory occupier charged with breach of the *Factories Act 1961* is that the Act itself, or more likely regulations made under it, placed the statutory duty on some person other than the occupier, e.g. *Reg 11* of the *Protection of Eyes Regulations 1974* (now revoked) which imposed a duty on an employee in prescribed circumstances to wear eye protection. The precise wording of the defence section is important. Thus, where there is a contravention by any person of any regulation or order under the *Factories Act 1961*, 'that person shall be guilty of an offence and the occupier or owner . . . shall not be guilty of an offence, by reason only of the contravention of the provision . . . unless it is proved that he failed to take all reasonable steps to prevent the contravention . . .'. [*Factories Act 1961, s 155(2)*].

Before this defence can be invoked by a factory occupier or company, it is necessary to show that:

(*a*)　a statutory duty had been laid on someone other than the factory occupier by a regulation or order passed under the Act, e.g. *Reg 11* of the *Protection of Eyes Regulations 1974* (now revoked by the *Personal Protective Equipment at Work Regulations 1992, 3 Sch*);

(*b*)　the factory occupier took all reasonable steps to prevent the contravention (a difficult test to satisfy).

NB. This statutory defence is not open to a building contractor (in his capacity as a notional factory occupier). Prosecution followed by conviction of an employee under this section, will not prevent a further prosecution (and possible conviction) against a building contractor who, for the purposes of *Sec 155(2)*, is not regarded as an occupier, although he is for the purposes of *Sec 127(4)*. That is, building contractors are subject to the requirements of the *Factories Act 1961* but cannot raise the general statutory defence under *Sec 155(2)* (*Davies v Camerons Industrial Services Ltd [1980] 2 AER 680*). The reason for this is that *Reg 3(1)* of the *Construction (Working Places) Regulations 1966* is outside *Sec 155(2)*, because it is caught by its proviso. In other words, building contractors must comply with all requirements of the *Construction Regulations*, regardless of whether an employee has done so.

Effect on civil liability

18.27 Whether conviction of an employee under *Sec 155(2)* would prejudice a subsequent claim for damages by him against a factory occupier, must be regarded as an open question. Thus, in *Potts v Reid [1942] 2 AER 161* the court said 'Criminal and civil liability are two separate things . . . The legislation (the *Factories Act 1937*) might well be unwilling to convict an owner who failed to carry out a statutory duty of a crime with which he was not himself directly concerned, but still be ready to leave the civil liability untouched'. Similarly in *Boyle v Kodak Ltd [1969] 2 AER 439* it was said, 'When considering the civil liability engrafted by judicial decision upon the criminal liability which has been imposed by statute, it is no good looking to the statute and seeing from it where the criminal liability would lie, for we are concerned only with civil liability. We must look to the cases' (per Lord Diplock). Moreover, a breach of general duties of *HSWA* gives rise only to civil liability at common law and not under statute. (Though this is not the position where there is a breach of a specific regulation under *HSWA*.) On the other hand, there is at least one isolated instance of an employee being denied damages where he was in breach of specific regulations (*ICI Ltd v Shatwell [1965] AC 656*). It is thought, however, that this decision would not apply in the case of breach of a *general* statutory duty, such as *Sec 155(2)*.

PART B

STRUCTURAL SAFETY AND HYGIENE IN FACTORIES

18.28 Accidents at work frequently occur as a result of people at work falling and slipping on floors, stairs, gangways and in passageways and injuring themselves. But it is not only for walking purposes that floors etc. must be strong and stable. They must be supportive for storage purposes and warehousing, as well as forklift trucks and heavy machinery used in the manufacturing process in the factory. Forklift trucks, in particular, put added pressure on floors (see Chapter 29 'Materials Handling') – a fact which should be borne in mind at factory or warehouse design stage. Whether floors are capable of carrying such extra load should be considered prior to installation and, if necessary, they should be strengthened. Failure to do so can result in civil liability for negligence as well as prosecution under the *Factories Act 1961, s 28(1)* and *HSWA s 6* (article for use at work) (*Greaves & Co (Contractors) Ltd v Baynham Meikle & Partners [1975] 3 AER 99* where a factory floor collapsed owing to poor design, in breach of a British Standard specification, when it had to support forklift trucks, and the design engineers were held to be liable for negligence). Ladders used in factories, offices and shops must be of sound construction and properly maintained. (For ladders on construction sites, see 7.45 CONSTRUCTION AND BUILDING OPERATIONS.) These duties are assiduously enforced by the HSE. In addition, the *HSWA* provides general cover in all places of work, including floors, stairs, gangways etc. (see 7.51 CONSTRUCTION AND BUILDING OPERATIONS). Where a person is injured as a result of an unsafe floor, stairway etc. on any premises, there is a separate right of action against the occupier, though employees are expected to take greater caution than ordinary visitors (see Chapter 32 'Occupiers' Liability').

Factories – safety provisions

18.29 There are two separate duties here. All floors, steps, stairs, passages and gangways:

  (*a*)   must be of sound construction and properly maintained; and

  (*b*)   so far as is reasonably practicable (see Chapter 15 'Employers' Duties' for the meaning of this expression), be kept free from:

(i)   any obstruction; and

(ii)   any substance likely to cause persons to slip.

[Factories Act 1961, s 28(1)] (remaining in force until 1 January 1996).

A loose plastic bag is a slippery substance (*McCart v Queen of Scots Knitwear Ltd, SLT, 24 April 1987*) and a duckboard is a floor or at least a passage or gangway and so has to be properly maintained (*Harper v Mander and Germain Ltd, The Times, 28 December 1992* where an employee's accident was caused by accumulation of slippery paste on duckboard. It was held that the employer was liable).

Sound construction and proper maintenance

18.30   These two duties are strict. Factory occupiers will be liable for breach even though all reasonable care has been taken in the manufacture of the floor, staircase etc. If, therefore, a worker is injured as a result of a breach of this duty, the factory occupier should seek indemnity against the manufacturer (assuming that the former commissioned the floor, stairway etc.) or by joining him as a third party in civil proceedings.

Freedom from obstruction and substances likely to cause persons to slip

18.31   This duty extends not only to cleaning the floor of slippery substances but also to preventing substances from getting on the floor in the first place (*Johnson v Caddies Wainwright [1983] ICR 407*). Liability under this second tier of *Sec 28(1)* is related to cost-effective criteria (*Latimer v AEC Ltd [1953] 2 AER 449* where part of a factory floor was treated after being flooded one weekend by a thunderstorm of unusual severity; the factory occupier was held not liable to an employee for injury, after he had slipped on the untreated part).

Obstruction

18.32   'Obstruction' is not defined in the *Factories Act 1961* but has been construed as something on the floor, stairs etc. which:

(*a*)   should not be there; and

(*b*)   would not normally be there.

Factories – health provisions

Cleaning of floors

18.33   All factories must be kept in a clean state and free from effluvia (i.e. minute particles or obnoxious vapours). *[Factories Act 1961, s 1(1)]*. Moreover, all accumulations of dust and refuse must be removed from floors or workrooms and every workroom floor must be cleaned, at least once a week, by washing or sweeping. *[Factories Act 1961, s 1(2)]* (remaining in force until 1 January 1996).

These are strict duties, with little or no defence to prosecution. In addition, if there is a breach of the health provisions of the *Factories Act 1961*, civil action for breach of statutory duty may well lie against the factory occupier, as well as at common law (*Nicholson v Atlas Steel Ltd [1957] 1 AER 776* concerning ventilation, and see also Chapter 43 'Ventilation').

Factory cleaning staff

18.34   A woman or young person employed *solely* in cleaning a factory, or any part of it, is not within the provisions of *Part VI* of the *Factories Act 1961*, relating to the 'Employment of Women and Young Persons' (and so is not protected by its provisions), unless the cleaning is incidental to, or connected with, any process. This is provided for in the *Factories Act 1961, s 176(4)*, which draws the distinction between cleaning effluvia or dust created by machines or some other process in the factory, and cleaning *per se*. In other words, a woman or young person employed to clean a factory is not deemed to be employed in the factory, and so not covered by the provisions of the *Factories Act 1961, Part VI*, unless he or she is engaged in cleaning factory machinery and workpieces (see also Chapter 45 'Women Workers'). Such a person would, however, be protected by *HSWA s 3(1)*, which states that it is the 'duty of every employer to conduct his undertaking in such a way as to ensure that persons not in his employment are not exposed to health and safety risks'.

Draining factory floors

18.35   Where a factory process renders the floor wet, effective means of drainage must be provided and maintained for draining off the wet. [*Factories Act 1961, s 6*]. The section does not specify 'effective means'; to that extent the matter is one for the discretion of the factory occupier. But whichever means are selected, there is a requirement to 'provide and maintain'. (For the meaning of these recurrent expressions, see Chapter 15 'Employers' Duties'.) This duty is strict. Whether, in addition to giving rise to criminal liability, an action for damages will lie, depends on the view of the section taken by the courts. If they consider it essentially safety-oriented, it probably will; whereas, if they consider that it is public health-oriented, it probably will not. (*Sec 6* remains in force until 1 January 1996.)

Staircases in factories

18.36   Where there is a staircase in a building, or a staircase which affords a means of exit from a building, a substantial hand-rail must be both provided and maintained. [*Factories Act 1961, s 28(2)*] (remaining in force until 1 January 1996).

Staircases with open sides

18.37   Where there is:

(*a*)   a staircase with an open side, the hand-rail must be on that side;

(*b*)   a staircase with two open sides, or a staircase which is specially liable to cause accidents (e.g. a circular staircase), a substantial hand-rail must be provided and maintained on both sides.

[*Factories Act 1961, s 28(2)*] (remaining in force until 1 January 1996).

This is a strict duty.

Guards

18.38   The open side of a staircase must be guarded by providing and maintaining a lower rail or other effective means. [*Factories Act 1961, s 28(3)*] (remaining in force until 1 January 1996).

Washing and painting

18.39   *(a)*   *Washing*. Where stairs and gangways in factories have smooth, impervious surfaces, they must be washed with hot water at least every 14 months, using soap or other detergent, or be cleaned in some other approved way.

(b)   *Painting*. Where stairs and gangways are painted, they must be repainted or revarnished at least every seven years; and they must be washed with hot water and soap or some other detergent at least every 14 months, or be cleaned in some other approved way.

[*Factories Act 1961, s 1(3)*] (remaining in force until 1 January 1996).

Ladders in factories

18.40   All ladders must be soundly constructed and properly maintained. [*Factories Act 1961, s 28(5)*]. This applies also to step ladders. This duty is strict (*Cole v Blackstone & Co* [*1943*] *KB 615*).

Ladders over containers of dangerous substances

18.41   The *Factories Act 1961* contains specific provisions for fixed vessels, structures, sumps and pits which contain scalding, corrosive or poisonous liquid and which are not securely covered. The requirements are that no *(a)* ladder, *(b)* stair, or *(c)* gangway must be placed (i) above, (ii) across, or (iii) inside any vessel etc. containing such a substance, unless the ladder, stair or gangway is:

(a)   at least 460 mm wide; and

(b)   securely fenced on both sides to a height of at least 920 mm; and

(c)   securely fixed.

[*Factories Act 1961, s 18(2)*] (remaining in force until 1 January 1996).

'Securely fenced' means 'provided with sheet fencing or an upper and lower rail and toeboards'. [*Factories Act 1961, s 18(4)*] (remaining in force until 1 January 1996).

Openings in floors

18.42   All openings in floors must be securely fenced, unless the nature of the work makes this impracticable. [*Factories Act 1961, s 28(4)*]. An 'opening' is not restricted to holes of such size and depth that they are capable of being fenced; three small pits 30 ins by 17 ins by 8 ins were held to be 'openings' (*Sanders v FH Lloyd & Co* [*1982*] *ICR 360*). Also, where the negligent act of an employee leads to temporary extinguishment of a lamp necessary for the maintenance of an adequate standard of lighting near a floor opening, an employer is in breach of *Sec 28(4)*, as well as the *Factories Act 1961, s 5(1)* (*Rawding v London Brick Co (1970) KIR 194*) (see Chapter 27 'Lighting'). A loading bay is not an 'opening in the floor' (*Hemmings v British Aerospace, The Times, 2 May 1986*). (*Sec 28(4)* remains in force until 1 January 1996.)

Chapter 19

Fire and Fire Precautions

Introduction

19.1   Statute law relating to fire and fire precautions is extensive and is located mainly in the *Fire Precautions Act 1971 (FPA)* (and regulations and orders made thereunder), the *Fire Safety and Safety of Places of Sport Act 1987*, the *Health and Safety at Work etc. Act 1974 (HSWA)*, the *Petroleum Acts* (and regulations made thereunder), the *Public Health Acts 1936–1961*, the *Building Act 1984* (and the *Building Regulations 1991* made thereunder), the *Fire Services Act 1947* and the *Fires Prevention (Metropolis) Act 1774* as well as certain regulations, made under the *Factories Act 1961*, such as the *Highly Flammable Liquids and Liquefied Petroleum Gases Regulations 1972* (see further Chapter 24 'Highly Flammable Liquids').

By way of implementation of both the general safety framework directive and the workplace minimum standards directive, the draft *Fire Precautions (Places of Work) Regulations* will probably come into effect in mid-1994, affecting both previously fire-certificated and non-fire-certificated work premises. Indeed, they will extend to practically *all workplaces*, including premises where the self-employed work and it will require employers to carry out an assessment to determine the nature and extent of fire precautionary measures.

The *Fire Precautions Act 1971* imposes requirements relating to fire precautions upon occupiers of premises (whether or not employers) where there is a fire risk. The *Fire Safety and Safety of Places of Sport Act 1987* is a de-regulating measure (see 19.11–19.21 below). Meanwhile, *HSWA* is concerned specifically with premises containing dangerous materials and/or where hazardous processes are carried on. The *Petroleum Spirit (Consolidation) Act 1928* imposes requirements on storage and transportation of petroleum spirit, whilst the *Public Health Acts* and, more particularly, the *Building Act 1984* (and *Building Regulations 1991*) apply health, safety and welfare requirements to *new* buildings (industrial, commercial and private) and buildings under construction and altered buildings, in the interests of occupants, both present and future. The *Fire Services Act 1947* specifies the duties of local fire authorities and the *Fires Prevention (Metropolis) Act 1774, inter alia,* regulates liability of occupiers of premises to adjoining occupiers for damage caused by fire spread.

The first four Acts, the *Fire Precautions Act 1971*, the *Fire Safety and Safety of Places of Sport Act 1987*, *HSWA 1974* and the *Public Health Acts 1936* and *1961* are predominantly penal measures, whilst the *Fires Prevention (Metropolis) Act 1774* concerns civil liability. More particularly, the *Fire Precautions Act 1971* (as amended by the *Fire Safety and Safety of Places of Sport Act 1987*) and *HSWA* specify fire precautions in relation to commercial and industrial (and a limited number of other) buildings already in existence (see 19.4 below), whilst the *Public Health Acts* and the *Building Regulations* apply mainly to *new* buildings – industrial, commercial and private, and *buildings under construction as well as altered buildings,* not to mention the *Smoke Detectors Act 1991*, which requires that private dwellings and flats under construction, are fitted with a smoke detector. Not to do so amounts to an offence, which, on conviction, carries a maximum fine of £1,000. [*Smoke Detectors Act 1991, ss 1, 2*].

This chapter is concerned with *industrial and commercial premises actually in existence* and to which the *Fire Precautions Act 1971* (as modified by the *Fire Safety and Safety of Places of Sport Act 1987*) and *HSWA* apply; but also considers how fires start and details some key fire prevention measures (see 19.54–19.78 below). The particular hazard of fires on construction sites receives separate attention (see 19.79–19.84 below).

Specific fire precautions legislation

19.2   The main legislation relating specifically to fire safety in workplaces is the *Fire Precautions Act 1971* (as amended by the *Fire Safety and Safety of Places of Sport Act 1987*). The effect of this latter Act is to de-regulate some fire precautions regulations (see 19.11–19.21 below). The principal regulations, made under the *Fire Precautions Act 1971, s 12* – the regulation-making power – are

(a)   the *Fire Precautions (Factories, Offices, Shops and Railway Premises) Order 1989 (SI 1989 No 76)*;

(b)   the *Fire Precautions (Hotels and Boarding Houses) Order 1972 (SIs 1972 Nos 238, 382)*;

(c)   the *Fire Certificates (Special Premises) Regulations 1976 (SI 1976 No 2003)* – hereafter referred to as the '*Special Premises Regulations*'.

[*Fire Precautions (Factories, Offices, Shops and Railway Premises) Order 1989 (SI 1989 No 76)*].

Fire-certificated (or designated premises)

19.3   'Designated' premises must be fire-certificated; hence the requirements of the proposed regulations regarding assessment and emergency plans are *in addition* to, rather than in substitution for, fire certificate requirements. In this latter connection, the *Fire Precautions Act 1971* envisioned that the following categories of 'designated' premises should become fire-certificated, namely, premises

(a)   involving provision of sleeping accommodation (hotels, boarding houses);

(b)   involving provision of treatment or care (hospitals, residential care homes);

(c)   involving provision of entertainment, recreation or instruction (theatres, cinemas);

(d)   involving provision of teaching, training or research (schools, universities);

(e)   for any purpose involving access by members of the public, for payment or otherwise, (e.g. libraries, museums, swimming baths – places of public worship were added later by the *Fire Safety and Safety of Places of Sport Act 1987, s 13*);

(f)   (perhaps most importantly) involving use as a place of work.

[*Fire Precautions Act 1971, s 1(2)*].

From this general enabling provision followed the regulations on fire certification mentioned earlier (see 19.2 above).

Work premises requiring a fire certificate

19.4   Under the *Fire Precautions (Factories, Offices, Shops and Railway Premises) Order 1989 (SI 1989 No 76)* a certificate must be applied for in the following situations:

(*a*)   (i)   where more than 20 people are at work, or

          (ii)   more than 10 are at work elsewhere than on the ground floor;

(*b*)   in buildings in multiple occupation containing two or more individual factory, office, shop or railway premises, when the aggregate of people at work exceeds the same totals;

(*c*)   in factories where explosive or highly flammable materials are stored, or used in or under the premises, unless, in the opinion of the fire authority, there is no serious risk to employees.

[*Fire Precautions (Factories, Offices, Shops and Railway Premises) Order 1989 (SI 1989 No 76)*].

In light of the amendment of the *Fire Precautions Act 1971* by the *Fire Safety and Safety of Places of Sport Act 1987*, some relaxation of earlier requirements is now possible (see 19.11 below).

Transitional arrangements regarding fire certificates issued under the Factories Act 1961 and OSRPA

19.5   As regards any premises in respect of which there is already in force a certificate under the *Factories Act 1961* or *OSRPA*, the existing certificate will continue in force, even though the statutory requirement under which it was issued has been repealed. Such existing certificates:

(*a*)   are deemed to be validly issued to cover the use or uses to which those premises were put at the time; and

(*b*)   may be amended or revoked under the *Fire Precautions Act 1971*.

[*HSWA s 78(10), 8 Sch 2*].

Applications for local authority fire certificate

19.6   Where a fire certificate is required in respect of premises, that is premises which have not been granted exemption, as low risk, from certification under the *Fire Safety and Safety of Places of Sport Act 1987*, applications for a fire certificate relating to appropriate premises (see 19.4 above) must be made to the local fire authority on the correct form (see 19.7 below), obtainable from each fire authority. Plans may be required and the premises will be inspected before issue of a certificate. If the fire authority is not satisfied as to existing arrangements, it will specify the steps to be taken before a certificate is issued, and notify the occupier or owner that they will not issue a certificate until such steps are taken within the specified time. [*Fire Precautions Act 1971, s 5*]. (Hospitals, NHS trusts and private hospitals must conform to the requirements of FIRECODE. For the position of hospitals, see generally 17.35 ENFORCEMENT and 19.19 below.)

Despite the fact that the *Fire Precautions Act 1971, s 5(3)* lays a duty on a fire authority to carry out an inspection of premises in respect of which an occupier has applied for a fire certificate, it seems that if the fire authority fails to do so it cannot be sued for negligence, as this would amount to provision of 'gratuitous insurance' for damage. Nor is the fire authority under a duty to advise hoteliers not to re-open (see 19.9 and 19.47, *Hallett v Nicholson*).

Form for application for fire certificate

19.7   Applications for a fire certificate must be made on the form prescribed by the *Fire Precautions (Application for Certificate) Regulations 1989 (SI 1989 No 77)*.

FIRE PRECAUTIONS ACT 1971, s.5

APPLICATION FOR A FIRE CERTIFICATE

For Official Use Only

To the Chief Executive of the Fire Authority*

I hereby apply for a fire certificate in respect of the premises of which details are given below. I make the application as, or on behalf of, the occupier/owner of the premises.

Signature ....

Name: Mr/Mrs/Miss..
(in block capitals)

If signing on behalf of a company or some other person, state the capacity in which

signing ....

Address..

Telephone number.................................... Date.....................

To be completed by the Applicant:–
1. Postal address of the premises ....
    ....
    ....
    ....

2. Name and address of the owner of the premises

Name ....

Address ....
....
....
....

(In the case of premises in plural ownership the names and addresses of all owners should be given.)

3. Details of the premises
(If the fire certificate is to cover the use of two or more sets of premises in the same building, details of each set of premises should be given on a separate sheet.)

(a) Name of occupier ....

(and any trading name, if different) ....

....

412

(b) Use(s) to which premises put ....

(c) Floor(s) in building on which premises situated (e.g. basement(s), ground floor, first floor etc.) ....

....

(d) Number of persons employed to work in the premises ....

(e) Maximum number of persons at work or it is proposed will work in the premises at any one time (including employees, self-employed persons and trainees)–

    (i) below the ground floor of the building ....

    (ii) on the ground floor of the building ....

    (iii) on the first floor of the building ....

    (iv) in the whole of the premises ....

(f) Maximum number of persons other than persons at work likely to be in the premises at any one time ....

(g) Number of persons (including staff, guests and other residents) for whom sleeping accommodation is provided in the premises–

    (i) below the ground floor of the building ....

    (ii) above the first floor of the building ....

    (iii) in the whole of the premises ....

4. If the premises consist of part only of a building, the uses to which the other parts of the building are put (on a floor by floor basis):

....

....

....

5. (a) Total number of floors (excluding basements) in the building in which the premises are situated ....

    (b) Total number of basements in that building ....

6. Approximate date of construction of the premises ....

7. Nature and quantity of any explosive or highly flammable materials stored or used in or under the premises

Materials	*Maximum quantity stored*	*Method of storage*	*Maximum quantity liable to be exposed at any one time*

(Continue on a separate sheet if necessary)

8. Details of fire-fighting equipment available for use in the premises

Nature of equipment	Number Provided	Where installed	Is the equipment regularly maintained?
(a) Hosereels			Yes/No
(b) Portable fire extinguishers			Yes/No
(c) Others			Yes/No
(specify types e.g. sand/water buckets, fire blanket)			

(Continue on a separate sheet if necessary)

[*Reg 2, Sch*].

Who should apply?

19.8   Application should normally be made by the occupier in the case of factories, offices and shops. In the following cases it must be made by the owner or owners:

(*a*)   premises consisting of part of a building, all parts of which are owned by the same person (i.e. multi-occupancy/single ownership situations);

(*b*)   premises consisting of part of a building, the different parts being owned by different persons (i.e. multi-occupancy/plural ownership situations).

[*Fire Precautions Act 1971, s 5, 2 Sch*].

Categories of fire risk premises

19.9   Where there is in the opinion of the fire authority a serious risk to persons from fire on premises, unless steps are taken to minimise that risk, and the fire authority thinks that a particular use of premises should be either prohibited or restricted, it may apply to the court for an order prohibiting or restricting that use of premises until remedial steps are taken. [*Fire Precautions Act 1971, s 10(2)*]. This requirement does not impose a duty on a fire authority to advise an occupier not to re-open; hence, if he re-opens and suffers loss from fire, the fire authority will not be liable (*Hallett v Nicholson*, see 19.47 below).

Premises are categorised as (*a*) high risk, (*b*) normal risk and (*c*) low risk.

(a) High risk establishments

These include:

(i)   premises providing sleeping accommodation, e.g. hotels, boarding houses, hostels, residential care premises, hospitals, training colleges;

(ii)   premises where materials are present which are easily ignitable (e.g.

414

factories, schools, shops retailing highly combustible products, warehouses, sports/leisure centres);

(iii) premises with unsatisfactory structural features (e.g. with long and complex escape routes, large expanses of flammable/smoke-producing surfaces, surfaces covered with a build-up of flammable paint, buildings with an absence of fire-resisting separation);

(iv) premises housing special occupants and/or visitors. Such premises present a substantial and not-so-obvious risk, including buildings:

(a) attracting a large number of the general public, who are unfamiliar with them, e.g. airports, railway terminals, sports stadia;

(b) where a large group of people is intermittently present, e.g. exhibitions, sales at department stores;

(c) where there is normally a large number of elderly and/or disabled people, e.g. hospitals, residential care homes, day centres;

(d) attracting a large number of children or young persons, e.g. pop concerts, leisure centres.

(b) Normal risk establishments

These comprise buildings of traditional structure with no unsatisfactory structural features, consisting of brick walls and timber floors, e.g. offices and shops not retailing combustible products. In other words, if a fire broke out, it would probably be localised.

(c) Low risk establishments

Low risk establishments consist of premises where the risk of fire spread is negligible, e.g. heavy engineering workplaces. Offices and shops are never considered 'low risk'.

Contents of a fire certificate

19.10 A fire certificate specifies:

(a) the particular use or uses of premises which it covers;

(b) the means of escape in the case of fire (as per plan);

(c) the means for securing that the means of escape can be safely and effectively used at all relevant times (e.g. direction signs/emergency lighting/fire or smoke stop doors);

(d) the means for fighting fire for use by persons in the building;

(e) the means for giving warnings in the case of fire;

(f) in the case of any factory, particulars as to any explosives or highly flammable materials stored or used on the premises.

[*Fire Precautions Act 1971, s 6(1)*].

In addition, a fire certificate may require:

(i) maintenance of the means of escape and their freedom from obstruction;

(ii) maintenance of other fire precautions set out in the certificate;

415

(iii)   training of employees on the premises as to what to do in the event of fire and keeping of suitable records of such training;

(iv)   limitation of number of persons who at any one time may be on the premises;

(v)   any other relevant fire precautions.

[*Fire Precautions Act 1971, s 6(2)*].

Waiver of certification

19.11   Under the insertions in the *Fire Safety and Safety of Places of Sport Act 1987*, a fire authority can grant exemption from certification requirements in the case of 'designated use' premises. [*Fire Precautions Act 1971, s 1(3A)*]. The powers to grant exemption are given to the local fire authority by the amended *Fire Precautions Act 1971, s 5A*. Exemption can be granted, either on application for a fire certificate, or at any time during the currency of a fire certificate. Fire certificates are not necessary, in the case of factory, office, shop and railway premises, where either

(a)   a fire authority has granted exemption (under *Sec 5A* of the *Fire Precautions Act 1971* (as amended)) in the case of 'low-risk' premises, or

(b)   there are fewer than

(i)   20 employees in buildings containing two or more factory and/or office premises at any one time, or

(ii)   10 employees in buildings containing two or more factory and/or office premises at any one time, elsewhere than on the ground floor.

(1989 Code of Practice for fire precautions in factories, offices, shops and railway premises not required to have a fire certificate, operational as from 1 April 1989.)

It is not necessary formally to apply for exemption. [*Fire Precautions Act 1971 (as amended), s 5A(2)*]. Normally, however, exemption would not be granted unless the fire authority had first carried out an inspection within the previous twelve months. Hence, if exemption is granted on application for a fire certificate, the grant disposes of the application; alternatively, if the grant is made during the currency of a fire certificate, the certificate ceases to have effect. Any exemption certificate must specify the greatest number of persons who can safely be in the premises at any one time. Such exemptions can be withdrawn by the fire authority without an inspection/inquiry as to the degree of seriousness of risk from fire to persons on the premises etc., in which case notice of withdrawal must be given.

Change of conditions affecting premises for which exemption is granted

19.12   If, while an exemption is in force an occupier proposes to carry out material changes in the premises, the occupier must inform the fire authority of the proposed changes. Not to do so is to commit an offence. [*Sec 8A(1)*]. This applies where it is proposed:

(a)   to make an extension of, or structural alteration to the premises which would affect the means of escape from the premises; or

(b)   to make an alteration in the internal arrangement of the premises, or in the furniture or equipment, which would affect the means of escape from the premises; or

(c)   to keep explosive or highly flammable materials under, in or on the premises, in a quantity or aggregate quantity greater than the prescribed maximum; or (*d*)   (where an exemption grant depends on a specified number of persons being on the premises) to make use of the premises which involves there being a greater number of persons on the premises.

Offences/penalties

19.13   Any person found guilty of any of these offences is liable:

(*a*)   on summary conviction to a maximum fine of £5,000 (see 17.29 ENFORCE-MENT);

(*b*)   on conviction on indictment, to an indefinite fine or imprisonment for up to two years (or both).

[*Sec 8A(3)*].

Duty to provide/maintain means of escape – exempted premises

19.14   Premises which are exempt from fire certification must be provided with:

(*a*)   means of escape in the case of fire; and

(*b*)   means of fighting fire;

as may reasonably be required by the fire authority. [*Sec 9A(1)*].

Breach of this duty carries with it a maximum fine of £5,000. However, it is important to note that there is no breach of duty to provide means of escape/fire-fighting equipment where the fire authority has served an *improvement notice* in respect of the premises (see 19.16 below). Moreover, it is anticipated that codes of practice relating to means of escape and fire-fighting methods and equipment, which are not themselves legally enforceable, will be issued. This means that an occupier who failed to follow a provision of a code of practice would have non-compliance taken into account under proceedings for breach of the Act. Compliance with such codes of practice will be admissible as a defence.

Definition of 'escape'

19.15   In relation to premises 'escape' means 'escape from them to some place of safety beyond the building, which constitutes or comprises the premises, and any area enclosed by it or within it; accordingly, conditions or requirements can be imposed as respects any place or thing by means of which a person escapes from premises to a place of safety'. [*Sec 5(5) as amended by FSSPSA 1987, s 4(2)*].

Improvement notices

19.16   Use of improvement notices, which have proved effective in general health and safety law for upgrading standards of health and safety at the workplace, has been duplicated in fire precautions law. Thus, where a fire authority is of the opinion that the duty to provide:

(*a*)   means of escape; and

(*b*)   means of fire-fighting;

has been breached, they can serve on the occupier an improvement notice, specifying, particularly by reference to a code of practice (see 19.14 above), what measures are necessary to remedy the breach and requiring the occupier to carry out this remedial work within three weeks, or alternatively appeal. [*Sec 9D*]. Service of such notice need not be recorded in a public register (see further 17.22 ENFORCEMENT).

Relevance of Building Regulations

19.17   Where premises are those to which, during erection, the *Building Regulations 1991* impose requirements as to means of escape in case of fire, and in consequence plans were deposited with the local authority, the fire authority cannot serve an improvement notice requiring structural or other alterations, unless the fire authority is satisfied that the means of escape in case of fire are inadequate, by reason of matters/circumstances of which particulars were not required by the *Building Regulations*. [*Sec 9D(3)*].

More particularly, the following requirements are specified in respect of new premises:

(1)   The building must be designed/constructed so that there are *means of escape* in case of fire, to a place of safety outside.

Internal fire spread

(2)   To inhibit internal fire spread, internal linings must:

(*a*)   resist flame spread over surfaces;

(*b*)   if ignited, have a reasonable rate of heat release.

(3)   The building must be designed and constructed so that, in the event of fire, its stability will be maintained for a reasonable period; and a common wall should be able to resist fire spread between the buildings.

(4)   The building must be designed and constructed so that unseen fire/smoke spread within concealed spaces in its fabric and structure, is inhibited.

External fire spread

(5)   External walls must be able to resist fire spread over walls and from one building to another.

(6)   A roof should be able to resist fire spread over the roof and from one building to another.

Finally:

(7)   The building must be designed and constructed to provide facilities to firefighters and enable fire appliances to gain access.

[*Building Regulations 1991, 1 Sch*].

Appeals against improvement notices

19.18   An appeal must be lodged against an improvement notice within 21 days from the date of service. Moreover, unlike prohibition notices, the effect of an appeal is to suspend operation of the improvement notice. Presumably, a ground of appeal would be that occupiers of 'low risk' premises have achieved satisfactory fire safety standards by means other than those specified in a code of practice.

If the appeal fails, the occupier must carry out the remedial work specified in the notice. Failure to do so carries with it:

(*a*)   on summary conviction a maximum fine of £5,000;

(*b*)   on conviction on indictment, an indefinite fine or imprisonment for up to two years (or both).

[*Secs 9E, 9F*].

Premises involving serious risk of injury to persons – prohibition notices

19.19   In places of work generally health and safety inspectors can serve prohibition notices requiring a hazardous activity to cease in cases where there is thought to be a serious risk of personal injury. Now, in the case of fire hazards where there is thought to be a serious risk of injury to persons from fire, the fire authority is in a similar way empowered to serve on the occupier a prohibition notice, requiring the occupier to carry out certain remedial work or else have the premises closed down. The original *Sec 10* of the *Fire Precautions Act 1971* is replaced by a new *Sec 10*, empowering fire authorities to issue prohibition notices. This replacement section applies to the following premises, in respect of which prohibition notices can be served, i.e. premises:

(*a*)   providing sleeping accommodation;

(*b*)   providing treatment/care;

(*c*)   for the purposes of entertainment, recreation or instruction, or for a club, society or association;

(*d*)   for teaching, training or research;

(*e*)   providing access to members of the public, whether for payment or otherwise;

(*f*)   places of work.

(This includes hospitals, factories and places of public worship, but not private dwellings. [*Fire Safety and Safety of Places of Sport Act 1987, s 13*]. Thus, a fire authority could restrict/prohibit the use of any part of a hospital, factory or place of religious worship, presenting a serious fire risk to persons – premises which are also subject to the *Building Act 1984* and *Building Regulations 1991* (see 18.12 FACTORIES AND WORKPLACES). In particular, after consultation with the fire authority, if a local authority is not satisfied with the means of escape in case of fire, it can serve a notice requiring the owner to carry out remedial work in residential premises of all kinds, including inns, hotels and nursing homes and certain commercial premises with sleeping accommodation above them, whether a fire certificate is in force or not. [*Building Act 1984, s 72*].)

The fire authority is most likely to serve prohibition notices in cases where it considers that means of escape are inadequate or could be improved. As with prohibition notices served generally in respect of workplaces, it can be immediate or deferred. Occupiers must lodge an appeal within 21 days; moreover, the appeal does not, as with improvement notices (above), suspend operation of the notice which remains in force.

Entry of such notices must appear in a public register. [*Environment and Safety Information Act 1988, ss 1, 3 and Sch*].

Offences/penalties

19.20   A person found guilty of contravening a prohibition notice is liable to:

(*a*)   a maximum fine of £5,000 on summary conviction; and (*b*)   on conviction on indictment, an indefinite fine or up to two years' imprisonment (or both).

[*Fire Safety and Safety of Places of Sport Act 1987, s 10B(3)*].

It is, however, a defence that the person did not know *and* had no reason to believe that the prohibition notice had been served. [*Fire Precautions Act 1971, s 10B(2) (as amended)*].

Civil liability/actionability

19.21   Any person suffering injury/damage as a result of breach of or failure to comply with the provisions of the *Fire Precautions Act 1971*, must in most cases prove negligence at common law if he wishes to secure compensation. There is an action for breach of statutory duty in the case of *Sec 9A* (duty as to means of escape and for fighting fire) but otherwise the Act excludes civil proceedings. The regulations made under the Act also exclude civil proceedings unless they provide otherwise. [*Fire Precautions Act 1971, s 27A (as amended)*]. This means that the decision in *Hallett v Nicholson* (19.47 below), which was concerned with fire certificate requirements, still stands.

Ultra-hazardous premises – 'special premises'

19.22   It was the view of the Robens Committee that general fire precautions law, e.g. fire certificates, means of escape etc., should be the responsibility of the fire authority, and that premises containing hazardous materials, particularly chemicals and processes, should be policed by the HSE. This view was translated into law by the *Fire Certificates (Special Premises) Regulations 1976 (SI 1976 No 2003)*. Here a fire certificate must be obtained from the relevant HSE inspectorate. This applies even if only a small number of persons is employed there. Exemption from this requirement may be granted where the regulations are inappropriate or not reasonably practicable of implementation.

When a certificate has been issued by the HSE the occupier of those premises must post a notice in those premises, stating:

(*a*)   that the certificate has been issued; and

(*b*)   the places where it (or a copy) can be inspected; and

(*c*)   the date of the posting of the notice.

[*Fire Certificates (Special Premises) Regulations 1976, Reg 5(5)(6)*].

These conditions do not override those applicable to a licence for the storage of petroleum spirit under the *Petroleum Spirit (Consolidation) Act 1928*.

'Special premises' for which a fire certificate is required from the HSE

19.23   The 'special premises' for which a fire certificate is required from the HSE are set out for reference in Table 16 below.

Table 16

'Special premises' for which a fire certificate is required by HSE

[*Special Premises Regulations, 1 Schedule Part I*].

1 Any premises at which are carried on any manufacturing processes in which the total quantity of any highly flammable liquid under pressure greater than atmospheric pressure and above its boiling point at atmospheric pressure may exceed 50 tonnes.

2 Any premises at which is carried on the manufacturing of expanded cellular plastics and at which the quantities manufactured are normally of, or in excess of, 50 tonnes per week.

3 Any premises at which there is stored, or there are facilities provided for the storage of, liquefied petroleum gas in quantities of, or in excess of, 100 tonnes except where the liquefied petroleum gas is kept for use at the premises either as a fuel, or for the production of an atmosphere for the heat-treatment of metals.

4 Any premises at which there is stored, or there are facilities provided for the storage of, liquefied natural gas in quantities of, or in excess of, 100 tonnes except where the liquefied natural gas is kept solely for use at the premises as a fuel.

5 Any premises at which there is stored, or there are facilities provided for the storage of, any liquefied flammable gas consisting predominantly of methyl acetylene in quantities of, or in excess of, 100 tonnes except where the liquefied flammable gas is kept solely for use at the premises as a fuel.

6 Any premises at which oxygen is manufactured and at which there are stored, or there are facilities provided for the storage of, quantities of liquid oxygen of, or in excess of, 135 tonnes.

7 Any premises at which there are stored, or there are facilities provided for the storage of, quantities of chlorine of, or in excess of, 50 tonnes except when the chlorine is kept solely for the purpose of water purification.

8 Any premises at which artificial fertilizers are manufactured and at which there are stored, or there are facilities provided for the storage of, quantities of ammonia of, or in excess of, 250 tonnes.

9 Any premises at which there are in process, manufacture, use or storage at any one time, or there are facilities provided for such processing, manufacture, use or storage of, quantities of any of the materials listed below in, or in excess of, the quantities specified —

Phosgene	5 tonnes
Ethylene oxide	20 tonnes
Carbon disulphide	50 tonnes
Acrylonitrile	50 tonnes
Hydrogen cyanide	50 tonnes
Ethylene	100 tonnes
Propylene	100 tonnes
Any highly flammable liquid not otherwise specified	4,000 tonnes

10 Explosives, factories or magazines which are required to be licensed under the Explosives Act 1875.

11 Any building on the surface at any mine within the meaning of the Mines and Quarries Act 1954.

12 Any premises in which there is comprised —
   (*a*) any undertaking on a site for which a licence is required in accordance with section 1 of the Nuclear Installations Act 1965 or for which a permit is required in accordance with section 2 of that Act; or
   (*b*) any undertaking which would, except for the fact that it is carried on by the United Kingdom Atomic Energy Authority, or by, or on behalf of, the Crown, be required to have a licence or permit in accordance with the provisions mentioned in sub-paragraph (*a*) above.

13 Any premises containing any machine or apparatus in which charged particles can be accelerated by the equivalent of a voltage of not less than 50 megavolts except where the premises are used as a hospital.

14 Premises to which Regulation 26 of the Ionising Radiations Regulations 1985 (SI 1985 No 1333) applies.

15 Any building, or part of a building, which either —
   (*a*) is constructed for temporary occupation for the purposes of building operations or works of engineering construction; or
   (*b*) is in existence at the first commencement there of any further such operations or works
   and which is used for any process of work ancillary to any such operations or works (but see 19.24 below).

Temporary buildings used for building operations or construction work – exempted

19.24 By virtue of the *Special Premises Regulations 1976, 1 Sch 15* a fire certificate is required in the case of buildings constructed for temporary occupation for the purposes of building operations or works of engineering construction (see Chapter 7 'Construction and Building Operations'), and buildings already in existence for such purposes when such operations or works begin. An exemption is available, however, if:

(*a*) fewer than 20 persons are employed at any one time, or fewer than 10 elsewhere than on the ground floor; and

(*b*) the nine conditions set out in *1 Sch Pt II* are satisfied.

[*Special Premises Regulations, Reg 3, 1 Sch 15*].

There must, however, be provided suitable means of escape in case of fire, adequate fire-fighting equipment, exit doorways that can be easily and immediately opened from inside, unobstructed passageways as well as distinctive and conspicuous marking of fire exits.

Other dangerous processes

19.25 Certain particularly dangerous processes are controlled, as far as fire prevention measures are concerned, by specific regulations. These are:

(*a*) the *Celluloid (Manufacture, etc.) Regulations 1921* – applying to the manufacture, manipulation and storage of celluloid and the disposal of celluloid waste;

(b)   the *Manufacture of Cinematograph Film Regulations 1928* – applicable to the manufacture, repair, manipulation or use of cinematograph film;

(c)   the *Cinematograph Film Stripping Regulations 1939* – applicable to the stripping, drying or storing of cinematograph film;

(d)   the *Highly Flammable Liquids and Liquefied Petroleum Gases Regulations 1972* – applicable to premises containing highly flammable liquids and liquefied petroleum gases (see further Chapter 24 'Highly Flammable Liquids');

(e)   the *Magnesium (Grinding of Castings and Other Articles) Special Regulations 1946* – prohibition on smoking, open lights and fires;

(f)   the *Factories (Testing of Aircraft Engines & Accessories) Special Regulations 1952* – applicable to the leakage or escape of petroleum spirit;

(g)   the *Electricity at Work Regulations 1989, Reg 6(d)* – electrical equipment which may reasonably foreseeably be exposed to any flammable or explosive substance, must be constructed or protected so as to prevent danger from exposure;

(h)   the *Dangerous Substances in Harbour Areas Regulations 1987* – applicable to risks of fire and explosion in harbour areas. A fire certificate is not required for these premises.

[Special Premises Regulations, Reg 3A, as amended].

Application for fire certificate for 'special premises'

19.26   In order to obtain a fire certificate for 'special premises' (see 19.23 above for definition), the occupier or owner (see 19.8 above) must apply to the relevant HSE inspectorate, e.g. the factory inspectorate in respect of factory premises. No form is prescribed but certain particulars must be provided, including:

(a)   the address and description of the premises;

(b)   the nature of the processes carried on or to be carried on there;

(c)   nature and approximate quantities of any explosive or highly flammable substance kept or to be kept on the premises;

(d)   the maximum number of persons likely to be present on the premises;

(e)   the name and address of the occupier.

Plans may be required to be deposited and premises will be inspected, and the occupier may well have to make improvements to the fire precautions before a certificate is issued. *[Special Premises Regulations, Reg 4]*.

Appeals relating to the issue of a fire certificate

19.27   An appeal may be made to the magistrates' court by an applicant for a fire certificate in relation to:

(a)   a requirement specified by a fire authority or the HSE; or

(b)   the fire authority or the HSE refusing to issue a certificate; or

(c)   the contents of a certificate.

An appeal must be lodged within 21 days of the date of notice from the fire authority. *[Special Premises Regulations, Reg 12]*.

Duty to keep fire certificate on the premises

19.28   Every fire certificate must be kept on the premises to which it relates (and preferably displayed), as long as it is in force. [*Fire Precautions Act 1971, s 6(8)*]. Failure to comply with this subsection is an offence. [*Fire Precautions Act 1971, s 7(6)*].

Notification of alteration to premises

19.29   Any proposed structural alterations or material internal alteration to premises for which a fire certificate has been issued, must first be notified to the local fire authority or inspectorate (as appropriate). Similarly, any proposed material alteration to equipment in the premises, or furniture, must be so notified. Not to do so is to commit an offence (see 19.30 below). The premises may be inspected by staff from the relevant enforcement agency at any reasonable time while the certificate is in force. [*Fire Precautions Act 1971, s 8(2)*].

Offences and penalties

Offences

19.30   A person (i.e. the occupier or, in some cases, the owner of the premises, see 19.8 above) who does not have a valid fire certificate, or who continues to use premises requiring a fire certificate when the certificate has been refused or cancelled, commits an offence. [*Fire Precautions Act 1971, s 7(1)*]. An offence is also committed if the relevant fire authority or inspectorate is not informed of a proposed structural or material alteration (see 19.12 above) before it is undertaken. [*Fire Precautions Act 1971, s 8*]. Other offences include obstruction of an inspector carrying out his duties and failing to keep a fire certificate on the premises.

Penalties

19.31   A person found guilty of an offence under the *Fire Precautions Act 1971, s 7(1)* is liable to:

(*a*)   a fine not exceeding £5,000 (on summary conviction); or

(*b*)   an unlimited fine or imprisonment for not more than two years, *or both* (on indictment).

[*Fire Precautions Act 1971, s 7(1) as amended by the Criminal Justice Act 1991, s 17(1)*].

Refusal of magistrates' licence

19.32   Some premises, other than work premises, which must have a current licence in order to operate, will have a licence refused or not renewed by the local magistrates if the local fire authority is not satisfied as to the fire precautions necessary in the premises. The premises mainly are:

Cinemas

19.33   Safety in cinemas is controlled by the *Cinematograph (Safety) Regulations 1955 (SI 1955 No 1129)* (as subsequently amended). Cinemas must be provided with:

(*a*)   adequate, clearly marked exits, so placed as to afford safe means of exit;

(*b*)   doors which are easily and fully openable outwards;

(*c*)   passages and stairways kept free from obstruction

[*Reg 2*];

(*d*)   suitable and properly maintained fire appliances;

(*e*)   proper instruction of licensee and staff on fire precautions;

(*f*)   treatment of curtains so that they will not readily catch fire;

(*g*)   use of non-inflammable substances for cleaning film or projectors

[*Reg 5*];

(*h*)   prohibition on smoking in certain parts of the premises [*Reg 6*];

(*j*)   appropriate siting of heating appliances [*Reg 24*].

Theatres

19.34   Under *Sec 12(1)* of the *Theatres Act 1968* premises used for the public performance of a play must be licensed. The conditions for obtaining or having renewed a licence include compliance with rules relating to safety of persons in the theatre, and particularly, staff fire drills, provision of fire-fighting equipment, maintenance of a safety curtain and communication with the fire service; gangways and seating correctly arranged and free from obstruction, doors and exits, marking and method of opening, lighting arrangements; also scenery and draperies must be non-inflammable and there are controls over smoking and overcrowding.

Gaming houses (casinos, bingo halls etc.)

19.35   Issue or retention of a licence to operate depends *inter alia* on compliance with fire requirements. [*Gaming Act 1968*].

Premises for music, dancing etc.

19.36   Issue or retention of a licence to operate premises for public music or entertainment depends on compliance with the fire requirements. [*Local Government (Miscellaneous Provisions) Act 1982, 1 Sch*].

Similarly, in the case of premises used for private music/dancing, e.g. dancing schools, there must be compliance with the fire requirements. [*Private Places of Entertainment (Licensing) Act 1967*].

Schools

19.37   In the case of local authority controlled schools, including special schools, the 'health and safety of their occupants, and in particular, their safe escape in the event of fire, must be reasonably assured', with particular reference to the design, construction, limitation of surface flame spread and fire resistance of structure and materials therein. [*Standards for School Premises Regulations 1972 (SI 1972 No 2051)*].

Children's and community homes

19.38   Both these local authority controlled establishments must carry out fire drills and practices and, in addition, consult with the fire authorities. [*Children's Homes Regulations 1991 (SI 1991 No 1506); Community Homes Regulations 1972 (SI 1972 No 319)*].

Residential and nursing homes

19.39   Similar requirements apply in the case of:

(a)   residential homes [*National Assistance (Conduct of Homes) Regulations 1962 (SI 1962 No 2000)*]; and

(b)   nursing homes [*Nursing Homes and Mental Nursing Homes Regulations 1981 (SI 1981 No 932) as amended*].

In particular, satisfactory arrangements must be made for the evacuation of patients and staff in the event of fire.

Crown premises

19.40   As with other health and safety duties and regulations, generally speaking, statutory fire duties and fire regulations apply to the Crown [*Fire Precautions Act 1971, s 40*] but, owing to Crown immunity in law – itself referable to the fiction that the king can do no wrong – proceedings cannot be enforced against the Crown (see further 17.35 ENFORCEMENT). This has the effect that Crown premises, that is, government buildings such as the Treasury and the Foreign Office as well as royal palaces, are required to be fire-certificated but, if they fail to apply for certification, they cannot, like other occupiers, be prosecuted. Secondly, failure to acquire fire-certificate status could prejudice the safety of firemen called upon to combat fires in Crown premises (see further 19.45 below). Moreover, fire certificates are not required in (a) prisons, (b) special hospitals for the mentally incapacitated and (c) premises occupied exclusively by the armed forces. [*Fire Precautions Act 1971, s 40(2)*].

Civil liability at common law and under the Fires Prevention (Metropolis) Act 1774 for fire damage

19.41   Civil liability, in respect of fire damage, can arise in one of several ways: an occupier of premises from which fire escapes and does damage can be liable to adjoining occupiers and/or firemen, or even members of the public injured or killed whilst fighting the fire on the premises; conversely, the occupier of premises may be injured as a consequence of damage negligently caused to his property by the fire authority whilst fighting a fire on his premises. Again, a fireman may be injured whilst fighting a fire owing to the negligence of his superior officers in failing to ascertain the dangerous state of the premises where the fire is to be fought, or a member of the public, assisting the fire authority to fight a fire on his premises, because he has not been given suitable equipment or proper fire-fighting instructions or protective clothing, may be injured. In addition, a fireman or third party, whether pedestrian or motorist, may be injured as a result of a fire appliance being driven dangerously on the way to a fire or as a result of crossing adverse traffic lights. All these situations are potential 'candidates' for the imposition of civil liability. Moreover, liability for damage done by fire spread is not necessarily confined to negligence; such liability can be strict if fire spread is within the rule in *Rylands v Fletcher* (see 19.44 below). In order to ensure therefore that occupiers and others involved may minimise their liability, insurance cover, though not compulsory, is highly desirable. The basic principles relating to fire cover are considered below (see 19.49 below).

Liability of occupier

19.42   An occupier of premises where fire breaks out can be liable to (a) lawful visitors to the premises injured by the fire or falling debris (and is also liable to unlawful visitors, i.e. trespassers, as the principle of 'common humanity', enunciated in

Herrington v British Railways Board applies, see Chapter 32 'Occupiers' Liability'); (*b*) firemen injured during fire-fighting operations; and (*c*) adjoining occupiers.

Firemen

19.43   The main principles established by case law are as follows:

(*a*)   The occupier owes a duty to a fireman not to expose him to unexpected hazards (i.e. hazards over and above that of fire – *Hartley v British Railways Board, The Times, 2 February 1981* where a fireman was injured whilst searching the roof space of the respondent's premises which had caught fire. He had been told that the station building was occupied when in fact it was not. The respondents were held liable for the confusion as to whether the station was occupied or not, the confusion having led to the hazardous situation causing injury).

(*b*)   The occupier is liable to a fireman for any hazard for which he is responsible, if the hazard is over and above the normal fire-fighting hazard (*Hartley v Mayoh [1953] 2 AER 525* where a fireman was killed whilst fighting a fire at a pickle manufacturing factory. The attempt to cut off electricity supply failed, owing to the novel construction of the switches, with the result that unknown to him power continued to flow. It was held that the occupier was liable because he should have known how the switches worked; the fact that he did not constituted an additional hazard for the fireman).

(*c*)   Decisions and conduct resulting from them which, in other circumstances, could well be regarded as negligent, may well not be negligent in an emergency (*Bull v London County Council, The Times, 29 January 1953* where an experienced fireman fell from the extension ladder at the height of a fire and was seriously injured. It was held that climbing the extension ladder in a fire emergency was not negligence on the part of the fireman).

(*d*)   More recently, occupiers, in the form of householders, were held liable to a fireman who was injured, on normal grounds of foreseeability and causation. The respondent, when burning off paint on his house, negligently set fire to roof timbers. The appellant, a fireman, sprayed water on the fire and the resulting steam caused him injuries. It was held that the appellant was so closely and directly affected by the respondent's act that the respondent ought reasonably to have had him in contemplation when directing his mind to the acts or omissions in question, namely, using the blowlamp without taking care to avoid setting the rafters alight (*Ogwo v Taylor [1987] 3 AER 961*). This includes the reasonably foreseeable *consequences* of an occupier's negligence, e.g. post-traumatic stress (*Hale v London Underground Ltd, The Times, 5 November 1992* concerning £147,000 damages awarded to a fireman injured going to the rescue of another fireman at the King's Cross fire in 1987).

Adjoining occupier

19.44   Originally liability for fire spread causing damage to adjoining property was strict (and in certain limited circumstances, still is (see below *Rylands v Fletcher*)). Current law, however, is traceable back to the *Fires Prevention (Metropolis) Act 1774, s 86* which provides that unless an occupier has been negligent he will not be liable for damage to adjoining property caused by fire spread. This extends to failure on the part of an occupier to take effective measures to prevent fire spread once a fire has started (*Goldman v Hargrave [1967] 1 AC 645*).

If, however, fire spreads and does damage in circumstances within the rule in *Rylands v Fletcher (1868) LR 3 HL 330*, liability is strict. The point here is that fire in itself is not regarded as ultra-hazardous and hence not governed by strict liability criteria; if however fire is caused by some activity/operation on land, or container capable of self-propulsion or explosion (e.g. petrol in storage), and it escapes and causes injury and/or damage to adjoining property, there will be liability irrespective of negligence. The main purpose of the rule in *Rylands v Fletcher* is to ensure that those putting land to ultra-hazardous use, e.g. electrical supply, water storage in bulk, petrol storage, keep the danger in 'at their peril'. Thus, 'Where a person for his own purposes brings and keeps on land in his occupation anything likely to do mischief if it escapes, (he) must keep it in at his peril, and if he fails to do so, he is liable for all damage naturally accruing from the escape' (Blackburn J). This applies to fire (*Emanuel v Greater London Council (1970) 114 SJ 653* where a contractor, who was an employee of the Ministry of Public Building and Works, removed prefabricated bungalows from the council's land. He then lit a fire and the sparks spread to the plaintiff's land, where buildings and products belonging to the plaintiff were damaged. It was held that, although the council had not been negligent, they were still liable). In fairness, however, it should be emphasised that the rule in *Rylands v Fletcher* has been interpreted restrictively. Thus, 'I should hesitate to hold that in these days and in an industrial community it was a non-natural use of land to build a factory on it and conduct there the manufacture of explosives' (per Lord Macmillan in *Read v J Lyons & Co Ltd [1947] AC 156*). Indeed, given the dominance of planning decisions in land development over the past forty years, presumptively, if planning permission has been obtained by an operator for a particular use(s) of land (as will be normal), it is impossible to say that use of said land is 'non-natural'; hence in most cases potentially dangerous activities are outside the scope of the rule of strict liability.

Liability of fire authority

Injury to firemen

19.45   Just as any other employer, a fire authority can be vicariously liable when a fireman is injured whilst being driven negligently to a fire; or when he suffers injuries fighting a fire, though in practice such cases are likely to be rare. Moreover, as an employer a fire authority has duties to its employees under *HSWA*, and particularly under *Sec 2*, to provide a safe system of work and adequate information/training in connection with fire-fighting. Thus, if a fire authority sent an insufficient number of men to fight a large fire this could be regarded as a defective system of work for the purposes of *HSWA s 2(2)(a)*; similarly, where a fireman was injured or killed whilst fire-fighting and it was shown that he had received inadequate training, there might well be breach of *HSWA s 2(2)(c)*.

Of course, a fireman can only be instructed and trained in fire-fighting and its hazards within the 'state of the art'. If the hazards of a particular type of fire are not known or not documented, the fire authority would not be liable for the fireman's injury (*Biggerstaff v Glasgow Corporation (1962) (unreported)* where a huge fire broke out in a bonded warehouse containing millions of gallons of whisky. Whilst the fire was being fought an explosion ripped out the walls, killing some firemen and injuring the plaintiff, the driver of a turntable ladder. He sued his employer, the fire authority, on two grounds: (*a*) that they had not removed non-essential personnel from the immediate area of the explosion, and (*b*) that training given to fire officers to fight hazards associated with whisky vapour fires was inadequate. The action failed, principally because this type of accident was (then) unique and the true hazards of whisky vapour were not appreciated).

Injury to members of the public fighting a fire

19.46   A fire authority could be liable to other persons legitimately and foreseeably fighting a fire who are injured or killed, e.g. ambulance staff, staff on the premises where a fire breaks out or spreads to, the in-house fire brigade (if any), or the owner or occupier of premises which have caught fire and who assists in fire-fighting. In such cases the fire authority can be liable if it fails to take similar precautions as it would take in respect of its own members (*Burrough v Berkshire & Reading Joint Fire Authority (1972) (unreported)* where the plaintiff suffered head injuries whilst helping to fight a fire at his barn. He had not been provided with a protective helmet. The fire authority was held to be liable).

Injury to visitors of the occupier's premises

19.47   Where a fire causes injury or death to visitors of an occupier, e.g. a hotelier, it is doubtful whether the fire authority can be sued for negligence for breach of the *Fire Precautions Act 1971, s 5(3)* (granting of a fire certificate to premises for particular use, following inspection, see 19.4, 19.5 above) (*Hallett v Nicholson 1979 SC 1* where hoteliers were sued by children whose parents had died in a fire at the hotel. The hoteliers had applied for a certificate under *FPA 1971, s 1* and they argued that the fire authority was under a duty under *Sec 5(3)* to inspect the hotel; and, in addition, that the fire authority had failed to advise the hotelier not to re-open, under *Sec 10(2)*. It was held that the fire authority was not liable because (*a*) acts/omissions on the part of a statutory authority in the proper exercise of its statutory duties were not actionable (but see now 12.29 EMISSIONS INTO THE ATMOSPHERE); (*b*) the failure of the fire authority to advise the hoteliers not to re-open under *Sec 10(2)* was not obligatory but discretionary; (*c*) the *Fire Precautions Act 1971* did not empower, even less impose, a duty on a fire authority to recommend interim measures; and (*d*) in the absence of a request on the part of the hoteliers for advice on interim measures, the fire authority was under no duty to give such advice). Moreover, a fire authority was not liable when a fireman deliberately drove very slowly during an industrial dispute and the plaintiff's premises were destroyed by a fire. Their manner of driving was not merely a wrongful and unauthorised mode of doing an act authorised by their employers, but was so unconnected with what they were authorised to do that it was not a mode of performing an authorised act at all (*General Engineering Services v Kingston & Saint Andrew Corporation [1988] 3 AER 867*).

Injury to third party road user, whilst speeding to scene of fire

19.48   An innocent third party road user is entitled to assume that a fire engine will stop at adverse traffic signals, and so, if he suffered injury or death as a result of their not stopping, the fire authority would be liable (*Ward v London County Council [1938] 2 AER 341*). The contrary is the position where, however, a fire engine stops and proceeds with caution at adverse traffic signals (*Buckoke v Greater London Council [1971] Ch 655* where the chief London Fire Brigade officer issued an order that adverse traffic lights could and should be passed through with caution; this order laid the onus of avoiding accidents on the driver of the fire engine. Some firemen went to court to test the order's legality. It was held by the Court of Appeal that the order was lawful).

Fire insurance

19.49   There is no statutory definition of fire, as there is of certain other insurable risks, e.g. theft, burglary. What is insured is loss or damage caused by fire. Hence, fire must be the proximate cause of loss/damage. This is not always easy to determine where there are several vying causes. For example, a shopkeeper insured his plateglass against loss/damage arising from any cause except fire. Fire broke out in a neighbour's property, in consequence of which a mob gathered. The mob rioted and broke the plateglass. It was held that the riot not the fire was the cause of the loss and so the insured was entitled to recover (*Marsden v City and County Insurance (1865) LR 1 CP 232*).

Where the fire insured against is imminent, loss caused to property by action taken to avert the risk, is covered. A cargo of cork insured against loss by fire and stored on a pier, was thrown into the sea in order to prevent an existing fire spreading. It was held that the damage by water loss was covered, since the dominant (or proximate) cause of the cork loss was the fire, itself an insured peril (*Symington v Union Insurance of Canton (1928) 97 LJKB 646*).

In order for there to be a fire, actual ignition is necessary. In *Austin v Drewe (1816) 6 Taunt 436*, stock in a sugar refinery was insured against loss by fire. A flue went up through all the floors of the refinery from a stove situated on the ground floor. There was a register, which was closed at night to retain heat, but opened when a fresh fire was lit in the morning. One morning an employee of the insured forgot to open the register. Intense heat in the flue damaged sugar on the top floor. There were smoke and sparks but the sugar did not ignite. It was held that there was no loss by fire.

In order to qualify for compensation for loss/damage caused by fire:

(*a*)   there must be actual ignition;

(*b*)   the outbreak of fire (from the insured's point of view) was accidental; and

(*c*)   something must be on fire which should not be on fire. Thus, a fire lit for a particular purpose would not qualify, e.g. fire to burn rubbish. But if such fire escaped, doing damage, the insurer would be liable (*Upjohn v Hitchens [1918] 2 KB 18*).

Fire prevention and control

Elements of fire

19.50   There are three prerequisites for fire:

(*a*)   oxygen;

(*b*)   fuel (or combustible substance);

(*c*)   source of energy;

the so-called 'fire triangle'.

Fire is a mixture in gaseous form of a combustible substance and oxygen, given sufficient energy to start a fire. Once a fire is under way, energy output guarantees a continuous source of sustainable energy, with excess taking the form of sensible heat. Fire takes place in a gaseous state, though it may be convenient to label fires as solids (e.g. wood), liquid (e.g. petrol) and gas (e.g. gas flame). In the former two cases, close inspection reveals that the flame burns a little way away from the wood or liquid.

This part of the chapter considers generally the practical aspects of fire prevention and control. It should be borne in mind that *special risks* involving flammable or toxic liquids, metal fires or other hazards should be separately evaluated for loss prevention and as regards control techniques. (For precautions against fire hazards from flammable liquids, see the *Highly Flammable Liquids and Liquefied Petroleum Gases Regulations 1972 (SI 1972 No 917)*, considered in Chapter 24 'Highly Flammable Liquids'.)

It is the responsibility of management to consider how safe is safe: that is, to balance the costs of improvement against the financial consequences of fire. Considerable improvement can often be made immediately at little or no cost. Other recommendations which may require a financial appraisal must be related to loss effect values. In certain cases, however, due to high loss effect, special protection may be needed almost regardless of cost.

Modern developments in fire prevention and protection can now provide a solution to most risk management problems within economic acceptability. It must be pointed out, however, that it is a waste of time and money installing protective equipment unless it is designed to be functional and the purpose of such equipment is understood and accepted by all personnel. The reasons for providing such equipment should, therefore, be fully covered in any fire training course. Fire routines should also be amended as necessary to ensure that full advantage is taken of any new measures implemented.

Common causes of fires

19.51   The following, in no particular order of significance, are the commonest causes of fires in industrial and non-industrial premises:

(*a*)   wilful fire raising and arson;

(*b*)   careless disposal of cigarettes, matches;

(*c*)   combustible material left near to sources of heat;

(*d*)   accumulation of easily ignitable rubbish or paper;

(*e*)   inadvertence on the part of contractors, maintenance workers;

(*f*)   electrical equipment left on inadvertently when not in use;

(*g*)   misuse of portable heaters;

(*h*)   obstructing ventilation of heaters, machinery or office equipment;

(*j*)   inadequate cleaning of work areas;

(*k*)   inadequate supervision of cooking activities.

Fire classification

19.52   There are four common categories of fire which are related to the fuel involved and the method of extinction, as follows.

(*a*)   *Class A*. Fires generally involving solid organic materials, such as coal, wood, paper and natural fibres, in which the combustion takes place with the formation of glowing embers. Extinction is achieved through the application of water in jet or spray form.

(*b*)   *Class B*. Fires involving:

   (i)   liquids, which can be separated into those liquids which mix with water e.g. acetone, acetic acid and methanol; and those which do not mix with water e.g. waxes, fats, petrol and solvents; and

   (ii)   liquefiable solids e.g. animal fats, solid waxes, certain plastics.

   Foam, vaporising liquids, carbon dioxide and dry powder can be used on all these types of fire. Water spray can be used on liquids that mix with water, but not on fats, petrol, etc. In all cases, extinction is principally achieved by smothering, with a certain degree of cooling in some cases.

(c)   *Class C*. Fires involving gases or liquefied gases e.g. butane, propane. Both foam and dry chemicals can be used on small fires following spillage, preferably supported by water to cool a leaking container or spillage collector. Extinguishers used on liquid gas fires work by smothering or inhibiting air for further combustion.

(d)   *Class D*. Fires involving certain flammable metals, such as aluminium or magnesium. In this case extinction is achieved by the use of dry powders which include soda ash, dry sand, limestone and talc. Such powders have a smothering effect.

Electrical fires

19.53   This classification is no longer used. Fires involving electrical apparatus must always be tackled by first isolating the electricity supply and then by the use of carbon dioxide, vaporising liquid or dry powder.

Table 17 below classifies fires which can be controlled by portable fire appliances (see also BS 5423 and BS 6643).

Table 17

Class of fire	Description	Appropriate extinguisher
A	Solid materials, usually organic, with glowing embers	Water, foam, dry powder, vaporising liquid, CO_2
B	Liquids and liquefiable solids:	
	miscible with water e.g. acetone, methanol	Water, foam (but must be stable on miscible solvents), CO_2, dry powder
	immiscible with water e.g. petrol, benzene, fats, waxes	Foam, dry powder, CO_2, vaporising liquid

Fire extinction – active fire protection measures

19.54   Extinction of a fire is achieved by one or more of the following:

(a)   *starvation* – this is achieved through a reduction in the concentration of the fuel. It can be effected by:

(i)   removing the fuel from the fire;

(ii)   isolating the fire from the fuel source; and

(iii)   reducing the bulk or quantity of fuel present;

(b)   *smothering* – this brings about a reduction in the concentration of oxygen available to support combustion. It is achieved by preventing the inward flow of more oxygen to the fire, or by adding an inert gas to the burning mixture;

(*c*)   *cooling* – this is the most common means of fire-fighting, using water. The addition of water to a fire results in vaporisation of some of the water to steam, which means that a substantial proportion of the heat is not being returned to the fuel to maintain combustion. Eventually, insufficient heat is added to the fuel and continuous ignition ceases. Water in spray form is more efficient for this purpose as the spray droplets absorb heat more rapidly than water in the form of a jet.

Classification of risk

19.55   There are three basic categories of risk:

(*a*)   areas of high loss effect value;

(*b*)   areas of high risk;

(*c*)   areas of infrequent use.

Certain areas could be classified in all categories, and need to be considered accordingly.

Areas of high loss effect value

19.56   'Loss effect values' are related to the effect a fire would have on certain specific areas. For example, an area where essential records or documents are stored is likely to have a high loss effect value should a fire occur; essential equipment, plant or stock which, if destroyed or severely damaged by fire, might be difficult to replace or have a serious effect on production would require special consideration, and often high fire protection requirements to minimise such an effect.

High loss effect values must be determined by management; they need to be identified, considered and evaluated. A report should be produced by each departmental head, outlining areas which may require special consideration. Such a report should also include protection of essential drawings, records and other essential documents.

A typical area of high loss effect would be the telephone equipment room. The loss of this equipment could have a serious and immediate effect upon communications generally. Fire separation (to keep a fire out) is therefore considered essential, and automatic fire suppression by self-contained extinguishing units should be strongly recommended.

Protection of files

19.57   An exercise should be carried out to determine the importance of the files held and the quantity of essential documents involved. This will then help to determine the manner in which they are to be stored.

Microfilming has now reduced greatly in cost and it may be considered economical to provide a microfilm unit and small approved fireproof cabinets. With this information available, decisions should be taken which account for the financial resources of the company, the direct and indirect importance of the assets involved, and the cost of protecting them, so that the best solutions, both financial and practical, can be found.

Areas of high risk

19.58   High risk areas include areas involving the use, conveyance and storage of flammable materials, especially highly flammable liquids, where fire spread could be rapid. A high risk would also include any areas where toxic fumes may be produced or gas cylinders, etc., are in use or stored. Such areas can create problems to fire-fighters and may result in delay in dealing with a fire. These may be a hazard to life and a danger to firemen.

Electrical control/distribution rooms

19.59   Electrical control and distribution rooms are both high risk and high loss effect areas. It is difficult to eliminate completely the possibility of fire in such areas. Therefore fire separation, protection and suppression should be considered.

The modern development of computer techniques and automation requires a new look at the protection of essential panels. Fire detection is often too late and it is necessary, therefore, to consider overheat protection of components and temperature control. A minimum of two warnings of an overheat condition should be provided before a fire occurs. Simple automatic fire suppression systems should be superimposed over the thermo-control systems.

Areas of infrequent use

19.60   Areas of infrequent use may allow a fire to develop unseen for some time. When it is finally discovered fire spread can be rapid. The size of a fire must also be related to the difficulties in dealing with it, when using the equipment readily available.

Smoke travel must also be taken into account, in that it may make the actual seat of the fire difficult to discover. Compartmentation, fire detection, audible alarms and fire suppression require special consideration in all areas of infrequent use.

All areas of infrequent use should be designated 'No smoking' areas and this should be strictly enforced. 'Housekeeping' must be maintained to a high standard at all times. The audibility of the fire alarm should be specially considered when persons are working in such areas. It is possible that even a small fire left undetected for some time could produce a large volume of smoke and in a short time make means of escape difficult. Such areas must always be considered for automatic fire detection, and possibly automatic suppression.

'Fire compartmentation' – passive fire protection technology

19.61   Fire safety can be achieved through two separate routes: (*a*) active fire protection (see 19.54, 19.63); and (*b*) passive fire protection. This latter, passive fire protection, is based on building compartmentation in order to restrict/minimise fire development and resist fire spread. In this connection, fire doors can be problematical, since 'overactive' closers may encourage workers, visiting suppliers, to leave doors wedged open, particularly if heavy loads are being carried inside. This practice should be condemned because, ultimately, fire pressure can only be contained by strong door closers. Fire doors should be fitted with requisite stiffness to BS 476 Part 22 'Methods for determination of fire-resistance of non-loadbearing elements of construction', preferably with swing-free closers, so as to close the door after fire detection.

Another significant recent development in passive fire protection is fire-resistant glass. Clear glass incorporating clear intumescent interlayers can offer fire resistance of up to 90 minutes, as well as complying with insulation requirements. Unfortunately, the higher the safety rating of glass – to BS 6262 'Glazing for buildings', the more incompatible it may be with fire tolerance needs.

Fire procedures and equipment

19.62 The need for effective and easily understood fire procedures cannot be over-emphasised. It may be necessary to provide a fire procedure manual, so arranged that it can be used for overall fire defence arrangements, and sectioned for use in individual departments or for special risks.

It is essential that three separate procedures are considered:

(*a*) procedure during normal working hours;

(*b*) procedure during restricted manning on shifts;

(*c*) procedure when only security staff are on the premises.

All procedures should take into consideration absence of personnel due to sickness, leave, etc. The fire brigade should be called immediately any fire occurs, irrespective of the size of the fire. Any delay in calling the fire brigade must be added to the delay before the fire brigade's actual arrival, which will be related to the traffic conditions or the local appliances already attending another fire.

A person should be given the responsibility for ensuring that pre-planned action is carried out when a fire occurs. Large fires often result from a delayed call, which may be due not to delayed discovery but to wrong action being taken in the early stages following discovery of a fire. A pre-planned fire routine is essential for fire safety. The fire brigade, when called, should be met on arrival by a designated person available to guide them directly to the area of the fire. It is essential that all fire routines, when finalised, be made known to the fire brigade.

Fire equipment

19.63 There has been a number of cases where a person using an extinguisher has been seriously injured. Investigations have shown that either the wrong type of extinguisher was supplied or the operator had no training in the correct use of the extinguisher. The latter should not need to be over-emphasised, especially in areas of special risk, oil dipping tanks, furnace areas, highly flammable liquids, gas or cylinder fires etc.

The fire authority will be responsible for determining the correct type of extinguisher for the building, and the siting of extinguishers will be entered on the fire certificate issued under the *FPA*. The following recommendations are given in order to allow an evaluation of an existing problem and may need to be related to process risks:

(*a*) it is essential that persons be trained in the use of extinguishers, especially in areas where special risks require a specific type of extinguisher to be provided;

(*b*) any person employed to work, who is requested to deal with a fire, should be clearly instructed that at no time should that person jeopardise his own safety or the safety of others;

(*c*) persons who may be wearing overalls contaminated with oil, grease, paint or solvents should not be instructed to attack a fire. Such contaminated materials may vaporise due to heat from the fire, and ignite.

Types of fire extinguisher

19.64 The type of extinguisher provided should be suitable for the risk involved, adequately maintained and appropriate records kept of all inspections, tests etc. All

435

fire extinguishers should be fitted on wall brackets. It has been found that if this is not done, extinguishers are removed or knocked over and damaged. Extinguishers should be sited near exits or on the line of exit.

Water extinguishers

19.65   This type of extinguisher is suitable for ordinary combustible fires, for example wood and paper, but are not suitable for flammable liquid fires. Such extinguishers should also be labelled 'not to be used on fires involving live electricity'. Water spray extinguishers are recommended.

Foam extinguishers

19.66   These are suitable for small liquid spill fires or small oil tank fires where it is possible for the foam to form a blanket over the surface of the flammable liquids involved. Foam extinguishers may not extinguish a flammable liquid fire on a vertical plane. Where foam is required for hydro-carbon fires, light water is recommended, preferably by spray applicator. Alcohols miscible with water, when on fire, will break down ordinary foam and should be considered a special risk.

Dry powder extinguishers

19.67   This type will deal effectively with flammable liquid fires and is recommended, as it is capable of quick knock-down of a fire. The size of the extinguisher is important and it must be capable of dealing effectively with the possible size of the spill fire which may occur, with some extinguishant in reserve. The recommended minimum size is a 20 lb trigger-controlled extinguisher with CO_2 discharge. (Dry powder extinguishers will also deal with fires involving electrical equipment.)

Bcf extinguishers

19.68   A Bcf extinguisher (Bromochlorordifluoromethane: a lightweight, efficient vaporising extinguisher) is suitable for fires where electrical or electronic equipment may be involved. This type of extinguisher can also be used on flammable liquid fires; such use may, however, produce large quantities of toxic irritant gases. The hotter the fire, the more toxic the vapours produced. Therefore, a quick knock-down is essential. Bcf extinguishers should not be used on high temperature, metal or deep fat fires, especially in confined areas.

Carbon dioxide extinguishers

19.69   For fires involving electrical equipment, carbon dioxide extinguishers are recommended. Carbon dioxide (CO_2) extinguishers are quite heavy and may be at high pressure. A minimum size of 10 lbs is recommended. CO_2 is not recommended for flammable liquid fires, except for small fires. Training in the use of CO_2 extinguishers is essential.

Dry powder or CO_2 extinguishers which are too small can be hazardous due to the danger of re-ignition or flash-back.

Colour coding of portable fire extinguishers

19.70   The following colour codes should be used for portable fire extinguishers:

Extinguisher	Colour code
Water	Red
Foam	Cream
Carbon dioxide	Black
Dry chemical powder	Blue
Vaporising liquid	Green

Fire alarms in 'certificated' premises

19.71 A manually operated fire alarm system is required in any 'certificated' premises (see 19.3 above), and will be indicated on the fire certificate. The system should comply with the British Standard Code of Practice for the installation of fire alarms, and any equipment used should comply with the appropriate British Standard specification. The system should be tested every three months, and the result recorded (see Appendix 2).

Means of escape in case of fire

19.72 In any certificated premises the means of escape certificate or fire certificate must be available on demand. The following are essential:

(a) all doors affording means of escape in case of fire should be maintained easily and readily available for use at all times that persons are on the premises;

(b) all doors not in continuous use, affording a means of escape in case of fire, should be clearly indicated;

(c) sliding doors should also clearly indicate the direction of opening;

(d) doors should be adequately maintained and should not be locked or fastened in such a way that they cannot be easily and immediately opened by persons leaving the premises. Moreover, all gangways and escape routes should be kept clear at all times.

Good 'housekeeping'

19.73 The need for good 'housekeeping' cannot be over-emphasised. Poor housekeeping is the greatest single cause of fire. A carelessly discarded cigarette end, especially into a container of combustible waste or amongst combustible storage, often results in fire. The risk is higher in an area which is infrequently used. The following are essential guidelines:

(a) where smoking is permitted, suitable deep metal ashtrays should be provided. Ashtrays should not be emptied into combustible waste unless the waste is to be removed from the building immediately;

(b) combustible waste and contaminated rags should be kept in separate metal bins with close fitting metal lids;

(c) cleaners should, preferably, be employed in the evenings when work ceases. This will ensure that combustible rubbish is removed from the building to a place of safety before the premises are left unoccupied;

(d) rubbish should not be kept in the building overnight, or stored in close proximity to the building;

(*e*) 'no smoking' areas should be strictly enforced, especially in places which are infrequently used, e.g. stationery stores, oil file stores, or GPO intake room. Suitable 'no smoking' notices should be displayed throughout such areas;

(*f*) where 'no smoking' is enforced due to legal requirements (for example, areas where flammable liquids are used or stored) or in areas of high risk or high loss effect, it is recommended that the notice read 'No smoking – dismissal offence'. (This presupposes that the threat of dismissal can be carried out if necessary, see Chapter 13 'Employee Safety Rights, Disciplinary Procedures and Unfair Dismissal'.)

Pre-planning of fire prevention

19.74 A pre-planned approach to fire prevention and control is essential. Fire spreads extremely fast, the temperature can rise to 1,000°C in only one minute. Smoke can be flammable and toxic. The essential factor is to re-evaluate the risk, identify areas of high loss effect or high risk, and plan accordingly to meet requirements and legal responsibilities.

Fire hazards at work probably account for more deaths and serious injuries than any others. Since fire spreads rapidly and smoke and fumes overcome easily and quickly, particular attention to fire precautions and prevention is a pre-requisite to operating a factory or workplace.

Means of escape

19.75 Means of escape should be designed and constructed around fire travel. This consists of three stages as follows:

(*a*) travel within rooms;

(*b*) travel from rooms to a stairway or exit;

(*c*) travel within stairways to a final exit.

In particular,

(i) total travel distance between any point in a building and the nearest final exit should not exceed

    (*a*) 18m, if there is only one exit, or

    (*b*) 45m, if more than one exit;

(ii) two or more exits are necessary

    (*a*) from a room in which more than 60 people work, or

    (*b*) if any point in the room is more than 12m from the nearest exit;

(iii) minimum width of exit should be 750mm;

(iv) (*a*) corridors should be at least 1m wide;

    (*b*) offices should be divided by fire-resisting doors whose corridors are longer than 45m;

(v) stairways should be at least 800mm wide and fire-resistant; so, too, should doors connecting them;

(vi) one stairway is adequate in a building of up to four storeys only; fire doors must open outwards only;

(vii) escape doors should never be locked. If, for security reasons, they have to be locked, panic bolts should be fitted or keys kept in designated key boxes;

(viii) fire exit notices should be affixed to or above fire escape doors;

(ix) corridors and stairways, which are a means of escape, should have half-hour fire resistance and be constructed from brick or concrete with a non-combustible surface;

(x) fire alarms should be audible all through the building. In multi-storey buildings such alarms will normally be electrically operated, whereas in smaller buildings a bell or gong is sufficient;

(xi) it should not normally be necessary for a person to travel more than 30m to the nearest alarm point.

Unsatisfactory means of escape

19.76 The following are unsatisfactory means of escape in case of fire:

(*a*) lifts;

(*b*) portable ladders;

(*c*) spiral staircases;

(*d*) escalators;

(*e*) lowering lines.

Fire drill

19.77 Although not a statutory requirement yet, as a matter of good housekeeping (in addition to being probably required as well by the fire certificate (see 19.10 above, 'Contents of a fire certificate')), employers should acquaint the workforce with the need for fire drill. This consists of putting up a notice in a prominent place stating the action employees should take on

(*a*) hearing the alarm, or

(*b*) discovering the fire.

Ideally, employees should receive regular fire drill, even though normal working is interrupted. Indeed, fire alarms should be sounded weekly so that employees may familiarise themselves with the sound, and evacuation drills should be carried out at least annually. Trained employees should be designated as fire wardens and carry out head counts on evacuation, as well as acting as last man out and generally advising and shepherding the public. In addition, selected employees should be trained in the proper use of fire extinguishers. Moreover, periodical visits by the local fire authority should be encouraged by employers, since this provides a valuable source of practical information on fire fighting, fire protection and training.

Typical fire drill notice

19.78 When the fire alarm sounds:

1. Close windows, switch off electrical equipment and leave room, closing doors behind you.

2. Walk quickly along escape route to open air.

3. Report to fire warden at assembly point.

4. Do not re-enter building.

When you discover a fire:

1. Raise alarm (normally by telephone, stating name and location).

2. Leave the room, closing doors behind you.

3. Leave the building by escape route.

4. Report to fire warden at assembly point.

5. Do not re-enter building.

Fires on construction sites

19.79 Each year there are numerous fires, of a major kind, on construction sites and in buildings undergoing refurbishment. For that reason the 'Joint Code of Practice on the Protection from Fire of Construction Sites and Buildings Undergoing Renovation' (published by the Loss Prevention Council, 140 Aldersgate St, EC1A 4HY) proposes that the main contractor should appoint a *site fire safety co-ordinator*, responsible for assessing the degree of fire risk and for formulating and regularly updating the *site fire safety plan*; he should liaise with the co-ordinator for the design phase (see 19.82 below). The site fire safety plan should detail:

(i) organisation of and responsibilities for fire safety;

(ii) general site precautions, fire detection and warning alarms;

(iii) requirements for a Hot Work Permit system;

(iv) site accommodation;

(v) fire escape and communications system (including evacuation plan and procedures for raising the fire brigade);

(vi) fire brigade access, facilities and co-ordination;

(vii) fire drill and training;

(viii) effective security measures to minimise the risk of arson;

(ix) materials storage and waste control system.

Role of site fire safety co-ordinator

19.80 The site fire safety co-ordinator must

(i) ensure that all procedures, precautionary measures and safety standards (as specified in the site fire safety plan) are clearly understood and complied with by all those on the project site;

(ii) ensure establishment of Hot Work Permit systems;

(iii) carry out weekly checks of firefighting equipment and test all alarm and detection devices;

(iv) conduct weekly inspections of escape routes, fire brigade access, firefighting facilities and work areas;

(v) liaise with local fire brigade for site inspections;

(vi) liaise with security personnel;

(vii) keep a written record of all checks, inspections, tests and fire drill procedures;

    (viii) monitor arrangements/procedures for calling the fire brigade;

    (ix) during the alarm, oversee safe evacuation of site, ensuring that all staff/visitors report to assembly points;

    (x) promote a safe working environment.

Emergency procedures

19.81   The following emergency procedures should be implemented, where necessary,

    (i) establish a means of warning of fire, e.g. handbells, whistles etc.;

    (ii) display written emergency procedures in prominent locations and give copies to all employees;

    (iii) maintain clear access to site and buildings;

    (iv) alert security personnel to unlock gates/doors in the event of an alarm;

    (v) instal clear signs in prominent positions, indicating locations of fire access routes, escape routes and positions of dry riser inlets and fire extinguishers.

Designing out fire

19.82   Construction works should be designed and sequenced to accommodate

    (i) permanent fire escape stairs, including compartment walls;

    (ii) fire compartments in buildings under construction, including installation of fire doors;

    (iii) fire protective materials to structural steelwork;

    (iv) planned firefighting shafts duly commissioned and maintained;

    (v) lightning conductors;

    (vi) automatic fire detection systems;

    (vii) automatic sprinkler and other fixed fire fighting installations.

Moreover, adequate water supplies should be available and hydrants suitably marked and kept clear of obstruction.

Other fire precautions on site

19.83   Portable fire extinguishers can represent the difference between a conflagration and a fire kept under control. Therefore, personnel must be trained in the use of portable firefighting equipment and adequate numbers of suitable types of portable extinguishers should be available. They should be located in conspicuous positions near exits on each floor. In the open, they should be 500 mm above ground bearing the sign 'Fire Point'. In addition, all mechanically-propelled site plant should carry an appropriate fire extinguisher, and extinguishers, hydrants and fire protection equipment should be maintained and regularly inspected by the site fire safety co-ordinator.

Plant on construction sites also constitutes a potential danger. All internal combustion engines of powered equipment, therefore, should be positioned in the open air or in a well-ventilated non-combustible enclosure. They should be separated from working areas and sited so that exhaust pipes/gases are kept clear of combustible materials. Moreover, fuel tanks should not be filled whilst engines are running and compressors should be housed singly away from other plant in separate enclosures.

Consequences of failure to comply with code

19.84 Non-compliance with the provisions of this code could well result in insurance ceasing to be available or being withdrawn, thereby constituting a breach of a Standard Form contract (see 7.7 CONSTRUCTION AND BUILDING OPERATIONS).

Chapter 20

First-Aid

Introduction

20.1   First-aid is the provision of treatment to preserve life and minimise the consequences of illness or injury until medical or nursing help is available. Provision of first-aid facilities in workplaces comes within the general duty under the *Health and Safety at Work etc. Act 1974 (HSWA)* which requires employers to ensure a safe and healthy workplace for their employees. This chapter deals with regulations made under *HSWA* which apply to all employers and to self-employed people, and the relevant code of practice. A booklet on this subject is produced by the HSE, 'First Aid at Work' (HS(R)11), which sets out the code of practice, guidance notes and the regulations. The regulations came into force on 1 July 1982 but the original (1982) approved code of practice has been revamped by the Approved Code of Practice 1990.

There is a general duty on all employers to ensure, so far as is reasonably practicable, the health, safety and welfare of all their employees. [*HSWA s 2(1)*]. (See further Chapter 15 'Employers' Duties'.) This obviously extends to the provision of appropriate first-aid facilities.

The specific law relating to the provision of first-aid facilities at work is to be found in the *Health and Safety (First-Aid) Regulations 1981 (SI 1981 No 917)* (the *'First-Aid Regulations'*).

Provision of first-aid equipment and facilities

20.2   An employer must provide, or ensure that there are provided, such equipment and facilities as are adequate and appropriate in the circumstances for enabling first-aid to be rendered to his employees if they either:

(*a*)   are injured at work; or

(*b*)   become ill at work.

[*First-Aid Regulations, Reg 3(1)*].

The four criteria for deciding what provision is adequate and appropriate are set out in the code of practice, paragraph 6, as follows: the number of employees, the nature of the undertaking, the size of the establishment and distribution of employees and, lastly, the location of the establishment and of the employees' places of work. However, under the revised code of 1990, less emphasis is now placed on numbers.

First-aiders and occupational first-aiders

20.3   The *First-Aid Regulations* require that an employer must provide, or ensure that there is provided, an adequate and appropriate number of suitable persons for rendering first-aid. A person is not 'suitable' unless he has undergone:

(1)   such training and has such qualifications as are approved by the Health and Safety Executive (HSE); or

(2)   additional training as may be appropriate in the particular circumstances.

[*Reg 3(2)*].

First-aid training should be given by

(*a*)   registered medical practitioners or nurses with knowledge and experience of first-aid in the workplace;

(*b*)   qualified teachers or graduate lecturers with current first-aid certificates from an HSE-approved organisation;

(*c*)   lay trainers holding a certificate from HSE-approved organisations, such certificate being renewable every three years.

By dint of the Approved Code of Practice 1990 (ACOP), 'occupational first-aiders' are no longer 'suitable persons' for administering first-aid. Employers should rather avail themselves of first-aiders trained in specific techniques required by their undertaking. More particularly, where there is a danger of poisoning by cyanide or of burns from hydrofluoric acid or a need for oxygen for resuscitation purposes, training should be done by HSE-approved organisations. Such training should include:

(i)   nature of hazards and method of preventing their effects;

(ii)   symptoms, signs and treatment of conditions produced by hazards;

(iii)   pharmacological action of antidotes;

(iv)   practical training in checking and use of appropriate equipment;

(v)   maintenance of detailed records where additional methods of first-aid treatment are used.

A first-aider is a person who has received training and who holds a current first-aid certificate from an organisation or employer whose training and qualifications for first-aiders are approved by the HSE (see paragraph 29(*a*) of the code). Establishments presenting a particular hazard are likely to require at least one occupational first-aider.

The provision of trained personnel will thus depend on the particular circumstances. In the case of shift-work, for example, an employer should ensure that sufficient first-aiders are appointed to provide adequate coverage for each shift in relation to the number of employees at work on each shift.

Low risk establishments

20.4   The code provides that in establishments with relatively low hazards, e.g. offices, shops, banks or libraries, there must be one first-aider per 50 employees. Where there are fewer than 50 employees, the employer must provide an 'appointed person'. (ACOP 1990, Reg 3(2)).

Establishments with greater risk

20.5   In establishments with greater risk, e.g. factories, dockyards, warehouses, farms, employers should decide how many first-aiders there should be to the workforce, but a minimum of one to every 50 employees is mandatory. (ACOP 1990, Reg 3(2)).

Provision of an occupational first-aider

20.6   Foreseeable absences of first-aiders (e.g. annual holidays) are no longer 'exceptional and temporary circumstances', justifying substitution by an 'appointed person' (ACOP 1990). Employers have to provide, as a minimum, an *appointed person* at all times when employees are at work. Such person should have basic knowledge of first-aid, though to a lesser extent than a trained first-aider.

First-aid room

20.7   The code provides that an employer should generally provide a suitably equipped and staffed first-aid room only where 400 or more employees are at work. However, exceptions to this are the following:

(*a*)   establishments with special hazards;

(*b*)   construction sites with more than 250 persons at work;

(*c*)   when access to casualty centres, or to emergency facilities, is difficult (e.g. owing to distance or inadequacy of transport facilities).

The first-aid room will be the responsibility of a suitably qualified person, who will normally be an occupational first-aider, but in the case of an establishment having a large number of employees (rather than special hazards), it will be the responsibility of the first-aider (see 20.3 above).

Access to the first-aid room should be available at all times when employees are at work, and it should be positioned as near as possible to access points for transport to hospital. It should contain suitable equipment and facilities, and be effectively ventilated, heated, lighted and maintained. The room should be cleaned each working day. It should be large enough to hold a couch, with access for a stretcher or wheelchair or carrying chair. The room should be clearly identified as the first-aid room, and the names and locations of the nearest first-aiders and occupational first-aiders and appointed persons should appear on the door of the room, and the times when they are available.

Contents of first-aid rooms

20.8   First-aid rooms in workplaces should contain a minimum of the following:

(*a*)   sink with running water and cold water always available;

(*b*)   drinking water when not available on tap and disposable cups;

(*c*)   soap;

(*d*)   paper towels;

(*e*)   smooth topped working surfaces;

(*f*)   suitable store for first-aid materials;

(*g*)   sufficient quantities of the following:

      (i)   one guidance card,

     (ii)   20 individually wrapped sterile adhesive dressings,

    (iii)   2 sterile eye pads, with attachment,

    (iv)   6 individually wrapped triangular bandages,

     (v)   6 safety pins,

(vi)   6 medium-sized individually wrapped unmedicated wound dressings,

(vii)   2 large sterile individually wrapped unmedicated wound dressings,

(viii)   3 extra large sterile individually wrapped unmedicated wound dressings;

(*h*)   suitable refuse containers lined with a disposable plastic bag;

(*j*)   a couch (with waterproof surface) and frequently cleaned pillow and blanket;

(*k*)   clean protective garments for use by first-aiders;

(*l*)   a chair;

(*m*)   an appropriate record book (see 20.20 'Format for recording first-aid treatment' below); and

(*n*)   a bowl.

Travelling first-aid kits

These should contain at least:

(i)   a card giving general first-aid guidance;

(ii)   6 individually wrapped sterile adhesive dressings;

(iii)   one large sterile unmedicated dressing;

(iv)   2 triangular bandages;

(v)   2 safety pins;

(vi)   individually wrapped moist cleaning wipes.

Employees to be informed

20.9   An employer must inform his employees of the arrangements made in connection with the provision of first-aid. This will include informing them where the first-aid equipment is kept, what facilities there are and the people appointed to provide the first-aid or take charge. [*Reg 4*].

Self-employed people

20.10   There is a similar duty for a self-employed person who must provide, or ensure that there is provided, adequate and appropriate first-aid equipment, so that he can render first-aid to himself while at work. [*Reg 5*]. This would probably extend to the provision of first-aid kits in cars and other vehicles used for work purposes.

Exemptions

20.11   If the HSE is satisfied that the health and safety of all concerned will not be prejudiced, exemption in writing from all or some of the regulations may be granted, subject to both conditions and a time limit, and may be revoked at any time. This will not happen unless the HSE is satisfied as to the health, safety and welfare of the following people:

(*a*)   employees;

(*b*)   self-employed persons;

(*c*)   other persons likely to be affected by the exemption.

[*Reg 6*].

Offshore work

20.12   The regulations apply to offshore employment, but not where the *Diving Operations at Work Regulations 1981 (SI 1981 No 399)* apply. [*First-Aid Regulations, Reg 9*]. (See further Chapter 34 'Offshore Operations'.)

Under the *Diving Operations at Work (Amendment) Regulations 1990 (SI 1990 No 996)*, divers and other persons working in compression chambers, must have a valid certificate of diving first-aid, issued by the HSE or some other approved body. [*Reg 2(h)*]. Also, diving contractors must provide facilities, medications and personnel which are adequate for rendering first-aid to persons who are injured whilst diving and must ensure that they are trained in first-aid to the satisfaction of the HSE. (See further Chapter 34 'Offshore Operations'.)

Registration of divers

20.13   A person cannot act as a diving contractor unless registered. Registration depends on

(*a*)   the following information being given to the HSE:

    (i)   diver's name and address,

    (ii)   diver's telephone number,

    (iii)   location of diving operation(s),

    (iv)   nature of work likely to be done during diving operation(s),

    (v)   level of competence likely to be required of divers; and

(*b*)   HSE issuing acknowledgment.

[*Diving Operations at Work Regulations 1981, Reg 5A (inserted by Amendment Regulations 1992 (SI 1992 No 608) and SI 1992 No 608, 1A Sch)*].

Registration expires either twelve months after

(*a*)   date of acknowledgment, or

(*b*)   date of expiry of existing registration.

Moreover, those engaging diving contractors must ensure that divers are, in fact, registered. [*Reg 5B*].

(As for notification of diving operations for offshore work, see 34.1 and 34.46 OFFSHORE OPERATIONS.)

Practical procedure

20.14   It is imperative that management ensure (possibly through induction training) that all employees are conversant with the procedure to be followed as and when they sustain injury. Generally, the accident causing the injury will be reported verbally by the injured person to his immediate supervisor prior to the treatment of the injured person either by a registered or enrolled nurse in the ambulance or first-aid room, or by a certificated and trained first-aider in charge of a first-aid box within a factory department or area.

The nurse or first-aider will then enter details of the accident on behalf of the injured person into the BI 510 Accident Book. The immediate supervisor should also be kept fully informed of the situation, to enable him to investigate the accident, together with the relevant safety representative, and raise and complete an internal accident report form for onward transmission to departmental management and the safety adviser, thus ensuring that prompt remedial action is taken to prevent a recurrence (see also Chapter 3 'Accident Reporting').

Principles of first-aid

20.15   In addition to its principal meaning (see 20.1 above), first-aid also includes the treatment of minor injuries which may otherwise receive no treatment or would not require treatment by a medical practitioner [*Health and Safety (First-Aid) Regulations 1981*]; that is 'the skilled application of accepted principles of treatment on the occurrence of an accident or in the case of sudden illness, using facilities and materials available at the time'.

As such, first-aid is given:

(*a*)   to sustain life;

(*b*)   to prevent deterioration in an existing condition; and

(*c*)   to promote recovery;

and the most important aspects of first-aid treatment are:

(i)   resuscitation (restoration of breathing);

(ii)   control of bleeding; and

(iii) prevention of collapse.

While the regulations specify the minimum number of first-aiders necessary for a given workforce and the inherent risks of the work processes, it is good practice for as many people as possible to be trained in elementary first-aid procedures. Not only does this ensure that casualties receive prompt attention but, in the event of a multiple casualty situation, there may not be sufficient first-aiders available if only the minimum statutory number have been trained.

First-aid training requirements

20.16   The guidance notes issued in conjunction with the regulations and approved code of practice indicate those areas of training necessary for first-aiders. These are:

(*a*)   resuscitation;

(*b*)   treatment and control of bleeding;

(*c*)   treatment of shock;

(*d*)   management of unconscious casualty;

(*e*)   contents of first-aid rooms (see 20.8 above);

(*f*)   purchasing first-aid supplies;

(*g*)   transport of casualties;

(*h*)   recognition of illness;

(*j*)   treatment of injuries to bones, muscles and joints;

(*k*)   treatment of minor injuries;

(*l*)   treatment of burns and scalds;

(*m*)   eye irritation;

(*n*)   poisons;

(*o*)   simple record keeping;

(*p*)   personal hygiene in treating wounds; and

(*q*)   communication and delegation in an emergency.

(Approved Code of Practice 1990).

In particular, the trainee should be able to demonstrate proficiency in resuscitation, control of bleeding and treatment of the unconscious patient.

A certificate of qualification as a first-aider is valid for three years, after which a two-day refresher course, followed by further examination, is necessary before the person can be granted a further certificate.

Occupational first-aiders need additional training covering:

(i)   safety and hygiene in treating the patient;

(ii)   detailed record keeping;

(iii)   particular aspects of first-aid specific to the undertaking; and

(iv)   chemical hazards and their treatment specific to the place of work.

All first-aid training must be undertaken by an organisation approved by the HSE.

First-aiders and AIDS

20.17   All first-aiders are potentially exposed to infectious diseases, notably HIV, causing AIDS and hepatitis B. Health care workers, handling blood products, are normally immunised against hepatitis B, though to date no vaccine has been developed against HIV.

Human immunodeficiency virus (HIV) (or AIDS) has a history of intransmissibility in the working environment, save for health care and research laboratories – and then as a result of exposure to the blood of an HIV-infected patient, e.g. blood on broken skin. Those most at risk, at least in theory, are first-aiders giving mouth-to-mouth resuscitation and trying to stop bleeding, since, in both cases, contact with body fluids of another person occurs. As for resuscitation, the World Health Organisation (WHO) recommends that resuscitation, an obvious life-saving procedure, should take priority over fear of contracting AIDS. As a precautionary measure, however, first-aiders are advised to use a clean cloth/handkerchief in order to wipe away any blood from the person's mouth. In the second situation, where a worker is bleeding, the first-aider should NOT render assistance. Better that he instruct the person to apply pressure to the wound himself, with a thick clean cloth. If, however, the latter is unconscious, the first-aider should apply pressure to the wound with a thick clean cloth, avoiding contact with blood, and using gloves. In all cases, first-aiders should prevent broken skin and eyes or mouth coming into contact with blood. Spilt blood should be soaked up with a cloth or rag, direct contact with blood being avoided. The contaminated area should then be disinfected, preferably by sodium hypochlorite, with rubber gloves being used. If a first-aider has any open cuts/wounds, these should be covered so as to prevent exposure to blood. All companies should have a procedure to deal with the possibility of first-aiders being exposed to contact with blood (see further Chapter 41 'Statements of Health and Safety Policy') and this should be written into the company health and safety policy and/or appended to it.

Precautions to be taken by first-aiders

20.18   First-aiders, exposed to blood on broken skin, should wash the contaminated area with hot water and soap as soon as possible. Similarly, a first-aider injured by an object itself contaminated with blood, should encourage bleeding, wash the wound with soap and water and apply a dressing. If a first-aider requests HIV antibody testing, this should be done immediately after exposure. If the initial test is negative, follow-up testing should be carried out three and six months later. Any interim counselling should include the low risk, on the part of the first-aider, of acquiring infection.

Training in first-aid

20.19   First-aid training is an ideal opportunity for disseminating accurate information on HIV infection and AIDS and first-aid trainers should inform workers of the methods by which AIDS cannot be transmitted. First-aiders should also be taught the precautions needed to avoid contact with blood or body fluids and the low risk of infection from HIV-infected blood.

Format for recording first-aid treatment

20.20

Full name & address of persons who suffered an accident	Occupation	Date when entry made	Date and time of accident	Place & circumstances of accident - (state clearly the work process being performed at the time of the accident)	Details of injury suffered and treatment given	Signature of person making this entry (state address if different from column 1)
(1)	(2)	(3)	(4)	(5)	(6)	(7)

Application of first-aid

20.21

Chapter 21

Food and Food Hygiene

Introduction

21.1   Traditionally, legislation controlling food has had two main aims: (*a*) the protection of the health of the consumer; and (*b*) the prevention of fraud. These two objectives have been largely achieved by an amalgam of primary legislation and more detailed regulations. The principal current Act, applicable in the United Kingdom (though not in Northern Ireland) is the *Food Safety Act 1990*, though, additionally, the *Food and Environment Protection Act 1985* prohibits sales of food where health hazards exist, for example, in the form of contaminants. Also important are the *Food Hygiene Regulations 1970 (SI 1970 No 1172)* (see 21.13 below).

The *Food Safety Act 1990* replaces much of the *Food Act 1984* (and the *Food and Drugs (Scotland) Act 1956*), which latter superseded the *Food and Drugs Act 1955* and its amendments, and seeks to ensure that food for sale is safe and not misleadingly labelled or presented and that new EC Directives on food are speedily implemented.

Under this Act several important regulations have already been passed (and more can confidently be expected), including (i) the *Food Premises (Registration) Regulations 1991 (SI 1991 No 2825)*, providing for registration of food premises (including vehicles) by food authorities (see 21.14 below); (ii) the *Food Labelling (Amendment) Regulations 1990 (SI 1990 No 2488)*, replacing 'sell by' dates with 'use by' dates on microbiologically perishable foodstuffs; (iii) the *Food Labelling (Amendment) (Irradiated Food) Regulations 1990 (SI 1990 No 2489)*, requiring the labelling of pre-packed food sold to consumers and catering establishments, to indicate irradiation; and (iv) the *Food (Control of Irradiation) Regulations 1990 (SI 1990 No 2490)*, permitting sale of certain types of irradiated food where irradiation has occurred under licence.

Development of regulations

21.2   Originally, the most effective consumer protection legislation, in the case of food, was thought to be 'compositional' standards or controls; but, more recently, emphasis has switched to more stringent labelling requirements, e.g. the *Food Labelling Regulations 1984*, reserving compositional controls for certain basic products. Most (but not all) food products are subject to the *Food Labelling Regulations 1984* (milk is an exception).

In addition, the maintenance of satisfactory hygiene practices is ensured by various food hygiene regulations. Whilst these are the most 'trusted' regulations, the great majority of cases involve small retailers, restaurants and catering establishments.

Enforcement

21.3   Enforcement of food legislation has traditionally been the province of local authorities. In particular, two types of trained professional are involved in the maintenance of food standards, namely environmental health officers and trading standards officers. Environmental health officers are responsible for enforcing those aspects of food law concerning health and hygiene. Thus, their main preoccupation is enforcement of food hygiene regulations and controls on unfit/unsafe food contained in the *Food Safety Act 1990*, as well as certain work at slaughterhouses. On the other hand, trading standards officers deal with enforcement of compositional and labelling controls and are also inspectors for the purposes of weights and measures legislation.

Food Safety Act 1990

21.4   To accommodate the rapid rate of technological change in food processing, this Act specifies:

(*a*)   tighter controls on unfit/unsafe food. In particular, certain enforcement procedures in the *Food Act 1984*, which have not been repealed, are extended to *possession* for sale as well as sale itself, so that powers can be exercised before products are put on sale; thus, supply of food, in the course of business, otherwise than on sale, constitutes a 'sale' of food. [*Food Safety Act 1990, s 2(1)*]. Moreover, the *Food Safety (Sampling and Qualifications) Regulations 1990 (SI 1990 No 2463)* lay down stringent qualifications for food examiners/analysts, e.g. first degree in microbiology, MSc. etc.;

(*b*)   that new enforcement procedures extend to food processing factories, with the result that whole batches of food can be condemned [*Secs 10-13*] and that, where food is likely to cause food poisoning, food can be seized and removed [*Sec 9(3)*] (see 'prescribed form' at 21.11 below);

(*c*)   registration of food premises so as to assist local authorities in enforcing food safety legislation [*Sec 19*] (see 21.14 below);

(*d*)   greater regulatory powers to control contaminants and residues [*Sec 16*];

(*e*)   greater regulatory powers to introduce control orders, on the part of Ministers, relating to adulterated imports [*Sec 13*];

(*f*)   a new 'diligence' defence, in place of the earlier 'warranty' defence, enshrined in the *Food Act 1984* [*Sec 21*];

(*g*)   the introduction of hygiene training for employees of food businesses, who handle food directly, whether frozen or chilled. This applies whether the businesses are manufacturing, wholesale, retail and/or catering (including hospitals and schools in the private and public sector). Excluded are employees handling only wrapped, canned or bottled food, packaged confectionery, fresh fruit, fresh vegetables and wet fish. Food handlers will be required to have a basic understanding of the ways and conditions in which bacteria multiply, the effects of food poisoning/ contamination, personal health and hygiene, pest control as well as legal duties, and environmental health officers can require proof of such training [*Sec 23*].

Presumption against seller of food

21.5   Any food commonly used for human consumption, if

(*a*)   sold, or

(*b*)   offered/kept for sale,

is presumed, until the contrary is proved, to have been

(i)   sold, or

(ii)   intended for sale for human consumption.

[*Food Safety Act 1990, s 3(2)*].

Food safety offences

Food safety offences are concerned with (*a*) protecting the health of the consumer, (*b*) giving the consumer value for money and (*c*) prevention of fraud.

Rendering food injurious to health

21.6   Any person who renders any food injurious to health, with intent that it be sold for human consumption, by

(*a*)   adding an article/substance (e.g. to increase weight/flavour),

(*b*)   using an article/substance as a preparation,

(*c*)   abstracting an ingredient from food, or

(*d*)   subjecting food to any other process/treatment,

is guilty of an offence. [*Sec 7(1)*].

Moreover, the onus is on the accused to show that the food was not intended for human consumption (see 21.5 above).

Selling unsafe food

21.7   Any person who

(*a*)   sells for human consumption,

(*b*)   offers (display in a shop window is probably not 'offering for sale') (*Fisher v Bell* [*1960*] *3 AER 731* concerning the display of a flick knife allegedly contrary to legislation prohibiting 'offering for sale' dangerous weapons),

(*c*)   exposes, or

(*d*)   advertises,

(*e*)   deposits with another, or

(*f*)   consigns to another,

for the purposes of sale, any food which does not comply with safety requirements, is guilty of an offence. [*Sec 8(1)*].

Food fails to comply with safety requirements if

(i)   it has been rendered injurious to health (as per *Sec 7* above);

(ii)   it is so contaminated that it would not be reasonable to expect it to be used for human consumption; and

(iii)   it is unfit for human consumption.

And where food is part of a batch, the presumption is that the whole batch is contaminated. [*Sec 8(2)(3)*].

Consumer protection

Substandard food

21.8   Any person who sells, to the purchaser's detriment, any food not of the nature and/or substance or quality demanded by the purchaser, is guilty of an offence. [*Sec 14(1)*].

Misleading labels

Any person who

(i)   gives with any food sold by him,

(ii)   displays with any food

   (a)   offered (see *Fisher v Bell* (21.7 above)),

   (b)   exposed for sale, or

   (c)   in his possession,

a label (attached or printed on a wrapper/container)

(a)   falsely describing food, or

(b)   likely to mislead as to the nature/substance/quality,

is guilty of an offence. [*Sec 15(1)*].

Penalties

21.9   A person found guilty of such offence is liable

(i)   on conviction on indictment, to a fine or imprisonment for up to two years, or even both;

(ii)   on summary conviction, to a fine of not more than £5,000 (for breach of *Secs 8* and *14*).

Companies, senior officers and managers can be prosecuted as well as individual non-corporate retailers (see also 17.32 ENFORCEMENT).

Enforcement powers/procedures

21.10   Enforcement of the *Food Safety Act 1990* is mainly by (a) improvement notices and/or (b) prohibition orders and/or (c) control orders. But, in addition, an environmental health officer can inspect or seize suspected food. [*Sec 9*].

Notices and orders

Improvement notice

21.11   If an environmental health officer reasonably believes that the proprietor of a food business is failing to comply with safety regulations, he can serve an improvement notice. Such notices (as with improvement notices generally – see Chapter 17 'Enforcement') must

(i)   state why he believes the proprietor to be in breach;

(ii)   specify matters which constitute the breach;

(iii)   specify matters which the proprietor must take to comply; and

Food Safety Act 1990—Section 9

DETENTION OF FOOD NOTICE

Reference Number:

1. To: ....
   Of: ....
   ....

2. Food to which this notice applies:
   Description   : ....
   Quantity   : ....
   Identification marks   : ....

3. *THIS FOOD IS NOT TO BE USED FOR HUMAN CONSUMPTION.*
   In my opinion, the food does not comply with food safety requirements because: ....
   ....
   ....

4. The food must not be removed from:
   ....
   ....
   *unless it is moved to:
   ....
   ....
   (*Officer to delete if not applicable)

5. Within 21 days, either this notice will be withdrawn and the food released, or the food will be seized to be dealt with by a justice of the peace, or in Scotland a sheriff or magistrate, who may condemn it.

Signed: ....Authorised Officer
Name in capitals: ....
Date: ....
Address: ....
....
....
Tel: .... Fax: ....

[Detention of Food (Prescribed Forms) Regulations 1990 (SI 1990 No 2614)].

(iv)   require the proprietor to take such measures within the period stipulated in the notice (of at least 14 days).

[Sec 10].

Failure to comply with an improvement notice is an offence (see 21.9 above, Penalties).

Prohibition order

If the proprietor of a food business is convicted of breach of food hygiene regulations and there is a health risk, the court can impose a prohibition order on such business, the effect of which is to close down the premises temporarily. *[Sec 11(1)]*. A 'health risk' can exist in respect of

(*a*)   use of any process/treatment;

(*b*)   construction of premises, or use of equipment;

(*c*)   state or condition of premises/equipment.

A prohibition order remains in effect until such time as the proprietor has taken steps to remove the health risk. Contravention is an offence (see 21.9 above, Penalties).

Emergency prohibition notices

Where an environmental health officer feels that there is an immediate health risk, he can serve an emergency prohibition notice on the proprietor which will be placed in a conspicuous place on the business premises *[Sec 12(5)(6)]*, and this remains in force until the latter has taken specified steps to remove the hazard. *[Sec 12]*.

Defence

General defence – due diligence

21.12   The 'warranty' defence associated with *Sec 102* of the *Food Act 1984* has been replaced by a general defence of 'due diligence'. Thus, it is a defence for an accused to show that he took all reasonable precautions *and* exercised all due diligence to avoid commission of the offence either by himself or by someone under his control. *[Sec 21(1)]* (see 21.15 below).

Defence to Secs 8, 14 and 15

More particularly, however, for the purposes of offences under *Secs 8, 14 and 15* (i.e. selling unsafe food, substandard food and falsely describing food) it is a defence that the person charged did not

(*a*)   prepare food, or

(*b*)   import food into Great Britain,

but the burden of establishing this particular defence is not discharged unless the accused can prove

(i)   that the commission of the offence was due to the act or default of another person not under his control, and

(ii)   he carried out such checks on food as were reasonable, or that he reasonably relied on checks carried out by the supplier of food, and

(iii)   he did not know or suspect that the act or omission was an offence.

[*Sec 21(2)(3)*]. (See further 33.19 OFFICES.)

The Food Hygiene Regulations

21.13   The *Food Hygiene Regulations 1970 (SI 1970 No 1172)* relating to any food intended for human consumption, except milk, provide for

(*a*)   the cleanliness of premises (and ships) used for the purposes of a food business and of the equipment that is used;

(*b*)   the hygienic handling of food;

(*c*)   the cleanliness of persons engaged in the handling of food and of their clothing, and the action to be taken where they suffer from or are the carrier of certain infections likely to cause food poisoning;

(*d*)   the construction of premises (and ships) used for the purposes of a food business and their repair and maintenance;

(*e*)   the provision of water supply and washing facilities;

(*f*)   the proper disposal of waste material;

(*g*)   the temperatures at which certain foods are to be kept on catering premises.

These regulations and other regulations relating to food, including milk, are enforced by local authorities (who may be either a county council or district council); though the *Food Hygiene Regulations* themselves are always enforced by environmental health departments of district councils.

Registration of food premises – Food Premises (Registration) Regulations 1991 (SI 1991 No 2825)

21.14   Registration (of food premises) is crucial to the operation of the *Food Safety Act 1990*. In particular, premises used as a food business on five (or more) consecutive (or non-consecutive) days in any period of five consecutive weeks, must be registered. [*Reg 2*]. Some important exceptions are:

—   production/packaging of eggs;

—   retail sale of food via automatic vending machines;

—   supply of beverages/biscuits to a business whose main activity is not the sale of food;

—   dairy farms;

—   slaughterhouses;

—   premises where food is stored/prepared for sale.

[*Reg 3*].

Contravention or permitting premises to be used as a food business is a summary offence, carrying a maximum penalty of £1,000.

Food safety critical procedures

21.15   The *Food Safety Act 1990* extends to all sectors of food distribution, from initial manufacture of animal foodstuffs, through primary production, such as farming, primary food processing operations, such as dairies and slaughterhouses, to food manufacture, wholesaling, retailing and catering to the public. In order to be able to raise 'due diligence' as a defence (see 21.12 above), food suppliers should establish a formal food safety policy (analogous with the company safety policy (see Chapter 41 'Statements of Health and Safety Policy')). This should set out a general statement of intent, organisation and arrangements for implementing the policy and specify individual responsibilities. A senior manager or even director should be identified as having ultimate responsibility for food safety and hygiene. Procedures and systems for implementing the policy should be documented in the Food Safety Manual.

Food Safety Manual

21.16   This should refer to:

(1)   *Monitoring arrangements* – including regular premises inspections, temperature of premises and products inspections, defects reporting system. In addition, contractors, such as cleaning contractors and pest controllers, should be monitored. As part of the contract of supply, suppliers' premises, processes and equipment should also be regularly monitored.

(2)   *Preventive maintenance* – a lot of the foreign bodies appearing regularly in food – pins, combs, nuts etc. – essentially emanate from indifferent maintenance. A planned maintenance programme, identifying each item of plant by number and record, should be retained (preferably) in a Plant Register. This register should specify the maintenance procedures, frequency of maintenance, necessary precautions and individual responsibility for overseeing maintenance operations.

(3)   *Cleaning operations* – cleaning operations for each area and item of plant and machinery as well as methods, materials and equipment to be used, frequency of cleaning and necessary precautions, should all be itemised.

(4)   *Product recall* – given the obvious consumer attraction of product liability laws (see Chapter 38 'Product Safety'), food manufacturers should set in train a formal and efficient product recall system so as to be able to withdraw an offending product or range of products from the market without scaremongering or exciting too much media attention. In particular, a senior manager, preferably the quality manager, should be appointed product recall liaison officer, to report directly to the managing director. He will also deal with the press and the media. Product recall in urgent cases – user level recall – can be expensive, involving recall from users, retailers and wholesalers; also owners' losses will have to be reimbursed. Less serious cases may warrant only wholesale or retail level recall. Moreover, insurance for product recall expenses can also be expensive.

(5)   *Training* – all staff should be regularly updated and receive induction training in food safety, hygiene and basic statutory requirements. For this reason, organisations have availed themselves of courses run by the Institution of Environmental Health Officers (IEH).

(6)   *Health surveillance* – pre-employment health screening and regular health examinations by an occupational health nurse (see Chapter 15 'Employers' Duties' and Chapter 31 'Occupational Health') coupled with periodical medical examinations can help to promote food hygiene awareness, underpin employee health and contribute to the wholesomeness of food being manufactured, prepared, sold, handled or transported. Such health surveillance procedures should be specified and itemised.

Chapter 22

Gas Safety

Introduction

22.1   Average deaths from carbon monoxide poisoning are three times those due to explosions and fire. This figure excludes injury to those at work from work activities, and such injuries occur mainly on domestic premises. Gas safety is of paramount importance in the maintenance of health and safety at work, as well as to the general consumer. Explosions caused by escaping gas have been responsible for large-scale damage to property and considerable personal injury, including death. Although escape of metered gas or gas in bulk holders might possibly have attracted civil liability under the rule in *Rylands v Fletcher* (see further 7.38 CONSTRUCTION AND BUILDING OPERATIONS and 19.44 FIRE AND FIRE PRECAUTIONS), statutory authority to perform a public utility (i.e. supply gas) used to constitute a defence in such proceedings, coupled with the fact that negligence had to be proved in order to establish liability for personal injury (*Read v J Lyons & Co Ltd [1947] AC 156*). This situation has now changed in favour of imposition of strict product liability for injury/damage caused by escape of gas (see 22.2 below).

Product liability

22.2   Injury or damage caused by escape of gas will be visited with strict liability, 'gas' being a product for the purposes of 'product liability' (along with electricity (see Chapter 11 'Electricity')). [*Consumer Protection Act 1987, s 10(7)(c)*]. Moreover, a statutory gas undertaker is 'absolutely liable' for loss of life, personal injury or damage to property caused as a result of underground storage of gas, except where damage etc. is suffered as a result of the fault of the plaintiff, his employees or agents. [*Gas Act 1965, s 14*]. (See further 12.30 EMISSIONS INTO THE ATMOSPHERE.)

Enforcement of gas safety

22.3   Maintenance and enforcement of gas safety in factories (for 'factories', see further Chapter 18 'Factories and Workplaces') is provided for by the *Factories Act 1961, s 31*, and in mines and quarries by the *Mines and Quarries Act 1954*, whilst public/consumer safety in connection with gas, is accommodated in the *Gas Act 1986, s 48* (re-enacting the *Gas Act 1972*), and the *Gas Safety Regulations 1972 (SI 1972 No 1178)* (as later amended by the *Gas Safety (Installation and Use) Regulations 1984*). Detailed regulation of gas is, however, contained in the *Gas Safety (Rights of Entry) Regulations 1983 (SI 1983 No 1575)* and, most importantly, the *Gas Safety (Installation and Use) Regulations 1984 (SI 1984 No 1358)*, which are considered in this chapter. In addition, the *Building Regulations 1991 (SI 1991 No 2768)*, enforceable by environmental health officers, are concerned with the location of appliances in buildings.

Gas Safety (Installation and Use) Regulations 1984

22.4   The *Gas Safety (Installation and Use) Regulations 1984 (SI 1984 No 1358)*, as amended by the *Gas Safety (Installation and Use) (Amendment) Regulations 1990 (SI 1990 No 824)*, specify requirements relating to installation and use of gas fittings and appliances, so as to ensure, so far as reasonably practicable (see further Chapter 15 'Employers' Duties'), that the general public is not exposed to personal injury, explosion or other damage emanating from gas in pipes. These regulations, which do not apply either in factories or in mines, and enforceable by HSE and local authorities, are concerned with safety in the use and/or installation of gas fittings (though not service pipes, unless part of a meter installation (see 22.5 below)), in domestic and/or commercial premises, irrespective of whether gas is natural gas, town or coal gas, synthetic natural gas and methane from waste; but not with liquefied petroleum gas (LPG) appliances (see further Chapter 24 'Highly Flammable Liquids'), though the Approved Code of Practice (ACOP) on Safety of Gas Installation is (see 22.16 below).

Gas fittings

22.5   A gas fitting is

(i)   a gas pipe (though not a service pipe, unless part of a primary meter installation);

(ii)   a gas fitting;

(iii)   a gas meter;

(iv)   apparatus/appliances designed for use by gas consumers.

[*Gas Act 1986, s 48(1)*].

Gas fitters

22.6   Work must not be carried out on a gas fitting/installation by anyone, unless competent, and employers must see that employees so engaged, are, in fact, competent. [*Gas Safety (Installation and Use) (Amendment) Regulations 1990, Reg 3*]. Competence generally refers to the Confederation of Registered Gas Installers (CORGI, 4 Elmwood, Chineham Business Park, Crockford Lane, Basingstoke RG24 0WG). If such persons are not competent, the employer is in breach of *HSWA s 2* and self-employed persons in breach of *HSWA s 3(1)* (see further Chapter 15 'Employers' Duties'). Moreover, no employer must allow any of his employees to carry out gas fitting, unless the employer is a member of a body approved by the HSE; the same requirements extend to self-employed persons. [*1990 Regulations, Reg 3(3)*].

Sound materials and work

22.7   Gas fittings must be of good construction, sound materials and of adequate strength and size to ensure safety; and pipes made of lead/lead alloy should never be installed; nor (normally) pipes made of non-metallic substance; and work carried out on gas fittings should be workmanlike. [*Reg 4*].

Safety precautions

22.8   (*a*)   Steps should be taken to prevent the escape of gas;

(*b*)   gas fittings must never be left unattended, unless every incomplete gasway has been so sealed as to be gas tight (or the gas fitting is otherwise safe);

(*c*)   where gas pipes are disconnected, every outlet of every pipe to which it was connected, must be sealed off with an appropriate fitting;

(*d*)   persons must not smoke whilst engaged on gas fitting;

(*e*)   sources of ignition must not be used by a person searching for an escape of gas;

(*f*)   where work might affect the tightness of the gas supply system, the person carrying out the work must test the system for gas tightness, at least as far as the nearest valves upstream/downstream are concerned

[*Reg 5*];

(*g*)   gas fittings must be properly supported and protected so as to avoid damage to them;

(*h*)   foreign bodies must not be allowed to block or interfere with the operation of a gas fitting, unless a filter has been fitted to the gas inlet;

(*j*)   gas fittings must not be exposed to corrosive substances, unless the fitting is made of corrosive-resistant materials

[*Reg 6*].

Emergency controls

22.9   Supply of gas must be accompanied by provision of emergency controls and access to them. Emergency controls should be sited:

(*a*)   in dwellings in buildings to be supplied with gas

(i)   as near as possible to the point where the supply pipe enters the dwelling, and

(ii)   if the supply pipe enters the building at a place outside the dwelling, as near as possible to the point of entry;

(*b*)   if there is no dwelling in the building, as near as possible to the point where the supply pipe enters the building.

Emergency controls must contain a key/lever securely attached to the operating spindle, and a person installing an emergency control (which is not part of a primary meter) must prominently display near the control apparatus, the words 'Gas Emergency Control'. The purpose of this is to ensure that the consumer

(i)   shuts off the gas supply in the event of an escape of gas;

(ii)   if gas continues to escape after the emergency control has been closed, notifies the supplier; and

(iii)   does not reopen the emergency control, until all steps have been taken to prevent the re-escape of gas.

The emergency control apparatus should also carry

(1)   name of gas supplier;

(2)   emergency telephone number of gas supplier;

(3)   date when notice was first displayed.

[*Reg 8*].

Gas meters

22.10   Gas meters must not be installed

(1)   (*a*)   on or under a stairway, or

(*b*)   in any other part of a building with two or more floors above the ground floor,

where the stairway/other part of the building, provides the only means of escape in the case of fire [*Reg 11(1)*];

(2)   in any building with only one floor above the ground floor,

(*a*)   on or under the stairway, or

(*b*)   in any other part of the building,

where the stairway, or other part of the building, provides the only means of escape in the case of fire, unless

(i)   the meter conforms with BS 476 'Fire tests on Building Materials and Structures, Part 8: 1972', and

(ii)   is of fire-resistant materials, or is housed in a compartment with automatic self-closing doors, which is fire-resistant and which conforms with BS 476, or

(iii)   the pipeline upstream of the meter can automatically cut off the flow of gas where the temperature exceeds 95°C;

(3)   the meter is installed in such a way that there is no risk of damage to it from electrical apparatus;

(4)   the meter is in a position readily accessible for inspection and maintenance;

(5)   following installation, meters and gas fittings are adequately tested for gas tightness and examined for compliance with these regulations;

(6)   test/examination is followed by purging so as to safely remove all air/gas (other than gas to be supplied)

[*Reg 11*];

(7)   all flammable materials are removed from the meter box;

(8)   the consumer is provided with a key to the meter lock labelled 'Gas Meter Box'

[*Reg 12*];

(9)   the primary meter installation contains a notice that consumers should

(i)   shut off the gas supply in the event of escape,

(ii)   give notice to the supplier in the event of further gas escaping,

(iii)   not re-open the supply until all steps have been taken to prevent the re-escape of gas;

(10)   the primary meter installation contains information relating to

(i)   the name of the supplier,

(ii)   emergency service telephone number of the supplier,

(iii)   the date when the notice was first displayed.

[*Reg 14*].

Moreover, pre-payment meters must never be installed as primary meters. [*Reg 15*].

Gas pipes

22.11   Gas pipes must be installed safely vis-à-vis other pipes, drains, sewers, cables, conduits and electrical apparatus and pipes must not be installed in walls or floors, unless protected against failure caused by movement. Further pipes must not be installed under the foundations of a building or in ground under the base of a wall or footings, or in an unventilated shaft, duct or void. [*Regs 17, 18*].

Gas appliances

22.12   Gas appliances (used by consumers for heating or lighting purposes) must not be installed

(1)   if the appliance and fittings, the means of ventilation, or the stability of the appliance, constitutes a danger to persons or property;

(2)   unless the appliance is verified as safe for further use;

(3)   if the appliance does not comply with safety regulations;

(4)   unless at the inlet there is a means of shutting off the gas supply

[*Reg 25*];

(5)   unless readily accessible for operation, inspection and maintenance [*Reg 28*];

(6)   unless the manufacturers' instructions for use of the appliance are left with the occupier [*Reg 29*].

Penalty

22.13   Breach of these regulations carries a maximum penalty, on summary conviction, of £5,000. [*Reg 36*].

Defences

22.14   It is a defence for

(*a*)   an employer, not employing competent gas fitters [*Reg 3(2)*];

(*b*)   a person installing a gas fitting made of unsuitable materials [*Reg 4(1)*];

(*c*)   a person installing a gas fitting where it is likely to corrode [*Reg 6(3)*];

(*d*)   a person failing to display an emergency notice [*Reg 14*];

(*e*)   a person failing to test/verify a gas appliance [*Reg 33*];

that all reasonable steps were taken to prevent a contravention. [*Reg 37*]. This may be a difficult test to satisfy, by analogy with comparable legislation (see *J H Dewhurst Ltd v Coventry Corporation*, Chapter 33 'Offices').

Gas safety requirements in factories

22.15   Where part of plant contains explosive/inflammable gas under pressure greater than atmospheric, that part must not be opened unless:

(i)   before the fastening of any joint of any pipe, connected with that part of the plant, any flow of gas has been stopped by a stop-valve;

(ii)   before such fastening is removed, all practicable steps have been taken to reduce the gas pressure in the pipe or part of the plant, to atmospheric pressure; and

(iii)   if such fastening is loosened or removed, inflammable gas is prevented from entering the pipe/part of the plant, until the fastening has been secured or securely replaced.

[*Factories Act 1961, s 31*].

Training of gas fitters

22.16   In order to achieve 'competence', for the purpose of *Reg 3* (above), Approved Code of Practice 'Standards of training in safe gas installation' (1988) specifies criteria for the training of gas fitters/installers. These require that gas fitters have sufficient knowledge, practical skill and experience to carry out gas installation safely in domestic or commercial premises as well as industrial installations of a similar nature, including work with portable/mobile LPG appliances (see further Chapter 24 'Highly Flammable Liquids') which need servicing/maintaining/repairing periodically, as well as mains gas.

Gas installation should only be carried out by an installer who has obtained an appropriate training qualification, or assessment test following a refresher course. To achieve competence in safe installation, training includes knowledge of purging, commissioning, testing, servicing, maintenance, repair, disconnection, modification and dismantling of gas systems, fittings and appliances. In addition, a sound knowledge of combustion and its technology is essential, including (i) properties of fuel gases, (ii) combustion, (iii) flame characteristics, (iv) control and measurement of fuel gases, (v) gas pressure and flow, (vi) construction and operation of burners and (vii) operation of flues and ventilation.

Installation

Gas systems

22.17   Gas fitters should know

(i)   where/how gas pipes/fittings (including valves, meters, governors and gas appliances) should be safely installed;

(ii)   how to site/install a gas system safely, with reference to safe ventilation/flueing;

(iii)   associated electrical work (e.g. appropriate electrical power supply circuits, that is, overcurrent and shock protection from electrical circuits, earthing and bonding);

(iv)   electrical controls appropriate to the system being installed/maintained/repaired;

(v)   when/how to check the whole system adequately before it is commissioned;

(vi)   how to commission the system, leaving it safe for use.

Gas appliances

22.18   Gas fitters should understand how various types of gas appliances (water heaters, cookers, space heaters, central heating boilers) should be safely installed, maintained and used; and should be trained to the standard appropriate for the type of appliance they are working with. Thus, they should understand

(*a*)   safety considerations in specifying appliances for domestic or commercial premises;

(*b*)　how to install/commission, safely and correctly, appliances to be installed;

(*c*)　that unsuitable appliances should not be installed;

(*d*)　that used appliances should be examined to verify that they are safe for further use;

(*e*)　basic design and construction criteria for the appliances he is working with;

(*f*)　the importance of manufacturers' instructions; and

(*g*)　basic electrical theory, control circuits, schematic and wiring diagrams, safe use of test instruments to measure insulation resistance and voltage, controls and control systems;

(*h*)　dangers of electrical equipment;

(*j*)　how to avoid danger from electrical equipment.

Servicing, maintenance and repair

22.19　Gas fitters should be able to service, maintain, repair, disconnect and reconnect appliances in use, including:

(*a*)　proper knowledge of servicing techniques for the gas appliances in question;

(*b*)　maintenance requirements;

(*c*)　basic fault-finding;

(*d*)　ability to follow manufacturers' instructions, fault diagnosis charts and wiring diagrams.

In addition, they should know how to recognise and test for conditions that might cause danger and take remedial action, as well as being able to show consumers how to use any equipment they have installed or modified, including how to shut off the gas supply in an emergency. They should also alert customers to the significance of inadequate ventilation and gas leaks and the need for regular maintenance/servicing.

Chapter 23

Health and Safety Commission and Executive

Introduction

23.1   One of the fundamental changes brought about by the *Health and Safety at Work etc. Act 1974* (*HSWA*) was (see further Chapter 1 'Introduction') the establishment of a new, unified system for the administration and enforcement of health and safety. The two bodies it created for this purpose were the Health and Safety Commission (HSC) and the Health and Safety Executive (HSE). The HSC is the body given overall responsibility for administering and overseeing health and safety matters, including the effective operation of health and safety law. It is a quasi-independent body, directly responsible to the relevant Secretary of State (the Secretary of State for Employment). In addition to keeping all aspects of health and safety under review, the HSC's specific functions include submitting proposals for regulations to the Secretary of State, and approval of codes of practice. The HSE is, in effect, the 'executive arm' of the HSC and is responsible to the HSC and the Secretary of State. The purpose of this chapter is to examine briefly the composition and functions of these two bodies.

Establishment and composition of the Commission and Executive

23.2   The Health and Safety Commission and the Health and Safety Executive were established by *HSWA s 10*. Both are bodies corporate. The HSC came into being on 1 October 1974, and the HSE on 1 January 1975.

The HSC consists of a Chairman and not fewer than six, nor more than nine, other members. Of the other members, three represent employers, three represent employees, and the remainder are from bodies such as local authorities and professional organisations. [*HSWA s 10(2)(3)*].

The HSE consists of three people. One is appointed by the HSC to be the Director of the HSE, and the other two are appointed by the HSC after consultation with the Director. All three appointments require the approval of the Secretary of State. [*HSWA s 10(5)*].

Before *HSWA*, there were seven separate Inspectorates, governing the following:

(*a*)   factories;

(*b*)   mines and quarries;

(*c*)   agriculture;

(*d*)   alkali;

(*e*)   explosives;

(*f*)   radiochemicals;

(*g*)   nuclear installations.

These have now all been brought under the unified control of the HSE.

The Commission has its own Secretariat, but in general the civil service staff which undertake the administration and enforcement of health and safety come under the wing of the Executive.

Functions of the Commission

23.3   The function of the HSC is to carry out the general purpose of *Part I* of *HSWA*. [*HSWA s 11(1); Employment Protection Act 1975, s 116, 15 Sch 4*]. In particular, the Commission has the following duties:

(*a*)   to assist and encourage people concerned with matters within *Part I* of *HSWA* to further those purposes;

(*b*)   to make appropriate arrangements for research, publication of the results of research and provision of training and information in connection with these purposes, including encouraging research and training by others;

(*c*)   to advise and keep informed as it considers appropriate, government departments, employers, employees, and organisations representing employers and employees, on matters relevant to these purposes;

(*d*)   to submit proposals for regulations to the relevant authority (see further 23.5 below);

(*e*)   to replace/update existing law and regulations and prepare approved codes of practice [*HSWA s 1(2)*].

[*HSWA s 11(2); Employment Protection Act 1975, s 116, 15 Sch 4*].

The HSC is given consequential powers to make agreements with other government departments, establish advisory committees, etc. for the purpose of discharging its functions. [*HSWA s 13*]. It may also delegate the exercise of certain of its functions to the HSE (see 23.11 below).

Relationship between HSC/HSE and the Secretary of State

23.4   The HSC and HSE are both independent of any government department. However, the HSC is under a continuing duty to submit particulars of its functions to the Secretary of State. [*HSWA s 11(3)(a)*]. The Secretary of State also has the power to give specific directions with which the HSC (and, if appropriate, HSE) must comply. [*HSWA s 11(3)(c),(4)*].

Power of HSC to propose regulations

23.5   The Secretary of State can approve, with or without modification, any proposals submitted to him by the HSC, but he has a duty to consult the HSC before making any regulations himself. [*HSWA s 50(2)*]. This is by far the most important function of the HSC; it means, in effect, that the HSC is responsible for all new statutory instruments, often emanating from EC directives (see Chapter 1 'Introduction'), relating to health and safety at work. Since its establishment several sets of regulations likely to have an important effect on health and safety at work have appeared, e.g. the *Safety Representatives and Safety Committees Regulations 1977*, the *Control of Lead at Work Regulations 1980*, the *Control of Asbestos at Work Regulations 1987* and the *Control of Substances Hazardous to Health Regulations 1988*. Such regulations are normally finalised following consultation with both sides of industry, particular trades and industries, and any other interested bodies e.g. local authorities and educational establishments. Publication of a consultative document and draft regulations precedes the final statutory instrument (see further 1.14 INTRODUCTION).

Nature of health and safety regulations

23.6   Health and safety regulations, proposed by the HSC, can do one of the following:

(*a*)   repeal or modify any of the 'relevant statutory provisions' (for definition of this expression, see Chapter 17 'Enforcement');

(*b*)   exclude or modify any of the 'existing statutory provisions'. An example of this is the *Employers' Health and Safety Policy Statements (Exception) Regulations 1975 (SI 1975 No 1584)*, which exempts employers employing fewer than *five* employees, from issuing a written company safety policy, as required by *HSWA s 2(3)* (see further Chapter 41 'Statements of Health and Safety Policy');

(*c*)   make a specified authority responsible for the enforcement of any of the relevant statutory provisions.

[*HSWA s 15(3)(c)*].

Areas likely to be the subject of future regulation are set out in *HSWA 3 Sch 3*.

Issue and approval of codes of practice

23.7   While it does not have the power to *make* regulations, the HSC is given the power to approve and issue codes of practice for the purpose of providing practical guidance on the requirements of health and safety legislation or regulations. [*HSWA s 1(2)*]. The HSC may arrange for such a code of practice to be prepared by some other body on its behalf, and it may also grant approval for any code of practice drawn up and issued by some other body. In all cases, the HSC is required to consult any appropriate government department, or other body, beforehand and it must also obtain the consent of the Secretary of State to its approval of the code. There are additional provisions relating to publicising approval of a code, revising codes, withdrawing approval in appropriate cases, etc. [*HSWA s 16*].

A code of practice approved in this way is an 'approved code of practice' [*HSWA s 16(7)*] a recent example being the Approved Code of Practice relating to First-Aid 1990 (see further 20.3 FIRST-AID). The important effect of approved codes of practice is considered further in Chapter 1 'Introduction'.

Investigations and inquiries

23.8   The HSC is given the following powers:

(*a*)   to request the HSE (or any other person) to investigate any accident, occurrence, situation or matter which the HSC considers ought to be investigated and present a special report to the HSC on the findings of the investigation;

(*b*)   if the Secretary of State consents, to direct that an inquiry be held into any accident, occurrence, situation or matter.

[*HSWA s 14*].

Functions of the Executive

Arrangements for enforcement of duties

23.9   The principal function of the HSE is to make adequate arrangements for the *enforcement* of the general duties of *HSWA* and any other relevant statutory provisions, contained in other protective Acts (or regulations passed thereunder), e.g. the *Factories Act 1961*, the *Offices, Shops and Railway Premises Act 1963* (*OSRPA*) and the *Fire Precautions Act 1971* (*FPA*), unless the responsibility for enforcement lies with some other enforcing body such as a local authority (see further Chapter 17 'Enforcement'). [*HSWA s 18(1)*].

Transfer of responsibilities

23.10   The Secretary of State may by regulation transfer responsibility for enforcing regulations from the HSE to local authorities and vice versa. [*HSWA s 18(2)(b)(i)*].

Duties delegated by the HSC

23.11   The HSC may direct the HSE to exercise certain functions, or perform certain duties on its behalf. [*HSWA s 11(4)(a)*]. These relate in practice to the carrying out of research into health and safety matters; provision for the education of persons concerned with health and safety, and publicity regarding health and safety at work.

Appointment of inspectors

23.12   In order to carry out its duty of enforcing the general duties under *HSWA* and other relevant legislation (see 23.5 above), the HSE is empowered to appoint inspectors (known as HSE inspectors), subject to their having the necessary suitable qualifications, and to terminate such appointments, if and when necessary. [*HSWA s 19(1)*]. Moreover, as an enforcing authority, the HSE may indemnify inspectors mistakenly acting outside their statutory powers against any damages, costs or expenses incurred if the HSE is satisfied that the inspector honestly believed that he was empowered to do what he did. [*HSWA s 26*]. (For the enforcement powers of inspectors, see Chapter 17 'Enforcement'.)

HSE publications

23.13   The HSE (through HMSO) publishes a series of guidance notes/advisory literature for employers, local authorities, trade unions, insurance companies etc. on most aspects of health and safety of concern to industry. These are divided into five main areas, i.e. Chemical Safety (CS); Environmental Hygiene (EH); General Series (GS); Medical Series (MS); and Plant and Machinery (PM).

In addition, there are the Health and Safety (Guidance) Series (HS(G)); the Health and Safety (Regulations) Series (HS(R)); Best Practicable Means Leaflets (BPM); Emission Test Methods (ETM); Health and Safety Commission Leaflets (HSC); Health and Safety Executive Leaflets (HSE); Industry General Leaflets (IND(G)); Industry Safety Leaflets (IND(S)); similarly, Methods for the Determination of Hazardous Substances (MDHS); Toxicity Reviews (TR); Occasional Papers; Agricultural Safety Leaflets (AS). (See further, Appendix 1.)

It is in the interests of employers to be familiar with these publications and their recommendations, or at least the more important ones. Since employers can be liable for negligence for injury/disease to employees (see Chapter 15 'Employers' Duties'), they will be liable for failure to take account, not only of developments which they were actually aware of, but also developments which, as good prudent employers, they ought to have known of. Thus, in a case concerning the death of an employee working with mineral oils in engineering from scrotal cancer, which occurred even though the dangers had been documented in two earlier prestigious medical 'reports': 'Whilst I am far from saying that every one of the welter of official and unofficial publications about safety that are published every year should be spotted and perused and followed by an employer even in such a large organisation, I do find that the defendant's organisation should have succeeded in acquiring and distributing this leaflet' (per Swanwick J in *Stokes v GKN Sankey (Nuts and Bolts) Ltd* [*1968*] *1 WLR 1776*). This stricture would extend, by way of analogy, to HSE publications.

23.14

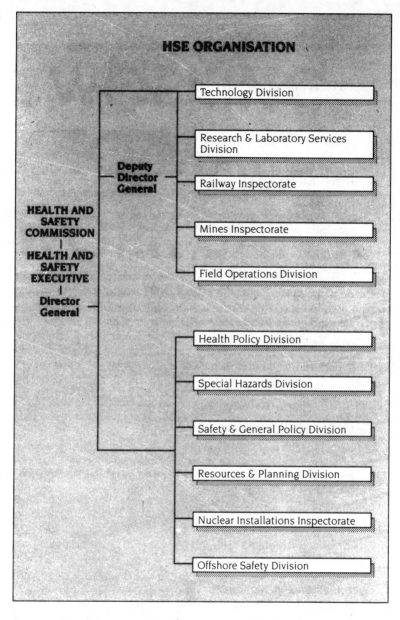

HSE ORGANISATION

Technology Division

Research & Laboratory Services Division

Railway Inspectorate

Mines Inspectorate

Field Operations Division

Health Policy Division

Special Hazards Division

Safety & General Policy Division

Resources & Planning Division

Nuclear Installations Inspectorate

Offshore Safety Division

Deputy Director General

HEALTH AND SAFETY COMMISSION

HEALTH AND SAFETY EXECUTIVE

Director General

Chapter 24

Highly Flammable Liquids and Liquefied Petroleum Gases

Introduction

24.1 The principal hazards arising from storage of flammable liquids (such as petroleum gases, liquid oxygen, chlorine, phosgene and sulphur dioxide, though not liquefied petroleum gas which is stored as a liquid under pressure) are fire and explosion involving either bulk liquid or escaping liquid/vapour. This could be caused by inadequate design, manufacture, installation, maintenance or equipment failure. To this end, storage of flammable liquids in fixed bulk tanks is preferable to storage in cans, drums, etc. and at ground level and in the open air, because leaks are more easily detectable and any resultant vapour is dispersed by natural ventilation. Buried or mounted tanks offer better fire protection but long-term corrosion is more difficult to control. In particular, tanks should not be situated

(a)   under buildings,

(b)   on roofs,

(c)   inside buildings,

(d)   high above ground level,

(e)   on top of one another,

but rather above ground, in the open, in a well-ventilated position away from sources of ignition. Moreover, there should be adequate distances between flammable liquid tanks and LPG storage as follows:

	distance from flammable liquid tank	distance outside bund wall
LPG cylinders	3 metres	3 metres
LPG vessel	6 metres	6 metres

A fire wall, often forming part of the bund wall, should be at least the height of the tank. This should be provided on one side of the tank only, to ensure adequate ventilation. The purpose of the bund wall is to limit the spread of spillage or leakage. They should be big enough to hold 110% of the capacity of the largest tank within the bund. Only in exceptional cases should storage tanks be sited inside buildings, but it is permissible to hold liquid in 'day tanks' where process conditions demand it, e.g. where mixing is taking place. Such tanks should be bunded, have tight-fitting lids and vented to a safe place. Tanks can be horizontal (top-discharge) or vertical (top-filled) storage tanks.

Hazardous areas – ignition dangers

24.2 Importantly, there should be no means of igniting flammable vapour in hazardous

474

areas where there are storage tanks, e.g. by welding and handlamps. Smoking (which is a criminal offence in such situations (see 13.13 EMPLOYEE SAFETY RIGHTS, DISCIPLINARY PROCEDURES AND UNFAIR DISMISSAL)) should be actively prohibited and 'No Smoking' signs posted. If hot work is necessary, a permit to work should be raised (see 1.32 INTRODUCTION). Hazardous areas in relation to equipment are classified (by BS 5345) into

(a)   Zone 0 – explosive vapour-air mixture is continuously present;

(b)   Zone 1 – explosive vapour-air mixture is likely to occur in normal operation;

(c)   Zone 2 – explosive vapour-air mixture is not likely to occur in normal operation.

Transport transfer facilities

24.3   Road transfer facilities should be at least 10 metres from occupied buildings and sources of ignition. Drainage should be provided on site for spills. Safe access to equipment and safe means of escape should be provided for work above ground level, e.g. access gantries with stairs or ladders for top loading of vehicles. Road transfer facilities should be at least 15 metres from any railway line in regular use. Means should be provided to control spillage and direct it to an evaporation area, catchment area or pit. Both road/rail transfer facilities should be supervised throughout the operation by an authorised person and, before any delivery is made from a road/rail tanker to a storage installation, an authorised site representative should be briefed. Written instructions should be provided covering all aspects of the operation.

Fire precautions

24.4   Since the major danger associated with storage or transfer of flammable liquids is fire or explosion, personnel involved should be trained and instructed in routine fire-fighting operations and emergency procedures, including passive fire-protection strategies. More particularly, plant design and layout should accommodate water supplies, fire protection equipment, fire fighting, means of escape, means of access for fire brigade, and protection of firefighters. A typical emergency procedure should include:

(a)   raising the fire alarm/calling the fire brigade;

(b)   tackling a fire/controlling spills and leaks;

(c)   evacuating the site.

Statutory requirements

General

24.5   The statutory requirements of *HSWA* relating to explosive or highly flammable or otherwise dangerous substances are designed to control the use and generally prevent the unlawful acquisition and possession of such substances. [*HSWA s 1 (1)(c)*].

Specific provisions

24.6   The *Highly Flammable Liquids and Liquefied Petroleum Gases Regulations 1972 (SI 1972 No 917)* (hereafter called the '*Highly Flammable Liquids Regulations*') lay down requirements for the following matters in relation to highly flammable liquids etc. used in a factory (see 24.7 below):

(*a*)   manner of storage;

(*b*)   marking of storage accommodation and vessels;

(*c*)   precautions to be observed for the prevention of fire and explosion;

(*d*)   provision of fire-fighting apparatus;

(*e*)   securing of means of escape in case of fire;

(*f*)   posting of the regulations*.

(See 9.4 *et seq.* DANGEROUS SUBSTANCES I for the site marking and notification requirements, and 9.8 *et seq.* for the classification, packaging and labelling of these substances.)

* A printed abstract of these regulations must be kept at the factory both where they can be read easily and on demand in factories where these liquids are employed (Form 2440). [*Factories Act 1961, s 139; Abstract of Special Regulations (Highly Flammable Liquids and Liquefied Petroleum Gases) Order 1974*].

Terms used in the regulations

'Highly flammable liquids'

24.7   The term 'highly flammable liquids' encompasses both liquefied flammable gas (see 24.8 below), although not aqueous ammonia, and liquefied petroleum gas (see 24.9 below) and therefore includes any liquid, liquid solution, emulsion or suspension which:

(*a*)   has a flashpoint of less than 32°C when tested in accordance with *Part III* of *Schedule 1* to the *Chemicals (Hazard Information and Packaging) Regulations 1993 (SI 1993 No 1746)* (see Table 18); and

(*b*)   supports combustion when tested in the manner set out in *Schedule 2* (see Table 19).

[*Highly Flammable Liquids Regulations, Reg 2(2A)*].

An abstract of *Schedules 1* and *2* of these Regulations are to be kept posted at the principal entrance to the factory where workers can conveniently read them. [*Factories Act 1961, s 139; Highly Flammable Liquids and Liquefied Petroleum Gases Order 1974*].

'Liquefied flammable gas'

24.8   This term refers to any substance which would be a flammable gas at a temperature of 20°C and a pressure of 760 millimetres of mercury, but which is in liquid form as a result of the application of pressure or refrigeration or both. [*Highly Flammable Liquids Regulations, Reg 2(2)*].

'Liquefied petroleum gas'

24.9   'Liquefied petroleum gas' covers:

(*a*)   commercial butane; and

(*b*)   commercial propane;

and any mixture of them. [*Highly Flammable Liquids Regulations, Reg 2(2)*].

Application of the regulations

24.10 The regulations apply to factories as defined in the *Factories Act 1961* (see Chapter 18 'Factories and Workplaces'). They impose duties on the occupier of the premises or, in some cases, the owner of the substances. They do not apply directly to premises subject to the *Offices, Shops and Railway Premises Act 1963* (see Chapter 33 'Offices') or to research premises, although *HSWA s 2* may well imply applicability to all places of work.

Storage of highly flammable liquids generally

24.11 When not in use or being conveyed, all highly flammable liquids (HFLs) should be stored in a safe manner. Specifically, all HFLs should be stored in one of the following ways:

(*a*) in suitable fixed storage tanks in safe positions; or

(*b*) in suitable closed vessels kept in a safe position in the open air and, where necessary, protected against direct sunlight; or

(*c*) in suitable closed vessels kept in a store room which either is in a safe position or is a fire-resisting structure; or

(*d*) in the case of a workroom where the aggregate quantity of HFL stored does not exceed 50 litres, in suitable closed vessels kept in a suitably placed cupboard or bin, being a cupboard or bin which is a fire resisting structure.

[*Highly Flammable Liquids Regulations, Reg 5(1)*]. (Certificate of Approval No 1 F2434 (HMSO) prescribes specifications for this purpose.)

Other precautions relating to storage include the following:

— *Bund walls.* Storage tanks should be provided with a bund wall enclosure which is capable of containing 110% of the capacity of the largest tank within the bund.

— *Ground beneath vessels.* The ground beneath storage vessels should be impervious to liquid and be so sloped that any minor spillage will not remain beneath the vessels, but will run away to the sides of the enclosure.

— *Bulk storage.* Bulk storage tanks should not be located inside buildings or on the roof of a building. Underground tanks should not be sited under the floors of process buildings.

— *Drum storage.* The area to be utilised for drum storage should be surrounded with a sill capable of containing the maximum spillage from the largest drum in store.

Marking of storerooms and containers (HFL)

24.12 Every storeroom, cupboard, bin, tank and vessel used for storing HFL should be clearly and boldly marked 'Highly Flammable' or 'Flashpoint below 32°C' or 'Flashpoint in the range of 22°C to 32°C'. [*Highly Flammable Liquids Regulations, Reg 6(1)*]. This is to ensure that all persons are made aware of the flammability of the contents of storerooms, tanks, vessels etc. (Signs complying with the *Safety Signs Regulations 1980 (SI 1980 No 1471)* should be utilised whenever relevant.) This would not in itself avoid strict liability in civil law for injury-causing product defects (see Chapter 38 'Product Safety'), or property damage coupled with personal injury, under the (restrictive) rule in *Rylands v Fletcher* (see Chapter 19 'Fire and Fire Precautions').

Specific provisions for the storage of liquefied petroleum gas

24.13   All LPG not in use must be stored in one of the following ways:

(*a*)   in suitable underground reservoirs or in suitable fixed storage tanks located in a safe position – either underground or in the open air; or

(*b*)   in suitable moveable storage tanks/vessels kept in safe positions in the open air; or

(*c*)   in pipelines and pumps forming part of an enclosed system; or

(*d*)   in suitable cylinders kept in safe positions in the open air or, where this is not reasonably practicable (for the meaning of 'reasonably practicable' see Chapter 15 'Employers' Duties'), in a storeroom constructed of non-combustible material, having adequate ventilation, being in a safe position, of fire-resisting structure, and being used solely for the storage of LPG and/or acetylene cylinders.

[*Highly Flammable Liquids Regulations, Reg 7(1)*].

LPG cylinders must be kept in store until they are required for use, and any expended cylinder must be returned to store as soon as is reasonably practicable. This should ensure that only the minimum amount of LPG is kept in any workplace. [*Reg 7(2)(3)*]. The effect of these regulations is that LPG cylinders connected up for use may remain in the workplace even though not actually in use. The keeping of additional or unnecessary cylinders in the workplace is, however, prohibited, whether such cylinders are full or have been used.

Marking of storerooms and containers (LPG)

24.14   Every tank, cylinder, storeroom, etc., used for the storage of LPG should be clearly and boldly marked 'Highly Flammable – LPG'. [*Highly Flammable Liquids Regulations, Reg 7*].

Precautions against spills and leaks (all HFLs)

24.15   Where HFLs are to be conveyed within a factory, a totally enclosed piped system should be used, where reasonably practicable. Where not reasonably practicable, a system using suitable closed 'non-spill' containers will be acceptable. *On no account should open buckets and tins be used.* Portable vessels, when emptied, should be removed without delay to a safe place. Where in any process or operation any HFL is liable to leak or be spilt, all reasonably practicable steps should be taken to ensure that any such HFL should be contained or immediately drained off to a suitable container, or to a safe place, or rendered harmless. [*Highly Flammable Liquids Regulations, Reg 8*].

Precautions against escaping vapours

24.16   No means likely to ignite vapour from any HFL should be present where a dangerous concentration of vapours from HFL may be present. [*Reg 9(1)*]. The regulations do not themselves require the use of specially protected electrical apparatus, but such apparatus will invariably be required in an area in which a dangerous concentration of vapour from HFL is likely to be present. Thus, electrical equipment which may reasonably foreseeably be exposed to any flammable or explosive substance, must be constructed or protected so far as is reasonably practicable so as to prevent danger arising from such exposure. [*Electricity at Work Regulations 1989 (SI 1989 No 635), Reg 6(d); Electrical Equipment for Explosive Atmospheres (Certification) Regulations 1990 (SI 1990 No 13)].* (See also Chapter 11 'Electricity'.)

Where any HFL is being utilised in the workplace, reasonably practicable steps should be taken so as to minimise the risk of escape of HFL vapours into the general workplace atmosphere. Where such escape cannot be avoided, then the safe dispersal of HFL vapours should be effected, so far as is reasonably practicable. [*Highly Flammable Liquids Regulations, Reg 10*].

An example of a situation where the problem of escaping HFL vapours cannot be avoided occurs during the filling of a container with HFL; flammable vapours will be created by displacement. The dangerous concentration of HFL vapour can be prevented by use of an exhaust ventilation system (see further Chapter 43 'Ventilation'). If the outlet of the ventilation system is near to possible ignition sources, then a flame arrestor should be provided on the outlet pipe. In any event, *all* sources of ignition should be removed from the area prior to any container-filling operation. [*Reg 9*]. (The HSE Health and Safety series booklet entitled 'Flame arrestors and explosion reliefs' HS(G) 11 should be consulted.)

Relaxation of fire-resistance specifications in certain circumstances

24.17 In cases where either explosion pressure relief or adequate natural ventilation are required in a fire-resistant structure, a relaxation of the specification of a fire-resistant structure (as defined in *Reg 2*) is allowable. [*Reg 11(1)*].

Fire escapes and fire certificates

24.18 The means of escape which are provided and which can be used at all material times, fire fighting means and fire warning precautions, which may reasonably be required, will be inspected before a fire certificate is issued where:

(*a*) highly flammable liquids are manufactured;

(*b*) liquefied petroleum gas is stored;

(*c*) liquefied flammable gas is stored.

[*Fire Certificates (Special Premises) Regulations 1976 (SI 1976 No 2003) 1 Sch Part I*]. (See further Chapter 19 'Fire and Fire Precautions'.)

Prevention of build-up of deposits

24.19 Whenever, as a result of any process or operation involving any HFL, a deposit of any solid waste residue liable to give rise to a risk of fire is liable to occur on any surface:

(*a*) steps must be taken to prevent the occurrence of all such deposits, so far as is reasonably practicable; and

(*b*) where any such deposits occur, effective steps must be taken to remove all such residues, as often as necessary, to prevent danger.

[*Highly Flammable Liquids Regulations, Reg 13(1)*].

No removal of any such residue containing cellulose nitrate must be carried out by the use of an iron or steel implement. [*Reg 13(2)*]. Because of the comparative ease of ignition of cellulose nitrate, the use of spark producing tools is prohibited. Scrapers constructed of wood or plastic should be used.

Smoking controls

24.20   No person may smoke in any place in which any HFL is present and where the circumstances are such that smoking will give rise to a risk of fire. [*Highly Flammable Liquids Regulations, Reg 14(1)*]. The occupier has a duty to display suitable 'No smoking' notices – designed to comply with the *Safety Signs Regulations 1980 (SI 1980 No 1471)* – at all places within the factory where the risk of fire exists. They should be circular with a red circle and cross bar over a symbol with a white background. [*Highly Flammable Liquids Regulations, Reg 14(2)*].

Provision of fire-fighting equipment

24.21   Appropriate fire-fighting equipment should be made readily available for use in all factories where HFL is manufactured, used or manipulated. [*Highly Flammable Liquids Regulations, Reg 17(1)*]. (See Chapter 19 'Fire and Fire Precautions'.)

Duties of employees

24.22   It is the duty of every employee to whom the regulations apply to comply with them (e.g. not to smoke [*Reg 14*]) and co-operate in carrying them out (for the consequences of failure to do so, see Chapters 13, 14 and 15). If an employee discovers any defect in plant, equipment or appliances, it is his duty to report the defect without delay to the occupier, manager or other responsible person. [*Highly Flammable Liquids Regulations, Reg 18*].

Liquefied gases in harbour areas

24.23   Liquid dangerous substances in bulk must not be carried, loaded or unloaded from a vessel in a harbour/harbour area unless:

(*a*)   the vessel has a valid certificate of fitness for carriage of the substance in bulk; or

(*b*)   the harbour master has given his permission in writing.

[*Dangerous Substances in Harbour Areas Regulations 1987, Reg 19*].

Liquid dangerous substances in bulk must not be transferred by pipeline from one vessel to another, unless the harbour master has given permission in writing. [*Reg 20*].

Furthermore, operators of berths where liquid dangerous substances are loaded or unloaded in bulk, must prepare a list of safety precautions to be taken. [*Reg 21*].

HSE guidance in connection with HFL and LPG

Guidance notes

24.24   CS1:   Industrial use of flammable gas detectors
        CS2:   The storage of highly flammable liquids
        CS4:   The keeping of LPG in cylinders and similar containers
        CS5:   The storage of LPG at fixed installations
        CS6:   Storage and use of LPG on construction sites
        EH9:   Spraying of highly flammable liquids

HS(G) series booklets

HS(G)3:	Highly flammable materials on construction sites
HS(G)4:	Highly flammable liquids in the paint industry
HS(G)5:	Hot work
HS(G)11:	Flame arrestors and explosion reliefs
HS(G)15:	Storage of LPG at factories
HS(G)22:	Electrical apparatus for use in potentially explosive atmospheres
HS(G)50:	Storage of flammable liquids in fixed tanks
HS(G)51:	Storage of flammable liquids in containers
HS(G)52:	Storage of flammable liquids in fixed tanks (exceeding 10,000 m^3 total capacity)

HSE guidance in connection with other flammable materials

Guidance notes

24.25   GS3:   Fire risk in the storage and industrial use of cellular plastics
          EH7:   Petroleum based adhesives in building operations

HS(G) series booklet

HS(G)1:   Polyurethane foam

Table 18

Methods for the Determination of Flash point

[*CHIP Regulations 1993, 1 Sch Part III*].

1. For the purpose of classifying a substance or preparation dangerous for supply or carriage in accordance with Part I of this Schedule or Part I of Schedule 3, the flash point shall be determined—
    (a)   by one of the equilibrium methods referred to in paragraph 3; or
    (b)   by one of the non-equilibrium methods referred to in paragraph 4, except that when the flash point so determined falls within one of the following ranges, namely:—
        (i)   −2°C to + 2°C,
        (ii)   19°C to 23°C, or
        (iii)   53°C to 57°C,
        that flash point shall be confirmed by one of the equilibrium methods referred to in paragraph 3 using like apparatus.

2. The use of any method or apparatus referred to in paragraphs 3, 4 and 5 is subject to the conditions specified in the appropriate standard particularly having regard to the nature of the substance (e.g. viscosity) and to the flash point range.

3. The equilibrium methods referred to in paragraph 1(a) are those defined in the following standards, namely International Standards ISO 1516, ISO 3680, ISO 1523 and ISO 3679.

4. The non-equilibrium methods referred to in paragraph 1(b) use the apparatus referred to below in accordance with the following standards namely:—

(a)   Abel Apparatus—
   (i)   British Standard BS 2000 Part 170,
   (ii)   French Standard NF M07–011,
   (iii)   French Standard NF T66–009;

(b)   Abel-Pensky Apparatus—
   (i)   German Standard DIN 51755, Part 1 (for temperatures from 5 to 65 degrees C),
   (ii)   German Standard DIN 51755, Part 2 (for temperatures below 5 degrees C),
   (iii)   French Standard NF M07–036,
   (iv)   European Standard EN 57;

(c)   Tag Apparatus—
   (i)   American Standard ASTM D-56;

(d)   Pensky-Martens Apparatus—
   (i)   British Standard BS 6664 Part 5,
   (ii)   International Standard ISO 2719,
   (iii)   American Standard ASTM D 93,
   (iv)   French Standard NF M07–019,
   (v)   German Standard DIN 51758,
   (vi)   European Standard EN 11.

5.   To determine the flash point of viscous liquids (paints, gums and similar) containing solvents, only apparatus and test methods suitable for determining the flash point of viscous liquids may be used namely:—
— International Standards ISO 3679, ISO 3680, ISO 1523 and German Standard DIN 53213, Part 1.

Table 19

Method of test for combustibility

[Highly Flammable Liquids Regulations, 2 Sch]

Scope

1   The method describes a procedure for determining if the product when heated under the conditions of test and exposed to an external source of flame applied in a standard manner supports combustion.

Principle of the method

2   (1) A block of aluminium alloy, or other non-rusting metal of suitable heat conductivity, with a concave depression (called the well) is heated to the required temperature. A standard source of flame capable of being swivelled over the centre of the well and at a given distance from it is attached to the metal block.
(2) Two millilitres of product under test are transferred to the well and its combustibility characteristics are noted in relation to the standard flame.

Apparatus

3   (1) A combustibility tester consisting of an aluminium alloy or non-rusting metal block of suitable heat conductivity fitted with a concave depression or well. The metal block has a thermometer embedded in it. A small gas jet on a swivel is attached to the metal block.
(2) A simple gauge to check height of gas jet above the top of the well.
(3) The thermometer in the metal block shall be a Celsius thermometer conforming to the dimensions and tolerances given in this Schedule.

(4) A hot plate fitted with a temperature controlling device or other means of heating the metal block.

(5) A stop watch or other suitable timing device.

(6) A graduated pipette or hypodermic syringe capable of delivering two millilitres to an accuracy of ± 0.1 ml.

Sampling

4 (1) The sample shall be representative of the material being tested and shall be kept prior to test in an airtight container.

(2) Because of the possibility of loss of volatile constituents the sample shall receive only the minimum treatment to ensure uniformity. After removing a portion for test the sample container shall be immediately closed tightly to ensure that no volatile flammable components escape from the container.

Procedure

5 (1) Set up the apparatus in a draught free area. Place the metal block on the hot plate fitted with a temperature controlling device or heat the metal block by other suitable means so that its temperature is maintained at 50°C (within an accuracy of −0 +5°C) or to the corrected temperature allowing for difference of barometric pressure from the standard (760 mm of mercury or 1013 millibar) by raising the test temperature for a higher or lowering the test temperature for a lower pressure at the rate of 1°C for each 30 mm of mercury (40 millibar) difference. Ensure that the top of the metal block is exactly level. Use a gauge to check that the jet is 2.2 mm above top of the well.

(2) Using the pipette or graduated hypodermic syringe withdraw from the sample container at least 2 ml. of the test material and transfer 2 ml. ± 0.1 ml. of it to the well of the combustibility tester.

(3) Immediately start the timing device.

(4) Light the test flame with the jet in the 'off' position away from the well. Adjust the size of the flame so that it is spherical and approximately 4 mm in diameter. The size of the flame is matched to a 4 mm diameter circle engraved on the surface of the combustibility tester.

(5) After exactly one minute (at this time the test-portion will be deemed to have reached the test temperature as indicated by the thermometer embedded in the metal block) swing the test flame into a position exactly central over the well. Hold it in this position for exactly 15 seconds and then return it to the 'off' position.

Interpretation of observation

6 For the purpose of these regulations a product will be deemed to support combustion if, when tested in the manner set out above, either:

> (*a*) when the flame is over the well the product ignites and the combustion is sustained for more than 15 seconds when the flame is removed, or
>
> (*b*) when the flame is in the 'off' position the product flashes and burns.

Report of test

7 The test report should include the following information:

(1) The type and identification of the material under test.

(2) The test temperature in °C and barometric pressure in mm of mercury or millibar.

(3) A statement as to whether the products support combustion as defined in paragraph 6 of this Schedule.

(4) The date of the test.

Chapter 25

Joint Consultation – Safety Representatives and Safety Committees

Introduction

25.1   A safety representative is an employee appointed by his trade union to represent the workforce in consultations with the employer on all matters concerning health and safety at work, and to carry out periodic inspections of the workplace for hazards (for unionised and non-unionised workforces, see below). Every employer has a duty to consult with such union-appointed safety representatives on health and safety arrangements (and, if they so request him, to establish a safety committee to review the arrangements, see 25.12 below). [*HSWA s 2*].

The duty, its enforcement and the details of the role and functions of safety representatives are dealt with in this chapter, along with the constitution and functions of safety committees.

The duty of the employer is to consult with union-appointed safety representatives as regards both making and maintaining arrangements that will enable the employer and his workforce to co-operate in promoting and developing health and safety at work, and monitoring its effectiveness. The *Safety Representatives and Safety Committees Regulations 1977 (SI 1977 No 500)* made under *HSWA s 2(6)* (hereafter referred to as the '*Safety Representatives Regulations*'), regulate matters relating to safety representatives. (See the Health and Safety Commission publications 'Safety Representatives and Safety Committees Regulations and Guidance Notes 1977', and the approved code of practice (HSC 9) 'Time Off for the Training of Safety Representatives', referred to in 25.8 below.)

As for offshore installations, not previously covered by the above regulations, provision is made for the appointment of (not necessarily unionised) safety representatives thereon by the *Offshore Installations (Safety Representatives and Safety Committees) Regulations 1989 (SI 1989 No 971)* (see further Chapter 34 'Offshore Operations').

It should be understood that these regulations do not allow Health and Safety Executive (HSE) inspectors to prosecute employers for failing to consult with union-appointed safety representatives in cases where a company is *not* unionised. Indeed, the essentially non-enforcement complexion of these regulations, which are industrial relations orientated, would rarely give rise to prosecutions by HSE inspectors before the magistrates. The only situation where prosecution is possible is where a company with a unionised workforce refuses to recognise and hence consult with union safety representatives. However, where an employer whose workforce is not unionised appoints safety representatives, such safety representatives would not have the powers and immunities of union appointees. In short, they would not be recognised by law.

The right, accorded to employees who are safety representatives, not to be victimised or subjected to detriment, for health and safety activities, with the consequential right to present a complaint to an industrial tribunal not to be dismissed, is a testament to the intrinsically industrial relations orientation of the *Safety Representatives and Safety Committees Regulations 1977* (see further 13.7–13.10 EMPLOYEE SAFETY RIGHTS, DISCIPLINARY PROCEDURES AND UNFAIR DISMISSAL).

Role of safety representatives

25.2   The *Safety Representatives Regulations* give a number of detailed functions to safety representatives (see 25.3 below) but, basically, safety representatives exist in order to:

(*a*)   represent their fellow employees; and

(*b*)   carry out investigations and inspections; and

(*c*)   deal with information.

These functions are inter-related, with the consequence that safety representatives should not be concerned exclusively with the health, safety and welfare of their members when accidents or near misses occur or at the time of periodic inspections. Safety representatives can and indeed should be engaged in representing the health and safety interests of their members on a continuing day-to-day basis. Indeed, the *Safety Representatives Regulations* state that safety representatives have the functions of investigating potential hazards and members' complaints *before* accidents, as well as investigating dangerous occurrences and the causes of accidents *after* they have occurred.

Specific functions

25.3   A person appointed as a safety representative has the following functions (which are only assumed when the employer has been notified in writing, see 25.4 below):

(*a*)   to investigate potential hazards and causes of accidents at the workplace;

(*b*)   to investigate employee complaints concerning health etc. at work;

(*c*)   to make representations to the employer on matters arising out of (*a*) and (*b*) and on general matters affecting the health etc. of the employees at the workplace;

(*d*)   to carry out the following inspections (and see 25.6 below):

> (i)   of the workplace (after giving reasonable written notice to the employer, see *Reg 5*);
>
> (ii)   of the relevant area after a reportable accident or dangerous occurrence (see Chapter 3 'Accident Reporting') or if a reportable disease is contracted, if it is safe to do so and in the interests of the employees represented (see *Reg 6*);
>
> (iii) of documents relevant to the workplace or the employees represented which the employer is required to keep (see *Reg 7*) – reasonable notice must be given (e.g. accident book, see Chapter 3 'Accident Reporting');

(*e*)   to represent the employees he was appointed to represent in consultations with the HSE inspectors, and to receive information from them (see 25.10 below);

(f)   to attend meetings of safety committees.

[*Reg 4(1)*].

Thus, safety representatives may possibly be closely involved not only in the technical aspects of health, safety and welfare matters at work, but also in those areas which could be described as quasi-legal. In other words, they may become involved in the interpretation and clarification of terminology in the *Safety Representatives Regulations*, as well as in discussion and negotiation with employers as to how and when the regulations may be applied. This would often happen in committee meetings.

The safety representative's terms of reference are, therefore, broad, and exceed the traditional 'accident prevention' area. *Reg 4(1)* for example, empowers safety representatives to investigate 'potential hazards' and to take up issues which affect standards of health, safety and welfare at work (see 25.3(*a*) and (*b*) above). In practice it is becoming clear that four broad areas are now engaging the attention of safety representatives and safety committees:

—   health;

—   safety;

—   environment;

—   welfare.

These four broad areas effectively mean that safety representatives can, and indeed often do, examine standards relating, for example, to noise, dust, heating, lighting, cleanliness, lifting and carrying, machine guarding, toxic substances, radiation, cloakrooms, toilets and canteens. The protective standards that are operating in the workplace, or the lack of them, are now coming under much closer scrutiny than hitherto.

Appointment of safety representatives

25.4   The right of appointment of safety representatives is restricted to independent trade unions who are recognised by employers for collective bargaining purposes. The terms 'independent' and 'recognised' are defined in the *Safety Representatives Regulations* and follow the definitions laid down in the *Trade Union and Labour Relations Act 1974* (and its amending Acts of 1976 and 1992) (*TULRA*) and the *Employment Protection Act 1975* (*EPA*). The regulations make no provision for dealing with disputes which may arise over questions of independence or recognition (this is dealt with elsewhere in the *Employment Protection (Consolidation) Act 1978* (*EPCA*)). Safety representatives must be trade union representatives and it is up to each union to decide on its arrangements for the appointment or election of its safety representatives. Employers are not involved in this matter, except that they must be informed in writing of the names of the safety representatives appointed and of the group or groups of employees they represent.

The *Safety Representatives Regulations, Reg 8* state that safety representatives must be employees except in the cases of members of the Musicians' Union and actors' Equity. In addition, safety representatives, where reasonably practicable, should have at least two years' employment with their present employer or two years' experience in similar employment. The HSC guidance notes advise that it is not reasonably practicable for safety representatives to have two years' experience or employment elsewhere, where:

(*a*)   the employer is newly established; or

(*b*)   the workplace is newly established; or

(c)   the work is of short duration; or

(d)   there is high labour turnover.

Number of representatives for workforce

25.5   The *Safety Representatives Regulations* do not lay down the number of safety representatives that unions are permitted to appoint for each workplace. This is a matter for unions themselves to decide, having regard to the number of workers involved and the hazards to which they are exposed. The HSC's view is that each safety representative should be regarded as responsible for the interests of a defined group of workers. This approach has not been found to conflict with existing workplace trade union organisation based on defined groups of workers. The size of these groups does vary from union to union and from workplace to workplace. While normally each workplace area or constituency would only need one safety representative, additional safety representatives are sometimes required where members are exposed to numerous or particularly severe hazards; where workers are distributed over a wide geographical area or over a variety of workplace locations; and where workers are employed on shiftwork.

Workplace inspections

25.6   Arrangements for three-monthly and other more frequent inspections and re-inspections should be by joint arrangement. The TUC advises that the issues to be discussed with the employer can include:

(a)   more frequent inspections of high risk or rapidly changing areas of work activity;

(b)   the precise timing and notice to be given for formal inspections by safety representatives;

(c)   the number of representatives taking part in any one formal inspection;

(d)   the breaking-up of plant-wide formal inspections into smaller, more manageable inspections;

(e)   provision for different groups of safety representatives to carry out inspections of different parts of the workplace;

(f)   the kind of inspections to be carried out, e.g. safety tours, safety sampling or safety surveys;

(g)   the calling in of independent technical advisers by the safety representatives.

While formal inspections are not intended to be a substitute for day-by-day observation, they have on a number of occasions provided an opportunity to carry out a full scale examination of all or part of the workplace and for discussion with employers' representatives about remedial action. They can also provide an opportunity to inspect documents required under health and safety legislation, e.g. certificates concerning the testing of equipment. It should be emphasised that, during inspections following reportable accidents or dangerous occurrences, employers are not required to be present when the safety representative talks with his members. In workplaces where more than one union is recognised, agreements with employers about inspections should involve all the unions concerned. It is generally agreed that safety representatives are also allowed under the regulations to investigate the following:

(a)   potential hazards;

(b)   dangerous occurrences;

(c)   the causes of accidents;

(d)   complaints from their members.

This means that imminent risks, or hazards which may affect their members, can be investigated right away by safety representatives without waiting for formal joint inspections. Following an investigation of a serious mishap, safety representatives are advised to complete a hazard report form, one copy being sent to the employer and one copy retained by the safety representative.

Rights and duties of safety representatives

Legal immunity

25.7   The *Safety Representatives Regulations* state that none of the functions of a safety representative confers legal duties, or responsibilities. [*Reg 4(1)*]. As safety representatives are not legally responsible for health, safety or welfare at work, they cannot be liable under either the criminal or civil law for anything they may do, or fail to do, as a safety representative under these regulations. This protection against criminal or civil liability does not, however, remove a safety representative's legal responsibility as an employee. Safety representatives must carry out their responsibilities under *HSWA s 7(a)(b)* if they are not to be liable for criminal prosecution by an HSE inspector. These duties as an employee are to take reasonable care for one's self and others, and to co-operate with one's employer as far as is necessary to enable him to carry out his statutory duties on health and safety. (See further Chapter 14 'Employees' Duties'.)

Time off with pay

25.8   Under the regulations, safety representatives are entitled to paid leave, both in order to carry out their statutory functions and to undergo training in accordance with a code of practice approved by the Health and Safety Commission. (Where the employer's refusal to allow paid time off is unreasonable, he must reimburse the employee for the time taken to attend (*Scarth v East Herts DC (HSIB 181)* – the test of reasonableness is to be judged at the time of the decision to refuse training).) [*Reg 4(2), Schedule*]. Details of these requirements are outlined in the code of practice attached to the *Safety Representatives Regulations* and the HSC approved code of practice on time off for training. Safety representatives who are refused time off to perform their functions or who are not paid for such time off are able to make a complaint to an industrial tribunal. [*Reg 11*]. The combined effect of the ACAS Code No 3: 'Time Off for Trade Union Duties and Activities' issued under *EPA 1975* and the HSC approved code on time off, is that shop stewards who have also been appointed as safety representatives are to be given time off by their employers to carry out both their industrial relations duties and their safety functions, and also paid leave to attend separate training courses on industrial relations and on health and safety at work. (This includes a TUC course on COSHH (*Gallagher v The Drum Engineering Co Ltd, COIT 1330/89*).) An employee is not entitled to be paid for time taken off in lieu of the time he had spent on a course. This was held in *Hairsine v Hull City Council, The Times, 9 December 1991 (EAT)* when a shift worker, whose shift ran from 3 p.m. to 11 p.m., attended a trade union course from 9 a.m. to 4 p.m. and then carried out his duties until 7 p.m. He was paid from 3 p.m. to 7 p.m. and he could claim no more. However, where more safety representatives have been appointed than there are sections of the workforce for which safety representatives could be responsible, it is not unreasonable for an employer to deny some safety representatives time off for fulfilling safety functions (*Howard and Peet v Volex plc (HSIB 181)*). A decision of the EAT seems to favour jointly sponsored in-house courses, except as regards the representational aspects of the functions of safety representatives, where the training is to be provided exclusively by the union (*White v Pressed Steel Fisher [1980] IRLR 176*). Moreover, one course per union per year is too rigid an approach (*Waugh v London Borough of Sutton (1983) HSIB 86*).

Facilities to be provided by employer

25.9   The type and number of facilities that employers are obliged to provide for safety representatives are not spelled out in the regulations, code of practice or guidance notes, other than a general requirement in the *Safety Representatives Regulations, Reg 5(3)* which states, inter alia, that 'the employer shall provide such facilities and assistance as the safety representative shall require'. Trade unions consider that the phrase 'facilities and assistance' includes the right to request the presence of an independent technical adviser or trade union official during an inspection, and for safety representatives to take samples of substances used at work for analysis outside the workplace. The TUC has recommended that the following facilities be made available to safety representatives:

(*a*)   a room and desk at the workplace;

(*b*)   facilities for storing correspondence;

(*c*)   inspection reports and other papers;

(*d*)   ready access to internal and external telephones;

(*e*)   access to typing and duplicating facilities;

(*f*)   provision of notice boards;

(*g*)   use of suitable room for reporting back to and consulting with members;

(*h*)   other facilities should include copies of all relevant statutes, regulations, approved codes of practice and HSC guidance notes; and copies of all legal or international standards which are relevant to the workplace.

Disclosure of information

25.10   Employers are required by the *Safety Representatives Regulations* to disclose information to safety representatives which it is necessary for them to carry out their functions. [*Reg 7(2)*] – paralleling *Regulation 8* of the *Management of Health and Safety at Work Regulations 1992* (see 15.34 EMPLOYERS' DUTIES). This wide requirement relating to information in the approved code of practice, includes not only technical information and consultants' reports, but also information concerning employers' future plans and proposed changes in so far as they affect the health, safety or welfare at work of their employees. (The decision in *Waugh v British Railways Board [1979] 2 AER 1169* established that where an employer seeks to withold a report made following an accident on grounds of privilege, he can only do so if its dominant purpose is related to actual or potential hostile legal proceedings. Here a report was commissioned for two purposes following the death of an employee: (*a*) to recommend improvements in safety measures and, (*b*) to gather material for employer's defence. It was held that the report was not privileged.) This was recently followed in *Lask v Gloucester Health Authority (1986) HSIB 123* where a circular 'Reporting Accidents in Hospitals' had to be discovered by order after an injury to an employee whilst he was walking along a path. The relevant information to be disclosed by employers is contained in paragraph 6 of the approved code of practice on Safety Representatives and Safety Committees. Where differences of opinion arise as to the evaluation or interpretation of technical aspects of safety information on health data, unions are advised to contact the local offices of the HSE, because of the HSE expertise and access to research.

Technical information

25.11   HSE inspectors are also obliged, by *HSWA s 28(8)*, to supply safety representatives with technical information – factual information obtained during their visits (i.e. any measurements, testing the results of sampling and monitoring), notices of prosecution, copies of correspondence and copies of any improvement or prohibition notices issued to their employer. The latter places an absolute duty on an inspector to disclose specific kinds of information to workers or their representatives concerning health, safety and welfare at work. This can also involve personal discussions between the HSE inspector and the safety representative. The inspector must also tell the representative what action he proposes to take as a result of his visit. Where local authority health inspectors are acting under powers granted by *HSWA* (see Chapter 17 'Enforcement') they are also required to provide appropriate information to safety representatives.

Safety committees

25.12   There is a duty on every employer, in cases where it is prescribed (see below), to establish a safety committee if requested to do so by safety representatives. The committee's purpose is to monitor health and safety measures at work. [*HSWA s 2(7)*]. Such cases are prescribed by the *Safety Representatives Regulations* and limit the duty to appoint a committee to requests made by trade union safety representatives.

Establishment of a safety committee

25.13   If requested by at least two safety representatives in writing, the employer must establish a safety committee. [*Safety Representatives Regulations, Reg 9(1)*].

When setting up a safety committee the employer must:

(*a*)   consult with both:

　　　(i)   the safety representatives who make the request; and

　　　(ii)   the representatives of recognised trade unions whose members work in any workplace where it is proposed that the committee will function;

(*b*)   post a notice, stating the composition of the committee and the workplace or workplaces to be covered by it, in a place where it can easily be read by employees;

(*c*)   establish the committee within three months after the request for it was made.

[*Reg 9(2)*].

Function of safety committees

25.14   In practical terms, trade union appointed safety representatives are now using the medium of safety committees to examine the implications of hazard report forms arising from inspections, and the results of investigations into accidents and dangerous occurrences, together with the remedial actions required. A similar procedure exists with respect to representatives for tests and measurements of noise, toxic substances or other harmful effects on the working environment.

Trade unions regard the function of safety committees as a forum for the discussion and resolution of problems that have failed to be solved initially through the intervention of the safety representative in discussion with line management. There is, therefore, from the trade unions' viewpoint, a large measure of negotiation with its consequent effect on collective bargaining agreements.

If safety representatives are unable to resolve a problem with management through the safety committee, or with the HSE, they can approach their own union for assistance – a number of unions have their own health and safety officers who can, and do, provide an extensive range of information on occupational health and safety matters. The unions, in turn, can refer to the TUC for further advice.

Chapter 26

Lifting Machinery and Equipment

Introduction

26.1 Prior to the *Health and Safety at Work etc. Act 1974* (*HSWA*) legislation centred round the place of work, and statutory requirements relating to hoists and lifting gear varied considerably, depending on the place of work. Moreover, British Standards were often at variance with comparable overseas standards. In addition to specific requirements, to be found in the *Factories Act 1961*, the *Offices, Shops and Railway Premises Act 1963* (*OSRPA*) and regulations passed thereunder, *HSWA* s 2(2)(a) imposes a *general* duty of care on employers which is applicable to all lifting appliances in all workplaces. Moreover, *HSWA s 40* states that, in the event of a prosecution, the burden of proving that it was not 'practicable' or not 'reasonably practicable' (depending on the statutory requirement) to do more than was in fact done, is on the defendant, though the general burden of proof (in criminal cases) remains with the prosecution (see further Chapter 17 'Enforcement'). In the light of all this, it is advisable that all items of plant and lifting gear or tackle used in hoisting or lowering goods, materials or persons, be treated analogously with statutory items, with tests and thorough examinations being carried out in accordance with the nearest specific statutory requirements reasonably applicable.

The principal provisions relating to safe use of hoists and lifting gear at work are contained in the *Factories Act 1961*, the *Construction (Lifting Operations) Regulations 1961 (SI 1961 No 1581)*, the *Offices, Shops and Railway Premises (Hoists and Lifts) Regulations 1968 (SIs 1968 No 849, 1974 No 1943)*, and certain other regulations of more limited scope such as the *Shipbuilding and Ship-repairing Regulations 1960 (SI 1960 No 1932)*, which are outside the ambit of this chapter. Some of these requirements, as from 1 January 1995, become disapplied – at least, as far as *supply* of machinery is concerned (though not as regards continuing use in service of such machinery or machinery parts [*Reg 33(3)*]) – by the *Supply of Machinery (Safety) Regulations 1992 (SI 1992 No 3073)*, which comes into operation on that date (see further 28.47 MACHINERY SAFETY): these are the *Factories Act 1961, s 26(1)*, certain of the *Construction (Lifting Operations) Regulations 1961* and the *Construction (General Provisions) Regulations 1961* as well as sundry parts of the *Docks Regulations 1988* and the *Shipbuilding and Ship-repairing Regulations 1960* relating to test before first use (see Table 22 below). Moreover, since 'machinery' qualifies as 'work equipment', for the purposes of the *Provision and Use of Work Equipment Regulations 1992 (SI 1992 No 2932), Reg 2(1)*, some of the requirements of these regulations will extend to lifting machinery and appliances – particularly, those concerning maintenance, stability and lighting. Machinery put into service before 1 January 1993 is not affected by these regulations. Also, until 31 December 1994, machinery which complies with existing UK requirements will not need an EC mark. Particulars relating to hoists/lifts, lifting machinery and lifting tackle, as specified in the *Lifting Plant and Equipment (Records of Test and Examination etc.) Regulations 1992* which remove the requirement to report results by a competent person on prescribed forms, are contained in 26.29–26.31 below and for particulars of lifting equipment on offshore installations, see 34.8 OFFSHORE OPERATIONS.

The chapter examines the *Factories Act 1961* (see 26.2-26.15 below) and the *Offices, Shops and Railway Premises Act 1963* (and regulations passed under *OSRPA*) (see 26.16, 26.17 below), concluding with a tabular reference to the main across the board safety requirements (see 26.27 below). The chapter also contains a section outlining the common causes of failure of cranes, hoists and lifting equipment (see 26.18-26.26 below).

Statutory requirements

Factories

26.2   The *Factories Act 1961* divides 'hoisting, lifting and lowering' appliances essentially into three parts, i.e. requirements relating to (*a*) hoists and lifts, (*b*) other lifting machinery, e.g. crane, crab etc., and (*c*) lifting tackle, e.g. chains, ropes etc. (It is not unusual to regard 'hoists and lifts' as part and parcel of conventional 'lifting machinery', although the statutory requirements relating to both are separate.)

Hoists and lifts (generally)

26.3   Statutory requirements relating to 'lifting machinery' are covered in the *Factories Act 1961, ss 22-25, 27*. (The special position of 'forklift trucks' is examined below.)

Special position of forklift trucks

In the case of hoists and lifts of *all* types (*Sec 22*) and lifts for carrying persons only (*Sec 23*) 'no lifting mechanism or appliance (is) deemed to be a lift or hoist unless it has a platform or cage the direction or movement of which is restricted by a guide or guides'. [*Factories Act 1961, s 25(1)*]. A forklift truck, therefore, of standard design is not a 'hoist or lift' for the purposes of *Secs 22* and *23* (*Oldfield v Reed & Smith Ltd* [*1972*] *2 AER 104* where the plaintiff, a chargehand fitter in a paper factory, saw that one of their forklift trucks seemed defective, in that the forks appeared to be tipping downwards. In order to test this he called in the company transport manager and contract service engineer, and a 30 cwt roll of paper was lifted to full height. The plaintiff went to inspect the truck for oil leaks when the load was at full height, and accordingly stood under the load. The forks tilted and the roll of paper fell, landing on his foot. It was held that there was no action for breach of *Sec 22(1)*, in that this particular forklift truck (Coventry Climax type) was not a 'hoist or lift'. Although *Sec 22(1)* did not apply to the Coventry Climax forklift truck, a motor lift with a flat platform, conversely, is probably a 'hoist or lift' for the purposes of *Sec 22(1)*). In addition, any forklift truck is 'machinery' for the purposes of the *Factories Act 1961, s 14(1)* (*British Railways Board v Liptrot* [*1967*] *3 AER 1072*, per Lord Reid) (see further Chapter 28 'Machinery Safety').

Regulations specifically applicable to self-propelled industrial trucks manufactured on or after 18 July 1989 – the *Self-Propelled Industrial Trucks (EC Requirements) Regulations 1988 (SI 1988 No 1736)* and *Amendment Regulations 1989 (SI 1989 No 1035)*, requiring that they undergo regular tests for stability, visibility and function – continue in force until 1 January 1996, as from which date they are revoked. [*Supply of Machinery (Safety) Regulations 1992, 1 Sch*].

Specific requirements

26.4   Requirements relating to 'hoists and lifts' specifically are laid down in *Secs 22* and *23* as follows:

Every hoist/lift (whether for carrying goods, persons or both) must be of good construction, sound materials, adequate strength and properly maintained. [*Sec 22(1)*].

(*a*)   *Good construction*

This duty is absolute and does not depend on proof of negligence (*Galashiels Gas Co Ltd v O'Donnell* [*1949*] *1 AER 319*). Thus the fact that a latent defect in a hoist/lift could not be discovered by reasonable inspection is not an available defence to a factory occupier/employer (*Whitehead v James Stott & Co Ltd* [*1949*] *1 AER 245* where a pinion supporting a pulley at the top of a lift shaft broke, and the cabin fell to the ground. The lift had operated normally for 25 years. In the fall some metal came away from the roof of the cabin and hit the plaintiff, causing him injury. Evidence showed that it would have required X-ray technology to detect this latent metal fatigue. It was held that the requirement was absolute and the employer was liable).

Hoists/lifts are of good mechanical construction if they are good when used for their normal purpose. There is no breach of statutory requirement if injury is caused when hoists/lifts are used for the wrong purpose (*Beadsley v United Steel Companies Ltd* [*1950*] *2 AER 872* where a slinger used the wrong set of tackle to move a heavy mould, although the right tackle was easily available. The mould fell when the lifting chains came free, killing the employee. His widow's action for breach of *Sec 22* failed).

(*b*)   *Adequate strength*

If lifts are strong enough for their normal purpose, the fact that they are unsuitable for that use does not amount to a breach of *Sec 22* (*Gledhill v Liverpool Abattoir Co Ltd* [*1957*] *3 AER 117* where a new pig-lifting device in the abattoir, although strong enough, did not provide a tight slip knot; a pig fell through the chains, injuring the plaintiff. It was held that the employer was not liable). What is important in the definition 'adequate strength' is the materials which are being used: any prescribed 'safe working loads' (for SWLs, see 26.6 below) are ancillary to the requirement of 'adequate strength'; in other words, whether SWLs are prescribed or not, is only marginally relevant in determining whether a hoist/lift is of 'adequate strength' (*Ball v Richard Thomas & Baldwins Ltd* [*1968*] *1 AER 389*).

(*c*)   *Properly maintained*

The duty of maintenance is also absolute. 'Maintain' means 'kept in efficient working order'. Once the mechanism fails to work efficiently, the burden of proving breach of statutory duty has been discharged (*Galashiels Gas Co Ltd v O'Donnell* [*1949*] *1 AER 319* where an employee was killed when he fell down a lift shaft, the brakes of the cage having failed. The failure of the brakes could not be explained. It was held that the employer was liable; the employee's widow did not have to show how the accident happened) (see further *res ipsa loquitur*, Chapter 40 'Shops').

(*d*)   *Examination by competent person*

Every hoist or lift must be thoroughly examined by a competent person (see below) once every six months at least and a record kept. The record of a test/examination need no longer be a written report; electronic storage/retrieval/transmission is sufficient, though a record must be capable of being reproduced as a written copy, when required by an inspector, for the purposes of *HSWA s 20(2)(l)*, *(m)*. [*Lifting Plant and Equipment (Records of Test and Examination etc.) Regulations 1992 (SI 1992 No 195), Reg 2*] (see 26.29 below for the particulars to be included in the report). Hence, a competent person can now use the same form on which to provide the written record for the majority of lifting plant/equipment to be used. (For details to be recorded, see 26.31 below.) Where defects indicate that the future operation of the equipment may be unsafe, the HSE must be notified by a 'competent person' within 28 days. [*Factories Act 1961, s 22(2)*].

Legislation relating to factories and offices consistently stresses the need for inspection and testing by a 'competent person'. It is exceedingly unfortunate, therefore, that there is no statutory definition of 'competent person' for most purposes, including the 'hoists and lifts' requirements. In order, therefore, to ensure that the organisation/individual *is* competent, the following questions should be asked:

(i)   What are the qualifications, experience and past training record of the person or persons who will carry out tests and a thorough examination?

(ii) What back-up services are available to monitor the work of the 'competent person' while maintaining and developing services to the optimum level, which will ensure continuing competency?

By initiating these inquiries, companies and managers could be going some way towards complying with their statutory duties.

Duty to prevent persons coming into contact with the hoist/lift

26.5   Every hoistway or liftway must be efficiently protected by a substantial enclosure fitted with gates of such design and layout as to prevent, when the gates are shut, any person (for the meaning of this expression, see Chapters 18 'Factories and Workplaces' and 28 'Machinery Safety') falling down the shaft or coming into contact with any moving parts of the equipment. Such a gate must be fitted with an efficient interlocking device. [*Factories Act 1961, s 22(4)*].

The duty to prevent any person (not merely an employee) coming into contact with moving parts of the lift is absolute. Thus, if a person can put his hands through the outer gates of a lift and reach the inner gates, the factory occupier is liable for breach of *Sec 22(4)* (*Blakely v C & H Clothing Co Ltd* [*1958*] *1 AER 297* where an employee put his hand through the lattice work of the outer gate of the works lift to check the inner gate of the lift. The lift moved, causing a guillotine effect between the inner and outer gates injuring the employee. It was held that the employer was liable; it was irrelevant whether the employee's conduct was foreseeable or not).

Similarly, every hoist or lift and every enclosure must be so constructed as to prevent any part of any person, or any goods carried, from being trapped between any part of the hoist or lift and any fixed structure, or between the counterbalance weight or any other moving part. [*Factories Act 1961, s 22(7)*].

Safe working loads (SWLs)

26.6   The safe working load of a hoist/lift must be conspicuously marked and not exceeded. [*Factories Act 1961, s 22(8)*]. This requirement is ancillary to the requirement of 'adequate strength' in *Sec 22(1)*. SWLs are only marginally relevant in determining whether a hoist/lift is of 'adequate strength' (*Ball v Richard Thomas & Baldwins Ltd* [*1968*] *1 AER 389*).

Hoists and lifts for carrying persons only

26.7   In addition to the requirements of the *Factories Act 1961, s 22* (see 26.4-26.6 above) in relation to *all* lifts/hoists in factories, the following requirements apply in relation to hoists/lifts for carrying persons:

(*a*)   efficient automatic devices must be provided to prevent the cage or platform over-running [*Sec 23(1)(a)*];

(*b*)   a gate must be provided on every side where access to a landing is afforded along with efficient devices to prevent the cage being set in motion when the gate is open *and* to ensure that the cage will come to rest when the gate is opened [*Sec 23(1)(b)*];

(*c*)   where the platform or cage is suspended by a rope or chain:

　　(i)   there must be at least two ropes or chains separately connected to the cage or platform;

　　(ii)   each rope or chain (and its attachments) must be capable of carrying the whole weight of the platform or cage and its maximum working load (MWL);

　　(iii) efficient devices must be 'provided and maintained' (see Chapter 15 'Employers' Duties' for the meaning of this expression) which will support the platform or cage with its MWL in the event of a breakage of the ropes or chains (or any attachments).

[*Factories Act 1961, s 23(3)*].

Teagle openings

26.8   A teagle opening is an opening in the fabric of a building through which goods can be hoisted into the building. Such openings are common in flour and agricultural mills in particular. They can also be found in older types of factories and warehouses. Every teagle opening or similar doorway used for hoisting or lowering goods or material by mechanical power or otherwise, must be securely fenced (see Chapter 28 'Machinery Safety' for the meaning of this expression) and provided with a secure hand-hold on each side. [*Factories Act 1961, s 24(1)*] (remaining in force until 1 January 1996). Such fencing must be properly maintained (see 26.5 above, *Blakely v C & H Clothing Co Ltd*) and kept in position, except when hoisting or lowering goods. [*Factories Act 1961, s 24(2)*].

Other lifting machinery

26.9   'Other lifting machinery' refers to (*a*) cranes, (*b*) crabs, (*c*) winches, (*d*) teagles, (*e*) pulley blocks, (*f*) gin wheels, (*g*) transporters and (*h*) runways. [*Factories Act 1961, s 27(9)*]. Statutory requirements relating to them are as follows:

(*a*)   all lifting machinery must comply with the requirements of the *Supply of Machinery (Safety) Regulations 1992*. For information on this see 28.47–28.65 MACHINERY SAFETY;

(*b*)   all parts and working gear must be examined by a 'competent person' (see 26.4(*d*) above) at least once every 14 months, and a report, containing particulars of the examination kept in a register (see 26.29 below for the relevant particulars). Where defects indicate that the operation of the equipment may be unsafe unless repairs can be carried out immediately or within a specified time, a copy must be sent to the HSE within 28 days [*Factories Act 1961, s 27(2)*];

(*c*)   all rails on which a travelling crane moves and every track on which a transporter or runway moves, must fulfil the following requirements:

　　(i)   be of proper size and adequate strength (see *Gledhill* above);

(ii)   have an even running surface;

(iii)   any rails on the track must be properly laid, adequately supported or suspended and properly maintained (see *Blakely* at 26.5 above) [*Factories Act 1961, s 27(3)*];

(iv)   the safe working load(s) must be plainly marked on every lifting machine. In the case of a jib crane (with a load that varies as the jib is raised or lowered), it must have attached to it either an SWL indicator or table indicating SWLs at corresponding inclinations of the jib or corresponding radii of the load [*Factories Act 1961, s 27(4)*];

(v)   no lifting machine must be loaded beyond its SWL (except for proof testing purposes) [*Factories Act 1961, s 27(5)*].

Cranes

26.10   If any person is employed or working on or near the wheeltrack of an overhead travelling crane in any place where he would be liable to be struck by the crane, effective measures must be taken to ensure that the crane does not approach within about six metres of that place. [*Factories Act 1961, s 27(7)*] .

A crane which travels on tracks laid on the ground but which has a high gantry and cabin is not an 'overhead travelling crane' (*Carrington v John Summers & Sons Ltd* [*1957*] *1 AER 457*. This case established that there is a difference between an 'overhead travelling crane' and an 'overhead crane travelling'. The word 'travelling' was qualified by the word 'overhead', indicating that the travelling gear had to be overhead. A crane, no matter how tall, was not 'overhead travelling' if its travelling gear was on the ground, e.g. very high gantry cranes in dockyards carrying very high loads. An overhead crane is one where it is not possible to raise the load higher than the lifting mechanism of the crane).

Moreover, the requirement that 'effective measures be taken' (above) imposes an absolute duty to ensure the safety of employees (and others) working on or near the wheeltrack of overhead cranes; the mere posting of a notice, warning employees not to approach nearer than 20 feet when a crane was passing, was not compliance with this requirement (*Lotinga v North Eastern Marine Engineering Co* [*1941*] *3 AER 1* where an employee was killed when working on the wheeltrack of an overhead crane. Notices were posted warning employees that they must tell the crane driver that they were working there because the crane was so constructed that the crane driver could not see whether employees were on the track or not. The company had not had a similar accident for the past 37 years. It was held that the employer was liable; his past safety record was irrelevant because safety duties cannot be delegated in this way to employees (see further generally Chapter 15 'Employers' Duties')). A person can be 'working on or near the wheeltrack of an overhead travelling crane', even though he is completely out of the path of an overhead travelling crane (*Holmes v Hadfield Ltd* [*1944*] *1 AER 235* where the employee was working on a platform near the wheeltrack of an overhead crane. The sides of the crane cab overhung the track. The crane driver stopped when he saw the plaintiff using a large drill on the platform. The plaintiff then got off the platform and climbed down to a girder eight feet below the platform and the wheeltrack. As the crane passed the platform, it knocked over the drill and it landed on the plaintiff. It was held that the factory occupier/employer was liable. 'Working on or near' referred to the whole area, i.e. places where the employee moves to and from in the course of carrying out his work. Moreover, the fact that he was struck by a tool knocked over by the crane (rather than the crane itself) was irrelevant).

Where any person is working at a place above floor level where he would be liable to be struck by an overhead travelling crane or its load, effective measures (see *Lotinga* above) must be taken to warn him of the approach of the crane, unless his work is so connected with or dependent on the movements of the crane as to make a warning unnecessary. [*Factories Act 1961, s 27(7)*]. (See further BS 7121: Safe use of cranes.)

Lifting tackle

26.11 'Lifting tackle' refers to (*a*) chain slings, (*b*) rope slings, (*c*) rings, (*d*) hooks, (*e*) shackles, and (*f*) swivels. [*Factories Act 1961, s 26(3)*].

Good construction/adequate strength

26.12 No chain, rope or lifting tackle must be used ('uses' are not limited to those only authorised by the employer – *Barry v Cleveland Bridge and Engineering Co Ltd* [*1963*] *1 AER 192*), unless it is of good construction, sound material, adequate strength and free from patent defect [*Factories Act 1961, s 26(1)(a)*] (see, in connection with hoists/lifts, the cases of *Galashiels Gas Co v O'Donnell*, *Gledhill v Liverpool Abattoir Co Ltd* and *Ball v RTB Ltd* at 26.4 above). (See 26.13 below for the EC mark for supply requirements.)

Safe working load

26.13 Unless the SWL is clearly marked on them [*Factories Act 1961, s 26(2)*], chains, ropes and lifting tackle must not be used, unless in the case of:

(*a*)   every kind and size of chain, rope or lifting tackle; and

(*b*)   multiple sling;

the SWL (at different angles of the legs) is posted in a prominent place in the store where the chains, ropes and lifting tackle are kept.

[*Factories Act 1961, s 26(1)(b)*].

The chains, ropes and lifting tackle must not be used for any load greater than the SWL. [*Factories Act 1961, s 26(1)(c)*]. The requirement relating to SWL is ancillary to that of 'adequate strength' (see *Ball v RTB Ltd* at 26.4 above).

Supply of machinery for this purpose must conform with the *Supply of Machinery (Safety) Regulations 1992*, that is, it must usually carry an EC mark.

Examinations/testing

26.14 (*a*)   All chains, ropes and lifting tackle must be examined by a 'competent person' (see 26.4(*d*) above) at least once every six months. [*Factories Act 1961, s 26(1)(d)*].

(*b*)   No chain, rope or lifting tackle (except a fibre rope or fibre rope sling) must be taken into use in any factory (for the meaning of this expression, see Chapter 18 'Factories and Workplaces') for the first time unless (i) it has been tested and (ii) thoroughly examined, by a 'competent person' and a certificate of test and examination, specifying the SWL and signed by that person, must be kept available for inspection. [*Factories Act 1961, s 26(1)(e)*]. (For details to be recorded, see 26.30 below.)

All chains, ropes and lifting tackle supplied for use in any factory must conform to the *Supply of Machinery (Safety) Regulations 1992* (see 28.47–28.65 MACHINERY SAFETY).

Annealing

26.15   (*a*)   Every chain and lifting tackle (but not a rope sling), must be annealed (i.e. heat treated) at least every 14 months (unless exempted because it cannot be subjected to heat treatment without damage) [*Factories Act 1961, s 26(1)(f)*];

   (*b*)   (i)   chains/slings of ½ inch bar (or smaller), or

        (ii)   chains used with molten metal or molten slag

   must be annealed every six months (except those in regular use) [*Factories Act 1961, s 26(1)(f)*];

   (*c*)   employers must keep a register containing all particulars relating to chains, ropes and lifting tackle (except fibre ropes) [*Factories Act 1961, s 26(1)(g)*].

Offices and shops – lifts suspended by ropes/chains

26.16   Statutory requirements relating to hoists and lifts in offices and shops (for the definition of 'office' and 'shop', see Chapters 33 and 40 respectively), are to be found in the *Offices, Shops and Railway Premises (Hoists and Lifts) Regulations 1968 (SI 1968 No 849; SI 1974 No 1943)*. The main duties are as follows (as laid down in the 1968 regulations):

   (*a*)   hoists/lifts must be of good mechanical construction, sound material, adequate strength and properly maintained. (In the absence of case law on the point, by way of analogy case law on the *Factories Act 1961, s 22* will apply; see above) [*Reg 5*];

   (*b*)   where hoists/lifts are mechanically powered, they must be examined by a 'competent person' every six months and a report signed by that person and the report should be sent within 28 days to the owner of the building or occupier in certain circumstances. The record must be kept for two years from the date of signing of the record [*Reg 6*] (for details to be recorded, see 26.31 below);

   (*c*)   in the case of continuous/manually operated hoists/lifts, they must be examined by a 'competent person' every twelve months [*Reg 3*];

   (*d*)   every liftway must be efficiently protected by a substantial enclosure fitted with gates; the enclosure must, when the gates are shut, prevent any person:

        (i)   falling down the way; or

        (ii)   coming into contact with any moving part of the lift (see *Blakely v C & H Clothing Co Ltd* at 26.5 above)

   [*Reg 7(1)*];

   (*e*)   except in the case of (i) a continuous lift, or (ii) a manually operated lift, such a gate must be fitted with an efficient interlocking device, so that:

        (i)   the gate cannot be opened, unless the cage or platform is at the landing; and

        (ii)   the cage or platform cannot be moved away from the landing till the gate is closed

   [*Reg 7(2)*];

(f)   the maximum working load (MWL) must be clearly marked on the lift, and no load greater than MWL must be carried [*Reg 8*];

(g)   if the lift cannot be used safely and repairs cannot be made immediately or within a specified time, notification of this fact must be made, within 28 days of the examination of the lift, to the competent authority.

Lifts for carrying persons

26.17   In the case of lifts for carrying persons (either exclusively or in addition to goods) the following additional requirements apply:

(a)   efficient automatic devices must be 'provided and maintained' (see Chapter 15 'Employers' Duties') to prevent the cage/platform overrunning; and

(b)   every cage must be fitted with a gate, and when persons are in the cage, devices must be fitted so that the cage cannot be raised or lowered, unless the gate is closed and will come to rest when the gate is opened

[*Reg 9(1)*];

(c)   where the platform/cage is suspended by a rope or chain, there must be at least two ropes or chains separately connected with the platform/cage, and each rope/chain (and attachments) must be capable of carrying the whole weight of the platform/cage and its MWL;

(d)   in the event of a breakage of ropes/chains (or attachments), efficient devices must be provided and maintained (see Chapter 15 'Employers' Duties') to support the platform/cage together with its MWL.

[*Reg 9(3)*].

Cranes, hoists and lifting equipment – common causes of failure

General

26.18   The principal cause of failure in all forms of lifting equipment is that of overloading, i.e. exceeding the specified Safe Working Load (SWL) of the crane, forklift truck, hoist, chain, etc. in use for a specific lifting job. Every year there are numerous accidents and scheduled dangerous occurrences reported which are caused as a result of overloading. A second common cause of failure, and one which is inexcusable, is associated with neglect of the equipment while not in use. Neglect may be associated with poor or inadequate maintenance of the fabric of a crane or its safety devices, or simply a failure to store rope slings properly while not in use. One of the results of neglect is corrosion of metal surfaces resulting in weakened crane structures, wire ropes and slings.

Specific causes of failure are outlined below.

Cranes

26.19   (a)   Failure to lift vertically, e.g. dragging a load sideways along the ground before lifting.

(b)   'Snatching' loads, i.e. not lifting slowly and smoothly.

(c)   Exceeding the maximum permitted moment, i.e. the product of the load and the radius of operation.

(d)   Excessive wind loading, resulting in crane instability.

(e)   Defects in the fabrication of the crane, e.g. badly welded joints.

(f)   Incorrect crane assembly in the case of tower cranes.

(g)   Brake failure (rail-mounted cranes).

(h)   In the case of mobile cranes:

    (i)   failure to use outriggers;

    (ii)   lifting on soft or uneven ground; and

    (iii)   incorrect tyre pressures.

Hoists and lifts

26.20   (a)   Excessive wear in wire ropes.

    (b)   Excessive broken wires in ropes.

    (c)   Failure of the overload protection device.

    (d)   Failure of the overrun device.

Ropes

Fibre ropes

26.21   (a)   Bad storage in wet or damp conditions resulting in rot and mildew.

    (b)   Inadequate protection of the rope when lifting loads with sharp edges.

    (c)   Exposure to direct heat to dry, as opposed to gradual drying in air.

    (d)   Chemical action.

Wire ropes

26.22   (a)   Excessive broken wires.

    (b)   Failure to lubricate regularly.

    (c)   Frequent knotting or kinking of the rope.

    (d)   Bad storage in wet or damp conditions which promotes rust.

Chains

26.23   (a)   Mechanical defects in individual links.

    (b)   Application of a static in excess of the breaking load.

    (c)   Snatch loading.

Slings

26.24   Slings are manufactured in natural or man-made fibre or chain. The safe working load of any sling varies according to the angle formed between the legs of the sling. (See diagram *fig. 6* below.)

Maximum safe working loads for slings at various angles

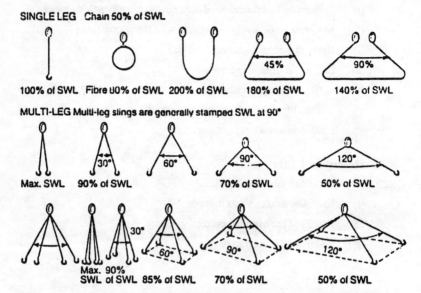

Select the correct size of a sling for the load taking into account the included angle and the possibility of unequal loading in the case of Multi-leg slings

fig. 6

Deviations from the criteria recommended in the above diagram will result in overloading of the sling. The relationship between sling angle and the distance between the legs of the sling is also important. (See Table 20 below.)

Table 20
Safe working load for slings

Sling Angle	Distance between legs
30°	½ leg length
60°	1 leg length
90°	1⅓ leg length
120°	1⅔ leg length

For a one tonne load, the tension in the leg increases as shown in Table 21 below.

Table 21

Safe working load for slings – increased tension

Sling leg angle	Tension in leg (tonnes)
90°	0.7
120°	1.0
151°	2.0
171°	6.0

Other causes of failure in slings are:

(*a*)   Cuts, excessive wear, kinking and general distortion of the sling legs.

(*b*)   Failure to lubricate wire slings.

(*c*)   Failure to pack sharp corners of a load, resulting in sharp bends in the sling and the possibility of cuts or damage to it.

(*d*)   Unequal distribution of the load between the legs of a multi-leg sling.

Hooks

26.25   (*a*)   Distortion of the hook due to overloading.

(*b*)   Use of a hook without a safety catch.

(*c*)   Stripping of the thread connecting the hook to the chain fixture.

Forklift trucks

26.26   (*a*)   Uneven floors, steeply inclined ramps or gradients, i.e. in excess of 1:10 gradient.

(*b*)   Inadequate room to manoeuvre.

(*c*)   Inadequate or poor maintenance of lifting gear.

(*d*)   The practice of driving forwards down a gradient with the load preceding the truck.

(*e*)   Load movement in transit.

(*f*)   Sudden or fast braking.

(*g*)   Hidden obstructions in the path of the truck.

(*h*)   Use of the forward tilt mechanism with a raised load.

(*j*)   Generally bad driving, including driving too fast, taking corners too fast, striking overhead obstructions, particularly when reversing and excessive use of the brakes.

Specific statutory provisions for hoists and lifting gear

26.27   Table 22 below contains a summary of the specific statutory provisions for hoists and lifting gear.

Table 22

Specific statutory provisions for hoists and lifting gear – summary

Part A
Hoists and lifts [*Factories Act 1961; OSRPA*]

Provision	Duty/requirement	Workplace
Factories Act 1961, s 22(1)	Hoists and lifts operated by mechanical power must be of good mechanical construction, sound material and adequate strength and properly maintained. This duty is strict (*Galashiels Gas Company Ltd v O'Donnell [1949] 1 AER 319*).	Factories as defined by the *Factories Act* (see Chapter 18 'Factories and Workplaces')
Factories Act 1961, s 22(2)	Examination and report by competent person every six months. (Mechanically powered only.)	Factories (as defined)
Factories Act 1961, s 25(2)(3)	Examination every twelve months. (Continuous/manually operated only.) (*N.B.* Various hoists are exempted from some or all these provisions by the *Hoists Exemption Order 1962 (SI 1962 No 715)*.)	Factories (as defined)
Factories Act 1961, s 22(4)	Provisions as to enclosure and gates.	Factories (as defined)
Factories Act 1961, s 22(8)	Conspicuous marking of maximum safe working load which must not be exceeded.	Factories (as defined)
Factories Act 1961, s 22(7)	Lifts and hoists used for carrying goods must be constructed in such a way as to ensure that goods and persons carried cannot be trapped between any part of the lift or hoist and a fixed structure (e.g. a wall).	Factories (as defined)
Factories Act 1961, s 23(1)	Lifts and hoists used for carrying people must have an automatic device to prevent the cage overrunning and an interlocked gate which allows the cage to move only if the gate is closed.	Factories (as defined)

Provision	Duty/requirement	Workplace

Specific requirements for lifts etc. suspended by rope/chain

Offices, Shops and
Railway Premises
(Hoists and Lifts)
Regulations 1968
(SI 1968 No 849;
SI 1974 No 1943):

Reg 5	Hoists and lifts must be of good mechanical construction, sound material, adequate strength and properly maintained. Presumably, by analogy with the *Factories Act 1961, s 22(1)* (see above), this duty is strict.	Offices, shops etc. as defined by *OSRPA* (see Chapter 33 'Offices')
Reg 6	Examination and report by competent person every six months. (Mechanically powered.)	Offices, shops etc. (as defined)
Reg 3	Examination and report by competent person every twelve months. (Continuous/manually operated.)	Offices, shops etc. (as defined)
Regs 7-9	Provisions relating to enclosure and gates, maximum safe working load and safety requirements for lifts used for carrying people.	Offices, shops etc. (as defined)
	(*N.B.* Schedule exempts certain types of hoist from various provisions.)	

Requirements for lifts suspended by rope/chain – on construction sites

Construction
(Lifting
Operations)
Regulations
1961 (SI 1961
No 1581):

Reg 41	Chain/lifting gear (other than those that cannot be annealed without risk of damage) not to be used for raising, lowering or for suspension purposes unless	Building operations and works of engineering construction
	(i) effectively annealed within previous fourteen months,	
	(ii) a report (F 91 Section K) relating to requisite annealing has been signed by the competent person, except	
	(*a*) chains made of malleable cast-iron,	
	(*b*) plate link chains,	

Table 22 (contd.)

Provision	Duty/requirement	Workplace
	(*c*) chains, rings, links, hooks, plate clamps, shackles, swivels and eye-bolts made of steel or any non-ferrous metal,	
	(*d*) pitched chains working on sprocket or pocketed wheels,	
	(*e*) rings, links, hooks, shackles and swivels permanently attached to pitched chains, pulley blocks or weighing machines,	
	(*f*) hooks, eye-bolts and swivels with screw-threaded parts or ball-bearings or other case-hardened parts,	
	(*g*) socket shackles secured to wire ropes by white metal cappings,	
	(*h*) bordeaux connections.	
Regs 42-44	General provisions relating to the safe operation of hoists.	Building operations and works of engineering construction (see Chapter 7 'Construction and Building Operations')
Reg 45	Safe working load and legible marking of hoists.	Building operations and works of engineering construction (see above)
Reg 46	Test and examination before use and after repair, and at least every six months by competent person.	Building operations and works of engineering construction (see above)
Reg 10	Weekly inspection of plant etc. should be recorded on form F 91, which should be available on site.	Building operations and works of engineering construction (see above)
	(*N.B.* 'Hoist' for these regulations means a lifting machine whether worked by mechanical power or not, but not a lifting appliance used for moving trucks etc. on rails.)	

Provision	Duty/requirement	Workplace

Part B
Other lifting machines – factories/construction sites

Factories Act 1961, *s 27(1)*	All parts of working gear (fixed or moveable, including anchoring) must be of good construction, of sound material, of adequate strength and free from patent defect. (If a part has a *latent* defect factory occupier could still be liable if the part was not, e.g., of good construction – *McNeill v Dickson & Mann 1957 SC 345*, but see also the duty of manufacturer and supplier in *HSWA s 6*.) All parts etc. must be adequately maintained (cf *Factories Act 1961, s 22(1)* in Part A above).	Factories (as defined)

(disapplied completely by the *Supply of Machinery (Safety) Regulations 1992*)

Factories Act 1961, *s 27(2)*	All parts and working gear must be thoroughly examined by a competent person at least once every 14 months and a register kept of prescribed particulars.	Factories (as defined)
Factories Act 1961, *s 27(4)(5)*	Safe working loads must be plainly marked on every lifting machine (not to be exceeded except for testing purposes).	Factories (as defined)
Factories Act 1961, *s 27(6)*	Testing, thorough examination and certification of lifting machine before first use.	Factories (as defined)

(disapplied completely by the *Supply of Machinery (Safety) Regulations 1992*)

Factories Act 1961, *s 27(3)(7)(8)*	Provisions relating to the safety of travelling cranes (including overhead travelling cranes).	Factories (as defined)
Construction (Lifting Operations) Regulations 1961 (SI 1961 No 1581), Reg 28(1)(2)	No crane, crab or winch shall be used unless it has been tested and thoroughly examined by a competent person within the last four years. Nor must a pulley block, gin wheel or sheer legs be used for loads of one ton or more unless tested and thoroughly examined by a competent person. A test and thorough examination must also be made in either case where the machine has undergone substantial alteration/repair.	Building operations and works of engineering construction (see Chapter 7 'Construction and Building Operations')
Construction (Lifting Operations) Regulations 1961, Reg 28(3)	Thorough examination of all such lifting appliances by a competent person at least every 14 months and after substantial alteration/repair. (Certificates of test and examination required in each case – *Reg 28(5)* (Form 80).)	Building operations and works of engineering construction (see above)

Table 22 (contd.)

Provision	Duty/requirement	Workplace
Construction (Lifting Operations) Regulations 1961, Reg 30	Inspection of automatic safe load indicator before first use, at weekly intervals, and, e.g., after adjustment/bad weather/ change of crane configuration (Form 91).	Building operations and works of engineering construction (see above)

(partly disapplied by the *Supply of Machinery (Safety) Regulations 1992, Reg 33*)

Construction (Lifting Operations) Regulations 1961, Reg 10(2)	Every lifting machine and every part of it (including all working gear) must be inspected at least once a week by a competent person (cf *Factories Act 1961, s 22(1)* in Part A above) (Form F 91).	Building operations and works of engineering construction (see above)
Construction (Lifting Operations) Regulations 1961, Reg 19(4)	Test and examination of anchorage and ballasting before first use and after, e.g., adjustment/bad weather/change of crane configuration.	Building operations and works of engineering construction (see above)
Construction (Lifting Operations) Regulations 1961, Reg 13	Provisions relating to the safety of crane platforms.	Building operations and works of engineering construction (see above)

(disapplied completely by the *Supply of Machinery (Safety) Regulations 1992, Reg 33* apart from *Reg 33(3)* relevant to guard rails and toe board use)

Construction (Lifting Operations) Regulations 1961, Regs 17, 19	Safe means of access to and stability of lifting machines.	Building operations and works of engineering construction (see above)
Construction (Lifting Operations) Regulations 1961, Reg 29(1)	The safe working load(s) and means of identification must be marked on every crane, crab and winch, and on every pulley block, gin wheel, sheer legs etc. used for loads of one ton or more.	Building operations and works of engineering cónstruction (see above)
Construction (Lifting Operations) Regulations 1961, Reg 29(2)	Safe working load is to be marked as specified on every crane of variable operating radius (including a crane with derricking jib) and such cranes to be fitted with an accurate indicator of radius and safe load.	Building operations and works of engineering construction (see above)

Provision	Duty/requirement	Workplace
Construction (Lifting Operations) Regulations 1961, Reg 30(2)(3)	Testing and inspection of load of jib cranes.	Building operations and works of engineering construction (see above)
Docks Regulations 1988 (SI 1988 No 1655), Regs 14, 15	Examination of lifting plant every twelve months by a competent person.	Docks, wharfs, quays
Shipbuilding and Ship-repairing Regulations 1960 (SI 1960 No 1932), Reg 34(2)	Thorough examination every twelve months.	Shipyards, harbours
Offshore Installations (Operational Safety, Health and Welfare) Regulations 1976 (SI 1976 No 1019), Reg 6	Every lifting appliance and piece of lifting gear must be thoroughly examined and tested: (a) before being used for the first time; and (b) before re-use after substantial alteration or repair; and (c) at set intervals and times given in *1 Sch Pt III* of the Regulations.	Fixed offshore installations, mobile offshore installations (excluding dredging vessels) (see further Chapter 34 'Offshore Operations')

Part C
Lifting tackle – factories/construction sites

Factories Act 1961, s 26(1)(a)	No chain, rope or lifting tackle must be used to raise or lower people, goods or materials unless it is of good construction, sound material, adequate strength and is free from patent defect. The requirement of adequate strength is judged in relation to the use to which the equipment is put. (*Milne v C F Wilson and Co (1960) SLT 162*).	Factories (as defined)
Factories Act 1961, s 26(1)(b)(c)	A table must be available showing the safe working loads (SWL) of all lifting tackle (unless item itself clearly marked) and this load must not be exceeded.	Factories (as defined)
Factories Act 1961, s 26(1)(d)	All lifting tackle must be examined thoroughly by a competent person at least every six months.	Factories (as defined)
Factories Act 1961, s 26(1)(e)	Testing and certification (of SWL) of all new equipment before use and re-examination every six months by a competent person (not fibre ropes/slings).	Factories (as defined)

Table 22 (contd.)

Provision	Duty/requirement	Workplace
Factories Act 1961, s 26(1)(f)	Metallic tackle must be annealed, i.e. heat-treated or stress-relieved, every 14 months (or, in case of small slings, every six months) unless exempted by certificate. (*Note*: The exemption certificate in fact applies to almost all tackle in use in industry today.)	Factories (as defined)

(all the above provisions relevant to the supply of machinery are disapplied by the *Supply of Machinery (Safety) Regulations 1992, Reg 33(3)*, as from 1 January 1995)

Provision	Duty/requirement	Workplace
Construction (Lifting Operations) Regulations 1961 (SI 1961 No 1581), Reg 34(2)	Thorough examination before first use (except fibre ropes/slings).	Building sites and works of engineering construction (see Chapter 7 'Construction and Building Operations')
Construction (Lifting Operations) Regulations 1961, Reg 40	Thorough examination every six months when in use.	Building sites and works of engineering construction (see above)
Construction (Lifting Operations) Regulations 1961, Reg 35	Test and thorough examination whenever lengthened, altered or repaired.	Building sites and works of engineering construction (see above)
Shipbuilding and Ship-repairing Regulations 1960, Reg 37	Thorough examination of all tackle, except rope slings, every six months.	Shipyards, harbours
Offshore Installations (Operational Safety, Health and Welfare) Regulations 1976, Reg 6	Same as detailed in Part B above.	Fixed offshore installations, mobile offshore installations (excluding dredging vessels)

26.28   The *Electrically Operated Lifts (EEC Requirements) Regulations 1986 (SI 1986 No 1500)* provide for the issue of EC type examination certificates and certificates of conformity and for EC inspections in Great Britain, in the case of electrically operated lifts, excluding:

(*a*)   lifts designed for military or research purposes, or those used as equipment on offshore prospecting and on drilling rigs and in mines, or for handling radioactive materials;

(*b*)   lifts intended exclusively for the transport of goods.

Records of test and examination of lifting plant and equipment

26.29   Particulars to be recorded for test and examination purposes of all types of hoist/lift and machinery are specified in the *Lifting Plant and Equipment (Records of Test and Examination etc.) Regulations 1992 (SI 1992 No 195)*. These regulations remove the necessity for competent persons to report results of testing and examination of lifting plant and equipment on prescribed forms, and to provide a written report, except when required by an inspector – though persons not wishing to devise their own means of recording such information can still do so on Form 2530 (and Form 91 for the purposes of *Regs 10, 30* and *41* of the *Construction (Lifting Operations) Regulations 1961* (see 26.27 above)). This allows for storage of records by electronic means. Thus, a competent person may provide the record by means that suit him and the owner/user of the equipment; in effect, using the same form on which to provide the written record for the majority of lifting plant and equipment likely to be tested. Alternatively, results can be recorded electronically.

(a) Particulars of examination/test to be recorded electronically or on Form 2531 – lifting machinery

[*Factories Act 1961, ss 26(1)(e), 27(2), (6)*]

The following details must be recorded following examination/test by a competent person.

(*a*)   Description of machinery, date of manufacture, identification mark, location of equipment;

(*b*)   safe working load;

(*c*)   details of examination/test;

(*d*)   date of completion of examination/test;

(*e*)   declaration that information is correct and equipment has been examined/tested;

(*f*)   name/address of owner;

(*g*)   name/address of competent person;

(*h*)   date that record of examination/test is made;

(*j*)   number/means of identifying record.

[*1 Sch Part III*].

(b) Particulars to be recorded electronically or on Form 2530 following thorough examination – lifting machinery

(*a*)   Description of machinery, identification mark, location;

(*b*)   date of last thorough examination and number of record thereof;

(*c*)   safe working load;

(*d*)   date of most recent test/thorough examination;

(*e*)   details of defects and rectification schedule;

(*f*)   latest date by which next thorough examination is to be carried out;

(*g*)   a declaration that the information is correct and that the equipment has been thoroughly examined in accordance with the appropriate provisions and is found free from any defect likely to affect safety;

(*h*)   name and address of the owner of the equipment;

(*j*)   name and address of the person responsible for the thorough examination;

(*k*)   date the record of the thorough examination is made;

(*l*)   name/address of the person who authenticates the record;

(*m*)   a number/other means of identifying the record.

[*1 Sch Part IV*].

Particulars to be recorded following examination/test – chains, ropes and lifting tackle electronically or on Form 2531

[*Factories Act 1961, s 26(1)(g)*]

26.30   (*a*)   Description, identification mark, location of machinery;

(*b*)   safe working load;

(*c*)   details and date of completion of last examination/test;

(*d*)   details and date of completion of each thorough examination;

(*e*)   details of defects and rectification schedule;

(*f*)   date of making current record and identifying number;

(*g*)   latest date by which next thorough examination is to be carried out;

(*h*)   name/address of owner;

(*j*)   name/address of competent person;

(*k*)   name/address of person authenticating record;

(*l*)   number/means of identifying record.

[*1 Sch Part V*].

Particulars to be recorded following thorough examination of (a) hoists/lifts in factories and (b) hoists/lifts in offices, shops and railway premises electronically or on Form 2530

[*Factories Act 1961, s 22(2); Offices, Shops and Railway Premises (Hoists and Lifts) Regulations 1968, Reg 6(1)*]

26.31   (*a*)   Description, identification mark, location of machinery;

(*b*)   date of last thorough examination and number of record;

(*c*)   safe working load;

(*d*)   details of inaccessible parts;

(*e*)   details of defects and rectification schedule;

(*f*)   date of completion of thorough examination;

(*g*)   latest date by which next thorough examination is to be carried out;

(*h*)   declaration that information is correct;

(*j*)   name/address of owner;

(*k*)   name/address of competent person;

(*l*)   date that record of thorough examination is made;

(*m*)   name/address of person authenticating the record;

(*n*)   number/other means of identifying record.

[*1 Sch Part VI*].

Chapter 27

Lighting

Introduction

27.1　Increasingly, over the last decade or so, employers have come to appreciate that indifferent lighting is both bad economics and bad ergonomics, not to mention potentially bad industrial relations; and conversely, good lighting uses energy efficiently and contributes to general workforce morale and profitability – that is, operating costs fall whilst productivity and quality improve. Alternatively, poor and indifferent lighting (both qualitative and quantitative, but principally the former since insufficiency of lighting is not a feature of modern industry) reduce efficiency, thereby increasing the risk of stress, denting workforce morale, promoting absenteeism and leading to accidents, injuries and even deaths at work.

Ideally, good lighting should 'guarantee' (*a*) employee safety, (*b*) acceptable job performance and (*c*) good workplace atmosphere, comfort and appearance. This is not just a matter of maintenance of correct lighting levels. Ergonomically relevant are:

(*a*)　horizontal illuminance;

(*b*)　uniformity of illuminance over the job area;

(*c*)　colour appearance;

(*d*)　colour rendering;

(*e*)　glare and discomfort;

(*f*)　ceiling, wall, floor reflectances;

(*g*)　job/environment illuminance ratios;

(*h*)　job and environment reflectances;

(*j*)　vertical illuminance.

To accommodate these 'requirements', a combination of general and localised lighting (not to be confused with 'local' lighting, e.g. desk light) is necessary. Moreover, state of the art visual display units have thrown up some occupational health problems (see 27.20 below) recently addressed by the *Health and Safety (Display Screen Equipment) Regulations 1992 (SI 1992 No 2792)* (see 27.20 and 27.22–27.29 below).

Statutory requirements in respect of lighting in places of work

27.2　Adequate standards of lighting in all places of work can be enforced under the general duties of the *Health and Safety at Work etc. Act 1974*, which require provision by an employer of a safe and healthy working environment (see further Chapter 15 'Employers' Duties'). As for factories, statutory duties vary slightly depending on whether the factory was in use before 1 January 1993 or not; if it was (i.e. *an existing factory*), *Sec 5* of the *Factories Act 1961* – to secure and maintain adequate lighting (natural or artificial) in all places where people work or pass through – although repealed as from 1 January 1993 [*Workplace (Health, Safety and Welfare) Regulations 1992, Reg 27, 2 Sch*], still applies until 1 January 1996 [*Workplace (Health, Safety and Welfare) Regulations 1992, Reg 1*]. Similarly, *Sec 8* of the *Offices, Shops and Railway Premises Act 1963* – provision and maintenance of adequate lighting in offices and shops – remains in force in *existing premises* until 1 January 1996, although repealed by *Regulation 27*. In the case of *new* factories and *new* offices and shop premises, there must be suitable and sufficient lighting, and, so far as reasonably practicable, provided by natural light. [*Workplace (Health, Safety and Welfare) Regulations 1992, Reg 8(1)(2)*].

Ideally, people should be able to work and move about without suffering eye strain and having to avoid shadows. Local lighting may be necessary at individual workstations and places of particular risk. Outdoor traffic routes used by pedestrians should be adequately lit after dark. Lights and light fittings should avoid dazzle and glare and be so positioned that they do not cause hazards, whether fire, radiation or electrical. Switches should be easily accessible and lights should be replaced, repaired or cleaned before lighting becomes insufficient. Moreover, where persons are particularly exposed to danger in the event of failure of artificial lighting, emergency lighting must be provided. [*Reg 8(3)*] (and ACOP).

In the case of existing factories, where *Sec 5* of the *Factories Act 1961* continues to apply, this duty is also strict. Thus, where the negligent act of an employee led to the temporary extinguishment of a lamp necessary for maintenance of an adequate standard of lighting, the employer was vicariously liable (*Rawding v London Brick Co Ltd (1970) KIR 194*) (see further 15.3 EMPLOYERS' DUTIES). *Sec 5(1)* places an *absolute* duty on employers to 'secure/maintain sufficient and suitable lighting'. Where an employer provides a reasonably efficient system of reporting defects in lighting arrangements, he can still be in breach of duty if a light bulb fails and an accident results because his duty is to secure suitable and sufficient lighting at all times (*Davies v Massey Ferguson Perkins Ltd [1983] ICR 580*). Statutory lighting requirements, applicable to woodworking machines, have (technically) been revoked but remain in force, in the case of *existing* equipment, until 1 January 1997, though, if new, such equipment will be governed by the *Provision and Use of Work Equipment Regulations 1992, Reg 21*. Lighting requirements for construction sites, in the form of the *Construction (General Provisions) Regulations 1961, Reg 47*, remain unaffected by revocation; so, too, do requirements in connection with electrical equipment. The 'suitable and sufficient' requirement is a strict liability in all workplaces covered by these regulations.

Lighting requirements for electrical equipment

27.3   So as to prevent injury, adequate lighting must be provided at all electrical equipment on which or near which work is being done in circumstances that may give rise to danger. [*Electricity at Work Regulations 1989 (SI 1989 No 635), Reg 15*].

Lighting requirements for woodworking machines

27.4   Lighting (whether natural or artificial) for every woodworking machine, must be sufficient and suitable for the purpose for which the machine is used; the means of artificial lighting for every woodworking machine must be so placed or shaded as to prevent glare, and so that direct rays of light do not impinge on the eyes of the operator whilst operating such a machine. [*Woodworking Machines Regulations 1974, Reg 43*] (remaining in force until 1 January 1997).

Lighting requirements on construction sites

27.5   (*a*)   Every working place (see further Chapter 7 'Construction and Building Operations'),

(*b*)   every approach to any working place,

(*c*)   every place where raising or lowering operations with the use of a lifting appliance are in progress, and

(*d*)   all openings dangerous to employees

must be adequately and suitably lighted. [*Construction (General Provisions) Regulations 1961, Reg 47*].

Sources of light

Natural lighting

27.6   Daylight is the natural, and cheapest, form of lighting, but it has only limited application to places of work where production is required beyond the hours of daylight, at all seasons, and where day-time visibility is restricted by climatic conditions. But, however good the outside daylight, windows can rarely provide adequate lighting alone for the interior of large floor areas. Single storey buildings can, of course, make use of insulated opaque roofing materials, but the most common provision of daylighting is by side windows. There is also the fact that the larger the glazing area of the building, the more other factors such as noise, heat loss in winter, and unsatisfactory thermal conditions in summer must be considered.

Modern conditions, where the creation of pleasant building interior environment requires the balanced integration of lighting, heating, air conditioning, acoustic treatment, etc., are such that lighting cannot be considered in isolation. At the very least, natural lighting will have to be supplemented for most of the time with artificial lighting, the most common source for which is electric lighting.

Electric lighting

27.7   Capital costs, running costs and replacement costs of various types of electric lighting have a direct bearing on the selection of the sources of electric lighting for particular application. Such costs are as important considerations as the size, heat and colour effects required of the lighting. The efficiency of any type of lamp used for lighting is measured as light output, in lumens, per watt of electricity. Typical values for various types of lamp are as follows (the term 'lumen' is explained in the discussion of standards of illuminance in 27.8 below).

Type of lamp	Lumens per watt
Incandescent lamps	10 to 18
Tungsten halogen	22
High pressure mercury	25 to 55
Tubular fluorescent	30 to 80 (depending on colour)
Mercury halide	60 to 80
High pressure sodium	100

In general, the common incandescent lamps (coiled filament lamps, the temperature of which is raised to white heat by the passage of current, thus giving out light) are relatively cheap to install but have relatively expensive running costs. A discharge or fluorescent lighting scheme (which works on the principle of electric current passing through certain gases and thereby producing an emission of light) has higher capital costs but higher running efficiency, lower running costs and longer lamp life. In larger places of work the choice is often between discharge and fluorescent lamps. The normal mercury discharge lamp and the low pressure sodium discharge lamp have restricted colour performance, although newly developed high pressure sodium discharge lamps and colour corrected mercury lamps do not suffer from this disadvantage.

Standards of lighting or 'illuminance'

The technical measurement of illuminance

27.8   The standard of illuminance (i.e. the amount of light) required for a given location or activity depends on a number of variables, including general comfort considerations and the visual efficiency required. The unit of illuminance is the 'lux' which equals one lumen per square metre: this unit has now replaced the 'foot candle' which was the number of lumens per square foot. The term 'lumen' is the unit of luminous flux, describing the quantity of light received by a surface or emitted by a source of light.

Light measuring instruments

27.9   For accurate measurement of the degree of illuminance at a particular working point, a reliable instrument is required. Such an instrument, suitable for most measurements, is a pocket lightmeter which incorporates the principle of the photo-electric cell, which generates a tiny electric current in proportion to the light at the point of measurement. This current deflects a pointer on a graduated scale measured in lux. Manufacturers' instructions should, of course, be followed in the care and use of such instruments.

Average illuminance and minimum measured illuminance

27.10   The recent HSE guidance note HS(G) 38 'Lighting at work' (1987) relates illuminance levels to the degree or extent of detail which needs to be seen in a particular task or situation. Recommended illuminances are shown in Table 23 in 27.11 below.

This guidance note makes recommendations both for average illuminance for the work area as a whole and for minimum measured illuminance at any position within it. As the illuminance produced by any lighting installation is rarely uniform, the use of the average illuminance figure alone could result in the presence of a few positions with much lower illuminance which pose a threat to health and safety. The minimum measured illuminance is therefore the lowest illuminance permitted in the work area taking health and safety requirements into account.

The planes on which the illuminances should be provided depend on the layout of the task. If predominantly on one plane, e.g. horizontal, as with an office desk, or vertical, as in a warehouse, the recommended illuminances are recommended for that plane. Where there is either no well defined plane or more than one, the recommended illuminances should be provided on the horizontal plane and care taken to ensure that the reflectances of surfaces in working areas are high.

Illuminance ratios

27.11   The relationship between the lighting of the work area and adjacent areas is significant. Large differences in illuminance between these areas may cause visual discomfort or even affect safety levels where there is frequent movement, e.g. forklift trucks. This problem arises most often where local or localised lighting in an interior exposes a person to a range of illuminance for a long period, or where there is movement between interior and exterior working areas exposing a person to a sudden change of illuminance. To reduce hazards and possible discomfort specific recommendations shown in Table 24 below should be followed.

Where there is conflict between the recommended average illuminances shown in Table 23 and maximum illuminance ratios shown in Table 24, the higher value should be taken.

Table 23

Average illuminances and minimum measured illuminances for different types of work

General activity	Typical locations/ types of work	Average illuminance (Lx)	Minimum measured illuminance (Lx)
Movement of people, machines and vehicles[1]	Lorry parks, corridors, circulation routes	20	5
Movement of people, machines and vehicles in hazardous areas; rough work not requiring any perception of detail	Construction site clearance, excavation and soil work, docks, loading bays, bottling and canning plants	50	20
Work requiring limited perception of detail[2]	Kitchens, factories, assembling large components, potteries	100	50
Work requiring perception of detail	Offices, sheet metal work, bookbinding	200	100
Work requiring perception of fine detail	Drawing offices, factories assembling electronic components, textile production	500	200

Notes

1. Only safety has been considered, because no perception of detail is needed and visual fatigue is unlikely. However, where it is necessary to see detail to recognise a hazard or where error in performing the task could put someone else at risk, for safety purposes as well as to avoid visual fatigue, the figure should be increased to that for work requiring the perception of detail.

2. The purpose is to avoid visual fatigue: the illuminances will be adequate for safety purposes.

Table 24

Maximum ratios of illuminance for adjacent areas

Situations to which recommendation applies	Typical location	Maximum ratio of illuminances	
		Working area	Adjacent area
Where each task is individually lit and the area around the task is lit to a lower illuminance	Local lighting in an office	5 :	1
Where two working areas are adjacent, but one is lit to a lower illuminance than the other	Localised lighting in a works store	5 :	1
Where two working areas are lit to different illuminances and are separated by a barrier but there is frequent movement between them	A storage area inside a factory and a loading bay outside	10 :	1

Maintenance of light fitments

27.12   The lighting output of a given lamp will reduce gradually in the course of its life but an improvement can be obtained by regular cleaning and maintenance, not only of the lamp itself but also of the reflectors, diffusers and other parts of the luminaire. A sensible and economic lamp replacement policy is called for (e.g. it may be more economical, in labour cost terms to change a batch of lamps than deal with them singly as they wear out).

Qualitative aspects of lighting and lighting design

27.13   While the quantity of lighting afforded to a particular location or task in terms of standard service illuminance is an important feature of lighting design, it is also necessary to consider the qualitative aspects of lighting, which have both direct and indirect effects on the way people perceive their work activities and dangers that may be present. The quality of lighting is affected by the presence or absence of glare, the distribution of the light, brightness, diffusion and colour rendition.

Glare

27.14   This is the effect of light which causes impaired vision or discomfort experienced when parts of the visual field are excessively bright compared with the general surroundings. It may be experienced in three different forms:

(*a*)   disability glare – the visually disabling effect caused by bright bare lamps directly in the line of vision;

(*b*)   discomfort glare – caused by too much contrast of brightness between an object and its background, and frequently associated with poor lighting design. It can cause discomfort without necessarily impairing the ability to see detail. Over a period it can cause visual fatigue, headaches and general fatigue;

(*c*)   reflected glare – is the reflection of bright light sources on shiny or wet work surfaces, such as plated metal or glass, which can almost entirely conceal the detail in or behind the object which is glinting.

N.B.   The Illuminating Engineering Society (IES) publishes a Limiting Glare Index for each of the effects in (*a*) and (*b*) above. This is an index representing the degree of discomfort glare which will be just tolerable in the process or location under consideration. If exceeded, occupants may suffer eye strain or headaches or both.

Distribution

27.15   Distribution is concerned with the way light is spread. The British Zonal Method classifies luminaires (light-fittings) according to the way they distribute light from BZ1 (all light downwards in a narrow column) to BZ10 (light in all directions). A fitting with a low BZ number does not necessarily imply less glare, however. Its positioning, the shape of the room and the reflective surfaces present are also significant.

The actual spacing of luminaires is also important when considering good lighting distribution. To ensure evenness of illuminance at operating positions, the ratio between the height of the luminaire and the spacing of it must be considered. The IES spacing: height ratio provides a basic guide to such arrangements. Under normal circumstances, e.g. offices, workshops and stores, this ratio should be between 1½:1 and 1:1 according to the type of luminaire.

Brightness

27.16   Brightness or 'luminosity' is very much a subjective sensation and, therefore, cannot be measured. However, it is possible to consider a brightness ratio, which is the ratio of apparent luminosity between a task object and its surroundings. To ensure the correct brightness ratio, the reflectance (i.e. the ability of a surface to reflect light) of all surfaces in the working area should be well maintained and consideration given to reflectance values in the design of interiors. Given a task illuminance factor (i.e. the recommended illuminance level for a particular task) of 1, the effective reflectance values should be ceilings – 0.6, walls – 0.3 to 0.8, and floors – 0.2 to 0.3.

Diffusion

27.17   This is the projection of light in all directions with no predominant direction. The directional flow of light can often determine the density of shadows, which may prejudice safety standards or reduce lighting efficiency. Diffused lighting will reduce the amount of glare experienced from bare luminaires.

Colour rendition

27.18 Colour rendition refers to the appearance of an object under a specific light source, compared to its colour under a reference illuminant, e.g. natural light. Good standards of colour rendition allow the colour appearance of an object to be properly perceived. Generally, the colour rendering properties of luminaires should not clash with those of natural light, and should be just as effective at night when there is no daylight contribution to the total illumination of the working area.

Stroboscopic effect

27.19 One aspect of lighting quality that formerly gave trouble was the stroboscopic effect of fluorescent tubes which gave the illusion of motion or even the illusion that a rotating part of machinery was stationary. With modern designs of fluorescent tubes, this effect has largely been eliminated.

Visual display units and lighting

Health factors (see also 33.25 OFFICES)

27.20 Introduction of new technology, in the form of VDUs, has ushered in, over the last decade, a rash of complaints from operators, the principal complaint being eye strain or visual fatigue. Compellingly, one in three VDU operators suffers from eye strain, back pain or general lethargy, and one in four from headaches attributable to glare discomfort and terminal reflections. Moreover, incidence of ocular discomfort among VDU operators, such as secretaries, journalists, finance dealers and graphic designers, remains twice that of the rest of the national workforce.

Visual fatigue is common to many tasks requiring a high degree of concentration and visual perception. Common symptoms are eye irritation, aggravated by rubbing; redness and soreness, together with temporary blurring and visual confusion. Spots, shapes in front of the eyes and chromatic effects (i.e. the sensation of coloured shapes before the eyes) surrounding viewed objects, also occur. Some people experience a fear or dislike of light or bright lights (photophobia), resulting in the need to wear dark glasses. Headaches are the most common symptom.

Generally, visual fatigue has a varied and complex pattern of symptoms, a component generally being anxiety. It is a temporary and reversible phenomenon, current optical wisdom arguing that it is impossible to damage eyes through the use of VDUs. Age, visual sharpness and performance are all significant in assessing whether an operator is likely to be affected by visual fatigue (see 27.21 below). VDU operators can also suffer from musculo-skeletal strain – stiffness and tenderness of the neck, shoulders and forearms as well as Repetitive Strain Injury (RSI) (see further Chapter 31 'Occupational Health') caused by repeated finger, hand/arm movements emanating from use of a keyboard, and also stress. More rarely, they may suffer from photogenic epilepsy. Compensation has recently been awarded to employees on this ground (see *McSherry and Lodge v British Telecom Ltd* (15.8 EMPLOYERS' DUTIES)).

Speaking generally, investment in the installation of a non-reflective, protective VDU glare filter screen is the best way of combating the incidence of visual fatigue, as well as varying employees' visual tasks, with only a specified percentage (say 50%) of a working day devoted to VDU work, and a specified maximum continuous period of work (say 1 hour), followed by a break (say of 15 minutes).

Operational considerations

27.21 Visual fatigue can be associated with:

(a)   poor legibility, due to factors in the VDU such as 'flicker', 'shimmer' and 'jitter', which are directly related to the 'refresh rate' (i.e. the rate at which the phosphors return to luminosity after they have faded) of the display system;

(b)   poor definition of the screen characters against the background field;

(c)   glare;

(d)   unsuitable background lighting;

(e)   poor quality source material; and

(f)   visual defects on the part of the operator.

Items (a) to (d) above can be corrected through good VDU and workplace design. Very few people, however, have perfect vision, the ability to see varying with age, and the presence or absence of visual defects, e.g. myopia (short-sightedness) and hypermetropia (long-sightedness). On this basis, it is recommended that vision screening should be a standard feature of any pre-employment health examination for VDU operators, followed by further vision screening at three-yearly intervals. Operators may need modifications to their prescription lenses to undertake such work. They should consult their optician whenever discomfort or visual fatigue is experienced, informing the optician of the type of work they perform (see 27.22, 27.23 below for the new eyetest rights).

Statutory requirements relating to VDUs – the Health and Safety (Display Screen Equipment) Regulations 1992

27.22   Applicable to new VDUs as from 1 January 1993 and existing VDUs as from 1 January 1996 (except for *Reg 3* – reducing risk – which applies as from 1 January 1993), the *Health and Safety (Display Screen Equipment) Regulations 1992 (SI 1992 No 2792)* impose the following duties on employers:

(1)   To assess (and review) health and safety risks to persons exposed at VDU workstations, whether or not provided by the employer, and reduce risks so identified [*Reg 2*]. (In the case of workstations put into service before 31 December 1992, these requirements must be met by 31 December 1996.)

Risk assessment

Given the health risks involved (see 27.20 above) and the possibility of liability being incurred by an employer for musculo-skeletal disorders (see 15.8 EMPLOYERS' DUTIES), employers will have to assess the extent of such risks in the case of display screen workers who are

(a)   employees, including home-workers,

(b)   employees of other employers ('temps'),

(c)   self-employed (e.g. self-employed temps, journalists).

Workstations used at home will also have to be assessed.

The risk assessment should be

(1)   systematic, with investigation of non-obvious causes, e.g. poor posture may be a response to glare rather than poor furniture,

(2)   appropriate to the foreseeable degree of risk – itself depending on duration, intensity or difficulty of work,

(3)   comprehensive, covering organisational, job, workplace and individual factors.

Probably the best form of assessment is an ergonomic checklist and employees must have received the necessary training (see 27.23 below) before completing such checklist. Once done, the assessment must be recorded, if necessary electronically, and kept readily accessible. Assessments should be reviewed in the following cases:

(i)   major change to software;

(ii)   major change to hardware;

(iii)   major change to workstation furniture;

(iv)   relocation of workstation;

(v)   significant modification of lighting.

(2)   To ensure that display screen equipment work is periodically interrupted by breaks or changes of activity so as to reduce the workload of employees. [*Reg 4*].

(3)   Provide employees with

(*a*)   initial eye/eyesight tests on request,

(*b*)   subsequent eye/eyesight tests at regular intervals, with consent of the operator,

(*c*)   additional eye/eyesight tests on request, where users are encountering visual difficulties,

(*d*)   special corrective appliances where tests show that normal corrective appliances cannot be used

[*Reg 5*];

(employees cannot, however, be required to take eyesight tests against their will [*Reg 5(6)*]);

(*e*)   adequate health and safety training in use of the workstation and whenever the workstation is substantially modified [*Reg 6*] (see further 27.23 below),

(*f*)   adequate health and safety information in connection with the workstation and in order to enable them to comply with *Regulations 2–6* [*Reg 7*].

Penalties for breach of these regulations coincide with those for breach of *HSWA* (see Chapter 17 'Enforcement').

Training and health and safety information

27.23 (*a*)   *Information* should be provided to all operators of VDUs or to employees and/or agency workers and should relate to:

(i) risks from display screen equipment	}	– employees
(ii) risk assessments (see 27.22 above) and measures to reduce risks and any risks resulting from changes to the workstation	}	– employees of others (e.g. agency workers or temps) – self-employed operators
(iii) breaks/activity changes	}	– employees

(iv)	eye/eyesight tests	– employees
(v)	initial training	– employees
(vi)	training following modification of workstation	– employees

(*b*)   *Training* which is only required to be given to employees should relate to:

(i)   comfort of posture and importance of postural change;

(ii) use of adjustment mechanisms, especially furniture;

(iii) use and arrangement of components for good posture and to prevent overreaching and avoid glare and reflections;

(iv) need for regular cleaning of screens and other equipment;

(v)   need for breaks and activity changes.

VDUs – User/Equipment Interface

①   SCREEN: READABLE AND STABLE IMAGE, ADJUSTABLE, GLARE FREE

②   KEYBOARD: USABLE, ADJUSTABLE, KEY TOPS LEGIBLE

③   WORK SURFACE: ALLOW FLEXIBLE ARRANGEMENT, SPACIOUS, GLARE FREE, DOCUMENT HOLDER AS APPROPRIATE

④   WORK CHAIR: APPROPRIATE ADJUSTABILITY PLUS FOOT REST

⑤   LEG ROOM AND CLEARANCES: TO FACILITATE POSTURAL CHANGE

⑥   LIGHTING: PROVISION OF ADEQUATE CONTRAST, NO DIRECT OR INDIRECT GLARE OR REFLECTIONS

⑦   DISTRACTING NOISE MINIMISED

⑧   NO EXCESSIVE HEAT, ADEQUATE HUMIDITY

⑨   SOFTWARE: APPROPRIATE TO THE TASK AND ADAPTED TO USER CAPABILITIES, PROVIDE FEEDBACK ON SYSTEM STATUS, NO CLANDESTINE MONITORING

fig. 7

Workstation equipment

27.24   (*a*)   *Display screens* must have

     (i)   well-defined, clean characters,

     (ii)   stable, flicker-free image,

     (iii)   adjustable brightness/contrast,

     (iv)   easy swivel/tilt, and

     (v)   be free of glare/reflections.

(*b*)   *Keyboards* must

     (i)   be tiltable and separate from display,

     (ii)   have space in front to support arms/hands,

     (iii)   have matt, non-reflective surfaces,

     (iv)   have adequately contrasted symbols.

(*c*)   *Work desks* must have

     (i)   a large, low reflectance surface,

     (ii)   a document holder,

     (iii)   adequate space for comfortable position.

(*d*)   *Work chairs* must

     (i)   be stable but allow worker easy freedom of movement,

     (ii)   be adjustable in backrest height/tilt and seat height,

     (iii)   have a footrest available.

Workstation environment

27.25   The following environmental conditions should be satisfied.

(*a*)   *Space* – it should be designed to allow for change of posture.

(*b*)   *Lighting* – there should be satisfactory lighting conditions, secondary adjustable lighting, and glare should be avoided by layout and design of light fittings.

(*c*)   *Heat* – equipment heat should not cause discomfort.

(*d*)   *Radiation* – all electromagnetic radiation (except visible light) should be reduced to negligible levels.

(*e*)   *Humidity* – an adequate level of humidity should be maintained.

(*f*)   *Operator/computer interface* – the workstation should:

     (i)   be easy to use,

     (ii)   be adapted to user's level of knowledge,

     (iii)   have a system to provide feedback to user,

     (iv)   have information displayed in a format and at a pace adapted to operator,

     (v)   accommodate the principles of software ergonomics.

Workstation design

27.26 For VDU operation, the head can be inclined 20° forward from the vertical. The centre of the field of view should therefore be at a point where the eyes are cast at an angle of 20° in a downward position. (This assumes that the field of vision is predominantly the screen plus document holder, rather than the keyboard.)

To ensure easy reading of documents and screen, the viewing distance from the eyes should be within the range 450 – 550 mm and should not exceed 700 mm. The distance from the eyes to the screen and from the eyes to the document should be identical to minimise frequent changes in focus.

Document holders should be used whenever possible as this will reduce the head and body movements when transferring gaze from documents to screen and back again.

Lighting

27.27 The VDU should, wherever possible, be positioned so that office lights or windows do not reflect directly on the face of the screen.

Office lighting should be adequate but not too bright to interfere with the screen image. For maximum comfort, the background lighting should be in the 300 to 500 lux (see 27.11 above) range, given that the VDU has a brightness control for use by the operator. The VDU can be operated below 300 lux or above 500 lux if required, depending upon the operator or the task. Local lighting can be introduced to facilitate the reading of documents in low background lighting conditions. Harsh lighting contrasts should be avoided.

Glare can be reduced by:

(*a*) changing the position of the VDU screen to eliminate reflections from the screen or other surfaces, e.g. by siting the VDU parallel to fluorescent light fittings;

(*b*) using a non-reflective VDU screen or filter over the screen;

(*c*) reducing the brightness of the light source;

(*d*) fitting lights with suitable diffusers; and

(*e*) as a last resort, changing the position of troublesome lights.

In certain cases, the provision of window blinds may be necessary where there is reflection from the screen face. Generally, any sort of light used by one operator whether emanating from the screen or otherwise, should be screened from other operators. [*Health and Safety (Display Screen Equipment) Regulations 1992, 1 Sch*].

Equipment maintenance

27.28 Regular maintenance and servicing of equipment should be undertaken in accordance with the manufacturer's instructions. Where there is evidence of screen flicker, poor contrast adjustment or other faults, the maintenance contractor or supplier should be contacted.

Display screens and the working environment

27.29 As regards *display screens*:

(*a*) characters on screen must be well-defined and clearly formed, of adequate size with adequate spacing between characters and lines;

(*b*)   the image on the screen must be stable, with no flickering;

(*c*)   brightness and contrast between characters must be easily adjustable;

(*d*)   the screen must swivel and tilt easily;

(*e*)   it must be possible to use a separate base for the screen or an adjustable table;

(*f*)   the screen must be free of reflective glare and discomfort-causing reflections.

As regards the *keyboard*:

(*a*)   it must be tiltable and separate from the screen so as to allow the user to find a comfortable working position;

(*b*)   the space in front of the keyboard must provide support for the hands/arms of the user;

(*c*)   it must have a matt surface and avoid reflective glare;

(*d*)   arrangement of keyboard/characteristics of keys must facilitate the use of the keyboard;

(*e*)   symbols on keys must be adequately contrasted and legible from the design working position.

As regards the *work desk or work surface*:

(*a*)   it must have a sufficiently large, low-reflectance surface and allow flexible arrangement of screen, keyboard, documents etc.;

(*b*)   the document holder must be stable and adjustable so as to minimise the need for uncomfortable head/eye movements;

(*c*)   there must be adequate space for users to find a comfortable position.

As regards the *work chair*:

(*a*)   it must be stable and allow the user freedom of movement and a comfortable position;

(*b*)   the seat must be adjustable in height;

(*c*)   the seat back must be adjustable in height and tilt;

(*d*)   a footrest must be available, if needed.

As regards the *working environment*:

(*a*)   the workstation must be dimensioned and designed so as to allow sufficient space for the user to change position/vary movements;

(*b*)   room lighting/spot lighting must ensure satisfactory lighting conditions and appropriate contrast between screen and background environment. Disturbing glare/reflections on the screen must be prevented by co-ordinating the workplace and the workstation layout with positioning of artificial light sources;

(*c*)   workstations must be so designed as to avoid glare from windows, transparent or translucent walls, as well as distracting reflections on screen;

(*d*)   equipment should not be too noisy or produce excess heat, and radiation, with the exception of the visible part of the electro-magnetic spectrum, must be reduced to negligible levels, and an adequate humidity level must be maintained.

As regards the *user/computer interface*:

(*a*)   software must be suitable;

(*b*)   software must be easy to use and adaptable to the user's level of knowledge or experience;

(*c*)   systems must provide feedback on the system's performance;

(*d*)   systems must display information in a format and at a pace adapted to users;

(*e*)   principles of software ergonomics must be applied, in particular to human data processing.

[*1 Sch*].

Chapter 28

Machinery Safety

Introduction

28.1 Legislation (generally) has accepted the premise that design of hazard-free machines is not realistic and that, in consequence, statutory duties should apply principally (along with complementary safety duties also placed on designers and manufacturers of industrial equipment – see Chapter 38 'Product Safety') to the guarding/fencing of machinery so as to minimise the risk of injury to the operator. Legal duty has, therefore, to date, tended to rest on employers, factory occupiers and occupiers of other workplaces, rather than on designers, producers and suppliers of machines, machinery and machine tools. Although not an ideal situation – in that the fencing requirements of the *Factories Act 1961* have been associated with a spate of irreconcilable case law, imposition of duty in relation to guarding/fencing of machinery does, nevertheless, underline the immediacy of the employer-employee relationship as compared with the more indirect relationship of the designer or manufacturer of the work equipment and employee – a fact itself denoted by the existence of compulsory employers' liability insurance (see Chapter 16 'Employers' Liability Insurance'), whereas product liability insurance, though highly desirable if not advisable, is, nevertheless, voluntary. That the status quo is beginning to shift in favour of engraftment of duty upon designers and manufacturers (and possible liability in consequence of breach of such duty) is underlined by the introduction of the *Supply of Machinery (Safety) Regulations 1992*, themselves embodying the tenets of BS 5304: 1988 as health and safety requirements (see 28.2, 28.5 below).

Other shortcomings of current law

28.2 1. There is not a *general* statutory requirement in relation to machinery safety applicable throughout industry; for instance, the fencing/guarding requirements of the *Factories Act 1961, ss 12–16* apply, strictly speaking, only to machinery in factories; whilst the regulations concerned with safety of agricultural machinery are out of date and the *Operations at Unfenced Machinery Regulations 1938* (as amended) do not extend to robots.

2. Terminology of certain 'key' requirements of the *Factories Act 1961* (e.g. *Sec 14(1)* concerning 'dangerous parts of other machinery'), if interpreted literally, quarantines whole classes of machinery (e.g. clicking presses in the footwear industry, lawn mowers in factory grounds), as a result of which fine and sometimes facile distinctions grew up around *Secs 12* and *13* of the *Factories Act 1961* on the one hand, and *Sec 14* on the other, leading (perhaps inevitably), at industry level, to universal reliance on 'current best practice', as reflected in BS 5304: 1988 (see 28.71–28.76 below). Hence, the tendency, in recent times, to issue codes of practice instead of regulations in relation to particular machinery dangers, e.g. codes on transfer machines, threading machines, sawing and cutting-off machines, turning machines and even passenger-carrying amusement devices.

3. Sometimes, advice bought in independently regarding safety of plant and appliances has been less than adequate, current liability, referable to negligence, for unsatisfactory advice being (perhaps) too low a standard.

4. The lack of attention to date shown towards the *producers* of machinery has recently been redressed by the introduction of the *Supply of Machinery (Safety) Regulations 1992 (SI 1992 No 3073)*. These regulations, applicable to new machinery and components (including components placed separately on the market as from 1 January 1995) coming into service after 1 January 1993, impose penalties on designers, manufacturers, importers and suppliers of machinery within EC parameters, if they fail to build 'health and safety requirements and specifications' into product design and construction. Indeed, given the similarity between these requirements and those placed on employers by the *Provision and Use of Work Equipment Regulations 1992* (see 28.4 below) as well as the strictures of BS 5304: 1988 (see 28.71 below), concededly, compliance with these new regulations, on the part of producers, will, in turn, enable employers and occupiers of workplaces with incoming and *in situ* machinery to comply with their duties under the *Provision and Use of Work Equipment Regulations 1992*, the key to which, in turn, is and will be specification to BS 5304: 1988.

Not surprisingly, therefore, some reform of machinery safety legislation is both desirable and imminent. In particular, the *Provision and Use of Work Equipment Regulations 1992 (SI 1992 No 2932)* introduces a general statutory requirement in respect of 'work equipment' (i.e. machinery, appliances, apparatus or tools), irrespective of the nature of the workplace, and inclusive of robots and programmable electric systems, with due emphasis on 'danger zones', and extending to work equipment in offices and shops, as well as agriculture. Consisting of both general and specific requirements, the former relating to selection/suitability of work equipment/maintenance/instruction and training, came into effect on 1 January 1993; whilst the specific requirements, *by way of replacement of existing machinery safety requirements*, in the *Factories Act 1961*, OSPRA and other regulations (see Table 25) come into effect on 1 January 1997 or, in the case of equipment used for the first time, on 1 January 1993. The overall effect of the new regulations will be to standardise safety criteria for all work equipment in all industries as per the specification of BS 5304: 1988 (see 28.71–28.76 below).

28.3 Given the (inevitable) overlap eventually between the *Provision and Use of Work Equipment Regulations 1992* on the one hand and the *Consumer Protection Act 1987* and the *Supply of Machinery (Safety) Regulations 1992* on the other, allowing the employer some leeway in sloughing off liability (or some of it) onto the manufacturer, current levels of mishap and injury associated with workplace machinery are set to improve. Failing this, at least, the devil will no longer be in the detail and fragment of the law as before and, in consequence, there will be a *general safety criterion applicable throughout industry to machinery*. Specifically, this chapter subdivides into:

(*a*) Duties on employers/occupiers regarding machinery safety, that is,

(i) the effect of the *Provision and Use of Work Equipment Regulations 1992*;

(ii) current requirements of the *Factories Act 1961* – fencing and guarding requirements.

(*b*) Duties of manufacturers and suppliers of machinery – the *Supply of Machinery (Safety) Regulations 1992* (as amended).

Duties of employers

28.4 Statutory duties of employers, in respect of machinery, used to be almost exclusively concerned with guarding, as witness the duties under the *Factories Act 1961* (see 28.16 below). Now, however, in light of the *Provision and Use of Work Equipment Regulations 1992*, employers are required to select suitably safe new or second-hand equipment for use at work, maintain it properly and inform operators of foreseeable dangers – a wider remit more consistent with their original common law duties (see 15.20 EMPLOYERS' DUTIES). Fulfilment of this duty presupposes, in turn, compliance, on the part of manufacturers, with their duties under the *Supply of Machinery (Safety) Regulations 1992* and BS 5304: 1988.

Provision and Use of Work Equipment Regulations 1992

28.5 As part and parcel of the on-going repeal of the *Factories Act 1961* (and other extant legislation) in accordance with the *Health and Safety at Work etc. Act 1974, s 1(2)* (duty of the HSC to update legislation) and, in furtherance of the general duty on employers, under *HSWA s 2(2)(a)* to 'provide and maintain' plant and systems of work that are safe and without health risks, the *Provision and Use of Work Equipment Regulations 1992* apply safeguards to any machine, appliance, apparatus or tool for use at work, including equipment for public use in non-domestic premises (e.g. a washing machine in a launderette) (see 28.8 below for the timetable for the implementation of these regulations).

Purpose of regulations

28.6 The general aim of the regulations is to encapsulate a duty to protect workers against 'dangerous parts of machinery'. Hence, there is a strict duty to

(a) prevent access to dangerous parts;

(b) stop movement of dangerous parts before a person (or any part of him/her) enters a danger zone.

Provision of guarding and establishment of safe systems of work should be an objective for all employers. If it is possible (that is, reasonably practicable) to provide a high standard of physical protection by guarding, employers should do so. Conversely, if dangerous parts cannot realistically be completely guarded, training courses and safe systems of work represent a fall-back alternative.

Scope

28.7 Covered are

(a) all activities involving work equipment (e.g. stopping/starting equipment); use, repair, transport, modification, maintenance, servicing and cleaning;

(b) all workplaces, including offices and service industries;

(c) employees, self-employed, members of the public using work equipment in public places.

These new regulations replace, as from 1 January 1997 or, in relation to equipment used for the first time, from 1 January 1993, the following regulations:

Table 25

List of repeals/revocations – continue to operate until 1 January 1997

(a) Repeals

    1. *Factories Act 1961, ss 12-16, 17(1)* and *19* (see 28.13–28.28 and 28.46–28.69 below)

    2. *OSRPA s 17*

(b) Revocations

(a) Total

    1. *Operations at Unfenced Machinery Regulations 1938 (SR&O 1938 No 641/SR&O 1946 No 156/SI 1976 No 955)*

    2. *Agriculture (Power Take-off) Regulations 1957 (SIs 1957 No 386/1976 No 1247/1981 No 1414)*

    3. *Agriculture (Stationary Machinery) Regulations 1959 (SIs 1959 No 1216/1976 No 1247/1981 No 1414)*

    4. *Agriculture (Field Machinery) Regulations 1962 (SIs 1962 No 1472/1976 No 1247/1981 No 1414)*

(b) Partial

    1. *Jute (Safety, Health and Welfare) Regulations 1948 (SI 1948 No 1696), Regs 27, 28 1 Sch*

2. *Abrasive Wheels Regulations 1970 (SI 1970 No 535)*	*part of Reg 3*
	Reg 4
	Regs 6-8
	Regs 10-16
	Regs 18, 19
3. *Woodworking Machines Regulations 1974 (SIs 1974 No 903/1978 No 1126)*	*part of Regs 1, 2 and 3*
	Regs 5-9
	Regs 14-43
4. *Construction (General Provisions) Regulations 1961 (SI 1961 No 1580)*	*Regs 42, 43*
5. *Shipbuilding and Ship-repairing Regulations (SI 1960 No 1932)*	*Reg 67*
6. *Agriculture (Circular Saws) Regulations 1959 (SI 1959 No 427)*	*parts of Reg 1*
	Regs 3, 4
	part of Reg 5
	1 Sch
7. *Agriculture (Threshers and Balers) Regulations 1960 (SIs 1960 No 1199/1976 No 1247/1981 No 1414)*	*parts of Schedule*

Timetable

28.8   The new regulations consist of (*a*) general requirements [*Regs 5-11*] and (*b*) specific requirements [*Regs 12-25*]. Both came into effect, in respect of work equipment first provided after 31 December 1992, on 1 January 1993. In respect of work equipment provided before 1 January 1993, general requirements came into effect on 1 January 1993 and specific requirements will come into effect on 1 January 1997. (In consequence, existing legislation, due for repeal (see Table 25 above) would operate alongside new specific requirements until final repeal takes effect on 1 January 1997.)

Hired, leased and second-hand equipment, after supply to a new owner, are all new equipment for the purposes of these regulations and must therefore conform with them from the date of acquisition.

General requirements (taking effect from 1 January 1993)

28.9   Every employer must ensure:

1.   (Selection of equipment) – that he has regard to the working conditions and hazards existing on premises, for the health and safety of persons and any additional hazards posed by use of work equipment. [*Reg 5*].

2.   (Suitability of work equipment) – that work equipment is

    (*a*)   constructed or adapted so as to be suitable for operations for which it is provided;

    (*b*)   provided/used only for operations for which, and under conditions for which, it is suitable (i.e. will not affect the health and safety of the user).

[*Reg 5*].

3.   (Maintenance) – that work equipment is properly maintained and, if necessary, a log kept up to date. [*Reg 6*].

4.   (Specific risks) – that where any use of work equipment is likely to involve a specific risk to the health or safety of any person

    (i)   use of work equipment must be restricted to those persons using it, and

    (ii)   repairs/modifications/maintenance/servicing be restricted to persons specifically designated to carry out such operations (whether or not authorised to carry them out) who must have received adequate training.

[*Reg 7*].

5.   (Information/instructions) – that all persons who use equipment or who supervise or manage work equipment must have available to them health and safety information and, if necessary, written instructions comprehensible to the workers concerned, including

    (*a*)   conditions in which/methods by which work equipment is to be used;

    (*b*)   foreseeable abnormal situations and the action to be taken;

    (*c*)   conclusions to be drawn from experience in using the equipment.

[*Reg 8*].

6.   (Training) – that all persons using work equipment or who supervise/manage

same must have adequate training and that special training is given to those responsible for special risk repairs, modifications, maintenance or servicing. [*Reg 9*].

7.   (Conformity with EC requirements) – every employer must ensure that work equipment complies with EC requirements [*Reg 10*] (see further 28.46 *et seq.* below).

Specific requirements (taking effect from 1 January 1997 and from 1 January 1993 in respect of equipment used for the first time after that date) (applicable also to offshore operations (see Chapter 34))

28.10   1.   (Dangerous parts of machinery) – in order

(*a*)   to prevent access to dangerous parts of machinery or rotating stock-bar, or

(*b*)   to stop movement of any dangerous parts of machinery or rotating stock-bar before any part of a person enters a danger zone (i.e. a zone where a person is exposed to risk from dangerous parts of machinery),

guards/protection devices must be provided, so far as practicable (see 15.18 EMPLOYERS' DUTIES).

A hierarchy of such measures consists of

(*a*)   fixed guards enclosing every dangerous part; if not practicable then –

(*b*)   other guards or protection devices where fixed guards are not possible; if not practicable then –

(*c*)   provision of jigs, holders, push-sticks or similar protection if practicable; if not practicable then –

(*d*)   information, instruction, training and supervision must be provided.

Guards must

(*a*)   be appropriate for purpose;

(*b*)   be of good construction, sound material, adequate strength and free from patent defect;

(*c*)   be properly maintained;

(*d*)   not create additional risks;

(*e*)   not be easily removed or rendered inoperative;

(*f*)   be situated at sufficient distance from a danger zone;

(*g*)   not restrict more than necessary any view of the operation of work equipment;

(*h*)   allow for fitting, replacing of parts, maintenance work, if possible, without removing the guard or protective device.

[*Reg 11*].

2.   (Protection against failure) – so far as is reasonably practicable (for meaning, see 15.19 EMPLOYERS' DUTIES), that work equipment is protected or, if it is not reasonably practicable, adequately controlled without the use of PPE against risks to health or safety from

—   ejected/falling objects;

535

— rupture/disintegration;

— overheating/catching fire;

— unintended/premature discharge or ejection of any article, gas, dust, liquid or vapour;

— unintended/premature explosion of work equipment or material produced, used or stored in it.

[*Reg 12*].

3. (High/low temperature) – that parts of work equipment and material produced or used on it, which might burn, scald or sear, be protected to prevent persons coming too close. [*Reg 13*].

4. (Controls for starting equipment) – that work equipment is provided with one or more controls to

   (*a*)   start equipment (as well as re-start),

   (*b*)   change speed, pressure or operating conditions,

   and it must not be possible to perform any of the above operations except by deliberate action (other than in the case of an automatic device). [*Reg 14*].

5. (Stop controls) – that work equipment is provided with readily accessible stop controls (including emergency stop controls [*Regs 15, 16*]), which

   (*a*)   must bring equipment to a complete stop safely, and

   (*b*)   if necessary, disconnect all energy sources, and

   (*c*)   must operate in priority over controls to start/change working conditions.

   [*Reg 15*].

6. (Position of controls) – that controls of work equipment are clearly visible and identifiable, have appropriate marking and are not in a danger zone (except where necessary). In particular, no-one should be in a danger zone *vis-à-vis* the position of any control affecting a danger zone hazard; but, if not reasonably practicable (see 15.19 EMPLOYERS' DUTIES), no-one should be in a danger zone when work equipment is about to start; but, if the latter is not reasonably practicable, audible/visible warning should be given when work equipment is about to start. [*Reg 17*].

7. Controls must be such that

   (*a*)   their operation does not create *increased* risk to health/safety;

   (*b*)   no fault in them can result in increased risk to health or safety;

   (*c*)   they do not hinder the operation of stop/emergency stop controls.

   [*Reg 18*].

8. (Isolation from energy sources) – that equipment must be provided with appropriate means to isolate it from its sources of energy; such means must be clearly identifiable and accessible. Re-connection of energy sources to work equipment must not expose operatives to risk. [*Reg 19*].

9. (Stability) – that work equipment is stabilised by clamping, etc. [*Reg 20*].

10. (Lighting) – that any place where work equipment is used, be adequately lit. [*Reg 21*].

11.   (Maintenance operations) – that, so far as is reasonably practicable, maintenance operations can be carried out while work is stopped, or without exposing anyone carrying them out to danger, or, alternatively, appropriate protective measures can be taken. [*Reg 22*].

12.   (Markings) – that equipment be appropriately marked (i.e. CE markings). [*Reg 23*].

13.   (Warnings) – that equipment incorporate clear and unambiguous warnings/ warning devices. [*Reg 24*].

Statutory requirements relating to general duties and existing work equipment

28.11   Current statutory requirements relating to machinery safety are contained in the general duties of the *Health and Safety at Work etc. Act 1974*, specific fencing/ guarding requirements of the *Factories Act 1961*, regulations relating to particular industries, e.g. the *Abrasive Wheels Regulations 1970*; the *Power Presses Regulations 1965*; the *Horizontal Milling Machines Regulations 1928, 1934* and the *Woodworking Machines Regulations 1974*; certain specific duties imposed on vendors or machinery, under the *Factories Act 1961*; and certain regulations relating to agricultural machinery (see 28.40–28.45 below) (see also 28.46 *et seq.* for current manufacturers' and suppliers' duties).

General duty under the Health and Safety at Work etc. Act 1974 (HSWA)

28.12   It is the duty of every employer to ensure, so far as reasonably practicable, the health, safety and welfare at work of all his employees. [*HSWA s 2(1)*]. This includes the 'provision and maintenance of plant and systems of work that are safe and without risks to health'. [*HSWA s 2(2)(a)*]. This duty extends to machine guarding and machine lay-out in all workplaces, including factories. It is assiduously enforced by the HSE by means of improvement/prohibition notices and prosecutions (see further *Belhaven Brewery Ltd v McLean* in Chapter 17 'Enforcement').

Fencing requirements of the Factories Act 1961 – the parameters

28.13   The principal fencing requirements of the *Factories Act 1961* are contained in:

—   *Sec 12* which deals with prime movers and their parts (see 28.26 below);

—   *Sec 13* which deals with transmission machinery (see 28.27 below);

—   *Sec 14* which deals with dangerous parts of other machinery (see 28.24 below);

—   *Sec 17* which deals with duties of suppliers/sellers of machinery (see 28.46-28.70 below);

—   *Sec 19* – self-acting machines (including robots, i.e. metal collar workers, whose main applications are handling, assembly work, hot forging, spot welding and finishing);

(all the above sections remaining in force until 1 January 1997, except for equipment used for the first time from 1 January 1993 when the new law will apply straightaway to that equipment). In this connection:

(a)   both mobile and static machinery are covered, once installed, even though not commercially operational;

(b)   statutory duties exist for the benefit of both employees and indirect workers;

(c)   only machinery which is 'in motion or use' has to be guarded/fenced;

(d)   the fencing requirements themselves do not specify what the machinery should be guarded against; case law has explained that the purpose is to prevent employees coming into contact with the machine and/or workpiece;

(e)   prime movers and transmission machinery (governed by *Secs 12, 13*) are deemed to be dangerous *per se* and so statutory duties relating to them are absolute; whereas, other parts of machinery are presumed safe until shown to be dangerous, i.e. foreseeably the cause of injury;

(f)   employees need not necessarily act within the course of their employment in order to qualify for compensation for breach of these sections;

(g)   the statutory defences of 'safety by construction/position' have probably been rendered obsolete by subsequent case law;

(h)   even though particular statutory duties may be inapplicable, employers can incur residual (i.e. secondary) liability at common law.

Machinery covered by the fencing requirements

28.14   Case law has established the following rules:

(a)   only machines used in the factory process (i.e. the manufacturing process), and not machines which are the end product of manufacture, are 'machinery' (*Parvin v Morton Machine Co Ltd [1952] AC 515* where a trainee was injured on a dough brake; the factory made baking equipment. It was held that there was no liability under the *Factories Act 1961, s 14*). However, when a machine was installed in a factory with the intention of modifying it and testing its suitability for the company's manufacturing process and an employee was injured by it whilst the machine was being modified, the employer was held liable for the employee's injuries resulting from the failure to fence under *Secs 14(1)* and *155(1)* of the *Factories Act 1961*. The machine, if the development was successful, was intended for use in the employer's manufacturing process and that brought the *Factories Act* liability into relevance (*TBA Industrial Products v Lainé [1987] ICR 75*);

(b)   mobile as well as static machinery/equipment is covered (*British Railways Board v Liptrot [1967] 2 AER 1072* where a mobile crane was held to be 'machinery' for the purposes of the *Factories Act 1961, s 14*); but the safety hook of an electrically powered hoist was not 'a dangerous part of machinery' (*Mirza v Ford Motor Co Ltd [1981] IRLR 544*);

(c)   machinery which itself is guarded but becomes dangerous when working on material requires fencing (*Midland and Low Moor Iron & Steel Co Ltd v Cross [1964] 3 AER 752* concerning a steel bar straightening machine); so, too, machinery which becomes dangerous owing to its proximity to other machinery (*FE Callow (Engineers) Ltd v Johnson [1971] AC 335* where the gap between a revolving workpiece and lathe created a hazard);

(d)   hand-held tools are not 'machinery' (*Sparrow v Fairey Aviation Co Ltd [1962] 3 AER 706* where a worker was injured when a hand-held scraping tool slipped and came into contact with the jaws of a chuck holding the workpiece. It was held that there was no liability);

(*e*)   there is no statutory duty to fence off a potential danger created by the interaction of a moving part of a machine and some completely independent stationary object (*Pearce v Stanley Bridges Ltd [1965] 2 AER 594* where an employee's arm was trapped between a lifting platform and the non-moving part of a conveyor belt system. It was held that there was no liability).

In motion or use

28.15   The fencing requirements only apply to machinery 'in motion or use' [*Factories Act 1961, s 16*] (though this is not the position with suppliers of machinery, who have duties under *Sec 17* (see 28.46-28.70 below)). 'In motion or use' includes:

(*a*)   motion *or* use for which the machine parts were intended, i.e. normal and/or a continuing state of motion – not just movement of any kind (*Richard Thomas & Baldwins Ltd v Cummings [1955] AC 321*);

(*b*)   machinery installed but not yet in commercial use, e.g. being tested or demonstrated prior to being put into operation (*Irwin v White, Tomkins & Courage Ltd [1964] 1 AER 545*); but installation must be complete (*Field v E E Jeavons & Co Ltd [1965] 2 AER 162* where a fitter almost lost an arm when he turned on the power to test a circular saw. It was held that there was no liability, since installation was not complete);

(*c*)   machinery which is in motion, though not in normal use (*Horne v Lec Refrigeration Ltd [1965] 2 AER 898* where the employee, who was installing a new mould into a power press, had to put his head and shoulders into the press. The safety routine specified that seven switches had to be turned off and the safety master key taken out of its socket. Only one switch was turned off. The lead of his electric drill caught the switch, causing the power press to operate, with fatal consequences. It was held that the machine was 'in motion', even though it was not 'in use', and the employer was liable);

(*d*)   machinery running slowly (as distinct from 'inching' (see (ii) below)) (*Joy v News of the World (1972) 13 KIR 57*).

'In motion or use' does *not* include:

(i)   movement of machinery by hand, if power-driven (see (*a*) above *Richard Thomas & Baldwins Ltd v Cummings*);

(ii)   rotation by inching (*Normille v News of the World (1975) 119 SJ 301*);

(iii)   quick on/off switching of power to advance action fractionally (*Mitchell v W S Westin Ltd [1965] 1 AER 657*).

General duty to fence machinery

28.16   Enforcement of the accident prevention regulations has not been facilitated by constantly subjecting them to 'clarification' in civil litigation. The result has been the emergence, to some extent, of irreconcilable case law. Nowhere is this more evident than in relation to the statutory duty to fence, particularly in the case of machinery/machine parts other than prime movers and transmission machinery, i.e. *Factories Act 1961, s 14*. Given some irreconcilability, the main points established by case law are as follows.

Absolute duty to fence if dangerous

28.17   If a machine is dangerous (see further *Walker v Bletchley-Flettons Ltd*, 28.23 below), it must be fenced. Putting up notices warning of dangers is not enough (*Chasteney v*

Michael Nairn & Co Ltd [1937] 1 AER 376). Nor can it be assumed that, if machinery is out of normal reach, there is no duty to fence (*Findlay v Newman, Hender & Co Ltd [1937] 4 AER 58* where a workman was injured when replacing a belt on a revolving shaft 12½ feet from the ground. It was held that the shaft was a source of danger, under the *Factory and Workshop Act 1901*, and so should have been securely fenced).

Duty to protect worker coming into contact with machine

28.18 The duty to fence/guard has traditionally been regarded as one to protect the worker from coming into contact with the machine (*Nicholls v Austin (F) (Leyton) Ltd [1946] 2 AER 92* where the appellant was injured when a piece of wood flew off a woodworking machine, cutting her fingers. The machine was fenced in a way which would have prevented an operator from coming into contact with the machine while it was in operation. It was held that the employer was not liable. In particular, the House of Lords was influenced by the *Factories Act 1937, s 14(2)*, (now the *Factories Act 1961, s 14(2)*), 'In so far as the safety of a dangerous part of any machinery cannot by reason of the nature of the operation be secured by means of a fixed guard, the requirements of subsection (1) . . . shall be deemed to have been complied with if a device is provided which automatically prevents the operator from coming into contact with that part').

This rule was followed by the House of Lords in *Carroll v Andrew Barclay & Sons Ltd [1948] 2 AER 386* where a drive belt (i.e. transmission machinery) broke and struck an employee. It was held that the employer was not liable, and a similar result occurred in *Close v Steel Company of Wales Ltd [1961] 2 AER 953*, where the bit of an electric drill, which the appellant was operating, shattered and a piece entered his eye. It was held that the employer was not liable. But later in *Wearing v Pirelli Ltd [1977] 1 AER 339* the House of Lords suggested more flexibility as a concession to practical necessity. Here the appellant, who was employed by the respondents to work on a machine which moulded and formed rubber to make tyres, had a bone in his wrist broken when it came into contact, after a hand tool snagged, with rubber fabric on a revolving drum (though not the drum itself). It was held that the employer was liable, since contact with the workpiece was contact with the machine itself. 'Where an injury is caused by material, it is not caused by a dangerous part of machinery but where a dangerous part of the machinery causes an injury by bringing a person into contact with the material or something that is not part of the machine, liability for breach of the statutory duty is established' (per Viscount Dilhorne).

Fencing to be of substantial construction and constantly maintained

28.19 While parts required to be fenced are 'in motion or use' (see 28.15 above), the fencing must be:

(a)   of substantial construction; and

(b)   constantly maintained and kept in position.

[*Factories Act 1961, s 16*] (remaining in force until 1 January 1997).

'Maintained' means 'maintained in an efficient state, in efficient working order, and in good repair'. [*Factories Act 1961, s 176(1)*].

When fencing can be removed

28.20 These requirements do not apply when parts are exposed for (a) examination, (b) lubrication or (c) adjustment purposes. This does not mean that, once an examination etc. has started, the machine can remain unfenced till complete; therefore, once exposure of machine parts is superfluous, fences/guards must be replaced (*Nash v High Duty Alloys Ltd [1947] 1 AER 363* where a press for making high quality metal pressings was turned off so that the supervisor could inspect the workpieces, the guard was put in the 'up' position. A test run was carried out. The supervisor was still not satisfied and further test pressing was done. As the supervisor was inspecting the dies, a toolmaker set the press in motion, crushing the supervisor's fingers. The guard was still in the 'up' position. It was held that the employer was liable, since the employee should have replaced the guard after the test).

For whose benefit duties exist

28.21   The *Factories Act 1961, ss 12-14* exist for the benefit of 'every person employed or working on premises' (i.e. direct employees and other persons working in the factory, e.g. an outside labour force), but this does not extend to persons doing their own work in the factory (i.e. self-employed people, or a fireman, HSE inspector or policeman) (*Flannigan v British Dyewood Ltd [1969] SLT 223* where a fireman failed in his action under the *Factories Act 1961, s 29*, relating to floors, stairs, gangways etc., when he was injured fighting a fire. The fact that the occupier had no control over the way in which he was injured may have influenced the judgment of the House of Lords). If an action, on behalf of the fireman/policeman fails under the *Factories Act 1961*, the factory occupier as *occupier* may be liable under the *Occupiers' Liability Act 1957* (see Chapter 32 'Occupiers' Liability'). Employees working outside working hours are not covered (*Napieralski v Curtis (Contractors) Ltd [1959] 2 AER 426*).

Prime movers and transmission machinery

28.22   *Prime movers* (and their moving parts) and *transmission machinery* are deemed to be dangerous (i.e. *dangerous per se*), with the result that the fencing/guarding duties are absolute, vitiating normally applicable defences (*Wheeler v New Merton Board Mills Ltd [1933] 2 KB 669* where the employee who was operating a cardboard cutting machine had his left arm cut off above the wrist, when trying to remove cardboard by hand from the machine when it clogged up; the machine had not been turned off, and did not have any fencing at all. It was held that the employer was liable and could not plead '*volenti non fit injuria*' (to one who is willing no harm is done) – see Chapter 15 'Employers' Duties'). Breach of the *Factories Act 1961, ss 12-14* is not like negligence where both *volenti* and contributory negligence can be pleaded. These duties are absolute and if inadequate fencing causes injury, the most the employer can do by way of defence is to plead contributory negligence and seek apportionment of damages (see further 28.26-28.28 below). (See further Chapter 15 'Employers' Duties' for details of these defences.)

Machinery presumed safe until proved dangerous

28.23   Other machinery/machine parts are *presumed to be safe until proved to be dangerous*, i.e. until associated with a reasonably foreseeable risk of injury/death. 'Danger' is not defined in the *Factories Act 1961* (or its predecessors) but case law suggests the following: 'A part of machinery is dangerous if it is a possible cause of injury to anybody in a way in which a human being may be reasonably expected to act in circumstances which may reasonably be expected to occur' (*Walker v Bletchley-Flettons Ltd [1937] 1 AER 170* per du Parcq J). This acknowledges that workers are (foreseeably) inattentive or careless at times or even perverse and so go beyond the authorised parameters of the job (*Uddin v Associated Portland Cement Manufacturers*

Ltd [1965] 2 AER 213 – see further Chapter 15 'Employers' Duties'). Whether machinery is 'dangerous' is to be judged, not by asking whether a similar accident has happened on it previously (i.e. retrospectively) but whether, given its current condition, an accident is likely to happen on it (foreseeably) (*Carr v Mercantile Produce Co Ltd [1949] 2 AER 531*). However, the fact that management had earlier warned of danger and/or taken steps to obviate it, is evidence of 'foreseeable' injury (*Woodley v Meason Freer & Co Ltd [1963] 3 AER 636* where iron bars had been placed over the top of a hopper, which itself was on top of a plastic grinding machine. The employee removed these bars and stood on boxes to clean the machine when it jammed; he lost four fingers when he put his hands into the machine).

Duty to fence dangerous machinery

28.24   'Every dangerous part of any machinery, other than prime movers and transmission machinery shall be securely fenced.' [*Factories Act 1961, s 14(1)*].

But,

'In so far as the safety of a dangerous part of any machinery cannot by reason of the nature of the operation be secured by means of a fixed guard, the requirements of subsection (1) . . . shall be deemed to have been complied with if a device is provided which automatically prevents the operator from coming into contact with that part'. [*Factories Act 1961, s 14(2)*].

The duty to 'fence securely' is absolute, in so far as the factory occupier, irrespective of commercial considerations and physical impracticability, must see that persons are completely protected against all foreseeable injuries.

If fencing/guards eliminate the possibility of risk of injury, the requirement is complied with (*John Summers & Sons Ltd v Frost [1955] 1 AER 870* where the respondent operated a power driven grinding machine. The employee's thumb got through a small gap between the guard and grinding wheel. It was held that the employer was liable for breach of *Sec 14(1)*). 'To my mind the natural meaning of the word "securely" used in regard to the fencing of a dangerous part of a machine is that the part must be so fenced that no part of the person or clothing of any person working the machine or passing it can come into contact with it' (per Viscount Simons). This includes danger to a (sometimes perforce) careless or inattentive worker (*Uddin v Associated Portland Cement* see 28.23 above), but not risk of injury from bits flying out of a machine (see 28.18 above *Nicholls v Austin, Carroll v Barclay*), because of the effect of *Sec 14(2)* on *Sec 14(1)* (above). In such circumstances, where the *Factories Act 1961, s 14(2)* has a vitiating effect on *Sec 14(1)*, an action will almost certainly lie at common law (*Hindle v Birtwhistle [1896] 1 QB 192, Kilgollan v Cooke Ltd [1956] 2 AER 294* – in the former case a factory owner was prosecuted for breach of a statutory duty to fence shuttles of a loom. It was held that the employer was liable for damages for breach of common law duty, where there was a risk of bits flying out and the plaintiff was injured).

Even though an employee is wholly to blame for his injury and hence loses the right to damages, the employer can still be prosecuted for failing to fence dangerous machinery (*Dunn v Birds Eye Foods Ltd [1959] 2 AER 403* where an employee was employed to clean machinery in a frozen vegetable factory. He had been clearly instructed never to clean the machine while it was in motion and never to use his hands, but rather a brush and hose. The drums of the conveyor were not fenced, since normally production staff would not come into contact with it. Instead of stopping the machine, the employee swept bean particles off with his hands while the conveyor was in motion and his hand got caught. The employer was convicted by the magistrates for failing to guard dangerous machinery (even though the employee's injury was his own fault)).

The defence of '*volenti non fit injuria*' (to one who is willing no harm is done) (see Chapter 15 'Employers' Duties') cannot be pleaded in answer to a breach of the *Factories Act 1961, ss 12-14*; the most that the employer can do is plead contributory negligence, a partial defence, resulting in reduction of damages for an employee (*Wheeler v New Merton Board Mills Ltd [1933] 2 KB 669*).

Exception – machinery safe by position or construction

28.25 An exception to the requirement to fence securely occurs if machinery is safe either by position or construction. [*Factories Act 1961, s 14(1)*]. (This is also the case with *Secs 12* and *13* (see 28.26, 28.27 below).) How far the effect of this defence has been diluted by case law (on *Sec 14*) establishing liability in favour of careless, inattentive or trespassing workers (see *Uddin*, 28.23 above) is a debatable point, but it is highly likely that this has happened – another step towards strict liability.

Duty to fence prime movers and transmission machinery

Prime movers

28.26 'Every flywheel directly connected to any prime mover and every moving part of any prime mover must be securely fenced.' [*Factories Act 1961, s 12(1)*]. A 'prime mover' refers to a source of mechanical power deriving from steam, water, wind or electricity. [*Factories Act 1961, s 176(1)*]. (This definition is not going to be repealed.)

The duty to fence extends to electric generators, motors and rotary converters, and every flywheel directly connected to them (unless safe by position/construction (see above)). [*Factories Act 1961, s 12(3)*].

Transmission machinery

28.27 Every part of transmission machinery must be securely fenced. [*Factories Act 1961, s 13(1)*]. 'Transmission machinery' means a 'shaft, wheel, drum, pulley, system of fast and loose pulleys, coupling, clutch, driving belt or other device by which the motion of a prime mover is transmitted to, or received by, any machine or appliance'. [*Factories Act 1961, s 176(1)*]. Safety by position/construction is again expressed to be a defence. (As for the requirements/prohibitions relating to cleaning factory machinery by young persons, see Chapter 5 'Children and Young Persons'.)

Cleaning machinery – Operations at Unfenced Machinery Regulations 1938 (SR&O 1938 No 641)

28.28 The *Factories Act 1961, s 15* accepts that dangerous parts of certain machines can only be (*a*) lubricated or (*b*) adjusted, while in motion. Some machines cannot be stopped without seriously interfering with manufacturing processes on which they are working. Such lubrication/adjustment operations can only be carried out by 'machinery attendants', who must:

(*a*)   be at least 18;

(*b*)   have received training; and

(*c*)   be specifically appointed in writing by the employer.

A copy of the certificate of appointment must be issued to each machinery attendant, specifying the operations which he has been appointed to carry out. Details of this must be entered in the general register (Factory Form 31). Moreover, machinery attendants must be instructed in the requirements of the *Operations at Unfenced Machinery Regulations 1938 (SR&O 1938 No 641)* and be issued with a precautionary leaflet (Factory Form 2487) which they must carry with them.

Regulations relating to machinery hazards in particular industries/processes

28.29   The following sets of regulations deal with hazards to employees from the use of particular machines, i.e. the *Abrasive Wheels Regulations 1970*, the *Horizontal Milling Machines Regulations 1928/1934*, the *Power Presses Regulations 1965*, the *Woodworking Machines Regulations 1974*, the *Construction (General Provisions) Regulations 1961* and various regulations on agriculture.

Abrasive Wheels Regulations 1970 (SI 1970 No 535)

28.30   These regulations are applicable expressly in factories, and by extension in similar workplaces, and provide for specific guarding in the case of abrasive wheels. They may be summarised as follows.

(*a*)   No abrasive wheel, with a diameter of more than 55 mm, must be used for the first time in any factory (see Chapter 18 'Factories and Workplaces' for the definition of 'factory'), unless:

    (i)   it is clearly marked with the maximum permissible speed (MPS) (as specified by the manufacturer) [*Reg 6(1)*]; and

    (ii)   the notice relating to MPS is permanently fixed in a room where grinding operations take place, stating maximum permissible speed, and in the case of a mounted wheel, the overhang permissible.

[*Reg 6(2)*].

(*b*)   No abrasive wheel must be opened at a speed greater than the MPS. [*Reg 6(3)*].

(*c*)   Every abrasive wheel must be properly mounted. [*Reg 8*].

(*d*)   Except in the case of persons:

    (i)   under supervision of a 'competent person'; and/or

    (ii)   mounting a mounted wheel or point;

abrasive wheels can only be mounted by a person who:

—   has been trained for this purpose;

—   is 'competent';

—   has been appointed by the factory occupier for this purpose.

[*Reg 9*]. (These regulations will remain in force until 1997; *Reg 9* indefinitely (see Table 25).)

Guarding abrasive wheels

28.31   Guards must be provided and kept in position at every abrasive wheel. [*Reg 10*]. Such a guard must (reversing the decision in *John Summers Ltd v Frost* (see 28.24 above)):

(*a*)   so far as is reasonably practicable, be of a sufficiently good design and construction as to contain the abrasive wheel, if it breaks whilst in motion;

(*b*)   be properly (i) maintained, and (ii) secured, so as to prevent displacement, if it breaks;

(*c*)   enclose the whole of the abrasive wheel (except such part as is necessarily exposed for the purposes of work being done at an abrasive wheel).

[*Reg 11*].

Horizontal Milling Machines Regulations 1928 and 1934 (SR&O 1928 No 548; SR&O 1934 No 207)

28.32   The requirements relating to the guarding of horizontal milling machines are as follows:

(*a*)   the cutters of every horizontal milling machine must be fenced by a strong guard enclosing the whole cutting surface, except the part necessarily exposed for milling work;

(*b*)   except in the case of face milling, the guard must:

    (i)   be provided with adequate side flanges; or

    (ii)   extend on each side of the cutters to the end of the arbor, or not less than half the diameter of the cutter

[*Reg 3*];

(*c*)   guards must be constantly kept in position while the cutter is 'in motion' (see 28.15 above for meaning), except when the machine is being set up [*Reg 6*];

(*d*)   there must be efficient starting and stopping devices readily accessible to the operator [*Reg 4*].

(These requirements will remain in force until 1997.)

Power Presses Regulations 1965 (SI 1965 No 1441; SI 1972 No 1512)

28.33   The main safety requirements relating to power presses are as follows.

(Except in the case of a person undergoing training), no person must:

(*a*)   set, re-set, adjust or try out tools on a power press; or

(*b*)   instal or adjust any safety device; or

(*c*)   carry out inspection and test a safety device; unless:

    (i)   he is 18 or over;

    (ii)   has been trained (in power press mechanisms, safety devices, accident causation and prevention, work of a tool setter and tool design);

    (iii)   is competent to perform the duties; and

    (iv)   has been appointed by the factory occupier to carry out the above duties.

[*Reg 4(1)(4)*].

Power presses and/or safety devices must not be used in any factory (see Chapter 18 'Factories and Workplaces' for the meaning of this expression), unless thoroughly examined and tested [*Reg 5(1)*]; power presses must be examined and tested by 'competent persons'; and defects reported [*Reg 6(1)*].

Power presses must not be used after (*a*) setting, (*b*) re-setting or (*c*) adjustment of tools, unless examined and tested and certified as safe [*Reg 7(1)*]; such certificates must be kept in the factory for six months for inspection [*Reg 7(5)*].

The maximum permissible flywheel speed (MPFS) (as certified by the manufacturer) and the direction of rotation of the flywheel, must be clearly marked, and power presses must not be driven at greater speeds than those specified [*Reg 10*].

(These regulations are not affected by revocation.)

Woodworking Machines Regulations 1974 (SI 1974 No 903)

28.34   Regulations can specify stricter duties than the parent Act (i.e. *Factories Act 1961*). The *Woodworking Machines Regulations 1974* are an example of this, where the guarding requirements have replaced those of the *Factories Act 1961, s 14* (see 28.24 above). A woodworking machine refers to the following types of machines (including portable ones):

(*a*)   any sawing machines designed to be fitted with one or more circular blades;

(*b*)   grooving machines;

(*c*)   a sawing machine, with a blade in the form of a continuous band or strip;

(*d*)   chain sawing machines;

(*e*)   mortising machines;

(*f*)   planing machines;

(*g*)   vertical spindle moulding machines;

(*h*)   multi-cutter moulding machines;

(*j*)   tenoning machines;

(*k*)   trenching machines;

(*l*)   automatic and semi-automatic lathes;

(*m*)   boring machines;

for use on wood, cork, fibre board etc. [*Woodworking Machines Regulations 1974, 1 Sch, Reg 2*]. (This definition will remain in force.)

The main duties under these regulations are as follows.

General

28.35   All woodworking machines (including cutters and cutter blocks) must be:

(*a*)   of good construction;

(*b*)   of sound material; and

(*c*)   properly maintained (see Chapter 26 'Lifting Machinery and Equipment' for meaning of these terms); and

(*d*)   securely fixed to the foundation floor.

[*Reg 42(2)*].

Guards

28.36   Cutters must be enclosed by a guard or guards to the greatest extent practicable, unless safe by position. (This duty does not extend to employees doing private work after working hours (see 28.21 above *Napieralski v Curtis (Contractors) Ltd*). [*Reg 5*].) Though in the case of vertical spindle moulding machines, where this sort of guard is impracticable, a jig or holder is sufficient. [*Reg 34*].

While cutters are in motion, no person must make an adjustment:

(*a*)   to a guard, unless means are provided whereby he can do so without endangering himself;

(*b*)   to a woodworking machine, except where it can be done safely.

[*Reg 6*].

While cutters are in motion, guards must be:

(i)   kept constantly in position;

(ii)   properly secured; and

(iii)   adjusted;

except where the work makes this impracticable (for the meaning of this expression, see Chapter 15 'Employers' Duties'). [*Reg 7(1)*].

The above exception does not apply in the following cases:

(*a*)   circular sawing machines for cutting rebate, tenon, mould or groove [*Reg 18(1)*];

(*b*)   multiple rip sawing machines and straight line edging machines [*Reg 21(1)*];

(*c*)   multiple rip sawing machines and straight line edging machines on which the saw spindle is mounted above the machine table [*Reg 21(2)*];

(*d*)   planing machines for cutting rebate, recess, tenon or mould [*Reg 23*];

(*e*)   planing machines for surfacing with adjustable guard for cutter block [*Reg 28*];

(*f*)   saw wheels of a narrow band sawing machine [*Reg 22*];

(*g*)   combined machines used for thicknessing [*Reg 28*];

(*h*)   planing machines used for thicknessing, with feed rollers to protect against ejected material [*Reg 31*].

Exceptions to guarding requirements

28.37   If a woodworking machine is provided with safeguards which make it as safe as if guards were provided, the guarding requirements can be dispensed with in the following cases:

(*a*)   cutters of all woodworking machines [*Reg 5*];

(*b*)   saw blades of all circular sawing machines [*Reg 16*];

(*c*)   multiple rip sawing machines and straight line edging machines [*Reg 21*];

(*d*)   saw wheels of narrow band sawing machines and blade [*Reg 22*];

(*e*)   bridge guards on planing machines [*Reg 26*];

(*f*)   cutter block guards on planing machines [*Reg 28*];

(*g*)   cutter block of a combined machine [*Reg 30*];

(*h*)   sectional feed rollers on planing machines [*Reg 31*];

(*j*)   back stops on vertical spindle moulding machines [*Reg 36*].

Duties of employees

28.38   No person must work on a woodworking machine unless he has been trained and instructed in the dangers involved. [*Reg 13*]. (For prohibitions on young persons operating woodworking machines, see Chapter 5 'Children and Young Persons'.) All employees operating a woodworking machine, must use:

(*a*)   the guards;

(*b*)   spikes, push-sticks, push-blocks, jigs, holders and back stops, unless impracticable; and

(*c*)   report any defect in a woodworking machine.

[*Reg 14*].

Failure to use push-sticks, resulting in injury to an employee, can mean that an employee will lose damages as there will be no liability on the part of the employer. In *Lewis v Denye* [*1940*] *3 AER 299* a 17-year-old trainee was operating a circular saw; he had been given detailed instructions and told about push-sticks to push pieces of wood through the saw and for cleaning off-cuts from the saw table. With the push-stick in his right hand, the employee cleared away off-cuts on the table with his left hand. He lost three fingers and a thumb when his hand came into contact with the saw blade. It was held that the employer was not liable for breach of the duty to fence; the material cause of the injury (see 15.23 EMPLOYERS' DUTIES) was the employee's failure to use a push-stick, in spite of instruction and training to the contrary. The absolute nature of the statutory duty to fence means, however, that even though an employee's injury is entirely his own fault, as in *Lewis v Denye*, this will not absolve an employer from prosecution (though it can absolve him from paying damages) (*Dunn v Birds Eye Foods Ltd*, see 28.24 above).

(These requirements will remain in force until 1997 but its training, circular saws and two-speed motors provisions will continue thereafter.)

Construction (General Provisions) Regulations 1961 (SI 1961 No 1580)

28.39   The *Construction (General Provisions) Regulations 1961* specify similar requirements in relation to machinery safety on construction sites (see Chapter 7 'Construction and Building Operations' for meaning of 'work of construction'). Thus:

(*a*)   every flywheel; and

(*b*)   moving part of any prime mover; and

(*c*)   every part of transmission machinery (whether mechanically driven or not);

must be securely fenced, unless safe by position and/or construction, to every person either (i) employed or (ii) working on site. (This covers indirect labour but not an employee doing private work after hours (see *Napieralski*, 28.21 above).) [*Reg 42*].

(This regulation remains in force until 1997.)

Agricultural machinery

28.40   Unlike other industries, agriculture has to accommodate the presence of children and elderly workers – two groups especially vulnerable to accidents, injuries and diseases. The following sets of regulations (some partially revoked (see Table 25)) specify statutory requirements in relation to agricultural machinery, i.e. the *Agriculture (Power Take-off) Regulations 1957*, the *Agriculture (Field Machinery) Regulations 1962*, the *Agriculture (Tractor Cabs) Regulations 1974* (as amended by *SI 1990 No 1075*), the *Agriculture (Stationary Machinery) Regulations 1959*, the *Agriculture (Circular Saws) Regulations 1959* and the *Agriculture (Threshers and Balers) Regulations 1960*. (These regulations remain in force until 1997.)

Power take-offs – guarding requirements

28.41   Under the *Agricultural (Power Take-off) Regulations 1957 (SI 1957 No 1386)*:

(*a*)   the tractor PTO must be covered while the engine is in motion by a shield made of metal (or other material) which, when attached to the tractor, must be able to support at least 113.4 kilograms. The shield must protect the worker and his clothing from coming into contact with the PTO from (i) above or (ii) either side, unless the PTO is enclosed by a fixed cover (in which case a shield is not necessary) [*Reg 3(1)*];

(*b*)   while in motion, the PTO shaft must be enclosed in a guard, extending along its whole length from the tractor to the first fixed bearing. Workers must not use tractors/machines not complying with these requirements [*Reg 4*].

Field machinery

28.42   The *Agriculture (Field Machinery) Regulations 1962 (SI 1962 No 1472)* specify that a field machine (i.e. loading trailers but not goods/passenger vehicles or aircraft, nor machinery for use in a stationary position):

(*a*)   must be properly maintained and its safety devices must be securely fixed [*Reg 15*]; and

(*b*)   workers must report defects in safety devices and not interfere with or misuse them.

[*Reg 17*].

Workers over 16:

(i)   can remove guards of machines which are not in motion for cleaning, repair, and adjustment; and

(ii)   if it cannot be done otherwise, do essential adjustment while it is in motion.

[*Reg 18*].

Tractor cabs

28.43   The *Agriculture (Tractor Cabs) Regulations 1974 (SI 1974 No 2034)* (as amended by *SI 1990 No 1075*) require:

(*a*)   all new wheeled tractors weighing 560 kilograms or more, and sold for use in agriculture, to be fitted with an approved safety cab [*Reg 4*];

(*b*)   all tractors, when used by agricultural workers, to be fitted with an approved safety cab [*Reg 5*];

(*c*)   new tractors sold for use in agriculture to be fitted with an approved safety cab with a noise level not greater than 90dBA at the driver's cab [*Reg 2(2)*].

(These regulations are not affected by revocation.)

Stationary machinery

28.44   The *Agriculture (Stationary Machinery) Regulations 1959 (SI 1959 No 1216)* specify fencing requirements in respect of stationary prime movers; though the transmission belt and stopping and disconnecting devices must be guarded even if the prime mover is not stationary. In addition, safety by situation is an alternative to fencing. More particularly, (i) shafting, (ii) pulleys, (iii) flywheels, (iv) gearing, (v) sprockets, (vi) chains, (vii) belts, (viii) wings or blades of a fan, must be:

(*a*)   either situated; or

(*b*)   guarded;

so as to prevent a worker or his clothing coming into contact with them [*Reg 2(3)*], except in the case of:

(i)   tractor take-off; or

(ii)   primary driving belt, where the prime mover and the machine driven by it are not permanently fixed.

Circular saws

28.45   The *Agriculture (Circular Saws) Regulations 1959 (SI 1959 No 427)* specify requirements in relation to circular saws. The main prohibitions are as follows:

(*a*)   saw blades with defects must not be 'knowingly' used [*Reg 3*];

(*b*)   as with circular saws used in factories, three separate guards are required to cover the full circle of the saw:

 (i)   below the table the blade must be guarded to the fullest extent practicable [*Reg 6*] (this requirement is not affected by revocation);

 (ii)   behind the blade, a riving knife [*Reg 4*];

 (iii)   over the top of the saw, a guard as close as practicable to the cutting edge [*Reg 5*] (this requirement is not affected by revocation);

(*c*)   workers must keep guards in position, except for adjustment purposes when the saw is not in motion [*Reg 8*]; and must not remove guards when the saw is in motion [*Reg 12*] (this requirement will remain in force); and must report defects [*Reg 9*] (this requirement is not affected by revocation);

(*d*)   no person must work at a saw unless he has received full instruction and demonstration in the working of the machine and safety rules applicable, from a person over 18 [*Reg 5*]. (As for prohibitions on young persons working circular saws, see Chapter 5 'Children and Young Persons'.)

Duties on manufacturers and suppliers

28.46   The principal duties on producers and suppliers of EC machinery and importers of non-EC manufactured machines are contained in the *Supply of Machinery (Safety) Regulations 1992 (SI 1992 No 3073)*. Of much less significance, in practice, is the specific duty on vendors of certain machinery under *Sec 17* of the *Factories Act 1961* (see 28.66 below), imposing both criminal and civil liability relevant to goods for private use, occupation and consumption. In addition, there is a general duty to make and supply safe and reliable products to the consuming public under the *Consumer Protection Act 1987* and to employees under amendments to *HSWA* contained in this Act (see Chapter 38 'Product Safety').

Supply of Machinery (Safety) Regulations 1992 (SI 1992 No 3073)

28.47   These regulations came into force on 1 January 1993, but they are not applicable to

(a)   machinery supplied before 1 January 1993 [*Reg 7*]; or

(b)   machinery complying with health and safety requirements as at 31 December 1992, which has been put into service before 31 December 1994 [*Reg 8*]; or

(c)   machinery exhibited at trade fairs, exhibitions and demonstrations;

but extend to

(d)   safety components marked separately (EC 89/392);

(e)   (i)   roll-over protective structures,

(ii)   falling-object protective structures,

(iii)   industrial trucks.

(These are excluded from these regulations until 1995, but after 1 July 1995, a supplier can comply with the requirements of either the *Supply of Machinery (Safety) Regulations 1992* or of the *Roll-Over Protective Structures/ Falling-Object Protective Structures for Construction Plant (EEC Requirements) Regulations 1988* or *Self-Propelled Industrial Trucks (EC Requirements) Regulations 1988* (see further 7.40 CONSTRUCTION AND BUILDING OPERATIONS.)

[*Reg 9*];

(f)   machinery covered by other directives (e.g. the Product Safety Directive, see further Chapter 38 'Product Safety');

(g)   electrical equipment.

[*Reg 10*].

The *Supply of Machinery (Safety) Regulations 1992, Regs 11, 12* provide that machinery cannot be supplied or put into service unless it complies with

(a)   essential health and safety requirements, and

(b)   appropriate conformity assessment procedures.

Moreover, manufacturers must issue

(i)   an EC declaration – to the effect that machinery satisfies the necessary 'health and safety' requirements, or

(ii)   in the case of machinery to be incorporated into other machinery – a declaration of incorporation.

[*Reg 12*].

Excluded machinery

28.48   Certain machinery is outside the ambit of the new regulations, namely,

(a)   machinery powered manually;

(b)   machinery for medical use;

(c)   machinery for use in fairgrounds;

(d)   steam boilers and pressure vessels;

(e)   machinery for nuclear purposes;

(*f*)   firearms;

(*g*)   storage tanks for petrol and dangerous substances;

(*h*)   vehicles/trailers for transporting passengers;

(*j*)   ships;

(*k*)   tractors;

(*l*)   machines for military use.

[5 *Sch*].

But included are

(i)   lifting equipment designed and constructed for raising and/or moving persons with/without loads as well as industrial trucks with elevating operation position;

(ii)   cableways (including funicular railways) for public or private transportation of persons;

(iii)   lifts permanently serving specific levels of buildings and constructions, with a car between guides, for transport of

(*a*)   persons,

(*b*)   persons and goods,

(*c*)   goods alone, if a person can enter without difficulty, and fitted with controls,

(*d*)   means of transport of persons using rack and pinion rail mounted vehicles,

(*e*)   mine winding gear,

(*f*)   theatre elevators,

(*g*)   construction site hoists for lifting

—   persons

—   persons and goods.

(EC 89/392).

General machinery and machinery posing special hazards

28.49   The regulations draw a distinction between general machinery and machinery posing special hazards, in that the latter's – machinery posing special hazards – technical file, which must be prepared in either case for relevant machinery, must be sent to

(i)   an approved body for retention/verification – in the case of machinery manufactured according to transposed harmonised standards [*Reg 14*], and

(ii)   an approved body, coupled with an example of machinery for EC-type-examination – in the case of machinery not manufactured according to transposed harmonised standards.

[*Regs 13, 15*].

Machinery posing special hazards – Schedule 4 machinery

28.50   Such machinery refers to:

(i)   circular saws (single or multi-blade) for working with wood or meat;

(ii)   sawing machines

    (*a*)   with fixed tool during operation, having fixed bed, with manual feed of workpiece or demountable power feed,

    (*b*)   having manually operated reciprocating saw-bench or carriage,

    (*c*)   having built-in mechanical feed device for workpieces, with manual loading and/or unloading,

    (*d*)   with movable tool during operation, with mechanical feed device and manual loading and/or unloading;

(iii)   hand-fed surface planing machines;

(iv)   thicknessing machines;

(v)   band-saws with fixed or mobile bed, or mobile carriage;

(vi)   hand-fed tenoning machines;

(vii)   hand-fed vertical spindle moulding machines for working with wood etc.;

(viii)   portable chain saws;

(ix)   presses;

(x)   injection/compression plastic and rubber moulding machines;

(xi)   machinery used underground, e.g. in mines;

(xii)   manually-loaded trucks for collection of household refuse;

(xiii)   guards/detachable transmission shafts;

(xiv)   vehicles servicing lifts;

(xv)   devices for lifting persons, involving a risk of falling from a vertical height of more than three metres;

(xvi)   machines for the manufacture of pyrotechnics;

(xvii)   (following safety components) – electro-sensitive devices for detecting persons so as to ensure their safety, e.g. sensor mats;

(xviii)   logic units;

(xix)   automatic movable screens for protecting presses (see (ix) and (x));

(xx)   roll-over protective structures;

(xxi)   falling-object protective structures.

[*4 Sch*] (EC 89/392).

(A) Technical file – machinery posing special hazards

28.51   The technical file must include:

(i)   an overall drawing of the machinery along with drawings of control circuits;

(ii)   full detailed drawings for conformity purposes with basic health and safety requirements;

(iii)   description of method for elimination of hazards together with list of transposed harmonised standards, or, alternatively, national standards (in the absence of transposed harmonised standards).

[*Regs 14, 15*].

(B) Technical file – general machinery

These technical files must be retained for the purposes of conformity assessment procedures. [*Reg 13(2)*].

The technical file should include:

   (i)   overall drawings of the machinery and control circuits;

   (ii)   full detailed drawings for conformity purposes with essential health and safety requirements;

   (iii) a list of

       (*a*)   essential health and safety requirements,

       (*b*)   transposed harmonised standards,

       (*c*)   relevant standards (national or international, e.g. BS 5304: 1988),

       (*d*)   technical specifications;

   (iv) description of methods for eliminating hazards;

   (v)   technical report and certificate of suitability from a competent body;

   (vi) machinery instructions (in the language of the country of the manufacturer *and* of the user), namely,

       (*a*)   name/address of manufacturer,

       (*b*)   CE mark,

       (*c*)   description of series,

       (*d*)   serial number,

       (*e*)   for foreseeable use of machinery,

       (*f*)   workstations likely to be occupied by operators,

       (*g*)   for putting into safe service,

       (*h*)   for use (and prohibited uses),

       (*j*)   for handling and transportation,

       (*k*)   for assembly, dismantling,

       (*l*)   for adjustment purposes,

       (*m*)   for maintenance purposes,

       (*n*)   for training purposes (see 28.33 above).

Essential health and safety requirements for general machinery and machinery posing special hazards

28.52   Essential health and safety features relate to:

   (1)   general design features;

   (2)   controls;

   (3)   mechanical hazards;

   (4)   non-mechanical hazards;

   (5)   maintenance;

   (6)   indicators.

Within state of the art parameters (see 38.34 PRODUCT SAFETY), the key objective of the new regulations, and its parent, the EC Machinery Directive as amended by EC 89/392, is to integrate safety into workplace machinery from initial drawing-board stage to eventual circulation in parallel with BS 5304: 1988.

(1) General design features

28.53   To that end the following general design features should be incorporated:

(*a*)   machinery must be constructed so as to be fit for function, and adjustable/ maintainable without endangering operators;

(*b*)   in order to do this, manufacturers should

  (i)   eliminate and/or reduce inherent risks as far as possible,

  (ii)   take necessary protection measures in relation to risks that cannot be eliminated,

  (iii)   inform users of residual risks owing to shortcomings in protection measures,

  (iv)   specify training needs,

  (v)   specify personal protection needs;

(*c*)   design of machinery should envisage not just normal use but also reasonably foreseeable use, and machinery should be designed to prevent reasonably foreseeable abnormal use;

(*d*)   discomfort, fatigue and psychological stress faced by an operator must be reduced to a minimum;

(*e*)   constraints upon operators must be accommodated, including requisite and foreseeable use of personal protective equipment;

(*f*)   supply of machinery must be accompanied by special equipment and accessories for use, adjustment and maintenance purposes;

(*g*)   machinery should not endanger the operator when being filled or used with or drained of fluids;

(*h*)   integral lighting should be supplied where there is a risk from lack of it, in spite of normal ambient lighting;

(*j*)   machinery must be capable of being handled and stored safely.

[*3 Sch*].

(2) Controls – starting and stopping

28.54   Control systems must be safe and reliable and be able to withstand normal use and external pressures. More particularly, they must be

(*a*)   clearly visible and appropriately marked;

(*b*)   positioned for safe operation;

(*c*)   located outside a danger zone, except for emergency stops or consoles;

(*d*)   powered so that operation cannot cause additional risk;

(*e*)   designed so that risk cannot occur without intentional operation;

(f)   made to withstand foreseeable strain, especially as regards emergency stop devices;

(g)   in the case of a multi-action control, the action to be performed, must be clearly displayed;

(h)   fitted with indicators which the operator can read;

(j)   prevented from exposing persons in danger zones – and the operator must be able to ensure this from the main control position; failing this, an acoustic and/or visual warning signal must be given whenever machinery is about to start.

Starting and stopping

(a) Starting

28.55   It must be possible to

(i)   start machinery;

(ii)   re-start machinery after stoppage;

(iii)   effect change in speed pressure only by voluntary action of control (though not from the normal sequence of the automatic cycle).

(b) Stopping

28.56   Stopping devices must accommodate both normal and emergency stopping.

(i)   *Normal stop.* Machinery must be fitted with a control to bring it safely to a complete stop and each workstation, too, to stop some or all of the moving parts, so that it is made safe. Stop controls must have priority over start controls, and, once machinery is stopped, energy supply must be cut off.

(ii)   *Emergency stop.* Emergency stops/devices must be easily identifiable, clearly visible and quickly accessible, and able to stop a dangerous process as quickly as possible. The emergency stop must remain engaged, and disengagement must not reactivate machinery. Further, stop controls must not trigger the stopping function before being in the engaged position. Once active operation of the emergency stop control has ceased following stop command, that command must be sustained by engagement of the emergency stop device until that engagement is specifically overridden. It must not be possible to engage the device without triggering a stop command. Disengaging the stop device must not reactivate machinery but only permit restarting.

(iii)   *Mode selection.* Control mode selected must override all other control systems, except the emergency stop. If, for certain operations, machinery has to operate with protection devices neutralised, the mode selector must simultaneously

(a)   disable automatic control mode;

(b)   permit movements only by controls requiring sustained action;

(c)   permit operation of dangerous moving parts only in enhanced safety conditions (e.g. reduced speed);

(d)   prevent any movement liable to pose a danger by acting voluntarily or involuntarily on a machine's internal sensors.

(iv) *Failure of power supply/failure of control circuit.* Neither failure of power supply or of control circuit must lead to:

    (*a*)   machinery starting unexpectedly;

    (*b*)   machinery being prevented from stopping if the command has been given;

    (*c*)   any moving part/piece falling out or being ejected;

    (*d*)   impeding of automatic or manual stopping of moving parts;

    (*e*)   protection devices becoming ineffective.

[*3 Sch*].

(3) Protection against mechanical hazards

28.57 Machinery must

    (i)   be stable enough for use without risk of overturning, falling or unexpected movement. If necessary, anchorage must be incorporated (and indicated);

    (ii)   be able to withstand workplace stresses and not be likely to break up, including fatigue, ageing, corrosion and abrasion. In particular, manufacturers must indicate the type and frequency of inspection and maintenance and specify the parts likely to need replacement. Where a workpiece comes into contact with a tool, the tool must be operating normally; when the tool starts or stops, intentionally or accidentally, feed and tool movement must be co-ordinated;

    (iii)   prevent objects, such as tools/workpieces, being ejected;

    (iv)   not have sharp edges/angles/rough surfaces;

    (v)   where intended to carry out various operations, be able to be used separately, and it must be possible to start and stop separately;

    (vi)   where designed to perform under different conditions or speeds, selection and adjustment must be able to be completed safely;

    (vii)   prevent hazards arising from moving parts of machinery, or if hazards are not avoidable, moving parts must be fixed with guards. In particular, manufacturers should indicate how, if necessary, equipment can be safely unblocked.

Guards

28.58 In order to ensure maximum safety with machinery, guards (or safety devices) should be used (see 28.75, 28.76 below for varieties) to protect the operator against the risk from

    (i)   moving transmission parts; and/or

    (ii)   moving parts directly involved in the work process.

In principle, machinery with moving transmission parts (e.g. belts/pulleys) can have fixed or movable guards – the latter being preferable where frequent access is foreseeable; but, whichever is used, it should always

    (*a*)   be fixed;

    (*b*)   be of strong construction;

    (*c*)   not be easily by-passable or rendered non-operational;

(d)   located at an adequate distance from a danger zone;

(e)   cause minimum obstruction to the view of those involved in the production process;

(f)   enable installation, replacement or maintenance work to be carried out, if possible, without the guard having to be dismantled.

But where moving parts cannot be made wholly or even partially inaccessible during operation, requiring operator intervention, either (a) fixed or (b) adjustable guards (i.e. incorporating an adjustable element which, once adjusted, remains *in situ* during operation) should be used.

Fixed guards – special requirements

Fixed guards should be

(a)   securely held in place;

(b)   fixed by systems that can be opened with tools;

(c)   where possible, unable to remain in place without their fixings.

Moveable guards – special requirements

(a) *Moveable guards offering protection against moving transmission parts*

These should

(i)   remain fixed to machinery when open, as far as possible;

(ii)   be interlocking

(a)   to prevent activation of moving parts, and

(b)   give stop command when they are no longer closed.

(b) *Moveable guards offering protection against moving parts directly involved in work process*

These should ensure that

(i)   moving parts cannot start up while within the operator's reach;

(ii)   the exposed person cannot reach the moving parts once activated;

(iii)   they can only be adjusted by a tool or key;

(iv)   the absence or failure of one of the component parts prevents starting, or stops moving parts;

(v)   the protection against any risk of ejection is proved by means of an appropriate barrier.

Adjustable guards (resisting access to parts involved)

These should

(i)   be adjustable manually or automatically;

(ii)   be readily adjustable without use of tools;

(iii)   reduce as far as possible the likelihood of ejection.

Interlocking systems may be mechanical, electrical (e.g. control interlocking, power interlocking), hydraulic, pneumatic (or any permutation) and should be 'fail-safe'.

Guards can also be automatic, in which case, they are activated by the mechanism of the machinery (see further 28.75 below). These are frequently used on power presses. [*3 Sch*].

(4) Protection against non-mechanical hazards

28.59   Additionally, machinery must protect against

(i)   electrical hazards – voltage limits must be observed;

(ii)   a build-up of electrostatic charges and/or be fitted with a discharging system;

(iii) if powered hydraulically or pneumatically or thermally, hydraulic, pneumatic or thermal dangers;

(iv)   fitting errors – in particular, incorrect fluid connections, electrical conductors, via information on pipes, cables etc.;

(v)   hazards of extreme temperatures, either high or low;

(vi)   fire, either through overheating of machinery or caused by gases, liquids, dusts, vapours;

(vii) explosion;

(viii) noise – airborne noise must be reduced to the lowest practicable level;

(ix)   vibration – must be reduced to the lowest practicable level;

(x)   radiation – the effects on exposed persons must be eliminated or reduced to safe levels;

(xi)   accidental radiation, in the case of laser equipment; as for optical equipment, this must not create health risks from laser rays; and laser equipment on machinery must not create health risks through reflection or diffusion;

(xii) emissions of dust, gases, liquids and vapours. If such hazard exists, machinery must be able to contain or evacuate it; and if not enclosed during normal operation, containment/evacuation devices must be as close as possible to emission source;

(xiii) the risk of being trapped – a person should be able to summon help;

(xiv) the risk of slipping or tripping or falling.

(5) Maintenance

28.60   (*a*)   Adjustment, maintenance, repair, cleaning and servicing must be able to be carried out while machinery is at a standstill; but if this is not possible, without risk. Diagnostic fault-finding equipment must be connectable to automated machinery. Automated machine components, which have to be changed frequently, must be easily and safely removeable and replaceable.

(*b*)   Safe means of access to areas of production, adjustment and maintenance should be provided and designed to prevent falls.

(*c*)   The machinery must be fitted with means of isolating it from all energy sources, clearly identifiable and capable of being locked where an operator cannot check whether energy is still cut off.

(*d*)   Need for operator intervention must be reduced to a minimum.

(e)   Cleaning of internal parts with dangerous substances or preparations must be possible without entry; and unblocking should take place from outside. If cleaning by entry is necessary, this should be able to be done with a minimum of danger.

[*3 Sch*].

(6) Indicators

28.61   Machinery must be fitted with indicators and the necessary unambiguous and intelligible information to control it easily. Indicators can consist of:

(i)   *Information devices.* These must be in clear, unambiguous and easily intelligible language, e.g. 'This machine emits radiation'.

(ii)   *Warning devices*, e.g. 'Warning. To be operated only by skilled personnel'.

(iii)   *Markings.* All machinery (including interchangeable equipment and safety components) must be marked legibly and indelibly as follows:

(a)   name/address of manufacturer;

(b)   CE mark, including year of construction;

(c)   designation of series or type;

(d)   use in an explosive atmosphere;

(e)   safe use specifications (e.g. maximum speed of rotating parts);

(f)   its mass, if machinery is to be handled.

(iv)   *Instructions.* Machinery must be accompanied by the following instructions:

(i)   marking information;

(ii)   maintenance information (e.g. address of importer);

(iii)   foreseeable use;

(iv)   likely workstation of operator;

(v)   instructions for

(a)   safe putting into service;

(b)   safe use,

(c)   safe handling,

(d)   safe assembly and dismantling,

(e)   safe maintenance, servicing, repair,

(f)   safe adjustment,

(g)   training instructions, if necessary (see 28.33 above),

(h)   properties of tools to be fitted,

(j)   incorrect use of machinery.

Instructions

28.62   (1)   The instructions should be in the language of the country of manufacture *and* user, except for specialised maintenance operations.

(2)   They must contain drawings and diagrams for putting into service, maintenance, inspection and repair as well as for safety purposes.

(3)   Installation and assembly requirements for reducing noise and vibration.

(4)   (With reference to airborne noise emissions):

—   equivalent continuous A-weighted sound pressure (see 30.6 NOISE AND VIBRATION) at workstations where this exceeds 70 dB(A); if not in excess of 70 dB(A), this must be shown;

—   peak C-weighted instantaneous sound pressure value at workstations, where this exceeds 63Pa (130 dB in relation to 20 μPa);

—   sound power level emitted by machinery where equivalent continuous A-weighted sound pressure level at workstations exceeds 85 dB(A).

(5)   If necessary, precautions relating to use in explosive atmospheres.

[*3 Sch*].

(7) Enforcement

28.63   Enforcement is by HSE, since these regulations qualify as 'relevant statutory provisions' (see Chapter 17 'Enforcement'). [*6 Sch 1(b)*].

Offences/Defences

Breach of these regulations, as well as failing to comply with the necessary marking requirements, is an offence under the *Health and Safety at Work etc. Act 1974*. [*Regs 11, 29 and 6 Sch*].

Defences

It is a defence that a person charged took all reasonable steps *and* exercised all due diligence to avoid committing the offence. [*Reg 31(1)*]. Where the substance of the defence is that commission of the offence was due either to

(*a*)   act or default of another, or

(*b*)   reliance on information given by another,

the accused cannot rely on this defence, unless

(i)   he served notice of this on the prosecutor at least seven days before the hearing,

(ii)   the notice sufficiently identifies the other person,

(iii)   it was reasonable for him to have relied on the information.

[*Reg 31*].

In such circumstances the 'other person' may be proceeded against, though this is no bar to prosecution against the original accused [*Reg 31(1)*] (see further 17.34 ENFORCEMENT). Similarly, offences may be committed by bodies corporate, companies and directors under these regulations (see 17.32 ENFORCEMENT).

Penalties

Breach of an offence under *Regulation 11* – duty to supply safe machinery – carries a maximum penalty

(*a*)   on summary conviction, of a fine of £5,000; or

(*b*)   on conviction on indictment, an indefinite fine, except for

> (i)   breach of an improvement/prohibition notice, or

> (ii)   failure to disclose information to the HSC or an enforcement officer

imprisonment for up to two years, or a fine (or both).

[*6 Sch 3*].

Disapplication of current law

28.64   The following statutory provisions/regulations, otherwise valid, are disapplied in respect of machinery to be supplied, though not as regards operation of machinery already in service. [*Regs 7, 33(2)(3)*].

(1)   *Factories Act 1961, s 26(1)* – chains, ropes and lifting tackle for raising/lowering *materials* with respect to supply (see 26.1–26.15 LIFTING MACHINERY AND EQUIPMENT);

(2)   *Factories Act, ss 27(1)(6)* and *28(1)(6)*;

(3)   the *Construction (General Provisions) Regulations 1961, Regs 26(1)(2), 29* and *31(1)*;

(4)   the *Construction (Lifting Operations) Regulations 1961, Regs 10(1)(a), 11(3), 13(1)(2), 14(1)(4), 15, 16, 20(2), 21, 22, 24, 30(1), 30(2) (part), 34(1)* (see also 26.27 LIFTING MACHINERY AND EQUIPMENT).

Civil liability

28.65   Breach of these regulations causing injury/damage will give rise to civil liability, even though the regulations, as here, are silent on the point, since they do not state otherwise – *HSWA s 47(2)* (see 1.14 INTRODUCTION).

Supply of factory machinery

28.66   In addition to the employers' duties (see 28.6 above) and the suppliers' duties, a duty is also imposed on a person supplying factory machinery. More particularly, with regard to any machine in a factory which is intended to be driven by mechanical power

(*a*)   every set-screw, bolt or key or any revolving shaft, spindle, wheel or pinion shall be sunk, encased or otherwise effectively guarded so as to prevent danger; and

(*b*)   all spur and other toothed friction gearing, which does not require frequent adjustment while in motion, shall be completely encased unless it is so situated as to be as safe as it would be if carefully encased.

[*Factories Act 1961, s 17(1)*] (repealed by the *Provision and Use of Work Equipment Regulations 1992, 2 Sch* – taking effect as from 1 January 1997).

Offences

28.67   Any person who:

(*a*)   sells;

(*b*)   lets on hire (either as principal or agent); or

(*c*)   causes or procures to be sold or hired;

machinery which does not comply with *Sec 17(1)* commits an offence. [*Factories Act 1961, s 17(2)*].

This extends to:

(*a*)　any abrasive wheel with a diameter of more than 55 mm (for use in a factory) not having the maximum permissible speed (MPS) clearly marked; and

(*b*)　any machine supplied with its prime mover as a unit having a spindle on which an abrasive wheel is mounted, which does not specify the maximum working speed of the spindle.

[*Abrasive Wheels Regulations 1970, Reg 19*].

Civil liability under the Factories Act 1961, s 17

28.68　Although the *Factories Act 1961, s 17(2)* imposes a duty on the machinery supplier (as distinct from the factory occupier), this is only true in respect of criminal liability (*Biddle v Truvox Engineering Co Ltd [1951] 2 AER 835* where the manufacturer was held not to be jointly liable in tort with the factory occupier for an injury to an employee who had been 'hoisted' on the platform of a truck and who, in order to save himself, clutched at a chain near a cog wheel and was injured when his hand was caught between them). This is a strange result and means that, in addition to the *Factories Act 1961, s 14*, *Sec 17* imposes a strict duty on factory occupiers. This duty will not be made any less strict by the introduction of strict product liability for injury-causing defects in industrial products (see Chapter 38 'Product Safety'). In addition, any employee injured by such machinery can automatically sue the employer/factory occupier under the *Employers' Liability (Defective Equipment) Act 1969*, which makes employers liable in tort for faults in supply subject to a contractual right of indemnity against the supplier (see further Chapter 15 'Employers' Duties').

Specific duties on suppliers

28.69　(*a*)　No one must sell to a purchaser for use in agriculture any field machine (e.g. power driven hand tool, trailer) not complying with the requirements of the *Agriculture (Field Machinery) Regulations 1962* (see 28.42 above). [*Agriculture (Field Machinery) Regulations 1962, Reg 4(1)*].

(*b*)　No person must:

(i)　sell; or

(ii)　let on hire;

a new tractor, for use in agriculture, unless it is properly fitted with a safety cab. [*Agriculture (Tractor Cabs) Regulations 1974, Reg 4, as amended by SI 1990 No 1075*]. (The *Agriculture (Tractor Cabs) Regulations* are not affected by revocation.)

General duty of suppliers under HSWA

28.70　A general duty is placed on producers and suppliers of articles and substances for use at work to produce and supply, so far as is reasonably practicable, safe products for use at work. [*HSWA s 6*].

In the context of machinery guarding, it is not yet clear whether *HSWA s 6* imposes a duty on makers of factory plant and machinery to guard, or whether the duty falls on the factory occupier, by virtue of the fencing requirements of the *Factories Act*

1961 (see 28.24 above). As yet there is little or no authoritative case law, but the Scottish case of *McConnachie v Danckearts Woodworking Machinery Ltd (1979 unreported)* suggests that there is not a duty on suppliers to fit guards, but there is no High Court ruling on the matter. This was consistent with *HSWA s 6(10)* which stated: 'for the purposes of this section an article or substance is not to be regarded as properly used where it is used without regard to any relevant information or advice relating to its use which has been made available by a person by whom it was designed, manufactured, imported or supplied'. This subsection has recently been revised by the *Consumer Protection Act 1987* (see further 38.15 PRODUCT SAFETY). The *Provision and Use of Work Equipment Regulations 1992* and the *Supply of Machinery (Safety) Regulations 1992* have added specific requirements to these general provisions.

The importance of design as regards machine safety

28.71   Because the legal requirements are generally stringent, Great Britain has a good accident record by international standards. Engineering design of safeguards, however, is often poor, indicating that the law is honoured in the breach rather than in the observance. The HSE states that about three-quarters of all moving machinery accidents are preventable with reasonably practicable precautions. Half the number of preventable accidents arise as a consequence of a failure on the part of employers to provide proper safeguards. The other half are largely caused by workmen removing safety devices.

Design of machine guards to date has not been particularly successful, though design standards, in recent years, were set by BS 5304: 1975 'Code of Practice for safe guarding of machinery'. Progress was made on certain machines, partly as a result of innovative guard design and partly as a result of operative training, thus minimising the level of serious injuries. Now that BS 5304: 1975 has been replaced by BS 5304: 1988 'Code of Practice for Safety of Machinery', together with the Product Safety Directive (see Chapter 38 'Product Safety') and the new regulations on the safety of machinery (see 28.5 above), operator injuries will be further reduced.

Responsibility for poor guard design rests predominantly with the fact that the law has laid emphasis on the user's obligations in respect of factory machinery, rather than considering the measure of involvement which designers and manufacturers of factory machinery should carry. It seems true to say that in some cases injured workmen have been blamed, or lost all or part of their compensation, for what amounts to lack of commitment on the part of design engineers. To some extent this regressive state of affairs has been ameliorated by the introduction of *HSWA s 6* placing for the first time, general duties regarding product safety upon designers, manufacturers, importers and suppliers, and by the *Consumer Protection Act 1987* (see Chapter 38 'Product Safety'). The stricter safeguards in the new legislation should make further improvements.

Practical control methods to prevent accidents

28.72   There are two main reasons why accidents happen: either because of a failure to identify danger or acknowledge the possibility of harm, or because control measures are inadequate. Historically three control methods have prevailed:

(a)   motivation of personnel at risk in an effort to make them cope better with danger;

(b)   provision of protective clothing (which complies with legal requirements but does not embrace machine operation and unpredictable behaviour);

(c) provision and maintenance of physical safeguards to meet the needs of those at risk and to cope with unpredictable behaviour.

The success of (a) and (b) depends on changing people's attitudes and skills regarding safety, or on employing people with the requisite attitudes and skills. Evidence shows overwhelmingly that the benefits here are likely to be short term. Conversely, adoption of the approach in (c) has proved highly successful, especially where it is written into legal requirement.

Machinery hazards

28.73   Hazards associated with machinery can be classified in the following categories.

Traps

Traps created by machinery are of three basic types:

(a) *In-running nips*: a common feature of conveyorised systems, traps are created where a moving chain meets a toothed wheel, where a moving belt meets a roller, or at the point where two revolving drums, rollers or toothed wheels meet. See *fig. 8* below:

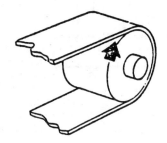

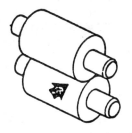

(*b*)   *Reciprocating traps*: these are a feature particularly of presses operating under vertical or horizontal motion. See *fig. 9* below:

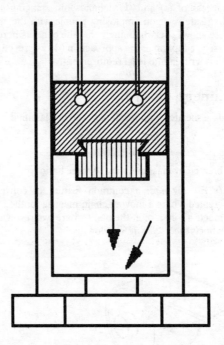

Vertical reciprocating
operation of a power
press

(*c*)   *Shearing traps*: where a moving part of machinery traverses a fixed part, or where two moving parts traverse each other, as with a pair of garden shears, and a guillotine effect is produced. See *fig. 10* below:

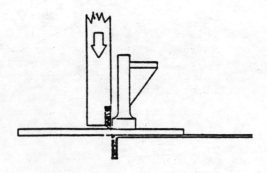

(*d*)   Shearing trap

Entanglement

The risk of entanglement of clothing, hair and limbs is associated with unfenced revolving shafts, pulleys, drills or chucks to drills. See *fig. 11* below:

Contact

Contact with machinery may cause injury, for instance abrasions due to contact with a grinding wheel, burns from hot surfaces, or amputations through contact with a circular saw.

Ejection

Machines may frequently eject particles of wood or metal during a processing operation, or parts of the machine may be thrown out of it.

Impact

Certain fast-moving machines could cause injury if an individual gets in the way during the cycle of the machine, e.g. certain types of meat slicing machine.

Classified dangerous parts of machinery

28.74 The HSE has classified certain parts of machinery as inherently dangerous and, as such, they must be securely fenced. These are listed below, with examples:

(*a*)   revolving shafts, spindles, mandrels and bars, e.g. line and counter shafts, machine shafts, drill spindles, chucks and drills, etc., boring bars, stock bars, traverse shafts;

(*b*)   in-running nips between pairs of rotating parts, e.g. gear wheels, friction wheels, calendar bowls, mangle rolls, metal manufacturing rolls, rubber washing, breaking and mixing rolls, dough brakes, printing machines, paper-making machines;

(*c*)   in-running nips of the belt and pulley type, e.g. belts and pulleys, plain, flanged or grooved, chain and sprocket gears, conveyor belts and pulleys, metal coiling and the like;

(*d*)   projections on revolving parts, e.g. key heads, set screws, cotter pins, coupling bolts;

(*e*)   discontinuous rotating parts, e.g. open arm pulleys, fan blades, spoked gear wheels and spoked flywheels;

(*f*)   revolving beaters, spiked cylinders and revolving drums, e.g. scutchers, rag flock teasers, cotton openers, carding engines, laundry washing machines;

(*g*)   revolving mixer arms in casing, e.g. dough mixers, rubber solution mixers;

(*h*)   revolving worms and spirals in casings, e.g. meat mincers, rubber extruders, spiral conveyors;

(*j*)   revolving high speed cages in casings, e.g. hydro-extractors, centrifuges;

(*k*)   abrasive wheels, e.g. manufactured wheels, natural sandstone wheels;

(*l*)   revolving cutting tools, e.g. circular saws, milling cutters, circular shears, wood slicers, routers, chaff cutters, woodworking machines such as spindle moulders, planing machines and tenoning machines;

(*m*)   reciprocating tools and dies, e.g. power presses, drop stamps, relief stamps, hydraulic and pneumatic presses, bending presses, hand presses, revolution presses;

(*n*)   reciprocating knives and saws, e.g. guillotines for metal, rubber and paper, trimmers, corner cutters, perforators;

(*o*)   closing nips between platen motions, e.g. letter press platen printing machines, paper and cardboard platen machine cutters, some power presses, foundry moulding machines;

(*p*)   projecting belt fasteners and fast-running belts, e.g. bolt and nut fasteners, wire pin fasteners and the like, woodworking machinery belts, textile machinery side belting, centrifuge belts;

(*q*)   nips between connecting rods or links, and rotating wheels, cranks or discs, e.g. side motion of certain flat-bed printing machines, jacquard motions or looms;

(*r*)   traps arising from the traversing carriages of self-acting machines, e.g. metal planing machines.

Machinery guards

28.75   A wide range of guard and guarding systems is available, according to the nature of the danger, the mode of operation of the machine and the method of operation to carry out the work for which the machine is designed. The various forms of machine guard are outlined below.

Fixed guard

BS 5304: 1988 'British Standard Code of Practice for Safety of Machinery' defines a fixed guard as 'a guard which has no moving parts'. A fixed guard should not be readily removable, other than through the use of a tool.

Interlocking guard

This is a guard which is movable or has a movable part, whose movement is interconnected with the power or control system of the machine. An interlocking guard should be so connected to the machine controls that:

(*a*)   until the guard is closed the interlock prevents the machinery from operating by interrupting the power medium;

(*b*)   either the guard remains locked closed until the risk of injury from the hazard has passed or opening the guard causes the hazard to be eliminated before access is possible.

(BS 5304: 1988)

Adjustable guard

This is defined as a fixed or movable guard which is adjustable as a whole or which incorporates an adjustable part or parts. The adjustment remains fixed during a particular operation. (BS 5304: 1988). Such guards are appropriate for band saws, drilling machines and circular saws.

Distance guard

Such a guard does not completely enclose a danger point or area but places that danger point or area out of normal reach. A common form of distance guard is the 'tunnel guard' used with metal cutting machinery. The strip metal can only be fed through the tunnel to the cutters and this prevents any access to the cutting mechanism. Distance guards can be interlocked or fixed.

Automatic guard

BS 5304: 1988 defines this form of guard as a guard which is moved into position automatically by the machine, thereby removing any part of a person from the danger area. Automatic guards are frequently installed on large power presses.

Self-adjusting guard

This is a fixed or movable guard which, either in whole or in part, adjusts itself to accommodate the passage of material. (BS 5304: 1988). Such types of guard are used in conjunction with cross-cutting sawing machines.

Safety devices

28.76   A safety device is a protective appliance, other than a guard, which eliminates or reduces danger before access to a danger point or area can be achieved. There are many forms of safety device available.

Trip device

A trip device is a device which causes working machinery to stop or assume an otherwise safe condition, to prevent injury when a person approaches a danger point or area beyond a safe limit. (BS 5304: 1988). Trip devices take a number of forms – mechanical, electro-sensitive safety systems and pressure sensitive mat systems.

Two-hand control device

This device requires both hands to operate the machinery controls, thus affording a measure of protection from danger to the machinery operator. BS 5304: 1988 lays down specific recommendations relating to the design of such devices.

Mechanical restraint device

Such a device applies mechanical restraint to a dangerous part of machinery which has been set in motion due to failure of the machinery controls or of other parts of the machinery, so as to prevent danger. (BS 5304: 1988).

Other aspects of machinery safety

Position of controls

28.77   Control should be so positioned and spaced as to provide safe and easy operation with ample clearance between each control. Two-hand control devices should not be used as an alternative to guarding, but as an extra safeguard. Push button start controls should be shrouded and pedal-operated controls should be protected to prevent accidental operation. Controls should be clearly identifiable and readily distinguishable from each other. (BS 3641: 1983 and BS 2771: 1986).

Emergency stops

An emergency stop device should be provided on all machine tools. Emergency push buttons should be of the mushroom head type, coloured red on a yellow background. Resetting emergency stop devices should not cause the machine to operate. Restarting should only be possible by operating the main start control. Where there is more than one normal working or operating position, each of these positions should be provided with an emergency stop.

Colour

It may be necessary to paint certain parts of machines a distinguishing colour which will only be visible when a danger exists, e.g. the insides of hinged or sliding covers which, when open, expose dangerous machine parts or a part of the machine which remains with the source of danger.

Spindles

Spindles should be able to be brought to rest quickly and consistently. Spindle brakes which are activated by mechanical, hydraulic, pneumatic or electrical means should bring the spindle to rest, or retain their capability of bringing the spindle to rest, in the event of a power failure. The braking system should be such that the spindle will not automatically rotate when power is resumed after a power failure. Rotating parts and equipment fastened to rotating parts should be so secured as to prevent dislodgement in consequence of the brake action.

Handles and handwheels

Cranked handles or handwheels used to operate a mechanism, which can also be operated under power at a peripheral speed of the handwheel of more than 20 metres per minute, should be designed to prevent rotation under power, be solid and be provided with a device that stalls rotation if obstructed. (Machine Tool Traders Association Standards Instruction Sheet No 11).

Power-operated workholding devices

These devices should be designed so that a dangerous situation is prevented in the event of failure of the power supply. On automatic machines the control system should be interlocked to prevent the machine from being operated until power is supplied to the workholding device and the workpiece is clamped. The control system should be such that the power-operating system for the workholding device cannot be operated to unclamp the workpiece whilst the machine is in operation.

Electrical equipment

Electrical equipment should comply with BS 2771: 1979. Hydraulic and pneumatic equipment should comply with BS 4575: 1987, Parts 1 and 2.

Coolants

Where a coolant is used, machines should be designed to contain the coolant at least during the more usual operations. It may also be necessary to add a bactericide to the coolant to prevent bacterial growth. Coolant reservoirs should be covered where possible. The coolant system should be designed so that coolant troughs, reservoirs, etc. can be easily cleaned. Nozzles should be designed so that they will stay firmly in position when set and not require adjustment by the operator during the machining process. On-off volume controls should not be adjacent to the nozzle and should be positioned so as to ensure operator safety when adjustments are made. Additional splash guards should be used where necessary. Means should be provided for the safe removal of swarf from the work area.

Lubrication

Lubrication points should be easily accessible. Care should be taken to avoid any accidental mixing of coolant, cutting fluids and lubricants. Excess lubricants should be prevented from reaching the surrounding floor area. On machines in which the failure of an automatic lubrication system could cause a hazard to the operator, such a lubrication system should incorporate a suitable indication of its correct functioning.

Counterweights and enclosures

Counterweights, related machine elements and their movements which constitute a hazard, should be safeguarded.

Enclosures used within the machine to house mechanical, electrical, hydraulic equipment, etc. which constitute a hazard should be provided with fixed covers and guards.

Lifting gear

All fixtures used on the machine and other externally-mounted devices should be provided with means for their safe loading and unloading. When a machine is provided with lifting gear and appliances, the supplier should provide details of the safe working load and notify the user of the need to obtain a certificate of test and examination. [*Factories Act 1961, s 27*] (disapplied with regard to supply of new machinery by the *Supply of Machinery (Safety) Regulations 1992*). Eyebolts and eyebolt holes should be identified to prevent mismatching. (HSE Guidance Note PM 16; BS 4278: 1984). (See Chapter 26 'Lifting Machinery and Equipment'.)

Non-mechanical machinery hazards

28.78   Other hazards associated with machinery operation, which can be a contributory factor in accidents and/or occupational ill-health, include:

(*a*)   inadequate temperature, lighting and ventilation control of the machine area, frequently resulting in steep temperature gradients, shadows, glare and general discomfort;

(*b*)   noise from machinery, which reduces the chance of operators hearing warning signals, such as the fire alarm or a forklift truck horn, and can result in operators going deaf over a period of time;

(*c*)   chemical substances used in machinery-operated processes, which can cause dermatitis or even result in a gassing accident;

(*d*)   ergonomic design faults, leading to postural fatigue, visual fatigue, back and other body strains, and an increased risk of operator error;

(*e*)   ionising radiation, due to inadequate containment of sealed and unsealed sources of radiation; and resulting in various occupational cancers; and

(*f*)   dust and fume emission, resulting in certain conditions of the respiratory tract, such as silicosis, and the potential for dust explosions.

All these factors should be considered in the assessment of machinery hazards in addition to the mechanical hazards outlined earlier in this chapter.

Checklist for machinery safeguards

28.79   The following is a list of safeguards for machine accident prevention:

(*a*)   Does the safeguard totally prevent dangerous access (or otherwise eliminate danger) when in its correct position and when working properly?

(*b*)   Is the guard reasonably convenient to use (i.e. does it interfere with either the speed or quality of the work); are there foreseeable reasons why it should be defeated?

(*c*)   How easy is it to defeat or misuse the safeguard? (The 'cost' of defeating a safeguard should always outweigh the benefits. It is wise never to underestimate the ingenuity of the man who spends all day, every day, working with what he believes is a perverse and unnecessary safety device.)

(*d*)   Are the components of the safeguard:
  (i)   reliable;
  (ii)   fail-safe?

(*e*)   Does the safeguard cope with foreseeable machine failures?

(*f*)   Is the safeguard straightforward to inspect and maintain?

(*g*)   Are all controls to the machine safely located, correctly designed and clearly identified?

(*h*)   Is there an efficient emergency stopping device? Is it clearly identified?

(*j*)   Does all electrical equipment comply with BS 2771? Is there an effective system for checking and maintaining such equipment?

(*k*)   Are coolant systems effective and easy to maintain?

(*l*)   Is access for lubrication readily and safely available? Are all lubrication points clearly identified?

(*m*)   Is the machine safely located so that other workers are not exposed to danger? Does the current layout of the machining area permit easy movement between machines, workbenches and other items?

(*n*)   What is the sound pressure level emitted by the machine? Is it in excess of 90 dBA? If so, what modifications must be made to control noise at source, or should the machine be installed in a soundproof enclosure? If hearing protection is provided for operators and other workers in the immediate vicinity, are they appropriate to the noise risks and are they being worn all the time during machine operation?

(*o*)   What is the procedure to ensure effective preventive maintenance? Is the procedure documented, including allocation of responsibilities? What are the mechanical and other hazards which may arise during routine maintenance of the machine?

(*p*)   What chemical substances are used in the machine process? Have they been checked for toxicity, flammability and other dangerous properties? Have operators been trained to recognise these hazards and to take suitable precautions?

(*q*)   Does the machine emit:

    (i)   dust;

    (ii)   fumes;

    (iii)   gases; or

    (iv)   other airborne contaminants?

What is the system for removing these contaminants at the point of emission? How frequently is the efficiency of the system checked to ensure it is operating effectively?

(*r*)   Is the general lighting in the machine area adequate? Is lighting at specific danger points adequate?

(*s*)   Does the machine emit heat? Are there hot surfaces which could cause burns on contact?

(*t*)   Is the level of ventilation in the machine area satisfactory?

Chapter 29

Materials Handling

Introduction

29.1 Back pain, which statistically is upwardly mobile, currently costs industry £3 billion a year; 67 million working days were lost as a result of bad backs. Most of this pain is work-related and reflects a marked increase in days lost through back pain by women. The main causes of back pain are heavy work – lifting, handling, forceful exertion, bending and twisting; prolonged sedentary work; prolonged stooping; vibration. Some of these losses could be saved by employment of a chiropractor (see 29.13 below); others by adherence to correct materials handling techniques and statutory requirement.

Materials handling is a fundamental activity in all work situations – factories, offices, shops, hospitals, farms, etc. The range of materials handled varies enormously as do the actual handling systems. This chapter examines the legal requirements relating to materials handling, both manual and mechanical, the hazards associated with these activities and the precautions necessary.

Broadly, materials handling can be categorised into three specific areas:

(a) manual handling and lifting, including the use of specific lifting aids;

(b) in-situ handling systems, such as conveyorised systems; and

(c) mobile handling equipment, such as forklift trucks.

The training of personnel in all the above operations should feature strongly in any organisation to ensure safe handling procedures.

Moreover, the *Manual Handling Operations Regulations 1992 (SI 1992 No 2793)* are concerned with all handling activities, regardless of weight. Avoidance of manual handling activities by mechanical equipment is the primary objective but, where this is not possible, employers should adopt 'appropriate organisational measures'. By way of replacement of the *Factories Act 1961, s 72* and *OSRPA s 23*, these new regulations, which came into effect on 1 January 1993, require employers to protect employees against manual handling injuries; similar duties are placed on self-employed persons in respect of themselves.

Before looking at the practical aspects of safety in materials handling, this chapter considers the specific statutory duties which may apply (see 29.3-29.5 below) and the possibility of action at common law (see 29.6 below). (For the specific requirements relating to lifting machinery/tackle, contained in the *Factories Act 1961, ss 22-27* (including forklift trucks), see Chapter 26 'Lifting Machinery and Equipment'.)

29.2 Over a quarter of all accidents, reported annually to the enforcing authorities, are connected with manual handling operations, costing industry billions of pounds. Back injuries are the most common but amputations, fractures, cuts and bruises are also of frequent occurrence, spanning the whole gamut of work activities from agriculture and construction to shops and warehouses. Moreover, manual handling injuries are not necessarily associated with routine work; maintenance work also quite often involves risk of injury.

Former protective legislation, that is, the *Factories Act 1961, s 72* and *OSRPA s 23*, were not especially suited to the task of avoiding and minimising injuries during manual handling, since they put too much accent on weight of load *per se*, instead of in tandem with other factors, such as working environment, individual capability etc. For that reason, the *Manual Handling Operations Regulations 1992*, which has replaced the two (above) sections, enjoin employers to avoid (where possible) manual handling operations; however, failing that, to make a suitable and sufficient assessment of any hazardous operations associated with manual handling, and based on the assessment, to reduce the risk of possible injury. *[Reg 4]*. The *Manual Handling Operations Regulations 1992* are concerned with all handling activities, regardless of weight or load.

General duties under the Health and Safety at Work Act

29.3   The general duty on employers under the *Health and Safety at Work etc. Act 1974 (HSWA)* applies generally to work involving materials handling as it applies to other kinds of work. The Act places a duty on every employer to ensure, so far as is reasonably practicable, the health, safety and welfare at work of all his employees. *[HSWA s 2(1)]*. Moreover, all employers must:

(*a*)   provide and maintain plant and systems of work that are, so far as is reasonably practicable, safe and free from health risks *[HSWA s 2(2)(a)]*; and

(*b*)   make arrangements for ensuring, so far as is reasonably practicable, safety and absence of health risks in connection with the use, handling, storage and transport of articles and substances *[HSWA s 2(2)(b)]*; and

(*c*)   provide such information, instruction, training and supervision as is necessary to ensure, so far as is reasonably practicable, the health and safety at work of their employees *[HSWA s 2(2)(c)]*.

Supplier's duty

29.4   Suppliers and manufacturers are also under a duty to see that their industrial products are safe and without health risks. *[HSWA s 6]*. This will apply to most articles and substances which are the subject of manual or mechanical handling, and also to the mechanical handling machines themselves (see Chapter 38 'Product Safety').

Specific legal requirements

Factories

Legal requirements – the Manual Handling Operations Regulations 1992

29.5   All employers must

(*a*)   so far as reasonably practicable, avoid the need for employees to undertake any manual handling operations involving a risk of injury;

(*b*)   where avoidance of manual handling activities is not reasonably practicable:

       (i)   make (and, if necessary, review) a formal assessment of manual handling operations;

      (ii)   reduce the risk of injury to those employees, to the lowest level reasonably practicable, and

    (iii)   provide employees involved in manual handling operations with general indications and, if possible, precise information on the weight of a load and the heaviest side of any load, where the centre of gravity is not centrally positioned.

[*Reg 4*].

All employees involved in manual handling operations must comply with the system of work provided. [*Reg 5*].

Assessment should address itself to (*a*) task, (*b*) load, (*c*) working environment and (*d*) individual capability [*1 Sch*] (see 29.9 below).

Civil liability for breach

29.6   Breach of health and safety regulations gives rise to civil liability, even if the regulations are silent on actionability (as here), unless the regulations state the contrary (see further 1.18 and 1.42 INTRODUCTION). If, therefore, breach of these duties causes injury/damage, there will be civil liability.

Manual handling injuries

29.7   Despite all the mechanisation of recent years, there still remains an enormous amount of manual handling with its risk of back trouble. Given that the number of days lost to industry is far greater than the certificated incapacity, it is clearly a considerable problem. Not all back trouble is caused by 'materials handling' and not all is through injury at work. But a very large proportion *is* caused by lifting; either by lifting too heavy a load, or by lifting it incorrectly.

Handling hazards

29.8   Typical injuries associated with manual handling activities include prolapsed intervertebral discs ('slipped discs'), hernias, damaged knee joints and general body strain; such injuries account for a high proportion of working days lost throughout the world. The need, therefore, for high standards of training in manual handling tasks, supported by constant supervision, cannot be over-emphasised. Conveyorised systems also represent a substantial hazard to operators if not adequately guarded. Conveyors may take many forms: belt conveyors, roller conveyors, chain conveyors, screw conveyors and slat conveyors. Typical hazards include:

    (*a*)   traps formed between the moving part of the conveyor and fixed parts of the structure;

    (*b*)   in-running nips created between belt and sprocket, between a conveyor chain and chain wheels, or between a moving belt and fixed rollers under the belt;

    (*c*)   traps created by drive mechanisms, e.g. V-belts and pulleys; and

    (*d*)   traps created at transfer points between two conveyors.

Effective guarding, to the standards outlined in BS 5304: 1988, is essential to prevent amputation of arms, hands and fingers (which are the most common form of accident associated with conveyorised systems). (See further Chapter 28 'Machinery Safety'.)

Mobile handling equipment, such as forklift trucks, can be lethal if not properly regulated in terms of driver training and supervision, truck maintenance, safe driving and frequent assessment of driver performance (see 29.20 below).

Handling technique

29.9   Failure to keep a load close to the body makes it less easy for the body weight to counterbalance it. Poor posture during manual handling operations increases the risk of loss of control of the load, and twisted trunk postures increase stress on the lower back. Combined with stooping and stretching, twisting can be exceedingly hazardous. Moreover, carrying loads for long distances over a continuous period of time can cause injury. A good rule of thumb is that, if a load can be safely lifted and lowered, it can also be carried without endangering the back. Injuries have also occurred where employees handle loads whilst seated, as a result of reaching or leaning forward, and unfixed seats tending to move backwards.

The shape of a load determines the way in which it should be held. Risk of injury increases if a load is not small enough to pass between the knees, when lifted. So, too, a bulky/unwieldy load can seriously impair vision and the centre of gravity of a load should always be positioned centrally. Loads which are difficult to grasp, either because they are too big, too smooth, too greasy, too hot, or cold, or too slippery, as well as loads whose contents are wont to shift about, all make for higher accident incidence potential at work and invite a more clinically ergonomic approach by both producers and employers to manual handling operations.

So, too, does the working environment. Uneven/slippery surfaces and floors inhibit smooth transit, along with undulating, swaying and unstable ones, on ships, trains and vans. Steps and steep slopes and the necessity of climbing ladders in order to convey loads add to the risk of injury to employees carrying loads and other employees who may be in the impact area of falling or rolling loads as well as having to reach up to very high pallets or delve into very deep bins. Similarly, stooping to pick up loads is necessitated by restricted headroom, and twisting and turning by the presence of fixtures, furniture and other obstructions on floors and surfaces. In addition, indifferent lighting conditions at the workplace and extremes of temperature in, say, furnaces and refrigeration warehouses, can cause rapid fatigue, thereby increasing risk of injury to those involved in manual handling. Ideally, loads should be stored around waist height.

Manual handling injuries are generally associated with the nature of the operation rather than with individual capabilities and idiosyncracies. Nevertheless, risk of injury is greater to employees in their teens and fifties and sixties, and pregnancy, associated with manual handling, is an obvious possible danger to women who are close to delivery or who have recently delivered. Throughout, close attention to personal protective equipment is essential – particularly, overalls, safety footwear, allied to a non-slip base, aprons and close-fitting gloves. In particular, at no time should personal protective clothing hinder the movement of those involved in manual handling (see also Chapter 36 'Personal Protective Equipment').

Ergonomic design

29.10   Ergonomic enlightenment also dictates that designers/producers of products that will have to be handled manually, design such products so that risk of injury, if not eliminated, is severely minimised. Thus, products with sharp edges or rough surfaces should be avoided, and advisability of handles, hand grips, hooks, straps and levers considered (see also Chapter 38 'Product Safety').

Repetitive strain injury (RSI)

29.11   Use of upper limbs to push, hold and grip are an indispensable part of everyday living and work. (These disorders are not covered by the new regulations.) Handling operations with relatively low weights, particularly with repetitive movements, are frequently identified with aches and pains, discomfort and disorder in the upper limbs. The problem, variously called golfer's elbow, tennis elbow, BMX wrist and repetitive strain injury (RSI), characterises assembly line work to packing operations, food preparation, the automotive and electronics industries as well as work in offices and supermarkets. Symptoms commonly affect tendons, ligaments, muscles, nerves and connective joints.

The condition is caused either simply or in combination by (*a*) awkward postures of upper limbs or shoulders, e.g. reaching up in consequence of bad stacking/ palletisation or tool handles too far apart; (*b*) excessive manual force (e.g. with static loadings, such as working above head height whilst painting a ceiling with a hand brush or roller); and (*c*) high rates of manual repetition.

The more repetitive the task, the more rapid and frequent are muscle contractions. Such tasks, therefore, require more time for recovery. Many work-induced upper limb disorders, such as beat elbow, tenosynovitis and carpal tunnel syndrome are prescribed occupational diseases (see 31.42 OCCUPATIONAL HEALTH) and also foreshadow an action against the employer at common law (see 15.8 EMPLOYERS' DUTIES and 31.45 OCCUPATIONAL HEALTH), which has recently happened in the case of RSI (£6,000 for pain and suffering awarded to two employees of BT). Guidance on the prevention of these disorders is available from the HSE entitled 'Work Related Upper Limb Disorders' HS(G) 30.

However, more recently, doubt was cast on the actual existence of such a condition, the High Court observing: 'There are so many diverse views about RSI that their very existence is a monument to doubt on the subject' (*Mughal v Reuters News Agency, The Times, 29 October 1993* – concerning a journalist suffering from painful joints as a result of keyboard working, who was forced to give up work and who was refused damages for RSI).

Mechanical materials handling

29.12   An important danger is evident where trucks and pedestrians work in the same area, and the objective should be to segregate them as far as possible. Narrow aisle stores and warehouses, and the ultimate automated warehouses where there are no operators near working machines, are preferable from a safety point of view. Segregation should also be the aim in container terminals (see also 29.25 below). The problem has been studied by a committee of the Health and Safety Executive which included employer and worker representatives. Based on the findings of the committee's working group – which studied operations both in the UK and several other European countries – a booklet has been published by the HSE setting out a code of practice for maintenance of safe and efficient systems of work. ('Container terminals: safe working practices', HSE Guidance booklet HS(G)7, HMSO).

Kinetic handling

29.13   The principles of kinetic handling have been known for some time but are currently receiving commendable promotion by the British Chiropractice Association.

Briefly, these principles include: proper balanced positioning of feet, arms in, chin in, load close to the body, and above all, a straight back. The Association has prepared an industrial training kit which includes booklets, posters, etc. ('Industrial Training Kit', British Chiropractice Association, Premier House, 10 Greycoat Place, Victoria SW1P 1SB. Tel: 071-222 8866).

The Royal Society for the Prevention of Accidents (RoSPA) also runs courses in kinetic handling. Information is available from RoSPA Training, 22 Summer Road, Acocks Green, Birmingham B27 7UT. Tel: 021-706 8121.

Safe stacking of materials

29.14   Once materials, containers etc. have been lifted, they must remain stable until it is necessary to bring them down again. Whether 'block stacked', i.e. self-supporting, or stored in shelving or racks, there is a hazard and attention to basic principles is important. A Health and Safety at Work booklet gives broad guidance on planned storage of goods and materials which are usually kept in store for a considerable period of time. It covers both bulk materials in heaps, bunkers and silos, and a very wide selection of particular units and packages ('Safety in the stacking of materials' HSE Health and Safety at Work booklet 47, HMSO).

Methods of storage depend on the shape and fragility of the material or package. Cylinders stored 'on the roll' are one of the more hazardous materials. The bottom layer must be properly secured to prevent movement; subsequent layers can rest on the one below, or be laid on battens and wedged. Progressively, as forklift trucks – and particularly reach trucks and narrow aisle stackers – lift to greater heights, so storage racking has been constructed higher. The Storage Equipment Manufacturers' Association has published a code of practice, which covers pallet racks, drive-in and drive-through racks and cantilever racks, setting out guidance to users. ('Code of practice for the use of static racking', Storage Equipment Manufacturers' Association, Bridge House, Smallbrook, Queensway, Birmingham B5 4JP. Tel: 021-643 3377).

Racking

29.15   A manufacturer will install racking to customer's requirements in terms of loading, pallet height and aisle width depending on the type of handling equipment used. Heavier loads must not be used; if there is to be a change of load stored, the manufacturer must be consulted. Racking has collapsed through either overloading or impact damage to an upright member.

Where trucks are used the following are to be recommended:

(*a*)   bolting to the floor; and

(*b*)   a column guard or guide rail to protect corners at the ends of aisles.

Pallets

29.16   Many types of load are carried on pallets and, whilst there are many metal pallets in use, the vast majority are of timber for economy of cost and weight. When damaged they are hazardous – and they are easily damaged by the dangerous forks of a truck. The pallet should, therefore, be designed according to the load it is to carry and, if it is to be stored in racking, the type of rack.

British Standard BS 2629 covers dimensions, materials and marking, pallets for use in freight containers, and performance requirements and methods of test. There is also a useful HSE Guidance Note which indicates some of the considerations of design, and makes recommendations for inspection of new and used pallets. ('Safety in the use of timber pallets', HSE Guidance Note PM 15, HMSO).

Access platforms

29.17   The *Construction (Working Places) Regulations 1966 (SI 1966 No 94)* impose requirements in respect of working platforms (see also Chapter 46 'Work at Heights'). Use of powered access or work platforms is growing rapidly, and whilst this is strictly a border-line form of materials handling (handling workers and their tools/equipment) it is worth a brief examination. In order to conform with the regulations, access platforms must be as safe, if not safer, than ladders and scaffolds when properly used. Various types are available with an articulated and /or telescopic boom which may rotate, or have vertical lift by scissor or straight hydraulic ram action. The most hazardous are those where the platform has horizontal projections beyond the base.

Forklift trucks

29.18   Forklift trucks (for legal requirements, see 26.3 LIFTING MACHINERY AND EQUIPMENT) are potentially hazardous for a variety of reasons:

(*a*)   they usually work in fairly congested areas;

(*b*)   when elevating a heavy load, stability is bound to be reduced;

(*c*)   there is always the possibility of a load falling down;

(*d*)   when travelling with a load in the lowered position, the driver's visibility is often impaired;

(*e*)   even when travelling unladen, the forks projecting at the front are dangerous.

Truck population in the UK is now reckoned to be more than a quarter of a million; there are, therefore, a great many older machines in use which can exhibit many faults. In recent years many manufacturers have been fitting load guards, overhead guards, and warning horns as standard. Some now include a transparent window in the overhead guard (a wise extra where there is a possibility of small items falling down and being able to pass through the guard members) and masts with improved forward visibility. There are British and International Standards Organisation (ISO) standards for stability testing and practically all manufacturers test accordingly. (British Standards BS 3726, BS 5777). Another safety move has been the introduction of standard control symbols, particularly useful now that more trucks are being imported. (BS 5829 'Specification for control symbols for powered industrial trucks').

Requirements for safe forklift truck operation

29.19   An analysis of safe truck operation identifies three principal aspects as the potential cause of truck accidents: the driver, the truck and the system of work.

The driver

29.20   Drivers should be in good health, with sound vision and hearing. They should be over 18 years of age and trained within an approved training scheme. Drivers should observe the following precautions:

(*a*)   regulate speed with visibility;

(*b*)   use the horn whenever turning a blind corner;

(*c*)   be constantly aware of pedestrians and vehicles on roadways, loading bays, storage areas and transfer points (the use of convex mirrors located at strategic points greatly reduces the risk of collision);

(*d*)   drive in reverse when the load obscures vision;

(*e*)   travel with the forks down, and not operate the forks when in motion;

(*f*)   use prescribed lanes/routes; *no short cuts*;

(*g*)   stick to factory speed limits, e.g. 10 mph;

(*h*)   slow down on wet or uneven surfaces;

(*j*)   use the handbrake and tilt mechanism correctly;

(*k*)   take care on ramps (max 1 : 10);

(*l*)   when leaving the truck at any time, put the controls in neutral position, switch the power off, apply the brakes, and ensure the key or connector plug is removed.

Drivers should not:

(i)   carry passengers;

(ii)   park in front of fire appliances or fire exits;

(iii)   turn around on ramps;

(iv)   permit unauthorised use, e.g. by contractors.

The truck

29.21   On no account should trucks in a defective or dangerous condition be used.

A daily check system should be operated, prior to starting or on handover to another driver, which covers brakes, lights, steering, horn, battery, hydraulics and speed controls.

The system of work

29.22   On no account should the maximum rated load capacity be exceeded. Loads should always be placed dead centre on the forks.

The truck should be driven with the forks well under the load, with the load located firmly against the fork carriage and the mast tilted to suit the stability of the load being carried.

The following general points should be observed:

(*a*)   slinging should be undertaken only at designated slinging points;

(*b*)   a load which looks unsafe should never be moved;

(*c*)   broken, defective or inadequate strength pallets should never be used;

(*d*)   care must be taken at overhead openings, pipework, ducting, conduits, etc.;

(*e*)   the stability of a stack should always be checked before moving the forks.

Training of truck operators

29.23   Although training in safe handling, storage and transportation is necessary under the general legal duties imposed by *HSWA* (see above), special hazards exist with respect to forklift trucks (see further 26.3 LIFTING MACHINERY AND EQUIPMENT). It has been proved over and over again that proper training of operators is the only way to safer use of lift trucks. The recognised guide here is the one published by the Road Transport Industry Training Board (RTITB), and agreed by a joint Committee of Industry Training Boards. ('Selection and training of fork truck operators', RTITB, Capitol House, Empire Way, Wembley, Middlesex). A number of centres are approved by the RTITB for operator training, and a smaller number for instructor training. Training is conducted in accordance with ACOP 'Rider operated lift trucks – Training of operators'.

After completing a course and receiving a certificate of competence, an operator needs proper supervision by a qualified person. Lamentably, many trainees (and so-called operators, in many cases) fail to understand the theory of counterbalancing. Most appreciate the effect of load weight, but not many grasp the effect of *load centre* which is equally essential to safe truck operation (e.g. the overturning moment: load weight × distance from pivot point, which is the front wheels).

Pedestrian-controlled lift trucks

29.24   Useful information for operators of pedestrian-controlled lift trucks is published by the British Industrial Truck Association in pocket book format. ('Operator's safety code for powered industrial trucks', British Industrial Truck Association, Buckhurst Hill, Ascot, Berks SL5 7NU). Features which are increasingly being built in by manufacturers are:

(*a*)   toe guards around the wheels; and

(*b*)   a safety button in the head of the control handle to reverse the machine in the event of the operator being trapped between the machine and some other object.

Other problem areas

Container terminals

29.25   Handling at docks is too complex to be dealt with here, but container terminals are now found inland as well as at docks. Freight containers pose special problems, whether handled by forklift truck, sideloader or straddle carrier. The principal problem is severely restricted operator visibility.

Overhead transfer systems

29.26   Special thought is needed when installing overhead transfer systems for loads, such as engine blocks, where the load actually hangs down. Speeds of operation are normally so slow that there is little danger of a load striking a person; a greater potential hazard is that a person may turn round and strike a load which was probably not there earlier.

Strapping

29.27   A common method of securing packages and unit loads to pallets is by manual or powered strapping equipment using steel or non-metallic strapping. There is an obvious hazard with such equipment where there is a possibility of fingers being caught under a strap. Steel strapping can result in more serious injury than non-metallic. A brief outline of safety aspects has been published by the manufacturers' association. ('Tensional strapping equipment and materials' –

health and safety guide leaflet, British Tensional Strapping Association, 133 Lichfield Street, Walsall, W. Midlands WS1 1SL. Tel: 0922 23515).

Loading bays

29.28 A loading bay with its sheer edge is self-evidently a potential hazard, particularly when industrial trucks are at work there. Where possible, guard rails should be installed, and the edges of the dock and dock levellers (when used) painted in bright 'safety' colours. Care is necessary when using any type of dock leveller, bridge plate or ramp, and a planned work system which is absolutely clear to warehouse staff and to road vehicle drivers is essential. This will include chocking (i.e. placing wedges under) trailer wheels, jacking trailers, and a routine which ensures that a vehicle does not pull away with leveller or bridge plate still in position.

Chapter 30

Noise and Vibration

Introduction

30.1   About 1 million workers in manufacturing industry are exposed to above the legal threshold for noise (85 dB(A)) – three-quarters of a million to 85–90 decibels and a further quarter million to 90–95 decibels. (A draft EC directive proposes to reduce the threshold level to 75 dB(A) and, as for exposure between 85 and 90 dB(A), noise assessments and control strategies are to become mandatory (see 30.11 below).) Understandably, much environmental and occupational stress can be attributed to noise. Control of noise and vibration, which might affect the health and safety of employees, is embraced in the general duties of employers under the *Health and Safety at Work etc. Act 1974 (HSWA)*; namely, the provision and maintenance of a working environment for employees that is, so far as is reasonably practicable, safe, without health risks and adequate as regards facilities and arrangements for their welfare at work. [*HSWA s 2(2)(e)*]. Moreover, there is power in *Sec 68* of the *Control of Pollution Act 1974* for regulations to be made, limiting noise levels from plant and machinery that might constitute a statutory nuisance under *Sec 79* of the *Environmental Protection Act 1990* (see 12.27 EMISSIONS INTO THE ATMOSPHERE). To date, no regulations have been made. However, if a local authority has designated its area as a noise abatement zone, the local authority has the power, after measuring and registering acceptable noise levels, to require the abatement of noise over the registered level. [*Control of Pollution Act 1974, ss 63–72*].

PART A

NOISE

Noise-induced hearing loss is an escalating problem for employers, with the threat of potential claims relating to deafness, tinnitus and other disorders; and, whilst employers are not specifically required to provide hearing tests under the *Noise at Work Regulations* (see 30.9 below), many employers are currently actively considering the introduction of audiometric programmes as part and parcel of good housekeeping and industrial relations programmes. Even more statistically compelling is the incidence of vibration white finger (VWF), currently the largest single category of occupational disease for benefit purposes (though not necessarily compensated in all cases) (see 30.24 below). Specific statutory controls are now proposed for hand, arm and whole body vibration (see 30.26 below). This chapter examines primarily occupational noise and statutory controls over it, the effect of vibration on groups of workers and benefits available for VWF, environmental controls over noise and the powers enjoyed by local authorities to suppress noise levels.

Hearing loss

30.2   Hearing loss is measured by audiometry. A person is asked to say whether he can hear a test signal applied to a headset, first in one ear then in another, the signal

584

being given at different frequencies (between 500Hz and 8KHz) and at different levels of loudness (dB).

Levels of loudness

0 – threshold of normal hearing
10 – leaf rustle
30 – whisper
60 – normal conversation
80 – busy traffic
90 – heavy goods vehicle
100 – factory floor
110 – grinding machine
120 – propeller aircraft
130 – rivetting hammer
140 – jet engine

Presbycusis (hearing disability through ageing), on average, gives a hearing loss of 30 dB in about 12% of the population by the age of 55. A working lifetime's exposure to 85 dB would increase this to 16%, whilst daily exposure to 90 dB would give a 30 dB hearing loss in 30% of the population. 30 dB hearing loss is enough to cause handicap (BS 5330: 4976 'Effects of noise exposure'), though 50 dB has to be established for 20% disablement benefit under the *Social Security (Industrial Injuries) (Prescribed Diseases) Regulations 1985* (see 30.15 below).

Sound and its measurement

30.3   Noise is often described as unwanted sound or a subjective response to sound. Industrial sound responsible for hearing damage constitutes noise in that sense. Sound travels through the air by moving the particles of air lying between the origin of the sound and the ear. It travels in waves and the vibrations of the air streams produce sound which, on reaching the human ear, vibrates the ear drum.

Sound may be 'pure tone', i.e. of one frequency only, such as that produced by a tuning fork. Most industrial sounds are, however, more highly complex, with components distributed over a wide range of frequencies (broadband sound/noise). In certain cases, where the noise may be produced by widely spaced impacts as from a cartridge-operated hand tool, this noise is known as 'impulse noise'.

Frequency and intensity are the two most important aspects of noise. Frequency refers to the number of vibrations made by sound in the air stream. This is measured in cycles per second or 'Hertz' (Hz). Sounds are generally a mixture of frequencies, i.e. high and low frequencies. Exposure to high frequency sounds, in particular, causes hearing damage. Intensity refers to the degree of strength with which sound vibrates the ear drum. This is measured in decibels (dB). Because more hearing damage is caused by high level frequencies, sound level meters are provided with a facility which makes them more responsive to higher frequencies. This adjustment is known as 'A-weighting of the decibel value' (indicated by 'dB(A)'). The magnitude of sound is measured as a pressure wave in Pascals (Pa), though for most purposes the decibel (dB) is used to measure and describe sound magnitude.

Effect of sound on the human ear

30.4   The human ear is sensitive to sounds between 20 and 20,000 Hz, but particularly to sounds of about 3,000 Hz and 6,000 Hz (speech frequencies) and less sensitive at

fig. 12

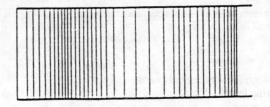

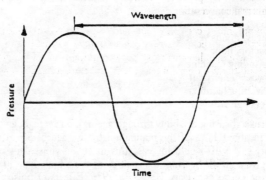

PURE TONE

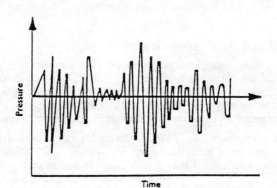

NORMAL SOUND SIGNAL – BROADBAND

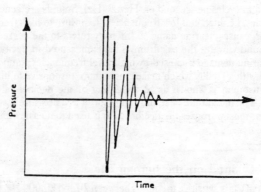

IMPULSE NOISE

lower and higher frequencies. Hearing damage is the result of sound dose; the product of magnitude and duration. To measure this, the equivalent continuous sound level (Leq) (see 30.6 below) is measured, which takes account of fluctuating levels common to most work situations, or even the daily personal exposure dose (Lepd). Although audiometry is not mandatory, by dint of the *Noise at Work Regulations 1989* (see 30.10 below), if an assessment has categorised the workplace as being in one of the action levels, audiometry is necessarily suggested by good occupational health practice. Indeed, audiometry is probably the best evidence that a hearing protection programme is working.

In addition, noise can have non-auditory effects, or nuisance effects, e.g. it interferes with speech, destroys concentration, causes irritation and annoyance. Whereas most people can accustom to continuous unvarying noise (e.g. hiss from an air-conditioning duct), intermittent and unpredictable noises (e.g. telephone ringing, burglar alarm) can be highly distracting.

Deafness

30.5   Hearing damage results from over-exposure to noise. The ear's sound receiver simply wears out. Having received sound waves the eardrum is activated by pressure from them. Eardrum vibrations are transmitted to the cochlea, a snail-shaped organ full of liquid. The motion of this liquid is detected by tiny hair cells and converted into electrical impulses transmitted to the brain. Hearing is damaged when these hair cells cease to respond to stimuli; the damage is irreparable.

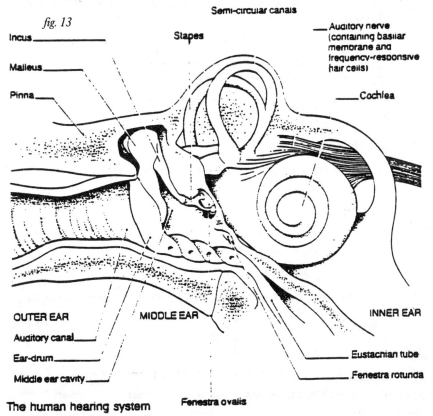

fig. 13

Semi-circular canals

Incus

Stapes

Malleus

Pinna

Auditory nerve (containing basilar membrane and frequency-responsive hair cells)

Cochlea

OUTER EAR   MIDDLE EAR   INNER EAR

Auditory canal

Ear-drum

Middle ear cavity

Eustachian tube

Fenestra rotunda

Fenestra ovalis

The human hearing system

Statistics

30.6   Noise-induced deafness becomes eligible for disablement benefit when the hearing loss exceeds 50 dB (see 30.18 below). The number of persons in every 100 likely to suffer 50 dB hearing loss is as follows:

Level of exposure dB(A) Leq (8hr)*	10 years' exposure No of persons per 100	Lifetime exposure No of persons per 100
100	17	32
90	5	11
80	1	3

* 'dB(A)' means that a particular 'A-weighted' filter is used when measuring the sound (see 30.3 above). The filter reduces the response to very high and very low frequencies. 'Leq (8hr)' means the 'equivalent continuous sound level normalised to eight hours' (i.e. a measure of the noise energy dose).

Hence, a reduction of the level from 100 to 90 dB(A) achieves a 'saving' of twenty-one persons in every 100; a reduction from 90 to 80 dB(A) achieves a further 'saving' of eight persons in every 100. The degree of reduction of risk achieved by reducing the level from 100 to 90 dB(A) is considerably greater than that achieved by reducing it from 90 to 80 dB(A). The major effect of the *Noise at Work Regulations 1989* (see 30.10 below) relates, therefore, to noise control in respect of workers exposed above 90 dB(A) Leq (8hr) (i.e. likely continuous equivalent exposure for eight hours per day to 90 dB(A)).

HSE estimates show the following figures in relation to manufacturing industry (they exclude office workers):

(*a*)   50% (approximately) of workers are exposed to 80 dB(A);

(*b*)   10% are exposed to 90 dB(A);

(*c*)   not more than 2% are exposed to 100 dB(A).

High noise levels exist also in construction, transport, shipping, agriculture, quarrying, forestry and entertainment.

Practical aspects of noise control

30.7   The four established ways of limiting or controlling noise are:

(*a*)   reduction of noise at source (see below);

(*b*)   isolation of the source of noise;

(*c*)   ear protection for workers at risk;

(*d*)   reduction of time to which personnel are exposed to noise.

Of these, reduction of noise at source represents the optimum approach, whereas provision of protective hearing equipment is, to some extent, an admission of failure. In engineering terms, it is eminently feasible to produce quieter machines. For example, pressure put on manufacturers by employers within the industry has resulted in quieter woodworking machines. But this is an improvement in a small area only, and cost is always the overall inhibiting factor.

Statutory controls over occupational and environmental noise

30.8   Control of occupational noise and vibration, which might adversely affect employees, is embraced within the general duties of employers under the *Health and Safety at Work etc. Act 1974* (*HSWA*); namely, the provision and maintenance of a working environment for employees that is, so far as is reasonably practicable, safe, without health risks and adequate as regards facilities and arrangements for their welfare at work [*HSWA s 2(2)(e)*] (see further 30.9 below). By contrast, controls over environmental noise are contained mainly in the *Control of Pollution Act 1974*, and regulations made thereunder, and the *Environmental Protection Act 1990* (see 30.27 below).

Legal requirements

30.9   Statutory requirements relating to noise at work *generally* are contained in the *Noise at Work Regulations 1989 (SI 1989 No 1790)*. Replacing the previous Department of Employment (voluntary) Code of Practice on Noise (1972), these regulations require employers to take reasonably practicable measures, on a long-term on-going basis, to reduce employees' exposure to noise at work to the lowest possible level, and to lower noise exposure where employees are exposed to levels of 90 dB(A) or above, or to peak action level or above (200 pascals). In addition, ear protectors must be provided and worn and ear protection zones designated. Estimates throughout industry overall suggest that about 1.7 million workers may be exposed above 85 dB(A) – first action level and 630,000 above 90 dB(A) – second action level.

Control of noise and vibration is important for the well-being of the workforce, and the dangers of exposure to high noise levels and certain forms of vibration have long been acknowledged. The need for noise control depends, of course, on the type of work, the dose of noise received by workers, the frequency range of the noise and the number of workers exposed at any one time. Work involving the use of a pneumatic drill or percussive tool is clearly at one end of the scale and machine-free office work at the other.

In addition to the general statutory requirements, noise levels are *specifically* controlled in the case of:

(*a*)   tractor cabs (see 30.12 below);

(*b*)   offshore operations (see 30.13 below);

(*c*)   construction sites (see 30.14 below).

At present, there are no specific provisions relating to *vibration* other than those contained in the *Social Security (Industrial Injuries) (Prescribed Diseases) Regulations 1985* and the *Reporting of Injuries, Diseases and Dangerous Occurrences Regulations 1985*. Occupational deafness and certain forms of vibration-induced conditions, i.e. vibration-induced white finger, are prescribed industrial diseases for which disablement benefit is payable. Damages may also be awarded against the employer (though the 14% disablement rule will obviously limit the number of successful claimants (see 6.10 COMPENSATION FOR WORK INJURIES/DISEASES)). (See further 30.19 below.)

Noise at Work Regulations 1989 (SI 1989 No 1790)

30.10   The following duties are laid on employers.

1. To make (and update where necessary) a formal noise assessment, where employees are likely to be exposed to

(*a*)   first action level or above (85 dB(A)),

589

(*b*)   peak action level or above (200 pascals).

Such assessment should be made by a competent person and adequately

(i)   identify which employees are exposed, and

(ii)   provide the employer with such information as will enable him to carry out his statutory duties, and

(iii)   when there is reason to suppose that the assessment is no longer valid, or when there has been a significant change in the work to which the assessment relates, review noise levels and make any changes recommended by the review.

[*Reg 4(2)*].

2. To keep an adequate record of such assessment until a further assessment is made. [*Reg 5*].

3. (As a long-term strategy, and on an on-going basis), to reduce the risk of damage to the hearing of their employees from exposure to noise to the lowest level reasonably practicable. [*Reg 6*]. (See further 'Practical aspects of noise control' (30.7 above).)

4. To reduce, so far as is reasonably practicable, the exposure to noise of employees (other than by provision of personal ear protectors), where employees are likely to be exposed to (*a*) 90 dB(A) or above or (*b*) peak action level (200 pascals) or above. [*Reg 7*].

5. To provide, at the request of an employee, suitable and efficient personal ear protectors where employees are likely to be exposed to 85 dB(A) or above but less than 90 dB(A). [*Reg 8(1)*].

Where employees are likely to be exposed to 90 dB(A) or above, or peak action level or above, they must be provided with suitable personal ear protectors, so as to keep risk of damage to employees' hearing below that arising from exposure to 90 dB(A) or peak action level. [*Reg 8(2)*].

6. To designate ear protection zones, indicating

(*a*)   that it is an ear protection zone, and

(*b*)   the need for employees to wear personal ear protectors whilst in such zone where any employee is likely to be exposed to 90 dB(A) or above, or to peak action level or above. Moreover, no employee should enter such zone unless he is wearing personal ear protectors.

[*Reg 9*].

Ear protection so provided must be maintained in an efficient state and employees must report any defects in it to the employer and see that it is fully and properly used. [*Reg 10*].

7. To provide employees, likely to be exposed to 85 dB(A) or above, or to peak action level or above, with adequate information, instruction and training with regard to

(*a*)   risk of damage to that employee's hearing,

(*b*)   steps the employee can take to minimise the risk,

(*c*)   the requirement on employees to obtain personal ear protectors from the employer, and

(d)   the employee's duties under the regulations.

[*Reg 11*].

In addition, there are specific legal requirements applying to tractor cabs and offshore installations and construction sites (see below).

fig. 14 Sign for informing that ear protectors must be worn (white on a circular blue background)

EAR PROTECTION ZONE

EAR PROTECTORS MUST BE WORN

(Based on British Standard 5378 Part 1: 1980)

Proposed tightening of controls over occupational noise

30.11   A draft EC directive (93/C77/02) proposes the following changes to noise controls:

(1)   the threshold level to be reduced to 75 dB(A) – at this level of exposure, workers must be given information about risks to hearing;

(2)   at exposure levels between 80 and 85 dB(A) workers would be entitled to hearing surveillance, if they wish, and also to personal protective equipment, on request; they should also be given information on protective and control measures;

(3)   at exposure levels between 85 and 90 dB(A) noise assessments and audiometry become mandatory – copies to be given to safety representatives; also employers would have to establish a regime of control strategies;

(4)   at levels between 90 and 105 dB(A) use of ear protectors would become mandatory, accompanied by systematic health surveillance and designation of hazard areas;

(5)   at levels over 105 dB(A) offending work activities would have to be notified to HSE, which would take appropriate remedial steps.

Specific legal requirements

Agriculture

30.12   The *Agriculture (Tractor Cabs) Regulations 1974 (SI 1974 No 2034)* (as amended by *SI 1990 No 1075*) provide that noise levels in tractor cabs must not exceed 90 dB(A) or 86 dB depending which annex is relevant in the certificate under Directive 77/311/EEC. [*Reg 3(3)*].

Offshore installations

30.13   The *Offshore Installations (Construction and Survey) Regulations 1974 (SI 1974 No 289), 2 Sch 8.1(e)* (likely to be revoked shortly, see Chapter 34 'Offshore Operations') and the *Offshore Installations (Operational Safety, Health and Welfare) Regulations 1976 (SI 1976 No 1019), Reg 16* require:

(a)   the suitable insulation of every item of equipment capable of causing noise or vibration which:

  (i)   is injurious to health, or

  (ii)   is likely to be injurious to health;

(b)   the provision of suitable protective equipment (including ear protectors) for all persons engaged in operations where they are exposed to risk of injury or disease.

Construction sites

30.14   There are both UK and EC requirements affecting noise emanating from construction equipment and sites.

A code of practice has been made under the *Control of Noise (Codes of Practice for Construction and Open Sites) Order 1984 (SI 1984 No 1992)* to provide guidance on controls on noise emanating from construction sites. The code is entitled 'Code of Practice for basic information and procedures for noise control' published on 31 May 1984 (BS 5228).

Under the *Construction Plant and Equipment (Harmonisation of Noise) Regulations 1985 (SI 1985 No 1968, amended by SI 1992 No 488)* and the *Construction Plant and Equipment (Harmonisation of Noise) Regulations 1988 (SI 1988 No 361),* marketing of various construction plant equipment is prohibited unless a relevant EC-type certificate has been obtained for the equipment and an EEC mark has been placed on it in accordance with the examination provisions in the regulations. There is an appeal and review procedure available for equipment which fails the test.

The first set of regulations apply to construction plant defined as compressors, tower cranes, welding generators, powered hand-held concrete breakers and picks. A certificate relevant to any of these types of equipment lasts for five years from the date of the certificate.

The second set applies to earth-moving machines, and certificates relating to these last for seven years from the date of the certificate (see also 30.27 below for environmental aspects).

Compensation for occupational deafness

Social security

30.15 Prescription rules for occupational deafness have been extended twice, in 1980 and 1983. On each occasion the number of awards has increased substantially but then fallen back. Since the most recent extension, occupational deafness has been the largest single category of *compensated* occupational disease (1,128 cases in 1990 and 12,000 claimants in receipt of disablement benefit).

The most common condition associated with exposure to noise is occupational deafness. Deafness is prescribed occupational disease A 10 (see Chapter 31 'Occupational Health') and is defined as: 'sensorineural hearing loss amounting to at least 50 dB in each ear being the average of hearing losses at 1, 2 and 3 kHz frequencies, and being due, in the case of at least one ear, to occupational noise'. [*Social Security (Industrial Injuries) (Prescribed Diseases) Amendment Regulations 1989 (SI 1989 No 1207), Reg 4(5)*]. Thus, the former requirement for hearing loss to be measured by pure tone audiometry no longer applies. Extensions of benefit criteria relating to occupational deafness are contained in the *Social Security (Industrial Injuries) (Prescribed Diseases) Regulations 1985 (SI 1985 No 967)*, which are amended, as regards assessment of disablement for benefit purposes, by the *Social Security (Industrial Injuries) (Prescribed Diseases) Amendment Regulations 1989, Reg 4*.

Conditions for which deafness is prescribed

30.16 Any occupation involving:

(*a*) the use of powered (but not hand-powered) grinding tools on cast metal (other than weld metal) or on billets or blooms in the metal producing industry, or work wholly or mainly in the immediate vicinity of those tools whilst they are being so used; or

(*b*) the use of pneumatic percussive tools on metal, or work wholly or mainly in the immediate vicinity of those tools whilst they are being so used; or

(*c*) the use of pneumatic percussive tools for drilling rock in quarries or underground or in mining coal, or work wholly or mainly in the immediate vicinity of those tools whilst they are being so used; or

(*d*) work wholly or mainly in the immediate vicinity of plant (excluding power press plant) engaged in the forging (including drop stamping) of metal by means of closed or open dies or drop hammers; or

(*e*) work in textile manufacturing where the work is undertaken wholly or mainly in rooms or sheds in which there are machines engaged in weaving man-made or natural (including mineral) fibres or in the high speed false twisting of fibres; or

(*f*) the use of, or work wholly or mainly in the immediate vicinity of, machines engaged in cutting, shaping or cleaning metal nails; or

(*g*) the use of, or work wholly or mainly in the immediate vicinity of, plasma spray guns engaged in the deposition of metal; or

(*h*) the use of, or work wholly or mainly in the immediate vicinity of, any of the following machines engaged in the working of wood or material composed partly of wood, that is to say: multi-cutter moulding machines. This does not extend to multi-cross cutting machines used for cutting newsprint (R(I) 2/92), planing machines, automatic or semi-automatic lathes, multiple cross-cut machines, automatic shaping machines, double-end tenoning machines, verticle spindle moulding machines (including high speed routing machines), edge banding machines, bandsawing machines with a blade width of not less than 75 millimetres and circular sawing machines in the operation of which the blade is moved towards the material being cut; or

(*j*)   the use of chain saws in forestry.

[*Social Security (Industrial Injuries) (Prescribed Diseases) Regulations 1985 (SI 1985 No 967); Social Security (Industrial Injuries) (Prescribed Diseases) Amendment No 2 Regulations 1987 (SI 1987 No 2112)*].

'Any occupation' covers activities in which an employee is engaged under his contract of employment. The fact that the workforce is designated, classified or graded by reference to function, training or skills (e.g. labourer, hot examiner, salvage and forge examiner) does not of itself justify a conclusion that each separate designation, classification or grading involves a separate occupation (*Decision of the Commissioner No R(I) 3/78*).

'Assistance in the use' of tools qualifies the actual *use* of tools, not the process in the course of which tools are employed. Thus, a crane driver who positions bogies to enable riveters to do work on them and then goes away, assists in the process of getting bogies repaired, which requires use of pneumatic tools, but this is not assistance in the actual use of tools, for the purposes of disablement benefit. The position is otherwise when a crane holds a bogie in suspension to enable riveters to work *safely* on them. Here the crane driver assists in the actual *use* of pneumatic percussive tools (*Decision of the Commissioner No R(I) 4/82*).

Conditions under which benefit is payable – 1985 Regulations

30.17   For a claimant to be entitled to disablement benefit for occupational deafness, the following conditions currently apply:

(*a*)   he must have been employed:

   (i)   at any time on or after 5 July 1948, and

   (ii)   for a period or periods amounting (in the aggregate) to at least ten years.

   [*Reg 25(2)(a)*];

(*b*)   there must be permanent sensorineural hearing loss, and loss in each ear must be at least 50 dB; and

(*c*)   at least loss of 50 dB in one ear must be attributable to noise at work.

[*1 Sch, Pt I*].

(There is a presumption that occupational deafness is due to the nature of employment [*1985 Regulations, Reg 4(5)*]);

(*d*)   the claim must be made within five years of the last date when the claimant worked in an occupation prescribed for deafness [*1985 Regulations, Reg 25(2)*];

(*e*)   any assessment of disablement at less than 20% is final [*1985 Regulations, Reg 33*].

Assessment of disablement benefit for social security purposes

30.18   The extent of disablement is the percentage calculated by (*a*)   determining the average total hearing loss due to all causes for each ear at 1, 2 and 3 kHz frequencies; and

(*b*)   determining the percentage degree of disablement for each ear; and then

(*c*)   determining the average percentage degree of binaural disablement.

[*Social Security (Industrial Injuries) (Prescribed Diseases) Amendment Regulations 1989, Reg 4(2)*].

Any degree of disablement, due to deafness at work, assessed at less than 20%, must be disregarded for benefit purposes. [*Social Security (Industrial Injuries) (Prescribed Diseases) Amendment Regulations 1990 (SI 1990 No 2269)*].

Action against employer at common law

30.19   There is no separate action for noise at common law; liability comes under the general heading of negligence (see further Chapter 15 'Employers' Duties'). Indeed, it was not until as late as 1972 that employers were made liable for deafness negligently caused to employees (*Berry v Stone Manganese Marine Ltd [1972] 1 Lloyd's Rep 182*). Absence of a previous general statutory requirement on employers regarding exposure of employees to noise sometimes led to the law being strained to meet the facts (*Carragher v Singer Manufacturing Co Ltd (1974) SLT (Notes) 28* relating to the *Factories Act 1961, s 29*: 'every place of work must, so far as is reasonably practicable, be made and kept safe for any person working there', to the effect that this is wide enough to provide protection against noise). Moreover, although there are specific statutory requirements to minimise exposure to noise (in agriculture and offshore operations and construction operations, see 30.12-30.14 above), these have generated little or no case law.

The main points established at common law are as follows.

(*a*)   As from 1963, the publication date by the (then) Factory Inspectorate of 'Noise and the Worker', employers have been 'on notice' of the dangers to hearing of their employees arising from over-exposure to noise (*McGuinness v Kirkstall Forge Engineering Ltd*, per Hodgson J, 1979 unreported). Hence, consistent with their common law duty to take reasonable care for the health and safety of their employees, employers should 'provide and maintain' (for the meaning of this expression, see Chapter 15 'Employers' Duties') a sufficient stock of ear muffs.

This was confirmed in *Thompson v Smiths* etc. (see (*d*) below). However, more recently, an employer was held liable for an employee's noise-induced deafness, even though the latter's exposure to noise, working in shipbuilding, had occurred *entirely before 1963*. The grounds were that the employer had done virtually nothing to combat the *known* noise hazard from 1954-1963 (apart from making earplugs available) (*Baxter v Harland & Woolf plc, Northern Ireland Court of Appeal 1990 (unreported)*).

This means that, as far as Northern Ireland is concerned, employers are liable at common law for noise-induced deafness as from 1 January 1954 – the earliest actionable date. Limitation statutes preclude employees suing prior to that date (*Arnold v CEGB [1988] AC 228*).

(*b*)   Because the true nature of deafness as a disability has not always been appreciated, damages have traditionally not been high (*Berry v Stone Manganese Marine Ltd [1972]* – £2,500 (halved because of time limitation obstacles); *Heslop v Metalock (Great Britain) Ltd (1981)* – £7,750;

O'Shea v Kimberley-Clark Ltd (1982) – £7,490 (tinnitus); Tripp v MOD [1982] – £7,500).

(c) Damages will be awarded for exposure to noise, even though the resultant deafness is not great, as in tinnitus (*O'Shea v Kimberley-Clark Ltd, The Guardian, 8 October 1982*).

(d) Originally the last employer of a succession of employers (for whom an employee had worked in noisy occupations) was exclusively liable for damages for deafness, even though damage (i.e. actual hearing loss) occurs in the early years of exposure (for which earlier employers would have been responsible) (*Heslop v Metalock (Great Britain) Ltd, The Observer, 29 November 1981*). More recently, however, the tendency is to *apportion* liability between offending employers (*Thompson, Gray, Nicholson v Smiths Ship Repairers (North Shields) Ltd; Blacklock, Waggott v Swan Hunter Shipbuilders Ltd; Mitchell v Vickers Armstrong Ltd [1984] IRLR 93-116*). This is patently fairer because some blame is then shared by the original employer(s), whose negligence would have been responsible for the actual hearing loss.

(e) Because of the current tendency to apportion liability, even in the case of pre-1963 employers (see above *McGuinness v Kirkstall Forge Engineering Ltd*), contribution will take place between earlier and later insurers.

(f) Although judges are generally reluctant to be swayed by scientific/statistical evidence, the trio of shipbuilding cases (see (d) above) demonstrates, at least in the case of occupational deafness, that this trend is being reversed (see below the 'Coles-Worgan classification'); in particular, it is relevant to consider the 'dose response' relationship published by the National Physical Laboratory (NPL), which relates long-term continuous noise exposure to expected resultant hearing loss. This graph always shows a rapid increase in the early years of noise exposure, followed by a trailing off (see 30.20 below 'Coles-Worgan scale').

(g) Current judicial wisdom identifies three separate evolutionary aspects of deafness, i.e. (i) hearing loss (measured in decibels at various frequencies); (ii) disability (i.e. difficulty/inability to receive everyday sounds); (iii) social handicap (attending musical concerts/meetings etc.). That social handicap is a genuine basis on which damages can be (*inter alia*) awarded, was reaffirmed in the recent case of *Bixby, Case, Fry and Elliott v Ford Motor Group (1990, unreported)*.

Relevance of Coles-Worgan scale

30.20 The Coles-Worgan scale (see Table 26 below) was used to assess disability in the trio of shipbuilding cases; this gives a better assessment of disability than reference to hearing loss alone. This scale takes account of hearing loss at 0.5, 1.0, 2.0 and 4.0 kHz and also clinical symptoms, the subject being assigned to one of ten classes or 'groups' of increasing severity, e.g. 'slight', 'moderate' etc. (0.5, 1.0, 2.0 and 4.0 kHz are the denoted 'frequencies of interest' from a hearing loss point of view. These are the frequencies at which normal speech takes place and are, therefore, significant in any assessment by audiometry of hearing loss).

Table 26
The Coles-Worgan classification for occupational deafness

Group O	– No significant auditory handicap.
Group I	– The hearing is not sufficiently impaired to affect the perception of speech, except for a slight (additional to normal) difficulty in noisy backgrounds.
Groups II & III	– Slight (II) and moderate (III) difficulty whenever listening to faint speech, but would usually understand normal speech. The subject would also have distinctly greater difficulty when trying to understand speech against a background of noise.
Groups IV & V	– Frequent difficulty with normal speech and would sometimes (IV) or often (V) have to ask people to 'speak up' in order to hear them, even in face-to-face conversation. Great (IV) or very great (V) difficulty in a background of noise.
Group VI	– Marked difficulties in communication since he would sometimes be unable to clearly understand even loud speech. In noise the subject would find it impossible to distinguish speech.
Groups VII & VIII	– Would only understand shouted or amplified speech, and then only moderately well (VII) or poorly (VIII).
Group IX	– Minimal speech intelligibility even with well amplified speech.
Group X	– Virtually totally deaf with respect to the understanding of speech.

Current hygiene standards for noise induced hearing loss (occupational deafness)

30.21 Audiometry measures hearing loss over a range of frequencies, measured in kHz. Current standards are based on hearing loss over the frequencies of interest, i.e. 0.5, 1.0, 2.0 kHz etc., at which normal human speech takes place.

These standards are based on noise induced deafness (sociocusis), age-based deafness (presbyacusis) and speech range over the frequencies of interest (speech range frequencies) i.e. 1000, 2000 and 3000 Hz (1, 2 and 3 kHz). These standards are as follows.

(a) *Social Security (Industrial Injuries) Commission*: 50 dB hearing loss averaged through 1, 2 and 3 kHz in the *better* ear.

(b) *American Academy of Ophthalmologists and Otolaryngolists*: 25 dB loss averaged through ½, 1 and 2 kHz in *both* ears.

(c) *British Association of Ophthalmologists*: 40 dB hearing loss averaged through 1, 2 and 3 kHz in *both* ears.

PART B

VIBRATION

General aspects of vibration

30.22   A body is said to vibrate when it describes an oscillating motion about a fixed position. The number of such complete oscillatory motions in a second is referred to as the 'frequency' of the vibration, which is measured in Hertz (Hz). Vibration amplitude, i.e. the maximum displacement of the vibratory motion, is the characteristic which determines the severity of the vibration. A graph showing the vibration amplitude as a function of frequency is known as a 'frequency spectrogram'.

The human body is most sensitive to vibration in the frequency range 1-80 Hz. There are two distinct conditions associated with exposure to vibration, namely the effects of whole body vibration and the condition known as 'vibration-induced white finger' (VWF).

Whole-body vibration

30.23   The general effects of exposure on the body are loss of balance, blurred vision and loss of concentration. This is particularly significant in the case of long distance lorry drivers who are subjected to whole body vibration, tractor drivers and drivers of vehicles used on construction sites. The International Standards Organisation (ISO) has published recommendations dealing with vibration and the human body (ISO 2631–1974). Recommendations cover cases where the human body is subjected to vibration on one of three supporting surfaces, i.e. the feet of a standing person, the buttocks of a person whilst sitting down and the areas supporting a lying person. Three severity criteria are specified, i.e.:

(*a*)   a boundary of reduced comfort, applying to fields such as passenger transportation;

(*b*)   a boundary of fatigue-decreased efficiency that is relevant to drivers of vehicles and to certain machine operators; and

(*c*)   an exposure limit boundary, which indicates danger to health.

Research into this problem indicates that in the longitudinal direction, i.e. head to feet, the human body is most sensitive to vibration in the frequency range 4-8 Hz, whilst in the transverse direction, i.e. finger tip to finger tip, the range is 1-2 Hz.

Vibration-induced white finger (VWF)

30.24   Since its recent addition, VWF has grown rapidly to become the largest single category of disease to date. Many of these claims – 35 out of 2,601 compensated in 1989/90 – will probably be a first step in suing employers at common law.

VWF is prescribed occupational disease A 11. It is described as: 'episodic blanching, occurring throughout the year, affecting the middle or proximate phalanges or in the case of a thumb the proximal phalanx, of:

(*a*)   in the case of a person with five fingers (including thumb) on one hand, any three of those fingers;

(*b*)   in the case of a person with only four such fingers, any two of those fingers; or

(c)   in the case of a person with less than four such fingers, any one of those fingers or . . . the remaining one finger.'

[*Social Security (Industrial Injuries) (Prescribed Diseases) Regulations 1985*].

VWF is also actionable at common law against the employer (*Heal v Garringtons Ltd (1984) unreported; McFaul v Garringtons Ltd (1985) HSIB 113*). Damages are awarded according to the stage of the disease at the time of the action from the date the employer should have known of the risk.

The principal cause of VWF is the use of vibrating hand tools, such as electrically-operated rotary tools, chain saws and vibrating hand tools. Extensive and prolonged exposure can lead to progressive loss of blood circulation in the hand and fingers, sometimes resulting in necrosis (death of tissue) and gangrene for which the only solution may be amputation of the affected areas or complete hand. Initial signs are mild tingling and numbness of the fingers. Further exposure results in blanching of the fingers, particularly in cold weather and early in the morning. The condition is progressive to the base of the fingers, sensitivity to attacks is reduced and the fingers take on a blue-black appearance. The development of the condition may take up to five years according to the degree of exposure to vibration and the duration of such exposure.

Vibratory hand tools

30.25   The energy level of the hand tool is significant. Percussive action tools, such as compressed air pneumatic hammers, operate within a frequency range of 33-50 Hz. These cause considerable damage whereas rotary hand tools, which operate within the frequency range 40-125 Hz, are less dangerous.

Use, either frequent or intermittent, of hand-held vibratory tools, can result in injury to the wrist. Carpal tunnel syndrome arising in this way is now prescribed occupational disease A12. [*Social Security (Industrial Injuries) (Prescribed Diseases) Amendment Regulations 1993 (SI 1993 No 862), Reg 6(2)*].

Proposed statutory controls over hand-arm and whole-body vibration

30.26   (a)   *Hand-arm vibration*

Daily exposure A(8):

(1) $1 m/s^2$ to be the threshold value and at this point workers are to be told of risks;

(2)   at $2.5 m/s^2$ vibration exposure assessments are to become mandatory – copies to be given to safety representatives. If vibration levels cannot be reliably quantified, action will have to be taken if exposure above $1 m/s^2$ cannot be ruled out. Also workers are entitled to information on protective and control measures and to on-going health surveillance;

(3)   at $5 m/s^2$ systematic health surveillance must be carried out.

Short term level exposure:

(1)   if vibration over a period of a few minutes reaches $10 m/s^2$, increased efforts are to be made to reduce vibration; if these are unsuccessful, work breaks may have to be introduced;

(2)   if vibration over a period of a few minutes reaches $20 m/s^2$, offending equipment must be marked and work activities declared to HSE.

(*b*)   *Whole-body vibration*

Daily exposure A(8):

(1) 0.25 m/s^2 is to be the threshold value; and workers are to be told of risks;

(2)   at 0.5 m/s^2 (or 1.25 m/s^2 – 1 hour average) employers must establish a regime of control strategies following vibration exposure assessments – copies of which must be given to safety representatives; also workers must be given information on protective and control measures and entitled to on-going health surveillance;

(3)   at 0.7 m/s^2 systematic health surveillance must be carried out;

(4)   at 1.25 m/s^2 offending work activities must be notified to HSE.

(EC draft Physical Agents at Work Directive 93/077/02).

Environmental noise – Sec 60 notices

30.27   Environmental noise, not necessarily constituting an actionable nuisance, emanating from construction sites, is subject to *discretionary* local authority control. In particular, works of

(i)   construction,

(ii)   inspection,

(iii)   maintenance,

(iv)   removal,

(v)   demolition,

(vi)   dredging,

involving

(*a*)   erecting,

(*b*)   constructing,

(*c*)   altering,

(*d*)   repairing,

(*e*)   maintaining

buildings, structures or roads, or

(*f*)   breaking up,

(*g*)   opening, or

(*h*)   boring under a road

can have notices served specifying requirements as to the manner of doing the works. [*Control of Pollution Act 1974, s 60*].

Requirements can specify

(i)   plant and machinery to be involved;

(ii)   permitted hours of working;

(iii)   permitted noise levels generally or in particular circumstances.

Also the local authority must ensure that operators comply with the provisions of any relevant code of practice, issued under *Part III* of the *Control of Pollution Act 1974* (i.e. BS 5228: 1984 'Basic information and procedures for noise control') and the *Control of Noise (Codes of Practice for Construction and Open Sites) Order 1984 (SI 1984 No 1992)* (see 30.14 above), as well as use the 'best practicable means' to minimise noise levels. Overall regard must be had to the need to protect persons in the vicinity against noise intrusion. Often *Sec 60* notices specify steps and time periods for compliance. Appellants have 21 days within which to appeal. [*Control of Noise (Appeals) Regulations 1975 (SI 1975 No 2116), Reg 5*].

Application for consent – Sec 61

30.28   A contractor intending to carry out works caught by *Sec 60*, can apply to the local authority for consent – which should be made simultaneously with a request for building regulations approval. The application should specify the works to be carried out, methods to be used in carrying them out and steps to minimise noise. [*Control of Pollution Act 1974, s 61*]. If the local authority is satisfied that it is not necessary to serve a *Sec 60* notice, consent to the application must be given, within 28 days of the receipt of the application, so long as the appellant agrees to abide by any relevant code of practice. Unconditional or conditional consent may be given, in which latter case, the appellant has a further 21 days in which to appeal to the magistrates. [*Control of Noise (Appeals) Regulations 1975, Reg 6*].

Defence

Where an operator is prosecuted for breach of *Sec 60*, it is a defence that the works were carried out in accordance with a *Sec 61* consent.

Noise abatement zones

30.29   A local authority can designate all or any part of its area a noise abatement zone. [*Control of Pollution Act 1974, s 63*]. Once made, the order takes effect after, at least, one month from the date that it was made. In such cases, the local authority must measure and record in a public register (the noise level register) the noise level emanating from premises within the zone. [*Control of Pollution Act 1974, s 64*]. The methods to be used in measuring levels are specified in the *Control of Noise (Measurements and Registers) Regulations 1976 (SI 1975 No 37)*. The level of noise recorded in the register in respect of any premises must not be exceeded, except with written consent of the local authority, which may be given unconditionally or conditionally. [*Control of Pollution Act 1974, s 65*]. Where, on conviction for this offence, the magistrates feel that the offence is likely to recur, they can require the offender to carry out preventive works – contravention of which, without reasonable excuse, is also an offence.

Noise reduction notice – Sec 66

30.30   Where a local authority feels that the noise level from premises subject to a noise abatement order is unacceptable and that a reduction in noise is practicable and for the public benefit, it can serve a noise reduction notice on the offender, allowing him six months in which to comply. [*Control of Pollution Act 1974, s 66*]. A noise reduction notice takes priority over a written consent issued under *Sec 65* (above). Appellants have three months in which to appeal to the magistrates. [*Control of Noise (Appeals) Regulations 1975, Reg 7*]. It is, however, a defence that 'best practicable means' were used to prevent or counteract the noise.

Buildings under construction

30.31   Where a building is going to be constructed, to which a noise abatement order will apply when finished, the local authority can, either on application from the owner/occupier, or on their own initiative, determine a noise emission level for that building, which must then be registered, and notify the owner/occupier within two months. [*Control of Pollution Act 1974, s 67*]. Appeals must be lodged within three months. [*Control of Noise (Appeals) Regulations 1975, Reg 9*]. If no noise level is determined under *Sec 67*, such noise reduction as is practicable at a reasonable cost, applies, by dint of *Sec 66* (see above).

Noise from plant and machinery

30.32   Regulations may be made to limit noise levels caused by plant machinery, or to require application of noise suppression devices. [*Control of Pollution Act 1974, s 68*]. To date no such regulations have been made. Such regulations would apply whether or not the plant/machinery was being used on a construction site.

Chapter 31

Occupational Health and Diseases

Introduction

31.1   Occupational health is a branch of preventive medicine examining:

(a)   the relationship of work to health; and

(b)   the effects of work upon the worker.

While it could be argued that the principal thrust of enforcement agencies, such as the Health and Safety Commission (HSC), has been directed at improving levels of occupational safety, there are clear indications in the *Health and Safety at Work etc. Act 1974 (HSWA)* and the *Management of Health and Safety at Work Regulations 1992* and other legislation of the need for employers and others to pay attention to the health of workers and to protect everyone, not only their workers, from risks to their health which may be associated with work activities. [*HSWA ss 1, 2(1)-(3)(6)(7), 3, 4, 6-8*]. Hence, the premium placed on the health of workers by recent regulations, such as the *Control of Lead Regulations 1980*, the *Ionising Radiations Regulations 1985*, the *Control of Asbestos at Work Regulations 1987* and the *Control of Substances Hazardous to Health Regulations 1988 (COSHH)*. Nor, although it is neither a reportable disease (see Chapter 3 'Accident Reporting') nor a prescribed occupational disease (see 31.42 below), should the dangers associated with legionella, both to the workforce and general public, from hot water systems and air conditioning plant, be forgotten (see 9.27 DANGEROUS SUBSTANCES I and 31.12 below).

In this connection, the role of the Industrial Injuries Advisory Council (IIAC) is an expansive one (see 31.43 below) and it seems that disablement benefit will progressively become payable on the basis of individual proof of occupational illness, as has happened in the case of occupational asthma, rather than prescription of substances. Moreover, chronic bronchitis and emphysema have recently been made prescribed occupational diseases for coal miners working underground for twenty years.

The workforce is an employer's greatest asset, and a healthy workforce is a pre-requisite for industrial efficiency. Effective occupational health procedures are, therefore, essential and should be welcomed by employers and employees. This chapter deals with the statutory provisions relating to occupational health procedures, as follows:

—   the Employment Medical Advisory Service (see 31.7, 31.8 below);

—   compulsory medical examination of factory workers (see 31.9 below);

—   periodic health checks for workers involved in certain hazardous operations (see 31.10 below);

—   statutory controls over dangerous substances (see 31.11 below);

—   legionnaire's disease (see 31.12 below);

— statutory payments during suspension from work on medical grounds (see 31.13 below);

— health surveillance (see 31.16 below);

— classification of occupational diseases (see 31.31 below);

— prescribed occupational diseases (see 31.41-31.45 below) and certain other conditions often associated with employment and collectively known as 'stress' (see 31.36 below).

(Although deafness and related conditions form an important prescribed occupational disease, details of this are dealt with in Chapter 30 'Noise and Vibration'.)

In addition, practical measures to ensure fitness at work as well as current good housekeeping practice are included (see 31.14, 31.15 below).

Occupational health procedures

31.2   Occupational health procedures cover a wide range of activities aimed at satisfying certain statutory requirements imposed on the employer, e.g. under the *Control of Lead at Work Regulations 1980*, to ensure the employee's fitness for work and in certain cases, such as the food manufacturing and catering industries, to ensure fitness of the product. They can extend from a health questionnaire completed by a prospective employee (see 31.14 below and the example reproduced at the end of this chapter) and health examination undertaken by an occupational health nurse to a complete medical examination by an occupational physician. Full-scale occupational health practice incorporates activities undertaken by three principal practitioners: the occupational physician, the occupational hygienist and the occupational health nurse, together with other specialists, such as ergonomists, toxicologists and epidemiologists.

Occupational medicine

31.3   This is the branch of preventive medicine concerned with the diagnosis and treatment of occupational diseases and conditions (see 31.42 below).

Occupational hygiene

31.4   Occupational hygiene is concerned with the identification, measurement, evaluation and control of contaminants and other phenomena, such as noise and radiation, which would have otherwise unacceptable adverse effects on the health of people exposed to them (see also 15.54 EMPLOYERS' DUTIES).

Occupational health nursing

31.5   The American Association of Occupational Health Nurses has defined occupational health nursing as 'the synthesis of public health principles, nursing practice, and occupational safety and health procedures for the purpose of conserving, promoting and restoring the health of workers. It includes the ability to identify the health needs of workers, to identify hazards and their potential for harm, to identify relationships between illness/injury and the job/work environment, to organise, co-ordinate and provide nursing care in a safe, efficient, therapeutically effective manner, consistent with established professional standards and company policy. It includes the ability to assist the worker to attain and maintain a high level of well-being and to work collaboratively and co-operatively with workers, their families and their unions, insurance companies, regulatory agencies, community agencies and other occupational safety and health professionals. Finally, it is both autonomous and independent, self-directed and self-motivated. It involves risk-taking and a willingness to be held accountable both legally and morally' (see also 15.51, 15.52 EMPLOYERS' DUTIES).

Health monitoring surveillance

31.6   Health monitoring or surveillance tends to take three specific forms:

(*a*)   pre-employment health screening;

(*b*)   periodic health examinations or health screening for certain groups of workers where there may be an on-going risk to them; and

(*c*)   health screening on return to work after illness or accident.

Health examinations should be related to the inherent risks to which workers may be exposed. They may include vision screening for visual display unit (VDU) operators (see 27.22, 27.27 and 27.29 LIGHTING), blood tests for workers exposed to lead, lung function tests for cotton workers or those exposed to isocyanates, together with other blood, urine, skin, allergy and sensitivity tests. Audiometry (i.e. the measurement, over a range of frequencies, of the ability of an individual to detect sound) is a typical form of on-going health screening where operators may be exposed to fluctuating sound pressure levels.

The more specific areas of occupational health practice are outlined later in this chapter.

Employment Medical Advisory Service

31.7   The Employment Medical Advisory Service (EMAS) was established by the *Employment Medical Advisory Service Act 1972*. It provides for expert groups of doctors engaged in industrial medicine to carry out selective examination of young persons, and the statutory examination of persons engaged in hazardous jobs or on hazardous tasks. The nucleus of the service is the Medical Services Division of the Health and Safety Executive (HSE). It consists of a national network of some 140 doctors and nurses accountable to nine Senior Medical Employment Advisers, and is headed by the Director of Medical Services of the HSE who takes advice from a team of specialists.

Statutory medical examinations

31.8   About 22,000 statutory examinations (i.e. examinations under the provisions below) are carried out by EMAS every year, for which employers must pay. [*Health and Safety (Fees) Regulations 1992 (SI 1992 No 1752)*]. A further 90,000 examinations a year are carried out by doctors employed by companies concerned who have been appointed for the purpose by EMAS. They are termed 'appointed doctors'. The fee for these examinations is a matter for agreement between the doctors and the employers concerned.

It is prescribed that:

(*a*)   the employer is officially informed of the fitness of a worker to undertake employment;

(*b*)   the employee has a duty to undergo examinations;

(*c*)   the employer cannot lawfully continue to employ any worker who is found to be unfit (see Chapter 13 'Employee Safety Rights, Disciplinary Procedures and Unfair Dismissal');

(d)   the employee must be removed from that particular job for the prescribed period and transferred to alternative work if it is available; and

(e)   the outcome of the medical examination must be recorded in a health register kept by the employer.

Medical examination of factory employees

31.9   The *Factories Act 1961, s 10A* gives an Employment Medical Adviser (EMA) the power to order medical examinations in the case of factory employees. (In the case of young persons employed in factories, an inspector can require that the employment of the young person be discontinued if he is of opinion that the work is prejudicial to his health, see Chapter 5 'Children and Young Persons'.) For the purposes of the *Factories Act 1961, s 10A*, the term 'medical examination' includes pathological, physiological, radiological and similar investigations. [*Factories Act 1961, s 10A*].

If, in the opinion of an EMA, the health of an employee in a factory (as defined by the *Factories Act 1961*, see Chapter 18 'Factories and Workplaces') has been, is being or will be injured, because of the nature of his work, he may serve a written notice on his employer requiring him to permit a medical examination of that employee. This will specify the time, date and place of the examination, and if the examination is to take place within the factory, the employer must make suitable accommodation available for the examination to take place. The examination should take place within seven days of the written notice. (The employee, however, is under no legal obligation to be examined.) [*Factories Act 1961, s 10A*].

Periodic compulsory examinations in hazardous occupations

31.10   There are a number of special regulations which provide for *compulsory* periodical medical examination and/or supervision. Much of the earlier statute law on this subject has been consolidated in the *Control of Lead at Work Regulations 1980* and, more recently, the *Control of Substances Hazardous to Health Regulations 1988* (*COSHH*).

More particularly, medical examination and/or supervision is compulsory for employees in the following operations/processes:

(a)   young persons employed in lifting/carrying work in pottery processes [*Pottery (Health and Welfare) Special Regulations 1950 (SI 1950 No 65), Reg 7*];

(b)   persons employed in compressed air operations [*Work in Compressed Air Special Regulations 1958 (SI 1958 No 61), Reg 14*];

(c)   persons employed in lead processes [*Control of Lead at Work Regulations 1980 (SI 1980 No 1248), Reg 16*];

(d)   persons employed as underwater divers [*Diving Operations at Work Regulations 1981 (SI 1981 No 399), Reg 11*];

(e)   persons employed in ionising radiations processes [*Ionising Radiations Regulations 1985 (SI 1985 No 1333), Reg 16(7)*];

(f)   persons covered by the *Control of Substances Hazardous to Health Regulations (SI 1988 No 1657), Reg 11*.

Statutory controls over dangerous substances and processes

31.11   As early as the (second) *Workmen's Compensation Act 1906*, it was recognised that certain diseases were either exclusively or predominantly employment-related (and hence gave rise to automatic no fault compensation); examples being lead poisoning, mercury poisoning, phosphorous poisoning and arsenic poisoning. During the twentieth century diseases have continued to be prescribed in accordance with occupation, with the result that there are now some sixty prescribed occupational diseases specified in the current *Social Security (Industrial Injuries) (Prescribed Diseases) Regulations 1985* (as amended) (see further 31.42–31.46 below).

Statutory controls over dangerous substances are designed principally to protect the worker from exposure to substances likely to cause disease, sometimes manifesting itself very tardily over a long incubation period, as, for instance, with asbestosis and/or mesothelioma. Failure on the part of employers to comply with regulations can lead to payment of a maximum fine of £5,000 on summary conviction. Moreover, if employees fail to co-operate with their employer, they can also be prosecuted and, in addition, dismissed from their employment.

There has been a spate of regulations in the last decade dealing with dangerous substances – particularly dangerous chemicals, e.g.

—   *Road Traffic (Carriage of Dangerous Substances in Road Tankers and Tank Containers) Regulations 1992* – controls over bulk transport by road of dangerous chemicals;

—   *Notification of Installations Handling Hazardous Substances Regulations 1982* – controls over dangerous chemicals on manufacturing sites and in pipelines;

—   *Notification of New Substances Regulations 1982* – duty to report dangerous chemicals to HSE;

—   *Road Traffic (Carriage of Dangerous Substances in Packages, etc.) Regulations 1992* – controls over transport of dangerous packages;

(see further Chapters 9 and 10 'Dangerous Substances I and II') and most recently,

—   *Control of Substances Hazardous to Health Regulations 1988* (*COSHH*);

—   *Radioactive Substances Act 1993* (see Chapter 9 'Dangerous Substances I'); and

—   *Chemicals (Hazard Information and Packaging) Regulations 1993* (see Chapter 9 'Dangerous Substances I');

(see further Chapter 9 'Dangerous Substances I').

Legionnaire's disease

31.12   Although not notifiable and/or reportable, legionnaire's disease is sufficiently serious to warrant the Medical Officer of Environmental Health (MOEH) being informed if there is an outbreak. Legionnaire's disease is a type of pneumonia. Infection is caused by inhaling airborne droplets containing visible legionella that are sufficiently small to pass into the lungs. It affects about one person in a hundred and has an incubation period of three to six days. Males are more likely to be affected than females, particularly those between 40 and 70. Smokers, alcoholics and those with respiratory conditions are especially vulnerable. (For conditions likely to produce legionella and precautions necessary, see further 9.31 DANGEROUS SUBSTANCES I.)

Suspension from work on medical grounds

31.13 Where an employee is suspended from work under one of the following provisions – but is otherwise able to work – he has a statutory right to be paid by his employer during the suspension, for up to 26 weeks. [*EPCA 1978, s 19(1)(b)*]. The purpose of medical suspension payments is *not* to top up sick pay, where employees are off work due to a work-related complaint; but rather to compensate workers removed from their normal work, owing to risks involved, from losing out financially (*Stallite Batteries Co Ltd v Appleton and Hopkinson (the Employment Appeal Tribunal, HSIB 147)*). But an employee will not be entitled to be paid unless he complies with any reasonable requirements specified by his employer or if he refuses to accept suitable alternative employment offered by the employer during the suspension period. If the employer does not pay, the employee can make a complaint to an industrial tribunal. The provisions are:

— *Control of Lead at Work Regulations 1980, Reg 16*;

— *Ionising Radiations Regulations 1985, Reg 16* (whereas under the *Ionising Radiations Regulations 1968* and *1969*, an employee who had received a radiation overdose was *automatically* suspended, under current regulations the decision whether to suspend or continue working under prescribed conditions rests exclusively with the Employment Medical Adviser (or appointed doctor));

— *Control of Substances Hazardous to Health Regulations 1988, Reg 11*, that is, where an employee requires surveillance for health reasons.

[*EPCA ss 19, 20 and 1 Sch; Employment Protection (Medical Suspension) Order 1980 (SI 1980 No 1581)*].

Where an employee is dismissed following doctors' orders prohibiting him from continuing work, under one of the provisions above, he only requires four weeks' service (not 52) in order to qualify to present a complaint of unfair dismissal (see Chapter 13 'Employee Safety Rights, Disciplinary Procedures and Unfair Dismissal'). [*EPCA s 64*].

Specific areas of occupational health practice

Pre-employment health screening

31.14 Pre-employment medical examinations for workers involved in traditionally high risk processes and activities have been a common feature of industrial practice for many years, e.g. lead workers, radiation workers, divers, pottery workers. It is in the interests of both the employer and employee that persons commencing new employment are both physically and mentally fit for the tasks they may be asked to undertake. Pre-employment health screening generally takes the form of completion of a specific health questionnaire by the employee, followed by assessment of the questionnaire and health examination by the occupational physician or occupational health nurse. (See example of pre-employment health questionnaire (*fig 15*) at the end of this chapter.) Health examinations of this type are a normal pre-requisite for entry into sick pay schemes, pension funds or maintenance of earnings schemes in the event of occupational disease. They may also be required by organisations who recognise that specific hazards may exist in their industries for which they wish to screen out certain workers who may be more vulnerable than others. The underlying purpose in these cases is often to satisfy insurance companies who underwrite such schemes and require medical examinations as part of their arrangements.

Common areas for pre-employment health screening are those involving food handling, diving work, contact with chemical substances, manual handling, close inspection work and contact with pathogens. The full range of recommended pre-employment and periodic medical examinations is defined in EMAS and HSE guidance notes (medical series).

The rejection rate from pre-employment screening should be expected to be very low; its aim is not to produce a superfit workforce, but to offer a form of protection. Screening should ensure that a worker is not suffering from a dangerous disease or is likely to endanger others through any illness from which he may suffer. It should determine whether a job will be of particular risk to the person concerned. Furthermore, the pre-employment screening should set a 'base-line' for the health of the worker from which future periodic checks can be assessed. In this way health examinations can act as a safety net to detect conditions which may be hazardous to health and have not been recorded by other means, such as monitoring of the environment.

Organisation of working time – night work/shift work

31.15 Occupational health is inextricably linked with organisation of working time. A draft EC directive (adopted 30 June 1993) proposes:

(*a*) a minimum daily rest period of 11 consecutive hours per 24-hour period;

(*b*) a minimum period of one rest day in every seven;

(*c*) all workers are to get an annual paid holiday;

(*d*) overtime does not interfere with minimum daily/weekly rest periods;

(*e*) normal hours of night work must not be greater than 8 hours in a 24-hour period over a 14-day period;

(*f*) where shift work involves night work, a prohibition on working two consecutive full-time shifts;

(*g*) no overtime is to be worked by night workers before or after a daily work period which includes either night work in hazardous occupations or heavy physical-mental strain;

(*h*) regular night workers be entitled to free health assessments prior to commencing work;

(*j*) where a night worker suffers health problems, he should be transferred to day work;

(*k*) employers regularly using night workers must inform the HSE;

(*l*) night workers and rotating shift workers be entitled to a minimum level of health/safety protection according to the nature of work;

(*m*) employers must see that changes in working patterns take account of health/safety.

Moreover, it is further proposed to extend health/safety protection to temporary workers (see Chapter 14 'Employees' Duties').

Health surveillance

31.16 This particular activity is directed at two groups of workers, namely those at risk of developing further ill health or disability by virtue of their current state of health and, secondly, those workers actually or potentially at risk by virtue of the form or type of work they undertake, e.g. radiation workers.

Health surveillance of these groups takes the form of periodic health examinations at, for instance, six-monthly or annual intervals according to the degree of risk. It allows for early detection of evidence of occupational disease and for subsequent treatment.

Health surveillance also covers medical or health examinations of workers on return to work following illness or accident, and is concerned with ensuring that the employee is now fit for such work.

There is now also a statutory duty on employers to ensure that employees are provided with health surveillance appropriate to the risks to health and safety resulting from their employment. The ACOP shows that knowledge of diseases which may arise in the relevant work and valid techniques for detecting such diseases will be required. The minimum requirement where surveillance is advisable is the keeping of an individual health record (see 31.26 below). The emphasis is on early detection and continuous monitoring. [*Management of Health and Safety at Work Regulations 1992, Reg 5*].

Treatment services

31.17   The efficient and speedy treatment of acute poisonings, injuries and work-associated conditions is an important feature of occupational health practice. Such treatment prevents future complications and assists rehabilitation. Moreover, this area of activity has an important role to play in keeping people at work, thereby reducing time lost through attendance at casualty departments or doctors' surgeries.

Primary and secondary monitoring

31.18   Primary monitoring involves the clinical observation of sick people who may seek treatment or advice. It assists in the identification of new risks which may not have been considered previously. Secondary monitoring, on the other hand, is concerned with controlling health hazards which already exist.

Avoiding potential risks

31.19   Here the principal emphasis is on prevention, whereby the occupational health practitioner can make a contribution to the design and planning of safe systems of work and the assessment and evaluation of potential environmental stressors, such as noise, vibration and fumes from processes.

Supervision of vulnerable groups

31.20   Certain groups are more vulnerable to occupational health risks than others, e.g. young persons, pregnant women, the disabled, the elderly and workers who may have had protracted periods of sickness absence. Routine health examinations to assess continuing fitness for work are essential here. Young persons must be continually advised of health risks which may exist in their work, e.g. occupational deafness through failure to wear hearing protection.

Monitoring for early evidence of non-occupational disease

31.21   Certain occupational diseases are specific to particular industries, e.g. byssinosis in the case of cotton workers, coal workers' pneumoconiosis in the case of miners.

Routine monitoring of workers not exposed to conditions which promote these diseases is an important feature of occupational health practice. In this activity the main aim is that of controlling disease prevalent in industrial populations with a view to their eventual eradication.

Counselling/Health education

(a) Counselling

31.22 Counselling on health-related matters and on personal, social and emotional problems is becoming increasingly more important with a view to reducing stress amongst workers. Stress can result in an inability to concentrate for long periods, fatigue, frustration and sickness absence. Occupational health practitioners are trained in many areas of counselling and the availability of a sympathetic ear, independent of management controls, can help the individual to come to terms with and cope with problems more easily.

(b) Health education

This is concerned with the education of employees towards healthier modes of living. It can also include training of staff in their individual responsibilities for health and safety at work, in healthy working techniques and the avoidance of health hazards. It may also be necessary to educate workers in the reasons for certain other areas of occupational health practice, such as annual health examinations, audiometry or blood tests.

First-aid and emergency services

31.23 The supervision of first-aid facilities and ancillary equipment such as breathing apparatus and other rescue equipment features strongly in occupational health practice, together with the design and preparation of contingency plans to cover major disasters, such as fire, explosion or gassing accidents. Many large organisations with occupational health services train their own first-aiders, rescue staff and key members of the management team in preparation for such disasters (see further Chapter 20 'First-Aid').

Welfare amenity provisions

31.24 The provision of advice on the design, layout and construction of amenity areas, together with legal requirements relating to sanitary conveniences, washing facilities, showers, drinking water and facilities for the storage and drying of clothing are a routine feature of occupational health practice. Such facilities assist in the maintenance of sound health standards (see Chapter 44 'Welfare Facilities').

Occupational hygiene and environmental control

31.25 Control of the working environment and the prevention of pollution in the general environment from workplace activities are normally included in occupational health procedures. The employer has a legal duty to provide a safe working environment, without risks to health, and to prevent emissions from the premises which may endanger the surrounding communities, or result in pollution of air, land, water, drainage system or watercourse. [*HSWA ss 2(1), 5*] (see further Chapter 12 'Emissions into the Atmosphere').

Health records

31.26   It is essential that suitable records relating to the state of health of each employee are kept. Such records should contain information derived from health questionnaires and examinations and screening undertaken, a full occupational history, including details of any disabilities and handicaps, details of any treatment received, injuries sustained or illness related to work, sickness absence record, correspondence with general practitioners or hospital consultants, and any counselling received (see 9.23 DANGER-OUS SUBSTANCES I for compulsory health records).

Liaison

31.27   Apart from liaising with medical and nursing advisers of the Medical Branch of the HSE, factories inspectors and staff of the Area Health Authority and even the Medical Officer of Environmental Health (in the case of legionella), occupational physicians and occupational health nurses frequently liaise with general medical practitioners subject (of course) to the agreement of the individual whose health state is under consideration. It is important that the general practitioner, who has primary responsibility for the health of individual workers registered with his practice, is kept informed of any matters of significance and is involved in the care of the patient whilst at work.

Confidentiality of information

31.28   Occupational health practitioners have a responsibility not only to their patients or clients, i.e. employees, but also to their employers. This dual responsibility can be a source of conflict if the practitioner or employer is in doubt about what information must remain confidential to the practitioner and what can be made known to management. In the case of occupational health nurses, the United Kingdom Co-ordinating Committee (UKCC) Code of Professional Conduct states that in the exercise of professional accountability each nurse shall 'respect confidential information obtained in the course of professional practice and refrain from disclosing such information without the consent of the patient/client, or a person entitled to act on his/her behalf, except where disclosure is required by law or by the order of a court or is necessary in the public interest'.

The preservation of confidentiality is an important feature of occupational health practice, particularly if the workforce is to obtain good standards of health protection. This preservation of confidentiality relates to information about employees of a clinical, social or personal nature, obtained verbally or recorded in written or computerised form. An important distinction must be made between this kind of information which is confidential and information representing opinion, advice or interpretation of facts, which is not so. It is, therefore, essential that an occupational health practitioner agrees with management the boundaries of confidentiality with regard to medical examinations, health assessments, interviews, pre-employment health screening, long term sickness absence, consultations with general medical practitioners, frequent short spells of absence and termination of service.

It is essential that employees are informed of the results of medical or health examinations, or of other forms of health surveillance undertaken by the occupational health practitioner, although health records are of course confidential between patient and practitioner. This applies whether or not the practitioner is employed by the company or provides a consultancy service. If the individual concerned is willing to allow access to his records, permission should be given in writing, naming the person or persons to whom access will be given.

HSE guidance on health surveillance

31.29   As a development of its own attention to health checks, the HSE has published a guidance note in its medical series entitled 'Health Surveillance by Routine Procedures'. Although no new legal requirements are imposed upon employers by this guidance, it does represent the current thinking of the HSE on the subject.

The methods of health surveillance described demonstrate how routine measures can guard the health of employees by making use of personnel trained to varying levels of competence, and using modern screening techniques. Various levels of surveillance are described ranging from basic record keeping by employers and simple 'self checks' by employees themselves, to full medical examinations by a doctor.

In order that the appropriate level or levels of health surveillance may be adopted in an establishment, employers are advised to make an assessment, together with employees and their trade union representatives, of work processes involved, substances used, and any other factors which may affect health. The HSE emphasises that the purpose of routine health surveillance is to identify at as early a stage as possible, any variations in the health of employees which may be related to working conditions. The note stresses therefore, that it is to the advantage of employees to co-operate in the carrying out of agreed procedures.

Prescribed occupational diseases

31.30   In the nineteenth century many occupations were dangerous, either because of the risk of injury, e.g. construction work, navvying, or more insidiously, because of the risk of disease, such as an acute poisoning (arising from work with lead, mercury, arsenic, phosphorus) or an infection (such as anthrax or glanders). Often the risk was self-evident from the nature of the occupation and because the disease or poisoning manifested itself dramatically and suddenly. Hence there was little need for a scientific demonstration of causation or to quantify the risk. The need was to protect the worker from the hazard and compensate workers afflicted. For this reason the earliest prescribed diseases were clearly and unmistakably employment-related and appeared in the schedule to the *Workmen's Compensation Act 1906*, which set out six industrial diseases for which compensation was automatically payable, namely anthrax, lead poisoning, mercury poisoning, phosphorus poisoning, arsenic poisoning and ankylostomiasis – coupled with a provision that more could be added. (Interestingly, the *Workmen's Compensation Act 1897*, the first 'no-fault' statute, made no provision for industrial disease (as distinct from injury).)

The importance of prescription lay originally (and still does) in the fact that the worker claiming compensation did not have to prove that his employment caused his disease (see further the liability of employers at common law, Chapter 15 'Employers' Duties'). Rather there was a presumption that his illness was employment-induced, though originally, this presumption could be rebutted by either the employer or doctor certifying the condition. This now forms *Regulation 4* of the *Social Security (Industrial Injuries) (Prescribed Diseases) Regulations 1985*.

During the remainder of the present century diseases have continued to be prescribed, a development resulting in the current 60 or so prescribed occupational diseases (see Table 27 in 31.42 below), with seven new sensitising agents having recently been prescribed for the purposes of occupational asthma (prescribed disease D7 see below) and the recent addition of carpal tunnel syndrome associated with use of hand-held vibrating tools, as well as emphysema and chronic bronchitis in the case of coal miners. [*Social Security (Industrial Injuries) (Prescribed Diseases) Amendment (No 2) Regulations 1993 (SI 1993 No 1985)*]. During the latter part of the present century, however, although health dangers still arise at work, the identification of occupationally induced diseases has grown more complicated. In particular, two epidemiological difficulties arise, (*a*) in relation to uncommon diseases, some instances of which may be due to occupation, e.g. bladder papilloma due to exposure to betanapthylamine, and mesothelioma due to asbestos exposure; (*b*) in relation to common diseases which may carry an occupational factor (e.g. lung cancer) – here the problem is to segregate the occupational factor from the common causatory factor (e.g. cigarette smoking).

Moreover, occupational asthma, a relatively recent addition to the list of prescribed occupational diseases, is not always recognised until it is too late for the worker. Symptoms of wheezing and chest tightness can come on after work, in the evening or at night. Thus, many cases of asthma go unchecked, as a result of which irreversible lung damage can occur. Where asthma is suspected, the worker should only be allowed to continue work at the offending process under strict medical supervision, until investigation is complete. Allowing a worker to become sensitised in this way, could precipitate an action for negligence against the employer (see 31.45 below).

Prescription of occupational diseases is likely to be speeded up in future by EC Directives/Recommendations (see further Chapter 1 'Introduction'). From the point of view of compensation, it is a very considerable 'bonus' for workers if a disease is prescribed, since this will obviate the necessity of proving negligence (see Chapter 6 'Compensation for Work Injuries/Diseases' and Chapter 15 'Employers' Duties'), since payment of disablement benefit does not depend on proof of fault.

Classification of occupational diseases

31.31   Occupational diseases are classified into four main aetiological categories by the *Social Security (Industrial Injuries) (Prescribed Diseases) Regulations 1985*, namely, (*a*) physical, (*b*) biological, (*c*) chemical and (*d*) miscellaneous – in practice, translating into (i) physical causes, (ii) biological causes, (iii) chemical causes and (iv) ergonomic causes.

(A) Physical causes

31.32   The principal physical agents responsible for occupational diseases are heat, lighting, noise, vibration, radiation, dust, pressure and electricity.

   (i)   *Heat.* Heat can cause heat cataract, heat stroke and heat cramps. The former, heat cataracts, caused by lengthy exposure to heat and microwaves, have tended to be associated with industries and processes such as glass blowing and chain making. Exposure to radiant heat results in the lens of the eye becoming opaque. Heat stroke has tended to afflict workers in hot processes, causing them to collapse unconscious. The last, heat cramp, occurs in workers involved in the heat treatment of metals, e.g. drop forging, as a result of heat transmitted by microwave radiation. The normal symptoms are muscle pain in the arms and calves, which can generally be eliminated by salt tablets. Heat cataract is prescribed disease A 2.

   (ii) *Lighting.* Although indifferent lighting conditions can be responsible for a variety of malaises, from headaches and vertigo to eye strain, only one occupational disease associated with lighting is prescribed, namely, miner's nystagmus. Symptomatic of this condition are frequent headaches, vertigo, insomnia and eyeball oscillation. The condition is caused by poor lighting conditions underground and generally ceases to afflict once underground work has ceased. Miner's nystagmus is prescribed disease A 9.

(iii) *Noise.* The normal condition associated with exposure to noise is occupational deafness (see for definition 30.15 NOISE AND VIBRATION). There are three ways in which noise can affect hearing, namely, (*a*) temporary threshold shift – a temporary reduction in hearing ability; (*b*) permanent threshold shift – here hearing impairment continues after 40 hours, with scant possibility of recovery; (*c*) acoustic trauma – this denotes sudden hearing damage from short-term intense exposure, e.g. exposure to explosives.

In most cases of occupational noise, intensity and duration of exposure are principally responsible for hearing loss, though, in addition, hearing ability deteriorates with age. Hearing loss is measured by audiometry, and, more specifically, pure tone audiometry, with the patient listening by earphone to a series of pure tone sounds in a sound-proof booth. Occupational deafness is prescribed disease A 10.

(iv) *Vibration.* The main condition associated with vibration is vibration-induced white finger (VWF) (for definition, see 31.42 below). In particular, it emanates from use of vibrating hand tools, such as chain saws, compressed air pneumatic hammers and rotary tools. The condition is characterised initially by a sensation of 'pins and needles' in the fingers. Subsequently, blanching of finger tips, exposed to vibration, occurs particularly in cold weather. Protracted and intense exposure can cause fingers to assume a blue-black appearance.

Other vibration-induced or vibration-aggravated conditions are osteoarthritis of the arm joints, Dupuytren's contracture (injury to the palm of the hand – occupational disease A 4), bursitis (occupational diseases A 6 and A 7) and carpal tunnel syndrome (occupational disease A 12). Percussive action tools, in the range 2000–3000 beats per minute (equal to a frequency range of 33–50 Hz) are the main culprits, for VWF purposes, whilst rotary tools, with a range 40–125 Hz also cause similar harm. Vibration white finger is prescribed disease A 11.

(v) *Dust.* Prolonged inhalation of dust can result in lung diseases of a chronically fibrotic nature (pneumoconiosis). Defined by the International Labour Office as the 'accumulation of dust in the lungs and the tissue reactions to its presence', pneumoconiosis can be collagenous or non-collagenous. Collagenous pneumoconiosis, often caused by inhalation of fibrogenic dusts, takes the following forms, namely, anthracosis (coal dust), silicosis (silica particles – in coal mining, zinc and tin mining as well as sandstone work and granite work); siderosis (iron particles); asbestosis (asbestos), byssinosis (cotton). Of these, asbestosis has received most media attention.

(*a*) *Asbestosis.* Resulting from prolonged exposure to asbestos dust, this is a fibrotic condition of the lung, causing breathlessness and coughing. Scarring of the lungs, along with emphysema, is a characteristic. Sufferers of asbestosis, particularly if they are smokers, may sometimes develop lung cancer and mesothelioma (occupational disease D 3). Asbestosis and related lung conditions are prescribed diseases D 8–D 12. (For compensation and benefits payable in respect of these conditions, see 4.30, 4.31 ASBESTOS and 6.28 COMPENSATION FOR WORK INJURIES/DISEASES).

(*b*) *Silicosis.* Caused by prolonged inhalation of respirable silica particles, silicosis results in fibrosis of the lung. Industries and processes at risk are mining, steel foundries, potteries, work with granite, furnaces and ceramics (occupational disease D 1).

(c) *Byssinosis.* Mainly confined to the textile industry, byssinosis is a chronic respiratory condition, caused by exposure to cotton dust and leading to bronchitis and eventually emphysema. Unless there is an onset of emphysema, byssinosis is not normally progressive, once exposure discontinues (occupational disease D 2).

(vi) *Pressure.* Decompression sickness, associated with work in compressed air, such as civil engineering excavations and diving, is caused by release within the blood of gases such as oxygen, carbon dioxide and nitrogen. Symptoms typically include pain in the limbs, vertigo and vomiting (occupational disease A 3).

(B) Biological causes

31.33 Certain occupational conditions can be contracted as a result of work with animals, birds, insects etc. Whilst incidence of such conditions is relatively low, some of the conditions are potentially serious. Classes of workers especially at risk are workers in zoos, pet shops and farms, as well as meat inspectors and veterinary surgeons. The following are the main risk areas:

(a) *Anthrax.* Occurring mainly through contact with cattle, the symptoms are toxaemia, shivering, vomiting and joint pains. If not treated early, anthrax may well be fatal. Anthrax is prescribed disease B 1.

(b) *Brucellosis.* Associated with work with cattle, sheep, goats and pigs, the symptoms are fever, insomnia, joint pains and headaches. The condition normally disappears after two weeks. Brucellosis is prescribed disease B 7.

(c) *Viral hepatitis.* Serum hepatitis (or hepatitis B) is associated with the medical profession and some hospital workers, particularly those handling and transporting blood and blood products, as well as those involved in renal dialysis. Symptoms typically include headache, vomiting, anorexia. Enlargement of the liver as well as jaundice are also features. Viral hepatitis is prescribed disease B 8.

(C) Chemical causes

31.34 Poisoning by exposure to chemical substances is the most extensive category of prescribed occupational disease. The principal culprits are lead, mercury, chromium, benzene, trichlorethylene and isocyanates.

(a) *Lead.* Lead enters the body mainly by inhalation, dust or fume. Symptoms of acute lead poisoning are a sweetish taste in the mouth, anorexia, headache and constipation. Additionally, there is (often) a dramatic effect on the nervous system characterised by muscular twitching, talkativeness and general restlessness. Most cases of acute lead poisoning are due to fume inhalation. Groups of workers particularly at risk are those involved in lead smelting, pottery glazing, vitreous enamelling, manufacture of lead accumulators. Lead poisoning is prescribed disease C 1.

(b) *Mercury.* Mercury normally enters the body through inhalation of vapour or dust, poisoning characteristically occurring from exposure to metallic mercury. Symptoms include tremors, lethargy and insomnia. Occupations at risk are mercury mining, thermometer and barometer manufacturing, manufacture of disinfectants and fungicides containing organic compounds of mercury. Mercury poisoning is prescribed disease C 5.

(c) *Chromium.* Ulceration of the skin can be caused by chromic acid as well as chromates and dichromates, this occurring mainly on hands and forearms owing to direct contact. It is a form of non-infective dermatitis and workers particularly at risk are those involved with metallic chromium in alloy formation, chromium plating and anodising as well as work with sensitisers in photography and dyestuff manufacture. Chromium poisoning is prescribed disease D 5.

(d) *Benzene.* Effectively prohibited from use in industry (see 9.34 DANGEROUS SUBSTANCES I) and replaced by toluene, benzene is potentially carcinogenic. Toluene and xylene are much less toxic. The effects of benzene poisoning can be serious, resulting in headache, vertigo, anaemia and even leukaemia. Benzene poisoning is prescribed disease C 7.

(e) *Chlorinated hydrocarbons.* Trichlorethylene, carbon tetrachloride, tetrachloroethane, methyl chloride, methyl bromide and perchlorethylene are all solvents, some more toxic than others. Tetrachloroethane vapour is highly toxic and exposure can have serious consequences, if not fatal. Use should, therefore, be restricted to well-ventilated areas. Poisoning affects the central nervous system and liver as well as producing delirium and oedema. Poisoning by tetrachloroethane is prescribed disease C 10.

Methyl bromide, an insecticide and fumigant, is a highly volatile liquid at a temperature above 4.5°C. Poisoning has tended to be associated with leakage from pipework and storage vessels in a variety of industries. Symptoms of poisoning typically include headache, vomiting, watering of the eyes, blurred and double vision. Methyl bromide poisoning is prescribed disease C 12.

(f) *Isocyanates.* Isocyanates are widely used throughout industry, mainly in the production of urethane foams and resins. The principal hazard arises from vapour evolved during foam manufacture. Some isocyanates also take powdered form, e.g. napthalene di-isocyanate, thereby producing a dust hazard. Workers particularly at risk are those in the furniture industry and involved with spraying urethane foams. Symptoms typically include dermatitis and asthma. Asthma due to exposure to isocyanate is prescribed disease D 7.

(D) Ergonomic causes

31.35 Ergonomic causes denote conditions associated with the nature of the job or work, and, in consequence, many ergonomic conditions arise from repetitive movements performed of necessity in the course of the job. The principal ergonomic conditions are cramp, beat hand, beat knee and beat elbow.

(a) *Cramp.* Known sometimes as writer's cramp, cramp arises from the performance of a regular act involving repeated muscular action. Eventually muscular fatigue takes over, making impossible performance of repetitive movements. Cramp is prescribed disease A 4. Writers and typists are mainly at risk.

(b) *Beat hand.* Beat hand occurs in consequence of damage to the skin and underlying tissues caused by manual labour, often following constant jarring of the hand, say, in the use of a pneumatic drill or pick and shovel etc. The friction and pressure of manual labour causes dirt and particles to lodge in the skin. Symptoms typically include acute inflammation in the palm of the hand accompanied by broken skin and pus release. Recovery depends largely on severity. Beat hand is prescribed disease A 5.

(c) *Beat knee.* Beat knee occurs in workers whose job involves frequent kneeling, e.g. carpet fitters. Infection of the skin may be followed by bursitis of the knee and enlargement of the knee joint. Normally the condition gives rise to incapacity for a few weeks. Beat knee is prescribed disease A 6.

(*d*) *Beat elbow.* Sometimes referred to as golfer's or tennis elbow, beat elbow occurs mainly in manual workers. Assembly line workers are particularly vulnerable. Typical symptoms include acute inflammation, with a swollen and painful elbow, and swelling spreading down the back to the forearm. Incapacity is similar to that for other beat conditions. Beat elbow is prescribed disease A 7.

Stress

31.36   Stress-induced and related conditions are responsible for more work absenteeism than any other single cause (assuming alcoholism – also stress-related – is included). Although predominantly and more severely afflicting executives and senior management, all echelons of workers are vulnerable in all industries. Not all stress, however, is bad. Indeed, some level of stress (or arousal) is good, producing positive results, e.g. salesman of the year competition. However, much occupational stress is negative, sometimes leading to incapacity and subsequent illness. Stress is not a prescribed occupational disease (perhaps for obvious reasons) nor, generally, have actions for damages against employers succeeded on this ground alone, no matter how compelling, though recently a fireman who suffered chronic post-traumatic stress, following attendance at the King's Cross fire in 1987, was awarded £147,000 (*Hale v London Underground Ltd, The Times, 5 November 1992*) (see further 19.43(*d*) FIRE AND FIRE PRECAUTIONS). Indeed, conceivably, stress could emerge as the leading occupational hazard.

Definition and aetiology

31.37   *Definition.* Stress may be defined in terms of the psychological, physiological and behavioural response on the part of a person to a situation where he is unable to cope with demands imposed upon him, leading eventually to incapacity and illness. Stress also has organisational facets indicative of faultlines within a company.

Aetiology. Some occupations are more stressful than others, for example, acting, advertising, broadcasting, civil aviation, construction, journalism, mining, personnel, the police service and prison duties; safety practitioners and social workers are particularly vulnerable. Conversely, accountancy, the law, book-writing, the Civil Service, the Church, horticulture and insurance and librarianship are less stressful.

Environmental factors

31.38   The principal environmental stressors are heat, cold, lighting, noise, humidity, darkness, dust/fibres, visual display units, static electricity, poor ventilation, atmospheric pollution, passive smoking, noxious chemicals and ergonomic 'indiscretions', such as uncomfortable chairs and inaccessible windows. Less obviously perhaps, nature of employment can cause stress, which may arise from work overload or underload; danger at work, either intrinsic or the result of a faulty system; introduction of new technology and its uncertainties; deadlines; monotonous and repetitive work or processes; working alone or in isolation or in a high crime risk area or industry; excessive travel and jet lag; working with uncooperative or unsympathetic colleagues. To date, deadlines and time pressures (including travel pressures) are the main causes of executive stress, followed closely by work overload or underload, or a combination of overload and underload (e.g. pilot, ambulance driver).

Organisational factors

31.39   Structure, culture and climate of an organisation may undermine individual motivation, in that interesting brain-jerking work may not be delegated, and employees do not participate in decision-making affecting them. This lack of influence will quickly result in antipathy and then apathy. Similarly, in times of change and flux, when senior management might expect support from all echelons, earlier identifiable hiatuses in communication and decision-making, resulting in low workforce morale, often continue to pervade. A climate of takeovers and buyouts, not untypical of the late 80s, is an ideal stress incubator.

Moreover, it is often quite impossible to divorce home and work situations. This combination of circumstances often results in the severest cases of stress, e.g. workers having to cope with a sudden redundancy simultaneously with a divorce or death of a member of the family or close relative. For this reason, redundancies and relocations can be particularly sensitive. Equally demoralising are racial and sexual harrassment at work, particularly in combination with personal factors, e.g. pregnancy, marital separation. The age of an employee is also important, as older employees tend to nurture greater worries about redundancy, compulsory early retirement, job security and demotion. Indeed, redundancy and job insecurity are the main causes of mid-life crisis. Wherever possible, therefore, companies should provide outplacement counselling and retraining facilities.

Role in organisation

31.40   The role of an employee in a corporate structure is also linked to stress – or rather, absence or ambiguity of role, especially the more senior the employee. In this context, employees/managers responsible for machines are less likely to be victims of stress than those responsible for people. Role demand subdivides into categories of role ambiguity and role conflict. Role ambiguity can be alleviated, particularly in the case of new staff unsure of what is expected of them, by induction training, clarifying relationships between peers, managers, supervisors etc. Again takeovers and buyouts pose role ambiguity problems. Role conflict is characterised by different expectations, coming from different directions, demanded of an employee, or emanating from a value system that is at variance with that of other employees, both resulting often in work overload (or sometimes underload).

Both role ambiguity and role conflict can (and not infrequently do) lead to interpersonal stress between peers and superiors. Again, induction training and regular grievance forums can identify, if not alleviate such problems. Telltale signs of role ambiguity and role conflict are hostility, angry tone, finger-wagging and aggressive body language. Stress-reducing change, democratically introduced, is often elusive, as more senior staff may well feel threatened. Interpersonal stress is also caused in many cases by the effect of behavioural traits and foibles, the latter often typified by

—   highly competitive attitude

—   quest for recognition or attention

—   impatience

—   superciliousness

—   quick talking, fast driving, fast eating and drinking

—   workaholic indifference to outside extracurricular influences.

One to one counselling and training can both help to identify and control such stressors.

Symptoms

31.41   As with causes, so the symptoms manifested by stress are (*a*) psychological, e.g. depression, anxiety, guilt, fear, indecision, lack of enthusiasm, apathy; (*b*) physiological, e.g. muscle tension, palpitations, nausea, high blood pressure, ulcers, skin disorders, allergies, excessive perspiration, rapid loss of weight; (*c*) behavioural, e.g. proneness to accidents and injuries, alcohol and drug abuse, aggressiveness, absenteeism, insomnia, restlessness; (*d*) organisational, e.g. low staff morale, health and injury claims, increased incidence of accidents and injuries, high rate of absenteeism, high staff turnover, low efficiency, poor quality control.

Current list of prescribed occupational diseases

31.42   The current list of prescribed occupational diseases is contained in the *Social Security (Industrial Injuries) (Prescribed Diseases) Regulations 1985 (SI 1985 No 967)* (the main regulations), the *Social Security (Industrial Injuries) (Prescribed Diseases) Amendment Regulations 1987 (SI 1987 No 335)*, the *Social Security (Industrial Injuries) (Prescribed Diseases) (Amendment No 2) Regulations 1987 (SI 1987 No 2112)*, the *Social Security (Industrial Diseases) (Prescribed Diseases) Amendment Regulations 1989 (SI 1989 No 1207)*, the *Social Security (Industrial Injuries) (Prescribed Diseases) Amendment Regulations 1990 (SI 1990 No 2269)*, the *Social Security (Industrial Injuries) (Prescribed Diseases) Amendment Regulations 1991 (SI 1991 No 1938)*, the *Social Security (Industrial Injuries) (Prescribed Diseases) Amendment Regulations 1993 (SI 1993 No 862)* and the *Social Security (Industrial Injuries) (Prescribed Diseases) Amendment (No 2) Regulations 1993 (SI 1993 No 1985)*. *Schedule 1* to the main regulations and occupations for which they are prescribed are reproduced in Table 27 below. Pneumoconiosis and the occupations for which it is prescribed are set out in *Schedule 2* to the main regulations and is also reproduced below.

The question whether a claimant is suffering from a prescribed disease is a diagnosis one, falling within the remit of the Medical Appeal Tribunal; the question whether a disease is prescribed is for the Adjudicating Officer, the Social Security Appeal Tribunal and the Commissioner. Where a claimant is suffering from a prescribed disease, it is open to the Adjudicating Officer to seek to show that the particular disease was not due to the nature of the claimant's employment (R(I) 4/91 – primary neoplasm C 23, invoking *Regulation 4* of the *Social Security (Industrial Injuries) (Prescribed Diseases) Regulations 1985*). In addition, a Medical Appeal Tribunal can decide disablement issues (R(I) 2/91 – disablement assessed at 7% in respect of vibration white finger, A 11).

Moreover, medical practitioners and specially qualified medical practitioners can now adjudicate upon matters relating to industrial injuries and prescribed diseases (hitherto the exclusive province of medical boards or special medical boards). [*Social Security (Industrial Injuries and Adjudication) Regulations 1993 (SI 1993 No 861; Social Security (Industrial Injuries) (Prescribed Diseases) Amendment (No 2) Regulations 1993 (SI 1993 No 1985)*].

Table 27
Current list of prescribed occupational diseases

Prescribed disease or injury	Occupation
A. *Conditions due to physical agents*	Any occupation involving:
1. Inflammation, ulceration or malignant disease of the skin or subcutaneous tissues or of the bones, or blood dyscrasia, or cataract, due to electro-magnetic radiations (other than radiant heat), or to ionising particles.	Exposure to electro-magnetic radiations (other than radiant heat) or to ionising particles.
2. Heat cataract.	Frequent or prolonged exposure to rays from molten or red-hot material.
3. Dysbarism, including decompression sickness, barotrauma and osteonecrosis.	Subjection to compressed or rarified air or other respirable gases or gaseous mixtures.
4. Cramp of the hand or forearm due to repetitive movements.	Prolonged periods of handwriting, typing or other repetitive movements of the fingers, hand or arm.
5. Subcutaneous cellulitis of the hand (Beat hand).	Manual labour causing severe or prolonged friction or pressure on the hand.
6. Bursitis or subcutaneous cellulitis arising at or about the knee due to severe or prolonged external friction or pressure at or about the knee (Beat knee).	Manual labour causing severe or prolonged external friction or pressure at or about the knee.
7. Bursitis or subcutaneous cellulitis arising at or about the elbow due to severe or prolonged external friction or pressure at or about the elbow (Beat elbow).	Manual labour causing severe or prolonged external friction or pressure at or about the elbow.
8. Traumatic inflammation of the tendons of the hand or forearm, or of the associated tendon sheaths.	Manual labour, or frequent or repeated movements of the hand or wrist.
9. Miner's nystagmus.	Work in or about a mine.
10. Substantial sensorineural hearing loss amounting to at least 50dB in each ear, being due in the case of at least one ear to occupational noise, and being the average of pure tone loss measured by audiometry over the 1, 2 and 3 kHz frequencies (occupational deafness).	(*a*) The use of, or work wholly or mainly in the immediate vicinity of, pneumatic percussive tools or high-speed grinding tools, in the cleaning, dressing or finishing of cast *metal* or of ingots, billets or blooms (but not stone/concrete used in road/railway construction [*Social Security Amendment Regulations 1990, SI 1990 No 2269*]); or

Any occupation involving:

(*b*) the use of, or work wholly or mainly in the immediate vicinity of, pneumatic percussive tools on metal in the shipbuilding or ship repairing industries; or

(*c*) the use of, or work in the immediate vicinity of, pneumatic percussive tools on metal, or for drilling rock in quarries or underground, or in mining coal, for at least an average of one hour per working day; or

(*d*) work wholly or mainly in the immediate vicinity of drop-forging plant (including plant for drop-stamping or drop-hammering) or forging press plant engaged in the shaping of metal; or

(*e*) work wholly or mainly in rooms or sheds where there are machines engaged in weaving man-made or natural (including mineral) fibres or in the bulking up of fibres in textile manufacturing; or

(*f*) the use of, or work wholly or mainly in the immediate vicinity of, machines engaged in cutting, shaping or cleaning metal nails; or

(*g*) the use of, or work wholly or mainly in the immediate vicinity of, plasma spray guns engaged in the deposition of metal; or

(*h*) the use of, or work wholly or mainly in the immediate vicinity of, any of the following machines engaged in the working of wood or material composed partly of wood, that is to say; multi-cutter moulding machines, planing machines, automatic or semi-automatic lathes, multiple cross-cut machines, automatic shaping machines, double-end tenoning machines, vertical spindle moulding machines (including high-speed routing machines), edge banding machines, bandsawing machines with a blade width of not less than 73 millimetres and circular sawing machines in the operation of which the blade is moved towards the material being cut; or

(*i*) the use of chain saws in forestry.

11. Episodic blanching, occurring throughout the year, affecting the middle or proximal phalanges or in the case of a thumb the proximal phalanx, of –
    (*a*) in the case of a person with 5 fingers (including thumb) on one hand, any 3 of those fingers, or
    (*b*) in the case of a person with only 4 such fingers, any 2 of those fingers, or
    (*c*) in the case of a person with less than 4 such fingers, any one of those fingers or, as the case may be, the one remaining finger (vibration white finger).

Any occupation involving:
    (*a*) The use of hand-held chain saws in forestry; or
    (*b*) the use of hand-held rotary tools in grinding or in the sanding or polishing of metal, or the holding of material being ground, or metal being sanded or polished, by rotary tools; or
    (*c*) the use of percussive metal-working tools, or the holding of metal being worked upon by percussive tools, in riveting, caulking, chipping, hammering, fettling or swaging; or
    (*d*) the use of hand-held powered percussive drills or hand-held powered percussive hammers in mining, quarrying, demolition, or on roads or footpaths, including road construction; or
    (*e*) the holding of material being worked upon by pounding machines in shoe manufacture.

12. Carpal tunnel syndrome.

Use of hand-held vibrating tools.

B. *Conditions due to biological agents*

Any occupation involving:

1. Anthrax.

Contact with animals infected with anthrax or the handling (including the loading or unloading or transport) of animal products or residues.

2. Glanders.

Contact with equine animals or their carcases.

3. Infection by leptospira. (See below*)

    (*a*) Work in places which are, or are liable to be, infested by rats, field mice or voles, or other small mammals; or
    (*b*) work at dog kennels or the care or handling of dogs; or
    (*c*) contact with bovine animals or their meat products or pigs or their meat products.

4. Ankylostomiasis.

Work in or about a mine.

5. Tuberculosis.

Contact with a source of tuberculosis infection.

6. Extrinsic allergic alveolitis (including farmer's lung).

Exposure to moulds or fungal spores or heterologous proteins by reason of employment in:
    (*a*) agriculture, horticulture, forestry, cultivation of edible fungi or maltworking; or

	Any occupation involving: (*b*) loading or unloading or handling in storage mouldy vegetable matter or edible fungi; or (*c*) caring for or handling birds; or (*d*) handling bagasse.
7. Infection by organisms of the genus brucella.	Contact with – (*a*) animals infected by brucella, or their carcases or parts thereof, or their untreated products; or (*b*) laboratory specimens or vaccines of, or containing, brucella.
8. Viral hepatitis.	Close and frequent contact with – (*a*) human blood or human blood products; or (*b*) a source of viral hepatitis.
9. Infection by *Streptococcus suis*.	Contact with pigs infected by *Streptococcus suis*, or with the carcases, products or residues of pigs so infected.
10. (*a*) Avian chlamydiosis	Contact with birds infected with chlamydia psittaci, or with the remains or untreated products of such birds.
(*b*) Ovine chlamydiosis.	Contact with sheep infected with chlamydia psittaci, or with the remains or untreated products of such sheep.
11. Q fever.	Contact with animals, their remains or their untreated products.
12. Orf.	Contact with sheep, goats or with the carcases of sheep or goats.
13. Hydatidosis.	Contact with dogs.

* (This can also give rise to liability at common law, where an employer fails to set up a system for killing off rats, or, alternatively fails to instruct employees to take proper precautions by washing their hands frequently (*Campbell v Percy Bilton Ltd (1988) (unreported)*).)

C. *Conditions due to chemical agents*	Any occupation involving:
1. Poisoning by lead or a compound of lead.	The use or handling of, or exposure to the fumes, dust or vapour of, lead or a compound of lead, or a substance containing lead.
2. Poisoning by manganese or a compound of manganese.	The use or handling of, or exposure to the fumes, dust or vapour of, manganese or a compound of manganese, or a substance containing manganese.

	Any occupation involving:
3. Poisoning by phosphorus or an inorganic compound or phosphorus or poisoning due to the anticholinesterase or pseudo anticholinesterase action of organic phosphorus compounds.	The use or handling of, or exposure to the fumes, dust or vapour of, phosphorus or a compound of phosphorus, or a substance containing phosphorus.
4. Poisoning by arsenic or a compound of arsenic.	The use or handling of, or exposure to the fumes, dust or vapour of, arsenic or a compound of arsenic, or a substance containing arsenic.
5. Poisoning by mercury or a compound of mercury.	The use or handling of, or exposure to the fumes, dust or vapour of, mercury or a compound of mercury, or a substance containing mercury.
6. Poisoning by carbon bisulphide.	The use or handling of, or exposure to the fumes or vapour of, carbon bisulphide or a compound of carbon bisulphide, or a substance containing carbon bisulphide.
7. Poisoning by benzene or a homologue of benzene.	The use or handling of, or exposure to the fumes of, or vapour containing benzene or any of its homologues.
8. Poisoning by nitro- or amino- or chloro- derivative of benzene or of a homologue of benzene, or poisoning by nitrochlorbenzene.	The use or handling of, or exposure to the fumes of, or vapour containing a nitro- or amino- or chloro- derivative of benzene, or of a homologue of benzene, or nitrochlorbenzene.
9. Poisoning by dinitrophenol or a homologue of dinitrophenol or by substituted dinitrophenols or by the salts of such substances.	The use or handling of, or exposure to the fumes of, or vapour containing, dinitrophenol or a homologue or substituted dinitrophenols or the salts of such substances.
10. Poisoning by tetrachloroethane.	The use or handling of, or exposure to the fumes of, or vapour containing, tetrachloroethane.
11. Poisoning by diethylene dioxide (dioxan).	The use or handling of, or exposure to the fumes of, or vapour containing, diethylene dioxide (dioxan).
12. Poisoning by methyl bromide.	The use or handling of, or exposure to the fumes of, or vapour containing, methyl bromide.
13. Poisoning by chlorinated naphthalene.	The use or handling of, or exposure to the fumes of, or dust or vapour containing, chlorinated naphthalene.
14. Poisoning by nickel carbonyl.	Exposure to nickel carbonyl gas.
15. Poisoning by oxides of nitrogen.	Exposure to oxides of nitrogen.

	Any occupation involving:
16. Poisoning by gonioma kamassi (African boxwood).	The manipulation of gonioma kamassi or any process in or incidental to the manufacture of articles therefrom.
17. Poisoning by beryllium or a compound of beryllium.	The use or handling of, or exposure to the fumes of, or dust or vapour of, beryllium or a compound of beryllium, or a substance containing beryllium.
18. Poisoning by cadmium.	Exposure to cadmium dust or fumes.
19. Poisoning by acrylamide monomer.	The use or handling of, or exposure to, acrylamide monomer.
20. Dystrophy of the cornea (including ulceration of the corneal surface) of the eye.	(*a*) The use or handling of, or exposure to, arsenic, tar, pitch, bitumen, mineral oil (including paraffin), soot or any compound, product or residue of any of these substances, except quinone or hydroquinone; or (*b*) exposure to quinone or hydroquinone during their manufacture.
21. (*a*) Localised new growth of the skin, papillomatous or keratotic; (*b*) squamous-celled carcinoma of the skin.	The use or handling of, or exposure to, arsenic, tar, pitch, bitumen, mineral oil (including paraffin), soot or any compound, product or residue of any of these substances, except quinone or hydroquinone.
22. (*a*) Carcinoma of the mucous membrane of the nose or associated air sinuses; (*b*) primary carcinoma of a bronchus or of a lung.	Work in a factory where nickel is produced by decomposition of a gaseous nickel compound which necessitates working in or about a building or buildings where that process or any other industrial process ancillary or incidental thereto is carried on.
23. Primary neoplasm (including papilloma, carcinoma-in-situ and invasive carcinoma) of the epithelial lining of the urinary tract (renal pelvis, ureter, bladder and urethra).	(*a*) Work in a building in which any of the following substances is produced for commercial purposes: (i) alpha-naphthylamine, beta-naphthylamine or methyl-ene-bis-orthochloroaniline; (ii) diphenyl substituted by at least one nitro or primary amino group or by at least one nitro and primary amino group (including benzidine); (iii) any of the substances mentioned in sub-paragraph (ii) above if further ring substituted by halogeno, methyl or methoxy groups, but not by other groups; (iv) the salts of any of the substances mentioned in sub-paragraphs (i) to (iii) above;

	Any occupation involving:
	(v) auramine or magenta; or
	(*b*) the use or handling of any of the substances mentioned in sub-paragraph (*a*) (i) to (iv), or work in a process in which any such substance is used, handled or liberated; or
	(*c*) the maintenance or cleaning of any plant or machinery used in any such process as is mentioned in sub-paragraph (*b*), or the cleaning of clothing used in any such building as is mentioned in sub-paragraph (*a*) if such clothing is cleaned within the works of which the building forms a part or in a laundry maintained and used solely in connection with such works; or
	(*d*) Soderberg aluminium smelting process. [*SI 1993 No 862*].
24. (*a*) Angiosarcoma of the liver; (*b*) osteolysis of the terminal phalanges of the fingers; (*c*) non-cirrhotic portal fibrosis.	(*a*) Work in or about machinery or apparatus used for the polymerization of vinyl chloride monomer, a process which, for the purposes of this provision, comprises all operations up to and including the drying of the slurry produced by the polymerization and the packaging of the dried product; or (*b*) work in a building or structure in which any part of that process takes place.
25. Occupational vitiligo.	The use or handling of, or exposure to, para-tertiary-butylphenol, para-tertiary-butylcatechol, para-amyl-phenol, hydroquinone or the monobenzyl or monobutyl ether of hydroquinone.
26. Damage to the liver or kidneys due to exposure to carbon tetrachloride.	Use of or handling of or exposure to the fumes of, or vapour containing carbon tetrachloride.
27. Damage to the liver or kidneys due to exposure to trichloromethane (chloroform).	Use of or handling of or exposure to fumes of or vapour containing trichloromethane (chloroform).
28. Central nervous system dysfunction and associated gastro-intestinal disorders due to exposure to chloromethane (methyl chloride).	Use of or handling of or exposure to fumes or vapours containing chloromethane (methyl chloride).

	Any occupation involving:
29. Peripheral neuropathy due to exposure to n-hexane or methyl n-butyl ketone.	Use of or handling of or exposure to the fumes of or vapours containing n-hexane or methyl n-butyl ketone.

D. *Miscellaneous Conditions*

1. Pneumoconiosis.

Any occupation involving –

(*a*) the mining, quarrying or working of silica rock or the working of dried quartzose sand or any dry deposit or dry residue of silica or any dry admixture containing such materials (including any occupation in which any of the aforesaid operations are carried out incidentally to the mining or quarrying of other minerals or to the manufacture of articles containing crushed or ground silica rock);

(*b*) the handling of any of the materials specified in the foregoing subparagraph in or incidental to any of the operations mentioned therein, or substantial exposure to the dust arising from such operations.

Any occupation involving the breaking, crushing or grinding of flint or the working or handling of broken, crushed or ground flint or materials containing such flint, or substantial exposure to the dust arising from any of such operations.

Any occupation involving sand blasting by means of compressed air with the use of quartzose sand or crushed silica rock or flint, or substantial exposure to the dust arising from sand and blasting.

Any occupation involving work in a foundry or the performance of, or substantial exposure to the dust arising from, any of the following operations:

(*a*) the freeing of steel castings from adherent siliceous substance;

(*b*) the freeing of metal castings from adherent siliceous substance–

   (i) by blasting with an abrasive propelled by compressed air, by steam or by a wheel; or

   (ii) by the use of power-driven tools.

	Any occupation in or incidental to the manufacture of china or earthenware (including sanitary earthenware, electrical earthenware and earthenware tiles), and any occupation involving substantial exposure to the dust arising therefrom.
	Any occupation involving the grinding of mineral graphite, or substantial exposure to the dust arising from such grinding.
	Any occupation involving the dressing of granite or any igneous rock by masons or the crushing of such materials, or substantial exposure to the dust arising from such operations.
	Any occupation involving the use, or preparation for use, of a grindstone, or substantial exposure to the dust arising therefrom.
	Any occupation involving– (*a*) the working or handling of asbestos or any admixture of asbestos; (*b*) the manufacture or repair of asbestos textiles or other articles containing or composed of asbestos; (*c*) the cleaning of any machinery or plant used in any foregoing operations and of any chambers, fixtures and appliances for the collection of asbestos dust; (*d*) substantial exposure to the dust arising from any of the foregoing operations.
	Any occupation involving– (*a*) work underground in any mine in which one of the objects of the mining operations is the getting of any mineral; (*b*) the working or handling above ground at any coal or tin mine of any minerals extracted therefrom, or any operation incidental thereto; (*c*) the trimming of coal in any ship, barge, or lighter, or in any dock or harbour or at any wharf or quay; (*d*) the sawing, splitting or dressing of slate, or any operation incidental thereto.
	Any occupation in or incidental to the manufacture of carbon electrodes by an industrial undertaking for use in the electrolytic extraction of aluminium from aluminium oxide, and any occupation involving substantial exposure to the dust arising therefrom.

	Any occupation involving boiler scaling or substantial exposure to the dust arising therefrom.
	[*Social Security (Industrial Injuries) (Prescribed Diseases) Regulations 1985 (SI 1985 No 967), 1 Sch, Part II*].
	Any occupation involving:
2. Byssinosis.	Work in any room where any process up to and including the weaving process is performed in a factory in which the spinning or manipulation of raw or waste cotton or of flax, or the weaving of cotton or flax, is carried on.
3. Diffuse mesothelioma (primary neoplasm of the mesothelium of the pleura or of the pericardium or of the peritoneum).	(*a*) The working or handling of asbestos or any admixture of asbestos; or (*b*) the manufacture or repair of asbestos textiles or other articles containing or composed of asbestos; or (*c*) the cleaning of any machinery or plant used in any of the foregoing operations and of any chambers, fixtures and appliances for the collection of asbestos dust; or (*d*) substantial exposure to the dust arising from any of the foregoing operations.
4. Inflammation or ulceration of the mucous membranes of the upper respiratory passages or mouth produced by dust, liquid or vapour.	Exposure to dust, liquid or vapour.
5. Non-infective dermatitis of external origin (including chrome ulceration of the skin but excluding dermatitis due to ionising particles or electro-magnetic radiations other than radiant heat).	Exposure to dust, liquid or vapour or any other external agent capable of irritating the skin (including friction or heat but excluding ionising particles or electro-magnetic radiations other than radiant heat).
6. Carcinoma of the nasal cavity or associated air sinuses (nasal carcinoma).	(*a*) Attendance for work in, on or about a building where wooden goods are manufactured or repaired; or (*b*) attendance for work in a building used for the manufacture of footwear or components of footwear made wholly or partly of leather or fibre board; or (*c*) attendance for work at a place used wholly or mainly for the repair of footwear made wholly or partly of leather or fibre board.

	Any occupation involving:
7. Asthma which is due to exposure to any of the following agents: (*a*) isocyanates; (*b*) platinum salts; (*c*) fumes or dusts arising from the manufacture, transport or use of hardening agents (including epoxy resin curing agents) based on phthalic anhydride, tetrachlorophthalic anhydride, trimellitic anhydride or triethylene-tetramine; (*d*) fumes arising from the use of rosin as a soldering flux; (*e*) proteolytic enzymes; (*f*) animals including insects and other anthropods used for the purposes of research or education or in laboratories; (*g*) dusts arising from the sowing, cultivation, harvesting, drying, handling, milling, transport or storage of barley, oats, rye, wheat or maize, or the handling, milling, transport or storage of meal or flour made therefrom; (*h*) antibiotics; (*i*) cimetidine; (*j*) wood dust; (*k*) ispaghula; (*l*) castor bean dust; (*m*) ipecacuanha; (*n*) azodicarbonamide; (*o*) animals including insects and other arthropods or their larval forms, used for the purposes of pest control or fruit cultivation, or the larval forms of animals used for the purposes of research, education or in laboratories; (*p*) glutaraldehyde; (*q*) persulphate salts or henna; (*r*) crustaceans or fish or products arising from these in the food processing industry; (*s*) reactive dyes; (*t*) soya bean; (*u*) tea dust; (*v*) green coffee bean dust; (*w*) fumes from stainless steel welding; (*x*) any other sensitising agent; (occupational asthma).	Exposure to any of the agents set out in column 1 of this paragraph.

Moreover, the time at which a person shall be treated as having developed prescribed diseases B.12 and B.13, or occupational asthma due to exposure to agents specified in D.7 (*o*) to (*x*), is the first day on which that person is incapable of work, or suffering from a loss of faculty as a result of those diseases after 25 September 1991.

8. Primary carcinoma of the lung where there is accompanying evidence of one or both of the following:
   (*a*) asbestosis;
   (*b*) bilateral diffuse pleural thickening.

Any occupation involving:
   (*a*) The working or handling of asbestos or any admixture of asbestos; or
   (*b*) the manufacture or repair of asbestos textiles or other articles containing or composed of asbestos; or
   (*c*) the cleaning of any machinery or plant used in any of the foregoing operations and of any chambers, fixtures and appliances for the collection of asbestos dust; or
   (*d*) substantial exposure to the dust arising from any of the foregoing operations.

9. Bilateral diffuse pleural thickening.

   (*a*) The working or handling of asbestos or any admixture of asbestos; or
   (*b*) the manufacture or repair of asbestos textiles or other articles containing or composed of asbestos; or
   (*c*) the cleaning of any machinery or plant used in any of the foregoing operations and of any chambers, fixtures and appliances for the collection of asbestos dust; or
   (*d*) substantial exposure to the dust arising from any of the foregoing operations.

10. Primary carcinoma of the lung.

    (*a*) Work underground in a tin mine; or
    (*b*) exposure to bis (chloromethyl) ether produced during the manufacture of chloromethyl methyl ether; or
    (*c*) exposure to pure zinc chromate, calcium chromate or strontium chromate.

11. Primary carcinoma of the lung with silicosis. (Presumed not to be recrudescent.) [*SI 1993 No 862, Reg 5*].

    Any occupation involving exposure to silica dust in the course of
    (*a*) manufacture of glass or pottery;
    (*b*) tunnelling in or quarrying sandstone or granite;
    (*c*) mining metal ores;
    (*d*) slate quarrying;
    (*e*) mining clay;
    (*f*) use of siliceous materials as abrasives;
    (*g*) cutting stone;
    (*h*) stonemasonry;
    (*j*) work in a factory.

	Any occupation involving:
12. Chronic bronchitis or emphysema (or both) (except where claimant is entitled to disablement benefit for pneumoconiosis, under *Reg 22(1)* – 'where a person is disabled by pneumoconiosis, or pneumoconiosis accompanied by tuberculosis – assessed at, at least, 50%, the effects of any emphysema and chronic bronchitis are to be treated as pneumoconiosis'). (In order to qualify for benefit a claimant must show (*a*) by means of a chest radiograph that he has coal dust retention to at least the level of Category 1 in the ILO's publication 'The Classification of Radiographs of Pneumoconioses' (Revised Edition 1980, 8th Impression 1992); (*b*) a forced expiratory volume in one second at least one litre below the mean value predicted in accordance with 'Lung function: Assessment and Application in Medicine' (Cotes, 4th Edition 1979) for a person of the claimant's age, height and sex, measured from the position of maximum inspiration with the claimant making maximum effort.)	Exposure to coal dust by reason of working underground in a coal mine for a period of, or periods amounting in the aggregate to, at least, 20 years (whether before or after 5 July 1948).

[*Social Security (Industrial Injuries) (Prescribed Diseases) Regulations 1985 (SI 1985 No 967), 1 Sch; Social Security (Industrial Injuries) (Prescribed Diseases) Amendment Regulations 1987 (SI 1987 No 335); Social Security (Industrial Injuries) (Prescribed Diseases) (Amendment No 2) Regulations 1987 (SI 1987 No 2112), Reg 2, Sch; Social Security (Industrial Injuries) (Prescribed Diseases) Amendment Regulations 1989 (SI 1989 No 1207), Reg 6, Sch; Social Security (Industrial Injuries) (Prescribed Diseases) Amendment Regulations 1990 (SI 1990 No 2269); Social Security (Industrial Injuries) (Prescribed Diseases) Amendment Regulations 1991 (SI 1991 No 1938); Social Security (Industrial Injuries) (Prescribed Diseases) Amendment Regulations 1993 (SI 1993 No 862); Social Security (Industrial Injuries) (Prescribed Diseases) Amendment (No 2) Regulations 1993 (SI 1993 No 1985)*].

Industrial Injuries Advisory Council (IIAC)

31.43   Inclusion of occupational diseases (of which there is no statutory definition), for the purposes of prescription under the *Social Security (Industrial Injuries) (Prescribed Diseases) Regulations 1985* etc., is the remit of the Industrial Injuries Advisory Council (IIAC), a body consisting of representation by the CBI, TUC and doctors, epidemiologists, toxicologists and lawyers.

Prescription can be a lengthy process. IIAC conducts a formal inquiry into a disease, following a recommendation from the research working group, calling evidence from relevant organisations/individuals. A report is then sent to the Secretary of State for Employment, who decides whether or not to publish it and whether the recommendations will be implemented. In order for a disease to be 'prescribed', it must be an *occupational risk*, as distinct from a 'risk common to all persons', and *attributable with reasonable certainty* to the nature of the occupation. Following a 1966 EC Recommendation, prescription may be more unfettered if, as seems possible, a system of individual proof is ushered in, whereby benefit would be paid wherever there was proof that a particular disease was caused by, and was a particular risk of an occupation (with the exception of certain common diseases). This has already happened in the case of occupational asthma, disablement benefit being payable where cause is attributable (*inter alia*) to 'any other sensitising agent inhaled at work' (see 31.30 above). Moreover, recently IIAC's recommendations have resulted in chronic bronchitis and emphysema both being prescribed for coal miners working underground for twenty years and lung cancer with silicosis in relation to workers exposed to silica dust from manufacture of glass/pottery, slate quarrying, mining clay etc.

Special cases of pneumoconiosis, byssinosis and diffuse mesothelioma

31.44   In the cases of (*a*) pneumoconiosis, (*b*) byssinosis and (*c*) diffuse mesothelioma, where an employee:

(*a*)   has been entitled to disablement benefit (whether or not it is actually being paid); and

(*b*)   is unable to recover damages against an employer (e.g. for breach of the *Factories Act 1961, s 4*, see Chapter 43 'Ventilation');

he is entitled to payment of a lump sum from the Secretary of State. [*Pneumoconiosis etc. (Workers' Compensation) Act 1979, s 1(1)*].

Furthermore, so long as no payment has been made to a deceased employee, payment can be made to a dependant of the deceased employee. [*Sec 1(2)*]. (See further Chapter 6 'Compensation for Work Injuries/Diseases'.) However, claimants are not entitled to disablement benefit for emphysema and chronic bronchitis (new prescribed disease D 12), if they are in receipt of benefit for pneumoconiosis, under the *Social Security (Industrial Injuries) (Prescribed Diseases) Regulations 1985* (see above).

Action against employer at common law for occupational diseases

31.45   As well as, or in lieu of statutory prescription, an employee can obtain damages for an occupational disease by suing his employer for negligence at common law. Thus, in recent years, employees have successfully sued employers at common law for

(*a*)   deafness – *Berry v Stone Manganese Marine Ltd [1972] 1 Lloyd's Rep 182*;

(*b*)   vibration-induced white finger – *McFaul v Garrington's Ltd [1985] HSIB 113*; and employers are 'on notice' of this as from 1 January 1971;

(*c*)   tenosynovitis (in the case of assembly workers) – *Burgess v Thorn Consumer Electronics Ltd (1983) HSIB 93*; carpal tunnel syndrome, if following on from tenosynovitis; and RSI – the recent *BT* case. This is particularly true where no improvements have been introduced by employers after complaints have been lodged – *Pepall & Ors v Thorn Consumers Electronics Ltd (1985, Queen's*

Bench Division, Law Society's Gazette, 9 January 1991): 'Where defendants did fall down on the duty which they owed to their employees to exercise reasonable care for their safety . . . was because the steps which ought to have been taken to combat the risk of tenosynovitis required a relatively sophisticated programme of educating and warning employees. . . . The problems needed consideration and implementation by management at a high level' (per Woolf J). Though in the more recent case of *Whitnall v Culrose Foods, Packaging Week, 20 June 1990*, where the employee's duties were to clean, label and pack 6oz to 12lb food cans, which involved repeatedly lifting and turning the cans, Judge J dismissed her claim for damages, on the ground that she had been negligent in failing to describe her condition to her employers;

but not

(*d*)   'anxiety' – *Fraser v Secretary of State for Social Services 1986 SLT 386.*

fig. 15

COMPANY PRE-EMPLOYMENT HEALTH SCREENING QUESTIONNAIRE

Surname _____   Unit _____

Forenames _____   Position Applied For _____

Date of Birth _____

SECTION A

Please tick if you are at present suffering from, or have suffered from:

Serious injury	Recurring stomach trouble	Back trouble
Serious operations	Recurring bowel trouble	Muscle or joint trouble
Giddiness	Stroke	Defective vision (not
Fainting attacks	Heart trouble	corrected by glasses
Epilepsy	High blood pressure	or contact lenses)
Fits or blackouts	Varicose veins	Defective colour vision
Mental illness	Severe hay fever	Diabetes
Anxiety or depression	Asthma	
	Recurring chest disease	Skin trouble
Recurring headaches	Recurring bladder trouble	Eye trouble
Hernia/rupture	Ear trouble or deafness	

SECTION B

Please tick if you have any disabilities that affect:

Standing	Lifting	Working at heights
Walking	Use of your hands	Climbing ladders
Climbing stairs	Driving a motor vehicle	Work on staging

SECTION C

How many working days have you lost during the last three years, due to illness or injury?   None/_____days

Are you at present having any medicine, injections, tablets or other treatment prescribed by a doctor?   YES/NO

Are you a Registered Disabled Person?   YES/NO

To the best of my knowledge the replies to the above questions are accurate. I accept that failure to disclose information or giving false information could lead to employment being terminated.

Signed_____Employee _____ Date _____ Manager

Chapter 32

Occupiers' Liability

Introduction

32.1   Inevitably, by far the greater part of this book details the duties of employers (and employees) both at common law and in the *Factories Act 1961* and other kindred legislation. This notwithstanding, duties are additionally laid on persons (including companies and local authorities) who merely *occupy* premises which other persons either visit or carry out work activities upon, e.g. repair work or servicing. More particularly, persons in control of premises (see below for meaning of 'control'), that is, occupiers of premises and employers, where others work (*although not their employees*), have a duty under *HSWA s 4* to take reasonable care towards such persons working on the premises. Failure to comply with this duty can lead to prosecution and a fine on conviction (see further Chapter 17 'Enforcement'). This duty applies to premises not *exclusively* used for private residence, e.g. lifts/ electrical installations in the *common parts* of a block of flats, and exists for the benefit of workmen repairing/servicing them (*Westminster CC v Select Management Ltd [1985] 1 AER 897*). Moreover, a person who is injured while working on or visiting premises, may be able to sue the occupier for damages, even though the injured person is not an employee. Statute law relating to this branch of civil liability (i.e. occupiers' liability) is to be found in the *Occupiers' Liability Act 1957* (*OLA*) and, as far as trespassers are concerned, in the *Occupiers' Liability Act 1984*. (In Scotland, the law is to be found in the *Occupiers' Liability (Scotland) Act 1960*.)

The long title to the Act (*OLA*) explains that it was passed to amend common law rather than introduce new law. The common law gave protection to lawful visitors to premises, based on proof of negligence against the occupier, but the degree of protection depended on whether the visitor was an invitee or licensee – a distinction now obsolete. Now one 'common' duty is owed under *OLA* to all lawful visitors (as regards trespassers, see 32.8 below), i.e. a 'common duty of care'. Otherwise, the common law position is preserved. 'Occupation of premises is a ground of liability and is not a ground of exemption from liability. It is a ground of liability because it gives some control over and knowledge of the state of the premises, and it is natural and right that the occupier should have some degree of responsibility for the safety of persons entering his premises with his permission . . . there is a "proximity" between the occupier and such persons (i.e. visitors), and they are his "neighbours". Thus arises a duty of care . . .' (per Lord Gardner, LC in *Commissioner for Railways v McDermott [1967] 1 AC 169*).

Duties owed under the Occupiers' Liability Act

32.2   An occupier of premises owes the same duty, the 'common duty of care', to all his lawful visitors. [*OLA s 2(1)*]. 'The common duty of care is a duty to take such care as in all the circumstances of the case is reasonable to see that the visitor will be reasonably safe in using the premises for the purposes for which he is invited or permitted by the occupier to be there.' [*OLA s 2(2)*]. Thus, a local authority which failed, in severe winter weather, to see that a path in school grounds was swept free

of snow and treated with salt and was not in a slippery condition, was in breach of
Sec 2, when a schoolteacher fell at 8.30 am and was injured (*Murphy v Bradford
Metropolitan Council* [*1992*] *PIQR 68*).

Nature of the duty

32.3   *OLA* is concerned only with tortious liability (i.e. negligence). This is made clear in
Sec 1 (3) of the Act: 'The rules so enacted in relation to an occupier of premises and
his visitors shall also apply, in like manner and to like extent as the principles
applicable at common law to an occupier of premises and his invitees or licensees
would apply. . .'. This, then, is different, indeed the reverse of the *Factories Act
1961* and *HSWA*, in that those two Acts are predominantly penal measures
enforced by the HSE (or some other 'enforcing authority'). *OLA* is concerned only
with civil liability and action under it must be brought in a private suit between
parties. It cannot be enforced by a state agency nor does it give rise to criminal
liability. The *Factories Act 1961*, in contrast, is principally a criminal measure but
can give rise to ancillary civil liability. The relationship created by *OLA* is different
from and less immediate than that existing under the *Factories Act 1961* or *HSWA*.
The latter are mainly concerned with the employer/employee relationship,
whereas *OLA* is designed to regulate the duties of occupiers of premises to lawful
visitors to those premises. [*OLA s 1(1)*].

The liability of an occupier towards lawful visitors at common law was (generally)
based on negligence; so, too, is the liability under *OLA*. It is never strict. This is not
always true of the *Factories Act 1961* (e.g. *Secs 12, 13* and the first half of *Sec 28(1)*).
Although the relationship of occupier and visitor is less immediate than that of
employer and employee, and is not, as far as occupiers' liability is concerned,
underwritten by compulsory insurance (but by public liability insurance, which is
not obligatory but advisable), in some ways the scope of liability under *OLA* is
wider than that under, for example, the *Factories Act 1961*; for instance, *OLA*
confers a right of action regarding damage to property: 'The rules enacted . . .
shall apply . . . to regulate the obligation of a person occupying or having control
over any premises or structure in respect of damage to property, including the
property of persons who are not themselves his visitors'. [*OLA s 1(3)*]. Few sections
of the *Factories Act 1961* confer such a right, an exception occurring in the case of
the *Factories Act 1961, s 59(1)*: 'There shall be provided and maintained for the use
of employed persons adequate and suitable accommodation for clothing not worn
during working hours'. This section has been held to give a worker a right of action
against the factory occupier (*McCarthy v Daily Mirror Newspapers Ltd* [*1949*] *1 AER
801*) (remaining in force until 1 January 1996 or, in the case of new buildings, until
1 January 1993) (see 44.1 WELFARE FACILITIES).

Who is an 'occupier'?

32.4   'Occupation' is not defined in the Act, which merely states that the 'rules regulate
the nature of the duty imposed by law in consequence of a person's occupation or
control of premises . . . but they (shall) not alter the rules of the common law as to
the persons on whom a duty is so imposed or to whom it is owed . . .'. [*OLA s 1(2)*].
The meaning of 'occupation' must, therefore, be gleaned from the rules of
common law. Where premises, including factory premises, are leased or subleased,
control is probably shared by lessor and lessee or by sublessor and sublessee.
'Wherever a person has a sufficient degree of control over premises that he ought to
realise that any failure on his part to use care may result in injury to a person coming
lawfully there, then he is an "occupier" and the person coming lawfully there is his
"visitor" and the "occupier" is under a duty to his "visitor" to use reasonable care.

In order to be an occupier it is not necessary for a person to have entire control over the premises. He need not have exclusive occupation. Suffice it that he has some degree of control with others' (per Lord Denning in *Wheat v E Lacon & Co Ltd* [*1965*] *2 AER 700*). In *Jordan v Achara (1989) Current Law 311*, the plaintiff, who was a meter reader, was injured when he fell down stairs in a basement of a house. The defendant landlord, who was the owner of the house, had divided it into flats. Because of arrears of payment, the electricity supply had been disconnected. The local authority, having arranged for it to be reconnected for the tenants, recovered payment by way of rents paid directly to the authority. It was held that the landlord was liable for the injury, under the *Occupiers' Liability Act 1957*, since he was the occupier of the staircase and the passageway (where the injury occurred) and his duties continued in spite of the local authority being in receipt of rents.

Liability associated with dangers arising from maintenance and repair of premises will be that of the person responsible, under the lease or sublease, for maintenance and/or repair. 'The duty of the defendants here arose not out of contract, but because they, as the requisitioning authority, were in law in possession of the house and were in practice responsible for repairs . . . and this control imposed upon them a duty to every person lawfully on the premises to take reasonable care to prevent damage through want of repair' (per Denning LJ in *Greene v Chelsea BC* [*1954*] *2 AER 318*, concerning a defective ceiling which collapsed, injuring the appellant, a licensee). Significantly also, managerial control constitutes 'occupation' (*Wheat v Lacon*, see above, concerning an injury to a customer at a public house owned by a brewery and managed by a manager – both were held to be 'in control'). Moreover, if a landlord leases part of a building but retains other parts, e.g. roof, common staircase, lifts, he remains liable for that part of the premises (*Moloney v Lambeth BC (1966) 64 LGR 440*, concerning a guest injured on a defective common staircase in a block of council flats).

Premises

32.5   *OLA* regulates the nature of the duty imposed by law in consequence of a person's occupation of premises. [*Sec 1(2)*]. This means that the duties are not *personal* duties but depend on occupation of premises; and extend to a 'person occupying, or having control over, any fixed or moveable structure, including any vessel, vehicle or aircraft' [*Sec 1(3)(a)*] (e.g. a car, *Houweling v Wesseler* [*1963*] *40 DLR(2d) 956-Canada*). In *Bunker v Charles Brand & Son Ltd* [*1969*] *2 AER 59* the defendants were contractors digging a tunnel for the construction of the Victoria Line of London Underground. To this end they used a large digging machine which moved forward on rollers. The plaintiff was injured when he slipped on the rollers. The defendants were held to be occupiers of the tunnel, even though it was owned by London Transport.

To whom duty owed

Visitors

32.6   Visitors to premises entitled to protection under the Act are both (*a*) invitees and (*b*) licensees. In effect, this means that protection is afforded to all lawful visitors, whether the visitors enter for the occupier's benefit (clients or customers) or for their own benefit (factory inspectors, policemen), though not to persons exercising a public or private way over premises. [*OLA s 2(6)*]. Moreover, occupiers are under a duty to erect a notice warning visitors of the immediacy of a danger (*Rae v Mars (UK) Ltd (1989) CLJ 284* where a deep pit was situated very close to the entrance of a dark shed, in which there was no artificial lighting, into which a visiting surveyor fell, sustaining injury. It was held that the occupier should have erected a warning). However, there is no duty on an employer to light premises at night, which are infrequently used by day and not occupied at night. It is sufficient to provide a torch (*Capitano v Leeds Eastern Health Authority, CLJ, October 1989* where a security officer was injured when he fell down a flight of stairs at night, while checking the premises following the sounding of a burglar alarm. The steps were formerly part of a fire escape route but were now infrequently used).

Trespassers

32.7   ' . . . a trespasser is not necessarily a bad man. A burglar is a trespasser; but so too is a law-abiding citizen who unhindered strolls across an open field. The statement that a trespasser comes upon land at his own risk has been treated as applying to all who trespass, to those who come for nefarious purposes and those who merely bruise the grass, to those who know their presence is resented and those who have no reason to think so.' (*Commissioner for Railways (NSW) v Cardy* [*1961*] *ALR 16*).

Common law defines a trespasser as a person who:

(*a*)   goes onto premises without invitation or permission; or

(*b*)   although invited or permitted to be on premises, goes to a part of the premises to which the invitation or permission does not extend; or

(*c*)   remains on premises after the invitation or permission to be there has expired; or

(*d*)   deposits goods on premises when not authorised to do so.

Duty owed to trespassers

32.8   Common law used to be that an occupier was not liable for injury caused to a trespasser, unless the injury was either intentional or done with reckless disregard for the trespasser's presence (*R Addie & Sons (Collieries) Ltd v Dumbreck* [*1929*] *AC 358*). In more recent times, however, the common law has adopted an attitude of humane conscientiousness towards simple (as distinct from aggravated) trespassers. ' . . . the question whether an occupier is liable in respect of an accident to a trespasser on his land would depend on whether a conscientious, humane man with his knowledge, skill and resources could reasonably have been expected to have done, or refrained from doing, before the accident, something which would have avoided it. If he knew before the accident that there was a substantial probability that trespassers would come I think that most people would regard as culpable failure to give any thought to their safety.' (*Herrington v British Railways Board* [*1972*] *1 AER 749*). More recently still, the *Occupiers' Liability Act 1984* has imposed a duty on an occupier in respect of trespassers, that is persons whether they have 'lawful authority to be in the vicinity or not' who may be at risk of injury on his premises. [*Sec 1*]. The duty can be discharged by issuing a warning, e.g. posting notices warning of hazards; these, however, must be explicit and not merely vague. Thus, 'Fire Hazards' would not be sufficient, whereas, 'Highly Flammable Liquid Vapours – No Smoking' would be (see 32.14 below). Moreover, under the *OLA 1984* there is no duty to persons who willingly accept risks (see 32.15 below). However, the fact that an occupier has taken precautions to prevent persons going on his land, where there is a danger, does not mean that the occupier has reason to believe that someone would be likely to come into the vicinity of the danger, thereby owing a duty to the trespasser, under the *Occupiers' Liability Act 1984, s 1(4)* (*White v St Albans City and District Council, The Times, 12 March 1990*).

Children

32.9 'An occupier must be prepared for children to be less careful than adults.' [*OLA 1957, s 2(3)(a)*]. Where an adult would be regarded as a trespasser, a child is likely to qualify as an implied licensee, and this in spite of the stricture that 'it is hard to see how infantile temptations can give rights however much they excuse peccadilloes' (per Hamilton LJ in *Latham v Johnson & Nephew Ltd [1913] 1 KB 398*). If there is something or some state of affairs on the premises (e.g. machinery, a pond, bright berries, a motor car, forklift truck, scaffolding), this constitutes a 'trap' to a child. If the child is then injured by the 'trap', the occupier will often be liable. Though sometimes the presence of a parent may be treated as an implied condition of the permission to enter premises (e.g. when children go on to premises at dusk – *Phipps v Rochester Corporation [1955] 1 AER 129*). Perhaps the current common law position regarding 'child-trespass' was best put as follows: 'The doctrine that a trespasser, however innocent, enters land at his own risk, that in no circumstances is he owed a duty of reasonable or any care by the owners or occupiers of the land, however conscious they may be of the likelihood of his presence and of the grave risk of terrible injury to which he will probably be exposed, may have been all very well when rights of property, particularly in land, were regarded as more sacrosanct than any other human right. . . It is difficult to see why today this doctrine should not be buried' (per Salmon LJ in *Herrington v British Railways Board*, concerning a six-year-old boy electrocuted on the defendant's electrified line) (but see 32.15 below, *Titchener v British Railways Board*).

Dangers to guard against

32.10 The duty owed by an occupier to his lawful visitors is a 'common duty of care', so called since the duty is owed to both invitees and licensees, i.e. those having an interest in common with the occupier (e.g. business associates, customers, clients, salesmen) and those permitted by regulation/statute to be on the premises, e.g. factory inspectors/policemen. That duty requires that the dangers against which the occupier must guard are twofold: (*a*) structural defects in the premises; and (*b*) dangers associated with works/operations carried out for the occupier on the premises.

Structural defects

32.11 As regards structural defects in premises, the occupier will only be liable if either he actually knew of a defect or foreseeably had reason to believe that there was a defect in the premises. Simply put, the occupier would not incur liability for the existence of latent defects causing injury or damage, unless he had *special* knowledge in that regard, e.g. a faulty electrical circuit, unless he were an electrician; whereas, he would be liable for patent (i.e. obvious) structural defects, e.g. an unlit hole in the road. This duty now extends to 'uninvited entrants', e.g. trespassers, under *OLA 1984, s 1*.

Workmen on occupier's premises

32.12 'An occupier may expect that a person, in the exercise of his calling, will appreciate and guard against any special risks ordinarily incident to it, so far as the occupier leaves him free to do so.' [*OLA 1957, s 2(3) (b)*]. This means that risks associated with the system or method of work on third party premises are the responsibility of the employer not the occupier (*General Cleaning Contractors Ltd v Christmas [1952] 2 AER 1110*, concerning a window cleaner who failed to take proper precautions in respect of a defective sash window: it was held that there was no liability on the part of the occupier, but liability on the part of the employer (see Chapter 15 'Employers' Duties')). The occupier will only incur liability for a structural defect in premises which the oncoming workman would not normally guard against as part of a safe system of doing his job, i.e. against 'unusual' dangers. 'And with respect to such a visitor at least, we consider it settled law that he, using reasonable care on his part for his own safety, is entitled to expect that the occupier shall on his part use reasonable care to prevent damage from unusual danger, which he knows or ought to know' (per Willes J in *Indermaur v Dames* [*1866*] *LR 1 CB 276*, concerning a gasfitter testing gas burners in a sugar refinery who fell into an unfenced shaft and was injured).

Case law has highlighted some liability on the part of occupiers to a particular class of employees, namely firemen, possibly by virtue of absence of actions reported against the fire authority (see Chapter 19 'Fire and Fire Precautions') and against factory occupiers under the *Factories Act 1961* (see 32.17 below, *Flannigan v British Dyewood Co Ltd* [*1969*] *SLT 223*).

Although the law is not entirely settled (*Sibbald v Sher Bros, The Times, 1 February 1981*): 'It (is) . . . very unlikely that the duty of care owed by the occupier to workers was the same as that owed to firemen,' (per Lord Fraser of Tullybelton), (but) it is arguable that a 'fireman (is) a "neighbour" of the occupier in the sense of Lord Atkin's famous dictum in *Donoghue v Stevenson* [*1932*] *AC 562*, so that the occupier owes him some duty of care, as for instance, to warn firemen of an unexpected danger or trap of which he knew or ought to know' (per Waller LJ in *Hartley v British Railways Board, The Times, 2 February 1981*). One's neighbour was defined in law as follows: 'persons who are so closely and directly affected by my act that I ought reasonably to have them in contemplation as being so affected when I am directing my mind to the acts or omissions which are called in question' (per Lord Atkin in *Donoghue v Stevenson* [*1932*] *AC 562*).

In consequence, an occupier will probably be liable if he exposes a fireman to a risk of injury/death over and above normal risks associated with fire-fighting (e.g. failing to inform a fireman that premises were empty (*Hartley v British Railways Board* above) or failing to understand how switches controlling electricity worked (*Hartley v Mayoh* [*1953*] *2 AER 525*) or the occupier failing to extinguish a light under a chip fryer in a fish and chip shop (*Salmon v Seafarer Restaurants* [*1983*] *1 WLR 1264*)). (See further Chapter 19 'Fire and Fire Precautions'.)

Dangers associated with works being done on premises

32.13   Where work is being done on premises by a contractor, the occupier is not liable if he:

(*a*)   took care in selecting a competent contractor; and

(*b*)   satisfied himself that the work was being properly done by the contractor.

[*OLA s 2(4)(b)*].

As regards (*b*) it may be highly desirable (indeed necessary) for an occupier to delegate the 'duty of satisfaction', especially where complicated building/engineering operations are being carried out, to a specialist, e.g. an architect, geotechnical engineer. Not to do so, in the interests of safety of visitors, is probably negligent. 'In the case of the construction of a substantial building, or of a ship, I should have thought that the building owner, if he is to escape subsequent tortious liability for faulty construction, should not only take care to contract with a competent contractor . . . but also cause that work to be supervised by a properly qualified professional . . such as an architect or surveyor . . . I cannot think that different principles can apply to precautions during the course of construction, if the building owner is going to invite a third party to bring valuable property on to the site during construction' (per Mocatta J in *AMF International Ltd v Magnet Bowling Ltd* [*1968*] *2 AER 789*).

Waiver of duty and the Unfair Contract Terms Act 1977 (UCTA)

32.14 Where damage was caused to a visitor by a danger of which he had been warned by the occupier (e.g. by notice), an explicit notice, e.g. 'Highly Flammable Liquid Vapours – No Smoking' (as distinct from a vague notice such as 'Fire Hazards') used to absolve an occupier from liability. Now, however, such notices are ineffective (except in the case of trespassers, see 32.8 above) and do not exonerate occupiers. Thus: 'a person cannot by reference to any contract term or to a notice given to persons generally or to particular persons exclude or restrict his liability for death or personal injury resulting from negligence'. [*UCTA s 2*]. Such explicit notices are, however, a defence to an occupier when sued for negligent injury by a simple trespasser under the *Occupiers' Liability Act 1984*. As regards negligent damage to property, a person can restrict or exclude his liability by a notice or contract term, but such notice or contract term must be 'reasonable', and it is incumbent on the occupier to prove that it is in fact reasonable. [*UCTA ss 2(2), 11*].

Risks willingly accepted – 'volenti non fit injuria'

32.15 'The common duty of care does not impose on an occupier any obligation to a visitor in respect of risks willingly accepted as his by the visitor'. [*OLA s 2(5)*]. It has earlier been pointed out (see Chapter 15 'Employers' Duties') that this 'defence' has generally not succeeded in industrial injuries claims. This is similarly the case with occupiers' liability claims (*Burnett v British Waterways Board [1973] 2 AER 631* where a lighterman was held not to be bound by the terms of a notice erected by the respondent, even though he had seen it many times and understood it). This decision has since been reinforced by the *Unfair Contract Terms Act 1977*. 'Where a contract term or notice purports to exclude or restrict liability for negligence a person's agreement to or awareness of it is not of itself to be taken as indicating his voluntary acceptance of any risk.' [*UCTA s 2(3)*]. This is not, however, the position with respect to trespassers. *OLA 1984, s 1(6)* states, 'No duty is owed . . . to any person in respect of risks willingly accepted as his by that person . . .'. This applies even if the trespasser is a child (see 32.9 above) (*Titchener v British Railways Board (1984) SLT 192* where a 15-year-old girl and her boyfriend aged 16 had been struck by a train. The boy was killed and the girl suffered serious injuries. They had squeezed through a gap in a fence to cross the line as a short-cut to a disused brickworks which was regularly used. It was held by the House of Lords that the respondent did not owe a duty to the girl to do more than they had done to maintain the fence. It would have been 'quite unreasonable' for the respondent to maintain an impenetrable and unclimbable fence. But the 'duty (to maintain fences) will tend to be higher with a very young or a very old person than with a normally active and intelligent adult or adolescent' (per Lord Fraser)).

Actions against factory occupiers

32.16 As far as civil actions are concerned, it is generally advisable for injured workmen, visiting premises of a third party to carry out work in the factory, to bring an action under the *Factories Act 1961*, since breach of many of the provisions of this Act gives rise to an action for breach of statutory duty and, in a limited number of cases, the liability is strict and not based on negligence (though the breach must have caused the injury, see Chapter 15 'Employers' Duties'), e.g. *Sec 28(1)*, where the duty is strict (see further *Dexter v Tenby Electrical Accessories Ltd* at 2.9 ACCESS).

Persons other than employees and outside workforce

32.17 Certain persons lawfully visiting factories are not deemed to be 'working' there,

and so would not have the protection of the *Factories Act 1961*. Thus, the definition
of 'any person' in the *Factories Act 1961, s 29(1)*, would not normally apply to a
fireman acting in the course of his employment within a factory (*Flannigan v British
Dyewood Co Ltd (1969) SLT 223, affirmed in (1970) SLT 285*). The reason for this is
that the fireman is doing his own work inside the factory, unlike an employee of an
outside contractor working in the factory. Presumably, the same argument applies
in the case of a policeman or HSE inspector. In such cases, if injury were suffered
by a fireman, policeman, or HSE inspector, he would have to sue the occupier of
the factory under *OLA*. (The occupier might also be criminally liable in such a case
for breach of *HSWA s 3*, see Chapter 15 'Employers' Duties', but that provision
confers no right of civil action for breach of statutory duty. [*HSWA s 47*].)

Occupier's duties under HSWA

32.18   In addition to civil liabilities under the *Occupiers' Liability Act 1957* and at common
law, occupiers of buildings also have duties, the failure of which to carry out can
lead to criminal liability under *HSWA*. More particularly, 'each person who has, to
any extent, control of premises (i.e. "non-domestic" premises) or the means of
access thereto or egress therefrom or of any plant or substance in such premises'
must do what is reasonably practicable to see that the premises, means of access
and egress and plant/substances on the premises, are safe and without health risks.
[*HSWA s 4(2)*]. This section applies in the case of (*a*) non-employees and (*b*)
non-domestic premises. [*HSWA s 4(1)*]. In other words, it places health and safety
duties on persons and companies letting or sub-letting premises for work purposes,
even though the persons working in those premises are not employees of the
lessor/sublessor, e.g. a local authority hiring out factory units on an industrial
estate. As with most other forms of leasehold tenure, the person who is responsible
for maintenance and repairs of the leased premises is the person who has 'control'
(see, by way of analogy, 32.4 above). [*HSWA s 4(3)*]. Included as 'premises' are
common parts of a block of flats. These are 'non-domestic' premises (*Westminster
CC v Select Management Ltd* [*1985*] *1 AER 897* which held that being a 'place' or
'installation on land', such areas are 'premises'; and they are not 'domestic', since
they are in common use by the occupants of more than one private dwelling).

Moreover, the reasonableness of the measures which a person is required to take to
ensure the safety of those premises is to be determined in the light of his knowledge
of the expected use for which the premises have been made available and of the
extent of his control and knowledge, if any, of the use thereafter. More particularly,
if premises were not a reasonably foreseeable cause of danger to anyone acting in a
way a person might reasonably be expected to act, in circumstances that might
reasonably be expected to occur during the carrying out of the work, further
measures would not be required against unknown and unexpected events (*Mailer v
Austin Rover Group* [*1989*] *2 AER 1087* where an employee of a firm of cleaning
contractors, whilst cleaning one of the appellant's paint spray booths and the sump
underneath it, was killed by escaping fumes. The contractors had been instructed
by the appellants not to use paint thinners from a pipe in the booth (which the
appellants had turned off but not capped) and only to enter the sump (where the
ventilator would have been turned off) with an approved safety lamp and when no
one was working above. Contrary to those instructions, an employee used thinners
from the pipe, which had then entered the sump below, where the deceased was
working with a non-approved lamp, and an explosion occurred. It was held that the
appellant was not liable for breach of *HSWA s 4(2)*).

Chapter 33

Offices

Introduction

33.1   Just as specific duties in the *Factories Act 1961* (and regulations thereunder) are gradually being repealed and revoked, and replaced by the *Health and Safety at Work etc. Act 1974* and regulations passed under it (see further Chapter 18 'Factories and Workplaces'), so, too, plenary duties under the *Offices, Shops and Railway Premises Act 1963 (OSRPA)*, in relation to offices and shops (and railway premises), are also being replaced by common provisions for health, safety and welfare. More particularly, *OSRPA ss 4-16* (concerning *inter alia* cleanliness, overcrowding, temperature, ventilation, sanitary conveniences) has been replaced by the *Workplace (Health, Safety and Welfare) Regulations 1992 (SI 1992 No 3004)* as from 1 January 1993. These new regulations came into force in respect of buildings used as offices for the first time from 1 January 1993 whilst existing offices will not need to comply with the new regulations until 1 January 1996. Until then, plenary duties, regarding health, safety, hygiene and welfare, as specified in *OSRPA ss 4- 16*, will continue to apply to occupiers of existing offices, shops (and some railway premises) in single or multi-occupation. The *Health and Safety at Work etc. Act 1974* will continue to apply and all other provisions of *OSRPA*. The provisions included in this chapter which will be subject to repeal appear at 33.14–33.17 below.

This chapter examines the meaning of 'office premises', to which *OSRPA* still applies; the categories of persons on whom duties are imposed; defences to breach and certain special cases, such as Crown premises. In addition, on the practical side, there is consideration of typical hazards and accidents in offices. (Statutory requirements in relation to VDUs are dealt with in Chapter 27 'Lighting' and 'Shops' are covered in Chapter 40.)

Application of the general duties under the Health and Safety at Work Act

33.2   The general statutory duties laid on all employers by *HSWA s 2(1)(2)* to ensure the health, safety and welfare of their employees and, *inter alia*, to maintain a safe place of work, without risks to health, and to provide and maintain a working environment that is safe and without risks to health and adequate as regards welfare arrangements, apply to offices as well as other workplaces.

'Office premises' covered by OSRPA

33.3   *OSRPA* applies to virtually all 'office premises' so long as persons are employed there. The Act has no application if only self-employed persons work on the premises. 'The premises to which this Act applies are office premises . . . being . . . premises in the case of which persons are employed to work therein.' [*OSRPA s 1(1)*]. The employed person or persons must work in total a minimum of 21 hours each week in the premises. [*OSRPA s 3*]. This may be the position, even though the greater part of the working week is spent away from the office, as might be the case with commercial travellers, for example.

The provisions of *OSRPA* can apply to an office in a factory (provided that it is not itself part of the 'factory', see Chapter 18 'Factories and Workplaces'), as well as offices which form part of a building used for other purposes, e.g. schools, clubs or places of entertainment. Hotels are not covered by *OSRPA* (except for offices in them), but restaurants and bars, as well as restaurants and bars in hotels are subject to its provisions and HSE inspectors or local authority officials can enforce *OSRPA* in such places, and any other premises where food and/or drink is sold for immediate consumption by the public (see further Chapter 21 'Food and Food Hygiene' and Chapter 40 'Shops').

Meaning of 'office premises'

33.4   'Office premises' means a building, or part of a building, the sole or principal use of which is an office or for office purposes. [*Sec 1(2)(a)*]. Thus, where there is an office in a building used for purposes other than an office, it will be covered by the Act, though the rest of the building would not be covered (e.g. an office in a hospital or hotel). Moreover, the term 'building' for this purpose includes a mere structure. [*Sec 90(1)*]. Thus, a building would qualify as an office even though it were without furniture, furnishings and carpets, etc. The size of the building, or room in the building, is irrelevant for definition purposes. A lift motor room in a telephone exchange qualified as office premises (*Westwood v The Post Office [1974] AC 1*). Whether premises qualify as 'office premises' so as to invite application of the Act depends on whether they are used, solely or principally as an office *or for 'office purposes'*.

In *Oxfordshire CC v Chancellor, Masters and Scholars of Oxford University, The Times, 10 December 1980* the test as to whether a room was 'part of a building' and so 'office premises' for the purposes of *OSRPA s 1(2)(a)* was:

(*a*)   was the area sufficiently well defined (for office purposes)?

(*b*)   was it an area where people were employed? and

(*c*)   was the sole or principal use 'office premises'? (libraries).

'Office purposes'

33.5   'Office purposes' includes the following:

(*a*)   administration;

(*b*)   clerical work (see below);

(*c*)   handling money;

(*d*)   telephone and telegraph operating.

[*Sec 1(2)(b)*].

'Clerical work' includes:

(*a*)   writing;

(*b*)   book-keeping;

(*c*)   sorting papers;

(*d*)   filing;

(*e*)   typing;

(*f*) duplicating;

(*g*) machine calculations;

(*h*) drawing and the editorial preparation of matter for publication.

[*Sec 1(2)(c)*].

Where the greater part of a building is not used for office purposes, a room satisfying the above criteria would still qualify as an office. The test is whether the sole use, or principal use, of the room was 'office purposes'. Take for example a laboratory where people make notes, type and even duplicate. This would not qualify as an office, since the making of notes, typing or duplicating is not generally its sole or principal purpose or use. However, if there were a separate room in the laboratory where nothing but duplicating was carried out, this room would be an office and the Act would apply. A room in a school where clerical staff are employed, or the head's room, is also an office, though a classroom or the staff common room is not.

Premises occupied in conjunction with office premises

33.6 Premises occupied together with office premises for office purposes are treated as part of the office premises. [*Sec 1(2)*]. Hence, stairs, steps, landings, galleries, entrance halls and yards are covered by the Act if they are used in connection with the business. Equally important, canteens are included, so the canteen staff have the same protection as the office staff.

Dangerous machines in offices

33.7 It is an offence to allow any person (compare the provisions of *Factories Act 1961, s 21*), employed to work in an office, shop or railway premises, to work at a dangerous machine, unless:

(*a*) he has been instructed as to dangers; and

(*b*) he is adequately supervised by a person with a thorough knowledge and experience of the machine.

[*OSRPA s 19(1)*].

The machines in question are:

(*a*) *Machines worked by mechanical power:*

    (i) worm-type mincing machines;

    (ii) rotary knife bowl-type chopping machines;

    (iii) dough brakes;

    (iv) dough mixers;

    (v) food mixing machines when used with attachments for mincing, slicing, chipping or any other cutting operation, or for crumbling;

    (vi) pie and tart making machines;

    (vii) vegetable slicing machines;

    (viii) wrapping and packing machines;

    (ix) garment presses;

    (x) opening or teasing machines used for upholstery or bedding work;

    (xi)   corner staying machines;

    (xii)   loose knife punching machines;

    (xiii) wire stitching machines;

    (xiv) machines of any type equipped with a circular saw blade;

    (xv)   machines of any type equipped with a saw in the form of a continuous band or strip;

    (xvi) planing machines, vertical spindle moulding machines and routing machines, being machines used for cutting wood, wood product, fibre-board, plastic or similar material.

(*b*)   *Machines worked by whatever means*:

    (i)   circular knife slicing machines used for cutting bacon and other foods (whether similar to bacon or not);

    (ii)   potato chipping machines;

    (iii) platen printing machines, including such machines when used for cutting and creasing;

    (iv) guillotine machines.

[*Prescribed Dangerous Machines Order 1964 (SI 1964 No 971)*].

Premises specifically excluded

33.8   The following premises are not covered by the provisions of *OSRPA*:

(*a*)   premises where only self-employed persons work. There must be at least one employed person [*Sec 1(1)*];

(*b*)   premises where the only employees are relatives of the employer [*Sec 2(1)*];

(*c*)   outworkers' dwellings [*Sec 2(2)*];

(*d*)   premises where the sum total of all hours worked by employees does not exceed 21 hours each week [*Sec 3(1)*];

(*e*)   premises occupied solely by the armed forces [*Sec 84*];

(*f*)   premises used for selling fish wholesale in the docks [*Sec 85(2)*];

(*g*)   parts of mines below ground [*Sec 85(3)*];

(*h*)   mobile offices and mobile shops [*Sec 1*];

(*j*)   premises used for a temporary purpose (see further 33.9 below) [*Sec 86*].

Premises used for a temporary purpose

33.9   It is a defence for a person charged with contravention of any provisions of *OSRPA* to prove that the premises were only being occupied for a temporary purpose, i.e. a purpose which will be accomplished within the following period:

(*a*)   six months, if the premises are a movable structure (this might apply in the case of a site office, for example, or a portable exhibition stand);

(*b*)   six weeks in other cases.

[*Sec 86(1)*].

In the case of a prosecution under *OSRPA s 49(1)* for failure to notify the appropriate authority that persons were employed, in order to establish the defence above the accused must prove both that the premises were occupied for a temporary purpose (as above) and that the employees concerned were there for that purpose. [*Sec 86(2)*].

Exemption for individual premises

33.10   If the enforcing authority (the HSE or the local authority, see Chapter 17 'Enforcement') is satisfied that compliance is not reasonably practicable, individual premises may be exempt from the following requirements of the Act (and the period of exemption should be used to bring premises up to the statutory standards):

(*a*)   room space [*Sec 5(2)*], for up to two years;

(*b*)   temperature [*Sec 6*], for up to two years;

(*c*)   provision of sanitary convenience [*Sec 9*], for up to two years;

(*d*)   the provision of running water [*Sec 10(1)*], with or without a time limit.

[*Sec 46*].

When the new provisions come into force this exemption will only apply to premises which have been specifically excluded from the new regulations.

Persons to whom the duties in OSRPA apply

33.11   Generally, responsibility for ensuring compliance with the provisions of *OSRPA* rests with the occupier of the premises, that is, the person or persons who have control over the buildings, or parts of them, rather than the owner (who may not be the occupier). In certain cases, though, responsibility does rest with the owner, i.e. the lessor or licensor. (The rules relating to the effect of occupation and ownership on compliance are dealt with immediately below.) Some of the duties under *OSRPA* are absolute upon an occupier. In *Wray v GLC CLJ June 1987* the plaintiff suffered injuries when the chair on which he was sitting broke. The chair was supported on a vertical metal member which rested on four splayed-out metal legs. One of the legs broke. The defendant argued that he was not liable, since he could not be shown to have known of the defect. It was held that the duty upon the defendant was absolute; he did not have to be shown to know of the defect. Moreover, these duties cannot be delegated to outside contractors in order to relieve the owner/occupier of liability (*Mitchell v Glenrothes Development Corporation and Northern Maintenance Cleaners Ltd (HSIB 186)* in which an employer was held liable for breach of (*inter alia*) *Sec 16* of *OSRPA* where an employee slipped on algal growth, injuring himself, and could not rely on the fact that he had delegated the cleaning of steps to an independent cleaning firm, since the terms of the contract did not specify a system for removing algal hazard).

Buildings in single ownership

33.12   The following are the provisions for buildings in single ownership.

(*a*)   Where a whole building is held under lease or licence by *one occupier* and consists entirely of premises to which the Act applies, the occupier must comply with the Act; though, if he were to sublet, his responsibility would be divided with the sublessee. [*Sec 63*].

(*b*)   Where a building is divided up into a number of sets of premises leased or licensed to different occupiers, the *owner*, in respect of the 'common parts' of the building, must:

(i) comply with the statutory requirements relating to cleanliness, lighting, floor safety, stairs, steps, passages and gangways [*Sec 42(2)-(5)*]; and

(ii) provide sanitary conveniences and washing facilities, as well as maintaining, lighting, and ventilating them [*Sec 42(6)(7)*];

but the *occupier* must:

(A) clean the sanitary conveniences and washing facilities provided for the sole use of one occupier; and

(B) provide soap and towels or other means of cleaning and drying.

[*Sec 42(6)(7)*].

Buildings in plural ownership

33.13 The owner has the responsibility for:

(*a*) cleanliness, lighting, floor safety, stairs, passages and gangways, regarding the 'common parts' of the building [*Sec 43(2)(3)*];

(*b*) provision of sanitary conveniences, washing facilities, including their maintenance, lighting, and ventilation [*Sec 43(4)(5)*];

(*c*) cleaning the sanitary conveniences and washing facilities provided for their joint use by two or more occupiers [*Sec 43(4)(5)*].

The occupier has the responsibility for:

(i) cleaning the sanitary conveniences and washing facilities provided for the sole use of one occupier;

(ii) provision of soap and towels or other means of cleaning and drying.

[*Sec 43(4)(5)*].

Health and safety duties in offices/shops

Cleanliness

33.14 All premises, furniture, furnishings and fittings must be kept in a clean state; and dirt and refuse must not be allowed to accumulate. Floors and steps must be cleaned, at least once a week, by washing, sweeping or other method. [*Sec 4(1)(2)*] (remaining in force until 1 January 1996).

Overcrowding

No room must be so overcrowded, whilst work is going on, as to cause risk of injury (regard being had to space occupied by furniture as well as the number of persons). [*Sec 5(1)*] (remaining in force until 1 January 1996). (See also 35.6 OVERCROWD-ING.)

Temperature

Effective provision must be made for securing and maintaining a reasonable temperature in every room where persons are employed to work otherwise than for short periods. Where a substantial proportion of the work done in a room does not involve severe physical effort, a temperature of more than 16°C must be maintained after the first hour, while work is going on. [*Sec 6(1)(2)*] (remaining in force until 1 January 1996). (See also 42.5 TEMPERATURE.)

Ventilation

Effective and suitable provision must be made, by the circulation of adequate supplies of fresh or artificially purified air, for securing and maintaining the ventilation of every room, where persons are employed to work. [*Sec 7(1)*] (remaining in force until 1 January 1996).

Lighting

Effective provision must be made for securing and maintaining sufficient and suitable lighting, whether natural or artificial. [*Sec 8(1)*] (remaining in force until 1 January 1996). (See also 27.2 LIGHTING.)

Floors in offices and shops

33.15 All floors in offices and shops must be of sound construction and properly maintained, and, so far as is reasonably practicable, be kept free from obstruction and any substance likely to cause persons to slip. [*OSRPA s 16(1)*]. To all intents and purposes, this section is a restatement of the *Factories Act 1961, s 28(1)* (see Chapter 18 'Factories and Workplaces') and case law attracted by the latter provision (presumably) will facilitate interpretation of this section.

This section gives protection only to employees in offices and shops and not to customers or clients (who would have to sue under the *Occupiers' Liability Act 1957* and/or common law, see Chapter 32 'Occupiers' Liability'), though the latter are given protection by *HSWA s 3* (a section which does not, however, confer a statutory right of action (see Chapter 15 'Employers' Duties')). It is not, however, essential that an employee be injured in the course of his employment in order to be able to sue for breach of duty under *OSRPA* (*Westwood v The Post Office [1974] AC 1* where a widow brought a successful action with regard to her husband who, while sun-bathing during the works' lunch hour, fell through a defective trap-door in the lift motor room and suffered fatal injuries). A specification in a cleaning contract between an office occupier and a contract cleaning firm to the effect that steps etc. be 'swept daily and thoroughly washed periodically' does not absolve the occupier from complete liability for breach of *Sec 16(1)* where an employee is injured as a result of slipping on the steps as a consequence of an obstruction (algae) (*Mitchell v Glenrothes Development Corporation and Northern Maintenance Cleaners Ltd* (see 33.11 above)) (remaining in force until 1 January 1996).

Staircases in offices and shops

33.16 Where there is a staircase in an office or shop, a substantial hand-rail must be provided and maintained (for the meaning of 'provide and maintain', see Chapter 15 'Employers' Duties').

Moreover, where there is:

(*a*) a staircase with an open side, the hand-rail must be on that side;

(*b*) a staircase with two open sides; or

(*c*) a staircase which is specially liable to cause accidents (e.g. a circular staircase), a hand-rail, or hand-hold must be provided and maintained on both sides.

[*OSRPA s 16(2)*] (remaining in force until 1 January 1996).

Guards

33.17   The open side of a staircase must be guarded by provision and maintenance of efficient means of preventing any person (not merely an employee) from falling through the space between the hand-rail or hand-hold and the staircase steps. [*OSRPA s 16(3)*] (remaining in force until 1 January 1996).

Crown premises

33.18   The health, safety and welfare provisions of *OSRPA ss 4-16, 19* are binding on the Crown to the extent that the provisions might give rise to liability in tort in the event of breach. [*OSRPA s 83*]. (See further 17.35, 17.36 ENFORCEMENT regarding the liability of the Crown.)

Defence of due diligence

33.19   It is a defence for a person charged with a contravention of a provision of *OSRPA* or of regulations thereunder to prove that he used all due diligence to secure compliance with that provision. [*OSRPA s 67*]. This defence has not been invoked with much success by those charged with breach of the provisions of *OSRPA*. It is a very difficult test to satisfy. Case law tends to identify situations where the test has not been satisfied. The only way of invoking this defence is to show that no matter how much care was taken by the occupier the injury would still have taken place (*Dewhurst (J H) Ltd v Coventry Corporation* [*1969*] *3 AER 1225* where a boy cut off the tip of his left index finger while cleaning a bacon slicer; the defendant's appeal against conviction under *OSRPA s 18(1)* was unsuccessful).

Moreover, *Sec 67* does not provide a defence in civil proceedings. The only complete bar to recovery of compensation is that the office worker caused the injury himself. Compliance with *Sec 67* on the part of an office occupier/employer may go some way towards establishing that the employee was responsible for his injury, though in itself it would not be enough. It would require a situation analogous with that in *ICI v Shatwell* [*1965*] *AC 656* for the employer to have a successful defence to such a civil action. (In that case, the employer raised the defence of consent, express or implied, by the employee to run the risk involved despite the fact that the statutory precautions had not been taken, see further Chapter 15 'Employers' Duties'.)

Penalties

33.20   The penalties for breach of *OSRPA* are those laid down in *HSWA s 33* (as the provisions of *OSRPA* are 'relevant statutory provisions', see Chapter 17 'Enforcement').

Hazards in offices

33.21   The average office would appear to be a relatively safe place compared, say, with a typical factory or workshop. Office work has traditionally been regarded as a low-risk activity, but every year there are numerous accidents and losses associated with poor safety standards in offices.

The risk of fire is perhaps the greatest office hazard. This may be associated with human carelessness, e.g. smoking and the careless disposal of cigarette ends, but other features are frequent causes of fire. The last 20 years have, for instance, seen great advances in office technology with the introduction of computerised equipment, word processors and a range of other electrically-operated equipment. Many of the older offices simply were not designed for this influx of electrically-operated equipment, with the result that there is frequent use of multi-point adaptors, extension leads and wiring of more than one appliance into a 13 amp plug. This results in overloading and increased potential for fire. Moreover, many offices still have no form of central heating with the result that freestanding electrical heating appliances are used during winter months resulting in further overloading of electrical systems.

A wide range of potentially flammable materials is used in offices: spirit-based cleaning fluids, floor polishes, paper of all types and the many forms of packaging materials. All these substances represent a fire hazard unless carefully controlled.

Whilst most offices now have some form of fire alarm which may be tested on a quarterly basis, the need for an annual fire drill goes virtually unrecognised in many offices and staff are rarely trained in the correct use of fire appliances. The need, therefore, to consider these aspects in normal management systems cannot be over-emphasised (see also Chapter 19 'Fire and Fire Precautions' and particularly 19.77).

Typical accidents in offices

33.22 Whilst the number of fatal and major injury accidents to office workers is relatively low each year, a great number of minor injury accidents take place, which may result in the need for first-aid treatment. Accidents associated with small items of equipment such as scissors, staplers, guillotines and letter openers are common, together with falls down stairways, or through tripping over an electrical flex. Such accidents may be associated with unsuitable footwear, badly treaded staircases, poor housekeeping, inadequate lighting or the absence of handrails to staircases. Many accidents, particularly to female office workers, are associated with lifting items such as electric typewriters, ledgers and items of office furniture.

Electrical safety in offices – general requirements

33.23 The following list suggests some general requirements for electrical safety in offices.

(*a*)   All accessible metal parts of electrically-operated machines should be efficiently earthed.

(*b*)   All live terminals should be adequately screened. It should be noted that operator access to parts of machinery should not allow access to live electrical parts at the same time.

(*c*)   Where interlock switches are provided to machinery guards, they should be of such design or construction as to prohibit inadvertent operation. The standard and frequency of maintenance should be specified in a specifically-written safe system of work for each machine.

(*d*)   All flexible cords, sockets and couplers should be of good quality and standard. Flexible cables need to be of adequate size, construction and protection, with proper connections and colour coding.

(*e*)   Mains input switches should be suitably placed on the machines and the 'on' and 'off' positions clearly identified and accessible. All phases should be disconnected by the operation of the switch.

(*f*)   An effective overcurrent protection device should be provided in each phase of the circuit and be so arranged as to disconnect the electricity supply to the machine in the event of overload or short circuit.

(*g*)   All high voltage terminals and live conductors should be securely screened and a suitable warning notice, indicating the possible danger, displayed in a prominent position.

(*h*)   Where fluids are used in any machine, they should be used and housed so that they do not come into contact with electrical conductors and components. In the case of flammable fluids, special attention should be given to the machine enclosure to prevent dangerous concentrations of fluid vapour. All electrical conductors and components should be specifically housed or constructed so as to avoid risk of fire or explosion.

(*j*)   Where heating elements are used in any machine, they should be placed and installed so as to cause no deterioration of electrical equipment or overheating that will create a hazard to people or plant.

Photocopying equipment

33.24   A number of hazards have been identified with photocopiers. These include the risk of contact with, or inhalation of fumes from, aqueous solutions of ammonia used as part of the processing operation; inhalation and fire risks associated with cleaning agents, many of which are solvent-based; and the risk of carbon dioxide gas being evolved due to overheating of the carbon-based toner. Certain developing agents used in dyeline copiers contain hydroquinone and resorcinol, both of which are powerful irritants. Further risks may result from the emission of ozone which is produced by the action of fuser lamps. Odours from this gas can be detected at a level of 0.02 ppm (parts per million) and at 0.05 ppm there can be irritation of the mucous membranes of the mouth, nose and eyes, possibly accompanied by headaches and reduced vision.

The following precautions are necessary where photocopying equipment is used, particularly if located in well-populated office locations.

(*a*)   The photocopier should be subject to regular maintenance, which should include the removal of residual toner from the drum and the replacement of the final filter to the exhaust. Servicing of this type may be necessary every 3,000 copies.

(*b*)   Staff who service the copier should be adequately trained, particularly in the procedure for cleaning the drum.

(*c*)   Where the copier is located in a relatively confined space and is subject to extensive use, there may be a need to install some form of local exhaust ventilation. Siting, therefore, is an important aspect in reducing hazards from such equipment.

(*d*)   Where staff are engaged in cleaning and maintenance, they should be provided with eye protection, in the form of goggles, gloves and respiratory protection.

Visual display units (VDUs)

33.25   Many VDU installations have been situated in existing offices with little consideration given to the needs of the operator. Operational stress is created through poor chair/desk design and positioning in relation to controls and displays, inadequate leg room, the need to regularly adjust body position, inadequate ventilation and noise from the terminal. New requirements on employers under the *Health and Safety (Display Screen Equipment) Regulations 1992* can be found in Chapter 27 'Lighting'.

VDU workstation check list

33.26   The following factors should be considered in VDU workstation design, with a view to reducing operator stress, and recognising the specific needs of operators.

VDU operators

33.27   Pre-employment health screening should incorporate vision screening for all operators, together with regular annual vision screening.

Where considered necessary by an optician, wearers of spectacles should be permitted free modifications to their prescription lenses. (For information on the new right to sight tests, see 27.22 LIGHTING.)

Operators should be aware of the fact that loss of visual sharpness and reduced visual performance is a feature of the ageing process, which may be exacerbated by VDU work.

VDU operators who have been prescribed medication, such as minor tranquillisers, should be aware of possible side effects from such medication such as dizziness or drowsiness which could result in erratic keyboard operation and even accidents.

VDU operators should be given regular rest periods during the working day.

Keyboard and screen characteristics

33.28   The luminance ratio between the screen and the rest of the work area should be not more than 1:10 (see further Chapter 27 'Lighting').

The screen should be capable of both horizontal and vertical adjustment.

Black keyboards should be avoided as they accentuate reflections from the work area.

Keyboards should, where practicable, be detachable. (The use of fixed keyboards can result in poor posture being adopted leading to general fatigue.)

The workstation

33.29   Chairs should incorporate an adjustable back rest, with no arm rests, and the height should also be adjustable.

Chairs should be of the swivel type, preferably mounted on castors.

The keyboard top should be set at approximately 0.7 m above floor level, with the screen approximately at right angles to the line of vision, but avoiding reflected light.

A simple document holder should be provided, set at an angle of 45° with the actual desk top.

A footrest should be made available with a minimum knee clearance of 0.2 m between seat and table.

Any wires to the screen should be positioned behind the table.

Chapter 34

Offshore Operations

Introduction

34.1 'Offshore operations' take place, broadly, in three specific stages:

(a) the initial stage, when the platform is under construction;

(b) the fitting out or 'hook-up' stage, when plant and equipment are being installed; and

(c) following commissioning, the operational stage of oil and gas production.

The initial stage is generally regarded as the most dangerous of the three stages.

Because offshore operations are generally regarded as potentially hazardous operations, a special Act was passed for the industry, namely, the *Mineral Workings (Offshore Installations) Act 1971*. This Act empowered the Secretary of State to make regulations to provide for the safety, health and welfare of persons on installations engaged in underwater exploitation and exploration of mineral resources. Regulations could provide for the safety, health and welfare of persons on offshore installations and for the safety of installations and prevention of accidents on or near them [*Sec 6*] (now repealed (see below)). The main regulations hitherto made under this provision were the *Offshore Installations (Operational Safety, Health and Welfare) Regulations 1976 (SI 1976 No 1019)* (the bulk of these regulations apply to safety on offshore installations and, to a much lesser extent, health and welfare) as well as the *Offshore Installations (Safety Representatives and Safety Committees) Regulations 1989 (SI 1989 No 971)* (see 34.33 below).

Following the Piper Alpha tragedy, however, in July 1988, the *Offshore Safety Act 1992*, which came into effect on 6 March 1992, transferred enforcement of the *Mineral Workings (Offshore Installations) Act 1971*, and regulations made under it, (from the Department of Energy) to the Health and Safety Executive, simultaneously converting that Act into an 'existing statutory provision' (see 17.2(c) ENFORCEMENT). Thus, instead of regulations being passed under the old *Sec 6* of the *Mineral Workings (Offshore Installations) Act 1971*, in future, they will be made under *Part I* of *HSWA* by HSC. [*Offshore Safety Act 1992, s 1(1); SI 1993 No 1823, Reg 4*]. However, any regulations previously made under *Sec 6* will remain in force. [*SI 1993 No 1823, Reg 6(1)*]. In this way, new regulations relating to offshore safety can be expected in this area in the near future, as the government intends to implement all of the Lord Cullen Report recommendations.

Moreover, the *Offshore Safety (Protection Against Victimisation) Act 1992* seeks to protect safety representatives on offshore installations from victimisation by conferring on them unfair dismissal rights if they are dismissed in connection with any functions conferred on them as safety representatives or members of a safety committee (see 34.33 below).

34.2 As far as insurance is concerned, the *Offshore Installations (Application of the Employers' Liability Compulsory Insurance) Act 1969 Regulations 1975 (SI 1975 No 1289)* extend to all offshore workers the provisions of the *Employers' Liability*

656

(Compulsory Insurance) Act 1969. Every employer of persons who work on, or in connection with, an offshore installation on the UK sector of the Continental Shelf is required to obtain insurance cover against claims for personal injury on the part of his employees. The requirement applies to foreign employers and employees as well as UK employers and nationals, except that foreign employees would need to work on an installation for more than seven days before their employer would be required to obtain cover. However, the employer does not need to insure employees personally or advise them to obtain insurance (see Chapter 16 'Employers' Liability Insurance').

34.3   In addition, the *Offshore Installations (Safety Representatives and Safety Committees) Regulations 1989 (SI 1989 No 971)* have placed duties on installation managers/owners/employers to arrange for the election of safety representatives (who need not be trade union appointees, unlike their on-shore namesakes) since most of the provisions of the *Health and Safety at Work Act 1974* extend to offshore installations and pipelines in territorial waters and to gas storage and accommodation installations and installations in transit. [*Health and Safety at Work etc. Act 1974 (Application outside Great Britain) (Variation) Order 1989 (SI 1989 No 672); Health and Safety at Work etc. Act 1974 (Application outside Great Britain) Order 1989 (SI 1989 No 840)*]. (See 34.33 below.) The *Offshore Installations and Pipeline Works (First-Aid) Regulations 1989 (SI 1989 No 1671)*, and accompanying code of practice, specify requirements and procedures relating to the provision of first-aid on offshore installations (see 34.21 below), and projects involving diving operations must be notified to the HSE. [*Diving Operations at Work Regulations 1981, Reg 5C as amended by SI 1992 No 608*].

There is a new code for standby vessels, which caused anxiety in the Piper Alpha disaster, the 'Assessment of the Suitability of Standby Vessels Attending Offshore Installations: Instructions for the Guidance of Surveyors', HMSO 1991. It came into operation on 16 July 1991. Owners and operators can demonstrate compliance with *HSWA s 2* by complying with this code.

The Offshore Installations (Operational Safety, Health and Welfare) Regulations 1976

Safety

Hazardous areas

34.4   The operations manual must contain drawings of the installation clearly and accurately showing any part where there is likely to be a danger of fire or explosion from gas, vapour or volatile liquid (i.e. 'a hazardous area'). [*Reg 2(1)*].

Any door or hatch giving access to a hazardous area must carry the words 'Hazardous Area' in large red capital letters at least 50 mm high. [*Reg 2(2)*].

Work permits

34.5   The following activities cannot be carried on without written instruction from the installation manager given to a responsible (i.e. competent) person (for further discussion of this expression, see 1.37 INTRODUCTION) (for permits to work generally see 1.32–1.36 INTRODUCTION);

(*a*)   welding;

(*b*)   flame cutting;

(*c*)   any work involving ignition;

(*d*)   work on electrical equipment;

(*e*)   work at any place where there is inadequate ventilation for diluting and dispelling

    (i)   flammable and/or

    (ii)   injurious (for the meaning of this term, see Chapter 43 'Ventilation') fumes, vapours or gases likely to be given off.

This instruction must specify:

(i)   the nature of the work;

(ii)   the period during which work may take place; and

(iii)   any precautions to be taken to avoid endangering the safety of the installation and persons on it.

[*Reg 3(1)*].

Dangerous substances

34.6   No substance which is:

(*a*)   radioactive;

(*b*)   corrosive;

(*c*)   toxic;

(*d*)   explosive; or

(*e*)   stored and/or used at a pressure greater than atmospheric;

must be kept on an offshore installation except in receptacles:

(i)   marked with contents; and

(ii)   so far as reasonably practicable, away from a hazardous area and any living accommodation.

[*Reg 4(1)*].

Moreover, no flammable substance must be kept unless in receptacles so far as reasonably practicable away from any other hazardous area and living accommodation. [*Reg 4(2)*].

Any door or hatch giving access to any place at which a 'dangerous substance' is kept, must carry the word 'Danger' in large red capital letters, with an adequate description of the substance. [*Reg 4(1)(4)*].

General maintenance

34.7   All parts of every offshore installation and its equipment must be maintained, so as to ensure the safety of the installation and persons on it [*Reg 5(1)*]; and there must be a scheme for providing systematic examination, maintenance and testing by a responsible person [*Reg 5(2)(3)*]; any part found to be defective and unsatisfactory must not be used [*Reg 5(4)*].

Independent examination of lifting machinery

34.8   Every lifting appliance and every piece of lifting gear must be thoroughly examined and tested by a competent person (see Chapter 26 'Lifting Machinery and Equipment'):

(*a*) before use for the first time;

(*b*) if already used, when substantially altered or repaired; and

(*c*) (in the case of examination) before being put into use after

  (i) installation,

  (ii) re-installation, or

  (iii) substantial alteration or repair,

 and at six-monthly intervals;

(*d*) (in the case of testing) before being put into use after

  (i) installation,

  (ii) re-installation, or

  (iii) substantial alteration or repair.

[*Reg 6(1), 1 Sch, Pt III*].

The record of the examination must be signed by the person who made it and a copy of it must be delivered or sent to the owner within fourteen days of the examination.

34.9 Examination and testing must be carried out as set out in Table 28 below.

Table 28

Intervals for Examination of Certain Equipment

(1) *Equipment*	(2) *Intervals for examination*
Those parts of lifting appliance wire-lines which are liable to suffer wear or other deterioration	Intervals of 7 days

Time or Intervals for Examination and Testing of Certain Equipment

Equipment	*Time or intervals for examination and testing*
Portable gas detection systems	Intervals of 28 days and immediately before use
Lifting appliance safety load indicators and alarms	Intervals of 7 days
Radiotelephone equipment	For correct operation – daily Thorough examination – intervals of 12 months

---

Time or Intervals for Thorough Examination and Testing of Certain Equipment

Equipment	*Time or intervals for examination*
Lifting appliances and lifting gear	Immediately before being put into use after installation, re-installation or substantial alteration or repair and subject thereto, intervals of 6 months

	Time or intervals for testing
Lifting appliances and lifting gear	Immediately before being put into use after installation, re-installation or substantial alteration or repair

[*1 Sch, Pts I, II and III*].

The following form of record of thorough examination of lifting appliances/gear must be used:

fig. 16

Form of Record of Thorough Examination of Lifting Appliance or Lifting Gear

Name and address of installation owner:	Name or designation of offshore installation:
1 Description and distinguishing mark or number of lifting appliance or lifting gear	
2 Maker and date of make	
3 Date of last record of examination (if seen) Name of person who conducted last examination, and of his employer	
4 Date first put into use (if known)	
5 Parts not accessible for thorough examination	
6 Parts that require opening up at the next examination	
7 Particulars of defects and remedy: particulars of any defect found in the lifting appliance or lifting gear which affects the safety of the appliance and the repairs (if any) required, either: (i) immediately, or (ii) within a specified time (which must be stated), to enable the lifting appliance or lifting gear to continue to be used with safety (*if no such repairs are required the word "NONE" is to be entered*)	

8 Safe Working Load subject to the repairs, renewals and alterations (if any) specified above In the case of a crane with a variable operating radius, including a crane with derricking jib, the safe working load at various radii of the jib, trolley, or crab is to be stated	

I hereby certify that on   (date) the item described in this report was thoroughly examined, so far as accessible, and the above particulars are correct.

Signature of person
conducting examination ....

Counter-signature on
behalf of employer.............................

Name of person
conducting examination ....

Name of employer.............................

Date

Date

Continuation sheet (please number items as above)

Details of component test certificates seen by person conducting examination.

[*1 Sch Pt IV*].

Practices to be observed

34.10   The installation owner must provide written instructions specifying the practices to be observed in the course of operations on the installation and the safe use of equipment. [*Reg 7(1)*]. He must, on demand of the Secretary of State, furnish him with a copy of the written instructions. [*Reg 7(3)*].

Table 29 below sets out which procedures must be included in written instructions.

Table 29

Matters to be Provided for in Written Instructions

Drilling production procedures

1. (*a*) Drilling operations on multiwell platforms.
   (*b*) Workover operations.
   (*c*) Installation of blowout preventers.
   (*d*) Operations on wellhead.
   (*e*) Venting of gas.
   (*f*) Venting of oil.
   (*g*) Formation testing.
   (*h*) Swabbing.
   (*i*) Plugging and abandonment.
   (*j*) Smoking and use of naked lights.
   (*k*) Detection of and protection from sour gases.
   (*l*) Transportation, storage, handling and use, including action to be taken in emergency, of –
      (i) acids and other dangerous chemicals,
      (ii) explosives,
      (iii) radioactive substances,
      (iv) flammable materials, including flammable waste, and
      (v) other dangerous materials.

Electrical procedures

2. (*a*) Access by persons.
   (*b*) Additions or alterations to the electrical supply system.
   (*c*) Precautions to be taken before and during the operation and maintenance of electrical equipment.
   (*d*) Use of portable insulating stands, screens and protective clothing.
   (*e*) Special precautions to be taken when working near bare conductors.
   (*f*) Use of portable equipment using electrical power.
   (*g*) Treatment of persons suffering from electrical shock.

Mechanical equipment procedures

3. (*a*) General operation of mechanical equipment.
   (*b*) Operation of lifting appliances, lifting gear, including use of slings, chains, wire ropes and other lifting tackle.
   (*c*) Handling and use of compressed air.
   (*d*) Handling and storage of loose tools.
   (*e*) Limitations on, and precautions during, welding and cutting.
   (*f*) Limitations on, and precautions during, operations involving cutting into live lines and the use of mechanical seal plugs.
   (*g*) Inspection or maintenance of dangerous machinery or apparatus when it is necessary to remove or render inoperative guards and other safety devices.

Personal procedures

4. (*a*) Liaison with medical practitioners.*
   (*b*) Arrangements for general medical advice and for medical treatment in the event of injury or disease.*

(c) General arrangements for safety of persons.
(d) Personal hygiene for kitchen staff and cleanliness of food rooms and kitchen.
(e) House-keeping and disposal of waste materials.
(f) Use of protective clothing and personal safety equipment.
(g) Working in exposed positions.
(h) Transfer of persons to and from vessels, aircraft and hovercraft.

Procedures to secure safety of the installation

5. (a) Communication with radio stations on land and attendant vessels.
(b) Obtaining meteorological information.
(c) Movement of the installation to and from station.
(d) Mooring of the installation.
(e) Monitoring sea-bed conditions.
(f) Jacking up and down or ballasting and de-ballasting.
(g) Monitoring accretions to the installation including marine growth, snow and ice.
(h) Keeping of records affecting safety of the installation.
(i) Procedures relating to movement of vessels, aircraft and hovercraft attending the installation.
(j) Transfer of equipment to and from vessels, aircraft and hovercraft.
(k) Refuelling of helicopters on the installation.

[*Sch 2*].

* These two requirements were revoked as from 13 September 1990 (except for installations maintained in tidal waters or in Northern Ireland up to the seaward limit of territorial waters).

Movement of offshore installations

34.11 Whilst an offshore installation is being (a) raised, (b) lowered or (c) dismantled, no person, not essential to the operation, must be present without consent from the installation manager. [*Reg 8*].

Construction of equipment

34.12 All equipment must be (a) of good construction, (b) sound material, (c) adequate strength, (d) free from patent defect and (e) suitable for the purpose. [*Reg 10*].

This provision will be revoked from 1 January 1997 and for new work equipment, this provision has already been revoked. The *Provision and Use of Work Equipment Regulations 1992* make rules about work equipment and these must be followed from the relevant date (see Chapter 28 'Machinery Safety' for details of the relevant provisions).

Moreover, all electrical equipment must be sufficient in size and power for the work and (a) constructed, (b) installed, (c) protected, (d) worked and (e) maintained so far as practicable (see Chapter 15 'Employers' Duties' for the meaning of this expression), so as to prevent danger. [*Reg 11*].

Dangerous machinery

34.13 Every dangerous part of any machinery or apparatus must be effectively guarded, so far as is practicable (for the meaning of 'dangerous' see Chapter 28 'Machinery Safety' and for the meaning of 'practicable' see 15.18 EMPLOYERS' DUTIES). More specifically, in the case of a *moving* dangerous part:

(*a*)   an enclosure which prevents any person (or his clothing) from coming into contact with that part; or

(*b*)   a device which encloses it in motion,

is necessary.

In the case of a dangerous *non-moving* part, a fixed enclosure is necessary. [*Reg 12(2)*].

(This requirement is wider than that in the *Factories Act 1961*, referring to (*a*) apparatus, as well as machinery and (*b*) fixed, as well as moving parts (see Chapter 28 'Machinery Safety').)

Guards and safety devices for moving dangerous parts must be constantly maintained and kept in position while parts are in motion (for the meaning of 'maintained' and 'in motion', see Chapter 28 'Machinery Safety'), except when necessarily exposed for (*a*) examination, (*b*) adjustment or (*c*) lubrication; all practicable (for the meaning of this term, see Chapter 15 'Employers' Duties') arrangements must be made to reduce to a minimum the risk of injury to all persons. [*Reg 12(3)*].

Moreover, removal of guards must only be done by a responsible person (i.e. competent person) *and* there must be another person, instructed in steps to be taken, who must be immediately available within sight or hearing. [*Reg 12*].

(As with 34.12 above, these provisions have been revoked from the dates mentioned in that paragraph.)

Lifting appliances

34.14   Every lifting appliance or gear must be plainly marked with the safe working load (SWL) or loads shown on the latest record of thorough examination. [*Reg 13*]. (For further discussion of the legal effect of SWLs, see Chapter 26 'Lifting Machinery and Equipment'.)

Table 30 below sets out the required marking of safe working loads for multiple slings.

Table 30

Marking of Safe Working Loads for Multiple Slings

Every multiple sling shall carry a mark in one of the forms below:

SWL x tonnes	or	SWL x t
0°−90°		0°−90°

where x is the safe working load ('SWL') in metric tonnes for any angle between the relevant sling legs ('the included angle') up to a limit of 90°.

For the purpose of this Schedule the included angle means–
(*a*)   in the case of 2-leg slings, the angle between the legs;
(*b*)   in the case of 3-leg slings, the angle between any two adjacent legs; and
(*c*)   in the case of 4-leg slings, the angle between any two diagonally opposite legs.

[*3 Sch*].

General safety

34.15   At all times all reasonably practicable steps must be taken to ensure the safety of persons at all places on the installation, including provision of safe means of access to and egress from (see Chapter 2 'Access' for the meaning of these expressions) any such place; in particular:

(*a*)   all scaffolding must be secured to prevent accidental displacement;

(*b*)   every ladder must be fixed so that the stiles or sides are evenly supported or suspended *and* secured to prevent slipping;

(*c*)   every working platform must be at least 65 centimetres wide *and* securely fastened to ledgers, standards or uprights or its movement prevented by other means;

(*d*)   any walking platform or walkway from which a person is liable to fall more than two metres, or into the sea, must where practicable be provided with:

    (i)   a toe-board not less than 15 centimetres high; and

    (ii)   suitable guard-rails of adequate strength of three courses, so arranged that:

        (A)   the lowest rail is not more than 76 centimetres above the toe-board, and

        (B)   the highest rail is at least one metre above the platform or walkway, and

        (C)   the openings between the rails are not more than 40 centimetres;

(*e*)   where any person is to work at any place from which he is liable to fall (i) into the sea or (ii) a distance of more than two metres (and compliance with (*d*) above is not practicable), safety nets/sheets must, if practicable, be provided so as to prevent that person falling, without causing injury to himself;

(*f*)   failing this, a suitable safety belt, coupled with lines, fittings and anchorages must be provided;

(*g*)   where any person (not just an employee), in getting to or from a place where he is to work, is liable to fall into the sea and (*e*) and (*f*) above are not practicable, he must be provided with a life jacket and wear it.

[*Reg 14*].

Personal safety equipment

34.16   There must be provided:

(*a*)   a safety helmet for every person;

(*b*)   sufficient protective clothing and equipment, including (i) eye protectors, (ii) ear protectors, (iii) welding masks or goggles, (iv) welding aprons, (v) breathing apparatus for use in toxic or oxygen deficient atmospheres, (vi) gloves, (vii) overalls, (viii) safety boots or shoes, for all persons exposed to risk of injury or disease, who must wear them, where necessary.

[*Reg 16(1)(3)*].

Electrical equipment

34.17 No unaccompanied person must (*a*) work on or (*b*) test electrical equipment, for which a work permit is required (see 34.5 above). Of the two persons at least one must be competent. [*Reg 17(1)*].

Signalling equipment

34.18 Signalling equipment must be provided and installed in a separate building or room. [*Reg 18*].

Radiotelephone operators

34.19 There must be, at any time when an installation is manned, at least:

(*a*)   one person fully trained as a radiotelephone operator [*Reg 19*];

(*b*)   a competent person responsible for the control of helicopter operations [*Reg 21*] (i.e. a helicopter landing officer), whose function it is to ensure, before a helicopter lands or takes off, that:

(i)   the helicopter landing area is clear of obstructions;

(ii)   any cranes nearby have ceased to operate;

(iii)   no persons, other than those necessary, are in the helicopter landing area;

(iv)   fire-fighting equipment (see Chapter 19 'Fire and Fire Precautions'), manned by adequately trained persons, is available;

(v)   any vessel standing by to render assistance is informed that helicopter operations are to take place; and

(vi)   safety nets are properly secured.

[*Reg 23*].

Health

34.20 *Drinking water*. Suitable drinking water must be provided and maintained (see Chapter 15 'Employers' Duties') and tested at least every three months. [*Reg 25*].

Sick bay. A sick bay must be provided and maintained on an offshore installation in tidal waters and parts of the sea in or adjacent to Northern Ireland up to the seaward limits of territorial waters. For other installations, the *Offshore Installations and Pipeline Works (First-Aid) Regulations 1989* (as appearing at 34.21 below) apply. [*Reg 27*].

First-aid

34.21 Installation managers/owners and those in control of pipeline works must make adequate arrangements for first-aid for persons at work. This includes provision of suitably trained personnel and advice or attendance of a registered medical practitioner when needed, and employees must be informed of these arrangements. [*Offshore Installations and Pipeline Works (First-Aid) Regulations 1989 (SI 1989 No 1671), Reg 5(1)*] and accompanying code of practice (ACOP).

The older provisions requiring at least one medically trained person to be on board or two where there are forty or more persons on board still apply to the installations mentioned in 34.20 above.

Manned installations – sick bays

In particular, *manned* offshore installations and all pipelaying barges and barges used in offshore construction, repair, maintenance, cleaning, demolition or dismantling activities must have a sick bay. The sick bay should:

(*a*)   be clearly identifiable;

(*b*)   be in the charge of a suitable person (e.g. offshore medic or first-aider) who should always be on call;

(*c*)   be available at all times and not used for other purposes;

(*d*)   be kept locked at all times when not in use (though suitable arrangements should be made for immediate access in cases of emergency);

(*e*)   have attached to the door a notice clearly showing names and locations of:

   (i)   offshore medics, or

   (ii)   offshore first-aiders

   (who should be easily identifiable, e.g. by arm bands) *and* means of contacting them (see further Duty of installation manager, 34.25 below);

(*f*)   contain suitable furniture, medications and equipment. Medications should be kept in a container and locked, the keys at all times being held by:

   (i)   the installation manager, or

   (ii)   the master, or

   (iii)   the offshore medic;

(*g*)   have facilities for effective two-way communication with onshore medical services.

(ACOP, para 6).

First-aid kits in sick bays

34.22   Sick bays should always contain a first-aid kit; but, in addition, offshore first-aiders must be provided with a first-aid kit readily available for use in emergency and located at the first-aider's place of work or around the installation.

Unmanned offshore installations need not have first-aid equipment, but, when persons are working there, they should contain:

(*a*)   a resuscitator with a 340 litre capacity oxygen cylinder; and

(*b*)   at least one box (or container) with a sufficient quantity of first-aid materials.

First-aid kits in sick bays should contain:

   (i)   12 individually wrapped sterile triangular bandages (90cm × 127cm);

   (ii)   20 packs of sterile gauze pads, each containing five pads (7.5cm × 7.5cm);

   (iii)   a suitable device for facilitating mouth to mouth resuscitation.

(ACOP, paras 3, 4).

Contents of sick bay

34.23   Sick bays on offshore installations should contain the following items:

(i) medications which an offshore medic can administer without the direction of a doctor, e.g. aluminium hydroxide tablets for indigestion, calamine lotion for irritating rashes;

(ii) standing orders relating to medications which can only be administered under the direction of a doctor, e.g. ampicillin capsules for infections, diazepam tablets for sedation;

(iii) dressings and bandages;

(iv) instruments and appliances, e.g. resuscitation devices, mouth gag, face masks;

(v) furnishings and equipment, e.g. alarm bell system, telephone, armchair, accident record book, daily treatment record book.

(ACOP, paras 31–36, Appendix 2, Parts 1, 2, 3).

Unmanned installations

34.24 Unmanned installations need not have first-aid equipment, but when persons are working there they should contain

(*a*) a resuscitator with a 340 litre capacity oxygen cylinder; and

(*b*) at least one box (or container) with sufficient first-aid material.

Duty of installation manager

34.25 Health and safety on offshore installations is controlled by the installation manager. He must see that all employees (and self-employed persons) are informed of the location of first-aid and medical equipment and how workers can contact the offshore medic or first-aiders rapidly in case of emergency. New workers, in particular, should be told this on first coming aboard. [*Reg 5(1)*].

To this end, notices should be put up (if necessary in various languages) in conspicuous positions (including sick bays), giving locations of first-aid and medical equipment and names and, if possible, locations of medic and first-aider. Offshore medics and first-aiders must be regularly supervised by fully registered medical practitioners and, where necessary, given medical advice [*Reg 5(1)(c)*], and written instructions should be drawn up, setting out arrangements for liaison with the medical practitioner. Copies of such instructions should be displayed in

(*a*) the sick bay;

(*b*) the radio operator's room; and

(*c*) the master or installation manager's office offshore.

(ACOP, paras 23-30).

Defence

34.26 It is a defence for a person charged with breach of these regulations to prove that he took all reasonable precautions *and* exercised all due diligence to avoid the commission of the offence. [*Reg 6*]. (This generally has proved a difficult test to satisfy (see further *Dewhurst v Coventry Corporation* at 33.19 OFFICES).)

Welfare

34.27   No person under 18 must be employed on offshore operations or installations. [*Offshore Installations (Operational Safety, Health and Welfare) Regulations 1976, Reg 28*].

Management

34.28   These safety, health, welfare and management duties are imposed on (*a*) installation managers, (*b*) owners of the installation and (*c*) concession owners (i.e. persons entitled to exploit/explore mineral resources). [*Reg 32(1)*]. Employers are *absolutely* liable for breach of these regulations on the part of their employees. It imposes not only vicarious liability (see 15.3 EMPLOYERS' DUTIES) but also a duty to guarantee compliance on the part of employees (*MacMillan v Wimpey Offshore Engineers and Constructors Ltd 1991 SLT 515* where an offshore worker was beaten up by a manager when discussing a job; the employer was held to be liable). Moreover, employers must ensure that employees comply with their duties. [*Reg 32(2)*]. (See Chapter 17 'Enforcement' for consequences of failing to do so.) In addition, breach of duty gives rise to statutory civil liability. [*Mineral Workings (Offshore Installations) Act 1971, s 11*]. (See further Chapter 1 'Introduction' and Chapter 6 'Compensation for Work Injuries/Diseases'.)

Life-saving procedures – Offshore Installations (Life-Saving Appliances) Regulations 1977

34.29   In both cases of fixed and mobile offshore installations (but not dredging installations) there must be provided life-saving appliances, such as survival craft, life rafts and life buoys as well as life jackets. These appliances are required by the *Offshore Installations (Life-Saving) Appliances Regulations 1977 (SI 1977 No 486)*. More particularly:

(*a*)   survival craft, life rafts, life buoys and life jackets must be properly constructed of suitable materials and of conspicuous colour [*Reg 4*]; and

(*b*)   every manned offshore installation must be provided with a totally enclosed motor propelled survival craft [*Reg 5(1)*].

Survival craft

34.30   There must be displayed near the survival craft/life raft launching apparatus, clear instructions for operating it in appropriate languages. The survival craft/life raft must be such that it can be lowered into water when loaded with the full complement of persons and equipment; and it must be clearly marked. [*Reg 5*]. In addition, the survival craft/life raft must be provided with the following:

(*a*)   waterproof electric hand lamp for signalling;

(*b*)   supply of wholesome drinking water;

(*c*)   suitable first-aid outfit.

[*Reg 5(8), as amended by the Offshore Installations (Operational Safety, Health and Welfare and Life-Saving Appliances) (Revocations) Regulations 1989 (SI 1989 No 1672)*].

Life buoys

34.31   Life buoys must be provided on every offshore installation and stowed in such places that one is readily accessible from any part of the deck from which a person is liable to fall; they must be clearly marked, and have attached a self-igniting light lit by an electric battery and inextinguishable in water. [*Reg 6*].

Other safety provisions

34.32 Offshore installations must be provided with:

(*a*) suitable and sufficient means of escape for persons to descend into the water [*Reg 8*];

(*b*) a general alarm system;

(*c*) a public address system

[*Reg 9*];

(*d*) a plan showing the position of all life-saving appliances (except life jackets issued to particular persons) [*Reg 10*].

Safety representatives

34.33 Although there have been safety representatives with statutory powers since the *Safety Representatives and Safety Committees Regulations 1977*, these regulations did not extend to offshore installations. This was (obviously) a key omission, since offshore installations qualify, along with construction sites and mining operations, as one of the most hazardous work activities.

Triggered off by the Piper Alpha disaster in the North Sea in July 1988, as well as other earlier 'near-misses', the *Offshore Installations (Safety Representatives and Safety Committees) Regulations 1989 (SI 1989 No 971)* make provision for the appointment of safety representatives (not necessarily union appointees) on offshore installations. More particularly, the regulations require that installation owners/managers ensure that the workforce is given the opportunity of nominating and electing safety representatives for the purposes of 'policing' safety and health and welfare on offshore installations. Moreover, such safety representatives are entitled to the same protection from unfair dismissal as safety representatives who are trade union appointees, under *Sec 1* of the *Offshore Safety (Protection Against Victimisation) Act 1992*.

Establishment of constituencies

34.34 The first stage in the appointment of safety representatives is the establishment of a system of constituencies by the installation manager in consultation with the safety committee. Constituencies will take account of

(*a*) areas of the offshore installation;

(*b*) activities undertaken on or from the installation;

(*c*) employees of the workforce;

(*d*) other objective criteria which appear to the installation manager to be appropriate to the circumstances of the installation.

There must be, at least, two constituencies and every worker can be assigned to one, but subject to a maximum of forty and a minimum of three. It is the duty of the installation manager to post particulars of a constituency in suitable places on the installation and, if necessary, in appropriate languages. This done, the workers comprising the constituency, can elect a safety representative. [*Reg 7*]. Election for a safety representative lasts five weeks (or less). [*Reg 8*]. Any worker can represent his constituency as a safety representative, provided that he

(i)   is a member of that constituency;

(ii)   is willing to stand as a candidate;

(iii)   has been nominated by a second member; and

(iv)   his nomination is seconded by a third member.

A list of duly nominated candidates must be posted within a week after nominations have expired. [*Reg 10*].

Functions of offshore safety representatives

34.35   Safety representatives on offshore installations have similar functions to safety representatives generally (see 34.33 above, 'Safety representatives'). More particularly, they can

(*a*)   investigate potential hazards/dangerous occurrences and examine causes of accidents;

(*b*)   investigate *bona fide* health and safety complaints from their members;

(*c*)   draw matters arising from (*a*) and (*b*) to the attention of the installation manager and any employer;

(*d*)   approach the installation manager/any employer about general health and safety matters;

(*e*)   attend meetings of the safety committee;

(*f*)   represent members in consultation with the Inspectorate;

(*g*)   consult members on any part of the above matters.

Exercise of these functions cannot give rise to criminal and/or civil liability on the part of a safety representative. [*Reg 16*].

Inspections

Inspection of equipment

34.36   A safety representative can inspect any part of the installation or its equipment, provided that he

(*a*)   has given the manager or if his employer is not the installation owner, also his employer, reasonable notice in writing, and

(*b*)   that part of the installation/equipment has not been inspected in the previous three months.

More frequent inspections, by agreement with the manager, can take place. [*Reg 17(2)*].

Inspection of documents

Safety representatives are entitled to inspect any documents relating to health and safety, except an individual's medical record. [*Reg 18*].

Notifiable incidents

34.37   A safety representative can inspect relevant parts of the installation or equipment so as to determine the cause of a 'notifiable incident', provided that he notifies the manager and, if practicable, his employer, if

(*a*)   there has been a notifiable incident (that is, 'notifiable' under the *Offshore Installations (Inspections and Casualties) Regulations 1973 (SI 1973 No 1842)*);

(*b*)   it is safe for an inspection; and

(*c*)   the interests of his members might be involved.

[*Reg 17(3)*].

Risk of serious personal injury

34.38   If two or more safety representatives think that there is an 'imminent risk of serious personal injury', arising from an installation activity, they can

(i)   make representations to the manager, who must send a written report to an inspector, and

(ii)   themselves send a written report to an inspector.

[*Reg 17(4)*].

Safety case documentation

34.39   A safety representative is entitled to be supplied with a written summary of the main features of a Safety Case (or its revision) or to see a copy of the Safety Case (or its revision). [*Offshore Installations (Safety Case) Regulations 1992 (SI 1992 No 2885), Reg 18A*].

Safety committees

34.40   Owners of offshore installations, with one or more safety representatives, must establish a safety committee. [*Reg 19*].

This must consist of

(*a*)   the installation manager (as chairman),

(*b*)   one other person (to be appointed by the owner or manager),

(*c*)   all safety representatives, and

(*d*)   persons who may be co-opted by unanimous vote, e.g. safety officer.

[*Reg 20*].

A safety committee must be convened by the chairman within six weeks of the date of its establishment, and afterwards at least once every three months. [*Reg 21*].

Functions of safety committees

34.41   Safety committees have the following functions:

(i)   to monitor health/safety at the workplace;

(ii)   to keep under review the constituency system;

(iii)   to monitor arrangements for the training of safety representatives;

(iv)   to monitor the frequency of safety committee meetings;

(v)   to consider representations from any member of a safety committee;

    (vi)   to consider the causes of accidents, dangerous occurrences and cases of ill-health;

    (vii)   to consider any statutory documents, e.g. registers (but not medical records);

    (viii)   to prepare and maintain a record of its business, with a copy being kept for one year from the date of the meeting.

[*Reg 22*].

Installation owners/managers must co-operate with safety committees and safety representatives to enable them to perform their functions and they must disclose relevant information to safety representatives. [*Regs 23, 24*].

Training

34.42   Employers must permit safety representatives time off from work, without loss of pay, to enable them

(*a*)   to perform their functions, and

(*b*)   to undertake training

[*Reg 26*], and employers must meet the cost of training, travel and subsistence expenses [*Reg 27*].

Offences/defences

Offence

34.43   If an installation owner, manager or employer fails to comply with any of his statutory duties, he commits an offence (punishable as with mainline *HSWA* offences – see Chapter 17 'Enforcement'). [*Reg 28(1)*].

Defence

34.44   It is a defence for the accused to prove

    (i)   that he exercised all due diligence to prevent the commission of the offence, and

    (ii)   the relevant failure to comply was committed without his consent, connivance, or wilful default.

[*Reg 28(2)*].

Hazards in offshore activities

34.45   The fact that offshore oil and gas production has attracted its own specific health and safety legislation is an indicator, as with agriculture and construction, of the high degree of risk associated with these activities and the need for sound levels of safety management and performance.

The principal hazards associated with offshore operations can be summarised as follows.

Diving operations

34.46   Those who engage diving contractors must notify the HSE of each project in which the diving contractor is involved and they must make sure that the diver is registered with the Executive. [*Diving Operations at Work Regulations 1981, Regs 5A, 5B, 5C(2) as amended by SI 1992 No 608*].

Notification consists of

(i) diver's name and address;

(ii) telephone number where the diver's contractor may be contacted;

(iii) date/dates of start of diving operation(s);

(iv) number of days on which operation(s) will take place;

(v) location(s) of diving operation(s) including any offshore installation or pipeline;

(vi) total number of persons in diving team;

(vii) whether breathing mixture will be air or diving will use saturation techniques;

(viii) name/identification of each diving support vessel, barge or installation or other place, and method of maintaining its position;

(ix) description of nature and purpose of operations so as to highlight risks involved;

(x) name of person able to make arrangements to facilitate inspection, and his telephone number.

[*Diving Operations at Work (Amendment) Regulations 1992, 1B Sch*].

Location of platforms

34.47   The very nature of the work location, directly above the sea, carries the perpetual risk of operators falling off the edge of, or through openings in, the platform into the sea below. In many cases the chance of rescue is remote, even with the use of helicopters. This risk is particularly common during the initial work stages in the establishment of the platform, prior to hook-up or fitting out work.

Fire

34.48   Work on operational platforms exposes operators to a far greater fire risk than their opposite numbers in industry and commerce. A well-established fire protection strategy is therefore essential, aimed principally at fire prevention. Such a strategy must incorporate adequate means of escape in the event of fire and the provision and maintenance of specialised fire-fighting equipment. Fire drill and emergency procedures should feature in induction training of operators prior to their commencing work on the platform, and there should be frequent drills following the establishment of the platform. In particular, control of potential sources of ignition is crucial to safe operation. Typical sources of ignition are welding torches, electrical equipment and matches and cigarette lighters carried by operators.

Radiation hazards

34.49   Site radiography techniques used to assess the integrity of pipeline joints implies the need for an exceptionally high level of radiological protection for operators. There must be total compliance with the *Ionising Radiations Regulations 1985* in terms of the designation of competent persons, authorised persons and classified workers, medical supervision, personal monitoring procedures following excessive exposure, control of sealed sources of radiation, equipment tests and the maintenance of records (see Chapter 9 'Dangerous Substances I').

Cranes and lifting equipment

34.50   The potential for crane and lifting equipment failures, including the use of helicopters in lifting operations during the initial work stage, represents a serious hazard in offshore work (see Chapter 26 'Lifting Machinery and Equipment').

Burns and eye injuries

34.51   These are the two most common forms of injury to operators, in many cases associated with a failure to wear personal protective equipment provided.

Noise and vibration

34.52   It was recognised in the early days of offshore work that operators were exposed to risk of occupational deafness and vibration-induced injury. Thus, the *Offshore Installations (Operational Safety, Health and Welfare) Regulations 1976* require suitable insulation of items of equipment producing noise or vibration which is dangerous to health or likely to be dangerous to health. Personal protective equipment (including hearing protection) must be provided for all operators where they may be exposed to risk of injury or disease (see 30.13 NOISE AND VIBRATION and Chapter 36 'Personal Protective Equipment').

Access hazards

34.53   Falls from scaffolds and ladders, particularly during the initial work stage, have been common in the past, emphasising the need for good systems of scaffold inspection and maintenance in particular.

Gassing accidents and incidents

34.54   Precautions against asphyxiation, oxygen enrichment and various fumes, dusts, gases and vapours are now a standard feature of the industry.

Offshore safety management

Management responsibility

34.55   Under the *Mineral Workings (Offshore Installations) Act 1971*, the owners of the offshore installation must appoint an installation manager, who has general responsibility for safety, health and welfare which, in certain cases, includes the maintenance of order and discipline (see *MacMillan v Wimpey* (34.28 above)). The installation manager has similar duties and powers to that of a ship's captain (see 34.25 above).

Written procedures

34.56   Detailed plans, procedures, safe systems of work and written instructions, including those covering the operation of permit to work systems, are a standard feature of offshore safety operations. Such procedures and safe systems of work may include the use of access equipment, e.g. scaffolding, boatswain's chairs, ladders, etc., work over the sea, the safe use of lifting equipment, helicopter operations and general fire and emergency procedures.

Contingency plans

34.57 A formal contingency plan to cover fire, explosion and other emergency situations must be readily available.

Operator training

34.58 High standards of operator training, prior to arrival on a working platform and at frequent intervals during their employment, are crucial to ensure safe operation.

Training programmes for operators

34.59 Induction training should incorporate the following aspects:

(*a*) *General safety* – dealing with the hazards of offshore work and the personal precautions necessary, in particular the correct use of all forms of personal protective equipment, i.e. foul weather protection, safety helmets, safety harnesses.

(*b*) *Safe working procedures* – the use of permit to work systems and safe systems of work covering electricity, welding and ionising radiation in particular; the use of scaffolding, working platforms, the use of plant and equipment, maintenance and inspection procedures and record keeping (see further 1.32 INTRODUCTION).

(*c*) *Health precautions* – including precautions against toxic dusts, fumes, gases and vapours, asbestos, the risk of asphyxiation and anoxia, and physical hazards associated with noise, electricity and radiation.

(*d*) *Survival* – instruction in the use of life jackets, survival capsules, life boats and rafts; emergency platform evacuation procedures, particularly in the event of fire or explosion.

(*e*) *Helicopter operations* – procedures for safe movement of personnel by helicopter to or from the platform.

(*f*) *Fire protection* – the correct use of fire appliances, platform evacuation procedure in the event of fire, platform fire alarm system.

(*g*) *First-aid* – elementary first-aid procedures.

(See also 34.73 below.)

Offshore Installations (Safety Case) Regulations 1992 (SI 1992 No 2885)

34.60 Following the recommendations of the Public Inquiry into the Piper Alpha tragedy in 1988 (the Lord Cullen Report), the current *Offshore Installations (Safety Case) Regulations 1992* were introduced. They came into operation (generally) on 31 May 1993 with one exception, and they require operators of fixed and mobile installations – and, additionally, where they are engaged in combined operations – to prepare a formal Safety Case, which must be accepted by HSE, before operations can begin; moreover, a fixed installation must not be decommissioned until similarly a Safety Case has been prepared and accepted.

A Safety Case is a document which contains the particulars specified in *Reg 8* and also *Schedule 1* of these regulations and the operator has to prepare this document containing the particulars and within the time limits and in accordance with the other requirements outlined below. Later Safety Cases may refer to the same particulars as earlier Safety Cases.

Before commencing operations

(i) *Fixed installations*

34.61   The operator or owner must prepare a Safety Case containing the relevant particulars and he must send it to HSE so that he will be able to comply with any design requirement raised by the Executive within three months of receipt of any design requirements.

No operations may be commenced until that has been done and six months have elapsed since he sent the Safety Case to the Executive and it has been accepted by the Executive. Commencement of an operation includes the first well drilling operation which may require the release of hydrocarbons beneath the sea bed or when hydrocarbons are brought onto the site for the first time. [*Reg 4*].

(ii) *Mobile installations*

Operators of mobile installations must not commence operations before a Safety Case has been sent to HSE at least three months before commencing the movement of the installation in the waters, and has been accepted by HSE. [*Reg 5*].

(iii) *Combined operations*

Operators of fixed installations must not engage in a combined operation with a mobile installation, and vice versa, unless

(*a*)   the joint operators have prepared a Safety Case and sent it to HSE

—   at least four weeks before operations commence where a mobile installation is to carry out an operation on a well connected to a fixed installation (but not a well beneath or immediately adjacent to the installation),

—   at least six weeks before operations commence in all other cases; and

(*b*)   HSE has accepted the Safety Case.

[*Reg 6*].

Safety cases must be revised as and when convenient and appropriate but, at least, every three years. [*Reg 9*].

Decommissioning fixed installations

34.62   Operators of a fixed installation must not decommission an installation unless they have

(*a*)   prepared a Safety Case,

(*b*)   sent it to HSE at least six months before the decommissioning starts, and

(*c*)   HSE has accepted the Safety Case.

[*Reg 7*].

Safety Case specifications

34.63   The particulars to be included in all Safety Cases are required to demonstrate that:

(a)   there is a management system that will make sure that the statutory provisions relating to the installation are complied with;

(b)   adequate arrangements have been made for audit and reporting of the management system;

(c)   all hazards that could cause a major accident have been identified;

(d)   risks have been evaluated and measures will be taken to keep these risks to the lowest level that is reasonably practicable.

[*Reg 8*].

(1) *Design of fixed installation*

PARTICULARS TO BE INCLUDED IN A SAFETY CASE FOR THE DESIGN OF A FIXED INSTALLATION

1. The name and address of the operator of the installation.

2. A general description of the means by which the management system of the operator, referred to in regulation 8, will ensure that the structure and plant of the installation will be designed, selected, constructed and commissioned in a way which will reduce risks to health and safety to the lowest level that is reasonably practicable.

3. A description, with diagrams, of–

   (a)   the main and secondary structure of the installation;

   (b)   its plant;

   (c)   the layout and configuration of its plant;

   (d)   the connections to be made to any pipe-line or installation; and

   (e)   any wells to be connected to the installation.

4. A scale plan of the intended location of the installation and of anything to be connected to it, and particulars of–

   (a)   the meteorological and oceanographic conditions to which the installation may foreseeably be subjected; and

   (b)   the properties of the sea-bed and subsoil at its location.

5. Particulars of the types of operation, and activities in connection with an operation, which the installation is to be capable of performing.

6. The maximum number of persons–

   (a)   expected to be on the installation at any time; and

   (b)   for whom accommodation is to be provided.

7. Particulars of the plant and arrangements for the control of operations on a well, including those–

   (a)   to control the pressure in a well;

   (b)   to prevent the uncontrolled release of hazardous substances; and

   (c)   to minimise the effects of damage to subsea equipment by drilling equipment.

8. A description of any pipe-line with the potential to cause a major accident, including–

    (*a*)   the fluid which it conveys;

    (*b*)   its dimensions and layout;

    (*c*)   its contained volume at declared maximum allowable operating pressure; and

    (*d*)   any apparatus and works intended to secure safety.

9. Particulars of plant and arrangements for–

    (*a*)   the detection of the presence of toxic or flammable gas; and

    (*b*)   the detection, prevention or mitigation of fires.

10. A description of the arrangements to be made for protecting persons on the installation from hazards of explosion, fire, heat, smoke, toxic gas or fumes during any period while they may need to remain on the installation following an incident which is beyond immediate control and for enabling such persons to be evacuated from the installation where necessary, including the provision for–

    (*a*)   temporary refuge;

    (*b*)   routes from locations where persons may be present to temporary refuge and for egress therefrom to points from where the installation may be evacuated;

    (*c*)   means of evacuation at these points; and

    (*d*)   facilities within temporary refuge for the monitoring and control of the incident and for organising evacuation.

11. A statement of performance standards which have been established in relation to the arrangements referred to in paragraph 10 (including performance standards which have been established for structures and plant provided pursuant to such arrangements), and a statement of the minimum period for which the arrangements as a whole are intended to be effective following an incident referred to in that paragraph.

12. A demonstration, by reference to the results of suitable and sufficient quantitative risk assessment, that the measures taken or to be taken in relation to the hazards referred to in paragraph 10, including the arrangements mentioned in that paragraph, will reduce risks to the health and safety of persons to the lowest level that is reasonably practicable.

13. Particulars of the intended methods of design and construction, and of the principal codes of practice to be observed in relation to them.

14. A description of–

    (*a*)   the principal features of the design of the installation, and the arrangements and procedures for its completion; and

    (*b*)   the arrangements and procedures for the construction and commissioning of the installation,

which are intended to ensure that risks from a major accident will be at the lowest level that is reasonably practicable.

[*1 Sch*].

(2) *Operation of fixed installation*

PARTICULARS TO BE INCLUDED IN A SAFETY CASE FOR THE OPERATION OF A FIXED INSTALLATION

1. The name and address of the operator of the installation.

2. A description, with scale diagrams, of

   (*a*) the main and secondary structure of the installation and its materials;

   (*b*) its plant;

   (*c*) the layout and configuration of its plant;

   (*d*) the connections to be made to any pipe-line or installation; and

   (*e*) any wells to be connected to the installation.

3. A scale plan of the location of the installation and of anything connected to it, and particulars of–

   (*a*) the meteorological and oceanographic conditions to which the installation may foreseeably be subjected; and

   (*b*) the properties of the sea-bed and subsoil at its location.

4. Particulars of the types of operation, and activities in connection with an operation, which the installation is capable of performing.

5. The maximum number of persons–

   (*a*) expected to be on the installation at any time; and

   (*b*) for whom accommodation is to be provided.

6. Particulars of the plant and arrangements for the control of operations on a well, including those–

   (*a*) to control the pressure in a well;

   (*b*) to prevent the uncontrolled release of hazardous substances; and

   (*c*) to minimise the effects of damage to subsea equipment by drilling equipment.

7. A description of any pipe-line with the potential to cause a major accident, including–

   (*a*) the fluid which it conveys;

   (*b*) its dimensions and layout;

   (*c*) its contained volume at declared maximum allowable operating pressure; and

   (*d*) any apparatus and works intended to secure safety.

8. Particulars of plant and arrangements for–

   (*a*) the detection of the presence of toxic or flammable gas; and

   (*b*) the detection, prevention or mitigation of fires.

9. A description of the arrangements made or to be made for protecting persons on the installation from hazards of explosion, fire, heat, smoke, toxic gas or fumes during any period while they may need to remain on the installation following an incident which is beyond immediate control and for enabling such persons to be

evacuated from the installation where necessary, including the provision for–

(*a*)   temporary refuge;

(*b*)   routes from locations where persons may be present to temporary refuge and for egress therefrom to points from where the installation may be evacuated;

(*c*)   means of evacuation at those points;

(*d*)   facilities within temporary refuge for the monitoring and control of the incident and for organising evacuation.

10. A statement of performance standards which have been established in relation to the arrangements referred to in paragraph 9 (including performance standards which have been established for structures and plant provided pursuant to such arrangements), and a statement of the minimum period for which the arrangements as a whole are intended to be effective following an incident referred to in that paragraph.

11. A demonstration, by reference to the results of suitable and sufficient quantitative risk assessment, that the measures taken or to be taken in relation to the hazards referred to in paragraph 9, including the arrangements mentioned in that paragraph, will reduce risks to the health and safety of persons to the lowest level that is reasonably practicable.

12. Particulars of the main requirements in the specification for the design of the installation and its plant, including any limits for safe operation or use specified therein.

13. Sufficient particulars to demonstrate that the design of the installation, its plant and the pipe-lines connected to it is such that the risks from a major accident are at the lowest level that is reasonably practicable.

14. Particulars concerning any remedial work to be carried out to the installation or the plant referred to in the preceeding paragraphs, and the time by which it will be done.

[*2 Sch*].

(3) *Mobile installation*

PARTICULARS TO BE INCLUDED IN A SAFETY CASE FOR A MOBILE INSTALLATION

1. The name of the owner of the installation.

2. A description, with scale diagrams, of:

(*a*)   the main and secondary structure of the installation and its materials;

(*b*)   its plant; and

(*c*)   the layout and configuration of its plant.

3. Particulars of the types of operation, and activities in connection with an operation, which the installation is capable of performing.

4. The maximum number of persons–

(*a*)   expected to be on the installation at any time; and

(*b*)   for whom accommodation is to be provided.

5. Particulars of the plant and arrangements for the control of operations on a well, including those–

    (*a*)   to control the pressure in a well;

    (*b*)   to prevent the uncontrolled release of hazardous substances; and

    (*c*)   to minimise the effects of damage to subsea equipment by drilling equipment.

6. Particulars of plant and arrangements for–

    (*a*)   the detection of the presence of toxic or flammable gas; and

    (*b*)   the detection, prevention or mitigation of fires.

7. A description of the arrangements made or to be made for protecting persons on the installation from hazards of explosion, fire, heat, smoke, toxic gas or fumes during any period while they may need to remain on the installation following an incident which is beyond immediate control and for enabling such persons to be evacuated from the installation where necessary, including the provision for–

    (*a*)   temporary refuge;

    (*b*)   routes from locations where persons may be present to temporary refuge and for egress therefrom to points from where the installation may be evacuated;

    (*c*)   means of evacuation at those points;

    (*d*)   facilities within temporary refuge for the monitoring and control of the incident and for organising evacuation.

8. A statement of performance standards which have been established in relation to the arrangements referred to in paragraph 7 (including performance standards which have been established for structures and plant provided pursuant to such arrangements), and a statement of the minimum period for which the arrangements as a whole are intended to be effective following an incident referred to in that paragraph.

9. A demonstration, by reference to the results of suitable and sufficient quantitative risk assessment, that the measures taken or to be taken in relation to the hazards referred to in paragraph 7, including the arrangements mentioned in that paragraph, will reduce risks to the health and safety of persons to the lowest level that is reasonably practicable.

10. Particulars of the main requirements in the specification for the design of the installation and its plant, including any limits for safe operation and use specified therein.

11. Particulars of–

    (*a*)   the limits of the environmental conditions beyond which the installation cannot safely be stationed or operated;

    (*b*)   the properties of the sea-bed and subsoil which are necessary for the safe stationing and operation of the installation; and

    (*c*)   the locations in which the installation may be stationed and operated safely.

12. Sufficient particulars to demonstrate that the design of the installation and its plant is such that the risks from a major accident are at the lowest level that is reasonably practicable.

13. Particulars concerning any remedial work to be carried out to the installation

or the plant referred to in the preceding paragraphs, and the time by which it will be done.

[*3 Sch*].

(4) Combined operations

PARTICULARS TO BE INCLUDED IN A SAFETY CASE FOR COMBINED OPERATIONS

1. The names and addresses of the operators and owners preparing the safety case.

2. Particulars which, were it not for regulation 6(1), would be contained in the safety cases prepared for the installations pursuant to regulation 4(2) or 5 or in a revision thereof pursuant to regulation 9.

3. Sufficient particulars to demonstrate that the management systems referred to in those safety cases pursuant to regulation 8 will be co-ordinated so as to reduce the risks from a major accident to the lowest level that is reasonably practicable.

4. Particulars of any plant installed solely for the purpose of permitting the installations to engage in the combined operation.

5. A demonstration that any limits for the safe operation or use of plant which are contained in the specifications for the design of the installations or their plant will not be exceeded while the installations are engaged in the combined operation.

6. A programme of work for the combined operation.

7. The date when the installation will cease to be engaged in the combined operation.

[*4 Sch*].

(5) Abandonment of fixed installation

PARTICULARS TO BE INCLUDED IN A SAFETY CASE FOR THE ABANDONMENT OF A FIXED INSTALLATION

1. The name and address of the operator of the installation.

2. A description, with scale diagrams, of–

   (*a*)   the main and secondary structure of the installation and its materials;

   (*b*)   its plant;

   (*c*)   the layout and configuration of its plant;

   (*d*)   the connections made to any pipe-line or installation; and

   (*e*)   any wells connected to the installation.

3. A scale plan of the location of the installation and of anything connected to it, and particulars of–

   (*a*)   the meteorological and oceanographic conditions to which the installation may foreseeably be subjected; and

   (*b*)   the properties of the sea-bed and subsoil at its location.

4. Particulars of the operations which were being carried out, including activities on and in connection with the installation relating to each operation.

5. The maximum number of persons at work on the installation during decommissioning.

6. Particulars of the plant and arrangements for the control of the operations on a well, including those–

(*a*)   to control the pressure in a well;

(*b*)   to prevent the uncontrolled release of hazardous substances; and

(*c*)   to minimise the effects of damage to subsea equipment by drilling equipment.

7. A description of any pipe-line with the potential to cause a major accident, including–

(*a*)   the fluid which it conveys;

(*b*)   its dimensions and layout;

(*c*)   its contained volume at declared maximum allowable operating pressure; and

(*d*)   any apparatus and works intended to secure safety.

8. Particulars of plant and arrangements for–

(*a*)   the detection of the presence of toxic or flammable gas;

(*b*)   the detection, prevention or mitigation of fires; and

(*c*)   the protection of persons from their consequences.

9. Particulars of escape routes, embarkation points and means of evacuation to enable the full and safe evacuation and rescue of persons to take place in an emergency.

10. Sufficient particulars to demonstrate that the proposed arrangements, methods and procedures for–

(*a*)   dealing, by way of abandonment or otherwise, with any wells to which the installation is connected;

(*b*)   decommissioning the installation and connected pipe-lines; and

(*c*)   demolishing or dismantling the installation and connected pipe-lines,

take adequate account of the design and method of construction of the installation and its plant, and reduce risks from a major accident to the lowest level that is reasonably practicable.

[*5 Sch*].

Construction activities

34.64   Construction activities may not be commenced unless notification of this is sent to the Executive at least 28 days before these occur and the particulars in *Schedule 7* below must be included in the notice. [*Reg 12*].

SCHEDULE 7

PARTICULARS TO BE INCLUDED IN NOTIFICATION OF CONSTRUCTION ACTIVITIES

1. The name and address of the operator of the installation.

2. The location at which the construction activity is to take place.

3. The name of any installation or heavy lift vessel to be involved in the construction activity (including one providing accommodation for persons engaged in the activity).

4. The dates on which the construction activity is expected to commence and finish.

5. A description of the nature of the construction activity and of the hazards with the potential to cause a major accident which it involves.

6. Particulars of the proposed programme of work.

7. The name of an individual who will be able to make arrangements to facilitate any inspection by an inspector of the construction activity, and details of how that person can be contacted.

Duty to comply with Safety Case and defences

34.65 Once prepared, or revised, an operator or owner must comply with the provisions of a Safety Case under threat of imposition of penalties (see 17.26 ENFORCEMENT). [*Reg 10(1)*].

Defences

There are two defences, namely,

(*a*) in the particular circumstances it was not in the best interests of health and safety to follow procedures specified and there was not sufficient time to revise the Safety Case; or

(*b*) commission of the offence was due to contravention by another (see below) of *Reg 14* (duty to co-operate with operator/owner) and

    (i) the accused had taken all reasonable precautions, and

    (ii) had exercised all due diligence to ensure that arrangements and procedures were followed.

[*Reg 10(2)*]. (See further 33.19 OFFICES for 'Due diligence' defence.)

'*Other person*' may refer to anyone required to co-operate with the operator/owner of the installation, namely,

(*a*) other party to a combined operation or party required to co-operate with the operator/owner;

(*b*) any other employer or self-employed person carrying out an activity on the installation;

(*c*) operator/owner of an installation connected by pipe-line to the installation in question;

(*d*) person in control of a stand-by vessel;

(*e*) person in control of a heavy lift vessel;

(*f*) owner of a pipe-line connected to the installation in question.

[*Reg 14(2)*].

Retention of documents

34.66 Operators/owners must keep a copy of the Safety Case, and any revision of it, for as long as it is current (normally three years – see 34.60 above). Any ensuing audit report and recommendations as well as any record of any action taken in consequence of such audit report, should be kept for, at least, three years at the address notified to the Executive which must be in Great Britain and on the installation to which it refers. [*Reg 15*].

(Provisions relevant to drilling of a well will not commence until 30 November 1995 and are not yet included here. [*Reg 11*].)

Permits to work

34.67   1.   Operators' permits to work should be part of the safety management system.

      2.   Operators and the HSE should pay particular attention to the competence of contractors' supervisors, who are to operate the permit to work system.

      3.   Standardisation of permit to work systems throughout the offshore industry is *not* necessary (or practicable), though some harmonisation is desirable.

      4.   Operators should be made responsible for ensuring that supervisors are trained in the permit to work system.

      5.   All permits to work should incorporate a mechanical isolation procedure, involving physical locking off and tagging of isolation valves.

      6.   Permits to work and their consequent isolations, both mechanical and electrical, should remain in force until work is sufficiently complete for the permit to be signed off and equipment returned to operation.

      7.   Copies of all issued permits should be displayed at a commencement location, so that operating staff can easily see and check which equipment is under maintenance.

(See further 1.32 INTRODUCTION.)

Fire and explosion protection procedures

34.68   1.   Operators should be compelled (by regulation) to submit a fire risk analysis to HSE.

      2.   Regulations and guidance notes should promote an approach to fire and explosion protection:

         (*a*)   encouraging active/passive fire protection; different forms of passive fire protection (e.g. fire insulation, platform layout and fire and explosion protection);

         (*b*)   in which location and resistance of fire and blast walls is determined by safety assessment rather than by regulation;

         (*c*)   in which the fire water deluge system is determined by safety assessment rather than by regulation;

         (*d*)   which provides an ability of the fire water deluge system (including the fire pump system) to survive severe accident conditions. (This should be a feature of the Safety Case.)

Escape routes

34.69   1.   External fire protection should be provided both to prevent a breach of accommodation and to maintain breathable air within it.

2. An integrated set of active/passive measures should be provided to prevent ingress of smoke into the accommodation.

3. Regulations should require that ventilation air intakes be provided with smoke and gas detectors, and that, on smoke or gas alarm sounding, ventilation and dampers should shut down.

4. Escape routes should be provided with adequate and reliable emergency lighting and photoluminescent direction signs.

5. Operators are to be required by HSE to carry out an assessment of the risk of smoke or gas ingress and to fit smoke and gas detectors and implement ventilation shutdown arrangements.

Emergency centres and systems

34.70 1. A radio room with facilities for external communications will have to be located in the temporary safe refuge. Where the radio room is not in the temporary safe refuge, such facility should be in the emergency radio room in the temporary safe refuge.

2. Emergency systems, including emergency power supplies, emergency shutdown and an emergency communications system, should be able to survive severe accident conditions (including fire, explosion and strong vibration) and this should feature in the Safety Case.

3. There should be standardisation of status lights and alarm systems for emergencies.

Evacuation, escape and rescue

34.71 1. Operators must submit to HSE evacuation, escape and rescue analysis. In particular, this should specify:

(*a*) formal command structure for the control of emergency;

(*b*) likely availability and capacity of helicopters for personnel evacuation;

(*c*) types, numbers, locations and accessibility of a totally enclosed motor-propelled survival craft for evacuation of personnel from the temporary safe refuge;

(*d*) types, numbers and locations of life rafts;

(*e*) specifications (i.e. speed, sea capability and accommodation), location and functions of standby and other vessels;

(*f*) types, numbers, locations and availability of fast rescue craft, whether on installation or on standby or other vessels;

(*g*) types, numbers and locations of personnel survival and escape equipment.

Escape to sea

34.72 1. Installations are to be provided with life rafts sufficient to accommodate safety personnel on the installation; and suitable ropes must give access to life rafts.

2. Means of descent into the sea are to be provided, including fixed ladders and stairways.

Personal survival and escape equipment

34.73 Each individual should be provided with

    (i)   personal survival (or immersion) suit,

    (ii)   life-jacket,

    (iii) smoke hood,

    (iv) torch,

    (v)   fireproof gloves,

and these must be kept in the accommodation. Other survival suits, life-jackets and smoke hoods for at least half the number of persons on site, are to be stored in containers.

Training

34.74 UKOOA (the Offshore Operators' Association) guidelines for offshore emergency safety training is to be the minimum requirement for survival and fire-fighting.

Chapter 35

Overcrowding

Introduction

35.1 Although generally associated with 'welfare' requirements, overcrowding in workplaces can cause injuries and health risks. Workrooms should have enough uncluttered space to allow people to go to and from workstations with relative ease. The number of people who may work in any particular room at any time will depend not only on the size of room but also on space given over to furniture, fittings, equipment and general room layout. Workrooms should be of sufficient height to afford staff safe access to workstations. If, however, the workroom is in an old building, say, with low beams or other possible obstructions, this should be clearly marked, e.g. 'Low beams, mind your head'. Current statutory requirements relating to overcrowding are contained in the *Workplace (Health, Safety and Welfare) Regulations 1992* (see 35.2 below) and, as regards existing factories, in the *Factories Act 1961, s 2* and existing offices/shops in *OSRPA s 5* (see 35.3–35.8 below).

There is sufficient compliance with the new obligations if the owner of an *existing* factory is already complying with *Sec 2* of the *Factories Act 1961*, provided that a minimum of 11 cubic metres per person is available. [*Workplace (Health, Safety and Welfare) Regulations 1992, Reg 10(2)*].

Current statutory requirements – all workplaces – workroom dimensions/space

35.2 Every room in which people work should have sufficient

(*a*)   floor area,

(*b*)   height, and

(*c*)   unoccupied space

for health, safety and welfare purposes (see also Chapter 18 'Factories and Workplaces' and Chapter 44 'Welfare Facilities'). [*Workplace (Health, Safety and Welfare) Regulations 1992, Reg 10*].

Total volume of the room (when empty), divided by the number of people normally working there, should be 11 cubic metres (minimum) per person – inapplicable to

(i)   retail sales kiosks, attendants' shelters etc.,

(ii)   lecture/meeting rooms etc.

[*1 Sch*].

Where furniture occupies a considerable part of the room, 11 metres may not be sufficient space per person. Here more careful planning and general room layout is required.

Existing factories – requirement until 1 January 1996

35.3 While work is being carried on, a factory must not be so overcrowded as to cause risk of injury to the health of persons employed in it. [*Factories Act 1961, s 2(1)*]. (For the definition of 'factory', see 18.16, 18.17 FACTORIES AND WORKPLACES.)

Minimum space per person

35.4 This general requirement is made more specific by the subsequent provisions of *Sec 2* which state that the number of persons employed at a time in any workroom must not be such that the amount of cubic space allowed for each one of them is less than 11 cubic metres. No space more than 4.2 metres from the floor is to be taken into account, and a gallery is treated as if it were a separate room. There must be posted in every workroom a notice (Form F 46) specifying the number of persons who may work in that workroom, unless the factory inspector of the district allows otherwise. [*Sec 2(2)(5)(6)*].

Exemption by certificate in case of explosive materials

35.5 If the chief inspector of factories is satisfied that, owing to special conditions in which work is carried on in a factory where explosive materials are either manufactured or handled, the application of the section is inappropriate, he may exempt it by certificate. [*Sec 2(3)*].

Existing offices/shops – requirement until 1 January 1996

35.6 While work is going on, no room comprised in or constituting an office or shop must be so overcrowded as to cause risk of injury to the health of persons working there.[*OSRPA s 5(1)*]. Moreover, in calculating whether a room is overcrowded, regard is to be had not only to the persons who may be expected to be working in the room at any given time, but also to the amount of space taken up by furniture, furnishings, fittings, machinery, plant, equipment, appliances and other things (whether similar to the preceding specified items or not). [*Sec 5(1)*]. (For the offices and shops covered by *OSRPA*, see Chapter 33 'Offices' (in particular, 33.14) and Chapter 40 'Shops'.)

Minimum space per person

35.7 Further, a room where people work must be of such a size that there is 3.7 sq m (40 sq ft) of floor space to each person habitually employed to work at any one time in the room and at least 11 cubic m of room space (400 cubic ft) to each person. This does not mean that each person must have his own space of 3.7 sq m, but it does mean that the total floor space must amount to 11.1 sq m, for example, if three people are employed in a room. [*OSRPA s 5(2); OSRPA (Metrication) Regulations 1982 (SI 1982 No 827), Reg 2*].

Exceptions

35.8 These numerical space standards do not apply to a room to which members of the public are invited to resort (e.g. a shop) [*Sec 5(3)(b)*], or hotel foyers or restaurants or switchrooms in public telephone exchanges [*OSRPA (Exemption No 5) Order 1968 (SI 1968 No 1047)*].

Chapter 36

Personal Protective Equipment

Introduction

36.1 Conventional wisdom suggests that 'safe place strategies' are more effective in combating health and safety risks than 'safe person strategies'. Safe systems of work, and control/prevention measures serve to protect everyone at work, whilst the advantages of personal protective equipment are limited to the individual(s) concerned. Given, however, the fallibility of any state of the art technology in endeavouring to achieve total protection, some level of personal protective equipment is inevitable in view of the obvious (and not so obvious) risks to head, face, neck, eyes, ears, lungs, skin, arms, hands and feet. Until very recently a gamut of occupation/process-based regulations, ranging from the *Aerated Water Regulations 1921* to the *Woodworking Machines Regulations 1974*, had specified personal protective equipment necessary in specified circumstances. Moreover, in tandem with statutory requirements, common law had gone a stage further by insisting not only that employers have requisite safety equipment at hand, or available in an accessible place, but also that management ensure that operators use it (see *Bux v Slough Metals Ltd*, 1.45 INTRODUCTION). That the hallowed duty to 'provide and maintain' has been getting progressively stricter is evidenced by *Crouch v British Rail Engineering Ltd [1988] IRLR 404* to the extent that employers could be in breach of either statutory or common law duty (or both) in the case of injury/disease to a member of the employee's immediate family involved, say, in cleaning protective clothing – but the injury/disease must have been foreseeable (*Hewett v Alf Brown's Transport Ltd, The Times, 4 January 1992*). This chapter deals with the requirements of the new *Personal Protective Equipment at Work Regulations 1992*, the *Personal Protective Equipment (EC Directive) Regulations 1992* (which have implemented the Personal Protective Equipment Directive) and the duties imposed on manufacturers and suppliers of personal protective equipment, the common law duty on employers to provide suitable personal protective equipment, and the main types of personal protective equipment and clothing and some relevant British Standards.

The Personal Protective Equipment at Work Regulations 1992 (SI 1992 No 2966)

36.2 With the advent of the *Personal Protective Equipment at Work Regulations 1992 (SI 1992 No 2966)*, all employers must make a formal assessment of the personal protective equipment needs of employees and provide ergonomically suitable equipment in relation to foreseeable risks at work (see further 36.7 below). However, employers cannot be expected to comply with their new statutory duties, unless manufacturers of personal protective equipment have complied with theirs under the requirements of the *Personal Protective Equipment (EC Directive) Regulations 1992 (SI 1992 No 3139)* – that is, had their products independently certified for EC accreditation purposes. Although imposing a considerable remit on manufacturers, EC accreditation is an indispensable condition precedent to sale and commercial circulation (see 36.13 below).

Employees must be made aware of the purpose of personal protective equipment, its limitations and the need for on-going maintenance. Thus, when assessing the need for, say, eye protection, employers should first identify the existence of workplace hazards (e.g. airborne dust, projectiles, liquid splashes, slippery floors, inclement weather in the case of outside work) and then the extent of danger (e.g. frequency/velocity of projectiles, frequency/severity of splashes). Selection can (and, indeed, should) then be made from the variety of CE-marked equipment available, in respect of which manufacturers must ensure that such equipment provides protection, and suppliers ascertain that it meets such requirements/ standards [*HSWA s 6*] (see further Chapter 38 'Product Safety'). Typically, most of the risks will have already been logged, located and quantified in a routine risk/safety audit (see 39.20 RISK ANALYSIS AND SAFETY MONITORING), and classified according to whether they are physical/chemical/biological in relation to the part(s) of the body affected (e.g. eyes, ears, skin).

36.3   Selection of personal protective equipment is a first stage in an on-going routine, followed by proper use and maintenance of equipment (on the part of both employers and employees) as well as training and supervision in personal protection techniques. Maintenance presupposes a stock of renewable spare parts coupled with regular inspection, testing, examination, repair, cleaning and disinfection schedules as well as keeping appropriate records. Depending on the particular equipment, some will require regular testing and examination (e.g. respiratory equipment), whilst others merely inspection (e.g. gloves, goggles). Generally, manufacturers' maintenance schedules should be followed and suitable accommodation provided for protective equipment in order to minimise loss or damage and prevent exposure to cold, damp or bright sunlight, e.g. pegs for helmets, pegs and lockers for clothing, spectacle cases for safety glasses.

On-going safety training (see 15.31 EMPLOYERS' DUTIES), often carried out by manufacturers for the benefit of users, identifying the need for personal protective equipment, should combine both theory and practice.

Work activities/processes requiring personal protective equipment

36.4   Examples abound of processes/activities of which personal protective equipment is a prerequisite, from construction work and mining, through work with ionising radiations, to work with lifting plant, cranes, as well as handling chemicals, tree felling and working from heights. Similarly, blasting operations, work in furnaces and drop forging all require a degree of personal protection.

Statutory requirements in connection with personal protective equipment

36.5   General statutory requirements relating to personal protective equipment are contained in *Sec 2* of the *Health and Safety at Work etc. Act 1974* (see further Chapter 15 'Employers' Duties'), and additionally *Sec 9* to the effect that employers cannot charge for provision of personal protective equipment. More specific statutory requirements concerning personal protective equipment exist in the *Personal Protective Equipment at Work Regulations 1992 (SI 1992 No 2966)* (in tandem with the *Personal Protective Equipment (EC Directive) Regulations 1992 (SI 1992 No 3139)*), and sundry other recent regulations applicable to particular industries/ processes, e.g. asbestos, noise, construction (see 36.8 below). As acknowledged, it is a characteristic of all statutory requirements that personal protective equipment is provided by employers to employees free of charge [*HSWA s 9; Personal Protective*

Equipment at Work Regulations 1992, Reg 11] (see also 15.1 EMPLOYERS' DUTIES for employer's duties towards immediate family of employee and 15.38 'Contributory negligence' for the position where employee fails to use protective equipment).

General statutory duties – HSWA 1974

36.6   Employers are under a general duty to ensure, so far as reasonably practicable, the health, safety and welfare at work of their employees – a duty which clearly implies provision/maintenance of personal protective equipment. [*HSWA s 2(1)*].

Specific statutory duties – Personal Protective Equipment at Work Regulations 1992 (SI 1992 No 2966)

(A) *Duties of employers*

36.7   Employers – and self-employed persons in cases (i), (ii), (iii), (iv) and (v) below, must

(i)   formally assess (and review periodically) provision and suitability of personal protective equipment. [*Personal Protective Equipment at Work Regulations 1992, Reg 6(1)(3)*].

The assessment should include

(*a*)   risks to health and safety not avoided by other means;

(*b*)   reference to characteristics which personal protective equipment must have.

[*Personal Protective Equipment at Work Regulations 1992, Reg 2*].

The aim of the assessment is to ensure that an employer knows which personal protective equipment to choose; it constitutes the first stage in a continuing programme, concerned also with proper use and maintenance of personal protective equipment and training and supervision of employees.

(ii)   provide suitable personal protective equipment to his employees, who may be exposed to health and safety risks while at work, except where the risk has either been adequately controlled by other equally or more effective means. [*Personal Protective Equipment at Work Regulations 1992, Reg 4(1)*].

Personal protective equipment is not suitable unless

(*a*)   it is appropriate for risks involved and conditions at the place of exposure;

(*b*)   it takes account of ergonomic requirements and the state of health of the person who wears it;

(*c*)   it is capable of fitting the wearer correctly; and

(*d*)   so far as reasonably practicable (for meaning, see Chapter 15 'Employers' Duties'), it is effective to prevent or adequately control risks involved without increasing the overall risk.

[*Personal Protective Equipment at Work Regulations 1992, Reg 4(3)*].

(iii)   provide compatible personal protective equipment – that is, that the use of more than one item of personal protective equipment is compatible with other personal protective equipment. [*Personal Protective Equipment at Work Regulations 1992, Reg 5*].

(iv)   maintain (as well as replace and clean) any personal protective equipment in an efficient state, efficient working order and in good repair. [*Personal Protective Equipment at Work Regulations 1992, Reg 7*].

(v)   provide suitable accommodation for personal protective equipment when not being used. [*Personal Protective Equipment at Work Regulations 1992, Reg 8*].

(vi)   provide employees with information, instruction and training to enable them to know

   (*a*)   the risks which personal protective equipment will avoid or minimise;

   (*b*)   the purpose for which and manner in which personal protective equipment is to be used;

   (*c*)   any action which the employee might take to ensure that personal protective equipment remains efficient.

   [*Personal Protective Equipment at Work Regulations 1992, Reg 9*].

(vii) ensure, taking all reasonable steps, that personal protective equipment is properly used. [*Personal Protective Equipment at Work Regulations 1992, Reg 10*]. (This important provision requires training of employees in the use of the equipment and in the instructions for use of it (ACOP).)

(B) *Duties of employees*

Every employee must

   (i)   use personal protective equipment in accordance with training and instructions [*Personal Protective Equipment at Work Regulations 1992, Reg 10(2)*];

   (ii)   return all personal protective equipment to the appropriate accommodation [*Personal Protective Equipment at Work Regulations 1992, Reg 10(4)*];

   (iii) report any defect or loss in the equipment to the employer [*Personal Protective Equipment at Work Regulations 1992, Reg 11*].

Summary of employer's duties

(*a*)   duty of assessment;

(*b*)   duty to provide suitable PPE;

(*c*)   duty to provide compatible PPE;

(*d*)   duty to maintain and replace PPE;

(*e*)   duty to provide suitable accommodation for PPE;

(*f*)   duty to provide information and training;

(*g*)   duty to see that PPE is correctly used.

Specific requirements for particular industries and processes

36.8   In addition to the general remit of the *Personal Protective Equipment at Work Regulations 1992*, the following regulations impose specific requirements on employers to provide personal protective equipment up to the EC level of the *Personal Protective Equipment at Work Regulations 1992* (e.g. equipment bearing the 'CE' mark).

(1)   *Factories Act 1961, s 30(6)* – supply of suitable breathing apparatus etc. for use in confined spaces (see further 2.11 ACCESS);

(2)   *Control of Lead at Work Regulations 1980, Regs 7, 8* – supply of suitable respiratory equipment where exposure is not insignificant; suitable protective clothing;

(3)   *Control of Asbestos at Work Regulations 1987, Reg 8* – supply of respiratory protective equipment/suitable protective clothing;

(4)   *Control of Substances Hazardous to Health Regulations 1988 (COSHH), Reg 7* – supply of suitable protective equipment where employees are foreseeably exposed to substances hazardous to health;

(5)   *Noise at Work Regulations 1989, Reg 8* – personal ear protectors;

(6)   *Construction (Head Protection) Regulations 1989, Reg 3* – suitable head protection (except Sikhs, see Chapter 7 'Construction and Building Operations');

(7)   *Ionising Radiations Regulations 1985, Reg 23* – supply of suitable respiratory protective equipment, film badges, dosemeters;

(8)   *Shipbuilding and Ship-repairing Regulations 1960, Regs 50, 51* – supply of suitable breathing apparatus, belts, eye protectors, gloves and gauntlets.

These earlier requirements still apply, with the addition of the new wider requirements of *SI 1992 No 2966* (see 36.6 above).

Increased importance of uniform European standards

36.9   To date, manufacturers of products, including personal protective equipment (PPE), have sought endorsement or approval for products, prior to commercial circulation, through reference to British Standards (BS), HSE or European standards, an example of the former being Kitemark and an example of the latter being CEN or CENELEC. Both are examples of *voluntary* national and international schemes enterable into by manufacturers and customers, under which both sides are 'advantaged' by conformity with such standards. Conformity is normally achieved following a level of testing appropriate to the level of protection offered by the product. With the introduction of the *Personal Protective Equipment (EC Directive) Regulations 1992* (see 36.13 below), on 1 January 1993, this voluntary system of approval will be replaced by a statutory certification procedure.

Towards certification

36.10   Certification as a condition of sale is probably some time away. Transition from adherence based on a wide range of voluntary national (and international) standards to a compulsory universal EC standard takes time and specialist expertise. Already, however, British Standards Institution (BSI) has adopted the form BS EN as a British version of a uniform European standard. But, generally speaking, uniformity of approach to design and testing, on the part of manufacturers, represents a considerable remit and so statutory compliance with tougher new European standards is probably not likely to happen immediately. Here, too, however, there is evidence of some progress, e.g. the EN 45000 series of standards on how test houses and certification bodies are to be established and independently accredited. In addition, a range of European standards on PPE is currently being prepared in relation, particularly, to eye protection, hearing protection, respiratory protection and falls from heights.

Interim measures

36.11 Because the testing and knowledge required is highly specialised, suitable inspection and testing houses may well not be in operation in time for the introduction of the *Personal Protective Equipment (EC Directive) Regulations 1992*, in early 1993. Thus, most manufacturers will probably elect to comply with the current CEN standard when seeking product certification. Alternatively, should a manufacturer so wish, the inspection body can verify by way of another route to certification – this latter might well be the case with an innovative product where standards did not exist. Generally, however, compliance with current CEN (European Standardisation Committee) or, alternatively, BS 5750: Quality Assurance, will, it is suspected, be the often well-trodden route to certification. To date, several UK organisations, including manufacturers and independent bodies, are setting up PPE test houses, which will be independently accredited by the National Measurement Accreditation Service (NAMAS). Such test houses will be open to all comers for verification of performance levels.

'CE' mark

36.12 The 'CE' mark is a new concept, indicating that a product has satisfied the necessary statutory criteria and requirements for commercial circulation – in other words, complies with the *Personal Protective Equipment (EC Directive) Regulations 1992 (SI 1992 No 3139)*. Indeed, affixation of the 'CE' mark is a condition of sale and manufacturers who put products into circulation without obtaining CE accreditation break the law. For the avoidance of doubt, CE accreditation is not synonymous with compliance with the CEN standard, since a manufacturer can opt for certification via an alternative route. Still less is it an approvals mark. It is more of a quality mark, since all products covered by the regulations are required to meet formal quality control or quality of production systems in their certification procedures (see below). [*Arts 8.4, 11*].

Personal Protective Equipment (EC Directive) Regulations 1992 (SI 1992 No 3139)

36.13 The *Personal Protective Equipment (EC Directive) Regulations 1992* require most types of PPE (for exceptions, see 36.19 below) to satisfy specified certification procedures [*Art 8*], pass EC type-examination (i.e. official inspection by an approved inspection body) [*Art 10*] and carry a 'CE' mark both on the product itself and its packaging [*Art 13*] before being put into commercial circulation. Indeed, failure on the part of a manufacturer to obtain affixation of a 'CE' mark on his product before putting it into circulation, is a criminal offence under *Sec 6* of the *Health and Safety at Work etc. Act 1974*, carrying a maximum fine, on summary conviction, of £20,000 (see Chapter 17 'Enforcement'). Enforcement is through trading standards officers, as from 1 January 1994.

CE Mark of conformity

[*Art 13, Annex IV*].

The *Personal Protective Equipment (EC Directive) Regulations 1992* specify procedures and criteria with which manufacturers must comply in order to be able to obtain certification. Essentially this involves incorporation into design and production basic health and safety requirements. [*Art 3*]. Hence, by compliance with health and safety criteria, affixation of the 'CE' mark becomes a condition of sale and approval. Moreover, compliance, on the part of manufacturers, with these regulations, will enable employers to comply with their duties under the *Personal*

Protective Equipment at Work Regulations 1992 (SI 1992 No 2966). Reg 4(3)(e) of the Personal Protective Equipment at Work Regulations 1992 requires the PPE provided by the employer to comply with this and any later EC directive requirements.

fig. 17

Certification procedures

36.14   In order to obtain certification, manufacturers must submit to an approved body the following documentation (except in the case of PPE of simple design, where risks are minimal, e.g. gardening gloves, thimble, aprons, headgear, footwear, helmets, sunglasses).

(1)   Technical file, i.e.

    (*a*)   overall and detailed plans, accompanied by calculation notes/results of prototype tests;

    (*b*)   exhaustive list of basic health and safety requirements and harmonised standards taken into account in the model's design.

(2)   Description of control and test facilities used to check compliance with harmonised standards.

(3)   Copy of information relating to

    (*a*)   storage, use, cleaning, maintenance, servicing and disinfection;

    (*b*)   performance recorded during technical tests to monitor levels of protection;

    (*c*)   suitable PPE accessories;

    (*d*)   classes of protection appropriate to different levels of risk and limits of use;

    (*e*)   obsolescence deadline;

    (*f*)   type of packaging suitable for transport;

    (*g*)   significance of markings;

[*Art 8.1, Annex III; Art 1.4, Annex II*].

This must be provided in the official language of the member state of destination.

PPE protection against mortal/serious dangers – requiring compliance with quality control system

36.15   This category of PPE, including

(i)   filtering, respiratory devices for protection against solid and liquid aerosols/irritant, dangerous, toxic or radiotoxic gases;

(ii)   respiratory protection devices providing full insulation from the atmosphere, and for use in diving;

(iii)   protection against chemical attack or ionising radiation;

(iv)   emergency equipment for use in high temperatures, whether with or without infrared radiation, flames or large amounts of molten metal (100°C or more);

(v)   emergency equipment for use in low temperatures (–50°C or less);

(vi)   protection against falls from heights;

(vii)   protection against electrical risks;

(viii)   motor cycle helmets and visors;

must satisfy either

(1)   (*a*)   an EC quality control system for the final product, or

(*b*)   a system for ensuring EC quality of production by means of monitoring;

and in either case,

(2)   an EC declaration of conformity.

[*Art 8.4*].

Basic health and safety requirements applicable to all PPE

36.16   All PPE must

(i)   be ergonomically suitable, that is, be able to perform a risk-related activity whilst providing the user with the highest possible level of protection;

(ii)   preclude risks and inherent nuisance factors, such as roughness, sharp edges and projections and must not cause movements endangering the user;

(iii)   provide comfort and efficiency by facilitating correct positioning on the user and remaining in place for the foreseeable period of use; and by being as light as possible without undermining design strength and efficiency;

(iv)   be accompanied by necessary information – that is, the name and address of the manufacturer and technical file (see 36.14 above).

[*Annex II*].

General purpose PPE – specific to several types of PPE

36.17   (*a*)   PPE incorporating adjustment systems must not become incorrectly adjusted without the user's knowledge;

(*b*)   PPE enclosing parts of the body must be sufficiently ventilated to limit perspiration or to absorb perspiration;

(c) PPE for the face, eyes and respiratory tracts must minimise risks to same and, if necessary, contain facilities to prevent moisture formation and be compatible with wearing spectacles or contact lenses;

(d) PPE subject to ageing must contain date of manufacture and date of obsolescence and must be indelibly inscribed, if possible; if the useful life of a product is not known, accompanying information must enable the user to establish a reasonable obsolescence date. In addition, the number of times it can be cleaned before being inspected or discarded must (if possible) be affixed to the product; or, failing this, be indicated in accompanying literature;

(e) PPE which may be caught up during use by a moving object must have a suitable resistance threshold above which a constituent part will break and eliminate danger;

(f) PPE for use in explosive atmospheres must not be likely to cause an explosive mixture to ignite;

(g) PPE for emergency use or rapid installation/removal must minimise the time required for attachment and/or removal;

(h) PPE for use in very dangerous situations (see 36.15 above) must be accompanied with data for exclusive use of competent trained individuals, and describe procedure to be followed to ensure that it is correctly adjusted and functional when worn;

(j) PPE incorporating components which are adjustable or removable by user, must facilitate adjustment, attachment and removal without tools;

(k) PPE for connection to an external complementary device must be mountable only on appropriate equipment;

(l) PPE incorporating a fluid circulation system must permit adequate fluid renewal in the vicinity of the entire part of the body to be protected;

(m) PPE bearing one or more identification or recognition marks relating to health and safety must preferably carry harmonised pictograms/ideograms which remain perfectly legible throughout the foreseeable useful life of the product;

(n) PPE in the form of clothing capable of signalling the user's presence visually must have one or more means of emitting direct or reflected visible radiation;

(o) multi-risk PPE must satisfy basic requirements specific to each risk.

[*Art 2, Annex II*].

Additional requirements for specific PPE for particular risks

36.18 There are additional requirements for PPE designed for certain particular risks as follows:

PPE protection against

(1) *Mechanical impact risks*

(i) impact caused by falling/projecting objects must be sufficiently shock-absorbent to prevent injury from crushing or penetration of the protected part of the body;

(ii) falls.

In the case of falls due to slipping, outsoles for footwear must ensure satisfactory adhesion by grip and friction, given the state and nature of the surface. In the case of falls from a height, PPE must incorporate a body harness and attachment system connectable to a reliable anchorage point. The vertical drop of the user must be minimised to prevent collision with obstacles and the braking force injuring, tearing or causing the operator to fall;

   (iii)   mechanical vibration. PPE must be capable of ensuring adequate attenuation of harmful vibration components for the part of the body at risk.

(2)   *(Static) compression of part of the body* – must be able to attenuate its effects so as to prevent serious injury of chronic complaints.

(3)   *Physical injury* – must be able to protect all or part of the body against superficial injury by machinery, e.g. abrasion, perforation, cuts or bites.

(4)   *Prevention of drowning* – (lifejackets, armbands etc.) must be capable of returning to the surface a user who is exhausted or unconscious, without danger to his health. Such PPE can be wholly or partially inherently buoyant or inflatable either by gas or orally. It should be able to withstand impact with liquid, and, if inflatable, able to inflate rapidly and fully.

(5)   *Harmful effects of noise* – must protect against exposure levels of the *Noise at Work Regulations 1989* (i.e. 85 and 90 dbA) and must indicate noise attenuation level.

(6)   *Heat and/or fire* – must possess sufficient thermal insulation capacity to retain most of the stored heat until after the user has left the danger area and removed PPE. Moreover, constituent materials which could be splashed by large amounts of hot product must possess sufficient mechanical-impact absorbency. In addition, materials which might accidentally come into contact with flame as well as being used in the manufacture of fire-fighting equipment, must possess a degree of non-flammability proportionate to the risk foreseeably arising during use and must not melt when exposed to flame or contribute to flame spread. When ready for use, PPE must be such that the quantity of heat transmitted by PPE to the user must not cause pain or health impairment. Second, ready-to-use PPE must prevent liquid or steam penetration and not cause burns. If PPE incorporates a breathing device, it must adequately protect the user. Accompanying manufacturers' notes must provide all relevant data for determination of maximum permissible user exposure to heat transmitted by equipment.

(7)   *Cold* – must possess sufficient thermal insulating capacity and retain the necessary flexibility for gestures and postures. In particular, PPE must protect tips of fingers and toes from pain or health impairment and prevent penetration by rain water. Manufacturers' accompanying notes must provide all relevant data concerning maximum permissible user exposure to cold transmitted by equipment.

(8)   *Electric shock* – must be sufficiently insulated against voltages to which the user is likely to be exposed under the most foreseeably adverse conditions. In particular, PPE for use during work with electrical installations (together with packaging), which may be under tension, must carry markings indicating either protection class and/or corresponding operating voltage, serial number and date of manufacture; in addition, date of entry into service must be inscribed as well as of periodic tests or inspections.

(9)   *Radiation*

(*a*)   Non-ionising radiation – must prevent acute or chronic eye damage from non-ionising radiation and be able to absorb/reflect the majority of energy radiated in harmful wavelengths without unduly affecting transmission of the innocuous part of the visible spectrum, perception of contrasts and distinguishment of colours. Thus, protective glasses must possess a spectral transmission factor so as to minimise radiant-energy illumination density capable of reaching the user's eye through the filter and ensure that it does not exceed permissible exposure value. Accompanying notes must indicate transmission curves, making selection of the most suitable PPE possible. The relevant protection-factor number must be marked on all specimens of filtering glasses.

(*b*)   Ionising radiation – must protect against external radioactive contamination. Thus, PPE should prevent penetration of radioactive dust, gases, liquids or mixtures under foreseeable use conditions. Moreover, PPE designed to provide complete user protection against external irradiation must be able to counter only weak electron or weak photon radiation.

(10)   *Dangerous substances and infective agents*

(*a*)   respiratory protection – must be able to supply the user with breathable air when exposed to polluted atmosphere or an atmosphere with inadequate oxygen concentration. Leak-tightness of the facepiece and pressure drop on inspiration (breath intake), as well as in the case of filtering devices purification capacity, must keep the contaminant penetration from the polluted atmosphere sufficiently low to avoid endangering health of the user. Instructions for use must enable a trained user to use the equipment correctly;

(*b*)   cutaneous and ocular contact (skin and eyes) – must be able to prevent penetration or diffusion of dangerous substances and infective agents. Therefore, PPE must be completely leak-tight but allow prolonged daily use or, failing that, of limited leak-tightness restricting the period of wear. In the case of certain dangerous substances/infective agents possessing high penetrative power and which limit duration of protection, such PPE must be tested for classification on the basis of efficiency. PPE conforming with test specifications must carry a mark indicating names or codes of substances used in tests and standard period of protection. Manufacturers' notes must contain an explanation of codes, detailed description of standard tests and refer to the maximum permissible period of wear under different foreseeable conditions of use.

(11)   *Safety devices for diving equipment* – must be able to supply the user with a breathable gaseous mixture, taking into account the maximum depth of immersion. If necessary, equipment must consist of

(*a*)   a suit to protect the user against pressure;

(*b*)   an alarm to give the user prompt warning of approaching failure in supply of breathable gaseous mixture;

(*c*)   life-saving suit to enable the user to return to the surface.

[*Art 3, Annex II*].

Excluded PPE

36.19 (i) PPE designed and manufactured for use specifically by the armed forces or in the maintenance of law and order (helmets, shields);

(ii) PPE for self-defence (aerosol canisters, personal deterrent weapons);

(iii) PPE designed and manufactured for private use against

— adverse weather (headgear, seasonal clothing, footwear, umbrellas),

— damp and water (dish-washing gloves),

— heat (e.g. gloves);

(iv) PPE intended for the protection or rescue of persons on vessels or aircraft, not worn all the time.

[Annex I].

Main types of personal protection

36.20 The main types of personal protection are (*a*) head protection, (*b*) eye protection, (*c*) hand/arm protection, (*d*) foot protection and (*e*) whole body protection.

(*a*) *Head protection* taking the form of:

(i) industrial safety helmets – to protect against falling objects,

(ii) scalp protectors (bump caps) – to protect against striking fixed obstacles,

(iii) caps/hairnets – to protect against scalping

is particularly suitable for the following activities:

(*a*) building work – particularly on scaffolds;

(*b*) civil engineering projects;

(*c*) blasting operations;

(*d*) work in pits and trenches;

(*e*) work near hoists/lifting plant;

(*f*) work in blast furnaces;

(*g*) work in industrial furnaces;

(*h*) ship-repairing;

(*j*) railway shunting;

(*k*) slaughterhouses;

(*l*) tree-felling;

(*m*) suspended access work, e.g. window cleaning.

(*b*) *Eye protection* takes the following forms:

(i) safety spectacles – these are the same as prescription spectacles but incorporating optional sideshields; lenses are made from tough plastic, such as polycarbonate – provide lateral protection;

(ii) eyeshields – these are heavier than safety spectacles and designed with a frameless one-piece moulded lens; can be worn over prescription spectacles;

    (iii)   safety goggles – these are heavier than spectacles or eye shields; they are made with flexible plastic frames and one-piece lens and have an elastic headband – they afford total eye protection;

    (iv)   faceshields – these are heavier than other eye protectors but comfortable if fitted with an adjustable head harness - faceshields protect the face but not fully the eyes and so are no protection against dusts, mist or gases.

(c)   *Hand/arm protection – gloves* provide protection against:

    (i)   cuts and abrasions,

    (ii)   extremes of temperature,

    (iii)   skin irritation/dermatitis,

    (iv)   contact with toxic/corrosive liquids

and are particularly useful in connection with the following activities/processes:

    (a)   manual handling;

    (b)   vibration;

    (c)   construction;

    (d)   hot and cold materials;

    (e)   electricity;

    (f)   chemicals;

    (g)   radioactivity.

(d)   *Foot protection* taking the form of:

    (i)   safety shoes/boots,

    (ii)   foundry boots,

    (iii)   clogs,

    (iv)   wellington boots,

    (v)   anti-static footwear,

    (vi)   conductive footwear

is particularly useful for the following activities:

    (a)   construction;

    (b)   mechanical/manual handling;

    (c)   electrical processes;

    (d)   working in cold conditions (thermal footwear);

    (e)   chemical processes;

    (f)   forestry;

    (g)   molten substances.

(e)   *Whole body protection* taking the form of

    (i)   coveralls, overalls, aprons,

    (ii)   outfits against cold and heat,

(iii)   protection against machinery and chainsaws,

(iv)   high visibility clothing,

(v)   life-jackets

is particularly useful in connection with the following activities:

(*a*)   laboratory work;

(*b*)   construction;

(*c*)   forestry;

(*d*)   work in cold-stores;

(*e*)   highway and road works;

(*f*)   food processing;

(*g*)   welding;

(*h*)   fire-fighting;

(*j*)   foundry work;

(*k*)   spraying pesticides.

Some relevant British Standards for protective clothing and equipment

36.21   Although not, strictly speaking, a condition of sale or approval, for the purposes of the *Personal Protective Equipment at Work (EC Directive) Regulations 1992 (SI 1992 No 3139)*, compliance with British Standards (e.g. BS 5750: 'Quality Assurance') may well become one of the well-tried verification routes to obtaining a 'CE' mark. For that reason, if for no other, the following British Standards on protective clothing and equipment should be of practical value to both manufacturers and users.

Table 31

Protective clothing

BS 697 : 1986   Specification for rubber gloves for electrical purposes
BS 1547: 1959   Flameproof industrial clothing (materials and design)
BS 1651: 1986   Specification for industrial gloves
BS 2653: 1955   Protective clothing for welders
BS 3314: 1982   Specification for protective aprons for wet work
BS 3791: 1970   Specification for clothing for protection against intense heat for short periods
BS 4724: 1986 Part 1 1988 Part 2   Method of test for resistance of air-impermeable clothing materials to penetration by harmful liquids
BS 5426: 1987   Specification for work wear
BS 5438: 1976   Methods of test for flammability of vertically oriented textile fabrics and fabric assemblies subject to a small igniting flame
1989   Methods of test for flammability of textile fabrics when subjected to a small igniting flame applied to the face or bottom edge of vertically oriented specimens

---

BS 6249: 1979   Materials and material assemblies used in clothing for protection against heat and flame – Part 1 – Specification for flammability testing and performance

BS 6308: 1982   Specification for men's uniforms

BS 6408: 1983   Specification for clothing made from coated fabrics for protection against wet weather

BS 6629: 1985   Specification for optical performance of high visibility garments and accessories for use on the highway

Protective footwear

BS 953 : 1988   Methods of test for safety and protective footwear

BS 1870:   Safety footwear –

     1986   Part 1 – Specification for safety footwear other than all-rubber and all-plastics moulded types

     1976   Part 2 – Lined rubber safety boots

     1981   Part 3 – Specification for polyvinyl chloride moulded safety footwear

BS 2723: 1956   Fireman's leather boots

BS 4676: 1983   Specification for gaiters and footwear for protection against burns and impact risks in foundries

BS 4972: 1973   Specification for women's protective footwear

BS 5145: 1989   Specification for lined industrial rubber boots

BS 5451: 1977   Specification for electrically conducting and antistatic rubber footwear

BS 5462: 1984   Specification for lined rubber boots with protective (penetration resistant) midsoles

BS 6159:   Polyvinyl chloride boots

     1987   Part 1 – Specification for general industrial lined or unlined boots

Head protection

BS 2495: 1977   Specification for protective helmets for vehicle users (high protection)

BS 6473: 1984   Protective hats for horse and pony riders

BS 3864: 1989   Specification for fireman's helmets

BS 4033: 1966   Specification for industrial scalp protectors (light duty)

BS 4423: 1969   Climber's helmets

BS 4472: 1988   Protective skull caps for jockeys

BS 5361: 1976   Specification for protective helmets for vehicle users

Face and eye protection

BS 679 : 1989   Filters for use during welding and similar industrial operations

BS 1542: 1982   Equipment for eye, face and neck protection against radiation arising during welding and similar operations

BS 2092: 1987   Specification for industrial eye protectors

BS 2724: 1987   Filters for protection against intense sunglaze (for general and industrial use)

BS 4110: 1979   Specification for eye-protectors for vehicle users

Respiratory protection

BS 2091: 1969 Specification for respirators for protection against harmful
dusts, gases and scheduled agricultural chemicals
BS 4001: Recommendations for the care and maintenance of
underwater breathing apparatus –
1981 Part 1 – Compressed air open circuit type
1967 Part 2 – Standard diving equipment
BS 4275: 1974 Recommendations for the selection, use and maintenance of
respiratory protective equipment
BS 4400: 1969 Method for sodium chloride particulate test for respirator
filters
BS 4555: 1970 Specification for high efficiency dust respirators
BS 4558: 1970 Specification for positive pressure, powered dust respirators
BS 4667: Specification for breathing apparatus –
1974 Part 1 – Closed-circuit breathing apparatus
1974 Part 2 – Open-circuit breathing apparatus
1974 Part 3 – Fresh air hose and compressed air line breathing
apparatus
1982 Part 4 – Specification for escape breathing apparatus
BS 4771: 1971 Specification for positive pressure powered dust hoods and
blouses
BS 5343: 1986 Gas detector tubes
BS 6016: 1980 Specification for filtering facepiece dust respirators
Aerospace standards
N1 – Specification for oxygen masks for use in demand
systems 1969
N2 – Specification for requirements for chemical oxygen
generators for aircraft 1989
N3 – Specification for gaseous breathing oxygen supplies 1973
N4 – Specification for full face mask assemblies for use in
contaminated atmospheres 1974
2N 100 – Specification for general requirements for aircraft
oxygen systems and equipment 1985
BS 7355: 1990 Specification for full masks for respiratory protective devices
BS 7356: 1990 Specification for half and quarter face masks for respiratory
protective devices

Radiation protection

BS 1542: 1982 Specification for equipment for eye, face and neck protection
against non-ionising radiation arising during welding and
similar operations
BS 3664: 1963 Specification for film badges for personnel radiation
monitoring

Common law requirements

36.22 In addition to general and/or specific statutory requirements, the residual
combined duty, on employers at common law, to provide and maintain a safe
system of work, including appropriate supervision of safety duties, still obtains,
extending, where necessary, to protection against foreseeable risk of eye injury (*Bux
v Slough Metals Ltd* (see 1.45 INTRODUCTION)) and dermatitis/facial eczema (*Pape
v Cumbria CC*).

Consequences of breach

36.23   Employers who fail to provide suitable personal protective equipment, commit a criminal offence, under the *Health and Safety at Work etc. Act 1974* and the *Personal Protective Equipment at Work Regulations 1992 (SI 1992 No 2966)* and sundry other regulations (see 36.8 above). In addition, if, as a result of failure to provide suitable equipment, an employee suffers foreseeable injury and/or disease, the employer will be liable to the employee for damages for negligence. Conversely, if, after instruction and, where necessary, training, an employee fails or refuses to wear and maintain suitable personal protective equipment, he too can be prosecuted and/or dismissed and, if injured or suffers a disease in consequence, will probably lose all or, certainly, part of his damages (see 14.12 EMPLOYEES' DUTIES).

Pressure Systems and Transportable Gas Containers

Introduction

37.1   Although boiler explosions are comparatively rare, when they occur, their consequences, as regards bodily injury and property damage, can be serious – indeed the Flixborough explosion in 1974, which precipitated the introduction of the *Health and Safety at Work etc. Act*, involved a pressure system. Legislation, however, concerning intrinsic safety of boilers is traceable back to the original *Boiler Explosions Act 1882*. Periodic examination of boilers became mandatory, following the *Factories and Workshops Act 1901*, a tradition perpetuated by the *Factories Act 1961*. Originally, examination concentrated on steam boilers, steam receivers and air receivers, that is, on the pressure vessel itself rather than the system incorporating it. The Flixborough tragedy, in tandem with inevitable advances in 'state of the art' (technological advancement), spotlighted the need for adjusting the ambit of statutory controls as well as the potential limitations of civil liability in connection with ensuing damage from ultra-hazardous activities (see 19.41 FIRE AND FIRE PRECAUTIONS). Moreover, controls over gas cylinders were largely limited to safe transport by road of certain gases. Now, however, the *Pressure Systems and Transportable Gas Containers Regulations 1989* impose strict controls (mainly) on designers, manufacturers and fillers of cylinders. Design and manufacturing duties (see 37.12 below) apply (perhaps obviously) to manufacturers of gas cylinders, whereas examination, filling, modification and repair duties fall on users (or employers) (see 37.6 below). As regards containers hired out (as most, in fact, are), less onerous duties relate to proper storage and user maintenance (see 37.33 below). Moreover, simple pressure vessels are separately controlled by regulation *(SI 1991 No 2749)* (see 37.2 below).

Pressure Systems and Transportable Gas Containers Regulations 1989 (SI 1989 No 2169)

37.2   Current statutory requirements relating to pressure systems are contained in the *Pressure Systems and Transportable Gas Containers Regulations 1989 (SI 1989 No 2169)* which, in the case of pressure systems and gas containers, came into operation on 1 July 1990 and 1 January 1991 respectively; and, as regards design/manufacture, written scheme of examination, operation and maintenance of pressure systems, will come into effect on 1 July 1994. These regulations and accompanying approved code of practice replace the earlier relevant sections of the *Factories Act 1961* – s 32 (steam boilers), s 35 (steam receivers and steam containers) and s 36 (air receivers) and attendant regulations *(SIs 1964 Nos 781, 1070)*. Moreover, the *Pressure Vessels (Verification) Regulations 1988 (SI 1988 No 896)* provide for the appointment by the HSE of inspection bodies to carry out inspection of gas cylinders; enable manufacturers to present gas cylinders to inspection bodies for EEC verification certificates; empower inspection bodies to carry out checks, examinations and tests for EEC verification and make it an offence for any person other than an inspection body to affix to a gas cylinder any of the EEC verification marks. [*Regs 3-6 and 9*]. Simple pressure vessels are also subject to certification requirements as an EC certificate of conformity must be obtained from UK approved bodies. [*Simple Pressure Vessels (Safety) Regulations 1991 (SI 1991 No 2749), Reg 13*].

Inspection bodies must send promptly a written notice of refusal to affix the appropriate EEC verification mark or to grant a certificate to the manufacturer and must state in the notice the grounds for the refusal and must also inform the manufacturer of his right of appeal. The appeal must be made to the Secretary of State within 14 days from the date on which the manufacturer received the notice of refusal. Copies of the notice of refusal and of the documents submitted to the relevant inspection body must accompany the review application. The Secretary of State may decide to hold a review. [*Reg 8*].

In addition, the *Simple Pressure Vessels (Safety) Regulations 1991 (SI 1991 No 2749)* require that manufacturers/suppliers/importers of simple pressure vessels (that is, welded vessels intended to contain air/nitrogen at a gauge pressure greater than 0.5 bar (but not intended for exposure to flame) and manufactured in series), meet certain safety criteria as regards pressurised components, steel, aluminium, welding materials, wall thickness, as well as identifying EC mark. [*1, 2 Schs*]. (Excluded are vessels for nuclear use/use in the propulsive system of a ship or aircraft, and fire extinguishers.) The regulations do not affect any vessel which was supplied or taken into service before 1 July 1992 and which complies with the existing UK safety requirements or, if exported to another EC country, with the requirements of that country. The regulations do not apply to exports of vessels outside the EC.

Application of regulations

37.3   Ever since the (original) *Boiler Explosions Act 1882* statutory requirement concentrated on safety of the pressure vessel itself – a pressure vessel being a closed vessel operating at a pressure greater than atmospheric, including steam boilers, steam receivers and containers and air receivers – rather than the system incorporating it. The *Pressure Systems and Transportable Gas Containers Regulations 1989*, which are adaptable to the advance in technology, are intended to prevent the risk of serious injury from stored energy, owing to the failure of a pressure system. Thus, apart from the risk of scalding from steam, these regulations deal with the contents of the pressure system, in so far as contents and operating procedures are liable to cause a rapid deterioration, leading to failure. More particularly, the regulations apply to steam gases under pressure or fluids artificially kept under pressure (i.e. 'relevant fluids' (see 37.9 below)), which become gases when led to atmosphere, that is, to steam systems and systems where gases exert a pressure greater than half a bar above atmospheric pressure (0.5 bar). Included, therefore, are chemicals such as ammonia and chlorine as well as air and hot water kept above boiling point.

Importantly, since the regulations are concerned with release of stored energy, ability of the fluid in the system to store such energy is paramount. The key to application of the regulations is '*relevant fluid*'. If the system does not contain a 'relevant fluid', that is, one which would release little energy, if it escaped, (e.g. hydraulic oils), the regulations do not apply. 'Pressure system', however, very definitely includes pipework as well as protective devices such as valves and guages.

Written schemes of examination – mandatory July 1994

37.4   Written schemes of examination must be prepared or certified by a '*competent person*', normally an engineering insurance company, though sometimes the user itself (if corporate). There must be an examination of every pressure vessel; pipework, valves, compressors, pumps, hoses etc. Also consideration must be given to whether repair work can be safely carried out without impeding inspection facilities or protective devices. An inventory of items to be included in the written scheme will often be prepared by the user-employer since he will often be more *au fait* with the system than the competent person, leaving the latter to agree the system and its extent. Pipework does not always have to be included, particularly if not failure-prone, or if it is of good condition or located in underground pipe ducts, so that, if there were a failure, it would not be likely to cause injury. The written scheme will need to be reviewed periodically, as environmental changes occur which can lead to pipework corrosion and erosion or, alternatively, where there have been alterations to the building itself housing the pressure system, with the result that servicing or maintenance could lead to scalding following a sudden release of energy. Such written schemes, however, can be computer-based [*Reg 8*], a fact which will facilitate updates and interrogations.

Safe operations and maintenance – documentation

37.5   It is essential to establish and maintain safe operating limits (SOL) for pressure systems. Systems previously examined (e.g. steam boilers, air receivers) will already possess these. But new pressure systems must be accompanied by manufacturers' information about the system's design, construction and operation. This includes knowledge of temperatures and flow rates as well as safe working pressures. In sum, the regulations impose compliance on user/owner of a system who must show, so far as is reasonably practicable, that he has taken steps to avoid/minimise risk of foreseeable serious injury from a failure of the system, including pipework. Since written schemes do not become mandatory until July 1994, this will, in all probability, include preparation *now* of appropriate schedules – referring to scope of system, its protective devices, safe operating limits as well as the system's category (major, intermediate or minor). Records and manuals relating to working pressure, temperature, rated flow, safety and relief valve settings, control system settings for normal operation, working levels, should be consulted, and pressure vessel serial numbers and inspection certificate numbers listed – all of which will facilitate subsequent external appraisal.

In addition, results of earlier examination should be kept in the schedule, and, in the case of a new pressure system, manufacturers should make available operating manuals, safe operating limits (SOL) and maintenance instructions. Tendering for new systems should be conducted with the requirements of these regulations in mind. Similarly, although filling, examination, modifications and record keeping of gas cylinders is the responsibility of cylinder owners, owners should nevertheless solicit copies of examination certificates from transferring owners of gas containers, particularly in the case of hire of 'fixed' pressure tanks – not to do so is to condone a faulty system.

Allocation of duties under regulations

37.6   Duties are allocated differently in the case of pressure systems, on the one hand, and transportable gas containers (see 37.10 below), on the other.

Whereas traditionally, health and safety legislation has tended to lay duties on occupiers (i.e. employers) of work premises, these regulations place duties (mainly) on users, in the case of installed systems (except in the case of leased installed systems, where the owner is prepared to assume the user's duties – typically bulk oxygen and/or LPG systems) though where a factory/workshop owner buys in a system, he would both own and control it. In addition, both *Regulations 4(6)* and *20* place duties on employers of persons who modify/repair pressure systems/ transportable gas containers. In the case of newly installed systems, designers/ manufacturers/importers and suppliers also have duties in respect of transportable gas containers and (from 1 July 1994) for pressure systems.

Pressure systems

37.7   Three types of pressure systems are covered by the regulations, namely:

(*a*)   systems comprising a pressure vessel, associated pipework and protective devices;

(*b*)   pipework with protective devices to which a gas cylinder is, or is intended, to be connected, containing high pressure gas at between 175 to 200 bar, but not pipework containing a 'relevant fluid' (see 37.9 below) at a pressure of 0.5 bar, or less; and

(*c*)   a pipeline with protective devices.

Throughout, the regulations attach importance to the integrity of the system, when initially installed, along with its subsequent maintenance; whereas (unlike the former position under the *Factories Act 1961*), subsequent examinations are limited to those parts of the system containing a defect and so dangerous; more particularly, periodic examination is restricted to parts identified in the written scheme of examination, as required by *Regulation 8* (see 37.18 below). See also *fig. 18*.

Protective devices

37.8   The regulations apply only to protective devices necessary to prevent danger. Thus, instrumentation/control equipment is included:

(*a*)   where it has to function to protect the system;

(*b*)   in process industries where it prevents safe operating limits (SOL) being exceeded where no other protective device is provided.

fig. 18 Pressure system

Relevant fluid

37.9   Only those parts of a pressure system containing a 'relevant fluid' are covered by the regulations. 'Relevant fluids' are fluids:

(*a*)   where pressure of 0.5 bar is greater than atmospheric – except in the case of steam;

(*b*)   compressed air as well as other compressed gases (e.g. nitrogen, acetylene and oxygen) and hot water above boiling point.

The regulations apply to fluids that are a mixture of gas and liquid, but *not* liquids with gas dissolved in them.

In all cases the criterion is, will the gaseous element separate out from the liquid with time to produce a pressure of more than 0.5 bar? Excluded, therefore, are motor gasoline and stabilised crude oils.

Transportable gas containers (gas cylinders)

37.10   Duties regarding gas cylinders fall (mainly) on manufacturers, suppliers and importers to ensure that new containers comply with approved designs, though employers of their repairers have duties. [*Reg 20*]. As regards existing gas cylinders, those who fill gas cylinders must ensure that such cylinders are safe for continued use before they are filled.

The types of gas cylinders involved are of between:

(*a*)   0.5 and 3,000 litres capacity – refillable containers which are transportable – that is, cylinders constructed to withstand rough handling during the course of transport (but not dewar flasks, containers for taking samples from static storage tanks or from road vehicles). Excluded also are portable fire extinguishers with a working pressure below 25 bar at 60°C and with a total mass not greater than 23 kilogrammes; and

(*b*)   1.4 and 5 litres in the case of cylinders designed to be discarded when the contents have been expended.

Responsibility for compliance

37.11   Primary responsibility for compliance with the regulations lies with the user, that is, the organisation in control of the pressure system, for example, the relevant engineering concern which services and repairs the system, as well as (or instead of) the employer or owner.

Specific duties

Design/manufacture of pressure systems and gas containers

37.12   Any person who designs/manufactures, imports or supplies

(i)   a pressure system, or

(ii)   a transportable gas container,

must ensure that the pressure system/gas container

(*a*)   is properly designed and constructed so as to prevent danger,

(*b*)   is designed and constructed so that all necessary examinations for preventing danger can be carried out (see 37.18 below, 'Written scheme of examination'),

(c)   in the case of a pressure system with means of access to the interior, that the means of access is designed and constructed so that access can be gained without danger,

(d)   is provided with protective devices necessary for preventing danger; and any device for releasing contents must do so safely, and

those who modify/repair pressure systems and/or gas containers must do so safely or, alternatively, ensure that the work is done safely.

[*Reg 4*] coming into effect on 1 July 1994 (except in the case of transportable gas containers when it came into force on 1 January 1991).

Relevant British Standards

37.13   For the purposes of *Regulation 4*, British Standards are a good basis for design of new pressurised plant; moreover, the HSE has not prosecuted where an article conforms with a relevant British Standard. The relevant British Standards are:

BS 806: 1986 – specification for the design and construction of ferrous piping installation for and in connection with land boilers;

BS 1113: 1989 – specification for the design and manufacture of water-tube steam generating plant;

BS 2790: 1989 – specification for the design and manufacture of shell boilers of welded construction;

BS 5169: 1975 – specification for welded steel air receivers;

BS 5500: 1988 – specification for unfired fusion welded pressure vessels;

BS 7005: 1988 – specification for the design and manufacture of carbon steel unfired pressure vessels for use in vapour compression refrigeration systems.

Duties regarding pressure systems
enforceable as from 1 July 1990

Information and marking requirements

Information requirements

37.14   Any person who designs or supplies, or the employer of any one who modifies or repairs, a pressure system or any article or component, must provide sufficient written information regarding its design, construction, examination, operation and maintenance as may reasonably foreseeably be necessary to comply with these regulations, such information to be provided with a pressure system and/or component when they are supplied. [*Reg 5*]. These information requirements do not, however, apply to simple pressure vessels, unless they were supplied before 1 July 1992. [*Simple Pressure Vessels (Safety) Regulations 1991, Reg 24*].

Marking requirements

37.15   Pressure vessels must be marked as follows:

(i)   manufacturer's name;

(ii)   serial number to identify the vessel;

(iii) date of manufacture;

(iv)   standard to which the vessel was built;

(v)   maximum design pressure of the vessel;

(vi)   minimum design pressure of the vessel when other than atmospheric;

(vii)   design temperature.

[*Reg 5, 4 Sch*].

In the case of steam boilers or air receivers, manufacturers should provide the written scheme of examination (as required by *Regulation 8* (see 37.18 below)). In this way, the user will know how the item has been designed to operate and the intended frequency of examinations. These requirements also do not apply to simple pressure vessels unless they were supplied before 1 July 1992.

From 1 July 1992, the EC mark which will be required for pressure vessels marketed or supplied after that date will have to be affixed after an EC type-examination certificate has been obtained and an EC verification certificate or certificate of conformity has been issued by a UK-approved body (see 37.2 above).

Installation requirements

37.16   Employers of persons who install pressure systems must ensure that an installation does not give rise to danger or impair the operation of a protective device and/or inspection facility. Thus, new vessels or equipment which have been carefully fabricated, subject to non-destructive testing, examination and certification, should not be carelessly handled or dropped when being connected up. Protective devices should be properly located. [*Reg 6*].

Safe operating limits

37.17   Users of an installed system and owners of a mobile system must not operate the system unless the safe operating limits (SOL) of that system are established.

Owners of mobile systems (if not also users) must:

(i)   supply the user with a written statement specifying the safe operating limits;

(ii)   ensure that the system is legibly and durably marked with safe operating limits and that the said mark is clearly visible.

[*Reg 7*].

'Safe operating limits' (SOL) corresponds with 'maximum permissible working pressure' (MPWP) in the case of boilers, and safe working pressure (SWP) in the case of air receivers.

Written scheme of examination (applicable to new and existing plant)
enforceable as from 1 July 1994

37.18   Users of an installed system, and owners of a mobile system must not operate the system, or allow it to be operated, unless they have a written scheme for periodic examination by a competent person. More particularly,

(i)   all protective devices,

(ii)   every pressure vessel/pipeline in which a defect may give rise to danger, and

(iii)   those parts of the pipework in which a defect may give rise to danger,

715

must be identified in the scheme.

In addition, users/owners must ensure that:

(*a*)   such a scheme has been drawn up, or, alternatively, certified as being suitable by a competent person;

(*b*)   the content of the scheme is reviewed periodically by a competent person;

(*c*)   the content of the scheme is modified in accordance with recommendations of a competent person (see 37.19 below).

The scheme of an examination must:

(i)   specify the nature/frequency of examinations;

(ii)   specify the steps necessary to prepare a pressure system for safe examination;

(iii)   (if necessary) provide for examination to be carried out before the system is used.

[*Reg 8*].

Thus, division of responsibility is as follows. The user (or owner of a mobile system) decides the scope of the scheme and a competent person specifies the nature and frequency of examinations and any special safety measures necessary to prepare the system for examination and certifies the scheme as suitable.

In the case of air and steam systems in industrial premises, which will have been subject to periodic examination for many years, if such systems are well maintained, some users will merely prepare a scheme to continue existing examinations. Moreover, although subject to the initial integrity/installation/operation and maintenance requirements, *pipework* is exempted from written examination requirements except where such pipework may give rise to danger. Such parts should be identified in the scheme. [*Reg 8(1)(c)*].

Competent persons

37.19   Although not defining a 'competent person' (see 1.37 INTRODUCTION), in addition to requiring examination of pressure systems, the regulations require a *competent person* to draw up or certify as suitable a written scheme of examination. Since the regulations are not only concerned with the limited range of pressure vessels covered by the *Factories Act 1961* but also with a wide range of pressure systems, 'competence' refers to corporate (or unincorporated) competence. Hence 'competence' requirements apply to companies and not individual employees. The accompanying approved code of practice suggests the attributes which a competent person is expected to have for each of the three classes of pressure system. Thus, 'competent person' can refer to independent inspection bodies and in-house technical groups. They may be part of a company's permanent organisation or appointed for a particular project (see also 37.4 above).

Examination as per written scheme
enforceable as from 1 July 1994

37.20   Users of installed systems and owners of mobile systems must:

(*a*)   ensure that parts of a pressure system included in the scheme of examination are examined by a competent person at the intervals specified and, if necessary, before the system is used for the first time;

(b)   before each examination, take all necessary steps to prepare the system for examination.

The competent person must then carry out an examination and make a written report of the examination and send it to the user of an installed system and to the owner of a mobile system, to arrive

(i)   within 28 days of the completion of the examination, or

(ii)   before the date specified for completion of repairs/modifications,

whichever is sooner. [*Reg 9*].

Contents of report

37.21   The report must specify:

(i)   which parts of a pressure system have been examined, the condition of those parts and the results of the examination;

(ii)   any repairs/modifications or changes in the established safe operating limits, which are necessary to prevent danger, as well as the completion date of repairs/modifications. In this connection, the system must not be operated, nor must a person supply a mobile system for operation, until repairs/ modifications and/or safe operating limits (SOL) have been made [*Reg 9(6)*];

(iii)   the date after which a pressure system cannot be operated without further examination. More particularly, a system must not be operated unless a further examination has been carried out. (In this connection, owners of mobile systems have to take greater care to see that examinations are carried out in the case of plant on long-term hire);

(iv)   the date beyond which a mobile system cannot be used without further examination, must be legibly and durably marked by the owner [*Reg 9(5)-(9)*].

Action in case of imminent danger
enforceable as from 1 July 1994

37.22   If the competent person thinks that the system will give rise to imminent danger, unless certain repairs/modifications are carried out and/or changes to operating conditions are made, he must make a written report to that effect, specifying the repairs, changes or modifications and give it to the user or owner, and within 14 days send a written report to the enforcing authority (see further Chapter 17 'Enforcement'). In such cases, installed or mobile systems must not be operated. [*Reg 10*]. This section only applies where there is a risk of imminent failure if repairs are not carried out immediately; it does not apply to gradual deterioration of the system.

Operation of system
enforceable as from 1 July 1994

37.23   Adequate and suitable instructions must be provided for persons operating the system to ensure

(i)   the safe operation of the system, and

(ii)   that action will be taken in the event of emergency.

[*Reg 11*].

Maintenance requirements
enforceable as from 1 July 1994

37.24   Users of installed systems and owners of mobile systems must ensure that the system is properly maintained so as to prevent danger. [*Reg 12*].

Precautions should ensure that vessels are adequately protected against over-pressure. And it should not be possible to isolate pressure relieving devices from any of the vessels that they are designed to protect unless:

(*a*)   in the case of *multiple* pressure relief devices, provision which is made for isolating any one relief device for testing or servicing, ensures that the remaining relief device, connected to the vessel, provides the full requisite capacity;

(*b*)   in the case of *single* pressure relief devices, provision made for removal/testing/servicing, by use of an automatic shut-off valve, where the valve is retained in the fully open position by the presence of the relief valve, closes before the relief valve is fully removed. The vessel must not be left unprotected and the replacement relief device must be fitted immediately;

(*c*)   in the case of *simultaneous isolation* of relief and pressure source, that the only source of pressure which could lead to an unsafe condition, originates from an external source and that this source is isolated from the vessel with the relief device.

Keeping of records
enforceable as from 1 July 1990

37.25   The user of an installed system and the owner of a mobile system must keep the following documents:

(*a*)   the last report relating to the system made by a competent person;

(*b*)   any previous reports containing information which will assist in assessing whether

(i)   the system is safe to operate, or

(ii)   any repairs or modifications can be carried out safely;

(*c*)   documents relating to the design or modification of pressure systems (for instance, to pressure vessels or protective devices supplied after the regulations came into force);

(*d*)   any agreement between the competent person and the user/owner relating to postponement of examination (see *Reg 8* at 37.18 above). (Moreover, where the user/owner changes, the previous user/owner must transfer documentation to the new user/owner.)

[*Reg 13*].

It is not necessary to keep all previous examination reports. What should be kept are any relevant manufacturer's records, initial examination report and the most recent examination report. Records of operating conditions do not need to be kept. But information relating to abnormal conditions may well be of use to a competent person at the next examination.

Duties regarding transportable gas containers (gas cylinders)

On whom the duties are imposed

37.26   (1)   Design/approval/certification requirements – manufacturers and suppliers.

(2)   Filling of gas containers – duties on employers/employees.

(3)   Examination of containers – duties on owners.

(4)   Modification of containers – duties on employers.

(5)   Repairs of containers – duties on employers.

(6)   Re-rating – duties on employers.

(7)   Keeping of records – duties on manufacturers.

Design/approval/certification requirements – manufacturers and suppliers

37.27   No person must

(i)   supply for the first time,

(ii)   import, or

(iii)   manufacture and use

a transportable gas container (including permanent fittings and valves) unless the container

(*a*)   has been verified as conforming with a design standard/specification approved by the HSE – that is, BS 5045: 1982-1989;

(*b*)   is an EC-type cylinder, that is,

(i)   there is an EC Verification Certificate in force in respect of it, and

(ii)   it bears all the marks and inscriptions required by the Framework Directive, that is, complies with the *Gas Cylinders (Pattern Approval) Regulations 1987 (SI 1987 No 116)*.

[*Reg 16*].

This requirement subjects gas cylinder designs to a positive approval regime, the two main routes for conformity being BS 5045 and EC Verification Certificate etc. (see 37.2 above). Moreover, the requirement to fit a relief device only applies, in general, to cylinders containing liquefied petroleum gas, carbon dioxide and halons (used as refrigerants and fire extinguishing media), since such cylinders are liable to become liquid full or develop very high pressures in case of overfill or overheat.

Filling of gas containers – duties on employers/employees

37.28   The employer of a person who is to fill a transportable gas container with a relevant fluid, must ensure that that person:

(*a*)   checks from the marks on the cylinder that

(i)   it has undergone proper examinations (unless the manufacturer's mark reveals that examination is not yet due (see above)), and

      (ii)   it is suitable for containing that fluid; and

(b)   makes other appropriate safety checks.

Also, that person must:

    (i)   check that, after filling, it is within the Safe Operating Limits;

    (ii)   check that it is not overfilled;

    (iii)   in the case of overfilling, remove excess fluid in a safe manner.

In addition, employers must ensure that no employee refills at work a non-refillable container with a relevant fluid (see 37.9 above, 'Relevant fluid'). [*Reg 17*].

Examination of containers – duties on owners

37.29   Owners of transportable gas containers must ensure that containers are examined for safety (to BS 5430, BS 6071 and BS 5306), at set intervals, by a competent person. If examination shows that the container is safe, the date of examination should be noted on the container by the competent person. [*Reg 18*].

Modification of containers – duties on employers

37.30   Employers must ensure that none of their employees modifies a transportable gas container

(a)   of seamless construction, or

(b)   which has contained acetylene.

[*Reg 19*].

Moreover, modified transportable gas containers must not be supplied unless they are certified by the HSE as fit for use, or, in the case of EC-type cylinders, they have been so certified by an appropriate inspection body. (This regulation does not prohibit the connection of a seamless gas cylinder to a pipework system for normal usage; and the remaking of threads is allowed, if carried out in accordance with BS 5430.)

Repairs of containers – duties on employers

37.31   Employers must ensure that employees do not do major repairs (i.e. hot work/welding but not heat treatment) to transportable gas containers

(a)   of seamless construction, or

(b)   which have contained acetylene, or

(c)   any other type of transportable gas container,

unless they are competent.

Transportable gas containers that have undergone major repair, must not be supplied unless marked/certified by the HSE as being fit for use or, in the case of EC-type cylinders, they have been marked/certified by the appropriate inspection body. [*Reg 20*].

Re-rating – duties on employers

37.32   Employers must ensure that employees do not re-rate transportable gas containers, unless competent to do so; moreover, such re-rating (i.e. reassessment of capability to contain compressed gas safely) must comply with the procedures prepared by the owner of the container; and re-rated transportable gas containers must not be supplied, unless certified as safe by the HSE. [*Reg 21*].

Keeping of records – duties on manufacturers

37.33 Manufacturers/their agents/importers of transportable gas containers *and* owners of hired-out transportable gas containers must keep records relating to such containers, if

(i) made to approved design specification (BS 5045),

(ii) made to approved design standard (BS 5045),

(iii) of EC-type cylinder (EC Verification Certificate).

In addition, owners of hired-out transportable gas containers must keep a copy of the design specification for the container, if it

(*a*) is a refillable container, and

(*b*) is used exclusively for liquefied petroleum gas, and

(*c*) has a water capacity up to and including 6.5 litres.

[*Reg 22*].

Penalties

37.34 Penalties for breach of the *Pressure Systems and Transportable Gas Containers Regulations 1989* are the same as for breach of *HSWA*. Penalties for breach of the *Simple Pressure Vessels (Safety) Regulations 1991* are as follows: on summary conviction, imprisonment for up to three months or a fine. [*Reg 20*].

Defences

37.35 It is a defence for an accused to show

(*a*) that the commission of the offence was due to the act or default of another person, who was not an employee, and

(*b*) that he took all reasonable precautions and exercised all due diligence to avoid commission of the offence.

[*Reg 23*].

If it is claimed that the default is due to the act or default of another, the person who it is claimed is responsible must be given written notice seven days before the hearing.

Moreover, notwithstanding that a defence has been successfully invoked, for the purposes of *Reg 23(1)*, by the accused (i.e. the employer), this will *not* prevent his being (simultaneously but separately) charged under *Sec 36* of *HSWA* – corporate bodies (nevertheless) being additionally liable for the acts/omissions of 'another person' (see further Chapter 17 'Enforcement').

Notable exceptions to regulations

37.36 The following are the main excepted systems:

(*a*) a pressure system forming part of a ship, spacecraft, aircraft, hovercraft;

(*b*)   a pressure system forming part of a weapons system;

(*c*)   a pressure system forming part of a braking, control or suspension system of a wheeled, track or rail mounted vehicle;

(*d*)   a pressure system subject to test, leak test, or pressurised unintentionally;

(*e*)   pipeline/protective devices in which pressure does not exceed 2 bar above atmospheric pressure;

(*f*)   pressure system/transportable gas container subject to research experiment;

(*g*)   plant/equipment used for diving at work operations (other than a transportable gas container);

(*h*)   working chamber for the purposes of *Work in Compressed Air (Special) Regulations 1958*;

(*j*)   road tanker/tank container;

(*k*)   water cooling system on an internal combustion engine or compressor;

(*l*)   a tyre used on a vehicle;

(*m*)   a vapour compression refrigeration system;

(*n*)   prime movers and turbines (but not steam locomotives or traction engines);

(*o*)   electrical or telecommunications cable;

(*p*)   pressure system containing sulphur hexafluoride gas, forming part of high voltage electrical apparatus;

(*q*)   water filled coupling used in power transmission;

(*r*)   portable fire extinguisher with working pressure below 25 bar at 60° with a total mass not more than 23 kilogrammes;

(*s*)   part of a tool or appliance which is a pressure vessel (e.g. small compressed air driven tool);

(*t*)   a road tanker or tank container to which the *Road Traffic (Carriage of Dangerous Substances in Road Tankers and Tank Containers) Regulations 1992* apply.

[*2 Sch*].

Chapter 38

Product Safety

Introduction

38.1   With the spate of EC directives, legislation and regulations aimed at manufacturers (including designers, importers and suppliers), product safety emerges as a fast growth area. Indeed, there is an identifiable trend away from legislation imposing duties on employers and occupiers to placement of duties on those involved in production (see 28.46 MACHINERY SAFETY, 36.13 PERSONAL PROTECTIVE EQUIPMENT and 37.2 PRESSURE SYSTEMS AND TRANSPORTABLE GAS CONTAINERS) and commercial circulation. More particularly, although there is no question of removal of duties from employers and occupiers and users of industrial plant, machinery and products, there is a current realisation that the *sine qua non* of compliance, on the part of employers and users, with their safety duties is compliance with health and safety specifications on the part of designers and manufacturers. This trend is likely to continue and, as far as civil liability at any rate is concerned, may well eventuate in considerable transfer of liability from employers and users of equipment to designers and producers, or, at least, joint (though not necessarily equal) liability on the part of both.

It was thalidomide that first focused serious attention on the ramifactory possibilities of product safety (and product liability), redress for its gross injuries and deformities not being available through the normal legal channels. This led to the Product Liability Directive, specifying strict liability for injury-causing defective products to consumers and legitimate users (see 38.18 below), subsequently implemented in the United Kingdom by the *Consumer Protection Act 1987*. More recently, the Product Safety Directive requires, *in a general way*, that producers place only safe products on the market. Whilst specific duties and regulations will take priority (e.g. duties specified in the *Consumer Protection Act 1987* and regulations passed thereunder or under earlier legislation), the general duties, introduced by way of implementation of the Product Safety Directive, will cover gaps in exisiting consumer protection legislation left by the *Consumer Protection Act 1987*. To date, legislation on product safety has divided into regulations dealing with industrial safety – passed mainly under the *Health and Safety at Work etc. Act 1974* and consumer safety – passed mainly under the *Consumer Protection Act 1987* and its predecessors (now repealed), such as the *Consumer Protection Acts 1961/1971* and the *Consumer Safety Act 1980*, still in force.

Consumer and industrial products

(a) Consumer products

38.2   The Product Safety Directive requires 'producers to place only safe products on the market', including notably food (though covered specifically by the *Food Safety Act 1990* – see 21.4 FOOD AND FOOD HYGIENE), tobacco, medicinal products and transport, such as aircraft and motor cars (all originally excluded by the *Consumer Protection Act 1987, s 10(7)*) as well as consumer durables generally. In tandem with the draft directive on Liability of Suppliers of Services (see 38.57 below) – the terms of which have not been entirely agreed upon – and the draft Unfair Contract Terms directive (to be implemented by 1 January 1995), requiring unfair terms (already incidentally outlawed by the *Unfair Contract Terms Act 1977*), to be couched in plain, simple and, particularly, uneuphemistic terminology, consumers will thus be afforded a greater measure of statutory protection. 'Safe' products are to be judged in relation to (*a*) composition, packaging, assembly and maintenance instructions; (*b*) effect on other products with which foreseeably they may come into contact (see 38.26 below); (*c*) presentation, labelling, instructions for use and disposal; and (*d*) consumer categories at serious risk, e.g. children.

(*b*) Industrial products

The *Health and Safety at Work etc. Act 1974* (*HSWA*) was the first Act to place a *general* duty on designers and manufacturers of industrial products to design and produce articles and substances that are safe and without health risks when used at work. Prior to this date legislation had tended to avoid this approach, e.g. the *Factories Act 1961*, on the premise that machinery could not be made design safe (see Chapter 28 'Machinery Safety'). Statutory requirements had tended to concentrate on duty to guard and fence machinery, and with placement of duty upon the user/employer to inspect and test inward products for safety. These duties to guard and fence still exist until 1996 under the *Factories Act 1961* and regulations made thereunder, and there is a general residual duty on the employers/users of industrial products to inspect and test them for safety under *Sec 2* of *HSWA*. These duties notwithstanding, the trend of legislation in recent years has been towards safer design and manufacture of products for industrial and domestic use. Thus, *HSWA s 6* lays down the duties of designers, manufacturers, importers and suppliers of products ('articles and substances') for use at work, to their immediate users. These duties have been to some extent revamped and updated by the *Consumer Protection Act 1987, 3 Sch* – applicable to both industrial and domestic products. Contravention of *Sec 6* carries with it a maximum fine, on summary conviction, of £20,000 (see 17.30 ENFORCEMENT). Additionally, a separate duty is laid on installers of industrial plant and machinery. However, because of their involvement in the key areas of design and manufacture, more onerous duties are placed upon designers and manufacturers of articles and substances for use at work than upon importers and suppliers, who are essentially concerned with distribution and retail of industrial products, though under *HSWA s 6(8A)* importers are made liable for the first time for the faults of *foreign* designers/manufacturers.

Actionability and insurance

38.3   Whilst legislation and regulations dealing with domestic and industrial safety are principally penal and enforceable by state agencies, such as trading standards officers and health and safety inspectors, if injury, death or damage occurs in consequence of breach of such statutory duties, there is civil liability. Such liability is strict – that is, it is not necessary to prove negligence against the manufacturer, though there are specified defences. Current law is contained in the *Consumer Protection Act 1987* (see 38.18 below). However, although civil liability for injuries is strict, product liability insurance, although eminently desirable, is not compulsory – unlike employers' liability insurance. More particularly, there is strict civil liability (subject to defences specified in *Sec 4*) for breach of duties to consumers in the *Consumer Protection Act 1987* and any regulations made under the Act [*Consumer Protection Act 1987, s 41*] (see also 1.18 INTRODUCTION and 38.26 below). Moreover, products defective by design or absence/inadequacy of warnings, pictorial and/or otherwise (see 38.26 below) may well attract group action, e.g. drugs.

This chapter deals with statutory duties which are penal (i.e. *HSWA s 6* as amended by the *Consumer Protection Act 1987, 3 Sch*), civil liability for injury-causing defective products under the *Consumer Protection Act 1987*, together with contractual liability for substandard products under the *Sale of Goods Act 1979*, the *Consumer Credit Act 1974* and the *Supply of Goods and Services Act 1982*.

Criminal liability for breach of statutory duties

38.4   This refers to duties laid down in *HSWA* as revised by *Schedule 3* of the *Consumer Protection Act 1987*. The duties exist in relation to articles and substances for use at work and fairground equipment. An article upon which first trials/demonstrations are carried out is not an article for use at work, but rather an article which *might* be used at work. The purpose of trial/demonstration was to determine whether the article could safely be later used at work (*McKay v Unwin Pyrotechnics Ltd, The Times, 5 March 1991* where a dummy mine exploded, causing the operator injury, when being tested to see if it would explode when hit by a flail attached to a vehicle. It was held that there was no breach of *HSWA s 6(1)(a)*). There is no civil liability available to employees under these provisions except for breach of safety regulations. (For the specific requirements now applicable to machinery for use at work, see Chapter 28 'Machinery Safety'.)

Definition of articles and substances

38.5   An article for use at work means:

(*a*)   any plant designed for use or operation (whether exclusively or not) by persons at work; and

(*b*)   any article designed for use as a component in any such plant.

[*HSWA s 53(1)*].

A substance for use at work means 'any natural or artificial substance, whether in solid or liquid form or gaseous form or in the form of a vapour, and includes substances comprised in or mixed with other goods'. [*Consumer Protection Act 1987, s 45*].

Duties in respect of articles and substances for use at work

38.6   *HSWA s 6* (as amended by the *Consumer Protection Act 1987, 3 Sch*) places duties upon manufacturers and designers, as well as importers and suppliers, of (*a*) articles and (*b*) substances for use at work, whether used exclusively at work or not (e.g. lawnmower, hair dryer).

Duties in respect of articles for use at work

38.7   Key changes in respect of duties regarding articles for use at work are contained in *Schedule 3* to the *Consumer Protection Act 1987*. These are detailed below.

Any person who designs, manufactures, imports or supplies any article for use at work (or any article of fairground equipment) must:

(*a*)   ensure, so far as is reasonably practicable (for the meaning of this expression see Chapter 15 'Employers' Duties'), that the article is so designed and constructed that it will be safe and without risks to health at all times when it is being (i) set, (ii) used, (iii) cleaned or (iv) maintained by a person at work;

(*b*)   carry out or arrange for the carrying out of such testing and examination as may be necessary for the performance of the above duty;

(*c*)   take such steps as are necessary to secure that persons supplied by that person with the article are provided with adequate information about the use for which the article is designed or has been tested and about any conditions necessary to ensure that it will be safe and without risks to health at all such times of (i) setting, (ii) using, (iii) cleaning, (iv) maintaining *and* when being (v) dismantled, or (vi) disposed of; and

(*d*)   take such steps as are necessary to secure, so far as is reasonably practicable, that persons so supplied are provided with all such revisions of information as are necessary by reason of it becoming known that anything gives rise to a serious risk to health or safety.

[*HSWA s 6(1) as amended by the Consumer Protection Act 1987, 3 Sch*].

(See 38.9 and 38.10 below for further duties relevant to articles for use at work.)

In the case of an article for use at work which is likely to cause an employee to be exposed to 85 dB(A) or above, or to peak action level (200 pascals) or above, adequate information must be provided about noise likely to be generated by that article. [*Noise at Work Regulations 1989, Reg 12*] (see further 30.10 NOISE AND VIBRATION).

Duties in respect of substances for use at work

38.8   Every person who manufactures, imports or supplies any substance must:

(*a*)   ensure, so far as is reasonably practicable that the substance will be safe and without risks to health at all times when it is being (i) used, (ii) handled, (iii) processed, (iv) stored, or (v) transported by any person at work or in premises where substances are being installed;

(*b*)   carry out or arrange for the carrying out of such testing and examination as may be necessary for the performance of the duty in (*a*);

(*c*)   take such steps as are necessary to secure that persons supplied by that person with the substance are provided with adequate information about:

    (i)   any risks to health or safety to which the inherent properties of the substance may give rise;

    (ii)   the results of any relevant tests which have been carried out on or in connection with the substance; and

    (iii)   any conditions necessary to ensure that the substance will be safe and without risks to health at all times when it is being (*a*) used, (*b*) handled, (*c*) processed, (*d*) stored, (*e*) transported and (*f*) disposed of; and

(*d*)   take such steps as are necessary to secure, so far as is reasonably practicable, that persons so supplied are provided with all such revisions of information as are necessary by reason of it becoming known that anything gives rise to a serious risk to health or safety.

[*HSWA s 6(4) as amended by the Consumer Protection Act 1987, 3 Sch*].

(See 38.11 below for further duties relevant to substances.)

Additional duty on designers and manufacturers to carry out research

38.9 Any person who undertakes the design or manufacture of any article for use at work must carry out, or arrange for the carrying out, of any necessary research with a view to the discovery and, so far as is reasonably practicable, the elimination or minimisation of any health or safety risks to which the design or article may give rise. [*HSWA s 6(2)*].

Duties on installers of articles for use at work

38.10 Any person who erects or instals any article for use at work in any premises where the article is to be used by persons at work, must ensure, so far as is reasonably practicable, that nothing about the way in which the article is erected or installed makes it unsafe or a risk to health when it is being (*a*) set, (*b*) used, (*c*) cleaned, or (*d*) maintained by someone at work. [*HSWA s 6(3) as amended by the Consumer Protection Act 1987, 3 Sch*].

Additional duty on manufacturers of substances to carry out research

38.11 Any person who manufactures any substance must carry out, or arrange for the carrying out, of any necessary research with a view to the discovery and, so far as is reasonably practicable, the elimination or minimisation of any health/safety risks at all times when the substance is being (*a*) used, (*b*) handled, (*c*) processed, (*d*) stored, or (*e*) transported by someone at work. [*HSWA s 6(5) as amended by the Consumer Protection Act 1987, 3 Sch*].

No duty on suppliers of industrial articles and substances to research

38.12 It is not necessary to repeat any testing, examination or research which has been carried out by designers and manufacturers of industrial products, on the part of importers and suppliers, in so far as it is reasonable to rely on the results. [*HSWA s 6(6)*].

Custom built articles

38.13 Where a person designs, manufactures, imports or supplies an article for or to another person on the basis of a written undertaking by that other to ensure that the article will be safe and without health risks when being (*a*) set, (*b*) used, (*c*) cleaned, or (*d*) maintained by a person at work, the undertaking will relieve the designer/manufacturer etc. from the duty specified in *HSWA s 6(1)(a)* (see 38.7 above), to such extent as is reasonable, having regard to the terms of the undertaking. [*HSWA s 6(8) as amended by the Consumer Protection Act 1987, 3 Sch*].

Importers liable for offences of foreign manufacturers/designers

38.14 In order to give added protection to industrial users from unsafe imported products, *Schedule 3* of the *Consumer Protection Act 1987* has introduced a new subsection (*HSWA s 6(8A)*) which, in effect makes importers of unsafe products liable for the acts/omissions of foreign designers and manufacturers. *Sec 6(8A)* states that nothing in (*inter alia*) *Sec 6(8)* is to relieve an importer of an article/substance from any of his duties, as regards anything done (or not done) by or within the control of:

(*a*)   a foreign designer; or

(*b*)   a foreign manufacturer of an article/substance.

[*HSWA s 6(8A)*].

Proper use

38.15   Current judicial interpretation of *HSWA s 6(10)* concerning 'proper use' excluded foreseeable user error as a defence, which had the consequence of favouring the supplier. Thus, if a supplier could demonstrate a degree of operator error, however reasonably foreseeable, the question of initial product safety was sidestepped. Moreover, 'when properly used' implied, as construed, that there could only be a breach of *Sec 6* once a product had actually been *used*. This was contrary to the spirit of *Sec 6* that safety should be built into design/production, rather than waiting until accidents later occurred. Thus, in future, only *unforeseeable* user/operator error will relieve the supplier from liability; he will no longer be able to rely on the strict letter of his operating instructions. [*Consumer Protection Act 1987, 3 Sch*].

New powers to deal with unsafe imported goods

38.16   Because *HSWA* does not empower enforcing authorities (see Chapter 17 'Enforcement') to stop the supply of unsafe products at source or prevent the sale of products after they have been found to be unsafe, enforcing officers have been given the power to act at the point of entry or anywhere else along the distribution chain in an effort to stop unsafe articles/substances being imported. Thus, the use of the prohibition notice to deal with both imported and domestically produced articles/substances where there is thought to be a hazard sufficiently serious to warrant preventing its sale/distribution is to be extended. Foreign and domestic suppliers are, therefore, to be treated in the same way, HM Customs being empowered to (*a*) detain articles/substances (in a manner similar to HSE inspectors) and (*b*) transmit information about unsafe products confidentially to HSE inspectors.

Thus, a customs officer can seize any imported article/substance, which is considered to be unsafe, and detain it for up to two (working) days. [*HSWA s 25(A) (incorporated by Schedule 3 to the Consumer Protection Act 1987)*].

In addition, customs officers can transmit information relating to unsafe imported products to HSE inspectors. [*HSWA s 27(A) (incorporated by Schedule 3 to the Consumer Protection Act 1987)*].

Civil liability for unsafe products – historical background

38.17   Originally at common law where defective products caused injury, damage and/or death, redress depended on whether the injured user had a contract with the seller or hirer of the product. This was often not the case, and in consequence many persons, including employees repairing and/or servicing products, were remediless. This rule of non-liability in tort, emanating from the decision of *Winterbottom v Wright (1842 10 M & W 109)*, remained unchanged till 1932, when *Donoghue v Stevenson [1932] AC 562* was decided by the House of Lords. This case was important because it established that manufacturers were liable in negligence (i.e. tort) if they failed to take reasonable care in the manufacturing and marketing of their products, and in consequence a user suffered injury when using the product in a reasonably foreseeable way. More particularly, a 'manufacturer of products, which he sells in such a form as to show that he intends them to reach the ultimate consumer in the form in which they left him with no reasonable possibility of intermediate inspection, and with the knowledge that the absence of reasonable care in the preparation or putting up of the products will result in an injury to the consumer's life or property, owes a duty to the consumer to take reasonable care' (per Lord Atkin). In this way, manufacturers of products which were defective were liable in negligence to users and consumers of their products, including those who as intermediaries, repair, maintain and service industrial products, it being irrelevant whether there was a contract between manufacturer and user (which normally there was not).

From a consumer standpoint, this compared unfavourably with litigational landmarks of consumerism in the USA, underpinning, first, an extended warranty of fitness (that is, extension to user beyond the contract parties) (*Henningsen v Bloomfield Motors Inc and Chrysler Corp* (1960 New Jersey)), and, currently, an inalienable liability in strict tort for injury-causing product defects – a development mirrored, to some extent, by the switch over to strict product liability, under the *Consumer Protection Act 1987*, and away from negligence.

'The purpose of such liability is to ensure that the costs of injuries resulting from defective products are borne by the manufacturers that put such products on the market rather than by the injured persons who are powerless to protect themselves. Sales warranties serve this purpose fitfully at best.' (*Greenman v Yuba Power Products, Inc 59 Cal 2d 57 (1962)*).

Consumer Protection Act 1987 – introduction of product liability

38.18   The introduction of strict product liability is enshrined within the *Consumer Protection Act 1987, s 2(1)*. Thus, where any damage is *caused* wholly or partly by a defect (see below) in a product (e.g. goods, electricity, a component product or raw materials), the following may be liable for damages (irrespective of negligence):

(*a*)   the producer;

(*b*)   any person who, by putting his name on the product or using a trade mark (or other distinguishing mark) has held himself out as the producer;

(*c*)   any person who has imported the product into a member state from outside the EC, in the course of trade/business.

[*Consumer Protection Act 1987, s 2(1)(2)*].

(These provisions apply to consumers (see 38.33 below). For criminal liability for protection of employees see 38.4–38.16 above.)

Producers

38.19   Producers are variously defined as:

(i)   the person who manufactured a product;

(ii)   in the case of a substance which has not been manufactured, but rather won or abstracted, the person who won or abstracted it;

(iii)   in the case of a product not manufactured, won or abstracted, but whose essential characteristics are attributable to an industrial process or agricultural process, the person who carried out the process.

[*Consumer Protection Act 1987, s 1(2)(c)*].

Liability of suppliers

38.20   Although producers are principally liable, suppliers can also be liable in certain circumstances. Thus, any person who supplied the product is liable for damages if:

(*a*)   the injured person requests the supplier to identify one (or more) of the following:

    (i)   the producer;

    (ii)   the person who put his trade mark on the product;

    (iii)   the importer of the product into the EC; and

(*b*)   the request is made within a reasonable time after damage/injury has occurred *and* it is not reasonably practicable for the requestor to identify the above three persons; and

(*c*)   within a reasonable time after receiving the request, the supplier fails either:

    (i)   to comply with the request; or

    (ii)   identify his supplier.

[*Consumer Protection Act 1987, s 2(3)*].

No liability attaches here to a supplier of game/agricultural produce, if the supply occurred before the product had undergone an industrial process. [*Consumer Protection Act 1987, s 2(4)*].

Defect – key to liability

38.21   Liability presupposes that there is a defect in the product, and indeed, existence of a defect is the key to liability. Defect is defined in terms of the absence of safety in the product. More particularly, there is a 'defect in a product . . . if the safety of the product is not such as persons generally are entitled to expect' (including products comprised in that product). [*Consumer Protection Act 1987, s 3(1)*].

The definition of 'defect' implies an entitlement to an expectation of safety on the part of the consumer, judged by reference to *general* consumer expectations not individual subjective ones. (The American case of *Webster v Blue Ship Tea Room Inc 347 Mass 421, 198 NE 2d 309 (1964)* is particularly instructive here. The plaintiff sued in a product liability action for a bone which had stuck in her throat, as a result of eating a fish chowder in the defendant's restaurant. It was held that there was no liability. Whatever her own expectations may have been, fish chowder would not be fish chowder without some bones and this is a general expectation.)

Consumer expectation of safety – criteria

38.22   The general consumer expectation of safety must be judged in relation to:

(*a*)   the marketing of the product, i.e.:

    (i)   the manner in which; and

    (ii)   the purposes for which the product has been marketed;

    (iii)   any instructions/warnings against doing anything with the product; and

(*b*)   by what might reasonably be expected to be done with or in relation to the product (e.g. the presupposition that pork chops will be cooked and that Coca-Cola will be removed from a can/bottle); and (*c*)   the time when the product was supplied.

In other words, a defect cannot arise retrospectively by virtue of the fact that, subsequently, a safer product is made and put into circulation. The consequences of 'defect by relation back' could be catastrophic, although such interpretations have occurred sometimes in American law. [*Consumer Protection Act 1987, s 3(2)*].

Types of defect

38.23   Defect can arise in one of three ways and is related to:

(*a*)   construction, manufacture, submanufacture, assembly;

(*b*)   absence or inadequacy of suitable warnings, or existence of misleading warnings or precautions;

(*c*)   design.

Time of supply

38.24   Liability attaches to the *supply* of a product (see 38.35 below). More particularly, the producer will be liable for any defects in the product existing at the time of supply (see 38.34(*d*) below); and where two or more persons collaborate in the manufacture of a product, say by submanufacture, either and both are liable, that is, severally and jointly (see 38.32 below).

Contributory negligence

38.25   A person who fails to follow clear instructions is probably guilty of contributory negligence and, thus, will risk a reduction in damages [*Consumer Protection Act 1987, s 6(4)*] (see also 15.38 EMPLOYERS' DUTIES).

Absence or inadequacy of suitable/misleading warnings

38.26   The common law required that the vendor of a product point out any latent dangers in a product which he either knew about or ought to have known about. Misleading terminology/labelling on a product or product container could result in liability for negligence (*Vacwell Engineering Ltd v BDH Chemicals Ltd [1969] 3 AER 1681* where ampoules containing boron tribromide, which carried the warning 'Harmful Vapours', exploded on contact with water, killing two scientists. It was held that this consequence was reasonably foreseeable and accordingly the defendants should have researched their product more thoroughly). In a similar product liability action, the manufacturers would be strictly liable (subject to statutory defences) and, if injury/damage followed the failure to issue a written/pictorial warning, as required by regulation (e.g. the *Chemicals (Hazard Information and Packaging) Regulations 1993 (CHIP)*), there will be liability. [*HSWA s 47(2); Consumer Protection Act 1987, s 41*].

Directions for use

38.27   The duty, on manufacturers, to research the safety of their products, before putting them into circulation (see *Vacwell Engineering Ltd v BDH Chemicals Ltd* (38.26 above)) is even more necessary and compulsory now, given the introduction of product liability. This includes safety in connection with directions for use on a product. A warning refers to something that can go wrong with the product; directions for use relate to the best results that can be obtained from products, if the directions are followed. In the absence of case law on the point it is reasonable to assume that in order to avoid actions for product liability, manufacturers should provide both warnings, indicating the worst results and dangers, and directions for use, indicating the best results; the warning, in effect, identifying the worst consequences that could follow if directions for use were not complied with. On this basis it is reasonably foreseeable that a product user would be injured by not following directions for use. Indeed American law may be regarded as persuasive on this point (*McClanahan v California Spray Chemical Corporation 75 SE 2d 712 (Va 1953)*).

Design

38.28   In the case of defects of construction or submanufacture the product does not turn out as planned; whereas, in the case of design defects, this is not so. Moreover, construction/production defects tend to apply to single products; a design defect runs through a whole range of products and is more expensive to rectify.

It is for this reason that American product liability litigation has drawn a distinction between design defects (including inadequate warnings), on the one hand, and manufacturing defects, on the other, reserving strict liability for manufacturing defects. This distinction was not followed in English law (see 38.23 above) but there is a relevant state of the art defence (see 38.34(*e*) below).

Defect must exist when the product left the manufacturer's possession

38.29   This situation tends to be spotlighted by alteration of, modification to or interference with a product on the part of an intermediary, for instance, a dealer or agent. If a product leaves an assembly line as per its intended design, but is subsequently altered, modified or generally interfered with by an intermediary, in a manner outside the product's specification, the manufacturer is probably not liable for any injury so caused. In *Sabloff v Yamaha Motor Co 113 NJ Super 279, 273 A 2d 606 (1971)*, the plaintiff was injured when the wheel of his motor-cycle locked, causing it to skid, then crash. The manufacturer's specification stipulated that the dealer attach the wheel of the motor-cycle to the front fork with a nut and bolt, and this had not been done properly. It was held that the dealer was liable for the motor-cyclist's injury (as well as the assembler, since the latter had delegated the function of tightening the nut to the dealer and it had not been properly carried out). In product liability litigation, as with negligence, much will depend on whether the defect was one which was foreseeable on the part of a legitimate intermediary.

Role of intermediaries

38.30   If a defect in a product is foreseeably detectable by a legitimate intermediary (e.g. a retailer in the case of a domestic product or an employer in the case of an industrial product), liability used to rest with the intermediary rather than the manufacturer, when liability was referable to negligence (*Donoghue v Stevenson [1932] AC 562*). This position probably does not duplicate under the *Consumer Protection Act 1987*, since the main object of the legislation is to fix producers with strict liability for injury-causing product defects to proper users. Nevertheless, there are statutory duties on employers to inspect/test inward plant and machinery for use at the workplace, under *HSWA s 2*, and failure to comply with this duty may make an employer liable at common law (see 1.43 INTRODUCTION). In addition, employers, in such circumstances, can incur liability under the *Employers' Liability (Defective Equipment) Act 1969* (see 15.13, 15.14 EMPLOYERS' DUTIES) and so should seek to exercise contractual indemnity against manufacturers.

Comparison with negligence

38.31 Product liability differs from negligence in that it is no longer necessary for injured users to prove absence of reasonable care on the part of manufacturers. All that is now necessary is proof of (*a*) defect (see 38.23 above) and (*b*) that the defect caused the injury (i.e. materially). It will, therefore, be no good for manufacturers to point to an unblemished safety record and/or excellent quality assurance programmes, since the user is not trying to establish negligence. How or why a defect arose is immaterial; what is important is the fact that it exists.

The similarity between product liability and negligence lies in causation. Defect must be the viable or material *cause* of injury, the main argument against this equation being, to date, subjective misuse of a product by a user (e.g. knowingly driving a car with defective brakes).

Joint and several liability

38.32 If two or more persons/companies are liable for the same damage, the liability is joint and several. This can, for example, refer to the situation where a product (e.g. an aircraft) is made partly in one country (e.g. England) and partly in another (e.g. France). Here both countries are liable (joint liability) but in the event of one party not being able to pay, the other can be made to pay all the compensation (several liability). [*Consumer Protection Act 1987, s 2(5)*].

Parameters of liability

38.33 Liability for certain types of damage including (*a*) death, (*b*) personal injury and (*c*) loss or damage to property [*Sec 5(1)*], is included relevant to private use, occupation and consumption by consumers. However, persons will not be liable for:

(*a*) damage/loss to the defective product itself, or any product supplied with the defective product [*Consumer Protection Act 1987, s 5(2)*];

(*b*) damage to property not 'ordinarily intended for private use, occupation or consumption' e.g. car/van used for business purposes [*Consumer Protection Act 1987, s 5(3)*]; and

(*c*) damage amounting to less than £275 (to be determined as early as possible after loss) [*Consumer Protection Act 1987, s 5(4)*].

Defences

38.34 The following defences are open to producers, etc.:

(*a*) the defect was attributable to compliance with any requirement imposed by law/regulation or a Community rule/regulation [*Consumer Protection Act 1987, s 4(1)(a)*];

(*b*) the defendant did not supply the product to another (i.e. did not sell/hire/lend/exchange for money/give goods as a prize etc. (see below 'supply')) [*Consumer Protection Act 1987, s 4(1)(b)*];

(*c*) the supply to another person was not in the course of that person's business [*Consumer Protection Act 1987, s 4(1)(c)*];

(*d*) the defect did not exist in the product at the relevant time (i.e. it came into existence after the product had left the possession of the defendant). This principally refers to the situation where, e.g. a retailer fails to follow the specification of the manufacturer [*Consumer Protection Act 1987, s 4(1)(d)*];

(e)   that the state of scientific and technical knowledge at the relevant time was not such that a producer 'might be expected to have discovered the defect if it had existed in his products while they were under his control' (i.e. development risk) [*Consumer Protection Act 1987, s 4(1)(e)*] (see 38.38 below);

(f)   that the defect was:

  (i)   a defect in a subsequent product (in which the product in question was comprised); and

  (ii)   was wholly attributable to:

    (A)   design of the subsequent product; or

    (B)   compliance by the producer with the instructions of the producer of the subsequent product.

[*Consumer Protection Act 1987, s 4(1)(f)*].

The meaning of 'supply'

38.35   Before there can be liability under the *Consumer Protection Act 1987*, that is, strict liability, a product must have been '*supplied*'. This is defined as follows:

(a)   selling, hiring out or lending goods;

(b)   entering into a hire-purchase agreement to furnish goods;

(c)   performance of any contract for work and materials to furnish goods (e.g. making/repairing teeth);

(d)   providing goods in exchange for a consideration other than money (e.g. trading stamps);

(e)   providing goods in or in connection with the performance of any statutory function/duty (e.g. supply of gas/electricity by public utilities);

(f)   giving the goods as a prize or otherwise making a gift of the goods.

[*Consumer Protection Act 1987, s 46(1)*].

Moreover, in the case of hire-purchase agreements/credit sales the effective supplier (i.e. the dealer) and not the ostensible supplier (i.e. the finance company) is the 'supplier' for the purposes of strict liability. [*Consumer Protection Act 1987, s 46(2)*].

Building work is only to be treated as a supply of goods in so far as it involves provision of any goods to any person by means of their incorporation into the building/structure, e.g. glass for windows. [*Consumer Protection Act 1987, s 46(3)*].

No contracting out of strict liability

38.36   The liability of a person who has suffered injury/damage under the *Consumer Protection Act 1987*, cannot be (a) limited or (b) excluded:

(a)   by any contract term; or

(b)   by any notice or other provision.

[*Consumer Protection Act 1987, s 7*].

Time limits for bringing product liability actions

38.37   No action can be brought under the *Consumer Protection Act 1987, Part I* (i.e. product liability actions) after the expiry of ten years from the time when the product was first put into circulation (i.e. supplied in the course of business/trade etc.). [*Limitation Act 1980, s 11(A)(3); Consumer Protection Act 1987, 1 Sch*].

In other words, ten years is the cut-off point of liability. Moreover, actions for personal injury caused by product defects must be initiated within three years of whichever event occurs later, namely:

(*a*) the date when the cause of action accrued (i.e. injury occurred); or

(*b*) the date when the injured person had knowledge of his injury/damage to property.

[*Limitation Act 1980, s 11(A)(4); Consumer Protection Act 1987, 1 Sch*].

But if during that period the injured person died, his personal representative has a further three years from his death to bring the action. (This coincides with actions for personal injuries against employers, except of course in that case there is no overall cut-off period of ten years.) [*Limitation Act 1980, s 11(A)(5)*].

Development risk

38.38 This will probably emerge as the most important defence to product liability actions. Manufacturers have argued that it would be wrong to hold them responsible for the consequences of defects which they could not reasonably have known about or discovered; moreover, that the absence of this defence would have the effect of increasing the cost of product liability insurance and so jeopardise the development of new products. On the other hand, consumers maintain that the existence of this defence threatens the whole basis of strict liability and allows manufacturers to escape liability by, in effect, pleading a defence associated with negligence. For this reason, not all EC states have allowed this defence; the states in favour of its retention are the United Kingdom, West Germany, Denmark, Italy and the Netherlands. The burden of proving development risk lies fairly and squarely on the producer and it seems likely that he will have to show that no producer of a product of that sort could be expected to have discovered the existence of the defect. 'It will not necessarily be enough to show that he (the producer) has done as many tests as his competitor, nor that he did all the tests required of him by a government regulation setting a minimum standard.' (Explanatory memorandum of EC Directive on Product Liability, Department of Trade and Industry, November 1985).

Additionally, the fact that judgments in product liability cases are 'transportable' could have serious implications for the retention of development risk in the United Kingdom (see 38.39 below).

Transportability of judgments

38.39 Under the *Foreign Judgments (Reciprocal Enforcement) Act 1933* judgments in certain civil proceedings in one country can be enforced in another, namely France, West Germany, Italy and the Netherlands as well as the United Kingdom. Moreover, the Brussels Convention of 17 September 1968 on Jurisdiction and Enforcement of Judgments in Civil and Commercial Matters requires judgments given in one of the original six EC member states to be enforced in another. The United Kingdom is now bound by this Convention, which, by virtue of the *Civil Jurisdiction and Judgments Act 1982*, is part of United Kingdom law. Where product liability actions are concerned, litigation would normally be initiated in the state where injury occurred and the judgment of that court 'transported' to another member state. This could pose a threat to retention of development risk in the United Kingdom and other states in favour of it from a state against it, e.g. France, Belgium, Luxembourg.

Contractual liability for substandard products

38.40   Contractual liability is concerned with defective products which are substandard. Liability is of statutory origin and is contained in the *Sale of Goods Act 1979*, where goods are sold; the *Consumer Credit Act 1974*, where goods are the subject of hire purchase and conditional and/or credit sale; and the *Supply of Goods and Services Act 1982*, where goods are supplied (but not sold and/or are the subject of hire purchase, credit sale etc.). Exemption or exclusion clauses in such contracts are generally invalid by dint of the *Unfair Contract Terms Act 1977*, which also applies to such transactions.

Significantly, contractual liability is strict. It is not necessary that negligence be established (*Frost v Aylesbury Dairy Co Ltd [1905] 1 KB 608* where the defendant supplied typhoid-infected milk to the plaintiff, who, after its consumption, became ill and required medical treatment. It was held that the defendant was liable, irrespective of the absence of negligence on his part).

Sale of Goods Acts

38.41   Conditions and warranties as to fitness for purpose, quality and merchantability were originally implied into contracts for the sale of goods at common law. Then those terms were codified in the *Sale of Goods Act 1893*, which, however, was not a blanket consumer protection measure, since sellers were still allowed to exclude liability by suitably worded exemption clauses in the contract. This practice was finally outlawed, at least as far as consumer contracts were excluded, by the *Supply of Goods (Implied Terms) Act 1973* and later still by the *Unfair Contract Terms Act 1977*, the current statute prohibiting contracting out of contractual liability and negligence.

Sale of Goods Act 1979

38.42   Moreover, in 1979 a consolidated *Sale of Goods Act* was passed and current law on quality and fitness of products is contained in that Act. Another equally important development has been the extension of implied terms, relating to quality and fitness of products, to contracts other than those for the sale of goods, that is, to credit sale/hire purchase contracts by the *Consumer Credit Act 1974*, and to straight hire contracts by the *Supply of Goods and Services Act 1982*. In addition, where services are performed under a contract, that is, a contract for work and materials, there is a statutory duty on the contractor to perform them with reasonable care and skill, that is, in the case of services (as distinct from products) liability is not strict, as with the sale and/or supply of products. This is laid down in *Sec 13* of the *Supply of Goods and Services Act 1982*. This applies whether products are simultaneously but separately supplied under any contract, e.g. after sales service, say, on a car or a contract to repair a window by a carpenter, in which latter case service is rendered irrespective of product supplied. However, the draft EC 'Services' Directive, which must be implemented by 31 December 1992, introduces strict liability for performance of services (see further 38.57 below).

Statutory duty to supply products of quality

38.43   Duties to supply products of the right quality and standard are enshrined within three separate statutes, namely, the *Sale of Goods Act 1979* in the case of sale of products, the *Supply of Goods and Services Act 1982* in the case of supply contracts (other than credit sale and hire purchase), and by the *Consumer Credit Act 1974* in the case of credit sale and hire purchase contracts.

Sale of products

38.44 The *Sale of Goods Act 1979* writes two quality conditions into all contracts for the sale of products, the first with regard to merchantability, the second with regard to fitness for purpose.

Products to be of merchantable quality

38.45 'Where the seller sells goods in the course of a business, there is an implied condition that the goods supplied under the contract are of merchantable quality, except that there is no such condition –

(*a*) as regards defects specifically drawn to the buyer's attention before the contract is made; or

(*b*) if the buyer examines the goods before the contract is made, as regards defects which that examination ought to reveal.'

[*Sale of Goods Act 1979, s 14(2)*].

Sale by sample

38.46 In the case of a contract for sale by sample, there is an implied condition '. . .

(*c*) that the goods will be free from any defect, rendering them unmerchantable, which would not be apparent on reasonable examination of the sample.'

[*Sale of Goods Act 1979, s 15(2)*].

Scope of liability

38.47 The condition of merchantability only arises in the case of sales by a dealer to a consumer, not in the case of private sales. *Sec 14(2)* also applies to second-hand as well as new products. It is not necessary, as it is with the 'fitness for purpose' condition (see 38.54 below) for the buyer in any way to rely on the skill and judgment of the seller in selecting his stock, in order to invoke *Sec 14(2)*. But if the buyer has examined the products, then, the seller will not be liable for any defects which the examination should have disclosed. Originally this applied if the buyer had been given opportunity to examine but had not, or only partially, exercised it. In *Thornett & Fehr v Beers & Son [1919] 1 KB 486*, a buyer of glue examined only the outside of some barrels of glue. The glue was defective. It was held that he had examined the glue and so was without redress.

Now, however, actual examination of the product must have taken place. Though, in the case of sale by sample, opportunity to carry out examination is enough to exclude the condition. [*Sale of Goods Act 1979, s 15(2)*].

Meaning of merchantability

38.48 'Merchantability' is defined in the *Sale of Goods Act 1979, s 14(6)* as follows: 'Goods of any kind are of merchantable quality . . . if they are as fit for the purpose or purposes for which goods of that kind are commonly bought as it is reasonable to expect, having regard to any description applied to them, the price (if relevant) and all the other relevant circumstances.'

Products to be reasonably fit for purpose

38.49   'Where the seller sells goods in the course of a business and the buyer, expressly or by implication, makes known

(a)   to the seller, or

(b)   where the purchase price or part of it is payable by instalments and the goods were previously sold by a credit-broker to the seller, to that credit-broker,

any particular purpose for which the goods are being bought, there is an implied condition that the goods supplied under the contract are reasonably fit for that purpose, whether or not that is a purpose for which such goods are commonly supplied, except where the circumstances show that the buyer does not rely or that it is unreasonable for him to rely, on the skill or judgment of the seller or credit-broker.' [*Sale of Goods Act 1979, s 14(3)*].

Reliance on the skill/judgment of the seller will generally be inferred from the buyer's conduct. The reliance will seldom be express: it will usually arise by implication from the circumstances; thus to take a case of a purchase from a retailer, the reliance will be in general inferred from the fact that a buyer goes to the shop in the confidence that the tradesman has selected his stock with skill and judgment (*Grant v Australian Knitting Mills Ltd [1936] AC 85*). Moreover, it is enough if the buyer relies partially on the seller's skill and judgment. But there will be no reliance where the seller can only sell goods of a particular brand. The plaintiff bought beer in a public house which he knew was a tied house. He later became ill as a result of drinking it. It was held that there was no reliance on the seller's skill and so no liability on the part of the seller (*Wren v Holt [1903] 1 KB 610*).

Even though products can only be used normally for one purpose, they will have to be reasonably fit for that particular purpose. The plaintiff bought a hot water bottle and was later scalded when using it because of its defective condition. It was held that the seller was liable because the hot water bottle was not suitable for its normal purpose (*Priest v Last [1903] 2 KB 148*). But, on the other hand, the buyer must not be hypersensitive to the effects of the product. The plaintiff bought a Harris Tweed coat from the defendants. She later contracted dermatitis from wearing it. Evidence showed that she had an exceptionally sensitive skin. It was held that the coat was reasonably fit for the purpose when worn by a person with an average skin (*Griffiths v Peter Conway Ltd [1939] 1 AER 685*).

Like *Sec 14(2)*, *Sec 14(3)* extends beyond the actual products themselves to their containers and labelling. The plaintiff was injured by a defective bottle containing mineral water, which she had purchased from the defendant, a retailer. The bottle remained the property of the seller because the plaintiff had paid the seller a deposit on the bottle, which would be returned to her, on return of the empty bottle. It was held that, although the bottle was the property of the seller, the seller was liable for the injury caused to the plaintiff by the defective container (*Geddling v Marsh [1920] 1 KB 668*).

Like *Sec 14(2)* (above), *Sec 14(3)* does not apply to private sales.

Strict liability under the Sale of Goods Act 1979, s 14

38.50   It should be emphasised that liability arising under the *Sale of Goods Act, s 14* is strict and does not depend on proof of negligence by the purchaser against the seller (*Frost v Aylesbury Dairy Co Ltd* (see 38.40 above)). This fact was stressed as follows in the important case of *Kendall v Lillico [1969] 2 AC 31*. 'If the law were always logical one would suppose that a buyer who has obtained a right to rely on the seller's skill and judgment, would only obtain thereby an assurance that proper skill and judgment had been exercised, and would only be entitled to a remedy if a defect in the goods was due to failure to exercise such skill and judgment. But the law has always gone further than that. By getting the seller to undertake his skill and judgment the buyer gets . . . an assurance that the goods will be reasonably fit for his purpose and that covers not only defects which the seller ought to have detected but also defects which are latent in the sense that even the utmost skill and judgment on the part of the seller would not have detected them' (per Lord Reid).

Dangerous products

38.51 As distinct from applying to merely substandard products, both these subsections, *Sec 14(2)* and *(3)* can be invoked where a product is so defective as to be unsafe, but the injury/damage must be a reasonably foreseeable consequence of breach of the implied condition. If, for instance, therefore, the chain of causation is snapped by contributory negligence on the part of the user, in using a product knowing it to be defective, there will be no liability. In *Lambert v Lewis [1982] AC 225*, manufacturers had made a defective towing coupling which was sold by retailers to a farmer. The farmer continued to use the coupling knowing that it was unsafe. As a result, an employee was injured and the farmer had to pay damages. He sought to recover these against the retailer for breach of *Sec 14(3)*. It was held that he could not do so.

Credit sale and supply of products

38.52 Similar duties to those under the *Sale of Goods Act 1979, s 14* exist, in the case of hire purchase/credit sale/conditional sale contracts, under the *Consumer Credit Act 1974*; and in the case of straight hire and deposit contracts, under the *Supply of Goods and Services Act 1982*. This chapter confines itself to the latter Act.

Merchantable quality

38.53 Where, under such a contract, the transferor transfers the property in goods in the course of a business, there is an implied condition that the goods supplied under the contract are of merchantable quality. [*Supply of Goods and Services Act 1982, s 4(2)*].

'There is no such condition . . .

(*a*) as regards defects specifically drawn to the transferee's attention before the contract is made; or

(*b*) if the transferee examines the goods before the contract is made, as regards defects which that examination ought to reveal.'

[*Supply of Goods and Services Act 1982, s 4(3)*].

Fitness for purpose

38.54 ' . . . where, under a contract for the transfer of goods, the transferor transfers the property in goods in the course of a business and the transferee, expressly or by implication, makes known

(*a*) to the transferor, or

(*b*) where the consideration or part of the consideration for the transfer is a sum payable by instalments and the goods were previously sold by a credit-broker to the transferor, to that credit-broker, any particular purpose for which the goods are being acquired, . . . there is . . . an implied condition that the goods supplied under the contract are reasonably fit for that purpose, whether or not that is a purpose for which such goods are commonly supplied . . . (except) where the circumstances show that the transferee does not rely, or that it is unreasonably for him to rely, on the skill or judgment of the transferor or credit-broker.'

[*Supply of Goods and Services Act 1982, s 4(4)(5) and (6)*].

Supply of goods by sample

38.55   In the case of supply of goods by sample, there is an implied condition that

(*a*)   the bulk will correspond with the sample in quality; and

(*b*)   the transferee will have a reasonable opportunity of comparing the bulk with the sample; and

(*c*)   the goods will be free from any defect, rendering them unmerchantable, which would not be apparent on reasonable examination of the sample.

[*Supply of Goods and Services Act 1982, s 5(2)*].

Product information request

38.56   In spite of the *Chemicals (Hazard Information and Packaging) Regulations 1993* (*CHIP*) and other similarly-oriented regulations as well as the *Consumer Protection Act 1987*, there is still considerable room for improvement in the quality/quantity of information provided to users by manufacturers in respect of their products. Where data given is inadequate, a product information request may be a satisfactory vehicle for the acquisition of such information in a standardised form.

PRODUCT INFORMATION
Serial No . . . .

1. IDENTIFICATION   Date of issue . . . .

Commercial Name and Synonyms_____

Chemical Name and Synonyms_____

Constituent Parts_____

Supplier/Manufacturer_____ Tel No._____

2. PHYSICAL PROPERTIES

Appearance_____ Colour_____ Odour_____

B.P.°C_____ M.P.°C_____ S.G. at 15°C_____

Vapour Pressure (mm Mercury at   °C)_____ Vapour Density_____

Solubility – in water_____ in organic solvents_____

Flash Point °C_____ Auto-Ignition Temp. °C___ Flammability Limits – Upper_____
                                          (% by volume)   – Lower_____

Corrosive   YES/NO

pH Value_____ % Volatiles_____ Evaporation Rate (Butyl Acetate-1)_____

Stability STABLE/UNSTABLE   Conditions to Avoid_____

Hazardous Decomposition   Hazardous Combustion
Products_____ Products_____

Hazardous Polymerisation WILL OCCUR/WILL NOT OCCUR

Conditions to Avoid_____

Incompatibility (Materials to Avoid)_____
Threshold Limit Values of Active Ingredients _____ ppm._____mg/m^3

_____ ppm._____mg/m^3

_____ ppm._____mg/m^3

3. PROCESS USES
                 YES/NO   YES/NO

    Solvent   Disinfectant
    Lubricant   Cleansing Agent/Detergent
    Adhesive   Sterilising Agent
    Heat Treatment
    Paint
    Other uses (specify)_____

4. RISK FACTORS

    (a) FIRE/EXPLOSION

    Fire Extinguishing Media_____

    Special Fire Fighting Procedures_____

Unusual Fire/Explosion Hazards_____

(b)   SPILLAGE/LEAKAGE

Measures in the event of Spillage/Leakage_____

_____

Waste Disposal Method_____

_____

(c)   HANDLING

Protective Clothing and Type_____

_____

Respiratory Protection_____

Ventilation_____

Other precautions_____

(d)   TRANSPORT/STORAGE

Transport/Storage Temp (°C)_____ Loading/Unloading Temp °C_____

CEFIC Tremcard No._____

5.   HEALTH AND FIRST AID

Inhalation_____

Eye Contact_____

Skin Contact_____

Ingestion_____

Other_____

Special Precautions_____

6.   REMARKS AND/OR ADDITIONAL INFORMATION

7.   LEGISLATION   APPLIES

Consumer Protection Act 1987   YES/NO
Health and Safety at Work etc. Act 1974   YES/NO
Factories Act 1961   YES/NO
Environmental Protection Act 1990   YES/NO
Radioactive Material (Road Transport) Act 1991   YES/NO
Chemicals (Hazard Information and
   Packaging) Regulations 1993   YES/NO
Highly Flammable Liquids & Liquefied Petroleum
   Gases Regulations 1972   YES/NO

```
Road Traffic (Carriage of Dangerous
  Substances in Road Tankers and Tank
  Containers) Regulations 1992              YES/NO
Road Traffic (Carriage of Dangerous
  Substances in Packages, etc.) Regulations 1992   YES/NO
Road Traffic (Carriage of Explosives)
  Regulations 1989                         YES/NO
Control of Asbestos at Work
  Regulations 1987                         YES/NO
Ionising Radiations Regulations 1985       YES/NO
Control of Substances Hazardous to Health
  Regulations 1988                         YES/NO
Pressure Systems and Transportable Gas Containers
  Regulations 1989                         YES/NO
Noise at Work Regulations 1990             YES/NO
Manual Handling Operations Regulations 1992 YES/NO
Provision and Use of Work Equipment
  Regulations 1992                         YES/NO
Personal Protective Equipment at Work
  Regulations 1992                         YES/NO
Personal Protective Equipment (EC Directive)
  Regulations 1992                         YES/NO
Supply of Machinery (Safety)
  Regulations 1992                         YES/NO
Construction Products Regulations 1991     YES/NO
Other Legislation_____

        _____

        _____

                        Signed_____

                        Position_____

Date_____  Company_____

        _____

        _____
```

Services provided with products

38.57 A recent EC directive proposes that repairers and installers of products and equipment are to be liable for faulty service unless they can prove that there was no fault on their part (as distinct from the current position, where negligence must be proved by the consumer).

Chapter 39

Risk Analysis and Safety Monitoring

Introduction

39.1   The clear identification and operation of health and safety procedures and systems is an important feature of any business. Accidents, occupational ill-health, dangerous occurrences and other forms of incident represent substantial losses to an organisation. It is essential therefore that individual managers appreciate their responsibilities for preventing losses, that levels of safety performance by management are regularly assessed, perhaps as a feature of a management appraisal, that performance objectives are established in areas of health and safety activity, and that the achievement or non-achievement of such objectives is recognised in the reward structure of the organisation. Managers at all levels should know the principal risks associated with their operation together with procedures necessary to avert these risks. No longer should they consider health and safety in isolation. Good standards of health and safety are a direct indication of good management performance, and vice versa. All employers are required to carry out regular assessments by competent personnel of risks to the health and safety of their employees, by dint of the *Management of Health and Safety at Work Regulations 1992* (see 15.29 EMPLOYERS' DUTIES).

Risk and risk analysis

39.2   Research into risk has shown there are a number of factors which influence the degree of risk in a particular situation. These factors include:

(*a*)   the probability of an adverse outcome;

(*b*)   the severity of the risk, i.e. the number of people at risk;

(*c*)   the maximum potential loss, e.g. fatal injury, major injury, minor injury; and

(*d*)   the frequency of the risk arising, e.g. once per day, once per minute.

Risk analysis seeks to identify and measure risks within these parameters, embracing the potential for danger increasing to a point where there is an imminent risk and the behavioural factors associated with individual risk-taking by people.

Crucial to good standards of safety performance is the design and operation of safe systems of work. (A safe system of work is defined as 'the integration of men, machinery and materials in the correct environment to provide the safest possible working conditions for a particular task or operation'.) Before safe systems of work can be designed and implemented, however, a careful review of the hazards present in the workplace is necessary. This implies the undertaking of risk analysis of each task. This chapter examines the procedures involved in such analysis, together with the subsequent safety monitoring necessary, including the use of safety audits.

Safety objectives

39.3   Before risk analysis is undertaken, it is essential that the board of directors establish

744

the safety objectives for the organisation. These objectives should not only reflect the attitude of the firm to health and safety at work, but also ensure compliance with legal requirements, particularly those of the employer under the *Health and Safety at Work etc. Act 1974, s 2*, which would be clearly stated in the Statement of Health and Safety Policy (see Chapter 41 'Statements of Health and Safety Policy'). Typical objectives are:

(*a*)   compliance with all relevant health and safety legislation: the competent person will have safety expertise and will immediately be able to identify problems (see 15.29 EMPLOYERS' DUTIES);

(*b*)   a policy of protection for all employees, visitors, contractors and members of the public who could be exposed to death, injury or ill-health from the firm's processes, products, buildings, plant, materials or substances used at work (see further Chapter 41 'Statements of Health and Safety Policy');

(*c*)   provision of all appropriate personal protective equipment (see further Chapter 36 'Personal Protective Equipment');

(*d*)   the development and implementation of sound safety practices and safe systems of work;

(*e*)   the implementation of staff safety training as needs are identified; and

(*f*)   ensuring safety projects are given financial priority.

Establishment of these objectives is a necessary declaration of the organisation's intent, indicating practical commitment and establishing the overall parameters within which risk analysis and safety monitoring are to be conducted.

Persons involved in risk analysis

39.4   The next stage is to determine who should carry out the risk analysis. The ideal arrangement is to adopt a team approach, the team to be led by an internal co-ordinator of the programme, such as the safety adviser/manager or a senior line manager. The co-ordinator should not attempt to undertake the risk analysis by himself. He should act as a catalyst within the organisation ensuring that the review is properly and fully carried out.

The task of carrying out risk analysis should be delegated to the *line manager* who, in theory, knows most about the operations under his control. In conducting the analysis, the line manager will realise that there are many others who have important information to provide, and their views and co-operation must be sought.

The *employee* can identify the aspects of any job which create physical or other difficulties in carrying out the task. There is more likely to be inherent danger in the stages of a job which are presenting recognisable problems.

The *supervisor* will know the day-to-day complaints of the workforce and will have looked into many minor problems over the years. He knows how the job is actually done as distinct from how it should be done and may have ideas as to more efficient and safer methods.

The *maintenance engineer* will know from the maintenance records which items of plant are a regular source of trouble. Machines which break down too frequently can lead to unsafe practices by the workforce as they attempt to minimise the inconvenience.

The *first-aider* (see Chapter 20 'First-Aid') will be able to pinpoint areas giving rise to regular injury-producing accidents. In this connection, however, an historical absence of accidents is no guarantee for the future.

In addition to internal assistance, the line manager should make himself aware of the *external* sources of help which are available. Health and Safety Executive inspectors, fire brigade officers, local authority environmental health officers can be very useful in pinpointing problem areas and assisting in producing an appropriate solution.

An approach to risk analysis

39.5   Risk analysis implies an initial careful examination of the tasks undertaken, perhaps using the technique of task analysis, followed by an assessment of the hazards to operators and others. The analysis may be job-based, e.g. machinery operation, or activity-based, e.g. track assembly of vehicles, where operators may be working in teams.

Suggested framework

39.6   Documentation for the analysis should incorporate the following:

(*a*)   job or activity title;

(*b*)   scope and function of task/activity;

(*c*)   possible hazards or dangers involved:

   (i)   mechanical;

   (ii)   electrical;

   (iii)   chemical;

   (iv)   environmental;

   (v)   physical;

(*d*)   influences on behaviour;

(*e*)   precautions necessary to avert danger;

(*f*)   safety equipment required;

(*g*)   training requirements; and

(*h*)   detailed description of the safe system of work or working method.

The job or activity title should be specific to the task under review and must be reserved for the task to avoid confusion. Code numbering of specifically identified tasks would be appropriate in certain cases.

Scope and function of the task or activity should identify the task objectives, e.g. assembly of certain parts correctly to produce a finished product which complies with a performance specification; range of articles, parts, substances, tools and equipment to be used; commencement and finishing stages of the task; any testing necessary and certification as to completion.

Possible hazards

39.7   Detailed analysis of each task is then carried out with specific reference to possible mechanical, electrical, chemical, environmental and physical hazards, including manual handling hazards.

Mechanical

39.8   This involves an analysis of all machinery and mechanical handling aids employed in the task. The review should concentrate on identifying any portion of the equipment likely to give rise to injuries (such as gear wheels, revolving shafts, conveyor belts) when the plant is operating normally; in addition, mechanical dangers arising from the product, such as broken glass or metal fragments.

This assessment naturally leads to a decision as to steps which are necessary to avoid injury. This may involve provision of guards, either fixed or automatic, or the use of trip or interlocking devices. Consideration should be given also to protective clothing and equipment necessary to combat the hazards, e.g. goggles, visors and gloves (see Chapter 36 'Personal Protective Equipment').

Electrical

39.9   Similarly, each location and item of plant (not forgetting portable appliances) should be reviewed to ascertain whether or not there is any danger from the use of electricity. Voltage ratings, cable condition, vicinity of steam pipes are examples of items to be fully checked out. Necessary precautions, protective clothing and equipment should be itemised.

Chemical

39.10   The chemical hazards arising from the materials being used in the process need to be fully known. This involves obtaining full details of every substance. Such information should be available from the supplier or manufacturer and detail should be as specific as possible. It is recommended that each supplier be asked to detail the chemical composition of any substance sold under a trade name, rather than merely accepting the supplier's statement on hazards associated with the product. The problem of incompatibility between certain chemicals has to be considered and, at some stage of the review, this aspect will have to be considered in relation to all other chemicals used within the workplace to ensure that accidents cannot arise through the use of an incorrect substance which, for example, has been wrongly delivered from stores.

Environmental

39.11   The possible adverse effects on the work environment must be assessed, e.g. noise, dust, or fumes. Possible ways of mitigating these adverse factors should be considered both as regards the employee and others (see Chapter 12 'Emissions into the Atmosphere' for penalties for failure to do so).

Physical

39.12   The physical hazards associated with processes can include the risk of contact injuries associated with the structure, mobile equipment, such as forklift trucks, or the nature of the raw materials being used. Moreover, there may be hazards created by poor lighting, excessive temperatures or radiation.

Influences on behaviour

39.13   The task may require a high degree of discipline amongst operators, together with the ability to concentrate and work carefully in order to produce the product. The potential for human error, resulting in hazards being created, must also be considered. People may be distracted, they may try to save time and effort, they may have personal problems which reduce their ability to concentrate or they may simply not be physically or mentally fit for the task. Other influences on behaviour can be the discomfort associated with various forms of personal protective equipment, space limitations for the task, the quality of supervision and even the current rate for the job. There are many direct and indirect influences on human behaviour which should be considered at the risk analysis stage. A careful perusal of previous accident reports may identify many of these adverse influences.

Precautions necessary to avert danger

39.14   Once the risks have been identified and quantified, the appropriate precautions necessary should be considered. Such precautions could include improving environmental conditions, introducing a better level of supervision, providing a more appropriate form of personal protection, improving the guarding system to a machine, replacing a potentially dangerous substance with a less dangerous one or improving fire protection measures in the area.

Safety equipment required

39.15   Certain tasks may require provision of specific safety equipment, such as emergency shower and eye wash stations, a certain form of lifting equipment or atmospheric monitoring devices.

Training requirements

39.16   Most new tasks will require some form of training input. Here it is essential that training needs are identified, training objectives established and a training programme devised. In high risk activities, it should be a condition of employment in the job that the individual has completed the appropriate training programme satisfactorily.

Formulation of safe systems of work/working procedures

39.17   The final stage is the formal documentation of the safe system of work or working procedure. This should be written on a stage-by-stage basis, with the various hazards and precautions necessary at each stage clearly identified. Individual responsibilities of managers, supervisors, operators and contractors (where appropriate) should also be clearly stated in the document. All persons should be trained in the system and its correct implementation monitored regularly.

During the risk assessment it is necessary constantly to bear in mind the safety objectives, (see 39.3 above) to ensure that the final system accords with them.

When the analysis of all tasks has been completed, it will be found that decisions have been taken and standards adopted covering the complete range of the organisation's activities. In particular, detailed arrangements will have been promulgated regarding:

(*a*)   safe systems of work and working procedures;

(*b*)   induction and job training;

(*c*)   fire prevention;

(*d*)   emergency procedures;

(*e*)   control of hazardous substances;

(*f*)   environmental control;

(*g*)   maintenance of plant, buildings and equipment;

(*h*)   medical and health supervision requirements;

(*j*)   care of visitors and contractors; and

(*k*)   statutory records.

This position is secured by the interlocking of the various tasks within each area of the organisation. Care must be exercised to ensure that decisions taken regarding one task or area do not impinge adversely on others.

Departmental policies

39.18   In effect, the achievement of acceptable practices and standards creates a series of departmental safety policies detailing arrangements and responsibilities which have to be maintained at the agreed levels.

This involves management in a further set of consultations to determine how best to ensure that agreed standards are kept. Systems will have to be developed covering such aspects as employee involvement and workplace inspections. The latter may be carried out by means of safety sampling or by the use of safety check lists. The former covers such matters as liaison with safety representatives, safety committees and the practical utilisation of employees in general safety activities.

Safety monitoring

39.19   The last stage of the operation is the introduction of a specific safety monitoring procedure as a continuing tool of management. This is frequently undertaken by use of safety audits, together with other forms of monitoring, such as safety surveys, inspections and sampling exercises.

Safety audits

39.20   Safety audits are required by the *Management of Health and Safety at Work Regulations 1992 (SI 1992 No 2051)* (see 15.29, 15.47 EMPLOYERS' DUTIES) and should be carried out by accredited auditors with specified qualifications. A safety audit is a detailed inspection of the workplace for the purposes of identifying actual and potential hazards to the workforce and the environment. It subjects each area of an organisation's activities to a systematic critical examination with the objective of minimising injury and loss. It is fundamentally designed to measure management effectiveness in producing and maintaining a safe place of work.

The safety audit is carried out on a department by department basis. Ideally, it should be conducted by the same individual to ensure uniformity of judgment. Each component part of the audit should reflect the various aspects of safety arrangements and practices which the organisation has decided are important to the overall success of the safety programme. There is no point in attempting to audit factors which have not been adopted by the organisation, although the evaluator might think them important. Consequently the number of areas or activities to be evaluated will vary from firm to firm.

Areas of audit

39.21   Examples of the areas to be audited are:

(*a*)   management involvement;

(*b*)   employee involvement;

(*c*)   provision of protective equipment;

(*d*)   safety training;

(*e*)   control of hazardous substances;

(*f*)   fire prevention standards;

(*g*)   maintenance;

(*h*)   medical facilities.

These examples mirror the arrangements specified in the departmental safety policy. The safety auditor will interview the departmental manager and attempt to assess how successful he has been in developing standards to meet company requirements. The auditor will bear in mind company standards, accepted good practices and legislative requirements. Table 32 below demonstrates the nature of the questions which may be asked during the audit, but are not exhaustive.

Table 32

Questions relevant to a safety audit

Management involvement

(*c*)   Does he discuss safety performance with his superiors and subordinates?

(*d*)   Does he receive reports of accidents?

(*e*)   Does he attend safety committee meetings?

(*f*)   Does he personally conduct safety inspections?

(*g*)   Does he receive reports of all safety inspections?

(*h*)   Does he receive safety training records?

(*i*)   Does he sign personally approved safe systems of work?

Provision of protective equipment

(*a*)   Are all jobs requiring protective equipment identified?

(*b*)   Is an attempt made to 'engineer out' the need for protective equipment where practicable?

(*c*)   What system is used to issue protective equipment?

(*d*)   Are all employees aware of the need to wear protective equipment?

(*e*)   Is the protective equipment supplied effective in use? How often are employees' views sought?

(*f*)   Is any charge made for supplying protective equipment?

(*g*)   Is the non-wearing of protective equipment a disciplinary offence?

(*h*)   What steps are taken to ensure that employees are aware of the reasons for protective equipment being supplied?

(*j*)   Is spare protective equipment held?

(*k*)   Is protective equipment issued to visitors as appropriate?

Safety training

(*a*)   Whose responsibility is it to identify safety training needs?

(b)   Is on-the-job safety training carried out? By whom? When?

(c)   Are records of on-the-job safety training kept?

(d)   Are safety representatives involved in developing appropriate on-the-job safety training?

(e)   What off-the-job safety training is given, e.g. safety legislation? company safety policy? fire prevention?

(f)   Is a record of off-the-job safety training kept?

(g)   Is there a recognised programme for off-the-job safety training?

(h)   Is safety training given to all managers, supervisors and staff?

(j)   What safety training have you received?

(k)   Do you review safety training with your direct subordinates?

Ratings of safety effectiveness and remedial action

39.22   Based on the answers to the above questions the manager will be given a rating, the evaluation of which is a real challenge to the auditor, as he will find himself in an area of value judgments (to be given as objectively as possible) rather than absolute fact. Ratings are given in each area, which produce an overall picture of the manager's safety effectiveness. By looking at his rating the manager immediately knows where he is failing to meet company safety standards and can then take remedial action. When all departmental reviews are complete, an overall company picture emerges for the board of directors, showing areas of success or failure within the company and indicating where group action is necessary. The response in many areas will be a call for improved risk analysis.

Safety surveys

39.23   A survey is a detailed examination of a number of critical areas of operation or an in-depth study of the total health and safety operation of a factory or other premises. It would cover procedures for health and safety administration and management, the working environment, provisions relating to occupational health and hygiene, general and specific aspects of safety and accident prevention and systems for health and safety training of staff, contractors and other groups.

A survey report generally makes short, medium term and long term recommendations, many of which may involve capital expenditure, such as improvements to amenities, replacement of buildings, plant and equipment which may be dangerous or unsuitable, improvements to ventilation and lighting systems, etc. Short term recommendations would incorporate improvements to machinery safety and other items where there is a direct breach of the law, and recommendations not involving capital expenditure.

It is normal to produce a progress report on the implementation of the safety survey recommendations at quarterly or six monthly intervals.

Safety inspections

39.24   This is a scheduled inspection of premises or part of premises by personnel within that organisation, possibly accompanied by an external specialist. Inspections may examine housekeeping standards, compliance with formally written safe systems of work, environmental control, machinery safety standards, etc. Depending upon the system agreed for reporting deficiencies, it would be normal for an inspection report to be submitted to and discussed with senior management, with a view to establishing targets for implementation of safety recommendations made.

Safety sampling

39.25 Safety sampling is designed to measure, by random sampling, the accident potential in a specific workplace or process by identifying safety defects or omissions. Observers follow a prescribed route through a specific area noting safety defects on a sampling sheet with a limited number of points to be deserved. It is normal to cover, say, 15 or 20 specific points, such as structural hazards, noise control and access equipment, awarding points up to a certain maximum for degrees of safety performance. Areas with low scores will need immediate attention, whereas those with high scores may not need such attention, as a good standard of performance is already being achieved. Safety sampling can be an excellent means of increasing safety awareness amongst staff, particularly if an element of competition is introduced. Thus, many companies give a prize or shield for the best weekly or monthly performance in the safety sampling exercise.

Damage control

39.26 This technique aims to ensure a safe working environment, and is based on the philosophy that damage accidents are an indicator of poor safety performance. In other words, non-injury accidents are considered as significant as those causing injury, and the elimination of non-injury or damage only accidents will frequently remove the potential for other forms of injury accident. The technique calls for keen observation and co-operation by staff who see or experience a condition which may lead to an accident. There must be an effective inspection and reporting system for all damage and defects supported by a programme of preventive maintenance.

Chapter 40

Shops

Introduction

40.1 Although obviously not so hazardous and accident-prone as factories and manufacturing establishments, shops should, by way of self-advertisement, maintain high health and safety standards in the interests of both employees and the general visiting and consuming public. Nothing generates adverse publicity more for retailing organisations than inevitable press coverage concerned with indifferent hygiene standards or breach of the offices and shops legislation. In order, therefore, to project a favourable corporate image, if for no other more compelling reason, shops should treat compliance with minimal health and safety standards as a leading priority. In particular, large multi-storey retail 'own-branding' outlets, with a wide variety of consumer products, ranging from toys, through clothes, confectionery, to toiletries, electrical gadgetry, garden equipment to food and drink, are an obvious attraction to children. (For the implications of this, see 40.5 below).

Shop management should also consider the dangers associated with continual use of escalators between floors and lifts, particularly to the elderly, disabled and children, and inform customers accordingly with boldly worded notices. Similarly, entrance and exit points, as well as means of escape in case of fire, should be clearly identified. Shop entrances and exits to and from, in many cases, a main street or busy thoroughfare, should at all times be kept clear from obstructions as well as delivery points, often at the rear of commercial premises, and members of the public should be prohibited from parking in such restricted areas. Staff should be made aware, as part of induction training, of their health and safety duties to the general public and the possibility of liability, both criminal and civil, if potentially dangerous situations arise or someone is accidentally injured. Where necessary, staff should see that wandering trolleys are returned to ranks and spillages eliminated as soon as possible (see 40.4 below). Out of bounds areas, such as lift motor rooms and staff offices should be clearly signposted and marked 'Private. No admittance except for staff'. Latent structural hazards should be clearly identified, e.g. a dark or unlit staircase, and even patent dangers should be drawn to the attention of unattended children (see 32.9 OCCUPIERS' LIABILITY). Where repairs are being carried out or remedial or decorative work is going on above, customers and visitors should be alerted to this. Wherever possible, particularly in large multi-storey stores, lighting should be evenly distributed.

More so than with factories and offices, shop staff – in constant contact with the general public – should be au fait with risks to the public (and especially babies and children) and, where necessary, briefed as to first-aid location and provision. Moreover, since fire hazard and risk of fire spread is one of the deadliest dangers in shops, staff should be briefed in fire hazards and routine fire fighting techniques (see also Chapter 19 'Fire and Fire Precautions'). A knowledge of the location of fire extinguishers and how to operate them is essential, as well as any dangerous cutting machines at food counters. Employees operating bacon slicers and similar food processing machines should be instructed in the inherent dangers of such machines and management should make failure to comply with guarding requirements an instantly dismissible offence (see further Chapters 33 'Offices' and 13 'Employee Safety Rights, Disciplinary Procedures and Unfair Dismissal'). Prominent signs should prohibit smoking (by staff on duty as well as customers) and the introduction of product liability for injury-causing defective products underlines a need for on-going staff familiarisation with use of sophisticated tier products (see further Chapter 38 'Product Safety').

Maintenance of high health and safety and public hygiene standards in shops (as well as restaurants and hotels) is required by a variety of overlapping statutes and regulations. Apart from the *Health and Safety at Work etc. Act 1974*, which applies in a general way to shops, the principal legislation applicable to shops, hotels and restaurants is the *Offices, Shops and Railway Premises Act 1963* and regulations made under it (see further Chapter 33 'Offices'), the *Food Safety Act 1990* and subsequent regulations (see further Chapter 21 'Food and Food Hygiene') and the *Consumer Protection Act 1987* (see further Chapter 38 'Product Safety'), as well as a host of regulations still operational under the defunct *Consumer Safety Act 1978*.

Law in shops is enforced by environmental health officers, except for the fire regulations which are enforced by the local fire authority, with whom on-going consultation and co-operation by shop management is strongly advised. Since much of the liability associated with shops legislation is criminal and depends on either 'sale' having taken place or with 'offering for sale' products, case law has instructively established that display of products in a supermarket, hypermarket or shop for self-service purposes is not an 'offer for sale' (*Pharmaceutical Society of Great Britain v Boots Cash Chemists Ltd [1953] 1 QB 401*) (see also *Fisher v Bell* relating to the display of a flick knife (21.7 FOOD AND FOOD HYGIENE)). Actual sale takes place when money is handed over at the check-out in return for goods.

Application of the general duties under the Health and Safety at Work Act

40.2   Every employer must ensure, so far as is reasonably practicable, the health, safety and welfare at work of all his employees. [*HSWA s 2(1)*]. Various components of this general duty are specified in more detail in *HSWA s 2(2)*. These general duties apply to all employers, and therefore clearly extend to employees working in shops, hotels, restaurants, cafeterias and similar premises, to which the specific requirements of the *Workplace (Health, Safety and Welfare) Regulations 1992* will also apply, as from 1 January 1996, unless the workplace is new, that is, used for the first time, in which case the same requirements will apply from 1 January 1993 (see further Chapters 18 'Factories and Workplaces' and 33 'Offices').

'Shop premises' covered by the specific legislation

40.3   There are two principal Acts relating to shops, the *Shops Act 1950* and *OSPRA*. The former deals with hours of closing, conditions of employment and Sunday trading. *OSRPA* deals with health, safety and welfare of personnel employed in shops. A 'shop' for the purposes of the 1950 Act is 'any premises where any retail trade or business is carried on'. [*Shops Act 1950, s 74(1)*]. For *OSRPA*, however, the definition is rather wider; for example, it includes wholesale premises as well.

'Shop premises' for the purposes of *OSRPA* are:

(*a*)   a 'shop' (the term 'shop' is not further defined in *OSRPA*);

(*b*)   a building, or part of a building, which is not a shop under (*a*) but whose sole or principal use is the carrying on of retail trade or business, including:

(i)   sale to members of the public food and drink for immediate consumption, e.g. a restaurant;

(ii)   lending of books and periodicals, e.g. a library;

(*c*)   a building where goods are kept for wholesale sale or part of such a building (but not a warehouse belonging to a dock, which is covered by the *Factories Act 1961*);

(*d*)   a building or part of a building:

(i)   to which members of the public are invited to deliver goods for repair or some other treatment; or

(ii)   where they carry out the repairs themselves;

(*e*)   fuel storage premises, where solid fuel is stored before being sold, but not dock or colliery storage premises (the latter being governed by the *Factories Act 1961* and the *Mines and Quarries Act 1954*).

[*OSRPA s 1(3)*].

Although restaurants are covered by *OSRPA*, hotels are not (with the exception of their offices, shops, bars and public restaurants). They would, of course, be covered by *HSWA* (see 40.2 above).

Injuries on shop premises – liability in tort

40.4   Under normal circumstances negligence must be proved before there will be liability on the part of an employer/occupier for work injuries but in the case of injuries occurring on shop premises where the general public is involved liability can be strict. In such cases the burden of proof is reversed and '*res ipsa loquitur*' applies, with the result that the shopkeeper must disprove negligence (see further Chapter 1 'Introduction'). Thus, 'The duty of the shopkeeper in this class of case is well established. It may be said to be a duty to use reasonable care to see that the shop-floor, on which people are invited, is kept reasonably safe, and if an unusual danger is present of which the injured person is unaware, and the danger is one which would not be expected and ought not to be present, the onus of proof is on the defendants to explain how it was that the accident happened' (per Lord Goddard CJ in *Turner v Arding & Hobbs Ltd* [*1949*] *2 AER 911*).

In *Ward v Tesco Stores Ltd* [*1976*] *1 AER 219* the appellant slipped, while shopping, on some yoghourt which had spilled onto the floor, was injured and sued the respondent for negligence. It was held that it was the duty of the respondents, through their employees, to see that floors were kept clean and free from spillages. Since the appellant's injury was not one which, in the ordinary course of things, would have happened if the floor had been kept clean and spillages dealt with as soon as they occurred, it was for the respondents to demonstrate that the accident had not arisen from lack of reasonable care on their part. In the absence, therefore, of a satisfactory explanation as to how yoghourt got onto the floor, the inference was that the spillage had occurred because the respondents had failed to exercise reasonable care. The law on *res ipsa loquitur* was authoritatively laid down by Erle CJ in *Scott v London and St Katherine Docks Co* (*1865*) *3 H & C 596*: 'But where the thing is shewn to be under the management of the defendant or his servants, and the accident is such as in the ordinary course of things does not happen if those who have the management use proper care, it affords reasonable evidence, in the absence of explanation by the defendants, that the accident arose from want of care'. Thus, there are four circumstances in which *res ipsa loquitur* applies:

(*a*)   the 'thing' causing the accident must be under the control of the employer, or under his management;

(b) the injury-causing accident must be one which does not happen in the ordinary course of things (e.g. sugar barrels falling from an upper window);

(c) the accident would not have happened if management had been exercising reasonable care;

(d) absence of explanation, on the part of the defendant, to show that they used reasonable care.

Application of Occupiers' Liability Act 1957

40.5 A shop, supermarket or hypermarket is 'premises' for the purposes of the *Occupiers' Liability Act 1957* and customers who visit the shop are 'lawful visitors' and so entitled to the protection of that Act, unless they go or stray to places or parts of the premises (e.g. staff room) to which they are not invited, or excluded (see further Chapter 33 'Occupiers' Liability'). In particular, an enormous variety of gadgetry in shops and supermarkets is a fertile source of attraction for children, from sweets to medicines and from coat hangers to lifts and escalators. As such, these constitute 'traps' and children, although ostensibly trespassers, will be treated as 'implied licensees' entitled to the protection of the *Occupiers' Liability Act 1957*. In particular, children unattended by parents, guardians or teachers should be forbidden entrance or removed from shop premises.

Chapter 41

Statements of Health and Safety Policy

Introduction

41.1　Employers are under a statutory duty under the *Health and Safety at Work etc. Act 1974 (HSWA)* to prepare and keep revised a written statement of health and safety policy. [*HSWA s 2(3)*]. There is an exception for small businesses (see 41.3 below). To this end, the *Management of Health and Safety at Work Regulations 1992 (SI 1992 No 2051), Regs 3* and *4* require that employers formally assess risks to their employees whilst at work (including a written assessment where there are five or more employees) and implement arrangements for protective/preventive measures. This includes making known to all employees, and first-aiders, procedures for dealing with AIDS (see Chapter 20 'First-Aid') and fire hazards (and advisably the attendant emergency plan, as required by the draft *Fire Precautions (Places of Work) Regulations* (see Chapter 19 'Fire and Fire Precautions')).

This chapter outlines the format which a written statement should follow and then considers in more detail the matters that it should cover. A checklist for writing and revising statements of health and safety policy, produced by the Health and Safety Commission (HSC) in 1985 is shown at the end of the chapter as well as a typical health and safety policy.

An important feature of the statement of health and safety policy is that it should be, in the words of the HSC, 'a living document', which implies that it should be subject to regular revision, updating and modification in accordance with changes in duties and responsibilities, processes and practices, systems of work and other aspects of an organisation's activities. The statement is the key to regulating health and safety activity and should be directly related to other forms of health and safety documentation, such as company codes of practice and working instructions. It may incorporate a number of appendices covering specific aspects aimed at extending the self-regulation process. Most significantly, the statement must be seen as an important tool of the business operation which permits health and safety to be related to the establishment and achievement of business objectives.

Requirement to prepare a written policy statement

41.2　Every employer must prepare, and if necessary revise, a written statement of his general policy regarding the health and safety of his employees. In particular, the policy statement should refer to the organisation, in terms of manpower, and the arrangements, in terms of systems, for implementing the policy. The general policy statement and any revision of it, must be brought to the attention of all employees. [*HSWA s 2(3)*]. This last may be achieved by notification and posters throughout the workplace, backed up by training, briefing sessions and, in the case of new employees, induction.

Exception

41.3　Those employers carrying on an undertaking in which, for the time being, fewer than five persons are being employed, are excepted from the provisions of *Sec 2(3)*. [*Employers' Health and Safety Policy Statements (Exception) Regulations 1975 (SI 1975 No 1584)*]. Regard is to be given only to employees actually present on the premises, i.e. 'employees for the time being'. This has been held not to include relief staff (*Osborne v Bill Taylor of Huyton [1982] IRLR 17*).

Essential format and content of the policy statement

41.4   The key words or phrases in *Sec 2(3)* are 'written statement', 'general policy', 'organisation', 'arrangements', and 'bring to the notice of all employees'. This breakdown of *Sec 2(3)* indicates the basic format of a health and safety policy statement. Essentially, a policy statement should consist of three parts, as follows:

—   *A general statement of intent.* This should outline in broad terms the organisation's overall philosophy in relation to the management of health and safety. It should also include reference to the broad responsibilities of both management and workforce.

—   *Organisation (people and their duties).* This part outlines the chain of command in terms of health and safety management. Who is responsible to whom and for what? How is the accountability fixed so as to ensure that delegated responsibilities are undertaken? How is the policy implementation monitored? Other organisational features should include: individual job descriptions having a safety content; details of specific safety responsibilities; the role and function of safety committee(s); the role and function of safety representatives; and a management chart clearly showing the lines of responsibility and accountability in terms of health and safety management. The competent person who is to assist with compliance with health and safety requirements should also be included. [*Management of Health and Safety at Work Regulations 1992, Reg 6*].

—   *Arrangement (systems and procedures).* This part of the policy deals with the practical arrangements by which the policy will be effectively implemented. These include: safety training; safe systems of work; environmental control; safe place of work; machine/area guarding; housekeeping; safe plant and equipment; noise control; radiation safety; dust control; use of toxic materials; internal communication/participation; utilisation of safety committee(s) and safety representatives; fire safety and prevention; medical facilities and welfare; maintenance of records; accident reporting and investigation; emergency procedures; and workplace monitoring. (Records of arrangements are also required to be kept where more than five employees are employed. [*Management of Health and Safety at Work Regulations 1992, Reg 4*].)

HSE guidance on policy statements

41.5   The HSE has published a review of health and safety policies in industry and commerce drawn from the work and experience of the Accident Prevention Advisory Unit (APAU) of HM Factory Inspectorate. (Health and Safety Executive 'Effective Policies for Health and Safety' (1980)). The APAU states that complex health and safety problems can be solved by efficient managements if they specify their objectives; organise to meet those objectives; make effective arrangements to deal with risks; and monitor the effectiveness of the organisation and arrangements. These four aspects are considered further in the following paragraphs.

Basic objectives and general content of statement

41.6   The APAU details those characteristics which are the hallmarks of successful policies as follows:

(*a*)   The policy should state its main objectives.

(*b*)   It should specify that health and safety are management responsibilities ranking equally with responsibilities for production, sales, costs, and similar matters.

(*c*)   It should indicate that it is the duty of management to see that everything reasonably practicable is done to prevent personal injury in the processes of production, and in the design, construction, and operation of all plant, machinery and equipment, and to maintain a safe and healthy place of work.

(*d*)   It should indicate that it is the duty of all employees to act responsibly, and to do everything they can to prevent injury to themselves and fellow workers. Although the implementation of policy is a management responsibility, it will rely heavily on the co-operation of those who actually produce the goods and take the risks.

(*e*)   It should identify the main board director or managing board director (or directors) who have prime responsibility for health and safety, in order to make the commitment of the board precise, and provide points of reference for any manager who is faced with a conflict between the demands of safety and the demands of production.

(*f*)   The policy should be dated so as to ensure that it is periodically revised in the light of current conditions, and be signed by the chairman, managing director, chief executive, or whoever speaks for the organisation at the highest level and with the most authority on all matters of general concern.

(*g*)   It should clearly state how and by whom its operation is to be monitored.

Organisation (people and their duties)

41.7   In respect of the second part of the policy, the APAU suggests that suitable policies will demonstrate – both in written and diagrammatic form (where appropriate) – the following features:

(*a*)   The unbroken and logical delegation of duties through line management and supervisors who operate where the hazards arise and the majority of the accidents occur.

(*b*)   The identification of key personnel (by name and/or job title) who are accountable to top management for ensuring that detailed arrangements for safe working are drawn up, implemented and maintained.

(*c*)   The definition of the roles of both line and functional management. Specific job descriptions should be formulated.

(*d*)   The provision of adequate support for line management via relevant functional management such as safety advisers, engineers, medical advisers, designers, hygienists, chemists, ergonomists, etc.

(*e*)   The nomination of persons with the competence and authority to measure and monitor safety performance.

(*f*)   The provision of the means to deal with failures in order to meet job requirements.

(g)   The fixing of accountability for the management of health and safety in a similar manner to other management functions.

(h)   The organisation must unambiguously indicate to the individual exactly what he must do to fulfil his role. Thereafter a failure is a failure to manage effectively.

(j)   The organisation should make it known – both in terms of time and money – what resources are available for health and safety. The individual must be certain of the extent to which he is realistically supported by the policy and by the organisation needed to fulfil it.

Arrangements (systems and procedures)

41.8   When developing the third part of the policy, the APAU recommends that it is vital to establish safe and healthy systems of work designed to counteract the identified risks within a business. The following aspects should be used as a guide when preparing arrangements for health and safety at work:

(a)   The involvement of the safety adviser and relevant line/functional management at the planning/design stage.

(b)   The provision of health and safety performance criteria for articles, and product safety data for substances, prior to purchase.

(c)   The provision of specific instructions for using machines, for maintaining safety systems, and for the control of health hazards.

(d)   The development of specific health and safety training for all employees.

(e)   The undertaking of medical examinations and biological monitoring.

(f)   The provision of suitable protective equipment.

(g)   The development and utilisation of permit-to-work systems.

(h)   The provision of first-aid/emergency procedures, including aspects of fire safety/prevention.

(j)   The provision of written procedures in respect of contractors and visitors.

(k)   The formulation of written safe systems of work for use by all levels of management and workforce.

Appendices to statements

41.9   There are a number of reasons for incorporating appendices to statements of health and safety policy (although this is not a statutory requirement). For instance, there may be a need to detail in depth the organisation's intentions, arrangements and procedures for dealing with a hazard specific to a process, e.g. the risk of back injury associated with a particular handling operation. It may be necessary to formally declare the company's policy on asbestos in existing buildings or on the provision of prescription lens eye protection to certain groups of operators. Fundamentally, an appendix qualifies in depth certain provisions outlined in the statement.

Policy monitoring

41.10   Finally, in connection with the overall monitoring of policy implementation, APAU highlights four key areas:

(*a*)   The accident and ill-health record.

(*b*)   The standards of compliance with legal requirements and codes of practice.

(*c*)   The extent to which organisations specify and *achieve* – within a given time scale – certain clearly defined objectives (of both short-term and long-term nature).

(*d*)   The extent of compliance with the 'organisation' and 'arrangements' parts of the organisation's own policy statement (discussed earlier), including in particular the written safe systems of work that have been developed by the organisation to meet its individual needs.

HSC checklist for statements of health and safety policy

41.11   In 1985 the Health and Safety Commission (HSC) produced a checklist giving further guidance on statements of health and safety policy, the main features of which are summarised below.

Questions that need to be asked

Does the statement express a commitment to health and safety and are the organisation's obligations towards its employees made clear?

Does it say which senior officer is responsible for seeing that it is implemented and for keeping it under review, and how this will be done?

Is it signed and dated by a partner or senior director?

Have the views of managers and supervisors, the competent person, safety representatives and the safety committee been taken into account?

Were the duties set out in the statement discussed with the people concerned in advance, and accepted by them, and do they understand how their performance is to be assessed and what resources they have at their disposal?

Does the statement make clear that co-operation on the part of all employees is vital to the success of the health and safety policy?

Does it say how employees are to be involved in health and safety matters, for example by being consulted, by taking part in inspections and by sitting on a safety committee?

Does it show clearly how the duties for health and safety are allocated and are the responsibilities at different levels described?

Does it say who is responsible for the following matters (including deputies where appropriate)?

—   reporting investigations and recording accidents;

—   fire precautions, fire drill, evacuation procedures;

—   first-aid;

—   safety inspections;

—   the training programme;

—   ensuring that legal requirements are met, for example, regular testing of lifts and notifying accidents to the health and safety inspector.

Arrangements that need to be considered

General

Keeping the workplace, including staircases, floors, ways in and out, washrooms, etc. in a safe and clean condition by cleaning, maintenance and repair.

Plant and substances

Maintenance of equipment such as tools, ladders, etc. Are they in safe condition?

Maintenance and proper use of safety equipment such as helmets, boots, goggles, respirators, etc.

Maintenance and proper use of plant, machinery and guards.

Regular testing and maintenance of lifts, hoists, cranes, pressure systems, boilers and other dangerous machinery, emergency repair work, and safe methods of doing it.

Maintenance of electrical installations and equipment.

Safe storage, handling and, where applicable, packaging, labelling and transport of dangerous substances (see Chapter 9 'Dangerous Substances I').

Controls on work involving harmful substances, such as lead and asbestos.

The introduction of new plant, equipment or substances into the workplace – by examination, testing and consultation with the workforce.

Other hazards

Noise problems – wearing ear protection and control of noise at source.

Preventing unnecessary or unauthorised entry into hazardous areas.

Lifting of heavy or awkward loads.

Protecting the safety of employees against assault when handling or transporting the employer's money or valuables.

Special hazards to employees when working on unfamiliar sites, including discussions with site manager where necessary.

Control of works transport, e.g. forklift trucks, by restricting use to experienced and authorised operators or operators under instruction (which should deal fully with safety aspects).

Emergencies

Ensuring that fire exits are marked, unlocked and free from obstruction (see Chapter 19 'Fire and Fire Precautions').

Maintenance and testing of fire-fighting equipment, fire drills and evacuation procedures.

First-aid, including the name and location of the person responsible for first-aid and the deputy, and the location of the first-aid box (see also Chapter 20 'First-Aid').

Communication

Giving employees information about the general duties under *HSWA* and specific legal requirements relating to their work.

Giving employees necessary information about substances, plant, machinery and equipment with which they come into contact.

Discussing with contractors, before they come on site, how they plan to do their job, whether they need the organisation's equipment to help them, whether they can operate in a segregated area or when part of the plant is shut down and, if not, what hazards they may create for employees and vice versa.

Training

Training employees, supervisors and managers to enable them to work safely and carry out their health and safety responsibilities.

Supervising

Supervising employees as far as necessary for their safety – especially young workers, new employees and employees carrying out unfamiliar tasks.

Keeping check

Regular inspections and checks of the workplace, machinery, appliances and working methods.

(From the HSC leaflet: 'Writing a safety policy statement: advice to employers'.)

(For the connection between company health and safety policy statements, works' rules, terms of a contract of employment and disciplinary procedures that can result in dimissal, see Chapter 13 'Employee Safety Rights, Disciplinary Procedures and Unfair Dismissal'. The most commonly held view would seem to be, by way of analogy with a trade union rule book, that statements in a health and safety policy statement are not implied terms of a contract of employment (*Secretary of State for Employment v ASLEF (No 2)* [*1972*] *2 AER 949* – a case involving a go-slow) (see 13.12 EMPLOYEE SAFETY RIGHTS, DISCIPLINARY PROCEDURES AND UNFAIR DISMISSAL).)

Comprehensive company health and safety policy document

41.12   1. The Company recognises its health and safety duties under the Health and Safety at Work Act 1974 and the Management of Health and Safety at Work Regulations 1992 and concomitant protective legislation, including the Environmental Protection Act 1990 and the Fire Precautions Act 1971, both as an Employer and as a Company and to that end has appointed (the following member(s) of staff) to be responsible for health and safety maintenance at the company, to keep workplace procedures relating to health and safety under constant review and to liaise with the Health and Safety Executive wherever necessary, so as to keep the Company and its Board of Directors updated on any new legislation affecting them, EC Directives, regulations and British Standards, in order to ensure compliance with same.

2. In recognition of its duties under the Reporting of Injuries, Diseases and Dangerous Occurrences Regulations 1985 (RIDDOR), the Company has instituted a system for reporting accidents, diseases and dangerous occurrences to the Health and Safety Executive, including injury to any trainee, and this is in addition to its statutory duty to keep an Accident Book available for inspection by an inspector of the Health and Safety Executive.

3. In furtherance of (1), the Company proposes always to comply with its duties

under s 2 of the Health and Safety at Work Act and the Management of Health and Safety at Work Regulations 1992, regs 3-6, towards its employees and, more particularly, so far as is reasonably practicable, to

(a)   provide and maintain a safe place of work, a safe system of work, safe appliances for work and a safe and healthy working environment;

(b)   provide such information and instruction as may be necessary to ensure the health and safety at work of its employees and also compliance with the Health and Safety Information for Employees Regulations 1989, the Personal Protective Equipment at Work Regulations 1992, the Provision and Use of Work Equipment Regulations 1992, the Workplace (Health, Safety and Welfare) Regulations 1992, the Health and Safety (Display Screen Equipment) Regulations 1992, the Trade Union Reform and Employment Rights Act 1993 (TURERA) and the Management of Health and Safety at Work Regulations 1992 and to promote awareness and understanding of health and safety throughout the workforce;

(c)   ensure safety and absence of health risks in connection with use, handling, storage and transport of articles and substances;

(d)   make regular risk assessments to employees;

(e)   take appropriate preventive/protective measures;

(f)   provide employees with health surveillance;

(g)   appoint competent personnel to secure compliance with statutory duties.

4. In further recognition of its statutory and common law duties, the Company has taken out insurance, with an approved insurer, against liability for death, injury and/or disease suffered by any of its employees and arising out of and in the course of employment, provided only that it was caused by the negligence and/or breach of statutory duty on the part of the Company; such certificate of insurance being prominently displayed so as to be available for inspection at all reasonable times by employees and a health and safety inspector.

5. All employees of the Company agree, as a term of their contract of employment, to comply with their individual duties under s 7 of the Health and Safety at Work Act, reg 12 of the Management of Health and Safety at Work Regulations 1992 and generally co-operate with their Employer so as to enable the Employer to carry out his health and safety duties towards them. Failure to comply with health and safety duties, regulations, works rules and procedures regarding health and safety, on the part of any Employee, can lead to dismissal from employment; in the case of serious breaches, or repeated breaches, such dismissal may be instant without prior warning.

6. Prime responsibility for health and safety lies with the Managing Director(s) of the Company and Board of Directors and the Company regards itself as bound by any acts and/or omissions of the Managing Director(s), any executive director or senior manager, giving rise to liability, provided only that such acts and/or omissions arise out of and in the course of company business, and prosecution of any director or senior manager shall not prevent a further prosecution against the Company.

7. In recognition of its duties under s 6 of the Health and Safety at Work Act and the Consumer Protection Act 1987, towards its Customers, the Company proposes (expressed as a normal term/condition of trade in its Terms/Conditions of Trade) to always supply machinery and parts which, so far as is reasonably practicable, are safe for normal operational use and free from foreseeable health and hygiene risks to Customers. To that end the Company will provide on an on-going basis Customers with such official and trade information, including relevant EC

Standards and British Standards, relating to new and existing health and safety risks that may, or indeed, have come to its attention in the normal course of trade, and which can reasonably be obtained from HSE, British Standards Institution and the EC.

8. In recognition of its duties towards the general public and all lawful visitors to the Company's premises, the Company regards the extent of its duties as compatible with sections 2 and 5 of the Health and Safety at Work Act and the Occupiers' Liability Acts 1957 and 1984. In particular, where visitors are under a statutory duty to wear personal protective clothing, or otherwise to take reasonable precautions for their own health and safety, failure to do so will be regarded as a breach of Company policy, entitling the Company to take such measures as it considers appropriate, including asking the Visitor to leave the premises.

9. This Policy has been prepared in furtherance of s 2(3) of the Health and Safety at Work Act 1974 and binds all Directors, Managers and Employees, in the interests of Employees and Customers. We request that our Customers and Visitors respect this Policy, a copy of which can be obtained on demand.

Signed

Managing Director

Dated

Chapter 42

Temperature

Introduction

42.1 Temperature relates to comfort. Although comfort is subjective and personal, workroom temperature should be sufficient to enable people to work (and visit sanitary conveniences) in reasonable comfort, without having to put on extra or special clothing. The *minimum* acceptable temperature is 16°C at the workstation (and not by open windows), except where work involves considerable physical effort, when it reduces to 13°C (dry bulb thermometer reading). Optimum air temperatures or comfort ranges, however, are as follows:

Sedentary/office work:	comfort range	19.4 to 22.8°C
Light work:	optimum temperature	18.3°C
	comfort range	15.5 to 20°C
Heavy work:	comfort range	12.8 to 15.6°C

Sometimes maintenance of such temperatures may not be feasible, as, for instance, where hot/cold production/storage processes are involved, or where food has to be stored. In such cases, an *approximate* temperature should be maintained. With cold storage, this may be achievable by keeping a small chilling area separate or by insulating the product; whereas in the case of hot processes, by insulation of hot plant or pipes, provision of cooling plant, window shading and positioning of workstations away from radiant heat. Moreover, where it is necessary from time to time to work in rooms normally unoccupied (e.g. storerooms), temporary heating should be installed. Current statutory requirements are contained in *HSWA* (general) and the *Workplace (Health, Safety and Welfare) Regulations 1992* (specific) – as well as the *Factories Act 1961* and *OSRPA* in existing factories/offices, shops until 1 January 1996. Failure to comply with these requirements, particularly in hot workplaces, can result in heat exhaustion, dehydration, heat cramps and heat strokes (see further Chapter 31 'Occupational Health').

Statutory requirements

(a) General

42.2 Under *Sec 2* of the *Health and Safety at Work etc. Act 1974* employers must provide and maintain a safe and healthy working environment – temperature and humidity control included. Thus, employers can incur penalties if they fail to take reasonably practicable steps to instal heating, fans, ventilation etc.

(b) Specific

During working hours, temperature in all workplaces must be reasonable (16°C). But cooling/heating methods which emit injurious fumes/gases/vapours must not be installed. In addition, thermometers must be provided, so that workers can periodically check the temperature. [*Workplace (Health, Safety and Welfare) Regulations 1992 (SI*

1992 No 3004), Reg 7]. (This requirement applies to new workplaces as from 1 January 1993 and existing factories/offices etc. as from 1 January 1996.)

Existing factories – requirement until 1 January 1996

42.3   *Sec 3* of the *Factories Act 1961* (repealed by the *Workplace (Health, Safety and Welfare) Regulations 1992, Reg 27*) requires every factory occupier to make effective provision for securing and maintaining a reasonable temperature, though not by methods emitting fumes, gases and vapours that are injurious. Moreover, a minimum temperature of 16°C is necessary for workrooms where a substantial portion of the work is done sitting and does not involve serious physical effort. The minimum temperature must be reached (and maintained) after the first hour of work, and a thermometer provided and maintained in a suitable position in every such workroom. [*Sec 3(2)*].

Humid factories

42.4   There are special provisions relating to 'humid' factories. A humid factory is one in which atmospheric humidity is artificially produced either by steaming or by other means in connection with any textile process. The factory occupier must notify the local factory inspectorate before any artificial humidity is produced. [*Factories Act 1961, ss 68(1), 176(1)*].

Generally, in every room in which artificial humidity is produced, two hygrometers must be both provided and maintained with accurate thermometers either on or near to the hygrometers. One must be kept in the middle and one at the side of the room and regular readings made and recorded on a prescribed table. No artificial humidity may be produced once a wet bulb reading of 22.5°C is reached in most cases, nor if the difference between the wet and dry bulb readings becomes too small as measured by the *First Schedule* to the *Factories Act 1961, 2 Sch*. (Where the humidity will never exceed the limits, the occupier may apply for exemption from the requirement to take the regular readings.) [*Factories Act 1961, s 68(4)(8)*]. The occupier must keep records of wet bulb temperatures and hygrometer readings for two years from when they were made and employees must be given access to these records. (These provisions will not be repealed by the new regulations *(SI 1992 No 3004)*.)

Existing offices and shops – requirement until 1 January 1996

42.5   As in factory premises (see 42.3 above), provision must be made for securing and maintaining a reasonable temperature in every room in an office or shop (as defined, see Chapter 33 'Offices', Chapter 40 'Shops'). Where a substantial portion of the work done in a room does not require 'severe' physical effort, then a temperature of at least 16°C should be maintained after the first hour. A lower temperature is not deemed reasonable, and a thermometer must be kept where it can be easily seen and read by the employees. [*OSRPA s 6(1)(2); Offices, Shops and Railway Premises Act 1963 etc. (Metrication) Regulations 1982 (SI 1982 No 827), Reg 2(2) and Schedule*].

The requirements of *Sec 6* do not apply to a room in premises:

(*a*)   to which members of the public are invited to come (office premises); or

(*b*)   where the maintenance of a reasonable temperature (as above) is not reasonably practicable or would cause deterioration of goods (shops).

In these cases there must be provided for employees conveniently accessible and effective means of enabling them to keep warm [*OSRPA s 6(3)(a)(b)*] (see also 33.14 OFFICES).

Special regulations

Textiles

42.6   The following provisions apply to the flax, tow, spinning and weaving industries:

(*a*)   minimum temperatures for specified operations, e.g. 10°C for hand hackling;

(*b*)   provision of wet and dry bulb thermometers;

(*c*)   keeping of records;

(*d*)   control of humidity levels and quality of water used.

[*Factories (Flax and Tow Spinning and Weaving) Regulations 1906 (SR&O 1906 No 177)*] (remaining in force until 1 January 1996).

These regulations will continue indefinitely with respect to hygrometers and humidity requirements and record-keeping, but the temperature requirements will only remain in force until 1 January 1996. Certain textile processes under the humidity provisions in *Sec 68* of the *Factories Act 1961* will also continue in force indefinitely. The same applies to the *Cotton Cloth Factories Regulations 1929* below.

Provisions relating to the cotton industries require the following:

(*a*)   control of artificial humidification;

(*b*)   provision of hygrometers according to number of sheds and looms;

(*c*)   keeping of records in regard to hygrometer readings (e.g. Forms 81 and 317);

(*d*)   minimum temperatures for weaving sheds and absence of direct draughts from air inlets;

(*e*)   control of steam pipes in weaving sheds;

(*f*)   design of humid sheds erected after 1912;

(*g*)   arrangements for ventilation;

(*h*)   control of carbon dioxide levels.

[*Cotton Cloth Factories Regulations 1929 (SR&O 1929 No 300)*].

Work with woodworking machines

42.7   The heating provisions applying specifically to work involving the use of woodworking machines are as follows:

(*a*)   minimum temperatures in machine rooms;

(*b*)   provision of effective means for people to warm themselves if it is impracticable to maintain the minimum temperature of 13°C;

(*c*)   control of heating method to prevent ignition of materials and the release of fumes.

[*Woodworking Machines Regulations 1974 (SI 1974 No 903), Reg 12*] (remaining in force until 1 January 1996).

Potteries

42.8 Provisions regulating heating in potteries are as follows:

(*a*) maximum and minimum temperatures for specified operations and processes;

(*b*) provision of suitable thermometers;

(*c*) controls for drying of pottery articles by means of heat.

[*Pottery (Health and Welfare) Special Regulations 1950 (SI 1950 No 65), Reg 16*] (remaining in force until 1 January 1996).

Chapter 43

Ventilation

Introduction

43.1 Because air is invisible and intangible, there is a constant tendency to take it for granted. Given, however, that an average individual needs an intake of over thirty pounds of air per day (or about six pints of air every minute), the dangers to employees of inadequate or polluted air supply are obvious. The object of good ventilation is replacement of stale or hot or humid air (often associated with production processes or equipment) with fresh air free from impurity. Normally this is achievable by means of windows (or other similar openings or apertures) as well as by recirculated air, particularly in warmer weather or hot workplaces. Air recirculated via mechanical ventilation or air conditioning systems, should be adequately filtered and impurities removed (see 'Legionella' at 9.27 DANGEROUS SUBSTANCES I), with purified air being impregnated with fresh air prior to recirculation. To that end, ventilation systems should be designed with fresh air inlets and kept open, regularly and properly cleaned, tested and maintained. To avoid uncomfortable draughts, the velocity of ventilation systems may have to be controlled. Current statutory requirements are contained in the *Health and Safety at Work etc. Act 1974* (general) and the *Workplace (Health, Safety and Welfare) Regulations 1992* (specific) – as well as the *Factories Act 1961* and *OSRPA* in respect of existing factories/offices until 1 January 1996.

Statutory requirements

(A) General – HSWA 1974

43.2 The general duty upon employers under the *Health and Safety at Work etc. Act 1974 (HSWA)* to 'ensure, so far as reasonably practicable, the health, safety and welfare at work of all their employees' [*HSWA s 2(1)*], must be regarded as including a duty to provide employees with an adequate and renewable supply of pure and uncontaminated air. Employers must also provide and maintain a safe working environment. [*HSWA s 2(2)*]. In consequence, employers may be in breach if the workplace is not adequately ventilated and specific dust and fume hazards not controlled. In addition, all employers must inform, instruct and train their employees in health and safety procedures. This means that they, or their representatives, must know how to use, test and maintain equipment for ensuring air purity and ventilation as well as dust control (*R v Swan Hunter Shipbuilders Ltd [1981] ICR 831*, where the deaths of the subcontractor employees might have been avoided, had they been properly instructed and trained in the use of respirators).

(B) Specific – Workplace (Health, Safety and Welfare) Regulations 1992 (SI 1992 No 3004)

Effective and suitable provision must be made to ensure that every enclosed workplace is ventilated by a sufficient quantity of fresh or purified air. Plant designed and used for such purposes must be accompanied with visible and/or audible means of warning of any failure, which might affect health or safety. [*Workplace (Health, Safety and Welfare) Regulations 1992, Reg 6*].

Air purification requirements in existing factories – requirement until 1 January 1996

43.3   In all factories (for the definition of 'factory', see Chapter 18 'Factories and Workplaces') effective and suitable provision must be made, by circulation of fresh air, for securing and maintaining adequate ventilation of workrooms. [*Factories Act 1961, s 4(1)*].

This section is restricted to ventilation; it does not extend to respirators (*Ebbs v Whitson & Co Ltd [1952] 2 QB 877*). Nor does it extend to fumes in a boiler room, since this is not a 'work room' or 'process', as required by the *Factories Act 1961 (Brophy v Bradfield & Co Ltd [1955] 3 AER 286)*, though these excluded matters would be within the ambit of *HSWA s 2*. The aim of *Sec 4* is to ensure circulation of fresh air; it does not extend to preventing dust from settling and, in consequence, (possibly) causing dermatitis (*Graham v Co-operative Wholesale Society Ltd [1957] 1 AER 654*).

Air purification requirements in existing offices/shops – requirement until 1 January 1996

43.4   The equivalent provision for offices and shops (to the *Factories Act 1961, s 4(1)*) is *Sec 7(1)* of the *Offices, Shops and Railway Premises Act 1963 (OSRPA)*. In premises regulated by *OSRPA* (see Chapter 33 'Offices') effective and suitable provision must be made for securing and maintaining ventilation of premises by circulation of adequate supplies of fresh or artificially purified air. [*OSRPA s 7(1)*]. For these purposes, ventilation was held to be adequate when a shop door was mostly open, since this provided adequate supplies of fresh air (*Zetland Park Garage v Douglas, Middlesbrough COIT No 2/19 Case No HS 20716/78*).

Specific processes or industries

(1) Highly flammable liquids and liquefied petroleum gases

43.5   Where a dangerous concentration of vapours from a highly flammable liquid may be expected, the process must be carried on within a cabinet or other enclosure, which is:

(*a*)   effective to prevent the escape of such vapours into the general atmosphere;

(*b*)   adequately ventilated; and

(*c*)   fire-resistant.

[*Highly Flammable Liquids and Liquefied Petroleum Gases Regulations 1972, Reg 10(2)*].

Where compliance with this requirement is not reasonably practicable the workroom must have exhaust ventilation adequate to remove vapours from the workroom. [*Reg 10(3)*]. (See further Chapter 24 'Highly Flammable Liquids'.)

(2) Lead processes

43.6   Control of fumes produced by lead processes is governed by the *Control of Lead at Work Regulations 1980*. These regulations are of a general nature, as distinct from the earlier very specific provisions, and apply to all industries where lead is used, linking biological monitoring and medical surveillance to information, instruction and training of employees. (Their operation is unaffected by the new regulations.) More specifically, they require:

(*a*)   the control of employee exposure to lead, primarily by means other than use of protective equipment;

(*b*)   monitoring for concentrations of lead in the air; and

(*c*)   keeping of adequate records which will be available for inspection by employees or their representatives (see further Chapter 9 'Dangerous Substances I').

(3) Control of Lead at Work Regulations 1980

43.7   So far as reasonably practicable (see Chapter 15 'Employers' Duties' for the meaning of this expression), employers must provide measures for controlling exposure of employees to lead otherwise than by use of respiratory protective equipment or protective clothing [*Control of Lead at Work Regulations 1980, Reg 6*], including:

(*a*)   substitution by lead-free materials or low solubility lead compounds;

(*b*)   use of lead or lead compounds in emulsion or paste form to prevent or minimise dust formation;

(*c*)   use of temperature controls to control the temperature of molten lead to below 500°C, at which levels fume emission is insignificant;

(*d*)   containment of lead in totally enclosed plant and in enclosed containers, such as drums and bags;

(*e*)   where total enclosure is not reasonably practicable, an effective exhaust ventilation system, consisting of:

   (i)   partial enclosures, such as booths;

   (ii)   various types of hoods which, when enclosure of the source of pollution is not reasonably practicable, are to be placed as near as practicable to the point of origin of lead dust, fume or vapour, and draw the dust, fume or vapour away from any person's breathing zone;

   (iii)   duct work with an airflow of adequate conveying velocity;

   (iv)   dust and/or fume collection unit with filtration or arrestment equipment;

   (v)   fans placed in the system after collection and filtration unit, so that the unit is kept under negative pressure, thus minimising the escape of lead;

   (vi)   wet methods, including:

      (A)   the wetting of lead and lead materials, e.g. wet grinding and pasting processes;

      (B)   the wetting of floors and work benches while certain types of work are carried out, e.g. work with dry lead compounds and pasting processes in the manufacture of batteries.

Wetting should be thorough enough to prevent dust formation and wetted materials or surfaces should not be allowed to dry out, since this can create dry lead dust, which, if airborne, can be hazardous. Water sprays should not normally be used to control an airborne dust cloud. Moreover, wetting should not be used where such a method could be unsafe, e.g. at furnaces where it might constitute an explosion risk; or in the case of lead materials containing arsenides or antimonides, which might produce, on contact with water, arsine or stibine gases, both of which are highly toxic. [*Reg 6*].

(4) Ventilation of working places in excavations, pits etc., construction sites

43.8   Subject to physical conditions making it possible and as far as reasonably practicable [*Reg 21(3)*], there must be provided and maintained adequate ventilation of every working place in the following areas and their approaches:

(*a*)   any excavation;

(*b*)   pit;

(*c*)   hole;

(*d*)   adit;

(*e*)   tunnel;

(*f*)   shaft;

(*g*)   caisson; or

(*h*)   other enclosed or confined space;

in order to:

(i)   maintain an atmosphere fit for respiration; and

(ii)   render harmless, so far as is reasonably practicable, all fumes, dust or other impurities which:

(A)   may be injurious to health, and

(B)   are generated, produced or released by explosives or any other means in the working place or its approach.

[*Construction (General Provisions) Regulations 1961, Reg 21(1)*] (unrevoked). (For requirements relating to confined spaces generally, see 2.11 ACCESS.)

(5) Asbestos

43.9   No process must be carried on in any factory unless exhaust equipment is provided, maintained and used, which prevents the entry into air of asbestos dust. [*Control of Asbestos at Work Regulations 1987, Reg 13(2)*].

In addition, where it is not reasonably practicable to reduce exposure of employees to below the 'control limits', employers must provide employees concerned with suitable respiratory protective equipment. [*Control of Asbestos at Work Regulations 1987, Reg 8(2)*].

Moreover, where the concentration of asbestos is likely to exceed any 'control limit', the employer must designate that area a 'respirator zone' and ensure that only permitted employees enter/remain in that zone. [*Control of Asbestos at Work Regulations 1987, Reg 14(2)*]. (See further Chapter 4 'Asbestos'.)

Measurement and control of air purity

Composition of pure air

43.10   The composition of pure dry air is as follows:

Oxygen	20.94%
Carbon dioxide	0.03%
Nitrogen and other inert gases	79.03%

Normal air also contains a variable quantity of water vapour.

Occupational exposure limits

43.11   Up to 1981, threshold limit values (TLVs), the principal form of exposure limit, were published annually by HSE in Guidance Note EH 15. However, threshold limit values have now been replaced by Maximum Exposure Limits (MELs) and Occupational Exposure Standards (OESs), establishing tighter administrative and statutory controls on occupational exposure to toxic substances. An occupational exposure standard (OES) is set at a level where there is no indication of risk to health; whereas, in the case of a maximum exposure limit (MEL), there may be a residual risk (see further Appendix A DANGEROUS SUBSTANCES I). Maximum exposure limits and occupational exposure standards are particularly relevant in connection with the *COSHH Regulations* which impose duties on employers where there is a risk of exposure to toxic substances or substances hazardous to health. Employers who fail to ventilate effectively and follow relevant official guidance on medical surveillance of workers can be liable at common law if an employee becomes sensitised to a respiratory sensitiser in the workplace, even in the absence of evidence that the relevant occupational exposure limits have been exceeded (*Douglas Reilly v Robert Kellie & Sons Ltd (1989) HSIB 166* where the employee contracted occupational asthma whilst working with low levels of isocyanate fumes. It was held that the employer was liable at common law and for breach of the *Factories Act 1961, s 63* (now abolished), since hazards associated with isocyanate fumes have been known since the early 1980s).

Comfort

43.12   The sensation of comfort varies with age, state of health and vitality and is a subjective assessment of the conditions at work, whilst relaxing at home, travelling or sleeping. Ventilation has an important part to play in the maintenance of comfort, as well as reduction of pollution in the working environment, along with relative humidity, temperature and radiated heat. (See further Chapter 42 'Temperature'.)

Pollution of the working environment

43.13   Pollution of the workplace environment may take place through the generation of airborne particulates, such as dusts, fumes, mists and vapours. These are defined below.

Particulate: a collection of solid particles, each of which is an aggregation of many molecules.

Dust: an aerosol composed of solid inanimate particles. (Standard ILO definition).

Fumes: airborne fine solid particulates formed from a gaseous state, usually by vaporisation or oxidation of metals.

Mist: airborne liquid droplets.

Vapour: a substance in the form of a mist, fume or smoke emitted from a liquid.

Control of airborne particulates

Substitution replacement

43.14 The use of a less harmful toxic substance or modification to a process may minimise or totally eliminate the hazard. For example, substitution of soap solutions for organic solvents is sometimes possible in cleaning operations.

Suppression

The use of a wet process for handling powders or other particulates is an effective form of control. In the cleaning process, it may be possible to damp down floors prior to removal of dust sooner than resorting to dry sweeping.

Isolation

This form of control entails enclosure of all or part of a process or the actual point of dust production and may be incorporated in machinery/plant, in which case it is necessary to ensure seals are maintained. Total enclosure of large processes involving grinding of metals or other materials, linked to an extract ventilation system, is an effective method of isolating dust from the operator's breathing zone.

Extract/exhaust ventilation

Removal of dust or fume at the point of emission by entraining it in a path of fresh air and taking it to an extract hood or other collection device is the role of extract/exhaust ventilation. The air velocity required to provide this movement depends upon the type of material, varying from about 0.5 metres per second for gases to 10 metres per second or above for some dusts. In fact for large dense dust particles from grinding or cutting operations, it may be necessary to arrange for the trajectory of the emitted particles to be encompassed by the exhaust hood so that the material is literally thrown into the hood by its own energy.

Extract ventilation systems generally take three distinct forms:

(*a*) *Receptor systems*: the contaminant enters the system without inducement, and is transported from the hood through ducting to a collection point by the use of a fan.

(*b*) *Captor systems*: in this system moving air captures the contaminant at some point outside the hood and induces its flow into it. The rate of air flow must be sufficient to capture the contaminant at the furthest point of origin, and the air velocity induced at this point must be high enough to overcome the effects of cross currents created by open doors, windows or moving parts of machinery.

(*c*) *High velocity low volume systems*: dusts from high speed grinding machines in particular require very high capture velocities. With an HVLV system high velocities at the source are created by extracting from small apertures very close to the source of the contaminant. These high velocities can be achieved with quite low air flow rates.

Dilution ventilation

In certain cases, it may not be possible to extract particulates close to their point of origin. Where the quantity of contaminant is small, uniformly evolved and of low toxicity, it may be possible to dilute it by inducing large volumes of air to flow through the contaminated region. Dilution ventilation is most successfully used to control vapours from low toxicity solvents, but is seldom satisfactory in the control of dust and fumes.

Cleaning procedures

Whilst the above methods may be effective in preventing environmental contamination of the workplace, there will inevitably be a need for efficient cleaning procedures wherever dusty processes are operated. Hand sweeping should be replaced by the use of industrial vacuum cleaning equipment, or in situ (ring main) systems which incorporate hand-held suction devices connected via ducting to a central collection point.

Air cleaning

Air cleaning is often employed, either to prevent emission of noxious substances into the atmosphere or to enable some of the air to be recirculated during winter months, thus reducing heated air costs and lowering fuel bills. For particulates such as dusts and grit, air cleaning may involve some form of inertial separator, such as settling chambers or cyclones, usually followed by bag filters. For very fine dusts and fumes, bag filters are often used as the pre-filter, followed by absolute or electrostatic filters. For gases and vapours, the cleaning is usually achieved by wet scrubbers (device where the air is passed in close contact with a liquid) to take the gas into solution or react chemically with it. Scrubbers can also be used for particulate material. The selection of air cleaning types will depend upon the properties of the materials emitted and the size ranges of the particulates.

To generate air flow in the duct, various types of fans are available. The type of fan must be suitable for the system in which it is installed. This requires a knowledge of the system resistance and the fan characteristics in order to generate the desired air flow with minimum noise and power consumption.

For systems with little ducting and airflow resistance, axial fans may be used to generate high air flows. For ducted systems, centrifugal fans are often used, creating generally lower air flows per size, but at the higher air pressures required to overcome the resistances imposed by ducting and air cleaners. The fan should not be used outside its duty range. It should be sited either outside the building or as near to the discharge as possible, so that air cleaners and all ducting within the building are on the negative static pressure side of the fan, thus preventing leakage of the contaminant through cracks or defects in the duct.

Respiratory protection – the last resort

43.15   Respiratory protection implies the provision and use of equipment such as dust masks, general purpose dust respirators, positive pressure powered dust respirators, self-contained breathing apparatus or other forms of such protection. Where dust emission is intermittent or other controls are not available (as above), then resort may be made to respiratory protection. The work and care required in the selection and establishment of a respiratory protection programme, including the training of operators in the correct use of the equipment, is likely to be at least as great as any other control system. The protection must be selected to give adequate cover and minimum discomfort and the need for other personal protective devices should not be ignored. (See also Chapter 36 'Personal Protective Equipment'.)

Chapter 44

Welfare Facilities

Introduction

44.1 'Welfare facilities' is a wide term, embracing both sanitary and washing accommodation at workplaces, provision of drinking water, clothing accommodation (including facilities for changing clothes) and facilities for rest and eating meals (see 44.14 below). In the past, breach of welfare duties, being public health-oriented, has tended not to give rise to additional civil liability (see 1.18 INTRODUCTION), though breach of current welfare requirements would probably, if injury ensued, be actionable as a breach of statutory duty (see 1.18, 1.43 and 1.44 INTRODUCTION).

The need for sufficient suitable hygienic lavatory and washing facilities in all workplaces is obvious. Sufficient facilities must be provided to enable everyone at work to use them without undue delay. They do not have to be in the actual workplace but ideally should be situated in the building(s) containing them and they should provide protection from the weather, be well-ventilated, well-lit and enjoy a reasonable temperature. Where disabled workers are employed, special provision should be made for their sanitary and washing requirements. Wash basins should allow washing of hands, face and forearms and, where work is particularly strenuous, dirty, or results in skin contamination (e.g. molten metal work), showers or baths should be provided. In the case of showers, they should be fed by hot and cold water and fitted with a thermostatic mixer valve. Washing facilities should ensure privacy for the user and be separate from the water closet, with a door that can be secured from the inside; nor should it be possible to see urinals or the communal shower from outside the facilities when the entrance/exit door opens. Entrance/exit doors should be fitted to both washing and sanitary facilities (unless there are other means of ensuring privacy). Windows to sanitary accommodation, showers/bathrooms should be obscured either by being frosted, or by blinds or curtains (unless it is impossible to see into them from outside).

This chapter examines (*a*) current statutory requirements in all workplaces as from 1 January 1993 (44.2–44.5), (*b*) current statutory requirements in connection with construction sites (44.10) and (*c*) current statutory requirements in existing factories, offices and shops until 1 January 1996 (44.7–44.9 and 44.11–44.13).

Current specific statutory requirements in relation to welfare

44.2 Apart from the general duty under *HSWA* to provide and maintain a safe and healthy working environment [*HSWA s 2(2)(e)*], current statutory requirements are contained in the *Workplace (Health, Safety and Welfare) Regulations 1992*, applying to all *new* workplaces as from 1 January 1993 and to *existing* factories, offices and shops as from 1 January 1996. Until the new *Workplace (Health,*

Safety and Welfare) Regulations 1992 come to apply to *existing* factories, offices and shops, *Sec 7* of the *Factories Act 1961* and the *Sanitary Accommodation Regulations 1938* (as amended in 1974) will continue to apply to factories until 1 January 1996 and *Sec 9* of *OSRPA* to offices and shops (although technically repealed by *Reg 27* of the *Workplace (Health, Safety and Welfare) Regulations 1992*).

As from 1 January 1993 in all *new* workplaces and from 1 January 1996 in *existing* factories, offices/shops, employers must provide the following sanitary conveniences and washing facilities:

(A) Sanitary conveniences in all workplaces – Workplace (Health, Safety and Welfare) Regulations 1992 (SI 1992 No 3004)

Suitable and sufficient sanitary conveniences must be provided at readily accessible places. In particular,

(i)   the rooms containing them must be adequately ventilated and lit;

(ii)   they (and the rooms in which they are situate) must be kept clean and in an orderly condition;

(iii) separate rooms containing conveniences must be provided for men and women except where the convenience is in a separate room which can be locked from the inside.

[Workplace (Health, Safety and Welfare) Regulations 1992, Reg 20].

(B) Washing facilities in all workplaces – Workplace (Health, Safety and Welfare) Regulations 1992 (SI 1992 No 3004)

Suitable and sufficient washing facilities (including showers where necessary (see 44.1 above)), must be provided at readily accessible places or points. In particular, facilities must

(i)   be provided in the immediate vicinity of every sanitary convenience (whether or not provided elsewhere);

(ii)   be provided in the vicinity of any changing rooms – whether or not provided elsewhere;

(iii) include a supply of clean hot and cold or warm water (if possible, running water);

(iv)   include soap (or something similar);

(v)   include towels (or the equivalent);

(vi)   be in rooms sufficiently well-ventilated and well-lit;

(vii) be kept clean and in an orderly condition (including rooms in which they are situate);

(viii) be separate for men and women (except for the purposes of washing hands, forearms and face only, where separate provision is not necessary).

[Workplace (Health, Safety and Welfare) Regulations 1992, Reg 21].

Minimum number of facilities – sanitary conveniences and washing facilities

(a) People at work

44.3

Number of people at work	Number of WCs	Number of wash stations
1 to 5	1	1
6 to 25	2	2
26 to 50	3	3
51 to 75	4	4
76 to 100	5	5

(b) Men at work

Number of men at work	Number of WCs	Number of urinals
1 to 15	1	1
16 to 30	2	1
31 to 45	2	2
46 to 60	3	2
61 to 75	3	3
76 to 90	4	3
91 to 100	4	4

For every 25 people above 100 an additional WC and wash station should be provided; in the case of WCs used only by *men*, an additional WC per every 50 men above 100 is sufficient (provided that at least an equal number of additional urinals is provided). Those factories which comply with the *Factories Act 1961* requirements, and also workplaces where there are only 25 females or 25 males respectively, may use only one water closet (see 44.7 below).

Particularly dirty work etc.

44.4   Where work results in heavy soiling of hands, arms and forearms, there should be one wash station for every 10 people at work up to 50 people; and one extra for every additional 20 people. And where sanitary and wash facilities are also used by members of the public, the number of conveniences and facilities should be increased so that workers can use them without undue delay.

Temporary work sites

44.5   At temporary work sites suitable and sufficient sanitary conveniences and washing facilities should be provided so far as is reasonably practicable (see Chapter 15 'Employers' Duties' for meaning). If possible, these should incorporate flushing sanitary conveniences and washing facilities with running water.

Extra cost of compliance with new regulations – offices/shops

44.6   *Regs 20* and *21* of the *Workplace (Health, Safety and Welfare) Regulations 1992* may well involve some extra costs for some offices and shops. Ventilation and lighting requirements are added and must be provided in the immediate vicinity of every sanitary convenience and also of any changing rooms. Separate facilities must be provided for men and women but not as regards washing the face, hands and forearms.

Sanitary conveniences in existing factories

44.7   Sufficient and suitable sanitary conveniences for the persons employed in the factory must be provided, maintained and kept clean, and effective provision must be made for lighting them. Where persons of both sexes are, or are intended to be, employed on the premises, the conveniences must afford proper separate accommodation for persons of each sex. [*Factories Act 1961, s 7(1)*].

Minimum number of conveniences

The present sanitary requirements are laid down in the *Sanitary Accommodation Regulations 1938 (SR&O 1938 No 611)* as amended by the *Sanitary Accommodation (Amendment) Regulations 1974 (SI 1974 No 426)*. They are as follows:

(a)   where females are employed, one sanitary convenience for every 25 females;

(b)   where males are employed, one sanitary convenience for every 25 males;

(c)   where the number of males employed exceeds 100 and sufficient urinal accommodation is also provided, one convenience for every 25 males up to the first 100, and one for every 40 thereafter;

(d)   where the number of males employed exceeds 500, one convenience for every 60 males, provided also that there is sufficient urinal accommodation (this rule does not apply to any factory constructed, enlarged or converted after 30 June 1938 and can only apply where the local authority has issued a certificate that it applies).

In counting the number of employees for this purpose, any odd number of persons less than 25, or 40, is regarded as 25, or 40.

[*Regs 2-4*].

Significantly, *Reg 20* of the *Workplace (Health, Safety and Welfare) Regulations 1992* provides that if the *Factories Act 1961* obligations relating to washing facilities are complied with in an existing factory, this will be sufficient compliance with the new provisions. Benefit of the duty will extend to all workers on the premises, whether employees of the owner or not, as from 1 January 1996. Exemption certificates will not be valid from 1 January 1996 and will not apply at all to factories used for the first time from 1 January 1993.

Liability for breach

44.8   *Factories Act 1961, s 7* and the regulations above give rise only to criminal liability. It has been established that, as far as civil liability is concerned, the section is oriented towards public health rather than towards safety; hence, there would be no civil liability for damages on the ground of breach of statutory duty (as distinct from negligence, see Chapter 15 'Employers' Duties') for any injury or disease caused by breach of the provisions (*Hands v Rolls Royce Ltd (1972) 122 NLJ 474*). It will be possible, however, to take civil proceedings under the *Workplace (Health, Safety and Welfare) Regulations 1992* for breach of statutory duty in addition to the criminal liability in them (see 44.1 above).

Washing facilities in existing factories

44.9   There is an obligation to provide and maintain for the use of 'employed persons' adequate and suitable facilities for washing, including a supply of clean, running hot and cold or warm water and, in addition, soap and clean towels or other suitable means of cleaning or drying. These facilities must be conveniently accessible and kept in a clean and orderly condition. [*Factories Act 1961, s 58(1)*] (to be replaced by *Regs 21* and *22* of the *Workplace (Health, Safety and Welfare) Regulations 1992*, as from 1 January 1996). If the existing rules are being complied with, this will be satisfactory for the new regulations. [*Reg 21(4)*]. The exemption rights mentioned below will no longer be available when the new regulations come into force.

Exemption

By virtue of the *Washing Facilities (Running Water) Exemption Regulations 1960 (SI 1960 No 1029)*, the inspector for the district may exempt, by certificate, any factory from the requirement that the water be running water where he is satisfied that:

(*a*)   accommodation is restricted and adequate and suitable facilities for washing in clean hot and cold or warm water are otherwise conveniently available; or

(*b*)   provision of a piped water supply or of drainage facilities or of facilities for heating running water would not be reasonably practicable.

[*Reg 3*] (remaining in force until 1 January 1996).

Construction sites – sanitary conveniences and washing facilities

(a) Sanitary conveniences

44.10   Construction workers (who are not covered by *SI 1992 No 3004*) are entitled to be provided with one sanitary convenience per 25 on site unless there are more than 100 on site, when one per 25 for the first 100 and one per 35 above that number is the requirement. [*Construction (Health and Welfare) Regulations 1966, Reg 13*].

(b) Washing facilities

Where contractors have one or more employees on site for more than four hours, they must provide them with adequate and suitable washing facilities. On operations of six weeks or less, troughs, basins or buckets, soap, towels and hot water must be provided, if there are more than 20 persons on site. Where there are more than 100 employees, wash basins will be required if the operation will not be finished within twelve months, on the basis of one per 100 and one more for every 35 extra employees. [*Construction (Health and Welfare) Regulations 1966, Reg 12*].

Sanitary conveniences in existing offices and shops

44.11   In relation to offices, shops and railway premises, there is a requirement to provide, at places conveniently accessible to the persons employed to work in the premises, suitable and sufficient sanitary conveniences for their use. Such conveniences must be kept clean and properly maintained. Effective provision must also be made for lighting and ventilating them. [*OSRPA s 9(1)(2)*] (remaining in force until 1 January 1996). The expression 'conveniently accessible' has been considered from time to time. Thus, for example, it was held that a toilet in a flat above a shop in which women were working was 'conveniently accessible' (*A C Davis & Sons v Environmental Health Department of Leeds City Council* [*1976*] *IRLR 282*).

As with the corresponding provision of the *Factories Act 1961*, this provision exists for the benefit of direct employees, though members of an outside workforce working on the premises could obviously avail themselves of the facilities. Also by analogy with the *Factories Act 1961*, it is doubtful whether this section would give rise to an action for damages, as it would probably be construed as being public health oriented.

Duty on owner

With regard to buildings in single and plural ownership, by virtue of *OSRPA ss 42(6), 43(3)*, the duty of providing sanitary conveniences rests with the owner, that is, the lessor or licensor.

Washing facilities in existing offices and shops

44.12   There is a statutory requirement to provide, at places conveniently accessible to the persons employed to work in the premises, suitable and sufficient washing facilities, including a supply of clean running hot and cold or warm water and, in addition, soap and clean towels or other suitable means of cleaning or drying. The place where the washing facilities are provided must be effectively lighted and kept clean. Moreover, any apparatus used for washing or drying must be kept clean and properly maintained. [*OSRPA s 10(1)(2)*] (remaining in force until 1 January 1996).

Division of duties under OSRPA – existing offices and shops

44.13   With regard to buildings in single and plural ownership, the duty of providing sanitary conveniences and washing facilities rests with the owner (i.e. lessor or licensor) and not with the occupier. [*OSRPA ss 42(6), 43(3)*] – sanitary conveniences; [*ss 42(7), 43(5)*] – washing facilities.

Drinking water/clothing accommodation/facilities for changing clothes – all workplaces

44.14   Additionally, employers should, as part and parcel of their welfare duties, provide wholesome drinking water as well as clothing accommodation and facilities for changing clothes along with facilities for rest in smoke-free rooms and for eating meals. These requirements apply in new workplaces as from 1 January 1993 and in existing ones from 1 January 1996.

(a) Drinking water

An adequate supply of wholesome drinking water must be provided for all persons at work in the workplace. It must be readily accessible at suitable places and conspicuously marked, unless non-drinkable cold water supplies are clearly marked. In addition, there must be provided a sufficient number of suitable cups (or other drinking vessels), unless the water supply is in a jet. [*Workplace (Health, Safety and Welfare) Regulations 1992, Reg 22*].

Where water cannot be obtained from the mains supply, it should only be provided in refillable containers. The containers should be enclosed to prevent contamination and refilled at least daily. So far as reasonably practicable, drinking water taps should not be installed in sanitary accommodation, or in places where contamination is likely, for instance, in a workshop containing lead processes.

(b) Clothing accommodation

Suitable and sufficient accommodation must be provided for

(*a*)   any person at work's own clothing which is not worn during working hours, and

(*b*)   special clothing which is worn by any person at work but which is not taken home.

[*Workplace (Health, Safety and Welfare) Regulations 1992, Reg 23(1)*].

Accommodation is not suitable unless it

  (i)   provides suitable security for the person's own clothing;

 (ii)   includes separate accommodation for clothing worn at work and for other clothing, where necessary to avoid risks to health or damage to clothing;

(iii)   is in a suitable location.

[*Workplace (Health, Safety and Welfare) Regulations 1992, Reg 23(2)*].

Work clothing is overalls, uniforms, thermal clothing and hats worn for hygiene purposes. Workers' own clothing should be able to hang in a clean, warm, dry, well-ventilated place. If this is not possible in the workroom, then it should be put elsewhere. Accommodation should take the form of a separate hook or peg. Clothing which is dirty, damp or contaminated owing to work should be accommodated separately from the worker's own clothes.

(*c*) Facilities for changing clothing

Suitable and sufficient facilities must be provided for any person at work in the workplace to change clothing where

  (i)   the person has to wear special clothing for work, and

 (ii)   the person cannot be expected to change in another room.

Facilities are not suitable unless they include

(*a*)   separate facilities for men and women, or

(*b*)   separate use of facilities by men and women.

[*Workplace (Health, Safety and Welfare) Regulations 1992, Reg 24*].

Changing rooms (or room) should be provided for workers who change into special work clothing and where they remove more than outer clothing; also where it is necessary to prevent workers' own clothes being contaminated by a harmful substance. Changing facilities should be easily accessible from workrooms and eating places. They should contain adequate seating and clothing accommodation, and showers or baths (see 44.1 above). Privacy of user should be ensured. The facilities should be large enough to cater for the maximum number of persons at work expected to use them at any one time without overcrowding or undue delay.

(*d*) Facilities for rest and eating meals

For workers who have to stand to carry out their work, suitable seats should be provided, if their work allows them to sit from time to time. Also, suitable seats should be provided for workers during breaks. In offices (and other clean workplaces) work seats or other seats in the work area will suffice generally. In other cases *separate* rest areas should be provided when necessary for health and safety or a *separate* rest room. Moreover, where workers regularly eat meals at work, suitable and sufficient facilities must be provided for them to eat; also, where food would otherwise become contaminated by dust or water etc., e.g. cement works, clay works, foundries, potteries, laundries. Seats in work areas count as eating facilities, provided that they are in a sufficiently clean place and there is a suitable surface on which to place food. Eating facilities should include a facility for preparing or obtaining a hot drink, e.g. vending machine. Workers who work during hours or at places where hot food cannot be obtained in or near to the workplace, should be provided with the means of heating their own food. Eating facilities should be kept clean and free from contamination brought in on clothing or footwear. Ideally, adequate washing and changing facilities should be provided nearby. Canteens or restaurants qualify as rest areas, so long as purchase of food is not compulsory.

Rest and eating facilities – all workplaces

(a) Rest facilities

44.15   In all new workplaces, as from 1 January 1993 (and in existing workplaces, as from 1 January 1996) suitable and sufficient rest facilities must be provided at readily accessible places. [*Workplace (Health, Safety and Welfare) Regulations 1992, Reg 25(1)*].

A rest facility is

(i)   in the case of a new workplace, extension or conversion – a rest room (or rooms);

(ii)   in other cases, a rest room (or rooms) or rest area; including

(iii)   (in both cases):

   (*a*)   appropriate facilities for eating meals where food eaten in the workplace would otherwise be likely to become contaminated;

   (*b*)   suitable arrangements for protecting non-smokers from tobacco smoke;

   (*c*)   a facility for a pregnant or nursing mother to rest in.

Canteens or restaurants may be used as rest rooms provided that there is no obligation to buy food there (ACOP). [*Workplace (Health, Safety and Welfare) Regulations 1992, Regs 25(2)(3) and (4)*].

(b) Eating facilities

Where workers regularly eat meals at work, facilities must be provided for them to eat meals. [*Workplace (Health, Safety and Welfare) Regulations 1992, Reg 25(5)*].

Chapter 45

Women Workers

Introduction

45.1 Women are an integral part of the industrialised workforce, occupying a variety of positions, both supervisory and manual, on the shopfloor and elsewhere. Generally, they are subject to the same duties as men, more so now in the wake of recent repeals, first by the *Sex Discrimination Act 1986*, of certain restrictions on employment laid down in the *Factories Act 1961*, particularly *Secs 86-94* relating to holidays, nightwork etc.; and subsequently by the *Employment Act 1989*, of certain restrictions relating to health and safety, specified in the *Factories Act 1961* (e.g. *Sec 20* – cleaning of machinery (remaining in force until 1 January 1997)) and regulations passed under it (e.g. *Woollen and Worsted Textiles Regulations 1926*).

Moreover, as pregnant women are a particularly sensitive risk group, a recent EC directive (November 1992) proposes that employers formally assess risks of exposure to pregnant women and those who have just given birth or who are breast feeding, from certain physical, biological and chemical agents and decide what protective measures to take. When the nature of the activity can endanger their health and safety, their working hours and conditions should be adapted to alternative duties without a pay reduction or modification of employment rights. If alternative work is not possible, a worker should be entitled to 14 uninterrupted weeks' leave from work on full pay and/or a corresponding allowance. The main risks to be avoided are:

(*a*) *Physical*
shocks/vibration/movement
handling of loads
ionising/non-ionising radiations
extremes of heat and cold

(*b*) *Biological*
listeria
rubella and chicken pox virus
toxoplasma
cytomegalo virus

(*c*) *Chemical*
thiophosphoric esters
mercury
nitro/chlorite derivatives of benzene hydrocarbons
asbestos

This notwithstanding, there are still a number of regulations specifying prohibitions in respect of work done by women. This chapter deals specifically with (*a*) the general statutory requirements applicable to men and women and (*b*) specific prohibitions in the interests of health and safety, on certain work being done by women (and young persons). (For detailed statutory requirements relating to prohibitions on work by young persons, see Chapter 5 'Children and Young Persons'.)

General statutory requirements

45.2   The *Health and Safety at Work etc. Act 1974 (HSWA), s 2* lays a duty on all employers to ensure, so far as is reasonably practicable (for the meaning of this expression, see Chapter 15 'Employers' Duties'), the health, safety and welfare of all their employees. This necessarily includes women. Moreover, although the *Sex Discrimination Act (SDA) 1975* prohibits discrimination on grounds of sex, *SDA s 5(1)* provides that any action taken to comply with existing legislation (e.g. *HSWA*) will *not* amount to unlawful discrimination (*Page v Freight Hire (Tank Haulage) Ltd [1981] IRLR 13* where the claimant was an HGV driver driving vehicles carrying the chemical dimethylformamide (DMF). The company had a policy that women of child-bearing age should not be employed driving lorries carrying DMF. The claimant was dismissed from this employment and sued for unlawful dismissal. It was held that the employer's duty to ensure safety of women from certain processes or chemicals had priority over the duty not to discriminate).

All statutory requirements emphasise the need for safety consciousness, supervision and training in safe methods of work by women (and young persons) though, unlike *HSWA*, the *Factories Act 1961* does not apply to women in managerial positions *not* engaged in manual labour. [*Factories Act 1961, s 95*]. More particularly, the following groups of women workers are excluded from the protection of the *Factories Act 1961* (but are, of course, within the scope of protection of *HSWA*), i.e.:

(a)   women employed solely in cleaning the factory [*Factories Act 1961, s 176(4)*];

(b)   women in responsible management positions who are not ordinarily engaged in manual labour [*Factories Act 1961, s 95*].

Effect of Sex Discrimination Acts 1975 and 1986

45.3   Not unnaturally, perhaps, the effect of the *Sex Discrimination Acts 1975* and *1986* has been to remove some of the restrictions on women and their employment generally and health and safety specifically. In particular, the *Sex Discrimination Act 1975* allowed machine attendants, for the purposes of the *Operations at Unfenced Machinery Regulations 1938* (remaining in force until 1 January 1997), to be women. Moreover, restrictions on the employment of women by night imposed in the *Hours of Employment (Conventions) Act 1936* have been removed by the *Sex Discrimination Act 1986, s 7(1)*. The further restrictions on employment of women as regards hours of employment, holidays etc. specified in the *Factories Act 1961, ss 86-94* (and the corresponding restrictions of the *Mines and Quarries Act 1954*) have also been repealed by *Sec 7*. However, some restrictions/prohibitions on certain types of employment by women, in the interests of health and safety at work, still remain (see 45.4 below) in spite of the fact that the *Employment Act 1989* has removed the prohibition on women cleaning machinery (see 45.6 below).

Specific prohibitions on certain types of employment

45.4   The main health and safety statutory prohibitions on types of work done by women are as follows (for the corresponding health and safety prohibitions on young persons see Chapter 5 'Children and Young Persons'):

(a)   manipulation of raw oxide of lead or pasting [*Electric Accumulator Regulations 1925(SR&O 1925 No 28), Reg 1(ii)*];

(b)   (i)   any lead process (women under 18); or

(ii)   incorporating dry compound of lead with indiarubber

[*Indiarubber Regulations 1922 (SR&O 1922 No 329), Reg 1*];

(c)   lead manufacture other than in factories [*Factories Act 1961, s 128; Control of Lead at Work Regulations 1980 (SI 1980 No 1248), 1 Sch*];

(d)   painting of factory buildings or parts with lead paint [*Factories Act 1961, s 131*]. (In fact, the supply and use of lead paint has been prohibited from 28 February 1992 except in connection with historic buildings and works of art [*Environmental Protection (Controls on Injurious Substances) Regulations 1992 (SI 1992 No 31)*] (see also 45.7 below).)

Effect of Employment Act 1989 – removal of prohibitions

45.5   The *Employment Act 1989* removes the restriction on cleaning of factory machinery by women, by repealing the relevant part of *Sec 20* of the *Factories Act 1961*. In addition, it has repealed, wholly or in part, the following prohibitions affecting women workers engaged in:

(a)   annealing of glass [*Factories Act 1961, s 73*];

(b)   brine evaporation [*Factories Act 1961, s 73*];

(c)   lifting of heavy weights – jute [*Jute (Safety, Health and Welfare) Regulations 1948, Reg 4*]; and

(d)   pottery processes [*Pottery (Health and Welfare) Special Regulations, Reg 6(1)(6)*].

Prohibition on cleaning machinery

45.6   The absolute duty to fence (see further Chapter 28 'Machinery Safety') does not apply when machinery must be (a) examined, (b) cleaned or (c) lubricated, whilst in motion [*Factories Act 1961, ss 15, 16*] (remaining in force until 1 January 1997). Here there is a total prohibition on such work being done by young persons but the (former) restrictions on the cleaning of machinery by women in *Sec 20* of the *Factories Act 1961*, have been removed. [*Employment Act 1989, 7 Sch, Part II*].

Lead processes

45.7   No woman must be employed in the following processes:

(a)   work at a furnace where reduction or treatment of zinc or lead ores is carried on;

(b)   manipulation, treatment or reduction of ashes containing lead, desilverising of lead, or melting of scrap lead or zinc;

(c)   manufacture of solder or alloys containing more than 10% lead;

(d)   manufacture of any oxide, carbonate, sulphate, chromate, acetate, nitrate or silicate of lead;

(e)   mixing or pasting in connection with the manufacture or repair of electric accumulators;

(f)   cleaning of workrooms where any of the above processes are carried on

[*Factories Act 1961, s 74*]; or

(g) painting of factory buildings or parts with lead paint [*Factories Act 1961, s 131*];

(h) manufacture of lead colour [*Lead Paint Manufacture Regulations 1907 (SR&O 1907 No 17), Reg 3*] (see 45.4 above for the new statutory provisions relating to lead paint);

(j) in a lead process (i.e. manipulation, movement or treatment of lead material) [*Factories (Lead Smelting, etc.) Regulations 1911 (SR&O 1911 No 752), Reg 10*];

(k) in any room where manipulation of raw oxide of lead or pasting is carried on [*Electric Accumulator Regulations 1925 (SR&O 1925 No 28), Reg 1*].

Chapter 46

Work at Heights

Introduction

46.1   Two-fifths of all reported major injuries are caused by falls from a height; and half the fatal injuries to workers in construction are caused by falls from a height. Indeed, falls from heights are the most common cause of fatality to employees.

Work at heights is a feature of many occupations – construction and maintenance workers, installers of plant and equipment, people who service passenger lifts, heating and air conditioning systems, window cleaners etc. The risk of a fall, with often fatal results, is a common hazard in these activities. There are two salient causes of this type of accident. First, there is the means of access to the working position (see Chapter 2 'Access'). This may be a portable ladder, roof ladder or powered working platform. In many cases, the means of access has proved to be totally inadequate or unsuitable for the job being undertaken, resulting in falls through fragile roofs, from the edge of a roof or from an item of plant located above floor level. New workplaces (and existing factories and workplaces as from 1 January 1996 – temporary as well as permanent) must have suitable and effective safeguards for preventing persons being injured by falling a distance likely to cause personal injury (see 46.2 below). [*Workplace (Health, Safety and Welfare) Regulations 1992 (SI 1992 No 3004), Reg 13*]. Building operations and works of engineering construction are *not* covered by these regulations – temporary and mobile construction sites will be addressed by the draft directive on temporary and mobile construction sites. The current law is summarised in 46.6–46.14 below.

The second most common cause of accident/fatality is the system of work adopted once the working position is reached. If the system has been correctly planned, operators briefed in the system and the appropriate precautions to be taken prior to commencement of work, should be able to work safely at a height. Such system will include compulsory provision, maintenance, replacement and wearing of safety helmets to protect those working at heights and those working or visiting below, by dint of the *Construction (Head Protection) Regulations 1989 (SI 1989 No 2209)*, and bump caps for those working in confined spaces. However, work at heights is frequently undertaken in a situation of emergency or crisis. For instance, a fault may have developed on an item of plant which needs immediate attention for production to continue or the factory roof may be leaking, resulting in damage to stored products below. In both cases, urgent action is required and there is insufficient time to consider any precautions necessary to ensure safe working at height; therefore there should be emergency procedures planned and in force to deal with this sort of contingency.

Another thorny aspect of work at heights is window cleaning. Windows in factories, workplaces and high-rise commercial and office blocks must be regularly and periodically cleaned (see 46.32 below) [*Workplace (Health, Safety and Welfare) Regulations 1992, Reg 16*], as well as windows in *existing* factories [*Factories Act 1961, s 5(4)*], and offices/shops [*OSRPA s 8(3)*]. Frequency of cleaning depends on type of establishment, whether office, shop or factory etc. (see 46.32 below) – but in any case

789

the method selected should ensure protection for window cleaners (see 46.31, 46.33 below). The inescapable fact is that window cleaning, particularly in high-rise commercial properties with vast oceans of glass has posed serious safety problems for contract window cleaning companies and self-employed window cleaners, requiring, on the one hand, contract cleaning companies to use best available window cleaning equipment and methods, and, on the other, building owners/occupiers to make safety anchorage points, in so far as they are permitted to do so, conveniently accessible on the building (see further BS 8213 for excellent guidance). Crucially, in this connection, buildings, windows and skylights on new buildings may need to be fitted with suitable devices (see 46.15–46.17 below) to allow windows and skylights to be securely cleaned to satisfy the safety requirements. [*Workplace (Health, Safety and Welfare) Regulations 1992, Reg 16(1)*]. Other buildings must comply with *Reg 16(1)* by 1 January 1996. Falls from heights accounting for by far the greater majority of major injuries, the need to comply with fall-preventive statutory requirements and window cleaning regulations at all times is paramount.

Current statutory requirements

46.2   Current statutory requirements relating to falls from heights are contained in the *Workplace (Health, Safety and Welfare) Regulations 1992, Reg 13* and, as far as *existing* factories are concerned (until 1 January 1996) in the *Factories Act 1961, s 29(2)*; there are also specific requirements relating to prevention of falls on construction sites, in the form of the *Construction (Working Places) Regulations 1966, Regs 35, 36* which remain intact and unaffected by the *Workplace (Health, Safety and Welfare) Regulations 1992*. Requirements relating to windows and window cleaning are contained (for the first time) in the *Workplace (Health, Safety and Welfare) Regulations 1992, Regs 14–16*.

Falls from a height – all new workplaces

46.3   So far as reasonably practicable (for meaning, see Chapter 15 'Employers' Duties'), suitable and effective measures must be taken (other than by provision of personal protective equipment, training, information, supervision etc.) to prevent

(*a*)   any person falling a distance likely to cause personal injury (e.g. deep hole);

(*b*)   any person being struck by a falling object likely to cause personal injury.

Any area from which this might happen must be clearly indicated – particularly in the case of pits or tanks. (As to the possible effect of such notices in civil cases see 32.14 OCCUPIERS' LIABILITY.) [*Workplace (Health, Safety and Welfare) Regulations 1992, Reg 13*].

Suitable and effective measures are

(i)   fencing,

(ii)   covering,

(iii)   fixed ladders.

(i) *Fencing*

This should primarily prevent people falling from edges and objects falling onto people, and where it has to be removed temporarily (as where goods/materials are admitted), temporary measures should be put in train (e.g. provision of handholds). Except in the case of roof edges or points to which there is no general legitimate access, secure fencing should be provided where a person might fall (*a*)   2 metres or more, or

(*b*)   less than 2 metres, where the risk of injury is otherwise greater (e.g. internal traffic route below).

Fencing should be sufficiently high to prevent falls, both of people and objects, over or through it. Minimally, it should consist of two guard-rails at suitable heights. The top of the fencing should generally be at least 1,100 mm above the surface from which a person might fall. It should be of adequate strength and stability to restrain any person or object liable to fall against it. (As for civil liability for injury following breach, see particularly the case of *Bailey v Ayr Engineering* at 7.43 CONSTRUCTION AND BUILDING OPERATIONS, where comparable requirements apply to construction sites).

(ii) *Covers*

Pits, tanks, vats, sumps, kiers etc. can be securely covered (instead of fenced). Covers must be strong and able to support loads imposed on them as well as passing traffic; nor should they be easily detachable and removable. They should be kept securely *in situ* except for purposes of inspection or access. Uncovered tanks, pits or structures must be fenced if there is a traffic route over them.

(iii) *Fixed ladders*

Assuming a staircase is impractical, fixed ladders – sloping ones are safer than vertical ones – (which should be provided in pits etc.) should be

(*a*)   of sound construction,

(*b*)   properly maintained,

(*c*)   securely fixed.

Rungs should be horizontal and provide adequate foothold without reliance on nails or screws. In the absence of an adequate handhold, stiles should extend to at least 1,100 mm above any landing (or the highest rung) to step or stand on. Fixed ladders with a vertical distance of more than 6 m should normally have a landing at every 6 m point. Where possible, each run should be out of line with the previous run to reduce falling distance. And where a ladder passes through a floor, the opening should be as small as possible, fenced (if possible) and a gate provided to prevent falls.

(For ladders on construction sites, see 7.45 CONSTRUCTION AND BUILDING OPERATIONS.)

Pits, tanks, vats, kiers etc. – new workplaces

46.4   Serious accidents have occurred as a result of workers, often maintenance workers, falling into or overreaching or overbalancing (and falling) into pits etc. containing dangerous corrosive or scalding substances. Thus, so far as is reasonably practicable, (for meaning, see Chapter 15 'Employers' Duties') pits, tanks or similar vessels attendant with a risk of a person falling into a dangerous substance, must be securely (*a*) fenced or (*b*) covered (for meaning of 'securely fenced' in connection with analogous requirements of the *Factories Act 1961, ss 12–14*, see 28.24 MACHINERY SAFETY). And as a means of access/egress into pits, tanks etc. fixed ladders (or the equivalent) should be provided. [*Workplace (Health, Safety and Welfare) Regulations 1992, Reg 13(5)*].

Existing factories – Factories Act 1961, s 29 – requirement until 1 January 1996

46.5   All means of access to every place at which any person (e.g. indirect workers) has at any time to work, and every such place, must, so far as is reasonably practicable, be kept safe. [*Factories Act 1961, s 29(1)*]. (For the strict nature of this duty, see 2.7 ACCESS.)

Moreover, if the place at which any person has to work is a place from which he will be liable to fall a distance of more than 2 metres, the place must be provided, so far as is reasonably practicable, with fencing (or other means e.g. covering) to ensure an employee's safety, unless there are secure footholds and handholds. [*Factories Act 1961, s 29(2)*]. This provision applies to every workplace in a factory, so that it will cover not only all the permanent parts of the premises but also temporary scaffolding or staging used as a place of work or to reach a place of work.

Construction sites – sloping roofs/fragile materials/scaffolds etc.

46.6   A fair proportion of serious accidents occur as a result of workers falling off sloping roofs or through roofs with fragile materials – a situation addressed by *Regs 35* and *36* of the *Construction (Working Places) Regulations 1966 (SI 1966 No 94)* (not affected and unrevoked by the *Workplace (Health, Safety and Welfare) Regulations 1992*).

Sloping roofs

46.7   A sloping roof is a roof (or part of a roof) having a pitch of more than 10 degrees, including one which is covered (wholly or partly), and is either

(*a*)   in the course of construction, maintenance, repair or demolition; or

(*b*)   used as a means of access to or egress from a roof (or part of a roof) where operations are being carried on.

[*Reg 35(1)*].

Where the sloping roof is a means of access or egress, sufficient and suitable crawling ladders, or crawling boards, must be provided on the sloping roof, unless the battens or similar members of the roof structure provide adequate handhold and foothold. [*Reg 35(3)(6)*].

Certain work on certain roofs must be carried out only by workmen who are suitable for such work – that is, where a sloping roof has a pitch:

(*a*)   of more than 30 degrees; or

(*b*)   of 30 degrees or less and a surface on or from which a person is liable to slip or to fall from the edge of the roof, owing to the nature or condition of the surface, or to the weather.

[*Reg 35(2)*].

Where any work is done on or from any sloping roof, sufficient and suitable crawling ladders or crawling boards must be provided on the sloping roof. Furthermore, except where the work is not extensive or the fall from the eaves of the roof is not more than 2 metres, either:

(*a*)   the work must be done from a securely supported working platform not less than 430 mm wide; or (*b*)   a barrier must be provided at the lower edge of the sloping roof (other than the upper surface of a tank or similar structure of metal construction) which is of such design and construction as to prevent any person falling from the edge.

[*Reg 35(4)(7)*].

Crawling ladders and boards

46.8   Crawling boards are boards with battens across (*Jenner v Allen West & Co Ltd* [*1959*] *2 AER 115*). These must be:

(*a*)   of good construction, suitable and sound material, adequate strength, free from patent defect and properly maintained;

(*b*)   properly supported; and

(*c*)   (i)   securely fixed or anchored to the sloping surface or over the roof ridge; or

(ii)   otherwise securely fixed so as to prevent slipping.

[*Reg 35(5)*].

Work on fragile materials

46.9   No person must pass across or work on or from material which would be liable to fracture if his weight were applied to it *and* from which (if it so fractured) he might fall more than 2 metres, unless ladders, crawling ladders or crawling boards and duck boards are both provided and used. The ladders and boards must be securely supported and, if necessary, secured so as to prevent slipping. They must be used in such a way that the weight of the person passing or working is wholly or mainly supported by the ladders or boards *unless* his weight is supported by other equally safe and sufficient means. [*Reg 36(1)*]. Moreover,

(*a*)   suitable guard-rails,

(*b*)   suitable coverings, and

(*c*)   any other suitable means

must be provided to prevent, so far as is reasonably practicable, any person passing over or working on the material, from falling through it. [*Reg 36(2)*].

Warning notices

Where any person passes across or near, or works on or near fragile materials, warning notices (Factory Form 901) must be affixed at approaches to the place where the material is situated, except where the material consists wholly of glass.[*Reg 36(3)*]. (As to how far such notices might absolve occupiers from liability in the event of injury, see Chapter 32 'Occupiers' Liability'.)

Scaffolds, working platforms, gangways etc.

46.10   Where work is done from scaffolds, working platforms, gangways and runs, boatswain's chairs, or on sloping roofs or fragile material, there are specific regulations for the provision of safety precautions (e.g. *Regs 35* and *36* considered in 46.6-46.9 above). However, where it is impracticable to comply with the specific requirements owing, for example, to the special nature of the work, the particular requirements must be complied with, so far as practicable and, in addition, suitable safety nets or sheets must be provided. [*Reg 38(1)*]. Where it is impracticable or not reasonably practicable to provide all the necessary safety nets or sheets, or where the work will last such a short time as to make provision of the necessary safety nets unreasonable, safety nets and safety sheets must be provided (in compliance with *Reg 38(1)*) so far as reasonably practicable, and, in addition, safety belts or other suitable and sufficient equipment. [*Reg 38(3)*]. Since, however, it is now incumbent on employers to provide a safe system of work and train employees in health and safety procedures, under the *Management of Health and Safety at Work Regulations 1992*, this situation is probably obsolescent.

Where all the persons working or using the access and egress points are able to do so using safety belts, it is not necessary to provide safety nets or sheets. Such safety belts must be provided and used, and attached continuously to a suitable and secure fixed anchorage. [*Reg 38(2)*]. Workmen who do such work without using safety belts provided are in danger of losing all their compensaton for injury (*McWilliams v Sir William Arrol Ltd [1962] 1 AER 623*) (see further Chapter 15 'Employers' Duties').

Work on temporary structures

46.11   To prevent danger to any person employed through the collapse of any part of a building or other structure during any temporary state of weakness or instability prior to completion, all practicable precautions must be taken by way of temporary guys, stays, supports and fixings or in any other way. [*Construction (General Provisions) Regulations 1961 (SI 1961 No 1580), Reg 50(1)*].

Guard-rails etc., where falling is a risk

46.12   Where a person is liable to fall more than 2 metres from where he is working, every working platform or place must be provided with a suitable, adequately strong, guard-rail or rails of a height between 910 mm and 1.15 metres above the platform. Toe-boards or other barriers of a sufficient height, but not less than 150 mm, must be provided as well. The guard-rails, toe-boards and other barriers must be placed so as to prevent, as far as possible, the fall of persons, materials and articles. [*Reg 28(1)*].

Even where the above provision does not apply (see immediately below):

(*a*)   the platform must be at least 800 mm;

(*b*)   there must be adequate handhold;

(*c*)   the platform must not be used for the deposit of materials or articles otherwise than in boxes or receptacles, to prevent the contents falling.

[*Reg 28(6)(c)*].

The provisions in *Reg 28(1)* do not apply, *inter alia*, to:

(*a*)   the platform of a ladder scaffold, if a secure handhold is provided along its full length;

(*b*)   the platform of a trestle scaffold, when the platform is supported on folding trestles (indeed, a trestle scaffold must *not* be used if the scaffold is so situated that a person is liable to fall more than 4.50 metres) [*Reg 21(2)*];

(*c*)   a platform used only for erecting any framework or prefabricated unit for the purpose of jointing, bolting up, riveting or welding work, for such a short period as to make the provision of guard-rails, toe-boards or barriers unreasonable.

[*Reg 28(6)*].

Guard-rails for stairs, gangways etc.

46.13 Handrails or other efficient means to prevent the fall of persons must be provided throughout the length of stairs, and if necessary to prevent danger, continued beyond the end of the stairs. [*Reg 29(1)*]. These preventive means may be interrupted for the passage of persons and materials. (The provisions relating to the safety of gangways and stairs are dealt with in detail in Chapter 18 'Factories and Workplaces'.)

Lifting appliances on construction sites – examinations

46.14 The *Construction (Lifting Operations) Regulations 1961 (SI 1961 No 1581)* provide that when a person is examining, repairing or lubricating a lifting appliance and would be liable to fall more than 2 metres whilst doing so, he must be provided so far as is reasonably practicable with safe means of access to and egress from the area of work. This may necessitate the provision of suitable handholds and footholds. [*Reg 17*]. (See further Chapter 2 'Access'.)

Practical guidelines

46.15 The underlying principle is that if it is not possible to work safely from the ground or other part of a building or structure, suitable access equipment or other safeguards must be provided and attention paid to the following general aspects.

(*a*) Who is in control and the amount of co-ordination necessary, i.e. have the responsibilities of the occupier, employer and contractor been clearly defined?

(*b*) What level of supervision and training is required with regard to the type of hazard and level of risk? (including selection of the appropriate method, and the use of approved equipment).

(*c*) What other considerations are necessary, e.g. is there any danger to works employees from the contractors' operations, or vice-versa?

Many of these matters may seem obvious, but lives have been lost because the contractor or maintenance worker did not appreciate the fragile nature of a roof or the fact that it had been weakened owing to the nature of the process. The factory occupier should also bear in mind that many building contractors have a high labour turnover, i.e. many of these employees are taken on locally for the duration of the contract. Thus, they are virtually untried until work has been in progress for some time; accordingly, if the necessary action is not taken at the start of the contract the chances are that some employees will not complete the contract.

Most large employers will include all these aspects as an integral part of their accident prevention programmes and in their contract documents, etc. The smaller employer may simply rely on the use of a check list to remind himself of the key points before a contractor starts work in his premises. For example:

(*a*) a pre-operational safety survey on the part of the contractor carried out by a responsible person before the work starts;

(*b*) close liaison and supervision throughout the contract and the occupier must not overlook the fact that the supervision on a small building job on a roof may not be up to the standard required to appreciate the industrial hazards in the area of the roof or at the work place below;

(*c*) early lighting arrangements;

(*d*)   display of warning notices, especially in regard to fragile roofs (see 46.9 above);

(*e*)   precautions with regard to fire services and issuance of fire permits, etc.;

(*f*)   potential risks associated with adverse weather conditions, such as a sudden downpour, dense fog, snow laying on a roof or high winds; in particular, the responsibility for calling operators off a roof or high level position given adverse weather conditions;

(*g*)   the provision of safety harnesses and belts, including the necessary anchorage points for them, or safety nets in certain situations (see below, 'Windows and window cleaning');

(*h*)   the personal protection needs of individuals, such as hard hats, gloves, eye and face protection in certain cases, non-slip safety shoes or boots. (See further 7.19-7.27 CONSTRUCTION AND BUILDING OPERATIONS and Chapter 36 'Personal Protective Equipment'.)

In addition the occupier/employer should ensure that his maintenance supervisor or clerk of works, etc. has access to the information contained in the health and safety at work booklets. He may also provide simple check lists to cover his own operations.

Windows and window cleaning – all workplaces

46.16   Window cleaning hazards occur principally in high-rise properties such as office blocks and residential tower blocks. These contain vast areas of glass which must be maintained in a clean state on both inner and outer surfaces. Cleaning the interior surfaces generally presents no difficulties, though accidents have arisen from the unsafe practice of window cleaners reaching up to clean windows from step ladders which have not been securely placed on highly-polished office floors and, in consequence, falling through the glass windows and injuring themselves. It is the cleaning of outer surfaces that can present serious hazards if precautions are not taken, and this part of the chapter is concerned with the duty of factory occupiers in relation to windows on their premises (see 46.19 below) and the similar duty applying to occupiers of offices, shops and railway premises (see 46.20 below). In addition, the liability of employers at common law in relation to window cleaning personnel is mentioned in 46.28 below. Methods of protection for window cleaners and methods of cleaning are also covered (see 46.30-46.36 below).

Statutory requirements relevant to windows in new workplaces – the Workplace (Health, Safety and Welfare) Regulations 1992 (SI 1992 No 3004)

(i) *Composition of windows*

46.17   Every window (and every transparent/translucent surface in a door or gate) must be

(*a*)   (i)   of safety material (e.g. polycarbonates, glass blocks, glass which breaks safely (laminated glass) or ordinary annealed glass meeting certain minimal criteria),

(ii)   protected against breakage of transparent/translucent material (e.g. by a screen or barrier);

(*b*)   appropriately (and conspicuously) marked so as to make it apparent (e.g. with coloured lines/patterns).

[*Workplace (Health, Safety and Welfare) Regulations 1992, Reg 14*].

(ii) *Position and use of windows*

No window, skylight or ventilator, capable of being opened, must be likely to be

(i)   opened,

(ii) closed,

(iii) adjusted, or

(iv) in a position when open,

so as to expose the operator to risk of injury. [*Workplace (Health, Safety and Welfare) Regulations 1992, Reg 15*].

In other words, it must be possible to reach openable windows safely; and window poles or a stable platform should be kept ready nearby. Window controls should be so positioned that people are not likely to fall out of or through the window. And where there is a danger of falling from a height, devices should prevent the window opening too far. In order to prevent people colliding with them, the bottom edge of opening windows should generally be 800 mm above floor level (unless there is a barrier to stop or cushion falls). Staircase windows should have controls accessible from a safe foothold, and window controls beyond normal reach should be gear-operated or accessible by pole (see BS 8213 and GS 25 1983). Manually operated window controls should not be higher than 2 metres above floor level.

(iii) *Cleaning windows*

All windows and skylights in workplaces must be designed and constructed to allow safe cleaning. [*Workplace (Health, Safety and Welfare) Regulations 1992, Reg 16*]. If they cannot be cleaned from the ground (or similar surface), the building should be fitted with suitable safety devices to be able to comply with the general safety requirement (see above). [*Workplace (Health, Safety and Welfare) Regulations 1992, Reg 16*].

Civil liability in connection with fall-preventive regulations

46.18   Because regulations give rise to civil liability when breached, even if silent (which these are), if breach leads to injury/damage, an action for breach of statutory duty would lie (see further 1.18, 1.43 and 1.44 INTRODUCTION).

Clean windows in existing factories – requirements until 1 January 1996

46.19   All glazed windows and skylights used for lighting workrooms must, so far as practicable, be kept clean on both inner and outer surfaces and obstruction-free. [*Factories Act 1961, s 5(4)*]. Moreover, glazing should be adequate by design and in thickness to afford protection in the event of accidental impact (BS 6292: 1982). Also, windows and skylights in factories may be whitewashed or shaded in order to cut down glare and heat. [*Factories Act 1961, s 5(4)*]. (For current lighting requirements, see 27.2 LIGHTING.)

Clean windows in existing offices/shops and whitewashing and shading – requirement until 1 January 1996

46.20   All glazed windows and skylights which light offices, shops and railway premises where persons work (or pass through in order to work) must, so far as is reasonably practicable, be kept clean on both inner and outer surfaces and free from obstruction. [*OSRPA s 8(3)*]. Unlike the requirement applying to factories (see 46.19 above), this provision requires the duty to be carried out 'so far as reasonably practicable' (for the difference between 'reasonably practicable' and 'practicable' see Chapter 15 'Employers' Duties').

As with factories (see 46.19 above), windows and/or skylights in offices, shops etc. may be whitewashed or shaded in order to mitigate heat or glare. [*OSRPA s 8(3)*].

Window cleaners as employees or self-employed contractors

46.21   Where window cleaners are employees of a contract window cleaning company, the company as employer owes a duty to its employees, under *HSWA s 2(1)* and *(2)*, to provide a safe method of work, and instruction and training in job safety, e.g. provision of information as to how to tackle the job and the use of safety harnesses etc. In addition, as from 1 January 1993, in all *new* workplaces, buildings, windows and skylights should be fitted with suitable devices to allow the window or skylight to be cleaned safely, to comply with *Reg 16* of the *Workplace (Health, Safety and Welfare) Regulations 1992* (see 46.17 above).

Alternatively, window cleaners may be self-employed. In such cases they themselves commit an offence if they fail to provide themselves with adequate protection, e.g. safety harnesses, because of the requirement of *HSWA s 3(2)* (see 1.27 INTRODUCTION).

Who provides protection to window cleaners on high-rise properties?

46.22   Where multi-storey properties are concerned, the duty of protection may fall upon one of three parties (or, at least, there may be division of responsibility between them):

(*a*)   the contract window cleaning firm or the self-employed window cleaner;

(*b*)   the building owner;

(*c*)   the building occupier or business operator (i.e. the building occupier who is not the owner of the building).

Contract window cleaning firms and self-employed window cleaners

46.23   Both the contract window cleaning firm and the self-employed window cleaner have a statutory duty to provide protection (under *HSWA ss 2(1)(2), 3(2)*) and the employer/occupier, under *Regs 15* and *16* of the *Workplace (Health, Safety and Welfare) Regulations 1992* (see 46.17 above). This applies to contract cleaning companies (not just of windows) in respect of equipment left on the occupier's premises and used by the occupier's employees, even though the contract cleaning company is not actually working (*R v Mara [1987] 1 WLR 87* where one of the occupier's employees was electrocuted when using polisher/scrubber, which had a defective cable, to clean loading bay on a Saturday afternoon, when cleaning company did not operate its undertaking. It was held that the director of the cleaning company was in breach of *HSWA s 3(1)*). In addition, if an accident arose from the work, the window cleaning company could, as employer, be liable at common law, if it failed to take reasonable care and exercise control. There is no action for damages for breach of statutory duty under *HSWA* (see Chapter 15 'Employers' Duties'). In this connection, any employer, when prosecuted under *HSWA* or sued at common law would have to show that he had clearly instructed employees not to clean windows where no proper safety precautions had been taken, in order to avoid liability. Also, window cleaning companies would have to satisfy themselves, before instructing employees to clean windows, as to what safety precautions (if any) were provided, and that, if necessary, employees were told to test for defective sashes (*General Cleaning Contractors Ltd v Christmas [1952] 2 AER 1110*).

Division of responsibility between window cleaning firm or self-employed window cleaner and building owner or occupier (i.e. employer)

46.24   Although a window cleaner, whether an employee or self-employed, would be expected to have his own safety harness (as a tool of his trade), it would be up to the contractor to provide fixing points for harness attachment. The responsibility for provision of harness anchorage points (e.g. safe rings, i.e. eyebolts) will be with either the building owner or building occupier (business operator) whose windows are being cleaned. Two situations are possible here:

(*a*)   the building occupier is the owner of the building; or

(*b*)   the building occupier (as is usual) is not the owner of the building.

Where the building occupier is the building owner

46.25   Here, the window cleaning contract is placed by the building occupier/owner and the latter, having control of the building, is therefore responsible under *HSWA s 3(1)*, *Regs 15* and *16* of the *Workplace (Health, Safety and Welfare) Regulations 1992*, and at common law (and under the contract) to protect window cleaning personnel on his premises. Courts may also be prepared to imply terms into such contracts that such premises be reasonably safe to work on.

This position (that is, where the building owner and the building occupier are the same person) is not, however, the norm. On the contrary, the position normally obtaining is that the building owner and business operator are separate persons or companies.

Where the building occupier (that is, the employer) is not the building owner

46.26   Given that the employee or self-employed window cleaner must provide his own safety harness (see 46.24 above), the responsibility of providing a safe ring for harness attachment lies with the building owner or occupier. More precisely, where the building owner employs a contract window cleaning firm, then it is up to the building owner (*inter alia*, as an implied contractual term) to make safety anchorage provision. He cannot escape from this contractual obligation owing to the strictures of the *Unfair Contract Terms Act 1977* (see Chapter 32 'Occupiers' Liability'). He would also be required to do so by virtue of *HSWA s 3(1)* – the duty towards persons working on premises who are not one's employees (see Chapter 15 'Employers' Duties').

But this is the exception, not the norm. Generally, window cleaning contracts are placed by building occupiers (business operators), and so in the great majority of cases it is the *building occupier* who is responsible under *HSWA s 3(1)* and under the *Workplace (Health, Safety and Welfare) Regulations 1992*, under the express or implied terms of a contract, and/or at common law (should an accident occur) for ensuring the safety of window cleaning personnel. Thus, the building occupier would have to provide a safety ring for harness attachment. A problem could arise here if the building owner refused permission for such attachment – resort to legal action would be, it is thought, the only ultimate solution. And occupiers should be under no illusion that failure to provide safety anchorage points can (and will, in all probability) result in the imposition of heavy fines! (By way of consolation, however, the cost of making available certain types of protection to window cleaners may often be less than the penalty incurred for failing to provide it.)

Applicability of the Construction Regulations

46.27   Although 'building operation' is a wide expression, covering 'external cleaning of a structure' (see Chapter 7 'Construction and Building Operations'), the term 'external cleaning of a structure' does *not* extend to window cleaning (*Lavender v Diamints [1949] 1 AER 532*). It does, however, apply to cleaning a glass roof which forms a large part of the roof area. This is regarded as a 'building operation' and so the *Construction Regulations* (e.g. *Working Places Regulations*) can be enforced (*Bowie v Great International Plate Glass Insurance Cleaning Co Ltd [1981] CLY 1207*).

Common law liability to window cleaners

46.28   At common law (and under *HSWA s 2(2)*), an employer must provide and maintain a safe system of work. This extends to provision of safe appliances, tools etc. and giving information/training in how to carry out tasks safely (see Chapter 15 'Employers' Duties'). Nevertheless, there is a division of responsibility between employer and occupier of premises where a window cleaner is working. The former, the employer, must see that the employee is provided with a safe method of work; he is not liable for defects in the premises (e.g. window sills) of the occupier causing injury to employees (*General Cleaning Contractors Ltd v Christmas [1952] 2 AER 1110* where an experienced employee window cleaner was injured whilst cleaning windows at a club. There were no fittings on the building to which safety belts could have been attached. A defective sash dropped onto the employee's hand, causing him to lose his handhold and fall. It was held that the employer was liable; he should have provided wedges to prevent sashes from falling and also instructed employees to test for dangerous sashes). But in *Wilson v Tyneside Window Cleaning Co Ltd [1958] 2 AER 265* an experienced window cleaner was cleaning windows at a brewery, something which he had done quarterly for ten years. The employee was cleaning a window 12 feet from the ground which overlooked a street with a steep slope. He grasped a handle with his right hand, underneath the upper sash, and placed the fingers of his left hand over the putty on the bottom bar of the top sash in order to pull the sash down. He pulled the handle and it came away. He lost his balance and fell off the ladder, sustaining serious injuries. Woodwork surrounding the window was rotten, a fact with which the employee was familiar. It was held that the employer was not liable. He had taken reasonable care because the danger was apparent to the employee who was very experienced. Moreover, the employer had instructed the employee not to clean windows which it was not safe to clean.

Much of the extant common law liability will, in all probability, be replaced in due course by case law arising in connection with breach of duty under the *Workplace (Health, Safety and Welfare) Regulations 1992*; such duties are strict.

Accidents to window cleaners – typical causes

46.29   Information obtained from accident reports and similar sources by the Health and Safety Executive (HSE) indicates that:

(*a*) the most common fatal accident is that of a cleaner falling from an external window sill, ledge, or similar part of a building, due to loss of balance as the result of a slip, or the breakage of part of a sill, or the failure of a pull handle or part of a building being used as a handhold;

(*b*) other fatalities have been due to falls through fragile roofing where cleaners have relied upon the roof for support when cleaning or glazing windows, or gaining access for such work, and falls from suspended scaffolds or boatswain's chairs due to failure of the equipment;

(*c*) falls from ladders, which account for a substantial proportion of injuries, are occasionally fatal; they include falls due to the unexpected movement of a ladder such as the top sliding sideways or the foot slipping outwards, failure of part of the ladder, and falls when stepping on or off it.

Methods of protection for window cleaners

46.30 (*a*) If the building was designed with totally self-pivoting windows, this is probably the ideal situation in terms of safeguarding the window cleaner. However, a wide variety of window designs are used in buildings – sliding sashes, louvred sashes, hinged casements and fixed lights. All require a slightly different technique for cleaning.

(*b*) Ordinary ladders are not suitable (and should not be used) for multi-storey properties of more than two storeys.

(*c*) Hydraulic platforms are effective but work can only safely proceed at a relatively slow rate; moreover, their maximum reach is sometimes limited, and they cause nuisance to passers-by.

(*d*) Gondola cages are used on high-rise buildings with good results, but are of little use for low and medium-rise blocks. They can also be dangerous to window cleaning personnel, as they are inclined to sway about in high winds. Moreover, this method of window cleaning is expensive.

Probably the most practical and economical method of complying with legal requirements for the safety of window cleaning personnel is provision of safe ring/harness combinations. These have proved satisfactory for most kinds of multi-storey properties. These bolts can be installed rapidly, without damaging the building structurally, and without impairing its aesthetic appearance. Such bolts must, however, comply with British Standard BS 970: 1980 Part 1 (high tensile carbon steel) or Part 4 (premium stainless steel); also the whole anchorage system must comply with BS 5845: 1980.

Safety rings should be installed by a specialist company operating in the field. In this way a window cleaner can clip his harness onto the ring and step onto the window ledge and clean the window safely. After proper installation, anchorage points should be professionally examined from time to time to ensure that they remain firm and safe.

Another (relatively inexpensive) device for use in cleaning outer surfaces on high-rise office blocks and industrial multi-storey properties is the new mobile safety anchor. The cost is often shared between the contract window cleaning company (or self-employed window cleaner) and the building owner or occupier.

Suspended scaffolds are commonly used for window cleaning in high-rise buildings. Guidance on the design, construction and use of suspended scaffolds is given in:

(*a*) HSE guidance Plant and Machinery Series 30/198 'Suspended access equipment';

(b)   BS 6037: 1981 'Code of Practice for permanently installed suspended access equipment'; and

(c)   BS 5974: 1982 'Code of practice for temporarily installed suspended scaffolds and access equipment'.

Whether a suspended scaffold is used, either permanently or temporarily installed, it is essential to ensure that:

(a)   safe means of access to and egress from the cradle are provided;

(b)   properly planned inspection and maintenance procedures for each installation are carried out;

(c)   there are instructions that work shall be carried out only from the cradle; and

(d)   operatives are properly trained in the use of the cradle.

Where power-driven equipment is used, operatives should be familiar with:

(a)   relevant instructions from the manufacturer or supplier;

(b)   any limitations on use, for example, due to wind conditions or length of suspension rope;

(c)   the correct operation of the controls, particularly those affecting the raising or lowering of the cradle;

(d)   the safety devices fitted to the equipment; and

(e)   the procedure if the equipment does not work properly.

Precautions against the failure of a cradle having a single suspension rope at each end are described in BS 6037 (Clause 14.3), for example, the provision at each suspension point of a second rope (safety rope) and an automatic device to support the platform. In some cases, protection against suspension rope failure at the cradle end can be obtained by fitting a manually operated clamping device.

Travelling ladders are permanently installed in some buildings. In other cases a ladder can be suspended from a specially designed frame on the roof. In such cases, the cleaner should wear a safety harness or belt, attached to an automatic fall arrest device on the side of the ladder, and have a safe place at which he can step on or off the ladder.

Boatswain's chairs, frequently used in window cleaning operations, should:

(a)   conform to BS 2830:1973 'Suspended safety chairs and cradles for use in the construction industry';

(b)   not be used by a person, unless he is either:

   (i)   experienced in its use and has an adequate knowledge of the precautions which should be taken; or

   (ii)   is being trained and is under the immediate supervision of a person who has such experience and knowledge;

(c)   where an outrigger and counterweights are used, the counterweights must be sufficient to hold the outrigger in place and allow for an adequate factor of safety (which is calculated from a specific formula).

[*Construction (Working Places) Regulations 1966, Reg 20(1)*].

Cleaning methods

46.31   Window glass can normally be cleaned satisfactorily using plain water, liberally applied, followed by leather off and polishing with a scrim. The use of squeegees is on the increase and, although they cannot safely be used by a person standing on a window sill, they can be safely operated from the ground. Very dirty glazing in factories, foundries or railway premises may need treatment with ammonia or strong soda solution; and hydrofluoric acid in diluted solution may be necessary when cleaning skylights or roof glazing which has remained uncleaned for a long time. Here the working area should be adequately sheeted to protect passers-by, and, in the case of roof glazing, the interior of the building should be protected against penetrating drops. Stringent personal precautions are necessary when handling acids (e.g. eye shields, rubber gloves, boots (see further Chapter 36 'Personal Protective Equipment'), which should only be used as a last resort) and such work should only be carried out by specialist firms. Hydrofluoric acid should never be used on vertical glazing.

Frequency of cleaning

46.32   The recommended frequencies of external and internal cleaning, as dictated by current good practice, are as follows:

Shops	weekly
Banks	twice a month
Offices/hotels	monthly
Hospitals	monthly
Factories – light industry	monthly
Heavy industry	every two months
Schools	every two months

Access for cleaning

46.33   There are three ways in which windows can be cleaned, affecting access:

(*a*)   external cleaning (with access exclusively from the outside);

(*b*)   internal cleaning;

(*c*)   a mixed system, whereby windows accessible from the inside are cleaned internally, and the rest are cleaned externally, access being through the opening lights of the facade.

Moreover, in factories and other industrial concerns windows are, not infrequently, obstructed by machines, this reflecting in plant lay-out at initial design. Also safety officers and safety representatives will be concerned with this matter when carrying out safety audits (see Chapter 25 'Joint Consultation – Safety Representatives and Safety Committees').

(A) Cleaning from the outside

46.34   Assuming windows cannot be cleaned from inside the workplace or building, as a matter of design, there should be safe external access in the form of permanent walkways, with guard-rails or other protective devices to prevent cleaners (and other users) from falling down. Such walkways should be at least 400 mm wide and guard-rails at least 900 mm above the walkway, with a knee rail. Safety of window cleaners is best guaranteed by installation of totally self-pivoting windows (see 46.30(*a*) above). However, a wide variety of window designs is currently in use in buildings – sliding sashes, louvred sashes, fixed lights and hinged casements, all requiring different cleaning techniques.

(1) Cleaning from ladders

Portable ladders, aluminium or timber, should rest on a secure base and reasonably practicable precautions, to avoid sliding outwards at the base and sideways at the top, should be taken to

(*a*)   secure fixing at the top to preclude lateral or outward movement, e.g. by fastening to an eyebolt/ringbolt;

(*b*)   fasten rung to eyebolt/ringbolt or other anchorage point (see further 46.30 above) at a height of 2 metres;

(*c*)   failing this, a person should be stationed at the base in order to steady the ladder.

The '1 out 4 up' rule (for ladders) suggests that ladders are safest when placed at an angle of 75° to the horizontal; lesser angles indicate that the ladder is more likely to slide outwards at the base. Moreover, window cleaners (and other users) should avoid

(i)   overreaching (as this can unbalance the ladder);

(ii)   proximity with moving objects either above or below (e.g. overhead travelling crane or vehicles operating in the workplace or delivering to the workplace);

(iii)   positioning near to vats or tanks containing dangerous fluids/substances or near to unguarded machinery or exposed electrical equipment. (As for *in situ* travelling ladders, see 46.30 above.)

(2) *Safety harnesses*

In the absence of other, more satisfactory means of cleaning windows, e.g. suspended scaffolds, hydraulic platforms etc., the other reasonably practicable alternative is a safety harness. However, this has the shortcoming that, if a window cleaner falls, he is still likely to be injured. For this reason, harnesses and safety belts must be up to 'free fall' distance (that is, the distance preceding arrest of fall) of, at least,

(i)   2 metres – safety harness, or

(ii)   0.6 metres – safety belt.

(BS 1397: 'Specification for industrial safety belts, harnesses etc.').

Because some walls may not be strong enough or otherwise suitable, inspection by a competent person should always precede selection of permanent fixed anchorage points. Permanent fixed anchorages should comply with BS 5845 (see 46.30 above) and be periodically inspected and tested for exposure to elements. Failing this, temporary anchorage or even mobile anchorage, given the same built-in safeguards, may suffice (see 46.30 above).

(B) *Cleaning from the inside*

46.35   Outer surfaces by design should be able to be cleaned from inside the workplace without use of steps or stepladders. Also, size of aperture and weight of window is relevant. Different types of windows present different dangers; for example, in the case of reversible pivoted/projecting windows, a safety catch is necessary to maintain the window in a fully reversed position; in the case of louvres, there should be sufficient space for a cleaner's hand to pass between the blades, which should incorporate a positive hold-open position to avoid the danger of blowing shut (see BS 8213, Part 1 1991: 'Safety in use and during cleaning of windows').

Maximum safe reach to clean glass immediately beneath an open window is 610 mm downwards (that is, 2' 0"), 510 mm upwards (1' 8") and 560 mm sideways

(1'10"). Horizontally or vertically pivoted windows, reversible for cleaning purposes, are probably the best safety option (see 46.30 above). Given that windows should be accessible without resort to a ladder, short-of-stature window cleaners should invariably make use of cleaning aids to reach further up glazing panels. Built-in furniture should never be placed near windows to obstruct access; nor should blinds or pelmets inhibit the operation of windows and window controls.

Mixed system of cleaning

46.36 Where window cleaners clean windows externally without facilities for ladders or cradles, the building designer should appreciate that the cleaner's safety depends on good foothold and good handhold. The practice of cleaners having to balance, like trapeze artists, on narrow sills or transoms, is dangerous. Owing to the frequency of failure of apparently safe and adequate footholds and handholds, it is imperative that suitable and convenient safety bolts or fixings, to which the cleaner may fix his safety belt, should be provided. Where possible, the safety eyebolt should be fitted on the inside of the wall. Moreover, internal bolts are not weakened by the weather. Where safety eyebolts are fitted to the window frame, architects should pay particular regard at design stage to the fixing of the frame to the building structure, so as to ensure that fixings can withstand the extra load, imposed on the frame, in the event of the cleaner falling.

Where glazing areas are incorporated in roofs, provision should be made for cleaning both sides of the glass, and, where possible, walkways should be provided, both externally and internally. Internal walkways can also be designed to serve for maintenance of electric lighting installations. Where walkways are not feasible, access by permanent travelling ladders should be considered (see 46.30 above).

Appendix 1

Current HSE Publications

Guidance Notes

There are 5 principal series of guidance notes available. These are: Chemical Safety; Environmental Hygiene; General Series; Medical Series; and Plant and Machinery.

Chemical safety

CS 1	Industrial use of flammable gas detectors. 1987
CS 3	Storage and use of sodium chlorate and other similar strong oxidants. 1985
$CS 4	Keeping of LPG in cylinders and similar containers. 1986
$CS 6	Storage and use of LPG on construction sites. 1981
CS 7	Odorisation of bulk oxygen supplies in shipyards. 1983
CS 8	Small scale storage and display of LPG at retail premises. 1985
CS 9	Bulk storage and use of liquid carbon dioxide: hazards and procedures. 1985
CS 10	Fumigation using phosphine. 1986
CS 11	Storage and use of LPG at metered estates. 1987
CS 12	Fumigation using methyl bromide (bromomethane). 1986
CS 15	Cleaning and gas freeing of tanks containing flammable residues. 1985
CS 16	Chlorine vaporisers. 1985
CS 17	Storage of packaged dangerous substances. 1986
CS 18	Storage and handling of ammonium nitrate. 1986
$CS 19	Storage of approved pesticides: guidance for farmers and other professional users. 1988
CS 20	Sulphuric acid used in agriculture. 1990
CS 21	Storage and handling of organic peroxides. 1990

Environmental hygiene

$$EH 1	Cadmium – health and safety precautions. 1986
$$EH 2	Chromium – health and safety precautions. 1977 O/P
$EH 4	Aniline – health and safety precautions. 1979
EH 5	Trichloroethylene – health and safety precautions. 1985
EH 6	Chromic acid concentrations in air: electrolytic chromium processes: monitoring chromic acid mists. 1990
$EH 7	Petroleum based adhesives in building operations. 1977
EH 8	Arsenic – toxic hazards and precautions. 1987
$EH 9	Spraying of highly flammable liquids. 1977
$EH 10	Asbestos – exposure limits and measurement of airborne dust concentrations. 1988
$EH 11	Arsenic – health and safety precautions. 1977 O/P
$EH 12	Stibine – health and safety precautions. 1977
$EH 13	Beryllium – health and safety precautions. 1977

EH 14	Level of training for technicians making noise surveys. 1977
$$EH 16	Isocyanates: toxic hazards and precautions. 1984
$EH 17	Mercury – health and safety precautions. 1977
$EH 19	Antimony – health and safety precautions. 1978
$EH 20	Phosphine – health and safety precautions. 1979
$EH 21	Carbon dust – health and safety precautions. 1979
$EH 22	Ventilation of the workplace. 1988
$EH 23	Anthrax: health hazards. 1979
$EH 24	Dust and accidents in malthouses. 1979
$EH 25	Cotton dust sampling. 1980
$$EH 26	Occupational skin diseases: health and safety precautions. 1981
$EH 27	Acrylonitrile: personal protective equipment. 1981
EH 28	Control of lead: air sampling techniques and strategies. 1986
EH 29	Control of lead: outside workers. 1981
$EH 31	Control of exposure to polyvinyl chloride dust. 1982
$EH 33	Atmospheric pollution in car parks. 1982
$$EH 34	Benzidine based dyes. Health and safety precautions. 1982
EH 35	Probable asbestos dust concentrations at construction processes. 1989
EH 36	Work with asbestos cement. 1990
EH 37	Work with asbestos insulating board. 1989
$EH 38	Ozone: health hazards and precautionary measures. 1983
EH 40/93	Occupational exposure limits. 1993
EH 41	Respiratory protective equipment for use against asbestos. 1985
EH 42	Monitoring strategies for toxic substances. 1989
$$EH 43	Carbon monoxide. 1984
$$EH 44	Dust in the workplace: general principles of protection. 1984 O/P
$EH 45	Carbon disulphide: control of exposure in the viscose industry. 1984
$EH 46	Exposure to mineral wools. 1986
EH 47	Provision, use and maintenance of hygiene facilities for work with asbestos insulation and coatings. 1986
EH 48	Legionnaires' disease. 1987
$EH 49	Nitrosamines in synthetic metal cutting and grinding fluids. 1987
EH 50	Training operatives and supervisors for work with asbestos insulation and coatings. 1988
EH 51	Enclosures provided for work with asbestos insulation, coatings and insulating board. 1989
EH 52	Removal techniques for asbestos insulation. 1989
EH 53	Respiratory protective equipment for use against airborne radioactivity. 1990
EH 54	Assessment of exposure to fumes from welding and allied processes. 1990
EH 55	Control of exposure to fumes from welding and allied processes. 1990
EH 56	Biological monitoring for toxic substances. 1990
EH 57	Asbestos removal at high temperatures. 1993
EH 58	Carcinogenicity of mineral oils. 1990
EH 59	Crystalline silica. 1990
EH 60	Nickel and its inorganic compounds. 1991
EH 62	Metalworking fluids. 1991
EH 64	Occupational exposure limits. 1993

EH 65/1	Trimethylbenzene . . . criteria for occupational exposure limit. 1992
EH 65/2	Pulverised fuel ash; criteria for occupational exposure limit. 1992
EH 65/3	N_1N^-Dimethylacetamide; criteria for occupational exposure limit. 1992
EH 65/4	Dichlorethane; criteria for occupational exposure limit. 1992
EH 65/6	Epichlorohydrin; criteria for occupational exposure limits. 1992
EH 66	Grain dust. 1992
EH 67	Grain dust in maltings. 1992

General series

GS 2	Metrication of construction safety regs. 1976
$GS 3	Fire risk in the storage and industrial use of cellular plastics. 1976
GS 4	Safety in pressure testing. 1976
$$GS 5	Entry into confined spaces. 1977
GS 6	Avoidance of danger from overhead electrical lines. 1980
*GS 7	Accidents to children on construction sites. 1989
GS 9	Road transport in factories. 1978
GS 11	Whisky cask racking. 1980
$$GS 12	Effluent storage on farms. 1981
GS 15	General access scaffolds. 1982
$GS 16	Gaseous fire extinguishing systems: precautions for toxic and asphyxiating hazards. 1984
$GS 17	Safe custody and handling of stock bulls on farms and at artificial insemination centres. 1982 O/P see GS 35
$GS 18	Commercial ultra violet tanning equipment. 1982
GS 19	General fire precautions aboard ships being fitted out or under repair. 1983
GS 20	Fire precautions in pressurised workings. 1983
GS 21	Assessment of the radio frequency ignition hazard to process plants where flammable atmospheres may occur. 1983 O/P replaced by BS 6656: 1986
GS 23	Electrical safety in schools. 1983
GS 24	Electricity on construction sites. 1983
GS 25	Prevention of falls to window cleaners. 1983
GS 26	Access to road tankers. 1983
GS 27	Protection against electric shock. 1984
GS 28/1	Safe erection of structures. Part 1: initial planning and design. 1984
GS 28/2	Safe erection of structures. Part 2: site management and procedures. 1985
GS 28/3	Safe erection of structures. Part 3: working places and access. 1986
GS 28/4	Safe erection of structures. Part 4: legislation and training. 1986
$GS 29/1	Health and safety in demolition work. Part 1: preparation and planning. 1988
$GS 29/2	Health and safety in demolition work. Part 2: legislation. 1984 O/P
GS 29/3	Health and safety in demolition work. Part 3: techniques. 1984
$GS 29/4	Health and safety in demolition work. Part 4: health hazards. 1985
$GS 30	Health and safety hazards associated with pig husbandry. 1984

GS 31	Safe use of ladders, step ladders and trestles. 1984
$GS 32	Health and safety in shoe repair premises. 1984
GS 33	Avoiding danger from buried electricity cables. 1985
GS 34	Electrical safety in departments of electrical engineering. 1986
$GS 35	Safe custody and handling of bulls on farms and similar premises. 1985
$GS 36	Safe custody and handling of bulls at agricultural shows, markets and similar premises off the farm. 1985
GS 37	Flexible leads, plugs, sockets, etc. 1985
GS 38	Electrical test equipment for use by electricians. 1986
GS 39	Training of crane drivers and slingers. 1986
$GS 40	Loading and unloading of bulk flammable liquids and gases at harbours and inland waterways. 1986
GS 41	Radiation safety in underwater radiography. 1986
GS 42	Tower scaffolds. 1987
GS 43	Lithium batteries. 1987
$GS 46	In situ timber treatment using timber preservatives: health, safety and environmental precautions. 1989
GS 47	Safety of electrical distribution systems on factory premises. 1990
GS 48	Training and standards of competence for users of chain saws in agriculture. 1990
GS 49	Pre-stress concrete. 1990
GS 51	Facade retention. 1992

Medical series

MS 4	Organic dust surveys. 1977
MS 5	Lung function. 1977
MS 6	Chest X-rays in dust diseases. 1977
MS 7	Colour vision. 1987
MS 8	Isocyanates: medical surveillance. 1983
MS 9	Byssinosis. 1977
MS 10	Beat conditions, tenosynovitis. 1977
MS 12	Mercury – medical surveillance. 1978
MS 13	Asbestos. 1988
MS 15	Welding. 1978
MS 16	Training of offshore sick-bay attendants ('rig-medics'). 1978
MS 17	Biological monitoring of workers exposed to organo-phosphorus pesticides. 1987
MS 20	Pre-employment health screening. 1982
$MS 21	Precautions for the safe handling of cytotoxic drugs. 1983
MS 22	Medical monitoring of workers exposed to platinum salts. 1983
*MS 23	Health aspects of job placement and rehabilitation – advice to employers. 1989
MS 24	Health surveillance of occupational skin disease. 1990
MS 25	Occupational asthma. 1990

Plant and machinery

PM 1	Guarding of portable pipe-threading machines. 1984
PM 2	Guards for planing machines. 1976
PM 3	Erection and dismantling of tower cranes. 1976
PM 4	High temperature dyeing machines. 1980
PM 5	Automatically controlled steam and hot water boilers. 1977

PM 6	Dough dividers. 1976
PM 7	Lifts: thorough examination and testing. 1982
PM 8	Passenger-carrying paternosters. 1977
PM 9	Access to tower cranes. 1979
PM 10	Tripping devices for radial and heavy vertical drilling machines. 1987
PM 13	Zinc embrittlement of austenitic stainless steel. 1977
PM 14	Safety in the use of cartridge operated tools. 1978 O/P
PM 15	Safety in the use of timber pallets. 1978
PM 16	Eyebolts. 1978
PM 17	Pneumatic nailing and stapling tools. 1979
PM 19	Use of lasers for display purposes. 1980
PM 20(rev)	Cable laid slings and grommets. 1987
PM 21	Safety in the use of woodworking machines. 1981
PM 22	Training advice on the mounting of abrasive wheels. 1983
PM 23	Photo-electric safety systems. 1981
PM 24	Safety at rack and pinion hoists. 1981
PM 25	Vehicle finishing units: fire and explosion hazards. 1981
PM 26	Safety at lift landings. 1981
PM 27	Construction hoists. 1981
PM 28	Working platforms on fork lift trucks. 1981
PM 29(rev)	Electrical hazards from steam/water pressure cleaners etc. 1988
PM 30	Suspended access equipment. 1983
PM 31	Chain saws. 1982
PM 32(rev)	Safe use of portable electrical apparatus (electrical safety). 1983
PM 33	Safety of bandsaws in the food industry. 1983
PM 34	Safety in the use of escalators. 1983
PM 35	Safety in the use of reversing dough brakes. 1983
PM 36	Weld defect acceptance levels for in service non- destructive examination of set-in endplate to furnace and shell connections of shell boilers. 1984
PM 37	Electrical installations in motor vehicle repair premises and amendment sheet. 1984
PM 38	Selection and use of electric handlamps. 1984
PM 39	Hydrogen embrittlement of grade T chain. 1984
PM 40	Protection of workers at welded steel tube mills. 1984
PM 41	Application of photo-electric safety systems to machinery. 1984
PM 42	Excavators used as cranes. 1984
PM 43	Scotch derrick cranes. 1984
PM 45	Escalators: periodic thorough examination. 1984
PM 46	Wedge and socket anchorages for wire ropes. 1985
PM 47	Safe operation of passenger carrying amusement devices – the waltzer. 1985
PM 48	Safe operation of passenger carrying amusement devices – the octopus. 1985
PM 49	Safe operation of passenger carrying amusement devices – the cyclone twist. 1985
PM 51	Safety in the use of radio-frequency dielectric heating equipment. 1986
PM 52	Safety in the use of refuse compaction vehicles. 1985
PM 53	Emergency private generation: electrical safety. 1985
PM 54	Lifting gear standards. 1985
PM 55	Safe working with overhead travelling cranes. 1985
PM 56	Noise from pneumatic systems. 1985

PM 57	Safe operation of passenger carrying amusement devices – the big wheel. 1986
PM 58	Diesel engined lift trucks in hazardous areas. 1986
PM 59	Safe operation of passenger carrying amusement devices – the paratrooper. 1986
PM 60	Steam boiler blowdown systems. 1987
PM 61	Safe operation of passenger carrying amusement devices – the chair-o-plane. 1986
PM 62	Expanded polystyrene moulding machines. 1986
PM 63	Inclined hoists used in building and construction work. 1987
PM 64	Electrical safety in arc welding. 1986
PM 65	Worker protection at crocodile (alligator) shears. 1986
PM 66	Scrap baling machines. 1986
PM 68	Safe operation of passenger carrying amusement devices – roller coasters. 1987
PM 69	Safety in the use of freight containers. 1987
PM 70	Safe operation of passenger carrying amusement devices – Ark/speedways. 1988
PM 71	Safe operation of passenger carrying amusement devices – water chutes. 1989
PM 73	Safety of autoclaves. 1990
PM 74	Forced air filtration units for agricultural vehicles. 1990
PM 75	Glass reinforced plastic vessels and tanks. 1991
PM 76	Safe operation of passenger carrying amusement devices – inflatable bouncing devices. 1991
PM 77	Fitness of equipment used for medical exposure to ionising radiation. 1992

Health and Safety: Guidance Booklets

HS(G) 1	Safe use and storage of flexible polyurethane foam. 1978 O/P
$HS(G) 3	Highly flammable materials on construction sites. 1978
$HS(G) 4	Highly flammable liquids in the paint industry. 1978
HS(G) 5	Hot work: welding and cutting on plant containing flammable materials. 1979
HS(G) 6	Safety in working with lift trucks. (rev 1992)
HS(G) 7	Container terminals: safe working practice. 1980
HS(G) 8	Fabric production: safety in the cotton and allied fibres industry. 1980
HS(G) 9	Spinning, winding and sizing: safety in the cotton and allied fibres industry. 1980
$HS(G) 10	Cloakroom accommodation and washing facilities. 1980
HS(G) 11	Flame arresters and explosion reliefs. 1980
HS(G) 12	Off-shore construction: health, safety and welfare. 1980
HS(G) 13	Electrical testing: safety in electrical testing. 1980
HS(G) 14	Opening processes: cotton and allied fibres. 1980
HS(G) 16	Evaporating and other ovens. 1981
HS(G) 17	Safety in the use of abrasive wheels. 1984
$$HS(G) 18	Portable grinding machines: control of dust. 1982
HS(G) 19	Safety in working with power operated mobile work platforms. 1982
$HS(G) 20	Guidelines for occupational health services. 1980
HS(G) 21	Safety in the cotton and allied fibres industry: cardroom processes. 1986

HS(G) 22	Electrical apparatus for use in potentially explosive atmospheres. 1984 O/P
HS(G) 23	Safety at power operated mast work platforms. 1985
HS(G) 24	Guarding of cutters of horizontal milling machines. 1985
$HS(G) 25	Control of Industrial Major Accident Hazards Regulations 1984 (CIMAH): further guidance on emergency plans. 1985
$HS(G) 26	Transport of dangerous substances in tank containers. 1986
$HS(G) 27	Substances for use at work: the provision of information. 1989
$HS(G) 28	Safety advice for bulk chlorine installations. 1986
HS(G) 29	Locomotive boilers. 1986
HS(G) 30	Storage of anhydrous ammonia under pressure in the United Kingdom: spherical and cylindrical vessels. 1986
HS(G) 31	Pie and tart machines. 1986. (updates and revises information in TDN 30)
HS(G) 32	Safety in falsework for in situ beams and slabs. 1987
HS(G) 33	Safety in roofwork. 1987 (Supersedes Guidance Note GS10: Roofwork, prevention of falls)
HS(G) 34	Storage of LPG at fixed installations. 1987
$HS(G) 35	Catering safety: food preparation machinery. 1987
HS(G) 36	Disposal of explosives waste and the decontamination of explosives plant. 1987
$$HS(G) 37	Introduction to local exhaust ventilation. 1987
HS(G) 38	Lighting at work. 1987
HS(G) 39	Compressed air safety. 1990
$HS(G) 40	Chlorine from drums and cylinders. 1987
HS(G) 41	Petrol filling stations: construction and operation. 1990
HS(G) 42	Safety in the use of metal cutting guillotines and shears. 1988
HS(G) 43	Industrial robot safety. 1988
HS(G) 44	Drilling machines: guarding of spindles and attachments. 1988
HS(G) 45	Safety in meat preparation: guidance for butchers. 1988
*HS(G) 46	A guide for small contractors. Site safety and concrete construction. 1989
HS(G) 47	Avoiding danger from underground services. 1989
HS(G) 48	Human factors in industrial safety. 1989
HS(G) 49	Examination and testing of portable radiation instruments for external radiations. 1990
HS(G) 50	Storage of flammable liquids in fixed tanks. 1990
HS(G) 51	Storage of flammable liquids in containers. 1990
HS(G) 52	Storage of flammable liquids in fixed tanks. 1990
HS(G) 53	Respiratory protective equipment: a practical guide for users. 1990
HS(G) 54	Maintenance, examination and testing of local exhaust ventilation. 1990
HS(G) 55	Health and safety in kitchens and food preparation areas. 1990
HS(G) 56	Noise at work. Noise assessment, information and control. Noise guides 3 to 8. 1990 (Noise guides 1 and 2 appear in the Unnumbered Reports series.)
HS(G) 57	Seating at work. 1991
HS(G) 58	Evaluation and inspection of buildings and structures. 1990
HS(G) 60	Work related upper limb disorders: a guide to prevention. 1990
HS(G) 61	Surveillance of people exposed to health risks at work. 1990
HS(G) 62	Health and safety in tyre/exhaust fitting premises. 1991
HS(G) 63	Radiation protection off-site for emergency services in the event of a nuclear accident. 1991

HS(G) 64	Assessment of fire hazards from solid materials. 1991
HS(G) 65	Successful health and safety management. 1991
HS(G) 66	Protection of workers and the general public during development of contaminated land. 1991
HS(G) 67	Health and safety in motor vehicle repair. 1991
HS(G) 70	Control of legionellosis. 1991
HS(G) 71	Storage of packaged dangerous substances. 1992
HS(G) 72	Control of respirable silica dust in heavy clay and refractory processes. 1992
HS(G) 73	Control of respirable crystalline silica in quarries. 1992
HS(G) 74	Control of silica dust in foundries. 1992
HS(G) 76	Health and safety in retail and wholesale warehouses. 1992
HS(G) 77	COSHH and peripatetic workers. 1992
HS(G) 78	Container packing: packing and transporting dangerous goods in cargo transport units for carriage by sea. 1992
HS(G) 81	Code of safe practice at fairgrounds and amusement parks. 1992
HS(G) 83	Training woodworking machinists. 1992
HS(G) 84	Safe systems: Guidance for shopping trolleys. 1992
HS(G) 85	Electricity at work: safe working practices. 1992
HS(G) 86	Veterinary medicines – safe use by farmers. 1992
HS(G) 89	Safeguarding agricultural machinery: moving parts. 1992
HS(G) 91	Restriction of occupational exposure to ionising radiation. 1993
HS(G) 93	Assessment of pressure vessels operating at low temperature. 1993
HS(G) 96	Cost of accidents at work. 1993
HS(G) 97	Step by step guide to COSHH assessments. 1993

Health and Safety: Regulations Booklets

HS(R) 1	Packaging and labelling of dangerous substances – regulations and guidance notes. 1978
$HS(R) 2	Guide to agricultural legislation. 1978 O/P
HS(R) 4	Guide to the OSRP Act 1963. 1989
HS(R) 8	Guide to the Diving Operations at Work Regulations 1981. 1981
HS(R) 9	Guide to Woodworking Regulations 1974. 1981
HS(R) 11	First-aid at work. 1981
HS(R) 12	Guide to the Health and Safety (Dangerous Pathogens) Regulations 1981. 1981
HS(R) 13	Guide to the Dangerous Substances (Conveyance by Road in Road Tankers and Tank Containers) Regulations 1981. 1981
HS(R) 14	Guide to the Notification of New Substances Regulations. 1989
HS(R) 15	Administrative guidance on the European Community 'Explosive Atmospheres' directive (76/117/EEC and 79/196/EEC) and related directives. 1987
HS(R) 16	Guide to the Notification of Installations Handling Hazardous Substances Regulations 1982. 1983
HS(R) 17	Guide to the Classification and Labelling of Explosives Regulations 1983. 1983
HS(R) 18	Administrative guidance on the application of the European Community 'Low Voltage' directive (73/23/EEC) to electrical equipment for use at work in the United Kingdom. 1984

*HS(R) 19	Guide to the Asbestos (Licensing) Regulations 1983. 1989
HS(R) 21	Guide to the Control of Industrial Major Accident Hazards Regulations 1984. 1985
HS(R) 22	Guide to the Classification, Packaging and Labelling of Dangerous Substances Regulations 1984. 1985
HS(R) 23	Guide to the Reporting of Injuries, Diseases and Dangerous Occurrences Regulations 1985. 1986
HS(R) 24	Guide to the Road Traffic (Carriage of Dangerous Substances in Packages etc.) Regulations 1986. 1987
*HS(R) 25	Memorandum of guidance on the Electricity at Work Regulations 1989. 1989
HS(R) 26	Guidance on the legal and administrative measures taken to implement the European Community Directives on Lifting and Mechanical Handling Appliances and Electrically Operated Lifts. 1987
HS(R) 27	A guide to Dangerous Substances in Harbour Areas Regulations 1987. 1988
HS(R) 28	A guide to the Loading and Unloading of Fishing Vessels Regulations 1988. 1988
HS(R) 29	Notification and marking of sites. The Dangerous Substances (Notification and Marking of Sites) Regulations 1990. 1990
HS(R) 30	A guide to the Pressure Systems and Transportable Gas Containers Regulations 1989. 1990

Appendix 2

Some Relevant British Standards

(For the relevance of British Standards to legal requirement, see 1.30
INTRODUCTION.)

Access equipment	BS 6037
Acoustic measurement/machine tools	BS 4813
Agriculture, protective cabs and frames	BS 4063
Airborne noise emission	
earth-moving machinery	BS 6812
hydraulic transmission systems	BS 5944
portable chain saws	BS 6916
Anchorages	
industrial safety harnesses	BS 5845
self-locking, industrial	BS 5062
Arc welding equipment	BS 638
Artificial daylight lamps	
colour assessment	BS 950
for sensitometry	BS 1380
Artificial lighting	BS 8206
Bromochlorodifluoromethane	
fire extinguishing systems	BS 5306
fire extinguishers	BS 6535
Carbon steel welded horizontal	
cylindrical storage tanks	BS 2594
Carpet cleaners, electric, industrial use	BS 5415
Cellulose fibres	BS 1771
Chain lever hoists	BS 4898
Chain pulley blocks, hand-operated	BS 3243
Chain slings	
alloy steel	BS 3458
high tensile steel	BS 2902
steel use and maintenance	BS 6968
welded	BS 6304
Chairs	
adjustable office furniture	BS 5459
office furniture, design/dimensions	BS 5940
office furniture, ergonomic design	BS 3044
Chemical protective clothing	
against gases and vapours	pr EN 464
liquid chemicals	pr EN 463, 465, 466, 467, 468
Circular saws	
hand-held electric	BS 2769
safeguarding	BS 6854
woodworking	BS 411
Cleaning and surface repair of buildings	BS 6270

Closed circuit escape breathing apparatus	BS 4667
Clothing for protection against intense heat	BS 3791
Construction equipment	
hoists	BS 7212
suspended safety chairs, cradles	BS 2830
Control of noise (construction and open sites)	BS 5228
Cranes, safe use	BS 5744, 7121
Disabled people, means of escape	BS 5588
Dust	
high efficiency respirators	BS 4555
particulate emission	BS 3405
particulate emission, high accuracy	BS 893
Ear protectors, sound attenuation measurement	BS 5108
Earphones	
audiometry, calibration, acoustic couplers	BS 4668
audiometry, calibration ears	BS 4669
Earthing	BS 7430
Electrical equipment	
explosive atmospheres	BS 4683, 5501, 5345, 6941
fire hazard testing	BS 6458
impedance measurement	BS 6161
Electrical resistance materials	
arc suppression coils, for electric power systems	BS 4994
bare fine resistance wires	BS 1117
conductor sizes, low-voltage industrial switchgear and	
controlgear	BS 6733
double electrical insulation	BS 2754
earth-leakage circuit-breakers	
— AC voltage operated	BS 842
— current-operated	BS 4293
— portable RCDs	BS 7071
effects of current on human body	PD 6519
electric shock protection, construction of electrical	
equipment	BS 2754
enclosures for high-voltage cable terminations, transformers	
and reactors	BS 6435
fans, industrial	BS 848
industrial electric plugs	BS 4343
industrial machines	BS 2771
marking for low-voltage industrial switchgear/controlgear	BS 6272
metallic	BS 115
resistivity measurement	BS 5714
static electricity	BS 5958
switchgear	BS 162
test for resistance per unit length	BS 3466
Emergency exits	BS 5725
Emergency lighting	BS 5266
Environmental management systems	BS 7750
Ergonomic requirements for office work with VDUs	BS EN 29241
Eye protection	
equipment for eye, face and neck protection against non-	
ionising radiation during welding operations	BS 1542
glossary of terms	BS 6967
guide for selection and use	BS 7028

Eye protectors	BS 2092
Fabrics, curtains and drapes	BS 5867
Face shields	BS 7028
Falling-object protective structures	BS 5495
Falsework, code of practice	BS 5975
Filters	
specification for infra-red filters used in personal eye protection equipment	BS EN 171
specification for personal eye protection equipment in welding	BS EN 169
specification for ultra-violet filters used in personal eye protection equipment	BS EN 170
Fire blankets	BS 6575
Fire classification	BS 4547
Fire detection/alarm systems	BS 5839
Fire door assemblies	BS 8214
Fire extinguishers	
disposable aerosol type	BS 6165
media	BS 6535
on premises	BS 5306
portable	BS 5423
portable, recharging	BS 6643
Fire hose reels (water)	BS 5274
Fire point determination, petroleum products	
Cleveland open cup method	BS 4689
Pensky-Martens apparatus method	BS 2000(35)
Fire precautions in design/construction of buildings	BS 5588
Fire protection measures, code of practice for operation	BS 7273
Fire safety signs	BS 5499
Fire tests	BS 476
Fire tests for furniture	BS 5852
Firefighters gloves	pr EN 659
First-aid reel/hoses	BS 3269
Flameproof industrial clothing	BS 1547
Flammability testing and performance	BS 6249
Flammable liquids	BS 476
Footwear	
footwear with midsole protection	BS 5462
general and industrialised lined or unlined boots	BS 6159 Pt 1
lined industrialised vulcanised rubber boots	BS 5143
lined rubber safety boots	BS 1870 Pt 2
methods of test for safety	BS 953
other than all rubber and plastic moulded compounds	BS 1870 Pt 1
polyvinyl chloride boots	BS 6159
protective clothing for users of hand-held chain saws	pr EN 381
PVC moulded safety footwear	BS 1870 Pt 3
requirements/test methods for safety protective and occupational footwear for professional use	pr EN 344
specification for safety footwear for professional use	pr EN 347
women's protective footwear	BS 4972
Freight containers	BS 3951
Gaiters and footwear for protection against burns and impact risks in foundries	BS 4676
Gas detector tubes	BS 5343
Gas fired hot water boilers	BS 6798

817

Glazing	BS 6262
Gloves: rubber gloves for electrical purposes	BS 697
Goggles, industrial/non-industrial use	BS 2092
Grinding machines	
hand-held electric	BS 2769
pneumatic, portable	BS 4390
spindle noses	BS 1089
Head protection	BS 3864
High visibility warning clothing	pr EN 471
Hoisting slings	BS 6166
alloy steel, chain	BS 3458
chain, welded	BS 6304
high tensile, steel chain	BS 2902
textile	BS 6668
wire rope	BS 1290
Hoists	
construction, safe use	BS 7212
electric, passenger/materials	BS 4465
working platforms	BS 6289
Industrial gloves	BS 1651
Industrial safety helmets, firemen's	BS 3864
Industrial trucks	
hand-operated stillage trucks, dimensions	BS 4337
pallet trucks, dimensions	BS 4155
pedals, construction/layout	BS 7178
Ionising radiation	
exposure rate calculation	BS 4094
units of measurement	BS 5775
Jib cranes	
high pedestal and portal	BS 2452
power-driven, mobile	BS 1757
power-driven, travelling	BS 367
power-driven derricks	BS 327
Ladders	
code of practice	BS 5395
permanent for chimneys, high structures	BS 4211
portable aluminium	BS 2037
portable timber	BS 1129
Lamps, artificial daylight, for colour assessment	BS 950
Life jackets	BS 3595
Lifting chains	
alloy, steel	BS 3113
high tensile steel	BS 1663
safe working on lifts	BS 7255
Machine guards	
chain saws	BS 6916
conveyors and elevators	BS 5667
earth-moving equipment	BS 5945
woodworking machines	BS 6854
Machine tools	
emergency stop equipment, functional aspects	BS EN 418
noise measurement methods	BS 4813
safeguarding	BS 5304
Machinery, safety of, drafting and presentation	BS EN 414

Machinery, safety of, minimum gaps to avoid crushing parts of
body   BS EN 349
Machines, vibration   BS 4675
Materials handling
    conveyor belts   BS 5767
    freight containers   BS 3951
    used in clothing for protection against heat and flame   BS 6249
Mobile cranes   BS 1757
Mortising machines, single chain   BS 4361
Natural fibre ropes   BS 2052
    cords, lines, twines   BS 6125
Nets, safety   BS 3913
Noise
    airborne, chain saws   BS 6916
    airborne, earth-moving equipment   BS 6812
    airborne, hydraulic transmission systems   BS 5944
    effects on hearing handicap   BS 5330
    industrial noise, method for rating   BS 4142
    industrial premises, measurement   BS 4142
    machine tools, measurement methods   BS 4813
    sound exposure meters   BS 6402
Noise induced hearing loss
    effects of noise exposure   BS 5330
    pure tone air conduction threshold audiometry   BS 6655
Office buildings, fire precautions   BS 5588
Office furniture, design/dimensions   BS 5940
Office machines
    electrically energised, safety   BS 5850, 7002
    keyboards, control keys   BS 5231
    noise measurement   BS 7135
Oil burning equipment   BS 799
Oil firing   BS 5410
Overhead travelling cranes
    power-driven   BS 466
    safe use   BS 5744
Packaging, pictorial marking for handling of goods   BS EN 20780
Particulate air pollutants
    in effluent gases, measurement   BS 3415
    in effluent gases, measurement, high accuracy   BS 893
Passenger hoists
    electric, building sites   BS 4465
    vehicular   BS 6109
    working platforms   BS 6289
    working platforms, mobile, elevating   BS 7171
Patent glazing   BS 5516
Performance of windows   BS 6375
Personal eye protection
    filters for welding and related techniques   BS EN 169
    infrared filters   BS EN 171
    non-optical test methods   pr EN 168
    optical test methods   pr EN 167
    specifications   pr EN 166
    ultraviolet filters   BS EN 170
    vocabulary   pr EN 165
Pipelines, identification marking   BS 1710, 4800

Pneumatic tools
    portable grinding machines   BS 4390
Portable fire extinguishers   BS 5423
Portable tools
    electric, radio interference limits and measurements   BS 800
    pneumatic grinding machines   BS 4390
Powder fire extinguishers
    disposable, aerosol type   BS 6165
    extinguishing powders for   BS 6535
    on premises   BS 5306
    portable, recharging   BS 6643
Power take-off
    agricultural tractors, front-mounted   BS 6818
    agricultural tractors, rear-mounted   BS 5861
Powered industrial trucks
    controls, symbols   BS 5829
    high-lift rider trucks, overhead guards   BS 5933
Pressure vessels   BS 5500
Protective barriers   BS 6180
Protective cabs
    agricultural tractors   BS 4063
    controls for external equipment   BS 5731
Protective clothing
    against cold weather   pr EN 342
    against foul weather   pr EN 343
    against heat and fire   pr EN 366
    against molten metal splash   pr EN 373
    against risk of being caught up in moving parts   pr EN 510
    eye, face and neck protection, welding   BS 1542
    flameproof   BS 1547
    for firefighters   pr EN 469
    for use where there is risk of entanglement   BS EN 510
    for users of hand-held chain saws   pr EN 381
    for welders   pr EN 470
    for workers exposed to heat   pr EN 531
    gaiters for foundries   BS 4676
    general requirements   pr EN 340
    protection against heat and fire   BS EN 366
    protection against intense heat   BS 3791
    protection against liquid chemicals   BS EN 369
    welding   BS 2653
Protective footwear
    antistatic rubber   BS 5451
    firemen's leather boots   BS 2723
    for foundries   BS 4676
    lined industrialised rubber boots   BS 5145
    polyvinyl chloride boots   BS 6159
    women's   BS 4972
Protective gloves
    against chemicals and micro-organisms   pr EN 374
    against cold   pr EN 511
    against ionising radiation   BS EN 421
    against thermal hazards   pr EN 407
    for users of hand-held chain saws   pr EN 381
    general requirements   pr EN 420

welded steel low pressure boilers	BS 855
Step ladders	
portable aluminium alloy	BS 2037
portable timber	BS 1129
Storage tanks	
carbon steel welded horizontal cylindrical	BS 2594
vertical steel welded non-refrigerated butt-welded shells	BS 2654
Suspended access equipment, permanently installed	BS 6037
Suspended safety chairs	BS 2830
Suspended scaffolds, temporarily installed	BS 5974
Tables, office furniture, ergonomic design	BS 3044
Textile floor coverings	BS 5287
Transportable gas containers	
acetylene containers	BS 6071
periodic inspection, testing and maintenance	BS 5430
welded steel tanks for road transport of liquefiable gases	BS 7122
Travelling cranes, power-driven jib	BS 357, 5744
Vertical steel welded non-refrigerated storage tanks, manufacture of	BS 2654
Vibration measurement	
chain saws	BS 6916
rotating shafts	BS 6749
Visual display terminals, ergonomics and design	BS 7179
Water absorption and translucency of china or porcelain	BS 5416
Water services, installation, testing and maintenance	BS 6700
Welders, protective clothing	BS 2653
Window cleaning	BS 8213
Windows, performance of	BS 6375
Woodworking machines	BS 6854
Wool and wool blends	BS 1771
Working platforms	
mobile	BS 6289
mobile, elevating	BS 7171
permanent, suspended access	BS 6037
Workwear and career wear	BS 5426

Table of Cases

This table is referenced to paragraph numbers in the book.

Table of Statutes

Table of Statutory Instruments

Index

References are to chapters and paragraph numbers of this book.